MODERN
OPERATING SYSTEMS

SECOND EDITION

Other bestselling titles by Andrew S. Tanenbaum

Structured Computer Organization, 4th edition

This widely-read classic, now in its fourth edition, provides the ideal introduction to computer architecture. It covers the topic in an easy-to-understand way, bottom up. There is a chapter on digital logic for beginners, followed by chapters on microarchitecture, the instruction set architecture level, operating systems, assembly language, and parallel computer architectures.

Computer Networks, 3rd edition

This widely-read classic, now in its third edition, provides the ideal introduction to today's and tomorrow's networks. It explains in detail how modern networks are structured. Starting with the physical layer and working up to the application layer, the book covers a vast number of important topics, including wireless communication, fiber optics, data link protocols, Ethernet, routing algorithms, network performance, security, DNS, electronic mail, USENET news, the World Wide Web, and multimedia. The book has especially thorough coverage of TCP/IP and the Internet.

Operating Systems: Design and Implementation, 2nd edition

This popular text on operating systems is the only book covering both the principles of operating systems and their application to a real system. All the traditional operating systems topics are covered in detail. In addition, the principles are carefully illustrated with MINIX, a free POSIX-based UNIX-like operating system for personal computers. Each book contains a free CD-ROM containing the complete MINIX system, including all the source code. The source code is listed in an appendix to the book amd explained in detail in the text.

Distributed Operating Systems

This text covers the fundamental concepts of distributed operating systems. Key topics include communication and synchronization, processes and processors, distributed shared memory, distributed file systems, and distributed real-time systems. The principles are illustrated using four chapter-long examples.

MODERN OPERATING SYSTEMS

SECOND EDITION

ANDREW S. TANENBAUM

Vrije Universiteit
Amsterdam, The Netherlands

PRENTICE HALL INTERNATIONAL

Vice President and Editorial Director, ECS: *Marcia Horton*
Publisher: *Alan Apt*
Associate Editor: *Toni D. Holm*
Editorial Assistant: *Amy K. Todd*
Vice President and Director of Production and Manufacturing, ESM: *David W. Riccardi*
Executive Managing Editor: *Vince O'Brien*
Managing Editor: *David A. George*
Senior Production Editor: *Camille Trentacoste*
Director of Creative Services: *Paul Belfanti*
Creative Director: *Carole Anson*
Art Director: *Heather Scott*
Cover Art: *Don Martinetti*
Cover Design: *Joseph Sengotta*
Assistant to Art Director: *John Christiana*
Interior Illustration: *Patricia Gutièrrez*
Interior Design and Typesetting; Cover Illustration Concept: *Andrew S. Tanenbaum*
Manufacturing Manager: *Trudy Pisciotti*
Manufacturing Buyer: *Pat Brown*
Marketing Manager: *Jennie Burger*

© 2001 by Prentice-Hall, Inc.
Upper Saddle River, New Jersey 07458

10 9 8 7 6 5

ISBN 0-13-092641-8

To Suzanne, Barbara, Marvin, and the memory of Bram and Sweetie π

CONTENTS

2   PROCESSES AND THREADS   71

4 MEMORY MANAGEMENT   189

6 FILE SYSTEMS   379

7 MULTIMEDIA OPERATING SYSTEMS   453

10 CASE STUDY 1: UNIX AND LINUX   671

11 CASE STUDY 2: WINDOWS 2000   **763**

12 OPERATING SYSTEM DESIGN   855

13 READING LIST AND BIBLIOGRAPHY 901

PREFACE

The world has changed a great deal since the first edition of this book appeared in 1992. Computer networks and distributed systems of all kinds have become very common. Small children now roam the Internet, where previously only computer professionals went. As a consequence, this book has changed a great deal, too.

The most obvious change is that the first edition was about half on single-processor operating systems and half on distributed systems. I chose that format in 1991 because few universities then had courses on distributed systems and whatever students learned about distributed systems had to be put into the operating systems course, for which this book was intended. Now most universities have a separate course on distributed systems, so it is not necessary to try to combine the two subjects into one course and one book. This book is intended for a first course on operating systems, and as such focuses mostly on traditional single-processor systems.

I have coauthored two other books on operating systems. This leads to two possible course sequences.

Practically-oriented sequence:
  1. Operating Systems Design and Implementation by Tanenbaum and Woodhull
  2. Distributed Systems by Tanenbaum and Van Steen

Traditional sequence:
  1. Modern Operating Systems by Tanenbaum
  2. Distributed Systems by Tanenbaum and Van Steen

The former sequence uses MINIX and the students are expected to experiment with MINIX in an accompanying laboratory supplementing the first course. The latter sequence does not use MINIX. Instead, some small simulators are available that can be used for student exercises during a first course using this book. These simulators can be found starting on the author's Web page: *www.cs.vu.nl/~ast/* by clicking on <u>Software and supplementary material for my books</u> .

In addition to the major change of switching the emphasis to single-processor operating systems in this book, other major changes include the addition of entire chapters on computer security, multimedia operating systems, and Windows 2000, all important and timely topics. In addition, a new and unique chapter on operating system design has been added.

Another new feature is that many chapters now have a section on research about the topic of the chapter. This is intended to introduce the reader to modern work in processes, memory management, and so on. These sections have numerous references to the current research literature for the interested reader. In addition, Chapter 13 has many introductory and tutorial references.

Finally, numerous topics have been added to this book or heavily revised. These topics include: graphical user intefaces, multiprocessor operating systems, power management for laptops, trusted systems, viruses, network terminals, CD-ROM file systems, mutexes, RAID, soft timers, stable storage, fair-share scheduling, and new paging algorithms. Many new problems have been added and old ones updated. The total number of problems now exceeds 450. A solutions manual is available to professors using this book in a course. They can obtain a copy from their local Prentice Hall representative. In addition, over 250 new references to the current literature have been added to bring the book up to date.

Despite the removal of more than 400 pages of old material, the book has increased in size due to the large amount of new material added. While the book is still suitable for a one-semester or two-quarter course, it is probably too long for a one-quarter or one-trimester course at most universities. For this reason, the book has been designed in a modular way. Any course on operating systems should cover chapters 1 through 6. This is basic material that every student show know.

If additional time is available, additional chapters can be covered. Each of them assumes the reader has finished chapters 1 through 6, but Chaps. 7 through 12 are each self contained, so any desired subset can be used and in any order, depending on the interests of the instructor. In the author's opinion, Chaps. 7 through 12 are much more interesting than the earlier ones. Instructors should tell their students that they have to eat their broccoli before they can have the double chocolate fudge cake dessert.

I would like to thank the following people for their help in reviewing parts of the manuscript: Rida Bazzi, Riccardo Bettati, Felipe Cabrera, Richard Chapman, John Connely, John Dickinson, John Elliott, Deborah Frincke, Chandana Gamage, Robbert Geist, David Golds, Jim Griffioen, Gary Harkin, Frans Kaashoek, Mukkai Krishnamoorthy, Monica Lam, Jussi Leiwo, Herb Mayer, Kirk McKusick, Evi Nemeth, Bill Potvin, Prasant Shenoy, Thomas Skinner, Xian-He Sun, William Terry, Robbert Van Renesse, and Maarten van Steen. Jamie Hanrahan, Mark Russinovich, and Dave Solomon were enormously knowledgeable about Windows 2000 and very helpful. Special thanks go to Al Woodhull for valuable reviews and thinking of many new end-of-chapter problems.

My students were also helpful with comments and feedback, especially Staas de Jong, Jan de Vos, Niels Drost, David Fokkema, Auke Folkerts, Peter Groenewegen, Wilco Ibes, Stefan Jansen, Jeroen Ketema, Joeri Mulder, Irwin Oppenheim, Stef Post, Umar Rehman, Daniel Rijkhof, Maarten Sander, Maurits van der Schee, Rik van der Stoel, Mark van Driel, Dennis van Veen, and Thomas Zeeman.

Barbara and Marvin are still wonderful, as usual, each in a unique way. Finally, last but not least, I would like to thank Suzanne for her love and patience, not to mention all the *druiven* and *kersen*, which have replaced the *sinasappelsap* in recent times.

Andrew S. Tanenbaum

1

INTRODUCTION

A modern computer system consists of one or more processors, some main memory, disks, printers, a keyboard, a display, network interfaces, and other input/output devices. All in all, a complex system. Writing programs that keep track of all these components and use them correctly, let alone optimally, is an extremely difficult job. For this reason, computers are equipped with a layer of software called the **operating system**, whose job is to manage all these devices and provide user programs with a simpler interface to the hardware. These systems are the subject of this book.

The placement of the operating system is shown in Fig. 1-1. At the bottom is the hardware, which, in many cases, is itself composed of two or more levels (or layers). The lowest level contains physical devices, consisting of integrated circuit chips, wires, power supplies, cathode ray tubes, and similar physical devices. How these are constructed and how they work are the provinces of the electrical engineer.

Next comes the **microarchitecture level**, in which the physical devices are grouped together to form functional units. Typically this level contains some registers internal to the CPU (Central Processing Unit) and a data path containing an arithmetic logic unit. In each clock cycle, one or two operands are fetched from the registers and combined in the arithmetic logic unit (for example, by addition or Boolean AND). The result is stored in one or more registers. On some machines, the operation of the data path is controlled by software, called the **microprogram**. On other machines, it is controlled directly by hardware circuits.

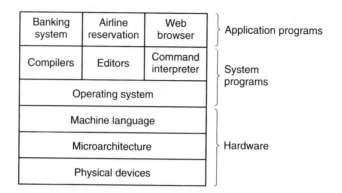

Figure 1-1. A computer system consists of hardware, system programs, and application programs.

The purpose of the data path is to execute some set of instructions. Some of these can be carried out in one data path cycle; others may require multiple data path cycles. These instructions may use registers or other hardware facilities. Together, the hardware and instructions visible to an assembly language programmer form the **ISA** (**Instruction Set Architecture**) level. This level is often called **machine language**.

The machine language typically has between 50 and 300 instructions, mostly for moving data around the machine, doing arithmetic, and comparing values. In this level, the input/output devices are controlled by loading values into special **device registers**. For example, a disk can be commanded to read by loading the values of the disk address, main memory address, byte count, and direction (read or write) into its registers. In practice, many more parameters are needed, and the status returned by the drive after an operation is highly complex. Furthermore, for many I/O (Input/Output) devices, timing plays an important role in the programming.

To hide this complexity, an operating system is provided. It consists of a layer of software that (partially) hides the hardware and gives the programmer a more convenient set of instructions to work with. For example, read block from file is conceptually simpler than having to worry about the details of moving disk heads, waiting for them to settle down, and so on.

On top of the operating system is the rest of the system software. Here we find the command interpreter (shell), window systems, compilers, editors, and similar application-independent programs. It is important to realize that these programs are definitely not part of the operating system, even though they are typically supplied by the computer manufacturer. This is a crucial, but subtle, point. The operating system is (usually) that portion of the software that runs in **kernel mode** or **supervisor mode**. It is protected from user tampering by the hardware (ignoring for the moment some older or low-end microprocessors that do not have hardware protection at all). Compilers and editors run in **user mode**. If a user does not like a particular compiler, he† is free to write his own if he so chooses; he is not free to write his own clock interrupt handler, which is part of the operating system and is normally protected by hardware against attempts by users to modify it.

This distinction, however, is sometimes blurred in embedded systems (which may not have kernel mode) or interpreted systems (such as Java-based operating systems that use interpretation, not hardware, to separate the components). Still, for traditional computers, the operating system is what runs in kernel mode.

That said, in many systems there are programs that run in user mode but which help the operating system or perform privileged functions. For example, there is often a program that allows users to change their passwords. This program is not part of the operating system and does not run in kernel mode, but it clearly carries out a sensitive function and has to be protected in a special way.

In some systems, this idea is carried to an extreme form, and pieces of what is traditionally considered to be the operating system (such as the file system) run in user space. In such systems, it is difficult to draw a clear boundary. Everything running in kernel mode is clearly part of the operating system, but some programs running outside it are arguably also part of it, or at least closely associated with it.

Finally, above the system programs come the application programs. These programs are purchased or written by the users to solve their particular problems, such as word processing, spreadsheets, engineering calculations, or storing information in a database.

1.1 WHAT IS AN OPERATING SYSTEM?

Most computer users have had some experience with an operating system, but it is difficult to pin down precisely what an operating system is. Part of the problem is that operating systems perform two basically unrelated functions, extending the machine and managing resources, and depending on who is doing the talking, you hear mostly about one function or the other. Let us now look at both.

1.1.1 The Operating System as an Extended Machine

As mentioned earlier, the **architecture** (instruction set, memory organization, I/O, and bus structure) of most computers at the machine language level is primitive and awkward to program, especially for input/output. To make this point more concrete, let us briefly look at how floppy disk I/O is done using the NEC

---

† "He" should be read as "he or she" throughout the book.

PD765 compatible controller chips used on most Intel-based personal computers. (Throughout this book we will use the terms "floppy disk" and "diskette" interchangeably.) The PD765 has 16 commands, each specified by loading between 1 and 9 bytes into a device register. These commands are for reading and writing data, moving the disk arm, and formatting tracks, as well as initializing, sensing, resetting, and recalibrating the controller and the drives.

The most basic commands are **read** and **write**, each of which requires 13 parameters, packed into 9 bytes. These parameters specify such items as the address of the disk block to be read, the number of sectors per track, the recording mode used on the physical medium, the intersector gap spacing, and what to do with a deleted-data-address-mark. If you do not understand this mumbo jumbo, do not worry; that is precisely the point—it is rather esoteric. When the operation is completed, the controller chip returns 23 status and error fields packed into 7 bytes. As if this were not enough, the floppy disk programmer must also be constantly aware of whether the motor is on or off. If the motor is off, it must be turned on (with a long startup delay) before data can be read or written. The motor cannot be left on too long, however, or the floppy disk will wear out. The programmer is thus forced to deal with the trade-off between long startup delays versus wearing out floppy disks (and losing the data on them).

Without going into the *real* details, it should be clear that the average programmer probably does not want to get too intimately involved with the programming of floppy disks (or hard disks, which are just as complex and quite different). Instead, what the programmer wants is a simple, high-level abstraction to deal with. In the case of disks, a typical abstraction would be that the disk contains a collection of named files. Each file can be opened for reading or writing, then read or written, and finally closed. Details such as whether or not recording should use modified frequency modulation and what the current state of the motor is should not appear in the abstraction presented to the user.

The program that hides the truth about the hardware from the programmer and presents a nice, simple view of named files that can be read and written is, of course, the operating system. Just as the operating system shields the programmer from the disk hardware and presents a simple file-oriented interface, it also conceals a lot of unpleasant business concerning interrupts, timers, memory management, and other low-level features. In each case, the abstraction offered by the operating system is simpler and easier to use than that offered by the underlying hardware.

In this view, the function of the operating system is to present the user with the equivalent of an **extended machine** or **virtual machine** that is easier to program than the underlying hardware. How the operating system achieves this goal is a long story, which we will study in detail throughout this book. To summarize it in a nutshell, the operating system provides a variety of services that programs can obtain using special instructions called system calls. We will examine some of the more common system calls later in this chapter.

1.1.2 The Operating System as a Resource Manager

The concept of the operating system as primarily providing its users with a convenient interface is a top-down view. An alternative, bottom-up, view holds that the operating system is there to manage all the pieces of a complex system. Modern computers consist of processors, memories, timers, disks, mice, network interfaces, printers, and a wide variety of other devices. In the alternative view, the job of the operating system is to provide for an orderly and controlled allocation of the processors, memories, and I/O devices among the various programs competing for them.

Imagine what would happen if three programs running on some computer all tried to print their output simultaneously on the same printer. The first few lines of printout might be from program 1, the next few from program 2, then some from program 3, and so forth. The result would be chaos. The operating system can bring order to the potential chaos by buffering all the output destined for the printer on the disk. When one program is finished, the operating system can then copy its output from the disk file where it has been stored to the printer, while at the same time the other program can continue generating more output, oblivious to the fact that the output is not really going to the printer (yet).

When a computer (or network) has multiple users, the need for managing and protecting the memory, I/O devices, and other resources is even greater, since the users might otherwise interfere with one another. In addition, users often need to share not only hardware, but information (files, databases, etc.) as well. In short, this view of the operating system holds that its primary task is to keep track of who is using which resource, to grant resource requests, to account for usage, and to mediate conflicting requests from different programs and users.

Resource management includes multiplexing (sharing) resources in two ways: in time and in space. When a resource is time multiplexed, different programs or users take turns using it. First one of them gets to use the resource, then another, and so on. For example, with only one CPU and multiple programs that want to run on it, the operating system first allocates the CPU to one program, then after it has run long enough, another one gets to use the CPU, then another, and then eventually the first one again. Determining how the resource is time multiplexed—who goes next and for how long—is the task of the operating system. Another example of time multiplexing is sharing the printer. When multiple print jobs are queued up for printing on a single printer, a decision has to be made about which one is to be printed next.

The other kind of multiplexing is space multiplexing. Instead of the customers taking turns, each one gets part of the resource. For example, main memory is normally divided up among several running programs, so each one can be resident at the same time (for example, in order to take turns using the CPU). Assuming there is enough memory to hold multiple programs, it is more efficient to hold several programs in memory at once rather than give one of them all of it, especially if it only needs a small fraction of the total. Of course, this raises issues of fairness, protection, and so on, and it is up to the operating system to solve them. Another resource that is space multiplexed is the (hard) disk. In many systems a single disk can hold files from many users at the same time. Allocating disk space and keeping track of who is using which disk blocks is a typical operating system resource management task.

1.2 HISTORY OF OPERATING SYSTEMS

Operating systems have been evolving through the years. In the following sections we will briefly look at a few of the highlights. Since operating systems have historically been closely tied to the architecture of the computers on which they run, we will look at successive generations of computers to see what their operating systems were like. This mapping of operating system generations to computer generations is crude, but it does provide some structure where there would otherwise be none.

The first true digital computer was designed by the English mathematician Charles Babbage (1792–1871). Although Babbage spent most of his life and fortune trying to build his "analytical engine," he never got it working properly because it was purely mechanical, and the technology of his day could not produce the required wheels, gears, and cogs to the high precision that he needed. Needless to say, the analytical engine did not have an operating system.

As an interesting historical aside, Babbage realized that he would need software for his analytical engine, so he hired a young woman named Ada Lovelace, who was the daughter of the famed British poet Lord Byron, as the world's first programmer. The programming language Ada® is named after her.

1.2.1 The First Generation (1945–55) Vacuum Tubes and Plugboards

After Babbage's unsuccessful efforts, little progress was made in constructing digital computers until World War II. Around the mid-1940s, Howard Aiken at Harvard, John von Neumann at the Institute for Advanced Study in Princeton, J. Presper Eckert and William Mauchley at the University of Pennsylvania, and Konrad Zuse in Germany, among others, all succeeded in building calculating engines. The first ones used mechanical relays but were very slow, with cycle times measured in seconds. Relays were later replaced by vacuum tubes. These machines were enormous, filling up entire rooms with tens of thousands of vacuum tubes, but they were still millions of times slower than even the cheapest personal computers available today.

In these early days, a single group of people designed, built, programmed, operated, and maintained each machine. All programming was done in absolute machine language, often by wiring up plugboards to control the machine's basic functions. Programming languages were unknown (even assembly language was unknown). Operating systems were unheard of. The usual mode of operation was for the programmer to sign up for a block of time on the signup sheet on the wall, then come down to the machine room, insert his or her plugboard into the computer, and spend the next few hours hoping that none of the 20,000 or so vacuum tubes would burn out during the run. Virtually all the problems were straightforward numerical calculations, such as grinding out tables of sines, cosines, and logarithms.

By the early 1950s, the routine had improved somewhat with the introduction of punched cards. It was now possible to write programs on cards and read them in instead of using plugboards; otherwise, the procedure was the same.

1.2.2 The Second Generation (1955–65) Transistors and Batch Systems

The introduction of the transistor in the mid-1950s changed the picture radically. Computers became reliable enough that they could be manufactured and sold to paying customers with the expectation that they would continue to function long enough to get some useful work done. For the first time, there was a clear separation between designers, builders, operators, programmers, and maintenance personnel.

These machines, now called **mainframes**, were locked away in specially air conditioned computer rooms, with staffs of professional operators to run them. Only big corporations or major government agencies or universities could afford the multimillion dollar price tag. To run a **job** (i.e., a program or set of programs), a programmer would first write the program on paper (in FORTRAN or assembler), then punch it on cards. He would then bring the card deck down to the input room and hand it to one of the operators and go drink coffee until the output was ready.

When the computer finished whatever job it was currently running, an operator would go over to the printer and tear off the output and carry it over to the output room, so that the programmer could collect it later. Then he would take one of the card decks that had been brought from the input room and read it in. If the FORTRAN compiler was needed, the operator would have to get it from a file cabinet and read it in. Much computer time was wasted while operators were walking around the machine room.

Given the high cost of the equipment, it is not surprising that people quickly looked for ways to reduce the wasted time. The solution generally adopted was the **batch system**. The idea behind it was to collect a tray full of jobs in the input room and then read them onto a magnetic tape using a small (relatively) inexpensive computer, such as the IBM 1401, which was very good at reading cards, copying tapes, and printing output, but not at all good at numerical calculations.

Other, much more expensive machines, such as the IBM 7094, were used for the real computing. This situation is shown in Fig. 1-2.

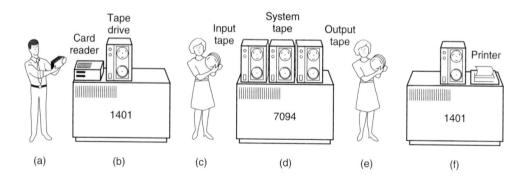

Figure 1-2. An early batch system. (a) Programmers bring cards to 1401. (b) 1401 reads batch of jobs onto tape. (c) Operator carries input tape to 7094. (d) 7094 does computing. (e) Operator carries output tape to 1401. (f) 1401 prints output.

After about an hour of collecting a batch of jobs, the tape was rewound and brought into the machine room, where it was mounted on a tape drive. The operator then loaded a special program (the ancestor of today's operating system), which read the first job from tape and ran it. The output was written onto a second tape, instead of being printed. After each job finished, the operating system automatically read the next job from the tape and began running it. When the whole batch was done, the operator removed the input and output tapes, replaced the input tape with the next batch, and brought the output tape to a 1401 for printing **off line** (i.e., not connected to the main computer).

The structure of a typical input job is shown in Fig. 1-3. It started out with a $JOB card, specifying the maximum run time in minutes, the account number to be charged, and the programmer's name. Then came a $FORTRAN card, telling the operating system to load the FORTRAN compiler from the system tape. It was followed by the program to be compiled, and then a $LOAD card, directing the operating system to load the object program just compiled. (Compiled programs were often written on scratch tapes and had to be loaded explicitly.) Next came the $RUN card, telling the operating system to run the program with the data following it. Finally, the $END card marked the end of the job. These primitive control cards were the forerunners of modern job control languages and command interpreters.

Large second-generation computers were used mostly for scientific and engineering calculations, such as solving the partial differential equations that often occur in physics and engineering. They were largely programmed in FORTRAN and assembly language. Typical operating systems were FMS (the Fortran Monitor System) and IBSYS, IBM's operating system for the 7094.

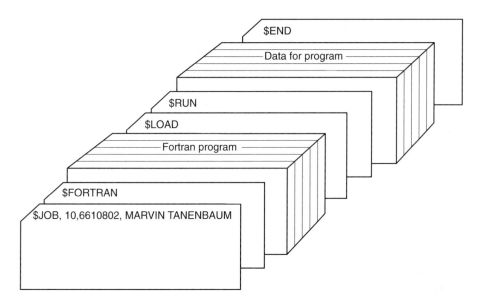

Figure 1-3. Structure of a typical FMS job.

1.2.3 The Third Generation (1965–1980) ICs and Multiprogramming

By the early 1960s, most computer manufacturers had two distinct, and totally incompatible, product lines. On the one hand there were the word-oriented, large-scale scientific computers, such as the 7094, which were used for numerical calculations in science and engineering. On the other hand, there were the character-oriented, commercial computers, such as the 1401, which were widely used for tape sorting and printing by banks and insurance companies.

Developing and maintaining two completely different product lines was an expensive proposition for the manufacturers. In addition, many new computer customers initially needed a small machine but later outgrew it and wanted a bigger machine that would run all their old programs, but faster.

IBM attempted to solve both of these problems at a single stroke by introducing the System/360. The 360 was a series of software-compatible machines ranging from 1401-sized to much more powerful than the 7094. The machines differed only in price and performance (maximum memory, processor speed, number of I/O devices permitted, and so forth). Since all the machines had the same architecture and instruction set, programs written for one machine could run on all the others, at least in theory. Furthermore, the 360 was designed to handle both scientific (i.e., numerical) and commercial computing. Thus a single family of machines could satisfy the needs of all customers. In subsequent years, IBM has come out with compatible successors to the 360 line, using more modern technology, known as the 370, 4300, 3080, and 3090 series.

The 360 was the first major computer line to use (small-scale) Integrated Circuits (ICs), thus providing a major price/performance advantage over the second-generation machines, which were built up from individual transistors. It was an immediate success, and the idea of a family of compatible computers was soon adopted by all the other major manufacturers. The descendants of these machines are still in use at computer centers today. Nowadays they are often used for managing huge databases (e.g., for airline reservation systems) or as servers for World Wide Web sites that must process thousands of requests per second.

The greatest strength of the "one family" idea was simultaneously its greatest weakness. The intention was that all software, including the operating system, **OS/360** had to work on all models. It had to run on small systems, which often just replaced 1401s for copying cards to tape, and on very large systems, which often replaced 7094s for doing weather forecasting and other heavy computing. It had to be good on systems with few peripherals and on systems with many peripherals. It had to work in commercial environments and in scientific environments. Above all, it had to be efficient for all of these different uses.

There was no way that IBM (or anybody else) could write a piece of software to meet all those conflicting requirements. The result was an enormous and extraordinarily complex operating system, probably two to three orders of magnitude larger than FMS. It consisted of millions of lines of assembly language written by thousands of programmers, and contained thousands upon thousands of bugs, which necessitated a continuous stream of new releases in an attempt to correct them. Each new release fixed some bugs and introduced new ones, so the number of bugs probably remained constant in time.

One of the designers of OS/360, Fred Brooks, subsequently wrote a witty and incisive book (Brooks, 1996) describing his experiences with OS/360. While it would be impossible to summarize the book here, suffice it to say that the cover shows a herd of prehistoric beasts stuck in a tar pit. The cover of Silberschatz et al. (2000) makes a similar point about operating systems being dinosaurs.

Despite its enormous size and problems, OS/360 and the similar third-generation operating systems produced by other computer manufacturers actually satisfied most of their customers reasonably well. They also popularized several key techniques absent in second-generation operating systems. Probably the most important of these was **multiprogramming**. On the 7094, when the current job paused to wait for a tape or other I/O operation to complete, the CPU simply sat idle until the I/O finished. With heavily CPU-bound scientific calculations, I/O is infrequent, so this wasted time is not significant. With commercial data processing, the I/O wait time can often be 80 or 90 percent of the total time, so something had to be done to avoid having the (expensive) CPU be idle so much.

The solution that evolved was to partition memory into several pieces, with a different job in each partition, as shown in Fig. 1-4. While one job was waiting for I/O to complete, another job could be using the CPU. If enough jobs could be held in main memory at once, the CPU could be kept busy nearly 100 percent of the time. Having multiple jobs safely in memory at once requires special hardware to protect each job against snooping and mischief by the other ones, but the 360 and other third-generation systems were equipped with this hardware.

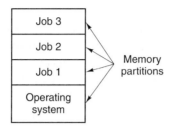

Figure 1-4. A multiprogramming system with three jobs in memory.

Another major feature present in third-generation operating systems was the ability to read jobs from cards onto the disk as soon as they were brought to the computer room. Then, whenever a running job finished, the operating system could load a new job from the disk into the now-empty partition and run it. This technique is called **spooling** (from Simultaneous Peripheral Operation On Line) and was also used for output. With spooling, the 1401s were no longer needed, and much carrying of tapes disappeared.

Although third-generation operating systems were well suited for big scientific calculations and massive commercial data processing runs, they were still basically batch systems. Many programmers pined for the first-generation days when they had the machine all to themselves for a few hours, so they could debug their programs quickly. With third-generation systems, the time between submitting a job and getting back the output was often several hours, so a single misplaced comma could cause a compilation to fail, and the programmer to waste half a day.

This desire for quick response time paved the way for **timesharing**, a variant of multiprogramming, in which each user has an online terminal. In a timesharing system, if 20 users are logged in and 17 of them are thinking or talking or drinking coffee, the CPU can be allocated in turn to the three jobs that want service. Since people debugging programs usually issue short commands (e.g., compile a five-page procedure†) rather than long ones (e.g., sort a million-record file), the computer can provide fast, interactive service to a number of users and perhaps also work on big batch jobs in the background when the CPU is otherwise idle. The first serious timesharing system, **CTSS** (**Compatible Time Sharing System**), was developed at M.I.T. on a specially modified 7094 (Corbató et al., 1962). However, timesharing did not really become popular until the necessary protection hardware became widespread during the third generation.

---

†We will use the terms "procedure," "subroutine," and "function" interchangeably in this book.

After the success of the CTSS system, MIT, Bell Labs, and General Electric (then a major computer manufacturer) decided to embark on the development of a "computer utility," a machine that would support hundreds of simultaneous timesharing users. Their model was the electricity distribution system—when you need electric power, you just stick a plug in the wall, and within reason, as much power as you need will be there. The designers of this system, known as **MULTICS** (**MULTiplexed Information and Computing Service**), envisioned one huge machine providing computing power for everyone in the Boston area. The idea that machines far more powerful than their GE-645 mainframe would be sold for a thousand dollars by the millions only 30 years later was pure science fiction. Sort of like the idea of supersonic trans-Atlantic undersea trains now.

MULTICS was a mixed success. It was designed to support hundreds of users on a machine only slightly more powerful than an Intel 386-based PC, although it had much more I/O capacity. This is not quite as crazy as it sounds, since people knew how to write small, efficient programs in those days, a skill that has subsequently been lost. There were many reasons that MULTICS did not take over the world, not the least of which is that it was written in PL/I, and the PL/I compiler was years late and barely worked at all when it finally arrived. In addition, MULTICS was enormously ambitious for its time, much like Charles Babbage's analytical engine in the nineteenth century.

To make a long story short, MULTICS introduced many seminal ideas into the computer literature, but turning it into a serious product and a major commercial success was a lot harder than anyone had expected. Bell Labs dropped out of the project, and General Electric quit the computer business altogether. However, M.I.T. persisted and eventually got MULTICS working. It was ultimately sold as a commercial product by the company that bought GE's computer business (Honeywell) and installed by about 80 major companies and universities worldwide. While their numbers were small, MULTICS users were fiercely loyal. General Motors, Ford, and the U.S. National Security Agency, for example, only shut down their MULTICS systems in the late 1990s, 30 years after MULTICS was released.

For the moment, the concept of a computer utility has fizzled out but it may well come back in the form of massive centralized Internet servers to which relatively dumb user machines are attached, with most of the work happening on the big servers. The motivation here is likely to be that most people do not want to administrate an increasingly complex and finicky computer system and would prefer to have that work done by a team of professionals working for the company running the server. E-commerce is already evolving in this direction, with various companies running e-malls on multiprocessor servers to which simple client machines connect, very much in the spirit of the MULTICS design.

Despite its lack of commercial success, MULTICS had a huge influence on subsequent operating systems.It is described in (Corbató et al., 1972; Corbató and Vyssotsky, 1965; Daley and Dennis, 1968; Organick, 1972; and Saltzer, 1974). It also has a still-active Web site, *www.multicians.org*, with a great deal of information about the system, its designers, and its users.

Another major development during the third generation was the phenomenal growth of minicomputers, starting with the DEC PDP-1 in 1961. The PDP-1 had only 4K of 18-bit words, but at $120,000 per machine (less than 5 percent of the price of a 7094), it sold like hotcakes. For certain kinds of nonnumerical work, it was almost as fast as the 7094 and gave birth to a whole new industry. It was quickly followed by a series of other PDPs (unlike IBM's family, all incompatible) culminating in the PDP-11.

One of the computer scientists at Bell Labs who had worked on the MULTICS project, Ken Thompson, subsequently found a small PDP-7 minicomputer that no one was using and set out to write a stripped-down, one-user version of MULTICS. This work later developed into the **UNIX**® operating system, which became popular in the academic world, with government agencies, and with many companies.

The history of UNIX has been told elsewhere (e.g., Salus, 1994). Part of that story will be given in Chap. 10. For now, suffice it to say, that because the source code was widely available, various organizations developed their own (incompatible) versions, which led to chaos. Two major versions developed, **System V**, from AT&T, and **BSD**, (Berkeley Software Distribution) from the University of California at Berkeley. These had minor variants as well. To make it possible to write programs that could run on any UNIX system, IEEE developed a standard for UNIX, called **POSIX**, that most versions of UNIX now support. POSIX defines a minimal system call interface that conformant UNIX systems must support. In fact, some other operating systems now also support the POSIX interface.

As an aside, it is worth mentioning that in 1987, the author released a small clone of UNIX, called **MINIX,** for educational purposes. Functionally, MINIX is very similar to UNIX, including POSIX support. A book describing its internal operation and listing the source code in an appendix is also available (Tanenbaum and Woodhull, 1997). MINIX is available for free (including all the source code) over the Internet at URL *www.cs.vu.nl/~ast/minix.html*.

The desire for a free production (as opposed to educational) version of MINIX led a Finnish student, Linus Torvalds, to write **Linux**. This system was developed on MINIX and originally supported various MINIX features (e.g., the MINIX file system). It has since been extended in many ways but still retains a large amount of underlying structure common to MINIX, and to UNIX (upon which the former was based). Most of what will be said about UNIX in this book thus applies to System V, BSD, MINIX, Linux, and other versions and clones of UNIX as well.

1.2.4 The Fourth Generation (1980–Present) Personal Computers

With the development of LSI (Large Scale Integration) circuits, chips containing thousands of transistors on a square centimeter of silicon, the age of the personal computer dawned. In terms of architecture, personal computers (initially called **microcomputers**) were not all that different from minicomputers of the PDP-11 class, but in terms of price they certainly were different. Where the minicomputer made it possible for a department in a company or university to have its own computer, the microprocessor chip made it possible for a single individual to have his or her own personal computer.

In 1974, when Intel came out with the 8080, the first general-purpose 8-bit CPU, it wanted an operating system for the 8080, in part to be able to test it. Intel asked one of its consultants, Gary Kildall, to write one. Kildall and a friend first built a controller for the newly-released Shugart Associates 8-inch floppy disk and hooked the floppy disk up to the 8080, thus producing the first microcomputer with a disk. Kildall then wrote a disk-based operating system called **CP/M (Control Program for Microcomputers**) for it. Since Intel did not think that disk-based microcomputers had much of a future, when Kildall asked for the rights to CP/M, Intel granted his request. Kildall then formed a company, Digital Research, to further develop and sell CP/M.

In 1977, Digital Research rewrote CP/M to make it suitable for running on the many microcomputers using the 8080, Zilog Z80, and other CPU chips. Many application programs were written to run on CP/M, allowing it to completely dominate the world of microcomputing for about 5 years.

In the early 1980s, IBM designed the IBM PC and looked around for software to run on it. People from IBM contacted Bill Gates to license his BASIC interpreter. They also asked him if he knew of an operating system to run on the PC. Gates suggested that IBM contact Digital Research, then the world's dominant operating systems company. Making what was surely the worst business decision in recorded history, Kildall refused to meet with IBM, sending a subordinate instead. To make matters worse, his lawyer even refused to sign IBM's nondisclosure agreement covering the not-yet-announced PC. Consequently, IBM went back to Gates asking if he could provide them with an operating system.

When IBM came back, Gates realized that a local computer manufacturer, Seattle Computer Products, had a suitable operating system, **DOS (Disk Operating System**). He approached them and asked to buy it (allegedly for $50,000), which they readily accepted. Gates then offered IBM a DOS/BASIC package, which IBM accepted. IBM wanted certain modifications, so Gates hired the person who wrote DOS, Tim Paterson, as an employee of Gates' fledgling company, Microsoft, to make them. The revised system was renamed **MS-DOS (MicroSoft Disk Operating System**) and quickly came to dominate the IBM PC market. A key factor here was Gates' (in retrospect, extremely wise) decision to sell MS-DOS to computer companies for bundling with their hardware, compared to Kildall's attempt to sell CP/M to end users one at a time (at least initially).

By the time the IBM PC/AT came out in 1983 with the Intel 80286 CPU, MS-DOS was firmly entrenched and CP/M was on its last legs. MS-DOS was later widely used on the 80386 and 80486. Although the initial version of MS-DOS was fairly primitive, subsequent versions included more advanced features, including many taken from UNIX. (Microsoft was well aware of UNIX, even selling a microcomputer version of it called XENIX during the company's early years.)

CP/M, MS-DOS, and other operating systems for early microcomputers were all based on users typing in commands from the keyboard. That eventually changed due to research done by Doug Engelbart at Stanford Research Institute in the 1960s. Engelbart invented the **GUI** (**Graphical User Interface**), pronounced "gooey," complete with windows, icons, menus, and mouse. These ideas were adopted by researchers at Xerox PARC and incorporated into machines they built.

One day, Steve Jobs, who co-invented the Apple computer in his garage, visited PARC, saw a GUI, and instantly realized its potential value, something Xerox management famously did not (Smith and Alexander, 1988). Jobs then embarked on building an Apple with a GUI. This project led to the Lisa, which was too expensive and failed commercially. Jobs' second attempt, the Apple Macintosh, was a huge success, not only because it was much cheaper than the Lisa, but also because it was **user friendly**, meaning that it was intended for users who not only knew nothing about computers but furthermore had absolutely no intention whatsoever of learning.

When Microsoft decided to build a successor to MS-DOS, it was strongly influenced by the success of the Macintosh. It produced a GUI-based system called Windows, which originally ran on top of MS-DOS (i.e., it was more like a shell than a true operating system). For about 10 years, from 1985 to 1995, Windows was just a graphical environment on top of MS-DOS. However, starting in 1995 a freestanding version of Windows, Windows 95, was released that incorporated many operating system features into it, using the underlying MS-DOS system only for booting and running old MS-DOS programs. In 1998, a slightly modified version of this system, called Windows 98 was released. Nevertheless, both Windows 95 and Windows 98 still contain a large amount of 16-bit Intel assembly language.

Another Microsoft operating system is **Windows NT** (NT stands for New Technology), which is compatible with Windows 95 at a certain level, but a complete rewrite from scratch internally. It is a full 32-bit system. The lead designer for Windows NT was David Cutler, who was also one of the designers of the VAX VMS operating system, so some ideas from VMS are present in NT. Microsoft expected that the first version of NT would kill off MS-DOS and all other versions of Windows since it was a vastly superior system, but it fizzled. Only with Windows NT 4.0 did it finally catch on in a big way, especially on corporate networks. Version 5 of Windows NT was renamed Windows 2000 in early 1999. It was intended to be the successor to both Windows 98 and Windows NT 4.0. That did not quite work out either, so Microsoft came out with yet another version of Windows 98 called **Windows Me** (**Millennium edition**).

The other major contender in the personal computer world is UNIX (and its various derivatives). UNIX is strongest on workstations and other high-end computers, such as network servers. It is especially popular on machines powered by high-performance RISC chips. On Pentium-based computers, Linux is becoming a popular alternative to Windows for students and increasingly many corporate users. (As an aside, throughout this book we will use the term "Pentium" to mean the Pentium I, II, III, and 4.)

Although many UNIX users, especially experienced programmers, prefer a command-based interface to a GUI, nearly all UNIX systems support a windowing system called the **X Windows** system produced at M.I.T. This system handles the basic window management, allowing users to create, delete, move, and resize windows using a mouse. Often a complete GUI, such as **Motif**, is available to run on top of the X Windows system giving UNIX a look and feel something like the Macintosh or Microsoft Windows, for those UNIX users who want such a thing.

An interesting development that began taking place during the mid-1980s is the growth of networks of personal computers running **network operating systems** and **distributed operating systems** (Tanenbaum and Van Steen, 2002). In a network operating system, the users are aware of the existence of multiple computers and can log in to remote machines and copy files from one machine to another. Each machine runs its own local operating system and has its own local user (or users).

Network operating systems are not fundamentally different from single-processor operating systems. They obviously need a network interface controller and some low-level software to drive it, as well as programs to achieve remote login and remote file access, but these additions do not change the essential structure of the operating system.

A distributed operating system, in contrast, is one that appears to its users as a traditional uniprocessor system, even though it is actually composed of multiple processors. The users should not be aware of where their programs are being run or where their files are located; that should all be handled automatically and efficiently by the operating system.

True distributed operating systems require more than just adding a little code to a uniprocessor operating system, because distributed and centralized systems differ in critical ways. Distributed systems, for example, often allow applications to run on several processors at the same time, thus requiring more complex processor scheduling algorithms in order to optimize the amount of parallelism.

Communication delays within the network often mean that these (and other) algorithms must run with incomplete, outdated, or even incorrect information. This situation is radically different from a single-processor system in which the operating system has complete information about the system state.

1.2.5 Ontogeny Recapitulates Phylogeny

After Charles Darwin's book *The Origin of the Species* was published, the German zoologist Ernst Haeckel stated that "Ontogeny Recapitulates Phylogeny." By this he meant that the development of an embryo (ontogeny) repeats (i.e., recapitulates) the evolution of the species (phylogeny). In other words, after fertilization, a human egg goes through stages of being a fish, a pig, and so on before turning into a human baby. Modern biologists regard this as a gross simplification, but it still has a kernel of truth in it.

Something analogous has happened in the computer industry. Each new species (mainframe, minicomputer, personal computer, embedded computer, smart card, etc.) seems to go through the development that its ancestors did. The first mainframes were programmed entirely in assembly language. Even complex programs, like compilers and operating systems, were written in assembler. By the time minicomputers appeared on the scene, FORTRAN, COBOL, and other high-level languages were common on mainframes, but the new minicomputers were nevertheless programmed in assembler (for lack of memory). When microcomputers (early personal computers) were invented, they, too, were programmed in assembler, even though by then minicomputers were also programmed in high-level languages. Palmtop computers also started with assembly code but quickly moved on to high-level languages (mostly because the development work was done on bigger machines). The same is true for smart cards.

Now let us look at operating systems. The first mainframes initially had no protection hardware and no support for multiprogramming, so they ran simple operating systems that handled one manually-loaded program at a time. Later they acquired the hardware and operating system support to handle multiple programs at once, and then full timesharing capabilities.

When minicomputers first appeared, they also had no protection hardware and ran one manually-loaded program at a time, even though multiprogramming was well established in the mainframe world by then. Gradually, they acquired protection hardware and the ability to run two or more programs at once. The first microcomputers were also capable of running only one program at a time, but later acquired the ability to multiprogram. Palmtops and smart cards went the same route.

Disks first appeared on large mainframes, then on minicomputers, microcomputers, and so on down the line. Even now, smart cards do not have hard disks, but with the advent of flash ROM, they will soon have the equivalent of it. When disks first appeared, primitive file systems sprung up. On the CDC 6600, easily the most powerful mainframe in the world during much of the 1960s, the file system consisted of users having the ability to create a file and then declare it to be permanent, meaning it stayed on the disk even after the creating program exited. To access such a file later, a program had to attach it with a special command and give its password (supplied when the file was made permanent). In effect, there was a single directory shared by all users. It was up to the users to avoid file name conflicts. Early minicomputer file systems had a single directory shared by all users and so did early microcomputer file systems.

Virtual memory (the ability to run programs larger than the physical memory) had a similar development. It first appeared in mainframes, minicomputers, microcomputers and gradually worked its way down to smaller and smaller systems. Networking had a similar history.

In all cases, the software development was dictated by the technology. The first microcomputers, for example, had something like 4 KB of memory and no protection hardware. High-level languages and multiprogramming were simply too much for such a tiny system to handle. As the microcomputers evolved into modern personal computers, they acquired the necessary hardware and then the necessary software to handle more advanced features. It is likely that this development will continue for years to come. Other fields may also have this wheel of reincarnation, but in the computer industry it seems to spin faster.

1.3 THE OPERATING SYSTEM ZOO

All of this history and development has left us with a wide variety of operating systems, not all of which are widely known. In this section we will briefly touch upon seven of them. We will come back to some of these different kinds of systems later in the book.

1.3.1 Mainframe Operating Systems

At the high end are the operating systems for the mainframes, those room-sized computers still found in major corporate data centers. These computers distinguish themselves from personal computers in terms of their I/O capacity. A mainframe with 1000 disks and thousands of gigabytes of data is not unusual; a personal computer with these specifications would be odd indeed. Mainframes are also making something of a comeback as high-end Web servers, servers for large-scale electronic commerce sites, and servers for business-to-business transactions.

The operating systems for mainframes are heavily oriented toward processing many jobs at once, most of which need prodigious amounts of I/O. They typically offer three kinds of services: batch, transaction processing, and timesharing. A batch system is one that processes routine jobs without any interactive user present. Claims processing in an insurance company or sales reporting for a chain of stores is typically done in batch mode. Transaction processing systems handle large numbers of small requests, for example, check processing at a bank or airline reservations. Each unit of work is small, but the system must handle hundreds or thousands per second. Timesharing systems allow multiple remote users to run jobs on the computer at once, such as querying a big database. These functions are closely related; mainframe operating systems often perform all of them. An example mainframe operating system is OS/390, a descendant of OS/360.

1.3.2 Server Operating Systems

One level down are the server operating systems. They run on servers, which are either very large personal computers, workstations, or even mainframes. They serve multiple users at once over a network and allow the users to share hardware and software resources. Servers can provide print service, file service, or Web service. Internet providers run many server machines to support their customers and Web sites use servers to store the Web pages and handle the incoming requests. Typical server operating systems are UNIX and Windows 2000. Linux is also gaining ground for servers.

1.3.3 Multiprocessor Operating Systems

An increasingly common way to get major-league computing power is to connect multiple CPUs into a single system. Depending on precisely how they are connected and what is shared, these systems are called parallel computers, multicomputers, or multiprocessors. They need special operating systems, but often these are variations on the server operating systems, with special features for communication and connectivity.

1.3.4 Personal Computer Operating Systems

The next category is the personal computer operating system. Their job is to provide a good interface to a single user. They are widely used for word processing, spreadsheets, and Internet access. Common examples are Windows 98, Windows 2000, the Macintosh operating system, and Linux. Personal computer operating systems are so widely known that probably little introduction is needed. In fact, many people are not even aware that other kinds exist.

1.3.5 Real-Time Operating Systems

Another type of operating system is the real-time system. These systems are characterized by having time as a key parameter. For example, in industrial process control systems, real-time computers have to collect data about the production process and use it to control machines in the factory. Often there are hard deadlines that must be met. For example, if a car is moving down an assembly line, certain actions must take place at certain instants of time. If a welding robot welds too early or too late, the car will be ruined. If the action absolutely *must* occur at a certain moment (or within a certain range), we have a **hard real-time system**.

Another kind of real-time system is a **soft real-time system**, in which missing an occasional deadline is acceptable. Digital audio or multimedia systems fall in this category. VxWorks and QNX are well-known real-time operating systems.

1.3.6 Embedded Operating Systems

Continuing on down to smaller and smaller systems, we come to palmtop computers and embedded systems. A palmtop computer or **PDA** (**Personal Digital Assistant**) is a small computer that fits in a shirt pocket and performs a small number of functions such as an electronic address book and memo pad. Embedded systems run on the computers that control devices that are not generally thought of as computers, such as TV sets, microwave ovens, and mobile telephones. These often have some characteristics of real-time systems but also have size, memory, and power restrictions that make them special. Examples of such operating systems are PalmOS and Windows CE (Consumer Electronics).

1.3.7 Smart Card Operating Systems

The smallest operating systems run on smart cards, which are credit card-sized devices containing a CPU chip. They have very severe processing power and memory constraints. Some of them can handle only a single function, such as electronic payments, but others can handle multiple functions on the same smart card. Often these are proprietary systems.

Some smart cards are Java oriented. What this means is that the ROM on the smart card holds an interpreter for the Java Virtual Machine (JVM). Java applets (small programs) are downloaded to the card and are interpreted by the JVM interpreter. Some of these cards can handle multiple Java applets at the same time, leading to multiprogramming and the need to schedule them. Resource management and protection also become an issue when two or more applets are present at the same time. These issues must be handled by the (usually extremely primitive) operating system present on the card.

1.4 COMPUTER HARDWARE REVIEW

An operating system is intimately tied to the hardware of the computer it runs on. It extends the computer's instruction set and manages its resources. To work, it must know a great deal about the hardware, at least, about how the hardware appears to the programmer.

Conceptually, a simple personal computer can be abstracted to a model resembling that of Fig. 1-5. The CPU, memory, and I/O devices are all connected by a system bus and communicate with one another over it. Modern personal computers have a more complicated structure, involving multiple buses, which we will look at later. For the time being, this model will be sufficient. In the following sections, we will briefly review these components and examine some of the hardware issues that are of concern to operating system designers.

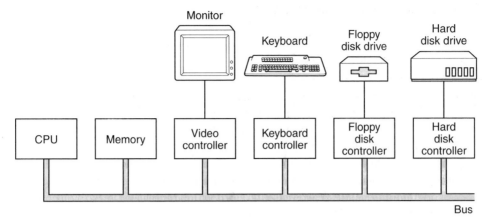

Figure 1-5. Some of the components of a simple personal computer.

1.4.1 Processors

The "brain" of the computer is the CPU. It fetches instructions from memory and executes them. The basic cycle of every CPU is to fetch the first instruction from memory, decode it to determine its type and operands, execute it, and then fetch, decode, and execute subsequent instructions. In this way, programs are carried out.

Each CPU has a specific set of instructions that it can execute. Thus a Pentium cannot execute SPARC programs and a SPARC cannot execute Pentium programs. Because accessing memory to get an instruction or data word takes much longer than executing an instruction, all CPUs contain some registers inside to hold key variables and temporary results. Thus the instruction set generally contains instructions to load a word from memory into a register, and store a word from a register into memory. Other instructions combine two operands from registers, memory, or both into a result, such as adding two words and storing the result in a register or in memory.

In addition to the general registers used to hold variables and temporary results, most computers have several special registers that are visible to the programmer. One of these is the **program counter**, which contains the memory address of the next instruction to be fetched. After that instruction has been fetched, the program counter is updated to point to its successor.

Another register is the **stack pointer**, which points to the top of the current stack in memory. The stack contains one frame for each procedure that has been entered but not yet exited. A procedure's stack frame holds those input parameters, local variables, and temporary variables that are not kept in registers.

Yet another register is the **PSW** (**Program Status Word**). This register contains the condition code bits, which are set by comparison instructions, the CPU priority, the mode (user or kernel), and various other control bits. User programs may normally read the entire PSW but typically may write only some of its fields. The PSW plays an important role in system calls and I/O.

The operating system must be aware of all the registers. When time multiplexing the CPU, the operating system will often stop the running program to (re)start another one. Every time it stops a running program, the operating system must save all the registers so they can be restored when the program runs later.

To improve performance, CPU designers have long abandoned the simple model of fetching, decoding, and executing one instruction at a time. Many modern CPUs have facilities for executing more than one instruction at the same time. For example, a CPU might have separate fetch, decode, and execute units, so that while it was executing instruction n, it could also be decoding instruction $n + 1$ and fetching instruction $n + 2$. Such an organization is called a **pipeline** and is illustrated in Fig. 1-6(a) for a pipeline with three stages. Longer pipelines are common. In most pipeline designs, once an instruction has been fetched into the pipeline, it must be executed, even if the preceding instruction was a conditional branch that was taken. Pipelines cause compiler writers and operating system writers great headaches because they expose the complexities of the underlying machine to them.

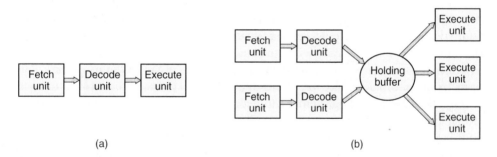

(a)　　　　　　　　　　　　　　　　　　　　(b)

Figure 1-6. (a) A three-stage pipeline. (b) A superscalar CPU.

Even more advanced than a pipeline design is a **superscalar** CPU, shown in Fig. 1-6(b). In this design, multiple execution units are present, for example, one for integer arithmetic, one for floating-point arithmetic, and one for Boolean operations. Two or more instructions are fetched at once, decoded, and dumped into a holding buffer until they can be executed. As soon as an execution unit is free, it looks in the holding buffer to see if there is an instruction it can handle, and if so, it removes the instruction from the buffer and executes it. An implication of this design is that program instructions are often executed out of order. For the most part, it is up to the hardware to make sure the result produced is the same one a sequential implementation would have produced, but an annoying amount of the complexity is foisted onto the operating system, as we shall see.

Most CPUs, except very simple ones used in embedded systems, have two modes, kernel mode and user mode, as mentioned earlier. Usually a bit in the

PSW controls the mode. When running in kernel mode, the CPU can execute every instruction in its instruction set and use every feature of the hardware. The operating system runs in kernel mode, giving it access to the complete hardware.

In contrast, user programs run in user mode, which permits only a subset of the instructions to be executed and a subset of the features to be accessed. Generally, all instructions involving I/O and memory protection are disallowed in user mode. Setting the PSW mode bit to kernel mode is also forbidden, of course.

To obtain services from the operating system, a user program must make a **system call**, which traps into the kernel and invokes the operating system. The TRAP instruction switches from user mode to kernel mode and starts the operating system. When the work has been completed, control is returned to the user program at the instruction following the system call. We will explain the details of the system call process later in this chapter. As a note on typography, we will use the lower case Helvetica font to indicate system calls in running text, like this: read.

It is worth noting that computers have traps other than the instruction for executing a system call. Most of the other traps are caused by the hardware to warn of an exceptional situation such as an attempt to divide by 0 or a floating-point underflow. In all cases the operating system gets control and must decide what to do. Sometimes the program must be terminated with an error. Other times the error can be ignored (an underflowed number can be set to 0). Finally, when the program has announced in advance that it wants to handle certain kinds of conditions, control can be passed back to the program to let it deal with the problem.

1.4.2 Memory

The second major component in any computer is the memory. Ideally, a memory should be extremely fast (faster than executing an instruction so the CPU is not held up by the memory), abundantly large, and dirt cheap. No current technology satisfies all of these goals, so a different approach is taken. The memory system is constructed as a hierarchy of layers, as shown in Fig. 1-7.

The top layer consists of the registers internal to the CPU. They are made of the same material as the CPU and are thus just as fast as the CPU. Consequently, there is no delay in accessing them. The storage capacity available in them is typically 32×32-bits on a 32-bit CPU and 64×64-bits on a 64-bit CPU. Less than 1 KB in both cases. Programs must manage the registers (i.e., decide what to keep in them) themselves, in software.

Next comes the cache memory, which is mostly controlled by the hardware. Main memory is divided up into **cache lines**, typically 64 bytes, with addresses 0 to 63 in cache line 0, addresses 64 to 127 in cache line 1, and so on. The most heavily used cache lines are kept in a high-speed cache located inside or very close to the CPU. When the program needs to read a memory word, the cache hardware checks to see if the line needed is in the cache. If it is, called a **cache**

Typical access time

Typical capacity

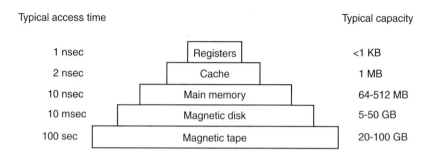

1 nsec	<1 KB
2 nsec	1 MB
10 nsec	64-512 MB
10 msec	5-50 GB
100 sec	20-100 GB

Figure 1-7. A typical memory hierarchy. The numbers are very rough approximations.

hit, the request is satisfied from the cache and no memory request is sent over the bus to the main memory. Cache hits normally take about two clock cycles. Cache misses have to go to memory, with a substantial time penalty. Cache memory is limited in size due to its high cost. Some machines have two or even three levels of cache, each one slower and bigger than the one before it.

Main memory comes next. This is the workhorse of the memory system. Main memory is often called **RAM** (**Random Access Memory**). Old timers sometimes call it **core memory**, because computers in the 1950s and 1960s used tiny magnetizable ferrite cores for main memory. Currently, memories are tens to hundreds of megabytes and growing rapidly. All CPU requests that cannot be satisfied out of the cache go to main memory.

Next in the hierarchy is magnetic disk (hard disk). Disk storage is two orders of magnitude cheaper than RAM per bit and often two orders of magnitude larger as well. The only problem is that the time to randomly access data on it is close to three orders of magnitude slower. This low speed is due to the fact that a disk is a mechanical device, as shown in Fig. 1-8.

A disk consists of one or more metal platters that rotate at 5400, 7200, or 10,800 rpm A mechanical arm pivots over the platters from the corner, similar to the pickup arm on an old 33 rpm phonograph for playing vinyl records. Information is written onto the disk in a series of concentric circles. At any given arm position, each of the heads can read an annular region called a **track**. Together, all the tracks for a given arm position form a **cylinder**.

Each track is divided into some number of sectors, typically 512 bytes per sector. On modern disks, the outer cylinders contain more sectors than the inner ones. Moving the arm from one cylinder to the next one takes about 1 msec. Moving it to a random cylinder typically takes 5 msec to 10 msec, depending on the drive. Once the arm is on the correct track, the drive must wait for the needed sector to rotate under the head, an additional delay of 5 msec to 10 msec, depending on the drive's rpm. Once the sector is under the head, reading or writing occurs at a rate of 5 MB/sec on low-end disks to 160 MB/sec on faster ones.

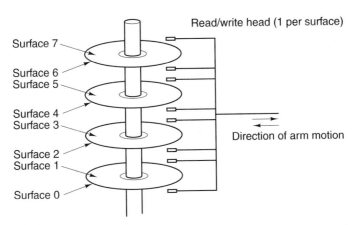

Surface 7

Surface 6
Surface 5

Surface 4
Surface 3

Surface 2
Surface 1

Surface 0

Read/write head (1 per surface)

Direction of arm motion

Figure 1-8. Structure of a disk drive.

The final layer in the memory hierarchy is magnetic tape. This medium is often used as a backup for disk storage and for holding very large data sets. To access a tape, it must first be put into a tape reader, either by a person or a robot (automated tape handling is common at installations with huge databases). Then the tape may have to be spooled forwarded to get to the requested block. All in all, this could take minutes. The big plus of tape is that it is exceedingly cheap per bit and removable, which is important for backup tapes that must be stored off-site in order to survive fires, floods, earthquakes, etc.

The memory hierarchy we have discussed is typical, but some installations do not have all the layers or have a few different ones (such as optical disk). Still, in all of them, as one goes down the hierarchy, the random access time increases dramatically, the capacity increases equally dramatically, and the cost per bit drops enormously. Consequently, it is likely that memory hierarchies will be around for years to come.

In addition to the kinds of memory discussed above, many computers have a small amount of nonvolatile random access memory. Unlike RAM, nonvolatile memory does not lose its contents when the power is switched off. **ROM (Read Only Memory)** is programmed at the factory and cannot be changed afterward. It is fast and inexpensive. On some computers, the bootstrap loader used to start the computer is contained in ROM. Also, some I/O cards come with ROM for handling low-level device control.

EEPROM (Electrically Erasable ROM) and **flash RAM** are also nonvolatile, but in contrast to ROM can be erased and rewritten. However, writing them takes orders of magnitude more time than writing RAM, so they are used in the same way ROM is, only with the additional feature that it is now possible to correct bugs in programs they hold by rewriting them in the field.

Yet another kind of memory is CMOS, which is volatile. Many computers use CMOS memory to hold the current time and date. The CMOS memory and the clock circuit that increments the time in it are powered by a small battery, so the time is correctly updated, even when the computer is unplugged. The CMOS memory can also hold the configuration parameters, such as which disk to boot from. CMOS is used because it draws so little power that the original factory-installed battery often lasts for several years. However, when it begins to fail, the computer can appear to have Alzheimer's disease, forgetting things that it has known for years, like which hard disk to boot from.

Let us now focus on main memory for a little while. It is often desirable to hold multiple programs in memory at once. If one program is blocked waiting for a disk read to complete, another program can use the CPU, giving a better CPU utilization. However, with two or more programs in main memory at once, two problems must be solved:

1. How to protect the programs from one another and the kernel from them all.

2. How to handle relocation.

Many solutions are possible. However, all of them involve equipping the CPU with special hardware.

The first problem is obvious, but the second one is a bit more subtle. When a program is compiled and linked, the compiler and linker do not know where in physical memory it will be loaded when it is executed. For this reason, they usually assume it will start at address 0, and just put the first instruction there. Suppose that the first instruction fetches a word from memory address 10,000. Now suppose that the entire program and data are loaded starting at address 50,000. When the first instruction executes, it will fail because it will reference the word at 10,000, instead of the word at 60,000. To solve this problem, we need to either relocate the program at load time, finding all the addresses and modifying them (which is doable, but expensive), or have relocation done on-the-fly during execution.

The simplest solution is shown in Fig. 1-9(a). In this figure we see a computer equipped with two special registers, the **base register** and the **limit register**. (Please note that in this book, numbers beginning with 0x are in hexadecimal—the C language convention. Similarly, numbers beginning with a leading zero are in octal.) When a program is run, the base register is set to point to the start of its program text and the limit register tells how large the combined program text and data are. When an instruction is to be fetched, the hardware checks to see if the program counter is less than the limit register, and if it is, adds it to the base register and sends the sum to memory. Similarly, when the program wants to fetch a data word (e.g., from address 10,000), the hardware automatically adds the contents of the base register (e.g., 50,000) to that address and sends the sum (60,000) to the memory. The base register makes it impossible for a program to reference any part of memory below itself. Furthermore, the limit register makes it impossible to reference any part of memory above itself. Thus this scheme solves both the protection and the relocation problem at the cost of two new registers and a slight increase in cycle time (to perform the limit check and addition).

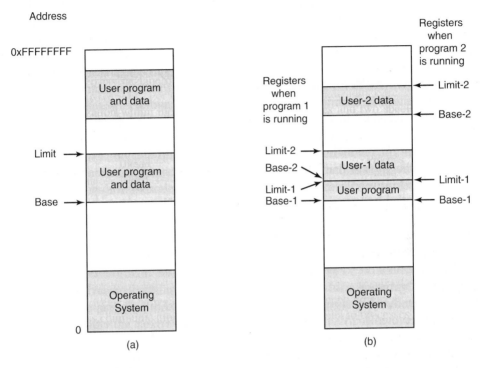

Figure 1-9. (a) Use of one base-limit pair. The program can access memory between the base and the limit. (b) Use of two base-limit pairs. The program code is between Base-1 and Limit-1 whereas the data are between Base-2 and Limit-2.

The check and mapping result in converting an address generated by the program, called a **virtual address**, into an address used by the memory, called a **physical address**. The device that performs the check and mapping is called the **MMU (Memory Management Unit)**. It is located on the CPU chip or close to it, but is logically between the CPU and the memory.

A more sophisticated MMU is illustrated in Fig. 1-9(b). Here we have an MMU with two pairs of base and limit registers, one for the program text and one for the data. The program counter and all other references to the program text use pair 1 and data references use pair 2. As a consequence, it is now possible to have multiple users share the same program with only one copy of it in memory, something not possible with the first scheme. When program 1 is running, the four registers are set as indicated by the arrows to the left of Fig. 1-9(b). When program 2 is running, they are set as indicated by the arrows to the right of the figure. Much more sophisticated MMUs exist. We will study some of them later in this book. The thing to note here is that managing the MMU must be an operating system function, since users cannot be trusted to do it correctly.

Two aspects of the memory system have a major effect on performance. First, caches hide the relatively slow speed of memory. When a program has been running for a while, the cache is full of that program's cache lines, giving good performance. However, when the operating system switches from one program to another, the cache remains full of the first program's cache lines. The ones needed by the new program must be loaded one at a time from physical memory. This operation can be a major performance hit if it happens too often.

Second, when switching from one program to another, the MMU registers have to be changed. In Fig. 1-9(b), only four registers have to be reset, which is not a problem, but in real MMUs, many more registers have to be reloaded, either explicitly or dynamically, as needed. Either way, it takes time. The moral of the story is that switching from one program to another, called a **context switch**, is an expensive business.

1.4.3 I/O Devices

Memory is not the only resource that the operating system must manage. I/O devices also interact heavily with the operating system. As we saw in Fig. 1-5, I/O devices generally consist of two parts: a controller and the device itself. The controller is a chip or a set of chips on a plug-in board that physically controls the device. It accepts commands from the operating system, for example, to read data from the device, and carries them out.

In many cases, the actual control of the device is very complicated and detailed, so it is the job of the controller to present a simpler interface to the operating system. For example, a disk controller might accept a command to read sector 11,206 from disk 2. The controller then has to convert this linear sector number to a cylinder, sector, and head. This conversion may be complicated by the fact that outer cylinders have more sectors than inner ones and that some bad sectors have been remapped onto other ones. Then the controller has to determine which cylinder the disk arm is on and give it a sequence of pulses to move in or out the requisite number of cylinders. It has to wait until the proper sector has rotated under the head and then start reading and storing the bits as they come off the drive, removing the preamble and computing the checksum. Finally, it has to assemble the incoming bits into words and store them in memory. To do all this work, controllers often contain small embedded computers that are programmed to do their work.

The other piece is the actual device itself. Devices have fairly simple interfaces, both because they cannot do much and to make them standard. The latter is needed so that any IDE disk controller can handle any IDE disk, for example. **IDE** stands for **Integrated Drive Electronics** and is the standard type of disk on Pentiums and some other computers. Since the actual device interface is hidden behind the controller, all that the operating system sees is the interface to the controller, which may be quite different from the interface to the device.

Because each type of controller is different, different software is needed to control each one. The software that talks to a controller, giving it commands and accepting responses, is called a **device driver**. Each controller manufacturer has to supply a driver for each operating system it supports. Thus a scanner may come with drivers for Windows 98, Windows 2000, and UNIX, for example.

To be used, the driver has to be put into the operating system so it can run in kernel mode. Theoretically, drivers can run outside the kernel, but few current systems support this possibility because it requires the ability to allow a user-space driver to be able to access the device in a controlled way, a feature rarely supported. There are three ways the driver can be put into the kernel. The first way is to relink the kernel with the new driver and then reboot the system. Many UNIX systems work like this. The second way is to make an entry in an operating system file telling it that it needs the driver and then reboot the system. At boot time, the operating system goes and finds the drivers it needs and loads them. Windows works this way. The third way is for the operating system to be able to accept new drivers while running and install them on-the-fly without the need to reboot. This way used to be rare but is becoming much more common now. Hot pluggable devices, such as USB and IEEE 1394 devices (discussed below) always need dynamically loaded drivers.

Every controller has a small number of registers that are used to communicate with it. For example, a minimal disk controller might have registers for specifying the disk address, memory address, sector count, and direction (read or write). To activate the controller, the driver gets a command from the operating system, then translates it into the appropriate values to write into the device registers.

On some computers, the device registers are mapped into the operating system's address space, so they can be read and written like ordinary memory words. On such computers, no special I/O instructions are needed and user programs can be kept away from the hardware by not putting these memory addresses within their reach (e.g., by using base and limit registers). On other computers, the device registers are put in a special I/O port space, with each register having a port address. On these machines, special IN and OUT instructions are available in kernel mode to allow drivers to read and write the registers. The former scheme eliminates the need for special I/O instructions but uses up some of the address space. The latter uses no address space but requires special instructions. Both systems are widely used.

Input and output can be done in three different ways. In the simplest method, a user program issues a system call, which the kernel then translates into a procedure call to the appropriate driver. The driver then starts the I/O and sits in a tight loop continuously polling the device to see if it is done (usually there is some bit that indicates that the device is still busy). When the I/O has completed, the driver puts the data where they are needed (if any), and returns. The operating system then returns control to the caller. This method is called **busy waiting** and has the disadvantage of tying up the CPU polling the device until it is finished.

The second method is for the driver to start the device and ask it to give an interrupt when it is finished. At that point the driver returns. The operating system then blocks the caller if need be and looks for other work to do. When the controller detects the end of the transfer, it generates an **interrupt** to signal completion.

Interrupts are very important in operating systems, so let us examine the idea more closely. In Fig. 1-10(a) we see a three-step process for I/O. In step 1, the driver tells the controller what to do by writing into its device registers. The controller then starts the device. When the controller has finished reading or writing the number of bytes it has been told to transfer, it signals the interrupt controller chip using certain bus lines in step 2. If the interrupt controller is prepared to accept the interrupt (which it may not be if it is busy with a higher priority one), it asserts a pin on the CPU chip informing it, in step 3. In step 4, the interrupt controller puts the number of the device on the bus so the CPU can read it and know which device has just finished (many devices may be running at the same time).

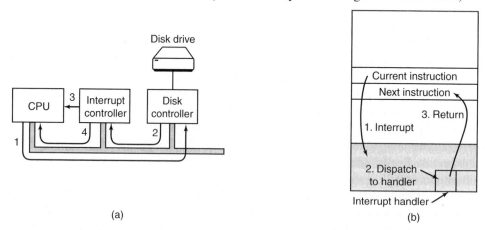

(a)   (b)

Figure 1-10. (a) The steps in starting an I/O device and getting an interrupt. (b) Interrupt processing involves taking the interrupt, running the interrupt handler, and returning to the user program.

Once the CPU has decided to take the interrupt, the program counter and PSW are typically then pushed onto the current stack and the CPU switched into kernel mode. The device number may be used as an index into part of memory to find the address of the interrupt handler for this device. This part of memory is called the **interrupt vector**. Once the interrupt handler (part of the driver for the interrupting device) has started, it removes the stacked program counter and PSW and saves them, then queries the device to learn its status. When the handler is all finished, it returns to the previously-running user program to the first instruction that was not yet executed. These steps are shown in Fig. 1-10(b).

The third method for doing I/O makes use of a special **DMA** (**Direct Memory Access**) chip that can control the flow of bits between memory and some controller without constant CPU intervention. The CPU sets up the DMA chip, telling it how many bytes to transfer, the device and memory addresses involved, and the direction, and lets it go. When the DMA chip is done, it causes an interrupt, which is handled as described above. DMA and I/O hardware in general will be discussed in more detail in Chap. 5.

Interrupts can often happen at highly inconvenient moments, for example, while another interrupt handler is running. For this reason, the CPU has a way to disable interrupts and then reenable them later. While interrupts are disabled, any devices that finish continue to assert their interrupt signals, but the CPU is not interrupted until interrupts are enabled again. If multiple devices finish while interrupts are disabled, the interrupt controller decides which one to let through first, usually based on static priorities assigned to each device. The highest priority device wins.

1.4.4 Buses

The organization of Fig. 1-5 was used on minicomputers for years and also on the original IBM PC. However, as processors and memories got faster, the ability of a single bus (and certainly the IBM PC bus) to handle all the traffic was strained to the breaking point. Something had to give. As a result, additional buses were added, both for faster I/O devices and for CPU to memory traffic. As a consequence of this evolution, a large Pentium system currently looks something like Fig. 1-11.

This system has eight buses (cache, local, memory, PCI, SCSI, USB, IDE, and ISA), each with a different transfer rate and function. The operating system must be aware of all of them for configuration and management. The two main buses are the original IBM PC **ISA** (**Industry Standard Architecture**) bus and its successor, the **PCI** (**Peripheral Component Interconnect**) bus. The ISA bus, which was originally the IBM PC/AT bus, runs at 8.33 MHz and can transfer 2 bytes at once, for a maximum speed of 16.67 MB/sec. It is included for backward compatibility with old and slow I/O cards. The PCI bus was invented by Intel as a successor to the ISA bus. It can run at 66 MHz and transfer 8 bytes at a time, for a data rate of 528 MB/sec. Most high-speed I/O devices use the PCI bus now. Even some non-Intel computers use the PCI bus due to the large number of I/O cards available for it.

In this configuration, the CPU talks to the PCI bridge chip over the local bus, and the PCI bridge chip talks to the memory over a dedicated memory bus, often running at 100 MHz. Pentium systems have a level-1 cache on chip and a much larger level-2 cache off chip, connected to the CPU by the cache bus.

In addition, this system contains three specialized buses: IDE, USB, and SCSI. The IDE bus is for attaching peripheral devices such as disks and CD-

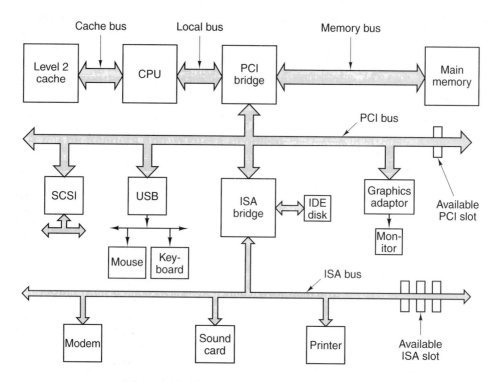

Figure 1-11. The structure of a large Pentium system

ROMs to the system. The IDE bus is an outgrowth of the disk controller interface on the PC/AT and is now standard on nearly all Pentium-based systems for the hard disk and often the CD-ROM.

The **USB** (**Universal Serial Bus**) was invented to attach all the slow I/O devices, such as the keyboard and mouse, to the computer. It uses a small four-wire connector, two of which supply electrical power to the USB devices. USB is a centralized bus in which a root device polls the I/O devices every 1 msec to see if they have any traffic. It can handle an aggregate load of 1.5 MB/sec. All the USB devices share a single USB device driver, making it unnecessary to install a new driver for each new USB device. Consequently, USB devices can be added to the computer without the need to reboot.

The **SCSI** (**Small Computer System Interface**) bus is a high-performance bus intended for fast disks, scanners, and other devices needing considerable bandwidth. It can run at up to 160 MB/sec. It has been present on Macintosh systems since they were invented and is also popular on UNIX and some Intel-based systems.

Yet another bus (not shown in Fig. 1-11) is **IEEE 1394**. Sometimes it is called FireWire, although strictly speaking, FireWire is the name Apple uses for its implementation of 1394. Like USB, IEEE 1394 is bit serial but is designed for packet transfers at speeds up to 50 MB/sec, making it useful for connecting digital camcorders and similar multimedia devices to a computer. Unlike USB, IEEE 1394 does not have a central controller. SCSI and IEEE 1394 face competition from a faster version of USB being developed.

To work in an environment such as that of Fig. 1-11, the operating system has to know what is out there and configure it. This requirement led Intel and Microsoft to design a PC system called **plug and play**, based on a similar concept first implemented in the Apple Macintosh. Before plug and play, each I/O card had a fixed interrupt request level and fixed addresses for its I/O registers. For example, the keyboard was interrupt 1 and used I/O addresses 0x60 to 0x64, the floppy disk controller was interrupt 6 and used I/O addresses 0x3F0 to 0x3F7, and the printer was interrupt 7 and used I/O addresses 0x378 to 0x37A, and so on.

So far, so good. The trouble came when the user bought a sound card and a modem card and both happened to use, say, interrupt 4. They would conflict and would not work together. The solution was to include DIP switches or jumpers on every I/O card and instruct the user to please set them to select an interrupt level and I/O device addresses that did not conflict with any others in the user's system. Teenagers who devoted their lives to the intricacies of the PC hardware could sometimes do this without making errors. Unfortunately, nobody else could, leading to chaos.

What plug and play does is have the system automatically collect information about the I/O devices, centrally assign interrupt levels and I/O addresses, and then tell each card what its numbers are. Very briefly, that works as follows on the Pentium. Every Pentium contains a parentboard (formerly called a motherboard before political correctness hit the computer industry). On the parentboard is a program called the system **BIOS (Basic Input Output System)** The BIOS contains low-level I/O software, including procedures to read the keyboard, write to the screen, and do disk I/O, among other things. Nowadays, it is held in a flash RAM, which is nonvolatile but which can be updated by the operating system when bugs are found in the BIOS.

When the computer is booted, the BIOS is started. It first checks to see how much RAM is installed and whether the keyboard and other basic devices are installed and responding correctly. It starts out by scanning the ISA and PCI buses to detect all the devices attached to them. Some of these devices are typically **legacy** (i.e., designed before plug and play was invented) and have fixed interrupt levels and I/O addresses (possibly set by switches or jumpers on the I/O card, but not modifiable by the operating system). These devices are recorded. The plug and play devices are also recorded. If the devices present are different from when the system was last booted, the new devices are configured.

The BIOS then determines the boot device by trying a list of devices stored in the CMOS memory. The user can change this list by entering a BIOS configuration program just after booting. Typically, an attempt is made to boot from the floppy disk. If that fails the CD-ROM is tried. If neither a floppy nor a CD-ROM is present, the system is booted from the hard disk. The first sector from the boot device is read into memory and executed. This sector contains a program that normally examines the partition table at the end of the boot sector to determine which partition is active. Then a secondary boot loader is read in from that partition. This loader reads in the operating system from the active partition and starts it.

The operating system then queries the BIOS to get the configuration information. For each device, it checks to see if it has the device driver. If not, it asks the user to insert a floppy disk or CD-ROM containing the driver (supplied by the device's manufacturer). Once it has all the device drivers, the operating system loads them into the kernel. Then it initializes its tables, creates whatever background processes are needed, and starts up a login program or GUI on each terminal. At least, this is the way it is supposed to work. In real life, plug and play is frequently so unreliable that many people call it plug and pray.

1.5 OPERATING SYSTEM CONCEPTS

All operating systems have certain basic concepts such as processes, memory, and files that are central to understanding them. In the following sections, we will look at some of these basic concepts ever so briefly, as an introduction. We will come back to each of them in great detail later in this book. To illustrate these concepts we will use examples from time to time, generally drawn from UNIX. Similar examples typically exist in other systems as well, however.

1.5.1 Processes

A key concept in all operating systems is the **process**. A process is basically a program in execution. Associated with each process is its **address space**, a list of memory locations from some minimum (usually 0) to some maximum, which the process can read and write. The address space contains the executable program, the program's data, and its stack. Also associated with each process is some set of registers, including the program counter, stack pointer, and other hardware registers, and all the other information needed to run the program.

We will come back to the process concept in much more detail in Chap. 2, but for the time being, the easiest way to get a good intuitive feel for a process is to think about timesharing systems. Periodically, the operating system decides to stop running one process and start running another, for example, because the first one has had more than its share of CPU time in the past second.

When a process is suspended temporarily like this, it must later be restarted in exactly the same state it had when it was stopped. This means that all information about the process must be explicitly saved somewhere during the suspension. For example, the process may have several files open for reading at once. Associated with each of these files is a pointer giving the current position (i.e., the number of the byte or record to be read next). When a process is temporarily suspended, all these pointers must be saved so that a read call executed after the process is restarted will read the proper data. In many operating systems, all the information about each process, other than the contents of its own address space, is stored in an operating system table called the **process table**, which is an array (or linked list) of structures, one for each process currently in existence.

Thus, a (suspended) process consists of its address space, usually called the **core image** (in honor of the magnetic core memories used in days of yore), and its process table entry, which contains its registers, among other things.

The key process management system calls are those dealing with the creation and termination of processes. Consider a typical example. A process called the **command interpreter** or **shell** reads commands from a terminal. The user has just typed a command requesting that a program be compiled. The shell must now create a new process that will run the compiler. When that process has finished the compilation, it executes a system call to terminate itself.

If a process can create one or more other processes (referred to as **child processes**) and these processes in turn can create child processes, we quickly arrive at the process tree structure of Fig. 1-12. Related processes that are cooperating to get some job done often need to communicate with one another and synchronize their activities. This communication is called **interprocess communication**, and will be addressed in detail in Chap. 2.

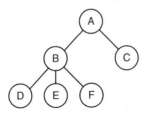

Figure 1-12. A process tree. Process *A* created two child processes, *B* and *C*. Process *B* created three child processes, *D*, *E*, and *F*.

Other process system calls are available to request more memory (or release unused memory), wait for a child process to terminate, and overlay its program with a different one.

Occasionally, there is a need to convey information to a running process that is not sitting around waiting for this information. For example, a process that is communicating with another process on a different computer does so by sending messages to the remote process over a computer network. To guard against the possibility that a message or its reply is lost, the sender may request that its own operating system notify it after a specified number of seconds, so that it can retransmit the message if no acknowledgement has been received yet. After setting this timer, the program may continue doing other work.

When the specified number of seconds has elapsed, the operating system sends an **alarm signal** to the process. The signal causes the process to temporarily suspend whatever it was doing, save its registers on the stack, and start running a special signal handling procedure, for example, to retransmit a presumably lost message. When the signal handler is done, the running process is restarted in the state it was in just before the signal. Signals are the software analog of hardware interrupts and can be generated by a variety of causes in addition to timers expiring. Many traps detected by hardware, such as executing an illegal instruction or using an invalid address, are also converted into signals to the guilty process.

Each person authorized to use a system is assigned a **UID** (User IDentification) by the system administrator. Every process started has the UID of the person who started it. A child process has the same UID as its parent. Users can be members of groups, each of which has a **GID** (**Group IDentification**).

One UID, called the **superuser** (in UNIX), has special power and may violate many of the protection rules. In large installations, only the system administrator knows the password needed to become superuser, but many of the ordinary users (especially students) devote considerable effort to trying to find flaws in the system that allow them to become superuser without the password.

We will study processes, interprocess communication, and related issues in Chap. 2.

1.5.2 Deadlocks

When two or more processes are interacting, they can sometimes get themselves into a stalemate situation they cannot get out of. Such a situation is called a deadlock.

Deadlocks can best be introduced with a real-world example everyone is familiar with, deadlock in traffic. Consider the situation of Fig. 1-13(a). Here four buses are approaching an intersection. Behind each one are more buses (not shown). With a little bit of bad luck, the first four could all arrive at the intersection simultaneously, leading to the situation of Fig. 1-13(b), in which they are deadlocked because none of them can go forward. Each one is blocking one of the others. They cannot go backward due to other buses behind them. There is no easy way out.

Processes in a computer can experience an analogous situation in which they cannot make any progress. For example, imagine a computer with a tape drive and CD-recorder. Now imagine that two processes each need to produce a CD-ROM from data on a tape. Process 1 requests and is granted the tape drive. Next process 2 requests and is granted the CD-recorder. Then process 1 requests the CD-recorder and is suspended until process 2 returns it. Finally, process 2 requests the tape drive and is also suspended because process 1 already has it. Here

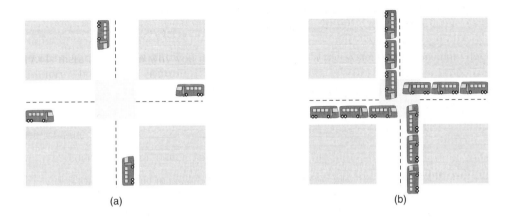

(a)   (b)

Figure 1-13. (a) A potential deadlock. (b) An actual deadlock.

we have a deadlock from which there is no escape. We will study deadlocks and what can be done about them in detail in Chap. 3.

1.5.3 Memory Management

Every computer has some main memory that it uses to hold executing programs. In a very simple operating system, only one program at a time is in memory. To run a second program, the first one has to be removed and the second one placed in memory.

More sophisticated operating systems allow multiple programs to be in memory at the same time. To keep them from interfering with one another (and with the operating system), some kind of protection mechanism is needed. While this mechanism has to be in the hardware, it is controlled by the operating system.

The above viewpoint is concerned with managing and protecting the computer's main memory. A different, but equally important memory-related issue, is managing the address space of the processes. Normally, each process has some set of addresses it can use, typically running from 0 up to some maximum. In the simplest case, the maximum amount of address space a process has is less than the main memory. In this way, a process can fill up its address space and there will be enough room in main memory to hold it all.

However, on many computers addresses are 32 or 64 bits, giving an address space of 2^{32} or 2^{64} bytes, respectively. What happens if a process has more address space than the computer has main memory and the process wants to use it all? In the first computers, such a process was just out of luck. Nowadays, a technique called virtual memory exists, in which the operating system keeps part of the address space in main memory and part on disk and shuttles pieces back and forth between them as needed. This important operating system function, and other memory management-related functions will be covered in Chap. 4.

1.5.4 Input/Output

All computers have physical devices for acquiring input and producing output. After all, what good would a computer be if the users could not tell it what to do and could not get the results after it did the work requested. Many kinds of input and output devices exist, including keyboards, monitors, printers, and so on. It is up to the operating system to manage these devices.

Consequently, every operating system has an I/O subsystem for managing its I/O devices. Some of the I/O software is device independent, that is, applies to many or all I/O devices equally well. Other parts of it, such as device drivers, are specific to particular I/O devices. In Chap. 5 we will have a look at I/O software.

1.5.5 Files

Another key concept supported by virtually all operating systems is the file system. As noted before, a major function of the operating system is to hide the peculiarities of the disks and other I/O devices and present the programmer with a nice, clean abstract model of device-independent files. System calls are obviously needed to create files, remove files, read files, and write files. Before a file can be read, it must be located on the disk and opened, and after it has been read it should be closed, so calls are provided to do these things.

To provide a place to keep files, most operating systems have the concept of a **directory** as a way of grouping files together. A student, for example, might have one directory for each course he is taking (for the programs needed for that course), another directory for his electronic mail, and still another directory for his World Wide Web home page. System calls are then needed to create and remove directories. Calls are also provided to put an existing file in a directory, and to remove a file from a directory. Directory entries may be either files or other directories. This model also gives rise to a hierarchy—the file system—as shown in Fig. 1-14.

The process and file hierarchies both are organized as trees, but the similarity stops there. Process hierarchies usually are not very deep (more than three levels is unusual), whereas file hierarchies are commonly four, five, or even more levels deep. Process hierarchies are typically short-lived, generally a few minutes at most, whereas the directory hierarchy may exist for years. Ownership and protection also differ for processes and files. Typically, only a parent process may control or even access a child process, but mechanisms nearly always exist to allow files and directories to be read by a wider group than just the owner.

Every file within the directory hierarchy can be specified by giving its **path name** from the top of the directory hierarchy, the **root directory**. Such absolute path names consist of the list of directories that must be traversed from the root directory to get to the file, with slashes separating the components. In Fig. 1-14,

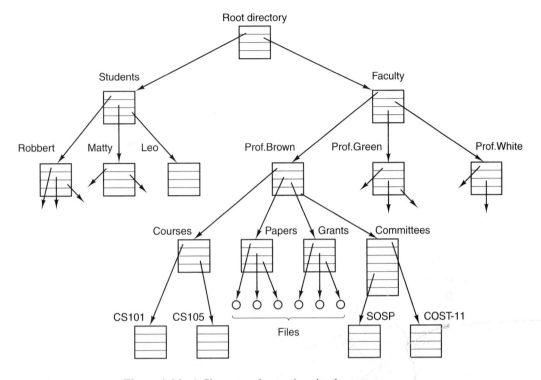

Figure 1-14. A file system for a university department.

the path for file *CS101* is */Faculty/Prof.Brown/Courses/CS101*. The leading slash indicates that the path is absolute, that is, starting at the root directory. As an aside, in MS-DOS and Windows, the backslash (\) character is used as the separator instead of the slash (/) character, so the file path given above would be written as *\Faculty\Prof.Brown\Courses\CS101*. Throughout this book we will generally use the UNIX convention for paths.

At every instant, each process has a current **working directory**, in which path names not beginning with a slash are looked for. As an example, in Fig. 1-14, if */Faculty/Prof.Brown* were the working directory, then use of the path name *Courses/CS101* would yield the same file as the absolute path name given above. Processes can change their working directory by issuing a system call specifying the new working directory.

Before a file can be read or written, it must be opened, at which time the permissions are checked. If the access is permitted, the system returns a small integer called a **file descriptor** to use in subsequent operations. If the access is prohibited, an error code is returned.

Another important concept in UNIX is the mounted file system. Nearly all personal computers have one or more floppy disk drives into which floppy disks can be inserted and removed. To provide an elegant way to deal with removable media (including CD-ROMs), UNIX allows the file system on a floppy disk to be attached to the main tree. Consider the situation of Fig. 1-15(a). Before the mount call, the **root file system**, on the hard disk, and a second file system, on a floppy disk, are separate and unrelated.

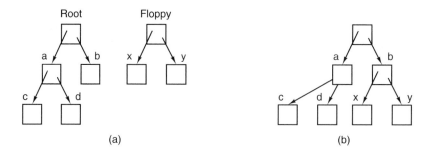

Figure 1-15. (a) Before mounting, the files on drive 0 are not accessible. (b) After mounting, they are part of the file hierarchy.

However, the file system on the floppy cannot be used, because there is no way to specify path names on it. UNIX does not allow path names to be prefixed by a drive name or number; that would be precisely the kind of device dependence that operating systems ought to eliminate. Instead, the mount system call allows the file system on the floppy to be attached to the root file system wherever the program wants it to be. In Fig. 1-15(b) the file system on the floppy has been mounted on directory *b*, thus allowing access to files */b/x* and */b/y*. If directory *b* had contained any files they would not be accessible while the floppy was mounted, since */b* would refer to the root directory of the floppy. (Not being able to access these files is not as serious as it at first seems: file systems are nearly always mounted on empty directories.) If a system contains multiple hard disks, they can all be mounted into a single tree as well.

Another important concept in UNIX is the **special file**. Special files are provided in order to make I/O devices look like files. That way, they can be read and written using the same system calls as are used for reading and writing files. Two kinds of special files exist: **block special files** and **character special files**. Block special files are used to model devices that consist of a collection of randomly addressable blocks, such as disks. By opening a block special file and reading, say, block 4, a program can directly access the fourth block on the device, without regard to the structure of the file system contained on it. Similarly, character special files are used to model printers, modems, and other devices that accept or output a character stream. By convention, the special files are kept in the */dev* directory. For example, */dev/lp* might be the line printer.

The last feature we will discuss in this overview is one that relates to both processes and files: pipes. A **pipe** is a sort of pseudofile that can be used to connect two processes, as shown in Fig. 1-16. If processes *A* and *B* wish to talk using a pipe, they must set it up in advance. When process *A* wants to send data to process *B*, it writes on the pipe as though it were an output file. Process *B* can read the data by reading from the pipe as though it were an input file. Thus, communication between processes in UNIX looks very much like ordinary file reads and writes. Stronger yet, the only way a process can discover that the output file it is writing on is not really a file, but a pipe, is by making a special system call. File systems are very important. We will have much more to say about them in Chap. 6 and also in Chaps. 10 and 11.

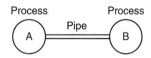

Figure 1-16. Two processes connected by a pipe.

1.5.6 Security

Computers contain large amounts of information that users often want to keep confidential. This information may include electronic mail, business plans, tax returns, and much more. It is up to the operating system to manage the system security so that files, for example, are only accessible to authorized users.

As a simple example, just to get an idea of how security can work, consider UNIX. Files in UNIX are protected by assigning each one a 9-bit binary protection code. The protection code consists of three 3-bit fields, one for the owner, one for other members of the owner's group (users are divided into groups by the system administrator), and one for everyone else. Each field has a bit for read access, a bit for write access, and a bit for execute access. These 3 bits are known as the **rwx bits**. For example, the protection code *rwxr-x--x* means that the owner can **r**ead, **w**rite, or e**x**ecute the file, other group members can read or execute (but not write) the file, and everyone else can execute (but not read or write) the file. For a directory, *x* indicates search permission. A dash means that the corresponding permission is absent.

In addition to file protection, there are many other security issues. Protecting the system from unwanted intruders, both human and nonhuman (e.g., viruses) is one of them. We will look at various security issues in Chap. 9.

1.5.7 The Shell

The operating system is the code that carries out the system calls. Editors, compilers, assemblers, linkers, and command interpreters definitely are not part of the operating system, even though they are important and useful. At the risk of confusing things somewhat, in this section we will look briefly at the UNIX command interpreter, called the **shell**. Although it is not part of the operating system, it makes heavy use of many operating system features and thus serves as a good example of how the system calls can be used. It is also the primary interface between a user sitting at his terminal and the operating system, unless the user is using a graphical user interface. Many shells exist, including *sh*, *csh*, *ksh*, and *bash*. All of them support the functionality described below, which derives from the original shell (*sh*).

When any user logs in, a shell is started up. The shell has the terminal as standard input and standard output. It starts out by typing the **prompt**, a character such as a dollar sign, which tells the user that the shell is waiting to accept a command. If the user now types

    date

for example, the shell creates a child process and runs the *date* program as the child. While the child process is running, the shell waits for it to terminate. When the child finishes, the shell types the prompt again and tries to read the next input line.

The user can specify that standard output be redirected to a file, for example,

    date >file

Similarly, standard input can be redirected, as in

    sort <file1 >file2

which invokes the sort program with input taken from *file1* and output sent to *file2*.

The output of one program can be used as the input for another program by connecting them with a pipe. Thus

    cat file1 file2 file3 | sort >/dev/lp

invokes the *cat* program to concatenate three files and send the output to *sort* to arrange all the lines in alphabetical order. The output of *sort* is redirected to the file */dev/lp*, typically the printer.

If a user puts an ampersand after a command, the shell does not wait for it to complete. Instead it just gives a prompt immediately. Consequently,

    cat file1 file2 file3 | sort >/dev/lp &

starts up the sort as a background job, allowing the user to continue working normally while the sort is going on. The shell has a number of other interesting features, which we do not have space to discuss here. Most books on UNIX discuss the shell at some length (e.g., Kernighan and Pike, 1984; Kochan and Wood, 1990; Medinets, 1999; Newham and Rosenblatt, 1998; and Robbins, 1999).

1.5.8 Recycling of Concepts

Computer science, like many fields, is largely technology driven. The reason the ancient Romans lacked cars is not that they liked walking so much. It is because they did not know how to build cars. Personal computers exist *not* because millions of people had some long pent-up desire to own a computer, but because it is now possible to manufacture them cheaply. We often forget how much technology affects our view of systems and it is worth reflecting on this point from time to time.

In particular, it frequently happens that a change in technology renders some idea obsolete and it quickly vanishes. However, another change in technology could revive it again. This is especially true when the change has to do with the relative performance of different parts of the system. For example, when CPUs became much faster than memories, caches became important to speed up the "slow" memory. If new memory technology some day makes memories much faster than CPUs, caches will vanish. And if a new CPU technology makes them faster than memories again, caches will reappear. In biology, extinction is forever, but in computer science, it is sometimes only for a few years.

As a consequence of this impermanence, in this book we will from time to time look at "obsolete" concepts, that is, ideas that are not optimal with current technology. However, changes in the technology may bring back some of the so-called "obsolete concepts." For this reason, it is important to understand why a concept is obsolete and what changes in the environment might bring it back again.

To make this point clearer, let us consider a few examples. Early computers had hardwired instruction sets. The instructions were executed directly by hardware and could not be changed. Then came microprogramming, in which an underlying interpreter carried out the instructions in software. Hardwired execution became obsolete. Then RISC computers were invented, and microprogramming (i.e., interpreted execution) became obsolete because direct execution was faster. Now we are seeing the resurgence of interpretation in the form of Java applets that are sent over the Internet and interpreted upon arrival. Execution speed is not always crucial because network delays are so great that they tend to dominate. But that could change, too, some day.

Early operating systems allocated files on the disk by just placing them in contiguous sectors, one after another. Although this scheme was easy to implement, it was not flexible because when a file grew, there was not enough room to store it any more. Thus the concept of contiguously allocated files was discarded as obsolete. Until CD-ROMs came around. There the problem of growing files did not exist. All of a sudden, the simplicity of contiguous file allocation was seen as a great idea and CD-ROM file systems are now based on it.

As our final idea, consider dynamic linking. The MULTICS system was designed to run day and night without ever stopping. To fix bugs in software, it was necessary to have a way to replace library procedures while they were being used. The concept of dynamic linking was invented for this purpose. After MULTICS died, the concept was forgotten for a while. However, it was rediscovered when modern operating systems needed a way to allow many programs to share the same library procedures without having their own private copies (because graphics libraries had grown so large). Most systems now support some form of dynamic linking once again. The list goes on, but these examples should make the point: an idea that is obsolete today may be the star of the party tomorrow.

Technology is not the only factor that drives systems and software. Economics plays a big role too. In the 1960s and 1970s, most terminals were mechanical printing terminals or 25×80 character-oriented CRTs rather than bitmap graphics terminals. This choice was not a question of technology. Bit-map graphics terminals were in use before 1960. It is just that they cost many tens of thousands of dollars each. Only when the price came down enormously could people (other than the military) think of dedicating one terminal to an individual user.

1.6 SYSTEM CALLS

The interface between the operating system and the user programs is defined by the set of system calls that the operating system provides. To really understand what operating systems do, we must examine this interface closely. The system calls available in the interface vary from operating system to operating system (although the underlying concepts tend to be similar).

We are thus forced to make a choice between (1) vague generalities ("operating systems have system calls for reading files") and (2) some specific system ("UNIX has a read system call with three parameters: one to specify the file, one to tell where the data are to be put, and one to tell how many bytes to read").

We have chosen the latter approach. It's more work that way, but it gives more insight into what operating systems really do. Although this discussion specifically refers to POSIX (International Standard 9945-1), hence also to UNIX, System V, BSD, Linux, MINIX, etc., most other modern operating systems have system calls that perform the same functions, even if the details differ. Since the actual mechanics of issuing a system call are highly machine dependent and often must be expressed in assembly code, a procedure library is provided to make it possible to make system calls from C programs and often from other languages as well.

It is useful to keep the following in mind. Any single-CPU computer can execute only one instruction at a time. If a process is running a user program in user mode and needs a system service, such as reading data from a file, it has to execute a trap or system call instruction to transfer control to the operating system. The operating system then figures out what the calling process wants by inspecting the parameters. Then it carries out the system call and returns control to the instruction following the system call. In a sense, making a system call is like making a special kind of procedure call, only system calls enter the kernel and procedure calls do not.

To make the system call mechanism clearer, let us take a quick look at the read system call. As mentioned above, it has three parameters: the first one specifying the file, the second one pointing to the buffer, and the third one giving the number of bytes to read. Like nearly all system calls, it is invoked from C programs by calling a library procedure with the same name as the system call: *read*. A call from a C program might look like this:

```
count = read(fd, buffer, nbytes);
```

The system call (and the library procedure) return the number of bytes actually read in *count*. This value is normally the same as *nbytes*, but may be smaller, if, for example, end-of-file is encountered while reading.

If the system call cannot be carried out, either due to an invalid parameter or a disk error, *count* is set to −1, and the error number is put in a global variable, *errno*. Programs should always check the results of a system call to see if an error occurred.

System calls are performed in a series of steps. To make this concept clearer, let us examine the read call discussed above. In preparation for calling the *read* library procedure, which actually makes the read system call, the calling program first pushes the parameters onto the stack, as shown in steps 1-3 in Fig. 1-17. C and C++ compilers push the parameters onto the stack in reverse order for historical reasons (having to do with making the first parameter to *printf*, the format string, appear on top of the stack). The first and third parameters are called by value, but the second parameter is passed by reference, meaning that the address of the buffer (indicated by &) is passed, not the contents of the buffer. Then comes the actual call to the library procedure (step 4). This instruction is the normal procedure call instruction used to call all procedures.

The library procedure, possibly written in assembly language, typically puts the system call number in a place where the operating system expects it, such as a register (step 5). Then it executes a TRAP instruction to switch from user mode to kernel mode and start execution at a fixed address within the kernel (step 6). The kernel code that starts examines the system call number and then dispatches to the correct system call handler, usually via a table of pointers to system call handlers indexed on system call number (step 7). At that point the system call handler runs (step 8). Once the system call handler has completed its work, control may be returned to the user-space library procedure at the instruction following the TRAP instruction (step 9). This procedure then returns to the user program in the usual way procedure calls return (step 10).

To finish the job, the user program has to clean up the stack, as it does after any procedure call (step 11). Assuming the stack grows downward, as it often does, the compiled code increments the stack pointer exactly enough to remove

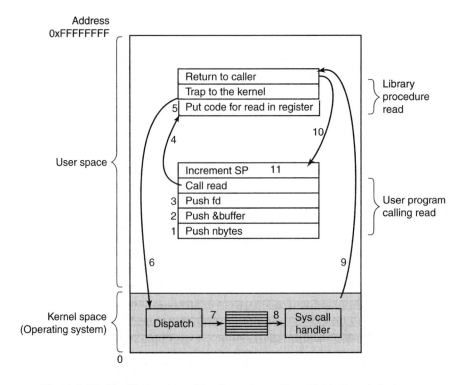

Figure 1-17. The 11 steps in making the system call read(fd, buffer, nbytes).

the parameters pushed before the call to *read*. The program is now free to do whatever it wants to do next.

In step 9 above, we said "may be returned to the user-space library procedure ..." for good reason. The system call may block the caller, preventing it from continuing. For example, if it is trying to read from the keyboard and nothing has been typed yet, the caller has to be blocked. In this case, the operating system will look around to see if some other process can be run next. Later, when the desired input is available, this process will get the attention of the system and steps 9–11 will occur.

In the following sections, we will examine some of the most heavily used POSIX system calls, or more specifically, the library procedures that make those system calls. POSIX has about 100 procedure calls. Some of the most important ones are listed in Fig. 1-18, grouped for convenience in four categories. In the text we will briefly examine each call to see what it does. To a large extent, the services offered by these calls determine most of what the operating system has to do, since the resource management on personal computers is minimal (at least compared to big machines with multiple users). The services include things like creating and terminating processes, creating, deleting, reading, and writing files, managing directories, and performing input and output.

Process management

Call	Description
pid = fork( )	Create a child process identical to the parent
pid = waitpid(pid, &statloc, options)	Wait for a child to terminate
s = execve(name, argv, environp)	Replace a process' core image
exit(status)	Terminate process execution and return status

File management

Call	Description
fd = open(file, how, ...)	Open a file for reading, writing or both
s = close(fd)	Close an open file
n = read(fd, buffer, nbytes)	Read data from a file into a buffer
n = write(fd, buffer, nbytes)	Write data from a buffer into a file
position = lseek(fd, offset, whence)	Move the file pointer
s = stat(name, &buf)	Get a file's status information

Directory and file system management

Call	Description
s = mkdir(name, mode)	Create a new directory
s = rmdir(name)	Remove an empty directory
s = link(name1, name2)	Create a new entry, name2, pointing to name1
s = unlink(name)	Remove a directory entry
s = mount(special, name, flag)	Mount a file system
s = umount(special)	Unmount a file system

Miscellaneous

Call	Description
s = chdir(dirname)	Change the working directory
s = chmod(name, mode)	Change a file's protection bits
s = kill(pid, signal)	Send a signal to a process
seconds = time(&seconds)	Get the elapsed time since Jan. 1, 1970

Figure 1-18. Some of the major POSIX system calls. The return code s is −1 if an error has occurred. The return codes are as follows: *pid* is a process id, *fd* is a file descriptor, *n* is a byte count, *position* is an offset within the file, and *seconds* is the elapsed time. The parameters are explained in the text.

As an aside, it is worth pointing out that the mapping of POSIX procedure calls onto system calls is not one-to-one. The POSIX standard specifies a number of procedures that a conformant system must supply, but it does not specify whether they are system calls, library calls, or something else. If a procedure can be carried out without invoking a system call (i.e., without trapping to the kernel), it will usually be done in user space for reasons of performance. However, most of the POSIX procedures do invoke system calls, usually with one procedure mapping directly onto one system call. In a few cases, especially where several required procedures are only minor variations of one another, one system call handles more than one library call.

1.6.1 System Calls for Process Management

The first group of calls in Fig. 1-18 deals with process management. Fork is a good place to start the discussion. Fork is the only way to create a new process in UNIX. It creates an exact duplicate of the original process, including all the file descriptors, registers—everything. After the fork, the original process and the copy (the parent and child) go their separate ways. All the variables have identical values at the time of the fork, but since the parent's data are copied to create the child, subsequent changes in one of them do not affect the other one. (The program text, which is unchangeable, is shared between parent and child.) The fork call returns a value, which is zero in the child and equal to the child's process identifier or **PID** in the parent. Using the returned PID, the two processes can see which one is the parent process and which one is the child process.

In most cases, after a fork, the child will need to execute different code from the parent. Consider the case of the shell. It reads a command from the terminal, forks off a child process, waits for the child to execute the command, and then reads the next command when the child terminates. To wait for the child to finish, the parent executes a waitpid system call, which just waits until the child terminates (any child if more than one exists). Waitpid can wait for a specific child, or for any old child by setting the first parameter to −1. When waitpid completes, the address pointed to by the second parameter, *statloc*, will be set to the child's exit status (normal or abnormal termination and exit value). Various options are also provided, specified by the third parameter.

Now consider how fork is used by the shell. When a command is typed, the shell forks off a new process. This child process must execute the user command. It does this by using the execve system call, which causes its entire core image to be replaced by the file named in its first parameter. (Actually, the system call itself is exec, but several different library procedures call it with different parameters and slightly different names. We will treat these as system calls here.) A highly simplified shell illustrating the use of fork, waitpid, and execve is shown in Fig. 1-19.

In the most general case, execve has three parameters: the name of the file to be executed, a pointer to the argument array, and a pointer to the environment array. These will be described shortly. Various library routines, including *execl*, *execv*, *execle*, and *execve*, are provided to allow the parameters to be omitted or

```
#define TRUE 1

while (TRUE) {                                  /* repeat forever */
    type_prompt( );                             /* display prompt on the screen */
    read_command(command, parameters);          /* read input from terminal */

    if (fork( ) != 0) {                         /* fork off child process */
        /* Parent code. */
        waitpid(−1, &status, 0);                /* wait for child to exit */
    } else {
        /* Child code. */
        execve(command, parameters, 0);         /* execute command */
    }
}
```

Figure 1-19. A stripped-down shell. Throughout this book, *TRUE* is assumed to be defined as 1.

specified in various ways. Throughout this book we will use the name exec to represent the system call invoked by all of these.

Let us consider the case of a command such as

    cp file1 file2

used to copy *file1* to *file2*. After the shell has forked, the child process locates and executes the file *cp* and passes to it the names of the source and target files.

The main program of *cp* (and main program of most other C programs) contains the declaration

    main(argc, argv, envp)

where *argc* is a count of the number of items on the command line, including the program name. For the example above, *argc* is 3.

The second parameter, *argv*, is a pointer to an array. Element *i* of that array is a pointer to the *i*-th string on the command line. In our example, *argv*[0] would point to the string "cp", *argv*[1] would point to the string "file1" and *argv*[2] would point to the string "file2".

The third parameter of *main*, *envp*, is a pointer to the environment, an array of strings containing assignments of the form *name* = *value* used to pass information such as the terminal type and home directory name to a program. In Fig. 1-19, no environment is passed to the child, so the third parameter of *execve* is a zero.

If exec seems complicated, do not despair; it is (semantically) the most complex of all the POSIX system calls. All the other ones are much simpler. As an example of a simple one, consider exit, which processes should use when they are finished executing. It has one parameter, the exit status (0 to 255), which is returned to the parent via *statloc* in the waitpid system call.

Processes in UNIX have their memory divided up into three segments: the **text segment** (i.e., the program code), the **data segment** (i.e., the variables), and the **stack segment**. The data segment grows upward and the stack grows downward, as shown in Fig. 1-20. Between them is a gap of unused address space. The stack grows into the gap automatically, as needed, but expansion of the data segment is done explicitly by using a system call, brk, which specifies the new address where the data segment is to end. This call, however, is not defined by the POSIX standard, since programmers are encouraged to use the *malloc* library procedure for dynamically allocating storage, and the underlying implementation of *malloc* was not thought to be a suitable subject for standardization since few programmers use it directly.

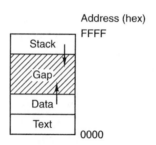

Figure 1-20. Processes have three segments: text, data, and stack.

1.6.2 System Calls for File Management

Many system calls relate to the file system. In this section we will look at calls that operate on individual files; in the next one we will examine those that involve directories or the file system as a whole.

To read or write a file, the file must first be opened using open. This call specifies the file name to be opened, either as an absolute path name or relative to the working directory, and a code of *O_RDONLY*, *O_WRONLY*, or *O_RDWR*, meaning open for reading, writing, or both. To create a new file, *O_CREAT* is used. The file descriptor returned can then be used for reading or writing. Afterward, the file can be closed by close, which makes the file descriptor available for reuse on a subsequent open.

The most heavily used calls are undoubtedly read and write. We saw read earlier. Write has the same parameters.

Although most programs read and write files sequentially, for some applications programs need to be able to access any part of a file at random. Associated with each file is a pointer that indicates the current position in the file. When reading (writing) sequentially, it normally points to the next byte to be read (written). The lseek call changes the value of the position pointer, so that subsequent calls to read or write can begin anywhere in the file.

Lseek has three parameters: the first is the file descriptor for the file, the second is a file position, and the third tells whether the file position is relative to the beginning of the file, the current position, or the end of the file. The value returned by lseek is the absolute position in the file after changing the pointer.

For each file, UNIX keeps track of the file mode (regular file, special file, directory, and so on), size, time of last modification, and other information. Programs can ask to see this information via the stat system call. The first parameter specifies the file to be inspected; the second one is a pointer to a structure where the information is to be put.

1.6.3 System Calls for Directory Management

In this section we will look at some system calls that relate more to directories or the file system as a whole, rather than just to one specific file as in the previous section. The first two calls, mkdir and rmdir, create and remove empty directories, respectively. The next call is link. Its purpose is to allow the same file to appear under two or more names, often in different directories. A typical use is to allow several members of the same programming team to share a common file, with each of them having the file appear in his own directory, possibly under different names. Sharing a file is not the same as giving every team member a private copy, because having a shared file means that changes that any member of the team makes are instantly visible to the other members—there is only one file. When copies are made of a file, subsequent changes made to one copy do not affect the other ones.

To see how link works, consider the situation of Fig. 1-21(a). Here are two users, *ast* and *jim*, each having their own directories with some files. If *ast* now executes a program containing the system call

```
link("/usr/jim/memo", "/usr/ast/note");
```

the file *memo* in *jim*'s directory is now entered into *ast*'s directory under the name *note*. Thereafter, */usr/jim/memo* and */usr/ast/note* refer to the same file. As an aside, whether user directories are kept in */usr*, */user*, */home*, or somewhere else is simply a decision made by the local system administrator.

Understanding how link works will probably make it clearer what it does. Every file in UNIX has a unique number, its i-number, that identifies it. This i-number is an index into a table of **i-nodes**, one per file, telling who owns the file, where its disk blocks are, and so on. A directory is simply a file containing a set of (i-number, ASCII name) pairs. In the first versions of UNIX, each directory entry was 16 bytes—2 bytes for the i-number and 14 bytes for the name. Now a more complicated structure is needed to support long file names, but conceptually a directory is still a set of (i-number, ASCII name) pairs. In Fig. 1-21, *mail* has i-number 16, and so on. What link does is simply create a new directory entry with a (possibly new) name, using the i-number of an existing file. In Fig. 1-21(b), two

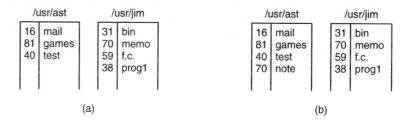

Figure 1-21. (a) Two directories before linking */usr/jim/memo* to ast's directory. (b) The same directories after linking.

entries have the same i-number (70) and thus refer to the same file. If either one is later removed, using the unlink system call, the other one remains. If both are removed, UNIX sees that no entries to the file exist (a field in the i-node keeps track of the number of directory entries pointing to the file), so the file is removed from the disk.

As we have mentioned earlier, the mount system call allows two file systems to be merged into one. A common situation is to have the root file system containing the binary (executable) versions of the common commands and other heavily used files, on a hard disk. The user can then insert a floppy disk with files to be read into the floppy disk drive.

By executing the mount system call, the floppy disk file system can be attached to the root file system, as shown in Fig. 1-22. A typical statement in C to perform the mount is

```
mount("/dev/fd0", "/mnt", 0);
```

where the first parameter is the name of a block special file for drive 0, the second parameter is the place in the tree where it is to be mounted, and the third parameter tells whether the file system is to be mounted read-write or read-only.

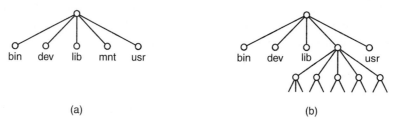

Figure 1-22. (a) File system before the mount. (b) File system after the mount.

After the mount call, a file on drive 0 can be accessed by just using its path from the root directory or the working directory, without regard to which drive it is on. In fact, second, third, and fourth drives can also be mounted anywhere in the tree. The mount call makes it possible to integrate removable media into a single integrated file hierarchy, without having to worry about which device a file is on. Although this example involves floppy disks, hard disks or portions of hard disks (often called **partitions** or **minor devices**) can also be mounted this way. When a file system is no longer needed, it can be unmounted with the umount system call.

1.6.4 Miscellaneous System Calls

A variety of other system calls exist as well. We will look at just four of them here. The chdir call changes the current working directory. After the call

```
chdir("/usr/ast/test");
```

an open on the file *xyz* will open */usr/ast/test/xyz*. The concept of a working directory eliminates the need for typing (long) absolute path names all the time.

In UNIX every file has a mode used for protection. The mode includes the read-write-execute bits for the owner, group, and others. The chmod system call makes it possible to change the mode of a file. For example, to make a file read-only by everyone except the owner, one could execute

```
chmod("file", 0644);
```

The kill system call is the way users and user processes send signals. If a process is prepared to catch a particular signal, then when it arrives, a signal handler is run. If the process is not prepared to handle a signal, then its arrival kills the process (hence the name of the call).

POSIX defines several procedures for dealing with time. For example, time just returns the current time in seconds, with 0 corresponding to Jan. 1, 1970 at midnight (just as the day was starting, not ending). On computers with 32-bit words, the maximum value time can return is $2^{32} - 1$ seconds (assuming an unsigned integer is used). This value corresponds to a little over 136 years. Thus in the year 2106, 32-bit UNIX systems will go berserk, imitating the famous Y2K problem. If you currently have a 32-bit UNIX system, you are advised to trade it in for a 64-bit one sometime before the year 2106.

1.6.5 The Windows Win32 API

So far we have focused primarily on UNIX. Now it is time to look briefly at Windows. Windows and UNIX differ in a fundamental way in their respective programming models. A UNIX program consists of code that does something or other, making system calls to have certain services performed. In contrast, a Windows program is normally event driven. The main program waits for some event to happen, then calls a procedure to handle it. Typical events are keys being struck, the mouse being moved, a mouse button being pushed, or a floppy disk inserted. Handlers are then called to process the event, update the screen and update the internal program state. All in all, this leads to a somewhat different style of programming than with UNIX, but since the focus of this book is on operating system function and structure, these different programming models will not concern us much more.

Of course, Windows also has system calls. With UNIX, there is almost a 1-to-1 relationship between the system calls (e.g., read) and the library procedures (e.g., *read*) used to invoke the system calls. In other words, for each system call, there is roughly one library procedure that is called to invoke it, as indicated in Fig. 1-17. Furthermore, POSIX has only about 100 procedure calls.

With Windows, the situation is radically different. To start with, the library calls and the actual system calls are highly decoupled. Microsoft has defined a set of procedures, called the **Win32 API** (**Application Program Interface**) that programmers are expected to use to get operating system services. This interface is (partially) supported on all versions of Windows since Windows 95. By decoupling the interface from the actual system calls, Microsoft retains the ability to change the actual system calls in time (even from release to release) without invalidating existing programs. What actually constitutes Win32 is also slightly ambiguous since Windows 2000 has many new calls that were not previously available. In this section, Win32 means the interface supported by all versions of Windows.

The number of Win32 API calls is extremely large, numbering in the thousands. Furthermore, while many of them do invoke system calls, a substantial number are carried out entirely in user space. As a consequence, with Windows it is impossible to see what is a system call (i.e., performed by the kernel) and what is simply a user-space library call. In fact, what is a system call in one version of Windows may be done in user space in a different version, and vice versa. When we discuss the Windows system calls in this book, we will use the Win32 procedures (where appropriate) since Microsoft guarantees that these will be stable over time. But it is worth remembering that not all of them are true system calls (i.e., traps to the kernel).

Another complication is that in UNIX, the GUI (e.g., X Windows and Motif) runs entirely in user space, so the only system calls needed for writing on the screen are write and a few other minor ones. Of course, there are a large number of calls to X Windows and the GUI, but these are not system calls in any sense.

In contrast, the Win32 API has a huge number of calls for managing windows, geometric figures, text, fonts, scrollbars, dialog boxes, menus, and other features of the GUI. To the extent that the graphics subsystem runs in the kernel (true on some versions of Windows but not on all), these are system calls; otherwise they are just library calls. Should we discuss these calls in this book or not? Since they are not really related to the function of an operating system, we have decided not to, even though they may be carried out by the kernel. Readers interested in the Win32 API should consult one of the many books on the subject, for example (Hart, 1997; Rector and Newcomer, 1997; and Simon, 1997).

Even introducing all the Win32 API calls here is out of the question, so we will restrict ourselves to those calls that roughly correspond to the functionality of the UNIX calls listed in Fig. 1-18. These are listed in Fig. 1-23.

UNIX	Win32	Description
fork	CreateProcess	Create a new process
waitpid	WaitForSingleObject	Can wait for a process to exit
execve	(none)	CreateProcess = fork + execve
exit	ExitProcess	Terminate execution
open	CreateFile	Create a file or open an existing file
close	CloseHandle	Close a file
read	ReadFile	Read data from a file
write	WriteFile	Write data to a file
lseek	SetFilePointer	Move the file pointer
stat	GetFileAttributesEx	Get various file attributes
mkdir	CreateDirectory	Create a new directory
rmdir	RemoveDirectory	Remove an empty directory
link	(none)	Win32 does not support links
unlink	DeleteFile	Destroy an existing file
mount	(none)	Win32 does not support mount
umount	(none)	Win32 does not support mount
chdir	SetCurrentDirectory	Change the current working directory
chmod	(none)	Win32 does not support security (although NT does)
kill	(none)	Win32 does not support signals
time	GetLocalTime	Get the current time

Figure 1-23. The Win32 API calls that roughly correspond to the UNIX calls of Fig. 1-18.

Let us now briefly go through the list of Fig. 1-23. CreateProcess creates a new process. It does the combined work of fork and execve in UNIX. It has many parameters specifying the properties of the newly created process. Windows does not have a process hierarchy as UNIX does so there is no concept of a parent process and a child process. After a process is created, the creator and createe are equals. WaitForSingleObject is used to wait for an event. Many possible events can be waited for. If the parameter specifies a process, then the caller waits for the specified process to exit, which is done using ExitProcess.

The next six calls operate on files and are functionally similar to their UNIX counterparts although they differ in the parameters and details. Still, files can be opened, closed, read, and written pretty much as in UNIX. The SetFilePointer and GetFileAttributesEx calls set the file position and get some of the file attributes.

Windows has directories and they are created with CreateDirectory and RemoveDirectory, respectively. There is also a notion of a current directory, set by SetCurrentDirectory. The current time is acquired using GetLocalTime.

The Win32 interface does not have links to files, mounted file systems, security, or signals, so the calls corresponding to the UNIX ones do not exist. Of course, Win32 has a huge number of other calls that UNIX does not have, especially for managing the GUI. And Windows 2000 has an elaborate security system and also supports file links.

One last note about Win32 is perhaps worth making. Win32 is not a terribly uniform or consistent interface. The main culprit here was the need to be backward compatible with the previous 16-bit interface used in Windows 3.x.

1.7 OPERATING SYSTEM STRUCTURE

Now that we have seen what operating systems look like on the outside (i.e., the programmer's interface), it is time to take a look inside. In the following sections, we will examine five different structures that have been tried, in order to get some idea of the spectrum of possibilities. These are by no means exhaustive, but they give an idea of some designs that have been tried in practice. The five designs are monolithic systems, layered systems, virtual machines, exokernels, and client-server systems.

1.7.1 Monolithic Systems

By far the most common organization, this approach might well be subtitled "The Big Mess." The structure is that there is no structure. The operating system is written as a collection of procedures, each of which can call any of the other ones whenever it needs to. When this technique is used, each procedure in the system has a well-defined interface in terms of parameters and results, and each one is free to call any other one, if the latter provides some useful computation that the former needs.

To construct the actual object program of the operating system when this approach is used, one first compiles all the individual procedures, or files containing the procedures, and then binds them all together into a single object file using the system linker. In terms of information hiding, there is essentially none—every procedure is visible to every other procedure (as opposed to a structure containing modules or packages, in which much of the information is hidden away inside modules, and only the officially designated entry points can be called from outside the module).

Even in monolithic systems, however, it is possible to have at least a little structure. The services (system calls) provided by the operating system are requested by putting the parameters in a well-defined place (e.g., on the stack) and then executing a trap instruction. This instruction switches the machine from user mode to kernel mode and transfers control to the operating system, shown as step 6 in Fig. 1-17. The operating system then fetches the parameters and determines which system call is to be carried out. After that, it indexes into a table that contains in slot k a pointer to the procedure that carries out system call k (step 7 in Fig. 1-17).

This organization suggests a basic structure for the operating system:

1. A main program that invokes the requested service procedure.

2. A set of service procedures that carry out the system calls.

3. A set of utility procedures that help the service procedures.

In this model, for each system call there is one service procedure that takes care of it. The utility procedures do things that are needed by several service procedures, such as fetching data from user programs. This division of the procedures into three layers is shown in Fig. 1-24.

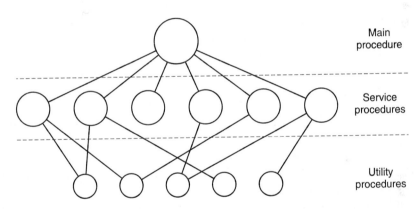

Figure 1-24. A simple structuring model for a monolithic system.

1.7.2 Layered Systems

A generalization of the approach of Fig. 1-24 is to organize the operating system as a hierarchy of layers, each one constructed upon the one below it. The first system constructed in this way was the THE system built at the Technische Hogeschool Eindhoven in the Netherlands by E. W. Dijkstra (1968) and his students. The THE system was a simple batch system for a Dutch computer, the Electrologica X8, which had 32K of 27-bit words (bits were expensive back then).

The system had 6 layers, as shown in Fig. 1-25. Layer 0 dealt with allocation of the processor, switching between processes when interrupts occurred or timers expired. Above layer 0, the system consisted of sequential processes, each of which could be programmed without having to worry about the fact that multiple processes were running on a single processor. In other words, layer 0 provided the basic multiprogramming of the CPU.

Layer	Function
5	The operator
4	User programs
3	Input/output management
2	Operator-process communication
1	Memory and drum management
0	Processor allocation and multiprogramming

Figure 1-25. Structure of the THE operating system.

Layer 1 did the memory management. It allocated space for processes in main memory and on a 512K word drum used for holding parts of processes (pages) for which there was no room in main memory. Above layer 1, processes did not have to worry about whether they were in memory or on the drum; the layer 1 software took care of making sure pages were brought into memory whenever they were needed.

Layer 2 handled communication between each process and the operator console. Above this layer each process effectively had its own operator console. Layer 3 took care of managing the I/O devices and buffering the information streams to and from them. Above layer 3 each process could deal with abstract I/O devices with nice properties, instead of real devices with many peculiarities. Layer 4 was where the user programs were found. They did not have to worry about process, memory, console, or I/O management. The system operator process was located in layer 5.

A further generalization of the layering concept was present in the MULTICS system. Instead of layers, MULTICS was described as having a series of concentric rings, with the inner ones being more privileged than the outer ones (which is effectively the same thing). When a procedure in an outer ring wanted to call a procedure in an inner ring, it had to make the equivalent of a system call, that is, a TRAP instruction whose parameters were carefully checked for validity before allowing the call to proceed. Although the entire operating system was part of the address space of each user process in MULTICS, the hardware made it possible to designate individual procedures (memory segments, actually) as protected against reading, writing, or executing.

Whereas the THE layering scheme was really only a design aid, because all the parts of the system were ultimately linked together into a single object program, in MULTICS, the ring mechanism was very much present at run time and enforced by the hardware. The advantage of the ring mechanism is that it can easily be extended to structure user subsystems. For example, a professor could write a program to test and grade student programs and run this program in ring n, with the student programs running in ring $n + 1$ so that they could not change their grades.

1.7.3 Virtual Machines

The initial releases of OS/360 were strictly batch systems. Nevertheless, many 360 users wanted to have timesharing, so various groups, both inside and outside IBM decided to write timesharing systems for it. The official IBM timesharing system, TSS/360, was delivered late, and when it finally arrived it was so big and slow that few sites converted to it. It was eventually abandoned after its development had consumed some $50 million (Graham, 1970). But a group at IBM's Scientific Center in Cambridge, Massachusetts, produced a radically different system that IBM eventually accepted as a product, and which is now widely used on its remaining mainframes.

This system, originally called CP/CMS and later renamed VM/370 (Seawright and MacKinnon, 1979), was based on an astute observation: a timesharing system provides (1) multiprogramming and (2) an extended machine with a more convenient interface than the bare hardware. The essence of VM/370 is to completely separate these two functions.

The heart of the system, known as the **virtual machine monitor**, runs on the bare hardware and does the multiprogramming, providing not one, but several virtual machines to the next layer up, as shown in Fig. 1-26. However, unlike all other operating systems, these virtual machines are not extended machines, with files and other nice features. Instead, they are *exact* copies of the bare hardware, including kernel/user mode, I/O, interrupts, and everything else the real machine has.

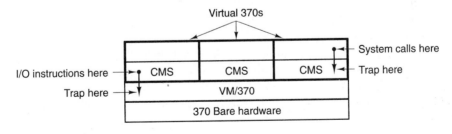

Figure 1-26. The structure of VM/370 with CMS.

Because each virtual machine is identical to the true hardware, each one can run any operating system that will run directly on the bare hardware. Different virtual machines can, and frequently do, run different operating systems. Some run one of the descendants of OS/360 for batch or transaction processing, while other ones run a single-user, interactive system called **CMS** (**Conversational Monitor System**) for interactive timesharing users.

When a CMS program executes a system call, the call is trapped to the operating system in its own virtual machine, not to VM/370, just as it would if it were running on a real machine instead of a virtual one. CMS then issues the normal hardware I/O instructions for reading its virtual disk or whatever is needed to carry out the call. These I/O instructions are trapped by VM/370, which then performs them as part of its simulation of the real hardware. By completely separating the functions of multiprogramming and providing an extended machine, each of the pieces can be much simpler, more flexible, and easier to maintain.

The idea of a virtual machine is heavily used nowadays in a different context: running old MS-DOS programs on a Pentium (or other 32-bit Intel CPU). When designing the Pentium and its software, both Intel and Microsoft realized that there would be a big demand for running old software on new hardware. For this reason, Intel provided a virtual 8086 mode on the Pentium. In this mode, the machine acts like an 8086 (which is identical to an 8088 from a software point of view), including 16-bit addressing with a 1-MB limit.

This mode is used by Windows and other operating systems for running MS-DOS programs. These programs are started up in virtual 8086 mode. As long as they execute normal instructions, they run on the bare hardware. However, when a program tries to trap to the operating system to make a system call, or tries to do protected I/O directly, a trap to the virtual machine monitor occurs.

Two variants on this design are possible. In the first one, MS-DOS itself is loaded into the virtual 8086's address space, so the virtual machine monitor just reflects the trap back to MS-DOS, just as would happen on a real 8086. When MS-DOS later tries to do the I/O itself, that operation is caught and carried out by the virtual machine monitor.

In the other variant, the virtual machine monitor just catches the first trap and does the I/O itself, since it knows what all the MS-DOS system calls are and thus knows what each trap is supposed to do. This variant is less pure than the first one, since it only emulates MS-DOS correctly, and not other operating systems, as the first one does. On the other hand, it is much faster, since it saves the trouble of starting up MS-DOS to do the I/O. A further disadvantage of actually running MS-DOS in virtual 8086 mode is that MS-DOS fiddles around with the interrupt enable/disable bit quite a lot, all of which must be emulated at considerable cost.

It is worth noting that neither of these approaches are really the same as VM/370, since the machine being emulated is not a full Pentium, but only an 8086. With the VM/370 system, it is possible to run VM/370, itself, in the virtual machine. With the Pentium, it is not possible to run, say, Windows in the virtual 8086 because no version of Windows runs on an 8086; a 286 is the minimum for even the oldest version, and 286 emulation is not provided (let alone Pentium emulation). However, by modifying the Windows binary slightly, this emulation is possible and even available in commercial products.

Another area where virtual machines are used, but in a somewhat different way, is for running Java programs. When Sun Microsystems invented the Java programming language, it also invented a virtual machine (i.e., a computer architecture) called the **JVM** (**Java Virtual Machine**). The Java compiler produces code for JVM, which then typically is executed by a software JVM interpreter. The advantage of this approach is that the JVM code can be shipped over the Internet to any computer that has a JVM interpreter and run there. If the compiler had produced SPARC or Pentium binary programs, for example, they could not have been shipped and run anywhere as easily. (Of course, Sun could have produced a compiler that produced SPARC binaries and then distributed a SPARC interpreter, but JVM is a much simpler architecture to interpret.) Another advantage of using JVM is that if the interpreter is implemented properly, which is not completely trivial, incoming JVM programs can be checked for safety and then executed in a protected environment so they cannot steal data or do any damage.

1.7.4 Exokernels

With VM/370, each user process gets an exact copy of the actual computer. With virtual 8086 mode on the Pentium, each user process gets an exact copy of a different computer. Going one step further, researchers at M.I.T. have built a system that gives each user a clone of the actual computer, but with a subset of the resources (Engler et al., 1995). Thus one virtual machine might get disk blocks 0 to 1023, the next one might get blocks 1024 to 2047, and so on.

At the bottom layer, running in kernel mode, is a program called the **exokernel**. Its job is to allocate resources to virtual machines and then check attempts to use them to make sure no machine is trying to use somebody else's resources. Each user-level virtual machine can run its own operating system, as on VM/370 and the Pentium virtual 8086s, except that each one is restricted to using only the resources it has asked for and been allocated.

The advantage of the exokernel scheme is that it saves a layer of mapping. In the other designs, each virtual machine thinks it has its own disk, with blocks running from 0 to some maximum, so the virtual machine monitor must maintain tables to remap disk addresses (and all other resources). With the exokernel, this remapping is not needed. The exokernel need only keep track of which virtual machine has been assigned which resource. This method still has the advantage of separating the multiprogramming (in the exokernel) from the user operating system code (in user space), but with less overhead, since all the exokernel has to do is keep the virtual machines out of each other's hair.

1.7.5 Client-Server Model

VM/370 gains much in simplicity by moving a large part of the traditional operating system code (implementing the extended machine) into a higher layer, CMS. Nevertheless, VM/370 itself is still a complex program because simulating a number of virtual 370s in their entirety is not *that* simple (especially if you want to do it reasonably efficiently).

A trend in modern operating systems is to take the idea of moving code up into higher layers even further and remove as much as possible from kernel mode, leaving a minimal **microkernel**. The usual approach is to implement most of the operating system in user processes. To request a service, such as reading a block of a file, a user process (now known as the **client process**) sends the request to a **server process**, which then does the work and sends back the answer.

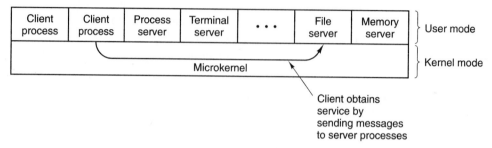

Figure 1-27. The client-server model.

In this model, shown in Fig. 1-27, all the kernel does is handle the communication between clients and servers. By splitting the operating system up into parts, each of which only handles one facet of the system, such as file service, process service, terminal service, or memory service, each part becomes small and manageable. Furthermore, because all the servers run as user-mode processes, and not in kernel mode, they do not have direct access to the hardware. As a consequence, if a bug in the file server is triggered, the file service may crash, but this will not usually bring the whole machine down.

Another advantage of the client-server model is its adaptability to use in distributed systems (see Fig. 1-28). If a client communicates with a server by sending it messages, the client need not know whether the message is handled locally in its own machine, or whether it was sent across a network to a server on a remote machine. As far as the client is concerned, the same thing happens in both cases: a request was sent and a reply came back.

The picture painted above of a kernel that handles only the transport of messages from clients to servers and back is not completely realistic. Some operating system functions (such as loading commands into the physical I/O device registers) are difficult, if not impossible, to do from user-space programs. There are two ways of dealing with this problem. One way is to have some critical server processes (e.g., I/O device drivers) actually run in kernel mode, with complete access to all the hardware, but still communicate with other processes using the normal message mechanism.

The other way is to build a minimal amount of **mechanism** into the kernel but leave the **policy** decisions up to servers in user space (Levin et al., 1975). For

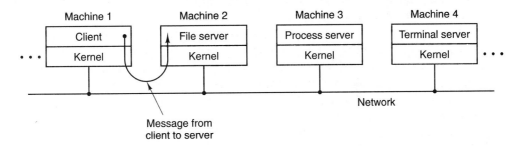

Figure 1-28. The client-server model in a distributed system.

example, the kernel might recognize that a message sent to a certain special address means to take the contents of that message and load it into the I/O device registers for some disk, to start a disk read. In this example, the kernel would not even inspect the bytes in the message to see if they were valid or meaningful; it would just blindly copy them into the disk's device registers. (Obviously, some scheme for limiting such messages to authorized processes only must be used.) The split between mechanism and policy is an important concept; it occurs again and again in operating systems in various contexts.

1.8 RESEARCH ON OPERATING SYSTEMS

Computer science is a rapidly advancing field and it is hard to predict where it is going. Researchers at universities and industrial research labs are constantly thinking up new ideas, some of which go nowhere but some of which become the cornerstone of future products and have massive impact on the industry and users. Telling which is which turns out to be easier to do in hindsight than in real time. Separating the wheat from the chaff is especially difficult because it often takes 20-30 years from idea to impact.

For example, when President Eisenhower set up the Dept. of Defense's Advanced Research Projects Agency (ARPA) in 1958, he was trying to keep the Army from killing the Navy and the Air Force over the Pentagon's research budget. He was not trying to invent the Internet. But one of the things ARPA did was fund some university research on the then-obscure concept of packet switching, which quickly led to the first experimental packet-switched network, the ARPANET. It went live in 1969. Before long, other ARPA-funded research networks were connected to the ARPANET, and the Internet was born. The Internet was then happily used by academic researchers for sending email to each other for 20 years. In the early 1990s, Tim Berners-Lee invented the World Wide Web at the CERN research lab in Geneva and Marc Andreesen wrote a graphical browser for it at the University of Illinois. All of a sudden the Internet was full of chatting teenagers. President Eisenhower is probably rolling over in his grave.

Research in operating systems has also led to dramatic changes in practical systems. As we discussed earlier, the first commercial computer systems were all batch systems, until M.I.T. invented interactive timesharing in the early 1960s. Computers were all text-based until Doug Engelbart invented the mouse and the graphical user interface at Stanford Research Institute in the late 1960s. Who knows what will come next?

In this section and in comparable sections throughout the book, we will take a brief look at some of the research in operating systems that has taken place during the past 5 to 10 years, just to give a flavor of what might be on the horizon. This introduction is certainly not comprehensive and is based largely on papers that have been published in the top research journals and conferences because these ideas have at least survived a rigorous peer review process in order to get published. Most of the papers cited in the research sections were published by either ACM, the IEEE Computer Society, or USENIX and are available over the Internet to (student) members of these organizations. For more information about these organizations and their digital libraries, see

ACM	http://www.acm.org
IEEE Computer Society	http://www.computer.org
USENIX	http://www.usenix.org

Virtually all operating systems researchers realize that current operating systems are massive, inflexible, unreliable, insecure, and loaded with bugs, certain ones more than others (*names withheld here to protect the guilty*). Consequently, there is a lot of research on how to build flexible and dependable systems. Much of the research concerns microkernel systems. These systems have a minimal kernel, so there is a reasonable chance they can be made reliable and be debugged. They are also flexible because much of the real operating system runs as user-mode processes, and can thus be replaced or adapted easily, possibly even during execution. Typically, all the microkernel does is handle low-level resource management and message passing between the user processes.

The first generation microkernels, such as Amoeba (Tanenbaum et al., 1990), Chorus (Rozier et al., 1988), Mach (Accetta et al., 1986), and V (Cheriton, 1988), proved that these systems could be built and made to work. The second generation is trying to prove that they can not only work, but with high performance as well (Ford et al., 1996; Hartig et al., 1997; Liedtke 1995, 1996; Rawson 1997; and Zuberi et al., 1999). Based on published measurements, it appears that this goal has been achieved.

Much kernel research is focused nowadays on building extensible operating systems. These are typically microkernel systems with the ability to extend or customize them in some direction. Some examples are Fluke (Ford et al., 1997), Paramecium (Van Doorn et al., 1995), SPIN (Bershad et al., 1995b), and Vino (Seltzer et al., 1996). Some researchers are also looking at how to extend existing systems (Ghormley et al., 1998). Many of these systems allow users to add their own code to the kernel, which brings up the obvious problem of how to allow user extensions in a secure way. Techniques include interpreting the extensions, restricting them to code sandboxes, using type-safe languages, and code signing (Grimm and Bershad, 1997; and Small and Seltzer, 1998). Druschel et al. (1997) present a dissenting view, saying that too much effort is going into security for user-extendable systems. In their view, researchers should figure out which extensions are useful and then just make those a normal part of the kernel, without the ability to have users extend the kernel on the fly.

Although one approach to eliminating bloated, buggy, unreliable operating systems is to make them smaller, a more radical one is to eliminate the operating system altogether. This approach is being taken by the group of Kaashoek at M.I.T. in their Exokernel research. Here the idea is to have a thin layer of software running on the bare metal, whose only job is to securely allocate the hardware resources among the users. For example, it must decide who gets to use which part of the disk and where incoming network packets should be delivered. Everything else is up to user-level processes, making it possible to build both general-purpose and highly-specialized operating systems (Engler and Kaashoek, 1995; Engler et al., 1995; and Kaashoek et al., 1997).

1.9 OUTLINE OF THE REST OF THIS BOOK

We have now completed our introduction and bird's-eye view of the operating system. It is time to get down to the details. Chapter 2 is about processes. It discusses their properties and how they communicate with one another. It also gives a number of detailed examples of how interprocess communication works and how to avoid some of the pitfalls.

Chapter 3 is about deadlocks. We briefly showed what deadlocks are in this chapter, but there is much more to say. Ways to prevent or avoid them are discussed.

In Chap. 4 we will study memory management in detail. The important topic of virtual memory will be examined, along with closely related concepts such as paging and segmentation.

Input/Output is covered in Chap. 5. The concepts of device independence and device dependence will be looked at. Several important devices, including disks, keyboards, and displays, will be used as examples.

Then, in Chap. 6, we come to the all-important topic of file systems. To a considerable extent, what the user sees is largely the file system. We will look at both the file system interface and the file system implementation.

At this point we will have completed our study of the basic principles of single-CPU operating systems. However, there is more to say, especially about advanced topics. In Chap. 7, we examine multimedia systems, which have a number of properties and requirements that differ from conventional operating systems. Among other items, scheduling and the file system are affected by the nature of multimedia. Another advanced topic is multiple processor systems, including multiprocessors, parallel computers, and distributed systems. These subjects are covered in Chap. 8.

A hugely important subject is operating system security, which is covered in Chap 9. Among the topics discussed in this chapter are threats (e.g., viruses and worms), protection mechanisms, and security models.

Next we have some case studies of real operating systems. These are UNIX (Chap. 10) and Windows 2000 (Chap. 11). The book concludes with some thoughts about operating system design in Chap. 12.

1.10 METRIC UNITS

To avoid any confusion, it is worth stating explicitly that in this book, as in computer science in general, metric units are used instead of traditional English units (the furlong-stone-fortnight system). The principal metric prefixes are listed in Fig. 1-29. The prefixes are typically abbreviated by their first letters, with the units greater than 1 capitalized. Thus a 1-TB database occupies 10^{12} bytes of storage and a 100 psec (or 100 ps) clock ticks every 10^{-10} seconds. Since milli and micro both begin with the letter "m," a choice had to be made. Normally, "m" is for milli and "μ" (the Greek letter mu) is for micro.

Exp.	Explicit	Prefix	Exp.	Explicit	Prefix
10^{-3}	0.001	milli	10^{3}	1,000	Kilo
10^{-6}	0.000001	micro	10^{6}	1,000,000	Mega
10^{-9}	0.000000001	nano	10^{9}	1,000,000,000	Giga
10^{-12}	0.000000000001	pico	10^{12}	1,000,000,000,000	Tera
10^{-15}	0.000000000000001	femto	10^{15}	1,000,000,000,000,000	Peta
10^{-18}	0.000000000000000001	atto	10^{18}	1,000,000,000,000,000,000	Exa
10^{-21}	0.000000000000000000001	zepto	10^{21}	1,000,000,000,000,000,000,000	Zetta
10^{-24}	0.000000000000000000000001	yocto	10^{24}	1,000,000,000,000,000,000,000,000	Yotta

Figure 1-29. The principal metric prefixes.

It is also worth pointing out that for measuring memory sizes, in common industry practice, the units have slightly different meanings. There Kilo means 2^{10} (1024) rather than 10^3 (1000) because memories are always a power of two. Thus a 1-KB memory contains 1024 bytes, not 1000 bytes. Similarly, a 1-MB memory contains 2^{20} (1,048,576) bytes and a 1-GB memory contains 2^{30} (1,073,741,824) bytes. However, a 1-Kbps communication line transmits 1000 bits per second and a 10-Mbps LAN runs at 10,000,000 bits/sec because these speeds are not powers of two. Unfortunately, many people tend to mix up these two systems, especially for disk sizes. To avoid ambiguity, in this book, we will use the symbols KB, MB, and GB for 2^{10}, 2^{20}, and 2^{30} bytes respectively, and the symbols Kbps, Mbps, and Gbps for 10^3, 10^6 and 10^9 bits/sec, respectively.

1.11 SUMMARY

Operating systems can be viewed from two viewpoints: resource managers and extended machines. In the resource manager view, the operating system's job is to manage the different parts of the system efficiently. In the extended machine view, the job of the system is to provide the users with a virtual machine that is more convenient to use than the actual machine.

Operating systems have a long history, starting from the days when they replaced the operator, to modern multiprogramming systems. Highlights include early batch systems, multiprogramming systems, and personal computer systems.

Since operating systems interact closely with the hardware, some knowledge of computer hardware is useful to understanding them. Computers are built up of processors, memories, and I/O devices. These parts are connected by buses.

The basic concepts on which all operating systems are built are processes, memory management, I/O management, the file system, and security. Each of these will be treated in a subsequent chapter.

The heart of any operating system is the set of system calls that it can handle. These tell what the operating system really does. For UNIX, we have looked at four groups of system calls. The first group of system calls relates to process creation and termination. The second group is for reading and writing files. The third group is for directory management. The fourth group contains miscellaneous calls.

Operating systems can be structured in several ways. The most common ones are as a monolithic system, a hierarchy of layers, a virtual machine system, an exokernel, or using the client-server model.

PROBLEMS

1. What are the two main functions of an operating system?

2. What is multiprogramming?

3. What is spooling? Do you think that advanced personal computers will have spooling as a standard feature in the future?

4. On early computers, every byte of data read or written was directly handled by the CPU (i.e., there was no DMA). What implications does this organization have for multiprogramming?

5. Why was timesharing not widespread on second-generation computers?

6. The family of computers idea was introduced in the 1960s with the IBM System/360 mainframes. Is this idea now dead as a doornail or does it live on?

7. One reason GUIs were initially slow to be adopted was the cost of the hardware needed to support them. How much video RAM is needed to support a 25 line × 80 row character monochrome text screen? How much for a 1024 × 768 pixel 24-bit color bitmap? What was the cost of this RAM at 1980 prices ($5/KB)? How much is it now?

8. Which of the following instructions should be allowed only in kernel mode?

   (a) Disable all interrupts.
   (b) Read the time-of-day clock.
   (c) Set the time-of-day clock.
   (d) Change the memory map.

9. List some differences between personal computer operating systems and mainframe operating systems.

10. A computer has a pipeline with four stages. Each stage takes the same time to do its work, namely, 1 nsec. How many instructions per second can this machine execute?

11. An alert reviewer notices a consistent spelling error in the manuscript of an operating systems textbook that is about to go to press. The book has approximately 700 pages, each with 50 lines of 80 characters each. How long will it take to electronically scan the text for the case of the master copy being in each of the levels of memory of Fig. 1-7? For internal storage methods, consider that the access time given is per character, for disk devices assume the time is per block of 1024 characters, and for tape assume the time given is to the start of the data with subsequent access at the same speed as disk access.

12. In Fig. 1-9, the MMU compares the incoming (virtual) address to the limit register, causing a fault if it is too large. An alternative design would be to first add the virtual address to the base register and then compare the result to the (physical) address in the limit register. Are the two methods logically equivalent? Are they equivalent in performance?

13. When a user program makes a system call to read or write a disk file, it provides an indication of which file it wants, a pointer to the data buffer, and the count. Control is then transferred to the operating system, which calls the appropriate driver. Suppose that the driver starts the disk and terminates until an interrupt occurs. In the case of reading from the disk, obviously the caller will have to be blocked (because there are no data for it). What about the case of writing to the disk? Need the caller be blocking awaiting completion of the disk transfer?

14. What is the key difference between a trap and an interrupt?

15. A computer uses the relocation scheme of Fig. 1-9(a). A program is 10,000 bytes long and is loaded at address 40,000. What values do the *base* and *limit* register get according to the scheme described in the text?

16. Why is the process table needed in a timesharing system? Is it also needed in personal computer systems in which only one process exists, that process taking over the entire machine until it is finished?

17. Is there any reason why you might want to mount a file system on a nonempty directory? If so, what is it?

18. For each of the following system calls, give a condition that causes it to fail: fork, exec, and unlink.

19. Can the

```
count = write(fd, buffer, nbytes);
```

call return any value in *count* other than *nbytes*? If so, why?

20. A file whose file descriptor is *fd* contains the following sequence of bytes: 3, 1, 4, 1, 5, 9, 2, 6, 5, 3, 5. The following system calls are made:

```
lseek(fd, 3, SEEK_SET);
read(fd, &buffer, 4);
```

where the lseek call makes a seek to byte 3 of the file. What does *buffer* contain after the read has completed?

21. What is the essential difference between a block special file and a character special file?

22. In the example given in Fig. 1-17, the library procedure is called *read* and the system call itself is called read. Is it essential that both of these have the same name? If not, which one is more important?

23. The client-server model is popular in distributed systems. Can it also be used in a single-computer system?

24. To a programmer, a system call looks like any other call to a library procedure. Is it important that a programmer know which library procedures result in system calls? Under what circumstances and why?

25. Figure 1-23 shows that a number of UNIX system calls have no Win32 API equivalents. For each of the calls listed as having no Win32 equivalent, what are the consequences for a programmer of converting a UNIX program to run under Windows?

26. Here are some questions for practicing unit conversions:

(a) How long is a microyear in seconds?
(b) Micrometers are often called microns. How long is a gigamicron?
(c) How many bytes are there in a 1-TB memory?
(d) The mass of the earth is 6000 yottagrams. What is that in kilograms?

27. Write a shell that is similar to Fig. 1-19 but contains enough code that it actually works so you can test it. You might also add some features such as redirection of input and output, pipes, and background jobs.

28. If you have a personal UNIX-like system (Linux, MINIX, Free BSD, etc.) available that you can safely crash and reboot, write a shell script that attempts to create an unlimited number of child processes and observe what happens. Before running the experiment, type sync to the shell to flush the file system buffers to disk to avoid ruining the file system. **Note**: Do not try this on a shared system without first getting permission from the system administrator. The consequences will be instantly obvious so you are likely to be caught and sanctions may follow.

29. Examine and try to interpret the contents of a UNIX-like or Windows directory with a tool like the UNIX *od* program or the MS-DOS *DEBUG* program. *Hint*: How you do this will depend upon what the OS allows. One trick that may work is to create a directory on a floppy disk with one operating system and then read the raw disk data using a different operating system that allows such access.

2

PROCESSES AND THREADS

We are now about to embark on a detailed study of how operating systems are designed and constructed. The most central concept in any operating system is the *process*: an abstraction of a running program. Everything else hinges on this concept, and it is important that the operating system designer (and student) have a thorough understanding of what a process is as early as possible.

2.1 PROCESSES

All modern computers can do several things at the same time. While running a user program, a computer can also be reading from a disk and outputting text to a screen or printer. In a multiprogramming system, the CPU also switches from program to program, running each for tens or hundreds of milliseconds. While, strictly speaking, at any instant of time, the CPU is running only one program, in the course of 1 second, it may work on several programs, thus giving the users the illusion of parallelism. Sometimes people speak of **pseudoparallelism** in this context, to contrast it with the true hardware parallelism of **multiprocessor** systems (which have two or more CPUs sharing the same physical memory). Keeping track of multiple, parallel activities is hard for people to do. Therefore, operating system designers over the years have evolved a conceptual model (sequential processes) that makes parallelism easier to deal with. That model, its uses, and some of its consequences form the subject of this chapter.

71

2.1.1 The Process Model

In this model, all the runnable software on the computer, sometimes including the operating system, is organized into a number of **sequential processes**, or just **processes** for short. A process is just an executing program, including the current values of the program counter, registers, and variables. Conceptually, each process has its own virtual CPU. In reality, of course, the real CPU switches back and forth from process to process, but to understand the system, it is much easier to think about a collection of processes running in (pseudo) parallel, than to try to keep track of how the CPU switches from program to program. This rapid switching back and forth is called **multiprogramming**, as we saw in Chap. 1.

In Fig. 2-1(a) we see a computer multiprogramming four programs in memory. In Fig. 2-1(b) we see four processes, each with its own flow of control (i.e., its own logical program counter), and each one running independently of the other ones. Of course, there is only one physical program counter, so when each process runs, its logical program counter is loaded into the real program counter. When it is finished for the time being, the physical program counter is saved in the process' logical program counter in memory. In Fig. 2-1(c) we see that viewed over a long enough time interval, all the processes have made progress, but at any given instant only one process is actually running.

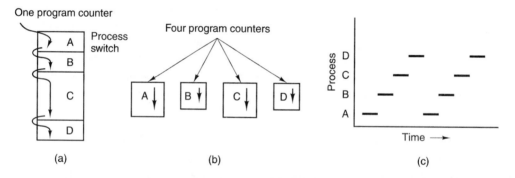

Figure 2-1. (a) Multiprogramming of four programs. (b) Conceptual model of four independent, sequential processes. (c) Only one program is active at once.

With the CPU switching back and forth among the processes, the rate at which a process performs its computation will not be uniform and probably not even reproducible if the same processes are run again. Thus, processes must not be programmed with built-in assumptions about timing. Consider, for example, an I/O process that starts a streamer tape to restore backed up files, executes an idle loop 10,000 times to let it get up to speed, and then issues a command to read the first record. If the CPU decides to switch to another process during the idle loop, the tape process might not run again until after the first record was already past the read head. When a process has critical real-time requirements like this, that is, particular events *must* occur within a specified number of milliseconds, special measures must be taken to ensure that they do occur. Normally, however, most processes are not affected by the underlying multiprogramming of the CPU or the relative speeds of different processes.

The difference between a process and a program is subtle, but crucial. An analogy make help here. Consider a culinary-minded computer scientist who is baking a birthday cake for his daughter. He has a birthday cake recipe and a kitchen well stocked with all the input: flour, eggs, sugar, extract of vanilla, and so on. In this analogy, the recipe is the program (i.e., an algorithm expressed in some suitable notation), the computer scientist is the processor (CPU), and the cake ingredients are the input data. The process is the activity consisting of our baker reading the recipe, fetching the ingredients, and baking the cake.

Now imagine that the computer scientist's son comes running in crying, saying that he has been stung by a bee. The computer scientist records where he was in the recipe (the state of the current process is saved), gets out a first aid book, and begins following the directions in it. Here we see the processor being switched from one process (baking) to a higher-priority process (administering medical care), each having a different program (recipe versus first aid book). When the bee sting has been taken care of, the computer scientist goes back to his cake, continuing at the point where he left off.

The key idea here is that a process is an activity of some kind. It has a program, input, output, and a state. A single processor may be shared among several processes, with some scheduling algorithm being used to determine when to stop work on one process and service a different one.

2.1.2 Process Creation

Operating systems need some way to make sure all the necessary processes exist. In very simple systems, or in systems designed for running only a single application (e.g., the controller in a microwave oven), it may be possible to have all the processes that will ever be needed be present when the system comes up. In general-purpose systems, however, some way is needed to create and terminate processes as needed during operation. We will now look at some of the issues.

There are four principal events that cause processes to be created:

1. System initialization.

2. Execution of a process creation system call by a running process.

3. A user request to create a new process.

4. Initiation of a batch job.

When an operating system is booted, typically several processes are created. Some of these are foreground processes, that is, processes that interact with (human) users and perform work for them. Others are background processes, which are not associated with particular users, but instead have some specific function. For example, one background process may be designed to accept incoming email, sleeping most of the day but suddenly springing to life when email arrives. Another background process may be designed to accept incoming requests for Web pages hosted on that machine, waking up when a request arrives to service the request. Processes that stay in the background to handle some activity such as email, Web pages, news, printing, and so on are called **daemons**. Large systems commonly have dozens of them. In UNIX, the *ps* program can be used to list the running processes. In Windows 95/98/Me, typing CTRL-ALT-DEL once shows what's running. In Windows 2000, the task manager is used.

In addition to the processes created at boot time, new processes can be created afterward as well. Often a running process will issue system calls to create one or more new processes to help it do its job. Creating new processes is particularly useful when the work to be done can easily be formulated in terms of several related, but otherwise independent interacting processes. For example, if a large amount of data is being fetched over a network for subsequent processing, it may be convenient to create one process to fetch the data and put them in a shared buffer while a second process removes the data items and processes them. On a multiprocessor, allowing each process to run on a different CPU may also make the job go faster.

In interactive systems, users can start a program by typing a command or (double) clicking an icon. Taking either of these actions starts a new process and runs the selected program in it. In command-based UNIX systems running X Windows, the new process takes over the window in which it was started. In Microsoft Windows, when a process is started it does not have a window, but it can create one (or more) and most do. In both systems, users may have multiple windows open at once, each running some process. Using the mouse, the user can select a window and interact with the process, for example, providing input when needed.

The last situation in which processes are created applies only to the batch systems found on large mainframes. Here users can submit batch jobs to the system (possibly remotely). When the operating system decides that it has the resources to run another job, it creates a new process and runs the next job from the input queue in it.

Technically, in all these cases, a new process is created by having an existing process execute a process creation system call. That process may be a running user process, a system process invoked from the keyboard or mouse, or a batch manager process. What that process does is execute a system call to create the new process. This system call tells the operating system to create a new process and indicates, directly or indirectly, which program to run in it.

In UNIX, there is only one system call to create a new process: fork. This call creates an exact clone of the calling process. After the fork, the two processes, the parent and the child, have the same memory image, the same environment strings, and the same open files. That is all there is. Usually, the child process then executes execve or a similar system call to change its memory image and run a new program. For example, when a user types a command, say, *sort*, to the shell, the shell forks off a child process and the child executes *sort*. The reason for this two-step process is to allow the child to manipulate its file descriptors after the fork but before the execve to accomplish redirection of standard input, standard output, and standard error.

In Windows, in contrast, a single Win32 function call, CreateProcess, handles both process creation and loading the correct program into the new process. This call has 10 parameters, which include the program to be executed, the command line parameters to feed that program, various security attributes, bits that control whether open files are inherited, priority information, a specification of the window to be created for the process (if any), and a pointer to a structure in which information about the newly created process is returned to the caller. In addition to CreateProcess, Win32 has about 100 other functions for managing and synchronizing processes and related topics.

In both UNIX and Windows, after a process is created, both the parent and child have their own distinct address spaces. If either process changes a word in its address space, the change is not visible to the other process. In UNIX, the child's initial address space is a *copy* of the parent's, but there are two distinct address spaces involved; no writable memory is shared (some UNIX implementations share the program text between the two since that cannot be modified). It is, however, possible for a newly created process to share some of its creator's other resources, such as open files. In Windows, the parent's and child's address spaces are different from the start.

2.1.3 Process Termination

After a process has been created, it starts running and does whatever its job is. However, nothing lasts forever, not even processes. Sooner or later the new process will terminate, usually due to one of the following conditions:

1. Normal exit (voluntary).
2. Error exit (voluntary).
3. Fatal error (involuntary).
4. Killed by another process (involuntary).

Most processes terminate because they have done their work. When a compiler has compiled the program given to it, the compiler executes a system call to tell the operating system that it is finished. This call is exit in UNIX and ExitProcess in Windows. Screen-oriented programs also support voluntary termination.

Word processors, Internet browsers and similar programs always have an icon or menu item that the user can click to tell the process to remove any temporary files it has open and then terminate.

The second reason for termination is that the process discovers a fatal error. For example, if a user types the command

cc foo.c

to compile the program *foo.c* and no such file exists, the compiler simply exits. Screen-oriented interactive processes generally do not exit when given bad parameters. Instead they pop up a dialog box and ask the user to try again.

The third reason for termination is an error caused by the process, often due to a program bug. Examples include executing an illegal instruction, referencing nonexistent memory, or dividing by zero. In some systems (e.g., UNIX), a process can tell the operating system that it wishes to handle certain errors itself, in which case the process is signaled (interrupted) instead of terminated when one of the errors occurs.

The fourth reason a process might terminate is that a process executes a system call telling the operating system to kill some other process. In UNIX this call is kill. The corresponding Win32 function is TerminateProcess. In both cases, the killer must have the necessary authorization to do in the killee. In some systems, when a process terminates, either voluntarily or otherwise, all processes it created are immediately killed as well. Neither UNIX nor Windows works this way, however.

2.1.4 Process Hierarchies

In some systems, when a process creates another process, the parent process and child process continue to be associated in certain ways. The child process can itself create more processes, forming a process hierarchy. Note that unlike plants and animals that use sexual reproduction, a process has only one parent (but zero, one, two, or more children).

In UNIX, a process and all of its children and further descendants together form a process group. When a user sends a signal from the keyboard, the signal is delivered to all members of the process group currently associated with the keyboard (usually all active processes that were created in the current window). Individually, each process can catch the signal, ignore the signal, or take the default action, which is to be killed by the signal.

As another example of where the process hierarchy plays a role, let us look at how UNIX initializes itself when it is started. A special process, called *init*, is present in the boot image. When it starts running, it reads a file telling how many terminals there are. Then it forks off one new process per terminal. These processes wait for someone to log in. If a login is successful, the login process executes a shell to accept commands. These commands may start up more processes, and so forth. Thus, all the processes in the whole system belong to a single tree, with *init* at the root.

In contrast, Windows does not have any concept of a process hierarchy. All processes are equal. The only place where there is something like a process hierarchy is that when a process is created, the parent is given a special token (called a **handle**) that it can use to control the child. However, it is free to pass this token to some other process, thus invalidating the hierarchy. Processes in UNIX cannot disinherit their children.

2.1.5 Process States

Although each process is an independent entity, with its own program counter and internal state, processes often need to interact with other processes. One process may generate some output that another process uses as input. In the shell command

    cat chapter1 chapter2 chapter3 | grep tree

the first process, running *cat*, concatenates and outputs three files. The second process, running *grep*, selects all lines containing the word "tree." Depending on the relative speeds of the two processes (which depends on both the relative complexity of the programs and how much CPU time each one has had), it may happen that *grep* is ready to run, but there is no input waiting for it. It must then block until some input is available.

When a process blocks, it does so because logically it cannot continue, typically because it is waiting for input that is not yet available. It is also possible for a process that is conceptually ready and able to run to be stopped because the operating system has decided to allocate the CPU to another process for a while. These two conditions are completely different. In the first case, the suspension is inherent in the problem (you cannot process the user's command line until it has been typed). In the second case, it is a technicality of the system (not enough CPUs to give each process its own private processor). In Fig. 2-2 we see a state diagram showing the three states a process may be in:

1. Running (actually using the CPU at that instant).

2. Ready (runnable; temporarily stopped to let another process run).

3. Blocked (unable to run until some external event happens).

Logically, the first two states are similar. In both cases the process is willing to run, only in the second one, there is temporarily no CPU available for it. The third state is different from the first two in that the process cannot run, even if the CPU has nothing else to do.

Four transitions are possible among these three states, as shown. Transition 1 occurs when a process discovers that it cannot continue. In some systems the

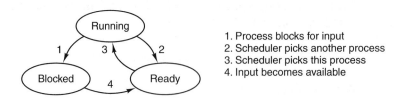

Figure 2-2. A process can be in running, blocked, or ready state. Transitions between these states are as shown.

process must execute a system call, such as block or pause, to get into blocked state. In other systems, including UNIX, when a process reads from a pipe or special file (e.g., a terminal) and there is no input available, the process is automatically blocked.

Transitions 2 and 3 are caused by the process scheduler, a part of the operating system, without the process even knowing about them. Transition 2 occurs when the scheduler decides that the running process has run long enough, and it is time to let another process have some CPU time. Transition 3 occurs when all the other processes have had their fair share and it is time for the first process to get the CPU to run again. The subject of scheduling, that is, deciding which process should run when and for how long, is an important one; we will look at it later in this chapter. Many algorithms have been devised to try to balance the competing demands of efficiency for the system as a whole and fairness to individual processes. We will study some of them later in this chapter.

Transition 4 occurs when the external event for which a process was waiting (such as the arrival of some input) happens. If no other process is running at that instant, transition 3 will be triggered and the process will start running. Otherwise it may have to wait in *ready* state for a little while until the CPU is available and its turn comes.

Using the process model, it becomes much easier to think about what is going on inside the system. Some of the processes run programs that carry out commands typed in by a user. Other processes are part of the system and handle tasks such as carrying out requests for file services or managing the details of running a disk or a tape drive. When a disk interrupt occurs, the system makes a decision to stop running the current process and run the disk process, which was blocked waiting for that interrupt. Thus, instead of thinking about interrupts, we can think about user processes, disk processes, terminal processes, and so on, which block when they are waiting for something to happen. When the disk has been read or the character typed, the process waiting for it is unblocked and is eligible to run again.

This view gives rise to the model shown in Fig. 2-3. Here the lowest level of the operating system is the scheduler, with a variety of processes on top of it. All the interrupt handling and details of actually starting and stopping processes are hidden away in what is here called the scheduler, which is actually not much code. The rest of the operating system is nicely structured in process form. Few real systems are as nicely structured as this, however.

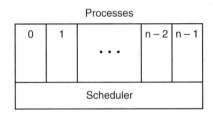

Figure 2-3. The lowest layer of a process-structured operating system handles interrupts and scheduling. Above that layer are sequential processes.

2.1.6 Implementation of Processes

To implement the process model, the operating system maintains a table (an array of structures), called the **process table**, with one entry per process. (Some authors call these entries **process control blocks**.) This entry contains information about the process' state, its program counter, stack pointer, memory allocation, the status of its open files, its accounting and scheduling information, and everything else about the process that must be saved when the process is switched from *running* to *ready* or *blocked* state so that it can be restarted later as if it had never been stopped.

Figure 2-4 shows some of the more important fields in a typical system. The fields in the first column relate to process management. The other two columns relate to memory management and file management, respectively. It should be noted that precisely which fields the process table has is highly system dependent, but this figure gives a general idea of the kinds of information needed.

Now that we have looked at the process table, it is possible to explain a little more about how the illusion of multiple sequential processes is maintained on a machine with one CPU and many I/O devices. Associated with each I/O device class (e.g., floppy disks, hard disks, timers, terminals) is a location (often near the bottom of memory) called the **interrupt vector**. It contains the address of the interrupt service procedure. Suppose that user process 3 is running when a disk interrupt occurs. User process 3's program counter, program status word, and possibly one or more registers are pushed onto the (current) stack by the interrupt hardware. The computer then jumps to the address specified in the disk interrupt vector. That is all the hardware does. From here on, it is up to the software, in particular, the interrupt service procedure.

All interrupts start by saving the registers, often in the process table entry for the current process. Then the information pushed onto the stack by the interrupt is removed and the stack pointer is set to point to a temporary stack used by the

Process management	Memory management	File management
Registers	Pointer to text segment	Root directory
Program counter	Pointer to data segment	Working directory
Program status word	Pointer to stack segment	File descriptors
Stack pointer		User ID
Process state		Group ID
Priority		
Scheduling parameters		
Process ID		
Parent process		
Process group		
Signals		
Time when process started		
CPU time used		
Children's CPU time		
Time of next alarm		

Figure 2-4. Some of the fields of a typical process table entry.

process handler. Actions such as saving the registers and setting the stack pointer cannot even be expressed in high-level languages such as C, so they are performed by a small assembly language routine, usually the same one for all interrupts since the work of saving the registers is identical, no matter what the cause of the interrupt is.

When this routine is finished, it calls a C procedure to do the rest of the work for this specific interrupt type. (We assume the operating system is written in C, the usual choice for all real operating systems.) When it has done its job, possibly making some process now ready, the scheduler is called to see who to run next. After that, control is passed back to the assembly language code to load up the registers and memory map for the now-current process and start it running. Interrupt handling and scheduling are summarized in Fig. 2-5. It is worth noting that the details vary somewhat from system to system.

```
1. Hardware stacks program counter, etc.
2. Hardware loads new program counter from interrupt vector.
3. Assembly language procedure saves registers.
4. Assembly language procedure sets up new stack.
5. C interrupt service runs (typically reads and buffers input).
6. Scheduler decides which process is to run next.
7. C procedure returns to the assembly code.
8. Assembly language procedure starts up new current process.
```

Figure 2-5. Skeleton of what the lowest level of the operating system does when an interrupt occurs.

2.2 THREADS

In traditional operating systems, each process has an address space and a single thread of control. In fact, that is almost the definition of a process. Nevertheless, there are frequently situations in which it is desirable to have multiple threads of control in the same address space running in quasi-parallel, as though they were separate processes (except for the shared address space). In the following sections we will discuss these situations and their implications.

2.2.1 The Thread Model

The process model as we have discussed it thus far is based on two independent concepts: resource grouping and execution. Sometimes it is useful to separate them; this is where threads come in.

One way of looking at a process is that it is way to group related resources together. A process has an address space containing program text and data, as well as other resources. These resource may include open files, child processes, pending alarms, signal handlers, accounting information, and more. By putting them together in the form of a process, they can be managed more easily.

The other concept a process has is a thread of execution, usually shortened to just **thread**. The thread has a program counter that keeps track of which instruction to execute next. It has registers, which hold its current working variables. It has a stack, which contains the execution history, with one frame for each procedure called but not yet returned from. Although a thread must execute in some process, the thread and its process are different concepts and can be treated separately. Processes are used to group resources together; threads are the entities scheduled for execution on the CPU.

What threads add to the process model is to allow multiple executions to take place in the same process environment, to a large degree independent of one another. Having multiple threads running in parallel in one process is analogous to having multiple processes running in parallel in one computer. In the former case, the threads share an address space, open files, and other resources. In the latter case, processes share physical memory, disks, printers, and other resources. Because threads have some of the properties of processes, they are sometimes called **lightweight processes**. The term **multithreading** is also used to describe the situation of allowing multiple threads in the same process.

In Fig. 2-6(a) we see three traditional processes. Each process has its own address space and a single thread of control. In contrast, in Fig. 2-6(b) we see a single process with three threads of control. Although in both cases we have three threads, in Fig. 2-6(a) each of them operates in a different address space, whereas in Fig. 2-6(b) all three of them share the same address space.

When a multithreaded process is run on a single-CPU system, the threads take turns running. In Fig. 2-1, we saw how multiprogramming of processes works.

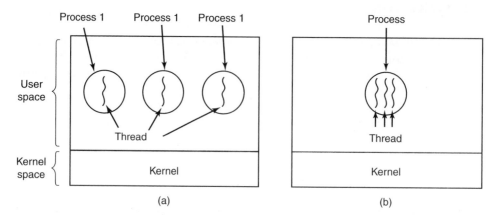

Figure 2-6. (a) Three processes each with one thread. (b) One process with three threads.

By switching back and forth among multiple processes, the system gives the illusion of separate sequential processes running in parallel. Multithreading works the same way. The CPU switches rapidly back and forth among the threads providing the illusion that the threads are running in parallel, albeit on a slower CPU than the real one. With three compute-bound threads in a process, the threads would appear to be running in parallel, each one on a CPU with one-third the speed of the real CPU.

Different threads in a process are not quite as independent as different processes. All threads have exactly the same address space, which means that they also share the same global variables. Since every thread can access every memory address within the process' address space, one thread can read, write, or even completely wipe out another thread's stack. There is no protection between threads because (1) it is impossible, and (2) it should not be necessary. Unlike different processes, which may be from different users and which may be hostile to one another, a process is always owned by a single user, who has presumably created multiple threads so that they can cooperate, not fight. In addition to sharing an address space, all the threads share the same set of open files, child processes, alarms, and signals, etc. as shown in Fig. 2-7. Thus the organization of Fig. 2-6(a) would be used when the three processes are essentially unrelated, whereas Fig. 2-6(b) would be appropriate when the three threads are actually part of the same job and are actively and closely cooperating with each other.

The items in the first column are process properties, not thread properties. For example, if one thread opens a file, that file is visible to the other threads in the process and they can read and write it. This is logical since the process is the unit of resource management, not the thread. If each thread had its own address space, open files, pending alarms, and so on, it would be a separate process. What we are trying to achieve with the thread concept is the ability for multiple threads

Per process items	Per thread items
Address space	Program counter
Global variables	Registers
Open files	Stack
Child processes	State
Pending alarms	
Signals and signal handlers	
Accounting information	

Figure 2-7. The first column lists some items shared by all threads in a process. The second one lists some items private to each thread.

of execution to share a set of resources so they can work together closely to perform some task.

Like a traditional process (i.e., a process with only one thread), a thread can be in any one of several states: running, blocked, ready, or terminated. A running thread currently has the CPU and is active. A blocked thread is waiting for some event to unblock it. For example, when a thread performs a system call to read from the keyboard, it is blocked until input is typed. A thread can block waiting for some external event to happen or for some other thread to unblock it. A ready thread is scheduled to run and will as soon as its turn comes up. The transitions between thread states are the same as the transitions between process states and are illustrated in Fig. 2-2.

It is important to realize that each thread has its own stack, as shown in Fig. 2-8. Each thread's stack contains one frame for each procedure called but not yet returned from. This frame contains the procedure's local variables and the return address to use when the procedure call has finished. For example, if procedure X calls procedure Y and this one calls procedure Z, while Z is executing the frames for X, Y, and Z will all be on the stack. Each thread will generally call different procedures and a thus a different execution history. This is why is thread needs its own stack.

When multithreading is present, processes normally start with a single thread present. This thread has the ability to create new threads by calling a library procedure, for example, *thread_create*. A parameter to *thread_create* typically specifies the name of a procedure for the new thread to run. It is not necessary (or even possible) to specify anything about the new thread's address space since it automatically runs in the address space of the creating thread. Sometimes threads are hierarchical, with a parent-child relationship, but often no such relationship exists, with all threads being equal. With or without a hierarchical relationship, the creating thread is usually returned a thread identifier that names the new thread.

When a thread has finished its work, it can exit by calling a library procedure, say, *thread_exit*. It then vanishes and is no longer schedulable. In some thread

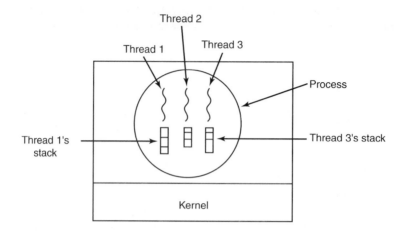

Figure 2-8. Each thread has its own stack.

systems, one thread can wait for a (specific) thread to exit by calling a procedure, for example, *thread_wait*. This procedure blocks the calling thread until a (specific) thread has exited. In this regard, thread creation and termination is very much like process creation and termination, with approximately the same options as well.

Another common thread call is *thread_yield*, which allows a thread to voluntarily give up the CPU to let another thread run. Such a call is important because there is no clock interrupt to actually enforce timesharing as there is with processes. Thus it is important for threads to be polite and voluntarily surrender the CPU from time to time to give other threads a chance to run. Other calls allow one thread to wait for another thread to finish some work, for a thread to announce that it has finished some work, and so on.

While threads are often useful, they also introduce a number of complications into the programming model. To start with, consider the effects of the UNIX fork system call. If the parent process has multiple threads, should the child also have them? If not, the process may not function properly, since all of them may be essential.

However, if the child process gets as many threads as the parent, what happens if a thread in the parent was blocked on a **read** call, say, from the keyboard? Are two threads now blocked on the keyboard, one in the parent and one in the child? When a line is typed, do both threads get a copy of it? Only the parent? Only the child? The same problem exists with open network connections.

Another class of problems is related to the fact that threads share many data structures. What happens if one thread closes a file while another one is still reading from it? Suppose that one thread notices that there is too little memory and starts allocating more memory. Part way through, a thread switch occurs, and the new thread also notices that there is too little memory and also starts allocating more memory. Memory will probably be allocated twice. These problems can be solved with some effort, but careful thought and design are needed to make multithreaded programs work correctly.

2.2.2 Thread Usage

Having described what threads are, it is now time to explain why anyone wants them. The main reason for having threads is that in many applications, multiple activities are going on at once. Some of these may block from time to time. By decomposing such an application into multiple sequential threads that run in quasi-parallel, the programming model becomes simpler.

We have seen this argument before. It is precisely the argument for having processes. Instead of thinking about interrupts, timers, and context switches, we can think about parallel processes. Only now with threads we add a new element: the ability for the parallel entities to share an address space and all of its data among themselves. This ability is essential for certain applications, which is why having multiple processes (with their separate address spaces) will not work.

A second argument for having threads is that since they do not have any resources attached to them, they are easier to create and destroy than processes. In many systems, creating a thread goes 100 times faster than creating a process. When the number of threads needed changes dynamically and rapidly, this property is useful.

A third reason for having threads is also a performance argument. Threads yield no performance gain when all of them are CPU bound, but when there is substantial computing and also substantial I/O, having threads allows these activities to overlap, thus speeding up the application.

Finally, threads are useful on systems with multiple CPUs, where real parallelism is possible. We will come back to this issue in Chap. 8.

It is probably easiest to see why threads are useful by giving some concrete examples. As a first example, consider a word processor. Most word processors display the document being created on the screen formatted exactly as it will appear on the printed page. In particular, all the line breaks and page breaks are in their correct and final position so the user can inspect them and change the document if need be (e.g., to eliminate widows and orphans—incomplete top and bottom lines on a page, which are considered esthetically unpleasing).

Suppose that the user is writing a book. From the author's point of view, it is easiest to keep the entire book as a single file to make it easier to search for topics, perform global substitutions, and so on. Alternatively, each chapter might be a separate file. However, having every section and subsection as a separate file is a real nuisance when global changes have to be made to the entire book since then hundreds of files have to be individually edited. For example, if proposed standard xxxx is approved just before the book goes to press, all occurrences of "Draft Standard xxxx" have to be changed to "Standard xxxx" at the last minute. If the entire book is one file, typically a single command can do all the substitutions. In contrast, if the book is spread over 300 files, each one must be edited separately.

Now consider what happens when the user suddenly deletes one sentence from page 1 of an 800-page document. After checking the changed page to make sure it is correct, the user now wants to make another change on page 600 and types in a command telling the word processor to go to that page (possibly by searching for a phrase occurring only there). The word processor is now forced to reformat the entire book up to page 600 on the spot because it does not know what the first line of page 600 will be until it has processed all the previous pages. There may be a substantial delay before page 600 can be displayed, leading to an unhappy user.

Threads can help here. Suppose that the word processor is written as a two-threaded program. One thread interacts with the user and the other handles reformatting in the background. As soon as the sentence is deleted from page 1, the interactive thread tells the reformatting thread to reformat the whole book. Meanwhile, the interactive thread continues to listen to the keyboard and mouse and responds to simple commands like scrolling page 1 while the other thread is computing madly in the background. With a little luck, the reformatting will be completed before the user asks to see page 600, so it can be displayed instantly.

While we are at it, why not add a third thread? Many word processors have a feature of automatically saving the entire file to disk every few minutes to protect the user against losing a day's work in the event of a program crash, system crash, or power failure. The third thread can handle the disk backups without interfering with the other two. The situation with three threads is shown in Fig. 2-9.

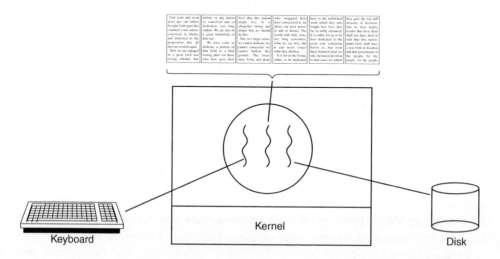

Figure 2-9. A word processor with three threads.

If the program were single-threaded, then whenever a disk backup started, commands from the keyboard and mouse would be ignored until the backup was finished. The user would perceive this as sluggish performance. Alternatively, keyboard and mouse events could interrupt the disk backup, allowing good performance but leading to a complex interrupt-driven programming model. With three threads, the programming model is much simpler. The first thread just interacts with the user. The second thread reformats the document when told to. The third thread writes the contents of RAM to disk periodically.

It should be clear that having three separate processes would not work here because all three threads need to operate on the document. By having three threads instead of three processes, they share a common memory and thus all have access to the document being edited.

An analogous situation exists with many other interactive programs. For example, an electronic spreadsheet is a program that allows a user to maintain a matrix, some of whose elements are data provided by the user. Other elements are computed based on the input data using potentially complex formulas. When a user changes one element, many other elements may have to be recomputed. By having a background thread do the recomputation, the interactive thread can allow the user to make additional changes while the computation is going on. Similarly, a third thread can handle periodic backups to disk on its own.

Now consider yet another example of where threads are useful: a server for a World Wide Web site. Requests for pages come in and the requested page is sent back to the client. At most Web sites, some pages are more commonly accessed than other pages. For example, Sony's home page is accessed far more than a page deep in the tree containing the technical specifications of some particular camcorder. Web servers use this fact to improve performance by maintaining a collection of heavily used pages in main memory to eliminate the need to go to disk to get them. Such a collection is called a **cache** and is used in many other contexts as well.

One way to organize the Web server is shown in Fig. 2-10(a). Here one thread, the **dispatcher**, reads incoming requests for work from the network. After examining the request, it chooses an idle (i.e., blocked) **worker thread** and hands it the request, possibly by writing a pointer to the message into a special word associated with each thread. The dispatcher then wakes up the sleeping worker, moving it from blocked state to ready state.

When the worker wakes up, it checks to see if the request can be satisfied from the Web page cache, to which all threads have access. If not, it starts a read operation to get the page from the disk and blocks until the disk operation completes. When the thread blocks on the disk operation, another thread is chosen to run, possibly the dispatcher, in order to acquire more work, or possibly another worker that is now ready to run.

This model allows the server to be written as a collection of sequential threads. The dispatcher's program consists of an infinite loop for getting a work

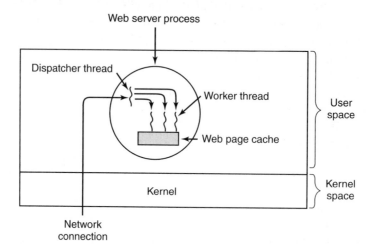

Figure 2-10. A multithreaded Web server.

request and handing it off to a worker. Each worker's code consists of an infinite loop consisting of accepting a request from the dispatcher and checking the Web cache to see if the page is present. If so, it is returned to the client and the worker blocks waiting for a new request. If not, it gets the page from the disk, returns it to the client, and blocks waiting for a new request.

A rough outline of the code is given in Fig. 2-11. Here, as in the rest of this book, *TRUE* is assumed to be the constant 1. Also, *buf* and *page* are structures appropriate for holding a work request and a Web page, respectively.

```
while (TRUE) {                       while (TRUE) {
    get_next_request(&buf);              wait_for_work(&buf);
    handoff_work(&buf);                  look_for_page_in_cache(&buf, &page);
}                                        if (page_not_in_cache(&page))
                                             read_page_from_disk(&buf, &page);
                                         return_page(&page);
                                     }

            (a)                                      (b)
```

Figure 2-11. A rough outline of the code for Fig. 2-10. (a) Dispatcher thread. (b) Worker thread.

Consider how the Web server could be written in the absence of threads. One possibility is to have it operate as a single thread. The main loop of the Web server gets a request, examines it, and carries it out to completion before getting the next one. While waiting for the disk, the server is idle and does not process any other incoming requests. If the Web server is running on a dedicated machine, as is commonly the case, the CPU is simply idle while the Web server is waiting for the disk. The net result is that many fewer requests/sec can be processed. Thus threads gain considerable performance, but each thread is programmed sequentially, in the usual way.

So far we have seen two possible designs: a multithreaded Web server and a single-threaded Web server. Suppose that threads are not available but the system designers find the performance loss due to single threading unacceptable. If a nonblocking version of the read system call is available, a third approach is possible. When a request comes in, the one and only thread examines it. If it can be satisfied from the cache, fine, but if not, a nonblocking disk operation is started.

The server records the state of the current request in a table and then goes and gets the next event. The next event may either be a request for new work or a reply from the disk about a previous operation. If it is new work, that work is started. If it is a reply from the disk, the relevant information is fetched from the table and the reply processed. With nonblocking disk I/O, a reply probably will have to take the form of a signal or interrupt.

In this design, the "sequential process" model that we had in the first two cases is lost. The state of the computation must be explicitly saved and restored in the table every time the server switches from working on one request to another. In effect, we are simulating the threads and their stacks the hard way. A design like this in which each computation has a saved state and there exists some set of events that can occur to change the state is called a **finite-state machine**. This concept is widely used throughout computer science.

It should now be clear what threads have to offer. They make it possible to retain the idea of sequential processes that make blocking system calls (e.g., for disk I/O) and still achieve parallelism. Blocking system calls make programming easier and parallelism improves performance. The single-threaded server retains the ease of blocking system calls but gives up performance. The third approach achieves high performance through parallelism but uses nonblocking calls and interrupts and is thus is hard to program. These models are summarized in Fig. 2-12.

Model	Characteristics
Threads	Parallelism, blocking system calls
Single-threaded process	No parallelism, blocking system calls
Finite-state machine	Parallelism, nonblocking system calls, interrupts

Figure 2-12. Three ways to construct a server.

A third example where threads are useful is in applications that must process very large amounts of data. The normal approach is to read in a block of data, process it, and then write it out again. The problem here is that if only blocking system calls are available, the process blocks while data are coming in and data are going out. Having the CPU go idle when there is lots of computing to do is clearly wasteful and should be avoided if possible.

Threads offer a solution. The process could be structured with an input thread, a processing thread, and an output thread. The input thread reads data into an input buffer. The processing thread takes data out of the input buffer, processes them, and puts the results in an output buffer. The output buffer writes these results back to disk. In this way, input, output, and processing can all be going on at the same time. Of course, this model only works if a system call blocks only the calling thread, not the entire process.

2.2.3 Implementing Threads in User Space

There are two main ways to implement a threads package: in user space and in the kernel. The choice is moderately controversial, and a hybrid implementation is also possible. We will now describe these methods, along with their advantages and disadvantages.

The first method is to put the threads package entirely in user space. The kernel knows nothing about them. As far as the kernel is concerned, it is managing ordinary, single-threaded processes. The first, and most obvious, advantage is that a user-level threads package can be implemented on an operating system that does not support threads. All operating systems used to fall into this category, and even now some still do.

All of these implementations have the same general structure, which is illustrated in Fig. 2-13(a). The threads run on top of a run-time system, which is a collection of procedures that manage threads. We have seen four of these already: *thread_create*, *thread_exit*, *thread_wait*, and *thread_yield*, but usually there are more.

When threads are managed in user space, each process needs its own private **thread table** to keep track of the threads in that process. This table is analogous to the kernel's process table, except that it keeps track only of the per-thread properties such the each thread's program counter, stack pointer, registers, state, etc. The thread table is managed by the run-time system. When a thread is moved to ready state or blocked state, the information needed to restart it is stored in the thread table, exactly the same way as the kernel stores information about processes in the process table.

When a thread does something that may cause it to become blocked locally, for example, waiting for another thread in its process to complete some work, it calls a run-time system procedure. This procedure checks to see if the thread must be put into blocked state. If so, it stores the thread's registers (i.e., its own) in the thread table, looks in the table for a ready thread to run, and reloads the machine registers with the new thread's saved values. As soon as the stack pointer and program counter have been switched, the new thread comes to life

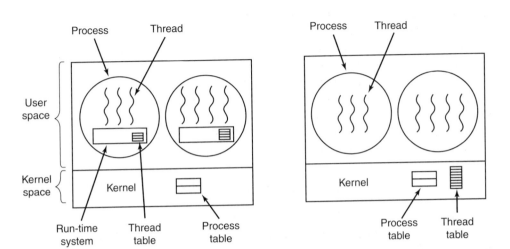

Figure 2-13. (a) A user-level threads package. (b) A threads package managed by the kernel.

again automatically. If the machine has an instruction to store all the registers and another one to load them all, the entire thread switch can be done in a handful of instructions. Doing thread switching like this is at least an order of magnitude faster than trapping to the kernel and is a strong argument in favor of user-level threads packages.

However, there is one key difference with processes. When a thread is finished running for the moment, for example, when it calls *thread_yield*, the code of *thread_yield* can save the thread's information in the thread table itself. Furthermore, it can then call the thread scheduler to pick another thread to run. The procedure that saves the thread's state and the scheduler are just local procedures, so invoking them is much more efficient than making a kernel call. Among other issues, no trap is needed, no context switch is needed, the memory cache need not be flushed, and so on. This makes thread scheduling very fast.

User-level threads also have other advantages. They allow each process to have its own customized scheduling algorithm. For some applications, for example, those with a garbage collector thread, not having to worry about a thread being stopped at an inconvenient moment is a plus. They also scale better, since kernel threads invariably require some table space and stack space in the kernel, which can be a problem if there are a very large number of threads.

Despite their better performance, user-level threads packages have some major problems. First among these is the problem of how blocking system calls are implemented. Suppose that a thread reads from the keyboard before any keys have been hit. Letting the thread actually make the system call is unacceptable, since this will stop all the threads. One of the main goals of having threads in the first place was to allow each one to use blocking calls, but to prevent one blocked thread from affecting the others. With blocking system calls, it is hard to see how this goal can be achieved readily.

The system calls could all be changed to be nonblocking (e.g., a read on the keyboard would just return 0 bytes if no characters were already buffered), but requiring changes to the operating system is unattractive. Besides, one of the arguments for user-level threads was precisely that they could run with *existing* operating systems. In addition, changing the semantics of read will require changes to many user programs.

Another alternative is possible in the event that it is possible to tell in advance if a call will block. In some versions of UNIX, a system call, select, exists, which allows the caller to tell whether a prospective read will block. When this call is present, the library procedure *read* can be replaced with a new one that first does a select call and then only does the read call if it is safe (i.e., will not block). If the read call will block, the call is not made. Instead, another thread is run. The next time the run-time system gets control, it can check again to see if the read is now safe. This approach requires rewriting parts of the system call library, is inefficient and inelegant, but there is little choice. The code placed around the system call to do the checking is called a **jacket** or **wrapper**.

Somewhat analogous to the problem of blocking system calls is the problem of page faults. We will study these in Chap. 4. For the moment, it is sufficient to say that computers can be set up in such a way that not all of the program is in main memory at once. If the program calls or jumps to an instruction that is not in memory, a page fault occurs and the operating system will go and get the missing instruction (and its neighbors) from disk. This is called a page fault. The process is blocked while the necessary instruction is being located and read in. If a thread causes a page fault, the kernel, not even knowing about the existence of threads, naturally blocks the entire process until the disk I/O is complete, even though other threads might be runnable.

Another problem with user-level thread packages is that if a thread starts running, no other thread in that process will ever run unless the first thread voluntarily gives up the CPU. Within a single process, there are no clock interrupts, making it impossible to schedule processes round-robin fashion (taking turns). Unless a thread enters the run-time system of its own free will, the scheduler will never get a chance.

One possible solution to the problem of threads running forever is to have the run-time system request a clock signal (interrupt) once a second to give it control, but this, too, is crude and messy to program. Periodic clock interrupts at a higher frequency are not always possible, and even if they are, the total overhead may be substantial. Furthermore, a thread might also need a clock interrupt, interfering with the run-time system's use of the clock.

Another, and probably the most devastating argument against user-level threads, is that programmers generally want threads precisely in applications where the threads block often, as, for example, in a multithreaded Web server.

These threads are constantly making system calls. Once a trap has occurred to the kernel to carry out the system call, it is hardly any more work for the kernel to switch threads if the old one has blocked, and having the kernel do this eliminates the need for constantly making select system calls that check to see if read system calls are safe. For applications that are essentially entirely CPU bound and rarely block, what is the point of having threads at all? No one would seriously propose computing the first n prime numbers or playing chess using threads because there is nothing to be gained by doing it that way.

2.2.4 Implementing Threads in the Kernel

Now let us consider having the kernel know about and manage the threads. No run-time system is needed in each, as shown in Fig. 2-13(b). Also, there is no thread table in each process. Instead, the kernel has a thread table that keeps track of all the threads in the system. When a thread wants to create a new thread or destroy an existing thread, it makes a kernel call, which then does the creation or destruction by updating the kernel thread table.

The kernel's thread table holds each thread's registers, state, and other information. The information is the same as with user-level threads, but it is now in the kernel instead of in user space (inside the run-time system). This information is a subset of the information that traditional kernels maintain about each of their single-threaded processes, that is, the process state. In addition, the kernel also maintains the traditional process table to keep track of processes.

All calls that might block a thread are implemented as system calls, at considerably greater cost than a call to a run-time system procedure. When a thread blocks, the kernel, at its option, can run either another thread from the same process (if one is ready), or a thread from a different process. With user-level threads, the run-time system keeps running threads from its own process until the kernel takes the CPU away from it (or there are no ready threads left to run).

Due to the relatively greater cost of creating and destroying threads in the kernel, some systems take an environmentally correct approach and recycle their threads. When a thread is destroyed, it is marked as not runnable, but its kernel data structures are not otherwise affected. Later, when a new thread must be created, an old thread is reactivated, saving some overhead. Thread recycling is also possible for user-level threads, but since the thread management overhead is much smaller, there is less incentive to do this.

Kernel threads do not require any new, nonblocking system calls. In addition, if one thread in a process causes a page fault, the kernel can easily check to see if the process has any other runnable threads, and if so, run one of them while waiting for the required page to be brought in from the disk. Their main disadvantage is that the cost of a system call is substantial, so if thread operations (creation, termination, etc.) are common, much more overhead will be incurred.

2.2.5 Hybrid Implementations

Various ways have been investigated to try to combine the advantages of user-level threads with kernel-level threads. One way is use kernel-level threads and then multiplex user-level threads onto some or all of the kernel threads, as shown in Fig. 2-14.

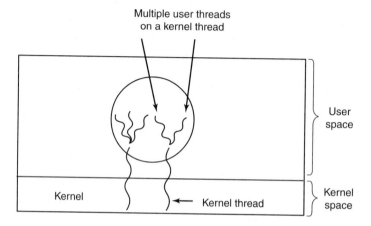

Figure 2-14. Multiplexing user-level threads onto kernel-level threads.

In this design, the kernel is aware of only the kernel-level threads and schedules those. Some of those threads may have multiple user-level threads multiplexed on top of them. These user-level threads are created, destroyed, and scheduled just like user-level threads in a process that runs on an operating system without multithreading capability. In this model, each kernel-level thread has some set of user-level threads that take turns using it.

2.2.6 Scheduler Activations

Various researchers have attempted to combine the advantage of user threads (good performance) with the advantage of kernel threads (not having to use a lot of tricks to make things work). Below we will describe one such approach devised by Anderson et al. (1992), called **scheduler activations**. Related work is discussed by Edler et al. (1988) and Scott et al. (1990).

The goals of the scheduler activation work are to mimic the functionality of kernel threads, but with the better performance and greater flexibility usually associated with threads packages implemented in user space. In particular, user threads should not have to make special nonblocking system calls or check in advance if it is safe to make certain system calls. Nevertheless, when a thread blocks on a system call or on a page fault, it should be possible to run other threads within the same process, if any are ready.

Efficiency is achieved by avoiding unnecessary transitions between user and kernel space. If a thread blocks waiting for another thread to do something, for example, there is no reason to involve the kernel, thus saving the overhead of the kernel-user transition. The user-space run-time system can block the synchronizing thread and schedule a new one by itself.

When scheduler activations are used, the kernel assigns a certain number of virtual processors to each process and lets the (user-space) run-time system allocate threads to processors. This mechanism can also be used on a multiprocessor where the virtual processors may be real CPUs. The number of virtual processors allocated to a process is initially one, but the process can ask for more and can also return processors it no longer needs. The kernel can also take back virtual processors already allocated in order to assign them to other, more needy, processes.

The basic idea that makes this scheme work is that when the kernel knows that a thread has blocked (e.g., by its having executed a blocking system call or caused a page fault), the kernel notifies the process' run-time system, passing as parameters on the stack the number of the thread in question and a description of the event that occurred. The notification happens by having the kernel activate the run-time system at a known starting address, roughly analogous to a signal in UNIX. This mechanism is called an **upcall**.

Once activated like this, the run-time system can reschedule its threads, typically by marking the current thread as blocked and taking another thread from the ready list, setting up its registers, and restarting it. Later, when the kernel learns that the original thread can run again (e.g., the pipe it was trying to read from now contains data, or the page it faulted over has been brought in from disk), it makes another upcall to the run-time system to inform it of this event. The run-time system, at its own discretion, can either restart the blocked thread immediately, or put it on the ready list to be run later.

When a hardware interrupt occurs while a user thread is running, the interrupted CPU switches into kernel mode. If the interrupt is caused by an event not of interest to the interrupted process, such as completion of another process' I/O, when the interrupt handler has finished, it puts the interrupted thread back in the state it was in before the interrupt. If, however, the process is interested in the interrupt, such as the arrival of a page needed by one of the process' threads, the interrupted thread is not restarted. Instead, the interrupted thread is suspended and the run-time system started on that virtual CPU, with the state of the interrupted thread on the stack. It is then up to the run-time system to decide which thread to schedule on that CPU: the interrupted one, the newly ready one, or some third choice.

An objection to scheduler activations is the fundamental reliance on upcalls, a concept that violates the structure inherent in any layered system. Normally, layer n offers certain services that layer $n + 1$ can call on, but layer n may not call procedures in layer $n + 1$. Upcalls do not follow this fundamental principle.

2.2.7 Pop-Up Threads

Threads are frequently useful in distributed systems. An important example is how incoming messages, for example requests for service, are handled. The traditional approach is to have a process or thread that is blocked on a receive system call waiting for an incoming message. When a message arrives, it accepts the message and processes it.

However, a completely different approach is also possible, in which the arrival of a message causes the system to create a new thread to handle the message. Such a thread is called a **pop-up thread** and is illustrated in Fig. 2-15. A key advantage of pop-up threads is that since they are brand new, they do not have any history—registers, stack, etc. that must be restored. Each one starts out fresh and each one is identical to all the others. This makes it possible to create such a thread quickly. The new thread is given the incoming message to process. The result of using pop-up threads is that the latency between message arrival and the start of processing can be made very short.

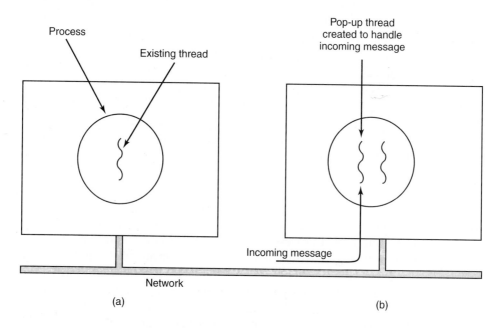

Figure 2-15. Creation of a new thread when a message arrives. (a) Before the message arrives. (b) After the message arrives.

Some advance planning is needed when pop-up threads are used. For example, in which process does the thread run? If the system supports threads running in the kernel's context, the thread may run there (which is why we have not shown the kernel in Fig. 2-15). Having the pop-up thread run in kernel space is usually easier and faster than putting it in user space. Also, a pop-up thread in kernel space can easily access all the kernel's tables and the I/O devices, which may be needed for interrupt processing. On the other hand, a buggy kernel thread can do more damage than a buggy user thread. For example, if it runs too long and there is no way to preempt it, incoming data may be lost.

2.2.8 Making Single-Threaded Code Multithreaded

Many existing programs were written for single-threaded processes. Converting these to multithreading is much trickier than it may at first appear. Below we will examine just a few of the pitfalls.

As a start, the code of a thread normally consists of multiple procedures, just like a process. These may have local variables, global variables, and procedure parameters. Local variables and parameters do not cause any trouble, but variables that are global to a thread but not global to the entire program do. These are variables that are global in the sense that many procedures within the thread use them (as they might use any global variable), but other threads should logically leave them alone.

As an example, consider the *errno* variable maintained by UNIX. When a process (or a thread) makes a system call that fails, the error code is put into *errno*. In Fig. 2-16, thread 1 executes the system call access to find out if it has permission to access a certain file. The operating system returns the answer in the global variable *errno*. After control has returned to thread 1, but before it has a chance to read *errno*, the scheduler decides that thread 1 has had enough CPU time for the moment and decides to switch to thread 2. Thread 2 executes an open call that fails, which causes *errno* to be overwritten and thread 1's access code to be lost forever. When thread 1 starts up later, it will read the wrong value and behave incorrectly.

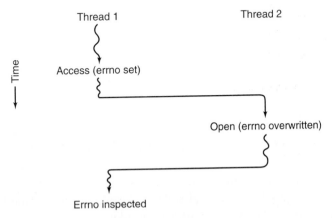

Figure 2-16. Conflicts between threads over the use of a global variable.

Various solutions to this problem are possible. One is to prohibit global variables altogether. However worthy this ideal may be, it conflicts with much existing software. Another is to assign each thread its own private global variables, as shown in Fig. 2-17. In this way, each thread has its own private copy of *errno* and other global variables, so conflicts are avoided. In effect, this decision creates a new scoping level, variables visible to all the procedures of a thread, in addition to the existing scoping levels of variables visible only to one procedure and variables visible everywhere in the program.

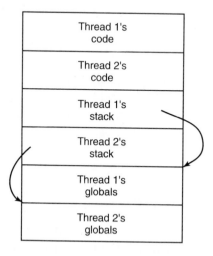

Figure 2-17. Threads can have private global variables.

Accessing the private global variables is a bit tricky, however, since most programming languages have a way of expressing local variables and global variables, but not intermediate forms. It is possible to allocate a chunk of memory for the globals and pass it to each procedure in the thread, as an extra parameter. While hardly an elegant solution, it works.

Alternatively, new library procedures can be introduced to create, set, and read these thread-wide global variables. The first call might look like this:

    create_global("bufptr");

It allocates storage for a pointer called *bufptr* on the heap or in a special storage area reserved for the calling thread. No matter where the storage is allocated, only the calling thread has access to the global variable. If another thread creates a global variable with the same name, it gets a different storage location that does not conflict with the existing one.

Two calls are needed to access global variables: one for writing them and the other for reading them. For writing, something like

    set_global("bufptr", &buf);

will do. It stores the value of a pointer in the storage location previously created by the call to *create_global.* To read a global variable, the call might look like

    bufptr = read_global("bufptr");

It returns the address stored in the global variable, so its data can be accessed.

The next problem turning a single-threaded program into a multithreaded program is that many library procedures are not reentrant. That is, they were not designed to have a second call made to any given procedure while a previous call has not yet finished. For example, sending a message over the network may well be programmed to assemble the message in a fixed buffer within the library, then to trap to the kernel to send it. What happens if one thread has assembled its message in the buffer, then a clock interrupt forces a switch to a second thread that immediately overwrites the buffer with its own message?

Similarly, memory allocation procedures, such as *malloc* in UNIX, maintain crucial tables about memory usage, for example, a linked list of available chunks of memory. While *malloc* is busy updating these lists, they may temporarily be in an inconsistent state, with pointers that point nowhere. If a thread switch occurs while the tables are inconsistent and a new call comes in from a different thread, an invalid pointer may be used, leading to a program crash. Fixing all these problems properly effectively means rewriting the entire library.

A different solution is to provide each procedure with a jacket that sets a bit to mark the library as in use. Any attempt for another thread to use a library procedure while a previous call has not yet completed is blocked. Although this approach can be made to work, it greatly eliminates potential parallelism.

Next, consider signals. Some signals are logically thread specific, whereas others are not. For example, if a thread calls alarm, it makes sense for the resulting signal to go to the thread that made the call. However, when threads are implemented entirely in user space, the kernel does not even know about threads and can hardly direct the signal to the right one. An additional complication occurs if a process may only have one alarm at a time pending and several threads call alarm independently.

Other signals, such as keyboard interrupt, are not thread specific. Who should catch them? One designated thread? All the threads? A newly created pop-up thread? Furthermore, what happens if one thread changes the signal handlers without telling other threads? And what happens if one thread wants to catch a particular signal (say, the user hitting CTRL-C), and another thread wants this signal to terminate the process? This situation can arise if one or more threads run standard library procedures and others are user-written. Clearly, these wishes are incompatible. In general, signals are difficult enough to manage in a single-threaded environment. Going to a multithreaded environment does not make them any easier to handle.

One last problem introduced by threads is stack management. In many systems, when a process' stack overflows, the kernel just provides that process with more stack automatically. When a process has multiple threads, it must also have multiple stacks. If the kernel is not aware of all these stacks, it cannot grow them automatically upon stack fault. In fact, it may not even realize that a memory fault is related to stack growth.

These problems are certainly not insurmountable, but they do show that just introducing threads into an existing system without a fairly substantial system redesign is not going to work at all. The semantics of system calls may have to be redefined and libraries have to be rewritten, at the very least. And all of these things must be done in such a way as to remain backward compatible with existing programs for the limiting case of a process with only one thread. For additional information about threads, see (Hauser et al., 1993; and Marsh et al., 1991).

2.3 INTERPROCESS COMMUNICATION

Processes frequently need to communicate with other processes. For example, in a shell pipeline, the output of the first process must be passed to the second process, and so on down the line. Thus there is a need for communication between processes, preferably in a well-structured way not using interrupts. In the following sections we will look at some of the issues related to this **InterProcess Communication** or **IPC**.

Very briefly, there are three issues here. The first was alluded to above: how one process can pass information to another. The second has to do with making sure two or more processes do not get into each other's way when engaging in critical activities (suppose two processes each try to grab the last 1 MB of memory). The third concerns proper sequencing when dependencies are present: if process A produces data and process B prints them, B has to wait until A has produced some data before starting to print. We will examine all three of these issues starting in the next section.

It is also important to mention that two of these issues apply equally well to threads. The first one—passing information—is easy for threads since they share a common address space (threads in different address spaces that need to communicate fall under the heading of communicating processes). However, the other two—keeping out of each other's hair and proper sequencing—apply equally well to threads. The same problems exist and the same solutions apply. Below we will discuss the problem in the context of processes, but please keep in mind that the same problems and solutions also apply to threads.

2.3.1 Race Conditions

In some operating systems, processes that are working together may share some common storage that each one can read and write. The shared storage may be in main memory (possibly in a kernel data structure) or it may be a shared file;

the location of the shared memory does not change the nature of the communication or the problems that arise. To see how interprocess communication works in practice, let us consider a simple but common example: a print spooler. When a process wants to print a file, it enters the file name in a special **spooler directory**. Another process, the **printer daemon**, periodically checks to see if there are any files to be printed, and if there are, it prints them and then removes their names from the directory.

Imagine that our spooler directory has a very large number of slots, numbered 0, 1, 2, ..., each one capable of holding a file name. Also imagine that there are two shared variables, *out*, which points to the next file to be printed, and *in*, which points to the next free slot in the directory. These two variables might well be kept on a two-word file available to all processes. At a certain instant, slots 0 to 3 are empty (the files have already been printed) and slots 4 to 6 are full (with the names of files queued for printing). More or less simultaneously, processes A and B decide they want to queue a file for printing. This situation is shown in Fig. 2-18.

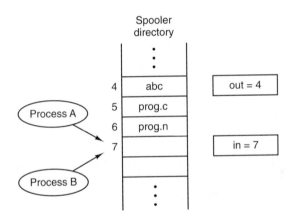

Figure 2-18. Two processes want to access shared memory at the same time.

In jurisdictions where Murphy's law† is applicable, the following might happen. Process A reads *in* and stores the value, 7, in a local variable called *next_free_slot*. Just then a clock interrupt occurs and the CPU decides that process A has run long enough, so it switches to process B. Process B also reads *in*, and also gets a 7. It too stores it in *its* local variable *next_free_slot*. At this instant both processes think that the next available slot is 7.

Process B now continues to run. It stores the name of its file in slot 7 and updates *in* to be an 8. Then it goes off and does other things.

Eventually, process A runs again, starting from the place it left off. It looks at *next_free_slot*, finds a 7 there, and writes its file name in slot 7, erasing the name

---

† If something can go wrong, it will.

that process *B* just put there. Then it computes *next_free_slot* + 1, which is 8, and sets *in* to 8. The spooler directory is now internally consistent, so the printer daemon will not notice anything wrong, but process *B* will never receive any output. User *B* will hang around the printer room for years, wistfully hoping for output that never comes. Situations like this, where two or more processes are reading or writing some shared data and the final result depends on who runs precisely when, are called **race conditions**. Debugging programs containing race conditions is no fun at all. The results of most test runs are fine, but once in a rare while something weird and unexplained happens.

2.3.2 Critical Regions

How do we avoid race conditions? The key to preventing trouble here and in many other situations involving shared memory, shared files, and shared everything else is to find some way to prohibit more than one process from reading and writing the shared data at the same time. Put in other words, what we need is **mutual exclusion**, that is, some way of making sure that if one process is using a shared variable or file, the other processes will be excluded from doing the same thing. The difficulty above occurred because process *B* started using one of the shared variables before process *A* was finished with it. The choice of appropriate primitive operations for achieving mutual exclusion is a major design issue in any operating system, and a subject that we will examine in great detail in the following sections.

The problem of avoiding race conditions can also be formulated in an abstract way. Part of the time, a process is busy doing internal computations and other things that do not lead to race conditions. However, sometimes a process have to access shared memory or files, or doing other critical things that can lead to races. That part of the program where the shared memory is accessed is called the **critical region** or **critical section**. If we could arrange matters such that no two processes were ever in their critical regions at the same time, we could avoid races.

Although this requirement avoids race conditions, this is not sufficient for having parallel processes cooperate correctly and efficiently using shared data. We need four conditions to hold to have a good solution:

1. No two processes may be simultaneously inside their critical regions.

2. No assumptions may be made about speeds or the number of CPUs.

3. No process running outside its critical region may block other processes.

4. No process should have to wait forever to enter its critical region.

In an abstract sense, the behavior that we want is shown in Fig. 2-19. Here process *A* enters its critical region at time T_1. A little later, at time T_2 process *B* attempts to enter its critical region but fails because another process is already in its critical region and we allow only one at a time. Consequently, B is temporarily suspended until time T_3 when A leaves its critical region, allowing B to enter immediately. Eventually B leaves (at T_4) and we are back to the original situation with no processes in their critical regions.

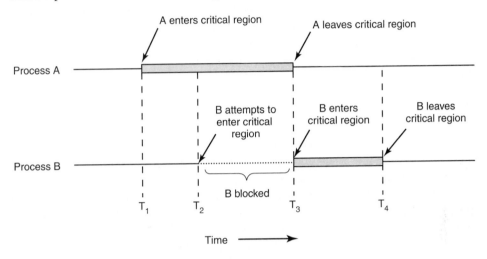

Figure 2-19. Mutual exclusion using critical regions.

2.3.3 Mutual Exclusion with Busy Waiting

In this section we will examine various proposals for achieving mutual exclusion, so that while one process is busy updating shared memory in its critical region, no other process will enter *its* critical region and cause trouble.

Disabling Interrupts

The simplest solution is to have each process disable all interrupts just after entering its critical region and re-enable them just before leaving it. With interrupts disabled, no clock interrupts can occur. The CPU is only switched from process to process as a result of clock or other interrupts, after all, and with interrupts turned off the CPU will not be switched to another process. Thus, once a process has disabled interrupts, it can examine and update the shared memory without fear that any other process will intervene.

This approach is generally unattractive because it is unwise to give user processes the power to turn off interrupts. Suppose that one of them did it, and never turned them on again? That could be the end of the system. Furthermore, if the system is a multiprocessor, with two or more CPUs, disabling interrupts affects only the CPU that executed the disable instruction. The other ones will continue running and can access the shared memory.

On the other hand, it is frequently convenient for the kernel itself to disable interrupts for a few instructions while it is updating variables or lists. If an interrupt occurred while the list of ready processes, for example, was in an inconsistent state, race conditions could occur. The conclusion is: disabling interrupts is often a useful technique within the operating system itself but is not appropriate as a general mutual exclusion mechanism for user processes.

Lock Variables

As a second attempt, let us look for a software solution. Consider having a single, shared (lock) variable, initially 0. When a process wants to enter its critical region, it first tests the lock. If the lock is 0, the process sets it to 1 and enters the critical region. If the lock is already 1, the process just waits until it becomes 0. Thus, a 0 means that no process is in its critical region, and a 1 means that some process is in its critical region.

Unfortunately, this idea contains exactly the same fatal flaw that we saw in the spooler directory. Suppose that one process reads the lock and sees that it is 0. Before it can set the lock to 1, another process is scheduled, runs, and sets the lock to 1. When the first process runs again, it will also set the lock to 1, and two processes will be in their critical regions at the same time.

Now you might think that we could get around this problem by first reading out the lock value, then checking it again just before storing into it, but that really does not help. The race now occurs if the second process modifies the lock just after the first process has finished its second check.

Strict Alternation

A third approach to the mutual exclusion problem is shown in Fig. 2-20. This program fragment, like nearly all the others in this book, is written in C. C was chosen here because real operating systems are virtually always written in C (or occasionally C++), but hardly ever in languages like Java, Modula 3, or Pascal. C is powerful, efficient, and predictable, characteristics critical for writing operating systems. Java, for example, is not predictable because it might run out of storage at a critical moment and need to invoke the garbage collector at a most inopportune time. This cannot happen in C because there is no garbage collection in C. A quantitative comparison of C, C++, Java, and four other languages is given in (Prechelt, 2000).

In Fig. 2-20, the integer variable *turn*, initially 0, keeps track of whose turn it is to enter the critical region and examine or update the shared memory. Initially, process 0 inspects *turn*, finds it to be 0, and enters its critical region. Process 1 also finds it to be 0 and therefore sits in a tight loop continually testing *turn* to see when it becomes 1. Continuously testing a variable until some value appears is called **busy waiting**. It should usually be avoided, since it wastes CPU time.

```
while (TRUE) {                              while (TRUE) {
    while (turn != 0)    /* loop */ ;           while (turn != 1)    /* loop */ ;
    critical_region( );                         critical_region( );
    turn = 1;                                   turn = 0;
    noncritical_region( );                      noncritical_region( );
}                                          }
```

            (a)   (b)

Figure 2-20. A proposed solution to the critical region problem. (a) Process 0. (b) Process 1. In both cases, be sure to note the semicolons terminating the while statements.

Only when there is a reasonable expectation that the wait will be short is busy waiting used. A lock that uses busy waiting is called a **spin lock**.

When process 0 leaves the critical region, it sets *turn* to 1, to allow process 1 to enter its critical region. Suppose that process 1 finishes its critical region quickly, so both processes are in their noncritical regions, with *turn* set to 0. Now process 0 executes its whole loop quickly, exiting its critical region and setting *turn* to 1. At this point *turn* is 1 and both processes are executing in their noncritical regions.

Suddenly, process 0 finishes its noncritical region and goes back to the top of its loop. Unfortunately, it is not permitted to enter its critical region now, because *turn* is 1 and process 1 is busy with its noncritical region. It hangs in its while loop until process 1 sets *turn* to 0. Put differently, taking turns is not a good idea when one of the processes is much slower than the other.

This situation violates condition 3 set out above: process 0 is being blocked by a process not in its critical region. Going back to the spooler directory discussed above, if we now associate the critical region with reading and writing the spooler directory, process 0 would not be allowed to print another file because process 1 was doing something else.

In fact, this solution requires that the two processes strictly alternate in entering their critical regions, for example, in spooling files. Neither one would be permitted to spool two in a row. While this algorithm does avoid all races, it is not really a serious candidate as a solution because it violates condition 3.

Peterson's Solution

By combining the idea of taking turns with the idea of lock variables and warning variables, a Dutch mathematician, T. Dekker, was the first one to devise a software solution to the mutual exclusion problem that does not require strict alternation. For a discussion of Dekker's algorithm, see (Dijkstra, 1965).

In 1981, G.L. Peterson discovered a much simpler way to achieve mutual exclusion, thus rendering Dekker's solution obsolete. Peterson's algorithm is shown in Fig. 2-21. This algorithm consists of two procedures written in ANSI C, which means that function prototypes should be supplied for all the functions defined and used. However, to save space, we will not show the prototypes in this or subsequent examples.

```
#define FALSE  0
#define TRUE   1
#define N      2                    /* number of processes */

int turn;                           /* whose turn is it? */
int interested[N];                  /* all values initially 0 (FALSE) */

void enter_region(int process);     /* process is 0 or 1 */
{
     int other;                     /* number of the other process */

     other = 1 − process;          /* the opposite of process */
     interested[process] = TRUE;    /* show that you are interested */
     turn = process;                /* set flag */
     while (turn == process && interested[other] == TRUE) /* null statement */ ;
}

void leave_region(int process)      /* process: who is leaving */
{
     interested[process] = FALSE;   /* indicate departure from critical region */
}
```

Figure 2-21. Peterson's solution for achieving mutual exclusion.

Before using the shared variables (i.e., before entering its critical region), each process calls *enter_region* with its own process number, 0 or 1, as parameter. This call will cause it to wait, if need be, until it is safe to enter. After it has finished with the shared variables, the process calls *leave_region* to indicate that it is done and to allow the other process to enter, if it so desires.

Let us see how this solution works. Initially neither process is in its critical region. Now process 0 calls *enter_region*. It indicates its interest by setting its array element and sets *turn* to 0. Since process 1 is not interested, *enter_region* returns immediately. If process 1 now calls *enter_region*, it will hang there until *interested*[0] goes to *FALSE*, an event that only happens when process 0 calls *leave_region* to exit the critical region.

Now consider the case that both processes call *enter_region* almost simultaneously. Both will store their process number in *turn*. Whichever store is done last is the one that counts; the first one is overwritten and lost. Suppose that process 1 stores last, so *turn* is 1. When both processes come to the while statement, process 0 executes it zero times and enters its critical region. Process 1 loops and does not enter its critical region until process 0 exits its critical region.

The TSL Instruction

Now let us look at a proposal that requires a little help from the hardware. Many computers, especially those designed with multiple processors in mind, have an instruction

TSL RX,LOCK

(Test and Set Lock) that works as follows. It reads the contents of the memory word *lock* into register RX and then stores a nonzero value at the memory address *lock*. The operations of reading the word and storing into it are guaranteed to be indivisible—no other processor can access the memory word until the instruction is finished. The CPU executing the TSL instruction locks the memory bus to prohibit other CPUs from accessing memory until it is done.

To use the TSL instruction, we will use a shared variable, *lock*, to coordinate access to shared memory. When *lock* is 0, any process may set it to 1 using the TSL instruction and then read or write the shared memory. When it is done, the process sets *lock* back to 0 using an ordinary move instruction.

How can this instruction be used to prevent two processes from simultaneously entering their critical regions? The solution is given in Fig. 2-22. There a four-instruction subroutine in a fictitious (but typical) assembly language is shown. The first instruction copies the old value of *lock* to the register and then sets *lock* to 1. Then the old value is compared with 0. If it is nonzero, the lock was already set, so the program just goes back to the beginning and tests it again. Sooner or later it will become 0 (when the process currently in its critical region is done with its critical region), and the subroutine returns, with the lock set. Clearing the lock is simple. The program just stores a 0 in *lock*. No special instructions are needed.

```
enter_region:
      TSL REGISTER,LOCK              | copy lock to register and set lock to 1
      CMP REGISTER,#0                | was lock zero?
      JNE enter_region               | if it was non zero, lock was set, so loop
      RET | return to caller; critical region entered


leave_region:
      MOVE LOCK,#0                   | store a 0 in lock
      RET | return to caller
```

Figure 2-22. Entering and leaving a critical region using the TSL instruction.

One solution to the critical region problem is now straightforward. Before entering its critical region, a process calls *enter_region*, which does busy waiting until the lock is free; then it acquires the lock and returns. After the critical region the process calls *leave_region*, which stores a 0 in *lock*. As with all solutions based on critical regions, the processes must call *enter_region* and *leave_region* at the correct times for the method to work. If a process cheats, the mutual exclusion will fail.

2.3.4 Sleep and Wakeup

Both Peterson's solution and the solution using TSL are correct, but both have the defect of requiring busy waiting. In essence, what these solutions do is this: when a process wants to enter its critical region, it checks to see if the entry is allowed. If it is not, the process just sits in a tight loop waiting until it is.

Not only does this approach waste CPU time, but it can also have unexpected effects. Consider a computer with two processes, *H*, with high priority and *L*, with low priority. The scheduling rules are such that *H* is run whenever it is in ready state. At a certain moment, with *L* in its critical region, *H* becomes ready to run (e.g., an I/O operation completes). *H* now begins busy waiting, but since *L* is never scheduled while *H* is running, *L* never gets the chance to leave its critical region, so *H* loops forever. This situation is sometimes referred to as the **priority inversion problem**.

Now let us look at some interprocess communication primitives that block instead of wasting CPU time when they are not allowed to enter their critical regions. One of the simplest is the pair sleep and wakeup. Sleep is a system call that causes the caller to block, that is, be suspended until another process wakes it up. The wakeup call has one parameter, the process to be awakened. Alternatively, both sleep and wakeup each have one parameter, a memory address used to match up sleeps with wakeups.

The Producer-Consumer Problem

As an example of how these primitives can be used, let us consider the **producer-consumer** problem (also known as the **bounded-buffer** problem). Two processes share a common, fixed-size buffer. One of them, the producer, puts information into the buffer, and the other one, the consumer, takes it out. (It is also possible to generalize the problem to have *m* producers and *n* consumers, but we will only consider the case of one producer and one consumer because this assumption simplifies the solutions).

Trouble arises when the producer wants to put a new item in the buffer, but it is already full. The solution is for the producer to go to sleep, to be awakened when the consumer has removed one or more items. Similarly, if the consumer wants to remove an item from the buffer and sees that the buffer is empty, it goes to sleep until the producer puts something in the buffer and wakes it up.

This approach sounds simple enough, but it leads to the same kinds of race conditions we saw earlier with the spooler directory. To keep track of the number of items in the buffer, we will need a variable, *count*. If the maximum number of items the buffer can hold is *N*, the producer's code will first test to see if *count* is *N*. If it is, the producer will go to sleep; if it is not, the producer will add an item and increment *count*.

The consumer's code is similar: first test *count* to see if it is 0. If it is, go to sleep; if it is nonzero, remove an item and decrement the counter. Each of the processes also tests to see if the other should be awakened, and if so, wakes it up. The code for both producer and consumer is shown in Fig. 2-23.

```
#define N 100                                /* number of slots in the buffer */
int count = 0;                               /* number of items in the buffer */

void producer(void)
{
    int item;

    while (TRUE) {                           /* repeat forever */
        item = produce_item( );              /* generate next item */
        if (count == N) sleep( );            /* if buffer is full, go to sleep */
        insert_item(item);                   /* put item in buffer */
        count = count + 1;                   /* increment count of items in buffer */
        if (count == 1) wakeup(consumer);    /* was buffer empty? */
    }
}


void consumer(void)
{
    int item;

    while (TRUE) {                           /* repeat forever */
        if (count == 0) sleep( );            /* if buffer is empty, got to sleep */
        item = remove_item( );               /* take item out of buffer */
        count = count - 1;                   /* decrement count of items in buffer */
        if (count == N - 1) wakeup(producer); /* was buffer full? */
        consume_item(item);                  /* print item */
    }
}
```

Figure 2-23. The producer-consumer problem with a fatal race condition.

To express system calls such as sleep and wakeup in C, we will show them as calls to library routines. They are not part of the standard C library but presumably would be available on any system that actually had these system calls. The procedures *insert_item* and *remove_item*, which are not shown, handle the book-keeping of putting items into the buffer and taking items out of the buffer.

Now let us get back to the race condition. It can occur because access to *count* is unconstrained. The following situation could possibly occur. The buffer is empty and the consumer has just read *count* to see if it is 0. At that instant, the scheduler decides to stop running the consumer temporarily and start running the producer. The producer inserts an item in the buffer, increments *count*, and notices that it is now 1. Reasoning that *count* was just 0, and thus the consumer must be sleeping, the producer calls *wakeup* to wake the consumer up.

Unfortunately, the consumer is not yet logically asleep, so the wakeup signal is lost. When the consumer next runs, it will test the value of *count* it previously read, find it to be 0, and go to sleep. Sooner or later the producer will fill up the buffer and also go to sleep. Both will sleep forever.

The essence of the problem here is that a wakeup sent to a process that is not (yet) sleeping is lost. If it were not lost, everything would work. A quick fix is to modify the rules to add a **wakeup waiting bit** to the picture. When a wakeup is sent to a process that is still awake, this bit is set. Later, when the process tries to go to sleep, if the wakeup waiting bit is on, it will be turned off, but the process will stay awake. The wakeup waiting bit is a piggy bank for wakeup signals.

While the wakeup waiting bit saves the day in this simple example, it is easy to construct examples with three or more processes in which one wakeup waiting bit is insufficient. We could make another patch and add a second wakeup waiting bit, or maybe 8 or 32 of them, but in principle the problem is still there.

2.3.5 Semaphores

This was the situation in 1965, when E. W. Dijkstra (1965) suggested using an integer variable to count the number of wakeups saved for future use. In his proposal, a new variable type, called a **semaphore**, was introduced. A semaphore could have the value 0, indicating that no wakeups were saved, or some positive value if one or more wakeups were pending.

Dijkstra proposed having two operations, down and up (generalizations of sleep and wakeup, respectively). The down operation on a semaphore checks to see if the value is greater than 0. If so, it decrements the value (i.e., uses up one stored wakeup) and just continues. If the value is 0, the process is put to sleep without completing the down for the moment. Checking the value, changing it, and possibly going to sleep, is all done as a single, indivisible **atomic action**. It is guaranteed that once a semaphore operation has started, no other process can access the semaphore until the operation has completed or blocked. This atomicity is absolutely essential to solving synchronization problems and avoiding race conditions.

The up operation increments the value of the semaphore addressed. If one or more processes were sleeping on that semaphore, unable to complete an earlier down operation, one of them is chosen by the system (e.g., at random) and is allowed to complete its down. Thus, after an up on a semaphore with processes sleeping on it, the semaphore will still be 0, but there will be one fewer process sleeping on it. The operation of incrementing the semaphore and waking up one process is also indivisible. No process ever blocks doing an up, just as no process ever blocks doing a wakeup in the earlier model.

As an aside, in Dijkstra's original paper, he used the names P and V instead of down and up, respectively, but since these have no mnemonic significance to people who do not speak Dutch (and only marginal significance to those who do), we will use the terms down and up instead. These were first introduced in Algol 68.

Solving the Producer-Consumer Problem using Semaphores

Semaphores solve the lost-wakeup problem, as shown in Fig. 2-24. It is essential that they be implemented in an indivisible way. The normal way is to implement up and down as system calls, with the operating system briefly disabling all interrupts while it is testing the semaphore, updating it, and putting the process to sleep, if necessary. As all of these actions take only a few instructions, no harm is done in disabling interrupts. If multiple CPUs are being used, each semaphore should be protected by a lock variable, with the TSL instruction used to make sure that only one CPU at a time examines the semaphore. Be sure you understand that using TSL to prevent several CPUs from accessing the semaphore at the same time is quite different from busy waiting by the producer or consumer waiting for the other to empty or fill the buffer. The semaphore operation will only take a few microseconds, whereas the producer or consumer might take arbitrarily long.

This solution uses three semaphores: one called *full* for counting the number of slots that are full, one called *empty* for counting the number of slots that are empty, and one called *mutex* to make sure the producer and consumer do not access the buffer at the same time. *Full* is initially 0, *empty* is initially equal to the number of slots in the buffer, and *mutex* is initially 1. Semaphores that are initialized to 1 and used by two or more processes to ensure that only one of them can enter its critical region at the same time are called **binary semaphores**. If each process does a down just before entering its critical region and an up just after leaving it, mutual exclusion is guaranteed.

Now that we have a good interprocess communication primitive at our disposal, let us go back and look at the interrupt sequence of Fig. 2-5 again. In a system using semaphores, the natural way to hide interrupts is to have a semaphore, initially set to 0, associated with each I/O device. Just after starting an I/O device, the managing process does a down on the associated semaphore, thus blocking immediately. When the interrupt comes in, the interrupt handler then does an up on the associated semaphore, which makes the relevant process ready to run again. In this model, step 5 in Fig. 2-5 consists of doing an up on the device's semaphore, so that in step 6 the scheduler will be able to run the device manager. Of course, if several processes are now ready, the scheduler may choose to run an

```
#define N 100                        /* number of slots in the buffer */
typedef int semaphore;              /* semaphores are a special kind of int */
semaphore mutex = 1;                /* controls access to critical region */
semaphore empty = N;                /* counts empty buffer slots */
semaphore full = 0;                 /* counts full buffer slots */

void producer(void)
{
    int item;

    while (TRUE) {                  /* TRUE is the constant 1 */
        item = produce_item( );     /* generate something to put in buffer */
        down(&empty);               /* decrement empty count */
        down(&mutex);               /* enter critical region */
        insert_item(item);          /* put new item in buffer */
        up(&mutex);                 /* leave critical region */
        up(&full);                  /* increment count of full slots */
    }
}


void consumer(void)
{
    int item;

    while (TRUE) {                  /* infinite loop */
        down(&full);                /* decrement full count */
        down(&mutex);               /* enter critical region */
        item = remove_item( );      /* take item from buffer */
        up(&mutex);                 /* leave critical region */
        up(&empty);                 /* increment count of empty slots */
        consume_item(item);         /* do something with the item */
    }
}
```

Figure 2-24. The producer-consumer problem using semaphores.

even more important process next. We will look at some of the algorithms used for scheduling later on in this chapter.

In the example of Fig. 2-24, we have actually used semaphores in two different ways. This difference is important enough to make explicit. The *mutex* semaphore is used for mutual exclusion. It is designed to guarantee that only one process at a time will be reading or writing the buffer and the associated variables. This mutual exclusion is required to prevent chaos. We will study mutual exclusion and how to achieve it more in the next section.

The other use of semaphores is for **synchronization**. The *full* and *empty* semaphores are needed to guarantee that certain event sequences do or do not occur. In this case, they ensure that the producer stops running when the buffer is full, and the consumer stops running when it is empty. This use is different from mutual exclusion.

2.3.6 Mutexes

When the semaphore's ability to count is not needed, a simplified version of the semaphore, called a mutex, is sometimes used. Mutexes are good only for managing mutual exclusion to some shared resource or piece of code. They are easy and efficient to implement, which makes them especially useful in thread packages that are implemented entirely in user space.

A **mutex** is a variable that can be in one of two states: unlocked or locked. Consequently, only 1 bit is required to represent it, but in practice an integer often is used, with 0 meaning unlocked and all other values meaning locked. Two procedures are used with mutexes. When a thread (or process) needs access to a critical region, it calls *mutex_lock*. If the mutex is current unlocked (meaning that the critical region is available), the call succeeds and the calling thread is free to enter the critical region.

On the other hand, if the mutex is already locked, the calling thread is blocked until the thread in the critical region is finished and calls *mutex_unlock*. If multiple threads are blocked on the mutex, one of them is chosen at random and allowed to acquire the lock.

Because mutexes are so simple, they can easily be implemented in user space if a TSL instruction is available. The code for *mutex_lock* and *mutex_unlock* for use with a user-level threads package are shown in Fig. 2-25.

```
mutex_lock:
        TSL REGISTER,MUTEX          | copy mutex to register and set mutex to 1
        CMP REGISTER,#0             | was mutex zero?
        JZE ok                      | if it was zero, mutex was unlocked, so return
        CALL thread_yield           | mutex is busy; schedule another thread
        JMP mutex_lock              | try again later
    ok: RET | return to caller; critical region entered


mutex_unlock:
        MOVE MUTEX,#0               | store a 0 in mutex
        RET | return to caller
```

Figure 2-25. Implementation of *mutex_lock* and *mutex_unlock*.

The code of *mutex_lock* is similar to the code of *enter_region* of Fig. 2-22 but with a crucial difference. When *enter_region* fails to enter the critical region, it keeps testing the lock repeatedly (busy waiting). Eventually, the clock runs out and some other process is scheduled to run. Sooner or later the process holding the lock gets to run and releases it.

With threads, the situation is different because there is no clock that stops threads that have run too long. Consequently, a thread that tries to acquire a lock by busy waiting will loop forever and never acquire the lock because it never allows any other thread to run and release the lock.

That is where the difference between *enter_region* and *mutex_lock* comes in. When the later fails to acquire a lock, it calls *thread_yield* to give up the CPU to another thread. Consequently there is no busy waiting. When the thread runs the next time, it tests the lock again.

Since *thread_yield* is just a call to the thread scheduler in user space, it is very fast. As a consequence, neither *mutex_lock* nor *mutex_unlock* requires any kernel calls. Using them, user-level threads can synchronize entirely in user space using procedures that require only a handful of instructions.

The mutex system that we have described above is a bare bones set of calls. With all software, there is always a demand for more features, and synchronization primitives are no exception. For example, sometimes a thread package offers a call *mutex_trylock* that either acquires the lock or returns a code for failure, but does not block. This call gives the thread the flexibility to decide what to do next if there are alternatives to just waiting.

Up until now there is an issue that we have glossed over lightly but which is worth at least making explicit. With a user-space threads package there is no problem with multiple threads having access to the same mutex since all the threads operate in a common address space. However, with most of the earlier solutions, such as Peterson's algorithm and semaphores, there is an unspoken assumption that multiple processes have access to at least some shared memory, perhaps only one word, but something. If processes have disjoint address spaces, as we have consistently said, how can they share the *turn* variable in Peterson's algorithm, or semaphores or a common buffer?

There are two answers. First, some of the shared data structures, such as the semaphores, can be stored in the kernel and only accessed via system calls. This approach eliminates the problem. Second, most modern operating systems (including UNIX and Windows) offer a way for processes to share some portion of their address space with other processes. In this way, buffers and other data structures can be shared. In the worst case, that nothing else is possible, a shared file can be used.

If two or more processes share most or all of their address spaces, the distinction between processes and threads becomes somewhat blurred but is nevertheless present. Two processes that share a common address space still have different open files, alarm timers, and other per-process properties, whereas the threads within a single process share them. And it is always true that multiple processes sharing a common address space never have the efficiency of user-level threads since the kernel is deeply involved in their management.

2.3.7 Monitors

With semaphores interprocess communication looks easy, right? Forget it. Look closely at the order of the downs before inserting or removing items from the buffer in Fig. 2-24. Suppose that the two downs in the producer's code were reversed in order, so *mutex* was decremented before *empty* instead of after it. If the buffer were completely full, the producer would block, with *mutex* set to 0. Consequently, the next time the consumer tried to access the buffer, it would do a down on *mutex*, now 0, and block too. Both processes would stay blocked forever and no more work would ever be done. This unfortunate situation is called a deadlock. We will study deadlocks in detail in Chap. 3.

This problem is pointed out to show how careful you must be when using semaphores. One subtle error and everything comes to a grinding halt. It is like programming in assembly language, only worse, because the errors are race conditions, deadlocks, and other forms of unpredictable and irreproducible behavior.

To make it easier to write correct programs, Hoare (1974) and Brinch Hansen (1975) proposed a higher-level synchronization primitive called a **monitor**. Their proposals differed slightly, as described below. A monitor is a collection of procedures, variables, and data structures that are all grouped together in a special kind of module or package. Processes may call the procedures in a monitor whenever they want to, but they cannot directly access the monitor's internal data structures from procedures declared outside the monitor. Figure 2-26 illustrates a monitor written in an imaginary language, Pidgin Pascal.

```
monitor example
     integer i;
     condition c;

     procedure producer( );
     .
     .
     end;

     procedure consumer( );
     .     .     .
     end;
end monitor;
```

Figure 2-26. A monitor.

Monitors have an important property that makes them useful for achieving mutual exclusion: only one process can be active in a monitor at any instant. Monitors are a programming language construct, so the compiler knows they are special and can handle calls to monitor procedures differently from other procedure calls. Typically, when a process calls a monitor procedure, the first few instructions of the procedure will check to see if any other process is currently active within the monitor. If so, the calling process will be suspended until the other process has left the monitor. If no other process is using the monitor, the calling process may enter.

It is up to the compiler to implement the mutual exclusion on monitor entries, but a common way is to use a mutex or binary semaphore. Because the compiler, not the programmer, is arranging for the mutual exclusion, it is much less likely that something will go wrong. In any event, the person writing the monitor does not have to be aware of how the compiler arranges for mutual exclusion. It is sufficient to know that by turning all the critical regions into monitor procedures, no two processes will ever execute their critical regions at the same time.

Although monitors provide an easy way to achieve mutual exclusion, as we have seen above, that is not enough. We also need a way for processes to block when they cannot proceed. In the producer-consumer problem, it is easy enough to put all the tests for buffer-full and buffer-empty in monitor procedures, but how should the producer block when it finds the buffer full?

The solution lies in the introduction of **condition variables**, along with two operations on them, wait and signal. When a monitor procedure discovers that it cannot continue (e.g., the producer finds the buffer full), it does a wait on some condition variable, say, *full*. This action causes the calling process to block. It also allows another process that had been previously prohibited from entering the monitor to enter now.

This other process, for example, the consumer, can wake up its sleeping partner by doing a signal on the condition variable that its partner is waiting on. To avoid having two active processes in the monitor at the same time, we need a rule telling what happens after a signal. Hoare proposed letting the newly awakened process run, suspending the other one. Brinch Hansen proposed finessing the problem by requiring that a process doing a signal *must* exit the monitor immediately. In other words, a signal statement may appear only as the final statement in a monitor procedure. We will use Brinch Hansen's proposal because it is conceptually simpler and is also easier to implement. If a signal is done on a condition variable on which several processes are waiting, only one of them, determined by the system scheduler, is revived.

As an aside, there is also a third solution, not proposed by either Hoare or Brinch Hansen. This is to let the signaler continue to run and allow the waiting process to start running only after the signaler has exited the monitor.

Condition variables are not counters. They do not accumulate signals for later use the way semaphores do. Thus if a condition variable is signaled with no one waiting on it, the signal is lost forever. In other words, the wait must come before the signal. This rule makes the implementation much simpler. In practice it is not a problem because it is easy to keep track of the state of each process with variables, if need be. A process that might otherwise do a signal can see that this operation is not necessary by looking at the variables.

A skeleton of the producer-consumer problem with monitors is given in Fig. 2-27 in an imaginary language, Pidgin Pascal. The advantage of using Pidgin Pascal here is that it is pure and simple and follows the Hoare/Brinch Hansen model exactly.

```
monitor ProducerConsumer
      condition full, empty;
      integer count;

      procedure insert(item: integer);
      begin
            if count = N then wait(full);
            insert_item(item);
            count := count + 1;
            if count = 1 then signal(empty)
      end;

      function remove: integer;
      begin
            if count = 0 then wait(empty);
            remove = remove_item;
            count := count − 1;
            if count = N − 1 then signal(full)
      end;

      count := 0;
end monitor;


procedure producer;
begin
      while true do
      begin
            item = produce_item;
            ProducerConsumer.insert(item)
      end
end;

procedure consumer;
begin
      while true do
      begin
            item = ProducerConsumer.remove;
            consume_item(item)
      end
end;
```

Figure 2-27. An outline of the producer-consumer problem with monitors. Only one monitor procedure at a time is active. The buffer has N slots.

You may be thinking that the operations wait and signal look similar to sleep and wakeup, which we saw earlier had fatal race conditions. They *are* very similar, but with one crucial difference: sleep and wakeup failed because while one process was trying to go to sleep, the other one was trying to wake it up. With monitors, that cannot happen. The automatic mutual exclusion on monitor procedures guarantees that if, say, the producer inside a monitor procedure discovers that the buffer is full, it will be able to complete the wait operation without having to worry about the possibility that the scheduler may switch to the consumer just before the wait completes. The consumer will not even be let into the monitor at all until the wait is finished and the producer has been marked as no longer runnable.

Although Pidgin Pascal is an imaginary language, some real programming languages also support monitors, although not always in the form designed by Hoare and Brinch Hansen. One such language is Java. Java is an object-oriented language that supports user-level threads and also allows methods (procedures) to be grouped together into classes. By adding the keyword synchronized to a method declaration, Java guarantees that once any thread has started executing that method, no other thread will be allowed to start executing any other synchronized method in that class.

A solution to the producer-consumer problem using monitors in Java is given in Fig. 2-28. The solution consists of four classes. The outer class, *ProducerConsumer*, creates and starts two threads, *p* and *c*. The second and third classes, *producer* and *consumer*, respectively, contain the code for the producer and consumer. Finally, the class *our_monitor*, is the monitor. It contains two synchronized threads that are used for actually inserting items into the shared buffer and taking them out. Unlike in the previous examples, we have finally shown the full code of *insert* and *remove* here.

The producer and consumer threads are functionally identical to their counterparts in all our previous examples. The producer has an infinite loop generating data and putting it into the common buffer. The consumer has an equally infinite loop taking data out of the common buffer and doing some fun thing with it.

The interesting part of this program is the class *our_monitor*, which contains the buffer, the administration variables, and two synchronized methods. When the producer is active inside *insert*, it knows for sure that the consumer cannot be active inside *remove*, making it safe to update the variables and the buffer without fear of race conditions. The variable *count* keeps track of how many items are in the buffer. It can take on any value from 0 through and including $N - 1$. The variable *lo* is the index of the buffer slot where the next item is to be fetched. Similarly, *hi* is the index of the buffer slot where the next item is to be placed. It is permitted that $lo = hi$, which means either that 0 items or N items are in the buffer. The value of *count* tells which case holds.

Synchronized methods in Java differ from classical monitors in an essential way: Java does not have condition variables. Instead, it offers two procedures, *wait* and *notify* that are the equivalent of *sleep* and *wakeup* except that when they are used inside synchronized methods, they are not subject to race conditions. In theory, the method *wait* can be interrupted, which is what the code surrounding it is all about. Java requires that the exception handling be made explicit. For our purposes, just imagine that *go_to_sleep* is the way to go to sleep.

By making the mutual exclusion of critical regions automatic, monitors make parallel programming much less error-prone than with semaphores. Still, they too have some drawbacks. It is not for nothing that our two examples of monitors were in Pidgin Pascal and Java instead of C, as are the other examples in this book. As we said earlier, monitors are a programming language concept. The compiler must recognize them and arrange for the mutual exclusion somehow. C, Pascal, and most other languages do not have monitors, so it is unreasonable to expect their compilers to enforce any mutual exclusion rules. In fact, how could the compiler even know which procedures were in monitors and which were not?

These same languages do not have semaphores either, but adding semaphores is easy: All you need to do is add two short assembly code routines to the library to issue the up and down system calls. The compilers do not even have to know that they exist. Of course, the operating systems have to know about the semaphores, but at least if you have a semaphore-based operating system, you can still write the user programs for it in C or C++ (or even assembly language if you are masochistic enough). With monitors, you need a language that has them built in.

Another problem with monitors, and also with semaphores, is that they were designed for solving the mutual exclusion problem on one or more CPUs that all have access to a common memory. By putting the semaphores in the shared memory and protecting them with TSL instructions, we can avoid races. When we go to a distributed system consisting of multiple CPUs, each with its own private memory, connected by a local area network, these primitives become inapplicable. The conclusion is that semaphores are too low level and monitors are not usable except in a few programming languages. Also, none of the primitives provide for information exchange between machines. Something else is needed.

2.3.8 Message Passing

That something else is **message passing**. This method of interprocess communication uses two primitives, send and receive, which, like semaphores and unlike monitors, are system calls rather than language constructs. As such, they can easily be put into library procedures, such as

    send(destination, &message);

and

    receive(source, &message);

The former call sends a message to a given destination and the latter one receives

```
public class ProducerConsumer {
    static final int N = 100;        // constant giving the buffer size
    static producer p = new producer( );   // instantiate a new producer thread
    static consumer c = new consumer( ); // instantiate a new consumer thread
    static our_monitor mon = new our_monitor( );     // instantiate a new monitor

    public static void main(String args[ ]) {
        p.start( );      // start the producer thread
        c.start( );      // start the consumer thread
    }

    static class producer extends Thread {
        public void run( )  {// run method contains the thread code
            int item;
            while (true) {     // producer loop
                item = produce_item( );
                mon.insert(item);
            }
        }
        private int produce_item( ) { ... }      // actually produce
    }

    static class consumer extends Thread {
        public void run( )  { run method contains the thread code
            int item;
            while (true) {     // consumer loop
                item = mon.remove( );
                consume_item (item);
            }
        }
        private void consume_item(int item) { ... }// actually consume
    }

    static class our_monitor {  // this is a monitor
        private int buffer[ ] = new int[N];
        private int count = 0, lo = 0, hi = 0;  // counters and indices

        public synchronized void insert(int val) {
            if (count == N) go_to_sleep( );     // if the buffer is full, go to sleep
            buffer [hi] = val; // insert an item into the buffer
            hi = (hi + 1) % N;       // slot to place next item in
            count = count + 1;      // one more item in the buffer now
            if (count == 1) notify( );      // if consumer was sleeping, wake it up
        }

        public synchronized int remove( ) {
            int val;
            if (count == 0) go_to_sleep( );     // if the buffer is empty, go to sleep
            val = buffer [lo]; // fetch an item from the buffer
            lo = (lo + 1) % N;       // slot to fetch next item from
            count = count − 1;      // one few items in the buffer
            if (count == N − 1) notify( ); // if producer was sleeping, wake it up
            return val;
        }
        private void go_to_sleep( ) { try{wait( );} catch(InterruptedException exc) {};}
    }
}
```

Figure 2-28. A solution to the producer-consumer problem in Java.

a message from a given source (or from *ANY*, if the receiver does not care). If no message is available, the receiver can block until one arrives. Alternatively, it can return immediately with an error code.

Design Issues for Message Passing Systems

Message passing systems have many challenging problems and design issues that do not arise with semaphores or monitors, especially if the communicating processes are on different machines connected by a network. For example, messages can be lost by the network. To guard against lost messages, the sender and receiver can agree that as soon as a message has been received, the receiver will send back a special **acknowledgement** message. If the sender has not received the acknowledgement within a certain time interval, it retransmits the message.

Now consider what happens if the message itself is received correctly, but the acknowledgement is lost. The sender will retransmit the message, so the receiver will get it twice. It is essential that the receiver be able to distinguish a new message from the retransmission of an old one. Usually, this problem is solved by putting consecutive sequence numbers in each original message. If the receiver gets a message bearing the same sequence number as the previous message, it knows that the message is a duplicate that can be ignored. Successfully communicating in the face of unreliable message passing is a major part of the study of computer networks. For more information, see (Tanenbaum, 1996).

Message systems also have to deal with the question of how processes are named, so that the process specified in a send or receive call is unambiguous. **Authentication** is also an issue in message systems: how can the client tell that he is communicating with the real file server, and not with an imposter?

At the other end of the spectrum, there are also design issues that are important when the sender and receiver are on the same machine. One of these is performance. Copying messages from one process to another is always slower than doing a semaphore operation or entering a monitor. Much work has gone into making message passing efficient. Cheriton (1984), for example, suggested limiting message size to what will fit in the machine's registers, and then doing message passing using the registers.

The Producer-Consumer Problem with Message Passing

Now let us see how the producer-consumer problem can be solved with message passing and no shared memory. A solution is given in Fig. 2-29. We assume that all messages are the same size and that messages sent but not yet received are buffered automatically by the operating system. In this solution, a total of N messages is used, analogous to the N slots in a shared memory buffer. The consumer

starts out by sending *N* empty messages to the producer. Whenever the producer
has an item to give to the consumer, it takes an empty message and sends back a
full one. In this way, the total number of messages in the system remains constant
in time, so they can be stored in a given amount of memory known in advance.

If the producer works faster than the consumer, all the messages will end up
full, waiting for the consumer; the producer will be blocked, waiting for an empty
to come back. If the consumer works faster, then the reverse happens: all the
messages will be empties waiting for the producer to fill them up; the consumer
will be blocked, waiting for a full message.

```
#define N 100                          /* number of slots in the buffer */

void producer(void)
{
     int item;
     message m;                        /* message buffer */

     while (TRUE) {
          item = produce_item( );      /* generate something to put in buffer */
          receive(consumer, &m);       /* wait for an empty to arrive */
          build_message(&m, item);     /* construct a message to send */
          send(consumer, &m);          /* send item to consumer */
     }
}

void consumer(void)
{
     int item, i;
     message m;

     for (i = 0; i < N; i++) send(producer, &m);  /* send N empties */
     while (TRUE) {
          receive(producer, &m);       /* get message containing item */
          item = extract_item(&m);     /* extract item from message */
          send(producer, &m);          /* send back empty reply */
          consume_item(item);          /* do something with the item */
     }
}
```

Figure 2-29. The producer-consumer problem with *N* messages.

Many variants are possible with message passing. For starters, let us look at
how messages are addressed. One way is to assign each process a unique address
and have messages be addressed to processes. A different way is to invent a new
data structure, called a **mailbox**. A mailbox is a place to buffer a certain number
of messages, typically specified when the mailbox is created. When mailboxes

are used, the address parameters in the send and receive calls are mailboxes, not processes. When a process tries to send to a mailbox that is full, it is suspended until a message is removed from that mailbox, making room for a new one.

For the producer-consumer problem, both the producer and consumer would create mailboxes large enough to hold N messages. The producer would send messages containing data to the consumer's mailbox, and the consumer would send empty messages to the producer's mailbox. When mailboxes are used, the buffering mechanism is clear: the destination mailbox holds messages that have been sent to the destination process but have not yet been accepted.

The other extreme from having mailboxes is to eliminate all buffering. When this approach is followed, if the send is done before the receive, the sending process is blocked until the receive happens, at which time the message can be copied directly from the sender to the receiver, with no intermediate buffering. Similarly, if the receive is done first, the receiver is blocked until a send happens. This strategy is often known as a **rendezvous**. It is easier to implement than a buffered message scheme but is less flexible since the sender and receiver are forced to run in lockstep.

Message passing is commonly used in parallel programming systems. One well-known message-passing system, for example, is **MPI** (**Message-Passing Interface**). It is widely used for scientific computing. For more information about it, see for example (Gropp et al., 1994; and Snir et al., 1996).

2.3.9 Barriers

Our last synchronization mechanism is intended for groups of processes rather than two-process producer-consumer type situations. Some applications are divided into phases and have the rule that no process may proceed into the next phase until all processes are ready to proceed to the next phase. This behavior may be achieved by placing a **barrier** at the end of each phase. When a process reaches the barrier, it is blocked until all processes have reached the barrier. The operation of a barrier is illustrated in Fig. 2-30.

In Fig. 2-30(a) we see four processes approaching a barrier. What this means is that they are just computing and have not reached the end of the current phase yet. After a while, the first process finishes all the computing required of it during the first phase. It then executes the barrier primitive, generally by calling a library procedure. The process is then suspended. A little later, a second and then a third process finish the first phase and also execute the barrier primitive. This situation is illustrated in Fig. 2-30(b). Finally, when the last process, C, hits the barrier, all the processes are released, as shown in Fig. 2-30(c).

As an example of a problem requiring barriers, consider a typical relaxation problem in physics or engineering. There is typically a matrix that contains some initial values. The values might represent temperatures at various points on a

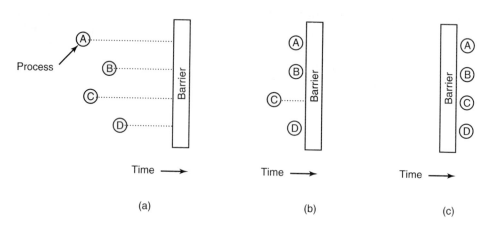

Figure 2-30. Use of a barrier. (a) Processes approaching a barrier. (b) All processes but one blocked at the barrier. (c) When the last process arrives at the barrier, all of them are let through.

sheet of metal. The idea might be to calculate how long it takes for the effect of a flame placed at one corner to propagate throughout the sheet.

Starting with the current values, a transformation is applied to the matrix to get the second version of the matrix, for example, by applying the laws of thermo-dynamics to see what all the temperatures are ΔT later. Then the processes is repeated over and over, giving the temperatures at the sample points as a function of time as the sheet heats up. The algorithm thus produces a series of matrices over time.

Now imagine that the matrix is very large (say, 1 million by 1 million), so that parallel processes are needed (possibly on a multiprocessor) to speed up the calcu-lation. Different processes work on different parts of the matrix, calculating the new matrix elements from the old ones according to the laws of physics. How-ever, no process may start on iteration $n + 1$ until iteration n is complete, that is, until all processes have finished their current work. The way to achieve this goal is to program each process to execute a barrier operation after it has finished its part of the current iteration. When all of them are done, the new matrix (the input to the next iteration) will be finished, and all processes will be simultaneously released to start the next iteration.

2.4 CLASSICAL IPC PROBLEMS

The operating systems literature is full of interesting problems that have been widely discussed and analyzed using a variety of synchronization methods. In the following sections we will examine three of the better-known problems.

2.4.1 The Dining Philosophers Problem

In 1965, Dijkstra posed and solved a synchronization problem he called the **dining philosophers problem**. Since that time, everyone inventing yet another synchronization primitive has felt obligated to demonstrate how wonderful the new primitive is by showing how elegantly it solves the dining philosophers problem. The problem can be stated quite simply as follows. Five philosophers are seated around a circular table. Each philosopher has a plate of spaghetti. The spaghetti is so slippery that a philosopher needs two forks to eat it. Between each pair of plates is one fork. The layout of the table is illustrated in Fig. 2-31.

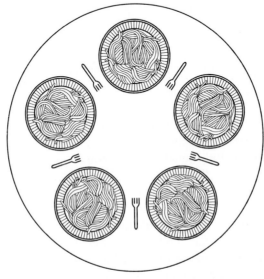

Figure 2-31. Lunch time in the Philosophy Department.

The life of a philosopher consists of alternate periods of eating and thinking. (This is something of an abstraction, even for philosophers, but the other activities are irrelevant here.) When a philosopher gets hungry, she tries to acquire her left and right fork, one at a time, in either order. If successful in acquiring two forks, she eats for a while, then puts down the forks, and continues to think. The key question is: Can you write a program for each philosopher that does what it is supposed to do and never gets stuck? (It has been pointed out that the two-fork requirement is somewhat artificial; perhaps we should switch from Italian food to Chinese food, substituting rice for spaghetti and chopsticks for forks.)

Figure 2-32 shows the obvious solution. The procedure *take_fork* waits until the specified fork is available and then seizes it. Unfortunately, the obvious solution is wrong. Suppose that all five philosophers take their left forks simultaneously. None will be able to take their right forks, and there will be a deadlock.

We could modify the program so that after taking the left fork, the program checks to see if the right fork is available. If it is not, the philosopher puts down

```
#define N 5                          /* number of philosophers */

void philosopher(int i)              /* i: philosopher number, from 0 to 4 */
{
    while (TRUE) {
        think( );                    /* philosopher is thinking */
        take_fork(i);                /* take left fork */
        take_fork((i+1) % N);        /* take right fork; % is modulo operator */
        eat( );                      /* yum-yum, spaghetti */
        put_fork(i);                 /* put left fork back on the table */
        put_fork((i+1) % N);         /* put right fork back on the table */
    }
}
```

Figure 2-32. A nonsolution to the dining philosophers problem.

the left one, waits for some time, and then repeats the whole process. This proposal too, fails, although for a different reason. With a little bit of bad luck, all the philosophers could start the algorithm simultaneously, picking up their left forks, seeing that their right forks were not available, putting down their left forks, waiting, picking up their left forks again simultaneously, and so on, forever. A situation like this, in which all the programs continue to run indefinitely but fail to make any progress is called **starvation**. (It is called starvation even when the problem does not occur in an Italian or a Chinese restaurant.)

Now you might think, "If the philosophers would just wait a random time instead of the same time after failing to acquire the right-hand fork, the chance that everything would continue in lockstep for even an hour is very small." This observation is true, and in nearly all applications trying again later is not a problem. For example, in the popular Ethernet local area network, if two computers send a packet at the same time, each one waits a random time and tries again; in practice this solution works fine. However, in a few applications one would prefer a solution that always works and cannot fail due to an unlikely series of random numbers. Think about safety control in a nuclear power plant.

One improvement to Fig. 2-32 that has no deadlock and no starvation is to protect the five statements following the call to *think* by a binary semaphore. Before starting to acquire forks, a philosopher would do a **down** on *mutex*. After replacing the forks, she would do an **up** on *mutex*. From a theoretical viewpoint, this solution is adequate. From a practical one, it has a performance bug: only one philosopher can be eating at any instant. With five forks available, we should be able to allow two philosophers to eat at the same time.

The solution presented in Fig. 2-33 is deadlock-free and allows the maximum parallelism for an arbitrary number of philosophers. It uses an array, *state*, to keep track of whether a philosopher is eating, thinking, or hungry (trying to acquire forks). A philosopher may move only into eating state if neither neighbor

```
#define N            5              /* number of philosophers */
#define LEFT         (i+N-1)%N      /* number of i's left neighbor */
#define RIGHT        (i+1)%N        /* number of i's right neighbor */
#define THINKING     0              /* philosopher is thinking */
#define HUNGRY       1              /* philosopher is trying to get forks */
#define EATING       2              /* philosopher is eating */
typedef int semaphore;             /* semaphores are a special kind of int */
int state[N];                      /* array to keep track of everyone's state */
semaphore mutex = 1;               /* mutual exclusion for critical regions */
semaphore s[N];                    /* one semaphore per philosopher */

void philosopher(int i)            /* i: philosopher number, from 0 to N-1 */
{
     while (TRUE) {                /* repeat forever */
          think( );               /* philosopher is thinking */
          take_forks(i);          /* acquire two forks or block */
          eat( );                 /* yum-yum, spaghetti */
          put_forks(i);           /* put both forks back on table */
     }
}

void take_forks(int i)             /* i: philosopher number, from 0 to N-1 */
{
     down(&mutex);                 /* enter critical region */
     state[i] = HUNGRY;            /* record fact that philosopher i is hungry */
     test(i);                      /* try to acquire 2 forks */
     up(&mutex);                   /* exit critical region */
     down(&s[i]);                  /* block if forks were not acquired */
}

void put_forks(i)                  /* i: philosopher number, from 0 to N-1 */
{
     down(&mutex);                 /* enter critical region */
     state[i] = THINKING;          /* philosopher has finished eating */
     test(LEFT);                   /* see if left neighbor can now eat */
     test(RIGHT);                  /* see if right neighbor can now eat */
     up(&mutex);                   /* exit critical region */
}

void test(i)                       /* i: philosopher number, from 0 to N-1 */
{
     if (state[i] == HUNGRY && state[LEFT] != EATING && state[RIGHT] != EATING) {
          state[i] = EATING;
          up(&s[i]);
     }
}
```

Figure 2-33. A solution to the dining philosophers problem.

is eating. Philosopher i's neighbors are defined by the macros *LEFT* and *RIGHT*. In other words, if i is 2, *LEFT* is 1 and *RIGHT* is 3.

The program uses an array of semaphores, one per philosopher, so hungry philosophers can block if the needed forks are busy. Note that each process runs the procedure *philosopher* as its main code, but the other procedures, *take_forks*, *put_forks*, and *test* are ordinary procedures and not separate processes.

2.4.2 The Readers and Writers Problem

The dining philosophers problem is useful for modeling processes that are competing for exclusive access to a limited number of resources, such as I/O devices. Another famous problem is the readers and writers problem (Courtois et al., 1971), which models access to a database. Imagine, for example, an airline reservation system, with many competing processes wishing to read and write it. It is acceptable to have multiple processes reading the database at the same time, but if one process is updating (writing) the database, no other processes may have access to the database, not even readers. The question is how do you program the readers and the writers? One solution is shown in Fig. 2-34.

In this solution, the first reader to get access to the database does a down on the semaphore *db*. Subsequent readers merely increment a counter, *rc*. As readers leave, they decrement the counter and the last one out does an up on the semaphore, allowing a blocked writer, if there is one, to get in.

The solution presented here implicitly contains a subtle decision that is worth commenting on. Suppose that while a reader is using the database, another reader comes along. Since having two readers at the same time is not a problem, the second reader is admitted. A third and subsequent readers can also be admitted if they come along.

Now suppose that a writer comes along. The writer cannot be admitted to the database, since writers must have exclusive access, so the writer is suspended. Later, additional readers show up. As long as at least one reader is still active, subsequent readers are admitted. As a consequence of this strategy, as long as there is a steady supply of readers, they will all get in as soon as they arrive. The writer will be kept suspended until no reader is present. If a new reader arrives, say, every 2 seconds, and each reader takes 5 seconds to do its work, the writer will never get in.

To prevent this situation, the program could be written slightly differently: when a reader arrives and a writer is waiting, the reader is suspended behind the writer instead of being admitted immediately. In this way, a writer has to wait for readers that were active when it arrived to finish but does not have to wait for readers that came along after it. The disadvantage of this solution is that it achieves less concurrency and thus lower performance. Courtois et al. present a solution that gives priority to writers. For details, we refer you to the paper.

```
typedef int semaphore;              /* use your imagination */
semaphore mutex = 1;                /* controls access to 'rc' */
semaphore db = 1;                   /* controls access to the database */
int rc = 0;                         /* # of processes reading or wanting to */

void reader(void)
{
     while (TRUE) {                 /* repeat forever */
          down(&mutex);             /* get exclusive access to 'rc' */
          rc = rc + 1;              /* one reader more now */
          if (rc == 1) down(&db);   /* if this is the first reader ... */
          up(&mutex);               /* release exclusive access to 'rc' */
          read_data_base( );        /* access the data */
          down(&mutex);             /* get exclusive access to 'rc' */
          rc = rc − 1;              /* one reader fewer now */
          if (rc == 0) up(&db);     /* if this is the last reader ... */
          up(&mutex);               /* release exclusive access to 'rc' */
          use_data_read( );         /* noncritical region */
     }
}


void writer(void)
{
     while (TRUE) {                 /* repeat forever */
          think_up_data( );         /* noncritical region */
          down(&db);                /* get exclusive access */
          write_data_base( );       /* update the data */
          up(&db);                  /* release exclusive access */
     }
}
```

Figure 2-34. A solution to the readers and writers problem.

2.4.3 The Sleeping Barber Problem

Another classical IPC problem takes place in a barber shop. The barber shop has one barber, one barber chair, and *n* chairs for waiting customers, if any, to sit on. If there are no customers present, the barber sits down in the barber chair and falls asleep, as illustrated in Fig. 2-35. When a customer arrives, he has to wake up the sleeping barber. If additional customers arrive while the barber is cutting a customer's hair, they either sit down (if there are empty chairs) or leave the shop (if all chairs are full). The problem is to program the barber and the customers without getting into race conditions. This problem is similar to various queueing situations, such as a multiperson helpdesk with a computerized call waiting system for holding a limited number of incoming calls.

Figure 2-35. The sleeping barber.

Our solution uses three semaphores: *customers*, which counts waiting customers (excluding the customer in the barber chair, who is not waiting), *barbers*, the number of barbers (0 or 1) who are idle, waiting for customers, and *mutex*, which is used for mutual exclusion. We also need a variable, *waiting*, which also counts the waiting customers. It is essentially a copy of *customers*. The reason for having *waiting* is that there is no way to read the current value of a semaphore. In this solution, a customer entering the shop has to count the number of waiting customers. If it is less than the number of chairs, he stays; otherwise, he leaves.

Our solution is shown in Fig. 2-36. When the barber shows up for work in the morning, he executes the procedure *barber*, causing him to block on the semaphore *customers* because it is initially 0. The barber then goes to sleep, as shown in Fig. 2-35. He stays asleep until the first customer shows up.

```
#define CHAIRS 5                    /* # chairs for waiting customers */

typedef int semaphore;             /* use your imagination */

semaphore customers = 0;           /* # of customers waiting for service */
semaphore barbers = 0;             /* # of barbers waiting for customers */
semaphore mutex = 1;               /* for mutual exclusion */
int waiting = 0;                   /* customers are waiting (not being cut) */

void barber(void)
{
    while (TRUE) {
        down(&customers);          /* go to sleep if # of customers is 0 */
        down(&mutex);              /* acquire access to 'waiting' */
        waiting = waiting - 1;     /* decrement count of waiting customers */
        up(&barbers);              /* one barber is now ready to cut hair */
        up(&mutex);                /* release 'waiting' */
        cut_hair( );               /* cut hair (outside critical region) */
    }
}


void customer(void)
{
    down(&mutex);                  /* enter critical region */
    if (waiting < CHAIRS) {        /* if there are no free chairs, leave */
        waiting = waiting + 1;     /* increment count of waiting customers */
        up(&customers);            /* wake up barber if necessary */
        up(&mutex);                /* release access to 'waiting' */
        down(&barbers);            /* go to sleep if # of free barbers is 0 */
        get_haircut( );            /* be seated and be serviced */
    } else {
        up(&mutex);                /* shop is full; do not wait */
    }
}
```

Figure 2-36. A solution to the sleeping barber problem.

When a customer arrives, he executes *customer*, starting by acquiring *mutex* to enter a critical region. If another customer enters shortly thereafter, the second one will not be able to do anything until the first one has released *mutex*. The customer then checks to see if the number of waiting customers is less than the number of chairs. If not, he releases *mutex* and leaves without a haircut.

If there is an available chair, the customer increments the integer variable, *waiting*. Then he does an up on the semaphore *customers*, thus waking up the barber. At this point, the customer and barber are both awake. When the customer releases *mutex*, the barber grabs it, does some housekeeping, and begins the haircut.

When the haircut is over, the customer exits the procedure and leaves the shop. Unlike our earlier examples, there is no loop for the customer because each one gets only one haircut. The barber loops, however, to try to get the next customer. If one is present, another haircut is given. If not, the barber goes to sleep.

As an aside, it is worth pointing out that although the readers and writers and sleeping barber problems do not involve data transfer, they are still belong to the area of IPC because they involve synchronization between multiple processes.

2.5 SCHEDULING

When a computer is multiprogrammed, it frequently has multiple processes competing for the CPU at the same time. This situation occurs whenever two or more processes are simultaneously in the ready state. If only one CPU is available, a choice has to be made which process to run next. The part of the operating system that makes the choice is called the **scheduler** and the algorithm it uses is called the **scheduling algorithm**. These topics form the subject matter of the following sections.

Many of the same issues that apply to process scheduling also apply to thread scheduling, although some are different. Initially we will focus on process scheduling. Later on we will explicitly look at thread scheduling.

2.5.1 Introduction to Scheduling

Back in the old days of batch systems with input in the form of card images on a magnetic tape, the scheduling algorithm was simple: just run the next job on the tape. With timesharing systems, the scheduling algorithm became more complex because there were generally multiple users waiting for service. Some mainframes still combine batch and timesharing service, requiring the scheduler to decide whether a batch job or an interactive user at a terminal should go next. (As an aside, a batch job may be a request to run multiple programs in succession, but for this section, we will just assume it is a request to run a single program.) Because CPU time is a scarce resource on these machines, a good scheduler can make a big difference in perceived performance and user satisfaction. Consequently, a great deal of work has gone into devising clever and efficient scheduling algorithms.

With the advent of personal computers, the situation changed in two ways. First, most of the time there is only one active process. A user entering a document on a word processor is unlikely to be simultaneously compiling a program in the background. When the user types a command to the word processor, the scheduler does not have to do much work to figure out which process to run—the word processor is the only candidate.

Second, computers have gotten so much faster over the years that the CPU is rarely a scarce resource any more. Most programs for personal computers are limited by the rate at which the user can present input (by typing or clicking), not by the rate the CPU can process it. Even compilations, a major sink of CPU cycles in the past, take just a few seconds at most nowadays. Even when two programs are actually running at once, such as a word processor and a spreadsheet, it hardly matters which goes first since the user is probably waiting for both of them to finish. As a consequence, scheduling does not matter much on simple PCs. [Of course, there are applications that practically eat the CPU alive: rendering one hour of high-resolution video may require industrial-strength image processing on each of 108,000 frames in NTSC (90,000 in PAL), but these applications are the exception rather than the rule.]

When we turn to high-end networked workstations and servers, the situation changes. Here multiple processes often do compete for the CPU, so scheduling matters again. For example, when the CPU has to choose between running a process that updates the screen after a user has closed a window and running a process that sends out queued email, it makes a huge difference in the perceived response. If closing the window were to take 2 sec while the email was being sent, the user would probably regard the system as extremely sluggish, whereas having the email delayed by 2 sec would not even be noticed. In this case, process scheduling matters very much.

In addition to picking the right process to run, the scheduler also has to worry about making efficient use of the CPU because process switching is expensive. To start with, a switch from user mode to kernel mode must occur. Then the state of the current process must be saved, including storing its registers in the process table so they can be reloaded later. In many systems, the memory map (e.g., memory reference bits in the page table) must be saved as well. Next a new process must be selected by running the scheduling algorithm. After that, the MMU must be reloaded with the memory map of the new process. Finally, the new process must be started. In addition to all that, the process switch usually invalidates the entire memory cache, forcing it to be dynamically reloaded from the main memory twice (upon entering the kernel and upon leaving it). All in all, doing too many process switches per second can chew up a substantial amount of CPU time, so caution is advised.

Process Behavior

Nearly all processes alternate bursts of computing with (disk) I/O requests, as shown in Fig. 2-37. Typically the CPU runs for a while without stopping, then a system call is made to read from a file or write to a file. When the system call completes, the CPU computes again until it needs more data or has to write more data, and so on. Note that some I/O activities count as computing. For example, when the CPU copies bits to a video RAM to update the screen, it is computing, not doing I/O, because the CPU is in use. I/O in this sense is when a process enters the blocked state waiting for an external device to complete its work.

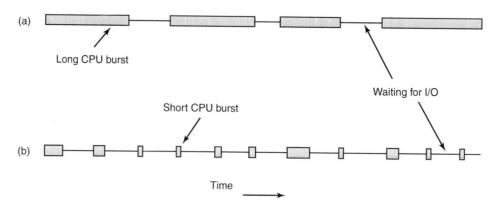

Figure 2-37. Bursts of CPU usage alternate with periods of waiting for I/O. (a) A CPU-bound process. (b) An I/O-bound process.

The important thing to notice about Fig. 2-37 is that some processes, such as the one in Fig. 2-37(a), spend most of their time computing, while others, such as the one in Fig. 2-37(b), spend most of their time waiting for I/O. The former are called **compute-bound**; the latter are called **I/O-bound**. Compute-bound processes typically have long CPU bursts and thus infrequent I/O waits, whereas I/O-bound processes have short CPU bursts and thus frequent I/O waits. Note that the key factor is the length of the CPU burst, not the length of the I/O burst. I/O-bound processes are I/O bound because they do not compute much between I/O requests, not because they have especially long I/O requests. It takes the same time to read a disk block no matter how much or how little time it takes to process the data after they arrive.

It is worth noting that as CPUs get faster, processes tend to get more I/O-bound. This effect occurs because CPUs are improving much faster than disks. As a consequence, the scheduling of I/O-bound processes is likely to become a more important subject in the future. The basic idea here is that if an I/O-bound process wants to run, it should get a chance quickly so it can issue its disk request and keep the disk busy.

When to Schedule

A key issue related to scheduling is when to make scheduling decisions. It turns out that there are a variety of situations in which scheduling is needed. First, when a new process is created, a decision needs to be made whether to run the parent process or the child process. Since both processes are in ready state, it is a normal scheduling decision and it can go either way, that is, the scheduler can legitimately choose to run either the parent or the child next.

Second, a scheduling decision must be made when a process exits. That process can no longer run (since it no longer exists), so some other process must be chosen from the set of ready processes. If no process is ready, a system-supplied idle process is normally run.

Third, when a process blocks on I/O, on a semaphore, or for some other reason, another process has to be selected to run. Sometimes the reason for blocking may play a role in the choice. For example, if *A* is an important process and it is waiting for *B* to exit its critical region, letting *B* run next will allow it to exit its critical region and thus let *A* continue. The trouble, however, is that the scheduler generally does not have the necessary information to take this dependency into account.

Fourth, when an I/O interrupt occurs, a scheduling decision may be made. If the interrupt came from an I/O device that has now completed its work, some process that was blocked waiting for the I/O may now be ready to run. It is up to the scheduler to decide if the newly ready process should be run, if the process that was running at the time of the interrupt should continue running, or if some third process should run.

If a hardware clock provides periodic interrupts at 50 Hz, 60 Hz, or some other frequency, a scheduling decision can be made at each clock interrupt or at every *k*-th clock interrupt. Scheduling algorithms can be divided into two categories with respect to how they deal with clock interrupts. A **nonpreemptive** scheduling algorithm picks a process to run and then just lets it run until it blocks (either on I/O or waiting for another process) or until it voluntarily releases the CPU. Even if it runs for hours, it will not be forceably suspended. In effect, no scheduling decisions are made during clock interrupts. After clock interrupt processing has been completed, the process that was running before the interrupt is always resumed.

In contrast, a **preemptive** scheduling algorithm picks a process and lets it run for a maximum of some fixed time. If it is still running at the end of the time interval, it is suspended and the scheduler picks another process to run (if one is available). Doing preemptive scheduling requires having a clock interrupt occur at the end of the time interval to give control of the CPU back to the scheduler. If no clock is available, nonpreemptive scheduling is the only option.

Categories of Scheduling Algorithms

Not surprisingly, in different environments different scheduling algorithms are needed. This situation arises because different application areas (and different kinds of operating systems) have different goals. In other words, what the scheduler should optimize for is not the same in all systems. Three environments worth distinguishing are

1. Batch.

2. Interactive.

3. Real time.

In batch systems, there are no users impatiently waiting at their terminals for a quick response. Consequently, nonpreemptive algorithms, or preemptive algorithms with long time periods for each process are often acceptable. This approach reduces process switches and thus improves performance.

In an environment with interactive users, preemption is essential to keep one process from hogging the CPU and denying service to the others. Even if no process intentionally ran forever, due to a program bug, one process might shut out all the others indefinitely. Preemption is needed to prevent this behavior.

In systems with real-time constraints, preemption is, oddly enough, sometimes not needed because the processes know that they may not run for long periods of time and usually do their work and block quickly. The difference with interactive systems is that real-time systems run only programs that are intended to further the application at hand. Interactive systems are general purpose and may run arbitrary programs that are not cooperative or even malicious.

Scheduling Algorithm Goals

In order to design a scheduling algorithm, it is necessary to have some idea of what a good algorithm should do. Some goals depend on the environment (batch, interactive, or real time), but there are also some that are desirable in all cases. Some goals are listed in Fig. 2-38. We will discuss these in turn below.

Under all circumstances, fairness is important. Comparable processes should get comparable service. Giving one process much more CPU time than an equivalent one is not fair. Of course, different categories of processes may be treated very differently. Think of safety control and doing the payroll at a nuclear reactor's computer center.

Somewhat related to fairness is enforcing the system's policies. If the local policy is that safety control processes get to run whenever they want to, even if it means the payroll is 30 sec late, the scheduler has to make sure this policy is enforced.

Another general goal is keeping all parts of the system busy when possible. If the CPU and all the I/O devices can be kept running all the time, more work gets done per second than if some of the components are idle. In a batch system, for example, the scheduler has control of which jobs are brought into memory to run. Having some CPU-bound processes and some I/O-bound processes in memory together is a better idea than first loading and running all the CPU-bound jobs and

All systems
    Fairness - giving each process a fair share of the CPU
    Policy enforcement - seeing that stated policy is carried out
    Balance - keeping all parts of the system busy

Batch systems
    Throughput - maximize jobs per hour
    Turnaround time - minimize time between submission and termination
    CPU utilization - keep the CPU busy all the time

Interactive systems
    Response time - respond to requests quickly
    Proportionality - meet users' expectations

Real-time systems
    Meeting deadlines - avoid losing data
    Predictability - avoid quality degradation in multimedia systems

Figure 2-38. Some goals of the scheduling algorithm under different circumstances.

then when they are finished loading and running all the I/O-bound jobs. If the latter strategy is used, when the CPU-bound processes are running, they will fight for the CPU and the disk will be idle. Later, when the I/O-bound jobs come in, they will fight for the disk and the CPU will be idle. Better to keep the whole system running at once by a careful mix of processes.

The managers of large computer centers that run many batch jobs typically look at three metrics to see how well their systems are performing: throughput, turnaround time, and CPU utilization. **Throughput** is the number of jobs per hour that the system completes. All things considered, finishing 50 jobs per hour is better than finishing 40 jobs per hour. **Turnaround time** is the statistically average time from the moment that a batch job is submitted until the moment it is completed. It measures how long the average user has to wait for the output. Here the rule is: Small is Beautiful.

A scheduling algorithm that maximizes throughput may not necessarily minimize turnaround time. For example, given a mix of short jobs and long jobs, a scheduler that always ran short jobs and never ran long jobs might achieve an excellent throughput (many short jobs per hour) but at the expense of a terrible turnaround time for the long jobs. If short jobs kept arriving at a steady rate, the long jobs might never run, making the mean turnaround time infinite while achieving a high throughput.

CPU utilization is also an issue with batch systems because on the big mainframes where batch systems run, the CPU is still a major expense. Thus computer center managers feel guilty when it is not running all the time. Actually though, this is not such a good metric. What really matters is how many jobs per hour come out of the system (throughput) and how long it takes to get a job back (turnaround time). Using CPU utilization as a metric is like rating cars based on how many times per hour the engine turns over.

For interactive systems, especially timesharing systems and servers, different goals apply. The most important one is to minimize **response time**, that is the time between issuing a command and getting the result. On a personal computer where a background process is running (for example, reading and storing email from the network), a user request to start a program or open a file should take precedence over the background work. Having all interactive requests go first will be perceived as good service.

A somewhat related issue is what might be called **proportionality**. Users have an inherent (but often incorrect) idea of how long things should take. When a request that is perceived as complex takes a long time, users accept that, but when a request that is perceived as simple takes a long time, users get irritated. For example, if clicking on a icon that calls up an Internet provider using an analog modem takes 45 seconds to establish a connection, the user will probably accept that as a fact of life. On the other hand, if clicking on an icon that breaks the connection takes 45 seconds, the user will probably be swearing a blue streak by the 30-sec mark and frothing at the mouth by 45 sec. This behavior is due to the common user perception that placing a phone call and getting a connection is *supposed* to take a lot longer than just hanging up. In some cases (such as this one), the scheduler cannot do anything about the response time, but in other cases it can, especially when the delay is due to a poor choice of process order.

Real-time systems have different properties than interactive systems, and thus different scheduling goals. They are characterized by having deadlines that must or at least should be met. For example, if a computer is controlling a device that produces data at a regular rate, failure to run the data-collection process on time may result in lost data. Thus the foremost need in a real-time system is meeting all (or most) deadlines.

In some real-time systems, especially those involving multimedia, predictability is important. Missing an occasional deadline is not fatal, but if the audio process runs too erratically, the sound quality will deteriorate rapidly. Video is also an issue, but the ear is much more sensitive to jitter than the eye. To avoid this problem, process scheduling must be highly predictable and regular. We will study batch and interactive scheduling algorithms in this chapter but defer most of our study of real-time scheduling until we come to multimedia operating systems in Chap. 7.

2.5.2 Scheduling in Batch Systems

It is now time to turn from general scheduling issues to specific scheduling algorithms. In this section we will look at algorithms used in batch systems. In the following ones we will examine interactive and real-time systems. It is worth pointing out that some algorithms are used in both batch and interactive systems. We will study these later. Here we will focus on algorithms that are only suitable in batch systems.

First-Come First-Served

Probably the simplest of all scheduling algorithms is nonpreemptive **first-come first-served**. With this algorithm, processes are assigned the CPU in the order they request it. Basically, there is a single queue of ready processes. When the first job enters the system from the outside in the morning, it is started immediately and allowed to run as long as it wants to. As other jobs come in, they are put onto the end of the queue. When the running process blocks, the first process on the queue is run next. When a blocked process becomes ready, like a newly arrived job, it is put on the end of the queue.

The great strength of this algorithm is that it is easy to understand and equally easy to program. It is also fair in the same sense that allocating scarce sports or concert tickets to people who are willing to stand on line starting at 2 A.M. is fair. With this algorithm, a single linked list keeps track of all ready processes. Picking a process to run just requires removing one from the front of the queue. Adding a new job or unblocked process just requires attaching it to the end of the queue. What could be simpler?

Unfortunately, first-come first-served also has a powerful disadvantage. Suppose that there is one compute-bound process that runs for 1 sec at a time and many I/O-bound processes that use little CPU time but each have to perform 1000 disk reads to complete. The compute-bound process runs for 1 sec, then it reads a disk block. All the I/O processes now run and start disk reads. When the compute-bound process gets its disk block, it runs for another 1 sec, followed by all the I/O-bound processes in quick succession.

The net result is that each I/O-bound process gets to read 1 block per second and will take 1000 sec to finish. With a scheduling algorithm that preempted the compute-bound process every 10 msec, the I/O-bound processes would finish in 10 sec instead of 1000 sec, and without slowing down the compute-bound process very much.

Shortest Job First

Now let us look at another nonpreemptive batch algorithm that assumes the run times are known in advance. In an insurance company, for example, people can predict quite accurately how long it will take to run a batch of 1000 claims, since similar work is done every day. When several equally important jobs are sitting in the input queue waiting to be started, the scheduler picks the **shortest job first**. Look at Fig. 2-39. Here we find four jobs *A*, *B*, *C*, and *D* with run times of 8, 4, 4, and 4 minutes, respectively. By running them in that order, the turnaround time for A is 8 minutes, for B is 12 minutes, for C is 16 minutes, and for D is 20 minutes for an average of 14 minutes.

Figure 2-39. An example of shortest job first scheduling. (a) Running four jobs in the original order. (b) Running them in shortest job first order.

Now let us consider running these four jobs using shortest job first, as shown in Fig. 2-39(b). The turnaround times are now 4, 8, 12, and 20 minutes for an average of 11 minutes. Shortest job first is provably optimal. Consider the case of four jobs, with run times of a, b, c, and d, respectively. The first job finishes at time a, the second finishes at time $a + b$, and so on. The mean turnaround time is $(4a + 3b + 2c + d)/4$. It is clear that a contributes more to the average than the other times, so it should be the shortest job, with b next, then c, and finally d as the longest as it affects only its own turnaround time. The same argument applies equally well to any number of jobs.

It is worth pointing out that shortest job first is only optimal when all the jobs are available simultaneously. As a counterexample, consider five jobs, A through E, with run times of 2, 4, 1, 1, and 1, respectively. Their arrival times are 0, 0, 3, 3, and 3. Initially, only A or B can be chosen, since the other three jobs have not arrived yet. Using shortest job first we will run the jobs in the order A, B, C, D, E, for an average wait of 4.6. However, running them in the order B, C, D, E, A has an average wait of 4.4.

Shortest Remaining Time Next

A preemptive version of shortest job first is **shortest remaining time next**. With this algorithm, the scheduler always chooses the process whose remaining run time is the shortest. Again here, the run time has to be known in advance. When a new job arrives, its total time is compared to the current process' remaining time. If the new job needs less time to finish than the current process, the current process is suspended and the new job started. This scheme allows new short jobs to get good service.

Three-Level Scheduling

From a certain perspective, batch systems allow scheduling at three different levels, as illustrated in Fig. 2-40. As jobs arrive at the system, they are initially placed in an input queue stored on the disk. The **admission scheduler** decides which jobs to admit to the system. The others are kept in the input queue until they are selected. A typical algorithm for admission control might be to look for a mix of compute-bound jobs and I/O-bound jobs. Alternatively, short jobs could be admitted quickly whereas longer jobs would have to wait. The admission scheduler is free to hold some jobs in the input queue and admit jobs that arrive later if it so chooses.

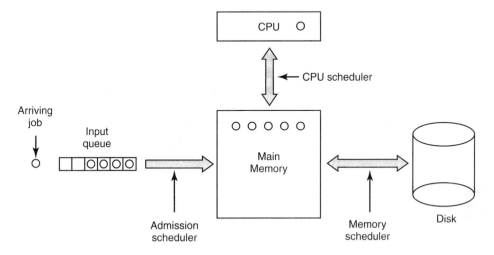

Figure 2-40. Three-level scheduling.

Once a job has been admitted to the system, a process can be created for it and it can contend for the CPU. However, it might well happen that the number of processes is so large that there is not enough room for all of them in memory. In that case, some of the processes have to be swapped out to disk. The second level of scheduling is deciding which processes should be kept in memory and which ones kept on disk. We will call this scheduler the **memory scheduler**, since it determines which processes are kept in memory and which on the disk.

This decision has to be reviewed frequently to allow the processes on disk to get some service. However, since bringing a process in from disk is expensive, the review probably should not happen more often than once per second, maybe less often. If the contents of main memory are shuffled too often, a large amount of disk bandwidth will be wasted, slowing down file I/O.

To optimize system performance as a whole, the memory scheduler might want to carefully decide how many processes it wants in memory, called the **degree of multiprogramming**, and what kind of processes. If it has information about which processes are compute bound and which are I/O bound, it can try to keep a mix of these process types in memory. As a very crude approximation, if a certain class of process computes about 20% of the time, keeping five of them around is roughly the right number to keep the CPU busy. We will look at a slightly better multiprogramming model in Chap. 4.

To make its decisions, the memory scheduler periodically reviews each process on disk to decide whether or not to bring it into memory. Among the criteria that it can use to make its decision are the following ones:

1. How long has it been since the process was swapped in or out?

2. How much CPU time has the process had recently?

3. How big is the process? (Small ones do not get in the way.)

4. How important is the process?

The third level of scheduling is actually picking one of the ready processes in main memory to run next. Often this is called the **CPU scheduler** and is the one people usually mean when they talk about the "scheduler." Any suitable algorithm can be used here, either preemptive or nonpreemptive. These include the ones described above as well as a number of algorithms to be described in the next section.

2.5.3 Scheduling in Interactive Systems

We will now look at some algorithms that can be used in interactive systems. All of these can also be used as the CPU scheduler in batch systems as well. While three-level scheduling is not possible here, two-level scheduling (memory scheduler and CPU scheduler) is possible and common. Below we will focus on the CPU scheduler.

Round-Robin Scheduling

Now let us look at some specific scheduling algorithms. One of the oldest, simplest, fairest, and most widely used algorithms is **round robin**. Each process is assigned a time interval, called its **quantum**, which it is allowed to run. If the process is still running at the end of the quantum, the CPU is preempted and given to another process. If the process has blocked or finished before the quantum has elapsed, the CPU switching is done when the process blocks, of course. Round robin is easy to implement. All the scheduler needs to do is maintain a list of runnable processes, as shown in Fig. 2-41(a). When the process uses up its quantum, it is put on the end of the list, as shown in Fig. 2-41(b).

The only interesting issue with round robin is the length of the quantum. Switching from one process to another requires a certain amount of time for doing the administration—saving and loading registers and memory maps, updating various tables and lists, flushing and reloading the memory cache, etc. Suppose that this **process switch** or **context switch**, as it is sometimes called, takes 1 msec, including switching memory maps, flushing and reloading the cache, etc. Also suppose that the quantum is set at 4 msec. With these parameters, after doing 4

Figure 2-41. Round-robin scheduling. (a) The list of runnable processes. (b) The list of runnable processes after *B* uses up its quantum.

msec of useful work, the CPU will have to spend 1 msec on process switching. Twenty percent of the CPU time will be wasted on administrative overhead. Clearly this is too much.

To improve the CPU efficiency, we could set the quantum to, say, 100 msec. Now the wasted time is only 1 percent. But consider what happens on a timesharing system if ten interactive users hit the carriage return key at roughly the same time. Ten processes will be put on the list of runnable processes. If the CPU is idle, the first one will start immediately, the second one may not start until 100 msec later, and so on. The unlucky last one may have to wait 1 sec before getting a chance, assuming all the others use their full quanta. Most users will perceive a 1-sec response to a short command as sluggish

Another factor is that if the quantum is set longer than the mean CPU burst, preemption will rarely happen. Instead, most processes will perform a blocking operation before the quantum runs out, causing a process switch. Eliminating preemption improves performance because process switches then only happen when they are logically necessary, that is, when a process blocks and cannot continue.

The conclusion can be formulated as follows: setting the quantum too short causes too many process switches and lowers the CPU efficiency, but setting it too long may cause poor response to short interactive requests. A quantum around 20-50 msec is often a reasonable compromise.

Priority Scheduling

Round robin scheduling makes the implicit assumption that all processes are equally important. Frequently, the people who own and operate multiuser computers have different ideas on that subject. At a university, the pecking order may be deans first, then professors, secretaries, janitors, and finally students. The need to take external factors into account leads to **priority scheduling**. The basic idea is straightforward: each process is assigned a priority, and the runnable process with the highest priority is allowed to run.

Even on a PC with a single owner, there may be multiple processes, some more important than others. For example, a daemon process sending electronic mail in the background should be assigned a lower priority than a process displaying a video film on the screen in real time.

To prevent high-priority processes from running indefinitely, the scheduler may decrease the priority of the currently running process at each clock tick (i.e., at each clock interrupt). If this action causes its priority to drop below that of the next highest process, a process switch occurs. Alternatively, each process may be assigned a maximum time quantum that it is allowed to run. When this quantum is used up, the next highest priority process is given a chance to run.

Priorities can be assigned to processes statically or dynamically. On a military computer, processes started by generals might begin at priority 100, processes started by colonels at 90, majors at 80, captains at 70, lieutenants at 60, and so on. Alternatively, at a commercial computer center, high-priority jobs might cost 100 dollars an hour, medium priority 75 dollars an hour, and low priority 50 dollars an hour. The UNIX system has a command, *nice*, which allows a user to voluntarily reduce the priority of his process, in order to be nice to the other users. Nobody ever uses it.

Priorities can also be assigned dynamically by the system to achieve certain system goals. For example, some processes are highly I/O bound and spend most of their time waiting for I/O to complete. Whenever such a process wants the CPU, it should be given the CPU immediately, to let it start its next I/O request, which can then proceed in parallel with another process actually computing. Making the I/O-bound process wait a long time for the CPU will just mean having it around occupying memory for an unnecessarily long time. A simple algorithm for giving good service to I/O-bound processes is to set the priority to $1/f$, where f is the fraction of the last quantum that a process used. A process that used only 1 msec of its 50 msec quantum would get priority 50, while a process that ran 25 msec before blocking would get priority 2, and a process that used the whole quantum would get priority 1.

It is often convenient to group processes into priority classes and use priority scheduling among the classes but round-robin scheduling within each class. Figure 2-42 shows a system with four priority classes. The scheduling algorithm is as follows: as long as there are runnable processes in priority class 4, just run each one for one quantum, round-robin fashion, and never bother with lower priority classes. If priority class 4 is empty, then run the class 3 processes round robin. If classes 4 and 3 are both empty, then run class 2 round robin, and so on. If priorities are not adjusted occasionally, lower priority classes may all starve to death.

Multiple Queues

One of the earliest priority schedulers was in CTSS (Corbató et al., 1962). CTSS had the problem that process switching was very slow because the 7094 could hold only one process in memory. Each switch meant swapping the current process to disk and reading in a new one from disk. The CTSS designers quickly

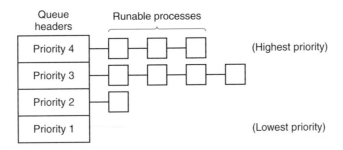

Figure 2-42. A scheduling algorithm with four priority classes.

realized that it was more efficient to give CPU-bound processes a large quantum once in a while, rather than giving them small quanta frequently (to reduce swapping). On the other hand, giving all processes a large quantum would mean poor response time, as we have already seen. Their solution was to set up priority classes. Processes in the highest class were run for one quantum. Processes in the next highest class were run for two quanta. Processes in the next class were run for four quanta, and so on. Whenever a process used up all the quanta allocated to it, it was moved down one class.

As an example, consider a process that needed to compute continuously for 100 quanta. It would initially be given one quantum, then swapped out. Next time it would get two quanta before being swapped out. On succeeding runs it would get 4, 8, 16, 32, and 64 quanta, although it would have used only 37 of the final 64 quanta to complete its work. Only 7 swaps would be needed (including the initial load) instead of 100 with a pure round-robin algorithm. Furthermore, as the process sank deeper and deeper into the priority queues, it would be run less and less frequently, saving the CPU for short, interactive processes.

The following policy was adopted to prevent a process that needed to run for a long time when it first started but became interactive later, from being punished forever. Whenever a carriage return was typed at a terminal, the process belonging to that terminal was moved to the highest priority class, on the assumption that it was about to become interactive. One fine day, some user with a heavily CPU-bound process discovered that just sitting at the terminal and typing carriage returns at random every few seconds did wonders for his response time. He told all his friends. Moral of the story: getting it right in practice is much harder than getting it right in principle.

Many other algorithms have been used for assigning processes to priority classes. For example, the influential XDS 940 system (Lampson, 1968), built at Berkeley, had four priority classes, called terminal, I/O, short quantum, and long quantum. When a process that was waiting for terminal input was finally awakened, it went into the highest priority class (terminal). When a process waiting for a disk block became ready, it went into the second class. When a process was still running when its quantum ran out, it was initially placed in the third class. However, if a process used up its quantum too many times in a row without blocking for terminal or other I/O, it was moved down to the bottom queue. Many other systems use something similar to favor interactive users and processes over background ones.

Shortest Process Next

Because shortest job first always produces the minimum average response time for batch systems, it would be nice if it could be used for interactive processes as well. To a certain extent, it can be. Interactive processes generally follow the pattern of wait for command, execute command, wait for command, execute command, and so on. If we regard the execution of each command as a separate "job," then we could minimize overall response time by running the shortest one first. The only problem is figuring out which of the currently runnable processes is the shortest one.

One approach is to make estimates based on past behavior and run the process with the shortest estimated running time. Suppose that the estimated time per command for some terminal is T_0. Now suppose its next run is measured to be T_1. We could update our estimate by taking a weighted sum of these two numbers, that is, $aT_0 + (1 - a)T_1$. Through the choice of a we can decide to have the estimation process forget old runs quickly, or remember them for a long time. With $a = 1/2$, we get successive estimates of

$$T_0, \quad T_0/2 + T_1/2, \quad T_0/4 + T_1/4 + T_2/2, \quad T_0/8 + T_1/8 + T_2/4 + T_3/2$$

After three new runs, the weight of T_0 in the new estimate has dropped to 1/8.

The technique of estimating the next value in a series by taking the weighted average of the current measured value and the previous estimate is sometimes called **aging**. It is applicable to many situations where a prediction must be made based on previous values. Aging is especially easy to implement when $a = 1/2$. All that is needed is to add the new value to the current estimate and divide the sum by 2 (by shifting it right 1 bit).

Guaranteed Scheduling

A completely different approach to scheduling is to make real promises to the users about performance and then live up to them. One promise that is realistic to make and easy to live up to is this: If there are n users logged in while you are working, you will receive about $1/n$ of the CPU power. Similarly, on a single-user system with n processes running, all things being equal, each one should get $1/n$ of the CPU cycles.

To make good on this promise, the system must keep track of how much CPU each process has had since its creation. It then computes the amount of CPU each one is entitled to, namely the time since creation divided by n. Since the amount of CPU time each process has actually had is also known, it is straightforward to compute the ratio of actual CPU time consumed to CPU time entitled. A ratio of 0.5 means that a process has only had half of what it should have had, and a ratio of 2.0 means that a process has had twice as much as it was entitled to. The algorithm is then to run the process with the lowest ratio until its ratio has moved above its closest competitor.

Lottery Scheduling

While making promises to the users and then living up to them is a fine idea, it is difficult to implement. However, another algorithm can be used to give similarly predictable results with a much simpler implementation. It is called **lottery scheduling** (Waldspurger and Weihl, 1994).

The basic idea is to give processes lottery tickets for various system resources, such as CPU time. Whenever a scheduling decision has to be made, a lottery ticket is chosen at random, and the process holding that ticket gets the resource. When applied to CPU scheduling, the system might hold a lottery 50 times a second, with each winner getting 20 msec of CPU time as a prize.

To paraphrase George Orwell: "All processes are equal, but some processes are more equal." More important processes can be given extra tickets, to increase their odds of winning. If there are 100 tickets outstanding, and one process holds 20 of them, it will have a 20 percent chance of winning each lottery. In the long run, it will get about 20 percent of the CPU. In contrast to a priority scheduler, where it is very hard to state what having a priority of 40 actually means, here the rule is clear: a process holding a fraction f of the tickets will get about a fraction f of the resource in question.

Lottery scheduling has several interesting properties. For example, if a new process shows up and is granted some tickets, at the very next lottery it will have a chance of winning in proportion to the number of tickets it holds. In other words, lottery scheduling is highly responsive.

Cooperating processes may exchange tickets if they wish. For example, when a client process sends a message to a server process and then blocks, it may give all of its tickets to the server, to increase the chance of the server running next. When the server is finished, it returns the tickets so the client can run again. In fact, in the absence of clients, servers need no tickets at all.

Lottery scheduling can be used to solve problems that are difficult to handle with other methods. One example is a video server in which several processes are feeding video streams to their clients, but at different frame rates. Suppose that the processes need frames at 10, 20, and 25 frames/sec. By allocating these processes 10, 20, and 25 tickets, respectively, they will automatically divide the CPU in approximately the correct proportion, that is, 10 : 20 : 25.

Fair-Share Scheduling

So far we have assumed that each process is scheduled on its own, without regard to who its owner is. As a result, if user 1 starts up 9 processes and user 2 starts up 1 process, with round robin or equal priorities, user 1 will get 90% of the CPU and user 2 will get only 10% of it.

To prevent this situation, some systems take into account who owns a process before scheduling it. In this model, each user is allocated some fraction of the CPU and the scheduler picks processes in such a way as to enforce it. Thus if two users have each been promised 50% of the CPU, they will each get that, no matter how many processes they have in existence.

As an example, consider a system with two users, each of which has been promised 50% of the CPU. User 1 has four processes, A, B, C, and D, and user 2 has only 1 process, E. If round-robin scheduling is used, a possible scheduling sequence that meets all the constraints is this one:

A E B E C E D E A E B E C E D E ...

On the other hand, if user 1 is entitled to twice as much CPU time as user 2, we might get

A B E C D E A B E C D E ...

Numerous other possibilities exist, of course, and can be exploited, depending on what the notion of fairness is.

2.5.4 Scheduling in Real-Time Systems

A **real-time** system is one in which time plays an essential role. Typically, one or more physical devices external to the computer generate stimuli, and the computer must react appropriately to them within a fixed amount of time. For example, the computer in a compact disc player gets the bits as they come off the drive and must convert them into music within a very tight time interval. If the calculation takes too long, the music will sound peculiar. Other real-time systems are patient monitoring in a hospital intensive-care unit, the autopilot in an aircraft, and robot control in an automated factory. In all these cases, having the right answer but having it too late is often just as bad as not having it at all.

Real-time systems are generally categorized as **hard real time**, meaning there are absolute deadlines that must be met, or else, and **soft real time**, meaning that missing an occasional deadline is undesirable, but nevertheless tolerable. In both cases, real-time behavior is achieved by dividing the program into a number of processes, each of whose behavior is predictable and known in advance. These processes are generally short lived and can run to completion in well under a second. When an external event is detected, it is the job of the scheduler to schedule the processes in such a way that all deadlines are met.

The events that a real-time system may have to respond to can be further categorized as **periodic** (occurring at regular intervals) or **aperiodic** (occurring unpredictably). A system may have to respond to multiple periodic event streams. Depending on how much time each event requires for processing, it may not even be possible to handle them all. For example, if there are m periodic events and event i occurs with period P_i and requires C_i seconds of CPU time to handle each event, then the load can only be handled if

$$\sum_{i=1}^{m} \frac{C_i}{P_i} \leq 1$$

A real-time system that meets this criteria is said to be **schedulable**.

As an example, consider a soft real-time system with three periodic events, with periods of 100, 200, and 500 msec, respectively. If these events require 50, 30, and 100 msec of CPU time per event, respectively, the system is schedulable because $0.5 + 0.15 + 0.2 < 1$. If a fourth event with a period of 1 sec is added, the system will remain schedulable as long as this event does not need more than 150 msec of CPU time per event. Implicit in this calculation is the assumption that the context-switching overhead is so small that it can be ignored.

Real-time scheduling algorithms can be static or dynamic. The former make their scheduling decisions before the system starts running. The latter make their scheduling decisions at run time. Static scheduling only works when there is perfect information available in advance about the work needed to be done and the deadlines that have to be met. Dynamic scheduling algorithms do not have these restrictions. We will defer our study of specific algorithms until we treat real-time multimedia systems in Chap. 7.

2.5.5 Policy versus Mechanism

Up until now, we have tacitly assumed that all the processes in the system belong to different users and are thus competing for the CPU. While this is often true, sometimes it happens that one process has many children running under its control. For example, a database management system process may have many children. Each child might be working on a different request, or each one might have some specific function to perform (query parsing, disk access, etc.). It is entirely possible that the main process has an excellent idea of which of its children are the most important (or time critical) and which the least. Unfortunately, none of the schedulers discussed above accept any input from user processes about scheduling decisions. As a result, the scheduler rarely makes the best choice.

The solution to this problem is to separate the **scheduling mechanism** from the **scheduling policy**. What this means is that the scheduling algorithm is parameterized in some way, but the parameters can be filled in by user processes. Let us consider the database example once again. Suppose that the kernel uses a priority scheduling algorithm but provides a system call by which a process can set (and change) the priorities of its children. In this way the parent can control in detail how its children are scheduled, even though it itself does not do the scheduling. Here the mechanism is in the kernel but policy is set by a user process.

2.5.6 Thread Scheduling

When several processes each have multiple threads, we have two levels of parallelism present: processes and threads. Scheduling in such systems differs substantially depending on whether user-level threads or kernel-level threads (or both) are supported.

Let us consider user-level threads first. Since the kernel is not aware of the existence of threads, it operates as it always does, picking a process, say, A, and giving A control for its quantum. The thread scheduler inside A decides which thread to run, say $A1$. Since there are no clock interrupts to multiprogram threads, this thread may continue running as long as it wants to. If it uses up the process' entire quantum, the kernel will select another process to run.

When the process A finally runs again, thread $A1$ will resume running. It will continue to consume all of A's time until it is finished. However, its antisocial behavior will not affect other processes. They will get whatever the scheduler considers their appropriate share, no matter what is going on inside process A.

Now consider the case that A's threads have relatively little work to do per CPU burst, for example, 5 msec of work within a 50-msec quantum. Consequently, each one runs for a little while, then yields the CPU back to the thread scheduler. This might lead to the sequence $A1$, $A2$, $A3$, $A1$, $A2$, $A3$, $A1$, $A2$, $A3$, $A1$, before the kernel switches to process B. This situation is illustrated in Fig. 2-43(a).

The scheduling algorithm used by the run-time system can be any of the ones described above. In practice, round-robin scheduling and priority scheduling are most common. The only constraint is the absence of a clock to interrupt a thread that has run too long.

Now consider the situation with kernel-level threads. Here the kernel picks a particular thread to run. It does not have to take into account which process the thread belongs to, but it can if it wants to. The thread is given a quantum and is forceably suspended if it exceeds the quantum. With a 50-msec quantum but threads that block after 5 msec, the thread order for some period of 30 msec might be $A1$, $B1$, $A2$, $B2$, $A3$, $B3$, something not possible with these parameters and user-level threads. This situation is partially depicted in Fig. 2-43(b).

A major difference between user-level threads and kernel-level threads is the performance. Doing a thread switch with user-level threads takes a handful of machine instructions. With kernel-level threads it requires a full context switch, changing the memory map, and invalidating the cache, which is several orders of

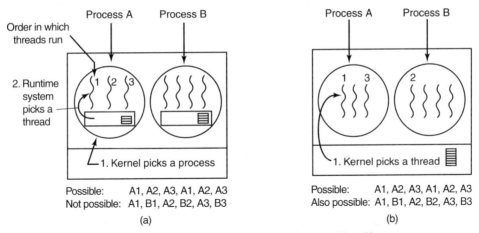

Possible: A1, A2, A3, A1, A2, A3
Not possible: A1, B1, A2, B2, A3, B3

(a)

Possible: A1, A2, A3, A1, A2, A3
Also possible: A1, B1, A2, B2, A3, B3

(b)

Figure 2-43. (a) Possible scheduling of user-level threads with a 50-msec process quantum and threads that run 5 msec per CPU burst. (b) Possible scheduling of kernel-level threads with the same characteristics as (a).

magnitude slower. On the other hand, with kernel-level threads, having a thread block on I/O does not suspend the entire process as it does with user-level threads.

Since the kernel knows that switching from a thread in process *A* to a thread in process *B* is more expensive that running a second thread in process *A* (due to having to change the memory map and having the memory cache spoiled), it can take this information into account when making a decision. For example, given two threads that are otherwise equally important, with one of them belonging to the same process as a thread that just blocked and one belonging to a different process, preference could be given to the former.

Another important factor is that user-level threads can employ an application-specific thread scheduler. Consider, for example, the Web server of Fig. 2-10. Suppose that a worker thread has just blocked and the dispatcher thread and two worker threads are ready. Who should run next? The run-time system, knowing what all the threads do, can easily pick the dispatcher to run next, so it can start another worker running. This strategy maximizes the amount of parallelism in an environment where workers frequently block on disk I/O. With kernel-level threads, the kernel would never know what each thread did (although they could be assigned different priorities). In general, however, application-specific thread schedulers can tune an application better than the kernel can.

2.6 RESEARCH ON PROCESSES AND THREADS

In Chap. 1, we looked at some of the current research in operating system structure. In this and subsequent chapters we will look at more narrowly focused research, starting with processes. As will become clear in time, some subjects are much more settled than others. Most of the research tends to be on the new topics, rather than ones that have been around for decades.

The concept of a process is an example of something that is well settled. Almost every system has some notion of a process as a container for grouping together related resources such as an address space, threads, open files, protection permissions, etc. Different systems do the grouping slightly differently, but these are just engineering differences. The basic idea is not very controversial any more and there is little new research on the subject.

Threads are a newer idea than processes, so there is still some research going on about them. Hauser et al. (1993) looked at how real programs actually use threads and came up with 10 different paradigms for thread usage. Thread scheduling (both uniprocessor and multiprocessor) is still a topic near and dear to the heart of some researchers (Blumofe and Leiserson, 1994; Buchanan and Chien, 1997; Corbalán et al., 2000; Chandra et al., 2000; Duda and Cheriton, 1999; Ford and Susarla, 1996; and Petrou et al., 1999). However, few actual system designers are walking around all day wringing their hands for lack of a decent thread scheduling algorithm, so it appears this type of research is more researcher-push than demand-pull.

Closely related to threads is thread synchronization and mutual exclusion. In the 1970s and 1980s, that subject was mined for all it was worth, so there is not much current work on the subject, and what there is tends to be focuses on performance (e.g., Liedtke, 1993) tools for detecting synchronization errors (Savage et al., 1997), or modifying old concepts in new ways (Tai and Carver, 1996; Trono, 2000). Finally, new POSIX-conformant threads packages are still being produced and reported on (Alfieri, 1994; and Miller, 1999).

2.7 SUMMARY

To hide the effects of interrupts, operating systems provide a conceptual model consisting of sequential processes running in parallel. Processes can be created and terminated dynamically. Each process has its own address space.

For some applications it is useful to have multiple threads of control within a single process. These threads are scheduled independently and each one has its own stack, but all the threads in a process share a common address space. Threads can be implemented in user space or in the kernel.

Processes can communicate with each other using interprocess communication primitives, such as semaphores, monitors, or messages. These primitives are used to ensure that no two processes are ever in their critical regions at the same time, a situation that leads to chaos. A process can be running, runnable, or blocked and can change state when it or another process executes one of the interprocess communication primitives. Interthread communication is similar.

Interprocess communication primitives can be used to solve such problems as the producer-consumer, dining philosophers, reader-writer, and sleeping barber. Even with these primitives, care has to be taken to avoid errors and deadlocks.

Many scheduling algorithms are known. Some of these are primarily used for batch systems, such as shortest job first. Others are common in both batch systems and interactive systems. These include round robin, priority scheduling, multilevel queues, guaranteed scheduling, lottery scheduling, and fair-share scheduling. Some systems make a clean separation between the scheduling mechanism and the scheduling policy, which allows users to have control of the scheduling algorithm.

PROBLEMS

1. In Fig. 2-2, three process states are shown. In theory, with three states, there could be six transitions, two out of each state. However, only four transitions are shown. Are there any circumstances in which either or both of the missing transitions might occur?

2. Suppose that you were to design an advanced computer architecture that did process switching in hardware, instead of having interrupts. What information would the CPU need? Describe how the hardware process switching might work.

3. On all current computers, at least part of the interrupt handlers are written in assembly language. Why?

4. When an interrupt or a system call transfers control to the operating system, a kernel stack area separate from the stack of the interrupted process is generally used. Why?

5. In the text it was stated that the model of Fig. 2-6(a) was not suited to a file server using a cache in memory. Why not? Could each process have its own cache?

6. In Fig. 2-7 the register set is listed as a per-thread rather than a per-process item. Why? After all, the machine has only one set of registers.

7. If a multithreaded process forks, a problem occurs if the child gets copies of all the parent's threads. Suppose that one of the original threads was waiting for keyboard input. Now two threads are waiting for keyboard input, one in each process. Does this problem ever occur in single-threaded processes?

8. In Fig. 2-10, a multithreaded Web server is shown. If the only way to read from a file is the normal blocking read system call, do you think user-level threads or kernel-level threads are being used for the Web server? Why?

9. Why would a thread ever voluntarily give up the CPU by calling *thread_yield*? After all, since there is no periodic clock interrupt, it may never get the CPU back.

10. Can a thread ever be preempted by a clock interrupt? If so, under what circumstances? If not, why not?

11. In this problem you are to compare reading a file using a single-threaded file server and a multithreaded server. It takes 15 msec to get a request for work, dispatch it, and do the rest of the necessary processing, assuming that the data needed are in the block cache. If a disk operation is needed, as is the case one-third of the time, an additional 75 msec is required, during which time the thread sleeps. How many requests/sec can the server handle if it is single threaded? If it is multithreaded?

12. In the text, we described a multithreaded Web server, showing why it is better than a single-threaded server and a finite-state machine server. Are there any circumstances in which a single-threaded server might be better? Give an example.

13. In the discussion on global variables in threads, we used a procedure *create_global* to allocate storage for a pointer to the variable, rather than the variable itself. Is this essential, or could the procedures work with the values themselves just as well?

14. Consider a system in which threads are implemented entirely in user space, with the run-time system getting a clock interrupt once a second. Suppose that a clock interrupt occurs while some thread is executing in the run-time system. What problem might occur? Can you suggest a way to solve it?

15. Suppose that an operating system does not have anything like the select system call to see in advance if it is safe to read from a file, pipe, or device, but it does allow alarm clocks to be set that interrupt blocked system calls. Is it possible to implement a threads package in user space under these conditions? Discuss.

16. Can the priority inversion problem discussed in Sec. 2.3.4 happen with user-level threads? Why or why not?

17. In a system with threads, is there one stack per thread or one stack per process when user-level threads are used? What about when kernel-level threads are used? Explain.

18. What is a race condition?

19. When a computer is being developed, it is usually first simulated by a program that runs one instruction at a time. Even multiprocessors are simulated strictly sequentially like this. Is it possible for a race condition to occur when there are no simultaneous events like this?

20. Does the busy waiting solution using the *turn* variable (Fig. 2-20) work when the two processes are running on a shared-memory multiprocessor, that is, two CPUs, sharing a common memory?

21. Does Peterson's solution to the mutual exclusion problem shown in Fig. 2-21 work when process scheduling is preemptive? How about when it is nonpreemptive?

22. Consider a computer that does not have a TSL instruction but does have an instruction to swap the contents of a register and a memory word in a single indivisible action. Can that be used to write a routine *enter_region* such as the one found in Fig. 2-22?

23. Give a sketch of how an operating system that can disable interrupts could implement semaphores.

24. Show how counting semaphores (i.e., semaphores that can hold an arbitrary value) can be implemented using only binary semaphores and ordinary machine instructions.

25. If a system has only two processes, does it make sense to use a barrier to synchronize them? Why or why not?

26. In Sec. 2.3.4, a situation with a high-priority process, H, and a low-priority process, L, was described, which led to H looping forever. Does the same problem occur if round-robin scheduling is used instead of priority scheduling? Discuss.

27. Can two threads in the same process synchronize using a kernel semaphore if the threads are implemented by the kernel? What if they are implemented in user space? Assume that no threads in any other processes have access to the semaphore. Discuss your answers.

28. Synchronization within monitors uses condition variables and two special operations, wait and signal. A more general form of synchronization would be to have a single primitive, waituntil, that had an arbitrary Boolean predicate as parameter. Thus, one could say, for example,

   waituntil $x < 0$ or $y + z < n$

The signal primitive would no longer be needed. This scheme is clearly more general than that of Hoare or Brinch Hansen, but it is not used. Why not? *Hint*: Think about the implementation.

29. A fast food restaurant has four kinds of employees: (1) order takers, who take customers' orders; (2) cooks, who prepare the food; (3) packaging specialists, who stuff the food into bags; and (4) cashiers, who give the bags to customers and take their money. Each employee can be regarded as a communicating sequential process. What form of interprocess communication do they use? Relate this model to processes in UNIX.

30. Suppose that we have a message-passing system using mailboxes. When sending to a full mailbox or trying to receive from an empty one, a process does not block. Instead, it gets an error code back. The process responds to the error code by just trying again, over and over, until it succeeds. Does this scheme lead to race conditions?

31. In the solution to the dining philosophers problem (Fig. 2-20), why is the state variable set to *HUNGRY* in the procedure *take_forks*?

32. Consider the procedure *put_forks* in Fig. 2-20. Suppose that the variable *state*[i] was set to *THINKING* after the two calls to *test*, rather than *before*. How would this change affect the solution?

33. The readers and writers problem can be formulated in several ways with regard to which category of processes can be started when. Carefully describe three different variations of the problem, each one favoring (or not favoring) some category of processes. For each variation, specify what happens when a reader or a writer becomes ready to access the database, and what happens when a process is finished using the database.

34. The CDC 6600 computers could handle up to 10 I/O processes simultaneously using an interesting form of round-robin scheduling called **processor sharing**. A process switch occurred after each instruction, so instruction 1 came from process 1, instruction 2 came from process 2, etc. The process switching was done by special hardware, and the overhead was zero. If a process needed T sec to complete in the absence of competition, how much time would it need if processor sharing was used with n processes?

35. Round-robin schedulers normally maintain a list of all runnable processes, with each process occurring exactly once in the list. What would happen if a process occurred twice in the list? Can you think of any reason for allowing this?

36. Can a measure of whether a process is likely to be CPU bound or I/O bound be determined by analyzing source code? How can this be determined at run time?

37. In the section "When to Schedule," it was mentioned that sometimes scheduling could be improved if an important process could play a role in selecting the next process to run when it blocks. Give a situation where this could be used and explain how.

38. Measurements of a certain system have shown that the average process runs for a time T before blocking on I/O. A process switch requires a time S, which is effectively wasted (overhead). For round-robin scheduling with quantum Q, give a formula for the CPU efficiency for each of the following:

(a) $Q = \infty$
(b) $Q > T$
(c) $S < Q < T$
(d) $Q = S$
(e) Q nearly 0

39. Five jobs are waiting to be run. Their expected run times are 9, 6, 3, 5, and X. In what order should they be run to minimize average response time? (Your answer will depend on X.)

40. Five batch jobs A through E, arrive at a computer center at almost the same time. They have estimated running times of 10, 6, 2, 4, and 8 minutes. Their (externally determined) priorities are 3, 5, 2, 1, and 4, respectively, with 5 being the highest priority. For each of the following scheduling algorithms, determine the mean process turnaround time. Ignore process switching overhead.

(a) Round robin.
(b) Priority scheduling.
(c) First-come, first-served (run in order 10, 6, 2, 4, 8).
(d) Shortest job first.

For (a), assume that the system is multiprogrammed, and that each job gets its fair share of the CPU. For (b) through (d) assume that only one job at a time runs, until it finishes. All jobs are completely CPU bound.

41. A process running on CTSS needs 30 quanta to complete. How many times must it be swapped in, including the very first time (before it has run at all)?

42. Can you think of a way to save the CTSS priority system from being fooled by random carriage returns?

43. The aging algorithm with $a = 1/2$ is being used to predict run times. The previous four runs, from oldest to most recent, are 40, 20, 40, and 15 msec. What is the prediction of the next time?

44. A soft real-time system has four periodic events with periods of 50, 100, 200, and 250 msec each. Suppose that the four events require 35, 20, 10, and x msec of CPU time, respectively. What is the largest value of x for which the system is schedulable?

45. Explain why two-level scheduling is commonly used.

46. Consider a system in which it is desired to separate policy and mechanism for the scheduling of kernel threads. Propose a means of achieving this goal.

47. Write a shell script that produces a file of sequential numbers by reading the last number in the file, adding 1 to it, and then appending it to the file. Run one instance of the script in the background and one in the foreground, each accessing the same file. How long does it take before a race condition manifests itself? What is the critical region? Modify the script to prevent the race (hint: use

> In file file.lock

to lock the data file).

48. Assume that you have an operating system that provides semaphores. Implement a message system. Write the procedures for sending and receiving messages.

49. Solve the dining philosophers problem using monitors instead of semaphores.

50. Suppose that a university wants to show off how politically correct it is by applying the U.S. Supreme Court's "Separate but equal is inherently unequal" doctrine to gender as well as race, ending its long-standing practice of gender-segregated bathrooms on campus. However, as a concession to tradition, it decrees that when a woman is in a bathroom, other women may enter, but no men, and vice versa. A sign with a sliding marker on the door of each bathroom indicates which of three possible states it is currently in:

- Empty
- Women present
- Men present

In your favorite programming language, write the following procedures: *woman_wants_to_enter*, *man_wants_to_enter*, *woman_leaves*, *man_leaves*. You may use whatever counters and synchronization techniques you like.

51. Rewrite the program of Fig. 2-20 to handle more than two processes.

52. Write a producer-consumer problem that uses threads and shares a common buffer. However, do not use semaphores or any other synchronization primitives to guard the shared data structures. Just let each thread access them when it wants to. Use sleep and wakeup to handle the full and empty conditions. See how long it takes for a fatal race condition to occur. For example, you might have the producer print a number once in a while. Do not print more than one number every minute because the I/O could affect the race conditions.

53. A process can be put into a round-robin queue more than once to give it a higher priority. Running multiple instances of a program each working on a different part of a data pool can have the same effect. First write a program that tests a list of numbers for primality. Then devise a method to allow multiple instances of the program to run

at once in such a way that no two instances of the program will work on the same number. Can you in fact get through the list faster by running multiple copies of the program? Note that your results will depend upon what else your computer is doing; on a personal computer running only instances of this program you would not expect an improvement, but on a system with other processes, you should be able to grab a bigger share of the CPU this way.

3

DEADLOCKS

Computer systems are full of resources that can only be used by one process at a time. Common examples include printers, tape drives, and slots in the system's internal tables. Having two processes simultaneously writing to the printer leads to gibberish. Having two processes using the same file system table slot will invariably lead to a corrupted file system. Consequently, all operating systems have the ability to (temporarily) grant a process exclusive access to certain resources.

For many applications, a process needs exclusive access to not one resource, but several. Suppose, for example, two processes each want to record a scanned document on a CD. Process A requests permission to use the scanner and is granted it. Process B is programmed differently and requests the CD recorder first and is also granted it. Now A asks for the CD recorder, but the request is denied until B releases it. Unfortunately, instead of releasing the CD recorder B asks for the scanner. At this point both processes are blocked and will remain so forever. This situation is called a **deadlock**.

Deadlocks can also occur across machines. For example, many offices have a local area network with many computers connected to it. Often devices such as scanners, CD recorders, printers, and tape drives are connected to the network as shared resources, available to any user on any machine. If these devices can be reserved remotely (i.e., from the user's home machine), the same kind of deadlocks can occur as described above. More complicated situations can cause deadlocks involving three, four, or more devices and users.

Deadlocks can occur in a variety of situations besides requesting dedicated I/O devices. In a database system, for example, a program may have to lock several records it is using, to avoid race conditions. If process A locks record R1 and process B locks record R2, and then each process tries to lock the other one's record, we also have a deadlock. Thus deadlocks can occur on hardware resources or on software resources.

In this chapter, we will look at deadlocks more closely, see how they arise, and study some ways of preventing or avoiding them. Although this material is about deadlocks in the context of operating systems, they also occur in database systems and many other contexts in computer science, so this material is actually applicable to a wide variety of multiprocess systems. A great deal has been written about deadlocks. Two bibliographies on the subject have appeared in *Operating Systems Review* and should be consulted for references (Newton, 1979; and Zobel, 1983). Although these bibliographies are old, most of the work on deadlocks was done well before 1980, so they are still useful.

3.1 RESOURCES

Deadlocks can occur when processes have been granted exclusive access to devices, files, and so forth. To make the discussion of deadlocks as general as possible, we will refer to the objects granted as **resources**. A resource can be a hardware device (e.g., a tape drive) or a piece of information (e.g., a locked record in a database). A computer will normally have many different resources that can be acquired. For some resources, several identical instances may be available, such as three tape drives. When several copies of a resource are available, any one of them can be used to satisfy any request for the resource. In short, a resource is anything that can be used by only a single process at any instant of time.

3.1.1 Preemptable and Nonpreemptable Resources

Resources come in two types: preemptable and nonpreemptable. A **preemptable resource** is one that can be taken away from the process owning it with no ill effects. Memory is an example of a preemptable resource. Consider, for example, a system with 32 MB of user memory, one printer, and two 32-MB processes that each want to print something. Process A requests and gets the printer, then starts to compute the values to print. Before it has finished with the computation, it exceeds its time quantum and is swapped out.

Process B now runs and tries, unsuccessfully, to acquire the printer. Potentially, we now have a deadlock situation, because A has the printer and B has the memory, and neither can proceed without the resource held by the other. Fortunately, it is possible to preempt (take away) the memory from *B* by swapping it out and swapping *A* in. Now *A* can run, do its printing, and then release the printer. No deadlock occurs.

A **nonpreemptable resource**, in contrast, is one that cannot be taken away from its current owner without causing the computation to fail. If a process has begun to burn a CD-ROM, suddenly taking the CD recorder away from it and giving it to another process will result in a garbled CD. CD recorders are not preemptable at an arbitrary moment.

In general, deadlocks involve nonpreemptable resources. Potential deadlocks that involve preemptable resources can usually be resolved by reallocating resources from one process to another. Thus our treatment will focus on non-preemptable resources.

The sequence of events required to use a resource is given below in an abstract form.

1. Request the resource.

2. Use the resource.

3. Release the resource.

If the resource is not available when it is requested, the requesting process is forced to wait. In some operating systems, the process is automatically blocked when a resource request fails, and awakened when it becomes available. In other systems, the request fails with an error code, and it is up to the calling process to wait a little while and try again.

A process whose resource request has just been denied will normally sit in a tight loop requesting the resource, then sleeping, then trying again. Although this process is not blocked, for all intents and purposes, it is as good as blocked, because it cannot do any useful work. In our further treatment, we will assume that when a process is denied a resource request, it is put to sleep.

The exact nature of requesting a resource is highly system dependent. In some systems, a request system call is provided to allow processes to explicitly ask for resources. In others, the only resources that the operating system knows about are special files that only one process can have open at a time. These are opened by the usual open call. If the file is already in use, the caller is blocked until its current owner closes it.

3.1.2 Resource Acquisition

For some kinds of resources, such as records in a database system, it is up to the user processes to manage resource usage themselves. One possible way of allowing user management of resources is to associate a semaphore with each resource. These semaphores are all initialized to 1. Mutexes can be used equally

well. The three steps listed above are then implemented as a down on the semaphore to acquire the resource, using the resource, and finally an up on the resource
to release it. These steps are shown in Fig. 3-1(a).

```
typedef int semaphore;              typedef int semaphore;
semaphore resource_1;               semaphore resource_1;
                                    semaphore resource_2;

void process_A(void) {              void process_A(void) {
    down(&resource_1);                  down(&resource_1);
    use_resource_1( );                  down(&resource_2);
    up(&resource_1);                    use_both_resources( );
}                                       up(&resource_2);
                                        up(&resource_1);
                                    }

            (a)                                     (b)
```

Figure 3-1. Using a semaphore to protect resources. (a) One resource. (b) Two resources.

Sometimes processes need two or more resources. They can be acquired
sequentially, as shown in Fig. 3-1(b). If more than two resources are needed, they
are just acquired one after another.

So far, so good. As long as only one process is involved, everything works
fine. Of course, with only one process, there is no need to formally acquire
resources, since there is no competition for them.

Now let us consider a situation with two processes, A and B, and two
resources. Two scenarios are depicted in Fig. 3-2. In Fig. 3-2(a), both processes
ask for the resources in the same order. In Fig. 3-2(b), they ask for them in a different order. This difference may seem minor, but it is not.

In Fig. 3-2(a), one of the processes will acquire the first resource before the
other one. That process will then successfully acquire the second resource and do
its work. If the other process attempts to acquire resource 1 before it has been
released, the other process will simply block until it becomes available.

In Fig. 3-2(b), the situation is different. It might happen that one of the
processes acquires both resources and effectively blocks out the other process
until it is done. However, it might also happen that process A acquires resource 1
and process B acquires resource 2. Each one will now block when trying the
acquire the other one. Neither process will ever run again. This situation is a
deadlock.

Here we see how what appears to be a minor difference in coding style—
which resource to acquire first—turns out to make the difference between the program working and the program failing in a hard-to-detect way. Because
deadlocks can occur so easily, a lot of research has gone into ways to deal them.
This chapter discusses deadlocks in detail and what can be done about them.

```
typedef int semaphore;
    semaphore resource_1;                semaphore resource_1;
    semaphore resource_2;                semaphore resource_2;

    void process_A(void) {               void process_A(void) {
        down(&resource_1);                   down(&resource_1);
        down(&resource_2);                   down(&resource_2);
        use_both_resources( );               use_both_resources( );
        up(&resource_2);                     up(&resource_2);
        up(&resource_1);                     up(&resource_1);
    }                                    }

    void process_B(void) {               void process_B(void) {
        down(&resource_1);                   down(&resource_2);
        down(&resource_2);                   down(&resource_1);
        use_both_resources( );               use_both_resources( );
        up(&resource_2);                     up(&resource_1);
        up(&resource_1);                     up(&resource_2);
    }                                    }

              (a)                                  (b)
```

Figure 3-2. (a) Deadlock-free code. (b) Code with a potential deadlock.

3.2 INTRODUCTION TO DEADLOCKS

Deadlock can be defined formally as follows:

A set of processes is deadlocked if each process in the set is waiting for an event that only another process in the set can cause.

Because all the processes are waiting, none of them will ever cause any of the events that could wake up any of the other members of the set, and all the processes continue to wait forever. For this model, we assume that processes have only a single thread and that there are no interrupts possible to wake up a blocked process. The no-interrupts condition is needed to prevent an otherwise deadlocked process from being awakened by, say, an alarm, and then causing events that release other processes in the set.

In most cases, the event that each process is waiting for is the release of some resource currently possessed by another member of the set. In other words, each member of the set of deadlocked processes is waiting for a resource that is owned by a deadlocked process. None of the processes can run, none of them can release any resources, and none of them can be awakened. The number of processes and the number and kind of resources possessed and requested are unimportant. This result holds for any kind of resource, including both hardware and software.

3.2.1 Conditions for Deadlock

Coffman et al. (1971) showed that four conditions must hold for there to be a deadlock:

1. Mutual exclusion condition. Each resource is either currently assigned to exactly one process or is available.

2. Hold and wait condition. Processes currently holding resources granted earlier can request new resources.

3. No preemption condition. Resources previously granted cannot be forcibly taken away from a process. They must be explicitly released by the process holding them.

4. Circular wait condition. There must be a circular chain of two or more processes, each of which is waiting for a resource held by the next member of the chain.

All four of these conditions must be present for a deadlock to occur. If one of them is absent, no deadlock is possible.

It is worth noting that each condition relates to a policy that a system can have or not have. Can a given resource be assigned to more than one process at once? Can a process hold a resource and ask for another? Can resources be preempted? Can circular waits exist? Later on we will see how deadlocks can be attacked by trying to negate some of these conditions.

3.2.2 Deadlock Modeling

Holt (1972) showed how these four conditions can be modeled using directed graphs. The graphs have two kinds of nodes: processes, shown as circles, and resources, shown as squares. An arc from a resource node (square) to a process node (circle) means that the resource has previously been requested by, granted to, and is currently held by that process. In Fig. 3-3(a), resource R is currently assigned to process A.

An arc from a process to a resource means that the process is currently blocked waiting for that resource. In Fig. 3-3(b), process B is waiting for resource S. In Fig. 3-3(c) we see a deadlock: process C is waiting for resource T, which is currently held by process D. Process D is not about to release resource T because it is waiting for resource U, held by C. Both processes will wait forever. A cycle in the graph means that there is a deadlock involving the processes and resources in the cycle (assuming that there is one resource of each kind). In this example, the cycle is $C–T–D–U–C$.

Now let us look at an example of how resource graphs can be used. Imagine that we have three processes, A, B, and C, and three resources, R, S, and T. The

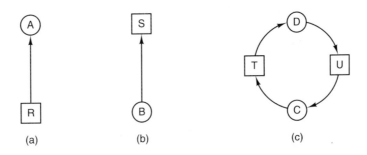

Figure 3-3. Resource allocation graphs. (a) Holding a resource. (b) Requesting a resource. (c) Deadlock.

requests and releases of the three processes are given in Fig. 3-4(a)-(c). The operating system is free to run any unblocked process at any instant, so it could decide to run A until A finished all its work, then run B to completion, and finally run C.

This ordering does not lead to any deadlocks (because there is no competition for resources) but it also has no parallelism at all. In addition to requesting and releasing resources, processes compute and do I/O. When the processes are run sequentially, there is no possibility that while one process is waiting for I/O, another can use the CPU. Thus running the processes strictly sequentially may not be optimal. On the other hand, if none of the processes do any I/O at all, shortest job first is better than round robin, so under some circumstances running all processes sequentially may be the best way.

Let us now suppose that the processes do both I/O and computing, so that round robin is a reasonable scheduling algorithm. The resource requests might occur in the order of Fig. 3-4(d). If these six requests are carried out in that order, the six resulting resource graphs are shown in Fig. 3-4(e)-(j). After request 4 has been made, A blocks waiting for S, as shown in Fig. 3-4(h). In the next two steps B and C also block, ultimately leading to a cycle and the deadlock of Fig. 3-4(j).

However, as we have already mentioned, the operating system is not required to run the processes in any special order. In particular, if granting a particular request might lead to deadlock, the operating system can simply suspend the process without granting the request (i.e., just not schedule the process) until it is safe. In Fig. 3-4, if the operating system knew about the impending deadlock, it could suspend B instead of granting it S. By running only A and C, we would get the requests and releases of Fig. 3-4(k) instead of Fig. 3-4(d). This sequence leads to the resource graphs of Fig. 3-4(l)-(q), which do not lead to deadlock.

After step (q), process B can be granted S because A is finished and C has everything it needs. Even if B should eventually block when requesting T, no deadlock can occur. B will just wait until C is finished.

Later in this chapter we will study a detailed algorithm for making allocation decisions that do not lead to deadlock. For the moment, the point to understand is

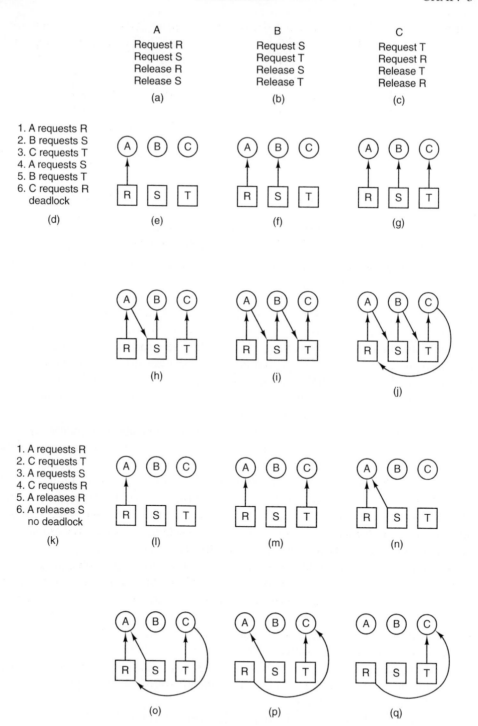

Figure 3-4. An example of how deadlock occurs and how it can be avoided.

that resource graphs are a tool that let us see if a given request/release sequence leads to deadlock. We just carry out the requests and releases step by step, and after every step check the graph to see if it contains any cycles. If so, we have a deadlock; if not, there is no deadlock. Although our treatment of resource graphs has been for the case of a single resource of each type, resource graphs can also be generalized to handle multiple resources of the same type (Holt, 1972).

In general, four strategies are used for dealing with deadlocks.

1. Just ignore the problem altogether. Maybe if you ignore it, it will ignore you.

2. Detection and recovery. Let deadlocks occur, detect them, and take action.

3. Dynamic avoidance by careful resource allocation.

4. Prevention, by structurally negating one of the four conditions necessary to cause a deadlock.

We will examine each of these methods in turn in the next four sections.

3.3 THE OSTRICH ALGORITHM

The simplest approach is the ostrich algorithm: stick your head in the sand and pretend there is no problem at all†. Different people react to this strategy in different ways. Mathematicians find it totally unacceptable and say that deadlocks must be prevented at all costs. Engineers ask how often the problem is expected, how often the system crashes for other reasons, and how serious a deadlock is. If deadlocks occur on the average once every five years, but system crashes due to hardware failures, compiler errors, and operating system bugs occur once a week, most engineers would not be willing to pay a large penalty in performance or convenience to eliminate deadlocks.

To make this contrast more specific, most operating systems potentially suffer from deadlocks that are not even detected, let alone automatically broken. The total number of processes in a system is determined by the number of entries in the process table. Thus process table slots are finite resources. If a fork fails because the table is full, a reasonable approach for the program doing the fork is to wait a random time and try again.

Now suppose that a UNIX system has 100 process slots. Ten programs are running, each of which needs to create 12 (sub)processes. After each process has

---

†Actually, this bit of folklore is nonsense. Ostriches can run at 60 km/hour and their kick is powerful enough to kill any lion with visions of a big chicken dinner.

created 9 processes, the 10 original processes and the 90 new processes have exhausted the table. Each of the 10 original processes now sits in an endless loop forking and failing—a deadlock. The probability of this happening is minuscule, but it *could* happen. Should we abandon processes and the fork call to eliminate the problem?

The maximum number of open files is similarly restricted by the size of the i-node table, so a similar problem occurs when it fills up. Swap space on the disk is another limited resource. In fact, almost every table in the operating system represents a finite resource. Should we abolish all of these because it might happen that a collection of n processes might each claim $1/n$ of the total, and then each try to claim another one?

Most operating systems, including UNIX and Windows, just ignore the problem on the assumption that most users would prefer an occasional deadlock to a rule restricting all users to one process, one open file, and one of everything. If deadlocks could be eliminated for free, there would not be much discussion. The problem is that the price is high, mostly in terms of putting inconvenient restrictions on processes, as we will see shortly. Thus we are faced with an unpleasant trade-off between convenience and correctness, and a great deal of discussion about which is more important, and to whom. Under these conditions, general solutions are hard to find.

3.4 DEADLOCK DETECTION AND RECOVERY

A second technique is detection and recovery. When this technique is used, the system does not attempt to prevent deadlocks from occurring. Instead, it lets them occur, tries to detect when this happens, and then takes some action to recover after the fact. In this section we will look at some of the ways deadlocks can be detected and some of the ways recovery from them can be handled.

3.4.1 Deadlock Detection with One Resource of Each Type

Let us begin with the simplest case: only one resource of each type exists. Such a system might have one scanner, one CD recorder, one plotter, and one tape drive, but no more than one of each class of resource. In other words, we are excluding systems with two printers for the moment. We will treat them later, using a different method.

For such a system, we can construct a resource graph of the sort illustrated in Fig. 3-3. If this graph contains one or more cycles, a deadlock exists. Any process that is part of a cycle is deadlocked. If no cycles exist, the system is not deadlocked.

As an example of a more complex system than the ones we have looked at so far, consider a system with seven processes, *A* though *G*, and six resources, *R* through *W*. The state of which resources are currently owned and which ones are currently being requested is as follows:

1. Process *A* holds *R* and wants *S*.

2. Process *B* holds nothing but wants *T*.

3. Process *C* holds nothing but wants *S*.

4. Process *D* holds *U* and wants *S* and *T*.

5. Process *E* holds *T* and wants *V*.

6. Process *F* holds *W* and wants *S*.

7. Process *G* holds *V* and wants *U*.

The question is: "Is this system deadlocked, and if so, which processes are involved?"

To answer this question, we can construct the resource graph of Fig. 3-5(a). This graph contains one cycle, which can be seen by visual inspection. The cycle is shown in Fig. 3-5(b). From this cycle, we can see that processes *D*, *E*, and *G* are all deadlocked. Processes *A*, *C*, and *F* are not deadlocked because *S* can be allocated to any one of them, which then finishes and returns it. Then the other two can take it in turn and also complete.

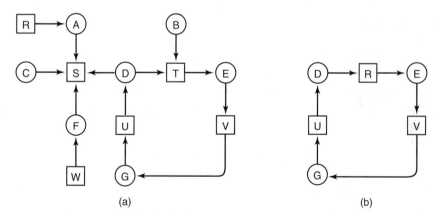

(a)   (b)

Figure 3-5. (a) A resource graph. (b) A cycle extracted from (a).

Although it is relatively simple to pick out the deadlocked processes by eye from a simple graph, for use in actual systems we need a formal algorithm for detecting deadlocks. Many algorithms for detecting cycles in directed graphs are known. Below we will give a simple one that inspects a graph and terminates either when it has found a cycle or when it has shown that none exist. It uses one data structure, *L*, a list of nodes. During the algorithm, arcs will be marked to indicate that they have already been inspected, to prevent repeated inspections.

The algorithm operates by carrying out the following steps as specified:

1. For each node, *N* in the graph, perform the following 5 steps with *N* as the starting node.

2. Initialize *L* to the empty list, and designate all the arcs as unmarked.

3. Add the current node to the end of *L* and check to see if the node now appears in *L* two times. If it does, the graph contains a cycle (listed in *L*) and the algorithm terminates.

4. From the given node, see if there are any unmarked outgoing arcs. If so, go to step 5; if not, go to step 6.

5. Pick an unmarked outgoing arc at random and mark it. Then follow it to the new current node and go to step 3.

6. We have now reached a dead end. Remove it and go back to the previous node, that is, the one that was current just before this one, make that one the current node, and go to step 3. If this node is the initial node, the graph does not contain any cycles and the algorithm terminates.

What this algorithm does is take each node, in turn, as the root of what it hopes will be a tree, and does a depth-first search on it. If it ever comes back to a node it has already encountered, then it has found a cycle. If it exhausts all the arcs from any given node, it backtracks to the previous node. If it backtracks to the root and cannot go further, the subgraph reachable from the current node does not contain any cycles. If this property holds for all nodes, the entire graph is cycle free, so the system is not deadlocked.

To see how the algorithm works in practice, let us use it on the graph of Fig. 3-5(a). The order of processing the nodes is arbitrary, so let us just inspect them from left to right, top to bottom, first running the algorithm starting at *R*, then successively, *A, B, C, S, D, T, E, F*, and so forth. If we hit a cycle, the algorithm stops.

We start at *R* and initialize *L* to the empty list. Then we add *R* to the list and move to the only possibility, *A*, and add it to *L*, giving *L* = [*R, A*]. From *A* we go to *S*, giving *L* = [*R, A, S*]. *S* has no outgoing arcs, so it is a dead end, forcing us to backtrack to *A*. Since *A* has no unmarked outgoing arcs, we backtrack to *R*, completing our inspection of *R*.

Now we restart the algorithm starting at *A*, resetting *L* to the empty list. This search, too, quickly stops, so we start again at *B*. From *B* we continue to follow outgoing arcs until we get to *D*, at which time *L* = [*B, T, E, V, G, U, D*]. Now we must make a (random) choice. If we pick *S* we come to a dead end and backtrack to *D*. The second time we pick *T* and update *L* to be [*B, T, E, V, G, U, D, T*], at which point we discover the cycle and stop the algorithm.

This algorithm is far from optimal. For a better one, see (Even, 1979). Nevertheless, it demonstrates that an algorithm for deadlock detection exists.

3.4.2 Deadlock Detection with Multiple Resource of Each Type

When multiple copies of some of the resources exist, a different approach is needed to detect deadlocks. We will now present a matrix-based algorithm for detecting deadlock among n processes, P_1 through P_n. Let the number of resource classes be m, with E_1 resources of class 1, E_2 resources of class 2, and generally, E_i resources of class i $(1 \leq i \leq m)$. E is the **existing resource vector**. It gives the total number of instances of each resource in existence. For example, if class 1 is tape drives, then $E_1 = 2$ means the system has two tape drives.

At any instant, some of the resources are assigned and are not available. Let A be the **available resource vector**, with A_i giving the number of instances of resource i that are currently available (i.e., unassigned). If both of our two tape drives are assigned, A_1 will be 0.

Now we need two arrays, C, the **current allocation matrix**, and R, the **request matrix**. The i-th row of C tells how many instances of each resource class P_i currently holds. Thus C_{ij} is the number of instances of resource j that are held by process i. Similarly, R_{ij} is the number of instances of resource j that P_i wants. These four data structures are shown in Fig. 3-6.

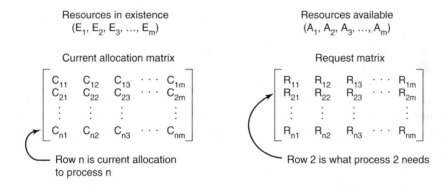

Figure 3-6. The four data structures needed by the deadlock detection algorithm.

An important invariant holds for these four data structures. In particular, every resource is either allocated or is available. This observation means that

$$\sum_{i=1}^{n} C_{ij} + A_j = E_j$$

In other words, if we add up all the instances of the resource j that have been allocated and to this add all the instances that are available, the result is the number of instances of that resource class that exist.

The deadlock detection algorithm is based on comparing vectors. Let us define the relation $A \leq B$ on two vectors A and B to mean that each element of A is less than or equal to the corresponding element of B. Mathematically, $A \leq B$ holds if and only if $A_i \leq B_i$ for $1 \leq i \leq m$.

Each process is initially said to be unmarked. As the algorithm progresses, processes will be marked, indicating that they are able to complete and are thus not deadlocked. When the algorithm terminates, any unmarked processes are known to be deadlocked.

The deadlock detection algorithm can now be given, as follows.

1. Look for an unmarked process, P_i, for which the i-th row of R is less than or equal to A.

2. If such a process is found, add the i-th row of C to A, mark the process, and go back to step 1.

3. If no such process exists, the algorithm terminates.

When the algorithm finishes, all the unmarked processes, if any, are deadlocked.

What the algorithm is doing in step 1 is looking for a process that can be run to completion. Such a process is characterized as having resource demands that can be met by the currently available resources. The selected process is then run until it finishes, at which time it returns the resources it is holding to the pool of available resources. It is then marked as completed. If all the processes are ultimately able to run, none of them are deadlocked. If some of them can never run, they are deadlocked. Although the algorithm is nondeterministic (because it may run the processes in any feasible order), the result is always the same.

As an example of how the deadlock detection algorithm works, consider Fig. 3-7. Here we have three processes and four resource classes, which we have arbitrarily labeled tape drives, plotters, scanner, and CD-ROM drive. Process 1 has one scanner. Process 2 has two tape drives and a CD-ROM drive. Process 3 has a plotter and two scanners. Each process needs additional resources, as shown by the R matrix .

To run the deadlock detection algorithm, we look for a process whose resource request can be satisfied. The first one cannot be satisfied because there is no CD-ROM drive available. The second cannot be satisfied either, because there is no scanner free. Fortunately, the third one can be satisfied, so process 3 runs and eventually returns all its resources, giving

$$A = (2\ 2\ 2\ 0)$$

At this point process 2 can run and return its resources, giving

$$A = (4\ 2\ 2\ 1)$$

Now the remaining process can run. There is no deadlock in the system.

$$E = (4 \quad 2 \quad 3 \quad 1) \qquad\qquad A = (2 \quad 1 \quad 0 \quad 0)$$

(Tape drives Plotters Scanners CD Roms)   (Tape drives Plotters Scanners CD Roms)

Current allocation matrix   Request matrix

$$C = \begin{bmatrix} 0 & 0 & 1 & 0 \\ 2 & 0 & 0 & 1 \\ 0 & 1 & 2 & 0 \end{bmatrix} \qquad R = \begin{bmatrix} 2 & 0 & 0 & 1 \\ 1 & 0 & 1 & 0 \\ 2 & 1 & 0 & 0 \end{bmatrix}$$

Figure 3-7. An example for the deadlock detection algorithm.

Now consider a minor variation of the situation of Fig. 3-7. Suppose that process 2 needs a CD-ROM drive as well as the two tape drives and the plotter. None of the requests can be satisfied, so the entire system is deadlocked.

Now that we know how to detect deadlocks, the question of when to look for them comes up. One possibility is to check every time a resource request is made. This is certain to detect them as early as possible, but it is potentially expensive in terms of CPU time. An alternative strategy is to check every k minutes, or perhaps only when the CPU utilization has dropped below some threshold. The reason for considering the CPU utilization is that if enough processes are deadlocked, there will be few runnable processes, and the CPU will often be idle.

3.4.3 Recovery from Deadlock

Suppose that our deadlock detection algorithm has succeeded and detected a deadlock. What next? Some way is needed to recover and get the system going again. In this section we will discuss various ways of recovering from deadlock. None of them are especially attractive, however.

Recovery through Preemption

In some cases it may be possible to temporarily take a resource away from its current owner and give it to another process. In many cases, manual intervention may be required, especially in batch processing operating systems running on mainframes.

For example, to take a laser printer away from its owner, the operator can collect all the sheets already printed and put them in a pile. Then the process can be suspended (marked as not runnable). At this point the printer can be assigned to another process. When that process finishes, the pile of printed sheets can be put back in the printer's output tray and the original process restarted.

The ability to take a resource away from a process, have another process use it, and then give it back without the process noticing it is highly dependent on the nature of the resource. Recovering this way is frequently difficult or impossible. Choosing the process to suspend depends largely on which ones have resources that can easily be taken back.

Recovery through Rollback

If the system designers and machine operators know that deadlocks are likely, they can arrange to have processes **checkpointed** periodically. Checkpointing a process means that its state is written to a file so that it can be restarted later. The checkpoint contains not only the memory image, but also the resource state, that is, which resources are currently assigned to the process. To be most effective, new checkpoints should not overwrite old ones but should be written to new files, so as the process executes, a whole sequence of checkpoint files are accumulated.

When a deadlock is detected, it is easy to see which resources are needed. To do the recovery, a process that owns a needed resource is rolled back to a point in time before it acquired some other resource by starting one of its earlier checkpoints. All the work done since the checkpoint is lost (e.g., output printed since the checkpoint must be discarded, since it will be printed again). In effect, the process is reset to an earlier moment when it did not have the resource, which is now assigned to one of the deadlocked processes. If the restarted process tries to acquire the resource again, it will have to wait until it becomes available.

Recovery through Killing Processes

The crudest, but simplest way to break a deadlock is to kill one or more processes. One possibility is to kill a process in the cycle. With a little luck, the other processes will be able to continue. If this does not help, it can be repeated until the cycle is broken.

Alternatively, a process not in the cycle can be chosen as the victim in order to release its resources. In this approach, the process to be killed is carefully chosen because it is holding resources that some process in the cycle needs. For example, one process might hold a printer and want a plotter, with another process holding a plotter and wanting a printer. These two are deadlocked. A third process may hold another identical printer and another identical plotter and be happily running. Killing the third process will release these resources and break the deadlock involving the first two.

Where possible, it is best to kill a process that can be rerun from the beginning with no ill effects. For example, a compilation can always be rerun because all it does is read a source file and produce an object file. If it is killed part way through, the first run has no influence on the second run.

On the other hand, a process that updates a database cannot always be run a second time safely. If the process adds 1 to some record in the database, running it once, killing it, and then running it again will add 2 to the record, which is incorrect.

3.5 DEADLOCK AVOIDANCE

In the discussion of deadlock detection, we tacitly assumed that when a process asks for resources, it asks for them all at once (the R matrix of Fig. 3-6). In most systems, however, resources are requested one at a time. The system must be able to decide whether granting a resource is safe or not and only make the allocation when it is safe. Thus the question arises: Is there an algorithm that can always avoid deadlock by making the right choice all the time? The answer is a qualified yes—we can avoid deadlocks, but only if certain information is available in advance. In this section we examine ways to avoid deadlock by careful resource allocation.

3.5.1 Resource Trajectories

The main algorithms for doing deadlock avoidance are based on the concept of safe states. Before describing the algorithms, we will make a slight digression to look at the concept of safety in a graphic and easy-to-understand way. Although the graphical approach does not translate directly into a usable algorithm, it gives a good intuitive feel for the nature of the problem.

In Fig. 3-8 we see a model for dealing with two processes and two resources, for example, a printer and a plotter. The horizontal axis represents the number of instructions executed by process A. The vertical axis represents the number of instructions executed by process B. At I_1 A requests a printer; at I_2 it needs a plotter. The printer and plotter are released at I_3 and I_4, respectively. Process B needs the plotter from I_5 to I_7 and the printer from I_6 to I_8.

Every point in the diagram represents a joint state of the two processes. Initially, the state is at p, with neither process having executed any instructions. If the scheduler chooses to run A first, we get to the point q, in which A has executed some number of instructions, but B has executed none. At point q the trajectory becomes vertical, indicating that the scheduler has chosen to run B. With a single processor, all paths must be horizontal or vertical, never diagonal. Furthermore, motion is always to the north or east, never to the south or west (processes cannot run backward).

When A crosses the I_1 line on the path from r to s, it requests and is granted the printer. When B reaches point t, it requests the plotter.

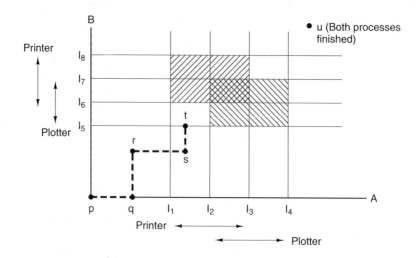

Figure 3-8. Two process resource trajectories.

The regions that are shaded are especially interesting. The region with lines slanting from southwest to northeast represents both processes having the printer. The mutual exclusion rule makes it impossible to enter this region. Similarly, the region shaded the other way represents both processes having the plotter, and is equally impossible.

If the system ever enters the box bounded by I_1 and I_2 on the sides and I_5 and I_6 top and bottom, it will eventually deadlock when it gets to the intersection of I_2 and I_6. At this point, A is requesting the plotter and B is requesting the printer, and both are already assigned. The entire box is unsafe and must not be entered. At point t the only safe thing to do is run process A until it gets to I_4. Beyond that, any trajectory to u will do.

The important thing to see here is at point t B is requesting a resource. The system must decide whether to grant it or not. If the grant is made, the system will enter an unsafe region and eventually deadlock. To avoid the deadlock, B should be suspended until A has requested and released the plotter.

3.5.2 Safe and Unsafe States

The deadlock avoidance algorithms that we will study use the information of Fig. 3-6. At any instant of time, there is a current state consisting of E, A, C, and R. A state is said to be **safe** if it is not deadlocked and there is some scheduling order in which every process can run to completion even if all of them suddenly request their maximum number of resources immediately. It is easiest to illustrate this concept by an example using one resource. In Fig. 3-9(a) we have a state in which A has 3 instances of the resource but may need as many as 9 eventually. B currently has 2 and may need 4 altogether, later. Similarly, C also has 2 but may need an additional 5. A total of 10 instances of the resource exist, so with 7 resources already allocated, there are 3 still free.

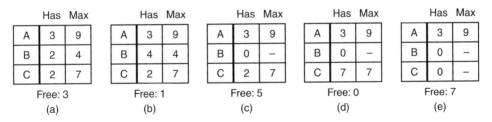

Figure 3-9. Demonstration that the state in (a) is safe.

The state of Fig. 3-9(a) is safe because there exists a sequence of allocations that allows all processes to complete. Namely, the scheduler could simply run B exclusively, until it asked for and got two more instances of the resource, leading to the state of Fig. 3-9(b). When B completes, we get the state of Fig. 3-9(c). Then the scheduler can run C, leading eventually to Fig. 3-9(d). When C completes, we get Fig. 3-9(e). Now A can get the six instances of the resource it needs and also complete. Thus the state of Fig. 3-9(a) is safe because the system, by careful scheduling, can avoid deadlock.

Now suppose we have the initial state shown in Fig. 3-10(a), but this time A requests and gets another resource, giving Fig. 3-10(b). Can we find a sequence that is guaranteed to work? Let us try. The scheduler could run B until it asked for all its resources, as shown in Fig. 3-10(c).

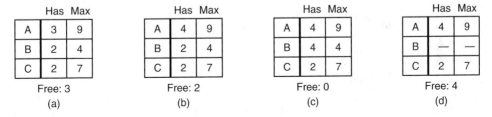

Figure 3-10. Demonstration that the state in (b) is not safe.

Eventually, B completes and we get the situation of Fig. 3-10(d). At this point we are stuck. We only have four instances of the resource free, and each of the active processes needs five. There is no sequence that guarantees completion. Thus the allocation decision that moved the system from Fig. 3-10(a) to Fig. 3-10(b) went from a safe state to an unsafe state. Running A or C next starting at Fig. 3-10(b) does not work either. In retrospect, A's request should not have been granted.

It is worth noting that an unsafe state is not a deadlocked state. Starting at Fig. 3-10(b), the system can run for a while. In fact, one process can even complete. Furthermore, it is possible that A might release a resource before asking for any more, allowing C to complete and avoiding deadlock altogether. Thus the difference between a safe state and an unsafe state is that from a safe state the system can *guarantee* that all processes will finish; from an unsafe state, no such guarantee can be given.

3.5.3 The Banker's Algorithm for a Single Resource

A scheduling algorithm that can avoid deadlocks is due to Dijkstra (1965) and is known as the **banker's algorithm** and is an extension of the deadlock detection algorithm given in Sec. 3.4.1. It is modeled on the way a small-town banker might deal with a group of customers to whom he has granted lines of credit. What the algorithm does is check to see if granting the request leads to an unsafe state. If it does, the request is denied. If granting the request leads to a safe state, it is carried out. In Fig. 3-11(a) we see four customers, A, B, C, and D, each of whom has been granted a certain number of credit units (e.g., 1 unit is 1K dollars). The banker knows that not all customers will need their maximum credit immediately, so he has reserved only 10 units rather than 22 to service them. (In this analogy, customers are processes, units are, say, tape drives, and the banker is the operating system.)

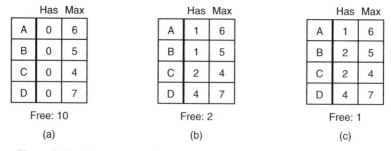

Figure 3-11. Three resource allocation states: (a) Safe. (b) Safe. (c) Unsafe.

The customers go about their respective businesses, making loan requests from time to time (i.e., asking for resources). At a certain moment, the situation is as shown in Fig. 3-11(b). This state is safe because with two units left, the banker can delay any requests except C's, thus letting C finish and release all four of his resources. With four units in hand, the banker can let either D or B have the necessary units, and so on.

Consider what would happen if a request from B for one more unit were granted in Fig. 3-11(b). We would have situation Fig. 3-11(c), which is unsafe. If all the customers suddenly asked for their maximum loans, the banker could not satisfy any of them, and we would have a deadlock. An unsafe state does not *have* to lead to deadlock, since a customer might not need the entire credit line available, but the banker cannot count on this behavior.

The banker's algorithm considers each request as it occurs, and see if granting it leads to a safe state. If it does, the request is granted; otherwise, it is postponed until later. To see if a state is safe, the banker checks to see if he has enough resources to satisfy some customer. If so, those loans are assumed to be repaid, and the customer now closest to the limit is checked, and so on. If all loans can eventually be repaid, the state is safe and the initial request can be granted.

3.5.4 The Banker's Algorithm for Multiple Resources

The banker's algorithm can be generalized to handle multiple resources. Figure 3-12 shows how it works.

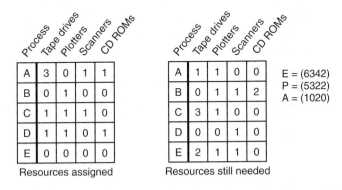

Figure 3-12. The banker's algorithm with multiple resources.

In Fig. 3-12 we see two matrices. The one on the left shows how many of each resource are currently assigned to each of the five processes. The matrix on the right shows how many resources each process still needs in order to complete. These matrices are just C and R from Fig. 3-6. As in the single resource case, processes must state their total resource needs before executing, so that the system can compute the right-hand matrix at each instant.

The three vectors at the right of the figure show the existing resources, E, the possessed resources, P, and the available resources, A, respectively. From E we see that the system has six tape drives, three plotters, four printers, and two CD-ROM drives. Of these, five tape drives, three plotters, two printers, and two CD-ROM drives are currently assigned. This fact can be seen by adding up the four resource columns in the left-hand matrix. The available resource vector is simply the difference between what the system has and what is currently in use.

The algorithm for checking to see if a state is safe can now be stated.

1. Look for a row, R, whose unmet resource needs are all smaller than or equal to A. If no such row exists, the system will eventually deadlock since no process can run to completion.

2. Assume the process of the row chosen requests all the resources it needs (which is guaranteed to be possible) and finishes. Mark that process as terminated and add all its resources to the A vector.

3. Repeat steps 1 and 2 until either all processes are marked terminated, in which case the initial state was safe, or until a deadlock occurs, in which case it was not.

If several processes are eligible to be chosen in step 1, it does not matter which one is selected: the pool of available resources either gets larger, or at worst, stays the same.

Now let us get back to the example of Fig. 3-12. The current state is safe. Suppose that process B now requests a printer. This request can be granted because the resulting state is still safe (process D can finish, and then processes A or E, followed by the rest).

Now imagine that after giving B one of the two remaining printers, E wants the last printer. Granting that request would reduce the vector of available resources to (1 0 0 0), which leads to deadlock. Clearly E's request must be deferred for a while.

The banker's algorithm was first published by Dijkstra in 1965. Since that time, nearly every book on operating systems has described it in detail. Innumerable papers have been written about various aspects of it. Unfortunately, few authors have had the audacity to point out that although in theory the algorithm is wonderful, in practice it is essentially useless because processes rarely know in advance what their maximum resource needs will be. In addition, the number of processes is not fixed, but dynamically varying as new users log in and out. Furthermore, resources that were thought to be available can suddenly vanish (tape drives can break). Thus in practice, few, if any, existing systems use the banker's algorithm for avoiding deadlocks.

3.6 DEADLOCK PREVENTION

Having seen that deadlock avoidance is essentially impossible, because it requires information about future requests, which is not known, how do real systems avoid deadlock? The answer is to go back to the four conditions stated by Coffman et al. (1971) to see if they can provide a clue. If we can ensure that at least one of these conditions is never satisfied, then deadlocks will be structurally impossible (Havender, 1968).

3.6.1 Attacking the Mutual Exclusion Condition

First let us attack the mutual exclusion condition. If no resource were ever assigned exclusively to a single process, we would never have deadlocks. However, it is equally clear that allowing two processes to write on the printer at the same time will lead to chaos. By spooling printer output, several processes can generate output at the same time. In this model, the only process that actually requests the physical printer is the printer daemon. Since the daemon never requests any other resources, we can eliminate deadlock for the printer.

Unfortunately, not all devices can be spooled (the process table does not lend itself well to being spooled). Furthermore, competition for disk space for spooling can itself lead to deadlock. What would happen if two processes each filled up half of the available spooling space with output and neither was finished producing output? If the daemon was programmed to begin printing even before all the output was spooled, the printer might lie idle if an output process decided to wait several hours after the first burst of output. For this reason, daemons are normally programmed to print only after the complete output file is available. In this case we have two processes that have each finished part, but not all, of their output, and cannot continue. Neither process will ever finish, so we have a deadlock on the disk.

Nevertheless, there is a germ of an idea here that is frequently applicable. Avoid assigning a resource when that is not absolutely necessary, and try to make sure that as few processes as possible may actually claim the resource.

3.6.2 Attacking the Hold and Wait Condition

The second of the conditions stated by Coffman et al. looks slightly more promising. If we can prevent processes that hold resources from waiting for more resources, we can eliminate deadlocks. One way to achieve this goal is to require all processes to request all their resources before starting execution. If everything is available, the process will be allocated whatever it needs and can run to completion. If one or more resources are busy, nothing will be allocated and the process would just wait.

An immediate problem with this approach is that many processes do not know how many resources they will need until they have started running. In fact, if they knew, the banker's algorithm could be used. Another problem is that resources will not be used optimally with this approach. Take, as an example, a process that reads data from an input tape, analyzes it for an hour, and then writes an output tape as well as plotting the results. If all resources must be requested in advance, the process will tie up the output tape drive and the plotter for an hour.

Nevertheless, some mainframe batch systems require the user to list all the resources on the first line of each job. The system then acquires all resources immediately and keeps them until the job finishes. While this method puts a burden on the programmer and wastes resources, it does prevent deadlocks.

A slightly different way to break the hold-and-wait condition is to require a process requesting a resource to first temporarily release all the resources it currently holds. Then it tries to get everything it needs all at once.

3.6.3 Attacking the No Preemption Condition

Attacking the third condition (no preemption) is even less promising than attacking the second one. If a process has been assigned the printer and is in the middle of printing its output, forcibly taking away the printer because a needed plotter is not available is tricky at best and impossible at worst.

3.6.4 Attacking the Circular Wait Condition

Only one condition is left. The circular wait can be eliminated in several ways. One way is simply to have a rule saying that a process is entitled only to a single resource at any moment. If it needs a second one, it must release the first one. For a process that needs to copy a huge file from a tape to a printer, this restriction is unacceptable.

Another way to avoid the circular wait is to provide a global numbering of all the resources, as shown in Fig. 3-13(a). Now the rule is this: processes can request resources whenever they want to, but all requests must be made in numerical order. A process may request first a printer and then a tape drive, but it may not request first a plotter and then a printer.

1. Imagesetter
2. Scanner
3. Plotter
4. Tape drive
5. CD Rom drive

(a)   (b)

Figure 3-13. (a) Numerically ordered resources. (b) A resource graph.

With this rule, the resource allocation graph can never have cycles. Let us see why this is true for the case of two processes, in Fig. 3-13(b). We can get a deadlock only if A requests resource j and B requests resource i. Assuming i and j are distinct resources, they will have different numbers. If $i > j$, then A is not allowed to request j because that is lower than what it already has. If $i < j$, then B is not allowed to request i because that is lower than what it already has. Either way, deadlock is impossible.

With multiple processes, the same logic holds. At every instant, one of the assigned resources will be highest. The process holding that resource will never ask for a resource already assigned. It will either finish, or at worst, request even higher numbered resources, all of which are available. Eventually, it will finish and free its resources. At this point, some other process will hold the highest resource and can also finish. In short, there exists a scenario in which all processes finish, so no deadlock is present.

A minor variation of this algorithm is to drop the requirement that resources be acquired in strictly increasing sequence and merely insist that no process request a resource lower than what it is already holding. If a process initially requests 9 and 10, and then releases both of them, it is effectively starting all over, so there is no reason to prohibit it from now requesting resource 1.

Although numerically ordering the resources eliminates the problem of deadlocks, it may be impossible to find an ordering that satisfies everyone. When the resources include process table slots, disk spooler space, locked database records, and other abstract resources, the number of potential resources and different uses may be so large that no ordering could possibly work.

The various approaches to deadlock prevention are summarized in Fig. 3-14.

Condition	Approach
Mutual exclusion	Spool everything
Hold and wait	Request all resources initially
No preemption	Take resources away
Circular wait	Order resources numerically

Figure 3-14. Summary of approaches to deadlock prevention.

3.7 OTHER ISSUES

In this section we will discuss a few miscellaneous issues related to deadlocks. These include two-phase locking, nonresource deadlocks, and starvation.

3.7.1 Two-Phase Locking

Although both avoidance and prevention are not terribly promising in the general case, for specific applications, many excellent special-purpose algorithms are known. As an example, in many database systems, an operation that occurs frequently is requesting locks on several records and then updating all the locked records. When multiple processes are running at the same time, there is a real danger of deadlock.

The approach often used is called **two-phase locking**. In the first phase, the process tries to lock all the records it needs, one at a time. If it succeeds, it begins the second phase, performing its updates and releasing the locks. No real work is done in the first phase.

If during the first phase, some record is needed that is already locked, the process just releases all its locks and starts the first phase all over. In a certain sense, this approach is similar to requesting all the resources needed in advance, or at least before anything irreversible is done. In some versions of two-phase locking, there is no release and restart if a lock is encountered during the first phase. In these versions, deadlock can occur.

However, this strategy is not applicable in general. In real-time systems and process control systems, for example, it is not acceptable to just terminate a process partway through because a resource is not available and start all over again. Neither is it acceptable to start over if the process has read or written messages to the network, updated files, or anything else that cannot be safely repeated. The algorithm works only in those situations where the programmer has very carefully arranged things so that the program can be stopped at any point during the first phase and restarted. Many applications cannot be structured this way.

3.7.2 Nonresource Deadlocks

All of our work so far has concentrated on resource deadlocks. One process wants something that another process has and must wait until the first one gives it up. Deadlocks can also occur in other situations, however, including those not involving resources at all.

For example, it can happen that two processes deadlock each waiting for the other one to do something. This often happens with semaphores. In Chap. 2 we saw examples in which a process had to do a down on two semaphores, typically *mutex* and another one. If these are done in the wrong order, deadlock can result.

3.7.3 Starvation

A problem closely related to deadlock is **starvation**. In a dynamic system, requests for resources happen all the time. Some policy is needed to make a decision about who gets which resource when. This policy, although seemingly reasonable, may lead to some processes never getting service even though they are not deadlocked.

As an example, consider allocation of the printer. Imagine that the system uses some kind of algorithm to ensure that allocating the printer does not lead to deadlock. Now suppose that several processes all want it at once. Which one should get it?

One possible allocation algorithm is to give it to the process with the smallest file to print (assuming this information is available). This approach maximizes the number of happy customers and seems fair. Now consider what happens in a busy system when one process has a huge file to print. Every time the printer is free, the system will look around and choose the process with the shortest file. If there is a constant stream of processes with short files, the process with the huge file will never be allocated the printer. It will simply starve to death (be post-poned indefinitely, even though it is not blocked).

Starvation can be avoided by using a first-come, first-serve, resource alloca-tion policy. With this approach, the process waiting the longest gets served next. In due course of time, any given process will eventually become the oldest and thus get the needed resource.

3.8 RESEARCH ON DEADLOCKS

If ever there was a subject that was investigated mercilessly during the early days of operating systems, it was deadlocks. The reason for this is that deadlock detection is a nice little graph theory problem that one mathematically-inclined graduate student can get his jaws around and chew on for 3 or 4 years. All kinds of algorithms were devised, each one more exotic and less practical than the pre-vious one. Essentially, all this research has died out, with only a very occasional new paper appearing (e.g., Karacali et al., 2000). When an operating system wants to do deadlock detection or prevention, which few of them do, they use one of the methods discussed in this chapter,

There is still a little research on distributed deadlock detection, however. We will not treat that here because (1) it is outside the scope of this book, and (2) none of it is even remotely practical in real systems. Its main function seems to be keeping otherwise unemployed graph theorists off the streets.

3.9 SUMMARY

Deadlock is a potential problem in any operating system. It occurs when a group of processes each have been granted exclusive access to some resources, and each one wants yet another resource that belongs to another process in the group. All of them are blocked and none will ever run again.

Deadlock can be avoided by keeping track of which states are safe and which are unsafe. A safe state is one in which there exists a sequence of events that guarantee that all processes can finish. An unsafe state has no such guarantee. The banker's algorithm avoids deadlock by not granting a request if that request will put the system in an unsafe state.

Deadlock can be structurally prevented by building the system in such a way that it can never occur by design. For example, by allowing a process to hold only one resource at any instant the circular wait condition required for deadlock is broken. Deadlock can also be prevented by numbering all the resources, and making processes request them in strictly increasing order. Starvation can be avoided by a first-come, first-served allocation policy.

PROBLEMS

1. Give an example of a deadlock taken from politics.

2. Students working at individual PCs in a computer laboratory send their files to be printed by a server which spools the files on its hard disk. Under what conditions may a deadlock occur if the disk space for the print spool is limited? How may the deadlock be avoided?

3. In the preceding question which resources are preemptable and which are nonpreemptable?

4. In Fig. 3-1 the resources are returned in the reverse order of their acquisition. Would giving them back in the other order be just as good?

5. Fig. 3-3 shows the concept of a resource graph. Do illegal graphs exist, that is graphs that structurally violate the model we have used of resource usage? If so, give an example of one.

6. The discussion of the ostrich algorithm mentions the possibility of process table slots or other system tables filling up. Can you suggest a way to enable a system administrator to recover from such a situation?

7. Consider Fig. 3-4. Suppose that in step (o) C requested S instead of requesting R. Would this lead to deadlock? Suppose that it requested both S and R?

8. At a crossroads with STOP signs on all four approaches, the rule is that each driver yields the right of way to the driver on his right. This rule is not adequate when four vehicles arrive simultaneously. Fortunately, humans are sometimes capable of acting more intelligently than computers and the problem is usually resolved when one driver signals the driver to his left to go ahead. Can you draw an analogy between this behavior and any of the ways of recovering from deadlock described in Sec. 3.4.3? Why is a problem with such a simple solution in the human world so difficult to apply to a computer system?

9. Suppose that in Fig. 3-6 $C_{ij} + R_{ij} > E_j$ for some i. What implications does this have for all the processes finishing without deadlock?

10. All the trajectories in Fig. 3-8 are horizontal or vertical. Can you envision any circumstances in which diagonal trajectories were also possible?

11. Can the resource trajectory scheme of Fig. 3-8 also be used to illustrate the problem of deadlocks with three processes and three resources? If so, how can this be done? If not, why not?

12. In theory, resource trajectory graphs could be used to avoid deadlocks. By clever scheduling, the operating system could avoid unsafe regions. Suggest a practical problem with actually doing this.

13. Take a careful look at Fig. 3-11(b). If D asks for one more unit, does this lead to a safe state or an unsafe one? What if the request came from C instead of D?

14. Can a system be in a state that is neither deadlocked nor safe? If so, give an example. If not, prove that all states are either deadlocked or safe.

15. A system has two processes and three identical resources. Each process needs a maximum of two resources. Is deadlock possible? Explain your answer.

16. Consider the previous problem again, but now with p processes each needing a maximum of m resources and a total of r resources available. What condition must hold to make the system deadlock free?

17. Suppose that process A in Fig. 3-12 requests the last tape drive. Does this action lead to a deadlock?

18. A computer has six tape drives, with n processes competing for them. Each process may need two drives. For which values of n is the system deadlock free?

19. The banker's algorithm is being run in a system with m resource classes and n processes. In the limit of large m and n, the number of operations that must be performed to check a state for safety is proportional to $m^a n^b$. What are the values of a and b?

20. A system has four processes and five allocatable resources. The current allocation and maximum needs are as follows:

	Allocated	Maximum	Available
Process A	1 0 2 1 1	1 1 2 1 3	0 0 x 1 1
Process B	2 0 1 1 0	2 2 2 1 0	
Process C	1 1 0 1 0	2 1 3 1 0	
Process D	1 1 1 1 0	1 1 2 2 1	

What is the smallest value of x for which this is a safe state?

21. A distributed system using mailboxes has two IPC primitives, send and receive. The latter primitive specifies a process to receive from and blocks if no message from that process is available, even though messages may be waiting from other processes. There are no shared resources, but processes need to communicate frequently about other matters. Is deadlock possible? Discuss.

22. Two processes, A and B, each need three records, 1, 2, and 3, in a database. If A asks for them in the order 1, 2, 3, and B asks for them in the same order, deadlock is not possible. However, if B asks for them in the order 3, 2, 1, then deadlock is possible. With three resources, there are 3! or 6 possible combinations each process can request the resources. What fraction of all the combinations are guaranteed to be deadlock free?

23. Now reconsider the above problem, but using two-phase locking. Will that eliminate the potential for deadlock? Does it have any other undesirable characteristics, however? If so, which ones?

24. In an electronic funds transfer system, there are hundreds of identical processes that work as follows. Each process reads an input line specifying an amount of money, the account to be credited, and the account to be debited. Then it locks both accounts and transfers the money, releasing the locks when done. With many processes running in parallel, there is a very real danger that having locked account x it will be unable to lock y because y has been locked by a process now waiting for x. Devise a scheme that avoids deadlocks. Do not release an account record until you have completed the

transactions. (In other words, solutions that lock one account and then release it immediately if the other is locked are not allowed.)

25. One way to prevent deadlocks is to eliminate the hold-and-wait condition. In the text it was proposed that before asking for a new resource, a process must first release whatever resources it already holds (assuming that is possible). However, doing so introduces the danger that it may get the new resource but lose some of the existing ones to competing processes. Propose an improvement to this scheme.

26. A computer science student assigned to work on deadlocks thinks of the following brilliant way to eliminate deadlocks. When a process requests a resource, it specifies a time limit. If the process blocks because the resource is not available, a timer is started. If the time limit is exceeded, the process is released and allowed to run again. If you were the professor, what grade would you give this proposal and why.

27. Cinderella and the Prince are getting divorced. To divide their property, they have agreed on the following algorithm. Every morning, each one may send a letter to the other's lawyer requesting one item of property. Since it takes a day for letters to be delivered, they have agreed that if both discover that they have requested the same item on the same day, the next day they will send a letter canceling the request. Among their property is their dog, Woofer, Woofer's doghouse, their canary, Tweeter, and Tweeter's cage. The animals love their houses, so it has been agreed that any division of property separating an animal from its house is invalid, requiring the whole division to start over from scratch. Both Cinderella and the Prince desperately want Woofer. So they can go on (separate) vacations, each spouse has programmed a personal computer to handle the negotiation. When they come back from vacation, the computers are still negotiating. Why? Is deadlock possible? Is starvation possible? Discuss.

28. A student majoring in anthropology and minoring in computer science has embarked on a research project to see if African baboons can be taught about deadlocks. He locates a deep canyon and fastens a rope across it, so the baboons can cross hand-over-hand. Several baboons can cross at the same time, provided that they are all going in the same direction. If eastward moving and westward moving baboons ever get onto the rope at the same time, a deadlock will result (the baboons will get stuck in the middle) because it is impossible for one baboon to climb over another one while suspended over the canyon. If a baboon wants to cross the canyon, he must check to see that no other baboon is currently crossing in the opposite direction. Write a program using semaphores that avoids deadlock. Do not worry about a series of eastward moving baboons holding up the westward moving baboons indefinitely.

29. Repeat the previous problem, but now avoid starvation. When a baboon that wants to cross to the east arrives at the rope and finds baboons crossing to the west, he waits until the rope is empty, but no more westward moving baboons are allowed to start until at least one baboon has crossed the other way.

30. Program a simulation of the banker's algorithm. Your program should cycle through each of the bank clients asking for a request and evaluating whether it is safe or unsafe. Output a log of requests and decisions to a file.

4

MEMORY MANAGEMENT

Memory is an important resource that must be carefully managed. While the average home computer nowadays has a thousand times as much memory as the IBM 7094, the largest computer in the world in the early 1960s, programs are getting bigger faster than memories. To paraphrase Parkinson's law, "Programs expand to fill the memory available to hold them." In this chapter we will study how operating systems manage memory.

Ideally, what every programmer would like is an infinitely large, infinitely fast memory that is also nonvolatile, that is, does not lose its contents when the electric power fails. While we are at it, why not also ask for it to be inexpensive, too? Unfortunately technology does not provide such memories. Consequently, most computers have a **memory hierarchy**, with a small amount of very fast, expensive, volatile cache memory, tens of megabytes of medium-speed, medium-price, volatile main memory (RAM), and tens or hundreds of gigabytes of slow, cheap, nonvolatile disk storage. It is the job of the operating system to coordinate how these memories are used.

The part of the operating system that manages the memory hierarchy is called the **memory manager**. Its job is to keep track of which parts of memory are in use and which parts are not in use, to allocate memory to processes when they need it and deallocate it when they are done, and to manage swapping between main memory and disk when main memory is too small to hold all the processes.

In this chapter we will investigate a number of different memory management schemes, ranging from very simple to highly sophisticated. We will start at the beginning and look first at the simplest possible memory management system and then gradually progress to more and more elaborate ones.

As we pointed out in Chap. 1, history tends to repeat itself in the computer world. While the simplest memory management schemes are no longer used on desktop computers, they are still used in some palmtop, embedded, and smart card systems. For this reason, they are still worth studying.

4.1 BASIC MEMORY MANAGEMENT

Memory management systems can be divided into two classes: those that move processes back and forth between main memory and disk during execution (swapping and paging), and those that do not. The latter are simpler, so we will study them first. Later in the chapter we will examine swapping and paging. Throughout this chapter the reader should keep in mind that swapping and paging are largely artifacts caused by the lack of sufficient main memory to hold all the programs at once. If main memory ever gets so large that there is truly enough of it, the arguments in favor of one kind of memory management scheme or another may become obsolete.

On the other hand, as mentioned above, software seems to be growing even faster than memory, so efficient memory management may always be needed. In the 1980s, there were many universities that ran a timesharing system with dozens of (more-or-less satisfied) users on a 4 MB VAX. Now Microsoft recommends having at least 64 MB for a single-user Windows 2000 system. The trend toward multimedia puts even more demands on memory, so good memory management is probably going to be needed for the next decade at least.

4.1.1 Monoprogramming without Swapping or Paging

The simplest possible memory management scheme is to run just one program at a time, sharing the memory between that program and the operating system. Three variations on this theme are shown in Fig. 4-1. The operating system may be at the bottom of memory in RAM (Random Access Memory), as shown in Fig. 4-1(a), or it may be in ROM (Read-Only Memory) at the top of memory, as shown in Fig. 4-1(b), or the device drivers may be at the top of memory in a ROM and the rest of the system in RAM down below, as shown in Fig. 4-1(c). The first model was formerly used on mainframes and minicomputers but is rarely used any more. The second model is used on some palmtop computers and embedded systems. The third model was used by early personal computers (e.g., running MS-DOS), where the portion of the system in the ROM is called the **BIOS** (Basic Input Output System).

When the system is organized in this way, only one process at a time can be running. As soon as the user types a command, the operating system copies the

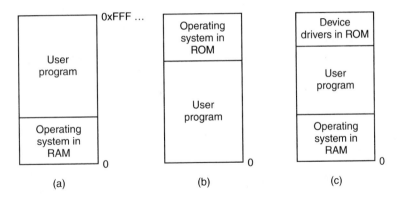

Figure 4-1. Three simple ways of organizing memory with an operating system and one user process. Other possibilities also exist.

requested program from disk to memory and executes it. When the process finishes, the operating system displays a prompt character and waits for a new command. When it receives the command, it loads a new program into memory, overwriting the first one.

4.1.2 Multiprogramming with Fixed Partitions

Except on simple embedded systems, monoprogramming is hardly used any more. Most modern systems allow multiple processes to run at the same time. Having multiple processes running at once means that when one process is blocked waiting for I/O to finish, another one can use the CPU. Thus multiprogramming increases the CPU utilization. Network servers always have the ability to run multiple processes (for different clients) at the same time, but most client (i.e., desktop) machines also have this ability nowadays.

The easiest way to achieve multiprogramming is simply to divide memory up into *n* (possibly unequal) partitions. This partitioning can, for example, be done manually when the system is started up.

When a job arrives, it can be put into the input queue for the smallest partition large enough to hold it. Since the partitions are fixed in this scheme, any space in a partition not used by a job is lost. In Fig. 4-2(a) we see how this system of fixed partitions and separate input queues looks.

The disadvantage of sorting the incoming jobs into separate queues becomes apparent when the queue for a large partition is empty but the queue for a small partition is full, as is the case for partitions 1 and 3 in Fig. 4-2(a). Here small jobs have to wait to get into memory, even though plenty of memory is free. An alternative organization is to maintain a single queue as in Fig. 4-2(b). Whenever a partition becomes free, the job closest to the front of the queue that fits in it could be loaded into the empty partition and run. Since it is undesirable to waste a large

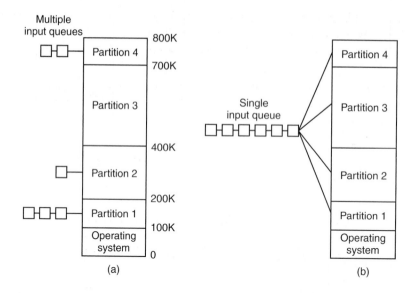

Figure 4-2. (a) Fixed memory partitions with separate input queues for each partition. (b) Fixed memory partitions with a single input queue.

partition on a small job, a different strategy is to search the whole input queue whenever a partition becomes free and pick the largest job that fits. Note that the latter algorithm discriminates against small jobs as being unworthy of having a whole partition, whereas usually it is desirable to give the smallest jobs (often interactive jobs) the best service, not the worst.

One way out is to have at least one small partition around. Such a partition will allow small jobs to run without having to allocate a large partition for them.

Another approach is to have a rule stating that a job that is eligible to run may not be skipped over more than k times. Each time it is skipped over, it gets one point. When it has acquired k points, it may not be skipped again.

This system, with fixed partitions set up by the operator in the morning and not changed thereafter, was used by OS/360 on large IBM mainframes for many years. It was called **MFT** (Multiprogramming with a Fixed number of Tasks or OS/MFT). It is simple to understand and equally simple to implement: incoming jobs are queued until a suitable partition is available, at which time the job is loaded into that partition and run until it terminates. Nowadays, few, if any, operating systems, support this model.

4.1.3 Modeling Multiprogramming

When multiprogramming is used, the CPU utilization can be improved. Crudely put, if the average process computes only 20 percent of the time it is sitting in memory, with five processes in memory at once, the CPU should be busy all the time. This model is unrealistically optimistic, however, since it assumes that all five processes will never be waiting for I/O at the same time.

A better model is to look at CPU usage from a probabilistic viewpoint. Suppose that a process spends a fraction p of its time waiting for I/O to complete. With n processes in memory at once, the probability that all n processes are waiting for I/O (in which case the CPU will be idle) is p^n. The CPU utilization is then given by the formula

$$\text{CPU utilization} = 1 - p^n$$

Figure 4-3 shows the CPU utilization as a function of n, which is called the **degree of multiprogramming**.

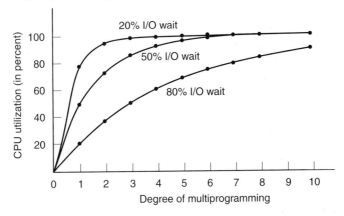

Figure 4-3. CPU utilization as a function of the number of processes in memory.

From the figure it is clear that if processes spend 80 percent of their time waiting for I/O, at least 10 processes must be in memory at once to get the CPU waste below 10 percent. When you realize that an interactive process waiting for a user to type something at a terminal is in I/O wait state, it should be clear that I/O wait times of 80 percent and more are not unusual. But even in batch systems, processes doing a lot of disk I/O will often have this percentage or more.

For the sake of complete accuracy, it should be pointed out that the probabilistic model just described is only an approximation. It implicitly assumes that all n processes are independent, meaning that it is quite acceptable for a system with five processes in memory to have three running and two waiting. But with a single CPU, we cannot have three processes running at once, so a process becoming ready while the CPU is busy will have to wait. Thus the processes are not independent. A more accurate model can be constructed using queueing theory, but the point we are making—multiprogramming lets processes use the CPU when it would be otherwise idle—is, of course, still valid, even if the true curves of Fig. 4-3 are slightly different.

Even though the model of Fig. 4-3 is simple-minded, it can nevertheless be used to make specific, although approximate, predictions about CPU performance.

Suppose, for example, that a computer has 32 MB of memory, with the operating system taking up 16 MB and each user program taking up 4 MB. These sizes allow four user programs to be in memory at once. With an 80 percent average I/O wait, we have a CPU utilization (ignoring operating system overhead) of $1 - 0.8^4$ or about 60 percent. Adding another 16 MB of memory allows the system to go from four-way multiprogramming to eight-way multiprogramming, thus raising the CPU utilization to 83 percent. In other words, the additional 16 MB will raise the throughput by 38 percent.

Adding yet another 16 MB would only increase CPU utilization from 83 percent to 93 percent, thus raising the throughput by only another 12 percent. Using this model the computer's owner might decide that the first addition is a good investment but that the second is not.

4.1.4 Analysis of Multiprogramming System Performance

The model discussed above can also be used to analyze batch systems. Consider, for example, a computer center whose jobs average 80 percent I/O wait time. On a particular morning, four jobs are submitted as shown in Fig. 4-4(a). The first job, arriving at 10:00 A.M., requires 4 minutes of CPU time. With 80 percent I/O wait, the job uses only 12 seconds of CPU time for each minute it is sitting in memory, even if no other jobs are competing with it for the CPU. The other 48 seconds are spent waiting for I/O to complete. Thus the job will have to sit in memory for at least 20 minutes in order to get 4 minutes of CPU work done, even in the absence of competition for the CPU.

From 10:00 A.M. to 10:10 A.M., job 1 is all by itself in memory and gets 2 minutes of work done. When job 2 arrives at 10:10 A.M., the CPU utilization increases from 0.20 to 0.36, due to the higher degree of multiprogramming (see Fig. 4-3). However, with round-robin scheduling, each job gets half of the CPU, so each job gets 0.18 minutes of CPU work done for each minute it is in memory. Notice that the addition of a second job costs the first job only 10 percent of its performance. It goes from getting 0.20 CPU minutes per minute of real time to getting 0.18 CPU minutes per minute of real time.

At 10:15 A.M. the third job arrives. At this point job 1 has received 2.9 minutes of CPU and job 2 has had 0.9 minutes of CPU. With three-way multiprogramming, each job gets 0.16 minutes of CPU time per minute of real time, as shown in Fig. 4-4(b). From 10:15 A.M. to 10:20 A.M. each of the three jobs gets 0.8 minutes of CPU time. At 10:20 A.M. a fourth job arrives. Fig. 4-4(c) shows the complete sequence of events.

4.1.5 Relocation and Protection

Multiprogramming introduces two essential problems that must be solved—relocation and protection. Look at Fig. 4-2. From the figure it is clear that different jobs will be run at different addresses. When a program is linked (i.e., the

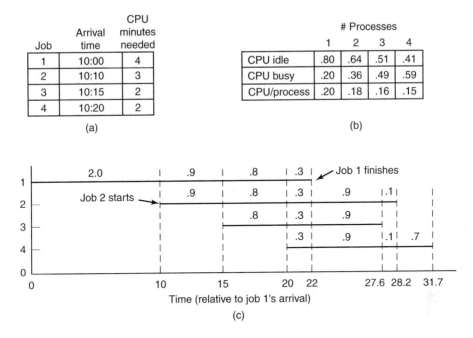

Figure 4-4. (a) Arrival and work requirements of four jobs. (b) CPU utilization for 1 to 4 jobs with 80 percent I/O wait. (c) Sequence of events as jobs arrive and finish. The numbers above the horizontal lines show how much CPU time, in minutes, each job gets in each interval.

main program, user-written procedures, and library procedures are combined into a single address space), the linker must know at what address the program will begin in memory.

For example, suppose that the first instruction is a call to a procedure at absolute address 100 within the binary file produced by the linker. If this program is loaded in partition 1 (at address 100K), that instruction will jump to absolute address 100, which is inside the operating system. What is needed is a call to 100K + 100. If the program is loaded into partition 2, it must be carried out as a call to 200K + 100, and so on. This problem is known as the **relocation** problem.

One possible solution is to actually modify the instructions as the program is loaded into memory. Programs loaded into partition 1 have 100K added to each address, programs loaded into partition 2 have 200K added to addresses, and so forth. To perform relocation during loading like this, the linker must include in the binary program a list or bitmap telling which program words are addresses to be relocated and which are opcodes, constants, or other items that must not be relocated. OS/MFT worked this way.

Relocation during loading does not solve the protection problem. A malicious program can always construct a new instruction and jump to it. Because programs in this system use absolute memory addresses rather than addresses relative to a register, there is no way to stop a program from building an instruction that reads or writes any word in memory. In multiuser systems, it is highly undesirable to let processes read and write memory belonging to other users.

The solution that IBM chose for protecting the 360 was to divide memory into blocks of 2-KB bytes and assign a 4-bit protection code to each block. The PSW (Program Status Word) contained a 4-bit key. The 360 hardware trapped any attempt by a running process to access memory whose protection code differed from the PSW key. Since only the operating system could change the protection codes and key, user processes were prevented from interfering with one another and with the operating system itself.

An alternative solution to both the relocation and protection problems is to equip the machine with two special hardware registers, called the **base** and **limit** registers. When a process is scheduled, the base register is loaded with the address of the start of its partition, and the limit register is loaded with the length of the partition. Every memory address generated automatically has the base register contents added to it before being sent to memory. Thus if the base register contains the value 100K, a CALL 100 instruction is effectively turned into a CALL 100K + 100 instruction, without the instruction itself being modified. Addresses are also checked against the limit register to make sure that they do not attempt to address memory outside the current partition. The hardware protects the base and limit registers to prevent user programs from modifying them.

A disadvantage of this scheme is the need to perform an addition and a comparison on every memory reference. Comparisons can be done fast, but additions are slow due to carry propagation time unless special addition circuits are used.

The CDC 6600—the world's first supercomputer—used this scheme. The Intel 8088 CPU used for the original IBM PC used a weaker version of this scheme—base registers, but no limit registers. Few computers use it any more though.

4.2 SWAPPING

With a batch system, organizing memory into fixed partitions is simple and effective. Each job is loaded into a partition when it gets to the head of the queue. It stays in memory until it has finished. As long as enough jobs can be kept in memory to keep the CPU busy all the time, there is no reason to use anything more complicated.

With timesharing systems or graphically oriented personal computers, the situation is different. Sometimes there is not enough main memory to hold all the currently active processes, so excess processes must be kept on disk and brought in to run dynamically.

Two general approaches to memory management can be used, depending (in part) on the available hardware. The simplest strategy, called **swapping**, consists of bringing in each process in its entirety, running it for a while, then putting it back on the disk. The other strategy, called **virtual memory**, allows programs to run even when they are only partially in main memory. Below we will study swapping; in Sec. 4.3 we will examine virtual memory.

The operation of a swapping system is illustrated in Fig. 4-5. Initially only process A is in memory. Then processes B and C are created or swapped in from disk. In Fig. 4-5(d) A is swapped out to disk. Then D comes in and B goes out. Finally A comes in again. Since A is now at a different location, addresses contained in it must be relocated, either by software when it is swapped in or (more likely) by hardware during program execution.

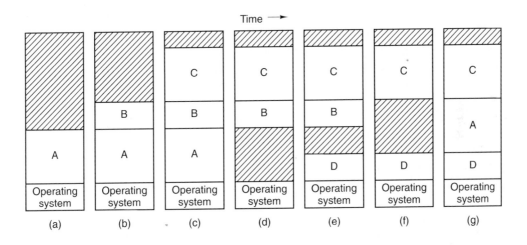

Figure 4-5. Memory allocation changes as processes come into memory and leave it. The shaded regions are unused memory.

The main difference between the fixed partitions of Fig. 4-2 and the variable partitions of Fig. 4-5 is that the number, location, and size of the partitions vary dynamically in the latter as processes come and go, whereas they are fixed in the former. The flexibility of not being tied to a fixed number of partitions that may be too large or too small improves memory utilization, but it also complicates allocating and deallocating memory, as well as keeping track of it.

When swapping creates multiple holes in memory, it is possible to combine them all into one big one by moving all the processes downward as far as possible. This technique is known as **memory compaction**. It is usually not done because it requires a lot of CPU time. For example, on a 256-MB machine that can copy 4 bytes in 40 nsec, it takes about 2.7 sec to compact all of memory.

A point that is worth making concerns how much memory should be allocated for a process when it is created or swapped in. If processes are created with a fixed size that never changes, then the allocation is simple: the operating system allocates exactly what is needed, no more and no less.

If, however, processes' data segments can grow, for example, by dynamically allocating memory from a heap, as in many programming languages, a problem occurs whenever a process tries to grow. If a hole is adjacent to the process, it can be allocated and the process allowed to grow into the hole. On the other hand, if the process is adjacent to another process, the growing process will either have to be moved to a hole in memory large enough for it, or one or more processes will have to be swapped out to create a large enough hole. If a process cannot grow in memory and the swap area on the disk is full, the process will have to wait or be killed.

If it is expected that most processes will grow as they run, it is probably a good idea to allocate a little extra memory whenever a process is swapped in or moved, to reduce the overhead associated with moving or swapping processes that no longer fit in their allocated memory. However, when swapping processes to disk, only the memory actually in use should be swapped; it is wasteful to swap the extra memory as well. In Fig. 4-6(a) we see a memory configuration in which space for growth has been allocated to two processes.

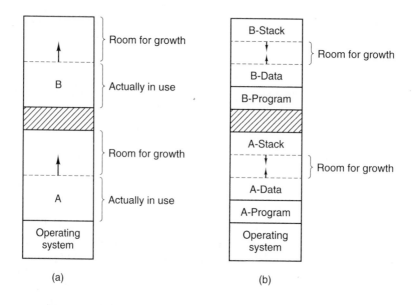

Figure 4-6. (a) Allocating space for a growing data segment. (b) Allocating space for a growing stack and a growing data segment.

If processes can have two growing segments, for example, the data segment being used as a heap for variables that are dynamically allocated and released and a stack segment for the normal local variables and return addresses, an alternative arrangement suggests itself, namely that of Fig. 4-6(b). In this figure we see that each process illustrated has a stack at the top of its allocated memory that is growing downward, and a data segment just beyond the program text that is growing upward. The memory between them can be used for either segment. If it runs out, either the process will have to be moved to a hole with enough space, swapped out of memory until a large enough hole can be created, or killed.

4.2.1 Memory Management with Bitmaps

When memory is assigned dynamically, the operating system must manage it. In general terms, there are two ways to keep track of memory usage: bitmaps and free lists. In this section and the next one we will look at these two methods in turn.

With a bitmap, memory is divided up into allocation units, perhaps as small as a few words and perhaps as large as several kilobytes. Corresponding to each allocation unit is a bit in the bitmap, which is 0 if the unit is free and 1 if it is occupied (or vice versa). Figure 4-7 shows part of memory and the corresponding bitmap.

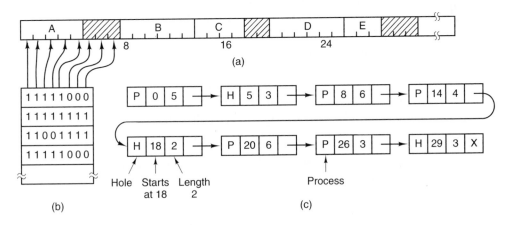

Figure 4-7. (a) A part of memory with five processes and three holes. The tick marks show the memory allocation units. The shaded regions (0 in the bitmap) are free. (b) The corresponding bitmap. (c) The same information as a list.

The size of the allocation unit is an important design issue. The smaller the allocation unit, the larger the bitmap. However, even with an allocation unit as small as 4 bytes, 32 bits of memory will require only 1 bit of the map. A memory of $32n$ bits will use n map bits, so the bitmap will take up only 1/33 of memory. If the allocation unit is chosen large, the bitmap will be smaller, but appreciable memory may be wasted in the last unit of the process if the process size is not an exact multiple of the allocation unit.

A bitmap provides a simple way to keep track of memory words in a fixed amount of memory because the size of the bitmap depends only on the size of memory and the size of the allocation unit. The main problem with it is that when it has been decided to bring a *k* unit process into memory, the memory manager must search the bitmap to find a run of *k* consecutive 0 bits in the map. Searching a bitmap for a run of a given length is a slow operation (because the run may straddle word boundaries in the map); this is an argument against bitmaps.

4.2.2 Memory Management with Linked Lists

Another way of keeping track of memory is to maintain a linked list of allocated and free memory segments, where a segment is either a process or a hole between two processes. The memory of Fig. 4-7(a) is represented in Fig. 4-7(c) as a linked list of segments. Each entry in the list specifies a hole (H) or process (P), the address at which it starts, the length, and a pointer to the next entry.

In this example, the segment list is kept sorted by address. Sorting this way has the advantage that when a process terminates or is swapped out, updating the list is straightforward. A terminating process normally has two neighbors (except when it is at the very top or bottom of memory). These may be either processes or holes, leading to the four combinations of Fig. 4-8. In Fig. 4-8(a) updating the list requires replacing a P by an H. In Fig. 4-8(b) and Fig. 4-8(c), two entries are coalesced into one, and the list becomes one entry shorter. In Fig. 4-8(d), three entries are merged and two items are removed from the list. Since the process table slot for the terminating process will normally point to the list entry for the process itself, it may be more convenient to have the list as a double-linked list, rather than the single-linked list of Fig. 4-7(c). This structure makes it easier to find the previous entry and to see if a merge is possible.

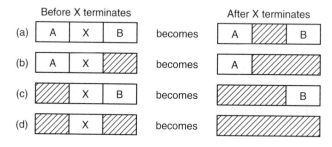

Figure 4-8. Four neighbor combinations for the terminating process, *X*.

When the processes and holes are kept on a list sorted by address, several algorithms can be used to allocate memory for a newly created process (or an existing process being swapped in from disk). We assume that the memory manager knows how much memory to allocate. The simplest algorithm is **first fit**. The memory manager scans along the list of segments until it finds a hole that is big enough. The hole is then broken up into two pieces, one for the process and one for the unused memory, except in the statistically unlikely case of an exact fit. First fit is a fast algorithm because it searches as little as possible.

A minor variation of first fit is **next fit**. It works the same way as first fit, except that it keeps track of where it is whenever it finds a suitable hole. The next time it is called to find a hole, it starts searching the list from the place where it left off last time, instead of always at the beginning, as first fit does. Simulations by Bays (1977) show that next fit gives slightly worse performance than first fit.

Another well-known algorithm is **best fit**. Best fit searches the entire list and takes the smallest hole that is adequate. Rather than breaking up a big hole that might be needed later, best fit tries to find a hole that is close to the actual size needed.

As an example of first fit and best fit, consider Fig. 4-7 again. If a block of size 2 is needed, first fit will allocate the hole at 5, but best fit will allocate the hole at 18.

Best fit is slower than first fit because it must search the entire list every time it is called. Somewhat surprisingly, it also results in more wasted memory than first fit or next fit because it tends to fill up memory with tiny, useless holes. First fit generates larger holes on the average.

To get around the problem of breaking up nearly exact matches into a process and a tiny hole, one could think about **worst fit**, that is, always take the largest available hole, so that the hole broken off will be big enough to be useful. Simulation has shown that worst fit is not a very good idea either.

All four algorithms can be speeded up by maintaining separate lists for processes and holes. In this way, all of them devote their full energy to inspecting holes, not processes. The inevitable price that is paid for this speedup on allocation is the additional complexity and slowdown when deallocating memory, since a freed segment has to be removed from the process list and inserted into the hole list.

If distinct lists are maintained for processes and holes, the hole list may be kept sorted on size, to make best fit faster. When best fit searches a list of holes from smallest to largest, as soon as it finds a hole that fits, it knows that the hole is the smallest one that will do the job, hence the best fit. No further searching is needed, as it is with the single list scheme. With a hole list sorted by size, first fit and best fit are equally fast, and next fit is pointless.

When the holes are kept on separate lists from the processes, a small optimization is possible. Instead of having a separate set of data structures for maintaining the hole list, as is done in Fig. 4-7(c), the holes themselves can be used. The first word of each hole could be the hole size, and the second word a pointer to the following entry. The nodes of the list of Fig. 4-7(c), which require three words and one bit (P/H), are no longer needed.

Yet another allocation algorithm is **quick fit**, which maintains separate lists for some of the more common sizes requested. For example, it might have a table with n entries, in which the first entry is a pointer to the head of a list of 4-KB holes, the second entry is a pointer to a list of 8-KB holes, the third entry a pointer to 12-KB holes, and so on. Holes of say, 21 KB, could either be put on the 20-KB list or on a special list of odd-sized holes. With quick fit, finding a hole of the required size is extremely fast, but it has the same disadvantage as all schemes that sort by hole size, namely, when a process terminates or is swapped out, finding its neighbors to see if a merge is possible is expensive. If merging is not done, memory will quickly fragment into a large number of small holes into which no processes fit.

4.3 VIRTUAL MEMORY

Many years ago people were first confronted with programs that were too big to fit in the available memory. The solution usually adopted was to split the program into pieces, called **overlays**. Overlay 0 would start running first. When it was done, it would call another overlay. Some overlay systems were highly complex, allowing multiple overlays in memory at once. The overlays were kept on the disk and swapped in and out of memory by the operating system, dynamically, as needed.

Although the actual work of swapping overlays in and out was done by the system, the work of splitting the program into pieces had to be done by the programmer. Splitting up large programs into small, modular pieces was time consuming and boring. It did not take long before someone thought of a way to turn the whole job over to the computer.

The method that was devised (Fotheringham, 1961) has come to be known as **virtual memory**. The basic idea behind virtual memory is that the combined size of the program, data, and stack may exceed the amount of physical memory available for it. The operating system keeps those parts of the program currently in use in main memory, and the rest on the disk. For example, a 16-MB program can run on a 4-MB machine by carefully choosing which 4 MB to keep in memory at each instant, with pieces of the program being swapped between disk and memory as needed.

Virtual memory can also work in a multiprogramming system, with bits and pieces of many programs in memory at once. While a program is waiting for part of itself to be brought in, it is waiting for I/O and cannot run, so the CPU can be given to another process, the same way as in any other multiprogramming system.

4.3.1 Paging

Most virtual memory systems use a technique called **paging**, which we will now describe. On any computer, there exists a set of memory addresses that programs can produce. When a program uses an instruction like

    MOV REG,1000

it does this to copy the contents of memory address 1000 to REG (or vice versa, depending on the computer). Addresses can be generated using indexing, base registers, segment registers, and other ways.

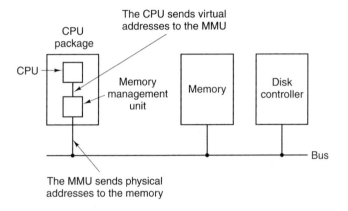

Figure 4-9. The position and function of the MMU. Here the MMU is shown as being a part of the CPU chip because it commonly is nowadays. However, logically it could be a separate chip and was in years gone by.

These program-generated addresses are called **virtual addresses** and form the **virtual address space**. On computers without virtual memory, the virtual address is put directly onto the memory bus and causes the physical memory word with the same address to be read or written. When virtual memory is used, the virtual addresses do not go directly to the memory bus. Instead, they go to an **MMU** (**Memory Management Unit**) that maps the virtual addresses onto the physical memory addresses as illustrated in Fig. 4-9.

A very simple example of how this mapping works is shown in Fig. 4-10. In this example, we have a computer that can generate 16-bit addresses, from 0 up to 64K. These are the virtual addresses. This computer, however, has only 32 KB of physical memory, so although 64-KB programs can be written, they cannot be loaded into memory in their entirety and run. A complete copy of a program's core image, up to 64 KB, must be present on the disk, however, so that pieces can be brought in as needed.

The virtual address space is divided up into units called **pages**. The corresponding units in the physical memory are called **page frames**. The pages and page frames are always the same size. In this example they are 4 KB, but page sizes from 512 bytes to 64 KB have been used in real systems. With 64 KB of virtual address space and 32 KB of physical memory, we get 16 virtual pages and 8 page frames. Transfers between RAM and disk are always in units of a page.

When the program tries to access address 0, for example, using the instruction

    MOV REG,0

virtual address 0 is sent to the MMU. The MMU sees that this virtual address falls

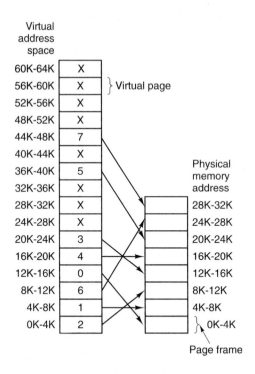

Figure 4-10. The relation between virtual addresses and physical memory addresses is given by the page table.

in page 0 (0 to 4095), which according to its mapping is page frame 2 (8192 to 12287). It thus transforms the address to 8192 and outputs address 8192 onto the bus. The memory knows nothing at all about the MMU and just sees a request for reading or writing address 8192, which it honors. Thus, the MMU has effectively mapped all virtual addresses between 0 and 4095 onto physical addresses 8192 to 12287.

Similarly, an instruction

    MOV REG,8192

is effectively transformed into

    MOV REG,24576

because virtual address 8192 is in virtual page 2 and this page is mapped onto physical page frame 6 (physical addresses 24576 to 28671). As a third example, virtual address 20500 is 20 bytes from the start of virtual page 5 (virtual addresses 20480 to 24575) and maps onto physical address 12288 + 20 = 12308.

By itself, this ability to map the 16 virtual pages onto any of the eight page frames by setting the MMU's map appropriately does not solve the problem that the virtual address space is larger than the physical memory. Since we have only eight physical page frames, only eight of the virtual pages in Fig. 4-10 are mapped onto physical memory. The others, shown as a cross in the figure, are not mapped. In the actual hardware, a **Present/absent bit** keeps track of which pages are physically present in memory.

What happens if the program tries to use an unmapped page, for example, by using the instruction

    MOV REG,32780

which is byte 12 within virtual page 8 (starting at 32768)? The MMU notices that the page is unmapped (indicated by a cross in the figure) and causes the CPU to trap to the operating system. This trap is called a **page fault**. The operating system picks a little-used page frame and writes its contents back to the disk. It then fetches the page just referenced into the page frame just freed, changes the map, and restarts the trapped instruction.

For example, if the operating system decided to evict page frame 1, it would load virtual page 8 at physical address 4K and make two changes to the MMU map. First, it would mark virtual page 1's entry as unmapped, to trap any future accesses to virtual addresses between 4K and 8K. Then it would replace the cross in virtual page 8's entry with a 1, so that when the trapped instruction is re-executed, it will map virtual address 32780 onto physical address 4108.

Now let us look inside the MMU to see how it works and why we have chosen to use a page size that is a power of 2. In Fig. 4-11 we see an example of a virtual address, 8196 (0010000000000100 in binary), being mapped using the MMU map of Fig. 4-10. The incoming 16-bit virtual address is split into a 4-bit page number and a 12-bit offset. With 4 bits for the page number, we can have 16 pages, and with 12 bits for the offset, we can address all 4096 bytes within a page.

The page number is used as an index into the **page table**, yielding the number of the page frame corresponding to that virtual page. If the *Present/absent* bit is 0, a trap to the operating system is caused. If the bit is 1, the page frame number found in the page table is copied to the high-order 3 bits of the output register, along with the 12-bit offset, which is copied unmodified from the incoming virtual address. Together they form a 15-bit physical address. The output register is then put onto the memory bus as the physical memory address.

4.3.2 Page Tables

In the simplest case, the mapping of virtual addresses onto physical addresses is as we have just described it. The virtual address is split into a virtual page number (high-order bits) and an offset (low-order bits). For example, with a 16-bit address and a 4-KB page size, the upper 4 bits could specify one of the 16 virtual pages and the lower 12 bits would then specify the byte offset (0 to 4095) within the selected page. However a split with 3 or 5 or some other number of bits for the page is also possible. Different splits imply different page sizes.

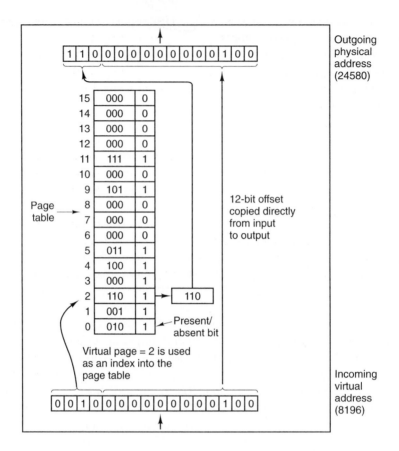

Figure 4-11. The internal operation of the MMU with 16 4-KB pages.

The virtual page number is used as an index into the page table to find the entry for that virtual page. From the page table entry, the page frame number (if any) is found. The page frame number is attached to the high-order end of the offset, replacing the virtual page number, to form a physical address that can be sent to the memory.

The purpose of the page table is to map virtual pages onto page frames. Mathematically speaking, the page table is a function, with the virtual page number as argument and the physical frame number as result. Using the result of this function, the virtual page field in a virtual address can be replaced by a page frame field, thus forming a physical memory address.

Despite this simple description, two major issues must be faced:

1. The page table can be extremely large.

2. The mapping must be fast.

The first point follows from the fact that modern computers use virtual addresses of at least 32 bits. With, say, a 4-KB page size, a 32-bit address space has 1 million pages, and a 64-bit address space has more than you want to contemplate. With 1 million pages in the virtual address space, the page table must have 1 million entries. And remember that each process needs its own page table (because it has its own virtual address space).

The second point is a consequence of the fact that the virtual-to-physical mapping must be done on every memory reference. A typical instruction has an instruction word, and often a memory operand as well. Consequently, it is necessary to make 1, 2, or sometimes more page table references per instruction. If an instruction takes, say, 4 nsec, the page table lookup must be done in under 1 nsec to avoid becoming a major bottleneck.

The need for large, fast page mapping is a significant constraint on the way computers are built. Although the problem is most serious with top-of-the-line machines, it is also an issue at the low end as well, where cost and the price/performance ratio are critical. In this section and the following ones, we will look at page table design in detail and show a number of hardware solutions that have been used in actual computers.

The simplest design (at least conceptually) is to have a single page table consisting of an array of fast hardware registers, with one entry for each virtual page, indexed by virtual page number, as shown in Fig. 4-11. When a process is started up, the operating system loads the registers with the process' page table, taken from a copy kept in main memory. During process execution, no more memory references are needed for the page table. The advantages of this method are that it is straightforward and requires no memory references during mapping. A disadvantage is that it is potentially expensive (if the page table is large). Having to load the full page table at every context switch hurts performance.

At the other extreme, the page table can be entirely in main memory. All the hardware needs then is a single register that points to the start of the page table. This design allows the memory map to be changed at a context switch by reloading one register. Of course, it has the disadvantage of requiring one or more memory references to read page table entries during the execution of each instruction. For this reason, this approach is rarely used in its most pure form, but below we will study some variations that have much better performance.

Multilevel Page Tables

To get around the problem of having to store huge page tables in memory all the time, many computers use a multilevel page table. A simple example is shown in Fig. 4-12. In Fig. 4-12(a) we have a 32-bit virtual address that is partitioned into a 10-bit *PT1* field, a 10-bit *PT2* field, and a 12-bit *Offset* field. Since offsets are 12 bits, pages are 4 KB, and there are a total of 2^{20} of them.

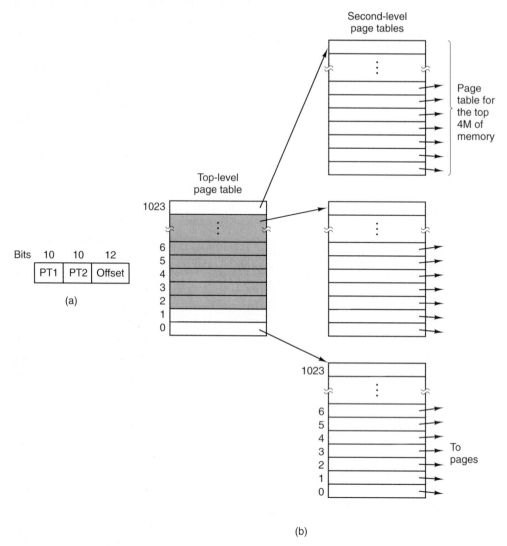

Figure 4-12. (a) A 32-bit address with two page table fields. (b) Two-level page tables.

The secret to the multilevel page table method is to avoid keeping all the page tables in memory all the time. In particular, those that are not needed should not be kept around. Suppose, for example, that a process needs 12 megabytes, the bottom 4 megabytes of memory for program text, the next 4 megabytes for data, and the top 4 megabytes for the stack. In between the top of the data and the bottom of the stack is a gigantic hole that is not used.

In Fig. 4-12(b) we see how the two-level page table works in this example. On the left we have the top-level page table, with 1024 entries, corresponding to the 10-bit $PT1$ field. When a virtual address is presented to the MMU, it first extracts the $PT1$ field and uses this value as an index into the top-level page table. Each of these 1024 entries represents 4M because the entire 4-gigabyte (i.e., 32-bit) virtual address space has been chopped into chunks of 1024 bytes.

The entry located by indexing into the top-level page table yields the address or the page frame number of a second-level page table. Entry 0 of the top-level page table points to the page table for the program text, entry 1 points to the page table for the data, and entry 1023 points to the page table for the stack. The other (shaded) entries are not used. The $PT2$ field is now used as an index into the selected second-level page table to find the page frame number for the page itself.

As an example, consider the 32-bit virtual address 0x00403004 (4,206,596 decimal), which is 12,292 bytes into the data. This virtual address corresponds to $PT1 = 1$, $PT2 = 2$, and $Offset = 4$. The MMU first uses $PT1$ to index into the top-level page table and obtain entry 1, which corresponds to addresses 4M to 8M. It then uses $PT2$ to index into the second-level page table just found and extract entry 3, which corresponds to addresses 12288 to 16383 within its 4M chunk (i.e., absolute addresses 4,206,592 to 4,210,687). This entry contains the page frame number of the page containing virtual address 0x00403004. If that page is not in memory, the *Present/absent* bit in the page table entry will be zero, causing a page fault. If the page is in memory, the page frame number taken from the second-level page table is combined with the offset (4) to construct a physical address. This address is put on the bus and sent to memory.

The interesting thing to note about Fig. 4-12 is that although the address space contains over a million pages, only four page tables are actually needed: the top-level table, and the second-level tables for 0 to 4M, 4M to 8M, and the top 4M. The *Present/absent* bits in 1021 entries of the top-level page table are set to 0, forcing a page fault if they are ever accessed. Should this occur, the operating system will notice that the process is trying to reference memory that it is not supposed to and will take appropriate action, such as sending it a signal or killing it. In this example we have chosen round numbers for the various sizes and have picked $PT1$ equal to $PT2$ but in actual practice other values are also possible, of course.

The two-level page table system of Fig. 4-12 can be expanded to three, four, or more levels. Additional levels give more flexibility, but it is doubtful that the additional complexity is worth it beyond three levels.

Structure of a Page Table Entry

Let us now turn from the structure of the page tables in the large, to the details of a single page table entry. The exact layout of an entry is highly machine dependent, but the kind of information present is roughly the same from machine to machine. In Fig. 4-13 we give a sample page table entry. The size varies from computer to computer, but 32 bits is a common size. The most important field is the *Page frame number*. After all, the goal of the page mapping is to locate this value. Next to it we have the *Present/absent* bit. If this bit is 1, the entry is valid and can be used. If it is 0, the virtual page to which the entry belongs is not currently in memory. Accessing a page table entry with this bit set to 0 causes a page fault.

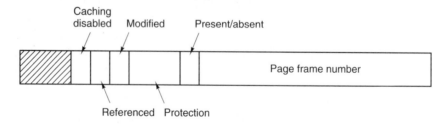

Figure 4-13. A typical page table entry.

The *Protection* bits tell what kinds of access are permitted. In the simplest form, this field contains 1 bit, with 0 for read/write and 1 for read only. A more sophisticated arrangement is having 3 bits, one bit each for enabling reading, writing, and executing the page.

The *Modified* and *Referenced* bits keep track of page usage. When a page is written to, the hardware automatically sets the *Modified* bit. This bit is of value when the operating system decides to reclaim a page frame. If the page in it has been modified (i.e., is "dirty"), it must be written back to the disk. If it has not been modified (i.e., is "clean"), it can just be abandoned, since the disk copy is still valid. The bit is sometimes called the **dirty bit**, since it reflects the page's state.

The *Referenced* bit is set whenever a page is referenced, either for reading or writing. Its value is to help the operating system choose a page to evict when a page fault occurs. Pages that are not being used are better candidates than pages that are, and this bit plays an important role in several of the page replacement algorithms that we will study later in this chapter.

Finally, the last bit allows caching to be disabled for the page. This feature is important for pages that map onto device registers rather than memory. If the operating system is sitting in a tight loop waiting for some I/O device to respond to a command it was just given, it is essential that the hardware keep fetching the word from the device, and not use an old cached copy. With this bit, caching can be turned off. Machines that have a separate I/O space and do not use memory mapped I/O do not need this bit.

Note that the disk address used to hold the page when it is not in memory is not part of the page table. The reason is simple. The page table holds only that information the hardware needs to translate a virtual address to a physical address. Information the operating system needs to handle page faults is kept in software tables inside the operating system. The hardware does not need it.

4.3.3 TLBs—Translation Lookaside Buffers

In most paging schemes, the page tables are kept in memory, due to their large size. Potentially, this design has an enormous impact on performance. Consider, for example, an instruction that copies one register to another. In the absence of paging, this instruction makes only one memory reference, to fetch the instruction. With paging, additional memory references will be needed to access the page table. Since execution speed is generally limited by the rate the CPU can get instructions and data out of the memory, having to make two page table references per memory reference reduces performance by 2/3. Under these conditions, no one would use it.

Computer designers have known about this problem for years and have come up with a solution. Their solution is based on the observation that most programs tend to make a large number of references to a small number of pages, and not the other way around. Thus only a small fraction of the page table entries are heavily read; the rest are barely used at all.

The solution that has been devised is to equip computers with a small hardware device for mapping virtual addresses to physical addresses without going through the page table. The device, called a **TLB** (**Translation Lookaside Buffer**) or sometimes an **associative memory**, is illustrated in Fig. 4-14. It is usually inside the MMU and consists of a small number of entries, eight in this example, but rarely more than 64. Each entry contains information about one page, including the virtual page number, a bit that is set when the page is modified, the protection code (read/write/execute permissions), and the physical page frame in which the page is located. These fields have a one-to-one correspondence with the fields in the page table. Another bit indicates whether the entry is valid (i.e., in use) or not.

Valid	Virtual page	Modified	Protection	Page frame
1	140	1	RW	31
1	20	0	R X	38
1	130	1	RW	29
1	129	1	RW	62
1	19	0	R X	50
1	21	0	R X	45
1	860	1	RW	14
1	861	1	RW	75

Figure 4-14. A TLB to speed up paging.

An example that might generate the TLB of Fig. 4-14 is a process in a loop that spans virtual pages 19, 20, and 21, so these TLB entries have protection codes for reading and executing. The main data currently being used (say, an array being processed) are on pages 129 and 130. Page 140 contains the indices used in the array calculations. Finally, the stack is on pages 860 and 861.

Let us now see how the TLB functions. When a virtual address is presented to the MMU for translation, the hardware first checks to see if its virtual page number is present in the TLB by comparing it to all the entries simultaneously (i.e., in parallel). If a valid match is found and the access does not violate the protection bits, the page frame is taken directly from the TLB, without going to the page table. If the virtual page number is present in the TLB but the instruction is trying to write on a read-only page, a protection fault is generated, the same way as it would be from the page table itself.

The interesting case is what happens when the virtual page number is not in the TLB. The MMU detects the miss and does an ordinary page table lookup. It then evicts one of the entries from the TLB and replaces it with the page table entry just looked up. Thus if that page is used again soon, the second time it will result in a hit rather than a miss. When an entry is purged from the TLB, the modified bit is copied back into the page table entry in memory. The other values are already there. When the TLB is loaded from the page table, all the fields are taken from memory.

Software TLB Management

Up until now, we have assumed that every machine with paged virtual memory has page tables recognized by the hardware, plus a TLB. In this design, TLB management and handling TLB faults are done entirely by the MMU hardware. Traps to the operating system occur only when a page is not in memory.

In the past, this assumption was true. However, many modern RISC machines, including the SPARC, MIPS, Alpha, and HP PA, do nearly all of this page management in software. On these machines, the TLB entries are explicitly loaded by the operating system. When a TLB miss occurs, instead of the MMU just going to the page tables to find and fetch the needed page reference, it just generates a TLB fault and tosses the problem into the lap of the operating system. The system must find the page, remove an entry from the TLB, enter the new one, and restart the instruction that faulted. And, of course, all of this must be done in a handful of instructions because TLB misses occur much more frequently than page faults.

Surprisingly enough, if the TLB is reasonably large (say, 64 entries) to reduce the miss rate, software management of the TLB turns out to be acceptably efficient. The main gain here is a much simpler MMU, which frees up a considerable amount of area on the CPU chip for caches and other features that can improve performance. Software TLB management is discussed by Uhlig et al. (1994).

Various strategies have been developed to improve performance on machines that do TLB management in software. One approach attacks both reducing TLB misses and reducing the cost of a TLB miss when it does occur (Bala et al., 1994). To reduce TLB misses, sometimes the operating system can use its intuition to figure out which pages are likely to be used next and to preload entries for them in the TLB. For example, when a client process sends a message to a server process on the same machine, it is very likely that the server will have to run soon. Knowing this, while processing the trap to do the send, the system can also check to see where the server's code, data, and stack pages are and map them in before they can cause TLB faults.

The normal way to process a TLB miss, whether in hardware or in software, is to go to the page table and perform the indexing operations to locate the page referenced. The problem with doing this search in software is that the pages holding the page table may not be in the TLB, which will cause additional TLB faults during the processing. These faults can be reduced by maintaining a large (e.g., 4-KB) software cache of TLB entries in a fixed location whose page is always kept in the TLB. By first checking the software cache, the operating system can substantially reduce TLB misses.

4.3.4 Inverted Page Tables

Traditional page tables of the type described so far require one entry per virtual page, since they are indexed by virtual page number. If the address space consists of 2^{32} bytes, with 4096 bytes per page, then over 1 million page table entries are needed. As a bare minimum, the page table will have to be at least 4 megabytes. On larger systems, this size is probably doable.

However, as 64-bit computers become more common, the situation changes drastically. If the address space is now 2^{64} bytes, with 4-KB pages, we need a page table with 2^{52} entries. If each entry is 8 bytes, the table is over 30 million gigabytes. Tying up 30 million gigabytes just for the page table is not doable, not now and not for years to come, if ever. Consequently, a different solution is needed for 64-bit paged virtual address spaces.

One such solution is the **inverted page table**. In this design, there is one entry per page frame in real memory, rather than one entry per page of virtual address space. For example, with 64-bit virtual addresses, a 4-KB page, and 256 MB of RAM, an inverted page table only requires 65,536 entries. The entry keeps track of which (process, virtual page) is located in the page frame.

Although inverted page tables save vast amounts of space, at least when the virtual address space is much larger than the physical memory, they have a serious downside: virtual-to-physical translation becomes much harder. When process n references virtual page p, the hardware can no longer find the physical page by using p as an index into the page table. Instead, it must search the entire inverted page table for an entry (n, p). Furthermore, this search must be done on every memory reference, not just on page faults. Searching a 64K table on every memory reference is not the way to make your machine blindingly fast.

The way out of this dilemma is to use the TLB. If the TLB can hold all of the heavily used pages, translation can happen just as fast as with regular page tables. On a TLB miss, however, the inverted page table has to be searched in software. One feasible way to accomplish this search is to have a hash table hashed on the virtual address. All the virtual pages currently in memory that have the same hash value are chained together, as shown in Fig. 4-15. If the hash table has as many slots as the machine has physical pages, the average chain will be only one entry long, greatly speeding up the mapping. Once the page frame number has been found, the new (virtual, physical) pair is entered into the TLB.

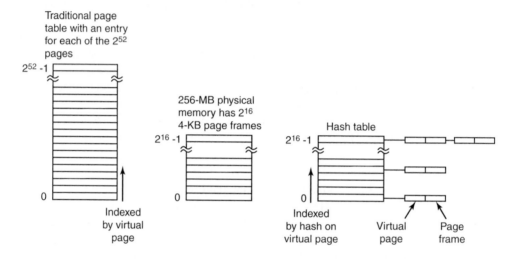

Figure 4-15. Comparison of a traditional page table with an inverted page table.

Inverted page tables are currently used on some IBM and Hewlett-Packard workstations and will become more common as 64-bit machines become widespread. Other approaches to handling large virtual memories can be found in (Huck and Hays, 1993; Talluri and Hill, 1994; and Talluri et al., 1995).

4.4 PAGE REPLACEMENT ALGORITHMS

When a page fault occurs, the operating system has to choose a page to remove from memory to make room for the page that has to be brought in. If the page to be removed has been modified while in memory, it must be rewritten to the disk to bring the disk copy up to date. If, however, the page has not been changed (e.g., it contains program text), the disk copy is already up to date, so no rewrite is needed. The page to be read in just overwrites the page being evicted.

While it would be possible to pick a random page to evict at each page fault, system performance is much better if a page that is not heavily used is chosen. If a heavily used page is removed, it will probably have to be brought back in quickly, resulting in extra overhead. Much work has been done on the subject of page replacement algorithms, both theoretical and experimental. Below we will describe some of the most important algorithms.

It is worth noting that the problem of "page replacement" occurs in other areas of computer design as well. For example, most computers have one or more memory caches consisting of recently used 32-byte or 64-byte memory blocks. When the cache is full, some block has to be chosen for removal. This problem is precisely the same as page replacement except on a shorter time scale (it has to be done in a few nanoseconds, not milliseconds as with page replacement). The reason for the shorter time scale is that cache block misses are satisfied from main memory, which has no seek time and no rotational latency.

A second example is in a Web server. The server can keep a certain number of heavily used Web pages in its memory cache. However, when the memory cache is full and a new page is referenced, a decision has to be made which Web page to evict. The considerations are similar to pages of virtual memory, except for the fact that the Web pages are never modified in the cache, so there is always a fresh copy on disk. In a virtual memory system, pages in main memory may be either clean or dirty.

4.4.1 The Optimal Page Replacement Algorithm

The best possible page replacement algorithm is easy to describe but impossible to implement. It goes like this. At the moment that a page fault occurs, some set of pages is in memory. One of these pages will be referenced on the very next instruction (the page containing that instruction). Other pages may not be referenced until 10, 100, or perhaps 1000 instructions later. Each page can be labeled with the number of instructions that will be executed before that page is first referenced.

The optimal page algorithm simply says that the page with the highest label should be removed. If one page will not be used for 8 million instructions and another page will not be used for 6 million instructions, removing the former pushes the page fault that will fetch it back as far into the future as possible. Computers, like people, try to put off unpleasant events for as long as they can.

The only problem with this algorithm is that it is unrealizable. At the time of the page fault, the operating system has no way of knowing when each of the pages will be referenced next. (We saw a similar situation earlier with the shortest job first scheduling algorithm—how can the system tell which job is shortest?) Still, by running a program on a simulator and keeping track of all page references, it is possible to implement optimal page replacement on the *second* run by using the page reference information collected during the *first* run.

In this way it is possible to compare the performance of realizable algorithms with the best possible one. If an operating system achieves a performance of, say, only 1 percent worse than the optimal algorithm, effort spent in looking for a better algorithm will yield at most a 1 percent improvement.

To avoid any possible confusion, it should be made clear that this log of page references refers only to the one program just measured and then with only one specific input. The page replacement algorithm derived from it is thus specific to that one program and input data. Although this method is useful for evaluating page replacement algorithms, it is of no use in practical systems. Below we will study algorithms that *are* useful on real systems.

4.4.2 The Not Recently Used Page Replacement Algorithm

In order to allow the operating system to collect useful statistics about which pages are being used and which ones are not, most computers with virtual memory have two status bits associated with each page. R is set whenever the page is referenced (read or written). M is set when the page is written to (i.e., modified). The bits are contained in each page table entry, as shown in Fig. 4-13. It is important to realize that these bits must be updated on every memory reference, so it is essential that they be set by the hardware. Once a bit has been set to 1, it stays 1 until the operating system resets it to 0 in software.

If the hardware does not have these bits, they can be simulated as follows. When a process is started up, all of its page table entries are marked as not in memory. As soon as any page is referenced, a page fault will occur. The operating system then sets the R bit (in its internal tables), changes the page table entry to point to the correct page, with mode READ ONLY, and restarts the instruction. If the page is subsequently written on, another page fault will occur, allowing the operating system to set the M bit and change the page's mode to READ/WRITE.

The R and M bits can be used to build a simple paging algorithm as follows. When a process is started up, both page bits for all its pages are set to 0 by the operating system. Periodically (e.g., on each clock interrupt), the R bit is cleared, to distinguish pages that have not been referenced recently from those that have been.

When a page fault occurs, the operating system inspects all the pages and divides them into four categories based on the current values of their R and M bits:

    Class 0: not referenced, not modified.
    Class 1: not referenced, modified.
    Class 2: referenced, not modified.
    Class 3: referenced, modified.

Although class 1 pages seem, at first glance, impossible, they occur when a class 3 page has its R bit cleared by a clock interrupt. Clock interrupts do not clear the M bit because this information is needed to know whether the page has to be rewritten to disk or not. Clearing R but not M leads to a class 1 page.

The **NRU** (**Not Recently Used**) algorithm removes a page at random from the lowest numbered nonempty class. Implicit in this algorithm is that it is better to remove a modified page that has not been referenced in at least one clock tick (typically 20 msec) than a clean page that is in heavy use. The main attraction of NRU is that it is easy to understand, moderately efficient to implement, and gives a performance that, while certainly not optimal, may be adequate.

4.4.3 The First-In, First-Out (FIFO) Page Replacement Algorithm

Another low-overhead paging algorithm is the **FIFO** (**First-In, First-Out**) algorithm. To illustrate how this works, consider a supermarket that has enough shelves to display exactly k different products. One day, some company introduces a new convenience food—instant, freeze-dried, organic yogurt that can be reconstituted in a microwave oven. It is an immediate success, so our finite supermarket has to get rid of one old product in order to stock it.

One possibility is to find the product that the supermarket has been stocking the longest (i.e., something it began selling 120 years ago) and get rid of it on the grounds that no one is interested any more. In effect, the supermarket maintains a linked list of all the products it currently sells in the order they were introduced. The new one goes on the back of the list; the one at the front of the list is dropped.

As a page replacement algorithm, the same idea is applicable. The operating system maintains a list of all pages currently in memory, with the page at the head of the list the oldest one and the page at the tail the most recent arrival. On a page fault, the page at the head is removed and the new page added to the tail of the list. When applied to stores, FIFO might remove mustache wax, but it might also remove flour, salt, or butter. When applied to computers the same problem arises. For this reason, FIFO in its pure form is rarely used.

4.4.4 The Second Chance Page Replacement Algorithm

A simple modification to FIFO that avoids the problem of throwing out a heavily used page is to inspect the R bit of the oldest page. If it is 0, the page is both old and unused, so it is replaced immediately. If the R bit is 1, the bit is cleared, the page is put onto the end of the list of pages, and its load time is updated as though it had just arrived in memory. Then the search continues.

The operation of this algorithm, called **second chance**, is shown in Fig. 4-16. In Fig. 4-16(a) we see pages A through H kept on a linked list and sorted by the time they arrived in memory.

Suppose that a page fault occurs at time 20. The oldest page is A, which arrived at time 0, when the process started. If A has the R bit cleared, it is evicted from memory, either by being written to the disk (if it is dirty), or just abandoned (if it is clean). On the other hand, if the R bit is set, A is put onto the end of the

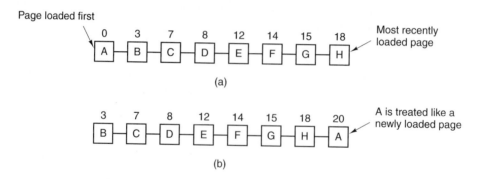

Figure 4-16. Operation of second chance. (a) Pages sorted in FIFO order. (b) Page list if a page fault occurs at time 20 and *A* has its *R* bit set. The numbers above the pages are their loading times.

list and its "load time" is reset to the current time (20). The *R* bit is also cleared. The search for a suitable page continues with *B*.

What second chance is doing is looking for an old page that has not been referenced in the previous clock interval. If all the pages have been referenced, second chance degenerates into pure FIFO. Specifically, imagine that all the pages in Fig. 4-16(a) have their *R* bits set. One by one, the operating system moves the pages to the end of the list, clearing the *R* bit each time it appends a page to the end of the list. Eventually, it comes back to page *A*, which now has its *R* bit cleared. At this point *A* is evicted. Thus the algorithm always terminates.

4.4.5 The Clock Page Replacement Algorithm

Although second chance is a reasonable algorithm, it is unnecessarily inefficient because it is constantly moving pages around on its list. A better approach is to keep all the page frames on a circular list in the form of a clock, as shown in Fig. 4-17. A hand points to the oldest page.

When a page fault occurs, the page being pointed to by the hand is inspected. If its *R* bit is 0, the page is evicted, the new page is inserted into the clock in its place, and the hand is advanced one position. If *R* is 1, it is cleared and the hand is advanced to the next page. This process is repeated until a page is found with $R = 0$. Not surprisingly, this algorithm is called **clock**. It differs from second chance only in the implementation.

4.4.6 The Least Recently Used (LRU) Page Replacement Algorithm

A good approximation to the optimal algorithm is based on the observation that pages that have been heavily used in the last few instructions will probably be heavily used again in the next few. Conversely, pages that have not been used for ages will probably remain unused for a long time. This idea suggests a realizable

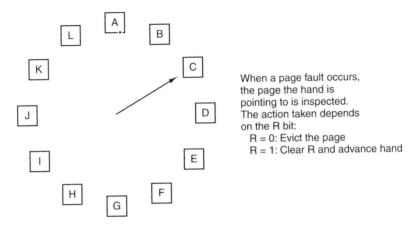

When a page fault occurs,
the page the hand is
pointing to is inspected.
The action taken depends
on the R bit:
  R = 0: Evict the page
  R = 1: Clear R and advance hand

Figure 4-17. The clock page replacement algorithm.

algorithm: when a page fault occurs, throw out the page that has been unused for the longest time. This strategy is called **LRU (Least Recently Used)** paging.

Although LRU is theoretically realizable, it is not cheap. To fully implement LRU, it is necessary to maintain a linked list of all pages in memory, with the most recently used page at the front and the least recently used page at the rear. The difficulty is that the list must be updated on every memory reference. Finding a page in the list, deleting it, and then moving it to the front is a very time consuming operation, even in hardware (assuming that such hardware could be built).

However, there are other ways to implement LRU with special hardware. Let us consider the simplest way first. This method requires equipping the hardware with a 64-bit counter, C, that is automatically incremented after each instruction. Furthermore, each page table entry must also have a field large enough to contain the counter. After each memory reference, the current value of C is stored in the page table entry for the page just referenced. When a page fault occurs, the operating system examines all the counters in the page table to find the lowest one. That page is the least recently used.

Now let us look at a second hardware LRU algorithm. For a machine with n page frames, the LRU hardware can maintain a matrix of $n \times n$ bits, initially all zero. Whenever page frame k is referenced, the hardware first sets all the bits of row k to 1, then sets all the bits of column k to 0. At any instant, the row whose binary value is lowest is the least recently used, the row whose value is next lowest is next least recently used, and so forth. The workings of this algorithm are given in Fig. 4-18 for four page frames and page references in the order

0 1 2 3 2 1 0 3 2 3

After page 0 is referenced, we have the situation of Fig. 4-18(a). After page 1 is reference, we have the situation of Fig. 4-18(b), and so forth.

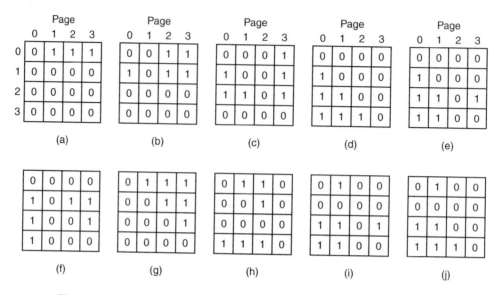

Figure 4-18. LRU using a matrix when pages are referenced in the order 0, 1, 2, 3, 2, 1, 0, 3, 2, 3.

4.4.7 Simulating LRU in Software

Although both of the previous LRU algorithms are realizable in principle, few, if any, machines have this hardware, so they are of little use to the operating system designer who is making a system for a machine that does not have this hardware. Instead, a solution that can be implemented in software is needed. One possibility is called the **NFU** (**Not Frequently Used**) algorithm. It requires a software counter associated with each page, initially zero. At each clock interrupt, the operating system scans all the pages in memory. For each page, the R bit, which is 0 or 1, is added to the counter. In effect, the counters are an attempt to keep track of how often each page has been referenced. When a page fault occurs, the page with the lowest counter is chosen for replacement.

The main problem with NFU is that it never forgets anything. For example, in a multipass compiler, pages that were heavily used during pass 1 may still have a high count well into later passes. In fact, if pass 1 happens to have the longest execution time of all the passes, the pages containing the code for subsequent passes may always have lower counts than the pass 1 pages. Consequently, the operating system will remove useful pages instead of pages no longer in use.

Fortunately, a small modification to NFU makes it able to simulate LRU quite well. The modification has two parts. First, the counters are each shifted right 1 bit before the R bit is added in. Second, the R bit is added to the leftmost, rather than the rightmost bit.

Figure 4-19 illustrates how the modified algorithm, known as **aging**, works. Suppose that after the first clock tick the R bits for pages 0 to 5 have the values 1,

0, 1, 0, 1, and 1, respectively (page 0 is 1, page 1 is 0, page 2 is 1, etc.). In other words, between tick 0 and tick 1, pages 0, 2, 4, and 5 were referenced, setting their R bits to 1, while the other ones remain 0. After the six corresponding counters have been shifted and the R bit inserted at the left, they have the values shown in Fig. 4-19(a). The four remaining columns show the six counters after the next four clock ticks.

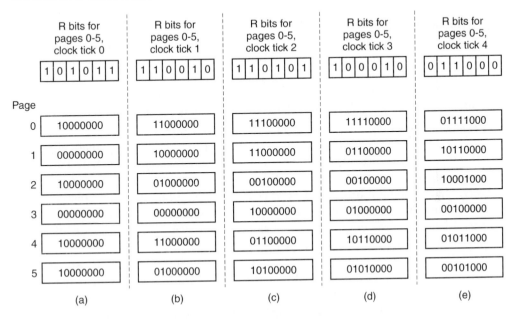

Figure 4-19. The aging algorithm simulates LRU in software. Shown are six pages for five clock ticks. The five clock ticks are represented by (a) to (e).

When a page fault occurs, the page whose counter is the lowest is removed. It is clear that a page that has not been referenced for, say, four clock ticks will have four leading zeros in its counter and thus will have a lower value than a counter that has not been referenced for three clock ticks.

This algorithm differs from LRU in two ways. Consider pages 3 and 5 in Fig. 4-19(e). Neither has been referenced for two clock ticks; both were referenced in the tick prior to that. According to LRU, if a page must be replaced, we should choose one of these two. The trouble is, we do not know which of these two was referenced last in the interval between tick 1 and tick 2. By recording only one bit per time interval, we have lost the ability to distinguish references early in the clock interval from those occurring later. All we can do is remove page 3, because page 5 was also referenced two ticks earlier and page 3 was not.

The second difference between LRU and aging is that in aging the counters have a finite number of bits, 8 bits in this example. Suppose that two pages each have a counter value of 0. All we can do is pick one of them at random. In reality, it may well be that one of the pages was last referenced 9 ticks ago and the other was last referenced 1000 ticks ago. We have no way of seeing that. In practice, however, 8 bits is generally enough if a clock tick is around 20 msec. If a page has not been referenced in 160 msec, it probably is not that important.

4.4.8 The Working Set Page Replacement Algorithm

In the purest form of paging, processes are started up with none of their pages in memory. As soon as the CPU tries to fetch the first instruction, it gets a page fault, causing the operating system to bring in the page containing the first instruction. Other page faults for global variables and the stack usually follow quickly. After a while, the process has most of the pages it needs and settles down to run with relatively few page faults. This strategy is called **demand paging** because pages are loaded only on demand, not in advance.

Of course, it is easy enough to write a test program that systematically reads all the pages in a large address space, causing so many page faults that there is not enough memory to hold them all. Fortunately, most processes do not work this way. They exhibit a **locality of reference**, meaning that during any phase of execution, the process references only a relatively small fraction of its pages. Each pass of a multipass compiler, for example, references only a fraction of all the pages, and a different fraction at that.

The set of pages that a process is currently using is called its **working set** (Denning, 1968a; Denning, 1980). If the entire working set is in memory, the process will run without causing many faults until it moves into another execution phase (e.g., the next pass of the compiler). If the available memory is too small to hold the entire working set, the process will cause many page faults and run slowly since executing an instruction takes a few nanoseconds and reading in a page from the disk typically takes 10 milliseconds. At a rate of one or two instructions per 10 milliseconds, it will take ages to finish. A program causing page faults every few instructions is said to be **thrashing** (Denning, 1968b).

In a multiprogramming system, processes are frequently moved to disk (i.e., all their pages are removed from memory) to let other processes have a turn at the CPU. The question arises of what to do when a process is brought back in again. Technically, nothing need be done. The process will just cause page faults until its working set has been loaded. The problem is that having 20, 100, or even 1000 page faults every time a process is loaded is slow, and it also wastes considerable CPU time, since it takes the operating system a few milliseconds of CPU time to process a page fault.

Therefore, many paging systems try to keep track of each process' working set and make sure that it is in memory before letting the process run. This approach is called the **working set model** (Denning, 1970). It is designed to greatly reduce the page fault rate. Loading the pages *before* letting processes run is also called **prepaging.** Note that the working set changes over time.

It has been long known that most programs do not reference their address space uniformly, but that the references tend to cluster on a small number of pages. A memory reference may fetch an instruction, it may fetch data, or it may store data. At any instant of time, t, there exists a set consisting of all the pages used by the k most recent memory references. This set, $w(k, t)$, is the working set. Because the $k = 1$ most recent references must have used all the pages used by the $k > 1$ most recent references, and possibly others, $w(k, t)$ is a monotonically nondecreasing function of k. The limit of $w(k, t)$ as k becomes large is finite because a program cannot reference more pages than its address space contains, and few programs will use every single page. Figure 4-20 depicts the size of the working set as a function of k.

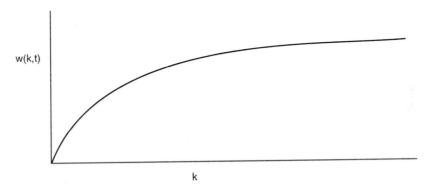

Figure 4-20. The working set is the set of pages used by the k most recent memory references. The function $w(k, t)$ is the size of the working set at time t.

The fact that most programs randomly access a small number of pages, but that this set changes slowly in time explains the initial rapid rise of the curve and then the slow rise for large k. For example, a program that is executing a loop occupying two pages using data on four pages, may reference all six pages every 1000 instructions, but the most recent reference to some other page may be a million instructions earlier, during the initialization phase. Due to this asymptotic behavior, the contents of the working set is not sensitive to the value of k chosen. To put it differently, there exists a wide range of k values for which the working set is unchanged. Because the working set varies slowly with time, it is possible to make a reasonable guess as to which pages will be needed when the program is restarted on the basis of its working set when it was last stopped. Prepaging consists of loading these pages before the process is allowed to run again.

To implement the working set model, it is necessary for the operating system to keep track of which pages are in the working set. Having this information also immediately leads to a possible page replacement algorithm: when a page fault occurs, find a page not in the working set and evict it. To implement such an algorithm, we need a precise way of determining which pages are in the working set and which are not at any given moment in time.

As we mentioned above, the working set is the set of pages used in the k most recent memory references (some authors use the k most recent page references, but the choice is arbitrary). To implement any working set algorithm, some value of k must be chosen in advance. Once some value has been selected, after every memory reference, the set of pages used by the previous k memory references is uniquely determined.

Of course, having an operational definition of the working set does not mean that there is an efficient way to monitor it in real time, during program execution. One could imagine a shift register of length k, with every memory reference shifting the register left one position and inserting the most recently referenced page number on the right. The set of all k page numbers in the shift register would be the working set. In theory, at a page fault, the contents of the shift register could be read out and sorted. Duplicate pages could then be removed. The result would be the working set. However, maintaining the shift register and processing it at a page fault would both be prohibitively expensive, so this technique is never used.

Instead, various approximations are used. One commonly used approximation is to drop the idea of counting back k memory references and use execution time instead. For example, instead of defining the working set as those pages used during the previous 10 million memory references, we can define it as the set of pages used during the past 100 msec of execution time. In practice, such a definition is just as good and much easier to use. Note that for each process, only its own execution time counts. Thus if a process starts running at time T and has had 40 msec of CPU time at real time $T + 100$ msec, for working set purposes, its time is 40 msec. The amount of CPU time a process has actually used has since it started is often called its **current virtual time**. With this approximation, the working set of a process is the set of pages it has referenced during the past τ seconds of virtual time.

Now let us look at a page replacement algorithm based on the working set. The basic idea is to find a page that is not in the working set and evict it. In Fig. 4-21 we see a portion of a page table for some machine. Because only pages that are in memory are considered as candidates for eviction, pages that are absent from memory are ignored by this algorithm. Each entry contains (at least) two items of information: the approximate time the page was last used and the R (Referenced) bit. The empty white rectangle symbolizes the other fields not needed for this algorithm, such as the page frame number, the protection bits, and the M (Modified) bit.

The algorithm works as follows. The hardware is assumed to set the R and M bits, as we have discussed before. Similarly, a periodic clock interrupt is assumed to cause software to run that clears the *Referenced* bit on every clock tick. On every page fault, the page table is scanned to look for a suitable page to evict.

As each entry is processed, the R bit is examined. If it is 1, the current virtual time is written into the *Time of last use* field in the page table, indicating that the page was in use at the time the fault occurred. Since the page has been referenced

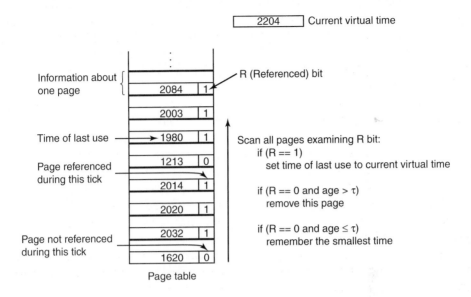

Figure 4-21. The working set algorithm.

during the current clock tick, it is clearly in the working set and is not a candidate for removal (τ is assumed to span multiple clock ticks).

If R is 0, the page has not been referenced during the current clock tick and may be a candidate for removal. To see whether or not it should be removed, its age, that is, the current virtual time minus its *Time of last use* is computed and compared to τ. If the age is greater than τ, the page is no longer in the working set. It is reclaimed and the new page loaded here. The scan continues updating the remaining entries, however.

However, if R is 0 but the age is less than or equal to τ, the page is still in the working set. The page is temporarily spared, but the page with the greatest age (smallest value of *Time of last use*) is noted. If the entire table is scanned without finding a candidate to evict, that means that all pages are in the working set. In that case, if one or more pages with $R = 0$ were found, the one with the greatest age is evicted. In the worst case, all pages have been referenced during the current clock tick (and thus all have $R = 1$), so one is chosen at random for removal, preferably a clean page, if one exists.

4.4.9 The WSClock Page Replacement Algorithm

The basic working set algorithm is cumbersome since the entire page table has to be scanned at each page fault until a suitable candidate is located. An improved algorithm, that is based on the clock algorithm but also uses the working set information is called **WSClock** (Carr and Hennessey, 1981). Due to its simplicity of implementation and good performance, it is widely used in practice.

The data structure needed is a circular list of page frames, as in the clock algorithm, and as shown in Fig. 4-22(a). Initially, this list is empty. When the first page is loaded, it is added to the list. As more pages are added, they go into the list to form a ring. Each entry contains the *Time of last use* field from the basic working set algorithm, as well as the *R* bit (shown) and the *M* bit (not shown).

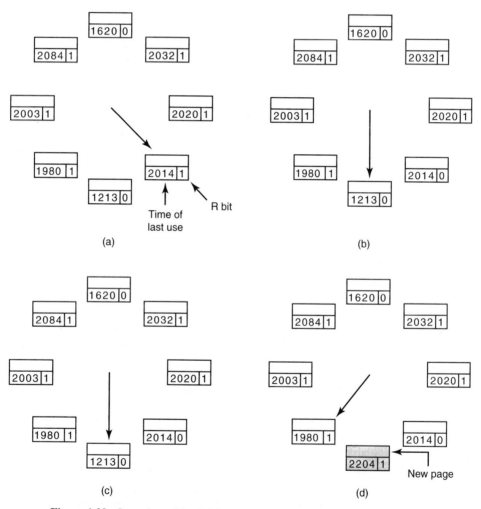

Figure 4-22. Operation of the WSClock algorithm. (a) and (b) give an example of what happens when $R = 1$. (c) and (d) give an example of $R = 0$.

As with the clock algorithm, at each page fault the page pointed to by the hand is examined first. If the *R* bit is set to 1, the page has been used during the current tick so it is not an ideal candidate to remove. The R bit is then set to 0, the hand advanced to the next page, and the algorithm repeated for that page. The state after this sequence of events is shown in Fig. 4-22(b).

Now consider what happens if the page pointed to has $R = 0$, as shown in Fig. 4-22(c). If the age is greater than τ and the page is clean, it is not in the working set and a valid copy exists on the disk. The page frame is simply claimed and the new page put there, as shown in Fig. 4-22(d). On the other hand, if the page is dirty, it cannot be claimed immediately since no valid copy is present on disk. To avoid a process switch, the write to disk is scheduled, but the hand is advanced and the algorithm continues with the next page. After all, there might be an old, clean page further down the line that can be used immediately.

In principle, all pages might be scheduled for disk I/O on one cycle around the clock. To reduce disk traffic, a limit might be set, allowing a maximum of n pages to be written back. Once this limit has been reached, no new writes are scheduled.

What happens if the hand comes all the way around to its starting point? There are two cases to distinguish:

1. At least one write has been scheduled.

2. No writes have been scheduled.

In the former case, the hand just keeps moving, looking for a clean page. Since one or more writes have been scheduled, eventually some write will complete and its page will be marked as clean. The first clean page encountered is evicted. This page is not necessarily the first write scheduled because the disk driver may reorder writes in order to optimize disk performance.

In the latter case, all pages are in the working set, otherwise at least one write would have been scheduled. Lacking additional information, the simplest thing to do is claim any clean page and use it. The location of a clean page could be kept track of during the sweep. If no clean pages exist, then the current page is chosen and written back to disk.

4.4.10 Summary of Page Replacement Algorithms

We have now looked at a variety of page replacement algorithms. In this section we will briefly summarize them. The list of algorithms discussed is given in Fig. 4-23.

The optimal algorithm replaces the page referenced last among the current pages. Unfortunately, there is no way to determine which page will be last, so in practice this algorithm cannot be used. It is useful as a benchmark against which other algorithms can be measured, however.

The NRU algorithm divides pages into four classes depending on the state of the R and M bits. A random page from the lowest numbered class is chosen. This algorithm is easy to implement, but it is very crude. Better ones exist.

Algorithm	Comment
Optimal	Not implementable, but useful as a benchmark
NRU (Not Recently Used)	Very crude
FIFO (First-In, First-Out)	Might throw out important pages
Second chance	Big improvement over FIFO
Clock	Realistic
LRU (Least Recently Used)	Excellent, but difficult to implement exactly
NFU (Not Frequently Used)	Fairly crude approximation to LRU
Aging	Efficient algorithm that approximates LRU well
Working set	Somewhat expensive to implement
WSClock	Good efficient algorithm

Figure 4-23. Page replacement algorithms discussed in the text.

FIFO keeps track of the order pages were loaded into memory by keeping them in a linked list. Removing the oldest page then becomes trivial, but that page might still be in use, so FIFO is a bad choice.

Second chance is a modification to FIFO that checks if a page is in use before removing it. If it is, the page is spared. This modification greatly improves the performance. Clock is simply a different implementation of second chance. It has the same performance properties, but takes a little less time to execute the algorithm.

LRU is an excellent algorithm, but it cannot be implemented without special hardware. If this hardware is not available, it cannot be used. NFU is a crude attempt to approximate LRU. It is not very good. However, aging is a much better approximation to LRU and can be implemented efficiently. It is a good choice.

The last two algorithms use the working set. The working set algorithm is reasonable performance, but it is somewhat expensive to implement. WSClock is a variant that not only gives good performance but is also efficient to implement.

All in all, the two best algorithms are aging and WSClock. They are based on LRU and the working set, respectively. Both give good paging performance and can be implemented efficiently. A few other algorithms exist, but these two are probably the most important in practice.

4.5 MODELING PAGE REPLACEMENT ALGORITHMS

Over the years, some work has been done on modeling page replacement algorithms from a theoretical perspective. In this section we will discuss some of these ideas, just to see how the modeling process works.

4.5.1 Belady's Anomaly

Intuitively, it might seem that the more page frames the memory has, the fewer page faults a program will get. Surprisingly enough, this is not always the case. Belady et al. (1969) discovered a counterexample, in which FIFO caused more page faults with four page frames than with three. This strange situation has become known as **Belady's anomaly**. It is illustrated in Fig. 4-24 for a program with five virtual pages, numbered from 0 to 4. The pages are referenced in the order

    0 1 2 3 0 1 4 0 1 2 3 4

In Fig. 4-24(a) we see how with three page frames a total of nine page faults are caused. In Fig. 4-24(b) we get ten page faults with four page frames.

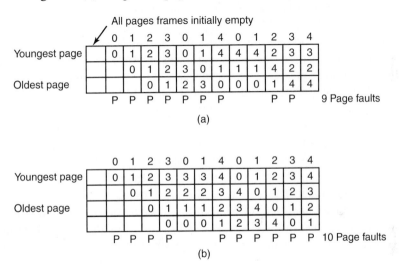

Figure 4-24. Belady's anomaly. (a) FIFO with three page frames. (b) FIFO with four page frames. The *P*'s show which page references cause page faults.

4.5.2 Stack Algorithms

Many researchers in computer science were dumbfounded by Belady's anomaly and began investigating it. This work led to the development of a whole theory of paging algorithms and their properties. While most of this work is beyond the scope of this book, we will give a brief introduction below. For more details see (Maekawa et al., 1987).

All of this work begins with the observation that every process generates a sequence of memory references as it runs. Each memory reference corresponds to a specific virtual page. Thus conceptually, a process' memory access can be characterized by an (ordered) list of page numbers. This list is called the **reference string**, and plays a central role in the theory. For simplicity, in the rest of this section we will consider only the case of a machine with one process, so each machine has a single, deterministic reference string (with multiple processes, we would have to take into account the interleaving of their reference strings due to the multiprogramming).

A paging system can be characterized by three items:

1. The reference string of the executing process.

2. The page replacement algorithm.

3. The number of page frames available in memory, m.

Conceptually, we can imagine an abstract interpreter that works as follows. It maintains an internal array, M, that keeps track of the state of memory. It has as many elements as the process has virtual pages, which we will call n. The array M is divided into two parts. The top part, with m entries, contains all the pages that are currently in memory. The bottom part, with $n - m$ pages, contains all the pages that have been referenced once but have been paged out and are not currently in memory. Initially, M is the empty set, since no pages have been referenced and no pages are in memory.

As execution begins, the process begins emitting the pages in the reference string, one at a time. As each one comes out, the interpreter checks to see if the page is in memory (i.e., in the top part of M). If it is not, a page fault occurs. If there is an empty slot in memory (i.e., the top part of M contains fewer than m entries), the page is loaded and entered in the top part of M. This situation arises only at the start of execution. If memory is full (i.e., the top part of M contains m entries), the page replacement algorithm is invoked to remove a page from memory. In the model, what happens is that one page is moved from the top part of M to the bottom part, and the needed page entered into the top part. In addition, the top part and the bottom part may be separately rearranged.

To make the operation of the interpreter clearer, let us look at a concrete example using LRU page replacement. The virtual address space has eight pages and the physical memory has four page frames. At the top of Fig. 4-25 we have a reference string consisting of the 24 pages:

0 2 1 3 5 4 6 3 7 4 7 3 3 5 5 3 1 1 1 7 2 3 4 1

Under the reference string, we have 25 columns of 8 items each. The first column, which is empty, reflects the state of M before execution begins. Each successive column shows M after one page has been emitted by the reference and processed by the paging algorithm. The heavy outline denotes the top of M, that is, the first four slots, which correspond to page frames in memory. Pages inside the heavy box are in memory, and pages below it have been paged out to disk.

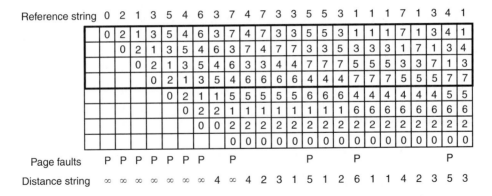

Figure 4-25. The state of the memory array, M, after each item in the reference string is processed. The distance string will be discussed in the next section.

The first page in the reference string is 0, so it is entered in the top of memory, as shown in the second column. The second page is 2, so it is entered at the top of the third column. This action causes 0 to move down. In this example, a newly loaded page is always entered at the top, and everything else moved down, as needed.

Each of the first seven pages in the reference string causes a page fault. The first four can be handled without removing a page, but starting with the reference to page 5, loading a new page requires removing an old page.

The second reference to page 3 does not cause a page fault, because 3 is already in memory. Nevertheless, the interpreter removes it from where it was and puts it on the top, as shown. The process continues for a while, until page 5 is referenced. This page is moved from bottom part of M to the top part (i.e., it is loaded into memory from disk). Whenever a page is referenced that is not within the heavy box, a page fault occurs, as indicated by the P's below the matrix.

Let us now briefly summarize some of the properties of this model. First, when a page is referenced, it is always moved to the top entry in M. Second, if the page referenced was already in M, all pages above it move down one position. A transition from within the box to outside of it corresponds to a page being evicted from memory. Third, pages that were below the referenced page are not moved. In this manner, the contents of M exactly represent the contents of the LRU algorithm.

Although this example uses LRU, the model works equally well with other algorithms. In particular, there is one class of algorithms that is especially interesting: algorithms that have the property

$$M(m, r) \subseteq M(m + 1, r)$$

where m varies over the page frames and r is an index into the reference string. What this says is that the set of pages included in the top part of M for a memory with m page frames after r memory references are also included in M for a memory with $m + 1$ page frames. In other words, if we increase memory size by one page frame and re-execute the process, at every point during the execution, all the pages that were present in the first run are also present in the second run, along with one additional page.

From examination of Fig. 4-25 and a little thought about how it works, it should be clear that LRU has this property. Some other algorithms (e.g., optimal page replacement) also have it, but FIFO does not. Algorithms that have this property are called **stack algorithms**. These algorithms do not suffer from Belady's anomaly and are thus much loved by virtual memory theorists.

4.5.3 The Distance String

For stack algorithms, it is often convenient to represent the reference string in a more abstract way than the actual page numbers. A page reference will be henceforth denoted by the distance from the top of the stack where the referenced page was located. For example, the reference to page 1 in the last column of Fig. 4-25 is a reference to a page at a distance 3 from the top of the stack (because page 1 was in third place *before* the reference). Pages that have not yet been referenced and thus are not yet on the stack (i.e., not yet in M) are said to be at a distance ∞. The distance string for Fig. 4-25 is given at the bottom of the figure.

Note that the distance string depends not only on the reference string, but also on the paging algorithm. With the same original reference string, a different paging algorithm would make different choices about which pages to evict. As a result, a different sequence of stacks arises.

The statistical properties of the distance string have a big impact on the performance of the algorithm. In Fig. 4-26(a) we see the probability density function for the entries in a (ficticious) distance string, d. Most of the entries in the string are between 1 and k. With a memory of k page frames, few page faults occur.

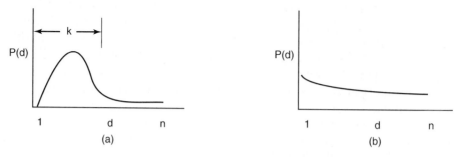

Figure 4-26. Probability density functions for two hypothetical distance strings.

In contrast, in Fig. 4-26(b), the references are so spread out that the only way to avoid a large number of page faults is to give the program as many page frames as it has virtual pages. Having a program like this is just bad luck.

4.5.4 Predicting Page Fault Rates

One of the nice properties of the distance string is that it can be used to predict the number of page faults that will occur with memories of different sizes. We will demonstrate how this computation can be made based on the example of Fig. 4-25. The goal is to make one pass over the distance string and, from the information collected, to be able to predict how many page faults the process would have in memories with 1, 2, 3, ..., n page frames, where n is the number of virtual pages in the process' address space.

The algorithm starts by scanning the distance string, page by page. It keeps track of the number of times 1 occurs, the number of times 2 occurs, and so on. Let C_i be the number of occurrences of i. For the distance string of Fig. 4-25, the C vector is illustrated in Fig. 4-27(a). In this example, it happens four times that the page referenced is already on top of the stack. Three times the reference is to the next-to-the-top page, and so forth. Let C_∞ be the number of times ∞ occurs in the distance string.

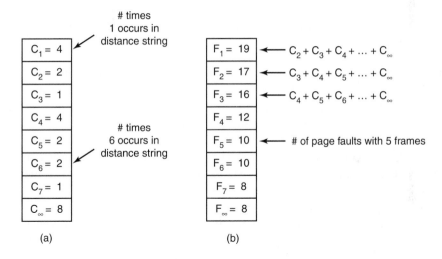

Figure 4-27. Computation of the page fault rate from the distance string. (a) The C vector. (b) F vector.

Now compute the F vector according to the formula

$$F_m = \sum_{k=m+1}^{n} C_k + C_\infty$$

The value of F_m is the number of page faults that will occur with the given distance string and m page frames. For the distance string of Fig. 4-25, Fig. 4-27(b) gives the F vector. For example, F_1 is 20, meaning that with a memory holding only 1 page frame, out of the 24 references in the string, all get page faults except the four that are the same as the previous page reference.

To see why this formula works, go back to the heavy box in Fig. 4-25. Let m be the number of page frames in the top part of M. A page fault occurs any time an element of the distance string is $m + 1$ or more. The summation in the formula above adds up the number of times such elements occur. This model can be used to make other predictions as well (Maekawa et al., 1987).

4.6 DESIGN ISSUES FOR PAGING SYSTEMS

In the previous sections we have explained how paging works and have given a few of the basic page replacement algorithms and shown how to model them. But knowing the bare mechanics is not enough. To design a system, you have to know a lot more to make it work well. It is like the difference between knowing how to move the rook, knight, bishop, and other pieces in chess, and being a good player. In the following sections, we will look at other issues that operating system designers must consider carefully in order to get good performance from a paging system.

4.6.1 Local versus Global Allocation Policies

In the preceding sections we have discussed several algorithms for choosing a page to replace when a fault occurs. A major issue associated with this choice (which we have carefully swept under the rug until now) is how memory should be allocated among the competing runnable processes.

Take a look at Fig. 4-28(a). In this figure, three processes, A, B, and C, make up the set of runnable processes. Suppose A gets a page fault. Should the page replacement algorithm try to find the least recently used page considering only the six pages currently allocated to A, or should it consider all the pages in memory? If it looks only at A's pages, the page with the lowest age value is $A5$, so we get the situation of Fig. 4-28(b).

On the other hand, if the page with the lowest age value is removed without regard to whose page it is, page $B3$ will be chosen and we will get the situation of Fig. 4-28(c). The algorithm of Fig. 4-28(b) is said to be a **local** page replacement algorithm, whereas that of Fig. 4-28(c) is said to be a **global** algorithm. Local algorithms effectively correspond to allocating every process a fixed fraction of the memory. Global algorithms dynamically allocate page frames among the runnable processes. Thus the number of page frames assigned to each process varies in time.

In general, global algorithms work better, especially when the working set size can vary over the lifetime of a process. If a local algorithm is used and the working set grows, thrashing will result, even if there are plenty of free page frames. If the working set shrinks, local algorithms waste memory. If a global algorithm is used, the system must continually decide how many page frames to assign to each process. One way is to monitor the working set size as indicated by

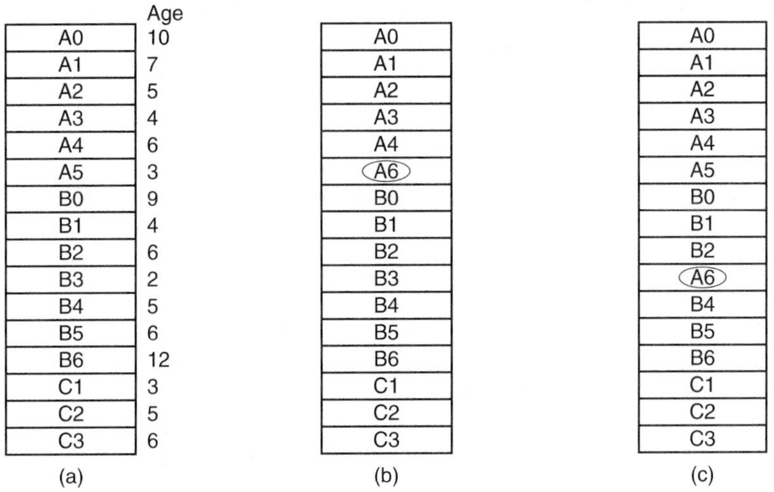

	Age
A0	10
A1	7
A2	5
A3	4
A4	6
A5	3
B0	9
B1	4
B2	6
B3	2
B4	5
B5	6
B6	12
C1	3
C2	5
C3	6

A0
A1
A2
A3
A4
(A6)
B0
B1
B2
B3
B4
B5
B6
C1
C2
C3

A0
A1
A2
A3
A4
A5
B0
B1
B2
(A6)
B4
B5
B6
C1
C2
C3

(a)   (b)   (c)

Figure 4-28. Local versus global page replacement. (a) Original configuration. (b) Local page replacement. (c) Global page replacement.

the aging bits, but this approach does not necessarily prevent thrashing. The working set may change size in microseconds, whereas the aging bits are a crude measure spread over a number of clock ticks.

Another approach is to have an algorithm for allocating page frames to processes. One way is to periodically determine the number of running processes and allocate each process an equal share. Thus with 12,416 available (i.e., non-operating system) page frames and 10 processes, each process gets 1241 frames. The remaining 6 go into a pool to be used when page faults occur.

Although this method seems fair, it makes little sense to give equal shares of the memory to a 10-KB process and a 300-KB process. Instead, pages can be allocated in proportion to each process' total size, with a 300-KB process getting 30 times the allotment of a 10-KB process. It is probably wise to give each process some minimum number, so it can run, no matter how small it is. On some machines, for example, a single two-operand instruction may need as many as six pages because the instruction itself, the source operand, and the destination operand may all straddle page boundaries. With an allocation of only five pages, programs containing such instructions cannot execute at all.

If a global algorithm is used, it may be possible to start each process up with some number of pages proportional to the process' size, but the allocation has to be updated dynamically as the processes run. One way to manage the allocation is to use the **PFF** (**Page Fault Frequency**) algorithm. It tells when to increase or decrease a process' page allocation but says nothing about which page to replace on a fault. It just controls the size of the allocation set.

For a large class of page replacement algorithms, including LRU, it is known that the fault rate decreases as more pages are assigned, as we discussed above. This is the assumption behind PFF. This property is illustrated in Fig. 4-29.

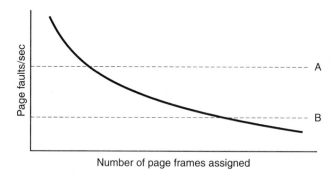

Figure 4-29. Page fault rate as a function of the number of page frames assigned.

Measuring the page fault rate is straightforward: just count the number of faults per second, possibly taking a running mean over past seconds as well. One easy way to do this is to add the present second's value to the current running mean and divide by two. The dashed line marked *A* corresponds to a page fault rate that is unacceptably high, so the faulting process is given more page frames to reduce the fault rate. The dashed line marked *B* corresponds to a page fault rate so low that it can be concluded that the process has too much memory. In this case page frames may be taken away from it. Thus, PFF tries to keep the paging rate for each process within acceptable bounds.

It is important to note that some page replacement algorithms can work with either a local replacement policy or a global one. For example, FIFO can replace the oldest page in all of memory (global algorithm) or the oldest page owned by the current process (local algorithm). Similarly, LRU or some approximation to it can replace the least recently page in all of memory (global algorithm) or the least recently used page owned by the current process (local algorithm). The choice of local versus global is independent of the algorithm in some cases.

On the other hand, for other page replacement algorithms, only a local strategy makes sense. In particular, the working set and WSClock algorithms refer to some specific process and must be applied in that context. There really is no working set for the machine as a whole and trying to use the union of all the working sets would lose the locality property and not work well.

4.6.2 Load Control

Even with the best page replacement algorithm and optimal global allocation of page frames to processes, it can happen that the system thrashes. In fact, whenever the combined working sets of all processes exceed the capacity of memory, thrashing can be expected. One symptom of this situation is that the PFF algorithm indicates that some processes need more memory but no processes need less memory. In this case there is no way to give more memory to those processes needing it without hurting some other processes. The only real solution is to temporarily get rid of some processes.

The way to reduce the number of processes competing for memory is to swap some of them to the disk and free up all the pages they are holding. For example, one process can be swapped to disk and its page frames divided up among other processes that are thrashing. If the thrashing stops, the system can run for a while this way. If it does not stop, another process has to be swapped out, and so on, until the thrashing stops. Thus even with paging, swapping is still needed, only now swapping is used to reduce potential demand for memory, rather than to reclaim blocks of it for immediate use.

Swapping processes out to relieve the load on memory is reminiscent of two-level scheduling, in which some processes are put on disk and a short-term scheduler is used to schedule the remaining processes. Clearly, the two ideas can be combined, with just enough processes swapped out to make the page-fault rate acceptable. Periodically, some processes are brought in from disk and other ones are swapped out there.

However, another factor to consider is the degree of multiprogramming. As we saw in Fig. 4-4, when the number of processes in main memory is too low, the CPU may be idle for substantial periods of time. This consideration argues for considering not only process size and paging rate when deciding which process to swap out, but also its characteristics, such as whether it is CPU bound or I/O bound, and what characteristics the remaining processes have as well.

4.6.3 Page Size

The page size is often a parameter that can be chosen by the operating system. Even if the hardware has been designed with, for example, 512-byte pages, the operating system can easily regard pages 0 and 1, 2 and 3, 4 and 5, and so on, as 1-KB pages by always allocating two consecutive 512-byte page frames for them.

Determining the best page size requires balancing several competing factors. As a result, there is no overall optimum. To start with, there are two factors that argue for a small page size. A randomly chosen text, data, or stack segment will not fill an integral number of pages. On the average, half of the final page will be empty. The extra space in that page is wasted. This wastage is called **internal fragmentation**. With n segments in memory and a page size of p bytes, $np/2$ bytes will be wasted on internal fragmentation. This reasoning argues for a small page size.

Another argument for a small page size becomes apparent if we think about a program consisting of eight sequential phases of 4 KB each. With a 32-KB page size, the program must be allocated 32 KB all the time. With a 16-KB page size, it needs only 16 KB. With a page size of 4 KB or smaller, it requires only 4 KB at any instant. In general, a large page size will cause more unused program to be in memory than a small page size.

On the other hand, small pages mean that programs will need many pages, hence a large page table. A 32-KB program needs only four 8-KB pages, but 64 512-byte pages. Transfers to and from the disk are generally a page at a time, with most of the time being for the seek and rotational delay, so that transferring a small page takes almost as much time as transferring a large page. It might take 64×10 msec to load 64 512-byte pages, but only 4×12 msec to load four 8-KB pages.

On some machines, the page table must be loaded into hardware registers every time the CPU switches from one process to another. On these machines having a small page size means that the time required to load the page registers gets longer as the page size gets smaller. Furthermore, the space occupied by the page table increases as the page size decreases.

This last point can be analyzed mathematically. Let the average process size be s bytes and the page size be p bytes. Furthermore, assume that each page entry requires e bytes. The approximate number of pages needed per process is then s/p, occupying se/p bytes of page table space. The wasted memory in the last page of the process due to internal fragmentation is $p/2$. Thus, the total overhead due to the page table and the internal fragmentation loss is given by the sum of these two terms:

$$\text{overhead} = se/p + p/2$$

The first term (page table size) is large when the page size is small. The second term (internal fragmentation) is large when the page size is large. The optimum must lie somewhere in between. By taking the first derivative with respect to p and equating it to zero, we get the equation

$$-se/p^2 + 1/2 = 0$$

From this equation we can derive a formula that gives the optimum page size (considering only memory wasted in fragmentation and page table size). The result is:

$$p = \sqrt{2se}$$

For $s = 1\text{MB}$ and $e = 8$ bytes per page table entry, the optimum page size is 4 KB. Commercially available computers have used page sizes ranging from 512 bytes to 64 KB. A typical value used to 1 KB, but nowadays 4 KB or 8 KB are more common. As memories get larger, the page size tends to get larger as well (but not linearly). Quadrupling the RAM size rarely even doubles the page size.

4.6.4 Separate Instruction and Data Spaces

Most computers have a single address space that holds both programs and data, as shown in Fig. 4-30(a). If this address space is large enough, everything works fine. However, it is often too small, forcing programmers to stand on their heads to fit everything into the address space.

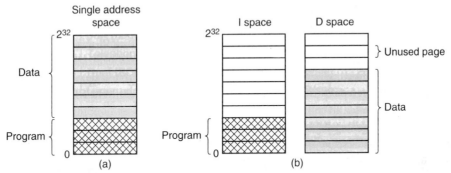

Figure 4-30. (a) One address space. (b) Separate I and D spaces.

One solution, pioneered on the (16-bit) PDP-11, is to have separate address spaces for instructions (program text) and data. These are called **I-space** and **D-space**, respectively. Each address space runs from 0 to some maximum, typically $2^{16} - 1$ or $2^{32} - 1$. In Fig. 4-30(b) we see both of them. The linker must know when separate I- and D-spaces are being used because when they are, the data are relocated to virtual address 0 instead of starting after the program.

In a computer with this design, both address spaces can be paged, independently from one another. Each one has its own page table, with its own mapping of virtual pages to physical page frames. When the hardware wants to fetch an instruction, it knows that it must use I-space and the I-space page table. Similarly, references to data must go through the D-space page table. Other than this distinction, having separate I- and D-spaces does not introduce any special complications and it does double the available address space.

4.6.5 Shared Pages

Another design issue is sharing. In a large multiprogramming system, it is common for several users to be running the same program at the same time. It is clearly more efficient to share the pages, to avoid having two copies of the same page in memory at the same time. One problem is that not all pages are sharable. In particular, pages that are read-only, such as program text, can be shared, but data pages cannot.

If separate I- and D-spaces are supported, it is relatively straightforward to share programs by having two or more processes use the same page table for their

I-space but different page tables for their D-spaces. Typically in an implementation that supports sharing in this way, page tables are data structures independent of the process table. Each process then has two pointers in its process table: one to the I-space page table and one to the D-space page table, as shown in Fig. 4-31. When the scheduler chooses a process to run, it uses these pointers to locate the appropriate page tables and sets up the MMU using them. Even without separate I- and D-spaces, processes can share programs (or sometimes, libraries), but the mechanism is more complicated.

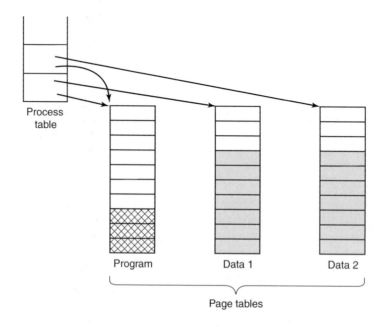

Figure 4-31. Two processes sharing the same program sharing its page table.

When two or more processes share some code, a problem occurs with the shared pages. Suppose that processes *A* and *B* are both running the editor and sharing its pages. If the scheduler decides to remove *A* from memory, evicting all its pages and filling the empty page frames with some other program will cause *B* to generate a large number of page faults to bring them back in again.

Similarly, when *A* terminates, it is essential to be able to discover that the pages are still in use so that their disk space will not be freed by accident. Searching all the page tables to see if a page is shared is usually too expensive, so special data structures are needed to keep track of shared pages, especially if the unit of sharing is the individual page (or run of pages), rather than an entire page table.

Sharing data is trickier than sharing code, but it is not impossible. In particular, in UNIX, after a fork system call, the parent and child are required to share both program text and data. In a paged system, what is often done is to give each of these processes its own page table and have both of them point to the same set of pages. Thus no copying of pages is done at fork time. However, all the data pages are mapped into both processes as READ ONLY.

As long as both processes just read their data, without modifying it, this situation can continue. As soon as either process updates a memory word, the violation of the read-only protection causes a trap to the operating system. A copy is then made of the page so that each process now has its own private copy. Both copies are now set to READ-WRITE so subsequent writes to either copy proceed without trapping. This strategy means that those pages that are never written (including all the program pages) need not be copied. Only the data pages that are actually written need be copied. This approach, called **copy on write**, improves performance by reducing copying.

4.6.6 Cleaning Policy

Paging works best when there are plenty of free page frames that can be claimed as page faults occur. If every page frame is full, and furthermore modified, before a new page can be brought in, an old page must first be written to disk. To insure a plentiful supply of free page frames, many paging systems have a background process, called the **paging daemon**, that sleeps most of the time but is awakened periodically to inspect the state of memory. If too few page frames are free, the paging daemon begins selecting pages to evict using the chosen page replacement algorithm. If these pages have been modified since being loaded, they are written to disk.

In any event, the previous contents of the page are remembered. In the event one of the evicted pages is needed again before its frame has been overwritten, it can be reclaimed by removing it from the pool of free page frames. Keeping a supply of page frames around yields better performance than using all of memory and then trying to find a frame at the moment it is needed. At the very least, the paging daemon ensures that all the free frames are clean, so they need not be written to disk in a big hurry when they are required.

One way to implement this cleaning policy is with a two-handed clock. The front hand is controlled by the paging daemon. When it points to a dirty page, that page it written back to disk and the front hand advanced. When it points to a clean page, it is just advanced. The back hand is used for page replacement, as in the standard clock algorithm. Only now, the probability of the back hand hitting a clean page is increased due to the work of the paging daemon.

4.6.7 Virtual Memory Interface

Up until now, our whole discussion has assumed that virtual memory is transparent to processes and programmers, that is, all they see is a large virtual address space on a computer with a small(er) physical memory. With many systems, that is true, but in some advanced systems, programmers have some control over the memory map and can use it in nontraditional ways to enhance program behavior. In this section, we will briefly look at a few of these.

One reason for giving programmers control over their memory map is to allow two or more processes to share the same memory. If programmers can name regions of their memory, it may be possible for one process to give another process the name of a memory region so that process can also map it in. With two (or more) processes sharing the same pages, high bandwidth sharing becomes possible—one process writes into the shared memory and another one reads from it.

Sharing of pages can also be used to implement a high-performance message-passing system. Normally, when messages are passed, the data are copied from one address space to another, at considerable cost. If processes can control their page map, a message can be passed by having the sending process unmap the page(s) containing the message, and the receiving process mapping them in. Here only the page names have to be copied, instead of all the data.

Yet another advanced memory management technique is **distributed shared memory** (Feeley et al., 1995; Li, 1986; Li and Hudak, 1989; and Zekauskas et al., 1994). The idea here is to allow multiple processes over a network to share a set of pages, possibly, but not necessarily, as a single shared linear address space. When a process references a page that is not currently mapped in, it gets a page fault. The page fault handler, which may be in the kernel or in user space, then locates the machine holding the page and sends it a message asking it to unmap the page and send it over the network. When the page arrives, it is mapped in and the faulting instruction is restarted. We will examine distributed shared memory in more detail in Chap. 8.

4.7 IMPLEMENTATION ISSUES

Implementers of virtual memory systems have to make choices among the major theoretical algorithms such as second chance versus aging, local versus global page allocation, and demand paging versus prepaging. But they also have to be aware of a number of practical implementation issues as well. In this section we will take a look at a few of the more common problems and some solutions.

4.7.1 Operating System Involvement with Paging

There are four times when the operating system has work to do relating to paging: process creation time, process execution time, page fault time, and process termination time. We will now briefly examine each of these to see what has to be done.

When a new process is created in a paging system, the operating system has to determine how large the program and data will be (initially) and create a page table for it. Space has to be allocated in memory for the page table and it has to be initialized. The page table need not be resident when the process is swapped out but has to be in memory when the process is running. In addition, space has to be allocated in the swap area on disk so that when a page is swapped out, it has somewhere to go. The swap area also has to be initialized with program text and data so that when the new process starts getting page faults, the pages can be brought in from disk. Some systems page the program text directly from the executable file, thus saving disk space and initialization time. Finally, information about the page table and swap area on disk must be recorded in the process table.

When a process is scheduled for execution, the MMU has to be reset for the new process and the TLB flushed, to get rid of traces of the previously executing process. The new process' page table has to be made current, usually by copying it or a pointer to it to some hardware register(s). Optionally, some or all of the process' pages can be brought into memory to reduce the number of page faults initially.

When a page fault occurs, the operating system has to read out hardware registers to determine which virtual address caused the fault. From this information, it must compute which page is needed and locate that page on disk. It must then find an available page frame to put the new page, evicting some old page if need be. Then it must read the needed page into the page frame. Finally, it must back up the program counter to have it point to the faulting instruction and let that instruction execute again.

When a process exits, the operating system must release its page table, its pages, and the disk space that the pages occupy when they are on disk. If some of the pages are shared with other processes, the pages in memory and on disk can only be released when the last process using them has terminated.

4.7.2 Page Fault Handling

We are finally in a position to describe what happens on a page fault in some detail. The sequence of events is as follows:

1. The hardware traps to the kernel, saving the program counter on the stack. On most machines, some information about the state of the current instruction is saved in special CPU registers.

2. An assembly code routine is started to save the general registers and other volatile information, to keep the operating system from destroying it. This routine calls the operating system as a procedure.

3. The operating system discovers that a page fault has occurred, and tries to discover which virtual page is needed. Often one of the hardware registers contains this information. If not, the operating system must retrieve the program counter, fetch the instruction, and parse it in software to figure out what it was doing when the fault hit.

4. Once the virtual address that caused the fault is known, the system checks to see if this address is valid and the protection consistent with the access. If not, the process is sent a signal or killed. If the address is valid and no protection fault has occurred, the system checks to see if a page frame is free. If no frames are free, the page replacement algorithm is run to select a victim.

5. If the page frame selected is dirty, the page is scheduled for transfer to the disk, and a context switch takes place, suspending the faulting process and letting another one run until the disk transfer has completed. In any event, the frame is marked as busy to prevent it from being used for another purpose.

6. As soon as the page frame is clean (either immediately or after it is written to disk), the operating system looks up the disk address where the needed page is, and schedules a disk operation to bring it in. While the page is being loaded, the faulting process is still suspended and another user process is run, if one is available.

7. When the disk interrupt indicates that the page has arrived, the page tables are updated to reflect its position, and the frame is marked as being in normal state.

8. The faulting instruction is backed up to the state it had when it began and the program counter is reset to point to that instruction.

9. The faulting process is scheduled, and the operating system returns to the assembly language routine that called it.

10. This routine reloads the registers and other state information and returns to user space to continue execution, as if no fault had occurred.

4.7.3 Instruction Backup

When a program references a page that is not in memory, the instruction causing the fault is stopped part way through and a trap to the operating system occurs. After the operating system has fetched the page needed, it must restart the instruction causing the trap. This is easier said than done.

To see the nature of this problem at its worst, consider a CPU that has instructions with two addresses, such as the Motorola 680x0, widely used in embedded systems. The instruction

```
MOV.L #6(A1),2(A0)
```

is 6 bytes, for example (see Fig. 4-32). In order to restart the instruction, the operating system must determine where the first byte of the instruction is. The value of the program counter at the time of the trap depends on which operand faulted and how the CPU's microcode has been implemented.

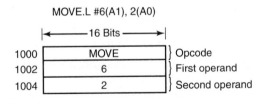

Figure 4-32. An instruction causing a page fault.

In Fig. 4-32, we have an instruction starting at address 1000 that makes three memory references: the instruction word itself, and two offsets for the operands. Depending on which of these three memory references caused the page fault, the program counter might be 1000, 1002, or 1004 at the time of the fault. It is frequently impossible for the operating system to determine unambiguously where the instruction began. If the program counter is 1002 at the time of the fault, the operating system has no way of telling whether the word in 1002 is a memory address associated with an instruction at 1000 (e.g., the location of an operand), or an instruction opcode.

Bad as this problem may be, it could have been worse. Some 680x0 addressing modes use autoincrementing, which means that a side effect of executing the instruction is to increment one or more registers. Instructions that use autoincrement mode can also fault. Depending on the details of the microcode, the increment may be done before the memory reference, in which case the operating system must decrement the register in software before restarting the instruction. Or, the autoincrement may be done after the memory reference, in which case it will not have been done at the time of the trap and must not be undone by the operating system. Autodecrement mode also exists and causes a similar problem. The precise details of whether autoincrements and autodecrements have or have not been done before the corresponding memory references may differ from instruction to instruction and from CPU model to CPU model.

Fortunately, on some machines the CPU designers provide a solution, usually in the form of a hidden internal register into which the program counter is copied just before each instruction is executed. These machines may also have a second register telling which registers have already been autoincremented or autodecremented, and by how much. Given this information, the operating system can unambiguously undo all the effects of the faulting instruction so it can be started all over again. If this information is not available, the operating system has to jump through hoops to figure out what happened and how to repair it. It is as though the hardware designers were unable to solve the problem, so they threw up their hands and told the operating system writers to deal with it. Nice guys.

4.7.4 Locking Pages in Memory

Although we have not discussed I/O much in this chapter, the fact that a computer has virtual memory does not mean that I/O is absent. Virtual memory and I/O interact in subtle ways. Consider a process that has just issued a system call to read from some file or device into a buffer within its address space. While waiting for the I/O to complete, the process is suspended and another process is allowed to run. This other process gets a page fault.

If the paging algorithm is global, there is a small, but nonzero, chance that the page containing the I/O buffer will be chosen to be removed from memory. If an I/O device is currently in the process of doing a DMA transfer to that page, removing it will cause part of the data to be written in the buffer where they belong, and part of the data to be written over the newly loaded page. One solution to this problem is to lock pages engaged in I/O in memory so that they will not be removed. Locking a page is often called **pinning** it in memory. Another solution is to do all I/O to kernel buffers and then copy the data to user pages later.

4.7.5 Backing Store

In our discussion of page replacement algorithms, we saw how a page is selected for removal. We have not said much about where on the disk it is put when it is paged out. Let us now describe some of the issues related to disk management.

The simplest algorithm for allocating page space on the disk is to have a special swap area on the disk. When the system is booted, this area is empty, and is represented in memory as a single entry giving its origin and size. When the first process is started, a chunk of the swap area the size of the first process is reserved and the remaining area reduced by that amount. As new processes are started, they are assigned chunks of the swap area equal in size to their core images. As they finish, their disk space is freed. The swap area is managed as a list of free chunks.

Associated with each process is the disk address of its swap area, kept in the process table. Calculating the address to write a page to becomes simple: just add the offset of the page within the virtual address space to the start of the swap area. However, before a process can start, the swap area must be initialized. One way is to copy the entire process image to the swap area, so that it can be brought *in* as needed. The other is to load the entire process in memory and let it be paged *out* as needed.

However, this simple model has a problem: processes can increase in size after starting. Although the program text is usually fixed, the data area can sometimes grow, and the stack can always grow. Consequently, it may be better to reserve separate swap areas for the text, data, and stack and allow each of these areas to consist of more than one chunk on the disk.

The other extreme is to allocate nothing in advance and allocate disk space for each page when it is swapped out and deallocate it when it is swapped back in. In this way, processes in memory do not tie up any swap space. The disadvantage is that a disk address is needed in memory to keep track of each page on disk. In other words, there must a table per process telling for each page on disk where it is. The two alternatives are shown in Fig. 4-33.

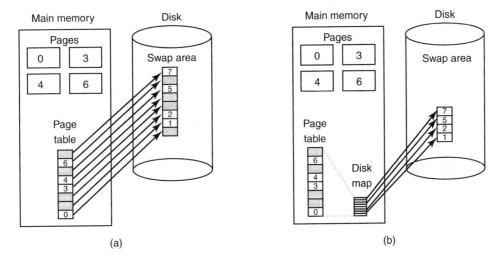

Figure 4-33. (a) Paging to a static swap area. (b) Backing up pages dynamically.

In Fig. 4-33(a), a page table with eight pages is illustrated. Pages 0, 3, 4, and 6 are in main memory. Pages 1, 2, 5, and 7 are on disk. The swap area on disk is as large as the process virtual address space (eight pages) with each page having a fixed location to which it is written when it is evicted from main memory. Calculation of this address requires knowing only where the process' paging area begins, since pages are stored in it contiguously in order of their virtual page number. Pages that are in memory always have a shadow copy on disk, but this copy may be out of date if the page has been modified since being loaded.

In Fig. 4-33(b), pages do not have fixed addresses on disk. When a page is swapped out, an empty disk page is chosen on the fly and the disk map (which has room for one disk address per virtual page) is updated accordingly. Pages that are in memory have no copy on disk. Their entries in the disk map contain an invalid disk address or a bit marking them as not in use.

4.7.6 Separation of Policy and Mechanism

An important tool for managing the complexity of any system is to separate the policy from the mechanism. This principle can be applied to memory management by having most of the memory manager run as a user-level process.

Such a separation was first done in Mach (Young et al., 1987) and in MINIX (Tanenbaum, 1987). The discussion below is loosely based on Mach.

A simple example of how policy and mechanism can be separated is shown in Fig. 4-34. Here the memory management system is divided into three parts:

1. A low-level MMU handler.

2. A page fault handler that is part of the kernel.

3. An external pager running in user space.

All the details of how the MMU works are encapsulated in the MMU handler, which is machine-dependent code and has to be rewritten for each new platform the operating system is ported to. The page-fault handler is machine independent code and contains most of the mechanism for paging. The policy is largely determined by the external pager, which runs as a user process.

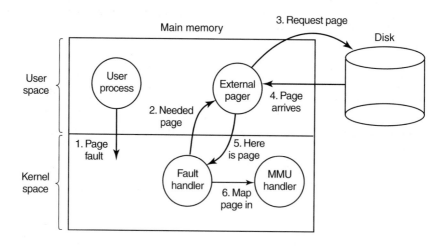

Figure 4-34. Page fault handling with an external pager.

When a process starts up, the external pager is notified in order to set up the process page map and allocate backing store on the disk if need be. As the process runs, it may map new objects into its address space, so the external pager is again notified.

Once the process starts running, it may get a page fault. The fault handler figures out which virtual page is needed and sends a message to the external pager, telling what the problem is. The external pager then reads the needed page in from the disk and copies it to a portion of its own address space. Then it tells the fault handler where the page is. The fault handler then unmaps the page from the external pager's address space and asks the MMU handler to put it into the user's address space at the right place. Then the user process can be restarted.

This implementation leaves open where the page replacement algorithm is put. It would be cleanest to have it in the external pager, but there are some problems with this approach. Principal among these is that the external pager does not have access to the R and M bits of all the pages. These bits play a role in many of the paging algorithms. Thus either some mechanism is needed to pass this information up to the external pager, or the page replacement algorithm must go in the kernel. In the latter case, the fault handler tells the external pager which page it has selected for eviction and provides the data, either by mapping it into the external pager's address space or including it in a message. Either way, the external pager writes the data to disk.

The main advantage of this implementation is more modular code and greater flexibility. The main disadvantage is the extra overhead of crossing the user-kernel boundary several times and the overhead of the various messages being sent between the pieces of the system. At the moment, the subject is highly controversial, but as computers get faster and faster, and the software gets more and more complex, in the long run sacrificing some performance for more reliable software will probably be acceptable to most implementers.

4.8 SEGMENTATION

The virtual memory discussed so far is one-dimensional because the virtual addresses go from 0 to some maximum address, one address after another. For many problems, having two or more separate virtual address spaces may be much better than having only one. For example, a compiler has many tables that are built up as compilation proceeds, possibly including

1. The source text being saved for the printed listing (on batch systems).

2. The symbol table, containing the names and attributes of variables.

3. The table containing all the integer and floating-point constants used.

4. The parse tree, containing the syntactic analysis of the program.

5. The stack used for procedure calls within the compiler.

Each of the first four tables grows continuously as compilation proceeds. The last one grows and shrinks in unpredictable ways during compilation. In a one-dimensional memory, these five tables would have to be allocated contiguous chunks of virtual address space, as in Fig. 4-35.

Consider what happens if a program has an exceptionally large number of variables but a normal amount of everything else. The chunk of address space allocated for the symbol table may fill up, but there may be lots of room in the other tables. The compiler could, of course, simply issue a message saying that the compilation cannot continue due to too many variables, but doing so does not seem very sporting when unused space is left in the other tables.

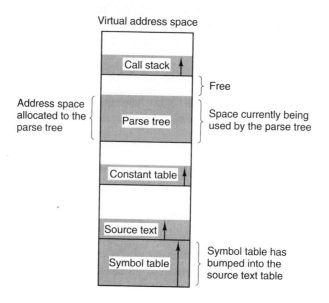

Figure 4-35. In a one-dimensional address space with growing tables, one table may bump into another.

Another possibility is to play Robin Hood, taking space from the tables with an excess of room and giving it to the tables with little room. This shuffling can be done, but it is analogous to managing one's own overlays—a nuisance at best and a great deal of tedious, unrewarding work at worst.

What is really needed is a way of freeing the programmer from having to manage the expanding and contracting tables, in the same way that virtual memory eliminates the worry of organizing the program into overlays.

A straightforward and extremely general solution is to provide the machine with many completely independent address spaces, called **segments**. Each segment consists of a linear sequence of addresses, from 0 to some maximum. The length of each segment may be anything from 0 to the maximum allowed. Different segments may, and usually do, have different lengths. Moreover, segment lengths may change during execution. The length of a stack segment may be increased whenever something is pushed onto the stack and decreased whenever something is popped off the stack.

Because each segment constitutes a separate address space, different segments can grow or shrink independently, without affecting each other. If a stack in a certain segment needs more address space to grow, it can have it, because there is nothing else in its address space to bump into. Of course, a segment can fill up but segments are usually very large, so this occurrence is rare. To specify an address in this segmented or two-dimensional memory, the program must supply a two-part address, a segment number, and an address within the segment.

Figure 4-36 illustrates a segmented memory being used for the compiler tables discussed earlier. Five independent segments are shown here.

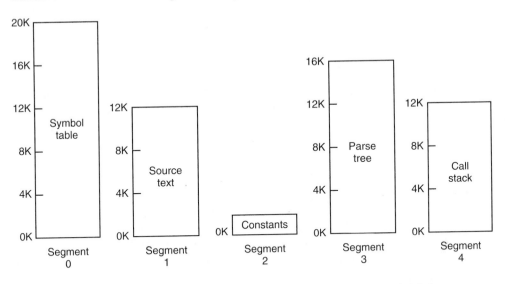

Figure 4-36. A segmented memory allows each table to grow or shrink independently of the other tables.

We emphasize that a segment is a logical entity, which the programmer is aware of and uses as a logical entity. A segment might contain a procedure, or an array, or a stack, or a collection of scalar variables, but usually it does not contain a mixture of different types.

A segmented memory has other advantages besides simplifying the handling of data structures that are growing or shrinking. If each procedure occupies a separate segment, with address 0 as its starting address, the linking up of procedures compiled separately is greatly simplified. After all the procedures that constitute a program have been compiled and linked up, a procedure call to the procedure in segment n will use the two-part address $(n, 0)$ to address word 0 (the entry point).

If the procedure in segment n is subsequently modified and recompiled, no other procedures need be changed (because no starting addresses have been modified), even if the new version is larger than the old one. With a one-dimensional memory, the procedures are packed tightly next to each other, with no address space between them. Consequently, changing one procedure's size can affect the starting address of other, unrelated procedures. This, in turn, requires modifying all procedures that call any of the moved procedures, in order to incorporate their new starting addresses. If a program contains hundreds of procedures, this process can be costly.

Segmentation also facilitates sharing procedures or data between several processes. A common example is the **shared library**. Modern workstations that run advanced window systems often have extremely large graphical libraries compiled into nearly every program. In a segmented system, the graphical library can be put in a segment and shared by multiple processes, eliminating the need for having it in every process' address space. While it is also possible to have shared libraries in pure paging systems, it is much more complicated. In effect, these systems do it by simulating segmentation.

Because each segment forms a logical entity of which the programmer is aware, such as a procedure, or an array, or a stack, different segments can have different kinds of protection. A procedure segment can be specified as execute only, prohibiting attempts to read from it or store into it. A floating-point array can be specified as read/write but not execute, and attempts to jump to it will be caught. Such protection is helpful in catching programming errors.

You should try to understand why protection makes sense in a segmented memory but not in a one-dimensional paged memory. In a segmented memory the user is aware of what is in each segment. Normally, a segment would not contain a procedure and a stack, for example, but one or the other. Since each segment contains only one type of object, the segment can have the protection appropriate for that particular type. Paging and segmentation are compared in Fig. 4-37.

Consideration	Paging	Segmentation
Need the programmer be aware that this technique is being used?	No	Yes
How many linear address spaces are there?	1	Many
Can the total address space exceed the size of physical memory?	Yes	Yes
Can procedures and data be distinguished and separately protected?	No	Yes
Can tables whose size fluctuates be accommodated easily?	No	Yes
Is sharing of procedures between users facilitated?	No	Yes
Why was this technique invented?	To get a large linear address space without having to buy more physical memory	To allow programs and data to be broken up into logically independent address spaces and to aid sharing and protection

Figure 4-37. Comparison of paging and segmentation.

The contents of a page are, in a sense, accidental. The programmer is unaware of the fact that paging is even occurring. Although putting a few bits in each entry of the page table to specify the access allowed would be possible, to utilize this feature the programmer would have to keep track of where in his address space the page boundaries were. That is precisely the sort of administration that paging was invented to eliminate. Because the user of a segmented memory has the illusion that all segments are in main memory all the time—that is, he can address them as though they were—he can protect each segment separately, without having to be concerned with the administration of overlaying them.

4.8.1 Implementation of Pure Segmentation

The implementation of segmentation differs from paging in an essential way: pages are fixed size and segments are not. Figure 4-38(a) shows an example of physical memory initially containing five segments. Now consider what happens if segment 1 is evicted and segment 7, which is smaller, is put in its place. We arrive at the memory configuration of Fig. 4-38(b). Between segment 7 and segment 2 is an unused area—that is, a hole. Then segment 4 is replaced by segment 5, as in Fig. 4-38(c), and segment 3 is replaced by segment 6, as in Fig. 4-38(d). After the system has been running for a while, memory will be divided up into a number of chunks, some containing segments and some containing holes. This phenomenon, called **checkerboarding** or **external fragmentation**, wastes memory in the holes. It can be dealt with by compaction, as shown in Fig. 4-38(e).

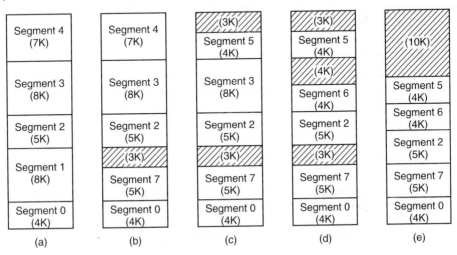

Figure 4-38. (a)-(d) Development of checkerboarding. (e) Removal of the checkerboarding by compaction.

4.8.2 Segmentation with Paging: MULTICS

If the segments are large, it may be inconvenient, or even impossible, to keep them in main memory in their entirety. This leads to the idea of paging them, so that only those pages that are actually needed have to be around. Several significant systems have supported paged segments. In this section we will describe the first one: MULTICS. In the next one we will discuss a more recent one: the Intel Pentium.

MULTICS ran on the Honeywell 6000 machines and their descendants and provided each program with a virtual memory of up to 2^{18} segments (more than 250,000), each of which could be up to 65,536 (36-bit) words long. To implement this, the MULTICS designers chose to treat each segment as a virtual memory and to page it, combining the advantages of paging (uniform page size and not having to keep the whole segment in memory if only part of it is being used) with the advantages of segmentation (ease of programming, modularity, protection, and sharing).

Each MULTICS program has a segment table, with one descriptor per segment. Since there are potentially more than a quarter of a million entries in the table, the segment table is itself a segment and is paged. A segment descriptor contains an indication of whether the segment is in main memory or not. If any part of the segment is in memory, the segment is considered to be in memory, and its page table will be in memory. If the segment is in memory, its descriptor contains an 18-bit pointer to its page table [see Fig. 4-39(a)]. Because physical addresses are 24 bits and pages are aligned on 64-byte boundaries (implying that the low-order 6 bits of page addresses are 000000), only 18 bits are needed in the descriptor to store a page table address. The descriptor also contains the segment size, the protection bits, and a few other items. Figure 4-39(b) illustrates a MULTICS segment descriptor. The address of the segment in secondary memory is not in the segment descriptor but in another table used by the segment fault handler.

Each segment is an ordinary virtual address space and is paged in the same way as the nonsegmented paged memory described earlier in this chapter. The normal page size is 1024 words (although a few small segments used by MULTICS itself are not paged or are paged in units of 64 words to save physical memory).

An address in MULTICS consists of two parts: the segment and the address within the segment. The address within the segment is further divided into a page number and a word within the page, as shown in Fig. 4-40. When a memory reference occurs, the following algorithm is carried out.

1. The segment number is used to find the segment descriptor.

2. A check is made to see if the segment's page table is in memory. If the page table is in memory, it is located. If it is not, a segment fault occurs. If there is a protection violation, a fault (trap) occurs.

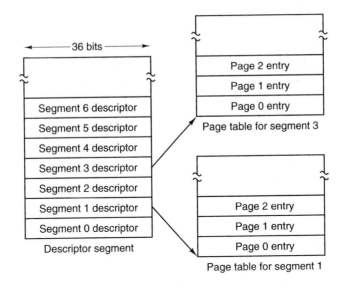

(a)

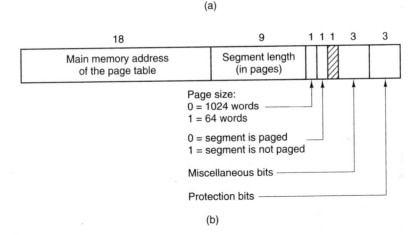

(b)

Figure 4-39. The MULTICS virtual memory. (a) The descriptor segment points to the page tables. (b) A segment descriptor. The numbers are the field lengths.

3. The page table entry for the requested virtual page is examined. If the page is not in memory, a page fault occurs. If it is in memory, the main memory address of the start of the page is extracted from the page table entry.

4. The offset is added to the page origin to give the main memory address where the word is located.

5. The read or store finally takes place.

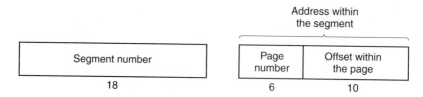

Figure 4-40. A 34-bit MULTICS virtual address.

This process is illustrated in Fig. 4-41. For simplicity, the fact that the descriptor segment is itself paged has been omitted. What really happens is that a register (the descriptor base register), is used to locate the descriptor segment's page table, which, in turn, points to the pages of the descriptor segment. Once the descriptor for the needed segment has been found, the addressing proceeds as shown in Fig. 4-41.

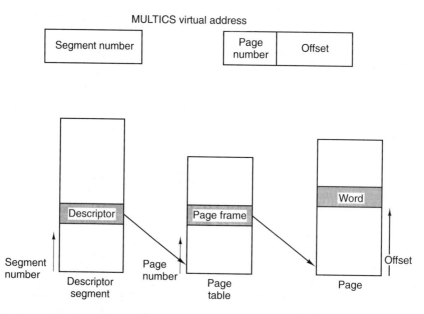

Figure 4-41. Conversion of a two-part MULTICS address into a main memory address.

As you have no doubt guessed by now, if the preceding algorithm were actually carried out by the operating system on every instruction, programs would not run very fast. In reality, the MULTICS hardware contains a 16-word high-speed TLB that can search all its entries in parallel for a given key. It is illustrated in Fig. 4-42. When an address is presented to the computer, the addressing hardware first checks to see if the virtual address is in the TLB. If so, it gets the page frame number directly from the TLB and forms the actual address of the referenced word without having to look in the descriptor segment or page table.

Comparison field				Is this entry used?	
Segment number	Virtual page	Page frame	Protection	Age	
4	1	7	Read/write	13	1
6	0	2	Read only	10	1
12	3	1	Read/write	2	1
					0
2	1	0	Execute only	7	1
2	2	12	Execute only	9	1

Figure 4-42. A simplified version of the MULTICS TLB. The existence of two page sizes makes the actual TLB more complicated.

The addresses of the 16 most recently referenced pages are kept in the TLB. Programs whose working set is smaller than the TLB size will come to equilibrium with the addresses of the entire working set in the TLB and therefore will run efficiently. If the page is not in the TLB, the descriptor and page tables are actually referenced to find the page frame address, and the TLB is updated to include this page, the least recently used page being thrown out. The age field keeps track of which entry is the least recently used. The reason that a TLB is used is for comparing the segment and page number of all the entries in parallel.

4.8.3 Segmentation with Paging: The Intel Pentium

In many ways, the virtual memory on the Pentium resembles MULTICS, including the presence of both segmentation and paging. Whereas MULTICS has 256K independent segments, each up to 64K 36-bit words, the Pentium has 16K independent segments, each holding up to 1 billion 32-bit words. Although there are fewer segments, the larger segment size is far more important, as few programs need more than 1000 segments, but many programs need large segments.

The heart of the Pentium virtual memory consists of two tables, the **LDT** (**Local Descriptor Table**) and the **GDT** (**Global Descriptor Table**). Each program has its own LDT, but there is a single GDT, shared by all the programs on the computer. The LDT describes segments local to each program, including its code, data, stack, and so on, whereas the GDT describes system segments, including the operating system itself.

To access a segment, a Pentium program first loads a selector for that segment into one of the machine's six segment registers. During execution, the CS register holds the selector for the code segment and the DS register holds the selector for the data segment. The other segment registers are less important. Each selector is a 16-bit number, as shown in Fig. 4-43.

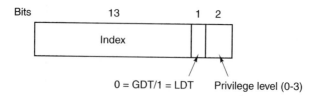

Figure 4-43. A Pentium selector.

One of the selector bits tells whether the segment is local or global (i.e., whether it is in the LDT or GDT). Thirteen other bits specify the LDT or GDT entry number, so these tables are each restricted to holding 8K segment descriptors. The other 2 bits relate to protection, and will be described later. Descriptor 0 is forbidden. It may be safely loaded into a segment register to indicate that the segment register is not currently available. It causes a trap if used.

At the time a selector is loaded into a segment register, the corresponding descriptor is fetched from the LDT or GDT and stored in microprogram registers, so it can be accessed quickly. A descriptor consists of 8 bytes, including the segment's base address, size, and other information, as depicted in Fig. 4-44.

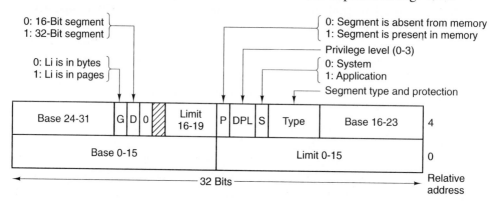

Figure 4-44. Pentium code segment descriptor. Data segments differ slightly.

The format of the selector has been cleverly chosen to make locating the descriptor easy. First either the LDT or GDT is selected, based on selector bit 2. Then the selector is copied to an internal scratch register, and the 3 low-order bits set to 0. Finally, the address of either the LDT or GDT table is added to it, to give a direct pointer to the descriptor. For example, selector 72 refers to entry 9 in the GDT, which is located at address GDT + 72.

Let us trace the steps by which a (selector, offset) pair is converted to a physical address. As soon as the microprogram knows which segment register is being used, it can find the complete descriptor corresponding to that selector in its internal registers. If the segment does not exist (selector 0), or is currently paged out, a trap occurs.

It then checks to see if the offset is beyond the end of the segment, in which case a trap also occurs. Logically, there should simply be a 32-bit field in the descriptor giving the size of the segment, but there are only 20 bits available, so a different scheme is used. If the *Gbit* (Granularity) field is 0, the *Limit* field is the exact segment size, up to 1 MB. If it is 1, the *Limit* field gives the segment size in pages instead of bytes. The Pentium page size is fixed at 4 KB, so 20 bits are enough for segments up to 2^{32} bytes.

Assuming that the segment is in memory and the offset is in range, the Pentium then adds the 32-bit *Base* field in the descriptor to the offset to form what is called a **linear address**, as shown in Fig. 4-45. The *Base* field is broken up into three pieces and spread all over the descriptor for compatibility with the 286, in which the *Base* is only 24 bits. In effect, the *Base* field allows each segment to start at an arbitrary place within the 32-bit linear address space.

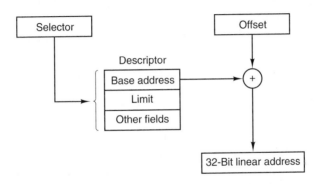

Figure 4-45. Conversion of a (selector, offset) pair to a linear address.

If paging is disabled (by a bit in a global control register), the linear address is interpreted as the physical address and sent to the memory for the read or write. Thus with paging disabled, we have a pure segmentation scheme, with each segment's base address given in its descriptor. Segments are permitted to overlap, incidentally, probably because it would be too much trouble and take too much time to verify that they were all disjoint.

On the other hand, if paging is enabled, the linear address is interpreted as a virtual address and mapped onto the physical address using page tables, pretty much as in our earlier examples. The only real complication is that with a 32-bit virtual address and a 4-KB page, a segment might contain 1 million pages, so a two-level mapping is used to reduce the page table size for small segments.

Each running program has a **page directory** consisting of 1024 32-bit entries. It is located at an address pointed to by a global register. Each entry in this directory points to a page table also containing 1024 32-bit entries. The page table entries point to page frames. The scheme is shown in Fig. 4-46.

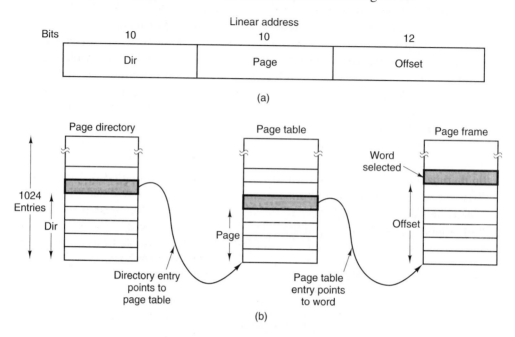

Figure 4-46. Mapping of a linear address onto a physical address.

In Fig. 4-46(a) we see a linear address divided into three fields, *Dir*, *Page*, and *Offset*. The *Dir* field is used to index into the page directory to locate a pointer to the proper page table. Then the *Page* field is used as an index into the page table to find the physical address of the page frame. Finally, *Offset* is added to the address of the page frame to get the physical address of the byte or word needed.

The page table entries are 32 bits each, 20 of which contain a page frame number. The remaining bits contain access and dirty bits, set by the hardware for the benefit of the operating system, protection bits, and other utility bits.

Each page table has entries for 1024 4-KB page frames, so a single page table handles 4 megabytes of memory. A segment shorter than 4M will have a page directory with a single entry, a pointer to its one and only page table. In this way, the overhead for short segments is only two pages, instead of the million pages that would be needed in a one-level page table.

To avoid making repeated references to memory, the Pentium, like MULTICS, has a small TLB that directly maps the most recently used *Dir−Page* combinations onto the physical address of the page frame. Only when the current combination is not present in the TLB is the mechanism of Fig. 4-46 actually carried out and the TLB updated. As long as TLB misses are rare, performance is good.

It is also worth noting that if some application does not need segmentation but is content with a single, paged, 32-bit address space, that model is possible. All the segment registers can be set up with the same selector, whose descriptor has *Base* = 0 and *Limit* set to the maximum. The instruction offset will then be the linear address, with only a single address space used—in effect, normal paging. In fact, all current operating systems for the Pentium work this way. OS/2 was the only one that used the full power of the Intel MMU architecture.

All in all, one has to give credit to the Pentium designers. Given the conflicting goals of implementing pure paging, pure segmentation, and paged segments, while at the same time being compatible with the 286, and doing all of this efficiently, the resulting design is surprisingly simple and clean.

Although we have covered the complete architecture of the Pentium virtual memory, albeit briefly, it is worth saying a few words about protection, since this subject is intimately related to the virtual memory. Just as the virtual memory scheme is closely modeled on MULTICS, so is the protection system. The Pentium supports four protection levels with level 0 being the most privileged and level 3 the least. These are shown in Fig. 4-47. At each instant, a running program is at a certain level, indicated by a 2-bit field in its PSW. Each segment in the system also has a level.

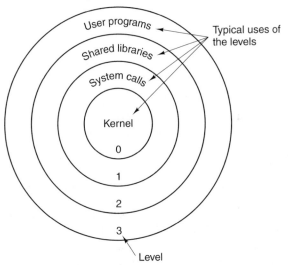

Figure 4-47. Protection on the Pentium.

As long as a program restricts itself to using segments at its own level, everything works fine. Attempts to access data at a higher level are permitted. Attempts to access data at a lower level are illegal and cause traps. Attempts to call procedures at a different level (higher or lower) are allowed, but in a carefully controlled way. To make an interlevel call, the CALL instruction must contain a selector instead of an address. This selector designates a descriptor called a **call**

gate, which gives the address of the procedure to be called. Thus it is not possible to jump into the middle of an arbitrary code segment at a different level. Only official entry points may be used. The concepts of protection levels and call gates were pioneered in MULTICS, where they were viewed as **protection rings**.

A typical use for this mechanism is suggested in Fig. 4-47. At level 0, we find the kernel of the operating system, which handles I/O, memory management, and other critical matters. At level 1, the system call handler is present. User programs may call procedures here to have system calls carried out, but only a specific and protected list of procedures may be called. Level 2 contains library procedures, possibly shared among many running programs. User programs may call these procedures and read their data, but they may not modify them. Finally, user programs run at level 3, which has the least protection.

Traps and interrupts use a mechanism similar to the call gates. They, too, reference descriptors, rather than absolute addresses, and these descriptors point to specific procedures to be executed. The *Type* field in Fig. 4-44 distinguishes between code segments, data segments, and the various kinds of gates.

4.9 RESEARCH ON MEMORY MANAGEMENT

Memory management, especially paging algorithms, was once a fruitful area for research, but most of that seems to have largely died off, at least for general-purpose systems. Most real systems tend to use some variation on clock, because it is easy to implement and relatively effective. One recent exception, however, is a redesign of the 4.4 BSD virtual memory system (Cranor and Parulkar, 1999).

There is still research going on concerning paging in special-purpose and newer kinds of systems though. Some of this work relates to allowing user processes to field their own page faults and handle their own memory management, possibly in an application-specific way (Engler et al., 1995). One area where applications may need to do their own paging in special ways is multimedia, so some research has looked at this (Hand, 1999). Another area that has some special requirements is hand-held personal communicators (Abutaleb and Li, 1997; and Wan and Lin, 1997). One final area is systems with 64-bit address spaces shared by many processes (Talluri et al., 1995).

4.10 SUMMARY

In this chapter we have examined memory management. We saw that the simplest systems do not swap or page at all. Once a program is loaded into memory, it remains there until it finishes. Some operating systems allow only one process at a time in memory, while others support multiprogramming.

The next step up is swapping. When swapping is used, the system can handle more processes than it has room for in memory. Processes for which there is no room are swapped out to the disk. Free space in memory and on disk can be kept track of with a bitmap or a hole list.

Modern computers often have some form of virtual memory. In the simplest form, each process' address space is divided up into uniform sized blocks called pages, which can be placed into any available page frame in memory. There are many page replacement algorithms; two of the better algorithms are aging and WSClock.

Paging systems can be modeled by abstracting the page reference string from the program and using the same reference string with different algorithms. These models can be used to make some predictions about paging behavior.

To make paging systems work well, choosing an algorithm is not enough; attention to issues such as determining the working set, memory allocation policy, and page size are required.

Segmentation helps in handling data structures that change size during execution and simplifies linking and sharing. It also facilitates providing different protection for different segments. Sometimes segmentation and paging are combined to provide a two-dimensional virtual memory. The MULTICS system and the Intel Pentium support segmentation and paging.

PROBLEMS

1. A computer system has enough room to hold four programs in its main memory. These programs are idle waiting for I/O half the time. What fraction of the CPU time is wasted?

2. In Fig. 4-21 we saw an example of how multiple jobs can run in parallel and finish faster than if they had run sequentially. Suppose that two jobs, each of which needs 10 minutes of CPU time, start simultaneously. How long will the last one take to complete if they run sequentially? How long if they run in parallel? Assume 50% I/O wait.

3. A swapping system eliminates holes by compaction. Assuming a random distribution of many holes and many data segments and a time to read or write a 32-bit memory word of 10 nsec, about how long does it take to compact 128 MB? For simplicity, assume that word 0 is part of a hole and that the highest word in memory contains valid data.

4. In this problem you are to compare the storage needed to keep track of free memory using a bitmap versus using a linked list. The 128-MB memory is allocated in units of

n bytes. For the linked list, assume that memory consists of an alternating sequence of segments and holes, each 64 KB. Also assume that each node in the linked list needs a 32-bit memory address, a 16-bit length, and a 16-bit next-node field. How many bytes of storage is required for each method? Which one is better?

5. Consider a swapping system in which memory consists of the following hole sizes in memory order: 10 KB, 4 KB, 20 KB, 18 KB, 7 KB, 9 KB, 12 KB, and 15 KB. Which hole is taken for successive segment requests of

(a) 12 KB
(b) 10 KB
(c) 9 KB

for first fit? Now repeat the question for best fit, worst fit, and next fit.

6. What is the difference between a physical address and a virtual address?

7. For each of the following decimal virtual addresses, compute the virtual page number and offset for a 4-KB page and for an 8 KB page: 20000, 32768, 60000.

8. Using the page table of Fig. 4-10, give the physical address corresponding to each of the following virtual addresses:

(a) 20
(b) 4100
(c) 8300

9. The Intel 8086 processor does not support virtual memory. Nevertheless, some companies previously sold systems that contained an unmodified 8086 CPU and do paging. Make an educated guess as to how they did it. *Hint*: Think about the logical location of the MMU.

10. The amount of disk space that must be available for page storage is related to the maximum number of processes, *n*, the number of bytes in the virtual address space, *v*, and the number of bytes of RAM, *r*. Give an expression for the worst case disk space requirements. How realistic is this amount?

11. If an instruction takes 10 nsec and a page fault takes an additional *n* nsec, give a formula for the effective instruction time if page faults occur every *k* instructions.

12. A machine has a 32-bit address space and an 8-KB page. The page table is entirely in hardware, with one 32-bit word per entry. When a process starts, the page table is copied to the hardware from memory, at one word every 100 nsec. If each process runs for 100 msec (including the time to load the page table), what fraction of the CPU time is devoted to loading the page tables?

13. A computer with a 32-bit address uses a two-level page table. Virtual addresses are split into a 9-bit top-level page table field, an 11-bit second-level page table field, and an offset. How large are the pages and how many are there in the address space?

14. Suppose that a 32-bit virtual address is broken up into four fields, *a*, *b*, *c*, and *d*. The first three are used for a three-level page table system. The fourth field, *d*, is the offset. Does the number of pages depend on the sizes of all four fields? If not, which ones matter and which ones do not?

15. A computer has 32-bit virtual addresses and 4-KB pages. The program and data together fit in the lowest page (0–4095) The stack fits in the highest page. How many entries are needed in the page table if traditional (one-level) paging is used? How many page table entries are needed for two-level paging, with 10 bits in each part?

16. Below is an execution trace of a program fragment for a computer with 512-byte pages. The program is located at address 1020, and its stack pointer is at 8192 (the stack grows toward 0). Give the page reference string generated by this program. Each instruction occupies 4 bytes (1 word) including immediate constants. Both instruction and data references count in the reference string.

> Load word 6144 into register 0
> Push register 0 onto the stack
> Call a procedure at 5120, stacking the return address
> Subtract the immediate constant 16 from the stack pointer
> Compare the actual parameter to the immediate constant 4
> Jump if equal to 5152

17. A computer whose processes have 1024 pages in their address spaces keeps its page tables in memory. The overhead required for reading a word from the page table is 5 nsec. To reduce this overhead, the computer has a TLB, which holds 32 (virtual page, physical page frame) pairs, and can do a look up in 1 nsec. What hit rate is needed to reduce the mean overhead to 2 nsec?

18. The TLB on the VAX does not contain an R bit. Why?

19. How can the associative memory device needed for a TLB be implemented in hardware, and what are the implications of such a design for expandability?

20. A machine has 48-bit virtual addresses and 32-bit physical addresses. Pages are 8 KB. How many entries are needed for the page table?

21. A computer with an 8-KB page, a 256-KB main memory, and a 64-GB virtual address space uses an inverted page table to implement its virtual memory. How big should the hash table be to ensure a mean hash chain length of less than 1? Assume that the hash table size is a power of two.

22. A student in a compiler design course proposes to the professor a project of writing a compiler that will produce a list of page references that can be used to implement the optimal page replacement algorithm. Is this possible? Why or why not? Is there anything that could be done to improve paging efficiency at run time?

23. If FIFO page replacement is used with four page frames and eight pages, how many page faults will occur with the reference string 0172327103 if the four frames are initially empty? Now repeat this problem for LRU.

24. Consider the page sequence of Fig. 4-16(b). Suppose that the R bits for the pages B through A are 11011011, respectively. Which page will second chance remove?

25. A small computer has four page frames. At the first clock tick, the R bits are 0111 (page 0 is 0, the rest are 1). At subsequent clock ticks, the values are 1011, 1010, 1101, 0010, 1010, 1100, and 0001. If the aging algorithm is used with an 8-bit counter, give the values of the four counters after the last tick.

26. Suppose that $\tau = 400$ in Fig. 4-21. Which page will be removed?

27. In the WSClock algorithm of Fig. 4-22(c), the hand points to a page with $R = 0$. If $\tau = 400$, will this page be removed? What about if $\tau = 1000$?

28. How long does it take to load a 64-KB program from a disk whose average seek time is 10 msec, whose rotation time is 10 msec, and whose tracks hold 32 KB

    (a) for a 2-KB page size?
    (b) for a 4-KB page size?

    The pages are spread randomly around the disk and the number of cylinders is so large that the chance of two pages being on the same cylinder is negligible.

29. A computer has four page frames. The time of loading, time of last access, and the R and M bits for each page are as shown below (the times are in clock ticks):

Page	Loaded	Last ref.	R	M
0	126	280	1	0
1	230	265	0	01
2	140	270	0	0
3	110	285	1	1

    (a) Which page will NRU replace?
    (b) Which page will FIFO replace?
    (c) Which page will LRU replace?
    (d) Which page will second chance replace?

30. One of the first timesharing machines, the PDP-1, had a memory of 4K 18-bit words. It held one process at a time in memory. When the scheduler decided to run another process, the process in memory was written to a paging drum, with 4K 18-bit words around the circumference of the drum. The drum could start writing (or reading) at any word, rather than only at word 0. Why do you suppose this drum was chosen?

31. A computer provides each process with 65,536 bytes of address space divided into pages of 4096 bytes. A particular program has a text size of 32,768 bytes, a data size of 16,386 bytes, and a stack size of 15,870 bytes. Will this program fit in the address space? If the page size were 512 bytes, would it fit? Remember that a page may not contain parts of two different segments.

32. Can a page be in two working sets at the same time? Explain.

33. If a page is shared between two processes, is it possible that the page is read-only for one process and read-write for the other? Why or why not?

34. It has been observed that the number of instructions executed between page faults is directly proportional to the number of page frames allocated to a program. If the available memory is doubled, the mean interval between page faults is also doubled. Suppose that a normal instruction takes 1 microsec, but if a page fault occurs, it takes 2001 μsec (i.e., 2 msec to handle the fault). If a program takes 60 sec to run, during which time it gets 15,000 page faults, how long would it take to run if twice as much memory were available?

35. A group of operating system designers for the Frugal Computer Company are thinking about ways of reducing the amount of backing store needed in their new operating system. The head guru has just suggested not bothering to save the program text in the swap area at all, but just page it in directly from the binary file whenever it is needed. Under what conditions, if any, does this idea work for the program text? Under what conditions, if any, does it work for the data?

36. A machine language instruction to load a 32-bit word into a register contains the 32-bit address of the word to be loaded. What is the maximum number of page faults this instruction can cause?

37. Explain the difference between internal fragmentation and external fragmentation. Which one occurs in paging systems? Which one occurs in systems using pure segmentation?

38. When segmentation and paging are both being used, as in MULTICS, first the segment descriptor must be looked up, then the page descriptor. Does the TLB also work this way, with two levels of lookup?

39. Plot a histogram and calculate the mean and median of the sizes of executable binary files on a computer to which you have access. On a Windows system, look at all .exe and .dll files; on a UNIX system look at all executable files in */bin*, */usr/bin*, and */local/bin* that are not scripts (or use the *file* utility to find all executables). Determine the optimal page size for this computer just considering the code (not data). Consider internal fragmentation and page table size, making some reasonable assumption about the size of a page table entry. Assume that all programs are equally likely to be run and thus should be weighted equally.

40. Small programs for MS-DOS can be compiled as *.COM* files. These files are always loaded at address 0x100 in a single memory segment that is used for code, data, and stack. Instructions that transfer control of execution, such as JMP and CALL, or that access static data from fixed addresses have the addresses compiled into the object code. Write a program that can relocate such a program file to run starting at an arbitrary address. Your program must scan through code looking for object codes for instructions that refer to fixed memory addresses, then modify those addresses that point to memory locations within the range to be relocated. You can find the object codes in an assembly language programming text. Note that doing this perfectly without additional information is, in general, an impossible task, because some data words may have values that mimic instruction object codes.

41. Write a program that simulates a paging system. At the start of the program, the user should be asked to choose a page replacement algorithm, choosing from FIFO, LRU, and at least one other. On each cycle, read the number of the referenced page from a file. Generate a listing similar to Fig. 4-25, except rotated 90 degrees so that each new page reference increases the length of the output file by one line.

42. Write a program that models the distance string algorithm described in the text. The input to the program is a list of page references (contained in a file), plus the number of page frames of physical memory available. If possible, use trace data from real programs instead of randomly-generated page references. The program should maintain the stack of pages, analogous to Fig. 4-25. At each page fault, a procedure should

be called to choose a replacement page. When the run is completed, the program should plot the distance string, analogous to Fig. 4-26. Make multiple runs for different values of the memory size and see what conclusions you can draw.

5

INPUT/OUTPUT

One of the main functions of an operating system is to control all the computer's I/O (Input/Output) devices. It must issue commands to the devices, catch interrupts, and handle errors. It should also provide an interface between the devices and the rest of the system that is simple and easy to use. To the extent possible, the interface should be the same for all devices (device independence). The I/O code represents a significant fraction of the total operating system. How the operating system manages I/O is the subject of this chapter.

This chapter is organized as follows. First we will look at some of the principles of I/O hardware, and then we will look at I/O software in general. I/O software can be structured in layers, with each layer having a well-defined task to perform. We will look at these layers to see what they do and how they fit together.

Following that introduction, we will look at several I/O devices in detail: disks, clocks, keyboards, and displays. For each device we will look at its hardware and software. Finally, we will consider power management.

5.1 PRINCIPLES OF I/O HARDWARE

Different people look at I/O hardware in different ways. Electrical engineers look at it in terms of chips, wires, power supplies, motors, and all the other physical components that make up the hardware. Programmers look at the interface presented to the software—the commands the hardware accepts, the functions it carries out, and the errors that can be reported back. In this book we are concerned with programming I/O devices, not designing, building, or maintaining them, so our interest will be restricted to how the hardware is programmed, not how it works inside. Nevertheless, the programming of many I/O devices is often intimately connected with their internal operation. In the next three sections we will provide a little general background on I/O hardware as it relates to programming. It may be regarded as a review and expansion of the introductory material in Sec. 1.4.

5.1.1 I/O Devices

I/O devices can be roughly divided into two categories: **block devices** and **character devices**. A block device is one that stores information in fixed-size blocks, each one with its own address. Common block sizes range from 512 bytes to 32,768 bytes. The essential property of a block device is that it is possible to read or write each block independently of all the other ones. Disks are the most common block devices.

If you look closely, the boundary between devices that are block addressable and those that are not is not well defined. Everyone agrees that a disk is a block addressable device because no matter where the arm currently is, it is always possible to seek to another cylinder and then wait for the required block to rotate under the head. Now consider a tape drive used for making disk backups. Tapes contain a sequence of blocks. If the tape drive is given a command to read block N, it can always rewind the tape and go forward until it comes to block N. This operation is analogous to a disk doing a seek, except that it takes much longer. Also, it may or may not be possible to rewrite one block in the middle of a tape. Even if it were possible to use tapes as random access block devices, that is stretching the point somewhat: they are normally not used that way.

The other type of I/O device is the character device. A character device delivers or accepts a stream of characters, without regard to any block structure. It is not addressable and does not have any seek operation. Printers, network interfaces, mice (for pointing), rats (for psychology lab experiments), and most other devices that are not disk-like can be seen as character devices.

This classification scheme is not perfect. Some devices just do not fit in. Clocks, for example, are not block addressable. Nor do they generate or accept character streams. All they do is cause interrupts at well-defined intervals. Memory-mapped screens do not fit the model well either. Still, the model of block and character devices is general enough that it can be used as a basis for making some of the operating system software dealing with I/O device independent. The file system, for example, deals just with abstract block devices and leaves the device-dependent part to lower-level software.

I/O devices cover a huge range in speeds, which puts considerable pressure on the software to perform well over many orders of magnitude in data rates. Fig. 5-1 shows the data rates of some common devices. Most of these devices tend to get faster as time goes on.

Device	Data rate
Keyboard	10 bytes/sec
Mouse	100 bytes/sec
56K modem	7 KB/sec
Telephone channel	8 KB/sec
Dual ISDN lines	16 KB/sec
Laser printer	100 KB/sec
Scanner	400 KB/sec
Classic Ethernet	1.25 MB/sec
USB (Universal Serial Bus)	1.5 MB/sec
Digital camcorder	4 MB/sec
IDE disk	5 MB/sec
40x CD-ROM	6 MB/sec
Fast Ethernet	12.5 MB/sec
ISA bus	16.7 MB/sec
EIDE (ATA-2) disk	16.7 MB/sec
FireWire (IEEE 1394)	50 MB/sec
XGA Monitor	60 MB/sec
SONET OC-12 network	78 MB/sec
SCSI Ultra 2 disk	80 MB/sec
Gigabit Ethernet	125 MB/sec
Ultrium tape	320 MB/sec
PCI bus	528 MB/sec
Sun Gigaplane XB backplane	20 GB/sec

Figure 5-1. Some typical device, network, and bus data rates.

5.1.2 Device Controllers

I/O units typically consist of a mechanical component and an electronic component. It is often possible to separate the two portions to provide a more modular and general design. The electronic component is called the **device controller** or **adapter**. On personal computers, it often takes the form of a printed circuit card that can be inserted into an expansion slot. The mechanical component is the device itself. This arrangement is shown in Fig. 1-5.

The controller card usually has a connector on it, into which a cable leading to the device itself can be plugged. Many controllers can handle two, four, or even eight identical devices. If the interface between the controller and device is a standard interface, either an official ANSI, IEEE, or ISO standard or a de facto one, then companies can make controllers or devices that fit that interface. Many companies, for example, make disk drives that match the IDE or SCSI interface.

The interface between the controller and the device is often a very low-level interface. A disk, for example, might be formatted with 256 sectors of 512 bytes per track. What actually comes off the drive, however, is a serial bit stream, starting with a **preamble**, then the 4096 bits in a sector, and finally a checksum, also called an **Error-Correcting Code** (**ECC**). The preamble is written when the disk is formatted and contains the cylinder and sector number, the sector size, and similar data, as well as synchronization information.

The controller's job is to convert the serial bit stream into a block of bytes and perform any error correction necessary. The block of bytes is typically first assembled, bit by bit, in a buffer inside the controller. After its checksum has been verified and the block declared to be error free, it can then be copied to main memory.

The controller for a monitor also works as a bit serial device at an equally low level. It reads bytes containing the characters to be displayed from memory and generates the signals used to modulate the CRT beam to cause it to write on the screen. The controller also generates the signals for making the CRT beam do a horizontal retrace after it has finished a scan line, as well as the signals for making it do a vertical retrace after the entire screen has been scanned. If it were not for the CRT controller, the operating system programmer would have to explicitly program the analog scanning of the tube. With the controller, the operating system initializes the controller with a few parameters, such as the number of characters or pixels per line and number of lines per screen, and lets the controller take care of actually driving the beam.

5.1.3 Memory-Mapped I/O

Each controller has a few registers that are used for communicating with the CPU. By writing into these registers, the operating system can command the device to deliver data, accept data, switch itself on or off, or otherwise perform some action. By reading from these registers, the operating system can learn what the device's state is, whether it is prepared to accept a new command, and so on.

In addition to the control registers, many devices have a data buffer that the operating system can read and write. For example, a common way for computers to display pixels on the screen is to have a video RAM, which is basically just a data buffer, available for programs or the operating system to write into.

The issue thus arises of how the CPU communicates with the control registers and the device data buffers. Two alternatives exist. In the first approach, each control register is assigned an **I/O port** number, an 8- or 16-bit integer. Using a special I/O instruction such as

IN REG,PORT,

the CPU can read in control register PORT and store the result in CPU register REG. Similarly, using

OUT PORT,REG

the CPU can write the contents of REG to a control register. Most early computers, including nearly all mainframes, such as the IBM 360 and all of its successors, worked this way.

In this scheme, the address spaces for memory and I/O are different, as shown in Fig. 5-2(a). The instructions

IN R0,4

and

MOV R0,4

are completely different in this design. The former reads the contents of I/O port 4 and puts it in R0 whereas the latter reads the contents of memory word 4 and puts it in R0. The 4s in these examples thus refer to different and unrelated address spaces.

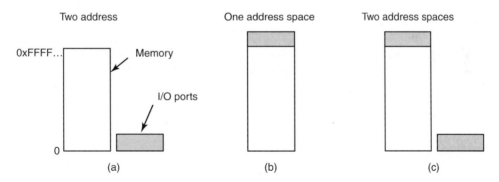

Figure 5-2. (a) Separate I/O and memory space. (b) Memory-mapped I/O. (c) Hybrid.

The second approach, introduced with the PDP-11, is to map all the control registers into the memory space, as shown in Fig. 5-2(b). Each control register is assigned a unique memory address to which no memory is assigned. This system is called **memory-mapped I/O**. Usually, the assigned addresses are at the top of the address space. A hybrid scheme, with memory-mapped I/O data buffers and separate I/O ports for the control registers is shown in Fig. 5-2(c). The Pentium uses this architecture, with addresses 640K to 1M being reserved for device data buffers in IBM PC compatibles, in addition to I/O ports 0 through 64K.

How do these schemes work? In all cases, when the CPU wants to read a word, either from memory or from an I/O port, it puts the address it needs on the bus' address lines and then asserts a READ signal on a bus' control line. A second signal line is used to tell whether I/O space or memory space is needed. If it is memory space, the memory responds to the request. If it is I/O space, the I/O device responds to the request. If there is only memory space [as in Fig. 5-2(b)], every memory module and every I/O device compares the address lines to the range of addresses that it services. It the address falls in its range, it responds to the request. Since no address is ever assigned to both memory and an I/O device, there is no ambiguity and no conflict.

The two schemes for addressing the controllers have different strengths and weaknesses. Let us start with the advantages of memory-mapped I/O. First, if special I/O instructions are needed to read and write the device control registers, access to them requires the use of assembly code since there is no way to execute an IN or OUT instruction in C or C++. Calling such a procedure adds overhead to controlling I/O. In contrast, with memory-mapped I/O, device control registers are just variables in memory and can be addressed in C the same way as any other variables. Thus with memory-mapped I/O, a I/O device driver can be written entirely in C. Without memory-mapped I/O, some assembly code is needed.

Second, with memory-mapped I/O, no special protection mechanism is needed to keep user processes from performing I/O. All the operating system has to do is refrain from putting that portion of the address space containing the control registers in any user's virtual address space. Better yet, if each device has its control registers on a different page of the address space, the operating system can give a user control over specific devices but not others by simply including the desired pages in its page table. Such a scheme can allow different device drivers to be placed in different address spaces, not only reducing kernel size but also keeping one driver from interfering with others.

Third, with memory-mapped I/O, every instruction that can reference memory can also reference control registers. For example, if there is an instruction, TEST, that tests a memory word for 0, it can also be used to test a control register for 0, which might be the signal that the device is idle and can accept a new command. The assembly language code might look like this:

```
LOOP:  TEST PORT_4        // check if port 4 is 0
       BEQ READY          // if it is 0, go to ready
       BRANCH LOOP        // otherwise, continue testing
READY:
```

If memory-mapped I/O is not present, the control register must first be read into the CPU, then tested, requiring two instructions instead of one. In the case of the loop given above, a fourth instruction has to be added, slightly slowing down the responsiveness of detecting an idle device.

In computer design, practically everything involves trade-offs, and that is the case here too. Memory-mapped I/O also has its disadvantages. First, most computers nowadays have some form of caching of memory words. Caching a device control register would be disastrous. Consider the assembly code loop given above in the presence of caching. The first reference to PORT_4 would cause it to be cached. Subsequent references would just take the value from the cache and not even ask the device. Then when the device finally became ready, the software would have no way of finding it out. Instead, the loop would go on forever.

To prevent this situation with memory-mapped I/O, the hardware has to be equipped with the ability to selectively disable caching, for example, on a per page basis. This feature adds extra complexity to both the hardware and the operating system, which has to manage the selective caching.

Second, if there is only one address space, then all memory modules and all I/O devices must examine all memory references to see which ones to respond to. If the computer has a single bus, as in Fig. 5-3(a), having everyone look at every address is straightforward.

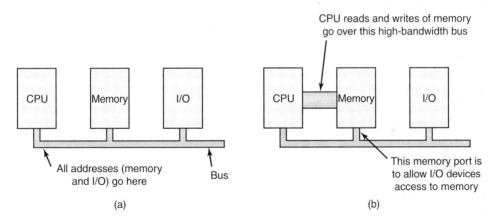

Figure 5-3. (a) A single-bus architecture. (b) A dual-bus memory architecture.

However, the trend in modern personal computers is to have a dedicated high-speed memory bus as shown in Fig. 5-3(b), a property also found in mainframes, incidentally. This bus is tailored for optimize memory performance, with no compromises for the sake of slow I/O devices. Pentium systems even have three external buses (memory, PCI, ISA), as shown in Fig. 1-11.

The trouble with having a separate memory bus on memory-mapped machines is that the I/O devices have no way of seeing memory addresses as they go by on the memory bus, so they have no way of responding. Again, special measures have to be taken to make memory-mapped I/O work on a system with multiple buses. One possibility is to first send all memory references to the memory. If the memory fails to respond, then the CPU tries the other buses. This design can be made to work but requires additional hardware complexity.

A second possible design is to put a snooping device on the memory bus to pass all addresses presented to potentially interested I/O devices. The problem here is that I/O devices may not be able to process requests at the speed the memory can.

A third possible design, which is the one used on the Pentium configuration of Fig. 1-11, is to filter addresses in the PCI bridge chip. This chip contains range registers that are preloaded at boot time. For example, 640K to 1M could be marked as a nonmemory range. Addresses that fall within one of the ranges marked as nonmemory are forwarded onto the PCI bus instead of to memory. The disadvantage of this scheme is the need for figuring out at boot time which memory addresses are not really memory addresses. Thus each scheme has arguments for and against it, so compromises and trade-offs are inevitable.

5.1.4 Direct Memory Access (DMA)

No matter whether a CPU does or does not have memory-mapped I/O, it needs to address the device controllers to exchange data with them. The CPU can request data from an I/O controller one byte at a time but doing so wastes the CPU's time, so a different scheme, called **DMA** (**Direct Memory Access**) is often used. The operating system can only use DMA if the hardware has a DMA controller, which most systems do. Sometimes this controller is integrated into disk controllers and other controllers, but such a design requires a separate DMA controller for each device. More commonly, a single DMA controller is available (e.g., on the parentboard) for regulating transfers to multiple devices, often concurrently.

No matter where it is physically located, the DMA controller has access to the system bus independent of the CPU, as shown in Fig. 5-4. It contains several registers that can be written and read by the CPU. These include a memory address register, a byte count register, and one or more control registers. The control registers specify the I/O port to use, the direction of the transfer (reading from the I/O device or writing to the I/O device), the transfer unit (byte at a time or word at a time), and the number of bytes to transfer in one burst.

To explain how DMA works, let us first look at how disk reads occur when DMA is not used. First the controller reads the block (one or more sectors) from the drive serially, bit by bit, until the entire block is in the controller's internal buffer. Next, it computes the checksum to verify that no read errors have occurred. Then the controller causes an interrupt. When the operating system starts running, it can read the disk block from the controller's buffer a byte or a word at a time by executing a loop, with each iteration reading one byte or word from a controller device register and storing it in main memory.

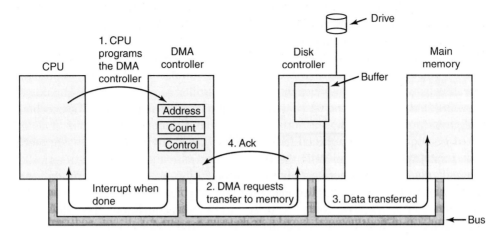

Figure 5-4. Operation of a DMA transfer.

When DMA is used, the procedure is different. First the CPU programs the DMA controller by setting its registers so it knows what to transfer where (step 1 in Fig. 5-4). It also issues a command to the disk controller telling it to read data from the disk into its internal buffer and verify the checksum. When valid data are in the disk controller's buffer, DMA can begin.

The DMA controller initiates the transfer by issuing a read request over the bus to the disk controller (step 2). This read request looks like any other read request, and the disk controller does not know or care whether it came from the CPU or from a DMA controller. Typically, the memory address to write to is on the bus' address lines so when the disk controller fetches the next word from its internal buffer, it knows where to write it. The write to memory is another standard bus cycle (step 3). When the write is complete, the disk controller sends an acknowledgement signal to the disk controller, also over the bus (step 4). The DMA controller then increments the memory address to use and decrements the byte count. If the byte count is still greater than 0, steps 2 through 4 are repeated until the count reaches 0. At that time, the DMA controller interrupts the CPU to let it know that the transfer is now complete. When the operating system starts up, it does not have to copy the disk block to memory; it is already there.

DMA controllers vary considerably in their sophistication. The simplest ones handle one transfer at a time, as described above. More complex ones can be programmed to handle multiple transfers at once. Such controllers have multiple sets of registers internally, one for each channel. The CPU starts by loading each set of registers with the relevant parameters for its transfer. Each transfer must use a different device controller. After each word is transferred (steps 2 through 4) in Fig. 5-4, the DMA controller decides which device to service next. It may be set up to use a round-robin algorithm, or it may have a priority scheme design to favor some devices over others. Multiple requests to different device controllers may be pending at the same time, provided that there is an unambiguous way to tell the acknowledgements apart. Often a different acknowledgement line on the bus is used for each DMA channel for this reason.

Many buses can operate in two modes: word-at-a-time mode and block mode. Some DMA controllers can also operate in either mode. In the former mode, the operation is as described above: the DMA controller requests for the transfer of one word and gets it. If the CPU also wants the bus, it has to wait. The mechanism is called **cycle stealing** because the device controller sneaks in and steals an occasional bus cycle from the CPU once in a while, delaying it slightly. In block mode, the DMA controller tells the device to acquire the bus, issue a series of transfers, then release the bus. This form of operation is called **burst mode**. It is more efficient than cycle stealing because acquiring the bus takes time and multiple words can be transferred for the price of one bus acquisition. The down side to burst mode is that it can block the CPU and other devices for a substantial period of time if a long burst is being transferred.

In the model we have been discussing, sometimes called **fly-by mode**, the DMA controller tells the device controller to transfer the data directly to main memory. An alternative mode that some DMA controllers use is to have the device controller send the word to the DMA controller, which then issues a second bus request to write the word to wherever it is supposed to go. This scheme requires an extra bus cycle per word transferred, but is more flexible in that it can also perform device-to-device copies and even memory-to-memory copies (by first issuing a read to memory and then issuing a write to memory at a different address).

Most DMA controllers use physical memory addresses for their transfers. Using physical addresses requires the operating system to convert the virtual address of the intended memory buffer into a physical address and write this physical address into the DMA controller's address register. An alternative scheme used in a few DMA controllers is to write virtual addresses into the DMA controller instead. Then the DMA controller must use the MMU to have the virtual-to-physical translation done. Only in the case that the MMU is part of the memory (possible, but rare) rather than part of the CPU, can virtual addresses be put on the bus.

We mentioned earlier that the disk first reads data into its internal buffer before DMA can start. You may be wondering why the controller does not just store the bytes in main memory as soon as it gets them from the disk. In other words, why does it need an internal buffer? There are two reasons. First, by doing internal buffering, the disk controller can verify the checksum before starting a transfer. If the checksum is incorrect, an error is signaled and no transfer is done.

The second reason is that once a disk transfer has started, the bits keep arriving from the disk at a constant rate, whether the controller is ready for them or not. If the controller tried to write data directly to memory, it would have to go over the system bus for each word transferred. If the bus were busy due to some other device using it (e.g., in burst mode), the controller would have to wait. If the next disk word arrived before the previous one had been stored, the controller would have to store it somewhere. If the bus were very busy, the controller might end up storing quite a few words and having a lot of administration to do as well. When the block is buffered internally, the bus is not needed until the DMA begins, so the design of the controller is much simpler because the DMA transfer to memory is not time critical. (Some older controllers did, in fact, go directly to memory with only a small amount of internal buffering, but when the bus was very busy, a transfer might have had to be terminated with an overrun error.)

Not all computers use DMA. The argument against it is that the main CPU is often far faster than the DMA controller and can do the job much faster (when the limiting factor is not the speed of the I/O device). If there is no other work for it to do, having the (fast) CPU wait for the (slow) DMA controller to finish is pointless. Also, getting rid of the DMA controller and having the CPU do all the work in software saves money, important on low-end (embedded) computers.

5.1.5 Interrupts Revisited

We briefly introduced interrupts in Sec. 1.4.3, but there is more to be said. In a typical personal computer system, the interrupt structure is as shown in Fig. 5-5. At the hardware level, interrupts work as follows. When an I/O device has finished the work given to it, it causes an interrupt (assuming that interrupts have been enabled by the operating system). It does this by asserting a signal on a bus line that it has been assigned. This signal is detected by the interrupt controller chip on the parentboard, which then decides what to do.

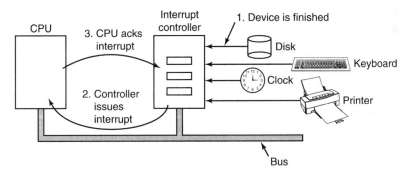

Figure 5-5. How an interrupt happens. The connections between the devices and the interrupt controller actually use interrupt lines on the bus rather than dedicated wires.

If no other interrupts are pending, the interrupt controller processes the interrupt immediately. If another one is in progress, or another device has made a simultaneous request on a higher-priority interrupt request line on the bus, the device is just ignored for the moment. In this case it continues to assert an interrupt signal on the bus until it is serviced by the CPU.

To handle the interrupt, the controller puts a number on the address lines specifying which device wants attention and asserts a signal that interrupts the CPU.

The interrupt signal causes the CPU to stop what it is doing and start doing something else. The number on the address lines is used as an index into a table called the **interrupt vector** to fetch a new program counter. This program counter points to the start of the corresponding interrupt service procedure. Typically traps and interrupts use the same mechanism from this point on, and frequently share the same interrupt vector. The location of the interrupt vector can be hardwired into the machine or it can be anywhere in memory, with a CPU register (loaded by the operating system) pointing to its origin.

Shortly after it starts running, the interrupt service procedure acknowledges the interrupt by writing a certain value to one of the interrupt controller's I/O ports. This acknowledgement tells the controller that it is free to issue another interrupt. By having the CPU delay this acknowledgement until it is ready to handle the next interrupt, race conditions involving multiple almost simultaneous interrupts can be avoided. As an aside, some (older) computers do not have a centralized interrupt controller chip, so each device controller requests its own interrupts.

The hardware always saves certain information before starting the service procedure. Which information is saved and where it is saved varies greatly from CPU to CPU. As a bare minimum, the program counter must be saved, so the interrupted process can be restarted. At the other extreme, all the visible registers and a large number of internal registers may be saved as well.

One issue is where to save this information. One option is to put it in internal registers that the operating system can read out as needed. A problem with this approach is that then the interrupt controller cannot be acknowledged until all potentially relevant information has been read out, lest a second interrupt overwrite the internal registers saving the state. This strategy leads to long dead times when interrupts are disabled and possibly lost interrupts and lost data.

Consequently, most CPUs save the information on the stack. However, this approach, too, has problems. To start with: whose stack? If the current stack is used, it may well be a user process stack. The stack pointer may not even be legal, which would cause a fatal error when the hardware tried to write some words at it. Also, it might point to the end of a page. After several memory writes, the page boundary might be exceeded and a page fault generated. Having a page fault occur during the hardware interrupt processing creates a bigger problem: where to save the state to handle the page fault?

If the kernel stack is used, there is a much better chance of the stack pointer being legal and pointing to a pinned page. However, switching into kernel mode may require changing MMU contexts and will probably invalidate most or all of the cache and TLB. Reloading all of these, statically or dynamically will increase the time to process an interrupt and thus waste CPU time.

Another problem is caused by the fact that most modern CPUs are heavily pipelined and often superscalar (internally parallel). In older systems, after each instruction was finished executing, the microprogram or hardware checked to see if there was an interrupt pending. If so, the program counter and PSW were pushed onto the stack and the interrupt sequence begun. After the interrupt handler ran, the reverse process took place, with the old PSW and program counter popped from the stack and the previous process continued.

This model makes the implicit assumption that if an interrupt occurs just after some instruction, all the instructions up to and including that instruction have been executed completely, and no instructions after it have executed at all. On older machines, this assumption was always valid. On modern ones it may not be.

For starters, consider the pipeline model of Fig. 1-6(a). What happens if an interrupt occurs while the pipeline is full (the usual case)? Many instructions are in various stages of execution. When the interrupt occurs, the value of the program counter may not reflect the correct boundary between executed instructions and nonexecuted instructions. More likely, it reflects the address of the next instruction to be fetched and pushed into the pipeline rather than the address of the instruction that just was processed by the execution unit.

As a consequence, there may be a well-defined boundary between instructions that have actually executed and those that have not, but the hardware may not know what it is. Consequently, when the operating system must return from an interrupt, it cannot just start filling the pipeline from the address contained in the program counter. It must figure out what the last executed instruction was, often a complex task that may require analyzing the state of the machine.

Although this situation is bad, interrupts on a superscalar machine, such as that of Fig. 1-6(b) are far worse. Because instructions may execute out of order, there may be no well-defined boundary between the executed and nonexecuted instructions. It may well be that instructions 1, 2, 3, 5, and 8 have executed, but instructions 4, 6, 7, 9, 10, and beyond have not. Furthermore, the program counter may now be pointing to instruction 9, 10, or 11.

An interrupt that leaves the machine in a well-defined state is called a **precise interrupt** (Walker and Cragon, 1995). Such an interrupt has four properties:

1. The PC (Program Counter) is saved in a known place.

2. All instructions before the one pointed to by the PC have fully executed.

3. No instruction beyond the one pointed to by the PC has been executed.

4. The execution state of the instruction pointed to by the PC is known.

Note that there is no prohibition on instructions beyond the one pointed to by the PC from starting. It is just that any changes they make to registers or memory must be undone before the interrupt happens. It is permitted that the instruction pointed to has been executed. It is also permitted that it has not been executed. However, it must be clear which case applies. Often, if the interrupt is an I/O interrupt, the instruction will not yet have started. However, if the interrupt is really a trap or page fault, then the PC generally points to the instruction that caused the fault so it can be restarted later.

An interrupt that does not meet these requirements is called an **imprecise interrupt** and makes life extremely unpleasant for the operating system writer, who now has to figure out what has happened and what still has to happen. Machines with imprecise interrupts usually vomit a large amount of internal state onto the stack to give the operating system the possibility of figuring out what was going on. Saving a large amount of information to memory on every interrupt makes interrupts slow and recovery even worse. This leads to the ironic situation of having very fast superscalar CPUs sometimes being unsuitable for real-time work due to slow interrupts.

Some computers are designed so that some kinds of interrupts and traps are precise and others are not. For example, having I/O interrupts be precise but traps due to fatal programming errors be imprecise is not so bad since no attempt need be made to restart the running process. Some machines have a bit that can be set to force all interrupts to be precise. The downside of setting this bit is that it forces the CPU to carefully log everything it is doing and maintain shadow copies of registers so it can generate a precise interrupt at any instant. All this overhead has a major impact on performance.

Some superscalar machines, such as the Pentium Pro and all of its successors, have precise interrupts to allow old 386, 486, and Pentium I programs to work correctly (superscalar was introduced in the Pentium Pro; the Pentium I just had two pipelines). The price paid for precise interrupts is extremely complex interrupt logic within the CPU to make sure that when the interrupt controller signals that it wants to cause an interrupt, all instructions up to some point are allowed to finish and none beyond that point are allowed to have any noticeable effect on the machine state. Here the price is paid not in time, but in chip area and in complexity of the design. If precise interrupts were not required for backward compatibility purposes, this chip area would be available for larger on-chip caches, making the CPU faster. On the other hand, imprecise interrupts make the operating system far more complicated and slower, so it is hard to tell which approach is really better.

5.2 PRINCIPLES OF I/O SOFTWARE

Let us now turn away from the I/O hardware and look at the I/O software. First we will look at the goals of the I/O software and then at the different ways I/O can be done from the point of view of the operating system.

5.2.1 Goals of the I/O Software

A key concept in the design of I/O software is known as **device indepen-dence**. What it means is that it should be possible to write programs that can access any I/O device without having to specify the device in advance. For exam-ple, a program that reads a file as input should be able to read a file on a floppy disk, on a hard disk, or on a CD-ROM, without having to modify the program for each different device. Similarly, one should be able to type a command such as

```
sort <input >output
```

and have it work with input coming from a floppy disk, an IDE disk, a SCSI disk, or the keyboard, and the output going to any kind of disk or the screen. It is up to the operating system to take care of the problems caused by the fact that these devices really are different and require very different command sequences to read or write.

Closely related to device independence is the goal of **uniform naming**. The name of a file or a device should simply be a string or an integer and not depend on the device in any way. In UNIX, all disks can be integrated in the file system hierarchy in arbitrary ways so the user need not be aware of which name corresponds to which device. For example, a floppy disk can be **mounted** on top of the directory */usr/ast/backup* so that copying a file to */usr/ast/backup/monday* copies the file to the floppy disk. In this way, all files and devices are addressed the same way: by a path name.

Another important issue for I/O software is **error handling**. In general, errors should be handled as close to the hardware as possible. If the controller discovers a read error, it should try to correct the error itself if it can. If it cannot, then the device driver should handle it, perhaps by just trying to read the block again. Many errors are transient, such as read errors caused by specks of dust on the read head, and will go away if the operation is repeated. Only if the lower layers are not able to deal with the problem should the upper layers be told about it. In many cases, error recovery can be done transparently at a low level without the upper levels even knowing about the error.

Still another key issue is **synchronous** (blocking) versus **asynchronous** (interrupt-driven) transfers. Most physical I/O is asynchronous—the CPU starts the transfer and goes off to do something else until the interrupt arrives. User pro-grams are much easier to write if the I/O operations are blocking—after a read system call the program is automatically suspended until the data are available in the buffer. It is up to the operating system to make operations that are actually interrupt-driven look blocking to the user programs.

Another issue for the I/O software is **buffering**. Often data that come off a device cannot be stored directly in its final destination. For example, when a packet comes in off the network, the operating system does not know where to put it until it has stored the packet somewhere and examined it. Also, some devices have severe real-time constraints (for example, digital audio devices), so the data must be put into an output buffer in advance to decouple the rate at which the buffer is filled from the rate at which it is emptied, in order to avoid buffer under-runs. Buffering involves considerable copying and often has a major impact on I/O performance.

The final concept that we will mention here is sharable versus dedicated devices. Some I/O devices, such as disks, can be used by many users at the same time. No problems are caused by multiple users having open files on the same disk at the same time. Other devices, such as tape drives, have to be dedicated to a single user until that user is finished. Then another user can have the tape drive. Having two or more users writing blocks intermixed at random to the same tape will definitely not work. Introducing dedicated (unshared) devices also introduces a variety of problems, such as deadlocks. Again, the operating system must be able to handle both shared and dedicated devices in a way that avoids problems.

5.2.2 Programmed I/O

There are three fundamentally different ways that I/O can be performed. In this section we will look at the first one (programmed I/O). In the next two sections we will examine the others (interrupt-driven I/O and I/O using DMA). The simplest form of I/O is to have the CPU do all the work. This method is called **programmed I/O**.

It is simplest to illustrate programmed I/O by means of an example. Consider a user process that wants to print the eight-character string "ABCDEFGH" on the printer. It first assembles the string in a buffer in user space, as shown in Fig. 5-6(a).

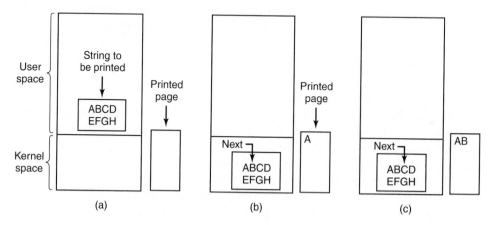

Figure 5-6. Steps in printing a string.

The user process then acquires the printer for writing by making a system call to open it. If the printer is currently in use by another process, this call will fail and return an error code or will block until the printer is available, depending on the operating system and the parameters of the call. Once it has the printer, the user process makes a system call telling the operating system to print the string on the printer.

The operating system then (usually) copies the buffer with the string to an array, say, *p*, in kernel space, where it is more easily accessed (because the kernel may have to change the memory map to get at user space). It then checks to see if the printer is currently available. If not, it waits until it is available. As soon as the printer is available, the operating system copies the first character to the printer's data register, in this example using memory-mapped I/O. This action activates the printer. The character may not appear yet because some printers buffer a line or a page before printing anything. In Fig. 5-6(b), however, we see that the first character has been printed and that the system has marked the "B" as the next character to be printed.

As soon as it has copied the first character to the printer, the operating system checks to see if the printer is ready to accept another one. Generally, the printer has a second register, which gives its status. The act of writing to the data register causes the status to become not ready. When the printer controller has processed the current character, it indicates its availability by setting some bit in its status register or putting some value in it.

At this point the operating system waits for the printer to become ready again. When that happens, it prints the next character, as shown in Fig. 5-6(c). This loop continues until the entire string has been printed. Then control returns to the user process.

The actions followed by the operating system are summarized in Fig. 5-7. First the data are copied to the kernel. Then the operating system enters a tight loop outputting the characters one at a time. The essential aspect of programmed I/O, clearly illustrated in this figure, is that after outputting a character, the CPU continuously polls the device to see if it is ready to accept another one. This behavior is often called **polling** or **busy waiting**.

```
copy_from_user(buffer, p, count);              /* p is the kernel bufer */
for (i = 0; i < count; i++) {                  /* loop on every character */
      while (*printer_status_reg != READY) ;   /* loop until ready */
      *printer_data_register = p[i];           /* output one character */
}
return_to_user( );
```

Figure 5-7. Writing a string to the printer using programmed I/O.

Programmed I/O is simple but has the disadvantage of tying up the CPU full time until all the I/O is done. If the time to "print" a character is very short (because all the printer is doing is copying the new character to an internal buffer), then busy waiting is fine. Also, in an embedded system, where the CPU has nothing else to do, busy waiting is reasonable. However, in more complex systems, where the CPU has other work to do, busy waiting is inefficient. A better I/O method is needed.

5.2.3 Interrupt-Driven I/O

Now let us consider the case of printing on a printer that does not buffer characters but prints each one as it arrives. If the printer can print, say 100 characters/sec, each character takes 10 msec to print. This means that after every character is written to the printer's data register, the CPU will sit in an idle loop for 10 msec waiting to be allowed to output the next character. This is more than enough time to do a context switch and run some other process for the 10 msec that would otherwise be wasted.

The way to allow the CPU to do something else while waiting for the printer to become ready is to use interrupts. When the system call to print the string is made, the buffer is copied to kernel space, as we showed earlier, and the first character is copied to the printer as soon as it is willing to accept a character. At that point the CPU calls the scheduler and some other process is run. The process that asked for the string to be printed is blocked until the entire string has printed. The work done on the system call is shown in Fig. 5-8(a).

```
copy_from_user(buffer, p, count);
enable_interrupts( );
while (*printer_status_reg != READY) ;
*printer_data_register = p[0];
scheduler( );
```

```
if (count == 0) {
    unblock_user( );
} else {
    *printer_data_register = p[i];
    count = count − 1;
    i = i + 1;
}
acknowledge_interrupt( );
return_from_interrupt( );
```

(a)   (b)

Figure 5-8. Writing a string to the printer using interrupt-driven I/O. (a) Code executed when the print system call is made. (b) Interrupt service procedure.

When the printer has printed the character and is prepared to accept the next one, it generates an interrupt. This interrupt stops the current process and saves its state. Then the printer interrupt service procedure is run. A crude version of this code is shown in Fig. 5-8(b). If there are no more characters to print, the interrupt handler takes some action to unblock the user. Otherwise, it outputs the next character, acknowledges the interrupt, and returns to the process that was running just before the interrupt, which continues from where it left off.

5.2.4 I/O Using DMA

An obvious disadvantage of interrupt-driven I/O is that an interrupt occurs on every character. Interrupts take time, so this scheme wastes a certain amount of CPU time. A solution is to use DMA. Here the idea is to let the DMA controller feed the characters to the printer one at time, without the CPU being bothered. In essence, DMA is programmed I/O, only with the DMA controller doing all the work, instead of the main CPU. An outline of the code is given in Fig. 5-9.

```
copy_from_user(buffer, p, count);          acknowledge_interrupt( );
set_up_DMA_controller( );                  unblock_user( );
scheduler( );                              return_from_interrupt( );
```

            (a)   (b)

Figure 5-9. Printing a string using DMA. (a) Code executed when the print system call is made. (b) Interrupt service procedure.

The big win with DMA is reducing the number of interrupts from one per character to one per buffer printed. If there are many characters and interrupts are slow, this can be a major improvement. On the other hand, the DMA controller is usually much slower than the main CPU. If the DMA controller is not capable of driving the device at full speed, or the CPU usually has nothing to do anyway while waiting for the DMA interrupt, then interrupt-driven I/O or even programmed I/O may be better.

5.3 I/O SOFTWARE LAYERS

I/O software is typically organized in four layers, as shown in Fig. 5-10. Each layer has a well-defined function to perform and a well-defined interface to the adjacent layers. The functionality and interfaces differ from system to system, so the discussion that follows, which examines all the layers starting at the bottom, is not specific to one machine.

5.3.1 Interrupt Handlers

While programmed I/O is occasionally useful, for most I/O, interrupts are an unpleasant fact of life and cannot be avoided. They should be hidden away, deep in the bowels of the operating system, so that as little of the operating system as possible knows about them. The best way to hide them is to have the driver starting an I/O operation block until the I/O has completed and the interrupt occurs. The driver can block itself by doing a **down** on a semaphore, a **wait** on a condition variable, a **receive** on a message, or something similar, for example.

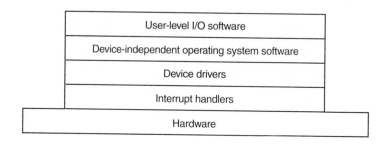

Figure 5-10. Layers of the I/O software system.

When the interrupt happens, the interrupt procedure does whatever it has to in order to handle the interrupt. Then it can unblock the driver that started it. In some cases it will just complete up on a semaphore. In others it will do a signal on a condition variable in a monitor. In still others, it will send a message to the blocked driver. In all cases the net effect of the interrupt will be that a driver that was previously blocked will now be able to run. This model works best if drivers are structured as kernel processes, with their own states, stacks, and program counters.

Of course, reality is not quite so simple. Processing an interrupt is not just a matter of taking the interrupt, doing an up on some semaphore, and then executing an IRET instruction to return from the interrupt to the previous process. There is a great deal more work involved for the operating system. We will now give an outline of this work as a series of steps that must be performed in software after the hardware interrupt has completed. It should be noted that the details are very system dependent, so some of the steps listed below may not be needed on a particular machine and steps not listed may be required. Also, the steps that do occur may be in a different order on some machines.

1. Save any registers (including the PSW) that have not already been saved by the interrupt hardware.

2. Set up a context for the interrupt service procedure. Doing this may involve setting up the TLB, MMU and a page table.

3. Set up a stack for the interrupt service procedure.

4. Acknowledge the interrupt controller. If there is no centralized interrupt controller, reenable interrupts.

5. Copy the registers from where they were saved (possibly some stack) to the process table.

6. Run the interrupt service procedure. It will extract information from the interrupting device controller's registers.

7. Choose which process to run next. If the interrupt has caused some high-priority process that was blocked to become ready, it may be chosen to run now.

8. Set up the MMU context for the process to run next. Some TLB set up may also be needed.

9. Load the new process' registers, including its PSW.

10. Start running the new process.

As can be seen, interrupt processing is far from trivial. It also takes a considerable number of CPU instructions, especially on machines in which virtual memory is present and page tables have to be set up or the state of the MMU stored (e.g., the R and M bits). On some machines the TLB and CPU cache may also have to be managed when switching between user and kernel modes, which takes additional machine cycles.

5.3.2 Device Drivers

Earlier in this chapter we looked at what device controllers do. We saw that each controller has some device registers used to give it commands or some device registers used to read out its status or both. The number of device registers and the nature of the commands vary radically from device to device. For example, a mouse driver has to accept information from the mouse telling how far it has moved and which buttons are currently depressed. In contrast, a disk driver has to know about sectors, tracks, cylinders, heads, arm motion, motor drives, head settling times, and all the other mechanics of making the disk work properly. Obviously, these drivers will be very different.

As a consequence, each I/O device attached to a computer needs some device-specific code for controlling it. This code, called the **device driver**, is generally written by the device's manufacturer and delivered along with the device. Since each operating system needs its own drivers, device manufacturers commonly supply drivers for several popular operating systems.

Each device driver normally handles one device type, or at most, one class of closely related devices. For example, a SCSI disk driver can usually handle multiple SCSI disks of different sizes and different speeds, and perhaps a SCSI CD-ROM as well. On the other hand, a mouse and joystick are so different that different drivers are usually required. However, there is no technical restriction on having one device driver control multiple unrelated devices. It is just not a good idea.

In order to access the device's hardware, meaning the controller's registers, the device driver normally has to be part of the operating system kernel, at least with current architectures. Actually, it would be possible to construct drivers that ran in user space, with system calls for reading and writing the device registers. In fact, this design would be a good idea, since it would isolate the kernel from the drivers and the drivers from each other. Doing this would eliminate a major source of system crashes—buggy drivers that interfere with the kernel in one way or another. However, since current operating systems expect drivers to run in the kernel, that is the model we will consider here.

Since the designers of every operating system know that pieces of code (drivers) written by outsiders will be installed in it, it needs to have an architecture that allows such installation. This means having a well-defined model of what a driver does and how it interacts with the rest of the operating system. Device drivers are normally positioned below the rest of the operating system, as illustrated in Fig. 5-11.

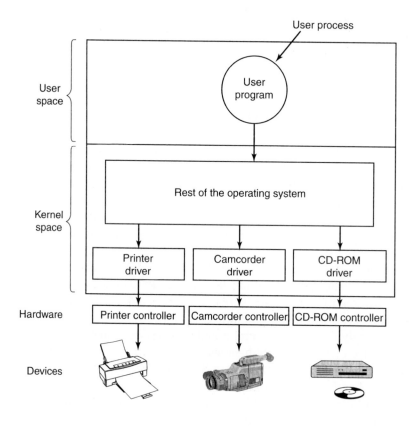

Figure 5-11. Logical positioning of device drivers. In reality all communication between drivers and device controllers goes over the bus.

Operating systems usually classify drivers into one of a small number of categories. The most common categories are the **block devices**, such as disks, which contain multiple data blocks that can be addressed independently, and the **character devices**, such as keyboards and printers, which generate or accept a stream of characters.

Most operating systems define a standard interface that all block drivers must support and a second standard interface that all character drivers must support. These interfaces consist of a number of procedures that the rest of the operating system can call to get the driver to do work for it. Typical procedures are those to read a block (block device) or write a character string (character device).

In some systems, the operating system is a single binary program that contains all of the drivers that it will need compiled into it. This scheme was the norm for years with UNIX systems because they were run by computer centers and I/O devices rarely changed. If a new device was added, the system administrator simply recompiled the kernel with the new driver to build a new binary.

With the advent of personal computers, with their myriad of I/O devices, this model no longer worked. Few users are capable of recompiling or relinking the kernel, even if they have the source code or object modules, which is not always the case. Instead, operating systems, starting with MS-DOS, went over to a model in which drivers were dynamically loaded into the system during execution. Different systems handle loading drivers in different ways.

A device driver has several functions. The most obvious one is to accept abstract read and write requests from the device-independent software above it and see that they are carried out. But there are also a few other functions they must perform. For example, the driver must initialize the device, if needed. It may also need to manage its power requirements and log events.

Many device drivers have a similar general structure. A typical driver starts out by checking the input parameters to see if they are valid. If not, an error is returned. If they are valid, a translation from abstract to concrete terms may be needed. For a disk driver, this may mean converting a linear block number into the head, track, sector, and cylinder numbers for the disk's geometry.

Next the driver may check if the device is currently in use. If it is, the request will be queued for later processing. If the device is idle, the hardware status will be examined to see if the request can be handled now. It may be necessary to switch the device on or start a motor before transfers can be begun. Once the device is on and ready to go, the actual control can begin.

Controlling the device means issuing a sequence of commands to it. The driver is the place where the command sequence is determined, depending on what has to be done. After the driver knows which commands it is going to issue, it starts writing them into the controller's device registers. After writing each command to the controller, it may be necessary to check to see if the controller accepted the command and is prepared to accept the next one. This sequence continues until all the commands have been issued. Some controllers can be given a linked list of commands (in memory) and told to read and process them all by itself without further help from the operating system.

After the commands have been issued, one of two situations will apply. In many cases the device driver must wait until the controller does some work for it, so it blocks itself until the interrupt comes in to unblock it. In other cases, however, the operation finishes without delay, so the driver need not block. As an example of the latter situation, scrolling the screen in character mode requires just writing a few bytes into the controller's registers. No mechanical motion is needed, so the entire operation can be completed in nanoseconds.

In the former case, the blocked driver will be awakened by the interrupt. In the latter case, it will never go to sleep. Either way, after the operation has been completed, the driver must check for errors. If everything is all right, the driver may have data to pass to the device-independent software (e.g., a block just read). Finally, it returns some status information for error reporting back to its caller. If any other requests are queued, one of them can now be selected and started. If nothing is queued, the driver blocks waiting for the next request.

This simple model is only a rough approximation to reality. Many factors make the code much more complicated. For one thing, an I/O device may complete while a driver is running, interrupting the driver. The interrupt may cause a device driver to run. In fact, it may cause the current driver to run. For example, while the network driver is processing an incoming packet, another packet may arrive. Consequently, drivers have to be **reentrant**, meaning that a running driver has to expect that it will be called a second time before the first call has completed.

In a hot pluggable system, devices can be added or removed while the computer is running. As a result, while a driver is busy reading from some device, the system may inform it that the user has suddenly removed that device from the system. Not only must the current I/O transfer be aborted without damaging any kernel data structures, but any pending requests for the now-vanished device must also be gracefully removed from the system and their callers given the bad news. Furthermore, the unexpected addition of new devices may cause the kernel to juggle resources (e.g., interrupt request lines), taking old ones away from the driver and giving it new ones in their place.

Drivers are not allowed to make system calls, but they often need to interact with the rest of the kernel. Usually, calls to certain kernel procedures are permitted. For example, there are usually calls to allocate and deallocate hardwired pages of memory for use as buffers. Other useful calls are needed to manage the MMU, timers, the DMA controller, the interrupt controller, and so on.

5.3.3 Device-Independent I/O Software

Although some of the I/O software is device specific, other parts of it are device independent. The exact boundary between the drivers and the device-independent software is system (and device) dependent, because some functions that could be done in a device-independent way may actually be done in the drivers, for efficiency or other reasons. The functions shown in Fig. 5-12 are typically done in the device-independent software.

Uniform interfacing for device drivers
Buffering
Error reporting
Allocating and releasing dedicated devices
Providing a device-independent block size

Figure 5-12. Functions of the device-independent I/O software.

The basic function of the device-independent software is to perform the I/O functions that are common to all devices and to provide a uniform interface to the user-level software. Below we will look at the above issues in more detail.

Uniform Interfacing for Device Drivers

A major issue in an operating system is how to make all I/O devices and drivers look more-or-less the same. If disks, printers, keyboards, etc., are all interfaced in different ways, every time a new device comes along, the operating system must be modified for the new device. Having to hack on the operating system for each new device is not a good idea.

One aspect of this issue is the interface between the device drivers and the rest of the operating system. In Fig. 5-13(a) we illustrate a situation in which each device driver has a different interface to the operating system. What this means is that the driver functions available for the system to call differ from driver to driver. It might also mean that the kernel functions that the driver needs also differ from driver to driver. Taken together, it means that interfacing each new driver requires a lot of new programming effort.

In contrast, in Fig. 5-13(b), we show a different design in which all drivers have the same interface. Now it becomes much easier to plug in a new driver, providing it conforms to the driver interface. It also means that driver writers know what is expected of them (e.g., what functions they must provide and what kernel functions they may call). In practice, not all devices are absolutely identical, but usually there are only a small number of device types and even these are generally almost the same. For example, even block and character devices have many functions in common.

Another aspect of having a uniform interface is how I/O devices are named. The device-independent software takes care of mapping symbolic device names onto the proper driver. For example, in UNIX a device name, such as */dev/disk0*, uniquely specifies the i-node for a special file, and this i-node contains the **major device number**, which is used to locate the appropriate driver. The i-node also

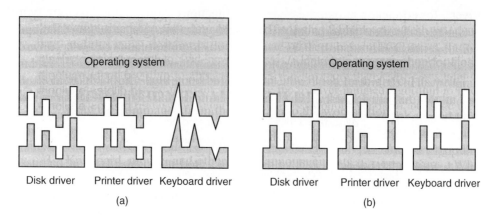

Figure 5-13. (a) Without a standard driver interface. (b) With a standard driver interface.

contains the **minor device number**, which is passed as a parameter to the driver in order to specify the unit to be read or written. All devices have major and minor numbers, and all drivers are accessed by using the major device number to select the driver.

Closely related to naming is protection. How does the system prevent users from accessing devices that they are not entitled to access? In both UNIX and Windows 2000 devices appears in the file system as named objects, which means that the usual protection rules for files also apply to I/O devices. The system administrator can then set the proper permissions for each device.

Buffering

Buffering is also an issue, both for block and character devices for a variety of reasons. To see one of them, consider a process that wants to read data from a modem. One possible strategy for dealing with the incoming characters is to have the user process do a read system call and block waiting for one character. Each arriving character causes an interrupt. The interrupt service procedure hands the character to the user process and unblocks it. After putting the character somewhere, the process reads another character and blocks again. This model is indicated in Fig. 5-14(a).

The trouble with this way of doing business is that the user process has to be started up for every incoming character. Allowing a process to run many times for short runs is inefficient, so this design is not a good one.

An improvement is shown in Fig. 5-14(b). Here the user process provides an *n*-character buffer in user space and does a read of *n* characters. The interrupt service procedure puts incoming characters in this buffer until it fills up. Then it

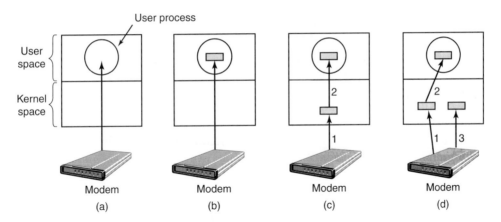

Figure 5-14. (a) Unbuffered input. (b) Buffering in user space. (c) Buffering in the kernel followed by copying to user space. (d) Double buffering in the kernel.

wakes up the user process. This scheme is far more efficient than the previous one, but it, too, has a drawback: what happens if the buffer is paged out when a character arrives? The buffer could be locked in memory, but if many processes start locking pages in memory, the pool of available pages will shrink and performance will degrade.

Yet another approach is to create a buffer inside the kernel and have the interrupt handler put the characters there, as shown in Fig. 5-14(c). When this buffer is full, the page with the user buffer is brought in, if needed, and the buffer copied there in one operation. This scheme is far more efficient.

However, even this scheme suffers from a problem: What happens to characters that arrive while the page with the user buffer is being brought in from the disk? Since the buffer is full, there is no place to put them. A way out is to have a second kernel buffer. After the first buffer fills up, but before it has been emptied, the second one is used, as shown in Fig. 5-14(d). When the second buffer fills up, it is available to be copied to the user (assuming the user has asked for it). While the second buffer is being copied to user space, the first one can be used for new characters. In this way, the two buffers take turns: while one is being copied to user space, the other is accumulating new input. A buffering scheme like this is called **double buffering**.

Buffering is also important on output. Consider, for example, how output is done to the modem without buffering using the model of Fig. 5-14(b). The user process executes a write system call to output *n* characters. The system has two choices at this point. It can block the user until all the characters have been written, but this could take a very long time over a slow telephone line. It could also release the user immediately and do the I/O while the user computes some more, but this leads to an even worse problem: how does the user process know that the output has been completed and it can reuse the buffer? The system could generate a signal or software interrupt, but that style of programming is difficult and prone to race conditions. A much better solution is for the kernel to copy the data to a kernel buffer, analogous in Fig. 5-14(c) (but the other way), and unblock the caller immediately. Now it does not matter when the actual I/O has been completed. The user is free to reuse the buffer the instant it is unblocked.

Buffering is a widely-used technique, but it has a downside as well. If data get buffered too many times, performance suffers. Consider, for example, the network of Fig. 5-15. Here a user does a system call to write to the network. The kernel copies the packet to a kernel buffer to allow the user to proceed immediately (step 1).

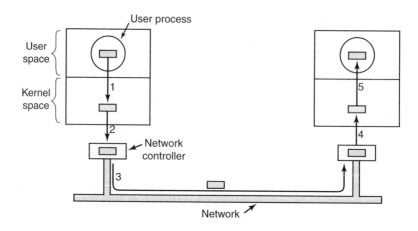

Figure 5-15. Networking may involve many copies of a packet.

When the driver is called, it copies the packet to the controller for output (step 2). The reason it does not output to the wire directly from kernel memory is that once a packet transmission has been started, it must continue at a uniform speed. The driver cannot guarantee that it can get to memory at a uniform speed because DMA channels and other I/O devices may be stealing many cycles. Failing to get a word on time would ruin the packet. By buffering the packet inside the controller, this problem is avoided.

After the packet has been copied to the controller's internal buffer, it is copied out onto the network (step 3). Bits arrive at the receiver shortly after being sent, so just after the last bit has been sent, that bit arrives at the receiver, where the packet has been buffered in the controller. Next the packet is copied to the receiver's kernel buffer (step 4). Finally, it is copied to the receiving process' buffer (step 5). Usually, the receiver then sends back an acknowledgement. When the sender gets the acknowledgement, it is free to send the next packet. However, it should be clear that all this copying is going to slow down the transmission rate considerably because all the steps must happen sequentially.

Error Reporting

Errors are far more common in the context of I/O than in other contexts. When they occur, the operating system must handle them as best it can. Many errors are device-specific and must be handled by the appropriate driver, but the framework for error handling is device independent.

One class of I/O errors are programming errors. These occur when a process asks for something impossible, such as writing to an input device (keyboard, mouse, scanner, etc.) or reading from an output device (printer, plotter, etc.). Other errors include providing an invalid buffer address or other parameter, and specifying an invalid device (e.g., disk 3 when the system has only two disks). The action to take on these errors is straightforward: just report back an error code to the caller.

Another class of errors is the class of actual I/O errors, for example, trying to write a disk block that has been damaged or trying to read from a camcorder that has been switched off. In these circumstances, it is up to the driver to determine what to do. If the driver does not know what to do, it may pass the problem back up to device-independent software.

What this software does depends on the environment and the nature of the error. If it is a simple read error and there is an interactive user available, it may display a dialog box asking the user what to do. The options may include retrying a certain number of times, ignoring the error, or killing the calling process. If there is no user available, probably the only real option is to have the system call fail with an error code.

However, some errors cannot be handled this way. For example, a critical data structure, such as the root directory or free block list, may have been destroyed. In this case, the system may have to display an error message and terminate.

Allocating and Releasing Dedicated Devices

Some devices, such as CD-ROM recorders, can be used only by a single process at any given moment. It is up to the operating system to examine requests for device usage and accept or reject them, depending on whether the requested device is available or not. A simple way to handle these requests is to require processes to perform opens on the special files for devices directly. If the device is unavailable, the open fails. Closing such a dedicated device then releases it.

An alternative approach is to have special mechanisms for requesting and releasing dedicated devices. An attempt to acquire a device that is not available blocks the caller instead of failing. Blocked processes are put on a queue. Sooner or later, the requested device becomes available and the first process on the queue is allowed to acquire it and continue execution.

Device-Independent Block Size

Different disks may have different sector sizes. It is up to the device-independent software to hide this fact and provide a uniform block size to higher layers, for example, by treating several sectors as a single logical block. In this way, the higher layers only deal with abstract devices that all use the same logical block size, independent of the physical sector size. Similarly, some character devices deliver their data one byte at a time (e.g., modems), while others deliver theirs in larger units (e.g., network interfaces). These differences may also be hidden.

5.3.4 User-Space I/O Software

Although most of the I/O software is within the operating system, a small portion of it consists of libraries linked together with user programs, and even whole programs running outside the kernel. System calls, including the I/O system calls, are normally made by library procedures. When a C program contains the call

```
count = write(fd, buffer, nbytes);
```

the library procedure *write* will be linked with the program and contained in the binary program present in memory at run time. The collection of all these library procedures is clearly part of the I/O system.

While these procedures do little more than put their parameters in the appropriate place for the system call, there are other I/O procedures that actually do real work. In particular, formatting of input and output is done by library procedures. One example from C is *printf*, which takes a format string and possibly some variables as input, builds an ASCII string, and then calls write to output the string. As an example of *printf*, consider the statement

```
printf("The square of %3d is  %6d\n", i, i*i);
```

It formats a string consisting of the 14-character string "The square of " followed by the value i as a 3-character string, then the 4-character string " is ", then i^2 as six characters, and finally a line feed.

An example of a similar procedure for input is *scanf* which reads input and stores it into variables described in a format string using the same syntax as *printf*. The standard I/O library contains a number of procedures that involve I/O and all run as part of user programs.

Not all user-level I/O software consists of library procedures. Another important category is the spooling system. **Spooling** is a way of dealing with dedicated I/O devices in a multiprogramming system. Consider a typical spooled device: a printer. Although it would be technically easy to let any user process open the character special file for the printer, suppose a process opened it and then did nothing for hours. No other process could print anything.

Instead what is done is to create a special process, called a **daemon**, and a special directory, called a **spooling directory**. To print a file, a process first generates the entire file to be printed and puts it in the spooling directory. It is up to the daemon, which is the only process having permission to use the printer's special file, to print the files in the directory. By protecting the special file against direct use by users, the problem of having someone keeping it open unnecessarily long is eliminated.

Spooling is not only used for printers. It is also used in other situations. For example, file transfer over a network often uses a network daemon. To send a file somewhere, a user puts it in a network spooling directory. Later on, the network daemon takes it out and transmits it. One particular use of spooled file transmission is the USENET News system. This network consists of millions of machines around the world communicating using the Internet. Thousands of news groups exist on many topics. To post a news message, the user invokes a news program, which accepts the message to be posted and then deposits it in a spooling directory for transmission to other machines later. The entire news system runs outside the operating system.

Figure 5-16 summarizes the I/O system, showing all the layers and the principal functions of each layer. Starting at the bottom, the layers are the hardware, interrupt handlers, device drivers, device-independent software, and finally the user processes.

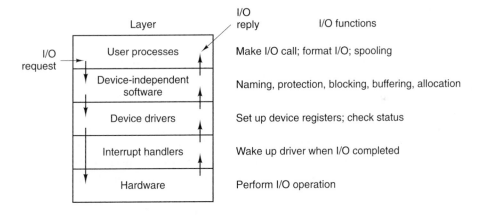

Figure 5-16. Layers of the I/O system and the main functions of each layer.

The arrows in Fig. 5-16 show the flow of control. When a user program tries to read a block from a file, for example, the operating system is invoked to carry out the call. The device-independent software looks for it in the buffer cache, for example. If the needed block is not there, it calls the device driver to issue the request to the hardware to go get it from the disk. The process is then blocked until the disk operation has been completed.

When the disk is finished, the hardware generates an interrupt. The interrupt handler is run to discover what has happened, that is, which device wants attention right now. It then extracts the status from the device and wakes up the sleeping process to finish off the I/O request and let the user process continue.

5.4 DISKS

Now we will begin studying some real I/O devices. We will begin with disks. After that we will examine clocks, keyboards, and displays.

5.4.1 Disk Hardware

Disks come in a variety of types. The most common ones are the magnetic disks (hard disks and floppy disks). They are characterized by the fact that reads and writes are equally fast, which makes them ideal as secondary memory (paging, file systems, etc.). Arrays of these disks are sometimes used to provide highly-reliable storage. For distribution of programs, data, and movies, various kinds of optical disks (CD-ROMs, CD-Recordables, and DVDs) are also important. In the following sections we will first describe the hardware and then the software for these devices.

Magnetic Disks

Magnetic disks are organized into cylinders, each one containing as many tracks as there are heads stacked vertically. The tracks are divided into sectors, with the number of sectors around the circumference typically being 8 to 32 on floppy disks, and up to several hundred on hard disks. The number of heads varies from 1 to about 16.

Some magnetic disks have little electronics and just deliver a simple serial bit stream. On these disks, the controller does most of the work. On other disks, in particular, **IDE** (**Integrated Drive Electronics**) disks, the drive itself contains a microcontroller that does some work and allows the real controller to issue a set of higher-level commands.

A device feature that has important implications for the disk driver is the possibility of a controller doing seeks on two or more drives at the same time. These are known as **overlapped seeks**. While the controller and software are waiting for a seek to complete on one drive, the controller can initiate a seek on another drive. Many controllers can also read or write on one drive while seeking on one or more other drives, but a floppy disk controller cannot read or write on two drives at the same time. (Reading or writing requires the controller to move bits on a microsecond time scale, so one transfer uses up most of its computing power.) The situation is different for hard disks with integrated controllers, and in a system with more than one of these hard drives they can operate simultaneously, at least to the extent of transferring between the disk and the controller's buffer memory. Only one transfer between the controller and the main memory is possible at once, however. The ability to perform two or more operations at the same time can reduce the average access time considerably.

Figure 5-17 compares parameters of the standard storage medium for the original IBM PC with parameters of a modern hard disk to show how much disks have changed in the past two decades. It is interesting to note that not all parameters have improved as much. Average seek time is seven times better, transfer rate is 1300 times better, while capacity is up by a factor of 50,000. This pattern has to do with relatively gradual improvements in the moving parts, but much higher bit densities on the recording surfaces.

Parameter	IBM 360-KB floppy disk	WD 18300 hard disk
Number of cylinders	40	10601
Tracks per cylinder	2	12
Sectors per track	9	281 (avg)
Sectors per disk	720	35742000
Bytes per sector	512	512
Disk capacity	360 KB	18.3 GB
Seek time (adjacent cylinders)	6 msec	0.8 msec
Seek time (average case)	77 msec	6.9 msec
Rotation time	200 msec	8.33 msec
Motor stop/start time	250 msec	20 sec
Time to transfer 1 sector	22 msec	17 μsec

Figure 5-17. Disk parameters for the original IBM PC 360-KB floppy disk and a Western Digital WD 18300 hard disk.

One thing to be aware of in looking at the specifications of modern hard disks is that the geometry specified, and used by the driver software, may be different than the physical format. On older disks, the number of sectors per track was the same for all cylinders. Modern disks are divided into zones with more sectors on the outer zones than the inner ones. Fig. 5-18(a) illustrates a tiny disk with two zones. The outer zone has 32 sectors per track; the inner one has 16 sectors per track. A real disk, such as the WD 18300, often has 16 zones, with the number of sectors increasing by about 4% per zone as one goes out from the innermost zone to the outermost zone.

To hide the details of how many sectors each track has, most modern disks have a virtual geometry that is presented to the operating system. The software is instructed to act as though there are x cylinders, y heads, and z sectors per track. The controller then remaps a request for (x, y, z) onto the real cylinder, head, and

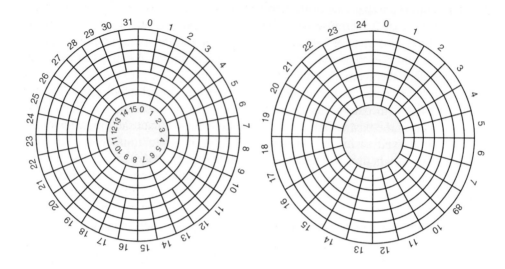

Figure 5-18. (a) Physical geometry of a disk with two zones. (b) A possible virtual geometry for this disk.

sector. A possible virtual geometry for the physical disk of Fig. 5-18(a) is shown in Fig. 5-18(b). In both cases the disk has 192 sectors, only the published arrangement is different than the real one.

For Pentium-based computers, the maximum values for these three parameters are often (65535, 16, and 63), due to the need to be backward compatible with the limitations of the original IBM PC. On this machine, 16-, 4-, and 6-bit fields were used to specify these numbers, with cylinders and sectors numbered starting at 1 and heads numbered starting at 0. With these parameters and 512 bytes per sector, the largest possible disk is 31.5 GB. To get around this limit, many disks now support a system called **logical block addressing**, in which disk sectors are just numbered consecutively starting at 0, without regard to the disk geometry.

RAID

CPU performance has been increasing exponentially over the past decade, roughly doubling every 18 months. Not so with disk performance. In the 1970s, average seek times on minicomputer disks were 50 to 100 msec. Now seek times are slightly under 10 msec. In most technical industries (say, automobiles or aviation), a factor of 5 to 10 performance improvement in two decades would be major news, but in the computer industry it is an embarrassment. Thus the gap between CPU performance and disk performance has become much larger over time.

As we have seen, parallel processing is being used more and more to speed up CPU performance. It has occurred to various people over the years that parallel

I/O might be a good idea too. In their 1988 paper, Patterson et al. suggested six specific disk organizations that could be used to improve disk performance, reliability, or both (Patterson et al., 1988). These ideas were quickly adopted by industry and have led to a new class of I/O device called a **RAID**. Patterson et al. defined RAID as **Redundant Array of Inexpensive Disks**, but industry redefined the I to be "Independent" rather than "Inexpensive" (maybe so they could use expensive disks?). Since a villain was also needed (as in RISC versus CISC, also due to Patterson), the bad guy here was the **SLED** (**Single Large Expensive Disk**).

The basic idea behind a RAID is to install a box full of disks next to the computer, typically a large server, replace the disk controller card with a RAID controller, copy the data over to the RAID, and then continue normal operation. In other words, a RAID should look like a SLED to the operating system but have better performance and better reliability. Since SCSI disks have good performance, low price, and the ability to have up to 7 drives on a single controller (15 for wide SCSI), it is natural that most RAIDs consist of a RAID SCSI controller plus a box of SCSI disks that appear to the operating system as a single large disk. In this way, no software changes are required to use the RAID, a big selling point for many system administrators.

In addition to appearing like a single disk to the software, all RAIDs have the property that the data are distributed over the drives, to allow parallel operation. Several different schemes for doing this were defined by Patterson et al., and they are now known as RAID level 0 through RAID level 5. In addition, there are a few other minor levels that we will not discuss. The term "level" is something of a misnomer since there is no hierarchy involved; there are simply six different organizations possible.

RAID level 0 is illustrated in Fig. 5-19(a). It consists of viewing the virtual single disk simulated by the RAID as being divided up into strips of k sectors each, with sectors 0 to $k-1$ being strip 0, sectors k to $2k-1$ as strip 1, and so on. For $k=1$, each strip is a sector; for $k=2$ a strip is two sectors, etc. The RAID level 0 organization writes consecutive strips over the drives in round-robin fashion, as depicted in Fig. 5-19(a) for a RAID with four disk drives. Distributing data over multiple drives like this is called **striping**. For example, if the software issues a command to read a data block consisting of four consecutive strips starting at a strip boundary, the RAID controller will break this command up into four separate commands, one for each of the four disks, and have them operate in parallel. Thus we have parallel I/O without the software knowing about it.

RAID level 0 works best with large requests, the bigger the better. If a request is larger than the number of drives times the strip size, some drives will get multiple requests, so that when they finish the first request they start the second one. It is up to the controller to split the request up and feed the proper commands to the proper disks in the right sequence and then assemble the results in memory correctly. Performance is excellent and the implementation is straightforward.

RAID level 0 works worst with operating systems that habitually ask for data one sector at a time. The results will be correct, but there is no parallelism and hence no performance gain. Another disadvantage of this organization is that the reliability is potentially worse than having a SLED. If a RAID consists of four disks, each with a mean time to failure of 20,000 hours, about once every 5000 hours a drive will fail and all the data will be completely lost. A SLED with a mean time to failure of 20,000 hours would be four times more reliable. Because no redundancy is present in this design, it is not really a true RAID.

The next option, RAID level 1, shown in Fig. 5-19(b), is a true RAID. It duplicates all the disks, so there are four primary disks and four backup disks. On a write, every strip is written twice. On a read, either copy can be used, distributing the load over more drives. Consequently, write performance is no better than for a single drive, but read performance can be up to twice as good. Fault tolerance is excellent: if a drive crashes, the copy is simply used instead. Recovery consists of simply installing a new drive and copying the entire backup drive to it.

Unlike levels 0 and 1, which work with strips of sectors, RAID level 2 works on a word basis, possibly even a byte basis. Imagine splitting each byte of the single virtual disk into a pair of 4-bit nibbles, then adding a Hamming code to each one to form a 7-bit word, of which bits 1, 2, and 4 were parity bits. Further imagine that the seven drives of Fig. 5-19(c) were synchronized in terms of arm position and rotational position. Then it would be possible to write the 7-bit Hamming coded word over the seven drives, one bit per drive.

The Thinking Machines' CM-2 computer used this scheme, taking 32-bit data words and adding 6 parity bits to form a 38-bit Hamming word, plus an extra bit for word parity, and spread each word over 39 disk drives. The total throughput was immense, because in one sector time it could write 32 sectors worth of data. Also, losing one drive did not cause problems, because loss of a drive amounted to losing 1 bit in each 39-bit word read, something the Hamming code could handle on the fly.

On the down side, this scheme requires all the drives to be rotationally synchronized, and it only makes sense with a substantial number of drives (even with 32 data drives and 6 parity drives, the overhead is 19 percent). It also asks a lot of the controller, since it must do a Hamming checksum every bit time.

RAID level 3 is a simplified version of RAID level 2. It is illustrated in Fig. 5-19(d). Here a single parity bit is computed for each data word and written to a parity drive. As in RAID level 2, the drives must be exactly synchronized, since individual data words are spread over multiple drives.

At first thought, it might appear that a single parity bit gives only error detection, not error correction. For the case of random undetected errors, this observation is true. However, for the case of a drive crashing, it provides full 1-bit error correction since the position of the bad bit is known. If a drive crashes, the controller just pretends that all its bits are 0s. If a word has a parity error, the bit from the dead drive must have been a 1, so it is corrected. Although both RAID levels

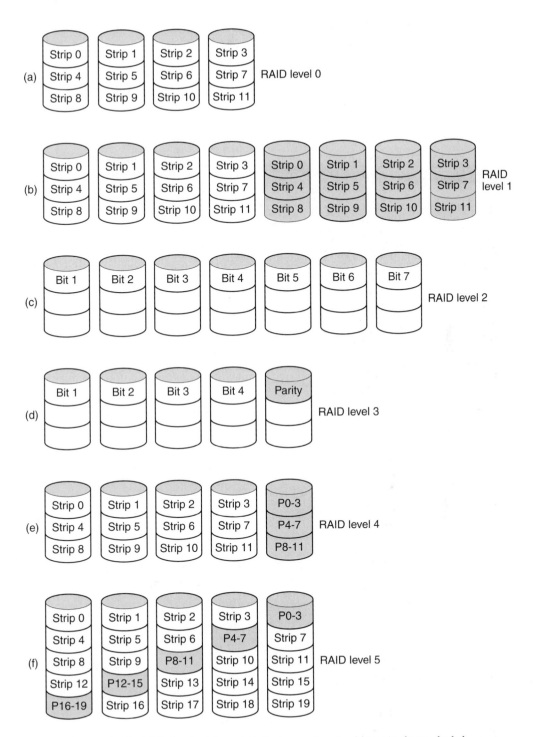

Figure 5-19. RAID levels 0 through 5. Backup and parity drives are shown shaded.

2 and 3 offer very high data rates, the number of separate I/O requests per second they can handle is no better than for a single drive.

RAID levels 4 and 5 work with strips again, not individual words with parity, and do not require synchronized drives. RAID level 4 [see Fig. 5-19(e)] is like RAID level 0, with a strip-for-strip parity written onto an extra drive. For example, if each strip is *k* bytes long, all the strips are EXCLUSIVE ORed together, resulting in a parity strip *k* bytes long. If a drive crashes, the lost bytes can be recomputed from the parity drive.

This design protects against the loss of a drive but performs poorly for small updates. If one sector is changed, it is necessary to read all the drives in order to recalculate the parity, which must then be rewritten. Alternatively, it can read the old user data and the old parity data and recompute the new parity from them. Even with this optimization, a small update requires two reads and two writes.

As a consequence of the heavy load on the parity drive, it may become a bottleneck. This bottleneck is eliminated in RAID level 5 by distributing the parity bits uniformly over all the drives, round robin fashion, as shown in Fig. 5-19(f). However, in the event of a drive crash, reconstructing the contents of the failed drive is a complex process.

CD-ROMs

In recent years, optical (as opposed to magnetic) disks have become available. They have much higher recording densities than conventional magnetic disks. Optical disks were originally developed for recording television programs, but they can be put to more esthetic use as computer storage devices. Due to their potentially enormous capacity, optical disks have been the subject of a great deal of research and have gone through an incredibly rapid evolution.

First-generation optical disks were invented by the Dutch electronics conglomerate Philips for holding movies. They were 30 cm across and marketed under the name LaserVision, but they did not catch on, except in Japan.

In 1980, Philips, together with Sony, developed the CD (Compact Disc), which rapidly replaced the 33 1/3-rpm vinyl record for music (except among connoisseurs, who still prefer vinyl). The precise technical details for the CD were published in an official International Standard (IS 10149), popularly called the **Red Book**, due to the color of its cover. (International Standards are issued by the International Organization for Standardization, which is the international counterpart of national standards groups like ANSI, DIN, etc. Each one has an IS number.) The point of publishing the disk and drive specifications as an International Standard is to allow CDs from different music publishers and players from different electronics manufacturers to work together. All CDs are 120 mm across and 1.2 mm thick, with a 15-mm hole in the middle. The audio CD was the first successful mass market digital storage medium. They are supposed to last 100 years. Please check back in 2080 for an update on how well the first batch did.

A CD is prepared by using a high-power infrared laser to burn 0.8-micron diameter holes in a coated glass master disk. From this master, a mold is made, with bumps where the laser holes were. Into this mold, molten polycarbonate resin is injected to form a CD with the same pattern of holes as the glass master. Then a very thin layer of reflective aluminum is deposited on the polycarbonate, topped by a protective lacquer and finally a label. The depressions in the polycarbonate substrate are called **pits**; the unburned areas between the pits are called **lands**.

When played back, a low-power laser diode shines infrared light with a wavelength of 0.78 micron on the pits and lands as they stream by. The laser is on the polycarbonate side, so the pits stick out toward the laser as bumps in the otherwise flat surface. Because the pits have a height of one-quarter the wavelength of the laser light, light reflecting off a pit is half a wavelength out of phase with light reflecting off the surrounding surface. As a result, the two parts interfere destructively and return less light to the player's photodetector than light bouncing off a land. This is how the player tells a pit from a land. Although it might seem simpler to use a pit to record a 0 and a land to record a 1, it is more reliable to use a pit/land or land/pit transition for a 1 and its absence as a 0, so this scheme is used.

The pits and lands are written in a single continuous spiral starting near the hole and working out a distance of 32 mm toward the edge. The spiral makes 22,188 revolutions around the disk (about 600 per mm). If unwound, it would be 5.6 km long. The spiral is illustrated in Fig. 5-20.

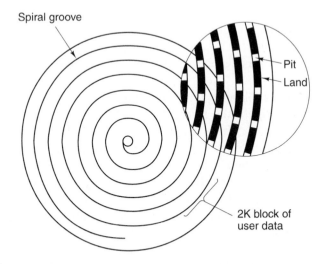

Figure 5-20. Recording structure of a compact disc or CD-ROM.

To make the music play at a uniform rate, it is necessary for the pits and lands to stream by at a constant linear velocity. Consequently the rotation rate of the

CD must be continuously reduced as the reading head moves from the inside of the CD to the outside. At the inside, the rotation rate is 530 rpm to achieve the desired streaming rate of 120 cm/sec; at the outside it has to drop to 200 rpm to give the same linear velocity at the head. A constant linear velocity drive is quite different than a magnetic disk drive, which operates at a constant angular velocity, independent of where the head is currently positioned. Also, 530 rpm is a far cry from the 3600 to 7200 rpm that most magnetic disks whirl at.

In 1984, Philips and Sony realized the potential for using CDs to store computer data, so they published the **Yellow Book** defining a precise standard for what are now called **CD-ROM**s (**Compact Disc - Read Only Memory**). To piggyback on the by-then already substantial audio CD market, CD-ROMs were to be the same physical size as audio CDs, mechanically and optically compatible with them, and produced using the same polycarbonate injection molding machines. The consequences of this decision were not only that slow variable-speed motors were required, but also that the manufacturing cost of a CD-ROM would be well under one dollar in moderate volume.

What the Yellow Book defined was the formatting of the computer data. It also improved the error-correcting abilities of the system, an essential step because although music lovers do not mind losing a bit here and there, computer lovers tend to be Very Picky about that. The basic format of a CD-ROM consists of encoding every byte in a 14-bit symbol. As we saw above, 14 bits is enough to Hamming encode an 8-bit byte with 2 bits left over. In fact, a more powerful encoding system is used. The 14-to-8 mapping for reading is done in hardware by table lookup.

At the next level up, a group of 42 consecutive symbols forms a 588-bit **frame**. Each frame holds 192 data bits (24 bytes). The remaining 396 bits are used for error correction and control. So far, this scheme is identical for audio CDs and CD-ROMs.

What the Yellow Book adds is the grouping of 98 frames into a **CD-ROM sector**, as shown in Fig. 5-21. Every CD-ROM sector begins with a 16-byte preamble, the first 12 of which are 00FFFFFFFFFFFFFFFFFFFF00 (hexadecimal), to allow the player to recognize the start of a CD-ROM sector. The next 3 bytes contain the sector number, needed because seeking on a CD-ROM with its single data spiral is much more difficult than on a magnetic disk with its uniform concentric tracks. To seek, the software in the drive calculates approximately where to go, moves the head there, and then starts hunting around for a preamble to see how good its guess was. The last byte of the preamble is the mode.

The Yellow Book defines two modes. Mode 1 uses the layout of Fig. 5-21, with a 16-byte preamble, 2048 data bytes, and a 288-byte error-correcting code (a crossinterleaved Reed-Solomon code). Mode 2 combines the data and ECC fields into a 2336-byte data field for those applications that do not need (or cannot afford the time to perform) error correction, such as audio and video. Note that to provide excellent reliability, three separate error-correcting schemes are used:

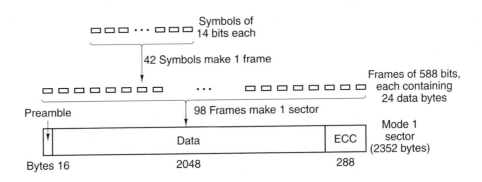

Figure 5-21. Logical data layout on a CD-ROM.

within a symbol, within a frame, and within a CD-ROM sector. Single-bit errors are corrected at the lowest level, short burst errors are corrected at the frame level, and any residual errors are caught at the sector level. The price paid for this reliability is that it takes 98 frames of 588 bits (7203 bytes) to carry a single 2048-byte payload, an efficiency of only 28 percent.

Single-speed CD-ROM drives operate at 75 sectors/sec, which gives a data rate of 153,600 bytes/sec in mode 1 and 175,200 bytes/sec in mode 2. Double-speed drives are twice as fast, and so on up to the highest speed. Thus a 40x drive can deliver data at a rate of $40 \times 153,600$ bytes/sec, assuming that the drive interface, bus, and operating system can all handle this data rate. A standard audio CD has room for 74 minutes of music, which, if used for mode 1 data, gives a capacity of 681,984,000 bytes. This figure is usually reported as 650 MB because 1 MB is 2^{20} bytes (1,048,576 bytes), not 1,000,000 bytes.

Note that even a 32x CD-ROM drive (4,915,200 bytes/sec) is no match for a fast SCSI-2 magnetic disk drive at 10 MB/sec, even though many CD-ROM drives use the SCSI interface (IDE CD-ROM drives also exist). When you realize that the seek time is usually several hundred milliseconds, it should be clear that CD-ROM drives are not in the same performance category as magnetic disk drives, despite their large capacity.

In 1986, Philips struck again with the **Green Book**, adding graphics and the ability to interleave audio, video and data in the same sector, a feature essential for multimedia CD-ROMs.

The last piece of the CD-ROM puzzle is the file system. To make it possible to use the same CD-ROM on different computers, agreement was needed on CD-ROM file systems. To get this agreement, representatives of many computer companies met at Lake Tahoe in the High Sierras on the California-Nevada boundary and devised a file system that they called **High Sierra**. It later evolved into an International Standard (IS 9660). It has three levels. Level 1 uses file names of up to 8 characters optionally followed by an extension of up to 3 characters (the

MS-DOS file naming convention). File names may contain only upper case letters, digits, and the underscore. Directories may be nested up to eight deep, but directory names may not contain extensions. Level 1 requires all files to be contiguous, which is not a problem on a medium written only once. Any CD-ROM conformant to IS 9660 level 1 can be read using MS-DOS, an Apple computer, a UNIX computer, or just about any other computer. CD-ROM publishers regard this property as being a big plus.

IS 9660 level 2 allows names up to 32 characters, and level 3 allows noncontiguous files. The Rock Ridge extensions (whimsically named after the town in the Gene Wilder film *Blazing Saddles*) allow very long names (for UNIX), UIDs, GIDs, and symbolic links, but CD-ROMs not conforming to level 1 will not be readable on all computers.

CD-ROMs have become extremely popular for publishing games, movies, encyclopedias, atlases, and reference works of all kinds. Most commercial software now comes on CD-ROMs. Their combination of large capacity and low manufacturing cost makes them well suited to innumerable applications.

CD-Recordables

Initially, the equipment needed to produce a master CD-ROM (or audio CD, for that matter) was extremely expensive. But as usual in the computer industry, nothing stays expensive for long. By the mid 1990s, CD recorders no bigger than a CD player were a common peripheral available in most computer stores. These devices were still different from magnetic disks because once written, CD-ROMs could not be erased. Nevertheless, they quickly found a niche as a backup medium for large hard disks and also allowed individuals or startup companies to manufacture their own small-run CD-ROMs or make masters for delivery to high-volume commercial CD duplication plants. These drives are known as **CD-R**s (**CD-Recordables**).

Physically, CD-Rs start with 120-mm polycarbonate blanks that are like CD-ROMs, except that they contain a 0.6-mm wide groove to guide the laser for writing. The groove has a sinusoidal excursion of 0.3 mm at a frequency of exactly 22.05 kHz to provide continuous feedback so the rotation speed can be accurately monitored and adjusted if need be. CD-Rs look like regular CD-ROMs, except that they are gold colored on top instead of silver colored. The gold color comes from the use of real gold instead of aluminum for the reflective layer. Unlike silver CDs, which have physical depressions on them, on CD-Rs the differing reflectivity of pits and lands has to be simulated. This is done by adding a layer of dye between the polycarbonate and the reflective gold layer, as shown in Fig. 5-22. Two kinds of dye are used: cyanine, which is green, and pthalocyanine, which is a yellowish orange. Chemists can argue endlessly about which one is better. These dyes are similar to those used in photography, which explains why Eastman Kodak and Fuji are major manufacturers of blank CD-Rs.

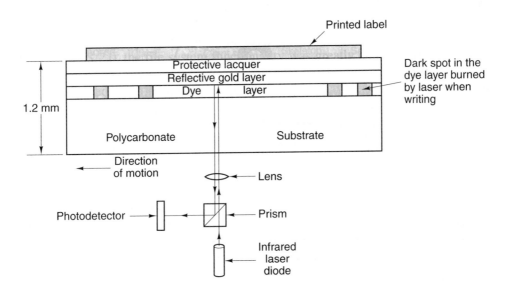

Figure 5-22. Cross section of a CD-R disk and laser (not to scale). A silver CD-ROM has a similar structure, except without the dye layer and with a pitted aluminum layer instead of a gold layer.

In its initial state, the dye layer is transparent and lets the laser light pass through and reflect off the gold layer. To write, the CD-R laser is turned up to high power (8–16 mW). When the beam hits a spot of dye, it heats up, breaking a chemical bond. This change to the molecular structure creates a dark spot. When read back (at 0.5 mW), the photodetector sees a difference between the dark spots where the dye has been hit and transparent areas where it is intact. This difference is interpreted as the difference between pits and lands, even when read back on a regular CD-ROM reader or even on an audio CD player.

No new kind of CD could hold up its head with pride without a colored book, so CD-R has the **Orange Book**, published in 1989. This document defines CD-R and also a new format, **CD-ROM XA**, which allows CD-Rs to be written incrementally, a few sectors today, a few tomorrow, and a few next month. A group of consecutive sectors written at once is called a **CD-ROM track**.

One of the first uses of CD-R was for the Kodak PhotoCD. In this system the customer brings a roll of exposed film and his old PhotoCD to the photo processor and gets back the same PhotoCD with the new pictures added after the old ones. The new batch, which is created by scanning in the negatives, is written onto the PhotoCD as a separate CD-ROM track. Incremental writing was needed because when this product was introduced, the CD-R blanks were too expensive to provide a new one for every film roll.

However, incremental writing creates a new problem. Prior to the Orange Book, all CD-ROMs had a single **VTOC** (**Volume Table of Contents**) at the start. That scheme does not work with incremental (i.e., multitrack) writes. The Orange Book's solution is to give each CD-ROM track its own VTOC. The files listed in the VTOC can include some or all of the files from previous tracks. After the CD-R is inserted into the drive, the operating system searches through all the CD-ROM tracks to locate the most recent VTOC, which gives the current status of the disk. By including some, but not all, of the files from previous tracks in the current VTOC, it is possible to give the illusion that files have been deleted. Tracks can be grouped into **sessions**, leading to **multisession** CD-ROMs. Standard audio CD players cannot handle multisession CDs since they expect a single VTOC at the start.

Each track has to be written in a single continuous operation without stopping. As a consequence, the hard disk from which the data are coming has to be fast enough to deliver it on time. If the files to be copied are spread all over the hard disk, the seek times may cause the data stream to the CD-R to dry up and cause a buffer underrun. A buffer underrun results in producing a nice shiny (but somewhat expensive) coaster for your drinks, or a 120 mm gold-colored frisbee. CD-R software usually offers the option of collecting all the input files into a single contiguous 650-MB CD-ROM image prior to burning the CD-R, but this process typically doubles the effective writing time, requires 650 MB of free disk space, and still does not protect against hard disks that panic and decide to do a thermal recalibration when they get too hot.

CD-R makes it possible for individuals and companies to easily copy CD-ROMs (and audio CDs), generally in violation of the publisher's copyright. Several schemes have been devised to make such piracy harder and to make it difficult to read a CD-ROM using anything other than the publisher's software. One of them involves recording all the file lengths on the CD-ROM as multigigabyte, thwarting any attempts to copy the files to hard disk using standard copying software. The true lengths are embedded in the publisher's software or hidden (possibly encrypted) on the CD-ROM in an unexpected place. Another scheme uses intentionally incorrect ECCs in selected sectors, in the expectation that CD copying software will "fix" the errors. The application software checks the ECCs itself, refusing to work if they are correct. Using nonstandard gaps between the tracks and other physical "defects" are also possibilities.

CD-Rewritables

Although people are used to other write-once media such as paper and photographic film, there is a demand for a rewritable CD-ROM. One technology now available is **CD-RW** (**CD-ReWritable**), which uses the same size media as CD-R. However, instead of cyanine or pthalocyanine dye, CR-RW uses an alloy of silver, indium, antimony, and tellurium for the recording layer. This alloy has two stable states: crystalline and amorphous, with different reflectivities.

CD-RW drives use lasers with three different powers. At high power, the laser melts the alloy, converting it from the high-reflectivity crystalline state to the low-reflectivity amorphous state to represent a pit. At medium power, the alloy melts and reforms in its natural crystalline state to become a land again. At low power, the state of the material is sensed (for reading), but no phase transition occurs.

The reason CD-RW has not replaced CD-R is that the CD-RW blanks are much more expensive than the CR-R blanks. Also, for applications consisting of backing up hard disks, the fact that once written, a CD-R cannot be accidentally erased is a big plus.

DVD

The basic CD/CD-ROM format has been around since 1980. The technology has improved since then, so higher-capacity optical disks are now economically feasible and there is great demand for them. Hollywood would dearly love to replace analog video tapes by digital disks, since disks have a higher quality, are cheaper to manufacture, last longer, take up less shelf space in video stores, and do not have to be rewound. The consumer electronics companies are looking for a new blockbuster product, and many computer companies want to add multimedia features to their software.

This combination of technology and demand by three immensely rich and powerful industries has led to **DVD**, originally an acronym for **Digital Video Disk**, but now officially **Digital Versatile Disk**. DVDs use the same general design as CDs, with 120-mm injection-molded polycarbonate disks containing pits and lands that are illuminated by a laser diode and read by a photodetector. What is new is the use of

1. Smaller pits (0.4 microns versus 0.8 microns for CDs).

2. A tighter spiral (0.74 microns between tracks versus 1.6 microns for CDs).

3. A red laser (at 0.65 microns versus 0.78 microns for CDs).

Together, these improvements raise the capacity sevenfold, to 4.7-GB. A 1x DVD drive operates at 1.4 MB/sec (versus 150 KB/sec for CDs). Unfortunately, the switch to the red lasers used in supermarkets means that DVD players will require a second laser or fancy conversion optics to be able to read existing CDs and CD-ROMs, something not all of them may provide. Also, reading CD-Rs and CD-RWs on a DVD drive may not be possible.

Is 4.7 GB enough? Maybe. Using MPEG-2 compression (standardized in IS 13346), a 4.7 GB DVD disk can hold 133 minutes of full-screen, full-motion video at high resolution (720×480), as well as soundtracks in up to eight languages and subtitles in 32 more. About 92 percent of all the movies Hollywood has ever made are under 133 minutes. Nevertheless, some applications such as multimedia games or reference works may need more, and Hollywood would like to put multiple movies on the same disk, so four formats have been defined:

1. Single-sided, single-layer (4.7 GB).

2. Single-sided, dual-layer (8.5 GB).

3. Double-sided, single-layer (9.4 GB).

4. Double-sided, dual-layer (17 GB).

Why so many formats? In a word: politics. Philips and Sony wanted single-sided, dual-layer disks for the high capacity version, but Toshiba and Time Warner wanted double-sided, single-layer disks. Philips and Sony did not think people would be willing to turn the disks over, and Time Warner did not believe putting two layers on one side could be made to work. The compromise: all combinations, but the market will determine which ones survive.

The dual layering technology has a reflective layer at the bottom, topped with a semireflective layer. Depending on where the laser is focused, it bounces off one layer or the other. The lower layer needs slightly larger pits and lands to be read reliably, so its capacity is slightly smaller than the upper layer's.

Double-sided disks are made by taking two 0.6-mm single-sided disks and gluing them together back to back. To make the thicknesses of all versions the same, a single-sided disk consists of a 0.6-mm disk bonded to a blank substrate (or perhaps in the future, one consisting of 133 minutes of advertising, in the hope that people will be curious as to what is down there). The structure of the double-sided, dual-layer disk is illustrated in Fig. 5-23.

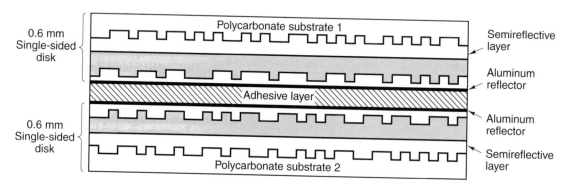

Figure 5-23. A double-sided, dual layer DVD disk.

DVD was devised by a consortium of 10 consumer electronics companies, seven of them Japanese, in close cooperation with the major Hollywood studios (some of which are owned by the Japanese electronics companies in the consortium). The computer and telecommunications industries were not invited to the picnic, and the resulting focus was on using DVD for movie rental and sales shows. For example, standard features include real-time skipping of dirty scenes (to allow parents to turn a film rated NC17 into one safe for toddlers), six-channel sound, and support for Pan-and-Scan. The latter feature allows the DVD player to dynamically decide how to crop the left and right edges off movies (whose width:height ratio is 3:2) to fit on current television sets (whose aspect ratio is 4:3).

Another item the computer industry probably would not have thought of is an intentional incompatibility between disks intended for the United States and disks intended for Europe and yet other standards for other continents. Hollywood demanded this "feature" because new films are always released first in the United States and then shipped to Europe when the videos come out in the United States. The idea was to make sure European video stores could not buy videos in the U.S. too early, thereby reducing new movies' European theater sales. If Hollywood had been running the computer industry, we would have had 3.5-inch floppy disks in the United States and 9-cm floppy disks in Europe.

5.4.2 Disk Formatting

A hard disk consists of a stack of aluminum, alloy, or glass platters 5.25 inch or 3.5 inch in diameter (or even smaller on notebook computers). On each platter is deposited a thin magnetizable metal oxide. After manufacturing, there is no information whatsoever on the disk.

Before the disk can be used, each platter must receive a **low-level format** done by software. The format consists of a series of concentric tracks, each containing some number of sectors, with short gaps between the sectors. The format of a sector is shown in Fig. 5-24.

| Preamble | Data | ECC |

Figure 5-24. A disk sector.

The preamble starts with a certain bit pattern that allows the hardware to recognize the start of the sector. It also contains the cylinder and sector numbers and some other information. The size of the data portion is determined by the low-level formatting program. Most disks use 512-byte sectors. The ECC field contains redundant information that can be used to recover from read errors. The size and content of this field varies from manufacturer to manufacturer, depending on how must disk space the designer is willing to give up for higher reliability and how complex an ECC code the controller can handle. A 16-byte ECC field is not unusual. Furthermore, all hard disks have some number of spare sectors allocated to be used to replace sectors with a manufacturing defect.

The position of sector 0 on each track is offset from the previous track when the low-level format is laid down. This offset, called **cylinder skew**, is done to improve performance. The idea is to allow the disk to read multiple tracks in one continuous operation without losing data. The nature of the problem can be seen by looking at Fig. 5-18(a). Suppose that a request needs 18 sectors starting at sector 0 on the innermost track. Reading the first 16 sectors takes one disk rotation, but a seek is needed to move outward one track to get the 17th sector. By the time the head has moved one track, sector 0 has rotated past the head so an entire rotation is needed until it comes by again. That problem is eliminated by offsetting the sectors as shown in Fig. 5-25.

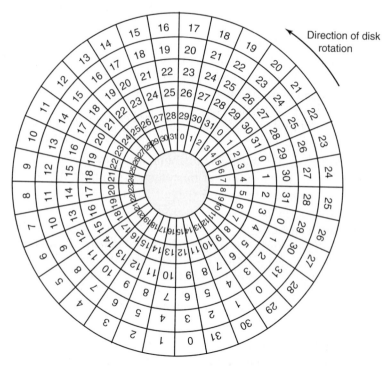

Figure 5-25. An illustration of cylinder skew.

The amount of cylinder skew depends on the drive geometry. For example, a 10,000-rpm drive rotates in 6 msec. If a track contains 300 sectors, a new sector passes under the head every 20 μsec. If the track-to-track seek time is 800 μsec, 40 sectors will pass by during the seek, so the cylinder skew should be 40 sectors, rather than the three sectors shown in Fig. 5-25. It is worth mentioning that switching between heads also takes a finite time, so there is **head skew** as well as cylinder skew, but head skew is not very large.

As a result of the low-level formatting, disk capacity is reduced, depending on the sizes of the preamble, intersector gap, and ECC, as well as the number of spare sectors reserved. Often the formatted capacity is 20% lower than the unformatted capacity. The spare sectors do not count toward the formatted capacity, so all disks of a given type have exactly the same capacity when shipped, independent of how many bad sectors they actually have (if the number of bad sectors exceeds the number of spares, the drive will be rejected and not shipped).

There is considerable confusion about disk capacity because some manufacturers advertised the unformatted capacity to make their drives look larger than they really are. For example, consider a drive whose unformatted capacity is 20×10^9 bytes. This might be sold as a 20-GB disk. However, after formatting, perhaps only $2^{34} \simeq 17.2 \times 10^9$ bytes are available for data. To add to the confusion, the operating system will probably report this capacity as 16.0 GB, not 17.2 GB because software considers 1 GB to be 2^{30} (1,073,741,824) bytes, not 10^9 (1,000,000,000) bytes.

To make things worse, in the data communication world, 1 Gbps means 1,000,000,000 bits/sec because the prefix *giga* really does mean 10^9 (a kilometer is 1000 meters, not 1024 meters, after all). Only with memory and disk sizes do kilo, mega, giga, and tera mean 2^{10}, 2^{20}, 2^{30}, and 2^{40}, respectively.

Formatting also affects performance. If a 10,000-rpm disk has 300 sectors per track of 512 bytes each, it takes 6 msec to read the 153,600 bytes on a track for a data rate of 25,600,000 bytes/sec or 24.4 MB/sec. It is not possible to go faster than this, no matter what kind of interface is present, even if it a SCSI interface at 80 MB/sec or 160 MB/sec.

Actually reading continuously at this rate requires a large buffer in the controller. Consider, for example, a controller with a one-sector buffer that has been given a command to read two consecutive sectors. After reading the first sector from the disk and doing the ECC calculation, the data must be transferred to main memory. While this transfer is taking place, the next sector will fly by the head. When the copy to memory is complete, the controller will have to wait almost an entire rotation time for the second sector to come around again.

This problem can be eliminated by numbering the sectors in an interleaved fashion when formatting the disk. In Fig. 5-26(a), we see the usual numbering pattern (ignoring cylinder skew here). In Fig. 5-26(b), we see **single interleaving**, which gives the controller some breathing space between consecutive sectors in order to copy the buffer to main memory.

If the copying process is very slow, the **double interleaving** of Fig. 5-27(c) may be needed. If the controller has a buffer of only one sector, it does not matter whether the copying from the buffer to main memory is done by the controller, the main CPU, or a DMA chip; it still takes some time. To avoid the need for interleaving, the controller should be able to buffer an entire track. Many modern controllers can do this.

After low-level formatting is completed, the disk is partitioned. Logically, each partition is like a separate disk. On the Pentium and most other computers, sector 0 contains the **master boot record**, which contains some boot code plus

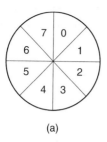
(a)
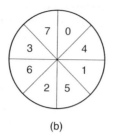
(b)
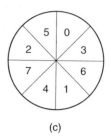
(c)

Figure 5-26. (a) No interleaving. (b) Single interleaving. (c) Double interleaving.

the partition table at the end. The partition table gives the starting sector and size of each partition. On the Pentium, the partition table has room for four partitions. If all of them are for Windows, they will be called C:, D:, E:, and F: and treated as separate drives. If three of them are for Windows and one is for UNIX, then Windows will call its partitions C:, D:, and E:. The first CD-ROM will then be F:. To be able to boot from the hard disk, one partition must be marked as active in the partition table.

The final step in preparing a disk for use is to perform a **high-level format** of each partition (separately). This operation lays down a boot block, the free storage administration (free list or bitmap), root directory, and an empty file system. It also puts a code in the partition table entry telling which file system is used in the partition because many operating systems support multiple incompatible file systems (for historical reasons). At this point the system can be booted.

When the power is turned on, the BIOS runs initially and then reads in the master boot record and jumps to it. This boot program then checks to see which partition is active. Then it reads in the boot sector from that partition and runs it. The boot sector contains a small program that searches the root directory for a certain program (either the operating system or a larger bootstrap loader). That program is loaded into memory and executed.

5.4.3 Disk Arm Scheduling Algorithms

In this section we will look at some issues related to disk drivers in general. First, consider how long it takes to read or write a disk block. The time required is determined by three factors:

1. Seek time (the time to move the arm to the proper cylinder).

2. Rotational delay (the time for the proper sector to rotate under the head).

3. Actual data transfer time.

For most disks, the seek time dominates the other two times, so reducing the mean seek time can improve system performance substantially.

If the disk driver accepts requests one at a time and carries them out in that order, that is, First-Come, First-Served (FCFS), little can be done to optimize seek time. However, another strategy is possible when the disk is heavily loaded. It is likely that while the arm is seeking on behalf of one request, other disk requests may be generated by other processes. Many disk drivers maintain a table, indexed by cylinder number, with all the pending requests for each cylinder chained together in a linked list headed by the table entries.

Given this kind of data structure, we can improve upon the first-come, first-served scheduling algorithm. To see how, consider an imaginary disk with 40 cylinders. A request comes in to read a block on cylinder 11. While the seek to cylinder 11 is in progress, new requests come in for cylinders 1, 36, 16, 34, 9, and 12, in that order. They are entered into the table of pending requests, with a separate linked list for each cylinder. The requests are shown in Fig. 5-27.

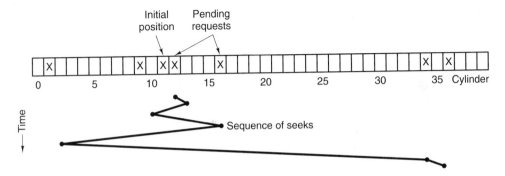

Figure 5-27. Shortest Seek First (SSF) disk scheduling algorithm.

When the current request (for cylinder 11) is finished, the disk driver has a choice of which request to handle next. Using FCFS, it would go next to cylinder 1, then to 36, and so on. This algorithm would require arm motions of 10, 35, 20, 18, 25, and 3, respectively, for a total of 111 cylinders.

Alternatively, it could always handle the closest request next, to minimize seek time. Given the requests of Fig. 5-27, the sequence is 12, 9, 16, 1, 34, and 36, as shown as the jagged line at the bottom of Fig. 5-27. With this sequence, the arm motions are 1, 3, 7, 15, 33, and 2, for a total of 61 cylinders. This algorithm, **Shortest Seek First** (SSF), cuts the total arm motion almost in half compared to FCFS.

Unfortunately, SSF has a problem. Suppose more requests keep coming in while the requests of Fig. 5-27 are being processed. For example, if, after going to cylinder 16, a new request for cylinder 8 is present, that request will have priority over cylinder 1. If a request for cylinder 13 then comes in, the arm will next go to 13, instead of 1. With a heavily loaded disk, the arm will tend to stay in the middle of the disk most of the time, so requests at either extreme will have to wait until a statistical fluctuation in the load causes there to be no requests near the middle. Requests far from the middle may get poor service. The goals of minimal response time and fairness are in conflict here.

Tall buildings also have to deal with this trade-off. The problem of scheduling an elevator in a tall building is similar to that of scheduling a disk arm. Requests come in continuously calling the elevator to floors (cylinders) at random. The computer running the elevator could easily keep track of the sequence in which customers pushed the call button and service them using FCFS. It could also use SSF.

However, most elevators use a different algorithm to reconcile the conflicting goals of efficiency and fairness. They keep moving in the same direction until there are no more outstanding requests in that direction, then they switch directions. This algorithm, known both in the disk world and the elevator world as the **elevator algorithm**, requires the software to maintain 1 bit: the current direction bit, *UP* or *DOWN*. When a request finishes, the disk or elevator driver checks the bit. If it is *UP*, the arm or cabin is moved to the next highest pending request. If no requests are pending at higher positions, the direction bit is reversed. When the bit is set to *DOWN*, the move is to the next lowest requested position, if any.

Figure 5-28 shows the elevator algorithm using the same seven requests as Fig. 5-27, assuming the direction bit was initially *UP*. The order in which the cylinders are serviced is 12, 16, 34, 36, 9, and 1, which yields arm motions of 1, 4, 18, 2, 27, and 8, for a total of 60 cylinders. In this case the elevator algorithm is slightly better than SSF, although it is usually worse. One nice property that the elevator algorithm has is that given any collection of requests, the upper bound on the total motion is fixed: it is just twice the number of cylinders.

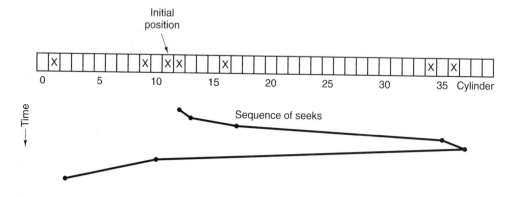

Figure 5-28. The elevator algorithm for scheduling disk requests.

A slight modification of this algorithm that has a smaller variance in response times (Teory, 1972) is to always scan in the same direction. When the highest numbered cylinder with a pending request has been serviced, the arm goes to the lowest-numbered cylinder with a pending request and then continues moving in an upward direction. In effect, the lowest-numbered cylinder is thought of as being just above the highest-numbered cylinder.

Some disk controllers provide a way for the software to inspect the current sector number under the head. With such a controller, another optimization is possible. If two or more requests for the same cylinder are pending, the driver can issue a request for the sector that will pass under the head next. Note that when multiple tracks are present in a cylinder, consecutive requests can be for different tracks with no penalty. The controller can select any of its heads instantaneously, because head selection involves neither arm motion nor rotational delay.

If the disk has the property that the seek time is much faster than the rotational delay, then a different optimization strategy should be used. Pending requests should be sorted by sector number, and as a soon as the next sector is about to pass under the head, the arm should be zipped over to the right track to read or write it.

With a modern hard disk, the seek and rotational delays so dominate performance that reading one or two sectors at a time is very inefficient. For this reason, many disk controllers always read and cache multiple sectors, even when only one is requested. Typically any request to read a sector will cause that sector and much or all the rest of the current track to be read, depending upon how much space is available in the controller's cache memory. The disk described in Fig. 5-17 has a 2-MB or 4-MB cache, for example. The use of the cache is determined dynamically by the controller. In its simplest mode, the cache is divided into two sections, one for reads and one for writes. If a subsequent read can be satisfied out of the controller's cache, it can return the requested data immediately.

It is worth noting that the disk controller's cache is completely independent of the operating system's cache. The controller's cache usually holds blocks that have not actually been requested, but which were convenient the read because they just happened to pass under the head as a side effect of some other read. In contrast, any cache maintained by the operating system will consist of blocks that were explicitly read and which the operating system thinks might be needed again in the near future (e.g., a disk block holding a directory block).

When several drives are present on the same controller, the operating should maintain a pending request table for each drive separately. Whenever any drive is idle, a seek should be issued to move its arm to the cylinder where it will be needed next (assuming the controller allows overlapped seeks). When the current transfer finishes, a check can be made to see if any drives are positioned on the correct cylinder. If one or more are, the next transfer can be started on a drive that is already on the right cylinder. If none of the arms is in the right place, the driver should issue a new seek on the drive that just completed a transfer and wait until the next interrupt to see which arm gets to its destination first.

It is important to realize that all of the above disk scheduling algorithms tacitly assume that the real disk geometry is the same as the virtual geometry. If it is not, then scheduling disk requests makes no sense because the operating system cannot really tell whether cylinder 40 or cylinder 200 is closer to cylinder 39. On the other hand, if the disk controller can accept multiple outstanding requests, it can use these scheduling algorithms internally. In that case, the algorithms are still valid, but one level down, inside the controller.

5.4.4 Error Handling

Disk manufacturers are constantly pushing the limits of the technology by increasing linear bit densities. A track midway out on a 5.25-inch disk has a circumference of about 300 mm. If the track holds 300 sectors of 512 bytes, the linear recording density may be about 5000 bits/mm taking into account the fact that some space is lost to preambles, ECCs, and intersector gaps. Recording 5000 bits/mm requires an extremely uniform substrate and a very fine oxide coating. Unfortunately, it is not possible to manufacture a disk to such specifications without defects. As soon as manufacturing technology has improved to the point where it is possible to operate flawlessly at such densities, disk designers will go to higher densities to increase the capacity. Doing so will probably reintroduce defects.

Manufacturing defects introduce bad sectors, that is, sectors that do not correctly read back the value just written to them. If the defect is very small, say, only a few bits, it is possible to use the bad sector and just let the ECC correct the errors every time. If the defect is bigger, the error cannot be masked.

There are two general approaches to bad blocks: deal with them in the controller or deal with them in the operating system. In the former approach, before the disk is shipped from the factory, it is tested and a list of bad sectors is written onto the disk. For each bad sector, one of the spares is substituted for it.

There are two ways to do this substitution. In Fig. 5-29(a), we see a single disk track with 30 data sectors and two spares. Sector 7 is defective. What the controller can do is remap one of the spares as sector 7 as shown in Fig. 5-29(b). The other way is to shift all the sectors up one, as shown in Fig. 5-29(c). In both cases the controller has to know which sector is which. It can keep track of this information through internal tables (one per track) or by rewriting the preambles to give the remapped sector numbers. If the preambles are rewritten, the method of Fig. 5-29(c) is more work (because 23 preambles must be rewritten) but ultimately gives better performance because an entire track can still be read in one rotation.

Errors can also develop during normal operation after the drive has been installed. The first line of defense upon getting an error that the ECC cannot handle is to just try the read again. Some read errors are transient, that is, are caused by specks of dust under the head and will go away on a second attempt. If the controller notices that it is getting repeated errors on a certain sector, it can switch to a spare before the sector has died completely. In this way, no data are lost and the operating system and user do not even notice the problem. Usually, the

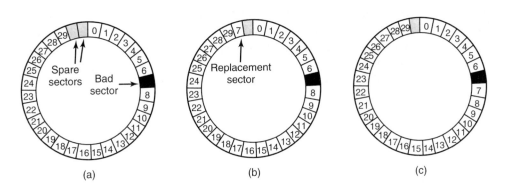

Figure 5-29. (a) A disk track with a bad sector. (b) Substituting a spare for the bad sector. (c) Shifting all the sectors to bypass the bad one.

method of Fig. 5-29(b) has to be used since the other sectors might now contain data. Using the method of Fig. 5-29(c) would require not only rewriting the preambles, but copying all the data as well.

Earlier we said there were two general approaches to handling errors: handle them in the controller or in the operating system. If the controller does not have the capability to transparently remap sectors as we have discussed, the operating system must do the same thing in software. This means that it must first acquire a list of bad sectors, either by reading them from the disk, or simply testing the entire disk itself. Once it knows which sectors are bad, it can build remapping tables. If the operating system wants to use the approach of Fig. 5-29(c), it must shift the data in sectors 7 through 29 up one sector.

If the operating system is handling the remapping, it must make sure that bad sectors do not occur in any files and also do not occur in the free list or bitmap. One way to do this is to create a secret file consisting of all the bad sectors. If this file is not entered into the file system, users will not accidentally read it (or worse yet, free it).

However, there is still another problem: backups. If the disk is backed up file by file, it is important that the backup utility not try to copy the bad block file. To prevent this, the operating system has to hide the bad block file so well that even a backup utility cannot find it. If the disk is backed up sector by sector rather than file by file, it will be difficult, if not impossible, to prevent read errors during backup. The only hope is that the backup program has enough smarts to give up after 10 failed reads and continue with the next sector.

Bad sectors are not the only source of errors. Seek errors caused by mechanical problems in the arm also occur. The controller keeps track of the arm position internally. To perform a seek, it issues a series of pulses to the arm motor, one pulse per cylinder, to move the arm to the new cylinder. When the arm gets to its destination, the controller reads the actual cylinder number from the preamble of the next sector. If the arm is in the wrong place, a seek error has occurred.

Most hard disk controllers correct seek errors automatically, but most floppy controllers (including the Pentium's) just set an error bit and leave the rest to the driver. The driver handles this error by issuing a recalibrate command, to move the arm as far out as it will go and reset the controller's internal idea of the current cylinder to 0. Usually this solves the problem. If it does not, the drive must be repaired.

As we have seen, the controller is really a specialized little computer, complete with software, variables, buffers, and occasionally, bugs. Sometimes an unusual sequence of events such as an interrupt on one drive occurring simultaneously with a recalibrate command for another drive will trigger a bug and cause the controller to go into a loop or lose track of what it was doing. Controller designers usually plan for the worst and provide a pin on the chip which, when asserted, forces the controller to forget whatever it was doing and reset itself. If all else fails, the disk driver can set a bit to invoke this signal and reset the controller. If that does not help, all the driver can do is print a message and give up.

Recalibrating a disk makes a funny noise but otherwise normally is not disturbing. However, there is one situation where recalibration is a serious problem: systems with real-time constraints. When a video is being played off a hard disk, or files from a hard disk are being burned onto a CD-ROM, it is essential that the bits arrive from the hard disk at a uniform rate. Under these circumstances, recalibrations insert gaps into the bit stream and are therefore unacceptable. Special drives, called **AV disks** (**Audio Visual disks**), which never recalibrate are available for such applications.

5.4.5 Stable Storage

As we have seen, disks sometimes make errors. Good sectors can suddenly become bad sectors. Whole drives can die unexpectedly. RAIDs protect against a few sectors going bad or even a drive falling out. However, they do not protect against write errors laying down bad data in the first place. They also do not protect against crashes during writes corrupting the original data without replacing them by newer data.

For some applications, it is essential that data never be lost or corrupted, even in the face of disk and CPU errors. Ideally, a disk should simply work all the time with no errors. Unfortunately, that is not achievable. What is achievable is a disk subsystem that has the following property: when a write is issued to it, the disk either correctly writes the data or it does nothing, leaving the existing data intact. Such as system is called **stable storage** and is implemented in software (Lampson and Sturgis, 1979). Below we will describe a slight variant of the original idea.

Before describing the algorithm, it is important to have a clear model of the possible errors. The model assumes that when a disk writes a block (one or more sectors), either the write is correct or it is incorrect and this error can be detected on a subsequent read by examining the values of the ECC fields. In principle, guaranteed error detection is never possible because with a, say, 16-byte ECC field guarding a 512-byte sector, there are 2^{4096} data values and only 2^{144} ECC values. Thus if a block is garbled during writing but the ECC is not, there are billions upon billions of incorrect combinations that yield the same ECC. If any of them occur, the error will not be detected. On the whole, the probability of random data having the proper 16-byte ECC is about 2^{-144}, which is small enough that we will call it zero, even though it is really not.

The model also assumes that a correctly written sector can spontaneously go bad and become unreadable. However, the assumption is that such events are so rare that having the same sector go bad on a second (independent) drive during a reasonable time interval (e.g., 1 day) is small enough to ignore.

The model also assumes the CPU can fail, in which case it just stops. Any disk write in progress at the moment of failure also stops, leading to incorrect data in one sector and an incorrect ECC that can later be detected. Under all these conditions, stable storage can be made 100% reliable in the sense of writes either working correctly or leaving the old data in place. Of course, it does not protect against physical disasters, such as an earthquake happening and the computer falling 100 meters into a fissure and landing in a pool of boiling magma. It is tough to recover from this condition in software.

Stable storage uses a pair of identical disks with the corresponding blocks working together to form one error-free block. In the absence of errors, the corresponding blocks on both drives are the same. Either one can be read to get the same result. To achieve this goal, the following three operations are defined:

1. **Stable writes**. A stable write consists of first writing the block on drive 1, then reading it back to verify that it was written correctly. If it was not written correctly, the write and reread are done again up to n times until they work. After n consecutive failures, the block is remapped onto a spare and the operation repeated until it succeeds, no matter how many spares have to be tried. After the write to drive 1 has succeeded, the corresponding block on drive 2 is written and reread, repeatedly if need be, until it, too, finally succeeds. In the absence of CPU crashes, when a stable write completes, the block has correctly been written onto both drives and verified on both of them.

2. **Stable reads**. A stable read first reads the block from drive 1. If this yields an incorrect ECC, the read is tried again, up to n times. If all of these give bad ECCs, the corresponding block is read from drive 2. Given the fact that a successful stable write leaves two good copies of the block behind, and our assumption that the probability of the same block spontaneously going bad on both drives in a reasonable time interval is negligible, a stable read always succeeds.

3. **Crash recovery**. After a crash, a recovery program scans both disks comparing corresponding blocks. If a pair of blocks are both good and the same, nothing is done. If one of them has an ECC error, the bad block is overwritten with the corresponding good block. If a pair of blocks are both good but different, the block from drive 1 is written onto drive 2.

In the absence of CPU crashes, this scheme always works because stable writes always write two valid copies of every block and spontaneous errors are assumed never to occur on both corresponding blocks at the same time. What about in the presence of CPU crashes during stable writes? It depends on precisely when the crash occur. There are five possibilities, as depicted in Fig. 5-30.

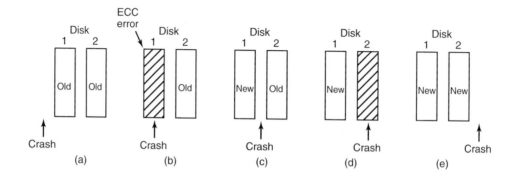

Figure 5-30. Analysis of the influence of crashes on stable writes.

In Fig. 5-30(a), the CPU crash happens before either copy of the block is written. During recovery, neither will be changed and the old value will continue to exist, which is allowed.

In Fig. 5-30(b), the CPU crashes during the write to drive 1, destroying the contents of the block. However the recovery program detects this error and restores the block on drive 1 from drive 2. Thus the effect of the crash is wiped out and the old state is fully restored.

In Fig. 5-30(c), the CPU crash happens after drive 1 is written but before drive 2 is written. The point of no return has been passed here: the recovery program copies the block from drive 1 to drive 2. The write succeeds.

Fig. 5-30(d) is like Fig. 5-30(b): during recovery, the good block overwrites the bad block. Again, the final value of both blocks is the new one.

Finally, in Fig. 5-30(e) the recovery program sees that both blocks are the same, so neither is changed and the write succeeds here too.

Various optimizations and improvements are possible to this scheme. For starters, comparing all the blocks pairwise after a crash is doable, but expensive. A huge improvement is to keep track of which block was being written during a stable write so that only one block has to be checked during recovery. Some computers have a small amount of **nonvolatile RAM** which is a special CMOS memory powered by a lithium battery. Such batteries last for years, possibly even the whole life of the computer. Unlike main memory, which is lost after a crash, nonvolatile RAM is not lost after a crash. The time of day is normally kept here (and incremented by a special circuit), which is why computers still know what time it is even after having been unplugged.

Suppose that a few bytes of nonvolatile RAM are available for operating system purposes. The stable write can put the number of the block it is about to update in nonvolatile RAM before starting the write. After successfully completing the stable write, the block number in nonvolatile RAM is overwritten with an invalid block number, for example, −1. Under these conditions, after a crash the recovery program can check the nonvolatile RAM to see if a stable write happened to be in progress during the crash, and if so, which block was being written when the crashed happened. The two copies of the block can then be checked for correctness and consistency.

If nonvolatile RAM is not available, it can be simulated as follows. At the start of a stable write, a fixed disk block on drive 1 is overwritten with the number of the block to be stably written. This block is then read back to verify it. After getting it correct, the corresponding block on drive 2 is written and verified. When the stable write completes correctly, both blocks are overwritten with an invalid block number and verified. Again here, after a crash it is easy to determine whether or not a stable write was in progress during the crash. Of course, this technique requires eight extra disk operations to write a stable block, so it should be used exceedingly sparingly.

One last point is worth making. We assumed that only one spontaneous decay of a good block to a bad block happens per block pair per day. If enough days go by, the other one might go bad too. Therefore, once a day a complete scan of both disks must be done repairing any damage. That way, every morning both disks are always identical. Even if both blocks in a pair go bad within a period of a few days, all errors are repaired correctly.

5.5 CLOCKS

Clocks (also called **timers**) are essential to the operation of any multiprogrammed system for a variety of reasons. They maintain the time of day and prevent one process from monopolizing the CPU, among other things. The clock software can take the form of a device driver, even though a clock is neither a block device, like a disk, nor a character device, like a mouse. Our examination of clocks will follow the same pattern as in the previous section: first a look at clock hardware and then a look at the clock software.

5.5.1 Clock Hardware

Two types of clocks are commonly used in computers, and both are quite different from the clocks and watches used by people. The simpler clocks are tied to the 110- or 220-volt power line and cause an interrupt on every voltage cycle, at 50 or 60 Hz. These clocks used to dominate, but are rare nowadays.

The other kind of clock is built out of three components: a crystal oscillator, a counter, and a holding register, as shown in Fig. 5-31. When a piece of quartz crystal is properly cut and mounted under tension, it can be made to generate a periodic signal of very high accuracy, typically in the range of several hundred megahertz, depending on the crystal chosen. Using electronics, this base signal can be multiplied by a small integer to get frequencies up to 1000 MHz or even more. At least one such circuit is usually found in any computer, providing a synchronizing signal to the computer's various circuits. This signal is fed into the counter to make it count down to zero. When the counter gets to zero, it causes a CPU interrupt.

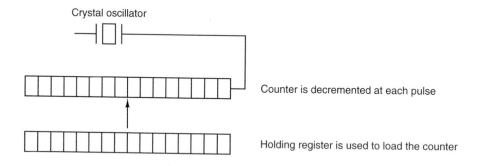

Figure 5-31. A programmable clock.

Programmable clocks typically have several modes of operation. In **one-shot mode**, when the clock is started, it copies the value of the holding register into the counter and then decrements the counter at each pulse from the crystal. When the counter gets to zero, it causes an interrupt and stops until it is explicitly started again by the software. In **square-wave mode**, after getting to zero and causing the interrupt, the holding register is automatically copied into the counter, and the whole process is repeated again indefinitely. These periodic interrupts are called **clock ticks**.

The advantage of the programmable clock is that its interrupt frequency can be controlled by software. If a 500-MHz crystal is used, then the counter is pulsed every 2 nsec. With (unsigned) 32-bit registers, interrupts can be programmed to occur at intervals from 2 nsec to 8.6 sec. Programmable clock chips usually contain two or three independently programmable clocks and have many other options as well (e.g., counting up instead of down, interrupts disabled, and more).

To prevent the current time from being lost when the computer's power is turned off, most computers have a battery-powered backup clock, implemented with the kind of low-power circuitry used in digital watches. The battery clock can be read at startup. If the backup clock is not present, the software may ask the user for the current date and time. There is also a standard way for a networked system to get the current time from a remote host. In any case the time is then translated into the number of clock ticks since 12 A.M. **UTC (Universal Coordinated Time**) (formerly known as Greenwich Mean Time) on Jan. 1, 1970, as UNIX does, or since some other benchmark. The origin of time for Windows is Jan. 1, 1980. At every clock tick, the real time is incremented by one count. Usually utility programs are provided to manually set the system clock and the backup clock and to synchronize the two clocks.

5.5.2 Clock Software

All the clock hardware does is generate interrupts at known intervals. Everything else involving time must be done by the software, the clock driver. The exact duties of the clock driver vary among operating systems, but usually include most of the following:

1. Maintaining the time of day.

2. Preventing processes from running longer than they are allowed to.

3. Accounting for CPU usage.

4. Handling the alarm system call made by user processes.

5. Providing watchdog timers for parts of the system itself.

6. Doing profiling, monitoring, and statistics gathering.

The first clock function, maintaining the time of day (also called the **real time**) is not difficult. It just requires incrementing a counter at each clock tick, as mentioned before. The only thing to watch out for is the number of bits in the time-of-day counter. With a clock rate of 60 Hz, a 32-bit counter will overflow in just over 2 years. Clearly the system cannot store the real time as the number of ticks since Jan. 1, 1970 in 32 bits.

Three approaches can be taken to solve this problem. The first way is to use a 64-bit counter, although doing so makes maintaining the counter more expensive since it has to be done many times a second. The second way is to maintain the time of day in seconds, rather than in ticks, using a subsidiary counter to count ticks until a whole second has been accumulated. Because 2^{32} seconds is more than 136 years, this method will work until the twenty-second century.

The third approach is to count in ticks, but to do that relative to the time the system was booted, rather than relative to a fixed external moment. When the backup clock is read or the user types in the real time, the system boot time is calculated from the current time-of-day value and stored in memory in any convenient form. Later, when the time of day is requested, the stored time of day is added to the counter to get the current time of day. All three approaches are shown in Fig. 5-32.

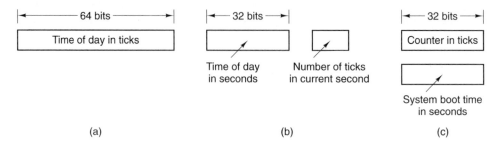

Figure 5-32. Three ways to maintain the time of day.

The second clock function is preventing processes from running too long. Whenever a process is started, the scheduler initializes a counter to the value of that process' quantum in clock ticks. At every clock interrupt, the clock driver decrements the quantum counter by 1. When it gets to zero, the clock driver calls the scheduler to set up another process.

The third clock function is doing CPU accounting. The most accurate way to do it is to start a second timer, distinct from the main system timer, whenever a process is started. When that process is stopped, the timer can be read out to tell how long the process has run. To do things right, the second timer should be saved when an interrupt occurs and restored afterward.

A less accurate, but much simpler, way to do accounting is to maintain a pointer to the process table entry for the currently running process in a global variable. At every clock tick, a field in the current process' entry is incremented. In this way, every clock tick is "charged" to the process running at the time of the tick. A minor problem with this strategy is that if many interrupts occur during a process' run, it is still charged for a full tick, even though it did not get much work done. Properly accounting for the CPU during interrupts is too expensive and is rarely done.

In many systems, a process can request that the operating system give it a warning after a certain interval. The warning is usually a signal, interrupt, message, or something similar. One application requiring such warnings is networking, in which a packet not acknowledged within a certain time interval must be retransmitted. Another application is computer-aided instruction, where a student not providing a response within a certain time is told the answer.

If the clock driver had enough clocks, it could set a separate clock for each request. This not being the case, it must simulate multiple virtual clocks with a single physical clock. One way is to maintain a table in which the signal time for all pending timers is kept, as well as a variable giving the time of the next one. Whenever the time of day is updated, the driver checks to see if the closest signal has occurred. If it has, the table is searched for the next one to occur.

If many signals are expected, it is more efficient to simulate multiple clocks by chaining all the pending clock requests together, sorted on time, in a linked list, as shown in Fig. 5-33. Each entry on the list tells how many clock ticks following the previous one to wait before causing a signal. In this example, signals are pending for 4203, 4207, 4213, 4215, and 4216.

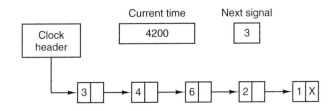

Figure 5-33. Simulating multiple timers with a single clock.

In Fig. 5-33, the next interrupt occurs in 3 ticks. On each tick, *Next signal* is decremented. When it gets to 0, the signal corresponding to the first item on the list is caused, and that item is removed from the list. Then *Next signal* is set to the value in the entry now at the head of the list, in this example, 4.

Note that during a clock interrupt, the clock driver has several things to do—increment the real time, decrement the quantum and check for 0, do CPU accounting, and decrement the alarm counter. However, each of these operations has been carefully arranged to be very fast because they have to be repeated many times a second.

Parts of the operating system also need to set timers. These are called **watchdog timers**. For example, floppy disks do not rotate when not in use, to avoid wear and tear on the medium and disk head. When data are needed from a floppy disk, the motor must first be started. Only when the floppy disk is rotating at full speed can I/O begin. When a process attempts to read from an idle floppy disk, the floppy disk driver starts the motor and then sets a watchdog timer to cause an interrupt after a sufficiently long time interval (because there is no up-to-speed interrupt from the floppy disk itself).

The mechanism used by the clock driver to handle watchdog timers is the same as for user signals. The only difference is that when a timer goes off, instead of causing a signal, the clock driver calls a procedure supplied by the caller. The procedure is part of the caller's code. The called procedure can do whatever is necessary, even causing an interrupt, although within the kernel interrupts are often inconvenient and signals do not exist. That is why the watchdog mechanism is provided. It is worth nothing that the watchdog mechanism works only when the clock driver and the procedure to be called are in the same address space.

The last thing in our list is profiling. Some operating systems provide a mechanism by which a user program can have the system build up a histogram of its program counter, so it can see where it is spending its time. When profiling is a possibility, at every tick the driver checks to see if the current process is being profiled, and if so, computes the bin number (a range of addresses) corresponding to the current program counter. It then increments that bin by one. This mechanism can also be used to profile the system itself.

5.5.3 Soft Timers

Most computers have a second programmable clock that can be set to cause timer interrupts at whatever rate a program needs. This timer is in addition to the main system timer whose functions were described above. As long as the interrupt frequency is low, there is no problem using this second timer for application-specific purposes. The trouble arrives when the frequency of the application-specific timer is very high. Below we will briefly describe a software-based timer scheme that works well under many circumstances, even at high frequencies. The idea is due to Aron and Druschel (1999). For more details, please see their paper.

Generally, there are two ways to manage I/O: interrupts and polling. Interrupts have low latency, that is, they happen immediately after the event itself with little or no delay. On the other hand, with modern CPUs, interrupts have a substantial overhead due to the need for context switching and their influence on the pipeline, TLB and cache.

The alternative to interrupts is to have the application poll for the event expected itself. Doing this avoids interrupts, but there may be substantial latency because an event may happen directly after a poll, in which case it waits almost a whole polling interval. On the average, the latency is half the polling interval.

For some applications, neither the overhead of interrupts nor the latency of polling is acceptable. Consider, for example, a high-performance network such as Gigabit Ethernet. This network is capable of accepting or delivering a full-size packet every 12 µsec. To run at optimal performance on output, one packet should be sent every 12 µsec.

One way to achieve this rate is to have the completion of a packet transmission cause an interrupt or to set the second timer to interrupt every 12 µsec. The problem is that this interrupt has been measured to take 4.45 µsec on a 300 MHz Pentium II (Aron and Druschel, 1999). This overhead is barely better than that of computers in the 1970s. On most minicomputers, for example, an interrupt took four bus cycles: to stack the program counter and PSW and to load a new program counter and PSW. Nowadays dealing with the pipeline, MMU, TLB, and cache, add a great deal to the overhead. These effects are likely to get worse rather than better in time, thus canceling out faster clock rates.

Soft timers avoid interrupts. Instead, whenever the kernel is running for some other reason, just before it returns to user mode it checks the real time clock to see if a soft timer has expired. If the timer has expired, the scheduled event (e.g., packet transmission or checking for an incoming packet) is performed, with no need to switch into kernel mode since the system is already there. After the work has been performed, the soft timer is reset to go off again. All that has to be done is copy the current clock value to the timer and add the timeout interval to it.

Soft timers stand or fall with the rate at which kernel entries are made for other reasons. These reasons include

1. System calls.

2. TLB misses.

3. Page faults.

4. I/O interrupts.

5. The CPU going idle.

To see how often these events happen, Aron and Druschel made measurements with several CPU loads, including a fully-loaded Web server, a Web server with a compute-bound background job, playing real-time audio from the Internet, and recompiling the UNIX kernel. The average entry rate into the kernel varied from 2 µsec to 18 µsec, with about half of these entries being system calls. Thus to a first-order approximation, having a soft timer go off every 12 µsec is doable, albeit with an occasional missed deadline. For applications like sending packets or polling for incoming packets, being 10 µsec late from time to time is better than having interrupts eat up 35% of the CPU.

Of course, there will be periods when there are no system calls, TLB misses, or page faults, in which case no soft timers will go off. To put an upper bound on these intervals, the second hardware timer can be set to go off, say, every 1 msec. If the application can live with only 1000 packets/sec for occasional intervals, then the combination of soft timers and a low-frequency hardware timer may be better than either pure interrupt-driven I/O or pure polling.

5.6 CHARACTER-ORIENTED TERMINALS

Every general-purpose computer has at least one keyboard and one display (monitor or flat screen) used to communicate with it. Although the keyboard and display on a personal computer are technically separate devices, they work closely together. On mainframes, there are frequently many remote users, each with a device containing a keyboard and an attached display. These devices have historically been called **terminals**. We will continue to use that term, even when discussing personal computers (mostly for lack of a better term).

Terminals come in many forms. Three of the types most commonly encountered in practice nowadays are

1. Standalone terminals with RS-232 serial interfaces for use on mainframes.

2. Personal computer displays with graphical user interfaces.

3. Network terminals.

Each type of terminal has its own ecological niche. In the following sections we will describe each of these types in turn.

5.6.1 RS-232 Terminal Hardware

RS-232 terminals are hardware devices containing both a keyboard and a display and which communicate using a serial interface, one bit at a time (see Fig. 5-34). These terminals use a 9-pin or 25-pin connector, of which one pin is used for transmitting data, one pin is for receiving data, and one pin is ground. The other pins are for various control functions, most of which are not used. Lines in which characters are sent one bit at a time (as opposed to 8 bits in parallel the way printers are interfaced to PCs) are called **serial lines**. All modems also use this interface. On UNIX, serial lines have names like */dev/tty1* and */dev/tty2*. On Windows they have names like *COM1* and *COM2*.

To send a character over a serial line to an RS-232 terminal or modem, the computer must transmit it 1 bit at a time, prefixed by a start bit, and followed by 1 or 2 stop bits to delimit the character. A parity bit which provides rudimentary error detection may also be inserted preceding the stop bits, although this is commonly required only for communication with mainframe systems.

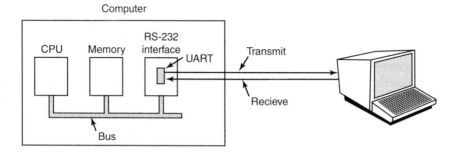

Figure 5-34. An RS-232 terminal communicates with a computer over a communication line, one bit at a time.

RS-232 terminals are still commonly used in the mainframe world to allow a remote user to communicate with the mainframe, sometimes using a modem and a telephone line. They are found in the airline, banking, and other industries. Even when they are replaced by personal computers, the PCs often simply emulate the old RS-232 terminals to avoid having to change the mainframe software.

These terminals also used to dominate the minicomputer world. A great deal of software for systems that grew up in this period are based on these terminals. For example, all UNIX systems support this kind of device.

However, even more important, many current UNIX systems (and other systems) provide the option of creating a window consisting of some number of lines of text. Many programmers work almost exclusively in text mode in such windows, even on personal computers or high-end workstations. These windows usually simulate some RS-232 terminal (or the ANSI standard for this type of terminal) so they can run the large existing software base that was written for such terminals. In the course of the years, this software, such as the *vi* and *emacs* editors, has become completely debugged and extremely stable, properties programmers value highly.

The keyboard and terminal software for these terminal emulation windows is the same as for the real terminals. Since these terminal emulators are in widespread use, the software is still important, so we will describe it in the following two sections.

RS-232 terminals are character oriented. What this means is that the screen or window displays a certain number of lines of text, each of a maximum size. A typical size is 25 lines of 80 characters each. While a few special characters are sometimes supported, these terminals (and the emulators) are basically text only.

Since both computers and terminals work internally with whole characters but must communicate over a serial line a bit at a time, chips have been developed to do the character-to-serial and serial-to-character conversions. They are called **UARTs** (Universal Asynchronous Receiver Transmitters). UARTs are attached to the computer by plugging RS-232 interface cards into the bus as illustrated in Fig. 5-34. On many computers, one or two serial ports are built into the parentboard.

To display a character, the terminal driver writes the character to the interface card, where it is buffered and then shifted out over the serial line one bit at a time by the UART. For example, for an analog modem operating at 56,000 bps, it takes just over 179 μsec to send a character. As a result of this slow transmission rate, the driver generally outputs a character to the RS-232 card and blocks, waiting for the interrupt generated by the interface when the character has been transmitted and the UART is able to accept another character. The UART can send and receive characters simultaneously. An interrupt is also generated when a character is received, and usually a small number of input characters can be buffered. The terminal driver must check a register when an interrupt is received to determine the cause of the interrupt. Some interface cards have a CPU and memory and can handle multiple lines, taking over much of the I/O load from the main CPU.

RS-232 terminals can be subdivided into three categories. The simplest ones are hardcopy (i.e., printing) terminals. Characters typed on the keyboard are transmitted to the computer. Characters sent by the computer are printed on the paper. These terminals are obsolete and rarely seen any more except as low-end printers.

Dumb CRT terminals work the same way, only with a screen instead of paper. These are often called "glass ttys" because they are functionally the same as hardcopy ttys. (The term "tty" is an abbreviation for Teletype®, a former company that pioneered in the computer terminal business; "tty" has come to mean any terminal.) Glass ttys are also obsolete.

Intelligent CRT terminals are in fact miniature, specialized computers. They have a CPU and memory and contain software, usually in ROM. From the operating system's viewpoint, the main difference between a glass tty and an intelligent terminal is that the latter understands certain escape sequences. For example, by sending the ASCII ESC character (0x1B), followed by various other characters, it may be possible to move the cursor to any position on the screen, insert text in the middle of the screen, and so forth. Intelligent terminals are the ones used in mainframe systems and are the ones emulated by other operating systems. It is their software that we will discuss below.

5.6.2 Input Software

The keyboard and display are almost independent devices, so we will treat them separately here. They are not quite independent, however, since typed characters generally are displayed on the screen.

The basic job of the keyboard driver is to collect input from the keyboard and pass it to user programs when they read from the terminal. Two possible philosophies can be adopted for the driver. In the first one, the driver's job is just to accept input and pass it upward unmodified. A program reading from the terminal gets a raw sequence of ASCII codes. (Giving user programs the key numbers is too primitive, as well as being highly machine dependent.)

This philosophy is well suited to the needs of sophisticated screen editors such as *emacs*, which allow the user to bind an arbitrary action to any character or sequence of characters. It does, however, mean that if the user types *dste* instead of *date* and then corrects the error by typing three backspaces and *ate*, followed by a carriage return, the user program will be given all 11 ASCII codes typed, as follows:

    d s t e ← ← ← a t e CR

Not all programs want this much detail. Often they just want the corrected input, not the exact sequence of how it was produced. This observation leads to the second philosophy: the driver handles all the intraline editing, and just delivers corrected lines to the user programs. The first philosophy is character-oriented; the second one is line oriented. Originally they were referred to as **raw mode** and **cooked mode**, respectively. The POSIX standard uses the less-picturesque term

canonical mode to describe line-oriented mode. **Noncanonical mode** is equivalent to raw mode, although many details of terminal behavior can be changed. POSIX-compatible systems provide several library functions that support selecting either mode and changing many aspects of terminal configuration.

The first task of the keyboard driver is to collect characters. If every keystroke causes an interrupt, the driver can acquire the character during the interrupt. If interrupts are turned into messages by the low-level software, it is possible to put the newly acquired character in the message. Alternatively, it can be put in a small buffer in memory and the message used to tell the driver that something has arrived. The latter approach is actually safer if a message can be sent only to a waiting process and there is some chance that the keyboard driver might still be busy with the previous character.

If the terminal is in canonical (cooked) mode, characters must be stored until an entire line has been accumulated, because the user may subsequently decide to erase part of it. Even if the terminal is in raw mode, the program may not yet have requested input, so the characters must be buffered to allow type ahead. (System designers who do not allow users to type far ahead ought to be tarred and feathered, or worse yet, be forced to use their own system.)

Two approaches to character buffering are common. In the first one, the driver contains a central pool of buffers, each buffer holding perhaps 10 characters. Associated with each terminal is a data structure, which contains, among other items, a pointer to the chain of buffers for input collected from that terminal. As more characters are typed, more buffers are acquired and hung on the chain. When the characters are passed to a user program, the buffers are removed and put back in the central pool.

The other approach is to do the buffering directly in the terminal data structure itself, with no central pool of buffers. Since it is common for users to type a command that will take a little while (say, recompiling and linking a large binary program) and then type a few lines ahead, to be safe the driver should allocate something like 200 characters per terminal. In a large-scale timesharing system with 100 terminals, allocating 20K all the time for type ahead is clearly overkill, so a central buffer pool with space for perhaps 5K is probably enough. On the other hand, a dedicated buffer per terminal makes the driver simpler (no linked list management) and is to be preferred on personal computers with only one keyboard. Figure 5-35 shows the difference between these two methods.

Although the keyboard and display are logically separate devices, many users have grown accustomed to seeing the characters they have just typed appear on the screen. Some (older) terminals oblige by automatically displaying (in hardware) whatever has just been typed, which is not only a nuisance when passwords are being entered but greatly limits the flexibility of sophisticated editors and other programs. Fortunately, with most terminals, nothing is automatically displayed when a key is struck. It is entirely up to the software in the computer to display the character, if desired. This process is called **echoing**.

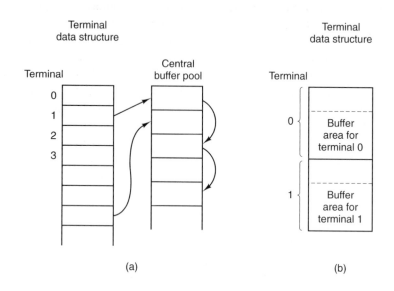

Figure 5-35. (a) Central buffer pool. (b) Dedicated buffer for each terminal.

Echoing is complicated by the fact that a program may be writing to the screen while the user is typing. At the very least, the keyboard driver has to figure out where to put the new input without it being overwritten by program output.

Echoing also gets complicated when more than 80 characters have to be displayed on a screen with 80-character lines (or some other number). Depending on the application, wrapping around to the next line may be appropriate. Some drivers just truncate lines to 80 characters by throwing away all characters beyond column 80.

Another problem is tab handling. It is usually up to the driver to compute where the cursor is currently located, taking into account both output from programs and output from echoing, and compute the proper number of spaces to be echoed.

Now we come to the problem of device equivalence. Logically, at the end of a line of text, one wants a carriage return, to move the cursor back to column 1, and a linefeed, to advance to the next line. Requiring users to type both at the end of each line would not sell well (although some terminals have a key which generates both, with a 50 percent chance of doing so in the order that the software wants them). It is up to the driver to convert whatever comes in to the standard internal format used by the operating system.

If the standard form is just to store a linefeed (the UNIX convention), then carriage returns should be turned into linefeeds. If the internal format is to store both (the Windows convention), then the driver should generate a linefeed when it gets a carriage return and a carriage return when it gets a linefeed. No matter what the internal convention, the terminal may require both a linefeed and a carriage return to be echoed in order to get the screen updated properly. Since a large computer may well have a wide variety of different terminals connected to it, it is up to the keyboard driver to get all the different carriage return/linefeed combinations converted to the internal system standard and arrange for all echoing to be done right.

When operating in canonical mode, a number of input characters have special meanings. Figure 5-36 shows all of the special characters required by POSIX. The defaults are all control characters that should not conflict with text input or codes used by programs, but all except the last two can be changed under program control.

Character	POSIX name	Comment
CTRL-H	ERASE	Backspace one character
CTRL-U	KILL	Erase entire line being typed
CTRL-V	LNEXT	Interpret next character literally
CTRL-S	STOP	Stop output
CTRL-Q	START	Start output
DEL	INTR	Interrupt process (SIGINT)
CTRL-\	QUIT	Force core dump (SIGQUIT)
CTRL-D	EOF	End of file
CTRL-M	CR	Carriage return (unchangeable)
CTRL-J	NL	Linefeed (unchangeable)

Figure 5-36. Characters that are handled specially in canonical mode.

The *ERASE* character allows the user to rub out the character just typed. It is usually the backspace (CTRL-H). It is not added to the character queue but instead removes the previous character from the queue. It should be echoed as a sequence of three characters, backspace, space, and backspace, in order to remove the previous character from the screen. If the previous character was a tab, erasing it depends on how it was processed when it was typed. If it is immediately expanded into spaces, some extra information is needed to determine how far to back up. If the tab itself is stored in the input queue, it can be removed and the entire line just output again. In most systems, backspacing will only erase characters on the current line. It will not erase a carriage return and back up into the previous line.

When the user notices an error at the start of the line being typed in, it is often convenient to erase the entire line and start again. The *KILL* character erases the entire line. Most systems make the erased line vanish from the screen, but a few echo it plus a carriage return and linefeed because some users like to see the old line. Consequently, how to echo *KILL* is a matter of taste. As with *ERASE* it is usually not possible to go further back than the current line. When a block of characters is killed, it may or may not be worth the trouble for the driver to return buffers to the pool, if one is used.

Sometimes the *ERASE* or *KILL* characters must be entered as ordinary data. The *LNEXT* character serves as an **escape character**. In UNIX CTRL-V is the default. As an example, older UNIX systems often used the @ sign for *KILL*, but the Internet mail system uses addresses of the form *linda@cs.washington.edu*. Someone who feels more comfortable with older conventions might redefine *KILL* as @, but then need to enter an @ sign literally to address email. This can be done by typing CTRL-V @. The CTRL-V itself can be entered literally by typing CTRL-V CTRL-V. After seeing a CTRL-V, the driver sets a flag saying that the next character is exempt from special processing. The *LNEXT* character itself is not entered in the character queue.

To allow users to stop a screen image from scrolling out of view, control codes are provided to freeze the screen and restart it later. In UNIX these are *STOP*, (CTRL-S) and *START*, (CTRL-Q), respectively. They are not stored but are used to set and clear a flag in the terminal data structure. Whenever output is attempted, the flag is inspected. If it is set, no output occurs. Usually, echoing is also suppressed along with program output.

It is often necessary to kill a runaway program being debugged. The *INTR* (DEL) and *QUIT* (CTRL-\) characters can be used for this purpose. In UNIX, DEL sends the SIGINT signal to all the processes started up from the terminal. Implementing DEL can be quite tricky. The hard part is getting the information from the driver to the part of the system that handles signals, which, after all, has not asked for this information. CTRL-\ is similar to DEL, except that it sends the SIGQUIT signal, which forces a core dump if not caught or ignored. When either of these keys is struck, the driver should echo a carriage return and linefeed and discard all accumulated input to allow for a fresh start. The default value for *INTR* is often CTRL-C instead of DEL, since many programs use DEL interchangeably with the backspace for editing.

Another special character is *EOF* (CTRL-D), which in UNIX causes any pending read requests for the terminal to be satisfied with whatever is available in the buffer, even if the buffer is empty. Typing CTRL-D at the start of a line causes the program to get a read of 0 bytes, which is conventionally interpreted as end-of-file and causes most programs to act the same way as they would upon seeing end-of-file on an input file.

Some terminal drivers allow much fancier intraline editing than we have sketched here. They have special control characters to erase a word, skip backward or forward characters or words, go to the beginning or end of the line being typed, inserting text in the middle of the line, and so forth. Adding all these functions to the terminal driver makes it much larger and, furthermore, is wasted when using fancy screen editors that work in raw mode anyway.

5.6.3 Output Software

Output is simpler than input. For the most part, the computer sends characters to the terminal and they are displayed there. Usually, a block of characters, for example, a line, is written to the terminal in one system call. The method that is commonly used for RS-232 terminals is to have output buffers associated with each terminal. The buffers can come from the same pool as the input buffers, or be dedicated, as with input. When a programs writes to the terminal, the output is first copied to the buffer. Similarly, output from echoing is also copied to the buffer. After all the output has been copied to the buffer, the first character is output, and the driver goes to sleep. When the interrupt comes in, the next character is output, and so on.

Screen editors and many other sophisticated programs need to be able to update the screen in complex ways such as replacing one line in the middle of the screen. To accommodate this need, most terminals support a a series of commands to move the cursor, insert and delete characters or lines at the cursor, etc. These commands are often called **escape sequences**. In the heyday of the RS-232 terminal, there were hundreds of terminal types, each with its own escape sequences. As a consequence, it was difficult to write software that worked on more than one terminal type.

One solution, which was introduced in Berkeley UNIX, was a terminal database called **termcap**. This software package defined a number of basic actions, such as moving the cursor to (*row, column*). To move the cursor to a particular location, the software, say, an editor, used a generic escape sequence which was then converted to the actual escape sequence for the terminal being written to. In this way, the editor worked on any terminal that had an entry in the termcap database.

Eventually, the industry saw the need for standardization of the escape sequence, so an ANSI standard was developed. A few of the values are shown in Fig. 5-37.

Consider how these escape sequences might be used by a text editor. Suppose that the user types a command telling the editor to delete all of line 3 and then close up the gap between lines 2 and 4. The editor might send the following escape sequence over the serial line to the terminal:

ESC [3 ; 1 H ESC [0 K ESC [1 M

(where the spaces are used above only to separate the symbols; they are not transmitted). This sequence moves the cursor to the start of line 3, erases the entire line, and then deletes the now-empty line, causing all the lines starting at 5 to move up 1 line. Then what was line 4 becomes line 3; what was line 5 becomes line 4, and so on. Analogous escape sequences can be used to add text to the middle of the display. Words and be added or removed in a similar way.

Escape sequence	Meaning
ESC [*n* A	Move up *n* lines
ESC [*n* B	Move down *n* lines
ESC [*n* C	Move right *n* spaces
ESC [*n* D	Move left *n* spaces
ESC [*m* ; *n* H	Move cursor to (*m*,*n*)
ESC [*s* J	Clear screen from cursor (0 to end, 1 from start, 2 all)
ESC [*s* K	Clear line from cursor (0 to end, 1 from start, 2 all)
ESC [*n* L	Insert *n* lines at cursor
ESC [*n* M	Delete *n* lines at cursor
ESC [*n* P	Delete *n* chars at cursor
ESC [*n* @	Insert *n* chars at cursor
ESC [*n* m	Enable rendition *n* (0=normal, 4=bold, 5=blinking, 7=reverse)
ESC M	Scroll the screen backward if the cursor is on the top line

Figure 5-37. The ANSI escape sequences accepted by the terminal driver on output. ESC denotes the ASCII escape character (0x1B), and *n*, *m*, and *s* are optional numeric parameters.

5.7 GRAPHICAL USER INTERFACES

PCs can use character-based interfaces. In fact, for years MS-DOS, which is character based, dominated the scene. However, nowadays most personal computers use a **GUI (Graphical User Interface)**. The acronym GUI is pronounced "gooey."

The GUI was invented by Douglas Engelbart and his research group at the Stanford Research Institute. It was then copied by researchers at Xerox PARC. One fine day, Steve Jobs, cofounder of Apple, was touring PARC and saw a GUI on a Xerox computer. This gave him the idea for a new computer, which became the Apple Lisa. The Lisa was too expensive and was a commercial failure, but its successor, the Macintosh, was a huge success. The Macintosh was the inspiration for Microsoft Windows and other GUI-based systems.

A GUI has four essential elements, denoted by the characters WIMP. These letters stand for Windows, Icons, Menus, and Pointing device, respectively. Windows are rectangular blocks of screen area used to run programs. Icons are little symbols that can be clicked on to cause some action to happen. Menus are lists of actions from which one can be chosen. Finally, a pointing device is a mouse, trackball, or other hardware device used to move a cursor around the screen to select items.

The GUI software can be implemented in either user-level code, as is done in UNIX systems, or in the operating system itself, as in the case in Windows. In the following sections we will look at the hardware, input software, and output software associated with personal computer GUIs with an emphasis on Windows, but the general ideas hold for other GUIs as well.

5.7.1 Personal Computer Keyboard, Mouse, and Display Hardware

Modern personal computers all have a keyboard and a bit-oriented memory-mapped display. These components are an integral part of the computer itself. However, the keyboard and screen are completely separated, each with their own driver.

The keyboard may be interfaced via a serial port, a parallel port, or a USB port. On every key action the CPU is interrupted, and the keyboard driver extracts the character typed by reading an I/O port. Everything else happens in software, mostly in the keyboard driver.

On a Pentium, the keyboard contains an embedded microprocessor which communicates through a specialized serial port with a controller chip on the parentboard. An interrupt is generated whenever a key is struck and also when one is released. Furthermore, all that the keyboard hardware provides is the key number, not the ASCII code. When the *A* key is struck, the key code (30) is put in an I/O register. It is up to the driver to determine whether it is lower case, upper case, CTRL-A, ALT-A, CTRL-ALT-A, or some other combination. Since the driver can tell which keys have been struck but not yet released (e.g., SHIFT), it has enough information to do the job.

For example, the key sequence

DEPRESS SHIFT, DEPRESS A, RELEASE A, RELEASE SHIFT

indicates an upper case A. However, the key sequence

DEPRESS SHIFT, DEPRESS A, RELEASE SHIFT, RELEASE A

also indicates an upper case A. Although this keyboard interface puts the full burden on the software, it is extremely flexible. For example, user programs may be interested in whether a digit just typed came from the top row of keys or the numeric key pad on the side. In principle, the driver can provide this information.

Most PCs have a mouse, or sometimes a trackball, which is just a mouse lying on its back. The most common type of mouse has a rubber ball inside that protrudes through a hole in the bottom and rotates as the mouse is moved over a rough surface. As the ball rotates, it rubs against rubber rollers placed on orthogonal shafts. Motion in the east-west direction causes the shaft parallel to the *y*-axis to rotate; motion in the north-south direction causes the shaft parallel to the *x*-axis to rotate. Whenever the mouse has moved a certain minimum distance in either direction or a button is depressed or released, a message is sent to the computer. The minimum distance is about 0.1 mm (although it can be set in software). Some people call this unit a **mickey**. Mice (or occasionally, mouses) can have one, two, or three buttons, depending on the designers' estimate of the users' intellectual ability to keep track of more than one button.

The message to the computer contains three items: Δx, Δy, buttons. The first item is the change in x position since the last message. Then comes the change in y position since the last message. Finally, the status of the buttons is included. The format of the message depends on the system and the number of buttons the mouse has. Usually, it takes 3 bytes. Most mice report back a maximum of 40 times/sec, so the mouse may have moved multiple mickeys since the last report.

Note that the mouse only indicates changes in position, not absolute position itself. If the mouse is picked up and put down gently without causing the ball to rotate, no messages will be sent.

Some GUIs distinguish between single clicks and double clicks of a mouse button. If two clicks are close enough in space (mickeys) and also close enough in time (milliseconds), a double click is signaled. The maximum for "close enough" is up to the software, with both parameters usually being user settable.

That is enough about the input hardware; let us now turn to the display hardware. Display devices can be divided into two categories. **Vector graphics** devices can accept and carry out commands such as drawing points, lines, geometric figures, and text. In contrast, **raster graphics** devices represent the output area as a rectangular grid of points called **pixels**, each of which has some grayscale value or some color. In the early days of computing, vector graphics devices were common, but now plotters are the only vector graphics devices around. Everything else uses raster graphics, sometimes called **bitmap graphics**.

Raster graphics displays are implemented by a hardware device called a **graphics adapter**. A graphics adapter contains a special memory called a **video RAM**, which forms part of the computer's address space and is addressed by the CPU the same way as the rest of memory (see Fig. 5-38). The screen image is stored here in either character mode or bit mode. In character mode, each byte (or 2 bytes) of video RAM contains one character to be displayed. In bitmap mode, each pixel on the screen is represented separately in the video RAM, with 1 bit per pixel for the simplest black and white display to 24 or more bits per pixel for a high quality color display.

Also part of the graphics adapter is a chip called a **video controller**. This chip pulls characters or bits out of the video RAM and generates the video signal used to drive the monitor. A monitor generates a beam of electrons that scans horizontally across the screen, painting lines on it. Typically the screen has 480 to 1024 lines from top to bottom, with 640 to 1200 pixels per line. The video controller signal modulates the electron beam, determining whether a given pixel will be light or dark. Color monitors have three beams, for red, green, and blue, which are independently modulated. Flat panel displays also use pixels in three colors, but how these displays work in detail is beyond the scope of this book.

Video controllers have two modes: character mode (used for simple text) and bit mode (for everything else). In character mode, the controller might fit each

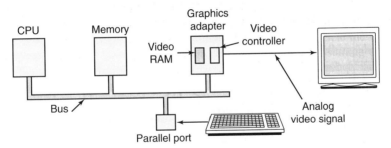

Figure 5-38. With memory-mapped displays, the driver writes directly into the display's video RAM.

character in a box 9 pixels wide by 14 pixels high (including the space between characters), and have 25 lines of 80 characters. The display would then have 350 scan lines of 720 pixels each. Each of these frames is redrawn 60 to 100 times a second to avoid flicker.

To display the text on the screen, the video controller might fetch the first 80 characters from the video RAM, generate 14 scan lines, fetch the next 80 characters from the video RAM, generate the following 14 scan lines, and so on. Alternatively, it could fetch each character once per scan line to eliminate the need for buffering in the controller. The 9-by-14 bit patterns for the characters are kept in a ROM used by the video controller. (RAM may also be used to support custom fonts.) The ROM is addressed by a 12-bit address, 8 bits from the character code and 4 bits to specify a scan line. The 8 bits in each byte of the ROM control 8 pixels; the 9th pixel between characters is always blank. Thus $14 \times 80 = 1120$ memory references to the video RAM are needed per line of text on the screen. The same number of references are made to the character generator ROM.

In Fig. 5-39(a) we see a portion of the video RAM for a display operating in character mode. Each character on the screen of Fig. 5-39(b) occupies two bytes in the RAM. The low-order character is the ASCII code for the character to be displayed. The high-order character is the attribute byte, which is used to specify the color, reverse video, blinking, and so on. A screen of 25 by 80 characters requires 4000 bytes of video RAM in this mode.

Operating in bitmap mode uses the same principle, except that each pixel on the screen is individually controlled and individually represented by 1 or more bits in the video RAM. In the simplest configuration for a monochrome display, each screen pixel has a corresponding bit in the video RAM. At the other extreme, each screen pixel is represented by a 24-bit number in the video RAM, with 8 bits each for the Red, Green, and Blue intensities. This RGB representation is used because red, green, and blue are the primary additive colors, from which all other colors can be constructed by summing various intensities of these colors.

Screen sizes vary, the most common being 640×480 (VGA), 800×600 (SVGA), 1024×768 (XGA), 1280×1024, and 1600×1200. All of these except

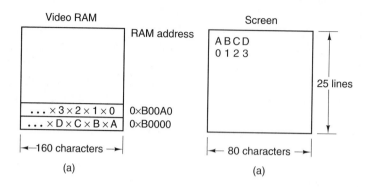

Figure 5-39. (a) A video RAM image for a simple monochrome display in character mode. (b) The corresponding screen. The ×s are attribute bytes.

1280×1024 are in the ratio of 4:3, which fits the aspect ratio of NTSC television sets and thus gives square pixels. 1280×1024 should have been 1280×960, but the lure of 1024 was apparently to great too resist, even though it distorts the pixels slightly and makes scaling to and from the other sizes harder. As an example, a 768×1024 color display with 24 bits per pixel requires 2.25 MB of RAM just to hold the image. If the full screen is refreshed 75 times/sec, the video RAM must be capable of delivering data continuously at 169 MB/sec.

To avoid having to manage such large screen images, some systems have the ability to trade off color resolution against image size. In the simplest scheme, each pixel is represented by an 8-bit number. Rather than indicating a color, this value is an index into a table of 256 entries, each holding a 24-bit (red, green, blue) value. This table, called a **color palette** and often stored in hardware, allows the screen to contain an arbitrary 256 colors at any instant. Changing, say, entry 7 in the color palette, changes the color of all the pixels in the image with a 7 as value. Using an 8-bit color palette reduces the amount of space needed to store the screen image from 3 bytes per pixel to 1 byte per pixel. The price paid is coarser color resolution. The GIF image compression scheme also works with a color palette like this.

It is also possible to use a color palette with 16 bits per pixel. In this case the color palette contains 65,536 entries so that up to 65,536 colors can be used at once. However, the saving in space is less since each pixel now requires 2 bytes in the video RAM. Also, if the color palette is kept in hardware (to avoid an expensive memory lookup on every pixel), more dedicated hardware is needed to store the color palette.

It is also possible to handle 16-bit color by storing the RGB values as three 5-bit numbers, with 1 bit left over (or to give green 6 bits, since the eye is more sensitive to green than to red or blue). In effect, this system is the same as 24-bit color, except with fewer shades of each color available.

5.7.2 Input Software

Once the keyboard driver has received the character, it must begin processing it. Since the keyboard delivers key numbers rather than the character codes used by application software, the driver must convert between the codes by using a table. Not all IBM ''compatibles'' use standard key numbering, so if the driver wants to support these machines, it must map different keyboards with different tables. A simple approach is to compile a table that maps between the codes provided by the keyboard and ASCII codes into the keyboard driver, but this is unsatisfactory for users of languages other than English. Keyboards are arranged differently in different countries, and the ASCII character set is not adequate even for the majority of people in the Western Hemisphere, where speakers of Spanish, Portuguese, and French need accented characters and punctuation marks not used in English.

To respond to the need for flexibility of keyboard layouts to provide for different languages, many operating systems provide for loadable **keymaps** or **code pages**, which make it possible to choose the mapping between keyboard codes and codes delivered to the application, either when the system is booted or later.

5.7.3 Output Software for Windows

Output software for GUIs is a massive topic. Many 1500-page books have been written about the Windows GUI alone (e.g., Petzold, 1999; Simon, 1997; and Rector and Newcomer, 1997). Clearly, in this section, we can only scratch the surface and present a few of the underlying concepts. To make the discussion concrete, we will describe the Win32 API, which is supported by all 32-bit versions of Windows. The output software for other GUIs is roughly comparable in a general sense, but the details are very different.

The basic item on the screen is a rectangular area called a **window**. A window's position and size are uniquely determined by giving the coordinates (in pixels) of two diagonally opposite corners. A window may contain a title bar, a menu bar, a tool bar, a vertical scroll bar, and a horizontal scroll bar. A typical window is shown in Fig. 5-40. Note that the Windows coordinate system puts the origin in the upper lefthand corner and has y increase downward, which is different from the Cartesian coordinates used in mathematics.

When a window is created, the parameters specify whether the window can be moved by the user, resized by the user, or scrolled (by dragging the thumb on the scroll bar) by the user. The main window produced by most programs can be moved, resized, and scrolled, which has enormous consequences for the way Windows programs are written. In particular, programs must be informed about changes to the size of their windows and must be prepared to redraw the contents of their windows at any time, even when they least expect it.

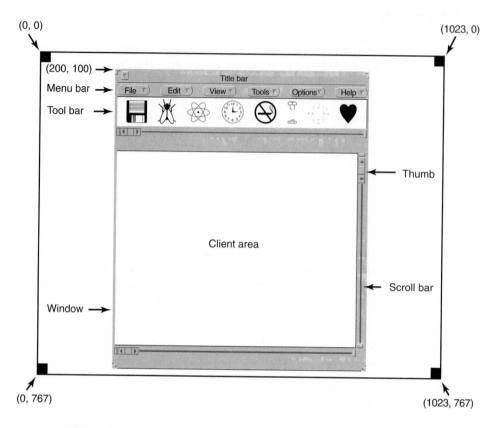

Figure 5-40. A sample window located at (200, 100) on an XGA display.

As a consequence, Windows programs are message oriented. User actions involving the keyboard or mouse are captured by Windows and converted into messages to the program owning the window being addressed. Each program has a message queue to which messages relating to all its windows are sent. The main loop of the program consists of fishing out the next message and processing it by calling an internal procedure for that message type. In some cases, Windows itself may call these procedures directly, bypassing the message queue. This model is quite different than the UNIX model of procedural code that makes system calls to interact with the operating system.

To make this programming model clearer, consider the example of Fig. 5-41. Here we see the skeleton of a main program for Windows. It is not complete and does no error checking, but it shows enough detail for our purposes. It starts by including a header file, *windows.h*, which contains many macros, data types, constants, function prototypes, and other information needed by Windows programs.

The main program starts with a declaration giving its name and parameters. The *WINAPI* macro is an instruction to the compiler to use a certain parameter

```
#include <windows.h>

int WINAPI WinMain(HINSTANCE h, HINSTANCE, hprev, char *szCmd, int iCmdShow)
{
     WNDCLASS wndclass;              /* class object for this window */
     MSG msg;                        /* incoming messages are stored here */
     HWND hwnd;                      /* handle (pointer) to the window object */

     /* Initialize wndclass */
     wndclass.lpfnWndProc = WndProc;          /* tells which procedure to call */
     wndclass.lpszClassName = "Program name";    /* Text for title bar */
     wndclass.hIcon = LoadIcon(NULL, IDI_APPLICATION);   /* load program icon */
     wndclass.hCursor = LoadCursor(NULL, IDC_ARROW);    /* load mouse cursor */

     RegisterClass(&wndclass);       /* tell Windows about wndclass */
     hwnd = CreateWindow ( ... )     /* allocate storage for the window */
     ShowWindow(hwnd, iCmdShow); /* display the window on the screen */
     UpdateWindow(hwnd);             /* tell the window to paint itself */

     while (GetMessage(&msg, NULL, 0, 0)) {    /* get message from queue */
          TranslateMessage(&msg);    /* translate the message */
          DispatchMessage(&msg);     /* send msg to the appropriate procedure */
     }
     return(msg.wParam);
}

long CALLBACK WndProc(HWND hwnd, UINT message, UINT wParam, long lParam)
{
     /* Declarations go here. */

     switch (message) {
          case WM_CREATE:     ... ;   return ... ;   /* create window */
          case WM_PAINT:      ... ;   return ... ;   /* repaint contents of window */
          case WM_DESTROY:  ... ;   return ... ;   /* destroy window */
     }
     return(DefWindowProc(hwnd, message, wParam, lParam));/* default */
}
```

Figure 5-41. A skeleton of a Windows main program.

passing convention and will not be of further concern to us. The first parameter, *h*, is an instance handle and is used to identify the program to the rest of the system. To some extent, Win32 is object oriented, which means that the system contains objects (e.g., programs, files, and windows) that have some state and associated code, called **methods**, that operate on that state. Objects are referred to using handles, and in this case, *h* identifies the program. The second parameter is present only for reasons of backward compatibility. It is no longer used. The third parameter, *szCmd*, is a zero-terminated string containing the command line that started the program, even if it was not started from a command line. The fourth parameter, *iCmdShow*, tells whether the program's initial window should occupy the entire screen, part of the screen, or none of the screen (task bar only).

This declaration illustrates a widely used Microsoft convention called **Hungarian notation**. The name is a pun on Polish notation, the postfix system invented by the Polish logician J. Lukasiewicz for representing algebraic formulas without using precedence or parentheses. Hungarian notation was invented by a Hungarian programmer at Microsoft, Charles Simonyi, and uses the first few characters of an identifier to specify the type. The allowed letters and types include c (character), w (word, now meaning an unsigned 16-bit integer), i (32-bit signed integer), l (long, also a 32-bit signed integer), s (string), sz (string terminated by a zero byte), p (pointer), fn (function), and h (handle). Thus *szCmd* is a zero-terminated string and *iCmdShow* is an integer, for example. Many programmers believe that encoding the type in variable names this way has little value and makes Windows code exceptionally hard to read. Nothing analogous to this convention is present in UNIX.

Every window must have an associated class object that defines its properties. In Fig. 5-41, that class object is *wndclass*. An object of type *WNDCLASS* has 10 fields, four of which are initialized in Fig. 5-41. In an actual program, the other six would be initialized as well. The most important field is *lpfnWndProc*, which is a long (i.e., 32-bit) pointer to the function that handles the messages directed to this window. The other fields initialized here tell which name and icon to use in the title bar, and which symbol to use for the mouse cursor.

After *wndclass* has been initialized, *RegisterClass* is called to pass it to Windows. In particular, after this call Windows knows which procedure to call when various events occur that do not go through the message queue. The next call, *CreateWindow*, allocates memory for the window's data structure and returns a handle for referencing it later. The program then makes two more calls in a row, to put the window's outline on the screen, and finally fill it in completely.

At this point we come to the program's main loop, which consists of getting a message, having certain translations done to it, and then passing it back to Windows to have Windows invoke *WndProc* to process it. To answer the question of whether this whole mechanism could have been made simpler, the answer is yes, but it was done this way for historical reasons and we are now stuck with it.

Following the main program is the procedure **WndProc**, which handles the various messages that can be sent to the window. The use of *CALLBACK* here, like *WINAPI* above, specifies the calling sequence to use for parameters. The first parameter is the handle of the window to use. The second parameter is the message type. The third and fourth parameters can be used to provide additional information when needed.

Message types *WM_CREATE* and *WM_DESTROY* are sent at the start and end of the program, respectively. They give the program the opportunity, for example, to allocate memory for data structures and then return it.

The third message type, *WM_PAINT*, is an instruction to the program to fill in the window. It is not only called when the window is first drawn, but often during program execution as well. In contrast to text-based systems, in Windows a program cannot assume that whatever it draws on the screen will stay there until it removes it. Other windows can be dragged on top of this one, menus can be pulled down over it, dialog boxes and tool tips can cover part of it, and so on. When these items are removed, the window has to be redrawn. The way Windows tells a program to redraw a window is to send it a *WM_PAINT* message. As a friendly gesture, it also provides information about what part of the window has been overwritten, in case it is easier to regenerate that part of the window instead of redrawing the whole thing.

There are two ways Windows can get a program to do something. One way is to post a message to its message queue. This method is used for keyboard input, mouse input, and timers that have expired. The other way, sending a message to the window, involves having Windows directly call *WndProc* itself. This method is used for all other events. Since Windows is notified when a message is fully processed, it can refrain from making a new call until the previous one is finished. In this way race conditions are avoided.

There are many more message types. To avoid erratic behavior should an unexpected message arrive, it is best to call *DefWindowProc* at the end of *WndProc* to let the default handler take care of the other cases.

In summary, a Windows program normally creates one or more windows with a class object for each one. Associated with each program is a message queue and a set of handler procedures. Ultimately, the program's behavior is driven by the incoming events, which are processed by the handler procedures. This is a very different model of the world than the more procedural view that UNIX takes.

The actual drawing to the screen is handled by a package consisting of hundreds of procedures that are bundled together to form the **GDI (Graphics Device Interface)**. It can handle text and all kinds of graphics and is designed to be platform and device independent. Before a program can draw (i.e., paint) in a window, it needs to acquire a **device context** which is an internal data structure containing properties of the window, such as the current font, text color, background color, etc. Most GDI calls use the device context, either for drawing or for getting or setting the properties.

Various ways exist to acquire the device context exist. A simple example of its acquisition and use is

```
hdc = GetDC(hwnd);
TextOut(hdc, x, y, psText, iLength);
ReleaseDC(hwnd, hdc);
```

The first statement gets a handle to a device content, *hdc*. The second one uses the device context to write a line of text on the screen, specifying the (*x*, *y*) coordinates of where the string starts, a pointer to the string itself, and its length. The third call releases the device context to indicate that the program is through drawing for the moment. Note that *hdc* is used in a way analogous to a UNIX file descriptor. Also note that *ReleaseDC* contains redundant information (the use of *hdc* uniquely specifies a window). The use of redundant information that has no actual value is common in Windows.

Another interesting note is that when *hdc* is acquired in this way, the program can only write in the client area of the window, not in the title bar and other parts of it. Internally, in the device context's data structure, a clipping region is maintained. Any drawing outside the clipping region is ignored. However, there is another way to acquire a device context, *GetWindowDC*, which sets the clipping region to the entire window. Other calls restrict the clipping region in other ways. Having multiple calls that do almost the same thing is another characteristic of Windows.

A complete treatment of the GDI is out of the question here. For the interested reader, the references cited above provide additional information. Nevertheless, a few words about the GDI are probably worthwhile given how important it is. GDI has various procedure calls to get and release device contexts, obtain information about device contexts, get and set device context attributes (e.g., the background color), manipulate GDI objects such as pens, brushes, and fonts, each of which has its own attributes. Finally, of course, there are a large number of GDI calls to actually draw on the screen.

The drawing procedures fall into four categories: drawing lines and curves, drawing filled areas, managing bitmaps, and displaying text. We saw an example of drawing text above, so let us take a quick look at one of the others. The call

```
Rectangle(hdc, xleft, ytop, xright, ybottom);
```

draws a filled rectangle whose corners are (*xleft*, *ytop*) and (*xright*, *ybottom*). For example,

```
Rectangle(hdc, 2, 1, 6, 4);
```

will draw the rectangle shown in Fig. 5-42. The line width and color and fill color are taken from the device context. Other GDI calls are similar in flavor.

BitMaps

The GDI procedures are examples of vector graphics. They are used to place geometric figures and text on the screen. They can be scaled easily to larger or smaller screens (provided the number of pixels on the screen is the same). They are also relatively device independent. A collection of calls to GDI procedures can be assembled in a file that can describe a complex drawing. Such a file is

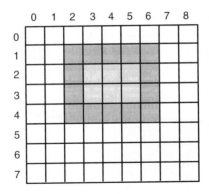

Figure 5-42. An example rectangle drawn using *Rectangle*. Each box represents one pixel.

called a Windows **metafile**, and is widely used to transmit drawings from one Windows program to another. Such files have extension *.wmf*.

Many Windows programs allow the user to copy (part of) a drawing and put in on the Windows clipboard. The user can then go to another program and paste the contents of the clipboard into another document. One way of doing this is for the first program to represent the drawing as a Windows metafile and put it on the clipboard in *.wmf* format. Other ways also exist.

Not all the images that computers manipulate can be generated using vector graphics. Photographs and videos, for example, do not use vector graphics. Instead, these items are scanned in by overlaying a grid on the image. The average red, green, and blue values of each grid square are then sampled and saved as the value of one pixel. Such a file is called a **bitmap**. There are extensive facilities in Windows for manipulating bitmaps.

Another use for bitmaps is for text. One way to represent a particular character in some font is as a small bitmap. Adding text to the screen then becomes a matter of moving bitmaps.

One general way to use bitmaps is through a procedure called *bitblt*. It is called as follows:

    bitblt(dsthdc, dx, dy, wid, ht, srchdc, sx, sy, rasterop);

In its simplest form, it copies a bitmap from a rectangle in one window to a rectangle in another window (or the same one). The first three parameters specify the destination window and position. Then come the width and height. Next come the source window and position. Note that each window has its own coordinate system, with (0, 0) in the upper left-hand corner of the window. The last parameter will be described below. The effect of

    BitBlt(hdc2, 1, 2, 5, 7, hdc1, 2, 2, SRCCOPY);

is shown in Fig. 5-43. Notice carefully that the entire 5×7 area of the letter A has been copied, including the background color.

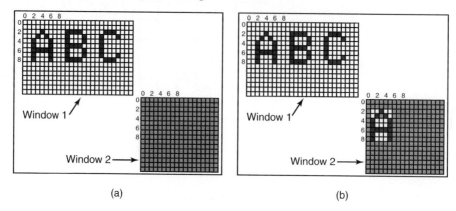

(a)   (b)

Figure 5-43. Copying bitmaps using *BitBlt*. (a) Before. (b) After.

BitBlt can do more than just copy bitmaps. The last parameter gives the possibility of performing Boolean operations to combine the source bitmap and the destination bitmap. For example, the source can be ORed into the destination to merge with it. It can also be EXCLUSIVE ORed into it, which maintains the characteristics of both source and destination.

A problem with bitmaps is that they do not scale. A character that is in a box of 8×12 on a display of 640×480 will look reasonable. However, if this bitmap is copied to a printed page at 1200 dots/inch, which is 10200 bits $\times$ 13200 bits, the character width (8 pixels) will be 8/1200 inch or 0.17 mm wide. In addition, copying between devices with different color properties or between monochrome and color does not work well.

For this reason, Windows also supports a data structure called a **DIB (Device Independent Bitmap)**. Files using this format use the extension *.bmp*. These files have file and information headers and a color table before the pixels. This information makes it easier to move bitmaps between dissimilar devices.

Fonts

In versions of Windows before 3.1. characters were represented as bitmaps and copied onto the screen or printer using *BitBlt*. The problem with that, as we just saw, is that a bitmap that makes sense on the screen is too small for the printer. Also, a different bitmap is needed for each character in each size. In other words, given the bitmap for A in 10-point type, there is no way to compute it for 12-point type. Because every character of every font might be needed for sizes ranging from 4 point to 120 point, a vast number of bitmaps were needed. The whole system was just too cumbersome for text.

The solution was the introduction of TrueType fonts, which are not bitmaps but outlines of the characters. Each TrueType character is defined by a sequence of points around its perimeter. All the points are relative to the (0, 0) origin. Using this system, it is easy to scale the characters up or down. All that has to be done is to multiply each coordinate by the same scale factor. In this way, a True-Type character can be scaled up or down to any point size, even fractional point sizes. Once at the proper size, the points can be connected using the well-known follow-the-dots algorithm taught in kindergarten (note that modern kindergartens use splines for smoother results). After the outline has been completed, the character can be filled in. An example of some characters scaled to three different point sizes is given in Fig. 5-44.

Figure 5-44. Some examples of character outlines at different point sizes.

Once the filled character is available in mathematical form, it can be rasterized, that is, converted to a bitmap at whatever resolution is desired. By first scaling and then rasterizing, we can be sure that the characters displayed on the screen and those that appear on the printer will be as close as possible, differing only in quantization error. To improve the quality still more, it is possible to embed hints in each character telling how to do the rasterization. For example, both serifs on the top of the letter T should be identical, something that might not otherwise be the case due to roundoff error.

5.8 NETWORK TERMINALS

Network terminals are used to connect a remote user to computer over a network, either a local area network or a wide area network. There are two different philosophies of how network terminals should work. In one view, the terminal should have a large amount of computing power and memory in order to run complex protocols to compress the amount of data sent over the network. (A **protocol** is a set of requests and responses that a sender and receiver agree upon in order to communicate over a network or other interface.) In the other view, the terminal should be extremely simple, basically displaying pixels and not doing much thinking in order to make it very cheap. In the following two sections we will discuss an example of each philosophy. First we will examine the sophisticated X Window System. Then we will look at the minimal SLIM terminal.

5.8.1 The X Window System

The ultimate in intelligent terminals is a terminal that contains a CPU as powerful as the main computer, along with megabytes of memory, a keyboard, and a mouse. One terminal of this type is the **X terminal**, which runs the X Window System (often just called X), developed at M.I.T. as part of project Athena. An X terminal is a computer that runs the X software and which interacts with programs running on a remote computer.

The program inside the X terminal that collects input from the keyboard or mouse and accepts commands from a remote computer is called the **X server**. It has to keep track of which window is currently selected (where the mouse pointer is), so it knows which client to send any new keyboard input to. It communicates over the network with **X clients** running on some remote host. It sends them keyboard and mouse input and accepts display commands from them.

It may seem strange to have the X server inside the terminal and the clients on the remote host, but the X server's job is to display bits, so it makes sense to be near the user. From the program's point of view, it is a client telling the server to do things, like display text and geometric figures. The server (in the terminal) just does what it is told, as do all servers. The arrangement of client and server is shown in Fig. 5-45.

It is also possible to run the X Window System on top of UNIX or another operating system. In fact, many UNIX systems run X as their standard windowing system, even on standalone machines or for accessing remote computers over the Internet. What the X Window System really defines is the protocol between the X client and the X server, as shown in Fig. 5-45. It does not matter whether the client and server are on the same machine, separated by 100 meters over a local area network, or are thousands of kilometers apart and connected by the Internet. The protocol and operation of the system is identical in all cases.

X is just a windowing system. It is not a complete GUI. To get a complete GUI, others layer of software are run on top of it. One layer is **Xlib**, which is a set of library procedures for accessing the X functionality. These procedures form the basis of the X Window System and are what we will examine below, but they are too primitive for most user programs to access directly. For example, each mouse click is reported separately, so that determining that two clicks really form a double click has to be handled above Xlib.

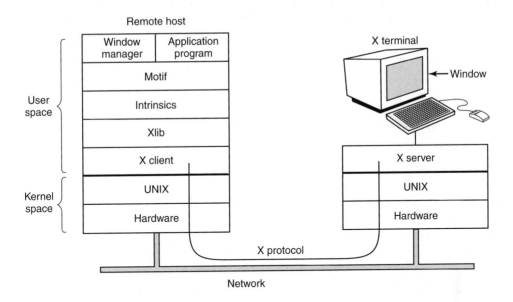

Figure 5-45. Clients and servers in the M.I.T. X Window System.

To make programming with X easier, a toolkit consisting of the **Intrinsics** is supplied as part of X. This layer manages buttons, scroll bars, and other GUI elements, called **widgets**. To make a true GUI interface, with a uniform look and feel, yet another layer is needed. The most popular one is called **Motif**. Most applications make use of calls to Motif rather than Xlib.

Also worth noting is that window management is not part of X itself. The decision to leave it out was fully intentional. Instead, a separate X client process, called a **window manager**, controls the creation, deletion, and movement of windows on the screen. To manage windows, it sends commands to the X server telling what to do. It often runs on the same machine as the X client, but in theory can run anywhere.

This modular design, consisting of several layers and multiple programs, makes X highly portable and flexible. It has been ported to most versions of UNIX, including Solaris, BSD, AIX, Linux, and so on, making it possible for application developers to have a standard user interface for multiple platforms. It has also been ported to other operating systems. In contrast, in Windows, the windowing and GUI systems are mixed together in the GDI and located in the kernel, which makes them harder to maintain. For example, the Windows 98 GUI is still fundamentally 16 bits, more than a decade after the Intel CPUs were 32 bits.

Now let us take a brief look at X as viewed from the Xlib level. When an X program starts, it opens a connection to one or more X servers— let us call them workstations even though they might be colocated on the same machine as the X program itself. X considers this connection to be reliable in the sense that lost and duplicate messages are handled by the networking software and it does not have to worry about communication errors. Usually, TCP/IP is used between the client and server.

Four kinds of messages go over the connection:

1. Drawing commands from the program to the workstation.

2. Replies by the workstation to program queries.

3. Keyboard, mouse, and other event announcements.

4. Error messages.

Most drawing commands are sent from the program to the workstation as one-way messages. No reply is expected. The reason for this design is that when the client and server processes are on different machines, it may take a substantial period of time for the command to reach the server and be carried out. Blocking the application program during this time would slow it down unnecessarily. On the other hand, when the program needs information from the workstation, it simply has to wait until the reply comes back.

Like Windows, X is highly event driven. Events flow from the workstation to the program, usually in response to some human action such as keyboard strokes, mouse movements, or a window being uncovered. Each event message is 32 bytes, with the first byte giving the event type and the next 31 bytes providing additional information. Several dozen kinds of events exist, but a program is sent only those events that it has said it is willing to handle. For example, if a program does not want to hear about key releases, it is not sent any key release events. As in Windows, events are queued, and programs read events from the queue. However, unlike Windows, the operating system never calls procedures within the application program on its own. It does not even know which procedure handles which event.

A key concept in X is the **resource**. A resource is a data structure that holds certain information. Application programs create resources on workstations. Resources can be shared among multiple processes on the workstation. Resources tend to be short lived and do not survive workstation reboots. Typical resources include windows, fonts, colormaps (color palettes), pixmaps (bitmaps), cursors, and graphic contexts. The latter are used to associate properties with windows and are similar in concept to device contexts in Windows.

A rough, incomplete skeleton of an X program is shown in Fig. 5-46. It begins by including some required headers and then declaring some variables. It then connects to the X server specified as the parameter to *XOpenDisplay*. Then it allocates a window resource and stores a handle to it in *win*. In practice, some initialization would happen here. After that it tells the window manager that the new window exists so the window manager can manage it.

```
#include <X11/Xlib.h>
#include <X11/Xutil.h>

main(int argc, char *argv[])
{
     Display disp;                              /* server identifier */
     Window win;                                /* window identifier */
     GC gc;                                     /* graphic context identifier */
     XEvent event;                              /* storage for one event */
     int running = 1;

     disp = XOpenDisplay("display_name");       /* connect to the X server */
     win = XCreateSimpleWindow(disp, ... );     /* allocate memory for new window */
     XSetStandardProperties(disp, ...);         /* announces window to window mgr */
     gc = XCreateGC(disp, win, 0, 0);           /* create graphic context */
     XSelectInput(disp, win, ButtonPressMask | KeyPressMask | ExposureMask);
     XMapRaised(disp, win);                     /* display window; send Expose event */

     while (running) {
          XNextEvent(disp, &event);        /* get next event */
          switch (event.type) {
               case Expose:       ...;  break;  /* repaint window */
               case ButtonPress:  ...;  break;  /* process mouse click */
               case Keypress:     ...;  break;  /* process keyboard input */
          }
     }

     XFreeGC(disp, gc);                         /* release graphic context */
     XDestroyWindow(disp, win);                 /* deallocate window's memory space */
     XCloseDisplay(disp);                       /* tear down network connection */
}
```

Figure 5-46. A skeleton of an X Window application program.

The call to *XCreateGC* creates a graphic context in which properties of the window are stored. In a more complete program, they might be initialized here. The next statement, the call to *XSelectInput*, tells the X server which events the program is prepared to handle. In this case it is interested in mouse clicks, keystrokes, and windows being uncovered. In practice, a real program would be interested in other events as well. Finally, the call to *XMapRaised* maps the new window onto the screen as the uppermost window. At this point the window becomes visible on the screen.

The main loop consists of two statements and is logically much simpler than the corresponding loop in Windows. The first statement here gets an event and the second one dispatches on the event type for processing. When some event indicates that the program has finished, *running* is set to 0 and the loop terminates. Before exiting, the program releases the graphic context, window, and connection.

It is worth mentioning that not everyone likes a GUI. Many programmers prefer a traditional command-line oriented interface of the type discussed in Sec. 5.6.2 above. X handles this via a client program called *xterm*. This program emulates an old VT102 intelligent terminal, complete with all the escape sequences. Thus editors such as *vi* and *emacs* and other software that uses termcap work in these windows without modification.

5.8.2 The SLIM Network Terminal

Over the years, the main computing paradigm has oscillated between centralized and decentralized computing. The first computers, such as the ENIAC, were, in fact, personal computers, albeit large ones, because only one person could use one at once. Then came timesharing systems, in which many remote users at simple terminals shared a big central computer. Next came the PC era, in which the users had their own personal computers again.

While the decentralized PC model has advantages, it also has some severe disadvantages that are only beginning to be taken seriously. Probably the biggest problem is that each PC has a large hard disk and complex software that must be maintained. For example, when a new release of the operating system comes out, a great deal of work has to be done to perform the upgrade on each machine separately. At most corporations, the labor costs of doing this kind of software maintenance dwarf the actual hardware and software costs. For home users, the labor is technically free, but few people are capable of doing it correctly and fewer still enjoy doing it. With a centralized system, only one or a few machines have to be updated and those machines have a staff of experts to do the work.

A related issue is that users should make regular backups of their gigabyte file systems, but few of them do. When disaster strikes, a great deal of moaning and wringing of hands tends to follow. With a centralized system, backups can be made every night by automated tape robots.

Another advantage is that resource sharing is easier with centralized systems. A system with 64 remote users, each with 64 MB of RAM will have most of that RAM idle most of the time. With a centralized system with 4 GB of RAM, it never happens that some user temporarily needs a lot of RAM but cannot get it because it is on someone else's PC. The same argument holds for disk space and other resources.

It is probably a fair conclusion to say that most users want high-performance interactive computing, but do not really want to administer a computer. This has led researchers to reexamine timesharing using dumb terminals (now politely called **thin clients**) that meet modern terminal expectations. X was a step in this direction, but an X server is still a complex system with megabytes of software that must be upgraded from time to time. The holy grail would be a high performance interactive computing system in which the user machines had no software at all. Interestingly enough, this goal is achievable. Below we will describe one such system, developed by researchers at Sun Microsystems and Stanford University and now commercially available from Sun (Schmidt et al., 1999).

The system is called **SLIM**, which stands for **Stateless Low-level Interface Machine**. The idea is based on traditional centralized timesharing as shown in Fig. 5-47. The client machines are just dumb 1280×1024 bitmap displays with a keyboard and mouse but no user-installable software. They are very much in the spirit of the old intelligent character-oriented terminals that had a little firmware to interpret escape codes, but no other software. Like the old character-oriented terminals, the only user control is an on-off switch. Terminals of this type that have little processing capacity are called **thin clients**.

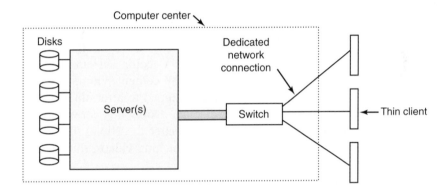

Figure 5-47. The architecture of the SLIM terminal system.

The simplest model—having the server ship bitmaps over the network to the SLIM clients 60 times a second—does not work. It requires about 2 Gbps of network bandwidth, which is far too much for current networks to handle. The next simplest model—storing the screen image in a frame buffer inside the terminal and having it refreshed 60 times a second locally— is much more promising. In particular, if the central server maintains a copy of each terminal's frame buffer and sends only updates (i.e., changes) to it as needed, the bandwidth requirements become quite modest. This is how the SLIM thin clients work.

Unlike the X protocol, which has hundreds of complex messages for managing windows, drawing geometric figures, and displaying text in many fonts, the SLIM protocol has only five display messages, listed in Fig. 5-48 (there are also a small number of control messages not listed). The first one, SET, just replaces a rectangle in the frame buffer with new pixels. Each pixel replaced requires 3 bytes in the message to specify its full (24-bit) color value. In theory, this message is sufficient to do the job; the other ones are just for optimization.

Message	Meaning
SET	Update a rectangle with new pixels
FILL	Fill a rectangle with one pixel value
BITMAP	Expand a bitmap to fill a rectangle
COPY	Copy a rectangle from one part of the frame buffer to another
CSCS	Convert a rectangle from television color (YUV) to RGB

Figure 5-48. Messages used in the SLIM protocol from the server to the terminals.

The FILL message fills an entire rectangle on the screen with a single pixel value. It is used for filling in uniform backgrounds. The BITMAP message fills an entire rectangle by repeating a pattern contained in a bitmap supplied in the message. This command is useful for filling in patterned backgrounds that have some texture and are not just a uniform color.

The COPY message instructs the terminal to copy a rectangle within the frame buffer to another part of the frame buffer. It is most useful for scrolling the screen and moving windows, for example.

Finally, the CSCS message converts the YUV color system used in U.S. (NTSC) television sets to the RGB system used by computer monitors. It is primarily used when a raw video frame has been shipped to a terminal in the YUV system and must be converted to RGB for display. Doing this conversion is algorithmically simple but time consuming, so it is better to offload the work to the terminals. If the terminals will not be used for watching videos, this message and its functionality are not needed.

The whole idea of dumb thin clients stands or falls with the performance, which Schmidt et al. extensively measured. In the prototype, 100-Mbps switched Fast Ethernet was used on both the server-to-switch segment and switch-to-terminal segments. Potentially a gigabit network could be used between the server and the switch because that segment is local to the central computer room.

The first measurement deals with character echoing to the screen. Each typed character is sent to the server, which computes which pixels have to be updated to place the character on the screen in the right position, font, and color. Measurements show that it takes 0.5 msec for the character to appear on the screen. In contrast, on a local workstation the echoing time is 30 msec due to kernel buffering.

The rest of the tests measured the performance with users running modern interactive application programs such as Adobe Photoshop (a program for retouching photographs), Adobe Framemaker (a desktop publishing program), and Netscape (a Web browser). It was observed that half the user commands required updating fewer than 10,000 pixels, which is 30,000 bytes uncompressed. At 100 Mbps, it takes 2.4 msec to pump 10,000 pixels out onto the wire. It takes another 2.7 msec to place them in the frame buffer upon arrival, for a total of 5.1 msec (but this varies a little depending on the circumstances). Since human reaction time is about 100 msec, such updates appear to be instantaneous. Even the larger updates were almost instantaneous. Furthermore, when compression is used, more than 85% of the updates are under 30,000 bytes.

The experiments were repeated with a 10-Mbps network, a 1-Mbps network, and a 128-Kbps network. At 10 Mbps the system was virtually instantaneous and 1 Mbps it was still good. At 128 Kbps it was too slow to use. Since 1 Mbps connections to the home are rapidly becoming a reality using cable TV networks and ADSL (Asymmetric Digital Subscriber Loop), it appears that this technology may be applicable to home users as well as business users.

5.9 POWER MANAGEMENT

The first general-purpose electronic computer, the ENIAC, had 18,000 vacuum tubes and consumed 140,000 watts of power. As a result, it ran up a non-trivial electricity bill. After the invention of the transistor, power usage dropped dramatically and the computer industry lost interest in power requirements. However, nowadays power management is back in the spotlight for several reasons, and the operating system is playing a role here.

Let us start with desktop PCs. A desktop PC often has a 200-watt power supply (which is typically 85% efficient, that is, loses 15% of the incoming energy to heat). If 100 million of these machines are turned on at once worldwide, together they use 20,000 megawatts of electricity. This is the total output of 20 average-sized nuclear power plants. If power requirements could be cut in half, we could get rid of 10 nuclear power plants. From an environmental point of view, getting rid of 10 nuclear power plants (or an equivalent number of fossil fuel plants) is a big win and well worth pursuing.

The other place where power is a big issue is on battery-powered computers, including notebooks, laptops, palmtops, and Webpads, among others. The heart of the problem is that the batteries cannot hold enough charge to last very long, a few hours at most. Furthermore, despite massive research efforts by battery companies, computer companies, and consumer electronics companies, progress is glacial. To an industry used to a doubling of the performance every 18 months (Moore's law), having no progress at all seems like a violation of the laws of physics, but that is the current situation. As a consequence, making computers use less energy so existing batteries last longer is high on everyone's agenda. The operating system plays a major role here, as we will see below.

There are two general approaches to reducing energy consumption. The first one is for the operating system to turn off parts of the computer (mostly I/O devices) when they are not in use because a device that is off uses little or no energy. The second one is for the application program to use less energy, possibly degrading the quality of the user experience, in order to stretch out battery time. We will look at each of these approaches in turn, but first we will say a little bit about hardware design with respect to power usage.

5.9.1 Hardware Issues

Batteries come in two general types: disposable and rechargeable. Disposable batteries (most commonly AAA, AA, and D cells) can be used to run handheld devices, but do not have enough energy to power laptop computers with large bright screens. A rechargeable battery, in contrast, can store enough energy to power a laptop for a few hours. Nickel cadmium batteries used to dominate here, but they gave way to nickel metal hydride batteries, which last longer and do not pollute the environment quite as badly when they are eventually discarded. Lithium ion batteries are even better, and may be recharged without first being fully drained, but their capacities are also severely limited.

The general approach most computer vendors take to battery conservation is to design the CPU, memory, and I/O devices to have multiple states: on, sleeping, hibernating, and off. To use the device, it must be on. When the device will not be needed for a short time, it can be put to sleep, which reduces energy consumption. When it is not expected to be needed for a longer interval, it can be made to hibernate, which reduces energy consumption even more. The trade-off here is that getting a device out of hibernation often takes more time and energy than getting it out of sleep state. Finally, when a device is off, it does nothing and consumes no power. Not all devices have all these states, but when they do, it is up to the operating system to manage the state transitions at the right moments.

Some computers have two or even three power buttons. One of these may put the whole computer in sleep state, from which it can be awakened quickly by typing a character or moving the mouse. Another may put the computer into hibernation, from which wakeup takes much longer. In both cases, these buttons typically do nothing except send a signal to the operating system, which does the rest in software. In some countries, electrical devices must, by law, have a mechanical power switch that breaks a circuit and removes power from the device, for safety reasons. To comply with this law, another switch may be needed.

Power management brings up a number of questions that the operating system must deal with. They include the following. Which devices can be controlled? Are they on/off, or do they have intermediate states? How much power is saved in the low-power states? Is energy expended to restart the device? Must some context be saved when going to a low-power state? How long does it take to go back to full power? Of course, the answers to these questions vary from device to device, so the operating system must be able to deal with a range of possibilities.

Various researchers have examined laptop computers to see where the power goes. Li et al. (1994) measured various workloads and came to the conclusions shown in Fig. 5-49. Lorch and Smith (1998) made measurements on other machines and came to the conclusions shown in Fig. 5-49. Weiser et al. (1994) also made measurements but did not publish the numerical values. They simply stated that the top three energy sinks were the display, hard disk, and CPU, in that order. While these numbers do not agree closely, possibly because the different brands of computers measured indeed have different energy requirements, it seems clear that the display, hard disk, and CPU are obvious targets for saving energy.

Device	Li et al. (1994)	Lorch and Smith (1998)
Display	68%	39%
CPU	12%	18%
Hard disk	20%	12%
Modem		6%
Sound		2%
Memory	0.5%	1%
Other		22%

Figure 5-49. Power consumption of various parts of a laptop computer.

5.9.2 Operating System Issues

The operating system plays a key role in energy management. It controls all the devices, so it must decide what to shut down and when to shut it down. If it shuts down a device and that device is needed again quickly, there may be an annoying delay while it is restarted. On the other hand, if it waits too long to shut down a device, energy is wasted for nothing.

The trick is to find algorithms and heuristics that let the operating system make good decisions about what to shut down and when. The trouble is that "good" is highly subjective. One user may find it acceptable that after 30 seconds of not using the computer it takes 2 seconds for it to respond to a keystroke. Another user may swear a blue streak under the same conditions. In the absence of audio input, the computer cannot tell these users apart.

The Display

Let us now look at the big spenders of the energy budget to see what can be done about each one. The biggest item in everyone's energy budget is the display. To get a bright sharp image, the screen must be backlit and that takes substantial energy. Many operating systems attempt to save energy here by shutting down the display when there has been no activity for some number of minutes. Often the user can decide what the shutdown interval is, pushing the trade-off between frequent blanking of the screen and using the battery up quickly back to the user (who probably really does not want it). Turning off the display is a sleep state because it can be regenerated (from the video RAM) almost instantaneously when any key is struck or the pointing device is moved.

One possible improvement was proposed by Flinn and Satyanarayanan (1999). They suggested having the display consist of some number of zones that can be independently powered up or down. In Fig. 5-50, we depict 16 zones using dashed lines to separate them. When the cursor is in window 2, as shown in Fig. 5-50(a), only the four zones in the lower righthand corner have to be lit up. The other 12 can be dark, saving 3/4 of the screen power.

When the user moves the cursor to window 1, the zones for window 2 can be darkened and the zones behind window 1 can be turned on. However, because window 1 straddles 9 zones, more power is needed. If the window manager can sense of what is happening, it can automatically move window 1 to fit into four zones, with a kind of snap-to-zone action, as shown in Fig. 5-50(b). To achieve this reduction from 9/16 of full power to 4/16 of full power, the window manager has to understand power management or be capable of accepting instructions from some other piece of the system that does. Even more sophisticated would be the ability to partially illuminate a window that was not completely full (e.g., a window containing short lines of text could be kept dark on the right hand side).

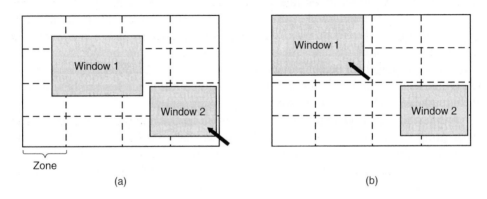

(a)   (b)

Figure 5-50. The use of zones for backlighting the display. (a) When window 2 is selected it is not moved. (b) When window 1 is selected, it moves to reduce the number of zones illuminated.

The Hard Disk

Another major villain is the hard disk. It takes substantial energy to keep it spinning at high speed, even if there are no accesses. Many computers, especially laptops, spin the disk down after a certain number of minutes of activity. When it is next needed, it is spun up again. Unfortunately, a stopped disk is hibernating rather than sleeping because it takes quite a few seconds to spin it up again, which causes noticeable delays for the user.

In addition, restarting the disk consumes considerable extra energy. As a consequence, every disk has a characteristic time, T_d, that is its break-even point, often in the range 5 to 15 sec. Suppose that the next disk access is expected to some time t in the future. If $t < T_d$, it takes less energy to keep the disk spinning rather than spin it down and then spin it up so quickly. If $t > T_d$, the energy saved makes it worth spinning the disk down and up again much later. If a good prediction could be made (e.g., based on past access patterns), the operating system could make good shutdown predictions and save energy. In practice, most systems are conservative and only spin down the disk after a few minutes of inactivity.

Another way to save disk energy is to have a substantial disk cache in RAM. If a needed block is in the cache, an idle disk does not have to be restarted to satisfy the read. Similarly, if a write to the disk can be buffered in the cache, a stopped disk does not have to restarted just to handle the write. The disk can remain off until the cache fills up or a read miss happens.

Another way to avoid unnecessary disk starts is for the operating system to keep running programs informed about the disk state by sending it messages or signals. Some programs have discretionary writes that can be skipped or delayed. For example, a word processor may be set up to write the file being edited to disk every few minutes. If the word processor knows that the disk is off at the moment it would normally write the file out, it can delay this write until the disk is next turned on or until a certain additional time has elapsed.

The CPU

The CPU can also be managed to save energy. A laptop CPU can be put to sleep in software, reducing power usage to almost zero. The only thing it can do in this state is wake up when an interrupt occurs. Therefore, whenever the CPU goes idle, either waiting for I/O or because there is no work to do, it goes to sleep.

On many computers, there is a relationship between CPU voltage, clock cycle, and power usage. The CPU voltage can often be reduced in software, which saves energy but also reduces the clock cycle (approximately linearly). Since power consumed is proportional to the square of the voltage, cutting the voltage in half makes the CPU about half as fast but at 1/4 the power.

This property can be exploited for programs with well-defined deadlines, such as multimedia viewers that have to decompress and display a frame every 40 msec, but go idle if they do it faster. Suppose that a CPU uses x joules while running full blast for 40 msec and $x/4$ joules running at half speed. If a multimedia viewer can decompress and display a frame in 20 msec, the operating system can run at full power for 20 msec and then shut down for 20 msec for a total energy usage of $x/2$ joules. Alternatively, it can run at half power and just make the deadline, but use only $x/4$ joules instead. A comparison of running at full speed and full power for some time interval and at half speed and one quarter power for twice as long is shown in Fig. 5-51. In both cases the same work is done, but in Fig. 5-51(b) only half the energy is consumed doing it.

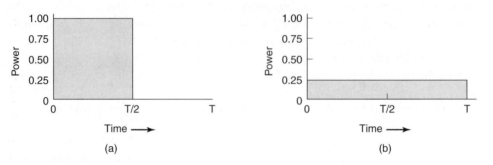

Figure 5-51. (a) Running at full clock speed. (b) Cutting voltage by two cuts clock speed by two and power consumption by four.

In a similar vein, if a user is typing at 1 char/sec, but the work needed to process the character takes 100 msec, it is better for the operating system to detect the long idle periods and slow the CPU down by a factor of 10. In short, running slowly is more energy efficient than running quickly.

The Memory

Two possible options exist for saving energy with the memory. First, the cache can be flushed and then switched off. It can always be reloaded from main memory with no loss of information. The reload can be done dynamically and quickly, so turning off the cache is entering a sleep state.

A more drastic option is to write the contents of main memory to the disk, then switch off the main memory itself. This approach is hibernation, since virtually all power can be cut to memory at the expense of a substantial reload time, especially if the disk is off too. When the memory is cut off, the CPU either has to be shut off as well or has to execute out of ROM. If the CPU is off, the interrupt that wakes it up has to cause it to jump to code in a ROM so the memory can be reloaded before being used. Despite all the overhead, switching off the memory for long periods of time (e.g., hours) may be worth it if restarting in a few seconds is considered much more desirable than rebooting the operating system from disk, which often takes a minute or more.

Wireless Communication

Increasingly many portable computers have a wireless connection to the outside world (e.g., the Internet). The radio transmitter and receiver required are often first-class power hogs. In particular, if the radio receiver is always on in order to listen for incoming email, the battery may drain fairly quickly. On the other hand, if the radio is switched off after, say, 1 minute of being idle, incoming messages may be missed, which is clearly undesirable.

One efficient solution to this problem has been proposed by Kravets and Krishnan (1998). The heart of their solution exploits the fact that mobile computers communicate with fixed base stations that have large memories and disks and no power constraints. What they propose is to have the mobile computer send a message to the base station when it is about to turn off the radio. From that time on, the base station buffers incoming messages on its disk. When the mobile computer switches on the radio again, it tells the base station. At that point any accumulated messages can be sent to it.

Outgoing messages that are generated while the radio is off are buffered on the mobile computer. If the buffer threatens to fill up, the radio is turned on and the queue transmitted to the base station.

When should the radio be switched off? One possibility is to let the user or the application program decide. Another is turn it off after some number of seconds of idle time. When should it be switched on again? Again, the user or program could decide, or it could be switched on periodically to check for inbound traffic and transmit any queued messages. Of course, it also should be switched on when the output buffer is close to full. Various other heuristics are possible.

Thermal Management

A somewhat different, but still energy-related issue, is thermal management. Modern CPUs get extremely hot due to their high speed. Desktop machines normally have an internal electric fan to blow the hot air out of the chassis. Since reducing power consumption is usually not a driving issue with desktop machines, the fan is usually on all the time.

With laptops, the situation is different. The operating system has to monitor the temperature continuously. When it gets close to the maximum allowable temperature, the operating system has a choice. It can switch on the fan, which makes noise and consumes power. Alternatively, it can reduce power consumption by reducing the backlighting of the screen, slowing down the CPU, being more aggressive about spinning down the disk, and so on.

Some input from the user may be valuable as a guide. For example, a user could specify in advance that the noise of the fan is objectionable, so the operating system would reduce power consumption instead.

Battery Management

In ye olde days, a battery just provided current until it was drained, at which time it stopped. Not any more. Laptops use smart batteries now, which can communicate with the operating system. Upon request they can report on things like maximum voltage, current voltage, maximum charge, current charge, maximum drain rate, current drain rate, and more. Most laptop computers have programs that can be run to query and display all these parameters. Smart batteries can also be instructed to change various operational parameters under control of the operating system.

Some laptops have multiple batteries. When the operating system detects that one battery is about to go, it has to arrange for a graceful cutover to the next one, without causing any glitches during the transition. When the final battery is on its last legs, it is up to the operating system to warn the user and then cause an orderly shutdown, for example, making sure that the file system is not corrupted.

Driver Interface

The Windows system has an elaborate mechanism for doing power management called **ACPI** (**Advanced Configuration and Power Interface**). The operating system can send any conformant driver commands asking it to report on the capabilities of its devices and their current states. This feature is especially important when combined with plug and play because just after it is booted, the operating system does not even know what devices are present, let alone their properties with respect to energy consumption or power manageability.

It can also sends commands to drivers instructing them to cut their power levels (based on the capabilities that it learned earlier, of course). There is also some traffic the other way. In particular, when a device such as a keyboard or a mouse detects activity after a period of idleness, this is a signal to the system to go back to (near) normal operation.

5.9.3 Degraded Operation

So far we have looked at ways the operating system can reduce energy usage by various kinds of devices. But there is another approach as well: tell the programs to use less energy, even if this means providing a poorer user experience (better a poorer experience than no experience when the battery dies and the lights go out). Typically, this information is passed on when the battery charge is below some threshold. It is then up to the programs to decide between degrading performance to lengthen battery life or to maintain performance and risk running out of energy.

One of the questions that comes up here is how can a program degrade its performance to save energy? This question has been studied by Flinn and Satyanarayanan (1999). They provided four examples of how degraded performance can save energy. We will now look at these.

In this study, information is presented to the user in various forms. When no degradation is present, the best possible information is presented. When degradation is present, the fidelity (accuracy) of the information presented to the user is worse than what it could have been. We will see examples of this shortly.

In order to measure energy usage, Flinn and Satyanarayanan devised a software tool called PowerScope. What it does is provide a power usage profile of a program. To use it, a computer must be hooked up to an external power supply through a software-controlled digital multimeter. Using the multimeter, software can read out the number of milliamperes coming in from the power supply and thus determine the instantaneous power being consumed by the computer. What PowerScope does is periodically sample the program counter and the power usage and write these data to a file. After the program has terminated the file is analyzed to give the energy usage of each procedure. These measurements formed the basis of their observations. Hardware energy saving measures were also used and formed the baseline against which the degraded performance was measured.

The first program measured was a video player. In undegraded mode, it plays 30 frames/sec in full resolution and in color. One form of degradation is to abandon the color information and display the video in black and white. Another form of degradation is to reduce the frame rate, which leads to flicker and gives the movie a jerky quality. Still another form of degradation is to reduce the number of pixels in both directions, either by lowering the spatial resolution or making the displayed image smaller. Measures of this type saved about 30% of the energy.

The second program was a speech recognizer. It sampled the microphone to construct a waveform. This waveform could either be analyzed on the laptop computer or sent over a radio link for analysis on a fixed computer. Doing this saves CPU energy but uses energy for the radio. Degradation was accomplished by using a smaller vocabulary and a simpler acoustic model. The win here was about 35%

The next example was a map viewer that fetched the map over the radio link. Degradation consisted of either cropping the map to smaller dimensions or telling the remote server to omit smaller roads, thus requiring fewer bits to be transmitted. Again here a gain of about 35% was achieved.

The fourth experiment was with transmission of JPEG images to a Web browser. The JPEG standard allows various algorithms, trading image quality against file size. Here the gain averaged only 9%. Still, all in all, the experiments showed that by accepting some quality degradation, the user can run longer on a given battery.

5.10 RESEARCH ON INPUT/OUTPUT

There is a fair amount of research on input/output, but most of it is focused on specific devices, rather than I/O in general. Often the goal is to improve performance in one way or another.

Disk systems are a case in point. Older disk arm scheduling algorithms use a disk model that is not really applicable any more, so Worthington et al. (1994) took a look at models that correspond to modern disks. RAID is a hot topic, with various researchers look at different aspects of it. Alvarez et al. (1997) looked at enhanced fault tolerance, as did Blaum et al. (1994). Cao et al. (1994) examined the idea of having a parallel controller on a RAID. Wilkes et al. (1996) described an advanced RAID system they built at HP. Having multiple drives requires good parallel scheduling, so that is also a research topic (Chen and Towsley, 1996; and Kallahalla and Varman, 1999). Lumb et al. (2000) argue for utilizing the idle time after the seek but before the sector needed rotates by the head to preload data. Even better than using the rotational latency to due useful work is to eliminate the rotation in the first place using a solid-state microelectromechanical storage device (Griffin et al., 2000; and Carley et al., 2000) or holographic storage (Orlov, 2000). Another new technology worth watching is magneto-optical storage (McDaniel, 2000).

The SLIM terminal provides a modern version of the old timesharing system, with all the computing done centrally and providing users with terminals that just manage the display, mouse, and keyboard, and nothing else (Schmidt et al., 1999). The main difference with old-time timesharing is that instead of connecting the terminal to the computer with a 9600-bps modem, a 10-Mbps Ethernet is used, which provides enough bandwidth for a full graphical interface at the user's end.

GUIs are fairly standard now, but there is still work continuing to go on in that area, for example, speech input (Malkewitz, 1998; Manaris and Harkreader, 1998; Slaughter et al., 1998; and Van Buskirk and LaLomia, 1995). Internal structure of the GUI is also a research topic (Taylor et al., 1995).

Given the large number of computer scientists with laptop computers and given the microscopic battery lifetime on most of them, it should come as no surprise that there is a lot of interest in using software techniques to manage and conserve battery power (Ellis, 1999; Flinn and Satyanarayanan, 1999; Kravets and Krishnan, 1998; Lebeck et al., 2000; Lorch and Smith, 1996; and Lu et al., 1999).

5.11 SUMMARY

Input/output is an often neglected, but important, topic. A substantial fraction of any operating system is concerned with I/O. I/O can be accomplished in one of three ways. First, there is programmed I/O, in which the main CPU inputs or outputs each byte or word and sits in a tight loop waiting until it can get or send the next one. Second, there is interrupt-driven I/O, in which the CPU starts an I/O transfer for a character or word and goes off to do something else until an interrupt arrives signaling completion of the I/O. Third, there is DMA, in which a separate chip manages the complete transfer of a block of data, given an interrupt only when the entire block has been transferred.

I/O can be structured in four levels: the interrupt service procedures, the device drivers, the device-independent I/O software, and the I/O libraries and spoolers that run in user space. The device drivers handle the details of running the devices and providing uniform interfaces to the rest of the operating system. The device-independent I/O software does things like buffering and error reporting.

Disks come in a variety of types, including magnetic disks, RAIDs, and various kinds of optical disks. Disk arm scheduling algorithms can often be used to improve disk performance, but the presence of virtual geometries complicates matters. By pairing two disks, a stable storage medium with certain useful properties can be constructed.

Clocks are used for keeping track of the real time, limiting how long processes can run, handling watchdog timers, and doing accounting.

Character-oriented terminals have a variety of issues concerning special characters that can be input and special escape sequences that can be output. Input can be in raw mode or cooked mode, depending on how much control the program wants over the input. Escape sequences on output control cursor movement and allow for inserting and deleting text on the screen.

Many personal computers use GUIs for their output. These are based on the WIMP paradigm: windows, icons, menus and a pointing device. GUI-based programs are generally event driven, with keyboard, mouse, and other events being sent to the program for processing as soon as they happen.

Network terminals come in several varieties. One of the most popular consists of those running X, a sophisticated system that can be used to build various GUIs. An alternative to X Windows is a low-level interface that simply ships raw pixels across the network. Experiments with the SLIM terminal show that this technique works surprisingly well.

Finally, power management is a major issue for laptop computers because battery lifetimes are limited. Various techniques can be employed by the operating system to reduce power consumption. Programs can also help out by sacrificing some quality for longer battery lifetimes.

PROBLEMS

1. Advances in chip technology have made it possible to put an entire controller, including all the bus access logic, on an inexpensive chip. How does that affect the model of Fig. 1-5?

2. Given the speeds listed in Fig. 5-1, is it possible to scan documents from a scanner onto an EIDE disk attached to an ISA bus at full speed? Defend your answer.

3. Figure 5-3(b) shows one way of having memory-mapped I/O even in the presence of separate buses for memory and I/O devices, namely, to first try the memory bus and if that fails try the I/O bus. A clever computer science student has thought of an improvement on this idea: try both in parallel, to speed up the process of accessing I/O devices. What do you think of this idea?

4. A DMA controller has four channels. The controller is capable of requesting a 32-bit word every 100 nsec. A response takes equally long. How fast does the bus have to be to avoid being a bottleneck?

5. Suppose that a computer can read or write a memory word in 10 nsec. Also suppose that when an interrupt occurs, all 32 CPU registers, plus the program counter and PSW are pushed onto the stack. What is the maximum number of interrupts per second this machine can process?

6. In Fig. 5-8(b), the interrupt is not acknowledged until after the next character has been output to the printer. Could it have equally well been acknowledged right at the start of the interrupt service procedure? If so, give one reason for doing it at the end, as in the text. If not, why not?

7. A computer has a three-stage pipeline as shown in Fig. 1-6(a). On each clock cycle, one new instruction is fetched from memory at the address pointed to by the PC and put into the pipeline and the PC advanced. Each instruction occupies exactly one memory word. The instructions already in the pipeline are each advanced one stage. When an interrupt occurs, the current PC is pushed onto the stack, and the PC is set to the address of the interrupt handler. Then the pipeline is shifted right one stage and the first instruction of the interrupt handler is fetched into the pipeline. Does this machine have precise interrupts? Defend your answer.

8. A typical printed page of text contains 50 lines of 80 characters each. Imagine that a certain printer can print 6 pages per minute and that the time to write a character to the printer's output register is so short it can be ignored. Does it make sense to run this printer using interrupt-driven I/O if each character printed requires an interrupt that takes 50 μsec all-in to service?

9. What is "device independence"?

10. In which of the four I/O software layers is each of the following done.

   (a) Computing the track, sector, and head for a disk read.
   (b) Writing commands to the device registers.
   (c) Checking to see if the user is permitted to use the device.
   (d) Converting binary integers to ASCII for printing.

11. Based on the data of Fig. 5-17, what is the transfer rate for transfers between the disk and the controller for a floppy disk and a hard disk? How does this compare with a 56-Kbps modem and 100-Mbps Fast Ethernet, respectively?

12. A local area network is used as follows. The user issues a system call to write data packets to the network. The operating system then copies the data to a kernel buffer. Then it copies the data to the network controller board. When all the bytes are safely inside the controller, they are sent over the network at a rate of 10 megabits/sec. The receiving network controller stores each bit a microsecond after it is sent. When the last bit arrives, the destination CPU is interrupted, and the kernel copies the newly arrived packet to a kernel buffer to inspect it. Once it has figured out which user the packet is for, the kernel copies the data to the user space. If we assume that each interrupt and its associated processing takes 1 msec, that packets are 1024 bytes (ignore the headers), and that copying a byte takes 1 μsec, what is the maximum rate

at which one process can pump data to another? Assume that the sender is blocked until the work is finished at the receiving side and an acknowledgement comes back. For simplicity, assume that the time to get the acknowledgement back is so small it can be ignored.

13. Why are output files for the printer normally spooled on disk before being printed?

14. How much cylinder skew is needed for a 7200-rpm disk with a track-to-track seek time of 1 msec? The disk has 200 sectors of 512 bytes each on each track.

15. Calculate the maximum data rate in MB/sec for the disk described in the previous problem.

16. RAID level 3 is able to correct single-bit errors using only one parity drive. What is the point of RAID level 2? After all, it also can only correct one error and takes more drives to do so.

17. A RAID can fail if two or more of its drives crash within a short time interval. Suppose that the probability of one drive crashing in a given hour is p. What is the probability of a k-drive RAID failing in a given hour?

18. Why are optical storage devices inherently capable of higher data density than magnetic storage devices? *Note*: This problem requires some knowledge of high-school physics and how magnetic fields are generated.

19. If a disk controller writes the bytes it receives from the disk to memory as fast as it receives them, with no internal buffering, is interleaving conceivably useful? Discuss.

20. A floppy disk is double interleaved, as in Fig. 5-26(c). It has eight sectors of 512 bytes per track, and a rotation rate of 300 rpm. How long does it take to read all the sectors of a track in order, assuming the arm is already correctly positioned, and 1/2 rotation is needed to get sector 0 under the head? What is the data rate? Now repeat the problem for a noninterleaved disk with the same characteristics. How much does the data rate degrade due to interleaving?

21. If a disk has double interleaving, does it also need cylinder skew in order to avoid missing data when making a track-to-track seek? Discuss your answer.

22. A disk manufacturer has two 5.25-inch disks that each have 10,000 cylinders. The newer one has double the linear recording density of the older one. Which disk properties are better on the newer drive and which are the same?

23. A computer manufacturer decides to redesign the partition table of a Pentium hard disk to provide more than four partitions. What are some consequences of this change?

24. Disk requests come in to the disk driver for cylinders 10, 22, 20, 2, 40, 6, and 38, in that order. A seek takes 6 msec per cylinder moved. How much seek time is needed for

(a) First-come, first served.
(b) Closest cylinder next.
(c) Elevator algorithm (initially moving upward).

In all cases, the arm is initially at cylinder 20.

25. A personal computer salesman visiting a university in South-West Amsterdam remarked during his sales pitch that his company had devoted substantial effort to making their version of UNIX very fast. As an example, he noted that their disk driver used the elevator algorithm and also queued multiple requests within a cylinder in sector order. A student, Harry Hacker, was impressed and bought one. He took it home and wrote a program to randomly read 10,000 blocks spread across the disk. To his amazement, the performance that he measured was identical to what would be expected from first-come, first-served. Was the salesman lying?

26. In the discussion of stable storage using nonvolatile RAM, the following point was glossed over. What happens if the stable write completes but a crash occurs before the operating system can write an invalid block number in the nonvolatile RAM? Does this race condition ruin the abstraction of stable storage? Explain your answer.

27. The clock interrupt handler on a certain computer requires 2 msec (including process switching overhead) per clock tick. The clock runs at 60 Hz. What fraction of the CPU is devoted to the clock?

28. Many versions of UNIX use an unsigned 32-bit integer to keep track of the time as the number of seconds since the origin of time. When will these systems wrap around (year and month)? Do you expect this to actually happen?

29. Some computers need to have large numbers of RS-232 lines, for example, servers or Internet providers. For this reason, plug-in cards with multiple RS-232 lines exist. Suppose that such a card contains a processor that must sample each incoming line at 8 times the baud rate to see if the incoming bit is a 0 or a 1. Also suppose that such a sample takes 1 μsec. For 28,800-bps lines operating at 3200 baud, how many lines can the processor support? Note: The baud rate of a line is the number of signal changes per second. A 3200-baud line can support 28,800 bps if each signaling interval encodes 9 bits using various amplitudes, frequencies, and phases. As an aside, 56K modems do not use RS-232, so are not a suitable example of RS-232 timing.

30. Why are RS232 terminals interrupt driven, but memory-mapped terminals not interrupt driven?

31. Consider the performance of a 56-Kbps modem. The driver outputs one character and then blocks. When the character has been printed, an interrupt occurs and a message is sent to the blocked driver, which outputs the next character and then blocks again. If the time to pass a message, output a character, and block is 100 μsec, what fraction of the CPU is eaten by the modem handling? Assume that each character has one start bit and one stop bit, for 10 bits in all.

32. A bitmap terminal contains 1280 by 960 pixels. To scroll a window, the CPU (or controller) must move all the lines of text upward by copying their bits from one part of the video RAM to another. If a particular window is 60 lines high by 80 characters wide (5280 characters, total), and a character's box is 8 pixels wide by 16 pixels high, how long does it take to scroll the whole window at a copying rate of 50 nsec per byte? If all lines are 80 characters long, what is the equivalent baud rate of the terminal? Putting a character on the screen takes 5 μsec. How many lines per second can be displayed?

33. After receiving a DEL (SIGINT) character, the display driver discards all output currently queued for that display. Why?

34. A user at an RS-232 terminal issues a command to an editor to delete the word on line 5 occupying character positions 7 through and including 12. Assuming the cursor is not on line 5 when the command is given, what ANSI escape sequence should the editor emit to delete the word?

35. Many RS232 terminals have escape sequences for deleting the current line and moving all the lines below it up one line. How do you think this feature is implemented inside the terminal?

36. On the original IBM PC's color display, writing to the video RAM at any time other than during the CRT beam's vertical retrace caused ugly spots to appear all over the screen. A screen image is 25 by 80 characters, each of which fits in a box 8 pixels by 8 pixels. Each row of 640 pixels is drawn on a single horizontal scan of the beam, which takes 63.6 μsec, including the horizontal retrace. The screen is redrawn 60 times a second, each of which requires a vertical retrace period to get the beam back to the top. What fraction of the time is the video RAM available for writing in?

37. The designers of a computer system expected that the mouse could be moved at a maximum rate of 20 cm/sec. If a mickey is 0.1 mm and each mouse message is 3 bytes, what is the maximum data rate of the mouse assuming that each mickey is reported separately?

38. The primary additive colors are red, green, and blue, which means that any color can be constructed from a linear superposition of these colors. Is it possible that someone could have a color photograph that cannot be represented using full 24-bit color?

39. One way to place a character on a bitmapped screen is to use bitblt from a font table. Assume that a particular font uses characters that are 16×24 pixels in true RGB color.

    (a) How much font table space does each character take?
    (b) If copying a byte takes 100 nsec, including overhead, what is the output rate to the screen in characters/sec?

40. Assuming that it takes 10 nsec to copy a byte, how much time does it take to completely rewrite the screen of an 80 character × 25 line text mode memory-mapped screen? What about a 1024×768 pixel graphics screen with 24-bit color?

41. In Fig. 5-41 there is a class to *RegisterClass*. In the corresponding X Window code, in Fig. 5-46, there is no such call or anything like it. Why not?

42. In the text we gave an example of how to draw a rectangle on the screen using the Windows GDI:

    Rectangle(hdc, xleft, ytop, xright, ybottom);

    Is there any real need for the first parameter (*hdc*), and if so, what? After all, the coordinates of the rectangle are explicitly specified as parameters.

43. A SLIM terminal is used to display a Web page containing an animated cartoon of size 400 pixels × 160 pixels running at 10 frames/sec. What fraction of a 100-Mbps Fast Ethernet is consumed by displaying the cartoon?

44. It has been observed that the SLIM system works well with a 1-Mbps network in a test. Are any problems likely in a multiuser situation? *Hint*: Consider a large number of users watching a scheduled TV show and the same number of users browsing the World Wide Web.

45. If a CPU's maximum voltage, V, is cut to V/n, its power consumption drops to $1/n^2$ of its original value and its clock speed drops to $1/n$ of its original value. Suppose that a user is typing at 1 char/sec, but the CPU time required to process each character is 100 msec. What is the optimal value of n and what is the corresponding energy saving in percent compared to not cutting the voltage? Assume that an idle CPU consumes no energy at all.

46. A laptop computer is set up to take maximum advantage of power saving features including shutting down the display and the hard disk after periods of inactivity. A user sometimes runs UNIX programs in text mode, and at other times uses the X Window System. She is surprised to find that battery life is significantly better when she uses text-only programs. Why?

47. Write a program that simulates stable storage. Use two large fixed-length files on your disk to simulate the two disks.

6

FILE SYSTEMS

All computer applications need to store and retrieve information. While a process is running, it can store a limited amount of information within its own address space. However, the storage capacity is restricted to the size of the virtual address space. For some applications this size is adequate, but for others, such as airline reservations, banking, or corporate record keeping, it is far too small.

A second problem with keeping information within a process' address space is that when the process terminates, the information is lost. For many applications, (e.g., for databases), the information must be retained for weeks, months, or even forever. Having it vanish when the process using it terminates is unacceptable. Furthermore, it must not go away when a computer crash kills the process.

A third problem is that it is frequently necessary for multiple processes to access (parts of) the information at the same time. If we have an online telephone directory stored inside the address space of a single process, only that process can access it. The way to solve this problem is to make the information itself independent of any one process.

Thus we have three essential requirements for long-term information storage:

1. It must be possible to store a very large amount of information.

2. The information must survive the termination of the process using it.

3. Multiple processes must be able to access the information concurrently.

The usual solution to all these problems is to store information on disks and other external media in units called **files**. Processes can then read them and write new ones if need be. Information stored in files must be **persistent**, that is, not be affected by process creation and termination. A file should only disappear when its owner explicitly removes it.

Files are managed by the operating system. How they are structured, named, accessed, used, protected, and implemented are major topics in operating system design. As a whole, that part of the operating system dealing with files is known as the **file system** and is the subject of this chapter.

From the users' standpoint, the most important aspect of a file system is how it appears to them, that is, what constitutes a file, how files are named and protected, what operations are allowed on files, and so on. The details of whether linked lists or bitmaps are used to keep track of free storage and how many sectors there are in a logical block are of less interest, although they are of great importance to the designers of the file system. For this reason, we have structured the chapter as several sections. The first two are concerned with the user interface to files and directories, respectively. Then comes a detailed discussion of how the file system is implemented. Finally, we give some examples of real file systems.

6.1 FILES

In the following pages we will look at files from the user's point of view, that is, how they are used and what properties they have.

6.1.1 File Naming

Files are an abstraction mechanism. They provide a way to store information on the disk and read it back later. This must be done in such a way as to shield the user from the details of how and where the information is stored, and how the disks actually work.

Probably the most important characteristic of any abstraction mechanism is the way the objects being managed are named, so we will start our examination of file systems with the subject of file naming. When a process creates a file, it gives the file a name. When the process terminates, the file continues to exist and can be accessed by other processes using its name.

The exact rules for file naming vary somewhat from system to system, but all current operating systems allow strings of one to eight letters as legal file names. Thus *andrea*, *bruce*, and *cathy* are possible file names. Frequently digits and special characters are also permitted, so names like *2*, *urgent!*, and *Fig.2-14* are often valid as well. Many file systems support names as long as 255 characters.

Some file systems distinguish between upper and lower case letters, whereas others do not. UNIX falls in the first category; MS-DOS falls in the second. Thus a UNIX system can have all of the following as three distinct files: *maria*, *Maria*, and *MARIA*. In MS-DOS, all these names refer to the same file.

An aside on file systems is probably in order here. Windows 95 and Windows 98 both use the MS-DOS file system, and thus inherit many of its properties, such as how file names are constructed. In addition, Windows NT and Windows 2000 support the MS-DOS file system and thus also inherit its properties. However, the latter two systems also have a native file system (NTFS) that has different properties (such as file names in Unicode). In this chapter, when we refer to the Windows file system, we mean the MS-DOS file system, which is the only file system supported by all versions of Windows. We will discuss the Windows 2000 native file system in Chap. 11.

Many operating systems support two-part file names, with the two parts separated by a period, as in *prog.c*. The part following the period is called the **file extension** and usually indicates something about the file. In MS-DOS, for example, file names are 1 to 8 characters, plus an optional extension of 1 to 3 characters. In UNIX, the size of the extension, if any, is up to the user, and a file may even have two or more extensions, as in *prog.c.Z*, where *.Z* is commonly used to indicate that the file (*prog.c*) has been compressed using the Ziv-Lempel compression algorithm. Some of the more common file extensions and their meanings are shown in Fig. 6-1.

Extension	Meaning
file.bak	Backup file
file.c	C source program
file.gif	Compuserve Graphical Interchange Format image
file.hlp	Help file
file.html	World Wide Web HyperText Markup Language document
file.jpg	Still picture encoded with the JPEG standard
file.mp3	Music encoded in MPEG layer 3 audio format
file.mpg	Movie encoded with the MPEG standard
file.o	Object file (compiler output, not yet linked)
file.pdf	Portable Document Format file
file.ps	PostScript file
file.tex	Input for the TEX formatting program
file.txt	General text file
file.zip	Compressed archive

Figure 6-1. Some typical file extensions.

In some systems (e.g., UNIX), file extensions are just conventions and are not enforced by the operating system. A file named *file.txt* might be some kind of text file, but that name is more to remind the owner than to convey any actual information to the computer. On the other hand, a C compiler may actually insist that files it is to compile end in *.c*, and it may refuse to compile them if they do not.

Conventions like this are especially useful when the same program can handle several different kinds of files. The C compiler, for example, can be given a list of several files to compile and link together, some of them C files and some of them assembly language files. The extension then becomes essential for the compiler to tell which are C files, which are assembly files, and which are other files.

In contrast, Windows is aware of the extensions and assigns meaning to them. Users (or processes) can register extensions with the operating system and specify for each one which program "owns" that extension. When a user double clicks on a file name, the program assigned to its file extension is launched with the file as parameter. For example, double clicking on *file.doc* starts Microsoft *Word* with *file.doc* as the initial file to edit.

6.1.2 File Structure

Files can be structured in any of several ways. Three common possibilities are depicted in Fig. 6-2. The file in Fig. 6-2(a) is an unstructured sequence of bytes. In effect, the operating system does not know or care what is in the file. All it sees are bytes. Any meaning must be imposed by user-level programs. Both UNIX and Windows use this approach.

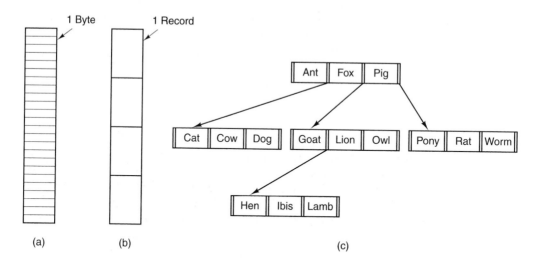

Figure 6-2. Three kinds of files. (a) Byte sequence. (b) Record sequence. (c) Tree.

Having the operating system regard files as nothing more than byte sequences provides the maximum flexibility. User programs can put anything they want in their files and name them any way that is convenient. The operating system does not help, but it also does not get in the way. For users who want to do unusual things, the latter can be very important.

The first step up in structure is shown in Fig. 6-2(b). In this model, a file is a sequence of fixed-length records, each with some internal structure. Central to the idea of a file being a sequence of records is the idea that the read operation returns one record and the write operation overwrites or appends one record. As a historical note, in decades gone by, when the 80-column punched card was king, many (mainframe) operating systems based their file systems on files consisting of 80-character records, in effect, card images. These systems also supported files of 132-character records, which were intended for the line printer (which in those days were big chain printers having 132 columns). Programs read input in units of 80 characters and wrote it in units of 132 characters, although the final 52 could be spaces, of course. No current general-purpose system works this way.

The third kind of file structure is shown in Fig. 6-2(c). In this organization, a file consists of a tree of records, not necessarily all the same length, each containing a **key** field in a fixed position in the record. The tree is sorted on the key field, to allow rapid searching for a particular key.

The basic operation here is not to get the "next" record, although that is also possible, but to get the record with a specific key. For the zoo file of Fig. 6-2(c), one could ask the system to get the record whose key is *pony*, for example, without worrying about its exact position in the file. Furthermore, new records can be added to the file, with the operating system, and not the user, deciding where to place them. This type of file is clearly quite different from the unstructured byte streams used in UNIX and Windows but is widely used on the large mainframe computers still used in some commercial data processing.

6.1.3 File Types

Many operating systems support several types of files. UNIX and Windows, for example, have regular files and directories. UNIX also has character and block special files. **Regular files** are the ones that contain user information. All the files of Fig. 6-2 are regular files. **Directories** are system files for maintaining the structure of the file system. We will study directories below. **Character special files** are related to input/output and used to model serial I/O devices such as terminals, printers, and networks. **Block special files** are used to model disks. In this chapter we will be primarily interested in regular files.

Regular files are generally either ASCII files or binary files. ASCII files consist of lines of text. In some systems each line is terminated by a carriage return character. In others, the line feed character is used. Some systems (e.g., MS-DOS) use both. Lines need not all be of the same length.

The great advantage of ASCII files is that they can be displayed and printed as is, and they can be edited with any text editor. Furthermore, if large numbers of programs use ASCII files for input and output, it is easy to connect the output of one program to the input of another, as in shell pipelines. (The interprocess plumbing is not any easier, but interpreting the information certainly is if a standard convention, such as ASCII, is used for expressing it.)

Other files are binary files, which just means that they are not ASCII files. Listing them on the printer gives an incomprehensible listing full of what is apparently random junk. Usually, they have some internal structure known to programs that use them.

For example, in Fig. 6-3(a) we see a simple executable binary file taken from a version of UNIX. Although technically the file is just a sequence of bytes, the operating system will only execute a file if it has the proper format. It has five sections: header, text, data, relocation bits, and symbol table. The header starts with a so-called **magic number**, identifying the file as an executable file (to prevent the accidental execution of a file not in this format). Then come the sizes of the various pieces of the file, the address at which execution starts, and some flag bits. Following the header are the text and data of the program itself. These are loaded into memory and relocated using the relocation bits. The symbol table is used for debugging.

Our second example of a binary file is an archive, also from UNIX. It consists of a collection of library procedures (modules) compiled but not linked. Each one is prefaced by a header telling its name, creation date, owner, protection code, and size. Just as with the executable file, the module headers are full of binary numbers. Copying them to the printer would produce complete gibberish.

Every operating system must recognize at least one file type: its own executable file, but some recognize more. The old TOPS-20 system (for the DECsystem 20) went so far as to examine the creation time of any file to be executed. Then it located the source file and saw if the source had been modified since the binary was made. If it had been, it automatically recompiled the source. In UNIX terms, the *make* program had been built into the shell. The file extensions were mandatory so the operating system could tell which binary program was derived from which source.

Having strongly typed files like this causes problems whenever the user does anything that the system designers did not expect. Consider, as an example, a system in which program output files have extension *.dat* (data files). If a user writes a program formatter that reads a *.c* file (C program), transforms it (e.g., by converting it to a standard indentation layout), and then writes the transformed file as output, the output file will be of type *.dat*. If the user tries to offer this to the C compiler to compile it, the system will refuse because it has the wrong extension. Attempts to copy *file.dat* to *file.c* will be rejected by the system as invalid (to protect the user against mistakes).

While this kind of "user friendliness" may help novices, it drives experienced users up the wall since they have to devote considerable effort to circumventing the operating system's idea of what is reasonable and what is not.

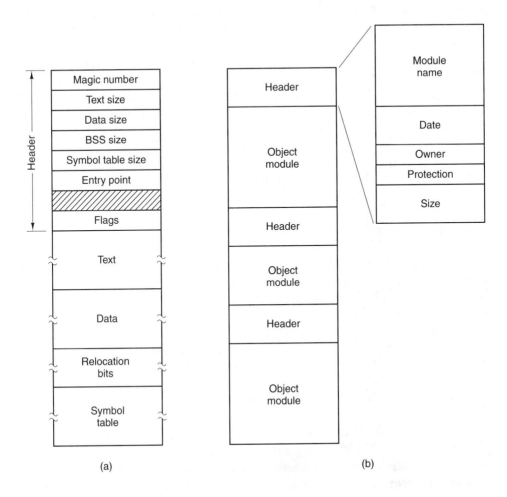

Figure 6-3. (a) An executable file. (b) An archive.

6.1.4 File Access

Early operating systems provided only one kind of file access: **sequential access**. In these systems, a process could read all the bytes or records in a file in order, starting at the beginning, but could not skip around and read them out of order. Sequential files could be rewound, however, so they could be read as often as needed. Sequential files were convenient when the storage medium was magnetic tape, rather than disk.

When disks came into use for storing files, it became possible to read the bytes or records of a file out of order, or to access records by key, rather than by position. Files whose bytes or records can be read in any order are called **random access files**. They are required by many applications.

Random access files are essential for many applications, for example, database systems. If an airline customer calls up and wants to reserve a seat on a particular flight, the reservation program must be able to access the record for that flight without having to read the records for thousands of other flights first.

Two methods are used for specifying where to start reading. In the first one, every read operation gives the position in the file to start reading at. In the second one, a special operation, seek, is provided to set the current position. After a seek, the file can be read sequentially from the now-current position.

In some older mainframe operating systems, files are classified as being either sequential or random access at the time they are created. This allows the system to use different storage techniques for the two classes. Modern operating systems do not make this distinction. All their files are automatically random access.

6.1.5 File Attributes

Every file has a name and its data. In addition, all operating systems associate other information with each file, for example, the date and time the file was created and the file's size. We will call these extra items the file's **attributes**. The list of attributes varies considerably from system to system. The table of Fig. 6-4 shows some of the possibilities, but other ones also exist. No existing system has all of these, but each one is present in some system.

The first four attributes relate to the file's protection and tell who may access it and who may not. All kinds of schemes are possible, some of which we will study later. In some systems the user must present a password to access a file, in which case the password must be one of the attributes.

The flags are bits or short fields that control or enable some specific property. Hidden files, for example, do not appear in listings of all the files. The archive flag is a bit that keeps track of whether the file has been backed up. The backup program clears it, and the operating system sets it whenever a file is changed. In this way, the backup program can tell which files need backing up. The temporary flag allows a file to be marked for automatic deletion when the process that created it terminates.

The record length, key position, and key length fields are only present in files whose records can be looked up using a key. They provide the information required to find the keys.

The various times keep track of when the file was created, most recently accessed and most recently modified. These are useful for a variety of purposes. For example, a source file that has been modified after the creation of the corresponding object file needs to be recompiled. These fields provide the necessary information.

The current size tells how big the file is at present. Some old mainframe operating systems require the maximum size to be specified when the file is created, in order to let the operating system reserve the maximum amount of storage in ad-

Attribute	Meaning
Protection	Who can access the file and in what way
Password	Password needed to access the file
Creator	ID of the person who created the file
Owner	Current owner
Read-only flag	0 for read/write; 1 for read only
Hidden flag	0 for normal; 1 for do not display in listings
System flag	0 for normal files; 1 for system file
Archive flag	0 for has been backed up; 1 for needs to be backed up
ASCII/binary flag	0 for ASCII file; 1 for binary file
Random access flag	0 for sequential access only; 1 for random access
Temporary flag	0 for normal; 1 for delete file on process exit
Lock flags	0 for unlocked; nonzero for locked
Record length	Number of bytes in a record
Key position	Offset of the key within each record
Key length	Number of bytes in the key field
Creation time	Date and time the file was created
Time of last access	Date and time the file was last accessed
Time of last change	Date and time the file has last changed
Current size	Number of bytes in the file
Maximum size	Number of bytes the file may grow to

Figure 6-4. Some possible file attributes.

vance. Workstation and personal computer operating systems are clever enough to do without this feature.

6.1.6 File Operations

Files exist to store information and allow it to be retrieved later. Different systems provide different operations to allow storage and retrieval. Below is a discussion of the most common system calls relating to files.

1. Create. The file is created with no data. The purpose of the call is to announce that the file is coming and to set some of the attributes.

2. Delete. When the file is no longer needed, it has to be deleted to free up disk space. There is always a system call for this purpose.

3. Open. Before using a file, a process must open it. The purpose of the open call is to allow the system to fetch the attributes and list of disk addresses into main memory for rapid access on later calls.

4. Close. When all the accesses are finished, the attributes and disk addresses are no longer needed, so the file should be closed to free up internal table space. Many systems encourage this by imposing a maximum number of open files on processes. A disk is written in blocks, and closing a file forces writing of the file's last block, even though that block may not be entirely full yet.

5. Read. Data are read from file. Usually, the bytes come from the current position. The caller must specify how much data are needed and must also provide a buffer to put them in.

6. Write. Data are written to the file, again, usually at the current position. If the current position is the end of the file, the file's size increases. If the current position is in the middle of the file, existing data are overwritten and lost forever.

7. Ap end. This call is a restricted form of write. It can only add data to .ie end of the file. Systems that provide a minimal set of system calls do not generally have append, but many systems provide multiple ways of doing the same thing, and these systems sometimes have append.

8. Seek. For random access files, a method is needed to specify from where to take the data. One common approach is a system call, seek, that repositions the file pointer to a specific place in the file. After this call has completed, data can be read from, or written to, that position.

9. Get attributes. Processes often need to read file attributes to do their work. For example, the UNIX *make* program is commonly used to manage software development projects consisting of many source files. When *make* is called, it examines the modification times of all the source and object files and arranges for the minimum number of compilations required to bring everything up to date. To do its job, it must look at the attributes, namely, the modification times.

10. Set attributes. Some of the attributes are user settable and can be changed after the file has been created. This system call makes that possible. The protection mode information is an obvious example. Most of the flags also fall in this category.

11. Rename. It frequently happens that a user needs to change the name of an existing file. This system call makes that possible. It is not always strictly necessary, because the file can usually be copied to a new file with the new name, and the old file then deleted.

6.1.7 An Example Program Using File System Calls

In this section we will examine a simple UNIX program that copies one file from its source file to a destination file. It is listed in Fig. 6-5. The program has minimal functionality and even worse error reporting, but it gives a reasonable idea of how some of the system calls related to files work.

The program, *copyfile*, can be called, for example, by the command line

    copyfile abc xyz

to copy the file *abc* to *xyz*. If *xyz* already exists, it will be overwritten. Otherwise, it will be created. The program must be called with exactly two arguments, both legal file names.

The four *#include* statements near the top of the program cause a large number of definitions and function prototypes to be included in the program. These are needed to make the program conformant to the relevant international standards, but will not concern us further. The next line is a function prototype for *main*, something required by ANSI C, but also not important for our purposes.

The first *#define* statement is a macro definition that defines the string *BUF_SIZE* as a macro that expands into the number 4096. The program will read and write in chunks of 4096 bytes. It is considered good programming practice to give names to constants like this and to use the names instead of the constants. Not only does this convention make programs easier to read, but it also makes them easier to maintain. The second *#define* statement determines who can access the output file.

The main program is called *main*, and it has two arguments, *argc*, and *argv*. These are supplied by the operating system when the program is called. The first one tells how many strings were present on the command line that invoked the program, including the program name. It should be 3. The second one is an array of pointers to the arguments. In the example call given above, the elements of this array would contain pointers to the following values:

    argv[0] = "copyfile"
    argv[1] = "abc"
    argv[2] = "xyz"

It is via this array that the program accesses its arguments.

Five variables are declared. The first two, *in_fd* and *out_fd*, will hold the **file descriptors**, small integers returned when a file is opened. The next two, *rd_count* and *wt_count*, are the byte counts returned by the read and write system calls, respectively. The last one, *buffer*, is the buffer used to hold the data read and supply the data to be written.

The first actual statement checks *argc* to see if it is 3. If not, it exits with status code 1. Any status code other than 0 means that an error has occurred. The

```
/* File copy program. Error checking and reporting is minimal. */

#include <sys/types.h>                    /* include necessary header files */
#include <fcntl.h>
#include <stdlib.h>
#include <unistd.h>

int main(int argc, char *argv[]);         /* ANSI prototype */

#define BUF_SIZE 4096                      /* use a buffer size of 4096 bytes */
#define OUTPUT_MODE 0700                   /* protection bits for output file */

int main(int argc, char *argv[])
{
     int in_fd, out_fd, rd_count, wt_count;
     char buffer[BUF_SIZE];

     if (argc != 3) exit(1);              /* syntax error if argc is not 3 */

     /* Open the input file and create the output file */
     in_fd = open(argv[1], O_RDONLY);    /* open the source file */
     if (in_fd < 0) exit(2);              /* if it cannot be opened, exit */
     out_fd = creat(argv[2], OUTPUT_MODE);  /* create the destination file */
     if (out_fd < 0) exit(3);             /* if it cannot be created, exit */

     /* Copy loop */
     while (TRUE) {
          rd_count = read(in_fd, buffer, BUF_SIZE); /* read a block of data */
          if (rd_count <= 0) break;              /* if end of file or error, exit loop */
          wt_count = write(out_fd, buffer, rd_count); /* write data */
          if (wt_count <= 0) exit(4);           /* wt_count <= 0 is an error */
     }

     /* Close the files */
     close(in_fd);
     close(out_fd);
     if (rd_count == 0)                   /* no error on last read */
          exit(0);
     else
          exit(5);                        /* error on last read */
}
```

Figure 6-5. A simple program to copy a file.

status code is the only error reporting present in this program. A production version would normally print error messages as well.

Then we try to open the source file and create the destination file. If the source file is successfully opened, the system assigns a small integer to *in_fd*, to identify the file. Subsequent calls must include this integer so the system knows which file it wants. Similarly, if the destination is successfully created, *out_fd* is given a value to identify it. The second argument to *creat* sets the protection mode. If either the open or the create fails, the corresponding file descriptor is set to −1, and the program exits with an error code.

Now comes the copy loop. It starts by trying to read in 4 KB of data to *buffer*. It does this by calling the library procedure *read*, which actually invokes the read system call. The first parameter identifies the file, the second gives the buffer, and the third tells how many bytes to read. The value assigned to *rd_count* gives the number of bytes actually read. Normally, this will be 4096, except if fewer bytes are remaining in the file. When end of file is reached, it will be 0. If *rd_count* is ever zero or negative, the copying cannot continue, so the *break* statement is executed to terminate the (otherwise endless) loop.

The call to *write* outputs the buffer to the destination file. The first parameter identifies the file, the second gives the buffer, and the third tells how many bytes to write, analogous to *read*. Note that the byte count is the number of bytes actually read, not *BUF_SIZE*. This point is important because the last read will not return 4096, unless the file just happens to be a multiple of 4 KB.

When the entire file has been processed, the first call beyond the end of file will return 0 to *rd_count*, which will make it exit the loop. At this point the two files are closed and the program exits with a status indicating normal termination.

Although the Windows system calls are different from those of UNIX, the general structure of a command-line Windows program to copy a file is moderately similar to that of Fig. 6-5. We will examine the Windows 2000 calls in Chap. 11.

6.1.8 Memory-Mapped Files

Many programmers feel that accessing files as shown above is cumbersome and inconvenient, especially when compared to accessing ordinary memory. For this reason, some operating systems, starting with MULTICS, have provided a way to map files into the address space of a running process. Conceptually, we can imagine the existence of two new system calls, map and unmap. The former gives a file name and a virtual address, which causes the operating system to map the file into the address space at the virtual address.

For example, suppose that a file, *f*, of length 64 KB, is mapped into the virtual address starting at address 512K. Then any machine instruction that reads the contents of the byte at 512K gets byte 0 of the file, and so on. Similarly, a write to address 512K + 21000 modifies byte 21000 of the file. When the process terminates, the modified file is left on the disk, just as though it had been changed by a combination of seek and write system calls.

What actually happens is that the system's internal tables are changed to make the file become the backing store for the memory region 512K to 576K. Thus a read from 512K causes a page fault, bringing in page 0 of the file. Similarly, a write to 512K + 1100 causes a page fault, bringing in the page containing that address, after which the write to memory can take place. If that page is ever evicted by the page replacement algorithm, it is written back to the appropriate place in the file. When the process finishes, all mapped, modified pages are written back to their files.

File mapping works best in a system that supports segmentation. In such a system, each file can be mapped onto its own segment so that byte k in the file is also byte k in the segment. In Fig. 6-6(a) we see a process that has two segments, text and data. Suppose that this process copies files, like the program of Fig. 6-5. First it maps the source file, say, *abc*, onto a segment. Then it creates an empty segment and maps it onto the destination file, *xyz* in our example. These operations give the situation shown in Fig. 6-6(b).

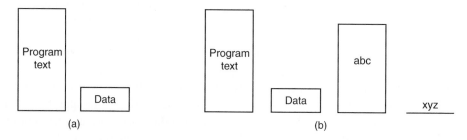

Figure 6-6. (a) A segmented process before mapping files into its address space. (b) The process after mapping an existing file *abc* into one segment and creating a new segment for file *xyz*.

At this point the process can copy the source segment into the destination segment using an ordinary copy loop. No read or write system calls are needed. When it is all done, it can execute the unmap system call to remove the files from the address space and then exit. The output file, *xyz*, will now exist, as though it had been created in the conventional way.

Although file mapping eliminates the need for I/O and thus makes programming easier, it introduces a few problems of its own. First, it is hard for the system to know the exact length of the output file, *xyz*, in our example. It can easily tell the number of the highest page written, but it has no way of knowing how many bytes in that page were written. Suppose that the program only uses page 0, and after execution all the bytes are still 0 (their initial value). Maybe *xyz* is a file consisting of 10 zeros. Maybe it is a file consisting of 100 zeros. Maybe it is a file consisting of 1000 zeros. Who knows? The operating system cannot tell. All it can do is create a file whose length is equal to the page size.

A second problem can (potentially) occur if a file is mapped in by one process and opened for conventional reading by another. If the first process modifies a page, that change will not be reflected in the file on disk until the page is evicted. The system has to take great care to make sure the two processes do not see inconsistent versions of the file.

A third problem with mapping is that a file may be larger than a segment, or even larger than the entire virtual address space. The only way out is to arrange the map system call to be able to map a portion of a file, rather than the entire file. Although this works, it is clearly less satisfactory than mapping the entire file.

6.2 DIRECTORIES

To keep track of files, file systems normally have **directories** or **folders**, which, in many systems, are themselves files. In this section we will discuss directories, their organization, their properties, and the operations that can be performed on them.

6.2.1 Single-Level Directory Systems

The simplest form of directory system is having one directory containing all the files. Sometimes it is called the **root directory**, but since it is the only one, the name does not matter much. On early personal computers, this system was common, in part because there was only one user. Interestingly enough, the world's first supercomputer, the CDC 6600, also had only a single directory for all files, even though it was used by many users at once. This decision was no doubt made to keep the software design simple.

An example of a system with one directory is given in Fig. 6-7. Here the directory contains four files. The file *owners* are shown in the figure, not the file *names* (because the owners are important to the point we are about to make). The advantages of this scheme are its simplicity and the ability to locate files quickly—there is only one place to look, after all.

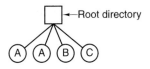

Figure 6-7. A single-level directory system containing four files, owned by three different people, *A*, *B*, and *C*.

The problem with having only one directory in a system with multiple users is that different users may accidentally use the same names for their files. For example, if user *A* creates a file called *mailbox*, and then later user *B* also creates a file called *mailbox*, *B*'s file will overwrite *A*'s file. Consequently, this scheme is not used on multiuser systems any more, but could be used on a small embedded system, for example, a system in a car that was designed to store user profiles for a small number of drivers.

6.2.2 Two-level Directory Systems

To avoid conflicts caused by different users choosing the same file name for their own files, the next step up is giving each user a private directory. In that way, names chosen by one user do not interfere with names chosen by a different user and there is no problem caused by the same name occurring in two or more directories. This design leads to the system of Fig. 6-8. This design could be used, for example, on a multiuser computer or on a simple network of personal computers that shared a common file server over a local area network.

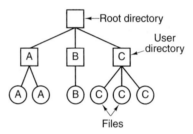

Figure 6-8. A two-level directory system. The letters indicate the owners of the directories and files.

Implicit in this design is that when a user tries to open a file, the system knows which user it is in order to know which directory to search. As a consequence, some kind of login procedure is needed, in which the user specifies a login name or identification, something not required with a single-level directory system.

When this system is implemented in its most basic form, users can only access files in their own directories. However, a slight extension is to allow users to access other users' files by providing some indication of whose file is to be opened. Thus, for example,

    open("x")

might be the call to open a file called x in the user's directory, and

    open("nancy/x")

might be the call to open a file x in the directory of another user, Nancy.

One situation in which users need to access files other than their own is to execute system binary programs. Having copies of all the utility programs present in each directory clearly is inefficient. At the very least, there is a need for a system directory with the executable binary programs.

6.2.3 Hierarchical Directory Systems

The two-level hierarchy eliminates name conflicts among users but is not satisfactory for users with a large number of files. Even on a single-user personal computer, it is inconvenient. It is quite common for users to want to group their files together in logical ways. A professor, for example, might have a collection of files that together form a book that he is writing for one course, a second collection of files containing student programs submitted for another course, a third group of files containing the code of an advanced compiler-writing system he is building, a fourth group of files containing grant proposals, as well as other files for electronic mail, minutes of meetings, papers he is writing, games, and so on. Some way is needed to group these files together in flexible ways chosen by the user.

What is needed is a general hierarchy (i.e., a tree of directories). With this approach, each user can have as many directories as are needed so that files can be grouped together in natural ways. This approach is shown in Fig. 6-9. Here, the directories *A*, *B*, and *C* contained in the root directory each belong to a different user, two of whom have created subdirectories for projects they are working on.

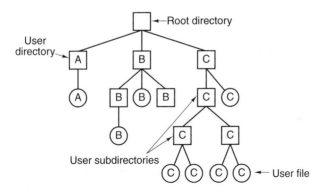

Figure 6-9. A hierarchical directory system.

The ability for users to create an arbitrary number of subdirectories provides a powerful structuring tool for users to organize their work. For this reason, nearly all modern file systems are organized in this manner.

6.2.4 Path Names

When the file system is organized as a directory tree, some way is needed for specifying file names. Two different methods are commonly used. In the first method, each file is given an **absolute path name** consisting of the path from the root directory to the file. As an example, the path */usr/ast/mailbox* means that the root directory contains a subdirectory *usr*, which in turn contains a subdirectory *ast*, which contains the file *mailbox*. Absolute path names always start at the root directory and are unique. In UNIX the components of the path are separated by /. In Windows the separator is \. In MULTICS it was >. Thus the same path name would be written as follows in these three systems:

```
Windows      \usr\ast\mailbox
UNIX         /usr/ast/mailbox
MULTICS      >usr>ast>mailbox
```

No matter which character is used, if the first character of the path name is the separator, then the path is absolute.

The other kind of name is the **relative path name**. This is used in conjunction with the concept of the **working directory** (also called the **current directory**). A user can designate one directory as the current working directory, in which case all path names not beginning at the root directory are taken relative to the working directory. For example, if the current working directory is */usr/ast*, then the file whose absolute path is */usr/ast/mailbox* can be referenced simply as *mailbox*. In other words, the UNIX command

```
cp /usr/ast/mailbox /usr/ast/mailbox.bak
```

and the command

```
cp mailbox mailbox.bak
```

do exactly the same thing if the working directory is */usr/ast*. The relative form is often more convenient, but it does the same thing as the absolute form.

Some programs need to access a specific file without regard to what the working directory is. In that case, they should always use absolute path names. For example, a spelling checker might need to read */usr/lib/dictionary* to do its work. It should use the full, absolute path name in this case because it does not know what the working directory will be when it is called. The absolute path name will always work, no matter what the working directory is.

Of course, if the spelling checker needs a large number of files from */usr/lib*, an alternative approach is for it to issue a system call to change its working directory to */usr/lib*, and then use just *dictionary* as the first parameter to open. By explicitly changing the working directory, it knows for sure where it is in the directory tree, so it can then use relative paths.

Each process has its own working directory, so when a process changes its working directory and later exits, no other processes are affected and no traces of the change are left behind in the file system. In this way it is always perfectly safe for a process to change its working directory whenever that is convenient. On the other hand, if a *library procedure* changes the working directory and does not change back to where it was when it is finished, the rest of the program may not work since its assumption about where it is may now suddenly be invalid. For this reason, library procedures rarely change the working directory, and when they must, they always change it back again before returning.

Most operating systems that support a hierarchical directory system have two special entries in every directory, "." and "..", generally pronounced "dot" and "dotdot." Dot refers to the current directory; dotdot refers to its parent. To see how these are used, consider the UNIX file tree of Fig. 6-10. A certain process has */usr/ast* as its working directory. It can use .. to go up the tree. For example, it can copy the file */usr/lib/dictionary* to its own directory using the command

    cp ../lib/dictionary .

The first path instructs the system to go upward (to the *usr* directory), then to go down to the directory *lib* to find the file *dictionary*.

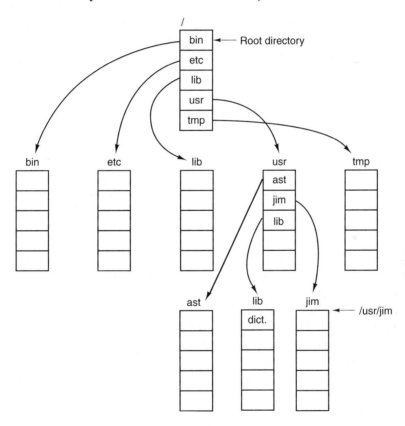

Figure 6-10. A UNIX directory tree.

The second argument (dot) names the current directory. When the *cp* command gets a directory name (including dot) as its last argument, it copies all the files there. Of course, a more normal way to do the copy would be to type

    cp /usr/lib/dictionary .

Here the use of dot saves the user the trouble of typing *dictionary* a second time. Nevertheless, typing

    cp /usr/lib/dictionary dictionary

also works fine, as does

    cp /usr/lib/dictionary /usr/ast/dictionary

All of these do exactly the same thing.

6.2.5 Directory Operations

The allowed system calls for managing directories exhibit more variation from system to system than system calls for files. To give an impression of what they are and how they work, we will give a sample (taken from UNIX).

1. Create. A directory is created. It is empty except for dot and dotdot, which are put there automatically by the system (or in a few cases, by the *mkdir* program).

2. Delete. A directory is deleted. Only an empty directory can be deleted. A directory containing only dot and dotdot is considered empty as these cannot usually be deleted.

3. Opendir. Directories can be read. For example, to list all the files in a directory, a listing program opens the directory to read out the names of all the files it contains. Before a directory can be read, it must be opened, analogous to opening and reading a file.

4. Closedir. When a directory has been read, it should be closed to free up internal table space.

5. Readdir. This call returns the next entry in an open directory. Formerly, it was possible to read directories using the usual read system call, but that approach has the disadvantage of forcing the programmer to know and deal with the internal structure of directories. In contrast, readdir always returns one entry in a standard format, no matter which of the possible directory structures is being used.

6. Rename. In many respects, directories are just like files and can be renamed the same way files can be.

7. Link. Linking is a technique that allows a file to appear in more than one directory. This system call specifies an existing file and a path name, and creates a link from the existing file to the name specified by the path. In this way, the same file may appear in multiple directories. A link of this kind, which increments the counter in the file's i-node (to keep track of the number of directory entries containing the file), is sometimes called a **hard link**.

8. Unlink. A directory entry is removed. If the file being unlinked is only present in one directory (the normal case), it is removed from the file system. If it is present in multiple directories, only the path name specified is removed. The others remain. In UNIX, the system call for deleting files (discussed earlier) is, in fact, unlink.

The above list gives the most important calls, but there are a few others as well, for example, for managing the protection information associated with a directory.

6.3 FILE SYSTEM IMPLEMENTATION

Now it is time to turn from the user's view of the file system to the implementor's view. Users are concerned with how files are named, what operations are allowed on them, what the directory tree looks like, and similar interface issues. Implementors are interested in how files and directories are stored, how disk space is managed, and how to make everything work efficiently and reliably. In the following sections we will examine a number of these areas to see what the issues and trade-offs are.

6.3.1 File System Layout

File systems are stored on disks. Most disks can be divided up into one or more partitions, with independent file systems on each partition. Sector 0 of the disk is called the **MBR** (**Master Boot Record**) and is used to boot the computer. The end of the MBR contains the partition table. This table gives the starting and ending addresses of each partition. One of the partitions in the table is marked as active. When the computer is booted, the BIOS reads in and executes the MBR. The first thing the MBR program does is locate the active partition, read in its first block, called the **boot block**, and execute it. The program in the boot block loads the operating system contained in that partition. For uniformity, every partition starts with a boot block, even if it does not contain a bootable operating system. Besides, it might contain one in the future, so reserving a boot block is a good idea anyway.

Other than starting with a boot block, the layout of a disk partition varies strongly from file system to file system. Often the file system will contain some of the items shown in Fig. 6-11. The first one is the **superblock**. It contains all the key parameters about the file system and is read into memory when the computer is booted or the file system is first touched. Typical information in the superblock includes a magic number to identify the file system type, the number of blocks in the file system, and other key administrative information.

Next might come information about free blocks in the file system, for example in the form of a bitmap or a list of pointers. This might be followed by the i-

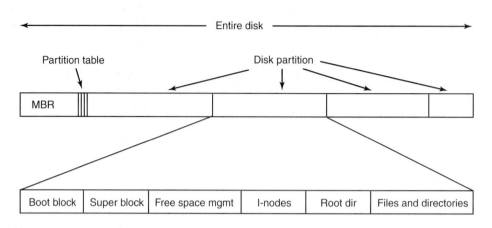

Figure 6-11. A possible file system layout.

nodes, an array of data structures, one per file, telling all about the file. After that might come the root directory, which contains the top of the file system tree. Finally, the remainder of the disk typically contains all the other directories and files.

6.3.2 Implementing Files

Probably the most important issue in implementing file storage is keeping track of which disk blocks go with which file. Various methods are used in different operating systems. In this section, we will examine a few of them.

Contiguous Allocation

The simplest allocation scheme is to store each file as a contiguous run of disk blocks. Thus on a disk with 1-KB blocks, a 50-KB file would be allocated 50 consecutive blocks. With 2-KB blocks, it would be allocated 25 consecutive blocks.

We see an example of contiguous storage allocation in Fig. 6-12(a). Here the first 40 disk blocks are shown, starting with block 0 on the left. Initially, the disk was empty. Then a file A, of length four blocks was written to disk starting at the beginning (block 0). After that a six-block file, B, was written starting right after the end of file A. Note that each file begins at the start of a new block, so that if file A was really 3½ blocks, some space is wasted at the end of the last block. In the figure, a total of seven files are shown, each one starting at the block following the end of the previous one. Shading is used just to make it easier to tell the files apart.

Contiguous disk space allocation has two significant advantages. First, it is simple to implement because keeping track of where a file's blocks are is reduced

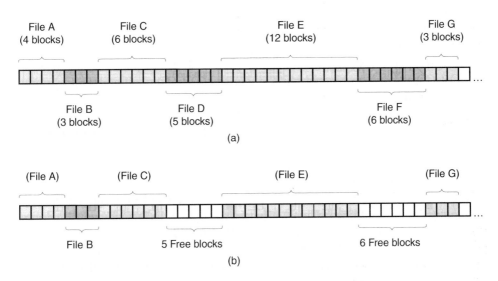

Figure 6-12. (a) Contiguous allocation of disk space for seven files. (b) The state of the disk after files *D* and *F* have been removed.

to remembering two numbers: the disk address of the first block and the number of blocks in the file. Given the number of the first block, the number of any other block can be found by a simple addition.

Second, the read performance is excellent because the entire file can be read from the disk in a single operation. Only one seek is needed (to the first block). After that, no more seeks or rotational delays are needed so data come in at the full bandwidth of the disk. Thus contiguous allocation is simple to implement and has high performance.

Unfortunately, contiguous allocation also has a significant drawback: in time, the disk becomes fragmented. To see how this comes about, examine Fig. 6-12(b). Here two files, *D* and F have been removed. When a file is removed, its blocks are freed, leaving a run of free blocks on the disk. The disk is not compacted on the spot to squeeze out the hole since that would involve copying all the blocks following the hole, potentially millions of blocks. As a result, the disk ultimately consists of files and holes, as illustrated in the figure.

Initially, this fragmentation is not a problem since each new file can be written at the end of disk, following the previous one. However, eventually the disk will fill up and it will become necessary to either compact the disk, which is prohibitively expensive, or to reuse the free space in the holes. Reusing the space requires maintaining a list of holes, which is doable. However, when a new file is to be created, it is necessary to know its final size in order to choose a hole of the correct size to place it in.

Imagine the consequences of such a design. The user starts a text editor or word processor in order to type a document. The first thing the program asks is how many bytes the final document will be. The question must be answered or the program will not continue. If the number given ultimately proves too small, the program has to terminate prematurely because the disk hole is full and there is no place to put the rest of the file. If the user tries to avoid this problem by giving an unrealistically large number as the final size, say, 100 MB, the editor may be unable to find such a large hole and announce that the file cannot be created. Of course, the user would be free to start the program again and say 50 MB this time, and so on until a suitable hole was located. Still, this scheme is not likely to lead to happy users.

However, there is one situation in which contiguous allocation is feasible and, in fact, widely used: on CD-ROMs. Here all the file sizes are known in advance and will never change during subsequent use of the CD-ROM file system. We will study the most common CD-ROM file system later in this chapter.

As we mentioned in Chap. 1, history often repeats itself in computer science as new generations of technology occur. Contiguous allocation was actually used on magnetic disk file systems years ago due to its simplicity and high performance (user friendliness did not count for much then). Then the idea was dropped due to the nuisance of having to specify final file size at file creation time. But with the advent of CD-ROMs, DVDs, and other write-once optical media, suddenly contiguous files are a good idea again. It is thus important to study old systems and ideas that were conceptually clean and simple because they may be applicable to future systems in surprising ways.

Linked List Allocation

The second method for storing files is to keep each one as a linked list of disk blocks, as shown in Fig. 6-13. The first word of each block is used as a pointer to the next one. The rest of the block is for data.

Unlike contiguous allocation, every disk block can be used in this method. No space is lost to disk fragmentation (except for internal fragmentation in the last block). Also, it is sufficient for the directory entry to merely store the disk address of the first block. The rest can be found starting there.

On the other hand, although reading a file sequentially is straightforward, random access is extremely slow. To get to block n, the operating system has to start at the beginning and read the $n - 1$ blocks prior to it, one at a time. Clearly, doing so many reads will be painfully slow.

Also, the amount of data storage in a block is no longer a power of two because the pointer takes up a few bytes. While not fatal, having a peculiar size is less efficient because many programs read and write in blocks whose size is a power of two. With the first few bytes of each block occupied to a pointer to the next block, reads of the full block size require acquiring and concatenating information from two disk blocks, which generates extra overhead due to the copying.

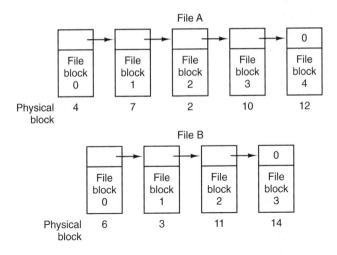

Figure 6-13. Storing a file as a linked list of disk blocks.

Linked List Allocation Using a Table in Memory

Both disadvantages of the linked list allocation can be eliminated by taking the pointer word from each disk block and putting it in a table in memory. Figure 6-14 shows what the table looks like for the example of Fig. 6-13. In both figures, we have two files. File *A* uses disk blocks 4, 7, 2, 10, and 12, in that order, and file *B* uses disk blocks 6, 3, 11, and 14, in that order. Using the table of Fig. 6-14, we can start with block 4 and follow the chain all the way to the end. The same can be done starting with block 6. Both chains are terminated with a special marker (e.g., −1) that is not a valid block number. Such a table in main memory is called a **FAT** (**File Allocation Table**).

Using this organization, the entire block is available for data. Furthermore, random access is much easier. Although the chain must still be followed to find a given offset within the file, the chain is entirely in memory, so it can be followed without making any disk references. Like the previous method, it is sufficient for the directory entry to keep a single integer (the starting block number) and still be able to locate all the blocks, no matter how large the file is.

The primary disadvantage of this method is that the entire table must be in memory all the time to make it work. With a 20-GB disk and a 1-KB block size, the table needs 20 million entries, one for each of the 20 million disk blocks. Each entry has to be a minimum of 3 bytes. For speed in lookup, they should be 4 bytes. Thus the table will take up 60 MB or 80 MB of main memory all the time, depending on whether the system is optimized for space or time. Conceivably the table could be put in pageable memory, but it would still occupy a great deal of virtual memory and disk space as well as generating extra paging traffic.

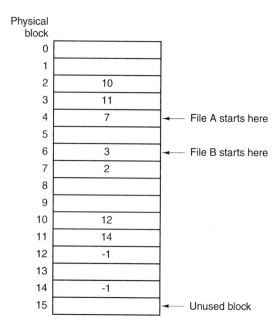

Figure 6-14. Linked list allocation using a file allocation table in main memory.

I-nodes

Our last method for keeping track of which blocks belong to which file is to associate with each file a data structure called an **i-node** (**index-node**), which lists the attributes and disk addresses of the file's blocks. A simple example is depicted in Fig. 6-15. Given the i-node, it is then possible to find all the blocks of the file. The big advantage of this scheme over linked files using an in-memory table is that the i-node need only be in memory when the corresponding file is open. If each i-node occupies n bytes and a maximum of k files may be open at once, the total memory occupied by the array holding the i-nodes for the open files is only kn bytes. Only this much space need be reserved in advance.

This array is usually far smaller than the space occupied by the file table described in the previous section. The reason is simple. The table for holding the linked list of all disk blocks is proportional in size to the disk itself. If the disk has n blocks, the table needs n entries. As disks grow larger, this table grows linearly with them. In contrast, the i-node scheme requires an array in memory whose size is proportional to the maximum number of files that may be open at once. It does not matter if the disk is 1 GB or 10 GB or 100 GB.

One problem with i-nodes is that if each one has room for a fixed number of disk addresses, what happens when a file grows beyond this limit? One solution is to reserve the last disk address not for a data block, but instead for the address

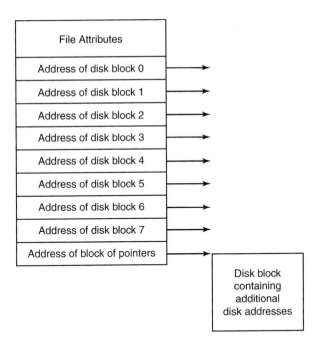

Figure 6-15. An example i-node.

of a block containing more disk block addresses, as shown in Fig. 6-15. Even more advanced would be two or more such blocks containing disk addresses or even disk blocks pointing to other disk blocks full of addresses. We will come back to i-nodes when studying UNIX later.

6.3.3　Implementing Directories

Before a file can be read, it must be opened. When a file is opened, the operating system uses the path name supplied by the user to locate the directory entry. The directory entry provides the information needed to find the disk blocks. Depending on the system, this information may be the disk address of the entire file (contiguous allocation), the number of the first block (both linked list schemes), or the number of the i-node. In all cases, the main function of the directory system is to map the ASCII name of the file onto the information needed to locate the data.

A closely related issue is where the attributes should be stored. Every file system maintains file attributes, such as each file's owner and creation time, and they must be stored somewhere. One obvious possibility is to store them directly in the directory entry. Many systems do precisely that. This option is shown in Fig. 6-16(a) In this simple design, a directory consists of a list of fixed-size entries, one per file, containing a (fixed-length) file name, a structure of the file attributes, and one or more disk addresses (up to some maximum) telling where the disk blocks are.

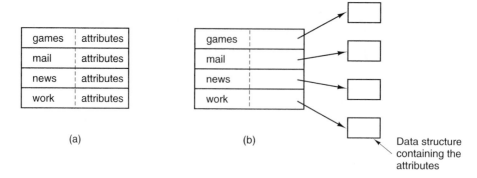

Figure 6-16. (a) A simple directory containing fixed-size entries with the disk addresses and attributes in the directory entry. (b) A directory in which each entry just refers to an i-node.

For systems that use i-nodes, another possibility for storing the attributes is in the i-nodes, rather than in the directory entries. In that case, the directory entry can be shorter: just a file name and an i-node number. This approach is illustrated in Fig. 6-16(b). As we shall see later, this method has certain advantages over putting them in the directory entry. The two approaches shown in Fig. 6-16 correspond to MS-DOS/Windows and UNIX, respectively, as we will see later in this chapter.

So far we have assumed that files have short, fixed-length names. In MS-DOS files have a 1-8 character base name and an optional extension of 1-3 characters. In UNIX Version 7, file names were 1-14 characters, including any extensions. However, nearly all modern operating systems support longer, variable-length file names. How can these be implemented?

The simplest approach is to set a limit on file name length, typically 255 characters, and then use one of the designs of Fig. 6-16 with 255 characters reserved for each file name. This approach is simple, but wastes a great deal of directory space, since few files have such long names. For efficiency reasons, a different structure is desirable.

One alternative is to give up the idea that all directory entries are the same size. With this method, each directory entry contains a fixed portion, typically starting with the length of the entry, and then followed by data with a fixed format, usually including the owner, creation time, protection information, and other attributes. This fixed-length header is followed by the actual file name, however long it may be, as shown in Fig. 6-17(a) in big-endian format (e.g., SPARC). In this example we have three files, *project-budget*, *personnel*, and *foo*. Each file name is terminated by a special character (usually 0), which is represented in the figure by a box with a cross in it. To allow each directory entry to begin on a word boundary, each file name is filled out to an integral number of words, shown by shaded boxes in the figure.

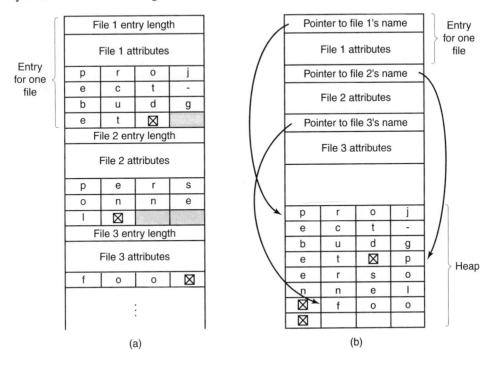

Figure 6-17. Two ways of handling long file names in a directory. (a) In-line. (b) In a heap.

A disadvantage of this method is that when a file is removed, a variable-sized gap is introduced into the directory into which the next file to be entered may not fit. This problem is the same one we saw with contiguous disk files, only now compacting the directory is feasible because it is entirely in memory. Another problem is that a single directory entry may span multiple pages, so a page fault may occur while reading a file name.

Another way to handle variable-length names is to make the directory entries themselves all fixed length and keep the file names together in a heap at the end of the directory, as shown in Fig. 6-17(b). This method has the advantage that when an entry is removed, the next file entered will always fit there. Of course, the heap must be managed and page faults can still occur while processing file names. One minor win here is that there is no longer any real need for file names to begin at word boundaries, so no filler characters are needed after file names in Fig. 6-17(b) and they are in Fig. 6-17(a).

In all of the designs so far, directories are searched linearly from beginning to end when a file name has to be looked up. For extremely long directories, linear searching can be slow. One way to speed up the search is to use a hash table in each directory. Call the size of the table n. To enter a file name, the name is hashed onto a value between 0 and $n - 1$, for example, by dividing it by n and taking the remainder. Alternatively, the words comprising the file name can be added up and this quantity divided by n, or something similar.

Either way, the table entry corresponding to the hash code is inspected. If it is unused, a pointer is placed there to the file entry. File entries follow the hash table. If that slot is already in use, a linked list is constructed, headed at that table entry and threading through all entries with the same hash value.

Looking up a file follows the same procedure. The file name is hashed to select a hash table entry. All the entries on the chain headed at that slot are checked to see if the file name is present. If the name is not on the chain, the file is not present in the directory.

Using a hash table has the advantage of much faster lookup, but the disadvantage of a more complex administration. It is only really a serious candidate in systems where it is expected that directories will routinely contain hundreds or thousands of files.

A completely different way to speed up searching large directories is to cache the results of searches. Before starting a search, a check is first made to see if the file name is in the cache. If so, it can be located quickly, avoiding a long lookup. Of course, caching only works if a relatively small number of files comprise the majority of the lookups.

6.3.4 Shared Files

When several users are working together on a project, they often need to share files. As a result, it is often convenient for a shared file to appear simultaneously in different directories belonging to different users. Figure 6-18 shows the file system of Fig. 6-9 again, only with one of C's files now present in one of B's directories as well. The connection between B's directory and the shared file is called a **link**. The file system itself is now a **Directed Acyclic Graph**, or **DAG**, rather than a tree.

Sharing files is convenient, but it also introduces some problems. To start with, if directories really do contain disk addresses, then a copy of the disk addresses will have to be made in B's directory when the file is linked. If either B or C subsequently appends to the file, the new blocks will be listed only in the directory of the user doing the append. The changes will not be visible to the other user, thus defeating the purpose of sharing.

This problem can be solved in two ways. In the first solution, disk blocks are not listed in directories, but in a little data structure associated with the file itself. The directories would then point just to the little data structure. This is the approach used in UNIX (where the little data structure is the i-node).

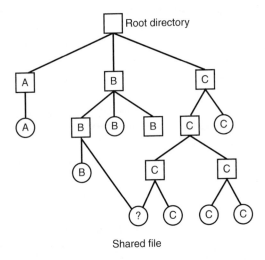

Figure 6-18. File system containing a shared file.

In the second solution, *B* links to one of *C*'s files by having the system create a new file, of type LINK, and entering that file in *B's* directory. The new file contains just the path name of the file to which it is linked. When *B* reads from the linked file, the operating system sees that the file being read from is of type LINK, looks up the name of the file, and reads that file. This approach is called **symbolic linking**.

Each of these methods has its drawbacks. In the first method, at the moment that *B* links to the shared file, the i-node records the file's owner as *C*. Creating a link does not change the ownership (see Fig. 6-19), but it does increase the link count in the i-node, so the system knows how many directory entries currently point to the file.

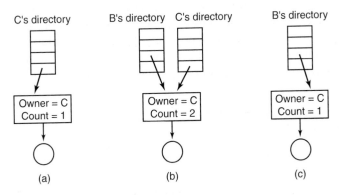

Figure 6-19. (a) Situation prior to linking. (b) After the link is created. (c) After the original owner removes the file.

If C subsequently tries to remove the file, the system is faced with a problem. If it removes the file and clears the i-node, B will have a directory entry pointing to an invalid i-node. If the i-node is later reassigned to another file, B's link will point to the wrong file. The system can see from the count in the i-node that the file is still in use, but there is no way for it to find all the directory entries for the file, in order to erase them. Pointers to the directories cannot be stored in the i-node because there can be an unlimited number of directories.

The only thing to do is remove C's directory entry, but leave the i-node intact, with count set to 1, as shown in Fig. 6-19(c). We now have a situation in which B is the only user having a directory entry for a file owned by C. If the system does accounting or has quotas, C will continue to be billed for the file until B decides to remove it, if ever, at which time the count goes to 0 and the file is deleted.

With symbolic links this problem does not arise because only the true owner has a pointer to the i-node. Users who have linked to the file just have path names, not i-node pointers. When the *owner* removes the file, it is destroyed. Subsequent attempts to use the file via a symbolic link will fail when the system is unable to locate the file. Removing a symbolic link does not affect the file at all.

The problem with symbolic links is the extra overhead required. The file containing the path must be read, then the path must be parsed and followed, component by component, until the i-node is reached. All of this activity may require a considerable number of extra disk accesses. Furthermore, an extra i-node is needed for each symbolic link, as is an extra disk block to store the path, although if the path name is short, the system could store it in the i-node itself, as an optimization. Symbolic links have the advantage that they can be used to link to files on machines anywhere in the world, by simply providing the network address of the machine where the file resides in addition to its path on that machine.

There is also another problem introduced by links, symbolic or otherwise. When links are allowed, files can have two or more paths. Programs that start at a given directory and find all the files in that directory and its subdirectories will locate a linked file multiple times. For example, a program that dumps all the files in a directory and its subdirectories onto a tape may make multiple copies of a linked file. Furthermore, if the tape is then read into another machine, unless the dump program is clever, the linked file will be copied twice onto the disk, instead of being linked.

6.3.5 Disk Space Management

Files are normally stored on disk, so management of disk space is a major concern to file system designers. Two general strategies are possible for storing an n byte file: n consecutive bytes of disk space are allocated, or the file is split up into a number of (not necessarily) contiguous blocks. The same trade-off is present in memory management systems between pure segmentation and paging.

As we have seen, storing a file as a contiguous sequence of bytes has the obvious problem that if a file grows, it will probably have to be moved on the disk. The same problem holds for segments in memory, except that moving a segment in memory is a relatively fast operation compared to moving a file from one disk position to another. For this reason, nearly all file systems chop files up into fixed-size blocks that need not be adjacent.

Block Size

Once it has been decided to store files in fixed-size blocks, the question arises of how big the block should be. Given the way disks are organized, the sector, the track and the cylinder are obvious candidates for the unit of allocation (although these are all device dependent, which is a minus). In a paging system, the page size is also a major contender.

Having a large allocation unit, such as a cylinder, means that every file, even a 1-byte file, ties up an entire cylinder. Studies (Mullender and Tanenbaum, 1984) have shown that the median file size in UNIX environments is about 1 KB, so allocating a 32-KB block for each file would waste 31/32 or 97 percent of the total disk space.

On the other hand, using a small allocation unit means that each file will consist of many blocks. Reading each block normally requires a seek and a rotational delay, so reading a file consisting of many small blocks will be slow.

As an example, consider a disk with 131,072 bytes per track, a rotation time of 8.33 msec, and an average seek time of 10 msec. The time in milliseconds to read a block of k bytes is then the sum of the seek, rotational delay, and transfer times:

$$10 + 4.165 + (k/131072) \times 8.33$$

The solid curve of Fig. 6-20 shows the data rate for such a disk as a function of block size. To compute the space efficiency, we need to make an assumption about the mean file size. A recent measurement at the author's department, which has 1000 users and over 1 million UNIX disk files, gives a median size of 1680 bytes, meaning that half the files are smaller than 1680 bytes and half are larger. As an aside, the median is a better metric than the mean because a very small number of files can influence the mean enormously, but not the median. (The mean is in fact 10,845 bytes, due in part to a few 100 MB hardware manuals that happen to be online). For simplicity, let us assume all files are 2 KB, which leads to the dashed curve in Fig. 6-20 for the disk space efficiency.

The two curves can be understood as follows. The access time for a block is completely dominated by the seek time and rotational delay, so given that it is going to cost 14 msec to access a block, the more data that are fetched, the better. Hence the data rate goes up with block size (until the transfers take so long that

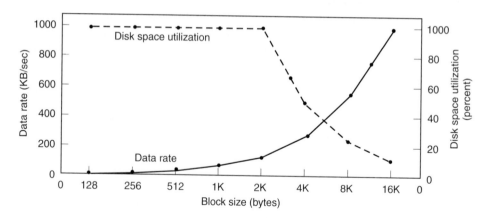

Figure 6-20. The solid curve (left-hand scale) gives the data rate of a disk. The dashed curve (right-hand scale) gives the disk space efficiency. All files are 2 KB.

the transfer time begins to dominate). With small blocks that are powers of two and 2-KB files, no space is wasted in a block. However, with 2-KB files and 4 KB or larger blocks, some disk space is wasted. In reality, few files are a multiple of the disk block size, so some space is always wasted in the last block of a file.

What the curves show, however, is that performance and space utilization are inherently in conflict. Small blocks are bad for performance but good for disk space utilization. A compromise size is needed. For this data, 4 KB might be a good choice, but some operating systems made their choices a long time ago, when the disk parameters and file sizes were different. For UNIX, 1 KB is commonly used. For MS-DOS the block size can be any power of two from 512 bytes to 32 KB, but is determined by the disk size and for reasons unrelated to these arguments (the maximum number of blocks on a disk partition is 2^{16}, which forces large blocks on large disks).

In an experiment to see if Windows NT file usage was appreciably different from UNIX file usage, Vogels made measurements on files at Cornell University (Vogels, 1999). He observed that NT file usage is more complicated than on UNIX. He wrote:

> *When we type a few characters in the* notepad *text editor, saving this to a file will trigger 26 system calls, including 3 failed open attempts, 1 file overwrite and 4 additional open and close sequences.*

Nevertheless, he observed a median size (weighted by usage) of files just read at 1 KB, files just written as 2.3 KB and files read and written as 4.2 KB. Given the fact that Cornell has much more large-scale scientific computing than the author's institution and the difference in measurement technique (static versus dynamic), the results are reasonably consistent with a median file size of around 2 KB.

Keeping Track of Free Blocks

Once a block size has been chosen, the next issue is how to keep track of free blocks. Two methods are widely used, as shown in Fig. 6-21. The first one consists of using a linked list of disk blocks, with each block holding as many free disk block numbers as will fit. With a 1-KB block and a 32-bit disk block number, each block on the free list holds the numbers of 255 free blocks. (One slot is needed for the pointer to the next block). A 16-GB disk needs a free list of maximum 16,794 blocks to hold all 2^{24} disk block numbers. Often free blocks are used to hold the free list.

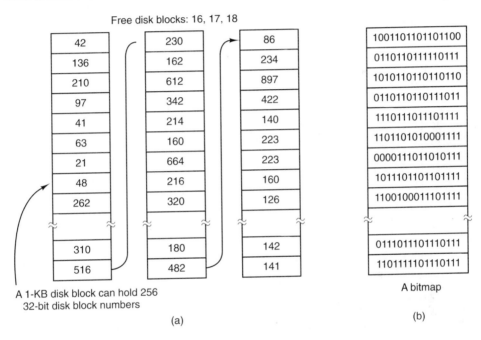

A 1-KB disk block can hold 256
32-bit disk block numbers

(a)

A bitmap

(b)

Figure 6-21. (a) Storing the free list on a linked list. (b) A bitmap.

The other free space management technique is the bitmap. A disk with n blocks requires a bitmap with n bits. Free blocks are represented by 1s in the map, allocated blocks by 0s (or vice versa). A 16-GB disk has 2^{24} 1-KB blocks and thus requires 2^{24} bits for the map, which requires 2048 blocks. It is not surprising that the bitmap requires less space, since it uses 1 bit per block, versus 32 bits in the linked list model. Only if the disk is nearly full (i.e., has few free blocks) will the linked list scheme require fewer blocks than the bitmap. On the other hand, if there are many blocks free, some of them can be borrowed to hold the free list without any loss of disk capacity.

When the free list method is used, only one block of pointers need be kept in main memory. When a file is created, the needed blocks are taken from the block of pointers. When it runs out, a new block of pointers is read in from the disk. Similarly, when a file is deleted, its blocks are freed and added to the block of pointers in main memory. When this block fills up, it is written to disk.

Under certain circumstances, this method leads to unnecessary disk I/O. Consider the situation of Fig. 6-22(a), in which the block of pointers in memory has room for only two more entries. If a three-block file is freed, the pointer block overflows and has to be written to disk, leading to the situation of Fig. 6-22(b). If a three-block file is now written, the full block of pointers has to be read in again, taking us back to Fig. 6-22(a). If the three-block file just written was a temporary file, when it is freed, another disk write is needed to write the full block of pointers back to the disk. In short, when the block of pointers is almost empty, a series of short-lived temporary files can cause a lot of disk I/O.

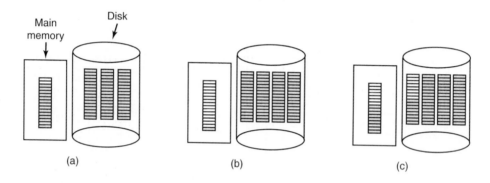

Figure 6-22. (a) An almost-full block of pointers to free disk blocks in memory and three blocks of pointers on disk. (b) Result of freeing a three-block file. (c) An alternative strategy for handling the three free blocks. The shaded entries represent pointers to free disk blocks.

An alternative approach that avoids most of this disk I/O is to split the full block of pointers. Thus instead of going from Fig. 6-22(a) to Fig. 6-22(b), we go from Fig. 6-22(a) to Fig. 6-22(c) when three blocks are freed. Now the system can handle a series of temporary files without doing any disk I/O. If the block in memory fills up, it is written to the disk and the half-full block from disk is read in. The idea here is to keep most of the pointer blocks on disk full (to minimize disk usage), but keep the one in memory about half full, so it can handle both file creation and file removal without disk I/O on the free list.

With a bitmap, it is also possible to keep just one block in memory, going to disk for another one only when it becomes full or empty. An additional benefit of this approach is that by doing all the allocation from a single block of the bitmap, the disk blocks will be close together, thus minimizing disk arm motion. Since the bitmap is a fixed-size data structure, if the kernel is (partially) paged, the bitmap can be put in virtual memory and have pages of it paged in as needed.

Disk Quotas

To prevent people from hogging too much disk space, multiuser operating systems often provide a mechanism for enforcing disk quotas. The idea is that the system administrator assigns each user a maximum allotment of files and blocks, and the operating system makes sure that the users do not exceed their quotas. A typical mechanism is described below.

When a user opens a file, the attributes and disk addresses are located and put into an open file table in main memory. Among the attributes is an entry telling who the owner is. Any increases in the file's size will be charged to the owner's quota.

A second table contains the quota record for every user with a currently open file, even if the file was opened by someone else. This table is shown in Fig. 6-23. It is an extract from a quota file on disk for the users whose files are currently open. When all the files are closed, the record is written back to the quota file.

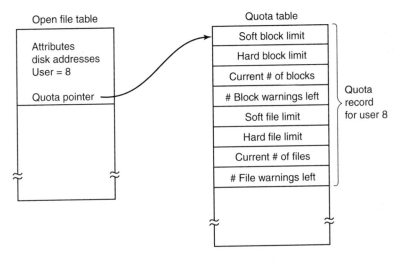

Figure 6-23. Quotas are kept track of on a per-user basis in a quota table.

When a new entry is made in the open file table, a pointer to the owner's quota record is entered into it, to make it easy to find the various limits. Every time a block is added to a file, the total number of blocks charged to the owner is incremented, and a check is made against both the hard and soft limits. The soft limit may be exceeded, but the hard limit may not. An attempt to append to a file when the hard block limit has been reached will result in an error. Analogous checks also exist for the number of files.

When a user attempts to log in, the system checks the quota file to see if the user has exceeded the soft limit for either number of files or number of disk blocks. If either limit has been violated, a warning is displayed, and the count of warnings remaining is reduced by one. If the count ever gets to zero, the user has ignored the warning one time too many, and is not permitted to log in. Getting permission to log in again will require some discussion with the system administrator.

This method has the property that users may go above their soft limits during a login session, provided they remove the excess before logging out. The hard limits may never be exceeded.

6.3.6 File System Reliability

Destruction of a file system is often a far greater disaster than destruction of a computer. If a computer is destroyed by fire, lightning surges, or a cup of coffee poured onto the keyboard, it is annoying and will cost money, but generally a replacement can be purchased with a minimum of fuss. Inexpensive personal computers can even be replaced within an hour by just going to the dealer (except at universities, where issuing a purchase order takes three committees, five signatures, and 90 days).

If a computer's file system is irrevocably lost, whether due to hardware, software, or rats gnawing on the floppy disks, restoring all the information will be difficult, time consuming, and in many cases, impossible. For the people whose programs, documents, customer files, tax records, databases, marketing plans, or other data are gone forever, the consequences can be catastrophic. While the file system cannot offer any protection against physical destruction of the equipment and media, it can help protect the information. In this section we will look at some of the issues involved in safeguarding the file system.

Floppy disks are generally perfect when they leave the factory, but they can develop bad blocks during use. Hard disks frequently have bad blocks right from the start: it is just too expensive to manufacture them completely free of all defects. As we saw in Chap. 5, bad blocks are generally handled by the controller by replacing bad sectors with spares provided for that purpose. Despite this technique, there are other reliability issues which we will consider below.

Backups

Most people do not think making backups of their files is worth the time and effort—until one fine day their disk abruptly dies, at which time most of them undergo a deathbed conversion. Companies, however, (usually) well understand the value of their data and generally do a backup at least once a day, usually to tape. Modern tapes hold tens or sometimes even hundreds of gigabytes and cost pennies per gigabyte. Nevertheless, Making backups is not quite as trivial as it sounds, so we will examine some of the related issues below.

Backups to tape are generally made to handle one of two potential problems:

1. Recover from disaster.

2. Recover from stupidity.

The first one covers getting the computer running again after a disk crash, fire, flood, or other natural catastrophe. In practice, these things do not happen very often, which is why many people do not bother with backups. These people also tend not to have fire insurance on their houses for the same reason.

The second reason is that users often accidentally remove files that they later need again. This problem occurs so often that when a file is "removed" in Windows, it is not deleted at all, but just moved to a special directory, the **recycle bin**, so it can be fished out and restored easily later. Backups take this principle further and allow files that were removed days, even weeks ago, to be restored from old backup tapes.

Making a backup takes a long time and occupies a large amount of space, so doing it efficiently and conveniently is important. These considerations raise the following issues. First, should the entire file system be backed up or only part of it? At many installations, the executable (binary) programs are kept in a limited part of the file system tree. It is not necessary to back up these files if they can all be reinstalled from the manufacturers' CD-ROMs. Also, most systems have a directory for temporary files. There is usually no reason to back it up either. In UNIX, all the special files (I/O devices) are kept in a directory /dev. Not only is backing up this directory not necessary, it is downright dangerous because the backup program would hang forever if it tried to read each of these to completion. In short, it is usually desirable to back up only specific directories and everything in them rather than the entire file system.

Second, it is wasteful to back up files that have not changed since the last backup, which leads to the idea of **incremental dumps**. The simplest form of incremental dumping is to make a complete dump (backup) periodically, say weekly or monthly, and to make a daily dump of only those files that have been modified since the last full dump. Even better is to dump only those files that have changed since they were last dumped. While this scheme minimizes dumping time, it makes recovery more complicated because first the most recent full dump has to be restored, followed by all the incremental dumps in reverse order. To ease recovery, more sophisticated incremental dumping schemes are often used.

Third, since immense amounts of data are typically dumped, it may be desirable to compress the data before writing them to tape. However, with many compression algorithms, a single bad spot on the backup tape can foil the decompression algorithm and make an entire file or even an entire tape unreadable. Thus the decision to compress the backup stream must be carefully considered.

Fourth, it is difficult to perform a backup on an active file system. If files and directories are being added, deleted, and modified during the dumping process, the resulting dump may be inconsistent. However, since making a dump may take hours, it may be necessary to take the system offline for much of the night to make the backup, something that is not always acceptable. For this reason, algorithms have been devised for making rapid snapshots of the file system state by copying critical data structures, and then requiring future changes to files and directories to copy the blocks instead of updating them in place (Hutchinson et al., 1999). In this way, the file system is effectively frozen at the moment of the snapshot, so it can be backed up at leisure afterward.

Fifth and last, making backups introduces many nontechnical problems into an organization. The best online security system in the world may be useless if the system administrator keeps all the backup tapes in his office and leaves it open and unguarded whenever he walks down the hall to get output from the printer. All a spy has to do is pop in for a second, put one tiny tape in his pocket, and saunter off jauntily. Goodbye security. Also, making a daily backup has little use if the fire that burns down the computers also burns up all the backup tapes. For this reason, backup tapes should be kept off-site, but that introduces more security risks. For a thorough discussion of these and other practical administration issues, see (Nemeth et al., 2000). Below we will discuss only the technical issues involved in making file system backups.

Two strategies can be used for dumping a disk to tape: a physical dump or a logical dump. A **physical dump** starts at block 0 of the disk, writes all the disk blocks onto the output tape in order, and stops when it has copied the last one. Such a program is so simple that it can probably be made 100% bug free, something that can probably not be said about any other useful program.

Nevertheless, it is worth making several comments about physical dumping. For one thing, there is no value in backing up unused disk blocks. If the dumping program can get access to the free block data structure, it can avoid dumping unused blocks. However, skipping unused blocks requires writing the number of each block in front of the block (or the equivalent), since it is no longer true that block k on the tape was block k on the disk.

A second concern is dumping bad blocks. If all bad blocks are remapped by the disk controller and hidden from the operating system as we described in Sec. 5.4.4, physical dumping works fine. On the other hand, if they are visible to the operating system and maintained in one or more "bad block files" or bitmaps, it is absolutely essential that the physical dumping program get access to this information and avoid dumping them to prevent endless disk read errors during the dumping process.

The main advantages of physical dumping are simplicity and great speed (basically, it can run at the speed of the disk). The main disadvantages are the inability to skip selected directories, make incremental dumps, and restore individual files upon request. For these reasons, most installations make logical dumps.

A **logical dump** starts at one or more specified directories and recursively dumps all files and directories found there that have changed since some given base date (e.g., the last backup for an incremental dump or system installation for a full dump). Thus in a logical dump, the dump tape gets a series of carefully identified directories and files, which makes it easy to restore a specific file or directory upon request.

Since logical dumping is the most common form, let us examine a common algorithm in detail using the example of Fig. 6-24 to guide us. Most UNIX systems use this algorithm. In the figure we see a file tree with directories (squares) and files (circles). The shaded items have been modified since the base date and thus need to be dumped. The unshaded ones do not need to be dumped.

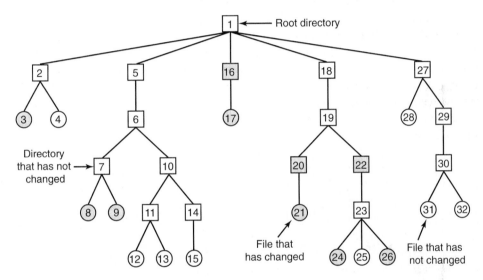

Figure 6-24. A file system to be dumped. The squares are directories and the circles are files. The shaded items have been modified since the last dump. Each directory and file is labeled by its i-node number.

This algorithm also dumps all directories (even unmodified ones) that lie on the path to a modified file or directory for two reasons. First, to make it possible to restore the dumped files and directories to a fresh file system on a different computer. In this way, the dump and restore programs can be used to transport entire file systems between computers.

The second reason for dumping unmodified directories above modified files is to make it possible to incrementally restore a single file (possibly to handle recovery from stupidity). Suppose that a full file system dump is done Sunday evening and an incremental dump is done on Monday evening. On Tuesday the directory */usr/jhs/proj/nr3* is removed, along with all the directories and files under it. On Wednesday morning bright and early the user wants to restore the file */usr/jhs/proj/nr3/plans/summary* However, is not possible to just restore the file *summary* because there is no place to put it. The directories *nr3* and *plans* must be restored first. To get their owners, modes, times, etc., correct, these directories must be present on the dump tape even though they themselves were not modified since the previous full dump.

The dump algorithm maintains a bitmap indexed by i-node number with several bits per i-node. Bits will be set and cleared in this map as the algorithm proceeds. The algorithm operates in four phases. Phase 1 begins at the starting directory (the root in this example) and examines all the entries in it. For each modified file, its i-node is marked in the bitmap. Each directory is also marked (whether or not it has been modified) and then recursively inspected.

At the end of phase 1, all modified files and all directories have been marked in the bitmap, as shown (by shading) in Fig. 6-25(a). Phase 2 conceptually recursively walks the tree again, unmarking any directories that have no modified files or directories in them or under them. This phase leaves the bitmap as shown in Fig. 6-25(b). Note that directories 10, 11, 14, 27, 29, and 30 are now unmarked because they contain nothing under them that has been modified. They will not be dumped. In contrast, directories 5 and 6 will be dumped even though they themselves have not been modified because they will be needed to restore today's changes to a fresh machine. For efficiency, phases 1 and 2 can be combined in one tree walk.

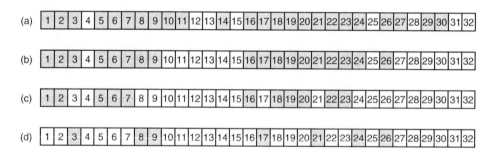

Figure 6-25. Bit maps used by the logical dumping algorithm.

At this point it is known which directories and files must be dumped. These are the ones marked in Fig. 6-25(b). Phase 3 consists of scanning the i-nodes in numerical order and dumping all the directories that are marked for dumping. These are shown in Fig. 6-25(c). Each directory is prefixed by the directory's attributes (owner, times, etc.) so they can be restored. Finally, in phase 4, the files marked in Fig. 6-25(d) are also dumped, again prefixed by their attributes. This completes the dump.

Restoring a file system from the dump tapes is straightforward. To start with, an empty file system is created on the disk. Then the most recent full dump is restored. Since the directories appear first on the tape, they are all restored first, giving a skeleton of the file system. Then the files themselves are restored. This process is then repeated with the first incremental dump made after the full dump, then the next one, and so on.

Although logical dumping is straightforward, there are a few tricky issues. For one, since the free block list is not a file, it is not dumped and hence it must be reconstructed from scratch after all the dumps have been restored. Doing so is always possible since the set of free blocks is just the complement of the set of blocks contained in all the files combined.

Another issue is links. If a file is linked to two or more directories, it is important that the file is restored only one time and that all the directories that are supposed to point to it do so.

Still another issue is the fact that UNIX files may contain holes. It is legal to open a file, write a few bytes, then seek to a distant file offset and write a few more bytes. The blocks in between are not part of the file and should not be dumped and not be restored. Core files often have a large hole between the data segment and the stack. If not handled properly, each restored core file will fill this area with zeros and thus be the same size as the virtual address space (e.g., 2^{32} bytes, or worse yet, 2^{64} bytes).

Finally, special files, named pipes, and the like should never be dumped, no matter in which directory they may occur (they need not be confined to */dev*). For more information about file system backups, see (Chervenak et al., 1998; and Zwicky, 1991).

File System Consistency

Another area where reliability is an issue is file system consistency. Many file systems read blocks, modify them, and write them out later. If the system crashes before all the modified blocks have been written out, the file system can be left in an inconsistent state. This problem is especially critical if some of the blocks that have not been written out are i-node blocks, directory blocks, or blocks containing the free list.

To deal with the problem of inconsistent file systems, most computers have a utility program that checks file system consistency. For example, UNIX has *fsck* and Windows has *scandisk*. This utility can be run whenever the system is booted, especially after a crash. The description below tells how *fsck* works. *Scandisk* is somewhat different because it works on a different file system, but the general principle of using the file system's inherent redundancy to repair it is still valid. All file system checkers verify each file system (disk partition) independently of the other ones.

Two kinds of consistency checks can be made: blocks and files. To check for block consistency, the program builds two tables, each one containing a counter for each block, initially set to 0. The counters in the first table keep track of how many times each block is present in a file; the counters in the second table record how often each block is present in the free list (or the bitmap of free blocks).

The program then reads all the i-nodes. Starting from an i-node, it is possible to build a list of all the block numbers used in the corresponding file. As each block number is read, its counter in the first table is incremented. The program then examines the free list or bitmap, to find all the blocks that are not in use. Each occurrence of a block in the free list results in its counter in the second table being incremented.

If the file system is consistent, each block will have a 1 either in the first table or in the second table, as illustrated in Fig. 6-26(a). However, as a result of a crash, the tables might look like Fig. 6-26(b), in which block 2 does not occur in either table. It will be reported as being a **missing block**. While missing blocks do no real harm, they do waste space and thus reduce the capacity of the disk. The solution to missing blocks is straightforward: the file system checker just adds them to the free list.

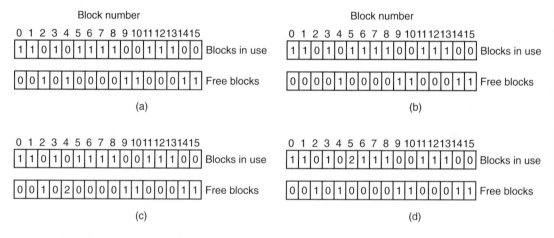

Figure 6-26. File system states. (a) Consistent. (b) Missing block. (c) Duplicate block in free list. (d) Duplicate data block.

Another situation that might occur is that of Fig. 6-26(c). Here we see a block, number 4, that occurs twice in the free list. (Duplicates can occur only if the free list is really a list; with a bitmap it is impossible.) The solution here is also simple: rebuild the free list.

The worst thing that can happen is that the same data block is present in two or more files, as shown in Fig. 6-26(d) with block 5. If either of these files is removed, block 5 will be put on the free list, leading to a situation in which the same block is both in use and free at the same time. If both files are removed, the block will be put onto the free list twice.

The appropriate action for the file system checker to take is to allocate a free block, copy the contents of block 5 into it, and insert the copy into one of the files.

In this way, the information content of the files is unchanged (although almost assuredly one is garbled), but the file system structure is at least made consistent. The error should be reported, to allow the user to inspect the damage.

In addition to checking to see that each block is properly accounted for, the file system checker also checks the directory system. It, too, uses a table of counters, but these are per file, rather than per block. It starts at the root directory and recursively descends the tree, inspecting each directory in the file system. For every file in every directory, it increments a counter for that file's usage count. Remember that due to hard links, a file may appear in two or more directories. Symbolic links do not count and do not cause the counter for the target file to be incremented.

When it is all done, it has a list, indexed by i-node number, telling how many directories contain each file. It then compares these numbers with the link counts stored in the i-nodes themselves. These counts start at 1 when a file is created and are incremented each time a (hard) link is made to the file. In a consistent file system, both counts will agree. However, two kinds of errors can occur: the link count in the i-node can be too high or it can be too low.

If the link count is higher than the number of directory entries, then even if all the files are removed from the directories, the count will still be nonzero and the i-node will not be removed. This error is not serious, but it wastes space on the disk with files that are not in any directory. It should be fixed by setting the link count in the i-node to the correct value.

The other error is potentially catastrophic. If two directory entries are linked to a file, but the i-node says that there is only one, when either directory entry is removed, the i-node count will go to zero. When an i-node count goes to zero, the file system marks it as unused and releases all of its blocks. This action will result in one of the directories now pointing to an unused i-node, whose blocks may soon be assigned to other files. Again, the solution is just to force the link count in the i-node to the actual number of directory entries.

These two operations, checking blocks and checking directories, are often integrated for efficiency reasons (i.e., only one pass over the i-nodes is required). Other checks are also possible. For example, directories have a definite format, with i-node numbers and ASCII names. If an i-node number is larger than the number of i-nodes on the disk, the directory has been damaged.

Furthermore, each i-node has a mode, some of which are legal but strange, such as 0007, which allows the owner and his group no access at all, but allows outsiders to read, write, and execute the file. It might be useful to at least report files that give outsiders more rights than the owner. Directories with more than, say, 1000 entries are also suspicious. Files located in user directories, but which are owned by the superuser and have the SETUID bit on, are potential security problems because such files acquire the powers of the superuser when executed by any user. With a little effort, one can put together a fairly long list of technically legal but still peculiar situations that might be worth reporting.

The previous paragraphs have discussed the problem of protecting the user against crashes. Some file systems also worry about protecting the user against himself. If the user intends to type

rm *.o

to remove all the files ending with *.o* (compiler generated object files), but accidentally types

rm * .o

(note the space after the asterisk), *rm* will remove all the files in the current directory and then complain that it cannot find *.o*. In MS-DOS and some other systems, when a file is removed, all that happens is that a bit is set in the directory or i-node marking the file as removed. No disk blocks are returned to the free list until they are actually needed. Thus, if the user discovers the error immediately, it is possible to run a special utility program that "unremoves" (i.e., restores) the removed files. In Windows, files that are removed are placed in the recycle bin, from which they can later be retrieved if need be. Of course, no storage is reclaimed until they are actually deleted from this directory.

6.3.7 File System Performance

Access to disk is much slower than access to memory. Reading a memory word might take 10 nsec. Reading from a hard disk might proceed at 10 MB/sec, which is forty times slower per 32-bit word, but to this must be added 5–10 msec to seek to the track and then wait for the desired sector to arrive under the read head. If only a single word is needed, the memory access is on the order of a million times as fast as disk access. As a result of this difference in access time, many file systems have been designed with various optimizations to improve performance. In this section we will cover three of them.

Caching

The most common technique used to reduce disk accesses is the **block cache** or **buffer cache**. (Cache is pronounced "cash" and is derived from the French *cacher*, meaning to hide.) In this context, a cache is a collection of blocks that logically belong on the disk but are being kept in memory for performance reasons.

Various algorithms can be used to manage the cache, but a common one is to check all read requests to see if the needed block is in the cache. If it is, the read request can be satisfied without a disk access. If the block is not in the cache, it is first read into the cache, and then copied to wherever it is needed. Subsequent requests for the same block can be satisfied from the cache.

Operation of the cache is illustrated in Fig. 6-27. Since there are many (often thousands of) blocks in the cache, some way is needed to determine quickly if a given block is present. The usual way is to hash the device and disk address and look up the result in a hash table. All the blocks with the same hash value are chained together on a linked list so the collision chain can be followed.

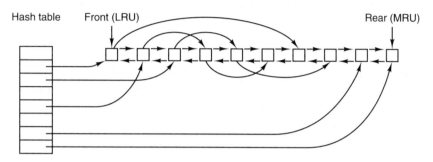

Figure 6-27. The buffer cache data structures.

When a block has to be loaded into a full cache, some block has to be removed (and rewritten to the disk if it has been modified since being brought in). This situation is very much like paging, and all the usual page replacement algorithms described in Chap. 3, such as FIFO, second chance, and LRU, are applicable. One pleasant difference between paging and caching is that cache references are relatively infrequent, so that it is feasible to keep all the blocks in exact LRU order with linked lists.

In Fig. 6-27, we see that in addition to the collision chains starting at the hash table, there is also a bidirectional list running through all the blocks in the order of usage, with the least recently used block on the front of this list and the most recently used block at the end of this list. When a block is referenced, it can be removed from its position on the bidirectional list and put at the end. In this way, exact LRU order can be maintained.

Unfortunately, there is a catch. Now that we have a situation in which exact LRU is possible, it turns out that LRU is undesirable. The problem has to do with the crashes and file system consistency discussed in the previous section. If a critical block, such as an i-node block, is read into the cache and modified, but not rewritten to the disk, a crash will leave the file system in an inconsistent state. If the i-node block is put at the end of the LRU chain, it may be quite a while before it reaches the front and is rewritten to the disk.

Furthermore, some blocks, such as i-node blocks, are rarely referenced two times within a short interval. These considerations lead to a modified LRU scheme, taking two factors into account:

1. Is the block likely to be needed again soon?
2. Is the block essential to the consistency of the file system?

For both questions, blocks can be divided into categories such as i-node blocks, indirect blocks, directory blocks, full data blocks, and partially full data blocks.

Blocks that will probably not be needed again soon go on the front, rather than the rear of the LRU list, so their buffers will be reused quickly. Blocks that might be needed again soon, such as a partly full block that is being written, go on the end of the list, so they will stay around for a long time.

The second question is independent of the first one. If the block is essential to the file system consistency (basically, everything except data blocks), and it has been modified, it should be written to disk immediately, regardless of which end of the LRU list it is put on. By writing critical blocks quickly, we greatly reduce the probability that a crash will wreck the file system. While a user may be unhappy if one of his files is ruined in a crash, he is likely to be far more unhappy if the whole file system is lost.

Even with this measure to keep the file system integrity intact, it is undesirable to keep data blocks in the cache too long before writing them out. Consider the plight of someone who is using a personal computer to write a book. Even if our writer periodically tells the editor to write the file being edited to the disk, there is a good chance that everything will still be in the cache and nothing on the disk. If the system crashes, the file system structure will not be corrupted, but a whole day's work will be lost.

This situation need not happen very often before we have a fairly unhappy user. Systems take two approaches to dealing with it. The UNIX way is to have a system call, sync, which forces all the modified blocks out onto the disk immediately. When the system is started up, a program, usually called *update*, is started up in the background to sit in an endless loop issuing sync calls, sleeping for 30 sec between calls. As a result, no more than 30 seconds of work is lost due to a crash.

The MS-DOS way is to write every modified block to disk as soon as it has been written. Caches in which all modified blocks are written back to the disk immediately are called **write-through caches**. They require more disk I/O than nonwrite-through caches. The difference between these two approaches can be seen when a program writes a 1-KB block full, one character at a time. UNIX will collect all the characters in the cache and write the block out once every 30 seconds, or whenever the block is removed from the cache. MS-DOS will make a disk access for every character written. Of course, most programs do internal buffering, so they normally write not a character, but a line or a larger unit on each write system call.

A consequence of this difference in caching strategy is that just removing a (floppy) disk from a UNIX system without doing a sync will almost always result in lost data, and frequently in a corrupted file system as well. With MS-DOS, no problem arises. These differing strategies were chosen because UNIX was developed in an environment in which all disks were hard disks and not removable, whereas MS-DOS started out in the floppy disk world. As hard disks became the norm, the UNIX approach, with its better efficiency, became the norm, and is also used now on Windows for hard disks.

Block Read Ahead

A second technique for improving perceived file system performance is to try to get blocks into the cache before they are needed to increase the hit rate. In particular, many files are read sequentially. When the file system is asked to produce block k in a file, it does that, but when it is finished, it makes a sneaky check in the cache to see if block $k + 1$ is already there. If it is not, it schedules a read for block $k + 1$ in the hope that when it is needed, it will have already arrived in the cache. At the very least, it will be on the way.

Of course, this read ahead strategy only works for files that are being read sequentially. If a file is being randomly accessed, read ahead does not help. In fact, it hurts by tying up disk bandwidth reading in useless blocks and removing potentially useful blocks from the cache (and possibly tying up more disk bandwidth writing them back to disk if they are dirty). To see whether read ahead is worth doing, the file system can keep track of the access patterns to each open file. For example, a bit associated with each file can keep track of whether the file is in "sequential access mode" or "random access mode." Initially, the file is given the benefit of the doubt and put in sequential access mode. However, whenever a seek is done, the bit is cleared. If sequential reads start happening again, the bit is set once again. In this way, the file system can make a reasonable guess about whether it should read ahead or not. If it gets it wrong once it a while, it is not a disaster, just a little bit of wasted disk bandwidth.

Reducing Disk Arm Motion

Caching and read ahead are not the only ways to increase file system performance. Another important technique is to reduce the amount of disk arm motion by putting blocks that are likely to be accessed in sequence close to each other, preferably in the same cylinder. When an output file is written, the file system has to allocate the blocks one at a time, as they are needed. If the free blocks are recorded in a bitmap, and the whole bitmap is in main memory, it is easy enough to choose a free block as close as possible to the previous block. With a free list, part of which is on disk, it is much harder to allocate blocks close together.

However, even with a free list, some block clustering can be done. The trick is to keep track of disk storage not in blocks, but in groups of consecutive blocks. If sectors consist of 512 bytes, the system could use 1-KB blocks (2 sectors) but allocate disk storage in units of 2 blocks (4 sectors). This is not the same as having a 2-KB disk blocks, since the cache would still use 1-KB blocks and disk transfers would still be 1 KB but reading a file sequentially on an otherwise idle system would reduce the number of seeks by a factor of two, considerably improving performance. A variation on the same theme is to take account of rotational positioning. When allocating blocks, the system attempts to place consecutive blocks in a file in the same cylinder.

Another performance bottleneck in systems that use i-nodes or anything equivalent to i-nodes is that reading even a short file requires two disk accesses: one for the i-node and one for the block. The usual i-node placement is shown in Fig. 6-28(a). Here all the i-nodes are near the beginning of the disk, so the average distance between an i-node and its blocks will be about half the number of cylinders, requiring long seeks.

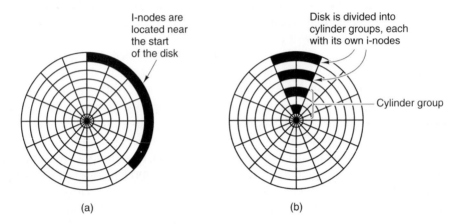

Figure 6-28. (a) I-nodes placed at the start of the disk. (b) Disk divided into cylinder groups, each with its own blocks and i-nodes.

One easy performance improvement is to put the i-nodes in the middle of the disk, rather than at the start, thus reducing the average seek between the i-node and the first block by a factor of two. Another idea, shown in Fig. 6-28(b), is to divide the disk into cylinder groups, each with its own i-nodes, blocks, and free list (McKusick et al., 1984). When creating a new file, any i-node can be chosen, but an attempt is made to find a block in the same cylinder group as the i-node. If none is available, then a block in a nearby cylinder group is used.

6.3.8 Log-Structured File Systems

Changes in technology are putting pressure on current file systems. In particular, CPUs keep getting faster, disks are becoming much bigger and cheaper (but not much faster), and memories are growing exponentially in size. The one parameter that is not improving by leaps and bounds is disk seek time. The combination of these factors means that a performance bottleneck is arising in many file systems. Research done at Berkeley attempted to alleviate this problem by designing a completely new kind of file system, LFS (the **Log-structured File System**). In this section we will briefly describe how LFS works. For a more complete treatment, see (Rosenblum and Ousterhout, 1991).

The idea that drove the LFS design is that as CPUs get faster and RAM memories get larger, disk caches are also increasing rapidly. Consequently, it is now possible to satisfy a very substantial fraction of all read requests directly from the file system cache, with no disk access needed. It follows from this observation, that in the future, most disk accesses will be writes, so the read-ahead mechanism used in some file systems to fetch blocks before they are needed no longer gains much performance.

To make matters worse, in most file systems, writes are done in very small chunks. Small writes are highly inefficient, since a 50-μsec disk write is often preceded by a 10-msec seek and a 4-msec rotational delay. With these parameters, disk efficiency drops to a fraction of 1 percent.

To see where all the small writes come from, consider creating a new file on a UNIX system. To write this file, the i-node for the directory, the directory block, the i-node for the file, and the file itself must all be written. While these writes can be delayed, doing so exposes the file system to serious consistency problems if a crash occurs before the writes are done. For this reason, the i-node writes are generally done immediately.

From this reasoning, the LFS designers decided to re-implement the UNIX file system in such a way as to achieve the full bandwidth of the disk, even in the face of a workload consisting in large part of small random writes. The basic idea is to structure the entire disk as a log. Periodically, and when there is a special need for it, all the pending writes being buffered in memory are collected into a single segment and written to the disk as a single contiguous segment at the end of the log. A single segment may thus contain i-nodes, directory blocks, and data blocks, all mixed together. At the start of each segment is a segment summary, telling what can be found in the segment. If the average segment can be made to be about 1 MB, almost the full bandwidth of the disk can be utilized.

In this design, i-nodes still exist and have the same structure as in UNIX, but they are now scattered all over the log, instead of being at a fixed position on the disk. Nevertheless, when an i-node is located, locating the blocks is done in the usual way. Of course, finding an i-node is now much harder, since its address cannot simply be calculated from its i-number, as in UNIX. To make it possible to find i-nodes, an i-node map, indexed by i-number, is maintained. Entry i in this map points to i-node i on the disk. The map is kept on disk, but it is also cached, so the most heavily used parts will be in memory most of the time.

To summarize what we have said so far, all writes are initially buffered in memory, and periodically all the buffered writes are written to the disk in a single segment, at the end of the log. Opening a file now consists of using the map to locate the i-node for the file. Once the i-node has been located, the addresses of the blocks can be found from it. All of the blocks will themselves be in segments, somewhere in the log.

If disks were infinitely large, the above description would be the entire story. However, real disks are finite, so eventually the log will occupy the entire disk, at which time no new segments can be written to the log. Fortunately, many existing segments may have blocks that are no longer needed, for example, if a file is overwritten, its i-node will now point to the new blocks, but the old ones will still be occupying space in previously written segments.

To deal with this problem, LFS has a **cleaner** thread that spends its time scanning the log circularly to compact it. It starts out by reading the summary of the first segment in the log to see which i-nodes and files are there. It then checks the current i-node map to see if the i-nodes are still current and file blocks are still in use. If not, that information is discarded. The i-nodes and blocks that are still in use go into memory to be written out in the next segment. The original segment is then marked as free, so the log can use it for new data. In this manner, the cleaner moves along the log, removing old segments from the back and putting any live data into memory for rewriting in the next segment. Consequently, the disk is a big circular buffer, with the writer thread adding new segments to the front and the cleaner thread removing old ones from the back.

The bookkeeping here is nontrivial, since when a file block is written back to a new segment, the i-node of the file (somewhere in the log) must be located, updated, and put into memory to be written out in the next segment. The i-node map must then be updated to point to the new copy. Nevertheless, it is possible to do the administration, and the performance results show that all this complexity is worthwhile. Measurements given in the papers cited above show that LFS outperforms UNIX by an order of magnitude on small writes, while having a performance that is as good as or better than UNIX for reads and large writes.

6.4 EXAMPLE FILE SYSTEMS

In the following sections we will discuss several example file systems, ranging from quite simple to highly sophisticated. Since modern UNIX file systems and Windows 2000's native file system are covered in the chapter on UNIX (Chap. 10) and the chapter on Windows 2000 (Chap. 11) we will not cover those systems here. We will, however, examine their predecessors below.

6.4.1 CD-ROM File Systems

As our first example of a file system, let us consider the file systems used on CD-ROMs. These systems are particularly simple because they were designed for write-once media. Among other things, for example, they have no provision for keeping track of free blocks because on a CD-ROM files cannot be freed or added after the disk has been manufactured. Below we will take a look at the main CD-ROM file system type and two extensions to it.

The ISO 9660 File System

The most common standard for CD-ROM file systems was adopted as an International Standard in 1988 under the name **ISO 9660**. Virtually every CD-ROM currently on the market is compatible with this standard, sometimes with the extensions to be discussed below. One of the goals of this standard was to make every CD-ROM readable on every computer, independent of the byte ordering used and independent of the operating system used. As a consequence, some limitations were placed on the file system to make it possible for the weakest operating systems then in use (such as MS-DOS) to read it.

CD-ROMs do not have concentric cylinders the way magnetic disks do. Instead there is a single continuous spiral containing the bits in a linear sequence (although seeks across the spiral are possible). The bits along the spiral are divided into logical blocks (also called logical sectors) of 2352 bytes. Some of these are for preambles, error correction, and other overhead. The payload portion of each logical block is 2048 bytes. When used for music, CDs have leadins, leadouts, and intertrack gaps, but these are not used for data CD-ROMs. Often the position of a block along the spiral is quoted in minutes and seconds. It can be converted to a linear block number using the conversion factor of 1 sec = 75 blocks.

ISO 9660 supports CD-ROM sets with as many as $2^{16} - 1$ CDs in the set. The individual CD-ROMs may also be partitioned into logical volumes (partitions). However, below we will concentrate on ISO 9660 for a single unpartitioned CD-ROM.

Every CD-ROM begins with 16 blocks whose function is not defined by the ISO 9660 standard. A CD-ROM manufacturer could use this area for providing a bootstrap program to allow the computer to be booted from the CD-ROM, or for some other purpose. Next comes one block containing the **primary volume descriptor**, which contains some general information about the CD-ROM. Among this information are the system identifier (32 bytes), volume identifier (32 bytes), publisher identifier (128 bytes), and data preparer identifier (128 bytes). The manufacturer can fill in these fields in any desired way, except that only upper case letters, digits, and a very small number of punctuation marks may be used to ensure cross-platform compatibility.

The primary volume descriptor also contains the names of three files, which may contain the abstract, copyright notice, and bibliographic information, respectively. In addition, certain key numbers are also present, including the logical block size (normally 2048, but 4096, 8192, and larger powers of two are allowed in certain cases), the number of blocks on the CD-ROM, and the creation and expiration dates of the CD-ROM. Finally, the primary volume descriptor also contains a directory entry for the root directory, telling where to find it on the CD-ROM (i.e., which block it starts at). From this directory, the rest of the file system can be located.

In addition to the primary volume descriptor, a CD-ROM may contain a supplementary volume descriptor. It contains similar information to the primary, but that will not concern us here.

The root directory, and all other directories for that matter, consists of a variable number of entries, the last of which contains a bit marking it as the final one.

The directory entries themselves are also variable length. Each directory entry consists of 10 to 12 fields, some of which are in ASCII and others of which are numerical fields in binary. The binary fields are encoded twice, once in little-endian format (used on Pentiums, for example) and once in big-endian format (used on SPARCs, for example). Thus a 16-bit number uses 4 bytes and a 32-bit number uses 8 bytes. The use of this redundant coding was necessary to avoid hurting anyone's feelings when the standard was developed. If the standard had dictated little endian, then people from companies with big-endian products would have felt like second-class citizens and would not have accepted the standard. The emotional content of a CD-ROM can thus be quantified and measured exactly in kilobytes/hour of wasted space.

The format of an ISO 9660 directory entry is illustrated in Fig. 6-29. Since directory entries have variable lengths, the first field is a byte telling how long the entry is. This byte is defined to have the high-order bit on the left to avoid any ambiguity.

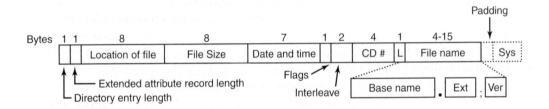

Figure 6-29. The ISO 9660 directory enty.

Directory entries may optionally have an extended attributes. If this feature is used for a directory entry, the second byte tells how long the extended attributes are.

Next comes the starting block of the file itself. Files are stored as contiguous runs of blocks, so a file's location is completely specified by the starting block and the size, which is contained in the next field.

The date and time that the CD-ROM was recorded is stored in the next field, with separate bytes for the year, month, day, hour, minute, second, and time zone. Years begin to count at 1900, which means that CD-ROMs will suffer from a Y2156 problem because the year following 2155 will be 1900. This problem could have been delayed by defining the origin of time to be 1988 (the year the standard was adopted). Had that been done, the problem would have been post-poned until 2244. Every 88 extra years helps.

The *Flags* field contains a few miscellaneous bits, including one to hide the entry in listings (a feature copied from MS-DOS), one to distinguish an entry that is a file from an entry that is a directory, one to enable the use of the extended attributes, and one to mark the last entry in a directory. A few other bits are also present in this field but they will not concern us here. The next field deals with interleaving pieces of files in a way that is not used in the simplest version of ISO 9660, so we will not consider it further.

The next field tells which CD-ROM the file is located on. It is permitted that a directory entry on one CD-ROM refers to a file located on another CD-ROM in the set. In this way it is possible to build a master directory on the first CD-ROM that lists all the files on all the CD-ROMs in the complete set.

The field marked L in Fig. 6-29 gives the size of the file name in bytes. It is followed by the file name itself. A file name consists of a base name, a dot, an extension, a semicolon, and a binary version number (1 or 2 bytes). The base name and extension may use upper case letters, the digits 0–9, and the underscore character. All other characters are forbidden to make sure that every computer can handle every file name. The base name can be up to eight characters; the extension can be up to three characters. These choices were dictated by the need to be MS-DOS compatible. A file name may be present in a directory multiple times, as long as each one has a different version number.

The last two fields are not always present. The *Padding* field is used to force every directory entry to be an even number of bytes, to align the numeric fields of subsequent entries on 2-byte boundaries. If padding is needed, a 0 byte is used. Finally, we have the *System use* field. Its function and size are undefined, except that it must be an even number of bytes. Different systems use it in different ways. The Macintosh keeps Finder flags here, for example.

Entries within a directory are listed in alphabetical order except for the first two entries. The first entry is for the directory itself. The second one is for its parent. In this respect, these entries are similar to the UNIX . and .. directory entries. The files themselves need not be in directory order.

There is no explicit limit to the number of entries in a directory. However, there is a limit to the depth of nesting. The maximum depth of directory nesting is eight.

ISO 9660 defines what are called three levels. Level 1 is the most restrictive and specifies that file names are limited to 8 + 3 characters as we have described, and also requires all files to be contiguous as we have described. Furthermore, it specifies that directory names be limited to eight characters with no extensions. Use of this level maximizes the chances that a CD-ROM can be read on every computer.

Level 2 relaxes the length restriction. It allows files and directories to have names of up to 31 characters, but still from the same set of characters.

Level 3 uses the same name limits as level 2, but partially relaxes the assumption that files have to be contiguous. With this level, a file may consist of several sections, each of which is a contiguous run of blocks. The same run may occur multiple times in a file and may also occur in two or more files. If large chunks of data are repeated in several files, level 3 provides some space optimization by not requiring the data to be present multiple times.

Rock Ridge Extensions

As we have seen, ISO 9660 is highly restrictive in several ways. Shortly after it came out, people in the UNIX community began working on an extension to make it possible to represent UNIX file systems on a CD-ROM. These extensions were named Rock Ridge, after a town in the Gene Wilder movie *Blazing Saddles*, probably because one of the committee members liked the film.

The extensions use the *System use* field in order to make Rock Ridge CD-ROMs readable on any computer. All the other fields retain their normal ISO 9660 meaning. Any system not aware of the Rock Ridge extensions just ignores them and sees a normal CD-ROM.

The extensions are divided up into the following fields:

1. PX - POSIX attributes.

2. PN - Major and minor device numbers.

3. SL - Symbolic link.

4. NM - Alternative name.

5. CL - Child location.

6. PL - Parent location.

7. RE - Relocation.

8. TF - Time stamps.

The *PX* field contains the standard UNIX *rwxrwxrwx* permission bits for the owner, group, and others. It also contains the other bits contained in the mode word, such as the SETUID and SETGID bits, and so on.

To allow raw devices to be represented on a CD-ROM, the *PN* field is present. It contains the major and minor device numbers associated with the file. In this way, the contents of the */dev* directory can be written to a CD-ROM and later reconstructed correctly on the target system.

The *SL* field is for symbolic links. It allows a file on one file system to refer to a file on a different file system.

Probably the most important field is *NM*. It allows a second name to be associated with the file. This name is not subject to the character set or length restrictions of ISO 9660, making it possible to express arbitrary UNIX file names on a CD-ROM.

The next three fields are used together to get around the ISO 9660 limit of directories that may only be nested eight deep. Using them it is possible to specify that a directory is to be relocated, and to tell where it goes in the hierarchy. It is effectively a way to work around the artificial depth limit.

Finally, the *TF* field contains the three timestamps included in each UNIX i-node, namely the time the file was created, the time it was last modified, and the time it was last accessed. Together, these extensions make it possible to copy a UNIX file system to a CD-ROM and then restore it correctly to a different system.

Joliet Extensions

The UNIX community was not the only group that wanted a way to extend ISO 9660. Microsoft also found it too restrictive (although it was Microsoft's own MS-DOS that caused most of the restrictions in the first place). Therefore Microsoft invented some extensions that were called **Joliet**. They were designed to allow Windows file systems to be copied to CD-ROM and then restored, in precisely the same way that Rock Ridge was designed for UNIX. Virtually all programs that run under Windows and use CD-ROMs support Joliet, including programs that burn CD-recordables. Usually, these programs offer a choice between the various ISO 9660 levels and Joliet.

The major extensions provided by Joliet are

1. Long file names.

2. Unicode character set.

3. Directory nesting deeper than eight levels.

4. Directory names with extensions

The first extension allows file names up to 64 characters. The second extension enables the use of the Unicode character set for file names. This extension is important for software intended for use in countries that do not use the Latin alphabet, such as Japan, Israel, and Greece. Since Unicode characters are two bytes, the maximum file name in Joliet occupies 128 bytes.

Like Rock Ridge, the limitation on directory nesting is removed by Joliet. Directories can be nested as deeply as needed. Finally, directory names can have extensions. It is not clear why this extension was included, since Windows directories virtually never use extensions, but maybe some day they will.

6.4.2 The CP/M File System

The first personal computers (then called microcomputers) came out in the early 1980s. A popular early type used the 8-bit Intel 8080 CPU and had 4 KB of RAM and a single 8-inch floppy disk with a capacity of 180 KB. Later versions used the slightly fancier (but still 8-bit) Zilog Z80 CPU, had up to 64 KB of RAM, and had a whopping 720-KB floppy disk as the mass storage device. Despite the slow speed and small amount of RAM, nearly all of these machines ran a surprisingly powerful disk-based operating system, called **CP/M (Control**

Program for Microcomputers) (Golden and Pechura, 1986). This system dominated its era as much as MS-DOS and later Windows dominated the IBM PC world. Two decades later, it has vanished without a trace (except for a small group of diehard fans), which gives reason to think that systems that now dominate the world may be essentially unknown when current babies become college students (Windows what?).

It is worth taking a look at CP/M for several reasons. First, it was a historically very important system and was the direct ancestor of MS-DOS. Second, current and future operating system designers who think that a computer needs 32 MB just to boot the operating system could probably learn a lot about simplicity from a system that ran quite well in 16 KB of RAM. Third, in the coming decades, embedded systems are going to be extremely widespread. Due to cost, space, weight, and power constraints, the operating systems used, for example, in watches, cameras, radios, and cellular telephones, are of necessity going to be lean and mean, not unlike CP/M. Of course, these systems do not have 8-inch floppy disks, but they may well have electronic disks using flash memory, and building a CP/M-like file system on such a device is straightforward.

The layout of CP/M in memory is shown in Fig. 6-30. At the top of main memory (in RAM) is the BIOS, which contains a basic library of 17 I/O calls used by CP/M (in this section we will describe CP/M 2.2, which was the standard version when CP/M was at the height of its popularity). These calls read and write the keyboard, screen, and floppy disk.

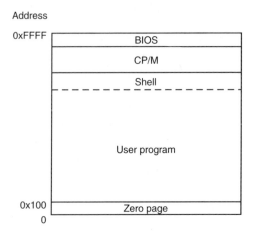

Figure 6-30. Memory layout of CP/M.

Just below the BIOS is the operating system proper. The size of the operating system in CP/M 2.2 is 3584 bytes. Amazing but true: a complete operating system in under 4 KB. Below the operating system comes the shell (command line processor), which chews up another 2 KB. The rest of memory is for user programs, except for the bottom 256 bytes, which are reserved for the hardware interrupt vectors, a few variables, and a buffer for the current command line so user programs can get at it.

The reason for splitting the BIOS from CP/M itself (even though both are in RAM) is portability. CP/M interacts with the hardware only by making BIOS calls. To port CP/M to a new machine, all that is necessary is to port the BIOS there. Once that has been done, CP/M itself can be installed without modification.

A CP/M system has only one directory, which contains fixed-size (32-byte) entries. The directory size, although fixed for a given implementation, may be different in other implementations of CP/M All files in the system are listed in this directory. After CP/M boots, it reads in the directory and computes a bitmap containing the free disk blocks by seeing which blocks are not in any file. This bitmap, which is only 23 bytes for a 180-KB disk, is kept in memory during execution. At system shutdown time it is discarded, that is, not written back to the disk. This approach eliminates the need for a disk consistency checker (like *fsck*) and saves 1 block on the disk (percentually equivalent to saving 90 MB on a modern 16-GB disk).

When the user types a command, the shell first copies the command to a buffer in the bottom 256 bytes of memory. Then it looks up the program to be executed and reads it into memory at address 256 (above the interrupt vectors), and jumps to it. The program then begins running. It discovers its arguments by looking in the command line buffer. The program is allowed to overwrite the shell if it needs the memory. When the program finishes, it makes a system call to CP/M telling it to reload the shell (if it was overwritten) and execute it. In a nutshell, that is pretty much the whole CP/M story.

In addition to loading programs, CP/M provides 38 system calls, mostly file services, for user programs. The most important of these are reading and writing files. Before a file can be read, it must be opened. When CP/M gets an **open** system call, it has to read in and search the one and only directory. The directory is not kept in memory all the time to save precious RAM. When CP/M finds the entry, it immediately has the disk block numbers, since they are stored right in the directory entry, as are all the attributes. The format of a directory entry is given in Fig. 6-31.

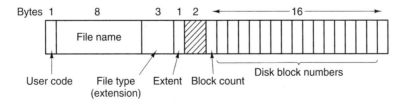

Figure 6-31. The CP/M directory entry format.

The fields in Fig. 6-31 have the following meanings. The *User code* field keeps track of which user owns the file. Although only one person can be logged into a CP/M at any given moment, the system supports multiple users who take turns using the system. While searching for a file name, only those entries belonging to the currently logged-in user are checked. In effect, each user has a virtual directory without the overhead of managing multiple directories.

The next two fields give the name and extension of the file. The base name is up to eight characters; an optional extension of up to three characters may be present. Only upper case letters, digits, and a small number of special characters are allowed in file names. This 8 + 3 naming using upper case only was later taken over by MS-DOS.

The *Block count* field tells how many bytes this file entry contains, measured in units of 128 bytes (because I/O is actually done in 128-byte physical sectors). The last 1-KB block may not be full, so the system has no way to determine the exact size of a file. It is up to the user to put in some END-OF-FILE marker if desired. The final 16 fields contain the disk block numbers themselves. Each block is 1 KB, so that maximum file size is 16 KB. Note that physical I/O is done in units of 128-byte sectors and sizes are kept track of in sectors, but file blocks are allocated in units of 1 KB (8 sectors at a time) to avoid making the directory entry too large.

However, the CP/M designer realized that some files, even on a 180-KB floppy disk, might exceed 16 KB, so an escape hatch was built around the 16-KB limit. A file that is between 16 KB and 32 KB uses not one directory entry, but two. The first entry holds the first 16 blocks; the second entry holds the next 16 blocks. Beyond 32 KB, a third directory entry is used, and so on. The *Extent* field keeps track of the order of the directory entries so the system knows which 16 KB comes first, which comes second, and so on.

After an open call, the addresses of all the disk blocks are known, making read straightforward. The write call is also simple. It just requires allocating a free block from the bitmap in memory and then writing the block. Consecutive blocks on a file are not placed in consecutive blocks on the disk because the 8080 cannot process an interrupt and start reading the next block on time. Instead, interleaving is used to allow several blocks to be read on a single rotation.

CP/M is clearly not the last word in advanced file systems, but it is simple, fast, and can be implemented by a competent programmer in less than a week. For many embedded applications, it may be all that is needed.

6.4.3 The MS-DOS File System

To a first approximation, MS-DOS is a bigger and better version of CP/M. It runs only on Intel platforms, does not support multiprogramming, and runs only in the PC's real mode (which was originally the only mode). The shell has more features and there are more system calls, but the basic function of the operating system is still loading programs, handling the keyboard and screen, and managing the file system. It is the latter functionality that interests us here.

The MS-DOS file system was patterned closely on the CP/M file system, including the use of 8 + 3 (upper case) character file names. The first version (MS-DOS 1.0) was even limited to a single directory, like CP/M. However, starting with MS-DOS 2.0, the file system functionality was greatly expanded. The biggest improvement was the inclusion of a hierarchical file system in which directories could be nested to an arbitrary depth. This meant that the root directory (which still had a fixed maximum size) could contain subdirectories, and these could contain further subdirectories ad infinitem. Links in the style of UNIX were not permitted, so the file system formed a tree starting at the root directory.

It is common for different application programs to start out by creating a subdirectory in the root directory and put all their files there (or in subdirectories thereof), so that different applications do not conflict. Since directories are themselves just stored as files, there are no limits on the number of directories or files that may be created. Unlike CP/M, however, there is no concept of different users in MS-DOS. Consequently, the logged in user has access to all files.

To read a file, an MS-DOS program must first make an open system call to get a handle for it. The open system call specifies a path, which may be either absolute or relative to the current working directory. The path is looked up component by component until the final directory is located and read into memory. It is then searched for the file to be opened.

Although MS-DOS directories are variable sized, like CP/M, they use a fixed-size 32-byte directory entry. The format of an MS-DOS directory entry is shown in Fig. 6-32. It contains the file name, attributes, creation date and time, starting block, and exact file size. File names shorter than 8 + 3 characters are left justified and padded with spaces on the right, in each field separately. The *Attributes* field is new and contains bits to indicate that a file is read-only, needs to be archived, is hidden, or is a system file. Read-only files cannot be written. This is to protect them from accidental damage. The archived bit has no actual operating system function (i.e., MS-DOS does not examine or set it). The intention is to allow user-level archive programs to clear it upon archiving a file and to have other programs set it when modifying a file. In this way, a backup program can just examine this attribute bit on every file to see which files to back up. The hidden bit can be set to prevent a file from appearing in directory listings. Its main use is to avoid confusing novice users with files they might not understand. Finally, the system bit also hides files. In addition, system files cannot accidentally be deleted using the *del* command. The main components of MS-DOS have this bit set.

The directory entry also contains the date and time the file was created or last modified. The time is accurate only to ±2 sec because it is stored in a 2-byte field, which can store only 65,536 unique values (a day contains 86,400 unique seconds). The time field is subdivided into seconds (5 bits), minutes (6 bits), and hours (5 bits). The date counts in days using three subfields: day (5 bits), month (4 bits), and year−1980 (7 bits). With a 7-bit number for the year and time

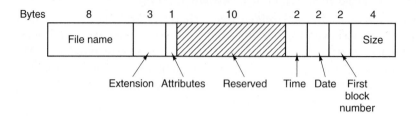

Figure 6-32. The MS-DOS directory entry.

beginning in 1980, the highest expressible year is 2107. Thus MS-DOS has a built-in Y2108 problem. To avoid catastrophe, MS-DOS users should begin with Y2108 compliance as early as possible. If MS-DOS had used the combined date and time fields as a 32-bit seconds counter, it could have represented every second exactly and delayed the catastrophe until 2116.

Unlike CP/M, which does not store the exact file size, MS-DOS does. Since a 32-bit number is used for the file size, in theory files can be as large as 4 GB. However, other limits (described below) restrict the maximum file size to 2 GB or less. A surprising large part of the entry (10 bytes) is unused.

Another way in which MS-DOS differs from CP/M is that it does not store a file's disk addresses in its directory entry, probably because the designers realized that large hard disks (by then common on minicomputers) would some day reach the MS-DOS world. Instead, MS-DOS keeps track of file blocks via a file allocation table in main memory. The directory entry contains the number of the first file block. This number is used as an index into a 64K entry FAT in main memory. By following the chain, all the blocks can be found. The operation of the FAT is illustrated in Fig. 6-14.

The FAT file system comes in three versions for MS-DOS: FAT-12, FAT-16, and FAT-32, depending on how many bits a disk address contains. Actually, FAT-32 is something of a misnomer since only the low-order 28 bits of the disk addresses are used. It should have been called FAT-28, but powers of two sound so much neater.

For all FATs, the disk block can be set to some multiple of 512 bytes (possibly different for each partition), with the set of allowed block sizes (called **cluster sizes** by Microsoft) being different for each variant. The first version of MS-DOS used FAT-12 with 512-byte blocks, giving a maximum partition size of $2^{12} \times 512$ bytes (actually only 4086×512 bytes because 10 of the disk addresses were used as special markers, such as end of file, bad block, etc. With these parameters, the maximum disk partition size was about 2 MB and the size of the FAT table in memory was 4096 entries of 2 bytes each. Using a 12-bit table entry would have been too slow.

This system worked well for floppy disks, but when hard disks came out, it became a problem. Microsoft solved the problem by allowing additional block sizes of 1 KB, 2 KB, and 4 KB. This change preserved the structure and size of the FAT-12 table, but allowed disk partitions of up to 16 MB.

Since MS-DOS supported four disk partitions per disk drive, the new FAT-12 file system worked up to 64-MB disks. Beyond that, something had to give. What happened was the introduction of FAT-16, with 16-bit disk pointers. Additionally, block sizes of 8 KB, 16 KB, and 32 KB were permitted. (32,768 is the largest power of two that can be represented in 16 bits.) The FAT-16 table now occupied 128 KB of main memory all the time, but with the larger memories by then available, it was widely used and rapidly replaced the FAT-12 file system. The largest disk partition that can be supported by FAT-16 is 2 GB (64K entries of 32 KB each) and the largest disk 8 GB, namely four partitions of 2 GB each.

For business letters, this limit is not a problem, but for storing digital video using the DV standard, a 2-GB file holds just over 9 minutes of video. As a consequence of the fact that a PC disk can support only four partitions, the largest video that can be stored on a disk is about 38 minutes, no matter how large the disk is. This limit also means that the largest video that can be edited on line is less than 19 minutes, since both input and output files are needed.

Starting with the second release of Windows 95, the FAT-32 file system, with its 28-bit disk addresses, was introduced and the version of MS-DOS underlying Windows 95 was adapted to support FAT-32. In this system, partitions could theoretically be $2^{28} \times 2^{15}$ bytes, but they are actually limited to 2 TB (2048 GB) because internally the system keeps track of partition sizes in 512-byte sectors using a 32-bit number and $2^9 \times 2^{32}$ is 2 TB. The maximum partition size for various block sizes and all three FAT types is shown in Fig. 6-33.

Block size	FAT-12	FAT-16	FAT-32
0.5 KB	2 MB		
1 KB	4 MB		
2 KB	8 MB	128 MB	
4 KB	16 MB	256 MB	1 TB
8 KB		512 MB	2 TB
16 KB		1024 MB	2 TB
32 KB		2048 MB	2 TB

Figure 6-33. Maximum partition size for different block sizes. The empty boxes represent forbidden combinations.

In addition to supporting larger disks, the FAT-32 file system has two other advantages over FAT-16. First, an 8-GB disk using FAT-32 can be a single partition. Using FAT-16 it has to be four partitions, which appears to the Windows user as the C:, D:, E:, and F: logical disk drives. It is up to the user to decide which file to place on which drive and keep track of what is where.

The other advantage of FAT-32 over FAT-16 is that for a given size disk partition, a smaller block size can be used. For example, for a 2-GB disk partition, FAT-16 must use 32-KB blocks, otherwise with only 64K available disk addresses, it cannot cover the whole partition. In contrast, FAT-32 can use, for example, 4-KB blocks for a 2-GB disk partition. The advantage of the smaller block size is that most files are much shorter than 32 KB. If the block size is 32 KB, a file of 10 bytes ties up 32 KB of disk space. If the average file is, say, 8 KB, then with a 32-KB block, ¾ of the disk will be wasted, not a terribly efficient way to use the disk. With an 8-KB file and a 4-KB block, there is no disk wastage, but the price paid is more RAM eaten up by the FAT. With a 4-KB block and a 2-GB disk partition, there are 512K blocks, so the FAT must have 512K entries in memory (occupying 2 MB of RAM).

MS-DOS uses the FAT to keep track of free disk blocks. Any block that is not currently allocated is marked with a special code. When MS-DOS needs a new disk block, it searches the FAT for an entry containing this code. Thus no bitmap or free list is required.

6.4.4 The Windows 98 File System

The original release of Windows 95 used the MS-DOS file system, including the use of 8 + 3 character file names and the FAT-12 and FAT-16 file systems. Starting with the second release of Windows 95, file names longer than 8 + 3 characters were permitted. In addition, FAT-32 was introduced, primarily to allow larger disk partitions larger than 2 GB and disks larger than 8 GB, which were then available. Both the long file names and FAT-32 were used in Windows 98 in the same form as in the second release of Windows 95. Below we will describe these features of the Windows 98 file system, which have been carried forward into Windows Me as well.

Since long file names are more exciting for users than the FAT structure, let us look at them first. One way to introduce long file names would have been to just invent a new directory structure. The problem with this approach is that if Microsoft had done this, people who were still in the process of converting from Windows 3 to Windows 95 or Windows 98 could not have accessed their files from both systems. A political decision was made within Microsoft that files created using Windows 98 must be accessible from Windows 3 as well (for dual-boot machines). This constraint forced a design for handling long file names that was backward compatible with the old MS-DOS 8 + 3 naming system. Since such backward compatibility constraints are not unusual in the computer industry, it is worth looking in detail at how Microsoft accomplished this goal.

The effect of this decision to be backward compatible meant that the Windows 98 directory structure had to be compatible with the MS-DOS directory structure. As we saw, this structure is just a list of 32-byte entries as shown in

Fig. 6-32. This format came directly from CP/M (which was written for the 8080), which goes to show how long (obsolete) structures can live in the computer world.

However, it was possible to now allocate the 10 unused bytes in the entries of Fig. 6-32, and that was done, as shown in Fig. 6-34. This change has nothing to do with long names, but it is used in Windows 98, so it is worth understanding.

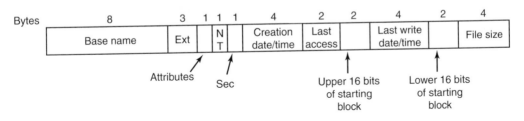

Figure 6-34. The extended MOS-DOS directory entry used in Windows 98.

The changes consist of the addition of five new fields where the 10 unused bytes used to be. The *NT* field is mostly there for some compatibility with Windows NT in terms of displaying file names in the correct case (in MS-DOS, all file names are upper case). The *Sec* field solves the problem that it is not possible to store the time of day in a 16-bit field. It provides additional bits so that the new *Creation time* field is accurate to 10 msec. Another new field is *Last access*, which stores the date (but not time) of the last access to the file. Finally, going to the FAT-32 file system means that block numbers are now 32 bits, so an additional 16-bit field is needed to store the upper 16 bits of the starting block number.

Now we come to the heart of the Windows 98 file system: how long file names are represented in a way that is backward compatible with MS-DOS. The solution chosen was to assign two names to each file: a (potentially) long file name (in Unicode, for compatibility with Windows NT), and an 8 + 3 name for compatibility with MS-DOS. Files can be accessed by either name. When a file is created whose name does not obey the MS-DOS naming rules (8 + 3 length, no Unicode, limited character set, no spaces, etc.), Windows 98 invents an MS-DOS name for it according to a certain algorithm. The basic idea is to take the first six characters of the name, convert them to upper case, if need be, and append ~1 to form the base name. If this name already exists, then the suffix ~2 is used, and so on. In addition, spaces and extra periods are deleted and certain special characters are converted to underscores. As an example, a file named *The time has come the walrus said* is assigned the MS-DOS name *THETIM~1*. If a subsequent file is created with the name *The time has come the rabbit said*, it is assigned the MS-DOS name *THETIM~2*, and so on.

Every file has an MS-DOS file name stored using the directory format of Fig. 6-34. If a file also has a long name, that name is stored in one or more directory entries directly preceding the MS-DOS file name. Each long-name entry holds up to 13 (Unicode) characters. The entries are stored in reverse order, with the start of the file name just ahead of the MS-DOS entry and subsequent pieces before it. The format of each long-name entry is given in Fig. 6-35.

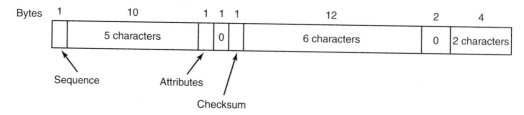

Figure 6-35. An entry for (part of) a long file name in Windows 98.

An obvious question is: "How does Windows 98 know whether a directory entry contains an MS-DOS file name or a (piece of a) long file name?" The answer lies in the *Attributes* field. For a long-name entry, this field has the value 0x0F, which represents an otherwise impossible combination of attributes. Old MS-DOS programs that read directories will just ignore it as invalid. Little do they know. The pieces of the name are sequenced using the first byte of the entry. The last part of the long name (the first entry in the sequence) is marked by adding 64 to the sequence number. Since only 6 bits are used for the sequence number, the theoretical maximum for file names is 63×13 or 819 characters. In fact they are limited to 260 characters for historical reasons.

Each long-name entry contains a *Checksum* field to avoid the following problem. First, a Windows 98 program creates a file with a long name. Second, the computer is rebooted to run MS-DOS or Windows 3. Third, an old program there then removes the MS-DOS file name from the directory but does not remove the long file name preceding it (because it does not know about it). Finally, some program creates a new file that reuses the newly-freed directory entry. At this point we have a valid sequence of long-name entries preceeding an MS-DOS file entry that has nothing to do with that file. The *Checksum* field allows Windows 98 to detect this situation by verifying that the MS-DOS file name following a long name does, in fact, belong to it. Of course, with only 1 byte being used, there is one chance in 256 that Windows 98 will not notice the file substitution.

To see an example of how long names work, consider the example of Fig. 6-36. Here we have a file called *The quick brown fox jumps over the lazy dog*. At 42-characters, it certainly qualifies as a long file name. The MS-DOS name constructed from it is *THEQUI~1* and is stored in the last entry.

Some redundancy is built into the directory structure to help detect problems in the event that an old Windows 3 program has made a mess of the directory. The sequence number byte at the start of each entry is not strictly needed since the 0x40 bit marks the first one, but it provides additional redundancy, for example. Also, the *Low* field of Fig. 6-36 (the lower half of the starting cluster) is 0 in all entries but the last one, again to avoid having old programs misinterpret it and

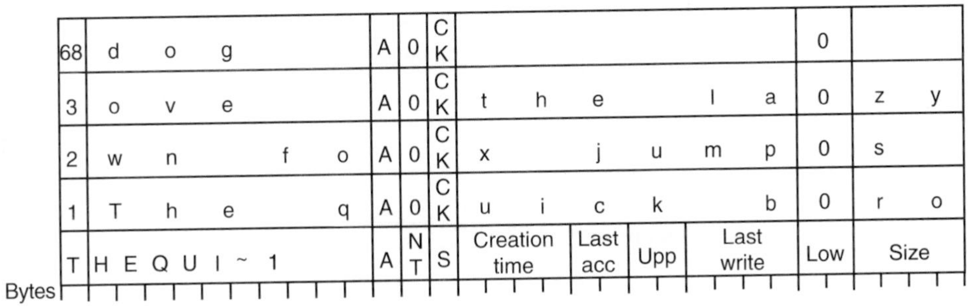

68	d	o	g			A	0	C K								0		
3	o	v	e			A	0	C K	t	h	e		l	a		0	z	y
2	w	n		f	o	A	0	C K	x		j	u	m	p		0	s	
1	T	h	e		q	A	0	C K	u	i	c	k		b		0	r	o
T	H	E	Q	U	I	~	1	A	N T	S	Creation time	Last acc	Upp	Last write	Low	Size		

Bytes

Figure 6-36. An example of how a long name is stored in Windows 98.

ruin the file system. The *NT* byte in Fig. 6-36 is used in NT and ignored in Windows 98. The *A* byte contains the attributes.

The implementation of the FAT-32 file system is conceptually similar to the implementation of the FAT-16 file system. However, instead of an array of 65,536 entries, there are as many entries as needed to cover the part of the disk with data on it. If the first million blocks are used, the table conceptually has 1 million entries. To avoid having all of them in memory at once, Windows 98 maintains a window into the table and keeps only in parts of it in memory at once.

6.4.5 The UNIX V7 File System

Even early versions of UNIX had a fairly sophisticated multiuser file system since it was derived from MULTICS. Below we will discuss the V7 file system, the one for the PDP-11 that made UNIX famous. We will examine modern versions in Chap. 10.

The file system is in the form of a tree starting at the root directory, with the addition of links, forming a directed acyclic graph. File names are up to 14 characters and can contain any ASCII characters except / (because that is the separator between components in a path) and NUL (because that is used to pad out names shorter than 14 characters). NUL has the numerical value of 0.

A UNIX directory entry contains one entry for each file in that directory. Each entry is extremely simple because UNIX uses the i-node scheme illustrated in Fig. 6-15. A directory entry contains only two fields: the file name (14 bytes) and the number of the i-node for that file (2 bytes), as shown in Fig. 6-37. These parameters limit the number of files per file system to 64K.

Like the i-node of Fig. 6-15, the UNIX i-nodes contains some attributes. The attributes contain the file size, three times (creation, last access, and last modification), owner, group, protection information, and a count of the number of directory entries that point to the i-node. The latter field is needed due to links. Whenever a new link is made to an i-node, the count in the i-node is increased. When a

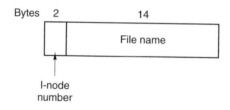

Figure 6-37. A UNIX V7 directory entry.

link is removed, the count is decremented. When it gets to 0, the i-node is reclaimed and the disk blocks are put back in the free list.

Keeping track of disk blocks is done using a generalization of Fig. 6-15 in order to handle very large files. The first 10 disk addresses are stored in the i-node itself, so for small files, all the necessary information is right in the i-node, which is fetched from disk to main memory when the file is opened. For somewhat larger files, one of the addresses in the i-node is the address of a disk block called a **single indirect block**. This block contains additional disk addresses. If this still is not enough, another address in the i-node, called a **double indirect block**, contains the address of a block that contains a list of single indirect blocks. Each of these single indirect blocks points to a few hundred data blocks. If even this is not enough, a **triple indirect block** can also be used. The complete picture is given in Fig. 6-38.

When a file is opened, the file system must take the file name supplied and locate its disk blocks. Let us consider how the path name */usr/ast/mbox* is looked up. We will use UNIX as an example, but the algorithm is basically the same for all hierarchical directory systems. First the file system locates the root directory. In UNIX its i-node is located at a fixed place on the disk. From this i-node, it locates the root directory which can be anywhere on the disk, but say block 1 in this case.

Then it reads the root directory and looks up the first component of the path, *usr*, in the root directory to find the i-node number of the file */usr*. Locating an i-node from its number is straightforward, since each one has a fixed location on the disk. From this i-node, the system locates the directory for */usr* and looks up the next component, *ast*, in it. When it has found the entry for *ast*, it has the i-node for the directory */usr/ast*. From this i-node it can find the directory itself and look up *mbox*. The i-node for this file is then read into memory and kept there until the file is closed. The lookup process is illustrated in Fig. 6-39.

Relative path names are looked up the same way as absolute ones, only starting from the working directory instead of starting from the root directory. Every directory has entries for . and .. which are put there when the directory is created. The entry . has the i-node number for the current directory, and the entry for .. has the i-node number for the parent directory. Thus, a procedure looking up *../dick/prog.c* simply looks up .. in the working directory, finds the i-node number

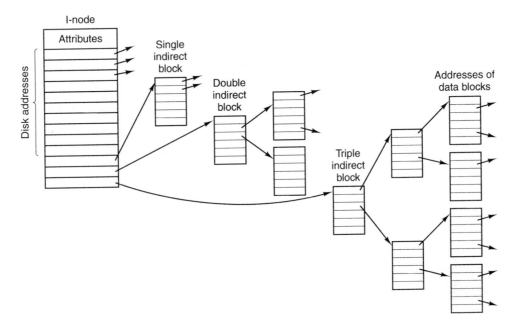

Figure 6-38. A UNIX i-node.

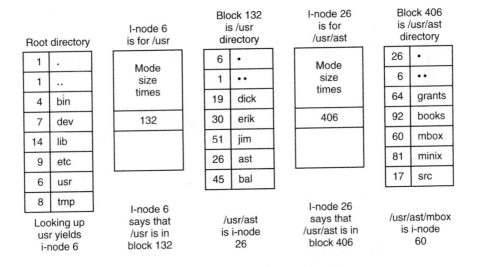

Figure 6-39. The steps in looking up */usr/ast/mbox*.

for the parent directory, and searches that directory for *dick*. No special mechanism is needed to handle these names. As far as the directory system is concerned, they are just ordinary ASCII strings, just the same as any other names.

6.5 RESEARCH ON FILE SYSTEMS

File systems have always attracted more research than other parts of the operating system and that is still the case. Some of this research relates to file system structure. Log-structured file systems and related topics are popular (Matthews et al., 1997; and Wang et al., 1999). The logical disk splits the file system into two distinct layers: the file system and the disk system (De Jonge et al., 1993). Building a file system from stackable layers is also a research topic (Heidemann and Popek, 1994).

Extensible file systems are analogous to the extensible kernels we saw in Chap 1. They allow new features to be added to the file system without having to redesign it from scratch (Karpovich et al., 1994; and Khalidi and Nelson, 1993).

Another research topic that has achieved a certain amount of popularity is making measurements of file system contents and use. People have measured what the file size distribution is, how long files live, whether all files are accessed equally, how reads compare to writes, and many other parameters (Douceur and Bolosky, 1999; Gill et al., 1994; Roselli and Lorch, 2000; and Vogels, 1999).

Other researchers have looked at file system performance and how to improve it using prefetching, caching, less copying, and other techniques. Usually, these researchers make measurements, find out where the bottlenecks are, eliminate at least one of them, and then make the measurements on the improved system to validate their results (Cao et al., 1995; Pai et al., 2000; and Patterson et al., 1995).

An area that many people rarely think about until disaster strikes is file system backup and recovery. Here, too, some new ideas have come up for better ways to do things (Chen et al., 1996; Devarakonda et al., 1996; and Hutchinson et al., 1999). Somewhat related to this is the question of what to do when a user removes a file—remove it or hide it? The Elephant file system, for example, never forgets (Santry et al., 1999a; and Santry et al., 1999b).

6.6 SUMMARY

When seen from the outside, a file system is a collection of files and directories, plus operations on them. Files can be read and written, directories can be created and destroyed, and files can be moved from directory to directory. Most modern file systems support a hierarchical directory system, in which directories may have subdirectories and these may have subsubdirectories ad infinitum.

When seen from the inside, a file system looks quite different. The file system designers have to be concerned with how storage is allocated, and how the system keeps track of which block goes with which file. Possibilities include contiguous files, linked lists, file allocation tables, and i-nodes. Different systems have different directory structures. Attributes can go in the directories or somewhere else (e.g., an i-node). Disk space can be managed using free lists of bitmaps. File system reliability is enhanced by making incremental dumps and by having a program that can repair sick file systems. File system performance is important and can be enhanced in several ways, including caching, read ahead, and carefully placing the blocks of a file close to each other. Log-structured file systems also improve performance by doing writes in large units.

Examples of file systems include ISO 9660, CP/M, MS-DOS, Windows 98, and UNIX. These differ in many ways, including how they keep track of which blocks go with which file, directory structure, and management of free disk space.

PROBLEMS

1. Give 5 different path names for the file */etc/passwd*. *Hint*: Think about the directory entries "." and "..".

2. In Windows, when a user double clicks on a file listed by Windows Explorer, a program is run and given that file as a parameter. List two different ways the operating system could know which program to run?

3. In early UNIX systems, executable files (*a.out* files) began with a very specific magic number, not one chosen at random. These files began with a header, followed by the text and data segments. Why do you think a very specific number was chosen for executable files, whereas other file types had a more-or-less random magic number as the first word?

4. In Fig. 6-4, one of the attributes is the record length. Why does the operating system ever care about this?

5. Is the open system call in UNIX absolutely essential? What would the consequences be of not having it?

6. Systems that support sequential files always have an operation to rewind files. Do systems that support random access files need this too?

7. Some operating systems provide a system call rename to give a file a new name. Is there any difference at all between using this call to rename a file, and just copying the file to a new file with the new name, followed by deleting the old one?

8. In some systems it is possible to map part of a file into memory. What restrictions must such systems impose? How is this partial mapping implemented?

9. A simple operating system only supports a single directory but allows that directory to have arbitrarily many files with arbitrarily long file names. Can something approximating a hierarchical file system be simulated? How?

10. In UNIX and Windows, random access is done by having a special system call that moves the "current position" pointer associated with a file to a given byte in the file. Propose an alternative way to do random access without having this system call.

11. Consider the directory tree of Fig. 6-10. If /usr/jim is the working directory, what is the absolute path name for the file whose relative path name is ../ast/x?

12. Contiguous allocation of files leads to disk fragmentation, as mentioned in the text, because some space in the last disk block will be wasted in files whose length is not an integral number of blocks. Is this internal fragmentation or external fragmentation? Make an analogy with something discussed in the previous chapter.

13. One way to use contiguous allocation of the disk and not suffer from holes is to compact the disk every time a file is removed. Since all files are contiguous, copying a file requires a seek and rotational delay to read the file, followed by the transfer at full speed. Writing the file back requires the same work. Assuming a seek time of 5 msec, a rotational delay of 4 msec, a transfer rate of 8 MB/sec, and an average file size of 8 KB, how long does it take to read a file into main memory then write it back to the disk at a new location? Using these numbers, how long would it take to compact half of a 16-GB disk?

14. In light of the answer to the previous question, does compacting the disk ever make any sense?

15. Some digital consumer devices need to store data, for example as files. Name a modern device that requires file storage and for which contiguous allocation would be a fine idea.

16. How does MS-DOS implement random access to files?

17. Consider the i-node shown in Fig. 6-15. If it contains 10 direct addresses of 4 bytes each and all disk blocks are 1024 KB, what is the largest possible file?

18. It has been suggested that efficiency could be improved and disk space saved by storing the data of a short file within the i-node. For the i-node of Fig. 6-15, how many bytes of data could be stored inside the i-node?

19. Two computer science students, Carolyn and Elinor, are having a discussion about i-nodes. Carolyn maintains that memories have gotten so large and so cheap that when a file is opened, it is simpler and faster just to fetch a new copy of the i-node into the i-node table, rather than search the entire table to see if it is already there. Elinor disagrees. Who is right?

20. Name one advantage of hard links over symbolic links and one advantage of symbolic links over hard links.

21. Free disk space can be kept track of using a free list or a bitmap. Disk addresses require D bits. For a disk with B blocks, F of which are free, state the condition under which the free list uses less space than the bitmap. For D having the value 16 bits, express your answer as a percentage of the disk space that must be free.

22. The beginning of a free space bitmap looks like this after the disk partition is first formatted: 1000 0000 0000 0000 (the first block is used by the root directory). The system always searches for free blocks starting at the lowest numbered block, so after writing file *A*, which uses 6 blocks, the bitmap looks like this: 1111 1110 0000 0000. Show the bitmap after each of the following additional actions:

    (a) File *B* is written, using 5 blocks
    (b) File *A* is deleted
    (c) File *C* is written, using 8 blocks
    (d) File *B* is deleted.

23. What would happen if the bitmap or free list containing the information about free disk blocks was completely lost due to a crash? Is there any way to recover from this disaster, or is it bye-bye disk? Discuss your answer for UNIX and the FAT-16 file system separately.

24. Oliver Owl's night job at the university computing center is to change the tapes used for overnight data backups. While waiting for each tape to complete, he works on writing his thesis that proves Shakespeare's plays were written by extraterrestrial visitors. His text processor runs on the system being backed up since that is the only one they have. Is there a problem with this arrangement?

25. We discussed making incremental dumps in some detail in the text. In Windows it is easy to tell when to dump a file because every file has an archive bit. This bit is missing in UNIX. How do UNIX backup programs know which files to dump?

26. Suppose that file 21 in Fig. 6-24 was not modified since the last dump. In what way would the four bitmaps of Fig. 6-25 be different?

27. It has been suggested that the first part of each UNIX file be kept in the same disk block as its i-node. What good would this do?

28. Consider Fig. 6-26. Is it possible that for some particular block number the counter in *both* lists have the value 2? How should this problem be corrected?

29. The performance of a file system depends upon the cache hit rate (fraction of blocks found in the cache). If it takes 1 msec to satisfy a request from the cache, but 40 msec to satisfy a request if a disk read is needed, give a formula for the mean time required to satisfy a request if the hit rate is h. Plot this function for values of h from 0 to 1.0.

30. A floppy disk has 40 cylinders. A seek takes 6 msec per cylinder moved. If no attempt is made to put the blocks of a file close to each other, two blocks that are logically consecutive (i.e., follow one another in the file) will be about 13 cylinders apart, on the average. If, however, the operating system makes an attempt to cluster related blocks, the mean interblock distance can be reduced to 2 cylinders (for example). How long does it take to read a 100-block file in both cases, if the rotational latency is 100 msec and the transfer time is 25 msec per block?

31. Consider the idea behind Fig. 6-20, but now for a disk with a mean seek time of 8 msec, a rotational rate of 15,000 rpm, and 262,144 bytes per track. What are the data rates for block sizes of 1 KB, 2 KB, and 4 KB, respectively?

32. A certain file system uses 2-KB disk blocks. The median file size is 1 KB. If all files were exactly 1 KB, what fraction of the disk space would be wasted? Do you think the wastage for a real file system will be higher than this number or lower than it? Explain your answer.

33. CP/M was designed to run with a small floppy disk as the mass storage device. Suppose that it were to be ported to a modern computer with a large hard disk. What is the largest possible disk that could be supported without changing the size of the directory format shown in Fig. 6-31? The fields within the directory and other system parameters may be changed if necessary. What changes would you make?

34. The MS-DOS FAT-16 table contains 64K entries. Suppose that one of the bits had been needed for some other purpose and that the table contained exactly 32,768 entries instead. With no other changes, what would the largest MS-DOS file have been under this conditions?

35. Files in MS-DOS have to compete for space in the FAT-16 table in memory. If one file uses k entries, that is k entries that are not available to any other file, what constraint does this place on the total length of all files combined?

36. A UNIX file system has 1-KB blocks and 4-byte disk addresses. What is the maximum file size if i-nodes contain 10 direct entries, and one single, double, and triple indirect entry each?

37. How many disk operations are needed to fetch the i-node for the file */usr/ast/courses/os/handout.t*? Assume that the i-node for the root directory is in memory, but nothing else along the path is in memory. Also assume that all directories fit in one disk block.

38. In many UNIX systems, the i-nodes are kept at the start of the disk. An alternative design is to allocate an i-node when a file is created and put the i-node at the start of the first block of the file. Discuss the pros and cons of this alternative.

39. Write a program that reverses the bytes of a file, so that the last byte is now first and the first byte is now last. It must work with an arbitrarily long file, but try to make it reasonably efficient.

40. Write a program that starts at a given directory and descends the file tree from that point recording the sizes of all the files it finds. When it is all done, it should print a histogram of the file sizes using a bin width specified as a parameter (e.g., with 1024, file sizes of 0 to 1023 go in one bin, 1024 to 2047 go in the next bin, etc.).

41. Write a program that scans all directories in a UNIX file system and finds and locates all i-nodes with a hard link count of two or more. For each such file, it lists together all file names that point to the file.

42. Write a new version of the UNIX *ls* program. This version takes as an argument one or more directory names and for each directory lists all the files in that directory, one line per file. Each field should be formatted in a reasonable way given its type. List only the first disk address, if any.

43. Write CP/M in C or C++. Look on the Web to find information about it.

7

MULTIMEDIA OPERATING SYSTEMS

Digital movies, video clips, and music are becoming an increasingly common way to present information and entertainment using a computer. Audio and video files can be stored on a disk and played back on demand. However, their characteristics are very different from the traditional text files that current file systems were designed for. As a consequence, new kinds of file systems are needed to handle them. Stronger yet, storing and playing back audio and video puts new demands on the scheduler and other parts of the operating system as well. In the sections that follow, we will study many of these issues and their implications for operating systems that are designed to handle multimedia.

Usually, digital movies go under the name **multimedia**, which literally means more than one medium. Under this definition, this book is a multimedia work. After all, it contains two media: text and images (the figures). However, most people use the term "multimedia" to mean a document containing two or more *continuous* media, that is media that must be played back over some time interval. In this book, we will use the term multimedia in this sense.

Another term that is somewhat ambiguous is "video." In a technical sense, it is just the image portion of a movie (as opposed to the sound portion). In fact, camcorders and televisions often have two connectors, one labeled "video" and one labeled "audio," since the signals are separate. However, the term "digital video" normally refers to the complete product, with both image and sound. Below we will use the term "movie" to refer to the complete product. Note that a movie in this sense need not be a two-hour long film produced by a Hollywood studio at a cost exceeding that of a Boeing 747. A 30-sec news clip downloaded from CNN's home page over the Internet is also a movie under our definition. We will also call these "video clips" when we are referring to very short movies.

7.1 INTRODUCTION TO MULTIMEDIA

Before getting into the technology of multimedia, a few words about its current and future uses are perhaps helpful to set the stage. On a single computer, multimedia often means playing a prerecorded movie from a **DVD** (**Digital Versatile Disk**). DVDs are optical disks that use the same 120-mm polycarbonate (plastic) blanks that CD-ROMs use, but are recorded at a higher density, giving a capacity of between 5 GB and 17 GB, depending on the format.

Another use of multimedia is for downloading video clips over the Internet. Many Web pages have items that can be clicked on to download short movies. At 56 Kbps, downloading even a short video clip takes a long time, but as faster distribution technologies take over, such as cable TV and **ADSL** (**Asymmetric Digital Subscriber Loop**), the presence of video clips on the Internet will skyrocket.

Another area in which multimedia must be supported is in the creation of videos themselves. Multimedia editing systems exist and for best performance need to run on an operating system that supports multimedia as well as traditional work.

Yet another arena where multimedia is becoming important is in computer games. Games often run short video clips to depict some kind of action. The clips are usually short, but there are many of them and the correct one is selected dynamically, depending on some action the user has taken. These are increasingly sophisticated

Finally, the holy grail of the multimedia world is **video on demand**, by which people mean the ability for consumers at home to select a movie using their television remote control (or mouse) and have it displayed on their TV set (or computer monitor) on the spot. To enable video on demand, a special infrastructure is needed. In Fig. 7-1 we see two possible video-on-demand infrastructures. Each one contains three essential components: one or more video servers, a distribution network, and a set-top box in each house for decoding the signal. The **video server** is a powerful computer that stores many movies in its file system and plays them back on demand. Sometimes mainframes are used as video servers, since connecting, say, 1000 large disks to a mainframe is straightforward, whereas connecting 1000 disks of any kind to a personal computer is a serious problem. Much of the material in the following sections is about video servers and their operating systems.

The distribution network between the user and the video server must be capable of transmitting data at high speed and in real time. The design of such networks is interesting and complex, but falls outside the scope of this book. We

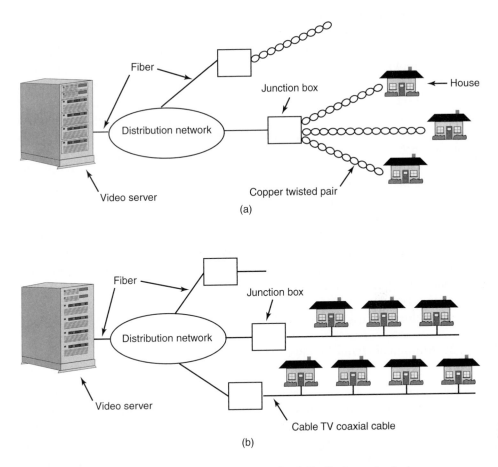

Figure 7-1. Video on demand using different local distribution technologies.
(a) ADSL. (b) Cable TV.

will not say any more about them except to note that these networks always use fiber optics from the video server down to a junction box in each neighborhood where customers live. In ADSL systems, which are provided by telephone companies, the existing twisted-pair telephone line provides the last kilometer or so of transmission. In cable TV systems, which are provided by cable operators, existing cable TV wiring is used for the local distribution. ADSL has the advantage of giving each user a dedicated channel, hence guaranteed bandwidth, but the bandwidth is low (a few megabits/sec) due to limitations of existing telephone wire. Cable TV uses high-bandwidth coaxial cable (at gigabits/sec), but many users have to share the same cable, giving contention for it and no guaranteed bandwidth to any individual user.

The last piece of the system is the **set-top box**, where the ADSL or TV cable terminates. This device is, in fact, a normal computer, with certain special chips for video decoding and decompression. As a minimum, it contains a CPU, RAM, ROM, and interface to ADSL or the cable.

An alternative to a set-top box is to use the customer's existing PC and display the movie on the monitor. Interestingly enough, the reason set-top boxes are even considered given that most customers probably already have a computer, is that video-on-demand operators expect that people will want to watch movies in their living rooms, which usually contain a TV but rarely a computer. From a technical perspective, using a personal computer instead of a set-top box makes far more sense since it is more powerful, has a large disk, and has a far higher resolution display. Either way, we will often make a distinction between the video server and the client process at the user end that decodes and displays the movie. In terms of system design, however, it does not matter much if the client process runs on a set-top box or on a PC. For a desktop video editing system, all the processes run on the same machine, but we will continue to use the terminology of server and client to make it clear which process is doing what.

Getting back to multimedia itself, it has two key characteristics that must be well understood to deal with it successfully:

1. Multimedia uses extremely high data rates.

2. Multimedia requires real-time playback.

The high data rates come from the nature of visual and acoustic information. The eye and the ear can process prodigious amounts of information per second, and have to be fed at that rate to produce an acceptable viewing experience. The data rates of a few digital multimedia sources and some common hardware devices are listed in Fig. 7-2. We will discuss some of these encoding formats later in this chapter. What should be noted is the high data rates multimedia requires, the need for compression, and the amount of storage that is required. For example, an uncompressed 2-hour HDTV movie fills a 570-GB file. A video server that stores 1000 such movies needs 570 TB of disk space, a nontrivial amount by current standards. What is also of note is that without data compression, current hardware cannot keep up with the data rates produced. We will examine video compression later in this chapter.

The second demand that multimedia puts on a system is the need for real-time data delivery. The video portion of a digital movie consists of some number of frames per second. The NTSC system, used in North and South America and Japan, runs at 30 frames/sec (29.97 for the purist), whereas the PAL and SECAM systems, used in most of the rest of the world, runs at 25 frames/sec (25.00 for the purist). Frames must be delivered at precise intervals of ca. 33.3 msec or 40 msec, respectively, or the movie will look choppy.

Officially NTSC stands for National Television Standards Committee, but the poor way color was hacked into the standard when color television was invented

Source	Mbps	GB/hr	Device	Mbps
Telephone (PCM)	0.064	0.03	Fast Ethernet	100
MP3 music	0.14	0.06	EIDE disk	133
Audio CD	1.4	0.62	ATM OC-3 network	156
MPEG-2 movie (640 × 480)	4	1.76	SCSI UltraWide disk	320
Digital camcorder (720 × 480)	25	11	IEEE 1394 (FireWire)	400
Uncompressed TV (640 × 480)	221	97	Gigabit Ethernet	1000
Uncompressed HDTV (1280 × 720)	648	288	SCSI Ultra-160 disk	1280

Figure 7-2. Some data rates for multimedia and high-performance I/O devices. Note that 1 Mbps is 10^6 bits/sec but 1 GB is 2^{30} bytes.

has led to the industry joke that it really stands for Never Twice the Same Color. PAL stands for Phase Alternating Line. Technically it is the best of the systems. SECAM is used in France (and was intended to protect French TV manufacturers from foreign competition) and stands for SEquentiel Couleur Avec Memoire. SECAM is also used in Eastern Europe because when television was introduced there, the then-Communist governments wanted to keep everyone from watching German (PAL) television, so they chose an incompatible system.

The ear is more sensitive than the eye, so a variance of even a few milliseconds in delivery times will be noticeable. Variability in delivery rates is called **jitter** and must be strictly bounded for good performance. Note that jitter is not the same as delay. If the distribution network of Fig. 7-1 uniformly delays all the bits by exactly 5.000 sec, the movie will start slightly later, but will look fine. On the other hand, if it randomly delays frames by between 100 and 200 msec, the movie will look like an old Charlie Chaplin film, no matter who is starring.

The real-time properties required to play back multimedia acceptably are often described by **quality of service** parameters. They include average bandwidth available, peak bandwidth available, minimum and maximum delay (which together bound the jitter), and bit loss probability. For example, a network operator could offer a service guaranteeing an average bandwidth of 4 Mbps, 99% of the transmission delays in the interval 105 to 110 msec, and a bit loss rate of 10^{-10}, which would be fine for MPEG-2 movies. The operator could also offer a cheaper, lower-grade service, with an average bandwidth of 1 Mbps (e.g., ADSL), in which case the quality would have to be compromised somehow, possibly by lowering the resolution, dropping the frame rate, or discarding the color information and showing the movie in black and white.

The most common way to provide quality of service guarantees is to reserve capacity in advance for each new customer. The resources reserved include a portion of the CPU, memory buffers, disk transfer capacity, and network bandwidth. If a new customer comes along and wants to watch a movie, but the video server or network calculates that it does not have sufficient capacity for another custo-mer, it has to reject the new customer to avoid degrading the service to current customers. As a consequence, multimedia servers need resource reservation schemes and an **admission control algorithm** to decide when they can handle more work.

7.2 MULTIMEDIA FILES

In most systems, an ordinary text file consists of a linear sequence of bytes without any structure that the operating system knows about or cares about. With multimedia, the situation is more complicated. To start with, video and audio are completely different. They are captured by distinct devices (CCD chip versus microphone), have a different internal structure (video has 25-30 frames/sec; audio has 44,100 samples/sec), and they are played back by different devices (monitor versus loudspeakers).

Furthermore, most Hollywood movies are now aimed at a worldwide audi-ence, most of which does not speak English. The latter point is dealt with in one of two ways. For some countries, an additional sound track is produced, with the voices dubbed into the local language (but not the sound effects). In Japan, all televisions have two sound channels to allow the viewer to listen to foreign films in either the original language or in Japanese. A button on the remote control is used for language selection. In still other countries, the original sound track is used, with subtitles in the local language.

In addition, many TV movies now provide closed-caption subtitles in English as well, to allow English-speaking but hearing-impaired people to watch the movie. The net result is that a digital movie may actually consist of many files: one video file, multiple audio files, and multiple text files with subtitles in various languages. DVDs have the capability for storing up to 32 language and subtitle files. A simple set of multimedia files is shown in Fig. 7-3. We will explain the meaning of fast forward and fast backward later in this chapter.

As a consequence, the file system needs to keep track of multiple "subfiles" per file. One possible scheme is to manage each subfile as a traditional file (e.g., using an i-node to keep track of its blocks) and to have a new data structure that lists all the subfiles per multimedia file. Another way is to invent a kind of two-dimensional i-node, with each column listing the blocks of each subfile. In gen-eral, the organization must be such that the viewer can dynamically choose which audio and subtitle tracks to use at the time the movie is viewed.

In all cases, some way to keep the subfiles synchronized is also needed so that when the selected audio track is played back it remains in sync with the video. If the audio and video get even slightly out of sync, the viewer may hear an actor's words before or after his lips move, which is easily detected and fairly annoying.

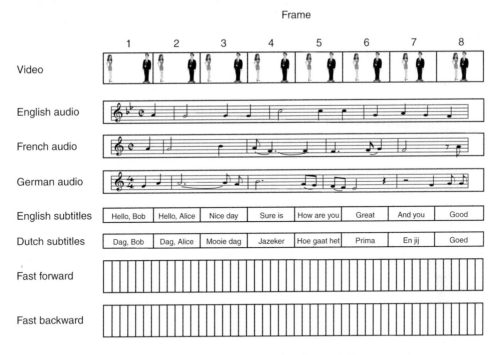

Figure 7-3. A movie may consist of several files.

To better understand how multimedia files are organized, it is necessary to understand how digital audio and video work in some detail. We will now give an introduction to these topics.

7.2.1 Audio Encoding

An audio (sound) wave is a one-dimensional acoustic (pressure) wave. When an acoustic wave enters the ear, the eardrum vibrates, causing the tiny bones of the inner ear to vibrate along with it, sending nerve pulses to the brain. These pulses are perceived as sound by the listener. In a similar way, when an acoustic wave strikes a microphone, the microphone generates an electrical signal, representing the sound amplitude as a function of time.

The frequency range of the human ear runs from 20 Hz to 20,000 Hz, although some animals, notably dogs, can hear higher frequencies. The ear hears logarithmically, so the ratio of two sounds with amplitudes A and B is conventionally expressed in **dB** (**decibels**) according to the formula

$$dB = 20 \log_{10}(A/B)$$

If we define the lower limit of audibility (a pressure of about 0.0003 dyne/cm^2) for a 1-kHz sine wave as 0 dB, an ordinary conversation is about 50 dB and the pain threshold is about 120 dB, a dynamic range of a factor of 1 million. To avoid any confusion, *A* and *B* above are *amplitudes*. If we were to use the power level, which is proportional to the square of the amplitude, the coefficient of the logarithm would be 10, not 20.

Audio waves can be converted to digital form by an **ADC** (**Analog Digital Converter**). An ADC takes an electrical voltage as input and generates a binary number as output. In Fig. 7-4(a) we see an example of a sine wave. To represent this signal digitally, we can sample it every ΔT seconds, as shown by the bar heights in Fig. 7-4(b). If a sound wave is not a pure sine wave, but a linear superposition of sine waves where the highest frequency component present is f, then it is sufficient to make samples at a frequency $2f$. This result was proven mathematically by H. Nyquist in 1924. Sampling more often is of no value since the higher frequencies that such sampling could detect are not present.

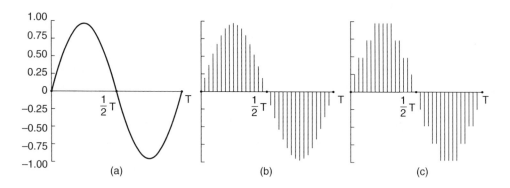

Figure 7-4. (a) A sine wave. (b) Sampling the sine wave. (c) Quantizing the samples to 4 bits.

Digital samples are never exact. The samples of Fig. 7-4(c) allow only nine values, from −1.00 to +1.00 in steps of 0.25. Consequently, 4 bits are needed to represent all of them. An 8-bit sample would allow 256 distinct values. A 16-bit sample would allow 65,536 distinct values. The error introduced by the finite number of bits per sample is called the **quantization noise**. If it is too large, the ear detects it.

Two well-known examples of sampled sound are the telephone and audio compact discs. **Pulse code modulation** is used within the telephone system and uses 7-bit (North America and Japan) or 8-bit (Europe) samples 8000 times per second. This system gives a data rate of 56,000 bps or 64,000 bps. With only 8000 samples/sec, frequencies above 4 kHz are lost.

Audio CDs are digital with a sampling rate of 44,100 samples/sec, enough to capture frequencies up to 22,050 Hz, which is good for people, bad for dogs. The samples are 16 bits each, and are linear over the range of amplitudes. Note that 16-bit samples allow only 65,536 distinct values, even though the dynamic range of the ear is about 1 million when measured in steps of the smallest audible sound. Thus using only 16 bits per sample introduces some quantization noise (although the full dynamic range is not covered—CDs are not supposed to hurt). With 44,100 samples/sec of 16 bits each, an audio CD needs a bandwidth of 705.6 Kbps for monaural and 1.411 Mbps for stereo (see Fig. 7-2). Audio compression is possible based on psychoacoustic models of how human hearing works. A compression of 10x is possible using the MPEG layer 3 (MP3) system. Portable music players for this format have been common in recent years.

Digitized sound can easily be processed by computers in software. Dozens of programs exist for personal computers to allow users to record, display, edit, mix, and store sound waves from multiple sources. Virtually all professional sound recording and editing is digital nowadays.

7.2.2 Video Encoding

The human eye has the property that when an image is flashed on the retina, it is retained for some number of milliseconds before decaying. If a sequence of images is flashed at 50 or more images/sec, the eye does not notice that it is looking at discrete images. All video- and film-based motion picture systems exploit this principle to produce moving pictures.

To understand video systems, it is best to start with simple, old-fashioned black-and-white television. To represent the two-dimensional image in front of it as a one-dimensional voltage as a function of time, the camera scans an electron beam rapidly across the image and slowly down it, recording the light intensity as it goes. At the end of the scan, called a **frame**, the beam retraces. This intensity as a function of time is broadcast, and receivers repeat the scanning process to reconstruct the image. The scanning pattern used by both the camera and the receiver is shown in Fig. 7-5. (As an aside, CCD cameras integrate rather than scan, but some cameras and all CRT monitors do scan.)

The exact scanning parameters vary from country to country. NTSC has 525 scan lines, a horizontal to vertical aspect ratio of 4:3, and 30 frames/sec. The European PAL and SECAM systems have 625 scan lines, the same aspect ratio of 4:3, and 25 frames/sec. In both systems, the top few and bottom few lines are not displayed (to approximate a rectangular image on the original round CRTs). Only 483 of the 525 NTSC scan lines (and 576 of the 625 PAL/SECAM scan lines) are displayed.

While 25 frames/sec is enough to capture smooth motion, at that frame rate many people, especially older ones, will perceive the image to flicker (because the old image has faded off the retina before the new one appears). Rather than increase the frame rate, which would require using more scarce bandwidth, a different approach is taken. Instead of displaying the scan lines in order fromtop to bottom, first all the odd scan lines are displayed, then the even ones are displayed. Each of these half frames is called a **field**. Experiments have shown that although

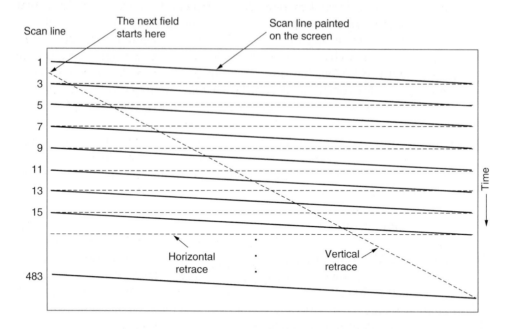

Figure 7-5. The scanning pattern used for NTSC video and television.

people notice flicker at 25 frames/sec, they do not notice it at 50 fields/sec. This technique is called **interlacing**. Noninterlaced television or video is said to be **progressive**.

Color video uses the same scanning pattern as monochrome (black and white), except that instead of displaying the image with one moving beam, three beams moving in unison are used. One beam is used for each of the three additive primary colors: red, green, and blue (RGB). This technique works because any color can be constructed from a linear superposition of red, green, and blue with the appropriate intensities. However, for transmission on a single channel, the three color signals must be combined into a single **composite** signal.

To allow color transmissions to be viewed on black-and-white receivers, all three systems linearly combine the RGB signals into a **luminance** (brightness) signal, and two **chrominance** (color) signals, although they all use different coefficients for constructing these signals from the RGB signals. Interestingly enough, the eye is much more sensitive to the luminance signal than to the chrominance signals, so the latter need not be transmitted as accurately. Consequently, the luminance signal can be broadcast at the same frequency as the old black-and-white signal, so it can be received on black-and-white television sets. The two chrominance signals are broadcast in narrow bands at higher frequencies. Some television sets have knobs or controls labeled brightness, hue, and saturation (or brightness, tint and color) for controlling these three signals separately.

Understanding luminance and chrominance is necessary for understanding how video compression works.

So far we have looked at analog video. Now let us turn to digital video. The simplest representation of digital video is a sequence of frames, each consisting of a rectangular grid of picture elements, or **pixels**. For color video, 8 bits per pixel are used for each of the RGB colors, giving 16 million colors, which is enough. The human eye cannot even distinguish this many colors, let alone more.

To produce smooth motion, digital video, like analog video, must display at least 25 frames/sec. However, since good quality computer monitors often rescan the screen from images stored in video RAM at 75 times per second or more, interlacing is not needed Consequently, all computer monitors use progressive scanning. Just repainting (i.e., redrawing) the same frame three times in a row is enough to eliminate flicker.

In other words, smoothness of motion is determined by the number of *different* images per second, whereas flicker is determined by the number of times the screen is painted per second. These two parameters are different. A still image painted at 20 frames/sec will not show jerky motion but it will flicker because one frame will decay from the retina before the next one appears. A movie with 20 different frames per second, each of which is painted four times in a row at 80 Hz, will not flicker, but the motion will appear jerky.

The significance of these two parameters becomes clear when we consider the bandwidth required for transmitting digital video over a network. Current computer monitors all use the 4:3 aspect ratio so they can use inexpensive, mass-produced picture tubes designed for the consumer television market. Common configurations are 640×480 (VGA), 800×600 (SVGA), and 1024×768 (XGA). An XGA display with 24 bits per pixel and 25 frames/sec needs to be fed at 472 Mbps. Doubling this rate to avoid flicker is not attractive. A better solution is to transmit 25 frames/sec and have the computer store each one and paint it twice. Broadcast television does not use this strategy because television sets do not have memory, and in any event, analog signals cannot be stored in RAM without first converting them to digital form, which requires extra hardware. As a consequence, interlacing is needed for broadcast television but not for digital video.

7.3 VIDEO COMPRESSION

It should be obvious by now that manipulating multimedia material in uncompressed form is completely out of the question—it is much too big. The only hope is that massive compression is possible. Fortunately, a large body of research over the past few decades has led to many compression techniques and algorithms that make multimedia transmission feasible. In this section we will study some methods for compressing multimedia data, especially images. For more detail, see (Fluckiger, 1995; and Steinmetz and Nahrstedt, 1995).

All compression systems require two algorithms: one for compressing the data at the source, and another for decompressing it at the destination. In the literature, these algorithms are referred to as the **encoding** and **decoding** algorithms, respectively. We will use this terminology here, too.

These algorithms have certain asymmetries that are important to understand. First, for many applications, a multimedia document, say, a movie will only be encoded once (when it is stored on the multimedia server) but will be decoded thousands of times (when it is viewed by customers). This asymmetry means that it is acceptable for the encoding algorithm to be slow and require expensive hardware provided that the decoding algorithm is fast and does not require expensive hardware. On the other hand, for real-time multimedia, such as video conferencing, slow encoding is unacceptable. Encoding must happen on-the-fly, in real time.

A second asymmetry is that the encode/decode process need not be invertible. That is, when compressing a file, transmitting it, and then decompressing it, the user expects to get the original back, accurate down to the last bit. With multimedia, this requirement does not exist. It is usually acceptable to have the video signal after encoding and then decoding be slightly different than the original. When the decoded output is not exactly equal to the original input, the system is said to be **lossy**. All compression systems used for multimedia are lossy because they give much better compression.

7.3.1 The JPEG Standard

The **JPEG** (**Joint Photographic Experts Group**) standard for compressing continuous-tone still pictures (e.g., photographs) was developed by photographic experts working under the joint auspices of ITU, ISO, and IEC, another standards body. It is important for multimedia because, to a first approximation, the multimedia standard for moving pictures, MPEG, is just the JPEG encoding of each frame separately, plus some extra features for interframe compression and motion compensation. JPEG is defined in International Standard 10918. It has four modes and many options, but we will only be concerned with the way it is used for 24-bit RGB video and will leave out many of the details.

Step 1 of encoding an image with JPEG is block preparation. For the sake of specificity, let us assume that the JPEG input is a 640×480 RGB image with 24 bits/pixel, as shown in Fig. 7-6(a). Since using luminance and chrominance gives better compression, the luminance and two chrominance signals are computed from the RGB values. For NTSC they are called Y, I, and Q, respectively. For PAL they are called Y, U, and V, respectively, and the formulas are different. Below we will use the NTSC names, but the compression algorithm is the same.

Separate matrices are constructed for Y, I, and Q, each with elements in the range 0 to 255. Next, square blocks of four pixels are averaged in the I and Q matrices to reduce them to 320×240. This reduction is lossy, but the eye barely

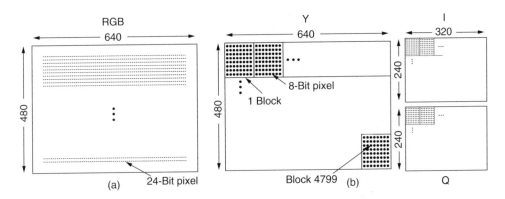

Figure 7-6. (a) RGB input data. (b) After block preparation.

notices it since the eye responds to luminance more than to chrominance. Nevertheless, it compresses the data by a factor of two. Now 128 is subtracted from each element of all three matrices to put 0 in the middle of the range. Finally, each matrix is divided up into 8×8 blocks. The Y matrix has 4800 blocks; the other two have 1200 blocks each, as shown in Fig. 7-6(b).

Step 2 of JPEG is to apply a DCT (Discrete Cosine Transformation) to each of the 7200 blocks separately. The output of each DCT is an 8×8 matrix of DCT coefficients. DCT element $(0, 0)$ is the average value of the block. The other elements tell how much spectral power is present at each spatial frequency. In theory, a DCT is lossless, but in practice using floating-point numbers and transcendental functions always introduces some roundoff error that results in a little information loss. Normally, these elements decay rapidly with distance from the origin, $(0, 0)$, as suggested by Fig. 7-7(b).

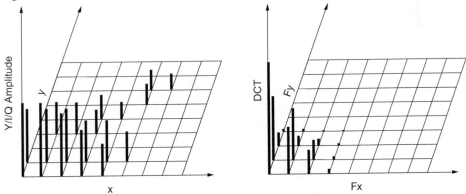

Figure 7-7. (a) One block of the Y matrix. (b) The DCT coefficients.

Once the DCT is complete, JPEG moves on to step 3, which is called **quantization**, in which the less important DCT coefficients are wiped out. This (lossy) transformation is done by dividing each of the coefficients in the 8×8 DCT matrix by a weight taken from a table. If all the weights are 1, the transformation does nothing. However, if the weights increase sharply from the origin, higher spatial frequencies are dropped quickly.

An example of this step is given in Fig. 7-8. Here we see the initial DCT matrix, the quantization table, and the result obtained by dividing each DCT element by the corresponding quantization table element. The values in the quantization table are not part of the JPEG standard. Each application must supply its own quantization table, giving it the ability to control its own loss-compression trade-off.

DCT Coefficients

150	80	40	14	4	2	1	0
92	75	36	10	6	1	0	0
52	38	26	8	7	4	0	0
12	8	6	4	2	1	0	0
4	3	2	0	0	0	0	0
2	2	1	1	0	0	0	0
1	1	0	0	0	0	0	0
0	0	0	0	0	0	0	0

Quantized coefficients

150	80	20	4	1	0	0	0
92	75	18	3	1	0	0	0
26	19	13	2	1	0	0	0
3	2	2	1	0	0	0	0
1	0	0	0	0	0	0	0
0	0	0	0	0	0	0	0
0	0	0	0	0	0	0	0
0	0	0	0	0	0	0	0

Quantization table

1	1	2	4	8	16	32	64
1	1	2	4	8	16	32	64
2	2	2	4	8	16	32	64
4	4	4	4	8	16	32	64
8	8	8	8	8	16	32	64
16	16	16	16	16	16	32	64
32	32	32	32	32	32	32	64
64	64	64	64	64	64	64	64

Figure 7-8. Computation of the quantized DCT coefficients.

Step 4 reduces the (0, 0) value of each block (the one in the upper left-hand corner) by replacing it with the amount it differs from the corresponding element in the previous block. Since these elements are the averages of their respective blocks, they should change slowly, so taking the differential values should reduce most of them to small values. No differentials are computed from the other values. The (0, 0) values are referred to as the DC components; the other values are the AC components.

Step 5 linearizes the 64 elements and applies run-length encoding to the list. Scanning the block from left to right and then top to bottom will not concentrate the zeros together, so a zig zag scanning pattern is used, as shown in Fig. 7-9. In this example, the zig zag pattern ultimately produces 38 consecutive 0s at the end of the matrix. This string can be reduced to a single count saying there are 38 zeros.

Now we have a list of numbers that represent the image (in transform space). Step 6 Huffman encodes the numbers for storage or transmission.

JPEG may seem complicated, but that is because it *is* complicated. Still, since it often produces a 20:1 compression or better, it is widely used. Decoding a JPEG image requires running the algorithm backward. JPEG is roughly symmetric: it takes about as long to decode an image as to encode it.

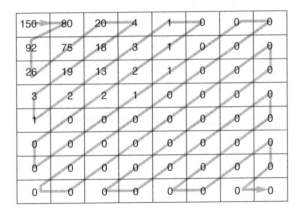

Figure 7-9. The order in which the quantized values are transmitted.

7.3.2 The MPEG Standard

Finally, we come to the heart of the matter: the **MPEG** (**Motion Picture Experts Group**) standards. These are the main algorithms used to compress videos and have been international standards since 1993. MPEG-1 (International Standard 11172) was designed for video recorder-quality output (352×240 for NTSC) using a bit rate of 1.2 Mbps. MPEG-2 (International Standard 13818) was designed for compressing broadcast quality video into 4 to 6 Mbps, so it could fit in a NTSC or PAL broadcast channel.

Both versions take advantages of the two kinds of redundancies that exist in movies: spatial and temporal. Spatial redundancy can be utilized by simply coding each frame separately with JPEG. Additional compression can be achieved by taking advantage of the fact that consecutive frames are often almost identical (temporal redundancy). The **DV** (**Digital Video**) system used by digital camcorders uses only a JPEG-like scheme because encoding has to be done in real time and it is much faster to just encode each frame separately. The consequences of this decision can be seen in Fig. 7-2: although digital camcorders have a lower data rate than uncompressed video, they are not nearly as good as full MPEG-2. (To keep the comparison honest, note that DV camcorders sample the luminance with 8 bits and each chrominance signal with 2 bits, but there is still a factor of five compression using the JPEG-like encoding.)

For scenes where the camera and background are stationary and one or two actors are moving around slowly, nearly all the pixels will be identical from frame to frame. Here, just subtracting each frame from the previous one and running JPEG on the difference would do fine. However, for scenes where the camera is panning or zooming, this technique fails badly. What is needed is some way to compensate for this motion. This is precisely what MPEG does; in fact, this is the main difference between MPEG and JPEG.

MPEG-2 output consists of three different kinds of frames that have to be processed by the viewing program:

1. I (Intracoded) frames: Self-contained JPEG-encoded still pictures.

2. P (Predictive) frames: Block-by-block difference with the last frame.

3. B (Bidirectional) frames: Differences with the last and next frame.

I-frames are just still pictures coded using JPEG, also using full-resolution luminance and half-resolution chrominance along each axis. It is necessary to have I-frames appear in the output stream periodically for three reasons. First, MPEG can be used for television broadcasting, with viewers tuning in at will. If all frames depended on their predecessors going back to the first frame, anybody who missed the first frame could never decode any subsequent frames. This would make it impossible for viewers to tune in after the movie had started. Second, if any frame were received in error, no further decoding would be possible. Third, without I-frames, while doing a fast forward or rewind, the decoder would have to calculate every frame passed over so it would know the full value of the one it stopped on. With I-frames, it is possible to skip forward or backward until an I-frame is found and start viewing there. For these reasons, I-frames are inserted into the output once or twice per second.

P-frames, in contrast, code interframe differences. They are based on the idea of **macroblocks**, which cover 16×16 pixels in luminance space and 8×8 pixels in chrominance space. A macroblock is encoded by searching the previous frame for it or something only slightly different from it.

An example of where P-frames would be useful is given in Fig. 7-10. Here we see three consecutive frames that have the same background, but differ in the position of one person. The macroblocks containing the background scene will match exactly, but the macroblocks containing the person will be offset in position by some unknown amount and will have to be tracked down.

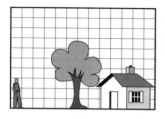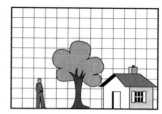

Figure 7-10. Three consecutive video frames.

The MPEG standard does not specify how to search, how far to search, or how good a match has to be to count. This is up to each implementation. For example, an implementation might search for a macroblock at the current position in the previous frame, and all other positions offset $\pm \Delta x$ in the x direction and $\pm \Delta y$

in the y direction. For each position, the number of matches in the luminance matrix could be computed. The position with the highest score would be declared the winner, provided it was above some predefined threshold. Otherwise, the macroblock would be said to be missing. Much more sophisticated algorithms are also possible, of course.

If a macroblock is found, it is encoded by taking the difference with its value in the previous frame (for luminance and both chrominances). These difference matrices are then subject to the JPEG encoding. The value for the macroblock in the output stream is then the motion vector (how far the macroblock moved from its previous position in each direction), followed by the JPEG-encoded differences with the one in the previous frame. If the macroblock is not located in the previous frame, the current value is encoded with JPEG, just as in an I-frame.

B-frames are similar to P-frames, except that they allow the reference macroblock to be in either a previous frame or in a succeeding frame, either in an I-frame or in a P-frame. This additional freedom allows improved motion compensation, and is also useful when objects pass in front of, or behind, other objects. For example, in a baseball game, when the third baseman throws the ball to first base, there may be some frame where the ball obscures the head of the moving second baseman in the background. In the next frame, the head may be partially visible to the left of the ball, with the next approximation of the head being derived from the following frame when the ball is now past the head. B-frames allow a frame to be based on a future frame.

To do B-frame encoding, the encoder needs to hold three decoded frames in memory at once: the past one, the current one, and the future one. To simplify decoding, frames must be present in the MPEG stream in dependency order, rather than in display order. Thus even with perfect timing, when a video is viewed over a network, buffering is required on the user's machine to reorder the frames for proper display. Due to this difference between dependency order and display order, trying to play a movie backward will not work without considerable buffering and complex algorithms.

7.4 MULTIMEDIA PROCESS SCHEDULING

Operating systems that support multimedia differ from traditional ones in three main ways: process scheduling, the file system, and disk scheduling. We will start with process scheduling here and continue with the other topics in subsequent sections.

7.4.1 Scheduling Homogeneous Processes

The simplest kind of video server is one that can support the display of a fixed number of movies, all using the same frame rate, video resolution, data rate, and other parameters. Under these circumstances, a simple, but effective scheduling algorithm is as follows. For each movie, there is a single process (or thread) whose job it is to read the movie from the disk one frame at a time and then transmit that frame to the user. Since all the processes are equally important, have the same amount of work to do per frame, and block when they have finished processing the current frame, round-robin scheduling does the job just fine. The only addition needed to standard scheduling algorithms is a timing mechanism to make sure each process runs at the correct frequency.

One way to achieve the proper timing is to have a master clock that ticks at, say, 30 times per second (for NTSC). At every tick, all the processes are run sequentially, in the same order. When a process has completed its work, it issues a suspend system call that releases the CPU until the master clock ticks again. When that happens, all the processes are run again in the same order. As long as the number of processes is small enough that all the work can be done in one frame time, round-robin scheduling is sufficient.

7.4.2 General Real-Time Scheduling

Unfortunately, this model is rarely applicable in reality. The number of users changes as viewers come and go, frame sizes vary wildly due to the nature of video compression (I-frames are much larger than P- or B-frames), and different movies may have different resolutions. As a consequence, different processes may have to run at different frequencies, with different amounts of work, and with different deadlines by which the work must be completed.

These considerations lead to a different model: multiple processes competing for the CPU, each with its own work and deadlines. In the following models, we will assume that the system knows the frequency at which each process must run, how much work it has to do, and what its next deadline is. (Disk scheduling is also an issue, but we will consider that later.) The scheduling of multiple competing processes, some or all of which have deadlines that must be met is called **real-time scheduling**.

As an example of the kind of environment a real-time multimedia scheduler works in, consider the three processes, A, B, and C shown in Fig. 7-11. Process A runs every 30 msec (approximately NTSC speed). Each frame requires 10 msec of CPU time. In the absence of competition, it would run in the bursts $A1$, $A2$, $A3$, etc., each one starting 30 msec after the previous one. Each CPU burst handles one frame and has a deadline: it must complete before the next one is to start.

Also shown in Fig. 7-11 are two other processes, B and C. Process B runs 25 times/sec (e.g., PAL) and process C runs 20 times/sec (e.g., a slowed down NTSC or PAL stream intended for a user with a low-bandwidth connection to the video server). The computation time per frame is shown as 15 msec and 5 msec for B and C, respectively, just to make the scheduling problem more general than having all of them the same.

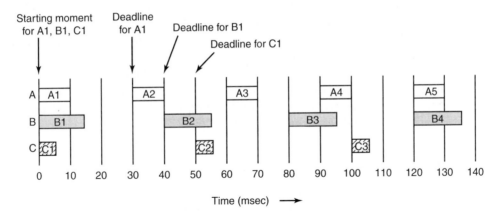

Figure 7-11. Three periodic processes, each displaying a movie. The frame rates and processing requirements per frame are different for each movie.

The scheduling question now is how to schedule *A*, *B*, and *C* to make sure they meet their respective deadlines. Before even looking for a scheduling algorithm, we have to see if this set of processes is schedulable at all. Recall from Sec. 2.5.4, that if process *i* has period P_i msec and requires C_i msec of CPU time per frame, the system is schedulable if and only if

$$\sum_{i=1}^{m} \frac{C_i}{P_i} \le 1$$

where *m* is the number of processes, in this case, 3. Note that P_i/C_i is just the fraction of the CPU being used by process *i*. For the example of Fig. 7-11, *A* is eating 10/30 of the CPU, *B* is eating 15/40 of the CPU, and *C* is eating 5/50 of the CPU. Together these fractions add to 0.808 of the CPU, so the system of processes is schedulable.

So far we assumed that there is one process per stream. Actually, there might be two (or more processes) per stream, for example, one for audio and one for video. They may run at different rates and may consume differing amounts of CPU time per burst. Adding audio processes to the mix does not change the general model, however, since all we are assuming is that there are *m* processes, each running at a fixed frequency with a fixed amount of work needed on each CPU burst.

In some real-time systems, processes are preemptable and in others they are not. In multimedia systems, processes are generally preemptable, meaning that a process that is in danger of missing its deadline may interrupt the running processes before the running process has finished with its frame. When it is done, the previous process can continue. This behavior is just multiprogramming, as we have seen before. We will study preemptable real-time scheduling algorithms because there is no objection to them in multimedia systems and they give better performance than nonpreemptable ones. The only concern is that if a transmission buffer is being filled in little bursts, the buffer is completely full by the deadline so it can be sent to the user in a single operation. Otherwise jitter might be introduced.

Real-time algorithms can be either static or dynamic. Static algorithms assign each process a fixed priority in advance and then do prioritized preemptive scheduling using those priorities. Dynamic algorithms do not have fixed priorities. Below we will study an example of each type.

7.4.3 Rate Monotonic Scheduling

The classic static real-time scheduling algorithm for preemptable, periodic processes is **RMS (Rate Monotonic Scheduling)** (Liu and Layland, 1973). It can be used for processes that meet the following conditions:

1. Each periodic process must complete within its period.

2. No process is dependent on any other process.

3. Each process needs the same amount of CPU time on each burst.

4. Any nonperiodic processes have no deadlines.

5. Process preemption occurs instantaneously and with no overhead.

The first four conditions are reasonable. The last one is not, of course, but it makes modeling the system much easier. RMS works by assigning each process a fixed priority equal to the frequency of occurrence of its triggering event. For example, a process that must run every 30 msec (33 times/sec) gets priority 33, a process that must run every 40 msec (25 times/sec) gets priority 25, and a process that must run every 50 msec (20 times/sec) gets priority 20. The priorities are thus linear with the rate (number of times/second the process runs). This is why it is called rate monotonic. At run time, the scheduler always runs the highest priority ready process, preempting the running process if need be. Liu and Layland proved that RMS is optimal among the class of static scheduling algorithms.

Figure 7-12 shows how rate monotonic scheduling works in the example of Fig. 7-11. Processes A, B, and C have static priorities, 33, 25, and 20, respectively, which means that whenever A needs to run, it runs, preempting any other process currently using the CPU. Process B can preempt C, but not A. Process C has to wait until the CPU is otherwise idle in order to run.

In Fig. 7-12, initially all three processes are ready to run. The highest priority one, A, is chosen, and allowed to run until it completes at 15 msec, as shown in the RMS line. After it finishes, B and C are run in that order. Together, these processes take 30 msec to run, so when C finishes, it is time for A to run again. This rotation goes on until the system goes idle at $t = 70$.

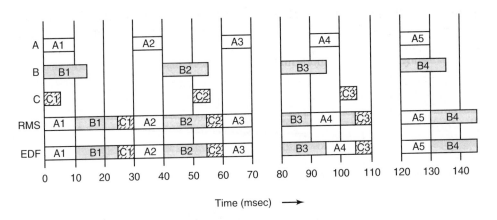

Figure 7-12. An example of RMS and EDF real-time scheduling.

At $t = 80$ B becomes ready and runs. However, at $t = 90$, a higher priority process, A, becomes ready, so it preempts B and runs until it is finished, at $t = 100$. At that point the system can choose between finishing B or starting C, so it chooses the highest priority process, B.

7.4.4 Earliest Deadline First Scheduling

Another popular real-time scheduling algorithm is **Earliest Deadline First**. EDF is a dynamic algorithm that does not require processes to be periodic, as does the rate monotonic algorithm. Nor does it require the same run time per CPU burst, as does RMS. Whenever a process needs CPU time, it announces its presence and its deadline. The scheduler keeps a list of runnable processes, sorted on deadline. The algorithm runs the first process on the list, the one with the closest deadline. Whenever a new process becomes ready, the system checks to see if its deadline occurs before that of the currently running process. If so, the new process preempts the current one.

An example of EDF is given in Fig. 7-12. Initially all three processes are ready. They are run in the order of their deadlines. A must finish by $t = 30$, B must finish by $t = 40$, and C must finish by $t = 50$, so A has the earliest deadline and thus goes first. Up until $t = 90$ the choices are the same as RMS. At $t = 90$, A becomes ready again, and its deadline is $t = 120$, the same as B's deadline. The scheduler could legitimately choose either one to run, but since in practice, preempting B has some nonzero cost associated with it, it is better to let B continue to run.

To dispel the idea that RMS and EDF always give the same results, let us now look at another example, shown in Fig. 7-13. In this example the periods of A, B, and C are the same as before, but now A needs 15 msec of CPU time per burst instead of only 10 msec. The schedulability test computes the CPU utilization as

$0.500 + 0.375 + 0.100 = 0.975$. Only 2.5% of the CPU is left over, but in theory the CPU is not oversubscribed and it should be possible to find a legal schedule.

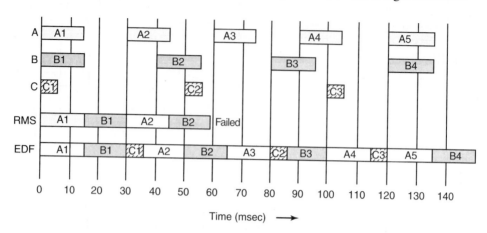

Figure 7-13. Another example of real-time scheduling with RMS and EDF.

With RMS, the priorities of the three processes are still 33, 25, and 20 as only the period matters, not the run time. This time, $B1$ does not finish until $t = 30$, at which time A is ready to roll again. By the time A is finished, at $t = 45$, B is ready again, so having a higher priority than C, it runs and C misses its deadline. RMS fails.

Now look at how EDF handles this case. At $t = 30$, there is a contest between $A2$ and $C1$. Because $C1$'s deadline is 50 and $A2$'s deadline is 60, C is scheduled. This is different from RMS, where A's higher priority wins.

At $t = 90$ A becomes ready for the fourth time. A's deadline is the same as that of the current process (120), so the scheduler has a choice of preempting or not. As before, it is better not to preempt if it is not needed, so $B3$ is allowed to complete.

In the example of Fig. 7-13, the CPU is 100% occupied up to $t = 150$. However, eventually a gap will occur because the CPU is only 97.5% utilized. Since all the starting and ending times are multiples of 5 msec, the gap will be 5 msec. In order to achieve the required 2.5% idle time, the 5 msec gap will have to occur every 200 msec, which is why it does not show up in Fig. 7-13.

An interesting question is why RMS failed. Basically, using static priorities only works if the CPU utilization is not too high. Liu and Layland (1973) proved that for any system of periodic processes, if

$$\sum_{i=1}^{m} \frac{C_i}{P_i} \le m(2^{1/m} - 1)$$

then RMS is guaranteed to work. For 3, 4, 5, 10, 20, and 100, the maximum permitted utilizations are 0.780, 0.757, 0.743, 0.718, 0.705, and 0.696. As $m \to \infty$, the maximum utilization is asymptotic to ln 2. In other words, Liu and Layland proved that for three processes, RMS always works if the CPU utilization is at or below 0.780. In our first example, it was 0.808 and RMS worked, but we were just lucky. With different periods and run times, a utilization of 0.808 might fail. In the second example, the CPU utilization was so high (0.975), there was no hope that RMS could work.

In contrast, EDF always works for any schedulable set of processes. It can achieve 100% CPU utilization. The price paid is a more complex algorithm. Thus in an actual video server, if the CPU utilization is below the RMS limit, RMS can be used. Otherwise EDF should be chosen.

7.5 MULTIMEDIA FILE SYSTEM PARADIGMS

Now that we have covered process scheduling in multimedia systems, let us continue our study by looking at multimedia file systems. These file systems use a different paradigm than traditional file systems. We will first review traditional file I/O, then turn our attention to how multimedia file servers are organized. To access a file, a process first issues an open system call. If this succeeds, the caller is given some kind of token, called a file descriptor in UNIX or a handle in Windows to be used in future calls. At that point the process can issue a read system call, providing the token, buffer address, and byte count as parameters. The operating system then returns the requested data in the buffer. Additional read calls can then be made until the process is finished, at which time it calls close to close the file and return its resources.

This model does not work well for multimedia on account of the need for real-time behavior. It works especially poorly for displaying multimedia files coming off a remote video server. One problem is that the user must make the read calls fairly precisely spaced in time. A second problem is that the video server must be able to supply the data blocks without delay, something that is difficult for it to do when the requests come in unplanned and no resources have been reserved in advance.

To solve these problems, a completely different paradigm is used by multimedia file servers: they act like VCRs (Video Cassette Recorders). To read a multimedia file, a user process issues a start system call, specifying the file to be read and various other parameters, for example, which audio and subtitle tracks to use. The video server then begins sending out frames at the required rate. It is up to the user to handle them at the rate they come in. If the user gets bored with the movie, the stop system call terminates the stream. File servers with this streaming model are often called **push servers** (because they push data at the user) and are contrasted with traditional **pull servers** where the user has to pull the data in one block at a time by repeatedly calling read to get one block after another. The difference between these two models is illustrated in Fig. 7-14.

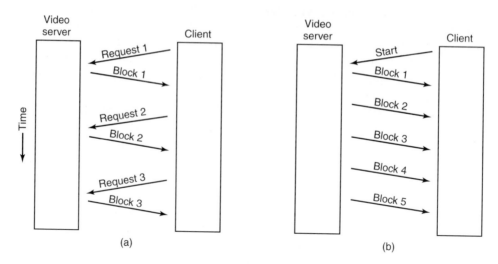

Figure 7-14. (a) A pull server. (b) A push server.

7.5.1 VCR Control Functions

Most video servers also implement standard VCR control functions, including pause, fast forward, and rewind. Pause is fairly straightforward. The user sends a message back to the video server that tells it to stop. All it has to do at that point is remember which frame goes out next. When the user tells the server to resume, it just continues from where it left off.

However, there is one complication here. To achieve acceptable performance, the server may reserve resources such as disk bandwidth and memory buffers for each outgoing stream. Continuing to tie these up while a movie is paused wastes resources, especially if the user is planning a trip to the kitchen to locate, microwave, cook, and eat a frozen pizza (especially an extra large). The resources can easily be released upon pausing, of course, but this introduces the danger that when the user tries to resume, they cannot be reacquired.

True rewind is actually easy, with no complications. All the server has to do is note that the next frame to be sent is 0. What could be easier? However, fast forward and fast backward (i.e., playing while rewinding) are much trickier. If it were not for compression, one way to go forward at 10x speed would be to just display every 10th frame. To go forward at 20x speed would require displaying every 20th frame. In fact, in the absence of compression, going forward or backward at any speed is easy. To run at k times normal speed, just display every k-th frame. To go backward at k times normal speed, do the same thing in the other direction. This approach works equally well for both pull servers and push servers.

Compression makes rapid motion either way more complicated. With a camcorder DV tape, where each frame is compressed independently of all the others, it is possible to use this strategy, provided that the needed frame can be found quickly. Since each frame compresses by a different amount, depending on its content, each frame is a different size, so skipping ahead k frames in the file cannot be done by doing a numerical calculation. Furthermore, audio compression is done independently of video compression, so for each video frame displayed in high-speed mode, the correct audio frame must also be located (unless sound is turned off when running faster than normal). Thus fast forwarding a DV file requires an index that allows frames to be located quickly, but it is at least doable in theory.

With MPEG, this scheme does not work, even in theory, due to the use of I-, P-, and B-frames. Skipping ahead k frames (assuming that can be done at all), might land on a P-frame that is based on an I-frame that was just skipped over. Without the base frame, having the incremental changes from it (which is what a P-frame contains) is useless. MPEG requires the file to be played sequentially.

Another way to attack the problem is to actually try to play the file sequentially at 10x speed. However, doing this requires pulling data off the disk at 10x speed. At that point, the server could try to decompress the frames (something it normally does not do), figure out which frame is needed, and recompress every 10th frame as an I-frame. However, doing this puts a huge load on the server. It also requires the server to understand the compression format, something it normally does not have to know.

The alternative of actually shipping all the data over the network to the user and letting the correct frames be selected out there requires running the network at 10x speed, possibly doable, but certainly not easy given the high speed at which it normally has to operate.

All in all, there is no easy way out. The only feasible strategy requires advance planning. What can be done is build a special file containing, say, every 10th frame, and compress this file using the normal MPEG algorithm. This file is what is shown in Fig. 7-3 as "fast forward." To switch to fast forward mode, what the server must do is figure out where in the fast forward file the user currently is. For example, if the current frame is 48,210 and the fast forward file runs at 10x, the server has to locate frame 4821 in the fast forward file and start playing there at normal speed. Of course, that frame might be a P- or B-frame, but the decoding process at the client can just skip frames until it sees an I-frame. Going backward is done in an analogous way using a second specially prepared file.

When the user switches back to normal speed, the reverse trick has to be done. If the current frame in the fast forward file is 5734, the server just switches back to the regular file and continues at frame 57,340. Again, if this frame is not an I-frame, the decoding process on the client side has to ignore all frames until an I-frame is seen.

While having these two extra files does the job, the approach has some disadvantages. First, some extra disk space is required to store the additional files. Second, fast forwarding and rewinding can only be done at speeds corresponding to the special files. Third, extra complexity is needed to switch back and forth between the regular, fast forward, and fast backward files.

7.5.2 Near Video on Demand

Having k users getting the same movie puts essentially the same load on the server as having them getting k different movies. However, with a small change in the model, great performance gains are possible. The problem with video on demand is that users can start streaming a movie at an arbitrary moment, so if there are 100 users all starting to watch some new movie at about 8 P.M., chances are that no two will start at exactly the same instant so they cannot share a stream. The change that makes optimization possible is to tell all users that movies only start on the hour and every (for example) 5 minutes thereafter. Thus if a user wants to see a movie at 8:02, he will have to wait until 8:05.

The gain here is that for a 2-hour movie, only 24 streams are needed, no matter how many customers there are. As shown in Fig. 7-15, the first stream starts at 8:00. At 8:05, when the first stream is at frame 9000, stream 2 starts. At 8:10, when the first stream is at frame 18,000 and stream 2 is at frame 9000, stream 3 starts, and so on up to stream 24, which starts at 9:55. At 10:00, stream 1 terminates and starts all over with frame 0. This scheme is called **near video on demand** because the video does not quite start on demand, but shortly thereafter.

The key parameter here is how often a stream starts. If one starts every 2 minutes, 60 streams will be needed for a two-hour movie, but the maximum waiting time to start watching will be 2 minutes. The operator has to decide how long people are willing to wait because the longer they are willing to wait, the more efficient the system, and the more movies can be shown at once. An alternative strategy is to also have a no-wait option, in which case a new stream is started on the spot, but to charge more for instant startup.

In a sense, video on demand is like using a taxi: you call it and it comes. Near video on demand is like using a bus: it has a fixed schedule and you have to wait for the next one. But mass transit only makes sense if there is a mass. In midtown Manhattan, a bus that runs every 5 minutes can count on picking up at least a few riders. A bus traveling on the back roads of Wyoming might be empty nearly all the time. Similarly, starting the latest Steven Spielberg release might attract enough customers to warrant starting a new stream every 5 minutes, but for *Gone with the Wind* it might be better to simply offer it on a demand basis.

With near video on demand, users do not have VCR controls. No user can pause a movie to make a trip to the kitchen. The best that can be done is upon returning from the kitchen, to drop back to a stream that started later, thereby repeating a few minutes of material.

Actually, there is another model for near video on demand as well. Instead of announcing in advance that some specific movie will start every 5 minutes, people can order movies whenever they want to. Every 5 minutes, the system sees which

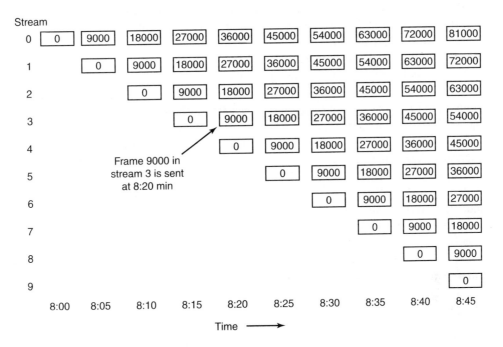

Figure 7-15. Near video on demand has a new stream starting at regular intervals, in this example every 5 minutes (9000 frames).

movies have been ordered and starts those. With this approach, a movie may start at 8:00, 8:10, 8:15, and 8:25, but not at the intermediate times, depending on demand. As a result, streams with no viewers are not transmitted, saving disk bandwidth, memory, and network capacity. On the other hand, attacking the freezer is now a bit of a gamble as there is no guarantee that there is another stream running 5 minutes behind the one the viewer was watching. Of course, the operator can provide an option for the user to display a list of all concurrent streams, but most people think their TV remote controls have more than enough buttons already and are not likely to enthusiastically welcome a few more.

7.5.3 Near Video on Demand with VCR Functions

The ideal combination would be near video on demand (for the efficiency) plus full VCR controls for every individual viewer (for the user convenience). With slight modifications to the model, such a design is possible. Below we will give a slightly simplified description of one way to achieve this goal (Abram-Profeta and Shin, 1998).

We start out with the standard near video-on-demand scheme of Fig. 7-15. However, we add the requirement that each client machine buffer the previous ΔT min and also the upcoming ΔT min locally. Buffering the previous ΔT min is easy: just save it after displaying it. Buffering the upcoming ΔT min is harder, but can be done if clients have the ability to read two streams at once.

One way to get the buffer set up can be illustrated using an example. If a user starts viewing at 8:15, the client machine reads and displays the 8:15 stream (which is at frame 0). In parallel, it reads and stores the 8:10 stream, which is currently at the 5-min mark (i.e., frame 9000). At 8:20, frames 0 to 17,999 have been stored and the user is expecting to see frame 9000 next. From that point on, the 8:15 stream is dropped, the buffer is filled from the 8:10 stream (which is at 18,000), and the display is driven from the middle of the buffer (frame 9000). As each new frame is read, one frame is added to the end of the buffer and one frame is dropped from the beginning of the buffer. The current frame being displayed, called the **play point**, is always in the middle of the buffer. The situation 75 min into the movie is shown in Fig. 7-16(a). Here all frames between 70 min and 80 min are in the buffer. If the data rate is 4 Mbps, a 10-min buffer requires 300 million bytes of storage. With current prices, the buffer can certainly be kept on disk and possibly in RAM. If RAM is desired, but 300 million bytes is too much, a smaller buffer can be used.

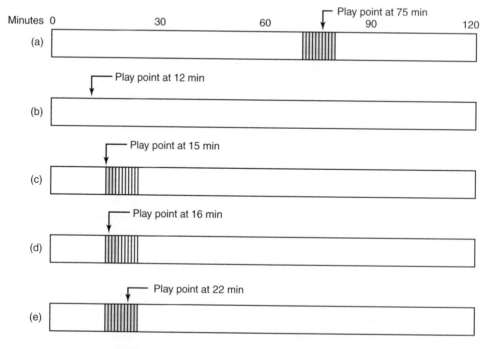

Figure 7-16. (a) Initial situation. (b) After a rewind to 12 min. (c) After waiting 3 min. (d) After starting to refill the buffer. (e) Buffer full.

Now suppose that the user decides to fast forward or fast reverse. As long as the play point stays within the range 70–80 min, the display can be fed from the buffer. However, if the play point moves outside that interval either way, we have a problem. The solution is to turn on a private (i.e., video-on-demand) stream to service the user. Rapid motion in either direction can be handled by the techniques discussed earlier.

Normally, at some point the user will settle down and decide to watch the movie at normal speed again. At this point we can think about migrating the user over to one of the near video-on-demand streams so the private stream can be dropped. Suppose, for example, that the user decides to go back to the 12 min mark, as shown in Fig. 7-16(b). This point is far outside the buffer, so the display cannot be fed from it. Furthermore, since the switch happened (instantaneously) at 75 min, there are streams showing the movie at 5, 10, 15, and 20 min, but none at 12 min.

The solution is to continue viewing on the private stream, but to start filling the buffer from the stream currently 15 minutes into the movie. After 3 minutes, the situation is as depicted in Fig. 7-16(c). The play point is now 15 min, the buffer contains minutes 15 to 18, and the near video-on-demand streams are at 8, 13, 18, and 23 min, among others. At this point the private stream can be dropped and the display can be fed from the buffer. The buffer continues to be filled from the stream now at 18 min. After another minute, the play point is 16 min, the buffer contains minutes 15 to 19, and the stream feeding the buffer is at 19 min, as shown in Fig. 7-16(d).

After an additional 6 minutes have gone by, the buffer is full and the play point is at 22 min. The play point is not in the middle of the buffer, although that can be arranged if necessary.

7.6 FILE PLACEMENT

Multimedia files are very large, are often written only once but read many times, and tend to be accessed sequentially. Their playback must also meet strict quality of service criteria. Together, these requirements suggest different file system layouts than traditional operating systems use. We will discuss some of these issues below, first for a single disk, then for multiple disks.

7.6.1 Placing a File on a Single Disk

The most important requirement is that data can be streamed to the network or output device at the requisite speed and without jitter. For this reason, having multiple seeks during a frame is highly undesirable. One way to eliminate intrafile seeks on video servers is to use contiguous files. Normally, having files be contiguous does not work well, but on a video server that is carefully preloaded in advance with movies that do not change afterward it can work.

One complication, however, is the presence of video, audio, and text, as shown in Fig. 7-3. Even if the video, audio, and text are each stored as separate contiguous files, a seek will be needed to go from the video file to an audio file and from there to a text file, if need be. This suggests a second possible storage arrangement, with the video, audio, and text interleaved as shown in Fig. 7-17, but the entire file still contiguous. Here, the video for frame 1 is directly followed by the various audio tracks for frame 1 and then the various text tracks for frame 1. Depending on how many audio and text tracks there are, it may be simplest just to read in all the pieces for each frame in a single disk read operation and only transmit the needed parts to the user.

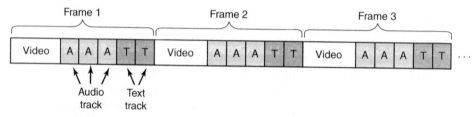

Figure 7-17. Interleaving video, audio, and text in a single contiguous file per movie.

This organization requires extra disk I/O for reading in unwanted audio and text, and extra buffer space in memory to store them. However it eliminates all seeks (on a single-user system) and does not require any overhead for keeping track of which frame is where on the disk since the whole movie is in one contiguous file. Random access is impossible with this layout, but if it is not needed, its loss is not serious. Similarly, fast forward and fast backward are impossible without additional data structures and complexity.

The advantage of having an entire movie as a single contiguous file is lost on a video server with multiple concurrent output streams because after reading a frame from one movie, the disk will have to read in frames from many other movies before coming back to the first one. Also, for a system in which movies are being written as well as being read (e.g., a system used for video production or editing), using huge contiguous files is difficult to do and not that useful.

7.6.2 Two Alternative File Organization Strategies

These observations lead to two other file placement organizations for multimedia files. The first of these, the small block model, is illustrated in Fig. 7-18(a). In this organization, the disk block size is chosen to be considerably smaller than the average frame size, even for P-frames and B-frames. For MPEG-2 at 4 Mbps with 30 frames/sec, the average frame is 16 KB, so a block size of 1 KB or 2 KB would work well. The idea here is to have a data structure, the frame index, per movie with one entry for each frame pointing to the start of the frame. Each frame itself consists of all the video, audio, and text tracks for that frame as a contiguous run of disk blocks, as shown. In this way, reading frame k consists of indexing into the frame index to find the k-th entry, and then reading in the entire frame in one disk operation. Since different frames have different sizes, the frame size (in blocks) is needed in the frame index, but even with 1-KB disk blocks, an 8-bit field can handle a frame up to 255 KB, which is enough for an uncompressed NTSC frame, even with many audio tracks.

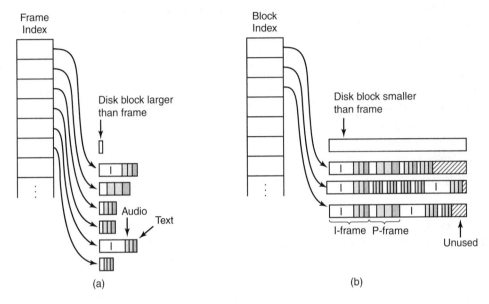

Figure 7-18. Noncontiguous movie storage. (a) Small disk blocks. (b) Large disk blocks.

The other way to store the movie is by using a large disk block (say 256 KB) and putting multiple frames in each block, as shown in Fig. 7-18(b). An index is still needed, but now it is a block index rather than a frame index. The index is, in fact, basically the same as the i-node of Fig. 6-15, possibly with the addition of information telling which frame is at the beginning of each block to make it possible to locate a given frame quickly. In general, a block will not hold an integral number of frames, so something has to be done to deal with this. Two options exist.

In the first option, which is illustrated in Fig. 7-18(b), whenever the next frame does not fit in the current block, the rest of the block is just left empty. This wasted space is internal fragmentation, the same as in virtual memory systems with fixed-size pages. On the other hand, it is never necessary to do a seek in the middle of a frame.

The other option is to fill each block to the end, splitting frames over blocks. This option introduces the need for seeks in the middle of frames, which can hurt performance, but saves disk space by eliminating internal fragmentation.

For comparison purposes, the use of small blocks in Fig. 7-18(a) also wastes some disk space because a fraction of the last block in each frame is unused. With a 1-KB disk block and a 2-hour NTSC movie consisting of 216,000 frames, the wasted disk space will only be about 108 KB out of 3.6 GB. The wasted space is harder to calculate for Fig. 7-18(b), but it will have to be much more because from time to time there will be 100 KB left at the end of a block with the next frame being an I-frame larger than that.

On the other hand, the block index is much smaller than the frame index. With a 256-KB block and an average frame of 16 KB, about 16 frames fit in a block, so a 216,000-frame movie needs only 13,500 entries in the block index, versus 216,000 for the frame index. For performance reasons, in both cases the index should list all the frames or blocks (i.e., no indirect blocks as UNIX), so tying up 13,500 8-byte entries in memory (4 bytes for the disk address, 1 byte for the frame size, and 3 bytes for the number of the starting frame) versus 216,000 5-byte entries (disk address and size only) saves almost 1 MB of RAM while the movie is playing.

These considerations lead to the following trade-offs:

1. Frame index: Heavier RAM usage while movie is playing; little disk wastage.

2. Block index (no splitting frames over blocks): Low RAM usage; major disk wastage.

3. Block index (splitting frames over blocks is allowed): Low RAM usage; no disk wastage; extra seeks

Thus the trade-offs involve RAM usage during playback, wasted disk space all the time, and performance loss during playback due to extra seeks. These problems can be attacked in various ways though. RAM usage can be reduced by paging in parts of the frame table just in time. Seeks during frame transmission can be masked by sufficient buffering, but this introduces the need for extra memory and probably extra copying. A good design has to carefully analyze all these factors and make a good choice for the application at hand.

Yet another factor here is that disk storage management is more complicated in Fig. 7-18(a) because storing a frame requires finding a consecutive run of blocks the right size. Ideally, this run of blocks should not cross a disk track boundary, but with head skew, the loss is not serious. Crossing a cylinder boundary should be avoided, however. These requirements mean that the disk's free storage has to be organized as a list of variable-sized holes, rather than a simple block list or bitmap, both of which can be used in Fig. 7-18(b).

In all cases, there is much to be said for putting all the blocks or frames of a movie within a narrow range, say a few cylinders, where possible. Such a placement means that seeks go faster so that more time will be left over for other (nonreal-time) activities or for supporting additional video streams. A constrained placement of this sort can be achieved by dividing the disk into cylinder groups and for each group keeping separate lists or bitmaps of the free blocks. If holes are used, for example, there could be one list for 1-KB holes, one for 2-KB holes, one for holes of 3 KB to 4 KB, another for holes of size 5 KB to 8 KB, and so on. In this way it is easy to find a hole of a given size in a given cylinder group.

Another difference between these two approaches is buffering. With the small-block approach, each read gets exactly one frame. Consequently, a simple double buffering strategy works fine: one buffer for playing back the current frame and one for fetching the next one. If fixed buffers are used, each buffer has to be large enough for the biggest possible I-frame. On the other hand, if a different buffer is allocated from a pool on every frame, and the frame size is known before the frame is read in, a small buffer can be chosen for a P-frame or B-frame.

With large blocks, a more complex strategy is required because each block contains multiple frames, possibly including fragments of frames on each end of the block (depending on which option was chosen earlier). If displaying or transmitting frames requires them to be contiguous, they must be copied, but copying is an expensive operation so it should be avoided where possible. If contiguity is not required, then frames that span block boundaries can be sent out over the network or to the display device in two chunks.

Double buffering can also be used with large blocks, but using two large blocks wastes memory. One way around wasting memory is to have a circular transmission buffer slightly larger than a disk block (per stream) that feeds the network or display. When the buffer's contents drop below some threshold, a new large block is read in from the disk, the contents copied to the transmission buffer, and the large block buffer returned to a common pool. The circular buffer's size must be chosen so that when it hits the threshold, there is room for another full disk block. The disk read cannot go directly to the transmission buffer because it might have to wrap around. Here copying and memory usage are being traded off against one another.

Yet another factor in comparing these two approaches is disk performance. Using large blocks runs the disk at full speed, often a major concern. Reading in little P-frames and B-frames as separate units is not efficient. In addition, striping large blocks over multiple drives (discussed below) is possible, whereas striping individual frames over multiple drives is not.

The small-block organization of Fig. 7-18(a) is sometimes called **constant time length** because each pointer in the index represents the same number of milliseconds of playing time. In contrast, the organization of Fig. 7-18(b) is sometimes called **constant data length** because the data blocks are the same size.

Another difference between the two file organizations is that if the frame types are stored in the index of Fig. 7-18(a), it may be possible to perform a fast forward by just displaying the I-frames. However, depending on how often I-frames appear in the stream, the rate may be perceived as too fast or too slow. In any case, with the organization of Fig. 7-18(b) fast forwarding is not possible this way. Actually reading the file sequentially to pick out the desired frames requires massive disk I/O.

A second approach is to use a special file that when played at normal speed gives the illusion of fast forwarding at 10x speed. This file can be structured the same as other files, using either a frame index or a block index. When opening a file, the system has to be able to find the fast forward file if needed. If the user hits the fast forward button, the system must instantly find and open the fast forward file and then jump to the correct place in the file. What it knows is the frame number it is currently at, but it needs the ability to locate the corresponding frame in the fast forward file. If it is currently at frame, say, 4816, and it knows the fast forward file is at 10x, then it must locate frame 482 in that file and start playing from there.

If a frame index is used, locating a specific frame is easy: just index into the frame index. If a block index is used, extra information in each entry is needed to identify which frame is in which block and a binary search of the block index has to be performed. Fast backward works in an analogous way to fast forward.

7.6.3 Placing Files for Near Video on Demand

So far we have looked at placement strategies for video on demand. For near video on demand, a different file placement strategy is more efficient. Remember that the same movie is going out as multiple staggered streams. Even if the movie is stored as a contiguous file, a seek is needed for each stream. Chen and Thapar (1997) have devised a file placement strategy to eliminate nearly all of those seeks. Its use is illustrated in Fig. 7-19 for a movie running at 30 frames/sec with a new stream starting every 5 min, as in Fig. 7-15. With these parameters, 24 concurrent streams are needed for a 2-hour movie.

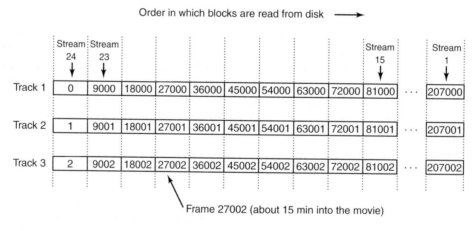

Figure 7-19. Optimal frame placement for near video on demand.

In this placement, frame sets of 24 frames are concatenated and written to the disk as a single record. They can also be read back on a single read. Consider the instant that stream 24 is just starting. It will need frame 0. Frame 23, which started 5 min earlier, will need frame 9000. Stream 22 will need frame 18,000, and so on back to stream 0 which will need frame 207,000. By putting these frames consecutively on one disk track, the video server can satisfy all 24 streams in reverse order with only one seek (to frame 0). Of course, the frames can be reversed on the disk if there is some reason to service the streams in ascending order. After the last stream has been serviced, the disk arm can move to track 2 to prepare servicing them all again. This scheme does not require the entire file to be contiguous, but still affords good performance to a number of streams at once.

A simple buffering strategy is to use double buffering. While one buffer is being played out onto 24 streams, another buffer is being loaded in advance. When the current one finishes, the two buffers are swapped and the one just used for playback is now loaded in a single disk operation.

An interesting question is how large to make the buffer. Clearly, it has to hold 24 frames. However, since frames are variable in size, it is not entirely trivial to pick the right size buffer. Making the buffer large enough for 24 I-frames is overkill, but making it large enough for 24 average frames is living dangerously.

Fortunately, for any given movie, the largest track (in the sense of Fig. 7-19) in the movie is known in advance, so a buffer of precisely that size can be chosen. However, it might just happen that in the biggest track, there are, say, 16 I-frames, whereas the next biggest track has only nine I-frames. A decision to choose a buffer large enough for the second biggest case might be wiser. Making this choice means truncating the biggest track, thus denying some streams one frame in the movie. To avoid a glitch, the previous frame can be redisplayed. No one will notice this.

Taking this approach further, if the third biggest track has only four I-frames, using a buffer capable of holding four I-frames and 20 P-frames is worth it. Introducing two repeated frames for some streams twice in the movie is probably acceptable. Where does this end? Probably with a buffer size that is big enough for 99% of the frames. Clearly, there is a trade-off here between memory used for buffers and quality of the movies shown. Note that the more simultaneous streams there are, the better the statistics are and the more uniform the frame sets will be.

7.6.4 Placing Multiple Files on a Single Disk

So far we have looked only at the placement of a single movie. On a video server, there will be many movies, of course. If they are strewn randomly around the disk, time will be wasted moving the disk head from movie to movie when multiple movies are being viewed simultaneously by different customers.

This situation can be improved by observing that some movies are more popular than others and taking popularity into account when placing movies on the disk. Although little can be said about the popularity of particular movies in general (other than noting that having big-name stars seems to help), something can be said about the relative popularity of movies in general.

For many kinds of popularity contests, such as movies being rented, books being checked out of a library, Web pages being referenced, even English words being used in a novel or the population of the largest cities, a reasonable approximation of the relative popularity follows a surprisingly predictable pattern. This pattern was discovered by a Harvard professor of linguistics, George Zipf (1902–1950) and is now called **Zipf's law**. What it states is that if the movies, books, Web pages, or words are ranked on their popularity, the probability that the next customer will choose the item ranked k-th in the list is C/k, where C is a normalization constant.

Thus the fraction of hits for the top three movies are $C/1$, $C/2$, and $C/3$, respectively, where C is computed such that the sum of all the terms is 1. In other words, if there are N movies, then

$$C/1 + C/2 + C/3 + C/4 + \cdots + C/N = 1$$

From this equation, C can be calculated. The values of C for populations with 10, 100, 1000, and 10,000 items are 0.341, 0.193, 0.134, and 0.102, respectively. For example, for 1000 movies, the probabilities for the top five movies are 0.134, 0.067, 0.045, 0.034, and 0.027, respectively.

Zipf's law is illustrated in Fig. 7-20. Just for fun, it has been applied to the populations of the 20 largest U.S. cities. Zipf's law predicts that the second largest city should have a population half of the largest city and the third largest city should be one third of the largest city, and so on. While hardly perfect, it is a surprisingly good fit.

For movies on a video server, Zipf's law states that the most popular movie is chosen twice as often as the second most popular movie, three times as often as the third most popular movie, and so on. Despite the fact that the distribution falls off fairly quickly at the beginning, it has a long tail. For example, movie 50 has a popularity of $C/50$ and movie 51 has a popularity of $C/51$, so movie 51 is 50/51 as popular as movie 50, only about a 2% difference. As one goes out further on the tail, the percent difference between consecutive movies becomes less and less. One conclusion is that the server needs a lot of movies since there is substantial demand for movies outside the top 10.

Knowing the relative popularities of the different movies makes it possible to model the performance of a video server and to use that information for placing files. Studies have shown that the best strategy is surprisingly simple and distribution independent. It is called the **organ-pipe algorithm** (Grossman and Silverman, 1973; and Wong, 1983). It consists of placing the most popular movie in the middle of the disk, with the second and third most popular movies on either side

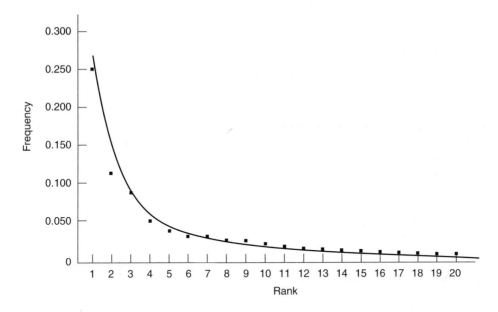

Figure 7-20. The curve gives Zipf's law for $N = 20$. The squares represent the populations of the 20 largest cities in the U.S., sorted on rank order (New York is 1, Los Angeles is 2, Chicago is 3, etc.).

of it. Outside of these come numbers four and five, and so on, as shown in Fig. 7-21. This placement works best if each movie is a contiguous file of the type shown in Fig. 7-17, but can also be used to some extent if each movie is constrained to a narrow range of cylinders. The name of the algorithm comes from the fact that a histogram of the probabilities looks like a slightly lopsided organ.

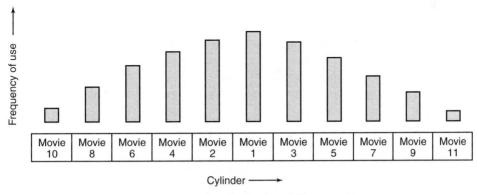

Figure 7-21. The organ-pipe distribution of files on a video server

What this algorithm does is try to keep the disk head in the middle of the disk. With 1000 movies and a Zipf's law distribution, the top five movies represent a total probability of 0.307, which means that the disk head will stay in the cylinders allocated to the top five movies about 30% of the time, a surprisingly large amount if 1000 movies are available.

7.6.5 Placing Files on Multiple Disks

To get higher performance, video servers often have many disks that can run in parallel. Sometimes RAIDs are used, but often not because what RAIDs offer is higher reliability at the cost of performance. Video servers generally want high performance and do not care so much about correcting transient errors. Also RAID controllers can become a bottleneck if they have too many disks to handle at once.

A more common configuration is simply a large number of disks, sometimes referred to as a **disk farm**. The disks do not rotate in a synchronized way and do not contain any parity bits, as RAIDS do. One possible configuration is to put movie *A* on disk 1, movie *B* on disk 2, and so on, as shown in Fig. 7-22(a). In practice, with modern disks several movies can be placed on each disk.

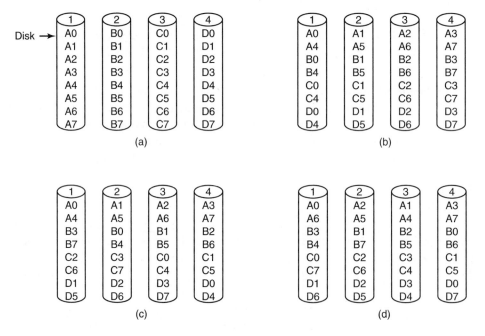

Figure 7-22. Four ways of organizing multimedia files over multiple disks. (a) No striping. (b) Same striping pattern for all files. (c) Staggered striping. (d) Random striping.

This organization is simple to implement and has straightforward failure characteristics: if one disk fails, all the movies on it become unavailable. Note that a company losing a disk full of movies is not nearly as bad as a company losing a disk full of data because the movies can easily be reloaded on a spare disk from a DVD. A disadvantage of this approach is that the load may not be well balanced. If some disks hold movies that are currently much in demand and other disks hold less popular movies, the system will not be fully utilized. Of course, once the usage frequencies of the movies are known, it may be possible to move some of them to balance the load by hand.

A second possible organization is to stripe each movie over multiple disks, four in the example of Fig. 7-22(b). Let us assume for the moment that all frames are the same size (i.e., uncompressed). A fixed number of bytes from movie A is written to disk 1, then the same number of bytes is written to disk 2, and so on until the last disk is reached (in this case with unit $A3$). Then the striping continues at the first disk again with $A4$ and so on until the entire file has been written. At that point movies B, C, and D are striped using the same pattern.

A possible disadvantage of this striping pattern is that because all movies start on the first disk, the load across the disks may not be balanced. One way to spread the load better is to stagger the starting disks, as shown in Fig. 7-22(c). Yet another way to attempt to balance the load is to use a random striping pattern for each file, as shown in Fig. 7-22(d).

So far we have assumed that all frames are the same size. With MPEG-2 movies, this assumption is false: I-frames are much larger than P-frames. There are two ways of dealing with this complication: stripe by frame or stripe by block. When striping by frame, the first frame of movie A goes on disk 1 as a contiguous unit, independent of how big it is. The next frame goes on disk 2, and so on. Movie B is striped in a similar way, either starting at the same disk, the next disk (if staggered), or a random disk. Since frames are read one at a time, this form of striping does not speed up the reading of any given movie. However, it spreads the load over the disks much better than in Fig. 7-22(a), which may behave badly if many people decide to watch movie A tonight and nobody wants movie C. On the whole, spreading the load over all the disks makes better use of the total disk bandwidth, and thus increases the number of customers that can be served.

The other way of striping is by block. For each movie, fixed-size units are written on each of the disks in succession (or at random). Each block contains one or more frames or fragments thereof. The system can now issue requests for multiple blocks at once for the same movie. Each request asks to read data into a different memory buffer, but in such a way that when all requests have been completed, a contiguous chunk of the movie (containing many frames) is now assembled in memory contiguously. These requests can proceed in parallel. When the last request has been satisfied, the requesting process can be signaled that the work has been completed. It can then begin transmitting the data to the user. A number of frames later, when the buffer is down to the last few frames, more requests are issued to preload another buffer. This approach uses large amounts of memory for buffering in order to keep the disks busy. On a system with 1000 active users and 1-MB buffers (for example, using 256-KB blocks on each of four disks), 1 GB of RAM is needed for the buffers. Such an amount is small potatoes on a 1000-user server and should not be a problem.

One final issue concerning striping is how many disks to stripe over. At one extreme, each movie is striped over all the disks. For example, with 2-GB movies and 1000 disks, a block of 2 MB could be written on each disk so that no movie uses the same disk twice. At the other extreme, the disks are partitioned into small groups (as in Fig. 7-22) and each movie is restricted to a single partition. The former, called **wide striping**, does a good job of balancing the load over the disks. Its main problem is that if every movie uses every disk and one disk goes down, no movie can be shown. The latter, called **narrow striping**, may suffer from hot spots (popular partitions), but loss of one disk only ruins the movies in its partition. Striping of variable-sized frames is analyzed in detail mathematically in (Shenoy and Vin, 1999).

7.7 CACHING

Traditional LRU file caching does not work well with multimedia files because the access patterns for movies are different from those of text files. The idea behind traditional LRU buffer caches is that after a block is used, it should be kept in the cache in case it is needed again quickly. For example, when editing a file, the set of blocks on which the file is written tend to be used over and over until the edit session is finished. In other words, when there is relatively high probability that a block will be reused within a short interval, it is worth keeping around to eliminate a future disk access.

With multimedia, the usual access pattern is that a movie is viewed from beginning to end sequentially. A block is unlikely to be used a second time unless the user rewinds the movie to see some scene again. Consequently, normal caching techniques do not work. However, caching can still help, but only if used differently. In the following sections we will look at caching for multimedia.

7.7.1 Block Caching

Although just keeping a block around in the hope that it may be reused quickly is pointless, the predictability of multimedia systems can be exploited to make caching useful again. Suppose that two users are watching the same movie, with one of them having started 2 sec after the other. After the first user has fetched and viewed any given block, it is very likely that the second user will need the same block 2 sec later. The system can easily keep track of which movies have only one viewer and which have two or more viewers spaced closely together in time.

Thus whenever a block is read on behalf of a movie that will be needed again shortly, it may make sense to cache it, depending on how long it has to be cached

and how tight memory is. Instead of keeping all disk blocks in the cache and discarding the least recently used one when the cache fills up, a different strategy
should be used. Every movie that has a second viewer within some time ΔT of the
first viewer can be marked as cachable and all its blocks cached until the second
(and possibly third) viewer has used them. For other movies, no caching is done
at all.

This idea can be taken a step further. In some cases it may be feasible to
merge two streams. Suppose that two users are watching the same movie but with
a 10-sec delay between them. Holding the blocks in the cache for 10 sec is possible but wastes memory. An alternative, but slightly sneaky, approach is to try to
get the two movies in sync. This can be done by changing the frame rate for both
movies. This idea is illustrated in Fig. 7-23.

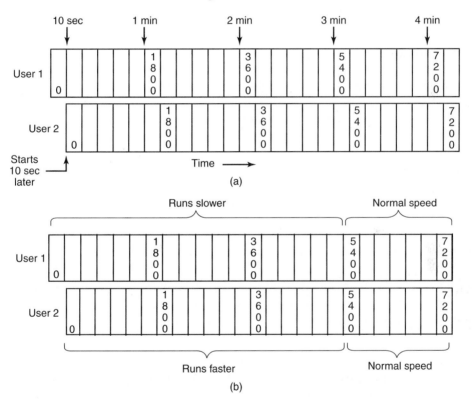

Figure 7-23. (a) Two users watching the same movie 10 sec out of sync. (b)
Merging the two streams into one.

In Fig. 7-23(a), both movies run at the standard NTSC rate of 1800
frames/min. Since user 2 started 10 sec later, he continues to be 10 sec beyond
for the entire movie. In Fig. 7-23(b), however, user 1's stream is slowed down
when user 2 shows up. Instead of running 1800 frames/min, for the next 3 min, it

runs at 1750 frames/min. After 3 minutes, it is at frame 5550. In addition, user 2's stream is played at 1850 frames/min for the first 3 min, also putting it at frame 5550. From that point on, both play at normal speed.

During the catch-up period, user 1's stream is running 2.8% slow and user 2's stream is running 2.8% fast. It is unlikely that the users will notice this. However, if that is a concern, the catch-up period can be spread out over a longer interval than 3 minutes.

An alternative way to slow down a user to merge with another stream is to give users the option of having commercials in their movies, presumably for a lower viewing price than commercial-free movies. The user can also choose the product categories, so the commercials will be less intrusive and more likely to be watched. By manipulating the number, length, and timing of the commercials, the stream can be held back long enough to get in sync with the desired stream (Krishnan, 1999).

7.7.2 File Caching

Caching can also be useful in multimedia systems in a different way. Due to the large size of most movies (2 GB), video servers often cannot store all their movies on disk, so they keep them on DVD or tape. When a movie is needed, it can always be copied to disk, but there is a substantial startup time to locate the movie and copy it to disk. Consequently, most video servers maintain a disk cache of the most heavily requested movies. The popular movies are stored in their entirety on disk.

Another way to use caching is to keep the first few minutes of each movie on disk. That way, when a movie is requested, playback can start immediately from the disk file. Meanwhile, the movie is copied from DVD or tape to disk. By storing enough of the movie on disk all the time, it is possible to have a very high probability that the next piece of the movie has been fetched before it is needed. If all goes well, the entire movie will be on disk well before it is needed. It will then go in the cache and stay on disk in case there are more requests later. If too much time goes by without another request, the movie will be removed from the cache to make room for a more popular one.

7.8 DISK SCHEDULING FOR MULTIMEDIA

Multimedia puts different demands on the disks than traditional text-oriented applications such as compilers or word processors. In particular, multimedia demands an extremely high data rate and real-time delivery of the data. Neither of these is trivial to provide. Furthermore, in the case of a video server, there is economic pressure to have a single server handle thousands of clients simultaneously. These requirements impact the entire system. Above we looked at the file system. Now let us look at disk scheduling for multimedia.

7.8.1 Static Disk Scheduling

Although multimedia puts enormous real-time and data-rate demands on all parts of the system, it also has one property that makes it easier to handle than a traditional system: predictability. In a traditional operating system, requests are made for disk blocks in a fairly unpredictable way. The best the disk subsystem can do is perform a one-block read ahead for each open file. Other than that, all it can do is wait for requests to come in and process them on demand. Multimedia is different. Each active stream puts a well-defined load on the system that is highly predictable. For NTSC playback, every 33.3 msec, each client wants the next frame in its file and the system has 33.3 msec to provide all the frames (the system needs to buffer at least one frame per stream so that the fetching of frame $k + 1$ can proceed in parallel with the playback of frame k).

This predictable load can be used to schedule the disk using algorithms tailored to multimedia operation. Below we will consider just one disk, but the idea can be applied to multiple disks as well. For this example we will assume that there are 10 users, each one viewing a different movie. Furthermore, we will assume that all movies have the same resolution, frame rate, and other properties.

Depending on the rest of the system, the computer may have 10 processes, one per video stream, or one process with 10 threads, or even one process with one thread that handles the 10 streams in round-robin fashion. The details are not important. What is important, is that time is divided up into **rounds**, where a round is the frame time (33.3 msec for NTSC, 40 msec for PAL). At the start of each round, one disk request is generated on behalf of each user, as shown in Fig. 7-24.

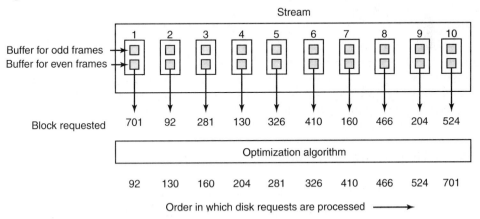

Figure 7-24. In one round, each movie asks for one frame.

After all the requests have come in at the start of the round, the disk knows what it has to do during that round. It also knows that no other requests will come in until these have been processed and the next round has begun. Consequently, it can sort the requests in the optimal way, probably in cylinder order (although conceivably in sector order in some cases) and then process them in the optimal order. In Fig. 7-24, the requests are shown sorted in cylinder order.

At first glance, one might think that optimizing the disk in this way has no value because as long as the disk meets the deadline, it does not matter if it meets it with 1 msec to spare or 10 msec to spare. However, this conclusion is false. By optimizing seeks in this fashion, the average time to process each request is diminished, which means that the disk can handle more streams per round on the average. In other words, optimizing disk requests like this increases the number of movies the server can transmit simultaneously. Spare time at the end of the round can also be used to service any nonreal-time requests that may exist.

If a server has too many streams, once in a while when it is asked to fetch frames from distant parts of the disk and miss a deadline. But as long as missed deadlines are rare enough, they can be tolerated in return for handling more streams at once. Note that what matters is the number of streams being fetched. Having two or more clients per stream does not affect disk performance or scheduling.

To keep the flow of data out to the clients moving smoothly, double buffering is needed in the server. During round 1, one set of buffers is used, one buffer per stream. When the round is finished, the output process or processes are unblocked and told to transmit frame 1. At the same time, new requests come in for frame 2 of each movie (there might be a disk thread and an output thread for each movie). These requests must be satisfied using a second set of buffers, as the first ones are still busy. When round 3 starts, the first set of buffers are now free and can be reused to fetch frame 3.

We have assumed that there is one round per frame. This limitation is not strictly necessary. There could be two rounds per frame to reduce the amount of buffer space required, at the cost of twice as many disk operations. Similarly, two frames could be fetched from the disk per round (assuming pairs of frames are stored contiguously on the disk). This design cuts the number of disk operations in half, at the cost of doubling the amount of buffer space required. Depending on the relative availability, performance, and cost of memory versus disk I/O, the optimum strategy can be calculated and used.

7.8.2 Dynamic Disk Scheduling

In the example above, we made the assumption that all streams have the same resolution, frame rate, and other properties. Now let us drop this assumption. Different movies may now have different data rates, so it is not possible to have one round every 33.3 msec and fetch one frame for each stream. Requests come in to the disk more or less at random.

Each read request specifies which block is to be read and in addition at what time the block is needed, that is, the deadline. For simplicity, we will assume that the actual service time for each request is the same (even though this is certainly not true). In this way we can subtract the fixed service time from each request to get the latest time the request can be initiated and still meet the deadline. This makes the model simpler because what the disk scheduler cares about is the deadline for scheduling the request.

When the system starts up, there are no disk requests pending. When the first request comes in, it is serviced immediately. While the first seek is taking place, other requests may come in, so when the first request is finished, the disk driver may have a choice of which request to process next. Some request is chosen and started. When that request is finished, there is again a set of possible requests: those that were not chosen the first time and the new arrivals that came in while the second request was being processed. In general, whenever a disk request completes, the driver has some set of requests pending from which it has to make a choice. The question is: "What algorithm does it use to select the next request to service?"

Two factors play a role in selecting the next disk request: deadlines and cylinders. From a performance point of view, keeping the requests sorted on cylinder and using the elevator algorithm minimizes total seek time, but may cause requests on outlying cylinders to miss their deadline. From a real-time point of view, sorting the requests on deadline and processing them in deadline order, earliest deadline first, minimizes the chance of missing deadlines, but increases total seek time.

These factors can be combined using the **scan-EDF algorithm** (Reddy and Wyllie, 1992). The basic idea of this algorithm is to collect requests whose deadlines are relatively close together into batches and process these in cylinder order. As an example, consider the situation of Fig. 7-25 at $t = 700$. The disk driver knows it has 11 requests pending for various deadlines and various cylinders. It could decide, for example, to treat the five requests with the earliest deadlines as a batch, sort them on cylinder number, and use the elevator algorithm to service these in cylinder order. The order would then be 110, 330, 440, 676, and 680. As long as every request is completed before its deadline, the requests can be safely rearranged to minimize the total seek time required.

When different streams have different data rates, a serious issue arises when a new customer shows up: should the customer be admitted. If admission of the customer will cause other streams to miss their deadlines frequently, the answer is probably no. There are two ways to calculate whether to admit the new customer or not. One way is to assume that each customer needs a certain amount of resources on the average, for example, disk bandwidth, memory buffers, CPU time, etc. If there is enough of each left for an average customer, the new one is admitted.

The other algorithm is more detailed. It takes a look at the specific movie the new customer wants and looks up the (precomputed) data rate for that movie, which differs for black and white versus color, cartoons versus filmed, and even

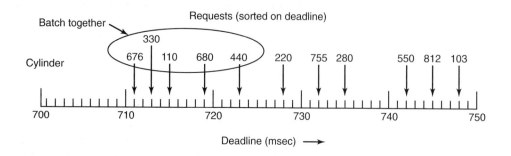

Figure 7-25. The scan-EDF algorithm uses deadlines and cylinder numbers for scheduling.

love stories versus war films. Love stories move slowly with long scenes and slow cross dissolves, all of which compress well whereas war films have many rapid cuts, and fast action, hence many I-frames and large P-frames. If the server has enough capacity for the specific film the new customer wants, then admission is granted; otherwise it is denied.

7.9 RESEARCH ON MULTIMEDIA

Multimedia is a hot topic these days, so there is a considerable amount of research about it. Much of this research is about the content, construction tools, and applications, all of which are beyond the scope of this book. However, some of it involves operating system structure, either writing a new multimedia operating system (Brandwein et al., 1994), or adding multimedia support to an existing operating system (Mercer, 1994). A related area is the design of multimedia servers (Bernhardt and Biersack, 1996; Heybey et al., 1996; Lougher et al., 1994; and Wong and Lee, 1997).

Some papers on multimedia are not about complete new systems, but about algorithms useful in multimedia systems. A popular topic has been real-time CPU scheduling for multimedia (Baker-Harvey, 1999; Bolosky et al., 1997; Dan et al., 1994; Goyal et al., 1996; Jones et al., 1997; Nieh and Lam, 1997; and Wu and Shu, 1996). Another topic that has been examined is disk scheduling for multimedia (Lee et al., 1997; Rompogiannakis et al., 1998; and Wang et al., 1999). File placement and load management on video servers are also important (Gafsi and Biersack, 1999; Shenoy and Vin, 1999; Shenoy et al., 1999; and Venkata-subramanian and Ramanathan, 1997) as is merging video streams to reduce bandwidth requirements (Eager et al., 1999).

In the text, we discussed how movie popularity affects placement on the video server. This topic is an ongoing area of research (Bisdikian and Patel, 1995; and

Griwodz et al., 1997). Finally, security and privacy in multimedia (e.g., in video-conferencing) are also subjects of research interest (Adams and Sasse, 1999; and Honeyman et. al, 1998)

7.10 SUMMARY

Multimedia is an up-and-coming use of computers. Due to the large sizes of multimedia files and their stringent real-time playback requirements, operating systems designed for text are not optimal for multimedia. Multimedia files consist of multiple, parallel tracks, usually one video and at least one audio and sometimes subtitle tracks as well. These must all be synchronized during playback.

Audio is recorded by sampling the volume periodically, usually 44,100 times/sec (for CD quality sound). Compression can be applied to the audio signal, giving a uniform compression rate of about 10x. Video compression uses both intraframe compression (JPEG) and interframe compression (MPEG). The latter represents P-frames as differences from the previous frame. B-frames can be based either on the previous frame or the next frame.

Multimedia needs real-time scheduling in order to meet its deadlines. Two algorithms are commonly used. The first is rate monotonic scheduling, which is a static preemptive algorithm that assigns fixed priorities to processes based on their periods. The second is earliest deadline first, which is a dynamic algorithm that always chooses the process with the closest deadline. EDF is more complicated, but it can achieve 100% utilization, something that RMS cannot achieve.

Multimedia file systems usually use a push model rather than a pull model. Once a stream is started, the bits come off the disk without further user requests. This approach is radically different from conventional operating systems, but is needed to meet the real-time requirements.

Files can be stored contiguously or not. In the latter case, the unit can be variable length (one block is one frame) or fixed length (one block is many frames). These approaches have different trade-offs.

File placement on the disk affects performance. When there are multiple files, the organ-pipe algorithm is sometimes used. Striping files across multiple disks, either wide or narrow, is common. Block and file caching strategies are also widely employed to improve performance.

PROBLEMS

1. What is the bit rate for uncompressed full-color XGA running at 25 frames/sec? Can a stream at this rate come off an UltraWide SCSI disk?

2. Can uncompressed black-and-white NTSC television be sent over fast Ethernet? If so, how many channels at once?

3. HDTV has twice the horizontal resolution of regular TV (1280 versus 640 pixels). Using information provided in the text, how much more bandwidth does it require than standard TV?

4. In Fig. 7-3, there are separate files for fast forward and fast reverse. If a video server is intended to support slow motion as well, is another file required for slow motion in the forward direction? What about in the backward direction?

5. A Compact Disc holds 74 min of music or 650 MB of data. Make an estimate of the compression factor used for music.

6. A sound signal is sampled using a signed 16-bit number (1 sign bit, 15 magnitude bits). What is the maximum quantization noise in percent? Is this a bigger problem for flute concertos or for rock and roll or is it the same for both? Explain your answer.

7. A recording studio is able to make a master digital recording using 20-bit sampling. The final distribution to listeners will use 16 bits. Suggest a way to reduce the effect of quantization noise, and discuss advantages and disadvantages of your scheme.

8. NTSC and PAL both use a 6-MHz broadcast channel, yet NTSC has 30 frames/sec whereas PAL has only 25 frames/sec. How is this possible? Does this mean that if both systems were to use the same color encoding scheme, NTSC would have inherently better quality than PAL? Explain your answer.

9. The DCT transformation uses an 8×8 block, yet the algorithm used for motion compensation uses 16×16. Does this difference cause problems, and if so, how are they solved in MPEG?

10. In Fig. 7-10 we saw how MPEG works with a stationary background and a moving actor. Suppose that an MPEG video is made from a scene in which the camera is mounted on a tripod and pans slowing from left to right at a speed such that no two consecutive frames are the same. Do all the frames have to be I-frames now? Why or why not?

11. Suppose that each of the three processes in Fig. 7-11 is accompanied by a process that supports an audio stream running with the same period as its video process, so audio buffers can be updated between video frames. All three of these audio processes are identical. How much CPU time is available for each burst of an audio process?

12. Two real-time processes are running on a computer. The first one runs every 25 msec for 10 msec. The second one runs every 40 msec for 15 msec. Will RMS always work for them?

13. The CPU of a video server has a utilization of 65%. How many movies can it show using RMS scheduling?

14. In Fig. 7-13, EDF keeps the CPU busy 100% of the time up to $t = 150$. It cannot keep the CPU busy indefinitely because there is only 975-msec work per second for it to do so. Extend the figure beyond 150 msec and determine when the CPU first goes idle with EDF.

15. A DVD can hold enough data for a full-length movie and the transfer rate is adequate to display a television-quality program. Why not just use a "farm" of many DVD drives as the data source for a video server?

16. The operators of a near video-on-demand system have discovered that people in a certain city are not willing to wait more than 6 minutes for a movie to start. How many parallel streams do they need for a 3-hour movie?

17. Consider a system using the scheme of Abram-Profeta and Shin in which the video server operator wishes customers to be able to search forward or backward for 1 min entirely locally. Assuming the video stream is MPEG-2 at 4 Mbps, how much buffer space must each customer have locally?

18. A video-on-demand system for HDTV uses the small block model of Fig. 7-18(a) with a 1-KB disk block. If the video resolution is 1280×720 and the data stream is 12 Mbps, how much disk space is wasted on internal fragmentation in a 2-hour movie using NTSC?

19. Consider the storage allocation scheme of Fig. 7-18(a) for NTSC and PAL. For a given disk block and movie size, does one of them suffer more internal fragmentation than the other? If so, which one is better and why?

20. Consider the two alternatives shown in Fig. 7-18. Does the shift toward HDTV favor either of these systems over the other? Discuss.

21. The near video-on-demand scheme of Chen and Thapar works best when each frame set is the same size. Suppose that a movie is being shown in 24 simultaneous streams and that one frame in 10 is an I-frame. Also assume that I-frames are 10 times larger than P-frames. B-frames are the same size as P-frames. What is the probability that a buffer equal to 4 I-frames and 20 P-frames will not be big enough? Do you think that such a buffer size is acceptable? To make the problem tractable, assume that frame types are randomly and independently distributed over the streams.

22. The end result of Fig. 7-16 is that the play point is not in the middle of the buffer any more. Devise a scheme to have at least 5 min behind the play point and 5 min ahead of it. Make any reasonable assumptions you have to, but state them explicitly.

23. The design of Fig. 7-17 requires that all language tracks be read on each frame. Suppose that the designers of a video server have to support a large number of languages, but do not want to devote so much RAM to buffers to hold each frame. What other alternatives are available, and what are the advantages and disadvantages of each one?

24. A small video server has eight movies. What does Zipf's law predict as the probabilities for the most popular movie, second most popular movie, and so on down to the least popular movie?

25. A 14-GB disk with 1000 cylinders is used to hold 1000 30-sec MPEG-2 video clips running at 4 Mbps. They are stored according to the organ-pipe algorithm. Assuming Zipf's law, what fraction of the time will the disk arm spend in the middle 10 cylinders?

26. Assuming that the relative demand for films A, B, C, and D is described by Zipf's law, what is the expected relative utilization of the four disks in Fig. 7-22 for the four striping methods shown?

27. Two video-on-demand customers started watching the same PAL movie 6 sec apart. If the system speeds up one stream and slows down the other to get them to merge, what percent speed up/down is needed to merge them in 3 min?

28. An MPEG-2 video server uses the round scheme of Fig. 7-24 for NTSC video. All the videos come off a single 10,800 rpm UltraWide SCSI disk with an average seek time of 3 msec. How many streams can be supported?

29. Repeat the previous problem, but now assume that scan-EDF reduces the average seek time by 20%. How many streams can now be supported?

30. Repeat the previous problem once more, but now assume that each frame is striped across four disks, with scan-EDF giving the 20% on each disk. How many streams can now be supported.

31. The text describes using a batch of five data requests to schedule the situation described in Fig. 7-25(a). If all requests take an equal amount of time, what is the maximum time per request allowable in this example?

32. Many of the bitmap images that are supplied for generating computer "wallpaper" use few colors and are easily compressed. A simple compression scheme is the following: choose a data value that does not appear in the input file, and use it as a flag. Read the file, byte by byte, looking for repeated byte values. Copy single values and bytes repeated up to three times directly to the output file. When a repeated string of 4 or more bytes is found, write to the output file a string of three bytes consisting of the flag byte, a byte indicating a count from 4 to 255, and the actual value found in the input file. Write a compression program using this algorithm, and a decompression program that can restore the original file. Extra credit: how can you deal with files that contain the flag byte in their data?

33. Computer animation is accomplished by displaying a sequence of slightly different images. Write a program to calculate the byte by byte difference between two uncompressed bitmap images of the same dimensions. The output will be the same size as the input files, of course. Use this difference file as input to the compression program of the previous problem, and compare the effectiveness of this approach with compression of individual images.

8

MULTIPLE PROCESSOR SYSTEMS

Since its inception, the computer industry has been driven by an endless quest for more and more computing power. The ENIAC could perform 300 operations per second, easily 1000 times faster than any calculator before it, yet people were not satisfied. We now have machines a million times faster than the ENIAC and still there is a demand for yet more horsepower. Astronomers are trying to make sense of the universe, biologists are trying to understand the implications of the human genome, and aeronautical engineers are interested in building safer and more efficient aircraft, and all want more CPU cycles. However much computing power there is, it is never enough.

In the past, the solution was always to make the clock run faster. Unfortunately, we are beginning to hit some fundamental limits on clock speed. According to Einstein's special theory of relativity, no electrical signal can propagate faster than the speed of light, which is about 30 cm/nsec in vacuum and about 20 cm/nsec in copper wire or optical fiber. This means that in a computer with a 10-GHz clock, the signals cannot travel more than 2 cm in total. For a 100-GHz computer the total path length is at most 2 mm. A 1-THz (1000 GHz) computer will have to be smaller than 100 microns, just to let the signal get from one end to the other and back once with a single clock cycle.

Making computers this small may be possible, but then we hit another fundamental problem: heat dissipation. The faster runs the computer, the more heat it generates, and the smaller the computer, the harder it is to get rid of this heat.

Already on high-end Pentium systems, the CPU cooler is bigger than the CPU itself. All in all, going from 1 MHz to 1 GHz simply required incrementally better engineering of the chip manufacturing process. Going from 1 GHz to 1 THz is going to require a radically different approach.

One approach to greater speed is through massively parallel computers. These machines consist of many CPUs, each of which runs at "normal" speed (whatever that may mean in a given year), but which collectively have far more computing power than a single CPU. Systems with 1000 CPUs are now commercially available. Systems with 1 million CPUs are likely to be built in the coming decade. While there are other potential approaches to greater speed, such as biological computers, in this chapter we will focus on systems with multiple conventional CPUs.

Highly parallel computers are often used for heavy number crunching. Problems such as predicting the weather, modeling airflow around an aircraft wing, simulating the world economy, or understanding drug-receptor interactions in the brain are all computationally intensive. Their solutions require long runs on many CPUs at once. The multiple processor systems discussed in this chapter are widely-used for these and similar problems in science and engineering, among other areas.

Another relevant development is the incredibly rapid growth of the Internet. It was originally designed as a prototype for a fault-tolerant military control system, then became popular among academic computer scientists, and has recently acquired many new uses. One of these is linking up thousands of computers all over the world to work together on large scientific problems. In a sense, a system consisting of 1000 computers spread all over the world is no different than one consisting of 1000 computers in a single room, although the delay and other technical characteristics are different. We will also consider these systems in this chapter.

Putting 1 million unrelated computers in a room is easy to do provided that you have enough money and a sufficiently large room. Spreading 1 million unrelated computers around the world is even easier since it finesses the second problem. The trouble comes in when you want them to communicate with one another to work together on a single problem. As a consequence, a great deal of work has been done on the interconnection technology, and different interconnect technologies have led to qualitatively different kinds of systems and different software organizations.

All communication between electronic (or optical) components ultimately comes down to sending messages—well-defined bit strings—between them. The differences are in the time scale, distance scale, and logical organization involved. At one extreme are the shared-memory multiprocessors, systems in which somewhere between two and about 1000 CPUs communicate via a shared memory. In this model, every CPU has equal access to the entire physical memory, and can read and write individual words using LOAD and STORE instructions. Accessing a memory word usually takes 10–50 nsec. While this model, illustrated in Fig. 8-1(a), sounds simple, actually implementing it is far from simple and usually involves considerable message passing under the covers, as we will explain shortly.

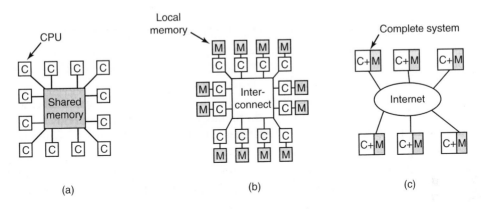

Figure 8-1. (a) A shared-memory multiprocessor. (b) A message-passing multicomputer. (c) A wide area distributed system.

Next comes the system of Fig. 8-1(b) in which a number of CPU-memory pairs are connected by some kind of high-speed interconnect. This kind of system is called a message-passing multicomputer. Each memory is local to a single CPU and can be accessed only by that CPU. The machines communicate by sending multiword messages over the interconnect. With a good interconnect, a short message can be sent in 10–50 μsec, but still far longer than the memory access time of Fig. 8-1(a). There is no shared global memory in this design. Multicomputers (i.e., message-passing systems) are much easier to build than (shared-memory) multiprocessors but they are harder to program. Thus each genre has its fans.

The third model, illustrated in Fig. 8-1(c), connects complete computer systems over a wide area network, such as the Internet, to form a **distributed system**. Each of these has its own memory, of course, and the systems communicate by message passing. The only real difference between Fig. 8-1(c) and Fig. 8-1(b) is that in the former, complete computers are used and message times are often 10–50 msec. This long delay forces these **loosely-coupled** systems to be used in different ways than the **tightly-coupled** systems of Fig. 8-1(b). The three types of systems differ in their delays by something like three orders of magnitude. That is the difference between a day and three years.

This chapter has three major sections, corresponding to the three models of Fig. 8-1. In each one, we start out with a brief introduction to the relevant hardware. Then we move on to the software, especially the operating system issues for that type of system. As we will see, in each case different issues are present.

8.1 MULTIPROCESSORS

A **shared-memory multiprocessor** (or just multiprocessor henceforth) is a computer system in which two or more CPUs share full access to a common RAM. A program running on any of the CPUs sees a normal (usually paged) virtual address space. The only unusual property this system has is that the CPU can write some value into a memory word and then read the word back and get a different value (because another CPU has changed it). When organized correctly, this property forms the basis of interprocessor communication: one CPU writes some data into memory and another one reads the data out.

For the most part, multiprocessor operating systems are just regular operating systems. They handle system calls, do memory management, provide a file system, and manage I/O devices. Nevertheless, there are some areas in which they have unique features. These include process synchronization, resource management, and scheduling. Below we will first take a brief look at multiprocessor hardware and then move on to these operating systems issues.

8.1.1 Multiprocessor Hardware

Although all multiprocessors have the property that every CPU can address all of memory, some multiprocessors have the additional property that every memory word can be read as fast as every other memory word. These machines are called **UMA (Uniform Memory Access)** multiprocessors. In contrast, **NUMA (Nonuniform Memory Access)** multiprocessors do not have this property. Why this difference exists will become clear later. We will first examine UMA multiprocessors and then move on to NUMA multiprocessors.

UMA Bus-Based SMP Architectures

The simplest multiprocessors are based on a single bus, as illustrated in Fig. 8-2(a). Two or more CPUs and one or more memory modules all use the same bus for communication. When a CPU wants to read a memory word, it first checks to see if the bus is busy. If the bus is idle, the CPU puts the address of the word it wants on the bus, asserts a few control signals, and waits until the memory puts the desired word on the bus.

If the bus is busy when a CPU wants to read or write memory, the CPU just waits until the bus becomes idle. Herein lies the problem with this design. With two or three CPUs, contention for the bus will be manageable; with 32 or 64 it will be unbearable. The system will be totally limited by the bandwidth of the bus, and most of the CPUs will be idle most of the time.

The solution to this problem is to add a cache to each CPU, as depicted in Fig. 8-2(b). The cache can be inside the CPU chip, next to the CPU chip, on the

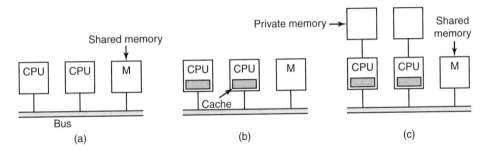

Figure 8-2. Three bus-based multiprocessors. (a) Without caching. (b) With caching. (c) With caching and private memories.

processor board, or some combination of all three. Since many reads can now be satisfied out of the local cache, there will be much less bus traffic, and the system can support more CPUs. In general, caching is not done on an individual word basis but on the basis of 32- or 64-byte blocks. When a word is referenced, its entire block is fetched into the cache of the CPU touching it.

Each cache block is marked as being either read-only (in which case it can be present in multiple caches at the same time), or as read-write (in which case it may not be present in any other caches). If a CPU attempts to write a word that is in one or more remote caches, the bus hardware detects the write and puts a signal on the bus informing all other caches of the write. If other caches have a "clean" copy, that is, an exact copy of what is in memory, they can just discard their copies and let the writer fetch the cache block from memory before modifying it. If some other cache has a "dirty" (i.e., modified) copy, it must either write it back to memory before the write can proceed or transfer it directly to the writer over the bus. Many cache transfer protocols exist.

Yet another possibility is the design of Fig. 8-2(c), in which each CPU has not only a cache, but also a local, private memory which it accesses over a dedicated (private) bus. To use this configuration optimally, the compiler should place all the program text, strings, constants and other read-only data, stacks, and local variables in the private memories. The shared memory is then only used for writable shared variables. In most cases, this careful placement will greatly reduce bus traffic, but it does require active cooperation from the compiler.

UMA Multiprocessors Using Crossbar Switches

Even with the best caching, the use of a single bus limits the size of a UMA multiprocessor to about 16 or 32 CPUs. To go beyond that, a different kind of interconnection network is needed. The simplest circuit for connecting n CPUs to k memories is the **crossbar switch**, shown in Fig. 8-3. Crossbar switches have been used for decades within telephone switching exchanges to connect a group of incoming lines to a set of outgoing lines in an arbitrary way.

At each intersection of a horizontal (incoming) and vertical (outgoing) line is a **crosspoint**. A crosspoint is a small switch that can be electrically opened or closed, depending on whether the horizontal and vertical lines are to be connected or not. In Fig. 8-3(a) we see three crosspoints closed simultaneously, allowing connections between the (CPU, memory) pairs (001, 000), (101, 101), and (110, 010) at the same time. Many other combinations are also possible. In fact, the number of combinations is equal to the number of different ways eight rooks can be safely placed on a chess board.

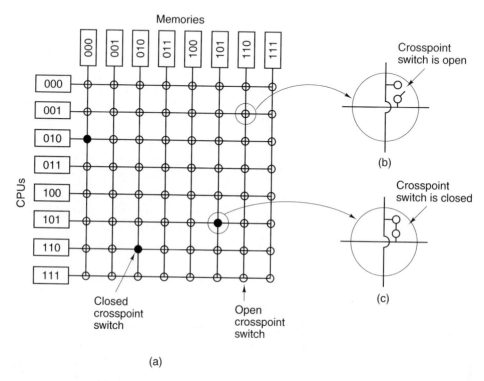

(a)

Figure 8-3. (a) An 8×8 crossbar switch. (b) An open crosspoint. (c) A closed crosspoint.

One of the nicest properties of the crossbar switch is that it is a **nonblocking network**, meaning that no CPU is ever denied the connection it needs because some crosspoint or line is already occupied (assuming the memory module itself is available). Furthermore, no advance planning is needed. Even if seven arbitrary connections are already set up, it is always possible to connect the remaining CPU to the remaining memory.

One of the worst properties of the crossbar switch is the fact that the number of crosspoints grows as n^2. With 1000 CPUs and 1000 memory modules we need a million crosspoints. Such a large crossbar switch is not feasible. Nevertheless, for medium-sized systems, a crossbar design is workable.

UMA Multiprocessors Using Multistage Switching Networks

A completely different multiprocessor design is based on the humble 2×2 switch shown in Fig. 8-4(a). This switch has two inputs and two outputs. Messages arriving on either input line can be switched to either output line. For our purposes, messages will contain up to four parts, as shown in Fig. 8-4(b). The *Module* field tells which memory to use. The *Address* specifies an address within a module. The *Opcode* gives the operation, such as READ or WRITE. Finally, the optional *Value* field may contain an operand, such as a 32-bit word to be written on a WRITE. The switch inspects the *Module* field and uses it to determine if the message should be sent on X or on Y.

(a)   (b)

Figure 8-4. (a) A 2×2 switch. (b) A message format.

Our 2×2 switches can be arranged in many ways to build larger **multistage switching networks** (Adams et al., 1987; Bhuyan et al., 1989; and Kumar and Reddy, 1987). One possibility is the no-frills, economy class **omega network**, illustrated in Fig. 8-5. Here we have connected eight CPUs to eight memories using 12 switches. More generally, for n CPUs and n memories we would need $\log_2 n$ stages, with $n/2$ switches per stage, for a total of $(n/2)\log_2 n$ switches, which is a lot better than n^2 crosspoints, especially for large values of n.

The wiring pattern of the omega network is often called the **perfect shuffle**, since the mixing of the signals at each stage resembles a deck of cards being cut in half and then mixed card-for-card. To see how the omega network works, suppose that CPU 011 wants to read a word from memory module 110. The CPU sends a READ message to switch 1D containing 110 in the *Module* field. The switch takes the first (i.e., leftmost) bit of 110 and uses it for routing. A 0 routes to the upper output and a 1 routes to the lower one. Since this bit is a 1, the message is routed via the lower output to 2D.

All the second-stage switches, including 2D, use the second bit for routing. This, too, is a 1, so the message is now forwarded via the lower output to 3D. Here the third bit is tested and found to be a 0. Consequently, the message goes out on the upper output and arrives at memory 110, as desired. The path followed by this message is marked in Fig. 8-5 by the letter *a*.

As the message moves through the switching network, the bits at the left-hand end of the module number are no longer needed. They can be put to good use by recording the incoming line number there, so the reply can find its way back. For

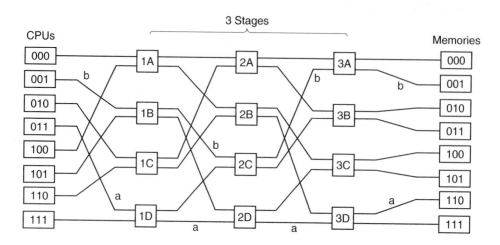

Figure 8-5. An omega switching network.

path *a*, the incoming lines are 0 (upper input to 1D), 1 (lower input to 2D), and 1 (lower input to 3D), respectively. The reply is routed back using 011, only reading it from right to left this time.

At the same time all this is going on, CPU 001 wants to write a word to memory module 001. An analogous process happens here, with the message routed via the upper, upper, and lower outputs, respectively, marked by the letter *b*. When it arrives, its *Module* field reads 001, representing the path it took. Since these two requests do not use any of the same switches, lines, or memory modules, they can proceed in parallel.

Now consider what would happen if CPU 000 simultaneously wanted to access memory module 000. Its request would come into conflict with CPU 001's request at switch 3A. One of them would have to wait. Unlike the crossbar switch, the omega network is a **blocking network**. Not every set of requests can be processed simultaneously. Conflicts can occur over the use of a wire or a switch, as well as between requests *to* memory and replies *from* memory.

It is clearly desirable to spread the memory references uniformly across the modules. One common technique is to use the low-order bits as the module number. Consider, for example, a byte-oriented address space for a computer that mostly accesses 32-bit words. The 2 low-order bits will usually be 00, but the next 3 bits will be uniformly distributed. By using these 3 bits as the module number, consecutively addressed words will be in consecutive modules. A memory system in which consecutive words are in different modules is said to be **interleaved**. Interleaved memories maximize parallelism because most memory references are to consecutive addresses. It is also possible to design switching networks that are nonblocking and which offer multiple paths from each CPU to each memory module, to spread the traffic better.

NUMA Multiprocessors

Single-bus UMA multiprocessors are generally limited to no more than a few dozen CPUs and crossbar or switched multiprocessors need a lot of (expensive) hardware and are not that much bigger. To get to more than 100 CPUs, something has to give. Usually, what gives is the idea that all memory modules have the same access time. This concession leads to the idea of NUMA multiprocessors, as mentioned above. Like their UMA cousins, they provide a single address space across all the CPUs, but unlike the UMA machines, access to local memory modules is faster than access to remote ones. Thus all UMA programs will run without change on NUMA machines, but the performance will be worse than on a UMA machine at the same clock speed.

NUMA machines have three key characteristics that all of them possess and which together distinguish them from other multiprocessors:

1. There is a single address space visible to all CPUs.

2. Access to remote memory is via LOAD and STORE instructions.

3. Access to remote memory is slower than access to local memory.

When the access time to remote memory is not hidden (because there is no caching), the system is called **NC-NUMA**. When coherent caches are present, the system is called **CC-NUMA (Cache-Coherent NUMA)**.

The most popular approach for building large CC-NUMA multiprocessors currently is the **directory-based multiprocessor**. The idea is to maintain a database telling where each cache line is and what its status is. When a cache line is referenced, the database is queried to find out where it is and whether it is clean or dirty (modified). Since this database must be queried on every instruction that references memory, it must be kept in extremely-fast special-purpose hardware that can respond in a fraction of a bus cycle.

To make the idea of a directory-based multiprocessor somewhat more concrete, let us consider as a simple (hypothetical) example, a 256-node system, each node consisting of one CPU and 16 MB of RAM connected to the CPU via a local bus. The total memory is 2^{32} bytes, divided up into 2^{26} cache lines of 64 bytes each. The memory is statically allocated among the nodes, with 0–16M in node 0, 16M–32M in node 1, and so on. The nodes are connected by an interconnection network, as shown in Fig. 8-6(a). Each node also holds the directory entries for the 2^{18} 64-byte cache lines comprising its 2^{24} byte memory. For the moment, we will assume that a line can be held in at most one cache.

To see how the directory works, let us trace a LOAD instruction from CPU 20 that references a cached line. First the CPU issuing the instruction presents it to its MMU, which translates it to a physical address, say, 0x24000108. The MMU splits this address into the three parts shown in Fig. 8-6(b). In decimal, the three

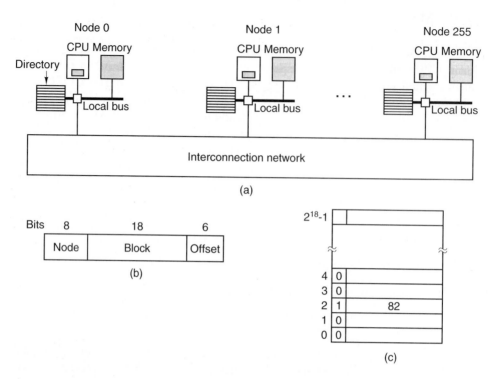

Figure 8-6. (a) A 256-node directory-based multiprocessor. (b) Division of a 32-bit memory address into fields. (c) The directory at node 36.

parts are node 36, line 4, and offset 8. The MMU sees that the memory word referenced is from node 36, not node 20, so it sends a request message through the interconnection network to the line's home node, 36, asking whether its line 4 is cached, and if so, where.

When the request arrives at node 36 over the interconnection network, it is routed to the directory hardware. The hardware indexes into its table of 2^{18} entries, one for each of its cache lines and extracts entry 4. From Fig. 8-6(c) we see that the line is not cached, so the hardware fetches line 4 from the local RAM, sends it back to node 20, and updates directory entry 4 to indicate that the line is now cached at node 20.

Now let us consider a second request, this time asking about node 36's line 2. From Fig. 8-6(c) we see that this line is cached at node 82. At this point the hardware could update directory entry 2 to say that the line is now at node 20 and then send a message to node 82 instructing it to pass the line to node 20 and invalidate its cache. Note that even a so-called "shared-memory multiprocessor" has a lot of message passing going on under the hood.

As a quick aside, let us calculate how much memory is being taken up by the directories. Each node has 16 MB of RAM and 2^{18} 9-bit entries to keep track of that RAM. Thus the directory overhead is about 9×2^{18} bits divided by 16 MB or about 1.76 percent, which is generally acceptable (although it has to be high-speed memory, which increases its cost). Even with 32-byte cache lines the overhead would only be 4 percent. With 128-byte cache lines, it would be under 1 percent.

An obvious limitation of this design is that a line can be cached at only one node. To allow lines to be cached at multiple nodes, we would need some way of locating all of them, for example, to invalidate or update them on a write. Various options are possible to allow caching at several nodes at the same time, but a discussion of these is beyond the scope of this book.

8.1.2 Multiprocessor Operating System Types

Let us now turn from multiprocessor hardware to multiprocessor software, in particular, multiprocessor operating systems. Various organizations are possible. Below we will study three of them.

Each CPU Has Its Own Operating System

The simplest possible way to organize a multiprocessor operating system is to statically divide memory into as many partitions as there are CPUs and give each CPU its own private memory and its own private copy of the operating system. In effect, the *n* CPUs then operate as *n* independent computers. One obvious optimization is to allow all the CPUs to share the operating system code and make private copies of only the data, as shown in Fig. 8-7.

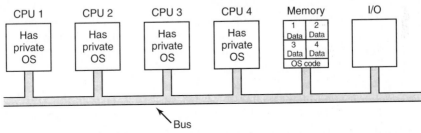

Figure 8-7. Partitioning multiprocessor memory among four CPUs, but sharing a single copy of the operating system code. The boxes marked Data are the operating system's private data for each CPU.

This scheme is still better than having *n* separate computers since it allows all the machines to share a set of disks and other I/O devices, and it also allows the memory to be shared flexibly. For example, if one day an unusually large program has to be run, one of the CPUs can be allocated an extra large portion of memory for the duration of that program. In addition, processes can efficiently communicate with one another by having, say a producer be able to write data into memory and have a consumer fetch it from the place the producer wrote it.

Still, from an operating systems' perspective, having each CPU have its own operating system is as primitive as it gets.

It is worth explicitly mentioning four aspects of this design that may not be obvious. First, when a process makes a system call, the system call is caught and handled on its own CPU using the data structures in that operating system's tables.

Second, since each operating system has its own tables, it also has its own set of processes that it schedules by itself. There is no sharing of processes. If a user logs into CPU 1, all of his processes run on CPU 1. As a consequence, it can happen that CPU 1 is idle while CPU 2 is loaded with work.

Third, there is no sharing of pages. It can happen that CPU 1 has pages to spare while CPU 2 is paging continuously. There is no way for CPU 2 to borrow some pages from CPU 1 since the memory allocation is fixed.

Fourth, and worst, if the operating system maintains a buffer cache of recently used disk blocks, each operating system does this independently of the other ones. Thus it can happen that a certain disk block is present and dirty in multiple buffer caches at the same time, leading to inconsistent results. The only way to avoid this problem is to eliminate the buffer caches. Doing so is not hard, but it hurts performance considerably.

Master-Slave Multiprocessors

For these reasons, this model is rarely used any more, although it was used in the early days of multiprocessors, when the goal was to port existing operating systems to some new multiprocessor as fast as possible. A second model is shown in Fig. 8-8. Here, one copy of the operating system and its tables are present on CPU 1 and not on any of the others. All system calls are redirected to CPU 1 for processing there. CPU 1 may also run user processes if there is CPU time left over. This model is called **master-slave** since CPU 1 is the master and all the others are slaves.

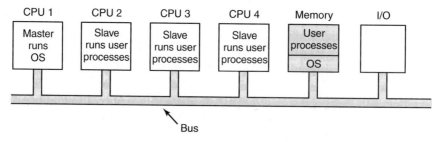

Figure 8-8. A master-slave multiprocessor model.

The master-slave model solves most of the problems of the first model. There is a single data structure (e.g., one list or a set of prioritized lists) that keeps track of ready processes. When a CPU goes idle, it asks the operating system for a process to run and it is assigned one. Thus it can never happen that one CPU is idle while another is overloaded. Similarly, pages can be allocated among all the processes dynamically and there is only one buffer cache, so inconsistencies never occur.

The problem with this model is that with many CPUs, the master will become a bottleneck. After all, it must handle all system calls from all CPUs. If, say, 10% of all time is spent handling system calls, then 10 CPUs will pretty much saturate the master, and with 20 CPUs it will be completely overloaded. Thus this model is simple and workable for small multiprocessors, but for large ones it fails.

Symmetric Multiprocessors

Our third model, the **SMP** (**Symmetric MultiProcessor**), eliminates this asymmetry. There is one copy of the operating system in memory, but any CPU can run it. When a system call is made, the CPU on which the system call was made traps to the kernel and processes the system call. The SMP model is illustrated in Fig. 8-9.

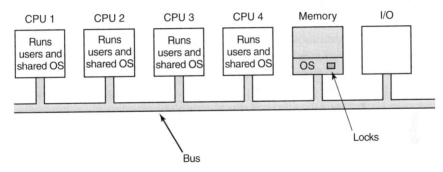

Figure 8-9. The SMP multiprocessor model.

This model balances processes and memory dynamically, since there is only one set of operating system tables. It also eliminates the master CPU bottleneck, since there is no master, but it introduces its own problems. In particular, if two or more CPUs are running operating system code at the same time, disaster will result. Imagine two CPUs simultaneously picking the same process to run or claiming the same free memory page. The simplest way around these problems is to associate a mutex (i.e., lock) with the operating system, making the whole system one big critical region. When a CPU wants to run operating system code, it must first acquire the mutex. If the mutex is locked, it just waits. In this way, any CPU can run the operating system, but only one at a time.

This model works, but is almost as bad as the master-slave model. Again, suppose that 10% of all run time is spent inside the operating system. With 20 CPUs, there will be long queues of CPUs waiting to get in. Fortunately, it is easy to improve. Many parts of the operating system are independent of one another. For example, there is no problem with one CPU running the scheduler while another CPU is handling a file system call and a third one is processing a page fault.

This observation leads to splitting the operating system up into independent critical regions that do not interact with one another. Each critical region is protected by its own mutex, so only one CPU at a time can execute it. In this way, far more parallelism can be achieved. However, it may well happen that some tables, such as the process table, are used by multiple critical regions. For example, the process table is needed for scheduling, but also for the fork system call and also for signal handling. Each table that may be used by multiple critical regions needs its own mutex. In this way, each critical region can be executed by only one CPU at a time and each critical table can be accessed by only one CPU at a time.

Most modern multiprocessors use this arrangement. The hard part about writing the operating system for such a machine is not that the actual code is so different from a regular operating system. It is not. The hard part is splitting it into critical regions that can be executed concurrently by different CPUs without interfering with one another, not even in subtle, indirect ways. In addition, every table used by two or more critical regions must be separately protected by a mutex and all code using the table must use the mutex correctly.

Furthermore, great care must be taken to avoid deadlocks. If two critical regions both need table *A* and table *B*, and one of them claims *A* first and the other claims *B* first, sooner or later a deadlock will occur and nobody will know why. In theory, all the tables could be assigned integer values and all the critical regions could be required to acquire tables in increasing order. This strategy avoids deadlocks, but it requires the programmer to think very carefully which tables each critical region needs to make the requests in the right order.

As the code evolves over time, a critical region may need a new table it did not previously need. If the programmer is new and does not understand the full logic of the system, then the temptation will be to just grab the mutex on the table at the point it is needed and release it when it is no longer needed. However reasonable this may appear, it may lead to deadlocks, which the user will perceive as the system freezing. Getting it right is not easy and keeping it right over a period of years in the face of changing programmers is very difficult.

8.1.3 Multiprocessor Synchronization

The CPUs in a multiprocessor frequently need to synchronize. We just saw the case in which kernel critical regions and tables have to be protected by mutexes. Let us now take a close look at how this synchronization actually works in a multiprocessor. It is far from trivial, as we will soon see.

To start with, proper synchronization primitives are really needed. If a process on a uniprocessor makes a system call that requires accessing some critical kernel table, the kernel code can just disable interrupts before touching the table. It can then do its work knowing that it will be able to finish without any other process sneaking in and touching the table before it is finished. On a multiprocessor, disabling interrupts affects only the CPU doing the disable. Other CPUs continue to run and can still touch the critical table. As a consequence, a proper mutex protocol must be used and respected by all CPUs to guarantee that mutual exclusion works.

The heart of any practical mutex protocol is an instruction that allows a memory word to be inspected and set in one indivisible operation. We saw how TSL (Test and Set Lock) was used in Fig. 2-22 to implement critical regions. As we discussed earlier, what this instruction does is read out a memory word and store it in a register. Simultaneously, it writes a 1 (or some other nonzero value) into the memory word. Of course, it takes two separate bus cycles to perform the memory read and memory write. On a uniprocessor, as long as the instruction cannot be broken off halfway, TSL always works as expected.

Now think about what could happen on a multiprocessor. In Fig. 8-10 we see the worst case timing, in which memory word 1000, being used as a lock is initially 0. In step 1, CPU 1 reads out the word and gets a 0. In step 2, before CPU 1 has a chance to rewrite the word to 1, CPU 2 gets in and also reads the word out as a 0. In step 3, CPU 1 writes a 1 into the word. In step 4, CPU 2 also writes a 1 into the word. Both CPUs got a 0 back from the TSL instruction, so both of them now have access to the critical region and the mutual exclusion fails.

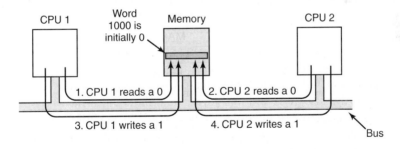

Figure 8-10. The TSL instruction can fail if the bus cannot be locked. These four steps show a sequence of events where the failure is demonstrated.

To prevent this problem, the TSL instruction must first lock the bus, preventing other CPUs from accessing it, then do both memory accesses, then unlock the bus. Typically, locking the bus is done by requesting the bus using the usual bus request protocol, then asserting (i.e., setting to a logical 1) some special bus line until *both* cycles have been completed. As long as this special line is being asserted, no other CPU will be granted bus access. This instruction can only be implemented on a bus that has the necessary lines and (hardware) protocol for using them. Modern buses have these facilities, but on earlier ones that did not, it was not possible to implement TSL correctly. This is why Peterson's protocol was invented, to synchronize entirely in software (Peterson, 1981).

If TSL is correctly implemented and used, it guarantees that mutual exclusion can be made to work. However, this mutual exclusion method uses a **spin lock** because the requesting CPU just sits in a tight loop testing the lock as fast as it can. Not only does it completely waste the time of the requesting CPU (or CPUs), but it may also put a massive load on the bus or memory, seriously slowing down all other CPUs trying to do their normal work.

At first glance, it might appear that the presence of caching should eliminate the problem of bus contention, but it does not. In theory, once the requesting CPU has read the lock word, it should get a copy in its cache. As long as no other CPU attempts to use the lock, the requesting CPU should be able to run out of its cache. When the CPU owning the lock writes a 1 to it to release it, the cache protocol automatically invalidates all copies of it in remote caches requiring the correct value to be fetched again.

The problem is that caches operate in blocks of 32 or 64 bytes. Usually, the words surrounding the lock are needed by the CPU holding the lock. Since the TSL instruction is a write (because it modifies the lock), it needs exclusive access to the cache block containing the lock. Therefore every TSL invalidates the block in the lock holder's cache and fetches a private, exclusive copy for the requesting CPU. As soon as the lock holder touches a word adjacent to the lock, the cache block is moved to its machine. Consequently, the entire cache block containing the lock is constantly being shuttled between the lock owner and the lock requester, generating even more bus traffic than individual reads on the lock word would have.

If we could get rid of all the TSL-induced writes on the requesting side, we could reduce cache thrashing appreciably. This goal can be accomplished by having the requesting CPU first do a pure read to see if the lock is free. Only if the lock appears to be free does it do a TSL to actually acquire it. The result of this small change is that most of the polls are now reads instead of writes. If the CPU holding the lock is only reading the variables in the same cache block, they can each have a copy of the cache block in shared read-only mode, eliminating all the cache block transfers. When the lock is finally freed, the owner does a write, which requires exclusive access, thus invalidating all the other copies in remote caches. On the next read by the requesting CPU, the cache block will be reloaded. Note that if two or more CPUs are contending for the same lock, it can happen that both see that it is free simultaneously, and both do a TSL simultaneously to acquire it. Only one of these will succeed, so there is no race condition here because the real acquisition is done by the TSL instruction, and this instruction is atomic. Seeing that the lock is free and then trying to grab it immediately with a CX u TSL does not guarantee that you get it. Someone else might win.

Another way to reduce bus traffic is to use the Ethernet binary exponential backoff algorithm (Anderson, 1990). Instead of continuously polling, as in Fig. 2-22, a delay loop can be inserted between polls. Initially the delay is one instruction. If the lock is still busy, the delay is doubled to two instructions, then four instructions and so on up to some maximum. A low maximum gives fast response when the lock is released, but wastes more bus cycles on cache thrashing. A high maximum reduces cache thrashing at the expense of not noticing that the lock is free so quickly. Binary exponential backoff can be used with or without the pure reads preceding the TSL instruction.

An even better idea is to give each CPU wishing to acquire the mutex its own private lock variable to test, as illustrated in Fig. 8-11 (Mellor-Crummey and Scott, 1991). The variable should reside in an otherwise unused cache block to avoid conflicts. The algorithm works by having a CPU that fails to acquire the lock allocate a lock variable and attach itself to the end of a list of CPUs waiting for the lock. When the current lock holder exits the critical region, it frees the private lock that the first CPU on the list is testing (in its own cache). This CPU then enters the critical region. When it is done, it frees the lock its successor is using, and so on. Although the protocol is somewhat complicated (to avoid having two CPUs attach themselves to the end of the list simultaneously), it is efficient and starvation free. For all the details, readers should consult the paper.

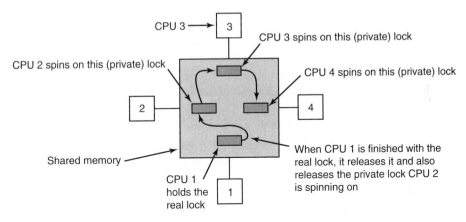

Figure 8-11. Use of multiple locks to avoid cache thrashing.

Spinning versus Switching

So far we have assumed that a CPU needing a locked mutex just waits for it, either by polling continuously, polling intermittently, or attaching itself to a list of waiting CPUs. In some cases, there is no real alternative for the requesting CPU to just waiting. For example, suppose that some CPU is idle and needs to access the shared ready list to pick a process to run. If the ready list is locked, the CPU cannot just decide to suspend what it is doing and run another process, because doing that would require access to the ready list. It *must* wait until it can acquire the ready list.

However, in other cases, there is a choice. For example, if some thread on a CPU needs to access the file system buffer cache and that is currently locked, the CPU can decide to switch to a different thread instead of waiting. The issue of whether to spin or whether to do a thread switch has been a matter of much research, some of which will be discussed below. Note that this issue does not occur on a uniprocessor because spinning does not make much sense when there is no other CPU to release the lock. If a thread tries to acquire a lock and fails, it is always blocked to give the lock owner a chance to run and release the lock.

Assuming that spinning and doing a thread switch are both feasible options, the trade-off is as follows. Spinning wastes CPU cycles directly. Testing a lock repeatedly is not productive work. Switching, however, also wastes CPU cycles, since the current thread's state must be saved, the lock on the ready list must be acquired, a thread must be selected, its state must be loaded, and it must be started. Furthermore, the CPU cache will contain all the wrong blocks, so many expensive cache misses will occur as the new thread starts running. TLB faults are also likely. Eventually, a switch back to the original thread must take place, with more cache misses following it. The cycles spent doing these two context switches plus all the cache misses are wasted.

If it is known that mutexes are generally held for, say, 50 μsec and it takes 1 msec to switch from the current thread and 1 msec to switch back later, it is more efficient just to spin on the mutex. On the other hand, if the average mutex is held for 10 msec, it is worth the trouble of making the two context switches. The trouble is that critical regions can vary considerably in their duration, so which approach is better?

One design is to always spin. A second design is to always switch. But a third design is to make a separate decision each time a locked mutex is encountered. At the time the decision has to be made, it is not known whether it is better to spin or switch, but for any given system, it is possible to make a trace of all activity and analyze it later offline. Then it can be said in retrospect which decision was the best one and how much time was wasted in the best case. This hindsight algorithm then becomes a benchmark against which feasible algorithms can be measured.

This problem has been studied by researchers (Karlin et al., 1989; Karlin et al., 1991; and Ousterhout, 1982). Most work uses a model in which a thread failing to acquire a mutex spins for some period of time. If this threshold is exceeded, it switches. In some cases the threshold is fixed, typically the known overhead for switching to another thread and then switching back. In other cases it is dynamic, depending on the observed history of the mutex being waited on.

The best results are achieved when the system keeps track of the last few observed spin times and assumes that this one will be similar to the previous ones.

For example, assuming a 1-msec context switch time again, a thread would spin for a maximum of 2 msec, but observe how long it actually spun. If it fails to acquire a lock and sees that on the previous three runs it waited an average of 200 µsec, it should spin for 2 msec before switching. However, it it sees that it spun for the full 2 msec on each of the previous attempts, it should switch immediately and not spin at all. More details can be found in (Karlin et al., 1991).

8.1.4 Multiprocessor Scheduling

On a uniprocessor, scheduling is one dimensional. The only question that must be answered (repeatedly) is: "Which process should be run next?" On a multiprocessor, scheduling is two dimensional. The scheduler has to decide which process to run and which CPU to run it on. This extra dimension greatly complicates scheduling on multiprocessors.

Another complicating factor is that in some systems, all the processes are unrelated whereas in others they come in groups. An example of the former situation is a timesharing system in which independent users start up independent processes. The processes are unrelated and each one can be scheduled without regard to the other ones.

An example of the latter situation occurs regularly in program development environments. Large systems often consist of some number of header files containing macros, type definitions, and variable declarations that are used by the actual code files. When a header file is changed, all the code files that include it must be recompiled. The program *make* is commonly used to manage development. When *make* is invoked, it starts the compilation of only those code files that must be recompiled on account of changes to the header or code files. Object files that are still valid are not regenerated.

The original version of *make* did its work sequentially, but newer versions designed for multiprocessors can start up all the compilations at once. If 10 compilations are needed, it does not make sense to schedule 9 of them quickly and leave the last one until much later since the user will not perceive the work as completed until the last one finishes. In this case it makes sense to regard the processes as a group and to take that into account when scheduling them.

Timesharing

Let us first address the case of scheduling independent processes; later we will consider how to schedule related processes. The simplest scheduling algorithm for dealing with unrelated processes (or threads) is to have a single system-wide data structure for ready processes, possibly just a list, but more likely a set of lists for processes at different priorities as depicted in Fig. 8-12(a). Here the 16 CPUs are all currently busy, and a prioritized set of 14 processes are waiting to run. The first CPU to finish its current work (or have its process block) is CPU 4, which then locks the scheduling queues and selects the highest priority process, A, as shown in Fig. 8-12(b). Next, CPU 12 goes idle and chooses process B, as illustrated in Fig. 8-12(c). As long as the processes are completely unrelated, doing scheduling this way is a reasonable choice.

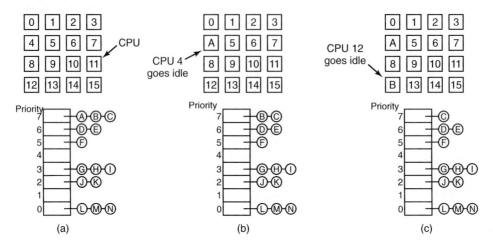

Figure 8-12. Using a single data structure for scheduling a multiprocessor.

Having a single scheduling data structure used by all CPUs timeshares the CPUs, much as they would be in a uniprocessor system. It also provides automatic load balancing because it can never happen that one CPU is idle while others are overloaded. Two disadvantages of this approach are the potential contention for the scheduling data structure as the numbers of CPUs grows and the usual overhead in doing a context switch when a process blocks for I/O.

It is also possible that a context switch happens when a process' quantum expires. On a multiprocessor, that has certain properties not present on a uniprocessor. Suppose that the process holds a spin lock, not unusual on multiprocessors, as discussed above. Other CPUs waiting on the spin lock just waste their time spinning until that process is scheduled again and releases the lock. On a uniprocessor, spin locks are rarely used so if a process is suspended while it holds a mutex, and another process starts and tries to acquire the mutex, it will be immediately blocked, so little time is wasted.

To get around this anomaly, some systems use **smart scheduling**, in which a process acquiring a spin lock sets a process-wide flag to show that it currently has a spin lock (Zahorjan et al., 1991). When it releases the lock, it clears the flag. The scheduler then does not stop a process holding a spin lock, but instead gives it a little more time to complete its critical region and release the lock.

Another issue that plays a role in scheduling is the fact that while all CPUs are equal, some CPUs are more equal. In particular, when process A has run for a long time on CPU k, CPU k's cache will be full of A's blocks. If A gets to run again soon, it may perform better if it is run on CPU k, because k's cache may still contain some of A's blocks. Having cache blocks preloaded will increase the cache hit rate and thus the process' speed. In addition, the TLB may also contain the right pages, reducing TLB faults.

Some multiprocessors take this effect into account and use what is called **affinity scheduling** (Vaswani and Zahorjan, 1991). The basic idea here is to make a serious effort to have a process run on the same CPU it ran on last time. One way to create this affinity is to use a **two-level scheduling algorithm**. When a process is created, it is assigned to a CPU, for example based on which one has the smallest load at that moment. This assignment of processes to CPUs is the top level of the algorithm. As a result, each CPU acquires its own collection of processes.

The actual scheduling of the processes is the bottom level of the algorithm. It is done by each CPU separately, using priorities or some other means. By trying to keep a process on the same CPU, cache affinity is maximized. However, if a CPU has no processes to run, it takes one from another CPU rather than go idle.

Two-level scheduling has three benefits. First, it distributes the load roughly evenly over the available CPUs. Second, advantage is taken of cache affinity where possible. Third, by giving each CPU its own ready list, contention for the ready lists is minimized because attempts to use another CPU's ready list are relatively infrequent.

Space Sharing

The other general approach to multiprocessor scheduling can be used when processes are related to one another in some way. Earlier we mentioned the example of parallel *make* as one case. It also often occurs that a single process creates multiple threads that work together. For our purposes, a job consisting of multiple related processes or a process consisting of multiple kernel threads are essentially the same thing. We will refer to the schedulable entities as threads here, but the material holds for processes as well. Scheduling multiple threads at the same time across multiple CPUs is called **space sharing**.

The simplest space sharing algorithm works like this. Assume that an entire group of related threads is created at once. At the time it is created, the scheduler checks to see if there are as many free CPUs as there are threads. If there are, each thread is given its own dedicated (i.e., nonmultiprogrammed) CPU and they all start. If there are not enough CPUs, none of the threads are started until enough CPUs are available. Each thread holds onto its CPU until it terminates, at which time the CPU is put back into the pool of available CPUs. If a thread blocks on I/O, it continues to hold the CPU, which is simply idle until the thread wakes up. When the next batch of threads appears, the same algorithm is applied.

At any instant of time, the set of CPUs is statically partitioned into some number of partitions, each one running the threads of one process. In Fig. 8-13, we have partitions of sizes 4, 6, 8, and 12 CPUs, with 2 CPUs unassigned, for example. As time goes on, the number and size of the partitions will change as processes come and go.

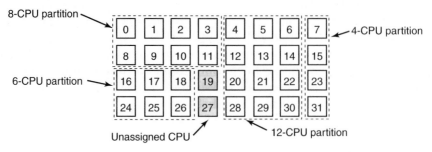

Figure 8-13. A set of 32 CPUs split into four partitions, with two CPUs available.

Periodically, scheduling decisions have to be made. In uniprocessor systems, shortest job first is a well-known algorithm for batch scheduling. The analogous algorithm for a multiprocessor is to choose the process needing the smallest number of CPU cycles, that is the process whose CPU-count × run-time is the smallest of the candidates. However, in practice, this information is rarely available, so the algorithm is hard to carry out. In fact, studies have shown that, in practice, beating first-come, first-served is hard to do (Krueger et al., 1994).

In this simple partitioning model, a process just asks for some number of CPUs and either gets them all or has to wait until they are available. A different approach is for processes to actively manage the degree of parallelism. One way to do manage the parallelism is to have a central server that keeps track of which processes are running and want to run and what their minimum and maximum CPU requirements are (Tucker and Gupta, 1989). Periodically, each CPU polls the central server to ask how many CPUs it may use. It then adjusts the number of processes or threads up or down to match what is available. For example, a Web server can have 1, 2, 5, 10, 20, or any other number of threads running in parallel. If it currently has 10 threads and there is suddenly more demand for CPUs and it is told to drop to 5, when the next 5 threads finish their current work, they are told to exit instead of being given new work. This scheme allows the partition sizes to vary dynamically to match the current workload better than the fixed system of Fig. 8-13.

Gang Scheduling

A clear advantage of space sharing is the elimination of multiprogramming, which eliminates the context switching overhead. However, an equally clear disadvantage is the time wasted when a CPU blocks and has nothing at all to do until it becomes ready again. Consequently, people have looked for algorithms that attempt to schedule in both time and space together, especially for processes that create multiple threads, which usually need to communicate with one another.

To see the kind of problem that can occur when the threads of a process (or processes of a job) are independently scheduled, consider a system with threads A_0 and A_1 belonging to process A and threads B_0 and B_1 belonging to process B. threads A_0 and B_0 are timeshared on CPU 0; threads A_1 and B_1 are timeshared on CPU 1. threads A_0 and A_1 need to communicate often. The communication pattern is that A_0 sends A_1 a message, with A_1 then sending back a reply to A_0, followed by another such sequence. Suppose that luck has it that A_0 and B_1 start first, as shown in Fig. 8-14.

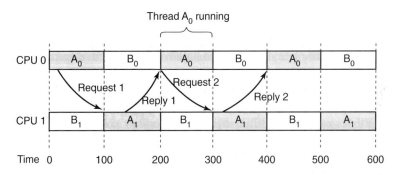

Figure 8-14. Communication between two threads belonging to process A that are running out of phase.

In time slice 0, A_0 sends A_1 a request, but A_1 does not get it until it runs in time slice 1 starting at 100 msec. It sends the reply immediately, but A_0 does not get the reply until it runs again at 200 msec. The net result is one request-reply sequence every 200 msec. Not very good.

The solution to this problem is **gang scheduling**, which is an outgrowth of **co-scheduling** (Ousterhout, 1982). Gang scheduling has three parts:

1. Groups of related threads are scheduled as a unit, a gang.

2. All members of a gang run simultaneously, on different timeshared CPUs.

3. All gang members start and end their time slices together.

The trick that makes gang scheduling work is that all CPUs are scheduled synchronously. This means that time is divided into discrete quanta as we had in Fig. 8-14. At the start of each new quantum, *all* the CPUs are rescheduled, with a new thread being started on each one. At the start of the following quantum, another scheduling event happens. In between, no scheduling is done. If a thread blocks, its CPU stays idle until the end of the quantum.

An example of how gang scheduling works is given in Fig. 8-15. Here we have a multiprocessor with six CPUs being used by five processes, A through E, with a total of 24 ready threads. During time slot 0, threads A_0 through A_6 are scheduled and run. During time slot 1, Threads B_0, B_1, B_2, C_0, C_1, and C_2 are scheduled and run. During time slot 2, D's five threads and E_0 get to run. The remaining six threads belonging to process E run in time slot 3. Then the cycle repeats, with slot 4 being the same as slot 0 and so on.

CPU

	0	1	2	3	4	5
0	A_0	A_1	A_2	A_3	A_4	A_5
1	B_0	B_1	B_2	C_0	C_1	C_2
2	D_0	D_1	D_2	D_3	D_4	E_0
3	E_1	E_2	E_3	E_4	E_5	E_6
4	A_0	A_1	A_2	A_3	A_4	A_5
5	B_0	B_1	B_2	C_0	C_1	C_2
6	D_0	D_1	D_2	D_3	D_4	E_0
7	E_1	E_2	E_3	E_4	E_5	E_6

Time slot (rows 0–7)

Figure 8-15. Gang scheduling.

The idea of gang scheduling is to have all the threads of a process run together, so that if one of them sends a request to another one, it will get the message almost immediately and be able to reply almost immediately. In Fig. 8-15, since all the A threads are running together, during one quantum, they may send and receive a very large number of messages in one quantum, thus eliminating the problem of Fig. 8-14.

8.2 MULTICOMPUTERS

Multiprocessors are popular and attractive because they offer a simple communication model: all CPUs share a common memory. Processes can write messages to memory that can then be read by other processes. Synchronization can be done using mutexes, semaphores, monitors, and other well-established techniques. The only fly in the ointment is that large multiprocessors are difficult to build and thus expensive.

To get around these problems, much research has been done on **multicomputers**, which are tightly-coupled CPUs that do not share memory. Each one has its own memory, as shown in Fig. 8-1(b). These systems are also known by a variety of other names, including **cluster computers**, and **COWS (Clusters of Workstations)**.

Multicomputers are easy to build because the basic component is just a stripped-down PC with the addition of a network interface card. Of course, the secret to getting high performance is to design the interconnection network and the interface card cleverly. This problem is completely analogous to building the shared memory in a multiprocessor. However, the goal is to send messages on a microsecond time scale, rather than access memory on a nanosecond time scale, so it is simpler, cheaper, and easier to accomplish.

In the following sections, we will first take a brief look at multicomputer hardware, especially the interconnection hardware. Then we will move onto the software, starting with low-level communication software, then high-level communication software. We will also look at a way shared memory can be achieved on systems that do not have it. Finally, we will examine scheduling and load balancing.

8.2.1 Multicomputer Hardware

The basic node of a multicomputer consists of a CPU, memory, a network interface, and sometimes a hard disk. The node may be packaged in a standard PC case, but the graphics adapter, monitor, keyboard, and mouse are nearly always absent. In some cases, the PC contains a 2-way or 4-way multiprocessor board instead of a single CPU, but for simplicity, we will assume that each node has one CPU. Often hundreds or even thousands of nodes are hooked together to form a multicomputer. Below we will say a little about how this hardware is organized.

Interconnection Technology

Each node has a network interface card with one or two cables (or fibers) coming out of it. These cables connect to either other nodes or to switches. In a small system, there may be one switch to which all the nodes are connected in the star topology of Fig. 8-16(a). Modern switched Ethernets use this topology.

As an alternative to the single switch design, the nodes may form a ring, with two wires coming out the network interface card, one going into the node on the left and one going into the node on the right, as shown in Fig. 8-16(b). In this topology, no switches are needed and none are shown.

The **grid** or **mesh** of Fig. 8-16(c) is a two-dimensional design that has been used in many commercial systems. It is highly regular and easy to scale up to large sizes. It has a **diameter**, which is the longest path between any two nodes, and which increases only as the square root of the number of nodes. A variant on the grid is the **double torus** of Fig. 8-16(d), which is a grid with the edges connected. Not only is it more fault tolerant than the grid, but the diameter is also less because the opposite corners can now communicate in only two hops.

The **cube** of Fig. 8-16(e) is a regular three-dimensional topology. We have illustrated a $2 \times 2 \times 2$ cube, but in the general case it could be a $k \times k \times k$ cube. In Fig. 8-16(f) we have a four-dimensional cube constructed from two three-dimensional cubes with the corresponding nodes connected. We could make a

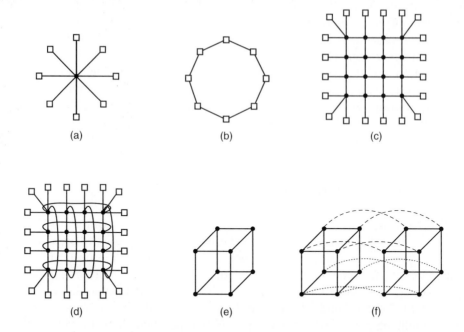

Figure 8-16. Various interconnect topologies. (a) A single switch. (b) A ring. (c) A grid. (d) A double torus. (e) A cube. (f) A 4D hypercube.

five-dimensional cube by cloning the structure of Fig. 8-16(f) and connecting the corresponding nodes to form a block of four cubes. To go to six dimensions, we could replicate the block of four cubes and interconnect the corresponding nodes, and so on. An *n*-dimensional cube formed this way is called a **hypercube**. Many parallel computers use this topology because the diameter grows linearly with the dimensionality. Put in other words, the diameter is the base 2 logarithm of the number of nodes, so, for example, a 10-dimensional hypercube has 1024 nodes but a diameter of only 10, giving excellent delay properties. Note that in contrast, 1024 nodes arranged as a 32×32 grid has a diameter of 62, more than six times worse than the hypercube. The price paid for the smaller diameter is that the fanout and thus the number of links (and the cost) is much larger for the hypercube.

Two kinds of switching schemes are used in multicomputers. In the first one, each message is first broken up (either by the user software or the network interface) into a chunk of some maximum length called a **packet**. The switching scheme, called **store-and-forward packet switching**, consists of the packet being injected into the first switch by the source node's network interface board, as shown in Fig. 8-17(a). The bits come in one at a time, and when the whole packet has arrived, it is copied to the next switch along the path, as shown in Fig. 8-17(b). When the packet arrives at the switch attached to the destination node, as shown in Fig. 8-17(c), the packet is copied to that node's network interface board and eventually to its RAM.

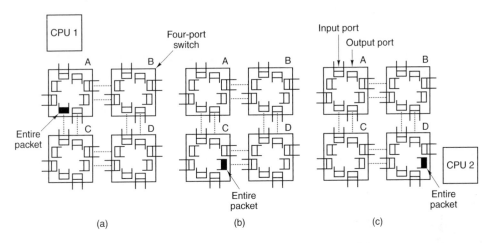

Figure 8-17. Store-and-forward packet switching.

While store-and-forward packet switching is flexible and efficient, it does have the problem of increasing latency (delay) through the interconnection network. Suppose that the time to move a packet one hop in Fig. 8-17 is T nsec. Since the packet must be copied four times to get it from CPU 1 to CPU 2 (to A, to C, to D, and to the destination CPU), and no copy can begin until the previous one is finished, the latency through the interconnection network is $4T$. One way out is to design a hybrid network, with some of the properties of circuit switching and some of the properties of packet switching. For example, each packet can be logically divided into smaller units. As soon as the first unit arrives at a switch, it can be moved to the next switch, even before the tail of the packet has arrived.

The other switching regime, **circuit switching**, consists of the first switch first establishing a path through all the switches to the destination switch. Once that path has been set up, the bits are pumped all the way from the source to the destination nonstop. There is no intermediate buffering at the intervening switches. Circuit switching requires a setup phase, which takes some time, but is faster once the setup has been completed. After the packet has been sent, the path must be torn down again. A variation on circuit switching, called **wormhole routing**, breaks each packet up into subpackets and allows the first subpacket to start flowing even before the full path has been built.

Network Interfaces

All the nodes in a multicomputer have a plug-in board containing the node's connection to the interconnection network that holds the multicomputer together. The way these boards are built and how they connect to the main CPU and RAM have substantial implications for the operating system. We will now briefly look at some of the issues here. This material is based in part on (Bhoedjang, 2000). Other references are (Buzzard et al., 1996; Pakin et al., 1997; Steenkiste, 1994; and Von Eicken et al., 1992).

In virtually all multicomputers, the interface board contains some RAM for holding outgoing and incoming packets. Usually, an outgoing packet has to be copied to the interface board's RAM before it can be transmitted to the first switch. The reason for this design is that many interconnection networks are synchronous, so that once a packet transmission has started, the bits must continue flowing at a constant rate. If the packet is in the main RAM, this continuous flow out onto the network cannot be guaranteed due to other traffic on the memory bus. Using a dedicated RAM on the interface board eliminates this problem. This design is shown in Fig. 8-18.

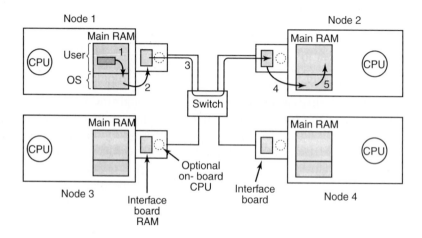

Figure 8-18. Position of the network interface boards in a multicomputer.

The same problem occurs with incoming packets. The bits arrive from the network at a constant and often extremely high rate. If the network interface board cannot store them in real time as they arrive, data will be lost. Again here, trying to go over the system bus (e.g., the PCI bus) to the main RAM is too risky. Since the network board is typically plugged into the PCI bus, this is the only connection it has to the main RAM, so competing for this bus with the disk and every other I/O device is inevitable. It is safer to store incoming packets in the interface board's private RAM and then copy them to the main RAM later.

The interface board may have one or more DMA channels or even a complete CPU on board. The DMA channels can copy packets between the interface board and the main RAM at high speed by requesting block transfers on the system bus, thus transferring several words without having to request the bus separately for each word. However, it is precisely this kind of block transfer, which ties up the system bus for multiple bus cycles, that makes the interface board RAM necessary in the first place.

Some interface boards have a full CPU on them, possibly in addition to one or more DMA channels. This design means that the main CPU can offload some work to the network board such as handling reliable transmission (if the underlying hardware can lose packets), multicasting (sending a packet to more than one destination), and taking care of protection in a system with multiple processes. However, having two CPUs means that they must synchronize to avoid race conditions, which adds extra overhead and means more work for the operating system.

8.2.2 Low-Level Communication Software

The enemy of high-performance communication in multicomputer systems is excess copying of packets. In the best case, there will be one copy from RAM to the interface board at the source node, one copy from the source interface board to the destination interface board (if no storing and forwarding along the path occurs), and one copy from there to the destination RAM, a total of three copies. However, in many systems it is even worse. In particular, if the interface board is mapped into kernel virtual address space and not user virtual address space, a user process can only send a packet by issuing a system call that traps to the kernel. The kernels may have to copy the packets to their own memory both on output and on input, for example, to avoid page faults while transmitting over the network. Also, the receiving kernel probably does not know where to put incoming packets until it has had a chance to examine them. These five copy steps are illustrated in Fig. 8-18.

If copies to and from RAM dominate the performance, the extra copies to and from the kernel may double the end-to-end delay and cut the bandwidth in half. To avoid this performance hit, many multicomputers map the interface board directly into user space and allow the user process to put the packets on the board directly, without the kernel being involved. While this approach definitely helps performance, it introduces two problems.

First, what if several processes are running on the node and need network access to send packets? Which one gets the interface board in its address space? Having a system call to map the board in and out of a virtual address space is expensive, but if only one process gets the board, how do the other ones send packets? And what happens if the board is mapped into process A's virtual address space and a packet arrives for process B, especially if A and B have different owners, neither of whom wants to put in any effort to help the other?

One solution is to map the interface board into all processes that need it, but then a mechanism is needed to avoid race conditions. For example if A claims a buffer on the interface board and then due to a time slice, B runs and claims the same buffer, disaster results. Some kind of synchronization mechanism is needed, but these mechanisms, such as mutexes, only work when the processes are assumed to be cooperating. In a timesharing environment with multiple users all in a hurry to get their work done, one user might just lock the mutex associated with the board and never release it. The conclusion here is that mapping the interface board into user space only really works well when there is just one user process running on each node unless special precautions are taken (for example, different processes get different portions of the interface RAM mapped into their address spaces).

The second problem is that the kernel may well need access to the interconnection network itself, for example, to access the file system on a remote node. Having the kernel share the interface board with any users is not a good idea, even on a timesharing basis. Suppose that while the board was mapped into user space, a kernel packet arrived? Or suppose that the user process sent a packet to a remote machine pretending to be the kernel? The conclusion is that the simplest design is to have two network interface boards, one mapped into user space for application traffic and one mapped into kernel space for use by the operating system. Many multicomputers do precisely this.

Node to Network Interface Communication

Another issue is how to get packets onto the interface board. The fastest way is to use the DMA chip on the board to just copy them in from RAM. The problem with this approach is that DMA uses physical rather than virtual addresses and runs independently of the CPU. To start with, although a user process certainly knows the virtual address of any packet it wants to send, it generally does not know the physical address. Making a system call to do the virtual-to-physical mapping is undesirable, since the point of putting the interface board in user space in the first place was to avoid having to make a system call for each packet to be sent.

In addition, if the operating system decides to replace a page while the DMA chip is copying a packet from it, the wrong data will be transmitted. Worse yet, if the operating system replaces a page while the DMA chip is copying an incoming packet to it, not only will the incoming packet be lost, but also a page of innocent memory will be ruined.

These problems can be avoided by having system calls to pin and unpin pages in memory, marking them as temporarily unpageable. However, having to make a system call to pin the page containing each outgoing packet and then having to make another call later to unpin it is expensive. If packets are small, say, 64 bytes or less, the overhead for pinning and unpinning every buffer is prohibitive. For large packets, say, 1 KB or more, it may be tolerable. For sizes in between, it depends on the details of the hardware (Bhoedjang, 2000).

In theory, the same problem occurs with DMA from a disk or other device, but since these are set up by the operating system to kernel buffers, it is easy for the system to avoid paging the buffers. The problem here is that the user is setting up and managing the DMA, and the operating system does not know that removing a page could be fatal, something it does know for I/O that it starts itself. The reason using kernel buffers is acceptable for disk I/O and not for multiprocessor communication is that an extra 20-μsec delay is tolerable for disk latency but not for process-to-process communication latency.

The DMA problem can be avoided by having the user process first pin one page at startup and asking for its physical address. Outgoing packets are first copied there and then to the network interface, but this extra copy is just as bad as copying to the kernel.

For these reasons, using programmed I/O to and from the interface board is usually the safest course, since any page faults encountered are just ordinary CPU page faults and can be handled in the usual way by the operating system. When a page fault occurs, the copy loop stops instantly and remains stopped until the operating system has handled the page fault. A more sophisticated scheme is to use programmed I/O for small packets and DMA with pinning and unpinning for large ones.

If the network interface boards have their own CPUs (e.g., as do Myrinet boards), these on-board CPUs can be used to speed up communication. However, care has to be taken to avoid race conditions between the main CPU and the on-board CPU. One way to avoid races is illustrated in Fig. 8-19, where we focus on node 1 sending packets and node 2 receiving them, not necessarily from each other. The key synchronization data structure for senders is the send ring; for receivers it is the receive ring. All nodes have both since they all send and receive. Each ring has room for n packets. There is also a bitmap per ring with n bits, possibly separate (as shown) or possibly integrated into the rings, telling which ring slots are currently valid.

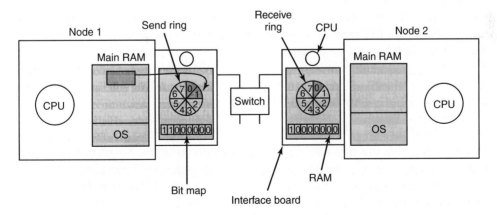

Figure 8-19. Use of send and receive rings to coordinate the main CPU with the on-board CPU.

When a sender has a new packet to send, it first checks to see if there is an available slot in the send ring. If not, it must wait, to prevent overrun. If there is a slot, it copies the packet to the next available slot, and after that is completed, sets the corresponding bit in the bitmap. When the on-board CPU has finished whatever it is doing, it checks the send ring. If it contains any packets, it takes the one there longest and transmits it. When it is done, it clears the corresponding bit in the bitmap. Since the main CPU is the only one that sets the bits and the on-board CPU is the only one that clears them, there are no race conditions. The receive ring works the other way, with the on-board CPU setting a bit to indicate packet arrival and the main CPU clearing it to indicate that it has copied the packet and freed the buffer.

This scheme can also be used even without programmed I/O done by the main CPU. In that case, the send ring entry does not contain the packet itself, but a pointer to the packet in the main RAM. When the on-board CPU is ready to transmit the packet, it fetches the packet to the interface board, either using programmed I/O itself or via DMA. In both cases, this approach works only if the page containing the packet is known to be pinned.

8.2.3 User-Level Communication Software

Processes on different CPUs on a multicomputer communicate by sending messages to one another. In the simplest form, this message passing is exposed to the user processes. In other words, the operating system provides a way to send and receive messages, and library procedures make these underlying calls available to user processes. In a more sophisticated form, the actual message passing is hidden from users by making remote communication look like a procedure call. We will study both of these methods below.

Send and Receive

At the barest minimum, the communication services provided can be reduced to two (library) calls, one for sending messages and one for receiving them. The calling for sending a message might be

    send(dest, &mptr);

and the call for receiving a message might be

    receive(addr, &mptr);

The former sends the message pointed to by *mptr* to a process identified by *dest* and causes the caller to be blocked until the message has been sent. The latter causes the caller to be blocked until a message arrives. When one does, the message is copied to the buffer pointed to by *mptr* and the caller is unblocked. The *addr* parameter specifies the address to which the receiver is listening. Many variants of these two procedures and their parameters are possible.

One issue is how addressing is done. Since multicomputers are static, with the number of CPUs fixed, the easiest way to handle addressing is to make *addr* a two-part address consisting of a CPU number and a process or port number on the addressed CPU. In this way each CPU can manage its own addresses without potential conflicts.

Blocking versus Nonblocking Calls

The calls described above are **blocking calls** (sometimes called **synchronous calls**). When a process calls *send*, it specifies a destination and a buffer to send to that destination. While the message is being sent, the sending process is blocked (i.e., suspended). The instruction following the call to *send* is not executed until the message has been completely sent, as shown in Fig. 8-20(a). Similarly, a call to *receive* does not return control until a message has actually been received and put in the message buffer pointed to by the parameter. The process remains suspended in *receive* until a message arrives, even if it takes hours. In some systems, the receiver can specify from whom it wishes to receive, in which case it remains blocked until a message from that sender arrives.

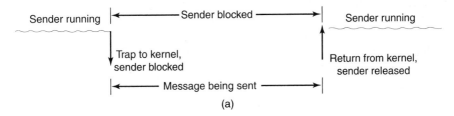

(a)

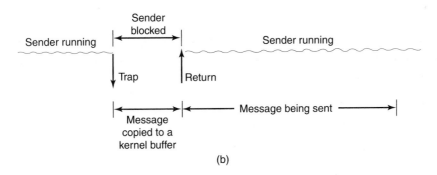

(b)

Figure 8-20. (a) A blocking send call. (b) A nonblocking send call.

An alternative to blocking calls are **nonblocking calls** (sometimes called **asynchronous calls**). If *send* is nonblocking, it returns control to the caller immediately, before the message is sent. The advantage of this scheme is that the sending process can continue computing in parallel with the message transmission, instead of having the CPU go idle (assuming no other process is runnable).

The choice between blocking and nonblocking primitives is normally made by the system designers (i.e., either one primitive is available or the other), although in a few systems both are available and users can choose their favorite.

However, the performance advantage offered by nonblocking primitives is offset by a serious disadvantage: the sender cannot modify the message buffer until the message has been sent. The consequences of the process overwriting the message during transmission are too horrible to contemplate. Worse yet, the sending process has no idea of when the transmission is done, so it never knows when it is safe to reuse the buffer. It can hardly avoid touching it forever.

There are three possible ways out. The first solution is to have the kernel copy the message to an internal kernel buffer and then allow the process to continue, as shown in Fig. 8-20(b). From the sender's point of view, this scheme is the same as a blocking call: as soon as it gets control back, it is free to reuse the buffer. Of course, the message will not yet have been sent, but the sender is not hindered by this fact. The disadvantage of this method is that every outgoing message has to be copied from user space to kernel space. With many network interfaces, the message will have to be copied to a hardware transmission buffer later anyway, so the first copy is essentially wasted. The extra copy can reduce the performance of the system considerably.

The second solution is to interrupt the sender when the message has been sent to inform it that the buffer is once again available. No copy is required here, which saves time, but user-level interrupts make programming tricky, difficult, and subject to race conditions, which makes them irreproducible and nearly impossible to debug.

The third solution is to make the buffer copy on write, that is, to mark it as read-only until the message has been sent. If the buffer is reused before the message has been sent, a copy is made. The problem with this solution is that unless the buffer is isolated on its own page, writes to nearby variables will also force a copy. Also, extra administration is needed because the act of sending a message now implicitly affects the read/write status of the page. Finally, sooner or later the page is likely to be written again, triggering a copy that may no longer be necessary.

Thus the choices on the sending side are

1. Blocking send (CPU idle during message transmission).

2. Nonblocking send with copy (CPU time wasted for the extra copy).

3. Nonblocking send with interrupt (makes programming difficult).

4. Copy on write (extra copy probably needed eventually).

Under normal conditions, the first choice is the best one, especially if multiple threads are available, in which case while one thread is blocked trying to send, other threads can continue working. It also does not require any kernel buffers to be managed. Furthermore, as can be seen from comparing Fig. 8-20(a) to Fig. 8-20(b), the message will usually be out the door faster if no copy is required.

For the record, we would like to point out that some authors use a different criterion to distinguish synchronous from asynchronous primitives. In the alternative view, a call is synchronous only if the sender is blocked until the message has been received and an acknowledgement sent back (Andrews, 1991). In the world of real-time communication, synchronous has yet another meaning, which can lead to confusion, unfortunately.

Just as *send* can be blocking or nonblocking, so can *receive*. A blocking call just suspends the caller until a message has arrived. If multiple threads are available, this is a simple approach. Alternatively, a nonblocking *receive* just tells the kernel where the buffer is and returns control almost immediately. An interrupt can be used to signal that a message has arrived. However, interrupts are difficult to program and are also quite slow, so it may be preferable for the receiver to poll for incoming messages using a procedure, *poll*, that tells whether any messages are waiting. If so, the caller can call *get_message*, which returns the first arrived message. In some systems, the compiler can insert poll calls in the code at appropriate places, although knowing how often to poll is tricky.

Yet another option is a scheme in which the arrival of a message causes a new thread to be created spontaneously in the receiving process' address space. Such a thread is called a **pop-up thread**. It runs a procedure specified in advance and whose parameter is a pointer to the incoming message. After processing the message, it simply exits and is automatically destroyed.

A variant on this idea is to run the receiver code directly in the interrupt handler, without going to the trouble of creating a pop-up thread. To make this scheme even faster, the message itself contains the address of the handler, so when a message arrives, the handler can be called in a few instructions. The big win here is that no copying at all is needed. The handler takes the message from the interface board and processes it on the fly. This scheme is called **active messages** (Von Eicken et al., 1992). Since each message contains the address of the handler, active messages only work when senders and receivers trust each other completely.

8.2.4 Remote Procedure Call

Although the message-passing model provides a convenient way to structure a multicomputer operating system, it suffers from one incurable flaw: the basic paradigm around which all communication is built is input/output. The procedures *send* and *receive* are fundamentally engaged in doing I/O and many people believe that I/O is the wrong programming model.

This problem has long been known, but little was done about it until a paper by Birrell and Nelson (1984) introduced a completely different way of attacking the problem. Although the idea is refreshingly simple (once someone has thought of it), the implications are often subtle. In this section we will examine the concept, its implementation, its strengths, and its weaknesses.

In a nutshell, what Birrell and Nelson suggested was allowing programs to call procedures located on other CPUs. When a process on machine 1 calls a procedure on machine 2, the calling process on 1 is suspended, and execution of the called procedure takes place on 2. Information can be transported from the caller to the callee in the parameters and can come back in the procedure result. No message passing or I/O at all is visible to the programmer. This technique is known as **RPC** (**Remote Procedure Call**) and has become the basis of a large amount of multicomputer software. Traditionally the calling procedure is known as the client and the called procedure is known as the server, and we will use those names here too.

The idea behind RPC is to make a remote procedure call look as much as possible like a local one. In the simplest form, to call a remote procedure, the client program must be bound with a small library procedure called the **client stub** that represents the server procedure in the client's address space. Similarly, the server is bound with a procedure called the **server stub**. These procedures hide the fact that the procedure call from the client to the server is not local.

The actual steps in making a RPC are shown in Fig. 8-21. Step 1 is the client calling the client stub. This call is a local procedure call, with the parameters pushed onto the stack in the normal way. Step 2 is the client stub packing the parameters into a message and making a system call to send the message. Packing the parameters is called **marshaling**. Step 3 is the kernel sending the message from the client machine to the server machine. Step 4 is the kernel passing the incoming packet to the server stub (which would normally have called *receive* earlier). Finally, step 5 is the server stub calling the server procedure. The reply traces the same path in the other direction.

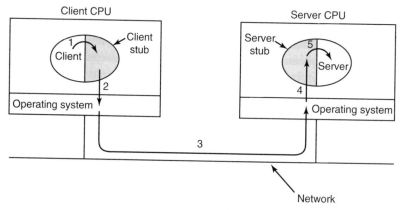

Figure 8-21. Steps in making a remote procedure call. The stubs are shaded gray.

The key item to note here is that the client procedure, written by the user, just makes a normal (i.e., local) procedure call to the client stub, which has the same name as the server procedure. Since the client procedure and client stub are in the same address space, the parameters are passed in the usual way. Similarly, the server procedure is called by a procedure in its address space with the parameters it expects. To the server procedure, nothing is unusual. In this way, instead of doing I/O using *send* and *receive*, remote communication is done by faking a normal procedure call.

Implementation Issues

Despite the conceptual elegance of RPC, there are a few snakes hiding under the grass. A big one is the use of pointer parameters. Normally, passing a pointer to a procedure is not a problem. The called procedure can use the pointer the same way the caller can because the two procedures reside in the same virtual address space. With RPC passing pointers is impossible because the client and server are in different address spaces.

In some cases, tricks can be used to make it possible to pass pointers. Suppose that the first parameter is a pointer to an integer, k. The client stub can marshal k and send it along to the server. The server stub then creates a pointer to k and passes it to the server procedure, just as it expects. When the server procedure returns control to the server stub, the latter sends k back to the client where the new k is copied over the old one, just in case the server changed it. In effect, the standard calling sequence of call-by-reference has been replaced by copy-restore. Unfortunately, this trick does not always work, for example, if the pointer points to a graph or other complex data structure. For this reason, some restrictions must be placed on parameters to procedures called remotely.

A second problem is that in weakly-typed languages, like C, it is perfectly legal to write a procedure that computes the inner product of two vectors (arrays), without specifying how large either one is. Each could be terminated by a special value known only to the calling and called procedure. Under these circumstances, it is essentially impossible for the client stub to marshal the parameters: it has no way of determining how large they are.

A third problem is that it is not always possible to deduce the types of the parameters, not even from a formal specification or the code itself. An example is *printf*, which may have any number of parameters (at least one), and they can be an arbitrary mixture of integers, shorts, longs, characters, strings, floating-point numbers of various lengths, and other types. Trying to call *printf* as a remote procedure would be practically impossible because C is so permissive. However, a rule saying that RPC can be used provided that you do not program in C (or C++) would not be popular.

A fourth problem relates to the use of global variables. Normally, the calling and called procedure may communicate using global variables, in addition to via parameters. If the called procedure is now moved to a remote machine, the code will fail because the global variables are no longer shared.

These problems are not meant to suggest that RPC is hopeless. In fact, it is widely used, but some restrictions and care are needed to make it work well in practice.

8.2.5 Distributed Shared Memory

Although RPC has its attractions, many programmers still prefer a model of shared memory and would like to use it, even on a multicomputer. Surprisingly enough, it is possible to preserve the illusion of shared memory reasonably well, even when it does not actually exist, using a technique called **DSM (Distributed Shared Memory)** (Li, 1986; and Li and Hudak, 1989). With DSM, each page is located in one of the memories of Fig. 8-1. Each machine has its own virtual memory and its own page tables. When a CPU does a LOAD or STORE on a page it does not have, a trap to the operating system occurs. The operating system then locates the page and asks the CPU currently holding it to unmap the page and send it over the interconnection network. When it arrives, the page is mapped in and the faulting instruction is restarted. In effect, the operating system is just satisfying page faults from remote RAM instead of from local disk. To the user, the machine looks as if it has shared memory.

The difference between actual shared memory and DSM is illustrated in Fig. 8-22. In Fig. 8-22(a), we see a true multiprocessor with physical shared memory implemented by the hardware. In Fig. 8-22(b), we see DSM, implemented by the operating system. In Fig. 8-22(c), we see yet another form of shared memory, implemented by yet higher levels of software. We will come back to this third option later in the chapter, but for now we will concentrate on DSM.

Let us now look in some detail at how DSM works. In a DSM system, the address space is divided up into pages, with the pages being spread over all the nodes in the system. When a CPU references an address that is not local, a trap occurs, and the DSM software fetches the page containing the address and restarts the faulting instruction, which now completes successfully. This concept is illustrated in Fig. 8-23(a) for an address space with 16 pages and four nodes, each capable of holding four pages.

In this example, if CPU 0 references instructions or data in pages 0, 2, 5, or 9, the references are done locally. References to other pages cause traps. For example, a reference to an address in page 10 will cause a trap to the DSM software, which then moves page 10 from node 1 to node 0, as shown in Fig. 8-23(b).

Replication

One improvement to the basic system that can improve performance considerably is to replicate pages that are read only, for example, program text, read-only constants, or other read-only data structures. For example, if page 10 in Fig. 8-23

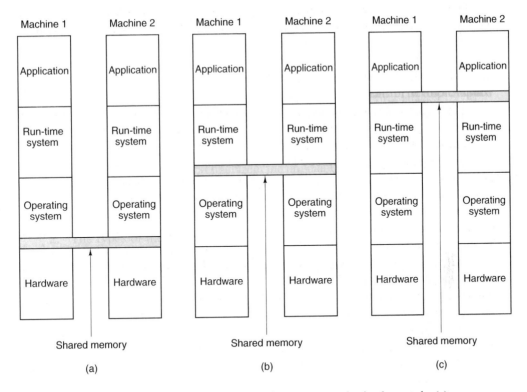

Figure 8-22. Various layers where shared memory can be implemented. (a) The hardware. (b) The operating system. (c) User-level software.

is a section of program text, its use by CPU 0 can result in a copy being sent to CPU 0, without the original in CPU 1's memory being disturbed, as shown in Fig. 8-23(c). In this way, CPUs 0 and 1 can both reference page 10 as often as needed without causing traps to fetch missing memory.

Another possibility is to replicate not only read-only pages, but also all pages. As long as reads are being done, there is effectively no difference between replicating a read-only page and replicating a read-write page. However, if a replicated page is suddenly modified, special action has to be taken to prevent having multiple, inconsistent copies in existence. How inconsistency is prevented will be discussed in the following sections.

False Sharing

DSM systems are similar to multiprocessors in certain key ways. In both systems, when a nonlocal memory word is referenced, a chunk of memory containing the word is fetched from its current location and put on the machine making the reference (main memory or cache, respectively). An important design issue is how big should the chunk be? In multiprocessors, the cache block size is usually

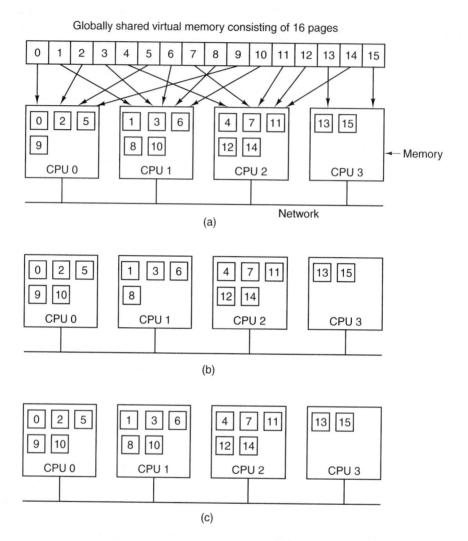

Figure 8-23. (a) Pages of the address space distributed among four machines. (b) Situation after CPU 1 references page 10. (c) Situation if page 10 is read only and replication is used.

32 or 64 bytes, to avoid tying up the bus with the transfer too long. In DSM systems, the unit has to be a multiple of the page size (because the MMU works with pages), but it can be 1, 2, 4, or more pages. In effect, doing this simulates a larger page size.

There are advantages and disadvantages to a larger page size for DSM. The biggest advantage is that because the startup time for a network transfer is fairly substantial, it does not really take much longer to transfer 4096 bytes than it does to transfer 1024 bytes. By transferring data in large units, when a large piece of address space has to be moved, the number of transfers may often be reduced. This property is especially important because many programs exhibit locality of reference, meaning that if a program has referenced one word on a page, it is likely to reference other words on the same page in the immediate future.

On the other hand, the network will be tied up longer with a larger transfer, blocking other faults caused by other processes. Also, too large an effective page size introduces a new problem, called **false sharing**, illustrated in Fig. 8-24. Here we have a page containing two unrelated shared variables, *A* and *B*. Processor 1 makes heavy use of *A*, reading and writing it. Similarly, process 2 uses *B* frequently. Under these circumstances, the page containing both variables will constantly be traveling back and forth between the two machines.

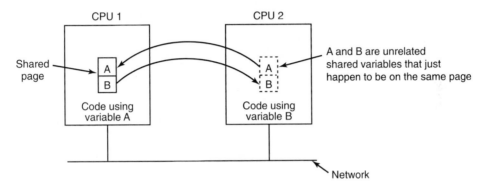

Figure 8-24. False sharing of a page containing two unrelated variables.

The problem here is that although the variables are unrelated, they appear by accident on the same page, so when a process uses one of them, it also gets the other. The larger the effective page size, the more often false sharing will occur, and conversely, the smaller the effective page size, the less often it will occur. Nothing analogous to this phenomenon is present in ordinary virtual memory systems.

Clever compilers that understand the problem and place variables in the address space accordingly can help reduce false sharing and improve performance. However, saying this is easier than doing it. Furthermore, if the false sharing consists of node 1 using one element of an array and node 2 using a different element of the same array, there is little that even a clever compiler can do to eliminate the problem.

Achieving Sequential Consistency

If writable pages are not replicated, achieving consistency is not an issue. There is exactly one copy of each writable page, and it is moved back and forth dynamically as needed. Since it is not always possible to see in advance which pages are writable, in many DSM systems, when a process tries to read a remote page, a local copy is made and both the local and remote copies are set up in their respective MMUs as read only. As long as all references are reads, everything is fine.

However, if any process attempts to write on a replicated page, a potential consistency problem arises because changing one copy and leaving the others alone is unacceptable. This situation is analogous to what happens in a multiprocessor when one CPU attempts to modify a word that is present in multiple caches. The solution there is for the CPU about to do the write to first put a signal on the bus telling all other CPUs to discard their copy of the cache block. DSM systems typically work the same way. Before a shared page can be written, a message is sent to all other CPUs holding a copy of the page telling them to unmap and discard the page. After all of them have replied that the unmap has finished, the original CPU can now do the write.

It is also possible to tolerate multiple copies of writable pages under carefully restricted circumstances. One way is to allow a process to acquire a lock on a portion of the virtual address space, and then perform multiple read and write operations on the locked memory. At the time the lock is released, changes can be propagated to other copies. As long as only one CPU can lock a page at a given moment, this scheme preserves consistency.

Alternatively, when a potentially writable page is actually written for the first time, a clean copy is made and saved on the CPU doing the write. Locks on the page can then be acquired, the page updated, and the locks released. Later, when a process on a remote machine tries to acquire a lock on the page, the CPU that wrote it earlier compares the current state of the page to the clean copy and builds a message listing all the words that have changed. This list is then sent to the acquiring CPU so it can update its copy instead of invalidating it (Keleher et al., 1994).

8.2.6 Multicomputer Scheduling

On a multiprocessor, all processes reside in the same memory. When a CPU finishes its current task, it picks a process and runs it. In principle, all processes are potential candidates. On a multicomputer the situation is quite different. Each node has its own memory and its own set of processes. CPU 1 cannot suddenly decide to run a process located on node 4 without first doing a fair amount of work to go get it. This difference means that scheduling on multicomputers is easier but allocation of processes to nodes is more important. Below we will study these issues.

Multicomputer scheduling is somewhat similar to multiprocessor scheduling, but not all of the former's algorithms apply to the latter. The simplest multiprocessor algorithm—maintaining a single central list of ready processes—does not work however, since each process can only run on the CPU it is currently located on. However, when a new process is created, a choice can be made where to place it, for example to balance the load.

Given that each node has its own processes, any local scheduling algorithm can be used. However, it is also possible to use gang scheduling, the same way it is used on a multiprocessor, since that merely requires an initial agreement on which process to run in which time slot, and some way to coordinate the start of the time slots.

8.2.7　Load Balancing

There is relatively little to say about multicomputer scheduling because once a process has been assigned to a node, any local scheduling algorithm will do, unless gang scheduling is being used. However, precisely because there is so little control once a process has been assigned to a node, the decision about which process should go on which node is important. This is in contrast to multiprocessor systems, in which all processes live in the same memory and can be scheduled on any CPU at will. Consequently, it is worth looking at how processes can be assigned to nodes in an effective way. The algorithms and heuristics for doing this assignment are known as **processor allocation algorithms**.

A large number of processor (i.e., node) allocation algorithms have been proposed over the years. They differ in what they assume is known and what the goal is. Properties that might be known about a process include the CPU requirements, memory usage, and amount of communication with every other process. Possible goals include minimizing wasted CPU cycles due to lack of local work, minimizing total communication bandwidth, and ensuring fairness to users and processes. Below we will examine a few algorithms to give an idea of what is possible.

A Graph-Theoretic Deterministic Algorithm

A widely-studied class of algorithms is for systems consisting of processes with known CPU and memory requirements, and a known matrix giving the average amount of traffic between each pair of processes. If the number of processes is greater than the number of CPUs, k, several processes will have to be assigned to each CPU. The idea is to perform this assignment such as to minimize network traffic.

The system can be represented as a weighted graph, with each vertex being a process and each arc representing the flow of messages between two processes. Mathematically, the problem then reduces to finding a way to partition (i.e., cut) the graph into k disjoint subgraphs, subject to certain constraints (e.g., total CPU and memory requirements below some limits for each subgraph). For each solution that meets the constraints, arcs that are entirely within a single subgraph represent intramachine communication and can be ignored. Arcs that go from one subgraph to another represent network traffic. The goal is then to find the partitioning that minimizes the network traffic while meeting all the constraints. As an example, Fig. 8-25 shows a system of nine processes, A through I, with each arc labeled with the mean communication load between those two processes (e.g., in Mbps).

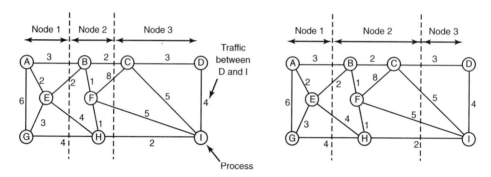

Figure 8-25. Two ways of allocating nine processes to three nodes.

In Fig. 8-25(a), we have partitioned the graph with processes A, E, and G on node 1, processes B, F, and H on node 2, and processes C, D, and I on node 3. The total network traffic is the sum of the arcs intersected by the cuts (the dashed lines), or 30 units. In Fig. 8-25(b) we have a different partitioning that has only 28 units of network traffic. Assuming that it meets all the memory and CPU constraints, this is a better choice because it requires less communication.

Intuitively, what we are doing is looking for clusters that are tightly coupled (high intracluster traffic flow) but which interact little with other clusters (low intercluster traffic flow). Some of the earliest papers discussing the problem are (Chow and Abraham, 1982; Lo, 1984; and Stone and Bokhari, 1978).

A Sender-Initiated Distributed Heuristic Algorithm

Now let us look at some distributed algorithms. One algorithm says that when a process is created, it runs on the node that created it unless that node is overloaded. The metric for overloaded might involve too many processes, too big a total working set, or some other metric. If it is overloaded, the node selects another node at random and asks it what its load is (using the same metric). If the probed node's load is below some threshold value, the new process is sent there (Eager et al., 1986). If not, another machine is chosen for probing. Probing does not go on forever. If no suitable host is found within N probes, the algorithm terminates and the process runs on the originating machine. The idea is for heavily loaded nodes to try to get rid of excess work, as shown in Fig. 8-26(a).

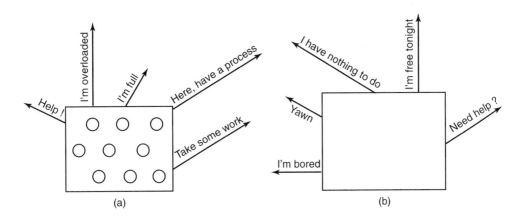

Figure 8-26. (a) An overloaded node looking for a lightly loaded node to hand off processes to. (b) An empty node looking for work to do.

Eager et al. (1986) constructed an analytical queueing model of this algorithm. Using this model, it was established that the algorithm behaves well and is stable under a wide range of parameters, including different threshold values, transfer costs, and probe limits.

Nevertheless, it should be observed that under conditions of heavy load, all machines will constantly send probes to other machines in a futile attempt to find one that is willing to accept more work. Few processes will be off loaded, but considerable overhead may be incurred in the attempt to do so.

A Receiver-Initiated Distributed Heuristic Algorithm

A complementary algorithm to the one given above, which is initiated by an overloaded sender, is one initiated by an underloaded receiver, as shown in Fig. 8-26(b). With this algorithm, whenever a process finishes, the system checks to see if it has enough work. If not, it picks some machine at random and asks it for work. If that machine has nothing to offer, a second, and then a third machine is asked. If no work is found with N probes, the node temporarily stops asking, does any work it has queued up, and tries again when the next process finishes. If no work is available, the machine goes idle. After some fixed time interval, it begins probing again.

An advantage of this algorithm is that it does not put extra load on the system at critical times. The sender-initiated algorithm makes large numbers of probes precisely when the system can least tolerate it—when it is heavily loaded. With the receiver-initiated algorithm, when the system is heavily loaded, the chance of a machine having insufficient work is small. However, when this does happen, it will be easy to find work to take over. Of course, when there is little work to do, the receiver-initiated algorithm creates considerable probe traffic as all the unemployed machines desperately hunt for work. However, it is far better to have the overhead go up when the system is underloaded than when it is overloaded.

It is also possible to combine both of these algorithms and have machines try to get rid of work when they have too much, and try to acquire work when they do not have enough. Furthermore, machines can perhaps improve on random polling by keeping a history of past probes to determine if any machines are chronically underloaded or overloaded. One of these can be tried first, depending on whether the initiator is trying to get rid of work or acquire it.

A Bidding Algorithm

Another class of algorithms tries to turn the computer system into a miniature economy, with buyers and sellers of services and prices set by supply and demand (Ferguson et al., 1988). The key players in the economy are the processes, which must buy CPU time to get their work done, and nodes, which auction their cycles off to the highest bidder.

Each node advertises its approximate price by putting it in a publicly readable file. This price is not guaranteed, but gives an indication of what the service is worth (actually, it is the price that the last customer paid). Different nodes may have different prices, depending on their speed, memory size, presence of fast floating-point hardware, and other features. An indication of the service provided, such as expected response time, can also be published.

When a process wants to start up a child process, it goes around and checks out who is currently offering the service that it needs. It then determines the set of nodes whose services it can afford. From this set, it computes the best candidate, where "best" may mean cheapest, fastest, or best price/performance, depending on the application. It then generates a bid and sends the bid to its first choice. The bid may be higher or lower than the advertised price.

Processors collect all the bids sent to them and make a choice, presumably by picking the highest one. The winners and losers are informed, and the winning process is executed. The published price of the server is then updated to reflect the new going rate.

Although Ferguson et al. do not go into the details, such an economic model raises all kinds of interesting questions, among them the following. Where do processes get money to bid? Do they get regular salaries? Does everyone get the same monthly salary, or do deans get more than professors, who in turn get more than students? If new users are introduced into the system without a corresponding increase in resources, do prices get bid up (inflation)? Can nodes form cartels to gouge users? Are users' unions allowed? Is disk space also chargeable? How about printer output? Does printing pictures cost more than printing text due to the additional ink or toner used? The list goes on and on.

8.3 DISTRIBUTED SYSTEMS

Having now completed our study of multiprocessors and multicomputers, it is time to turn to the third type of multiple processor system, the **distributed system**. These systems are similar to multicomputers in that each node has its own private memory, with no shared physical memory in the system. However, distributed systems are even more loosely coupled than multicomputers.

To start with, the nodes of a multicomputer generally have a CPU, RAM, a network interface, and perhaps a hard disk for paging. In contrast, each node in a distributed system is a complete computer, with a full complement of peripherals. Next, the nodes of a multicomputer are normally in a single room so they can communicate by a dedicated high-speed network, whereas the nodes of a distributed system may be spread around the world. Finally, all the nodes of a multicomputer run the same operating system, share a single file system, and are under a common administration, whereas the nodes of a distributed systems may run different operating systems, each have their own file system, and be under different administrations. A typical example of a multicomputer is 512 nodes in a single room at a company or university working on, say, pharmaceutical modeling, whereas a typical distributed system consists of thousands of machines loosely cooperating over the Internet. Figure 8-27 compares multiprocessors, multicomputers, and distributed systems on the points mentioned above.

Item	Multiprocessor	Multicomputer	Distributed System
Node configuration	CPU	CPU, RAM, net interface	Complete computer
Node peripherals	All shared	Shared exc. maybe disk	Full set per node
Location	Same rack	Same room	Possibly worldwide
Internode communication	Shared RAM	Dedicated interconnect	Traditional network
Operating systems	One, shared	Multiple, same	Possibly all different
File systems	One, shared	One, shared	Each node has own
Administration	One organization	One organization	Many organizations

Figure 8-27. Comparison of three kinds of multiple CPU systems.

Multicomputers are clearly in the middle using these metrics. An interesting question is: "Are multicomputers more like multiprocessors or more like distributed systems?" Oddly enough, the answer depends strongly on your perspective. From a technical perspective, multiprocessors have shared memory and the other two do not. This difference leads to different programming models and different mind sets. However, from an applications perspective, multiprocessors and multicomputers are just big equipment racks in a machine room. Both are used for solving computationally intensive problems, whereas a distributed system connecting computers all over the Internet is typically much more involved in communication than in computation and is used in a different way.

To some extent, loose coupling of the computers in a distributed system is both a strength and a weakness. It is a strength because the computers can be used for a wide variety of applications, but it is also a weakness, because programming these applications is difficult due to the lack of any common underlying model.

Typical Internet applications include access to remote computers (using *telnet* and *rlogin*), access to remote information (using the World Wide Web and FTP, the File Transfer Protocol), person-to-person communication (using email and chat programs), and many emerging applications (e.g., e-commerce, telemedicine, and distance learning). The trouble with all these applications is that each one has to reinvent the wheel. For example, email, FTP, and the World Wide Web all basically move files from point *A* to point *B*, but each one has its own way of doing it, complete with its own naming conventions, transfer protocols, replication techniques, and everything else. Although many Web browsers hide these differences from the average user, the underlying mechanisms are completely different. Hiding them at the user interface level is like having a person at a full-service travel agent Web site order a trip from New York to San Francisco, and only later discover whether she has purchased a plane, train, or bus ticket.

What distributed systems add to the underlying network is some common paradigm (model) that provides a uniform way of looking at the whole system. The intent of the distributed system is to turn a loosely-connected bunch of machines into a coherent system based on one concept. Sometimes the paradigm is simple and sometimes it is more elaborate, but the idea is always to provide something that unifies the system.

A simple example of a unifying paradigm in a slightly different context is found in UNIX, where all I/O devices are made to look like files. Having keyboards, printers, and serial lines all be operated on the same way, with the same primitives, makes it easier to deal with them than having them all be conceptually different.

One way a distributed system can achieve some measure of uniformity in the face of different underlying hardware and operating systems is to have a layer of software on top of the operating system. The layer, called **middleware**, is illustrated in Fig. 8-28. This layer provides certain data structures and operations that allow processes and users on far-flung machines to interoperate in a consistent way.

In a sense, middleware is like the operating system of a distributed system. That is why it is being discussed in a book on operating systems. On the other hand, it is *not* an operating system, so the discussion will not go into much detail. For a comprehensive, book-length treatment of distributed systems, see *Distributed Systems* (Tanenbaum and van Steen, 2002). In the remainder of this chapter, we will first look quickly at the hardware used in a distributed system (i.e., the underlying computer network), then its communication software (the network protocols). After that we will consider a variety of paradigms used in these systems.

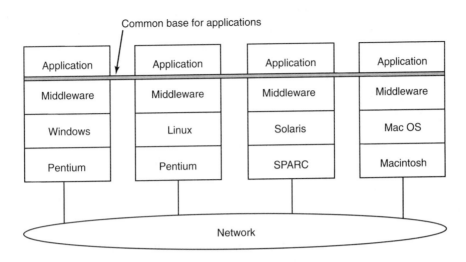

Figure 8-28. Positioning of middleware in a distributed system.

8.3.1 Network Hardware

Distributed systems are built on top of computer networks, so a brief introduction to the subject is in order. Networks come in two major varieties, **LANs (Local Area Networks)**, which cover a building or a campus, and **WANs (Wide Area Networks)**, that can be citywide, countrywide, or even worldwide. The most important kind of LAN is Ethernet, so we will examine that as an example LAN. As our example WAN, we will look at the Internet, even though technically, the Internet is not one network, but a federation of thousands of separate networks. However, for our purposes, it is sufficient to think of it as one WAN.

Ethernet

Classic Ethernet, which is described in IEEE Standard 802.3, consists of a coaxial cable to which a number of computers are attached. The cable is called the **Ethernet**, in reference to the *luminiferous ether*, through which electromagnetic radiation was once thought to propagate. (When the nineteenth-century British physicist James Clerk Maxwell discovered that electromagnetic radiation could be described by a wave equation, scientists assumed that space must be filled with some ethereal medium in which the radiation was propagating. Only after the famous Michelson-Morley experiment in 1887, which failed to detect the ether, did physicists realize that radiation could propagate in a vacuum.)

In the very first version of Ethernet, a computer was attached to the cable by literally drilling a hole halfway through the cable and screwing in a wire leading to the computer. This was called a **vampire tap**, and is shown symbolically in Fig. 8-29(a). The taps were hard to get right, so before long, proper connectors were used. Nevertheless, electrically, all the computers were connected as if the cables on their network interface cards were soldered together.

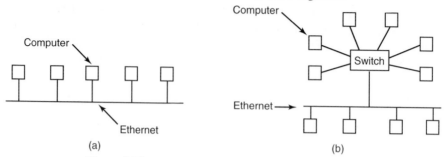

Figure 8-29. (a) Classic Ethernet. (b) Switched Ethernet.

To send a packet on an Ethernet, a computer first listens to the cable to see if any other computer is currently transmitting. If not, it just begins transmitting a packet, which consists of a short header followed by a 0- to 1500-byte payload. If the cable is in use, the computer simply waits until the current transmission finishes, then it begins sending.

If two computers start transmitting simultaneously, a collision results, which both of them detect. Both respond by terminating their transmissions, waiting a random amount of time between 0 and T μsec and then starting again. If another collision occurs, all colliding computers randomize the wait into the interval 0 to $2T$ μsec, and then try again. On each further collision, the maximum wait interval is doubled, reducing the chance of more collisions. This algorithm is called **binary exponential backoff**. We saw it earlier to reduce polling overhead on locks.

An Ethernet has a maximum cable length and also a maximum number of computers that can be connected to it. To exceed either of these limits, a large building or campus can be wired with multiple Ethernets, which are then connected by devices called **bridges**. A bridge allows traffic to pass from one Ethernet to another when the source is on one side and the destination is on the other.

To avoid the problem of collisions, modern Ethernets use switches, as shown in Fig. 8-29(b). Each switch has some number of ports, to which can be attached a computer, an Ethernet, or another switch. When a packet successfully avoids all collisions and makes it to the switch, it is buffered there and sent out on the port where the destination machine lives. By giving each computer its own port, all collisions can be eliminated, at the cost of bigger switches. Compromises, with just a few computers per port are also possible.

The Internet

The Internet evolved from the ARPANET, an experimental packet-switched network funded by the U.S. Dept. of Defense Advanced Research Projects Agency. It went live in Dec. 1969 with three computers in California and one in

Utah. It was designed to a be a highly fault-tolerant network that would continue to relay military traffic even in the event of direct nuclear hits on multiple parts of the network by automatically rerouting traffic around the dead machines.

The ARPANET grew rapidly in the 1970s, eventually encompassing hundreds of computers. Then a packet radio network, a satellite network, and eventually thousands of Ethernets were attached to it, leading to the federation of networks we now know as the Internet.

The Internet consists of two kinds of computers, hosts and routers. **Hosts** are PCs, laptops, palmtops, servers, mainframes, and other computers owned by individuals or companies that want to connect to the Internet. **Routers** are specialized switching computers that accept incoming packets on one of many incoming lines and send them on their way along one of many outgoing lines. A router is similar to the switch of Fig. 8-29(b), but also differs from it in ways that will not concern us here. Routers are connected together in large networks, with each router having wires or fibers to many other routers and hosts. Large national or worldwide router networks are operated by telephone companies and ISPs (Internet Service Providers) for their customers.

Figure 8-30 shows a portion of the Internet. At the top we have one of the backbones, normally operated by a backbone operator. It consists of a number of routers connected by high-bandwidth fiber optics, with connections to backbones operated by other (competing) telephone companies. Usually, no hosts connect directly to the backbone, other than maintenance and test machines run by the telephone company.

Attached to the backbone routers by medium-speed fiber optic connections are regional networks and routers at ISPs. In turn, corporate Ethernets each have a router on them and these are connected to regional network routers. Routers at ISPs are connected to modem banks used by the ISP's customers. In this way, every host on the Internet has at least one path, and often many paths, to every other host.

All traffic on the Internet is sent in the form of packets. Each packet carries its destination address inside it, and this address is used for routing. When a packet comes into a router, the router extracts the destination address and looks (part of) it up in a table to find which outgoing line to send the packet on and thus to which router. This procedure is repeated until the packet reaches the destination host. The routing tables are highly dynamic and are updated continuously as routers and links go down and come back up and as traffic conditions change.

8.3.2 Network Services and Protocols

All computer networks provide certain services to their users (hosts and processes), which they implement using certain rules about legal message exchanges. Below we will give a brief introduction to these topics.

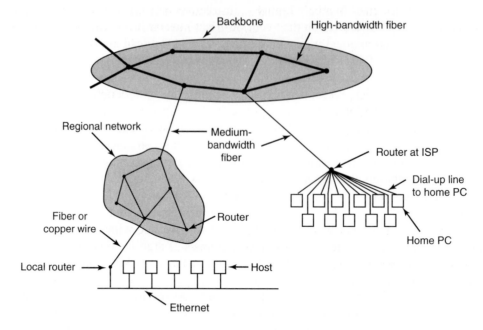

Figure 8-30. A portion of the Internet.

Network Services

Computer networks provide services to the hosts and processes using them. **Connection-oriented service** is modeled after the telephone system. To talk to someone, you pick up the phone, dial the number, talk, and then hang up. Similarly, to use a connection-oriented network service, the service user first establishes a connection, uses the connection, and then releases the connection. The essential aspect of a connection is that it acts like a tube: the sender pushes objects (bits) in at one end, and the receiver takes them out in the same order at the other end.

In contrast, **connectionless service** is modeled after the postal system. Each message (letter) carries the full destination address, and each one is routed through the system independent of all the others. Normally, when two messages are sent to the same destination, the first one sent will be the first one to arrive. However, it is possible that the first one sent can be delayed so that the second one arrives first. With a connection-oriented service this is impossible.

Each service can be characterized by a **quality of service**. Some services are reliable in the sense that they never lose data. Usually, a reliable service is implemented by having the receiver confirm the receipt of each message by sending back a special **acknowledgement packet** so the sender is sure that it arrived. The acknowledgement process introduces overhead and delays, which are necessary to detect packet loss, but which do slow things down.

A typical situation in which a reliable connection-oriented service is appropriate is file transfer. The owner of the file wants to be sure that all the bits arrive correctly and in the same order they were sent. Very few file transfer customers would prefer a service that occasionally scrambles or loses a few bits, even if it is much faster.

Reliable connection-oriented service has two minor variations: message sequences and byte streams. In the former, the message boundaries are preserved. When two 1-KB messages are sent, they arrive as two distinct 1-KB messages, never as one 2-KB message. In the latter, the connection is simply a stream of bytes, with no message boundaries. When 2K bytes arrive at the receiver, there is no way to tell if they were sent as one 2-KB message, two 1-KB messages, or 2048 1-byte messages. If the pages of a book are sent over a network to an imagesetter as separate messages, it might be important to preserve the message boundaries. On the other hand, with a terminal logging into a remote timesharing system, a byte stream from the terminal to the computer is all that is needed.

For some applications, the delays introduced by acknowledgements are unacceptable. One such application is digitized voice traffic. It is preferable for telephone users to hear a bit of noise on the line or a garbled word from time to time than to introduce a delay to wait for acknowledgements.

Not all applications require connections. For example, to test the network, all that is needed is a way to send a single packet that has a high probability of arrival, but no guarantee. Unreliable (meaning not acknowledged) connectionless service is often called **datagram service**, in analogy with telegram service, which also does not provide an acknowledgement back to the sender.

In other situations, the convenience of not having to establish a connection to send one short message is desired, but reliability is essential. The **acknowledged datagram service** can be provided for these applications. It is like sending a registered letter and requesting a return receipt. When the receipt comes back, the sender is absolutely sure that the letter was delivered to the intended party and not lost along the way.

Still another service is the **request-reply service**. In this service the sender transmits a single datagram containing a request; the reply contains the answer. For example, a query to the local library asking where Uighur is spoken falls into this category. Request-reply is commonly used to implement communication in the client-server model: the client issues a request and the server responds to it. Figure 8-31 summarizes the types of services discussed above.

Network Protocols

All networks have highly-specialized rules for what messages may be sent and what responses may be returned in response to these messages. For example, under certain circumstances (e.g., file transfer), when a message is sent from a source to a destination, the destination is required to send an acknowledgement

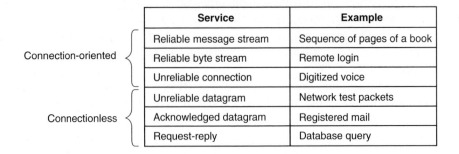

Figure 8-31. Six different types of network service.

back indicating correct receipt of the message. Under other circumstances (e.g., digital telephony), no such acknowledgement is expected. The set of rules by which particular computers communicate is called a **protocol**. Many protocols exist, including router-router protocols, host-host protocols, and others. For a thorough treatment of computer networks and their protocols, see *Computer Networks* (Tanenbaum, 1996).

All modern networks use what is called a **protocol stack** to layer different protocols on top of one another. At each layer, different issues are dealt with. For example, at the bottom level protocols define how to tell where in the bit stream a packet begins and ends. At a higher level, protocols deal with how to route packets through complex networks from source to destination. And at a still higher level, they make sure that all the packets in a multipacket message have arrived correctly and in the proper order.

Since most distributed systems use the Internet as a base, the key protocols these systems use are the two major Internet protocols: IP and TCP. **IP** (**Internet Protocol**) is a datagram protocol in which a sender injects a datagram of up to 64 KB into the network and hopes that it arrives. No guarantees are given. The datagram may be fragmented into smaller packets as it passes through the Internet. These packets travel independently, possibly along different routes. When all the pieces get to the destination, they are assembled in the correct order and delivered.

Two versions of IP are currently in use, v4 and v6. At the moment, v4 still dominates, so we will describe that here, but v6 is up and coming. Each v4 packet starts with a 40-byte header that contains a 32-bit source address and a 32-bit destination address among other fields. These are called **IP addresses** and form the basis of routing in the Internet. They are conventionally written as four decimal numbers in the range 0–255 separated by dots, as in 192.31.231.65. When a packet arrives at router, the router extracts the IP destination address and uses that for routing the packet.

Since IP datagrams are not acknowledged, IP alone is not sufficient for reliable communication in the Internet. To provide reliable communication, another protocol, **TCP (Transmission Control Protocol)**, is usually layered on top of IP. TCP uses IP to provide connection-oriented streams. To use TCP, a process first establishes a connection to a remote process. The process required is specified by the IP address of a machine and a port number on that machine, to which processes interested in receiving incoming connections listen. Once that has been done, it just pumps bytes into the connection and they are guaranteed to come out the other end undamaged and in the correct order. The TCP implementation achieves this guarantee by using sequence numbers, checksums, and retransmissions of incorrectly received packets. All of this is transparent to the sending and receiving processes. They just see reliable interprocess communication, just like a UNIX pipe .

To see how all these protocols interact, consider the simplest case of a very small message that does not need to be fragmented at any level. The host is on an Ethernet connected to the Internet. What happens exactly? The user process generates the message and makes a system call to send it on a previously established TCP connection. The kernel protocol stack adds a TCP header and then an IP header to the front. Then it goes to the Ethernet driver, which adds an Ethernet header directing the packet to the router on the Ethernet. This router then injects the packet into the Internet, as depicted in Fig. 8-32.

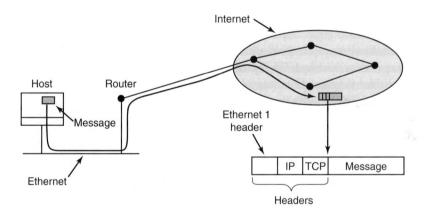

Figure 8-32. Accumulation of packet headers.

To establish a connection with a remote host (or even to send it a datagram), it is necessary to know its IP address. Since managing lists of 32-bit IP addresses is inconvenient for people, a scheme called **DNS (Domain Name System)** was invented as a database that maps ASCII names for hosts onto their IP addresses. Thus it is possible to use the DNS name *star.cs.vu.nl* instead of the corresponding IP address 130.37.24.6. DNS names are widely known because Internet email addresses are of the form *user-name@DNS-host-name*. This naming system allows the mail program on the sending host to look up the destination host's IP address in the DNS database, establish a TCP connection to the mail daemon process there, and send the message as a file. The *user-name* is sent along to identify which mailbox to put the message in.

8.3.3 Document-Based Middleware

Now that we have some background on networks and protocols, we can start looking at different middleware layers that can overlay the basic network to produce a consistent paradigm for applications and users. We will start with a simple, but well-known example: the World Wide Web. The Web was invented by Tim Berners-Lee at CERN, the European Nuclear Physics Research Center, in 1989 and has spread like wildfire all over the world since then.

The original paradigm behind the Web was very simple: every computer can hold one or more documents, called **Web pages**. Each Web page contains text, images, icons, sounds, movies, etc. as well as **hyperlinks** (pointers) to other Web pages. When a user requests a Web page using a program called a **Web browser**, the page is displayed on the screen. Clicking on a link causes the current page to be replaced on the screen by the page pointed to. Although many bells and whistles have been grafted onto the Web recently, the underlying paradigm is still clearly present: the Web is a great big directed graph of documents that can point to other documents, as shown in Fig. 8-33.

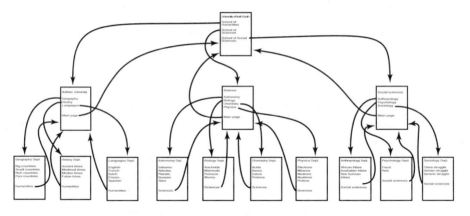

Figure 8-33. The Web is a big directed graph of documents.

Each Web page has a unique address, called a **URL** (**Uniform Resource Locator**), of the form *protocol://DNS-name/file-name*. The protocol is most commonly *http* (HyperText Transfer Protocol), but *ftp* and others also exist. Then comes the DNS name of the host containing the file. Finally, there is a local file name telling which file is needed.

The way the whole system hangs together is as follows. The Web is fundamentally a client-server system, with the user being the client and the Web site being the server. When the user provides the browser with a URL, either by typing it in or clicking on a hyperlink on the current page, the browser takes certain steps to fetch the requested Web page. As an example, suppose the URL provided is *http://www.acm.org/dl/faq.html* The browser then takes the following steps to get the page.

1. The browser asks DNS for the IP address of *www.acm.org*.

2. DNS replies with 199.222.69.151.

3. The browser makes a TCP connection to port 80 on 199.222.69.151.

4. It then sends a request asking for the file *dl/faq.html*.

5. The *www.acm.org* server sends the file *dl/faq.html*.

6. The TCP connection is released.

7. The browser displays all the text in *dl/faq.html*.

8. The browser fetches and displays all images in *dl/faq.html*.

To a first approximation, that is the basis of the Web and how it works. Many other features have since been added to the basic Web, including style sheets, dynamic Web pages that are generated on-the-fly, Web pages that contain small programs or scripts that execute on the client machine, and more, but they are outside the scope of this discussion.

8.3.4 File System-Based Middleware

The basic idea behind the Web is to make a distributed system look like a giant collection of hyperlinked documents. A second approach is to make a distributed system look like a great big file system. In this section we will look at some of the issues involved in designing a worldwide file system.

Using a file system model for a distributed system means that there is a single global file system, with users all over the world able to read and write files for which they have authorization. Communication is achieved by having one process write data into a file and having other ones read them back. Many of the standard file system issues arise here, but also some new ones related to distribution.

Transfer Model

The first issue is the choice between the **upload/download model** and the **remote access model**. In the former, shown in Fig. 8-34(a), a process accesses a file by first copying it from the remote server where it lives. If the file is only to be read, the file is then read locally, for high performance. If the file is to be written, it is written locally. When the process is done with it, the updated file is put back on the server. With the remote access model, the file stays on the server and the client sends commands there to get work done there, as shown in Fig. 8-34(b).

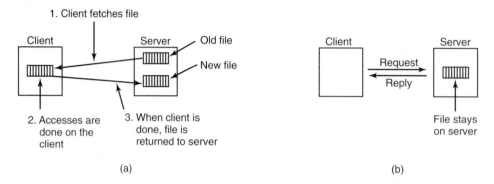

Figure 8-34. (a) The upload/download model. (b) The remote access model.

The advantages of the upload/download model are its simplicity, and the fact that transferring entire files at once is more efficient than transferring them in small pieces. The disadvantages are that there must be enough storage for the entire file locally, moving the entire file is wasteful if only parts of it are needed, and consistency problems arise if there are multiple concurrent users.

The Directory Hierarchy

Files are only part of the story. The other part is the directory system. All distributed file systems support directories containing multiple files. The next design issue is whether all clients have the same view of the directory hierarchy. As an example of what we mean by this remark, consider Fig. 8-35. In Fig. 8-35(a) we show two file servers, each holding three directories and some files. In Fig. 8-35(b) we have a system in which all clients (and other machines) have the same view of the distributed file system. If the path */D/E/x* is valid on one machine, it is valid on all of them.

In contrast, in Fig. 8-35(c), different machines can have different views of the file system. To repeat the preceding example, the path */D/E/x* might well be valid on client 1 but not on client 2. In systems that manage multiple file servers by remote mounting, Fig. 8-35(c) is the norm. It is flexible and straightforward to implement, but it has the disadvantage of not making the entire system behave like a single old-fashioned timesharing system. In a timesharing system, the file system looks the same to any process [i.e., the model of Fig. 8-35(b)]. This property makes a system easier to program and understand.

A closely related question is whether or not there is a global root directory, which all machines recognize as the root. One way to have a global root directory is to have the root contain one entry for each server and nothing else. Under these

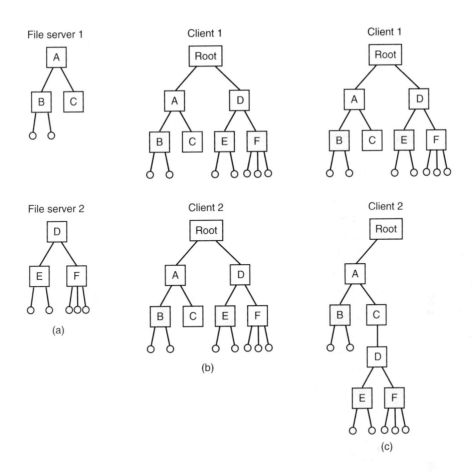

Figure 8-35. (a) Two file servers. The squares are directories and the circles are files. (b) A system in which all clients have the same view of the file system. (c) A system in which different clients may have different views of the file system.

circumstances, paths take the form */server/path*, which has its own disadvantages, but at least is the same everywhere in the system.

Naming Transparency

The principal problem with this form of naming is that it is not fully transparent. Two forms of transparency are relevant in this context and are worth distinguishing. The first one, **location transparency**, means that the path name gives no hint as to where the file is located. A path like */server1/dir1/dir2/x* tells everyone that *x* is located on server 1, but it does not tell where that server is located. The server is free to move anywhere it wants to in the network without the path name having to be changed. Thus this system has location transparency.

However, suppose that file *x* is extremely large and space is tight on server 1. Furthermore, suppose that there is plenty of room on server 2. The system might well like to move *x* to server 2 automatically. Unfortunately, when the first component of all path names is the server, the system cannot move the file to the other server automatically, even if *dir1* and *dir2* exist on both servers. The problem is that moving the file automatically changes its path name from */server1/dir1/dir2/x* to */server2/dir1/dir2/x*. Programs that have the former string built into them will cease to work if the path changes. A system in which files can be moved without their names changing is said to have **location independence**. A distributed system that embeds machine or server names in path names clearly is not location independent. One based on remote mounting is not either, since it is not possible to move a file from one file group (the unit of mounting) to another and still be able to use the old path name. Location independence is not easy to achieve, but it is a desirable property to have in a distributed system.

To summarize what we have said earlier, there are three common approaches to file and directory naming in a distributed system:

1. Machine + path naming, such as */machine/path* or *machine:path*.

2. Mounting remote file systems onto the local file hierarchy.

3. A single name space that looks the same on all machines.

The first two are easy to implement, especially as a way to connect existing systems that were not designed for distributed use. The latter is difficult and requires careful design, but makes life easier for programmers and users.

Semantics of File Sharing

When two or more users share the same file, it is necessary to define the semantics of reading and writing precisely to avoid problems. In single-processor systems the semantics normally state that when a read system call follows a write system call, the read returns the value just written, as shown in Fig. 8-36(a). Similarly, when two writes happen in quick succession, followed by a read, the value read is the value stored by the last write. In effect, the system enforces an ordering on all system calls and all processors see the same ordering. We will refer to this model as **sequential consistency**.

In a distributed system, sequential consistency can be achieved easily as long as there is only one file server and clients do not cache files. All reads and writes go directly to the file server, which processes them strictly sequentially.

In practice, however, the performance of a distributed system in which all file requests must go to a single server is frequently poor. This problem is often solved by allowing clients to maintain local copies of heavily used files in their private caches. However, if client 1 modifies a cached file locally and shortly thereafter client 2 reads the file from the server, the second client will get an obsolete file, as illustrated in Fig. 8-36(b).

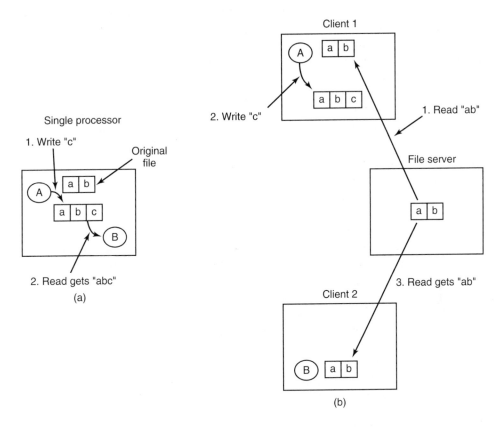

Figure 8-36. (a) Sequential consistency. (b) In a distributed system with caching, reading a file may return an obsolete value.

One way out of this difficulty is to propagate all changes to cached files back to the server immediately. Although conceptually simple, this approach is inefficient. An alternative solution is to relax the semantics of file sharing. Instead of requiring a read to see the effects of all previous writes, one can have a new rule that says: "Changes to an open file are initially visible only to the process that made them. Only when the file is closed are the changes visible to other processes." The adoption of such a rule does not change what happens in Fig. 8-36(b), but it does redefine the actual behavior (*B* getting the original value of the file) as being the correct one. When client 1 closes the file, it sends a copy back to the server, so that subsequent reads get the new value, as required. Effectively, this is the upload/download model of Fig. 8-34. This semantic rule is widely implemented and is known as **session semantics**.

Using session semantics raises the question of what happens if two or more clients are simultaneously caching and modifying the same file. One solution is to say that as each file is closed in turn, its value is sent back to the server, so the final result depends on who closes last. A less pleasant, but slightly easier to implement, alternative is to say that the final result is one of the candidates, but leave the choice of which one unspecified.

An alternative approach to session semantics is to use the upload/download model, but to automatically lock a file that has been downloaded. Attempts by other clients to download the file will be held up until the first client has returned it. If there is a heavy demand for a file, the server could send messages to the client holding the file, asking it to hurry up, but that may or may not help. All in all, getting the semantics of shared files right is a tricky business with no elegant and efficient solutions.

AFS

Several file-system based middleware systems have been built and deployed. Below we will briefly discuss one (AFS) based on the upload/download model of Fig. 8-34(a). In Chap. 10, we will discuss one (NFS) based on the remote access model of Fig. 8-34(b).

AFS was designed and implemented at Carnegie-Mellon University (Howard et al. 1988; Morris et al., 1986; and Satyanarayanan et al., 1985). It was originally called the **Andrew File System** in honor of the university's first benefactors, Andrew Carnegie and Andrew Mellon. The goal of the project, which started in the early 1980s, was to provide every student and faculty member at CMU with a powerful personal workstation running UNIX, but with a shared file system. Here the file system was being used as middleware to turn a collection of workstations into a coherent system.

Each AFS user has a private workstation running a slightly modified version of UNIX. The modifications consist of adding a piece of code called **venus** to the kernel and running a file server called **vice** in user space (originally, venus also ran in user space, but was later moved into the kernel for performance reasons). The positions of *venus* and *vice* are shown in Fig. 8-37(a). User workstations are grouped into **cells** for administrative purposes. A cell might be a LAN or a collection of interconnected LANs or even an entire academic department.

The name space visible to user programs looks like a traditional UNIX tree, with the addition of a directories */cmu* and */cache*, as depicted in Fig. 8-37(b). The */cache* directory contains cached remote files. The */cmu* directory contains the names of the shared remote cells, below which are their respective file systems. In effect, remote file systems are mounted in */cmu*. The other directories and files are strictly local and are not shared. Symbolic links from local file names to shared files are permitted, as indicated by *sh* in Fig. 8-37(b).

The basic idea behind AFS is for each user to do as much as possible locally and interact as little as possible with the rest of the system. When a file is opened, the *venus* code traps the open call and downloads the entire file (or if it is a huge file, a large chunk of it) to the local disk and inserts it into the */cache* directory.

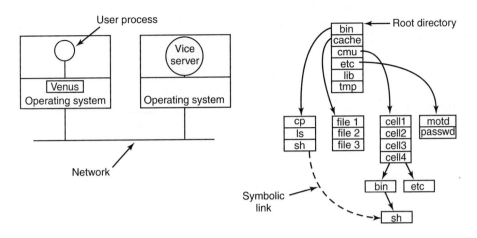

Figure 8-37. (a) The position of venus and vice in AFS. (b) A client's view of the file system.

The file descriptor returned by the open call refers to the file in /*cache* so that subsequent read and write calls use the cached file.

The semantics offered by AFS are close to session semantics. When a file is opened, it is fetched from the appropriate server and placed in /*cache* on the workstation's local disk. All reads and writes operate on the cached copy. When the file is closed, it is uploaded back to the server.

However, to prevent unsuspecting processes from using stale files in situations where it matters, when *venus* downloads a file into its cache, it tells *vice* whether or not it cares about subsequent opens by processes on other workstations. If it does, *vice* records the location of the cached file. If another process elsewhere in the system opens the file, *vice* sends a message to *venus* telling it to mark its cache entry as invalid and return the copy if it has been modified.

8.3.5 Shared Object-Based Middleware

Now let us take a look at a third paradigm. Instead of saying that everything is a document or everything is a file, we say that everything is an object. An **object** is a collection of variables that are bundled together with a set of access procedures, called **methods**. Processes are not permitted to access the variables directly. Instead, they are required to invoke the methods.

CORBA

Some programming languages, such as C++ and Java, are object oriented, but these are language-level objects rather than run-time objects. One well-known system based on run-time objects is **CORBA (Common Object Request Broker**

Architecture) (Vinoski, 1997). CORBA is a client-server system, in which client processes on client machines can invoke operations on objects located on (possibly remote) server machines. CORBA was designed for a heterogeneous system running a variety of hardware platforms and operating systems and programmed in a variety of languages. To make it possible for a client on one platform to invoke a server on a different platform, **ORBs** (**Object Request Brokers**) are interposed between client and server to allow them to match up. The ORBs play an important role in CORBA, even providing the system with its name.

Each CORBA object is defined by an interface definition in a language called **IDL** (**Interface Definition Language**), which tells what methods the object exports and what parameter types each one expects. The IDL specification can be compiled into a client stub procedure and stored in a library. If a client process knows in advance that it will need to access a certain object, it is linked with the object's client stub code. The IDL specification can also be compiled into a **skeleton** procedure that is used on the server side. If it is not known in advance which CORBA objects a process needs to use, dynamic invocation is also possible, but how that works is beyond the scope of our treatment.

When a CORBA object is created, a reference to it is also created and returned to the creating process. This reference is how the process identifies the object for subsequent invocations of its methods. The reference can be passed to other processes or stored in an object directory.

To invoke a method on an object, a client process must first acquire a reference to the object. The reference can either come directly from the creating process, or more likely, by looking it up by name or by function in some kind of a directory. Once the object reference is available, the client process marshals the parameters to the method calls into a convenient structure and then contacts the client ORB. In turn, the client ORB sends a message to the server ORB, which actually invokes the method on the object. The whole mechanism is similar to RPC.

The function of the ORBs is to hide all the low-level distribution and communication details from the client and server code. In particular, the ORBs hide from the client the location of the server, whether the server is a binary program or a script, what hardware and operating system the server runs on, whether the object is currently active, and how the two ORBs communicate (e.g., TCP/IP, RPC, shared memory, etc.).

In the first version of CORBA, the protocol between the client ORB and the server ORB was not specified. As a result, every ORB vendor used a different protocol and no two of them could talk to each other. In version 2.0, the protocol was specified. For communication over the Internet, the protocol is called **IIOP** (**Internet InterOrb Protocol**).

To make it possible to use objects that were not written for CORBA with CORBA systems, every object can be equipped with an **object adapter**. This is a wrapper that handles chores such as registering the object, generating object references, and activating the object if it is invoked when it is not active. The arrangement of all these CORBA parts is shown in Fig. 8-38.

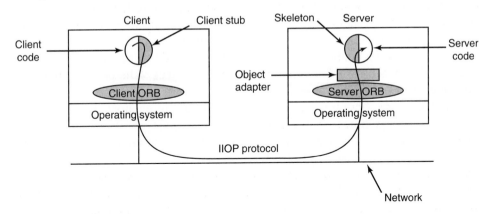

Figure 8-38. The main elements of a distributed system based on CORBA. The CORBA parts are shown in gray.

A serious problem with CORBA is that every object is located on only one server, which means the performance will be terrible for objects that are heavily used on client machines around the world. In practice, CORBA only functions acceptably in small-scale systems, such as to connect processes on one computer, one LAN or within a single company.

Globe

As an example of a distributed object system that was specifically designed to scale to a billion users and a trillion objects around the world, let us consider **Globe** (Van Steen et al., 1999a; Van Steen et al., 1999b). There are two key ideas to scaling to very large systems. The first is having replicated objects. If there is a single copy of a popular object that millions of users around the world want to access, the object will die under the weight of the requests. Think about an object that maintains stock prices or sports scores. Replicating this object allows the load to be spread over the replicas.

The second key idea is flexibility. In a worldwide system with a billion users, there is no way to get everyone to agree on one programming language, one replication strategy, one security model, or one anything else. The system has to allow different users and different objects to behave differently, while at the same time providing a coherent overall model. This is what Globe does.

Globe is also unusual in that, like DSM, it is based on the model of distributed shared memory, but now applied to a worldwide context. In principle, using normal page-based DSM on a worldwide system would work, only the performance would be horrible, so Globe takes a different approach. Conceptually, the basic idea is that the world is full of objects, each one containing some (hidden) internal state plus methods for accessing the internal state in controlled ways. The secret to making shared memory scalable worldwide is prohibiting direct LOADs and STOREs to an object's internal state and forcing all accesses to go through the methods. Because a Globe object can actively be shared by many processes at the same time, it is also called a **distributed shared object**. The positioning of systems like Globe is shown in Fig. 8-22(c).

Now let us see how scalability and flexibility are implemented. Every Globe object has a class object that contains the actual code for its methods. Every object also has one (or more) interfaces, each of which contains (method pointer, state pointer) pairs. Thus given an object interface, which is a table full of pointers present in memory at run time, a process can invoke the object's n-th method by making a call to the procedure pointed to by the n-th pair in the interface table and passing it the corresponding state pointer as a parameter. The state pointer is needed so that if there are, say, two objects of class mailbox in memory, each one has its own interface, with shared method pointers but private state pointers, as shown in Fig. 8-39. In this example, the process has two open mailboxes, each of which shares the code for the four mailbox methods, but each of which has its own private state (the messages stored in the mailbox instance). One mailbox might be for business mail and the other for personal mail, for example.

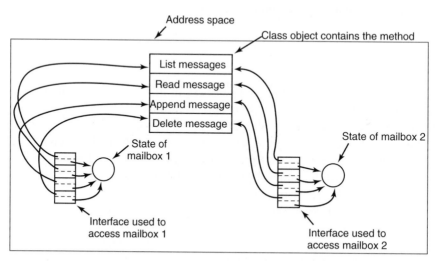

Figure 8-39. The structure of a Globe object.

The design of having interfaces be tables in memory at run time means that objects are not restricted to any particular language. This decision was made because a worldwide system will have many different people with many different favorite languages. An object's methods may be written in C, C++, Java, or even assembly language if the object's owner so desires. The interfaces are there to shield the process from what is behind the method pointers. This mix-and-match design is more flexible than a single-language design present in some systems (e.g., only Java or only C++).

To use a Globe object, a process must first bind to it by looking it up and finding at least one contact address (e.g., IP address and port). A security check is made at binding time, and if the process is authorized to bind to the object, the object's class object (i.e., its code) is loaded into the caller's address space, a copy of its state is instantiated and a pointer to its (standard) interface is returned. Using the interface pointer, the process can now invoke methods on this instance of the object. Depending on the object, the state may be the default state or a copy of the current state taken from one of the other live copies.

Imagine the simplest possible object. It has one integer as state and two methods: *read* and *write* that operate on the integer. If multiple processes in different countries are simultaneously bound to the object, all of them have an interface table pointing to the class object containing the two methods (which was loaded at bind time), as illustrated in Fig. 8-40. Each process (potentially) also has a copy of the integer comprising the state. Any *read* method is just invoked locally, but *write*s are more complicated. If the object wants to maintain sequential consistency, it must provide a mechanism for doing so.

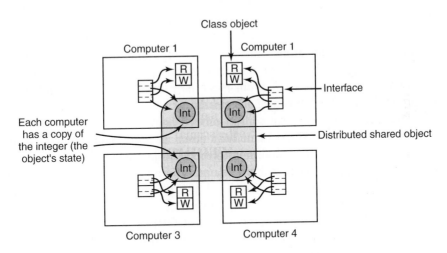

Figure 8-40. A distributed shared object can have its state copied on multiple computers at once.

One mechanism is to have a process called the **sequencer** whose job is to issue consecutive sequence numbers when requested to do so. To do a write, the *write* method might then first get a sequence number and then multicast a message containing the sequence number, operation name, and parameter to all the other processes bound to the object. If two processes invoked *write* simultaneously, they would be assigned different consecutive sequence numbers. All processes must apply incoming methods in sequence number order, not in message arrival order. If a process gets sequence number 26 and the previous one was 24, it must wait for 25 before applying 26. If 25 does not show up within a certain time, the process must take action to locate and get it. This scheme guarantees that all writes are done in the same order on all replicas of the object, ensuring sequential consistency.

Using this technique works reasonably well, but not all objects need sequential consistency. Consider, for example, an object maintaining stock prices. If the market maker for stock 1 issues an updated price for it concurrently with another market maker issuing an update for stock 2, it is not essential that all copies of the object apply those two updates in the same order because they are independent. It is probably sufficient that all processes apply the stream of updates from each market maker in the order they were sent, but this goal can be achieved by including a sequence number generated by the sending process. No object-wide sequencer is needed here.

The above replication scheme, namely a replicated object with all copies being equal and any copy being allowed to issue updates after first getting a sequence number is only one of many replication protocols. Another one has one master copy of each object, plus some number of slave copies. All updates are sent to the object's master copy, which then applies the update and sends out the new state to all the slave copies.

A third object replication strategy is having only one copy holding the object's state, with all the other copies being stateless proxies. When a *read* or *write* is done at a proxy (e.g., a client machine), the request is forwarded to the copy holding the state and executed there.

The strength of Globe is that each object can have its own replication policy. Some objects can use active replication at the same time other objects are using master-slave replication or any other strategy an object needs. Also, each object can have its own policy concerning consistency, replica creation and removal, security, etc. This is possible because all the policies are handled inside the object. Users of the object are not even aware of it, and neither are the system administrators. This approach is in contrast to CORBA, which does not hide any of these policies inside objects, making it difficult to have 1000 different objects with 1000 different policies.

A Globe object can be implemented as shown in Fig. 8-41. This figure illustrates the subobjects from which a Globe object is composed. The control object accepts incoming method invocations and uses the other subobjects to get them done. The semantics subobject actually does the work required by the object's interface. It is the only part of the object's code that must be written by the object's programmer; all the rest can be taken from standard libraries, unless the programmer wants a new strategy not currently available. The replication subobject's job is to manage replication. This module can be replaced to switch from active replication to master-slave replication or any other replication strategy without the rest of the object being affected. Similarly, the security subobject can be replaced to implement a new security policy (e.g., to switch from ACLs to capabilities) and the communication subobject can be replaced to change network protocols (e.g., from IP v4 to IP v6) without affecting the rest of the object.

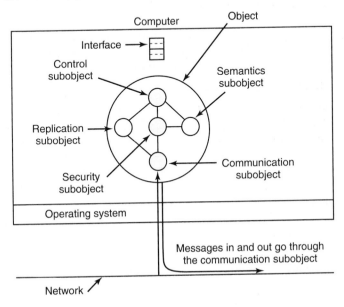

Figure 8-41. Structure of a Globe object.

To see how these subobjects interact, consider what happens when one of the object's methods is invoked. The code pointed to by the interface is in the control subobject, which then asks the replication subobject to do what it has to do. If the object is actively replicated, a sequence number is first acquired. Then the replication subobject tells all replicas (including its own) to actually do the work by invoking their semantics object. If the object is master-slave and the method invocation is on a slave, a message is sent to the master, and so on. At appropriate moments security checks are made by the security object (to see if the invocation is permitted, to see if outgoing data must be encrypted, etc.).

A key element of Globe is the **location service**, which allows objects to be looked up anywhere in the world. The location service is built as a tree, with object registrations being kept only in the node where the registration takes place. Pointers to this node are propagated up to the top of the tree so it is always possible to find the registration. Locality, partitioning of tree nodes, caching, and other techniques are used to make the scheme workable, even for mobile objects (Ballintijn et al., 2000; Van Steen et al., 1998a; and Van Steen et al., 1998b).

8.3.6 Coordination-Based Middleware

Our last paradigm for a distributed system is called **coordination-based middleware**. We will start with the Linda system, an academic research project that started the whole field, and then look at two commercial examples heavily inspired by it: publish/subscribe and Jini.

Linda

Linda is a novel system for communication and synchronization developed at Yale University by David Gelernter and his student Nick Carriero (Carriero and Gelernter, 1986; Carriero and Gelernter, 1989; and Gelernter, 1985). In Linda, independent processes communicate via an abstract **tuple space**. The tuple space is global to the entire system, and processes on any machine can insert tuples into the tuple space or remove tuples from the tuple space without regard to how or where they are stored. To the user, the tuple space looks like a big, global shared memory, as we have seen in various forms before [and in Fig. 8-22(c)].

A **tuple** is like a structure in C or a record in Pascal. It consists of one or more fields, each of which is a value of some type supported by the base language (Linda is implemented by adding a library to an existing language, such as C). For C-Linda, field types include integers, long integers, and floating-point numbers, as well as composite types such as arrays (including strings) and structures (but not other tuples). Unlike objects, tuples are pure data; they do not have any associated methods. Figure 8-42 shows three tuples as examples.

```
("abc", 2, 5)
("matrix-1", 1, 6, 3.14)
("family", "is-sister", "Stephany", "Roberta")
```

Figure 8-42. Three Linda tuples.

Four operations are provided on tuples. The first one, *out*, puts a tuple into the tuple space. For example,

```
out("abc", 2, 5);
```

puts the tuple ("abc", 2, 5) into the tuple space. The fields of *out* are normally constants, variables, or expressions, as in

```
out("matrix-1", i, j, 3.14);
```

which outputs a tuple with four fields, the second and third of which are determined by the current values of the variables i and j.

Tuples are retrieved from the tuple space by the *in* primitive. They are addressed by content rather than by name or address. The fields of *in* can be expressions or formal parameters. Consider, for example,

```
in("abc", 2, ?i);
```

This operation "searches" the tuple space for a tuple consisting of the string "abc", the integer 2, and a third field containing any integer (assuming that i is an integer). If found, the tuple is removed from the tuple space and the variable i is assigned the value of the third field. The matching and removal are atomic, so if two processes execute the same *in* operation simultaneously, only one of them will succeed, unless two or more matching tuples are present. The tuple space may even contain multiple copies of the same tuple.

The matching algorithm used by *in* is straightforward. The fields of the *in* primitive, called the **template**, are (conceptually) compared to the corresponding fields of every tuple in the tuple space. A match occurs if the following three conditions are all met:

1. The template and the tuple have the same number of fields.

2. The types of the corresponding fields are equal.

3. Each constant or variable in the template matches its tuple field.

Formal parameters, indicated by a question mark followed by a variable name or type, do not participate in the matching (except for type checking), although those containing a variable name are assigned after a successful match.

If no matching tuple is present, the calling process is suspended until another process inserts the needed tuple, at which time the caller is automatically revived and given the new tuple. The fact that processes block and unblock automatically means that if one process is about to output a tuple and another is about to input it, it does not matter which goes first. The only difference is that if the *in* is done before the *out*, there will be a slight delay until the tuple is available for removal.

The fact that processes block when a needed tuple is not present can be put to many uses. For example, it can be used to implement semaphores. To create or do an up on semaphore S, a process can execute

```
out("semaphore S");
```

To do a down, it does

```
in("semaphore S");
```

The state of semaphore S is determined by the number of ("semaphore S") tuples in the tuple space. If none exist, any attempt to get one will block until some other process supplies one.

In addition to *out* and *in*, Linda also has a primitive *read*, which is the same as *in* except that it does not remove the tuple from the tuple space. There is also a primitive *eval*, which causes its parameters to be evaluated in parallel and the resulting tuple to be put in the tuple space. This mechanism can be used to perform an arbitrary computation. This is how parallel processes are created in Linda.

Publish/Subscribe

Our next example of a coordination-based model was inspired by Linda and is called **publish/subscribe** (Oki et al., 1993). It consists of a number of processes connected by a broadcast network. Each process can be a producer of information, a consumer of information, or both.

When an information producer has a new piece of information (e.g., a new stock price), it broadcasts the information as a tuple on the network. This action is called **publishing**. Each tuple contains a hierarchical subject line containing multiple fields separated by periods. Processes that are interested in certain information can **subscribe** to certain subjects, including the use of wildcards in the subject line. Subscription is done by telling a tuple daemon process on the same machine that monitors published tuples what subjects to look for.

Publish/subscribe is implemented as illustrated in Fig. 8-43. When a process has a tuple to publish, it broadcasts it out onto the local LAN. The tuple daemon on each machine copies all broadcasted tuples into its RAM. It then inspects the subject line to see which processes are interested in it, forwarding a copy to each one that is. Tuples can also be broadcast over a wide area network or the Internet by having one machine on each LAN act as an information router, collecting all published tuples and then forwarding them to other LANs for rebroadcasting. This forwarding can also be done intelligently, only forwarding a tuple to a remote LAN if that remote LAN has at least one subscriber who wants the tuple. Doing this requires having the information routers exchange information about subscribers.

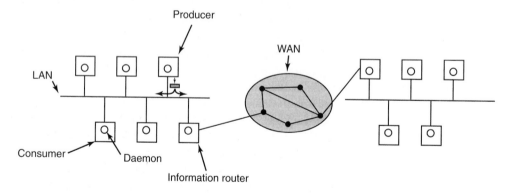

Figure 8-43. The publish/subscribe architecture.

Various kinds of semantics can be implemented, including reliable delivery and guaranteed delivery, even in the face of crashes. In the latter case, it is necessary to store old tuples in case they are needed later. One way to store them is to hook up a database system to the system and have it subscribe to all tuples. This can be done by wrapping the database system in an adapter, to allow an existing database to work with the publish/subscribe model. As tuples come by, the adapter captures all of them and puts them in the database.

The publish/subscribe model fully decouples producers from consumers, as does Linda. However, sometimes it is useful to know who else is out there. This information can be acquired by publishing a tuple that basically asks: "Who out there is interested in x?" Responses come back in the form of tuples that say: "I am interested in x."

Jini

For over 50 years, computing has been CPU-centric, with a computer being a freestanding device consisting of a CPU, some primary memory, and nearly always some mass storage such as a disk. Sun Microsystems' **Jini** (a variant spelling of genie) is an attempt to change that model to one that might be described as network-centric (Waldo, 1999).

The Jini world consists of a large number of self-contained Jini devices, each of which offers one or more services to the others. A Jini device can be plugged into a network and begin offering and using services instantly, with no complex installation procedure. Note that the devices are plugged into a *network*, not into a *computer* as is traditionally the case. A Jini device could be a traditional computer, but it could also be a printer, palmtop computer, cell phone, TV set, stereo, or other device with a CPU, some memory, and a (possibly wireless) network connection. A Jini system is a loose federation of Jini devices that may come and go at will, with no central administration.

When a Jini device wants to join the Jini federation, it broadcasts a packet on the local LAN or in the local wireless cell asking if there is a **lookup service** present. The protocol used to find a lookup service is the **discovery protocol** and is one of the few hardwired protocols in Jini. (Alternatively, the new Jini device can wait until one of the lookup service's periodic announcements comes by, but we will not treat this mechanism here.)

When the lookup service sees that a new device wants to register, it replies with a piece of code that can perform the registration. Since Jini is an all Java system, the code sent is in JVM (the Java Virtual Machine language), which all Jini devices must be capable of running, usually interpretively. The new device now runs the code, which contacts the lookup service and registers with it for some fixed period of time. Just before the time period expires, the device can reregister if it wishes. This mechanism means that a Jini device can just leave the system by shutting down and its previous existence will soon be forgotten, without the need for any central administration. The concept of registering for a fixed time interval is called acquiring a **lease**.

Note that since the code to register the device is downloaded into the device, it can be changed as the system evolves without affecting the hardware or software of the device. In fact, the device is not even aware of what the registration protocol is. A part of the registration process that the device is aware of consists of it providing some attributes and proxy code that other devices will later use to access it.

A device or user looking for a particular service can ask the lookup service if it knows about one. The request may involve some of the attributes that devices use when registering. If the request is successful, the proxy that the device provided at registration time is sent back to the requester and is run to contact the device. Thus a device or user can talk to another device without knowing where it is or even what protocol it speaks.

Jini clients and services (hardware or software devices) communicate and synchronize using **JavaSpaces**, which are modeled on the Linda tuple space but with some important differences. Each JavaSpace consists of some number of strongly typed entries. Entries are like Linda tuples, except that they are strongly typed, whereas Linda tuples are untyped. Each entry consists of some number of fields, each of which has a basic Java type. For example, an entry of type employee might consist of a string (for the name), an integer (for the department), a second integer (for the telephone extension), and a Boolean (for works-full-time).

Just four methods are defined on a JavaSpace (although two of them have a variant form):

1. **Write**: put a new entry into the JavaSpace.

2. **Read**: copy an entry that matches a template out of the JavaSpace.

3. **Take**: copy and remove an entry that matches a template.

4. **Notify**: notify the caller when a matching entry is written.

The *write* method provides the entry and specifies its lease time, that is when it should be discarded. In contrast, Linda tuples stay until removed. A JavaSpace may contain the same entry multiple times, so it is not a mathematical set (just as in Linda).

The *read* and *take* methods provide a template for the entry being sought. Each field in the template can contain a specific value that must be matched, or can contain a "don't care" wildcard that matches all values of the appropriate type. If a match is found, it is returned, and in the case of *take*, it is also removed from the JavaSpace. Each of these JavaSpace methods has two variants, which differ in the case that no entry matches. One variant returns with a failure indication immediately; the other one waits until a timeout (given as a parameter) has expired.

The *notify* method registers interest in a particular template. If a matching entry is later entered, the caller's *notify* method is invoked.

Unlike Linda's tuple space, JavaSpace supports atomic transactions. Using them, multiple methods can be grouped together. They will either all execute or none of them will execute. During the transaction, changes that are made to the JavaSpace are not visible outside the transaction. Only when the transaction commits, do they become visible to other callers.

JavaSpace can be used for synchronization between communicating processes. For example, in a producer-consumer situation, the producer puts items in a JavaSpace as it produces them. The consumer removes them with *take*, blocking if none are available. JavaSpace guarantees that each of the methods is executed atomically, so there is no danger of one process trying to read an entry that has only been half entered.

8.4 RESEARCH ON MULTIPLE PROCESSOR SYSTEMS

In this chapter we have looked at three kinds of multiple processor systems: multiprocessors, multicomputers, and distributed systems. Let us also look briefly at the research in these three areas. Most of the research on multiprocessors relates to the hardware, in particular, how to build the shared memory and keep it coherent. However, there has also been some research on using virtual machine monitors on multiprocessors (Bugnion et al., 1997) and on resource management on multiprocessors (Govil et al., 1999). Thread scheduling is also an issue in terms of the scheduling algorithm (Arora et al., 1998; and Philbin et al., 1996), and also in terms of contention for the run queue (Dandamudi, 1997).

Multicomputers are much easier to build than multiprocessors. All that is needed is a collection of PCs or workstations and a high-speed network. For this reason, they are a popular research topic at universities. A lot of the work relates to distributed shared memory in one form or another, sometimes page-based but sometimes entirely in software (Carter et al., 1995; Feeley et al., 1995; Johnson et al., 1995; Itzkovitz and Schuster, 1999; Scales and Gharachorloo, 1997; and Stets et al., 1997). Optimizing user-level communication is also a research topic (Von Eicken et al., 1995). So is load balancing (Harchol-Balter and Downey, 1996).

There are also many papers on distributed systems, for example on middleware (Bernstein, 1996), objects (Dogac et al., 1998), wireless systems (Liu et al., 1996), mobile agents (Chen et al., 2000), programming environments (Jo, 1999), distributed multimedia (Mourlas, 2000), theory (Buchs and Guelfi, 2000), and Web caching (Wolman et al., 1999), among others. Distributed file systems (Alexandrov et al., 1998; Hartman and Ousterhout, 1995; and Thekkath et al., 1997) and mobile file systems (Segarra and Andri, 1999) are also also popular.

8.5 SUMMARY

Computer systems can be made faster and more reliable by using multiple CPUs. Three organizations for multiCPU systems are multiprocessors, multicomputers, and distributed systems. Each of these has its own properties and issues.

A multiprocessor consists of two or more CPUs that share a common RAM. The CPUs can be interconnected by a bus, a crossbar switch, or a multistage switching network. Various operating system configurations are possible, including giving each CPU its own operating system, having one master operating system with the rest being slaves, or having a symmetric multiprocessor, in which there is one copy of the operating system that any CPU can run. In the latter case, locks are needed to provide synchronization. When a lock is not available, a CPU can spin or do a context switch. Various scheduling algorithms are possible, including timesharing, space sharing, and gang scheduling.

Multicomputers also have two or more CPUs, but these CPUs each have their own private memory. They do not share any common RAM, so all communication uses message passing. In some cases, the network interface board has its own CPU, in which case the communication between the main CPU and the interface board CPU has to be carefully organized to avoid race conditions. User-level communication on multicomputers often uses remote procedure call, but distributed shared memory can also be used. Load balancing of processes is an issue here, and the various algorithms used for it include sender-initiated algorithms, receiver-initiated algorithms, and bidding algorithms.

Distributed systems are loosely coupled systems each of whose nodes is a complete computer with a complete set of peripherals and its own operating system. Often these systems are spread over a large geographical area. Middleware is often put on top of the operating system to provide a uniform layer for applications to interact with. The various kinds of middleware include document-based, file-based, object-based, and coordination-based middleware. Some examples are the World Wide Web, AFS, CORBA, Globe, Linda, and Jini.

PROBLEMS

1. Can the USENET newsgroup system or the SETI@home project be considered distributed systems? (SETI@home uses several million idle personal computers to analyze radiotelescope data to search for extraterrestrial intelligence). If so, how do they relate to the categories described in Fig. 8-1?

2. What happens if two CPUs in a multiprocessor attempt to access exactly the same word of memory at exactly the same instant?

3. If a CPU issues one memory request every instruction and the computer runs at 200 MIPS, about how many CPUs will it take to saturate a 400-MHz bus? Assume that a memory reference requires one bus cycle. Now repeat this problem for a system in which caching is used and the caches have a 90% hit rate. Finally, what cache hit rate would be needed to allow 32 CPUs to share the bus without overloading it?

4. Suppose that the wire between switch 2A and switch 3B in the omega network of Fig. 8-5 breaks. Who is cut off from whom?

5. How is signal handling done in the model of Fig. 8-7?

6. When a system call is made in the model of Fig. 8-8, a problem has to be solved immediately after the trap that does not occur in the model of Fig. 8-7. What is the nature of this problem and how might it be solved?

7. Rewrite the enter_region code of Fig. 2-22 using the pure read to reduce thrashing induced by the TSL instruction.

8. Are critical regions on code sections really necessary in an SMP operating system to avoid race conditions or will mutexes on data structures do the job as well?

9. When the TSL instruction is used for multiprocessor synchronization, the cache block containing the mutex will get shuttled back and forth between the CPU holding the lock and the CPU requesting it if both of them keep touching the block. To reduce bus traffic, the requesting CPU executes one TSL every 50 bus cycles, but the CPU holding the lock always touches the cache block between TSL instructions. If a cache block consists of 16 32-bit words, each of which requires one bus cycle to transfer, and the bus runs at 400 MHz, what fraction of the bus bandwidth is eaten up by moving the cache block back and forth?

10. In the text, it was suggested that a binary exponential backoff algorithm be used between uses of TSL to poll a lock. It was also suggested to have a maximum delay between polls. Would the algorithm work correctly if there were no maximum delay?

11. Suppose that the TSL instruction was not available for synchronizing a multiprocessor. Instead, another instruction, SWP was provided that atomically swapped the contents of a register with a word in memory. Could that be used to provide multiprocessor synchronization? If so, how could it be used? If not, why does it not work?

12. In this problem you are to compute how much of a bus load a spin lock puts on the bus. Imagine that each instruction executed by a CPU takes 5 nsec. After an instruction has completed, any bus cycles needed, for example, for TSL are carried out. Each bus cycle takes an additional 10 nsec above and beyond the instruction execution time. If a process is attempting to enter a critical region using a TSL loop, what fraction of the bus bandwidth does it consume? Assume that normal caching is working so that fetching an instruction inside the loop consumes no bus cycles.

13. Fig. 8-12 was said to depict a timesharing environment. Why is only one process (*A*) shown in part (b)?

14. Affinity scheduling reduces cache misses. Does it also reduce TLB misses? What about page faults?

15. For each of the topologies of Fig. 8-16, what is the diameter of the interconnection network? Count all hops (host-router and router-router) equally for this problem.

16. Consider the double torus topology of Fig. 8-16(d) but expanded to size $k \times k$. What is the diameter of the network? *Hint*: Consider odd k and even k differently.

17. The bisection bandwidth of an interconnection network is often used as a measure of its capacity. It is computed by removing a minimal number of links that splits the network into two equal-size units. The capacity of the removed links is then added up. If there are many ways to make the split, the one with the minimum bandwidth is the bisection bandwidth. For an interconnection network consisting of an $8 \times 8 \times 8$ cube, what is the bisection bandwidth if each link is 1 Gbps?

18. Consider a multicomputer in which the network interface is in user mode, so only three copies are needed from source RAM to destination RAM. Assume that moving a 32-bit word to or from the network interface board takes 20 nsec and that the network itself operates at 1 Gbps. What would the delay for a 64-byte packet being sent from source to destination be if we could ignore the copying time? What is it with the copying time? Now consider the case where two extra copies are needed, to the kernel on the sending side and from the kernel on the receiving side. What is the delay in this case?

19. Repeat the previous problem for both the three-copy case and the five-copy case but this time compute the bandwidth rather than the delay.

20. How must the implementation of send and receive differ between a shared memory multiprocessor system and a multicomputer, and how does this affect performance?

21. When transferring data from RAM to a network interface, pinning a page can be used, but suppose that system calls to pin and unpin pages each take 1 μsec. Copying takes 5 byte/nsec using DMA but 20 nsec per byte using programmed I/O. How big does a packet have to be before pinning the page and using DMA is worth it?

22. When a procedure is scooped up from one machine and placed on another to called by RPC, some problems can occur. In the text, we pointed out four of these: pointers, unknown array sizes, unknown parameter types, and global variables. An issue not discussed is what happens if the (remote) procedure executes a system call. What problems might that cause and what might be done to handle them?

23. In a DSM system, when a page fault occurs, the needed page has to be located. List two possible ways to find the page.

24. Consider the processor allocation of Fig. 8-25. Suppose that process H is moved from node 2 to node 3. What is the total weight of the external traffic now?

25. Some multicomputers allow running processes to be migrated from one node to another. Is it sufficient to stop a process, freeze its memory image, and just ship that off to a different node? Name two nontrivial problems that have to be solved to make this work.

26. Why is there a limit to cable length on an Ethernet network?

27. In Fig. 8-28, the third and fourth layers are labeled Middleware and Application on all four machines. In what sense are they all the same across platforms and in what sense are they different?

28. Fig. 8-31 lists six different types of service. For each of the following applications, which service type is most appropriate?

(a) Video on demand over the Internet.
(b) Downloading a Web page.

29. DNS names have a hierarchical structure, such as *cs.uni.edu* or *sales.general-widget.com*. One way to maintain the DNS database would be as one centralized database, but that is not done because it would get too many requests/sec. Make a proposal how the DNS database could be maintained in practice.

30. In the discussion of how URLs are processed by a browser, it was stated that connections are made to port 80. Why?

31. Can the URLs used in the Web exhibit location transparency? Explain your answer.

32. When a browser fetches a Web page, it first makes a TCP connection to get the text on the page (in the HTML language). Then it closes the connection and examines the page. If there are figures or icons, it then makes a separate TCP connection to fetch each one. Suggest two alternative designs to improve performance here.

33. When session semantics are used, it is always true that changes to a file are immediately visible to the process making the change and never visible to processes on other machines. However, it is an open question as to whether or not they should be immediately visible to other processes on the same machine. Give an argument each way.

34. In AFS, whole files are cached on the client machines. Suppose that there is only so much disk space allocated for cached files and the allocation is full. When a new file is requested, what should be done? Give an algorithm for doing it.

35. When multiple processes need access to data, in what way is object-based access better than shared memory?

36. When a Linda *in* operation is done to locate a tuple, searching the entire tuple space linearly is very inefficient. Design a way to organize the tuple space that will speed up searches on all *in* operations.

37. Copying buffers takes time. Write a C program to find out how much time it takes on a system to which you have access. Use the *clock* or *times* functions to determine how long it takes to copy a large array. Test with different array sizes to separate copying time from overhead time.

38. Write C functions that could be used as client and server stubs to make an RPC call to the standard *printf* function, and a main program to test the functions. The client and server should communicate by means of a data structure that could be transmitted over a network. You may impose reasonable limits on the length of the format string and the number, types, and sizes of variables your client stub will accept.

39. Write two programs to simulate load balancing on a multicomputer. The first program should set up *m* processes distributed across *n* machines according to an initialization file. Each process should have running time chosen at random from a Gaussian distribuion whose mean and standard deviation are parameters of the simulation. At the end of each run, the process creates some number of new processes, chosen from a Poisson distribution. When a process exits, the CPU must decide whether to give away processes or try to find new processes. The first program should use the sender-initiated algorithm to give away work if it has more than k processes total on its machine. The second program should use the receiver-initiated algorithm to fetch work when needed. Make any other reasonable assumptions you need, but state them clearly.

9

SECURITY

Many companies possess valuable information that they guard closely. This information can be technical (e.g., a new chip design or software), commercial (e.g., studies of the competition or marketing plans), financial (e.g., plans for a stock offering), legal (e.g., documents about a potential merger or takeover), among many other possibilities. Frequently this information is protected by having a uniformed guard at the building entrance who checks to see that all people entering the building are wearing a proper badge. In addition, many offices may be locked and some file cabinets may be locked as well to ensure that only authorized people have access to the information.

As more and more of this information is stored in computer systems, the need to protect it is becoming increasingly important. Protecting this information against unauthorized usage is therefore a major concern of all operating systems. Unfortunately, it is also becoming increasingly difficult due to the widespread acceptance of system bloat as being a normal and acceptable phenomenon. In the following sections we will look at a variety of issues concerned with security and protection, some of which have analogies to real-world protection of information on paper, but some of which are unique to computer systems. In this chapter we will examine computer security as it applies to operating systems.

9.1 THE SECURITY ENVIRONMENT

Some people use the terms "security" and "protection" interchangeably. Nevertheless, it is frequently useful to make a distinction between the general problems involved in making sure that files are not read or modified by unauthorized persons, which include technical, administrative, legal, and political issues on the one hand, and the specific operating system mechanisms used to provide security, on the other. To avoid confusion, we will use the term **security** to refer to the overall problem, and the term **protection mechanisms** to refer to the specific operating system mechanisms used to safeguard information in the computer. The boundary between them is not well defined, however. First we will look at security to see what the nature of the problem is. Later on in the chapter we will look at the protection mechanisms and models available to help achieve security.

Security has many facets. Three of the more important ones are the nature of the threats, the nature of intruders, and accidental data loss. We will now look at these in turn.

9.1.1 Threats

From a security perspective, computer systems have three general goals, with corresponding threats to them, as listed in Fig. 9-1. The first one, **data confidentiality**, is concerned with having secret data remain secret. More specifically, if the owner of some data has decided that these data are only to be made available to certain people and no others, the system should guarantee that release of the data to unauthorized people does not occur. As a bare minimum, the owner should be able to specify who can see what, and the system should enforce these specifications.

Goal	Threat
Data confidentiality	Exposure of data
Data integrity	Tampering with data
System availability	Denial of service

Figure 9-1. Security goals and threats.

The second goal, **data integrity**, means that unauthorized users should not be able to modify any data without the owner's permission. Data modification in this context includes not only changing the data, but also removing data and adding false data as well. If a system cannot guarantee that data deposited in it remain unchanged until the owner decides to change them, it is not worth much as an information system.

The third goal, **system availability**, means that nobody can disturb the system to make it unusable. Such **denial of service** attacks are increasingly common.

For example, if a computer is an Internet server, sending a flood of requests to it may cripple it by eating up all of its CPU time just examining and discarding incoming requests. If it takes, say, 100 μsec to process an incoming request to read a Web page, then anyone who manages to send 10,000 requests/sec can wipe it out. Reasonable models and technology for dealing with attacks on confidentiality and integrity are available; foiling denial-of-services attacks is much harder.

Another aspect of the security problem is **privacy**: protecting individuals from misuse of information about them. This quickly gets into many legal and moral issues. Should the government compile dossiers on everyone in order to catch *X*-cheaters, where *X* is "welfare" or "tax," depending on your politics? Should the police be able to look up anything on anyone in order to stop organized crime? Do employers and insurance companies have rights? What happens when these rights conflict with individual rights? All of these issues are extremely important but are beyond the scope of this book.

9.1.2 Intruders

Most people are pretty nice and obey the law, so why worry about security? Because there are unfortunately a few people around who are not so nice and want to cause trouble (possibly for their own commercial gain). In the security literature, people who are nosing around places where they have no business being are called **intruders** or sometimes **adversaries**. Intruders act in two different ways. Passive intruders just want to read files they are not authorized to read. Active intruders are more malicious; they want to make unauthorized changes to data. When designing a system to be secure against intruders, it is important to keep in mind the kind of intruder one is trying to protect against. Some common categories are

1. Casual prying by nontechnical users. Many people have personal computers on their desks that are connected to a shared file server, and human nature being what it is, some of them will read other people's electronic mail and other files if no barriers are placed in the way. Most UNIX systems, for example, have the default that all newly created files are publicly readable.

2. Snooping by insiders. Students, system programmers, operators, and other technical personnel often consider it to be a personal challenge to break the security of the local computer system. They often are highly skilled and are willing to devote a substantial amount of time to the effort.

3. Determined attempts to make money. Some bank programmers have attempted to steal from the bank they were working for. Schemes have varied from changing the software to truncate rather than round interest, keeping the fraction of a cent for themselves, to siphoning

off accounts not used in years, to blackmail ("Pay me or I will destroy all the bank's records.").

4. Commercial or military espionage. Espionage refers to a serious and well-funded attempt by a competitor or a foreign country to steal programs, trade secrets, patentable ideas, technology, circuit designs, business plans, and so forth. Often this attempt will involve wiretapping or even erecting antennas directed at the computer to pick up its electromagnetic radiation.

It should be clear that trying to keep a hostile foreign government from stealing military secrets is quite a different matter from trying to keep students from inserting a funny message-of-the-day into the system. The amount of effort needed security and protection clearly depends on who the enemy is thought to be.

Another category of security pest that has manifested itself in recent years is the virus, which will be discussed at length below. Basically a virus is a piece of code that replicates itself and (usually) does some damage. In a sense, the writer of a virus is also an intruder, often with high technical skills. The difference between a conventional intruder and a virus is that the former refers to a person who is personally trying to break into a system to cause damage whereas the latter is a program written by such a person and then released into the world hoping it causes damage. Intruders try to break into specific systems (e.g., one belonging to some bank or the Pentagon) to steal or destroy particular data, whereas a virus usually causes more general damage. In a sense, an intruder is like someone with a gun who tries to kill a specific person; a virus writer is more like a terrorist bomber who just wants to kill people in general, rather than some particular person.

9.1.3 Accidental Data Loss

In addition to threats caused by malicious intruders, valuable data can be lost by accident. Some of the common causes of accidental data loss are

1. Acts of God: fires, floods, earthquakes, wars, riots, or rats gnawing tapes or floppy disks.

2. Hardware or software errors: CPU malfunctions, unreadable disks or tapes, telecommunication errors, program bugs.

3. Human errors: incorrect data entry, wrong tape or disk mounted, wrong program run, lost disk or tape, or some other mistake.

Most of these can be dealt with by maintaining adequate backups, preferably far away from the original data. While protecting data against accidental loss may seem mundane compared to protecting against clever intruders, in practice, probably more damage is caused by the former than the latter.

9.2 BASICS OF CRYPTOGRAPHY

A little knowledge of cryptography may be useful for understanding parts of this chapter and some subsequent ones. However, a serious discussion of cryptography is beyond the scope of this book. Many excellent books on computer security discuss the topic at length. The interested reader is referred to some of these (e.g., Kaufman et al., 1995; and Pfleeger, 1997). Below we give a very quick discussion of cryptography for readers not familiar with it at all.

The purpose of cryptography is to take a message or file, called the **plaintext**, and encrypt it into the **ciphertext** in such a way that only authorized people know how to convert it back to the plaintext. For all others, the ciphertext is just an incomprehensible pile of bits. Strange as it may sound to beginners in the area, the encryption and decryption algorithms (functions) should always be public. Trying to keep them secret never works and gives the people trying to keep the secrets a false sense of security. In the trade, this tactic is called **security by obscurity** and is employed only by security amateurs. Oddly enough, this category also includes many huge multinational corporations that really should know better.

Instead, the secrecy depends on parameters to the algorithms called **keys**. If P is the plaintext file, K_E is the encryption key, C is the ciphertext, and E is the encryption algorithm (i.e., function), then $C = E(P, K_E)$. This is the definition of encryption. It says that the ciphertext is obtained by using the (known) encryption algorithm, E, with the plaintext, P, and the (secret) encryption key, K_E, as parameters.

Similarly, $P = D(C, K_D)$ where D is the decryption algorithm and K_D is the decryption key. This says that to get the plaintext, P, back from the ciphertext, C, and the decryption key, K_D, one runs the algorithm D with C and K_D as parameters. The relation between the various pieces is shown in Fig. 9-2.

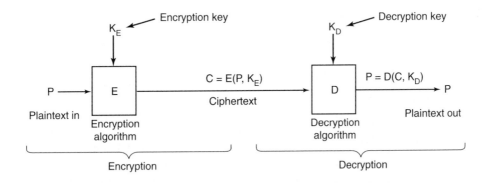

Figure 9-2. Relationship between the plaintext and the ciphertext.

9.2.1 Secret-Key Cryptography

To make this clearer, consider an encryption algorithm in which each letter is replaced by a different letter, for example, all *A*s are replaced by *Q*s, all *B*s are replaced by *W*s, all *C*s are replaced by *E*s, and so on like this:

    plaintext: A B C D E F G H I J K L M N O P Q R S T U V W X Y Z
    ciphertext: Q W E R T Y U I O P A S D F G H J K L Z X C V B N M

This general system is called a **monoalphabetic substitution**, with the key being the 26-letter string corresponding to the full alphabet. The encryption key in this example is *QWERTYUIOPASDFGHJKLZXCVBNM*. For the key above, the plaintext *ATTACK* would be transformed into the ciphertext *QZZQEA*. The decryption key tells how to get back from the ciphertext to the plaintext. In this example, the decryption key is *KXVMCNOPHQRSZYIJADLEGWBUFT* because an *A* in the ciphertext is a *K* in the plaintext, a *B* in the ciphertext is an *X* in the plaintext, etc.

At first glance this might appear to be a safe system because although the cryptanalyst knows the general system (letter for letter substitution), he does not know which of the 26! $\simeq 4 \times 10^{26}$ possible keys is in use. Nevertheless, given a surprisingly small amount of ciphertext, the cipher can be broken easily. The basic attack takes advantage of the statistical properties of natural languages. In English, for example, *e* is the most common letter, followed by *t, o, a, n, i*, etc. The most common two letter combinations, called **digrams**, are *th, in, er, re*, etc. Using this kind of information, breaking the cipher is easy.

Many cryptographic systems, like this one, have the property that given the encryption key it is easy to find the decryption key, and vice versa. Such systems are called **secret-key cryptography** or **symmetric-key cryptography**. Although monoalphabetic substitution ciphers are worthless, other symmetric key algorithms are known and are relatively secure if the keys are long enough. For serious security, probably 1024-bit keys should be used, giving a search space of $2^{1024} \simeq 2 \times 10^{308}$ keys. Shorter keys may thwart amateurs, but not major governments.

9.2.2 Public-Key Cryptography

Secret key systems are efficient because the amount of computation required to encrypt or decrypt a message is manageable, but have a big drawback: the sender and receiver must both be in possession of the shared secret key. They may even have to get together physically for one to give it to the other. To get around this problem, **public-key cryptography** is used (Diffie and Hellman, 1976). This system has the property that distinct keys are used for encryption and decryption and that given a well-chosen encryption key, it is virtually impossible to discover the corresponding decryption key. Under these circumstances, the encryption key can be made public and only the private decryption key kept secret.

Just to give a feel for public-key cryptography, consider the following two questions:

Question 1: How much is $314159265358979 \times 314159265358979$?
Question 2: What is the square root of 3912571506419387090594828508241?

Most sixth graders given a pencil, paper, and the promise of a really big ice cream sundae for the correct answer could answer question 1 in an hour or two. Most adults given a pencil, paper, and the promise of a lifetime 50% tax cut could not solve question 2 at all without using a calculator, computer, or other external help. Although squaring and square rooting are inverse operations, they differ enormously in their computational complexity. This kind of asymmetry forms the basis of public-key cryptography. Encryption makes use of the easy operation but decryption without the key requires you to perform the hard operation.

A public key system called **RSA** exploits the fact that multiplying big numbers is much easier for a computer to do than factoring big numbers, especially when all arithmetic is done using modulo arithmetic and all the numbers involved have hundreds of digits (Rivest et al., 1978). This system is widely used in the cryptographic world. Systems based on discrete logarithms are also used (El Gamal, 1985). The main problem with public-key cryptography is that it is a thousand times slower than symmetric cryptography.

The way public-key cryptography works is that everyone picks a (public key, private key) pair and publishes the public key. The public key is the encryption key; the private key is the decryption key. Usually, the key generation is automated, possibly with a user-selected password fed into the algorithm as a seed. To send a secret message to a user a correspondent encrypts the message with the receiver's public key. Since only the receiver has the private key, only the receiver can decrypt the message.

9.2.3 One-Way Functions

There are various situations that we will see later in which it is desirable to have some function, f, which has the property that given f and its parameter x, computing $y = f(x)$ is easy to do, but given only $f(x)$, finding x is computationally infeasible. Such a function typically mangles the bits in complex ways. It might start out by initializing y to x. Then it could have a loop that iterates as many times as there are 1 bits in x, with each iteration permuting the bits of y in an iteration-dependent way, adding in a different constant on each iteration, and generally mixing the bits up very thoroughly.

9.2.4 Digital Signatures

Frequently it is necessary to sign a document digitally. For example, suppose a bank customer instructs the bank to buy some stock for him by sending the bank an email message. An hour after the order has been sent and executed, the stock crashes. The customer now denies ever having sent the email. The bank can produce the email, of course, but the customer can claim the bank forged it in order to get a commission. How does a judge know who is telling the truth?

Digital signatures make it possible to sign email messages and other digital documents in such a way that they cannot be repudiated by the sender later. One common way is to first run the document through a one-way hashing algorithm that is very hard to invert. The hashing function typically produces a fixed-length result independent of the original document size. The most popular hashing functions used are **MD5** (**Message Digest**), which produces a 16-byte result (Rivest, 1992) and **SHA** (**Secure Hash Algorithm**), which produces a 20-byte result (NIST, 1995).

The next step assumes the use of public-key cryptography as described above. The document owner then applies his private key to the hash to get $D(hash)$. This value, called the **signature block**, is appended to the document and sent to the receiver, as shown in Fig. 9-3. The application of D to the hash is sometimes referred to as decrypting the hash, but it is not really a decryption because the hash has not been encrypted. It is just a mathematical transformation on the hash.

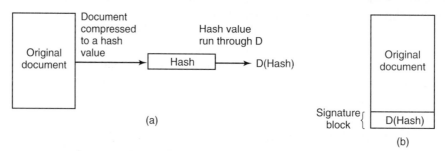

Figure 9-3. (a) Computing a signature block. (b) What the receiver gets.

When the document and hash arrive, the receiver first computes the hash of the document using MD5 or SHA, as agreed upon in advance. The receiver than applies the sender's public key to the signature block to get $E(D(hash))$. In effect, it encrypts the decrypted hash, canceling it out and getting the hash back. If the computed hash does not match the hash from the signature block, the document, the signature block, or both have been tampered with (or changed by accident). The value of this scheme is that it applies (slow) public-key cryptography only to a relatively small piece of data, the hash. Note carefully that this method works only if for all x

$$E(D(x)) = x$$

It is not guaranteed a priori that all encryption functions will have this property since all that we originally asked for was that

$$D(E(x)) = x$$

that is, E is the encryption function and D is the decryption function. To get the signature property in addition, the order of application must not matter, that is, D and E must be commutative functions. Fortunately, the RSA algorithm has this property.

To use this signature scheme, the receiver must know the sender's public key. Some users publish their public key on their Web page. Others do not because they may be afraid of an intruder breaking in and secretly altering their key. For them, an alternative mechanism is needed to distribute public keys. One common method is for message senders to attach a **certificate** to the message, which contains the user's name and public key and digitally signed by a trusted third party. Once the user has acquired the public key of the trusted third party, he can accept certificates from all senders who use this trusted third party to generate their certificates.

Above we have described how public-key cryptography can be used for digital signatures. It is worth mentioning that schemes that do not involve public-key cryptography also exist.

9.3 USER AUTHENTICATION

Now that we have some cryptographic background, let us start looking at security issues in operating systems. When a user logs into a computer, the operating system normally wishes to determine who the user is, a process called **user authentication**.

User authentication is one of those things we meant by "ontogeny recapitulates phylogeny" in Sec. 1.2.5. Early mainframes, such as the ENIAC, did not have an operating system, let alone a login procedure. Later mainframe batch and timesharing systems generally did have a login procedure for authenticating jobs and users.

Early minicomputers (e.g., PDP-1 and PDP-8) did not have a login procedure, but with the spread of UNIX on the PDP-11 minicomputer, logging in was again needed. Early personal computers (e.g., Apple II and the original IBM PC) did not have a login procedure, but more sophisticated personal computer operating systems, such as Windows 2000, again require a secure login. Using a personal computer to access servers on a LAN (local area network) or one's account at an e-commerce Web site always requires logging in. Thus the subject of secure login has gone through several cycles, and is once again an important subject.

Having determined that authentication is often important, the next step is to find a good way to achieve it. Most methods of authenticating users when they attempt to log in are based on one of three general principles, namely identifying

1. Something the user knows.

2. Something the user has.

3. Something the user is.

These principles lead to different authentication schemes with different complexities and security properties. In the following sections we will examine each of these in turn.

People who want to cause trouble on a particular system have to first log in to that system, which means getting past whichever authentication procedure is used. In the popular press, these people are called **hackers**. However, within the computer world, "hacker" is a term of honor reserved for great programmers. While some of these are rogues, most are not. The press got this one wrong. In deference to true hackers, we will use the term in the original sense and will call people who try to break into computer systems where they do not belong **crackers**.

9.3.1 Authentication Using Passwords

The most widely used form of authentication is to require the user to type a login name and a password. Password protection is easy to understand and easy to implement. The simplest implementation just keeps a central list of (login-name, password) pairs. The login name typed in is looked up in the list and the typed password is compared to the stored password. If they match, the login is allowed; if they do not match, the login is rejected.

It goes almost without saying that while a password is being typed in, the computer should not display the typed characters, to keep them from prying eyes near the terminal. With Windows 2000, as each character is typed, an asterisk is displayed. With UNIX, nothing at all is displayed while the password is being typed. These schemes have different properties. The Windows 2000 scheme may make it easy for absent-minded users to see how many characters they have typed so far, but it also discloses the password length to "eavesdroppers" (for some reason, English has a word for auditory snoopers but not for visual snoopers, other than perhaps Peeping Tom, which does not seem right in this context). From a security perspective, silence is golden.

Another area in which not quite getting it right has serious security implications is illustrated in Fig. 9-4. In Fig. 9-4(a), a successful login is shown, with system output in upper case and user input in lower case. In Fig. 9-4(b), a failed attempt by a cracker to log into System *A* is shown. In Fig. 9-4(c) a failed attempt by a cracker to log into System *B* is shown.

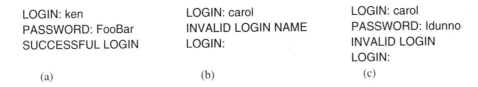

LOGIN: ken
PASSWORD: FooBar
SUCCESSFUL LOGIN

(a)

LOGIN: carol
INVALID LOGIN NAME
LOGIN:

(b)

LOGIN: carol
PASSWORD: Idunno
INVALID LOGIN
LOGIN:

(c)

Figure 9-4. (a) A successful login. (b) Login rejected after name is entered. (c) Login rejected after name and password are typed.

In Fig. 9-4(b), the system complains as soon as it sees an invalid login name. This is a mistake, as it allows the cracker to keep trying login names until she finds a valid one. In Fig. 9-4(c), the cracker is always asked for a password and gets no feedback about whether the login name itself is valid. All he learns is that the login name plus password combination tried is wrong.

How Crackers Break In

Most crackers break in by just calling up the target computer and trying many (login name, password) combinations until they find one that works. Many people use their name in one form or another as their login name. For Ellen Ann Smith, ellen, smith, ellen_smith, ellen-smith, ellen.smith, esmith, easmith, and eas are all reasonable candidates. Armed with one of those books entitled *4096 Names for Your New Baby*, plus a telephone book full of last names, a cracker can easily compile a computerized list of potential login names appropriate to the country being attacked (ellen_smith might work fine in the U.S. or England, but probably not in Japan).

Of course, guessing the login name is not enough. The password has to be guessed, too. How hard is that? Easier than you might think. The classic work on password security was done by Morris and Thompson (1979) on UNIX systems. They compiled a list of likely passwords: first and last names, street names, city names, words from a moderate-sized dictionary (also words spelled backward), license plate numbers, and short strings of random characters. They then compared their list to the system password file to see if there were any matches. Over 86% of all passwords turned up in their list. A similar result was obtained by Klein (1990).

Lest anyone think that better quality users pick better quality passwords, rest assured that they do not. A 1997 survey of passwords used in the financial district of London revealed that 82% could be guessed easily. Commonly used passwords were sexual terms, abusive expressions, people's names (often a family member or a sports star), vacation destinations, and common objects found around the office (Kabay, 1997). Thus a cracker can compile a list of potential login names and a list of potential passwords without much work.

Does it really matter if passwords are easy to guess? Yes. In 1998, the *San Jose Mercury News* reported that a Berkeley resident, Peter Shipley, had set up several unused computers as **war dialers**, which dial all 10,000 telephone numbers belonging to an exchange [e.g., (415) 770-xxxx], usually in random order to thwart telephone companies that frown upon such usage and try to detect it. After making 2.6 million calls, he located 20,000 computers in the Bay Area, 200 of which had no security at all. He estimated that a determined cracker could break into about 75% of the other ones (Denning, 1999).

The combination of a war dialer and password guessing can be deadly. An Australian cracker wrote a program that systematically dialed all the numbers at a telephone exchange and then attempted to break in using password guessing, notifying him when it succeeded. Among the many systems he broke into was a Citibank computer in Saudi Arabia, which allowed him to obtain credit card numbers and credit limits (in one case, $5 million) and transaction records (including at least one visit to a brothel). A cracker colleague of his also broke into the bank and collected 4000 credit card numbers (Denning, 1999). If such information were misused, the bank would undoubtedly emphatically and vigorously deny that it could possibly be at fault, claiming that the customer must have disclosed the information.

An alternative to using a war dialer is to attack computers over the Internet. Every computer on the Internet has a 32-bit IP address used to identify it. People usually write these addresses in **dotted decimal notation** as *w.x.y.z*, where each of the four components of the IP address is an integer from 0 to 255 in decimal. A cracker can easily test if some computer has this IP address and is up and running by typing

    ping w.x.y.z

If the computer is alive, it will respond and the *ping* program will tell how long the roundtrip time was in milliseconds (although some sites now disable *ping* to prevent this kind of attack). It is easy to write a program to ping large numbers of IP addresses systematically, analogous to what a war dialer does. If a live computer is found at *w.x.y.z*, the cracker can attempt to break in by typing

    telnet w.x.y.z

If the connection attempt is accepted (which it may not be, since not all system administrators welcome random logins over the Internet), the cracker can start trying login names and passwords from his lists. At first, it is trial and error. However, the cracker may eventually be able to break in a few times and capture the password file (located in */etc/passwd* on UNIX systems and often publicly readable). Then he will begin to collect statistical information about login name usage frequencies to optimize future searches.

Many telnet daemons break the underlying TCP connection after some number of unsuccessful login attempts in order to slow down crackers. Crackers respond to that by starting up many threads in parallel, working on different target machines at once. Their goal is to make as many tries per second as the outgoing bandwidth will allow. From their point of view, having to spray them over many machines being attacked simultaneously is not a serious disadvantage.

Instead of pinging machines in IP-address order, a cracker may wish to target a specific company, university, or other organization, say, the University of Foobar at *foobar.edu*. To find out what IP addresses they use, all he has to do is type

    dnsquery foobar.edu

and he will get a list of some of their IP addresses. (Alternatively, the programs *nslookup* or *dig* can also be used.) Since many organizations have 65,536 consecutive IP addresses (a common allocation unit in the past), once he knows the first 2 bytes of their IP addresses (which *dnsquery* supplies), it is straightforward to ping all 65,536 of them to see which ones respond and which ones accept telnet connections. From there on, it is back to guessing login names and passwords, a subject we have already discussed.

Needless to say, the entire process of starting with a domain name, finding the first 2 bytes of its IP addresses, pinging all of them to see which ones are alive, checking to see if any accept telnet connections, and then trying statistically likely (login name, password) pairs is a process that lends itself very well to automation. It will take many, many tries to break in, but if there is one thing that computers are very good at, it is repeating the same sequence of commands over and over until the cows come home. A cracker with a high-speed cable or DSL connection can program the break in process to run all day long and just check back once in a while to see what has showed up.

A telnet attack is clearly better than a war dialer attack since it goes much faster (no dialing time) and is much cheaper (no long distance telephone charges), but it only works for machines that are on the Internet and accept telnet connections. Nevertheless, many companies (and nearly all universities) do accept telnet connections so employees on a business trip or at a different branch office (or students at home) can log in remotely.

Not only are user passwords often weak, but sometimes the root password is too. In particular, some installations never bother to change the default passwords that systems are shipped with. Cliff Stoll, an astronomer at Berkeley, had observed irregularities on his system, and laid a trap for the cracker who had been trying to get in (Stoll, 1989). He observed the session shown in Fig. 9-5 typed by a cracker who had already broken into one machine at the Lawrence Berkeley Laboratory (LBL) and was trying to get into another one. The uucp (UNIX to UNIX Copy Program) account is used for intermachine network traffic and has superuser power, so the cracker was now in a U.S. Dept. of Energy machine as superuser. Fortunately, LBL does not design nuclear weapons although its sister lab at Livermore, does. One hopes their security is better, but there is little reason to believe that since another nuclear weapons lab, Los Alamos, lost a hard disk full of classified information in 2000.

```
LBL> telnet elxsi
ELXSI AT LBL
LOGIN: root
PASSWORD: root
INCORRECT PASSWORD, TRY AGAIN
LOGIN: guest
PASSWORD: guest
INCORRECT PASSWORD, TRY AGAIN
LOGIN: uucp
PASSWORD: uucp
WELCOME TO THE ELXSI COMPUTER AT LBL
```

Figure 9-5. How a cracker broke into a U.S. Dept. of Energy computer at LBL.

Once a cracker has broken into a system and become superuser, it may be possible to install a **packet sniffer**, software that examines all incoming and outgoing network packets looking for certain patterns. An especially interesting pattern to look for is people on the compromised machine logging into remote machines, especially as superuser there. This information can be squirreled away in a file for the cracker to pick up at his leisure later. In this way, a cracker who breaks into one machine with weak security can often leverage this into a way to break into other machines with stronger security.

Increasingly many break ins are being done by technically naive users who are just running scripts they found on the Internet. These scripts either use brute force attacks of the type described above, or try to exploit known bugs in specific programs. Real hackers refer to them as **script kiddies**.

Usually, the script kiddie has no particular target and no particular information he is trying to steal. He is just looking for machines that are easy to break into. Some of the scripts even pick a network to attack by chance, using a random network number (in the upper partof the IP address). They then probe all the machines on the network to see which ones respond. Once a database of valid IP addresses has been acquired, each machine is attacked in sequence. As a consequence of this methodology, it can happen that a brand new machine at a secure military installation can be attacked within hours of its being attached to the Internet, even though no one but the administrator even knows about it yet.

UNIX Password Security

Some (older) operating systems keep the password file on the disk in unencrypted form, but protected by the usual system protection mechanisms. Having all the passwords in a disk file in unencrypted form is just looking for trouble because all too often many people have access to it. These may include system administrators, machine operators, maintenance personnel, programmers, management, and maybe even some secretaries.

A better solution, used in UNIX, works like this. The login program asks the user to type his name and password. The password is immediately "encrypted" by using it as a key to encrypt a fixed block of data. Effectively, a one-way function is being run, with the password as input and a function of the password as output. This process is not really encryption, but it is easier to speak of it as encryption. The login program then reads the password file, which is just a series of ASCII lines, one per user, until it finds the line containing the user's login name. If the (encrypted) password contained in this line matches the encrypted password just computed, the login is permitted, otherwise it is refused. The advantage of this scheme is that no one, not even the superuser, can look up any users' passwords because they are not stored in unencrypted form anywhere in the system.

However, this scheme can also be attacked, as follows. A cracker first builds a dictionary of likely passwords the way Morris and Thompson did. At leisure, these are encrypted using the known algorithm. It does not matter how long this process takes because it is done in advance of the break in. Now armed with a list of (password, encrypted password) pairs, the cracker strikes. He reads the (publicly accessible) password file and strips out all the encrypted passwords. These are compared to the encrypted passwords in his list. For every hit, the login name and unencrypted password are now known. A simple shell script can automate this process so it can be carried out in a fraction of a second. A typical run of the script will yield dozens of passwords.

Recognizing the possibility of this attack, Morris and Thompson described a technique that renders the attack almost useless. Their idea is to associate an n-bit random number, called the **salt**, with each password. The random number is changed whenever the password is changed. The random number is stored in the password file in unencrypted form, so that everyone can read it. Instead of just storing the encrypted password in the password file, the password and the random number are first concatenated and then encrypted together. This encrypted result is stored in the password file, as shown in Fig. 9-6 for a password file with five users, Bobbie, Tony, Laura, Mark, and Deborah. Each user has one line in the file, with three entries separated by commas: login name, salt, and encrypted password+salt. The notation $e(Dog4238)$ represents the result of concatenating Bobbie's password, Dog, with her randomly assigned salt, 4238, and running it through the encryption function, e. It is the result of that encryption that is stored as the third field of Bobbie's entry.

Now consider the implications for a cracker who wants to build up a list of likely passwords, encrypt them, and save the results in a sorted file, f, so that any encrypted password can be looked up easily. If an intruder suspects that *Dog* might be a password, it is no longer sufficient just to encrypt *Dog* and put the result in f. He has to encrypt 2^n strings, such as *Dog0000*, *Dog0001*, *Dog0002*,

| Bobbie, 4238, e(Dog4238) |
| Tony, 2918, e(6%%TaeFF2918) |
| Laura, 6902, e(Shakespeare6902) |
| Mark, 1694, e(XaB@Bwcz1694) |
| Deborah, 1092, e(LordByron,1092) |

Figure 9-6. The use of salt to defeat precomputation of encrypted passwords.

and so forth and enter all of them in f. This technique increases the size of f by 2^n. UNIX uses this method with $n = 12$.

For additional security, some modern versions of UNIX make the password file itself unreadable but provide a program to look up entries upon request, adding just enough delay to greatly slow down any attacker. The combination of salting the password file and making it unreadable except indirectly (and slowly) can generally withstand most attacks on it.

Improving Password Security

Although salting the password file protects against crackers who try to precompute a large list of encrypted passwords and thus break many passwords at once, it does little to protect a user *David* whose password is also *David*. A cracker can still just try guessing passwords one at a time. Educating users about the need for strong passwords is critical, but few installations do it. One step further than user education is to have the computer help. Some computers have a program that generates random easy-to-pronounce nonsense words, such as *fotally*, *garbungy*, or *bipitty* that can be used as passwords (preferably with some upper case and special characters thrown in). The program that users call to install or change their password can also give a warning when a poor password is chosen. Among other items it might complain about are

1. Passwords should be a minimum of seven characters.

2. Passwords should contain both upper and lower case letters.

3. Passwords should contain at least one digit or special character.

4. Passwords should not be dictionary words, people's names, etc.

A lenient password program might just carp; a strict one could reject the password and demand a better one. The password program could also make a suggestion, as discussed above.

Some operating systems require users to change their passwords regularly, to limit the damage done if a password leaks out. The trade-off here is that if users have to change their password too often, they are going to run out of good ones and start picking easy ones. If prevented from picking easy ones, they will forget them and start writing them down on sticky notes attached to their monitors, which becomes a major security hole itself.

One-Time Passwords

The most extreme form of changing the passwords all the time is the **one-time password**. When one-time passwords are used, the user gets a book containing a list of passwords. Each login uses the next password in the list. If an intruder ever discovers a password, it will not do him any good, since next time a different password must be used. It is suggested that the user try to avoid losing the password book.

Actually, a book is not needed due to an elegant scheme devised by Leslie Lamport that allows a user to log in securely over an insecure network using one-time passwords (Lamport, 1981). Lamport's method can be used to allow a user running on a home PC to log in to a server over the Internet, even though intruders may see and copy down all the traffic in both directions. Furthermore, no secrets have to be stored in the file system of either the server or the user's PC.

The algorithm is based on a one-way function, that is, a function $y = f(x)$ that has the property that given x it is easy to find y but given y it is computational infeasible to find x. The input and output should be the same length, for example, 128 bits.

The user picks a secret password that he memorizes. He also picks an integer, n, which is how many one-time passwords the algorithm is able to generate. As an example, consider $n = 4$, although in practice a much larger value of n would be used. If the secret password is s, the first password is given by running the one-way function n times:

$$P_1 = f(f(f(f(s))))$$

The second password is given by running the one-way function $n - 1$ times:

$$P_2 = f(f(f(s)))$$

The third password runs f twice and the fourth password runs it once. In general, $P_{i-1} = f(P_i)$. The key fact to note here is that given any password in the sequence, it is easy to compute the *previous* one in the numerical sequence but impossible to compute the *next* one. For example, given P_2 it is easy to find P_1 but impossible to find P_3.

The server is initialized with P_0, which is just $f(P_1)$. This value is stored in the password file entry associated with the user's login name along with the integer 1, indicating that the next password required is P_1. When the user wants to log in for the first time, he sends his login name to the server, which responds by sending the integer in the password file, 1. The user's machine responds with P_1, which can be computed locally from s, which is typed in on the spot. The server then computes $f(P_1)$ and compares this to the value stored in the password file (P_0). If the values match, the login is permitted, the integer is incremented to 2, and P_1 overwrites P_0 in the password file.

On the next login, the server sends the user a 2, and the user's machine computes P_2. The server then computes $f(P_2)$ and compares it to the entry in the password file. If the values match, the login is permitted, the integer is incremented to 3, and P_2 overwrites P_1 in the password file. The property that makes this scheme work is that even though an intruder may capture P_i, he has no way to compute P_{i+1} from it, only P_{i-1} which has already been used and is now worthless. When all n passwords have been used up, the server is reinitialized with a new secret key.

Challenge-Response Authentication

A variation on the password idea is to have each new user provide a long list of questions and answers that are then stored on the server securely (e.g., in encrypted form). The questions should be chosen so that the user does not need to write them down. Possible questions are

1. Who is Marjolein's sister?

2. On what street was your elementary school?

3. What did Mrs. Woroboff teach?

At login, the server asks one of them at random and checks the answer. To make this scheme practical, though, many question-answer pairs would be needed.

Another variation is **challenge-response**. When this is used, the user picks an algorithm when signing up as a user, for example x^2. When the user logs in, the server sends the user an argument, say 7, in which case the user types 49. The algorithm can be different in the morning and afternoon, on different days of the week, and so on.

If the user's terminal has real computing power, such as a personal computer, a personal digital assistant, or a cellular telephone, a more powerful form of challenge-response can be used. In advance, the user selects a secret key, k, which is initially brought to the server system by hand. A copy is also kept (securely) on the user's computer. At login time, the server sends a random number, r to the user's computer, which then computes $f(r,k)$ and sends that back, where f is a publicly-known function. The server then does the computation itself and checks if the result sent back agrees with the computation. The advantage of this scheme over a password is that even if a wiretapper sees and records all the traffic in both directions, he will learn nothing that helps him next time. Of course, the function, f, has to be complicated enough that k cannot be deduced, even given a large set of observations.

9.3.2 Authentication Using a Physical Object

The second method for authenticating users is to check for some physical object they have rather than something they know. Metal door keys have been used for centuries for this purpose. Nowadays, the physical object used is often a plastic card that is inserted into a reader associated with the terminal or computer. Normally, the user must not only insert the card, but also type in a password, to prevent someone from using a lost or stolen card. Viewed this way, using a bank's ATM (Automated Teller Machine) starts out with the user logging in to the bank's computer via a remote terminal (the ATM machine) using a plastic card and a password (currently a 4-digit PIN code in most countries, but this is just to avoid the expense of putting a full keyboard on the ATM machine).

Information-bearing plastic cards come in two varieties: magnetic stripe cards and chip cards. Magnetic stripe cards hold about 140 bytes of information written on a piece of magnetic tape glued to the back of the card. This information can be read out by the terminal and sent to the central computer. Often the information contains the user's password (e.g., PIN code) so the terminal can do an identity check even if the link to the main computer is down. Typically the password is encrypted by a key known only to the bank. These cards cost about $0.10 to $0.50 each, depending on whether there is a hologram sticker on the front and the production volume. As a way to identify users in general, magnetic stripe cards are risky because the equipment to read and write them is cheap and widespread.

Chip cards contain an integrated circuit (chip) on them. These cards can be further subdivided into two categories: stored value cards and smart cards. **Stored value cards** contain a small amount of memory (usually less than 1 KB) using EEPROM technology to allow the value to be remembered when the card is removed from the reader and thus the power turned off. There is no CPU on the card, so the value stored must be changed by an external CPU (in the reader). These cards are mass produced by the millions for about $1 and are used, for example, as prepaid telephone cards. When a call is made, the telephone just decrements the value in the card, but no money actually changes hands. For this reason, these cards are generally issued by one company for use on only its machines (e.g., telephones or vending machines). They could be used for login authentication by storing a 1-KB password in them that the reader would send to the central computer, but this is rarely done.

However, nowadays, much security work is being focused on the **smart cards** which currently have something like a 4-MHz 8-bit CPU, 16 KB of ROM, 4 KB of EEPROM, 512 bytes of scratch RAM, and a 9600-bps communication channel to the reader. The cards are getting smarter in time, but are constrained in a variety of ways, including the depth of the chip (because it is embedded in the card), the width of the chip (so it does not break when the user flexes the card) and the cost (typically $5 to $50, depending on the CPU power, memory size, and presence or absence of a cryptographic coprocessor).

Smart cards can be used to hold money, as do stored value cards, but with much better security and universality. The cards can be loaded with money at an ATM machine or at home over the telephone using a special reader supplied by the bank. When inserted into a merchant's reader, the user can authorize the card to deduct a certain amount of money from the card (by typing YES), causing the card to send a little encrypted message to the merchant. The merchant can later turn the message over to a bank to be credited for the amount paid.

The big advantage of smart cards over, say, credit or debit cards, is that they do not need an online connection to a bank. If you do not believe this is an advantage, try the following experiment. Try to buy a single candy bar at a store and insist on paying with a credit card. If the merchant objects, say you have no cash with you and besides, you need the frequent flyer miles. You will discover that the merchant is not enthusiastic about the idea (because the associated costs dwarf the profit on the item). This makes smart cards useful for small store purchases, pay phones, parking meters, vending machines, and many other devices that normally require coins. They are in widespread use in Europe and spreading elsewhere.

Smart cards have many other potential uses (e.g., encoding the bearer's allergies and other medical conditions in a secure way for use in emergencies), but this is not the place to tell that story. Our interest here is how they can be used for secure login authentication. The basic concept is simple: a smart card is a small, tamperproof computer that can engage in a discussion (called a **protocol**) with a central computer to authenticate the user. For example, a user wishing to buy things at an e-commerce Web site could insert a smart card into a home reader attached to his PC. The e-commerce site would not only use the smart card to authenticate the user in a more secure way than a password, but could also deduct the purchase price from the smart card directly, eliminating a great deal of the overhead (and risk) associated with using a credit card for online purchases.

Various authentication schemes can be used with a smart card. A simple challenge-response works like this. The server sends a 512-bit random number to the smart card, which then adds the user's 512-bit password stored in the card's EEPROM to it. The sum is then squared and the middle 512 bits are sent back to the server, which knows the user's password and can compute whether the result is correct or not. The sequence is shown in Fig. 9-7. If a wiretapper sees both messages, he will not be able to make much sense out of them, and recording them for future use is pointless because on the next login, a different 512-bit random number will be sent. Of course, a much fancier algorithm than squaring can be used, and always is.

One disadvantage of any fixed cryptographic protocol is that over the course of time it could be broken, rendering the smart card useless. One way to avoid this fate is to use the ROM on the card not for a cryptographic protocol, but for a Java interpreter. The real cryptographic protocol is then downloaded onto the card as a Java binary program and run interpretively. In this way, as soon as one

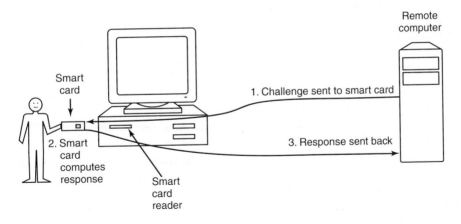

Figure 9-7. Use of a smart card for authentication.

protocol is broken, a new one can be installed worldwide instantly. A disadvantage of this approach is that it makes an already slow card even slower, but as technology improves, this method is very flexible. Another disadvantage of smart cards is that a lost or stolen one may be subject to a power analysis attack. By observing the electric power consumed during repeated encryption operations, an expert with the right equipment may be able to deduce the key. Measuring the time to encrypt with various specially-chosen keys may also provide valuable information about the key.

9.3.3 Authentication Using Biometrics

The third authentication method measures physical characteristics of the user that are hard to forge. These are called **biometrics** (Pankanti et al., 2000). For example, a fingerprint or a voiceprint reader in the terminal could verify the user's identity.

A typical biometrics system has two parts: enrollment and identification. During enrollment, the user's characteristics are measured and the results digitized. Then significant features are extracted and stored in a record associated with the user. The record can be kept in a central database (e.g., for logging in to a remote computer), or stored on a smart card that the user carries around and inserts into a remote reader (e.g., at an ATM machine).

The other part is identification. The user shows up and provides a login name. Then the system makes the measurement again. If the new values match the ones sampled at enrollment time, the login is accepted; otherwise it is rejected. The login name is needed because the measurements are not exact, so it is difficult to index them and then search the index. Also, two people may have the same characteristics, so requiring the measured characteristics to match those of a specific user is stronger than just requiring it to match those of any user.

The characteristic chosen should have enough variability that the system can distinguish among many people without error. For example hair color is not a good indicator because too many people share the same color. Also, the characteristic should not vary much over time. For example, a person's voice may be different due to a cold and a face may look different due to a beard or make-up not present at enrollment time. Since later samples are never going to match the enrollment values exactly, the system designers have to decide how good the match has to be to be accepted. In particular, they have to decide whether it is worse to reject a legitimate user once in a while or let an imposter get in once in a while. An e-commerce site might decide that rejecting a loyal customer might be worse than accepting a small amount of fraud, whereas a nuclear weapons site might decide that refusing access to a genuine employee was better than letting random strangers in twice a year.

Now let us take a brief look at some of the biometrics that are in actual use now. Finger length analysis is surprisingly practical. When this is used, each terminal has a device like the one of Fig. 9-8. The user inserts his hand into it, and the length of all his fingers is measured and checked against the database.

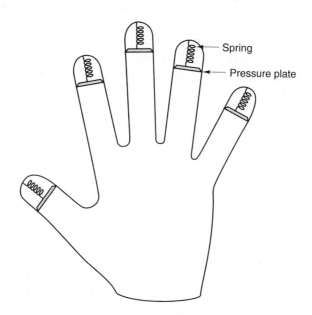

Figure 9-8. A device for measuring finger length.

Finger length measurements are not perfect however. The system can be attacked with hand molds made out of plaster of Paris or some other material, possibly with adjustable fingers to allow some experimentation.

Another biometric that is gaining in popularity is retinal pattern analysis. Every person has a different pattern of retinal blood vessels, even identical twins.

They can be accurately photographed by a camera 1 meter from the subject, without the person even being aware of it. The amount of information in a retinal scan is much more than in a fingerprint, and it can be coded in about 256 bytes,

Any technique that relies on images is subject to spoofing. For example, a person could approach the ATM machine camera wearing dark glasses to which photographs of someone else's retinas were attached. After all, if the ATM's camera can take a good retinal photo at 1 meter, other people can do it too, and at greater distances using telephoto lenses. For this reason, video cameras are generally used instead of still cameras, and the pulsations normally present in the retinal blood vessels are looked for.

A somewhat different technique is signature analysis. The user signs his name with a special pen connected to the terminal, and the computer compares it to a known specimen stored online or on a smart card. Even better is not to compare the signature, but compare the pen motions and pressure made while writing it. A good forger may be able to copy the signature, but will not have a clue as to the exact order in which the strokes were made or at what speed and what pressure.

A scheme that relies on minimal special hardware is voice biometrics (Markowitz, 2000). All that is needed is a microphone (or even a telephone); the rest is software. In contrast to voice recognition systems, which try to determine what the speaker is saying, these systems try to determine who the speaker is. Some systems just require the user to say a secret password, but these can be defeated by an eavesdropper who can tape record passwords and play them back later. More advanced systems say something to the user and ask that it be repeated back, with different texts used for each login. Some companies are starting to use voice identification for applications such as home shopping over the telephone because voice identification is less subject to fraud than using a PIN code for identification.

We could go on and on with more examples, but two more will help make an important point. Cats and other animals mark off their territory by urinating around its perimeter. Apparently cats can identify each other this way. Suppose that someone comes up with a tiny device capable of doing an instant urinalysis, thereby providing a foolproof identification. Each terminal could be equipped with one of these devices, along with a discreet sign reading: "For login, please deposit sample here." This might be an absolutely unbreakable system, but it would probably have a fairly serious user acceptance problem.

The same could be said of a system consisting of a thumbtack and a small spectrograph. The user would be requested to press his thumb against the thumbtack, thus extracting a drop of blood for spectrographic analysis. The point is that any authentication scheme must be psychologically acceptable to the user community. Finger-length measurements probably will not cause any problem, but even something as nonintrusive as storing fingerprints on line may be unacceptable to many people because they associate fingerprints with criminals.

9.3.4 Countermeasures

Computer installations that are really serious about security, something that frequently happens the day after an intruder has broken in and done major damage, often take steps to make unauthorized entry much harder. For example, a company could have a policy that people working in the patent department are only allowed to log in from 8 A.M. to 5 P.M. Monday through Friday and then only from a machine in the patent department connected to the company LAN. Any attempt by a patent department employee to log in at the wrong time or from the wrong place would be treated as an attempted break in.

Dial-up telephone lines can also be made secure as follows. Anyone can dial up and log in, but after a successful login, the system immediately breaks the connection and calls the user back at an agreed upon number. This measure means than an intruder cannot just try breaking in from any phone line; only the user's (home) phone will do. In any event, with or without call back, the system should take at least 5 seconds to check any password typed in on a dial-up line, and should increase this time after several consecutive unsuccessful login attempts, in order to reduce the rate at which intruders can try. After three failed login attempts, the line should be disconnected for 10 minutes and security personnel notified.

All logins should be recorded. When a user logs in, the system should report the time and terminal of the previous login, so he can detect possible break ins.

The next step up is laying baited traps to catch intruders. A simple scheme is to have one special login name with an easy password (e.g., login name: guest, password: guest). Whenever anyone logs in using this name, the system security specialists are immediately notified. All commands the intruder types are immediately displayed on the security manager's screen so he can see exactly what the intruder is up to.

Other traps can be easy-to-find bugs in the operating system and similar things, designed for the purpose of catching intruders in the act. Stoll (1989) has written an entertaining account of the traps he set to track down a spy who broke into a university computer in search of military secrets.

9.4 ATTACKS FROM INSIDE THE SYSTEM

Once a cracker has logged into a computer, he can start doing damage. If the computer has good security, it may only be possible to harm the user whose account has been broken, but often this initial entry can be leveraged to break into more accounts later. In the following sections, we will look at some attacks that can be set up by someone already logged in, either a cracker who has gotten in illictly or possibly a legitimate user with a grudge against someone.

9.4.1 Trojan Horses

One hoary insider attack is the **Trojan horse**, in which a seemingly innocent program contains code to perform an unexpected and undesirable function. This function might be modifying, deleting or encrypting the user's files, copying them to a place where the cracker can retrieve them later, or even sending them to the cracker or a temporary safe hiding place via email or FTP. To have the Trojan horse run, the person planting it first has to get the program carrying it executed. One way is to place the program on the Internet as a free, exciting new game, MP3 viewer, "special" porno viewer, or something else likely to attract attention, and encourage people to download it. When it runs, the Trojan horse procedure is called and can do anything the user can do (e.g., delete files, open network connections, etc.). Note that this ploy does not require the author of the Trojan horse to break into the victim's computer.

There are other ways to trick the victim into executing the Trojan horse program as well. For example, many UNIX users have an environment variable, *$PATH*, which controls which directories are searched for a command. It can be viewed by typing the following command to the shell:

    echo $PATH

A potential setting for the user *ast* on a particular system might consist of the following directories:

    :/usr/ast/bin:/usr/local/bin:/usr/bin:/bin:/usr/bin/X11:/usr/ucb:/usr/man\
    :/usr/java/bin:/usr/java/lib:/usr/local/man:/usr/openwin/man

Other users are likely to have a different search path. When the user types

    prog

to the shell, the shell first takes a look to see if there is a program named */usr/ast/bin/prog*. If there is, it is executed. If it is not there, the shell tries */usr/local/bin/prog*, */usr/bin/prog*, */bin/prog*, and so on, trying all 10 directories in turn before giving up. Suppose that just one of these directories was left unprotected so a cracker could put a program there. If this is the first occurrence of the program in the list, it will be executed and the Trojan horse will run.

Most common programs are in */bin* or */usr/bin*, so putting a Trojan horse in */usr/bin/X11/ls* does not work for a common program because the real one will be found first. However, suppose the cracker inserts *la* into */usr/bin/X11*. If a user mistypes *la* instead of *ls* (the directory listing program), now the Trojan horse will run, do its dirty work, and then issue the correct message that *la* does not exist. By inserting Trojan horses into complicated directories that hardly anyone ever looks at and giving them names that could represent common typing errors, there is a fair chance that someone will invoke one of them sooner or later. And that someone might be the superuser (even superusers make typing errors), in which case the Trojan horse now has the opportunity to replace */bin/ls* with a version containing a Trojan horse, so it will be invoked all the time now.

A malicious but legal user, Mal, could also lay a trap for the superuser as follows. He puts a version of *ls* containing a Trojan horse in his own directory and then does something suspicious that is sure to attract the superuser's attention, such as starting up 100 compute-bound processes at once. Chances are the superuser will check that out by typing

```
cd /usr/mal
ls –l
```

to see what Mal has in his home directory. Since some shells try the local directory before working through *$PATH*, the superuser may have just invoked Mal's Trojan horse with superuser power. The Trojan horse could make */usr/mal/bin/sh* SETUID root. All it takes is two system calls: chown to change the owner of */usr/mal/bin/sh* to root and chmod, to set its SETUID bit. Now Mal can become superuser at will by just running that shell.

If Mal finds himself frequently short of cash, he might use one of the following Trojan horse scams to help his liquidity position. In the first one, the Trojan horse checks to see if the victim has an online banking program, such as *Quicken*, installed. If so, the Trojan horse directs the program to transfer some money from the victim's account to a dummy account (preferably in a far-away country) for collection in cash later.

In the second scam, the Trojan horse first turns off the modem's sound, then dials a 900 (pay) number, again, preferably in a far-away country, such as Moldova (part of the former Soviet Union). If the user was online when the Trojan horse was started, then the 900 phone number in Moldova needs to be a (very expensive) Internet provider, so the user will not notice and perhaps stay online for hours. Neither of these techniques is hypothetical; both have happened and are reported in (Denning, 1999). In the latter one, 800,000 minutes of connect time to Moldova were run up before the U.S. Federal Trade Commission managed to get the plug pulled and filed suit against three people on Long Island. They eventually agreed to return $2.74 million to 38,000 victims.

9.4.2 Login Spoofing

Somewhat related to Trojan horses is **login spoofing**. It works as follows. Normally, when no one is logged in on a UNIX terminal or workstation on a LAN, a screen such as Fig. 9-9(a) is displayed. When a user sits down and types a login name, the system asks for a password. If it is correct, the user is logged in and a shell is started.

Now consider this scenario. Mal writes a program to display the screen of Fig. 9-9(b). It looks amazingly like the screen of Fig. 9-9(a), except that this is not the system login program running, but a phony one written by Mal. Mal now

Figure 9-9. (a) Correct login screen. (b) Phony login screen.

walks away to watch the fun from a safe distance. When a user sits down and types a login name, the program responds by asking for a password and disabling echoing. After the login name and password have been collected, they are written away to a file and the phony login program sends a signal to kill its shell. This action logs Mal out and triggers the real login program to start and display the prompt of Fig. 9-9(a). The user assumes that she made a typing error and just logs in again. This time it works. But in the meantime, Mal has acquired another (login name, password) pair. By logging in at many terminals and starting the login spoofer on all of them, he can collect many passwords.

The only real way to guard against this is to have the login sequence start with a key combination that user programs cannot catch. Windows 2000 uses CTRL-ALT-DEL for this purpose. If a user sits down at a terminal and starts out by typing CTRL-ALT-DEL, the current user is logged out and the system login program is started. There is no way to bypass this mechanism.

9.4.3 Logic Bombs

Another insider attack in these times of high employee mobility is the **logic bomb**. This device is a piece of code written by one of a company's (currently employed) programmers and secretly inserted into the production operating system. As long as the programmer feeds it its daily password, it does nothing. However, if the programmer is suddenly fired and physically removed from the premises without warning, the next day (or next week) the logic bomb does not get fed its daily password, so it goes off. Many variants on this theme are also possible. In one famous case, the logic bomb checked the payroll. If the personnel number of the programmer did not appear in it for two consecutive payroll periods, it went off (Spafford et al., 1989).

Going off might involve clearing the disk, erasing files at random, carefully making hard-to-detect changes to key programs, or encrypting essential files. In the latter case, the company has a tough choice about whether to call the police (which may or may not result in a conviction many months later but certainly does not restore the missing files) or to give in to this blackmail and to rehire the ex-programmer as a "consultant" for an astronomical sum to fix the problem (and hope that he does not plant new logic bombs while doing so).

9.4.4 Trap Doors

Another security hole caused by an insider is the **trap door**. This problem is created by code inserted into the system by a system programmer to bypass some normal check. For example, a programmer could add code to the login program to allow anyone to log in using the login name "zzzzz" no matter what was in the password file. The normal code in the login program might look something like Fig. 9-10(a). The trap door would be the change to Fig. 9-10(b). What the call to *strcmp* does is check if the login name is "zzzzz". If so, the login succeeds, no matter what password is typed. If this trap door code were inserted by a programmer working for a computer manufacturer and then shipped with its computers, the programmer could log into any computer made by his company, no matter who owned it or what was in the password file. The trap door simply bypasses the whole authentication process.

```
while (TRUE) {                          while (TRUE) {
    printf("login: ");                      printf("login: ");
    get_string(name);                       get_string(name);
    disable_echoing( );                     disable_echoing( );
    printf("password: ");                   printf("password: ");
    get_string(password);                   get_string(password);
    enable_echoing( );                      enable_echoing( );
    v = check_validity(name, password);     v = check_validity(name, password);
    if (v) break;                           if (v || strcmp(name, "zzzzz") == 0) break;
}                                       }
execute_shell(name);                    execute_shell(name);

        (a)                                     (b)
```

Figure 9-10. (a) Normal code. (b) Code with a trap door inserted.

One way for companies to prevent trap doors is to have **code reviews** as standard practice. With this technique, once a programmer has finished writing and testing a module, the module is checked into a code database. Periodically, all the programmers in a team get together and each one gets up in front of the group to explain what his code does, line by line. Not only does this greatly increase the chance that someone will catch a trap door, but it raises the stakes for the programmer, since being caught red-handed is probably not a plus for his career. If the programmers protest too much when this is proposed, having two coworkers check each other's code is also a possibility.

9.4.5 Buffer Overflow

One rich source of attacks has been due to the fact that virtually all operating systems and most systems programs are written in the C programming language (because programmers like it and it can be compiled extremely efficiently).

Unfortunately, no C compiler does array bounds checking. Consequently, the following code sequence, while not legal, is also not checked:

```
int i;
char c[1024];
i = 12000;
c[i] = 0;
```

The result is that some byte of memory 10,976 bytes outside the array c is overwritten, possibly with disastrous consequences. No check is performed at run time to prevent this error.

This property of C leads to attacks of the following kind. In Fig. 9-11(a), we see the main program running, with its local variables on the stack. At some point it calls a procedure A, as shown in Fig. 9-11(b). The standard calling sequence starts out by pushing the return address, (which points to the instruction following the call) onto the stack. It then transfers control to A, which decrements the stack pointer to allocate storage for its local variables.

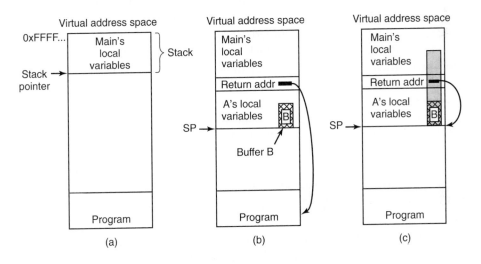

Figure 9-11. (a) Situation when the main program is running. (b) After the procedure A has been called. (c) Buffer overflow shown in gray.

Suppose that the job of A requires acquiring the full file path (possibly by concatenating the current directory path with a file name) and then opening it or doing something else with it. A has a fixed-size buffer (i.e., array) B to hold a file name, as shown in Fig. 9-11(b). Using a fixed-size buffer to hold the file name is much easier to program than first determining the actual size and then dynamically allocating enough storage. If the buffer is 1024 bytes, that should handle all file names, right? Especially if the operating system limits file names (or better yet, full paths) to a maximum of no more than 255 characters.

Unfortunately, this reasoning contains a fatal flaw. Suppose that the user of the program provides a file name that is 2000 characters long. When the file name is used, it will fail to open, but the attacker does not care. When the procedure copies the file name into the buffer, the name overflows the buffer and overwrites memory as shown in the gray area of Fig. 9-11(c). Worse yet, if the file name is long enough, it also overwrites the return address, so when A returns, the return address is taken from the middle of the file name. If this address is random junk, the program will jump to a random address and probably crash within a few instructions.

But what if the file name does not contain random junk? What if it contains a valid binary program and the layout has been very, very carefully made so that the word overlaying the return address just happens to be the address of the start of the program, for example, the address of B? What will happen is that when A returns, the program now in B will start executing. In effect, the attacker has inserted code into the program and gotten it executed.

This same trick works with things other than file names. It works with very long environment strings, user input, or anything else where the programmer has created a fixed-size buffer to handle a user-supplied string that was expected to be short. By providing a long handcrafted string containing a program, it may be possible to get the program onto the stack and then get it executed. The C library function *gets*, which reads a string (of unknown size) into a fixed-size buffer, but without checking for overflow, is notorious for being subject to this kind of attack. Some compilers even detect the use of *gets* and warn about it.

Now comes the really bad part. Suppose that the program being attacked is SETUID root in UNIX (or has administrator power in Windows 2000, which is effectively the same thing). The inserted code can now make a couple of system calls to convert the attacker's shell file on the disk into SETUID root, so that when it is executed it has superuser power. Alternatively, it can now map in a specially prepared shared library that can do all kinds of damage. Or it can simply issue an exec system call to overlay the current program with the shell, creating a shell with superuser powers. A substantial fraction of all security problems are due to this flaw, which is difficult to fix because there are so many existing C programs around that do not check for buffer overflow.

Detecting that a program has buffer overflow problems is easy: just feed it 10,000-character file names, 100-digit salaries, or something equally unexpected to see if it dumps core. The next step is to analyze the core dump to see where the long stream is stored. From there, figuring out which character overwrites the return address is not so difficult. If the source code is available, as it is for most UNIX programs, the attack is even easier because the layout of the stack is known in advance. The attack can be defended against by fixing the code to explicitly check the length of all user-supplied strings before stuffing them into fixed-length buffers. Unfortunately, the fact that some program is vulnerable to this kind of attack generally shows up after a successful attack.

9.4.6 Generic Security Attacks

The usual way to test a system's security is to hire a group of experts, known as **tiger teams** or **penetration teams**, to see if they can break in. Hebbard et al. (1980) tried the same thing with graduate students. In the course of the years, these penetration teams have discovered a number of areas in which systems are likely to be weak. Below we have listed some of the more common attacks that are often successful. While these were originally designed to attack timesharing systems, they can often also be used to attack LAN servers and other shared machines. When designing a system, be sure it can withstand attacks like these.

1. Request memory pages, disk space, or tapes and just read them. Many systems do not erase them before allocating them, and they may be full of interesting information written by the previous owner.

2. Try illegal system calls, or legal system calls with illegal parameters, or even legal system calls with legal but unreasonable parameters such as file names thousands of characters long. Many systems can easily be confused.

3. Start logging in and then hit DEL, RUBOUT or BREAK halfway through the login sequence. In some systems, the password checking program will be killed and the login considered successful.

4. Try modifying complex operating system structures kept in user space (if any). In some systems (especially on mainframes), to open a file, the program builds a large data structure containing the file name and many other parameters and passes it to the system. As the file is read and written, the system sometimes updates the structure itself. Changing these fields can wreak havoc with the security.

5. Look for manuals that say "Do not do X." Try as many variations of X as possible.

6. Convince a system programmer to add a trap door by skipping certain vital security checks for any user with your login name.

7. All else failing, the penetrator might find the system administrator's secretary and pose as a poor user who has forgotten his password and needs it quickly. An alternative approach is an out-and-out bribe of the secretary. The secretary probably has easy access to all kinds of wonderful information, and is usually poorly paid. Do not underestimate problems caused by personnel.

These and other attacks are discussed by Linde (1975). While this is an old paper, the attacks described in it often still work.

9.4.7 Famous Security Flaws

Just as the transportation industry has the *Titanic*, the *Hindenburg*, and the *Concorde* disasters, operating system designers also have a few things they would rather forget about. In this section we will look at some interesting security problems that have occurred in three different operating systems: UNIX, TENEX, and OS/360.

Famous Security Flaws in UNIX

The UNIX utility *lpr*, which prints a file on the line printer, has an option to remove the file after it has been printed. In early versions of UNIX it was possible for anyone to use *lpr* to print and then have the system remove the password file.

Another way to break into UNIX was to link a file called *core* in the working directory to the password file. The intruder then forced a core dump of a SETUID program, which the system wrote on the *core* file, that is, on top of the password file. In this way, a user could replace the password file with one containing a few strings of his own choosing (e.g., command arguments).

Yet another subtle flaw in UNIX involved the command

    mkdir foo

Mkdir, which was a SETUID program owned by the root, first created the i-node for the directory *foo* with the system call mknod and then changed the owner of *foo* from its effective UID (i.e., root) to its real UID (the user's UID). When the system was slow, it was sometimes possible for the user to quickly remove the directory i-node and make a link to the password file under the name *foo* after the mknod but before the chown. When *mkdir* did the chown, it made the user the owner of the password file. By putting the necessary commands in a shell script, they could be tried over and over until the trick worked.

Famous Security Flaws in TENEX

The TENEX operating system used to be very popular on the DEC-10 computers. It is no longer used, but it will live on forever in the annals of computer security due to the following design error. TENEX supported paging. To allow users to monitor the behavior of their programs, it was possible to instruct the system to call a user function on each page fault.

TENEX also used passwords to protect files. To access a file, a program had to present the proper password to the operating system at the time the file was opened. The operating system checked passwords one character at a time, stopping as soon as it saw that the password was wrong. To break into TENEX an intruder would carefully position a password as shown in Fig. 9-12(a), with the first character at the end of one page, and the rest at the start of the next page.

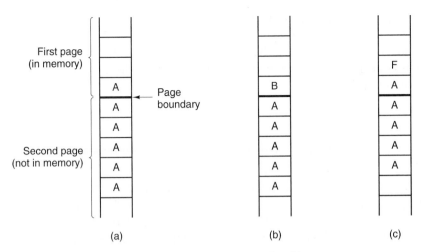

Figure 9-12. The TENEX password problem.

The next step was to make sure that the second page was not in memory, for example, by referencing so many other pages that the second page would surely be evicted to make room for them. Now the program tried to open the victim's file, using the carefully aligned password. If the first character of the real password was anything but A, the system would stop checking at the first character and report back with ILLEGAL PASSWORD. If, however, the real password did begin with A, the system continued reading and got a page fault, about which the intruder was informed.

If the password did not begin with A, the intruder changed the password to that of Fig. 9-12(b) and repeated the whole process to see if it began with B. It took at most 128 tries to go through the whole ASCII character set and thus determine the first character.

Suppose that the first character was an F. The memory layout of Fig. 9-12(c) allowed the intruder to test strings of the form FA, FB, and so on. Using this approach it took at most $128n$ tries to guess an *n-character* ASCII password, instead of 128^n.

Famous Security Flaws in OS/360

Our last flaw concerns OS/360. The description that follows is slightly simplified but preserves the essence of the flaw. In this system it was possible to start up a tape read and then continue computing while the tape drive was transferring data to the user space. The trick here was to carefully start up a tape read and then do a system call that required a user data structure, for example, a file to read and its password.

The operating system first verified that the password was indeed the correct one for the given file. After that it went back and read the file name again for the actual access (it could have saved the name internally, but it did not). Unfortunately, just before the system went to fetch the file name the second time, the file name was overwritten by the tape drive. The system then read the new file, for which no password had been presented. Getting the timing right took some practice, but it was not that hard.

9.4.8 Design Principles for Security

By now it should be clear that designing a secure operating system is not a trivial matter. People have been working on this problem for decades without much success. As far back as 1975, researchers have identified some general principles that should be used as a guide to designing secure systems (Saltzer and Schroeder, 1975). A brief summary of their ideas (based on experience with MULTICS) is given below. These ideas are as valid now as when they were first stated.

First, the system design should be public. Assuming that the intruders do not know how the system works serves only to delude the designers. The intruders will find out sooner or later, and if the protection is compromised by this knowledge, the system is sunk.

Second, the default should be no access. Errors in which legitimate access is refused will be reported much faster than errors in which unauthorized access is allowed. When in doubt, say "No."

Third, check for current authority. The system should not check for permission, determine that access is permitted, and then squirrel away this information for subsequent use. Many systems check for permission when a file is opened, and not afterward. This means that a user who opens a file, and keeps it open for weeks, will continue to have access, even if the owner has long since changed the file protection or maybe even tried to delete the file.

Fourth, give each process the least privilege possible. If an editor has only the authority to access the file to be edited (specified when the editor is invoked), editors with Trojan horses will not be able to do much damage. This principle implies a fine-grained protection scheme. We will discuss such schemes later in this chapter.

Fifth, the protection mechanism should be simple, uniform, and built into the lowest layers of the system. Trying to retrofit security to an existing insecure system is nearly impossible. Security, like correctness, is not an add-on feature.

Sixth, the scheme chosen must be psychologically acceptable. If users feel that protecting their files is too much work, they just will not do it. Nevertheless, they will complain loudly if something goes wrong. Replies of the form "It is your own fault" will generally not be well received.

To this list, we would like to add one other principle that has been gained by decades of hard-won experience:

Keep the design simple

If the system is elegant and simple, was designed by a single architect, and has a few guiding principles that determine the rest, it has a chance of being secure. If the design is a mess, with no coherence and many fundamental concessions to ancient insecure systems in the name of backward compatibility, it is going to be a security nightmare. You can design a system with many features (options, user-friendliness, etc.) but a system with many features is a big system. And a big system is potentially an insecure system. The more code there is, the more security holes and bugs there will be. From a security perspective, the simplest design is the best design.

9.5 ATTACKS FROM OUTSIDE THE SYSTEM

The threats discussed in the previous sections were largely caused from the inside, that is, perpetrated by users already logged in. However, for machines connected to the Internet or another network, there is a growing external threat. A networked computer can be attacked from a distant computer over the network. In nearly all cases, such an attack consists of some code being transmitted over the network to the target machine and executed there doing damage. As more and more computers join the Internet, the potential for damage keeps growing. In the following sections we will look at some of the operating systems aspects of these external threats, primarily focusing on viruses, worms, mobile code, and Java applets.

It is hard to open a newspaper these days without reading about another computer virus or worm attacking the world's computers. They are clearly a major security problem for individuals and companies alike. In the following sections we will examine how they work and what can be done about them.

I was somewhat hesitant to write this section in so much detail, lest it give some people bad ideas, but existing books give far more detail and even include real code (e.g., Ludwig, 1998). Also the Internet is full of information about viruses so the genie is already out of the bottle. In addition, it is hard for people to defend themselves against viruses if they do not know how they work. Finally, there are a lot of misconceptions about viruses floating around that need correction.

Unlike, say, game programmers, successful virus writers tend not to seek publicity after their products have made their debut. Based on the scanty evidence there is, it appears that most are high school or college students or recent graduates who wrote the virus as a technical challenge, not realizing (or caring) that a virus attack can cost the collective victims as much as a hurricane or earthquake. Let us call our antihero Virgil the virus writer. If Virgil is typical, his goals are to produce a virus that spreads quickly, is difficult to detect, and is hard to get rid of once detected.

What is a virus, anyway? To make a long story short, a **virus** is a program that can reproduce itself by attaching its code to another program, analogous to how biological viruses reproduce. In addition, the virus can also do other things in addition to reproducing itself. Worms are like viruses but are self replicating. That difference will not concern us here, so we will use the term "virus" to cover both for the moment. We will look at worms in Sec. 9.5.5.

9.5.1 Virus Damage Scenarios

Since a virus is just a program, it can do anything a program can do. For example, it can type a message, display an image on the screen, play music, or something else harmless. Unfortunately, it can also erase, modify, destroy, or steal files (by emailing them somewhere). Blackmail is also a possibility. Imagine a virus that encrypted all the files on the victim's hard disk, then displayed the following message:

GREETINGS FROM GENERAL ENCRYPTION!

TO PURCHASE A DECRYPTION KEY FOR YOUR HARD DISK, PLEASE SEND $100 IN SMALL, UNMARKED BILLS TO BOX 2154, PANAMA CITY, PANAMA. THANK YOU. WE APPRECIATE YOUR BUSINESS.

Another thing a virus can do is render the computer unusable as long as the virus is running. This is called a **denial of service attack**. The usual approach is consume resources wildly, such as the CPU, or filling up the disk with junk. Here is a one-line program that used to wipe out any UNIX system:

```
main( ) {while (1) fork( );}
```

This program creates processes until the process table is full, preventing any other processes from starting. Now imagine a virus that infected every program in the system with this code. To guard against this problem, many modern UNIX systems limit the number of children a process may have at once.

Even worse, a virus can permanently damage the computer's hardware. Many modern computers hold the BIOS in flash ROM, which can be rewritten under program control (to allow the manufacturer to distribute bug fixes electronically). A virus can write random junk in the flash ROM so that the computer will no longer boot. If the flash ROM chip is in a socket, fixing the problem requires opening up the computer and replacing the chip. If the flash ROM chip is soldered to the parentboard, probably the whole board has to be thrown out and a new one purchased. Definitely not a fun experience.

A virus can also be released with a specific target. A company could release a virus that checked if it was running at a competitor's factory and with no system administrator currently logged in. If the coast was clear, it would interfere with the production process, reducing product quality, thus causing trouble for the competitor. In all other cases it would do nothing, making it hard to detect.

Another example of a targeted virus is one that could be written by an ambitious corporate vice president and released onto the local LAN. The virus would check if it was running on the president's machine, and if so, go find a spreadsheet and swap two random cells. Sooner or later the president would make a bad decision based on the spreadsheet output and perhaps get fired as a result, opening up a position for you-know-who.

9.5.2 How Viruses Work

Enough for potential damage scenarios. Now let us see how viruses work. Virgil writes his virus, probably in assembly language, and then carefully inserts it into a program on his own machine using a tool called a **dropper**. That infected program is then distributed, perhaps by posting it to a bulletin board or a free software collection on the Internet. The program could be an exciting new game, a pirated version of some commercial software, or anything else likely to be considered desirable. People then begin to download the infected program.

Once installed on the victim's machine, the virus lies dormant until the infected program is executed. Once started, it usually begins by infecting other programs on the machine and then executing its **payload**. In many cases, the payload may do nothing until a certain date has passed to make sure that the virus is widespread before people begin noticing it. The date chosen might even send a political message (e.g., if it triggers on the 100th or 500th anniversary of some grave insult to the author's ethnic group).

In the discussion below, we will examine seven kinds of viruses based on what is infected. These are companion, executable program, memory, boot sector, device driver, macro, and source code viruses. No doubt new types will appear in the future.

Companion Viruses

A **companion virus** does not actually infect a program, but gets to run when the program is supposed to run. The concept is easiest to explain with an example. In MS-DOS, when a user types

    prog

MS-DOS first looks for a program named *prog.com*. If it cannot find one, it looks for a program named *prog.exe*. In Windows, when the user clicks on Start and then Run, the same thing happens. Nowadays, most programs are *.exe* files; *.com* files are very rare.

Suppose that Virgil knows that many people run *prog.exe* from an MS-DOS prompt or from Run on Windows. He can then simply release a virus called *prog.com*, which will get executed when anyone tries to run *prog* (unless he actually types the full name: *prog.exe*). When *prog.com* has finished its work, it then just executes *prog.exe* and the user is none the wiser.

A somewhat related attack uses the Windows desktop, which contains shortcuts (symbolic links) to programs. A virus can change the target of a shortcut to make it point to the virus. When the user double clicks on an icon, the virus is executed. When it is done, the virus just runs the original target program.

Executable Program Viruses

One step up in complexity are viruses that infect executable programs. The simplest of these viruses just overwrites the executable program with itself. These are called **overwriting viruses**. The infection logic of such a virus is given in Fig. 9-13.

```
#include <sys/types.h>                      /* standard POSIX headers */
#include <sys/stat.h>
#include <dirent.h>
#include <fcntl.h>
#include <unistd.h>
struct stat sbuf;                           /* for lstat call to see if file is sym link */

search(char *dir_name)
{                                           /* recursively search for executables */
     DIR *dirp;                             /* pointer to an open directory stream */
     struct dirent *dp;                     /* pointer to a directory entry */

     dirp = opendir(dir_name);              /* open this directory */
     if (dirp == NULL) return;              /* dir could not be opened; forget it */
     while (TRUE) {
          dp = readdir(dirp);               /* read next directory entry */
          if (dp == NULL) {                 /* NULL means we are done */
          chdir ("..");                     /* go back to parent directory */
          break;                            /* exit loop */
     }
     if (dp->d_name[0] == '.') continue;    /* skip the . and .. directories */
     lstat(dp->d_name, &sbuf);              /* is entry a symbolic link? */
     if (S_ISLNK(sbuf.st_mode)) continue;   /* skip symbolic links */
     if (chdir(dp->d_name) == 0) {          /* if chdir succeeds, it must be a dir */
          search(".");                      /* yes, enter and search it */
     } else {                               /* no (file), infect it */
          if (access(dp->d_name,X_OK) == 0) /* if executable, infect it */
               infect(dp->d_name);
     }
     closedir(dirp);                        /* dir processed; close and return */
}
```

Figure 9-13. A recursive procedure that finds executable files on a UNIX system.

The main program of this virus would first copy its binary program into an array by opening *argv*[0] and reading it in for safe keeping. Then it would traverse the entire file system starting at the root directory by changing to the root directory and calling *search* with the root directory as parameter.

The recursive procedure *search* processes a directory by opening it, then reading the entries one at a time using *readdir* until a *NULL* is returned, indicating that there are no more entries. If the entry is a directory, it is processed by changing to it and then calling *search* recursively; if it is an executable file, it is infected by calling *infect* with the name of the file to infect as parameter. Files starting with "." are skipped to avoid problems with the . and .. directories. Also, symbolic links are skipped because the program assumes that it can enter a directory using the chdir system call and then get back to where it was by going to .. , something that holds for hard links but not symbolic links. A fancier program could handle symbolic links, too.

The actual infection procedure, *infect* (not shown), merely has to open the file named in its parameter, copy the virus saved in the array over the file, and then close the file.

This virus could be "improved" in various ways. First, a test could be inserted into *infect* to generate a random number and just return in most cases without doing anything. In, say, one call out of 128, infection would take place, thereby reducing the chances of early detection, before the virus has had a good chance to spread. Biological viruses have the same property: those that kill their victims quickly do not spread nearly as fast as those that produce a slow, lingering death, giving the victims plenty of chance to spread the virus. An alternative design would be to have a higher infection rate (say, 25%) but a cutoff on the number of files infected at once to reduce disk activity and thus be less conspicuous.

Second, *infect* could check to see if the file is already infected. Infecting the same file twice just wastes time. Third, measures could be taken to keep the time of last modification and file size the same as it was to help hide the infection. For programs larger than the virus, the size will remain unchanged, but for programs smaller than the virus, the program will now be bigger. Since most viruses are smaller than most programs, this is not a serious problem.

Although this program is not very long (the full program is under one page of C and the text segment compiles to under 2 KB), an assembly code version of it can be even shorter. Ludwig (1998) gives an assembly code program for MS-DOS that infects all the files in its directory and is only 44 bytes when assembled.

Later in this chapter we will study antivirus programs, that is programs that track down and remove viruses. Nevertheless, it is interesting to note that the logic of Fig. 9-13, which a virus could use to find all the executable files to infect them could also be used by an antivirus program to track down all the infected programs in order to remove the virus. The technologies of infection and disinfection go hand in hand, which is why it is necessary to understand in detail how viruses work in order to be able to fight them effectively.

From Virgil's point of view, the problem with an overwriting virus is that it is too easy to detect. After all, when an infected program executes, it may spread the virus some more, but it does not do what it is supposed to do, and the user will notice this instantly. Consequently, most viruses attach themselves to the program and do their dirty work, but allow the program to function normally afterward. Such viruses are called **parasitic viruses**.

Parasitic viruses can attach themselves to the front, the back, or the middle of the executable program. If a virus attaches itself to the front of a program, it has to first copy the program to RAM, write itself at the front of the file, and then copy the program back from RAM following itself, as shown in Fig. 9-14(b). Unfortunately, the program will not run at its new virtual address, so either the virus has to relocate the program as it is moved, or slide it back to virtual address 0 after finishing its own execution.

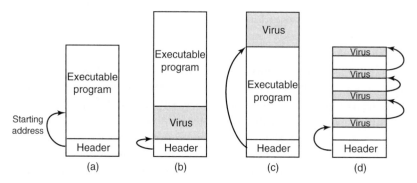

Figure 9-14. (a) An executable program. (b) With a virus at the front. (c) With a virus at the end. (d) With a virus spread over free space within the program.

To avoid either of the complex options required by these front loaders, most viruses are back loaders, attaching themselves to the end of the executable program instead of the front, changing the starting address field in the header to point to the start of the virus, as illustrated in Fig. 9-14(c). The virus will now execute at a different virtual address depending which infected program is running, but all this means is that Virgil has to make sure his virus is position independent, using relative instead of absolute addresses. That is not hard for an experienced programmer to do.

Complex executable program formats, such as *.exe* files on Windows and nearly all modern UNIX binary formats, allow a program to have multiple text and data segments, with the loader assembling them in memory and doing relocation on the fly. In some systems (Windows, for example), all segments (sections) are multiples of 512 bytes. If a segment is not full, the linker fills it out with 0s. A virus that understands this can try to hide itself in the holes. If it fits entirely, as in Fig. 9-14(d), the file size remains the same as that of the uninfected file, clearly a plus, since a hidden virus is a happy virus. Viruses that use this principle are called **cavity viruses**. Of course, if the loader does not load the cavity areas into memory, the virus will need another way of getting started.

Memory Resident Viruses

So far we have assumed that when an infected program is executed, the virus runs, passes control to the real program, and exits. In contrast, a **memory-resident virus** stays in memory all the time, either hiding at the very top of memory or perhaps down in the grass among the interrupt vectors, the last few hundred bytes of which are generally unused. A very smart virus can even modify the operating system's RAM bitmap to make the system think the virus' memory is occupied, to avoid the embarrassment of being overwritten.

A typical memory-resident virus captures one of the trap or interrupt vectors by copying the contents to a scratch variable and putting its own address there, thus directing that trap or interrupt to it. The best choice is the system call trap. In that way, the virus gets to run (in kernel mode) on every system call. When it is done, it just invokes the real system call by jumping to the saved trap address.

Why would a virus want to run on every system call? To infect programs, naturally. The virus can just wait until an exec system call comes along, and then, knowing that the file at hand is an executable binary (and probably a useful one at that), infect it. This process does not require the massive disk activity of Fig. 9-13 so it is far less conspicuous. Catching all system calls also gives the virus great potential for spying on data and performing all manner of mischief.

Boot Sector Viruses

As we discussed in Chap. 5, when most computers are turned on, the BIOS reads the master boot record from the start of the boot disk into RAM and executes it. This program determines which partition is active and reads in the first sector, the boot sector, from that partition and executes it. That program then either loads the operating system or brings in a loader to load the operating system. Unfortunately, many years ago one of Virgil's friends got the idea of creating a virus that could overwrite the master boot record or the boot sector, with devastating results. Such viruses, called **boot sector viruses**, are very common.

Normally, a boot sector virus, [which includes MBR (Master Boot Record) viruses], first copies the true boot sector to a safe place on the disk so it can boot the operating system when it is finished. The Microsoft disk formatting program, *fdisk*, skips the first track, so that is a good hiding place on Windows machines. Another option is to use any free disk sector and then update the bad sector list to mark the hideout as defective. In fact, if the virus is large, it can also disguise the rest of itself as bad sectors. If the root directory is large enough and in a fixed place, as it is in Windows 98, the end of the root directory is also a possibility. A really aggressive virus could even just allocate normal disk space for the true boot sector and itself and update the disk's bitmap or free list accordingly. Doing this requires an intimate knowledge of the operating system's internal data structures, but Virgil had a good professor for his operating systems course and studied hard.

When the computer is booted, the virus copies itself to RAM, either at the top or among the unused interrupt vectors. At this point the machine is in kernel mode, with the MMU off, no operating system, and no antivirus program running. Party time for viruses. When it is ready, it boots the operating system, usually staying memory resident.

One problem, however, is how to get control again later. The usual way is to exploit specific knowledge of how the operating system manages the interrupt vectors. For example, Windows does not overwrite all the interrupt vectors in one blow. Instead, it loads device drivers one at a time, and each one captures the interrupt vector it needs. This process can take a minute.

This design gives the virus the handle it needs. It starts out by capturing all the interrupt vectors as shown in Fig. 9-15(a). As drivers load, some of the vectors are overwritten, but unless the clock driver is loaded first, there will be plenty of clock interrupts later that start the virus. Loss of the printer interrupt is shown in Fig. 9-15(b). As soon as the virus sees that one of its interrupt vectors has been overwritten, it can overwrite that vector again, knowing that it is now safe (actually, some interrupt vectors are overwritten several times during booting, but the pattern is deterministic and Virgil knows it by heart). Recapture of the printer is shown in Fig. 9-15(c). When everything is loaded, the virus restores all the interrupt vectors and keeps only the system call trap vector for itself. After all, getting control on every system call is much more fun than getting control after every floppy disk operation, but during booting, it cannot take the risk of losing control forever. At this point we have a memory-resident virus in control of system calls. In fact, this is how most memory-resident viruses get started in life.

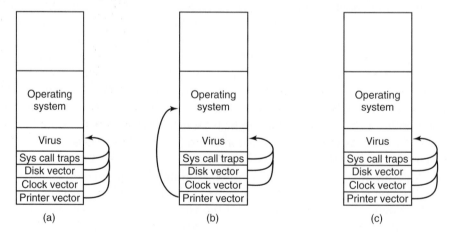

Figure 9-15. (a) After the virus has captured all the interrupt and trap vectors. (b) After the operating system has retaken the printer interrupt vector. (c) After the virus has noticed the loss of the printer interrupt vector and recaptured it.

Device Driver Viruses

Getting into memory like this is a little like spelunking (exploring caves)—you have to go through contortions and keep worrying about something falling down and landing on your head. It would be much simpler if the operating system would just kindly load the virus officially. With a little bit of work, that goal can be achieved. The trick is to infect a device driver, leading to a **device driver virus**. In Windows and some UNIX systems, device drivers are just executable programs that live on the disk and are loaded at boot time. If one of them can be infected using a parasitic virus, the virus will always be officially loaded at boot time. Even nicer, drivers run in kernel mode and after a driver is loaded, it is called, giving the virus a chance to capture the system call trap vector.

Macro Viruses

Many programs, such as *Word* and *Excel*, allow users to write macros to group several commands that can later be executed with a single keystroke. Macros can also be attached to menu items, so that when one of them is selected, the macro is executed. In Microsoft *Office*, macros can contain entire programs in Visual Basic, which is a complete programming language. The macros are interpreted rather than compiled, but that only affects execution speed, not what they can do. Since macros may be document specific, *Office* stores the macros for each document along with the document.

Now comes the problem. Virgil writes a document in *Word* and creates a macro that he attaches to the OPEN FILE function. The macro contains a **macro virus**. He then emails the document to the victim, who naturally opens it (assuming the email program has not already done this for him). Opening the document causes the OPEN FILE macro to execute. Since the macro can contain an arbitrary program, it can do anything, such as infect other *Word* documents, erase files, and more. In all fairness to Microsoft, *Word* does give a warning when opening a file with macros, but most users do not understand what this means and continue opening anyway. Besides, legitimate documents may also contain macros. And there are other programs that do not even give this warning, making it even harder to detect a virus.

With the growth of email, sending documents with viruses embedded in macros is an immense problem. Such viruses are much easier to write than concealing the true boot sector somewhere in the bad block list, hiding the virus among the interrupt vectors, and capturing the system call trap vector. This means that increasingly less skilled people can now write viruses, lowering the general quality of the product and giving virus writers a bad name.

Source Code Viruses

Parasitic and boot sector viruses are highly platform specific; document viruses are somewhat less so (*Word* runs on Windows and the Macintosh, but not on UNIX). The most portable viruses of all are **source code viruses**. Imagine the virus of Fig. 9-13, but with the modification that instead of looking for binary executable files, it looks for C programs, a change of only 1 line (the call to access). The *infect* procedure should be changed to insert the line

```
#include <virus.h>
```

at the top of each C source program. One other insertion is needed, the line

```
run_virus( );
```

to activate the virus. Deciding where to put this line requires some ability to parse C code, since it must be at a place that syntactically allows procedure calls and also not at a place where the code would be dead (e.g., following a return statement). Putting it in the middle of a comment does not work either, and putting it inside a loop might be too much of a good thing. Assuming the call can be placed properly (for example, just before the end of *main* or before the return statement if there is one), when the program is compiled, it now contains the virus, taken from *virus.h* (although *proj.h* might attract less attention should somebody see it).

When the program runs, the virus will be called. The virus can do anything it wants to, for example, look for other C programs to infect. If it finds one, it can include just the two lines given above, but this will only work on the local machine, where *virus.h* is assumed to be installed already. To have this work on a remote machine, the full source code of the virus must be included. This can be done by including the source code of the virus as an initialized character string, preferably as a list of 32-bit hexadecimal integers to prevent anyone from figuring out what it does. This string will probably be fairly long, but with today's multimegaline code, it might easily slip by.

To the uninitiated reader, all of these ways may look fairly complicated. One can legitimately wonder if they could be made to work in practice. They can be. Virgil is an excellent programmer and has a lot of free time on his hands. Check your local newspaper for proof.

9.5.3 How Viruses Spread

There are several scenarios for distribution. Let us start with the classical one. Virgil writes his virus, inserts it into some program he has written (or stolen), and starts distributing the program, for example, by putting it on a shareware Web site. Eventually, somebody downloads the program and runs it. At this point there are several options. To start with, the virus probably infects more files on the hard disk, just in case the victim decides to share some of these with a friend later. It can also try to infect the boot sector of the hard disk. Once the boot sector is infected, it is easy to start a kernel-mode memory-resident virus on subsequent boots.

In addition, the virus can check to see if there are any floppy disks in the drives, and if so, infect their files and boot sectors. Floppy disks are a good target because they get moved from machine to machine much more often than hard disks. If a floppy disk boot sector is infected and that disk is later used to boot a different machine, it can start infecting files and the hard disk boot sector on that machine. In the past, when floppy disks were the main transmission medium for programs, this mechanism was the main way viruses spread.

Nowadays, other options are available to Virgil. The virus can be written to check if the infected machine is on a LAN, something that is very likely on a machine belonging to a company or university. The virus can then start infecting unprotected files on the servers connected to this LAN. This infection will not extend to protected files, but that can be dealt with by making infected programs act strangely. A user who runs such a program will likely ask the system adminis-trator for help. The administrator will then try out the strange program himself to see what is going on. If the administrator does this while logged in as superuser, the virus can now infect the system binaries, device drivers, operating system, and boot sectors. All it takes is one mistake like this and all the machines on the LAN are compromised.

Often machines on a LAN have authorization to log onto remote machines over the Internet or a private corporate, or even authorization to execute com-mands remotely without logging in. This ability provides more opportunity for viruses to spread. Thus one innocent mistake can infect the entire company. To prevent this scenario, all companies should have a general policy telling adminis-trators never to make mistakes.

Another way to spread a virus is to post an infected program to a USENET newsgroup or bulletin board system to which programs are regularly posted. Also possible is to create a Web page that requires a special browser plug-in to view, and then make sure the plug-ins are infected.

A different attack is to infect a document and then email it to many people or broadcast it to a mailing list or USENET newsgroup, usually as an attachment. Even people who would never dream of running a program some stranger sent them might not realize that clicking on the attachment to open it can release a virus on their machine. To make matters worse, the virus can then look for the user's address book and then mail itself to everyone in the address book, usually with a Subject line that looks legitimate or interesting, like

```
Subject: Change of plans
Subject: Re: that last email
Subject: The dog died last night
Subject: I am seriously ill
Subject: I love you
```

When the email arrives, the receiver sees that the sender is a friend or colleague, and thus does not suspect trouble. Once the email has been opened, it is too late. The "I LOVE YOU" virus that spread around the world in June 2000 worked this way and did a billion dollars worth of damage.

Somewhat related to the actual spreading of active viruses is the spreading of virus technology. There are groups of virus writers who actively communicate over the Internet and help each other develop new technology, tools, and viruses. Most of these are probably hobbyists rather than career criminals, but the effects can be just as devastating. One other category of virus writers is the military, which sees viruses as a weapon of war potentially able to disable an enemy's computers.

Another issue related to spreading viruses is avoiding detection. Jails have notoriously bad computing facilities, so Virgil would prefer avoiding them. If he posts the initial virus from his home machine he is running a certain risk. If the attack is successful, the police might track him down by looking for the virus message with the youngest timestamp, since that is probably closest to the source of the attack.

To minimize his exposure, Virgil might go to an Internet cafe in a distant city and log in there. He can either bring the virus on a floppy disk and read it in himself, or if the machines do not all have floppy disk drives, ask the nice young lady at the desk to please read in the file *book.doc* so he can print it. Once it is on his hard disk, he renames the file *virus.exe* and executes it, infecting the entire LAN with a virus that triggers two weeks later, just in case the police decide to ask the airlines for a list of all people who flew in that week. An alternative is to forget the floppy disk and get the virus from a remote FTP site. Or bring a laptop and plug it in to an Ethernet or USB port that the Internet cafe has thoughtfully provided for laptop-toting tourists who want to read their email every day.

9.5.4 Antivirus and Anti-Antivirus Techniques

Viruses try to hide and users try to find them, which leads to a cat-and-mouse game. Let us now look at some of the issues here. To avoid showing up in directory listings, a companion virus, source code virus, or other file that should not be there can turn on the HIDDEN bit in Windows or use a file name beginning with the . character in UNIX. More sophisticated is to modify Windows' *explorer* or UNIX' *ls* to refrain from listing files whose names begin with *Virgil-*. Viruses can also hide in unusual and unsuspected places, such as the bad sector list on the disk or the Windows registry (an in-memory database available for programs to store uninterpreted strings). The flash ROM used to hold the BIOS and the CMOS memory are also possibilities although the former is hard to write and the latter is quite small. And, of course, the main workhorse of the virus world is infecting executable files and documents on the hard disk.

Virus Scanners

Clearly, the average garden-variety user is not going to find many viruses that do their best to hide, so a market has developed for antivirus software. Below we will discuss how this software works. Antivirus software companies have laboratories in which dedicated scientists work long hours tracking down and understanding new viruses. The first step is to have the virus infect a program that does nothing, often called a **goat file**, to get a copy of the virus in its purest form. The next step is to make an exact listing of the virus' code and enter it into the database of known viruses. Companies compete on the size of their databases. Inventing new viruses just to pump up your database is not considered sporting.

Once an antivirus program is installed on a customer's machine, the first thing it does is scan every executable file on the disk looking for any of the viruses in the database of known viruses. Most antivirus companies have a Web site from which customers can download the descriptions of newly-discovered viruses into their databases. If the user has 10,000 files and the database has 10,000 viruses, some clever programming is needed to make it go fast, of course.

Since minor variants of known viruses pop up all the time, a fuzzy search is needed, so a 3-byte change to a virus does not let it escape detection. However, fuzzy searches are not only slower than exact searches, but they may turn up false alarms, that is, warnings about legitimate files that happen to contain some code vaguely similar to a virus reported in Pakistan 7 years ago. What is the user supposed to do with the message:

WARNING! File xyz.exe may contain the lahore-9x virus. Delete?

The more viruses in the database and the broader the criteria for declaring a hit, the more false alarms there will be. If there are too many, the user will give up in disgust. But if the virus scanner insists on a very close match, it may miss some modified viruses. Getting it right is a delicate heuristic balance. Ideally, the lab should try to identify some core code in the virus that is not likely to change and use this as the virus signature to scan for.

Just because the disk was declared virus free last week does not mean that it still is, so the virus scanner has to be run frequently. Because scanning is slow, it is more efficient to check only those files that have been changed since the date of the last scan. The trouble is, a clever virus will reset the date of an infected file to its original date to avoid detection. The antivirus program's response to that is to check the date the enclosing directory was last changed. The virus' response to that is to reset the directory's date as well. This is the start of the cat-and-mouse game alluded to above.

Another way for the antivirus program to detect file infection is to record and store on the disk the lengths of all files. If a file has grown since the last check, it might be infected, as shown in Fig. 9-16(a-b). However, a clever virus can avoid detection by compressing the program and padding out the file to its original length. To make this scheme work, the virus must contain both compression and decompression procedures, as shown in Fig. 9-16(c).

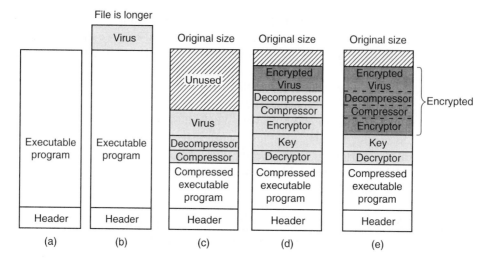

Figure 9-16. (a) A program. (b) An infected program. (c) A compressed infected program. (d) An encrypted virus. (e) A compressed virus with encrypted compression code.

Another way for the virus to try to escape detection is to make sure its representation on the disk does not look at all like its representation in the antivirus software's database. One way to achieve this goal is to encrypt itself with a different key for each file infected. Before making a new copy, the virus generates a random 32-bit encryption key, for example by XORing the current time with the contents of, say, memory words 72,008 and 319,992. It then XORs its code with this key, word by word to produce the encrypted virus stored in the infected file, as illustrated in Fig. 9-16(d). The key is stored in the file. For secrecy purposes, putting the key in the file is not ideal, but the goal here is to foil the virus scanner, not prevent the dedicated scientists at the antivirus lab from reverse engineering the code. Of course, to run, the virus has to first decrypt itself, so it needs a decrypting procedure in the file as well.

This scheme is still not perfect because the compression, decompression, encryption, and decryption procedures are the same in all copies, so the antivirus program can just use them as the virus signature to scan for. Hiding the compression, decompression, and encryption procedures is easy: they are just encrypted along with the rest of the virus, as shown in Fig. 9-16(e). The decryption code cannot be encrypted, however. It has to actually execute on the hardware to decrypt the rest of the virus so it must be present in plaintext form. Antivirus programs know this, so they hunt for the decryption procedure.

However, Virgil enjoys having the last word, so he proceeds as follows. Suppose that the decryption procedure needs to perform the calculation

$$X = (A + B + C - 4)$$

The straightforward assembly code for this calculation for a generic two-address computer is shown in Fig. 9-17(a). The first address is the source; the second is the destination, so MOV A,R1 moves the variable *A* to the register R1. The code in Fig. 9-17(b) does the same thing, only less efficiently due to the NOP (no operation) instructions interspersed with the real code.

MOV A,R1	MOV A,R1	MOV A,R1	MOV A,R1	MOV A,R1
ADD B,R1	NOP	ADD #0,R1	OR R1,R1	TST R1
ADD C,R1	ADD B,R1	ADD B,R1	ADD B,R1	ADD C,R1
SUB #4,R1	NOP	OR R1,R1	MOV R1,R5	MOV R1,R5
MOV R1,X	ADD C,R1	ADD C,R1	ADD C,R1	ADD B,R1
	NOP	SHL #0,R1	SHL R1,0	CMP R2,R5
	SUB #4,R1	SUB #4,R1	SUB #4,R1	SUB #4,R1
	NOP	JMP .+1	ADD R5,R5	JMP .+1
	MOV R1,X	MOV R1,X	MOV R1,X	MOV R1,X
			MOV R5,Y	MOV R5,Y
(a)	(b)	(c)	(d)	(e)

Figure 9-17. Examples of a polymorphic virus.

But we are not done yet. It is also possible to disguise the decryption code. There are many ways to represent NOP. For example, adding 0 to a register, ORing it with itself, shifting it left 0 bits, and jumping to the next instruction all do nothing. Thus the program of Fig. 9-17(c) is functionally the same as the one of Fig. 9-17(a). When copying itself, the virus could use Fig. 9-17(c) instead of Fig. 9-17(a) and still work later when executed. A virus that mutates on each copy is called a **polymorphic virus**.

Now suppose that R5 is not needed during this piece of the code. Then Fig. 9-17(d) is also equivalent to Fig. 9-17(a). Finally, in many cases it is possible to swap instructions without changing what the program does, so we end up with Fig. 9-17(e) as another code fragment that is logically equivalent to Fig. 9-17(a). A piece of code that can mutate a sequence of machine instructions without changing its functionality is called a **mutation engine**, and sophisticated viruses contain them to mutate the decryptor from copy to copy. The mutation engine itself can be hidden by encrypting it along with the body of the virus.

Asking the poor antivirus software to realize that Fig. 9-17(a) through Fig. 9-17(e) are all functionally equivalent is asking a lot, especially if the mutation engine has many tricks up its sleeve. The antivirus software can analyze the code to see what it does, and it can even try to simulate the operation of the code, but remember it may have thousands of viruses and thousands of files to analyze so it does not have much time per test or it will run horribly slowly.

As an aside, the store into the variable Y was thrown in just to make it harder to detect the fact that the code related to R5 is dead code, that is, does not do anything. If other code fragments read and write Y, the code will look perfectly legitimate. A well-written mutation engine that generates good polymorphic code can give antivirus software writers nightmares. The only bright side is that such an engine is hard to write, so Virgil's friends all use his code, which means there are not so many different ones in circulation—yet.

So far we have talked about just trying to recognize viruses in infected executable files. In addition, the antivirus scanner has to check the MBR, boot sectors, bad sector list, flash ROM, CMOS memory, etc., but what if there is a memory-resident virus currently running? That will not be detected. Worse yet, suppose the running virus is monitoring all system calls. It can easily detect that the antivirus program is reading the boot sector (to check for viruses). To thwart the antivirus program, the virus does not make the system call. Instead it just returns the true boot sector from its hiding place in the bad block list. It also makes a mental note to reinfect all the files when the virus scanner is finished.

To prevent being spoofed by a virus, the antivirus program could make hard reads to the disk, bypassing the operating system. However this requires having built-in device drivers for IDE, SCSI, and other common disks, making the antivirus program less portable and subject to failure on computers with unusual disks. Furthermore, since bypassing the operating system to read the boot sector is possible, but bypassing it to read all the executable files is not, there is also some danger that the virus can produce fraudulent data about executable files as well.

Integrity Checkers

A completely different approach to virus detection is **integrity checking**. An antivirus program that works this way first scans the hard disk for viruses. Once it is convinced that the disk is clean, it computes a checksum for each executable file and writes the list of checksums for all the relevant files in a directory to a file, *checksum*, in that directory. The next time it runs, it recomputes all the checksums and sees if they match what is in the file *checksum*. An infected file will show up immediately.

The trouble is Virgil is not going to take this lying down. He can write a virus that removes the checksum file. Worse yet, he can write a virus that computes the checksum of the infected file and replaces the old entry in the checksum file. To protect against this kind of behavior, the antivirus program can try to hide the checksum file, but that is not likely to work since Virgil can study the antivirus program carefully before writing the virus. A better idea is to encrypt it to make tampering easier to detect. Ideally, the encryption should involve use of a smart card with an externally stored key that programs cannot get at.

Behavioral Checkers

A third strategy used by antivirus software is **behavioral checking**. With this approach, the antivirus program lives in memory while the computer is running and catches all system calls itself. The idea is that it can then monitor all activity and try to catch anything that looks suspicious. For example, no normal program should attempt to overwrite the boot sector, so an attempt to do so is almost certainly due to a virus. Likewise, changing the flash ROM is highly suspicious.

But there are also cases that are less clear cut. For example, overwriting an executable file is a peculiar thing to do—unless you are a compiler. If the antivirus software detects such a write and issues a warning, hopefully the user knows whether overwriting an executable makes sense in the context of the current work. Similarly, *Word* overwriting a *.doc* file with a new document full of macros is not necessarily the work of a virus. In Windows, programs can detach from their executable file and go memory resident using a special system call. Again, this might be legitimate, but a warning might still be useful.

Viruses do not have to passively lie around waiting for an antivirus program to kill them, like cattle being led off to slaughter. They can fight back. A particularly interesting battle can occur if a memory-resident virus and a memory-resident antivirus meet up on the same computer. Years ago there was a game called Core Wars in which two programmers faced off by each dropping a program into an empty address space. The programs took turns probing memory, with the object of the game being to locate and wipe out your opponent before he wiped you out. The virus-antivirus confrontation looks a little like that, only the battlefield is the machine of some poor user who does not really want it to happen there. Worse yet, the virus has an advantage because its writer can find out a lot about the antivirus program by just buying a copy of it. Of course, once the virus is out there, the antivirus team can modify their program, forcing Virgil to go buy a new copy.

Virus Avoidance

Every good story needs a moral. The moral of this one is

Better safe than sorry.

Avoiding viruses in the first place is a lot easier than trying to track them down once they have infected a computer. Below are a few guidelines for individual users, but also some things that the industry as a whole can do to reduce the problem considerably.

What can users do to avoid a virus infection? First, choose an operating system that offers a high degree of security, with a strong kernel-user mode boundary and separate login passwords for each user and the system administrator. Under these conditions, a virus that somehow sneaks in cannot infect the system binaries.

Second, install only shrink-wrapped software bought from a reliable manufacturer. Even this is no guarantee since there have been cases where disgruntled employees have slipped viruses onto a commercial software product, but it helps a lot. Downloading software from Web sites and bulletin boards is risky behavior.

Third, buy a good antivirus software package and use it as directed. Be sure to get regular updates from the manufacturer's Web site.

Fourth, do not click on attachments to email and tell people not to send them to you. Email sent as plain ASCII text is always safe but attachments can start viruses when opened.

Fifth, make frequent backups of key files onto an external medium, such as floppy disk, CD-recordable, or tape. Keep several generations of each file on a series of backup media. That way, if you discover a virus, you may have a chance to restore files as they were before they were infected. Restoring yesterday's infected file does not help, but restoring last week's version might.

The industry should also take the virus threat seriously and change some dangerous practices. First, make simple operating systems. The more bells and whistles there are, the more security holes there are. That is a fact of life.

Second, forget active content. From a security point of view, it is a disaster. Viewing a document someone sends you should not require your running their program. JPEG files, for example, do not contain programs, and thus cannot contain viruses. All documents should work like that.

Third, there should be a way to selectively write protect specified disk cylinders to prevent viruses from infecting the programs on them. This protection could be implemented by having a bitmap inside the controller listing the write protected cylinders. The map should only be alterable when the user has flipped a mechanical toggle switch on the computer's front panel.

Fourth, flash ROM is a nice idea, but it should only be modifiable when an external toggle switch has been flipped, something that will only happen when the user is consciously installing a BIOS update. Of course, none of this will be taken seriously until a really big virus hits. For example, one that hit the financial world and reset all bank accounts to 0. Of course, by then it would be too late.

Recovery from a Virus Attack

When a virus is detected, the computer should be halted immediately since a memory-resident virus may still be running. The computer should be rebooted from a CD-ROM or floppy disk that has always been write protected, and which contains the full operating system to bypass the boot sector, hard disk copy of the operating system, and disk drivers, all of which may now be infected. Then an antivirus program should be run from its original CD-ROM, since the hard disk version may also be infected.

The antivirus program may detect some viruses and may even be able to eliminate them, but there is no guarantee that it will get them all. Probably the safest course of action at this point is to save all files that cannot contain viruses (like ASCII and JPEG files). Those files that might contain viruses (like *Word* files) should be converted to another format that cannot contain viruses, such as flat ASCII text (or at least the macros should be removed). All the saved files should be saved on an external medium. Then the hard disk should be reformatted using a format program taken from a write-protected floppy disk or a CD-ROM to insure that it itself is not infected. It is especially important that the MBR and boot sectors are also fully erased. Then the operating system should be reinstalled from the original CD-ROM. When dealing with virus infections, paranoia is your best friend.

9.5.5 The Internet Worm

The first large-scale Internet computer security violation began in the evening of Nov. 2, 1988 when a Cornell graduate student, Robert Tappan Morris, released a worm program into the Internet. This action brought down thousands of computers at universities, corporations, and government laboratories all over the world before it was tracked down and removed. It also started a controversy that has not yet died down. We will discuss the highlights of this event below. For more technical information see (Spafford, 1989). For the story viewed as a police thriller, see (Hafner and Markoff, 1991).

The story began sometime in 1988 when Morris discovered two bugs in Berkeley UNIX that made it possible to gain unauthorized access to machines all over the Internet. Working alone, he wrote a self replicating program, called a **worm**, that would exploit these errors and replicate itself in seconds on every machine it could gain access to. He worked on the program for months, carefully tuning it and having it try to hide its tracks.

It is not known whether the release on Nov. 2, 1988 was intended as a test, or was the real thing. In any event, it did bring most of the Sun and VAX systems on the Internet to their knees within a few hours of its release. Morris' motivation is unknown, but it is possible that he intended the whole idea as a high-tech practical joke, but which due to a programming error got completely out of hand.

Technically, the worm consisted of two programs, the bootstrap and the worm proper. The bootstrap was 99 lines of C called *ll.c*. It was compiled and executed on the system under attack. Once running, it connected to the machine from which it came, uploaded the main worm, and executed it. After going to some trouble to hide its existence, the worm then looked through its new host's routing tables to see what machines that host was connected to and attempted to spread the bootstrap to those machines.

Three methods were tried to infect new machines. Method 1 was to try to run a remote shell using the *rsh* command. Some machines trust other machines, and just run *rsh* without any further authentication. If this worked, the remote shell uploaded the worm program and continued infecting new machines from there.

Method 2 made use of a program present on all BSD systems called *finger* that allows a user anywhere on the Internet to type

finger name@site

to display information about a person at a particular installation. This information usually includes the person's real name, login, home and work addresses and telephone numbers, secretary's name and telephone number, FAX number, and similar information. It is the electronic equivalent of the phone book.

Finger works as follows. At every BSD site a background process called the **finger daemon** runs all the time fielding and answering queries from all over the Internet. What the worm did was call *finger* with a specially handcrafted 536-byte string as parameter. This long string overflowed the daemon's buffer and overwrote its stack, the way shown in Fig. 9-11(c). The bug exploited here was the daemon's failure to check for overflow. When the daemon returned from the procedure it was in at the time it got the request, it returned not to *main*, but to a procedure inside the 536-byte string on the stack. This procedure tried to execute *sh*. If it worked, the worm now had a shell running on the machine under attack.

Method 3 depended on a bug in the mail system, *sendmail*, which allowed the worm to mail a copy of the bootstrap and get it executed.

Once established, the worm tried to break user passwords. Morris did not have to do much research on how to accomplish this. All he had to do was ask his father, a security expert at the National Security Agency, the U.S. government's code breaking agency, for a reprint of a classic paper on the subject that Morris, Sr. and Ken Thompson wrote a decade earlier at Bell Labs (Morris and Thompson, 1979). Each broken password allowed the worm to log in on any machines the password's owner had accounts on.

Every time the worm gained access to a new machine, it checked to see if any other copies of the worm were already active there. If so, the new copy exited, except one time in seven it kept going, possibly in an attempt to keep the worm propagating even if the system administrator there started up his own version of the worm to fool the real worm. The use of 1 in 7 created far too many worms, and was the reason all the infected machines ground to a halt: they were infested with worms. If Morris had left this out and just exited whenever another worm was sighted, the worm would probably have gone undetected.

Morris was caught when one of his friends spoke with the *New York Times* computer reporter, John Markoff, and tried to convince Markoff that the incident was an accident, the worm was harmless, and the author was sorry. The friend inadvertently let slip that the perpetrator's login was *rtm*. Converting *rtm* into the owner's name was easy—all that Markoff had to do was to run *finger*. The next day the story was the lead on page one, even upstaging the presidential election three days later.

Morris was tried and convicted in federal court. He was sentenced to a fine of $10,000, 3 years probation, and 400 hours of community service. His legal costs probably exceeded $150,000. This sentence generated a great deal of controversy. Many in the computer community felt that he was a bright graduate student whose harmless prank had gotten out of control. Nothing in the worm suggested that Morris was trying to steal or damage anything. Others felt he was a serious criminal and should have gone to jail.

One permanent effect of this incident was the establishment of **CERT** (**Computer Emergency Response Team**), which provides a central place to report break-in attempts, and a group of experts to analyze security problems and design fixes. While this action was certainly a step forward, it also has its downside. CERT collects information about system flaws that can be attacked and how to fix them. Of necessity, it circulates this information widely to thousands of system administrators on the Internet. Unfortunately, the bad guys (possibly posing as system administrators) may also be able to get bug reports and exploit the loopholes in the hours (or even days) before they are closed.

9.5.6 Mobile Code

Viruses and worms are programs that get onto a computer without the owner's knowledge and against the owner's will. Sometimes, however, people more-or-less intentionally import and run foreign code on their machines. It usually happens like this. In the distant past (which, in the Internet world, means last year), most Web pages were just static HTML files with a few associated images. Nowadays, increasingly many Web pages contain small programs called **applets**. When a Web page containing applets is downloaded, the applets are fetched and executed. For example, an applet might contain a form to be filled out, plus interactive help in filling it out. When the form is filled out, it could be sent somewhere over the Internet for processing. Tax forms, customized product order forms, and many other kinds of forms could benefit from this approach.

Another example in which programs are shipped from one machine to another for execution on the destination machine are **agents**. These are programs that are launched by a user to perform some task and then report back. For example, an agent could be asked to check out some travel Web sites to find the cheapest flight from Amsterdam to San Francisco. Upon arriving at each site, the agent would run there, get the information it needs, then move on to the next Web site. When it was all done, it could come back home and report what it had learned.

A third example of mobile code is a PostScript file that is to be printed on a PostScript printer. A PostScript file is actually a program in the PostScript programming language that is executed inside the printer. It normally tells the printer to draw certain curves and then fill them in, but it can do anything else it wants to as well. Applets, agents, and PostScript files are just three examples of **mobile code**, but there are many others.

Given the long discussion about viruses and worms earlier, it should be clear that allowing foreign code to run on your machine is more than a wee bit risky.

Nevertheless, some people do want to run these foreign programs, thus the question arises: "Can mobile code be run safely"? The short answer is: "Yes, but not easily." The fundamental problem is that when a process imports an applet or other mobile code into its address space and runs it, that code is running as part of a valid user process and has all the power that user has, including the ability to read, write, erase or encrypt the user's disk files, email data to far-away countries, and much more.

Long ago, operating systems developed the process concept to build walls between users. The idea is that each process has its own protected address space and own UID, allowing it to touch files and other resources belonging to it, but not to other users. For providing protection against one part of the process (the applet) and the rest, the process concept does not help. Threads allow multiple threads of control within a process, but do nothing to protect one thread against another one.

In theory, running each applet as a separate process helps a little, but is often infeasible. For example, a Web page may contain two or more applets that interact with each other and with the data on the Web page. The Web browser may also need to interact with the applets, starting and stopping them, feeding them data, and so on. If each applet is put in its own process, the whole thing will not work. Furthermore, putting an applet in its own address space does not make it any harder for the applet to steal or damage data. If anything, it is easier since nobody is watching in there.

Various new methods of dealing with applets (and mobile code in general) have been proposed and implemented. Below we will look at three of these methods: sandboxing, interpretation, and code signing. Each one has its own strengths and weaknesses.

Sandboxing

The first method, called **sandboxing**, attempts to confine each applet to a limited range of virtual addresses enforced at run time (Wahbe et al., 1993). It works by dividing the virtual address space up into equal-size regions, which we will call sandboxes. Each sandbox must have the property that all of its addresses share some string of high-order bits. For a 32-bit address space, we could divide it up into 256 sandboxes on 16-MB boundaries so all addresses within a sandbox had a common upper 8 bits. Equally well, we could have 512 sandboxes on 8-MB boundaries, with each sandbox having a 9-bit address prefix. The sandbox size should be chosen to be large enough to hold the largest applet without wasting too much virtual address space. Physical memory is not an issue if demand paging is present, as it usually is. Each applet is given two sandboxes, one for the code and one for the data, as illustrated in for the case of 16 sandboxes of 16 MB each. Fig. 9-18(a),

The basic idea behind a sandbox is to guarantee that an applet cannot jump to code outside its code sandbox or reference data outside its data sandbox. The rea-

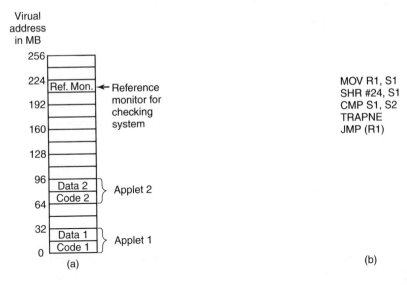

Figure 9-18. (a) Memory divided into 16-MB sandboxes. (b) One way of checking an instruction for validity.

son for having two sandboxes is to prevent an applet from modifying its code during execution to get around these restrictions. By preventing all stores into the code sandbox, we eliminate the danger of self-modifying code. As long as an applet is confined this way, it cannot damage the browser or other applets, plant viruses in memory, or otherwise do any damage to memory.

As soon as an applet is loaded, it is relocated to begin at the start of its sandbox. Then checks are made to see if code and data references are confined to the appropriate sandbox. In the discussion below, we will just look at code references (i.e., JMP and CALL instructions), but the same story holds for data references as well. Static JMP instructions that use direct addressing are easy to check: does the target address land within the boundaries of the code sandbox? Similarly, relative JMPs are also easy to check. If the applet has code that tries to leave the code sandbox, it is rejected and not executed. Similarly, attempts to touch data outside the data sandbox cause the applet to be rejected.

The hard part is dynamic JMPs. Most machines have an instruction in which the address to jump to is computed at run time, put in a register, and then jumped to indirectly, for example by JMP (R1) to jump to the address held in register 1. The validity of such instructions must be checked at run time. This is done by inserting code directly before the indirect jump to test the target address. An example of such a test is shown in Fig. 9-18(b). Remember that all valid addresses have the same upper k bits, so this prefix can be stored in a scratch register, say S2. Such a register cannot be used by the applet itself, which may require rewriting it to avoid this register.

The code works as follows: First the target address under inspection is copied to a scratch register, S1. Then this register is shifted right precisely the correct number of bits to isolate the common prefix in S1. Next the isolated prefix is compared to the correct prefix initially loaded into S2. If they do not match, a trap occurs and the applet is killed. This code sequence requires four instructions and two scratch registers.

Patching the binary program during execution requires some work, but it is doable. It would be simpler if the applet were presented in source form and then compiled locally using a trusted compiler that automatically checked the static addresses and inserted code to verify the dynamic ones during execution. Either way, there is some run-time overhead associated with the dynamic checks. Wahbe et al. (1993) have measured this as about 4%, which is generally acceptable.

A second problem that must be solved is what happens when an applet tries to make a system call? The solution here is straightforward. The system call instruction is replaced by a call to a special module called a **reference monitor** on the same pass that the dynamic address checks are inserted (or, if the source code is available, by linking with a special library that calls the reference monitor instead of making system calls). Either way, the reference monitor examines each attempted call and decides if it is safe to perform. If the call is deemed acceptable, such as writing a temporary file in a designated scratch directory, the call is allowed to proceed. If the call is known to be dangerous or the reference monitor cannot tell, the applet is killed. If the reference monitor can tell which applet called it, a single reference monitor somewhere in memory can handle the requests from all applets. The reference monitor normally learns about the permissions from a configuration file.

Interpretation

The second way to run untrusted applets is to run them interpretively and not let them get actual control of the hardware. This is the approach used by Web browsers. Web page applets are commonly written in Java, which is a normal programming language, or in a high-level scripting language such as safe-TCL or Javascript. Java applets are first compiled to a virtual stack-oriented machine language called **JVM** (**Java Virtual Machine**). It is these JVM applets that are put on the Web page. When they are downloaded, they are inserted into a JVM interpreter inside the browser as illustrated in Fig. 9-19.

The advantage of running interpreted code over compiled code, is that every instruction is examined by the interpreter before being executed. This gives the interpreter the opportunity to check if the address is valid. In addition, system calls are also caught and interpreted. How these calls are handled is a matter of the security policy. For example, if an applet is trusted (e.g., it came from the local disk), its system calls could be carried out without question. However, if an

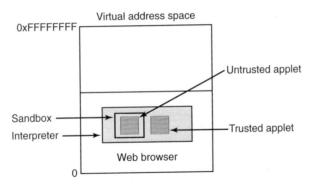

Figure 9-19. Applets can be interpreted by a Web browser.

applet is not trusted (e.g., it came in over the Internet), it could be put in what is effectively a sandbox to restrict its behavior.

High-level scripting languages can also be interpreted. Here no machine addresses are used, so there is no danger of a script trying to access memory in an impermissible way. The downside of interpretation in general is that it is very slow compared to running native compiled code.

Code

Yet another way to deal with applet security is to know where they came from and only accept applets from trusted sources. With this approach, a user can maintain a list of trusted applet vendors and only run applets from those vendors. Applets from all other sources are rejected as too dicey. In this approach, no actual security mechanisms are present at run time. Applets from trustworthy vendors are run as is and code from other vendors is not run at all or in a restricted way (sandboxed or interpreted with little or no access to user files and other system resources).

To make this scheme work, as a minimum, there has to be a way for a user to determine that an applet was written by a trustworthy vendor and not modified by anyone after being produced. This is done using a digital signature, which allows the vendor to sign the applet in such a way that future modifications can be detected.

Code signing is based on public-key cryptography. An applet vendor, typically a software company, generates a (public key, private key) pair, making the former public and zealously guarding the latter. To sign an applet, the vendor first computes a hash function of the applet to get a 128-bit or 160-bit number, depending on whether MD5 or SHA is used. It then signs the hash value by encrypting it with its private key (actually, decrypting it using the notation of Fig. 9-3). This signature accompanies the applet wherever it goes.

When the user gets the applet, the browser computes the hash function itself. It then decrypts the accompanying signature using the vendor's public key and compares what the vendor claims the hash function is with what the browser itself computed. If they agree, the applet is accepted as genuine. Otherwise it is rejected as a forgery. The mathematics involved makes it exceedingly difficult for anyone to tamper with the applet in such a way as its hash function will match the hash function that is obtained by decrypting the genuine signature. It is equally difficult to generate a new false signature that matches without having the private key. The process of signing and verifying is illustrated in Fig. 9-20.

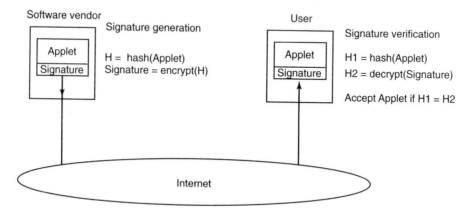

Figure 9-20. How code signing works.

9.5.7 Java Security

The Java programming language and accompanying run-time system were designed to allow a program to be written and compiled once and then shipped over the Internet in binary form and run on any machine supporting Java. Security was a part of the Java design from the beginning. In this section we will describe how it works.

Java is a type-safe language, meaning that the compiler will reject any attempt to use a variable in a way not compatible with its type. In contrast, consider the following C code:

```
naughty_func( )
{
    char *p;
    p = rand( );
    *p = 0;
}
```

It generates a random number and stores it in the pointer p. Then it stores a 0 byte at the address contained in p, overwriting whatever was there, code or data. In

Java, constructions that mix types like this are forbidden by the grammar. In addition, Java has no pointer variables, casts, user-controlled storage allocation (such as *malloc* and *free*) and all array references are checked at run time.

Java programs are compiled to an intermediate binary code called **JVM (Java Virtual Machine) byte code**. JVM has about 100 instructions, most of which push objects of a specific type onto the stack, pop them from the stack, or combine two items on the stack arithmetically. These JVM programs are typically interpreted, although in some cases they can be compiled into machine language for faster execution. In the Java model, applets sent over the Internet for remote execution are JVM programs.

When an applet arrives, it is run through a JVM byte code verifier that checks if the applet obeys certain rules. A properly compiled applet will automatically obey them, but there is nothing to prevent a malicious user from writing a JVM applet in JVM assembly language. The checks include

1. Does the applet attempt to forge pointers?

2. Does it violate access restrictions on private class members?

3. Does it try to use a variable of one type as another type?

4. Does it generate stack overflows or underflows?

5. Does it illegally convert variables of one type to another?

If the applet passes all the tests, it can be safely run without fear that it will access memory other than its own.

However, applets can still make system calls by calling Java methods (procedures) provided for that purpose. The way Java deals with that has evolved over time. In the first version of Java, **JDK (Java Development Kit) 1.0**. applets were divided into two classes: trusted and untrusted. Applets fetched from the local disk were trusted and allowed to make any system calls they wanted. In contrast, applets fetched over the Internet were untrusted. They were run in a sandbox, as shown in Fig. 9-19, and allowed to do practically nothing.

After some experience with this model, Sun decided that it was too restrictive. In JDK 1.1, code signing was employed. When an applet arrived over the Internet, a check was made to see if it was signed by a person or organization the user trusted (as defined by the user's list of trusted signers). If so, the applet was allowed to do whatever it wanted. If not, it was run in a sandbox and severely restricted.

After more experience, this proved unsatisfactory as well, so the security model was changed again. JDK 1.2 provides a configurable fine-grain security policy that applies to all applets, both local and remote. The security model is complicated enough that an entire book can be written describing it (Gong, 1999), so we will just briefly summarize some of the highlights.

Each applet is characterized by two things: where it came from and who signed it. Where it came from is its URL; who signed it is which private key was used for the signature. Each user can create a security policy consisting of a list of rules. A rule may list a URL, a signer, an object, and an action that the applet may perform on the object if the applet's URL and signer match the rule. Conceptually, the information provided is shown in the table of Fig. 9-21, although the actual formatting is different and is related to the Java class hierarchy.

URL	Signer	Object	Action
www.taxprep.com	TaxPrep	/usr/susan/1040.xls	Read
*		/usr/tmp/*	Read, Write
www.microsoft.com	Microsoft	/usr/susan/Office/–	Read, Write, Delete

Figure 9-21. Some examples of protection that can be specified with JDK 1.2.

One kind of action permits file access. The action can specify a specific file or directory, the set of all files in a given directory, or the set of all files and directories recursively contained in a given directory. The three lines of Fig. 9-21 correspond to these three cases. In the first line, the user, Susan, has set up her permissions file so that applets originating at her tax preparer's machine, *www.taxprep.com* and signed by the company, have read access to her tax data located in the file *1040.xls*. This is the only file they can read and no other applets can read this file. In addition, all applets from all sources, whether signed or not, can read and write files in */usr/tmp*.

Furthermore, Susan also trusts Microsoft enough to allow applets originating at its site and signed by Microsoft to read, write, and delete all the files below the *Office* directory in the directory tree, for example, to fix bugs and install new versions of the software. To verify the signatures, Susan must either have the necessary public keys on her disk or must acquire them dynamically, for example in the form of a certificate signed by a company she trusts and whose public key she already has.

Files are not the only resources that can be protected. Network access can also be protected. The objects here are specific ports on specific computers. A computer is specified by an IP address or DNS name; ports on that machine are specified by a range of numbers. The possible actions include asking to connect to the remote computer and accepting connections originated by the remote computer. In this way, an applet can be given network access, but restricted to talking only to computers explicitly named in the permissions list. Applets may dynamically load additional code (classes) as needed, but user-supplied class loaders can precisely control on which machines such classes may originate. Numerous other security features are also present.

9.6 PROTECTION MECHANISMS

In the previous sections we have looked at many potential problems, some of them technical, some of them not. In the following sections we will concentrate on some of the detailed technical ways that are used in operating systems to protect files and other things. All of these techniques make a clear distinction between policy (whose data are to be protected from whom) and mechanism (how the system enforces the policy). The separation of policy and mechanism is discussed in (Sandhu, 1993). Our emphasis will be on mechanisms, not policies.

In some systems, protection is enforced by a program called a **reference monitor**. Every time an access to a potentially protected resource is attempted, the system first asks the reference monitor to check its legality. The reference monitor then looks at its policy tables and makes a decision. Below we will describe the environment in which a reference monitor operates.

9.6.1 Protection Domains

A computer system contains many "objects" that need to be protected. These objects can be hardware (e.g., CPUs, memory segments, disk drives, or printers), or they can be software (e.g., processes, files, databases, or semaphores).

Each object has a unique name by which it is referenced, and a finite set of operations that processes are allowed to carry out on it. The read and write operations are appropriate to a file; up and down make sense on a semaphore.

It is obvious that a way is needed to prohibit processes from accessing objects that they are not authorized to access. Furthermore, this mechanism must also make it possible to restrict processes to a subset of the legal operations when that is needed. For example, process A may be entitled to read, but not write, file F.

In order to discuss different protection mechanisms, it is useful to introduce the concept of a domain. A **domain** is a set of (object, rights) pairs. Each pair specifies an object and some subset of the operations that can be performed on it. A **right** in this context means permission to perform one of the operations. Often a domain corresponds to a single user, telling what the user can do and not do, but a domain can also be more general than just one user.

Figure 9-22 shows three domains, showing the objects in each domain and the rights [Read, Write, eXecute] available on each object. Note that *Printer1* is in two domains at the same time. Although not shown in this example, it is possible for the same object to be in multiple domains, with *different* rights in each one.

At every instant of time, each process runs in some protection domain. In other words, there is some collection of objects it can access, and for each object it has some set of rights. Processes can also switch from domain to domain during execution. The rules for domain switching are highly system dependent.

To make the idea of a protection domain more concrete, let us look at UNIX. In UNIX, the domain of a process is defined by its UID and GID. Given any

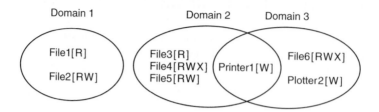

Figure 9-22. Three protection domains.

(UID, GID) combination, it is possible to make a complete list of all objects (files, including I/O devices represented by special files, etc.) that can be accessed, and whether they can be accessed for reading, writing, or executing. Two processes with the same (UID, GID) combination will have access to exactly the same set of objects. Processes with different (UID, GID) values will have access to a different set of files, although there may be considerable overlap in most cases.

Furthermore, each process in UNIX has two halves: the user part and the kernel part. When the process does a system call, it switches from the user part to the kernel part. The kernel part has access to a different set of objects from the user part. For example, the kernel can access all the pages in physical memory, the entire disk, and all the other protected resources. Thus, a system call causes a domain switch.

When a process does an **exec** on a file with the SETUID or SETGID bit on, it acquires a new effective UID or GID. With a different (UID, GID) combination, it has a different set of files and operations available. Running a program with SETUID or SETGID is also a domain switch, since the rights available change.

An important question is how the system keeps track of which object belongs to which domain. Conceptually, at least, one can envision a large matrix, with the rows being domains and the columns being objects. Each box lists the rights, if any, that the domain contains for the object. The matrix for Fig. 9-22 is shown in Fig. 9-23. Given this matrix and the current domain number, the system can tell if an access to a given object in a particular way from a specified domain is allowed.

				Object				
	File1	File2	File3	File4	File5	File6	Printer1	Plotter2
Domain								
1	Read	Read Write						
2			Read	Read Write Execute	Read Write		Write	
3						Read Write Execute	Write	Write

Figure 9-23. A protection matrix.

Domain switching itself can be easily included in the matrix model by realizing that a domain is itself an object, with the operation enter. Figure 9-24 shows the matrix of Fig. 9-23 again, only now with the three domains as objects themselves. Processes in domain 1 can switch to domain 2, but once there, they cannot go back. This situation models executing a SETUID program in UNIX. No other domain switches are permitted in this example.

		Object								
	File1	File2	File3	File4	File5	File6	Printer1	Plotter2	Domain1	Domain2	Domain3
Domain 1	Read	Read Write								Enter	
2			Read	Read Write Execute	Read Write		Write				
3						Read Write Execute	Write	Write			

Figure 9-24. A protection matrix with domains as objects.

9.6.2 Access Control Lists

In practice, actually storing the matrix of Fig. 9-24 is rarely done because it is large and sparse. Most domains have no access at all to most objects, so storing a very large, mostly empty, matrix is a waste of disk space. Two methods that are practical, however, are storing the matrix by rows or by columns, and then storing only the nonempty elements. The two approaches are surprisingly different. In this section we will look at storing it by column; in the next one we will study storing it by row.

The first technique consists of associating with each object an (ordered) list containing all the domains that may access the object, and how. This list is called the **Access Control List** or **ACL** and is illustrated in Fig. 9-25. Here we see three processes, each belonging to a different domain. *A*, *B*, and *C*, and three files *F1*, *F2*, and *F3*. For simplicity, we will assume that each domain corresponds to exactly one user, in this case, users *A*, *B*, and *C*. Often in the security literature, the users are called **subjects** or **principals**, to contrast them with the things owned, the **objects**, such as files.

Each file has an ACL associated with it. File *F1* has two entries in its ACL (separated by a semicolon). The first entry says that any process owned by user *A* may read and write the file. The second entry says that any process owned by user *B* may read the file. All other accesses by these users and all accesses by other users are forbidden. Note that the rights are granted by user, not by process. As far as the protection system goes, any process owned by user *A* can read and

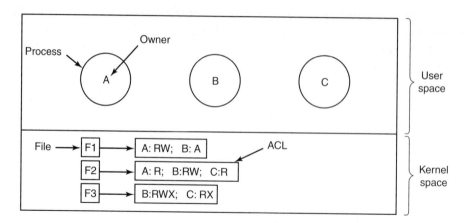

Figure 9-25. Use of access control lists to manage file access.

write file *F1*. It does not matter if there is one such process or 100 of them. It is the owner, not the process ID, that matters.

File *F2* has three entries in its ACL: *A*, *B*, and *C* can all read the file, and in addition *B* can also write it. No other accesses are allowed. File *F3* is apparently an executable program, since *B* and *C* can both read and execute it. *B* can also write it.

This example illustrates the most basic form of protection with ACLs. More sophisticated systems are often used in practice. To start with, we have only shown three rights so far: read, write, and execute. There may be additional rights as well. Some of these may be generic, that is, apply to all objects, and some may be object specific. Examples of generic rights are destroy object and copy object. These could hold for any object, no matter what type it is. Object-specific rights might include append message for a mailbox object and sort alphabetically for a directory object.

So far, our ACL entries have been for individual users. Many systems support the concept of a **group** of users. Groups have names and can be included in ACLs. Two variations on the semantics of groups are possible. In some systems, each process has a user ID (UID) and group ID (GID). In such systems, an ACL entry contains entries of the form

UID1, GID1: rights1; UID2, GID2: rights2; ...

Under these conditions, when a request is made to access an object, a check is made using the caller's UID and GID. If they are present in the ACL, the rights listed are available. If the (UID, GID) combination is not in the list, the access is not permitted.

Using groups this way effectively introduces the concept of a **role**. Consider an installation in which Tana is system administrator, and thus in the group *sysadm*. However, suppose that the company also has some clubs for employees and Tana is a member of the pigeon fanciers club. Club members belong to the group *pigfan* and have access to the company's computers for managing their pigeon database. A portion of the ACL might be as shown in Fig. 9-26.

File	Access control list
Password	tana, sysadm: RW
Pigeon_data	bill, pigfan: RW; tana, pigfan: RW; ...

Figure 9-26. Two access control lists.

If Tana tries to access one of these files, the result depends on which group she is currently logged in as. When she logs in, the system may ask her to choose which of her groups she is currently using, or there might even be different login names and/or passwords to keep them separate. The point of this scheme is to prevent Tana from accessing the password file when she currently has her pigeon fancier's hat on. She can only do that when logged in as the system administrator.

In some cases, a user may have access to certain files independent of which group she is currently logged in as. That case can be handled by introducing **wildcards**, which mean everyone. For example, the entry

tana, *: RW

for the password file would give Tana access no matter which group she was currently in as.

Yet another possibility is that if a user belongs to any of the groups that have certain access rights, the access is permitted. In this case, a user belonging to multiple groups does not have to specify which group to use at login time. All of them count all of the time. A disadvantage of this approach is that it provides less encapsulation: Tana can edit the password file during a pigeon club meeting.

The use of groups and wildcards introduces the possibility of selectively blocking a specific user from accessing a file. For example, the entry

virgil, *: (none); *, *: RW

gives the entire world except for Virgil read and write access to the file. This works because the entries are scanned in order, and the first one that applies is taken; subsequent entries are not even examined. A match is found for Virgil on the first entry and the access rights, in this case, (none) are found and applied. The search is terminated at that point. The fact that the rest of the world has access is never even seen.

The other way of dealing with groups is not to have ACL entries consist of (UID, GID) pairs, but to have each entry be a UID or a GID. For example, an entry for the file *pigeon_data* could be

debbie: RW; phil: RW; pigfan: RW

meaning that Debbie and Phil, and all members of the *pigfan* group have read and write access to the file.

It sometimes occurs that a user or a group has certain permissions with respect to a file that the file owner later wishes to revoke. With access control lists, it is relatively straightforward to revoke a previously granted access. All that has to be done is edit the ACL to make the change. However, if the ACL is checked only when a file is opened, most likely the change will only take effect on future calls to open. Any file that is already open will continue to have the rights it had when it was opened, even if the user is no longer authorized to access the file at all.

9.6.3 Capabilities

The other way of slicing up the matrix of Fig. 9-24 is by rows. When this method is used, associated with each process is a list of objects that may be accessed, along with an indication of which operations are permitted on each, in other words, its domain. This list is called a **capability list** or **C-list** and the individual items on it are called **capabilities** (Dennis and Van Horn, 1966; Fabry, 1974). A set of three processes and their capability lists is shown in Fig. 9-27.

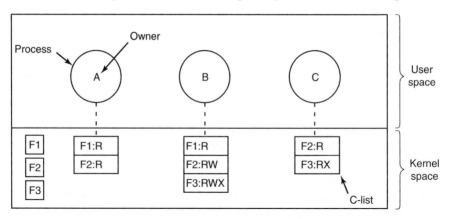

Figure 9-27. When capabilities are used, each process has a capability list.

Each capability grants the owner certain rights on a certain object. In Fig. 9-27, the process owned by user *A* can read files *F1* and *F2*, for example. Usually, a capability consists of a file (or more generally, an object) identifier and a bitmap for the various rights. In a UNIX-like system, the file identifier would probably be the i-node number. Capability lists are themselves objects and may be pointed to from other capability lists, thus facilitating sharing of subdomains.

It is fairly obvious that capability lists must be protected from user tampering. Three methods of protecting them are known. The first way requires a **tagged architecture**, a hardware design in which each memory word has an extra (or tag) bit that tells whether the word contains a capability or not. The tag bit is not used by arithmetic, comparison, or similar ordinary instructions, and it can be modified only by programs running in kernel mode (i.e., the operating system). Tagged-architecture machines have been built and can be made to work well (Feustal, 1972). The IBM AS/400 is a popular example.

The second way is to keep the C-list inside the operating system. Capabilities are then referred to by their position in the capability list. A process might say: "Read 1 KB from the file pointed to by capability 2." This form of addressing is similar to using file descriptors in UNIX. Hydra (Wulf et al., 1974) worked this way.

The third way is to keep the C-list in user space, but manage the capabilities cryptographically so that users cannot tamper with them. This approach is partic-ularly suited to distributed systems and works as follows. When a client process sends a message to a remote server, for example, a file server, to create an object for it, the server creates the object and generates a long random number, the check field, to go with it. A slot in the server's file table is reserved for the object and the check field is stored there along with the addresses of the disk blocks, etc. In UNIX terms, the check field is stored on the server in the i-node. It is not sent back to the user and never put on the network. The server then generates and returns a capability to the user of the form shown in Fig. 9-28.

Server	Object	Rights	f(Objects,Rights,Check)

Figure 9-28. A cryptographically-protected capability.

The capability returned to the user contains the server's identifier, the object number (the index into the server's tables, essentially, the i-node number), and the rights, stored as a bitmap. For a newly created object, all the rights bits are turned on. The last field consists of the concatenation of the object, rights, and check field run through a cryptographically-secure one-way function, f, of the kind we discussed earlier.

When the user wishes to access the object, it sends the capability to the server as part of the request. The server then extracts the object number to index into its tables to find the object. It then computes $f(Object, Rights, Check)$ taking the first two parameters from the capability itself and the third one from its own tables. If the result agrees with the fourth field in the capability, the request is honored; otherwise, it is rejected. If a user tries to access someone else's object, he will not be able to fabricate the fourth field correctly since he does not know the check field, and the request will be rejected.

A user can ask the server to produce a weaker capability, for example, for read-only access. First the server verifies that the capability is valid. If so, if computes $f(Object, New\_rights, Check)$ and generates a new capability putting this value in the fourth field. Note that the original *Check* value is used because other outstanding capabilities depend on it.

This new capability is sent back to the requesting process. The user can now give this to a friend by just sending it in a message. If the friend turns on rights bits that should be off, the server will detect this when the capability is used since the *f* value will not correspond to the false rights field. Since the friend does not know the true check field, he cannot fabricate a capability that corresponds to the false rights bits. This scheme was developed for the Amoeba system and used extensively there (Tanenbaum et al., 1990).

In addition to the specific object-dependent rights, such as read and execute, capabilities (both kernel and cryptographically-protected) usually have **generic rights** which are applicable to all objects. Examples of generic rights are

1. Copy capability: create a new capability for the same object.

2. Copy object: create a duplicate object with a new capability.

3. Remove capability: delete an entry from the C-list; object unaffected.

4. Destroy object: permanently remove an object and a capability.

A last remark worth making about capability systems is that revoking access to an object is quite difficult in the kernel-managed version. It is hard for the system to find all the outstanding capabilities for any object to take them back, since they may be stored in C-lists all over the disk. One approach is to have each capability point to an indirect object, rather than to the object itself. By having the indirect object point to the real object, the system can always break that connection, thus invalidating the capabilities. (When a capability to the indirect object is later presented to the system, the user will discover that the indirect object is now pointing to a null object.)

In the Amoeba scheme, revocation is easy. All that needs to be done is change the check field stored with the object. In one blow, all existing capabilities are invalidated. However, neither scheme allows selective revocation, that is, taking back, say, John's permission, but nobody else's. This defect is generally recognized to be a problem with all capability systems.

Another general problem is making sure the owner of a valid capability does not give a copy to 1000 of his best friends. Having the kernel manage capabilities, as in Hydra, solves this problem, but this solution does not work well in a distributed system such as Amoeba.

On the other hand, capabilities solve the problem of sandboxing mobile code very elegantly. When a foreign program is started, it is given a capability list containing only those capabilities that the machine owner wants to give it, such as the ability to write on the screen and the ability to read and write files in one scratch directory just created for it. If the mobile code is put into its own process with only these limited capabilities, it will not be able to access any other system resources and thus be effectively confined to a sandbox without the need to modify its code or run it interpretively. Running code with as few access rights as possible is known as the **principle of least privilege** and is a powerful guideline for producing secure systems.

Briefly summarized, ACLs and capabilities have somewhat complementary properties. Capabilities are very efficient because if a process says "Open the file pointed to by capability 3," no checking is needed. With ACLs, a (potentially long) search of the ACL may be needed. If groups are not supported, then granting everyone read access to a file requires enumerating all users in the ACL. Capabilities also allow a process to be encapsulated easily, whereas ACLs do not. On the other hand, ACLs allow selective revocation of rights, which capabilities do not. Finally, if an object is removed and the capabilities are not or the capabilities are removed and an object is not, problems arise. ACLs do not suffer from this problem.

9.7 TRUSTED SYSTEMS

Much of this chapter has been devoted to the fact that virtually all modern computer systems leak like a sieve. Estimates of the worldwide damage caused by viruses and similar problems exceed $1 trillion per year in wasted effort to repair problems, reconstruct damaged data, etc., not to mention lost business opportunities. A naive person might logically ask two questions concerning this state of affairs:

1. Is it possible to build a secure computer system?

2. If so, why is it not done?

The answer to the first one is basically yes. How to build a secure system has been known for decades. MULTICS, designed in the 1960s, for example, had security as one of its main goals and achieved that fairly well.

Why secure systems are not being built is more complicated, but it comes down to two fundamental reasons. First, current systems are not secure but users are unwilling to throw them out. If Microsoft were to announce that in addition to Windows it had a new product, SecureOS, that was guaranteed to be immune to viruses but did not run Windows applications, it is far from certain that every person and company would drop Windows like a hot potato and buy the new system immediately.

The second issue is more subtle. The only way to build a secure system is to keep it simple. Features are the enemy of security. System designers believe (rightly or wrongly) that what users want is more features. More features mean more complexity, more code, more bugs, and more security errors.

Here are two simple examples. The first email systems sent messages as ASCII text. They were completely secure. There is nothing an incoming ASCII message can do to damage a computer system. Then people got the idea to expand email to include other types of documents, for example, *Word* files, which can contain programs in macros. Reading such a document means running somebody else's program on your computer. No matter how much sandboxing is used, running a foreign program on your computer is inherently more dangerous than looking at ASCII text. Did users demand the ability to change email from passive documents to active programs? Probably not, but systems designers thought it would be a nifty idea, without worrying too much about the security implications.

The second example is the same thing for Web pages. When the Web consisted of passive HTML pages, it did not pose a major security problem (although illegal HTML could cause a buffer overflow attack). Now that many Web pages contain programs (applets) that the user has to run to view the content, one security leak after another pops up. As soon as one is fixed, another one takes its place. When the Web was entirely static, were users up in arms demanding dynamic content? Not that the author remembers, but its introduction brought with it a raft of security problems. It looks like the Vice-President-In-Charge-Of-Saying-No was asleep at the wheel.

Actually, there are some organizations that think good security is more important than nifty new features, the military being the prime example. In the following sections we will look some of the issues involved, but they can be summarized in one sentence. To build a secure system, have a security model at the core of the operating system that is simple enough that the designers can actually understand it, and resist all pressure to deviate from it in order to add new features.

9.7.1 Trusted Computing Base

In the security world, people often talk about **trusted systems** rather than secure systems. These are systems that have formally stated security requirements and meet these requirements. At the heart of every trusted system is a minimal **TCB** (**Trusted Computing Base**) consisting of the hardware and software necessary for enforcing all the security rules. If the trusted computing base is working to specification, the system security cannot be compromised, no matter what else is wrong.

The TCB typically consists of most of the hardware (except I/O devices that do not affect security), a portion of the operating system kernel, and most or all of the user programs that have superuser power (e.g., SETUID root programs in UNIX). Operating system functions that must be part of the TCB include process creation, process switching, memory map management, and part of file and I/O management. In a secure design, often the TCB will be quite separate from the rest of the operating system in order to minimize its size and verify its correctness.

An important part of the TCB is the reference monitor, as shown in Fig. 9-29. The reference monitor accepts all system calls involving security, such as opening files, and decides whether they should be processed or not. The reference monitor thus allows all the security decisions to be put in one place, with no possibility of bypassing it. Most operating systems are not designed this way, which is part of the reason they are so insecure.

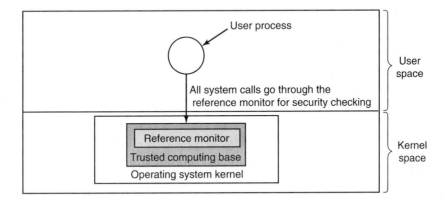

Figure 9-29. A reference monitor.

9.7.2 Formal Models of Secure Systems

Protection matrices, such as that of Fig. 9-23, are not static. They frequently change as new objects are created, old objects are destroyed, and owners decide to increase or restrict the set of users for their objects. A considerable amount of attention has been paid to modeling protection systems in which the protection matrix is constantly changing. In the remainder of this section, we will touch briefly upon some of this work.

Decades ago, Harrison et al. (1976) identified six primitive operations on the protection matrix that can be used as a base to model any protection system. These primitive operations are create object, delete object, create domain, delete domain, insert right, and remove right. The two latter primitives insert and remove rights from specific matrix elements, such as granting domain 1 permission to read *File6*.

These six primitives can be combined into **protection commands**. It is these protection commands that user programs can execute to change the matrix. They may not execute the primitives directly. For example, the system might have a command to create a new file, which would test to see if the file already existed, and if not, create a new object and give the owner all rights to it. There might also be a command to allow the owner to grant permission to read the file to everyone in the system, in effect, inserting the "read" right in the new file's entry in every domain.

At any instant, the matrix determines what a process in any domain can do, not what it is authorized to do. The matrix is what is enforced by the system; authorization has to do with management policy. As an example of this distinction, let us consider the simple system of Fig. 9-30 in which domains correspond to users. In Fig. 9-30(a) we see the intended protection policy: *Henry* can read and write *mailbox7*, *Robert* can read and write *secret*, and all three users can read and execute *compiler*.

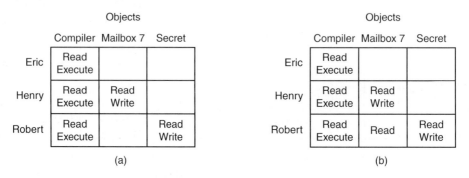

Figure 9-30. (a) An authorized state. (b) An unauthorized state.

Now imagine that *Robert* is very clever and has found a way to issue commands to have the matrix changed to Fig. 9-30(b). He has now gained access to *mailbox7*, something he is not authorized to have. If he tries to read it, the operating system will carry out his request because it does not know that the state of Fig. 9-30(b) is unauthorized.

It should now be clear that the set of all possible matrices can be partitioned into two disjoint sets: the set of all authorized states and the set of all unauthorized states. A question around which much theoretical research has revolved is this: "Given an initial authorized state and a set of commands, can it be proven that the system can never reach an unauthorized state?"

In effect, we are asking if the available mechanism (the protection commands) is adequate to enforce some protection policy. Given this policy, some initial state of the matrix, and the set of commands for modifying the matrix, what we would like is a way to prove that the system is secure. Such a proof turns out quite difficult to acquire; many general purpose systems are not theoretically secure. Harrison et al. (1976) proved that in the case of an arbitrary configuration for an arbitrary protection system, security is theoretically undecidable. However, for a specific system, it may be possible to prove whether the system can ever move from an authorized state to an unauthorized state. For more information, see Landwehr (1981).

9.7.3 Multilevel Security

Most operating systems allow individual users to determine who may read and write their files and other objects. This policy is called **discretionary access control**. In many environments this model works fine, but there are other environments where much tighter security is required, such as the military, corporate patent departments, and hospitals. In the latter environments, the organization has stated rules about who can see what, and these may not be modified by individual soldiers, lawyers, or doctors, at least not without getting special permission from the boss. These environments need **mandatory access controls** to ensure that the stated security policies are enforced by the system, in addition to the standard discretionary access controls. What these mandatory access controls do is regulate the flow of information, to make sure that it does not leak out in a way it is not supposed to.

The Bell-La Padula Model

The most widely used multilevel security model is the **Bell-La Padula model** so we will start there (Bell and La Padula, 1973). This model was designed for handling military security, but it is also applicable to other organizations. In the military world, documents (objects) can have a security level, such as unclassified, confidential, secret, and top secret. People are also assigned these levels, depending on which documents they are allowed to see. A general might be allowed to see all documents, whereas a lieutenant might be restricted to documents cleared as confidential and lower. A process running on behalf of a user acquires the user's security level. Since there are multiple security levels, this scheme is called a **multilevel security system**.

The Bell-La Padula model has rules about how information can flow:

1. **The simple security property:** A process running at security level k can read only objects at its level or lower. For example, a general can read a lieutenant's documents but a lieutenant cannot read a general's documents.

2. **The * property:** A process running at security level k can write only objects at its level or higher. For example, a lieutenant can append a message to a general's mailbox telling everything he knows, but a general cannot append a message to a lieutenant's mailbox telling everything he knows because the general may have seen top secret documents that may not be disclosed to a lieutenant.

Roughly summarized, processes can read down and write up, but not the reverse. If the system rigorously enforces these two properties, it can be shown that no information can leak out from a higher security level to a lower one. The * property was so named because in the original report, the authors could not think of a good name for it and used ∗ as a temporary placeholder until they could devise a better name. They never did and the report was printed with the ∗. In this model, processes read and write objects, but do not communicate with each other directly. The Bell-La Padula model is illustrated graphically in Fig. 9-31.

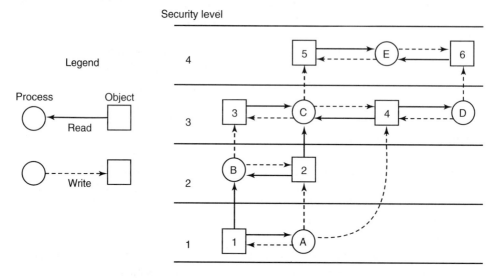

Figure 9-31. The Bell-La Padula multilevel security model.

In this figure a (solid) arrow from an object to a process indicates that the process is reading the object, that is, information is flowing from the object to the process. Similarly, a (dashed) arrow from a process to an object indicates that the process is writing into the object, that is, information is flowing from the process to the object. Thus all information flows in the direction of the arrows. For example, process *B* can read from object *1* but not from object *3*.

The simple security property says that all solid (read) arrows go sideways or up. The ∗ property says that all dashed (write) arrows also go sideways or up. Since information flows only horizontally or upward, any information that starts out at level *k* can never appear at a lower level. In other words, there is never a path that moves information downward, thus guaranteeing the security of the model.

The Biba Model

To summarize the Bell-La Padula model in military terms, a lieutenant can ask a private to reveal all he knows and then copy this information into a general's file without violating security. Now let us put the same model in civilian terms. Imagine a company in which janitors have security level 1, programmers have security level 3, and the president of the company has security level 5. Using Bell-La Padula, a programmer can query a janitor about the company's future plans, and then overwrite the President's files that contain corporate strategy. Not all companies might be equally enthusiastic about this model.

The problem with the Bell-La Padula model is that it was devised to keep secrets, not guarantee the integrity of the data. To guarantee the integrity of the data, we need precisely the reverse properties (Biba, 1977):

1. **The simple integrity principle:** A process running at security level k can write only objects at its level or lower (no write up).

2. **The integrity * property:** A process running at security level k can read only objects at its level or higher (no read down).

Together, these properties ensure that the programmer can update the janitor's files with information acquired from the president, but not vice versa. Of course, some organizations want both the Bell-La Padula properties and the Biba properties, but these are in direct conflict so they are hard to achieve simultaneously.

9.7.4 Orange Book Security

Given all this background, it should come as no surprise that the U.S. Dept. of Defense has put some effort into the area of secure systems. In particular, in 1985, it published a document formally known as Dept. of Defense standard DoD 5200.28, but usually called the **Orange Book** on account of its cover, which divides operating systems into seven categories based on their security properties. While the standard has since been replaced by another (and far more complex one), it is still a useful guide to some security properties. Also, one occasionally still sees vendor literature claiming conformance to some Orange Book security level. A table of the Orange Book requirements is given in Fig. 9-32. Below we will look at the security categories and point out some of the highlights.

Level D conformance is easy to achieve: it has no security requirements at all. It collects all the systems that have failed to pass even the minimum security tests. MS-DOS and Windows 95/98/Me are level D.

Level C is intended for environments with cooperating users. C1 requires a protected mode operating system, authenticated user login, and the ability for users to specify which files can be made available to other users and how (discretionary access control). Minimal security testing and documentation are also required.

C2 adds the requirement that discretionary access control is down to the level of the individual user. It also requires that objects (e.g., files, virtual memory pages) given to users must be initialized to all zeros, and a minimal amount of auditing is needed. The UNIX *rwx* scheme meets C1 but does not meet C2. For this, a more elaborate scheme, such as ACLs or equivalent, are needed.

Criterion	D	C1	C2	B1	B2	B3	A1
Security policy							
Discretionary access control		X	X	→	→	X	→
Object reuse			X	→	→	→	→
Labels				X	X	→	→
Label integrity				X	→	→	→
Exportation of labeled information				X	→	→	→
Labeling human readable output				X	→	→	→
Mandatory access control				X	X	→	→
Subject sensitivity labels					X	→	→
Device labels					X	→	→
Accountability							
Identification and authentication		X	X	X	→	→	→
Audit			X	X	X	X	→
Trusted path					X	X	→
Assurance							
System architecture		X	X	X	X	X	→
System integrity		X	→	→	→	→	→
Security testing		X	X	X	X	X	X
Design specification and verification				X	X	X	X
Covert channel analysis					X	X	X
Trusted facility management					X	X	→
Configuration management					X	→	X
Trusted recovery						X	→
Trusted distribution							X
Documentation							
Security features user's guide		X	→	→	→	→	→
Trusted facility manual		X	X	X	X	X	→
Test documentation		X	→	→	X	→	X
Design documentation		X	→	X	X	X	X

Figure 9-32. Orange Book security criteria. The symbol X means that there are new requirements here. The symbol → means that the requirements from the next lower category also apply here.

The B and A levels require all controlled users and objects to be assigned a security label, such as unclassified, secret, or top secret. The system must be capable of enforcing the Bell-La Padula information flow model.

B2 adds to this requirement that the system has been designed top-down in a modular way. The design must be presented in such a way that it can be verified. The possible covert channels (see the next section) must be analyzed.

B3 contains all of B2's features plus there must be ACLs with users and groups, a formal TCB must be presented, adequate security auditing must be present, and secure crash recovery must be included.

A1 requires a formal model of the protection system and a proof that the model is correct. It also requires a demonstration that the implementation conforms to the model. Covert channels must be formally analyzed.

9.7.5 Covert Channels

All these ideas about formal models and provably secure systems sound great, but do they actually work? In a word: No. Even in a system which has a proper security model underlying it and which has been proven to be secure and is correctly implemented, security leaks can still occur. In this section we discuss how information can still leak out even when it has been rigorously proven that such leakage is mathematically impossible. These ideas are due to Lampson (1973).

Lampson's model was originally formulated in terms of a single timesharing system, but the same ideas can be adapted to LANs and other multiuser environments. In the purest form, it involves three processes on some protected machine. The first process is the client, which wants some work performed by the second one, the server. The client and the server do not entirely trust each other. For example, the server's job is to help clients with filling out their tax forms. The clients are worried that the server will secretly record their financial data, for example, maintaining a secret list of who earns how much, and then selling the list. The server is worried that the clients will try to steal the valuable tax program.

The third process is the collaborator, which is conspiring with the server to indeed steal the client's confidential data. The collaborator and server are typically owned by the same person. These three processes are shown in Fig. 9-33. The object of this exercise is to design a system in which it is impossible for the server process to leak to the collaborator process the information that it has legitimately received from the client process. Lampson called this the **confinement problem**.

From the system designer's point of view, the goal is to encapsulate or confine the server in such a way that it cannot pass information to the collaborator. Using a protection matrix scheme we can easily guarantee that the server cannot communicate with the collaborator by writing a file to which the collaborator has read access. We can probably also ensure that the server cannot communicate with the collaborator using the system's interprocess communication mechanism.

Unfortunately, more subtle communication channels may be available. For example, the server can try to communicate a binary bit stream as follows. To send a 1 bit, it computes as hard as it can for a fixed interval of time. To send a 0 bit, it goes to sleep for the same length of time.

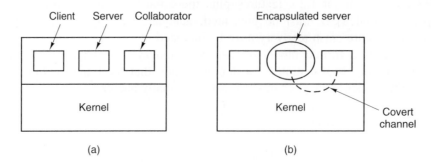

Figure 9-33. (a) The client, server, and collaborator processes. (b) The encapsulated server can still leak to the collaborator via covert channels.

The collaborator can try to detect the bit stream by carefully monitoring its response time. In general, it will get better response when the server is sending a 0 than when the server is sending a 1. This communication channel is known as a **covert channel**, and is illustrated in Fig. 9-33(b).

Of course, the covert channel is a noisy channel, containing a lot of extraneous information, but information can be reliably sent over a noisy channel by using an error-correcting code (e.g., a Hamming code, or even something more sophisticated). The use of an error-correcting code reduces the already low bandwidth of the covert channel even more, but it still may be enough to leak substantial information. It is fairly obvious that no protection model based on a matrix of objects and domains is going to prevent this kind of leakage.

Modulating the CPU usage is not the only covert channel. The paging rate can also be modulated (many page faults for a 1, no page faults for a 0). In fact, almost any way of degrading system performance in a clocked way is a candidate. If the system provides a way of locking files, then the server can lock some file to indicate a 1, and unlock it to indicate a 0. On some systems, it may be possible for a process to detect the status of a lock even on a file that it cannot access. This covert channel is illustrated in Fig. 9-34, with the file locked or unlocked for some fixed time interval known to both the server and collaborator. In this example, the secret bit stream 11010100 is being transmitted.

Locking and unlocking a prearranged file, S is not an especially noisy channel, but it does require fairly accurate timing unless the bit rate is very low. The reliability and performance can be increased even more using an acknowledgement protocol. This protocol uses two more files, $F1$ and $F2$, locked by the server and collaborator, respectively to keep the two processes synchronized. After the server locks or unlocks S, it flips the lock status of $F1$ to indicate that a bit has been sent. As soon as the collaborator has read out the bit, it flips $F2$'s lock status to tell the server it is ready for another bit and waits until $F1$ is flipped again to indicate that another bit is present in S. Since timing is no longer involved, this protocol is fully reliable, even in a busy system and can proceed as fast as the two

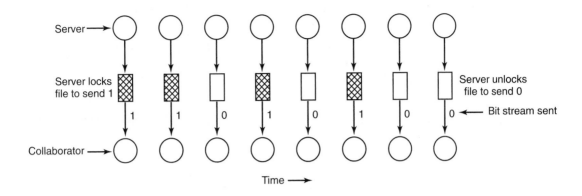

Figure 9-34. A covert channel using file locking.

processes can get scheduled. To get higher bandwidth, why not use two files per bit time, or make it a byte-wide channel with eight signaling files, *S0* through *S7*.

Acquiring and releasing dedicated resources (tape drives, plotters, etc.) can also be used for signaling. The server acquires the resource to send a 1 and releases it to send a 0. In UNIX, the server could create a file to indicate a 1 and remove it to indicate a 0; the collaborator could use the **access** system call to see if the file exists. This call works even though the collaborator has no permission to use the file. Unfortunately, many other covert channels exist.

Lampson also mentioned a way of leaking information to the (human) owner of the server process. Presumably the server process will be entitled to tell its owner how much work it did on behalf of the client, so the client can be billed. If the actual computing bill is, say, $100 and the client's income is $53,000 dollars, the server could report the bill as $100.53 to its owner.

Just finding all the covert channels, let alone blocking them, is extremely difficult. In practice, there is little that can be done. Introducing a process that causes page faults at random, or otherwise spends its time degrading system performance in order to reduce the bandwidth of the covert channels is not an attractive proposition.

So far we have assumed that the client and server are separate processes. Another case is where there is only one process, the client, which is running a program containing a Trojan horse. The Trojan horse might have been written by the collaborator with the purpose of getting the user to run it in order to leak out data that the protection system prevents the collaborator from getting at directly.

A slightly different kind of covert channel can be used to pass secret information between processes, even though a human or automated censor gets to inspect all messages between the processes and veto the suspicious ones. For example, consider a company that manually checks all outgoing email sent by company employees to make sure they are not leaking secrets to accomplices or competitors outside the company. Is there a way for an employee to smuggle substantial volumes of confidential information right out under the censor's nose? It turns out there is.

As a case in point, consider Fig. 9-35(a). This photograph, taken by the author in Kenya, contains three zebras contemplating an acacia tree. Fig. 9-35(b) appears to be the same three zebras and acacia tree, but it has an extra added attraction. It contains the complete, unabridged text of five of Shakespeare's plays embedded in it: *Hamlet*, *King Lear*, *Macbeth*, *The Merchant of Venice*, and *Julius Caesar*. Together, these plays total over 700 KB of text.

(a)   (b)

Figure 9-35. (a) Three zebras and a tree. (b) Three zebras, a tree, and the complete text of five plays by William Shakespeare.

How does this covert channel work? The original color image is 1024×768 pixels. Each pixel consists of three 8-bit numbers, one each for the red, green, and blue intensity of that pixel. The pixel's color is formed by the linear superposition of the three colors. The encoding method uses the low-order bit of each RGB color value as a covert channel. Thus each pixel has room for 3 bits of secret information, one in the red value, one in the green value, and one in the blue value. With an image of this size, up to $1024 \times 768 \times 3$ bits or 294,912 bytes of secret information can be stored in it.

The full text of the five plays and a short notice adds up to 734,891 bytes. This was first compressed to about 274 KB using a standard compression algorithm. The compressed output was then encrypted and inserted into the low-order bits of each color value. As can be seen (or actually, cannot be seen), the existence of the information is completely invisible. It is equally invisible in the large, full-color version of the photo. The eye cannot easily distinguish 7-bit color from 8-bit color. Once the image file has gotten past the censor, the receiver just strips off all the low-order bits, applies the decryption and decompression algorithms, and recovers the original 734,891 bytes. Hiding the existence of information like this is called **steganography** (from the Greek words for "covered writing"). Steganography is not popular with governments that try to restrict communication among their citizens, but it is popular with people who believe strongly in free speech.

Viewing the two images in black and white with low resolution does not do justice to how powerful the technique is. To get a better feel for how steganography works, the author has prepared a demonstration, including the full-color image of Fig. 9-35(b) with the five plays embedded in it. The demonstration can be found at *www.cs.vu.nl/~ast/* . Click on the <u>covered writing</u> link under the heading STEGANOGRAPHY DEMO. Then follow the instructions on that page to download the image and the steganography tools needed to extract the plays.

Another use of steganography is to insert hidden watermarks into images used on Web pages to detect their theft and reuse on other Web pages. If your Web page contains an image with the secret message: Copyright 2000, General Images Corporation, you might have a tough time convincing a judge that you produced the image yourself. Music, movies, and other kinds of material can also be watermarked in this way.

Of course, the fact that watermarks are used like this encourages some people to look for ways to remove them. A scheme that stores information in the low-order bits of each pixel can be defeated by rotating the image 1 degree clockwise, then converting it to a lossy system such as JPEG, then rotating it back by 1 degree. Finally, the image can be reconverted to the original encoding system (e.g., gif, bmp, tif). The lossy JPEG conversion will mess up the low-order bits and the rotations involve massive floating-point calculations, which introduce roundoff errrors, also adding noise to the low-order bits. The people putting in the watermarks know this (or should know this), so they put in their copyright information redundantly and use schemes besides just using the low-order bits of the pixels. In turn, this stimulates the attackers to look for better removal techniques, and so it goes.

9.8 RESEARCH ON SECURITY

Computer security is a very hot topic, with a great deal of research taking place, but most of it is not directly operating system related. Instead, it deals with network security (e.g., email, Web, and e-commerce security), cryptography, Java, or just managing a computer installation securely.

However, there is also some research closer to our subject. For example, user authentication is still important. Monrose and Rubin (1997) have studied it using keystroke dynamics, Pentland and Choudhury (2000) argue for face recognition, and Mark (2000) developed a way to model it, among others.

Some other operating systems related security work is as follows. Bershad et al. (1995a) have argued that protection is a software issue, not a hardware (i.e., MMU) issue. Mazieres et al. (1999) have looked at secure distributed file systems. Myers and Liskov (1997) studied secure information flow models. Chase et al. (1994) examined security in systems with a large address space occupied by multiple processes. Smart card security has been investigated by Clark and Hoffman (1994). Goldberg et al. (1998) have constructed virus phylogenies.

9.9 SUMMARY

Operating systems can be threatened in many ways, ranging from insider attacks to viruses coming in from the outside. Many attacks begin with a cracker trying to break into a specific system, often by just guessing passwords. These attacks often use dictionaries of common passwords and they are surprisingly successful. Password security can be made stronger using salt, one-time passwords, and challenge-response schemes. Smart cards and biometric indicators can also be used. Retinal scans are already practical.

Many different attacks on operating systems are known, including Trojan horse, login spoofing, logic bomb, trap door, and buffer overflow attacks. Generic attacks include asking for memory and snooping on it, making illegal system calls to see what happens, and even trying to trick insiders into revealing information they should not reveal.

Viruses are an increasingly serious problem for many users. Viruses come in many forms, including memory resident viruses, boot sector infectors, and macro viruses. Using a virus scanner to look for virus signatures is useful, but really good viruses can encrypt most of their code and modify the rest with each copy made, making detection very difficult. Some antivirus software works not by looking for specific virus signatures, but by looking for certain suspicious behavior. Avoiding viruses in the first place by safe computing practices is better than trying to deal with the aftermath of an attack. In short, do not load and execute programs whose origin is unknown and whose trustworthyness is questionable.

Mobile code is another issue that has to be dealt with these days. Putting it in a sandbox, interpreting it, and only running code signed by trusted vendors are possible approaches.

Systems can be protected using a matrix of protection domains (e.g., users) vertically and objects horizontally. The matrix can be sliced into rows, leading to capability-based systems or into columns, leading to ACL-based systems.

Secure systems can be designed, but that has to be a goal from the beginning. Probably the most important design rule is to have a minimal trusted computing base that cannot be bypassed whenever any resource is accessed. Multilevel security can be based on the Bell-La Padula model, designed for keeping secrets, or the Biba model, designed to maintaining system integrity. The Orange Book describes requirements trusted systems must meet. Finally, even if a system is provably secure, attention must be paid to covert channels, which can easily subvert the system by creating communication channels not included in the model.

PROBLEMS

1. Consider a secret-key cipher that has a 26×26 matrix with the columns headed by *ABC* ... *Z* and the rows are also *ABC* ... *Z*. Plaintext is encrypted two characters at a time. The first character is the column; the second is the row. The cell formed by the intersection of the row and column contains two ciphertext characters. What constraint must the matrix adhere to and how many keys are there?

2. Break the following monoalphabetic cipher. The plaintext, consisting of letters only, is a well-known excerpt from a poem by Lewis Carroll.

   kfd ktbd fzm eubd kfd pzyiom mztx ku kzyg ur bzha kfthcm
   ur mfudm zhx mftnm zhx mdzythc pzq ur ezsszcdm zhx gthcm
   zhx pfa kfd mdz tm sutythc fuk zhx pfdkfdi ntcm fzld pthcm
   sok pztk z stk kfd uamkdim eitdx sdruid pd fzld uoi efzk
   rui mubd ur om zid uok ur sidzkf zhx zyy ur om zid rzk
   hu foiia mztx kfd ezindhkdi kfda kfzhgdx ftb boef rui kfzk

3. Consider the following way to encrypt a file. The encryption algorithm uses two *n*-byte arrays, *A* and *B*. The first *n* bytes are read from the file into *A*. Then *A*[0] is copied to *B*[*i*], *A*[1] is copied to *B*[*j*], *A*[2] is copied to *B*[*k*], etc. After all *n* bytes are copied to the *B* array, that array is written to the output file and *n* more bytes are read into *A*. This procedure continues until the entire file has been encrypted. Note that here encryption is not being done by replacing characters with other ones, but by changing their order. How many keys have to be tried to exhaustively search the key space? Give an advantage of this scheme over a monoalphabetic substitution cipher?

4. Secret-key cryptography is more efficient than public-key cryptography, but requires the sender and receiver to agree on a key in advance. Suppose that the sender and receiver have never met, but there exists a trusted third party that shares a secret key with the sender and also shares a (different) secret key witht the receiver. How can the sender and receiver establish a new shared secret key under these circumstances?

5. Give a simple example of a mathematical function that to a first approximation will do as a one-way function.

6. Not having the computer echo the password is safer than having it echo an asterisk for each character typed since the latter discloses the password length to anyone nearby who can see the screen. Assuming that passwords consist of upper and lower case letters and digits only, and that passwords must be a minimum of five characters and a maximum of eight characters, how much safer is not displaying anything?

7. After getting your degree, you apply for a job as director of a large university computer center that has just put its ancient mainframe system out to pasture and switched over to a large LAN server running UNIX. You get the job. Fifteen minutes after starting work, your assistant bursts into your office screaming: "Some students have discovered the algorithm we use for encrypting passwords and posted it on the Internet." What should you do?

8. The Morris-Thompson protection scheme with the *n*-bit random numbers (salt) was designed to make it difficult for an intruder to discover a large number of passwords

by encrypting common strings in advance. Does the scheme also offer protection against a student user who is trying to guess the superuser password on his machine? Assume the password file is available for reading.

9. Name three characteristics that a good biometric indicator must have for it to be useful as a login authenticator.

10. Is there any feasible way to use the MMU hardware to prevent the kind of overflow attack shown in Fig. 9-11? Explain why or why not.

11. A computer science department has a large collection of UNIX machines on its local network. Users on any machine can issue a command of the form

    machine4 who

    and have the command executed on *machine4*, without having the user log in on the remote machine. This feature is implemented by having the user's kernel send the command and his UID to the remote machine. Is this scheme secure if the kernels are all trustworthy? What if some of the machines are students' personal computers, with no protection?

12. What property do the implementation of passwords in UNIX have in common with Lamport's scheme for logging in over an insecure network?

13. Lamport's one-time password scheme uses the passwords in reverse order. Would it not be simpler to use $f(s)$ the first time, $f(f(s))$ the second time, and so on?

14. As Internet cafes become more widespread, people are going to want ways of going to one anywhere in the world and conducting business from them. Describe a way to produce signed documents from one using a smart card (assume that all the computers are equipped with smart card readers). Is your scheme secure?

15. Can the Trojan horse attack work in a system protected by capabilities?

16. Name a C compiler feature that could eliminate a large number of security holes. Why is it not more widely implemented?

17. When a file is removed, its blocks are generally put back on the free list, but they are not erased. Do you think it would be a good idea to have the operating system erase each block before releasing it? Consider both security and performance factors in your answer, and explain the effect of each.

18. How could TENEX be modified to avoid the password problem described in the text?

19. How can a parasitic virus (a) ensure that it will be executed before its host program, and (b) pass control back to its host after doing whatever it does?

20. Some operating systems require that disk partitions must start at the beginning of a track. How does this make life easier for a boot sector virus?

21. Change the program of Fig. 9-13 so it finds all the C programs instead of all the executable files.

22. The virus in Fig. 9-16(d) is encrypted. How can the dedicated scientists at the antivirus lab tell which part of the file is the key so they can decrypt the virus and reverse engineer it? What can Virgil do to make their job a lot harder?

23. The virus of Fig. 9-16(c) has both a compressor and a decompressor. The decompressor is needed to expand and run the compressed executable program. What is the compressor for?

24. Name one disadvantage of a polymorphic encrypting virus *from the point of view of the virus writer.*

25. Often one sees the following instructions for recovering from a virus attack:

    1. Boot the infected system.
    2. Back up all files to an external medium.
    3. Run *fdisk* to format the disk.
    4. Reinstall the operating system from the original CD-ROM.
    5. Reload the files from the external medium.

    Name two serious errors in these instructions.

26. Are companion viruses (viruses that do not modify any existing files) possible in UNIX? If so, how? If not, why not?

27. What is the difference between a virus and a worm? How do they each reproduce?

28. Self-extracting archives, which contain one or more compressed files packaged with an extraction program, are frequently used to deliver programs or program updates. Discuss the security implications of this technique.

29. On some machines, the SHR instruction used in Fig. 9-18(b) fills the unused bits with zeros; on others the sign bit is extended to the right. For the correctness of Fig. 9-18(b), does it matter which kind of shift instruction is used? If so, which is better?

30. Represent the ownerships and permissions shown in this UNIX directory listing as a protection matrix. *Note*: asw is a member of two groups: *users* and *devel*; gmw is a member of only *users*. Treat each of the two users and two groups as a domain, so the matrix has four rows (one per domain) and four columns (one per file).

−rw−r−−r−−	2	gmw	users	908	May 26 16:45 PPP−Notes
−rwx r−x r−x	1	asw	devel	432	May 13 12:35 prog1
−rw−rw−−−−	1	asw	users	50094	May 30 17:51 project.t
−rw−r−−−−−	1	asw	devel	13124	May 31 14:30 splash.gif

31. Express the permissions shown in the directory listing of the previous problem as access control lists.

32. Modify the ACL for one file to grant or deny an access that cannot be expressed using the UNIX *rwx* system. Explain this modification.

33. To verify that an applet has been signed by a trusted vendor, the applet vendor may include a certificate signed by trusted third party that contains its public key. However, to read the certificate, the user needs the trusted third party's public key. This could be provided by a trusted fourth party, but then the user needs that public key. It appears that there is no way to bootstrap the verification system, yet existing browsers use it. How could it work?

34. In a full access control matrix, the rows are for domains and the columns are for objects. What happens if some object is needed in two domains?

35. Two different protection mechanisms that we have discussed are capabilities and access control lists. For each of the following protection problems, tell which of these mechanisms can be used.

   (a) Ken wants his files readable by everyone except his office mate.
   (b) Mitch and Steve want to share some secret files.
   (c) Linda wants some of her files to be public.

36. In the Amoeba scheme for protecting capabilities, a user can ask the server to produce a new capability with fewer rights, which can then be given to a friend. What happens if the friend asks the server to remove even more rights so the friend can give it to yet someone else?

37. In Fig. 9-31, there is no arrow from process *B* to object *1*. Would such an arrow be allowed? If not, what rule would it violate?

38. In Fig. 9-31, there is no arrow from object *2* to process *A*. Would such an arrow be allowed? If not, what rule would it violate?

39. If process to process messages were allowed in Fig. 9-31, what rules would apply to them? For process *B* in particular, to which processes could it send messages and which not?

40. Consider the steganographic system of Fig. 9-35. Each pixel can be represented in a color space by a point in the 3-dimensional system with axes for the R, G, and B values. Using this space, explain what happens to the color resolution when steganography is employed as it is in this figure.

41. Natural-language text in ASCII can be compressed by at least 50% using various compression algorithms. Using this knowledge, what is the steganographic carrying capacity for ASCII text (in bytes) of a 1600×1200 image stored using the low-order bits of each pixel? How much is the image size increased by the use of this technique (assuming no encryption or no expansion due to encryption)? What is the efficiency of the scheme, that is payload/(bytes transmitted)?

42. Suppose that a tightly-knit group of political dissidents living in a repressive country are using steganography to send out messages to the world about conditions in their country. The government is aware of this and is fighting them by sending out bogus images containing false steganographic messages. How can the dissidents try to help people tell the real messages from the false ones?

43. Write a pair of shell scripts to send and receive a text message by a covert channel on a UNIX system. (*Hint*: use the execution time of processes as your covert signal. The *sleep* command is guaranteed to run for a minimum time, set by its argument, and the *ps* command can be used to see all running processes).

44. Write a pair of programs, in C or as shell scripts, to send and receive a message by a covert channel on a UNIX system. *Hint*: A permission bit can be seen even when a file is otherwise inaccessible, and the *sleep* command or system call can is guaranteed to delay for a fixed time, set by its argument. Measure the data rate on an idle system. Then create an artificially heavy load by starting up numerous different background processes and measure the data rate again.

10

CASE STUDY 1: UNIX AND LINUX

In the previous chapters, we examined many operating system principles, abstractions, algorithms, and techniques in general. Now it is time to look at some concrete systems to see how these principles are applied in the real world. We will begin with UNIX because it runs on a wider variety of computers than any other operating system. It is the dominant operating system on high-end workstations and servers, but it is also used on systems ranging from notebook computers to supercomputers. It was carefully designed with a clear goal in mind, and despite its age, is still modern and elegant. Many important design principles are illustrated by UNIX. Quite a few of these have been copied by other systems.

Our discussion of UNIX will start with its history and evolution of the system. Then we will provide an overview of the system, to give an idea of how it is used. This overview will be of special value to readers familiar only with Windows, since the latter hides virtually all the details of the system from its users. Although graphical interfaces may be easy for beginners, they provide little flexibility and no insight into how the system works.

Next we come to the heart of this chapter, an examination of processes, memory management, I/O, the file system, and security in UNIX. For each topic we will first discuss the fundamental concepts, then the system calls, and finally the implementation.

One problem that we will encounter is that there are many versions and clones of UNIX, including AIX, BSD, 1BSD, HP-UX, Linux, MINIX, OSF/1, SCO UNIX, System V, Solaris, XENIX, and various others, and each of these has gone through many versions. Fortunately, the fundamental principles and system calls are pretty much the same for all of them (by design). Furthermore, the general implementation strategies, algorithms, and data structures are similar, but there are some differences. In this chapter we will draw upon several examples when discussing implementation, primarily 4.4BSD (which forms the basis for FreeBSD), System V Release 4, and Linux. Additional information about various implementations can be found in (Beck et al., 1998; Goodheart and Cox, 1994; Maxwell, 1999; McKusick et al., 1996; Pate, 1996; and Vahalia, 1996).

10.1 HISTORY OF UNIX

UNIX has a long and interesting history, so we will begin our study there. What started out as the pet project of one young researcher has become a multimillion dollar industry involving universities, multinational corporations, governments, and international standardization bodies. In the following pages we will tell how this story has unfolded.

10.1.1 UNICS

Back in the 1940s and 1950s, all computers were personal computers, at least in the sense that the then-normal way to use a computer was to sign up for an hour of time and take over the entire machine for that period. Of course, these machines were physically immense, but only one person (the programmer) could use them at any given time. When batch systems took over, in the 1960s, the programmer submitted a job on punched cards by bringing it to the machine room. When enough jobs had been assembled, the operator read them all in as a single batch. It usually took an hour or more after submitting a job until the output was returned. Under these circumstances, debugging was a time-consuming process, because a single misplaced comma might result in wasting several hours of the programmer's time.

To get around what almost everyone viewed as an unsatisfactory and unproductive arrangement, timesharing was invented at Dartmouth College and M.I.T. The Dartmouth system ran only BASIC and enjoyed a short-term commercial success before vanishing. The M.I.T. system, CTSS, was general purpose and was an enormous success among the scientific community. Within a short time, researchers at M.I.T. joined forces with Bell Labs and General Electric (then a computer vendor) and began designing a second generation system, **MULTICS (MULTiplexed Information and Computing Service**), as we discussed in Chap. 1.

Although Bell Labs was one of the founding partners in the MULTICS project, it later pulled out, which left one of the Bell Labs researchers, Ken Thompson, looking around for something interesting to do. He eventually decided to write a stripped down MULTICS by himself (in assembler this time) on a discarded PDP-7 minicomputer. Despite the tiny size of the PDP-7, Thompson's system actually worked and could support Thompson's development effort. Consequently, one of the other researchers at Bell Labs, Brian Kernighan, somewhat jokingly called it **UNICS (UNiplexed Information and Computing Service)**. Despite puns about "EUNUCHS" being a castrated MULTICS, the name stuck, although the spelling was later changed to **UNIX**.

10.1.2 PDP-11 UNIX

Thompson's work so impressed his colleagues at Bell Labs, that he was soon joined by Dennis Ritchie, and later by his entire department. Two major developments occurred around this time. First, UNIX was moved from the obsolete PDP-7 to the much more modern PDP-11/20 and then later to the PDP-11/45 and PDP-11/70. The latter two machines dominated the minicomputer world for much of the 1970s. The PDP-11/45 and PDP-11/70 were powerful machines with large physical memories for their era (256 KB and 2 MB, respectively). Also, they had memory protection hardware, making it possible to support multiple users at the same time. However, they were both 16-bit machines that limited individual processes to 64 KB of instruction space and 64 KB of data space, even though the machine may have had far more physical memory.

The second development concerned the language in which UNIX was written. By now it was becoming painfully obvious that having to rewrite the entire system for each new machine was no fun at all, so Thompson decided to rewrite UNIX in a high-level language of his own design, called **B**. B was a simplified form of BCPL (which itself was a simplified form of CPL, which, like PL/I, never worked). Due to weaknesses in B, primarily lack of structures, this attempt was not successful. Ritchie then designed a successor to B, (naturally) called **C**, and wrote an excellent compiler for it. Together, Thompson and Ritchie rewrote UNIX in C. C was the right language at the right time, and has dominated system programming ever since.

In 1974, Ritchie and Thompson published a landmark paper about UNIX (Ritchie and Thompson, 1974). For the work described in this paper they were later given the prestigious ACM Turing Award (Ritchie, 1984; Thompson, 1984). The publication of this paper stimulated many universities to ask Bell Labs for a copy of UNIX. Since Bell Labs' parent company, AT&T, was a regulated monopoly at the time and was not permitted to be in the computer business, it had no objection to licensing UNIX to universities for a modest fee.

In one of those coincidences that often shape history, the PDP-11 was the computer of choice at nearly all university computer science departments, and the operating systems that came with the PDP-11 were widely regarded as being dreadful by professors and students alike. UNIX quickly filled the void, not in the least because it was supplied with the complete source code, so people could, and did, tinker with it endlessly. Numerous scientific meetings were organized around

UNIX, with distinguished speakers getting up in front of the room to tell about some obscure kernel bug they had found and fixed. An Australian professor, John Lions, wrote a commentary on the UNIX source code of the type normally reserved for the works of Chaucer or Shakespeare (reprinted as Lions, 1996). The book described Version 6, so named because it was described in the sixth edition of the UNIX Programmer's Manual. The source code was 8200 lines of C and 900 lines of assembly code. As a result of all this activity, new ideas and improvements to the system spread rapidly.

Within a few years, Version 6 was replaced by Version 7, the first portable version of UNIX (it ran on the PDP-11 and the Interdata 8/32), by now 18,800 lines of C and 2100 lines of assembler. A whole generation of students was brought up on Version 7, which contributed to its spread after they graduated and went to work in industry. By the mid 1980s, UNIX was in widespread use on minicomputers and engineering workstations from a variety of vendors. A number of companies even licensed the source code to make their own version of UNIX. One of these was a small startup called Microsoft, which sold Version 7 under the name XENIX for a number of years until its interest turned elsewhere.

10.1.3 Portable UNIX

Now that UNIX was written in C, moving it to a new machine, known as porting it, was much easier than in the early days. A port requires first writing a C compiler for the new machine. Then it requires writing device drivers for the new machine's I/O devices, such as terminals, printers, and disks. Although the driver code is in C, it cannot be moved to another machine, compiled, and run there because no two disks work the same way. Finally, a small amount of machine-dependent code, such as the interrupt handlers and memory management routines, must be rewritten, usually in assembly language.

The first port beyond the PDP-11 was to the Interdata 8/32 minicomputer. This exercise revealed a large number of assumptions that UNIX implicitly made about the machine it was running on, such as the unspoken supposition that integers held 16 bits, pointers also held 16 bits (implying a maximum program size of 64 KB), and that the machine had exactly three registers available for holding important variables. None of these were true on the Interdata, so considerable work was needed to clean UNIX up .

Another problem was that although Ritchie's compiler was fast and produced good object code, it produced only PDP-11 object code. Rather than write a new compiler specifically for the Interdata, Steve Johnson of Bell Labs designed and implemented the **portable C compiler**, which could be retargeted to produce code for any reasonable machine with a only a moderate amount of effort. For years, nearly all C compilers for machines other than the PDP-11 were based on Johnson's compiler, which greatly aided the spread of UNIX to new computers.

The port to the Interdata initially went slowly because all the development work had to be done on the only working UNIX machine, a PDP-11, which happened to be on the fifth floor at Bell Labs. The Interdata was on the first floor. Generating a new version meant compiling it on the fifth floor and then physically carrying a magnetic tape down to the first floor to see if it worked. After several months, a great deal of interest arose in the possibility of connecting these two machines together electronically. UNIX networking traces its roots to this link. After the Interdata port, UNIX was ported to the VAX and other computers.

After AT&T was broken up in 1984 by the U.S. government, the company was legally free to set up a computer subsidiary, and did. Shortly thereafter, AT&T released its first commercial UNIX product, System III. It was not well received, so it was replaced by an improved version, System V, a year later. Whatever happened to System IV is one of the great unsolved mysteries of computer science. The original System V has since been replaced by System V, releases 2, 3, and 4, each one bigger and more complicated than its predecessor. In the process, the original idea behind UNIX, of having a simple, elegant system has gradually diminished. Although Ritchie and Thompson's group later produced an 8th, 9th, and 10th edition of UNIX, these were never widely circulated, as AT&T put all its marketing muscle behind System V. However, some of the ideas from the 8th, 9th, and 10th editions were eventually incorporated into System V. AT&T eventually decided that it wanted to be a telephone company, not a computer company, after all, and sold its UNIX business to Novell in 1993. Novell then sold it to the Santa Cruz Operation in 1995. By then it was almost irrelevant who owned it since all the major computer companies already had licenses.

10.1.4 Berkeley UNIX

One of the many universities that acquired UNIX Version 6 early on was the University of California at Berkeley. Because the complete source code was available, Berkeley was able to modify the system substantially. Aided by grants from ARPA, the U.S. Dept. of Defense's Advanced Research Projects Agency, Berkeley produced and released an improved version for the PDP-11 called **1BSD** (**First Berkeley Software Distribution**). This tape was followed quickly by 2BSD also for the PDP-11.

More important were 3BSD and especially its successor, 4BSD, for the VAX. Although AT&T had a VAX version of UNIX, called **32V**, it was essentially Version 7. In contrast, 4BSD (including 4.1BSD, 4.2BSD, 4.3BSD, and 4.4BSD) contained a large number of improvements. Foremost among these was the use of virtual memory and paging, allowing programs to be larger than physical memory by paging parts of them in and out as needed. Another change allowed file names to be longer than 14 characters. The implementation of the file system was also changed, making it considerably faster. Signal handling was made more reliable.

Networking was introduced, causing the network protocol that was used, **TCP/IP**, to become a de facto standard in the UNIX world, and later in the Internet, which is dominated by UNIX-based servers.

Berkeley also added a substantial number of utility programs to UNIX, including a new editor (*vi*), a new shell (*csh*), Pascal and Lisp compilers, and many more. All these improvements caused Sun Microsystems, DEC, and other computer vendors to base their versions of UNIX on Berkeley UNIX, rather than on AT&T's "official" version, System V. As a consequence, Berkeley UNIX became well established in the academic, research, and defense worlds. For more information about Berkeley UNIX, see (McKusick et al., 1996).

10.1.5 Standard UNIX

By the late 1980s, two different, and somewhat incompatible, versions of UNIX were in widespread use: 4.3BSD and System V Release 3. In addition, virtually every vendor added its own nonstandard enhancements. This split in the UNIX world, together with the fact that there were no standards for binary program formats, greatly inhibited the commercial success of UNIX because it was impossible for software vendors to write and package UNIX programs with the expectation that they would run on any UNIX system (as was routinely done with MS-DOS). Various attempts at standardizing UNIX initially failed. AT&T, for example, issued the **SVID** (**System V Interface Definition**), which defined all the system calls, file formats, and so on. This document was an attempt to keep all the System V vendors in line, but it had no effect on the enemy (BSD) camp, which just ignored it.

The first serious attempt to reconcile the two flavors of UNIX was initiated under the auspices of the IEEE Standards Board, a highly respected and, most important, neutral body. Hundreds of people from industry, academia, and government took part in this work. The collective name for this project was **POSIX**. The first three letters refer to Portable Operating System. The *IX* was added to make the name UNIXish.

After a great deal of argument and counterargument, rebuttal and counterrebuttal, the POSIX committee produced a standard known as **1003.1**. It defines a set of library procedures that every conformant UNIX system must supply. Most of these procedures invoke a system call, but a few can be implemented outside the kernel. Typical procedures are *open*, *read*, and *fork*. The idea of POSIX is that a software vendor who writes a program that uses only the procedures defined by 1003.1 knows that this program will run on every conformant UNIX system.

While it is true that most standards bodies tend to produce a horrible compromise with a few of everyone's pet features in it, 1003.1 is remarkably good considering the large number of parties involved and their respective vested interests. Rather than take the union of all features in System V and BSD as the starting point (the norm for most standards bodies), the IEEE committee took the intersection. Very roughly, if a feature was present in both System V and BSD, it was included in the standard; otherwise it was not. As a consequence of this algorithm, 1003.1 bears a strong resemblance to the direct ancestor of both System V and BSD, namely Version 7. The two areas in which it most strongly deviates from Version 7 are signals (which is largely taken from BSD) and terminal handling, which is new. The 1003.1 document is written in such a way that both operating system implementers and software writers can understand it, another novelty in the standards world, although work is already underway to remedy this.

Although the 1003.1 standard addresses only the system calls, related documents standardize threads, the utility programs, networking, and many other features of UNIX. In addition, the C language has also been standardized by ANSI and ISO.

Unfortunately, a funny thing happened on the way back from the standards meeting. Now that the System V versus BSD split had been dealt with, another one appeared. A group of vendors led by IBM, DEC, Hewlett-Packard, and many others did not like the idea that AT&T had control of the rest of UNIX, so they set up a consortium known as **OSF (Open Software Foundation)** to produce a system that met all the IEEE and other standards, but also contained a large number of additional features, such as a windowing system (X11), a graphical user interface (MOTIF), distributed computing (DCE), distributed management (DME), and much more.

AT&T's reaction was to set up its own consortium, **UI (UNIX International)** to do precisely the same thing. UI's version of UNIX was based on System V. The net result is that the world then had two powerful industry groups each offering their own version of UNIX, so the users were no closer to a standard than they were in the beginning. However, the marketplace decided that System V was a better bet than the OSF system, so the latter gradually vanished. Some companies have their own variants of UNIX, such as Sun's Solaris (based on System V).

10.1.6 MINIX

One property that all these systems have is that they are large and complicated, in a sense, the antithesis of the original idea behind UNIX. Even if the source code were freely available, which it is not in most cases, it is out of the question that a single person could understand it all any more. This situation led to the author of this book writing a new UNIX-like system that was small enough to understand, was available with all the source code, and could be used for educational purposes. That system consisted of 11,800 lines of C and 800 lines of assembly code. It was released in 1987, and was functionally almost equivalent to Version 7 UNIX, the mainstay of most computer science departments during the PDP-11 era.

MINIX was one of the first UNIX-like systems based on a microkernel design. The idea behind a microkernel is to provide minimal functionality in the kernel to make it reliable and efficient. Consequently, memory management and the file system were pushed out into user processes. The kernel handled message passing between the processes and little else. The kernel was 1600 lines of C and 800 lines of assembler. For technical reasons relating to the 8088 architecture, the I/O device drivers (2900 additional lines of C) were also in the kernel. The file system (5100 lines of C) and memory manager (2200 lines of C) ran as two separate user processes.

Microkernels have the advantage over monolithic systems that they are easy to understand and maintain due to their highly modular structure. Also, moving code from the kernel to user mode makes them highly reliable because the crash of a user-mode process does less damage than the crash of a kernel-mode component. Their main disadvantage is a slightly lower performance due to the extra switches between user mode and kernel mode. However, performance is not everything: all modern UNIX systems run X Windows in user mode and simply accept the performance hit to get the greater modularity (in contrast to Windows, where the entire GUI is in the kernel). Other well-known microkernel designs of this era were Mach (Accetta et al., 1986) and Chorus (Rozier et al., 1988). A discussion of microkernel performance issues is given in (Bricker et al., 1991).

Within a few months of its appearance, MINIX became a bit of a cult item, with its own newsgroup, *comp.os.minix*, and over 40,000 users. Many users contributed commands and other user programs, so MINIX became a collective undertaking done by large numbers of users over the Internet. It was a prototype of other collaborative efforts that came later. In 1997, Version 2.0 of MINIX, was released and the base system, now including networking, had grown to 62,200 lines of code. A book about operating systems principles illustrated using the 500-page MINIX source code given in an appendix and on an accompanying CD-ROM is (Tanenbaum and Woodhull, 1997). MINIX is also available for free on the World Wide Web at URL *www.cs.vu.nl/~ast/minix.html* .

10.1.7 Linux

During the early years of MINIX development and discussion on the Internet, many people requested (or in many cases, demanded) more and better features, to which the author often said "No" (to keep the system small enough for students to understand completely in a one-semester university course). This continuous "No" irked many users. At this time, FreeBSD was not available, so that was not an option. After a number of years went by like this, a Finnish student, Linus Torvalds, decided to write another UNIX clone, named **Linux,** which would be a full-blown production system with many features MINIX was (intentionally) lacking. The first version of Linux, 0.01, was released in 1991. It was cross-developed on a MINIX machine and borrowed some ideas from MINIX ranging from the structure of the source tree to the layout of the file system. However, it was a monolithic rather than a microkernel design, with the entire operating system in the kernel. The code size totaled 9,300 lines of C and 950 lines of assembler, roughly similar to MINIX version in size and also roughly comparable in functionality.

Linux rapidly grew in size and evolved into a full production UNIX clone as virtual memory, a more sophisticated file system, and many other features were added. Although it originally ran only on the 386 (and even had embedded 386 assembly code in the middle of C procedures), it was quickly ported to other platforms and now runs on a wide variety of machines, just as UNIX does. One difference with UNIX does stand out however: Linux makes use of many special features of the *gcc* compiler and would need a lot of work before it would compile with an ANSI standard C compiler with no extra features.

The next major release of Linux was version 1.0, issued in 1994. It was about 165,000 lines of code and included a new file system, memory-mapped files, and BSD-compatible networking with sockets and TCP/IP. It also included many new device drivers. Several minor revisions followed in the next two years.

By this time, Linux was sufficiently compatible with UNIX that a vast amount of UNIX software was ported to Linux, making it far more useful than it would have otherwise been. In addition, a large number of people were attracted to Linux and began working on the code and extending it in many ways under Torvalds' general supervision.

The next major release, 2.0, was made in 1996. It consisted of about 470,000 lines of C and 8000 lines of assembly code. It included support for 64-bit architectures, symmetric multiprogramming, new networking protocols, and numerous other features. A large fraction of the total code mass was taken up by an extensive collection of device drivers. Additional releases followed frequently.

A large array of standard UNIX software has been ported to Linux, including over 1000 utility programs, X Windows and a great deal of networking software. Two different GUIs (GNOME and KDE) have also been written for Linux. In short, it has grown to a full-blown UNIX clone with all the bells and whistles a UNIX lover might want.

One unusual feature of Linux is its business model: it is free software. It can be downloaded from various sites on the Internet, for example: *www.kernel.org*. Linux comes with a license devised by Richard Stallman, founder of the Free Software Foundation. Despite the fact that Linux is free, this license, the **GPL** (**GNU Public License**), is longer than Microsoft's Windows 2000 license and specifies what you can and cannot do with the code. Users may use, copy, modify, and redistribute the source and binary code freely. The main restriction is that all works derived from the Linux kernel may not be sold or redistributed in binary form only; the source code must either be shipped with the product or be made available on request.

Although Torvalds still controls the kernel fairly closely, a large amount of user-level software has been written by numerous other programmers, many of them originally migrated over from the MINIX, BSD, and GNU (Free Software

Foundation) online communities. However, as Linux evolves, a steadily smaller fraction of the Linux community want to hack source code (witness hundreds of books telling how to install and use Linux and only a handful discussing the code or how it works). Also, many Linux users now forego the free distribution on the Internet to buy one of many CD-ROM distributions available from numerous competing commercial companies. A Web site listing over 50 companies that sell different Linux packages is *www.linux.org*. As more and more software companies start selling their own versions of Linux and more and more hardware companies offer to preinstall it on the computers they ship, the line between commercial software and free software is beginning to blur a little.

As a footnote to the Linux story, it is interesting to note that just as the Linux bandwagon was gaining steam, it got a big boost from an unexpected source—AT&T. In 1992, Berkeley, by now running out of funding, decided to terminate BSD development with one final release, 4.4BSD, (which later formed the basis of FreeBSD). Since this version contained essentially no AT&T code, Berkeley issued the software under an open source license (not GPL) that let everybody do whatever they wanted with it except one thing—sue the University of California. The AT&T subsidiary controlling UNIX promptly reacted by—you guessed it—suing the University of California. It simultaneously sued a company, BSDI, set up by the BSD developers to package the system and sell support, much as Red Hat and other companies now do for Linux. Since virtually no AT&T code was involved, the lawsuit was based on copyright and trademark infringement, including items such as BSDI's 1-800-ITS-UNIX telephone number. Although the case was eventually settled out of court, this legal action kept FreeBSD off the market just long enough for Linux to get well established. Had the lawsuit not happened, starting around 1993 there would have been a serious competition between two free, open source UNIX systems: the reigning champion, BSD, a mature and stable system with a large academic following dating back to 1977 versus the vigorous young challenger, Linux, just two years old but with a growing following among individual users. Who knows how this battle of the free UNICES would have turned out?

Given this history, strict POSIX conformance, and overlap between the user communities, it should not come as a surprise that many of Linux' features, system calls, programs, libraries, algorithms, and internal data structures are very similar to those of UNIX. For example, over 80% of the ca. 150 Linux system calls are exact copies of the corresponding system calls in POSIX, BSD, or System V. Thus to a first approximation, much of the description of UNIX given in this chapter also applies to Linux. In places where there are substantial algorithmic differences between UNIX and Linux (e.g., the scheduling algorithm), we will point that out and cover both. Where they are essentially the same, for the sake of brevity we will just refer to UNIX. Be warned that Linux is evolving rapidly, and with thousands of people hacking away on it, some of this material (based on version 2.2) is sure to become obsolete before long.

10.2 OVERVIEW OF UNIX

In this section we will provide a general introduction to UNIX and how it is used, for the benefit of readers not already familiar with it. Although different versions of UNIX differ in subtle ways, the material presented here applies to all of them. The focus here is how UNIX appears at the terminal. Subsequent sections will focus on system calls and how it works inside.

10.2.1 UNIX Goals

UNIX is an interactive system designed to handle multiple processes and multiple users at the same time. It was designed by programmers, for programmers, to use in an environment in which the majority of the users are relatively sophisticated and are engaged in (often quite complex) software development projects. In many cases, a large number of programmers are actively cooperating to produce a single system, so UNIX has extensive facilities to allow people to work together and share information in controlled ways. The model of a group of experienced programmers working together closely to produce advanced software is obviously very different from the personal computer model of a single beginner working alone with a word processor, and this difference is reflected throughout UNIX from start to finish.

What is it that good programmers want in a system? To start with, most like their systems to be simple, elegant, and consistent. For example, at the lowest level, a file should just be a collection of bytes. Having different classes of files for sequential access, random access, keyed access, remote access, etc. (as mainframes do) just gets in the way. Similarly, if the command

　　ls A*

means list all the files beginning with "A" then the command

　　rm A*

should mean remove all the files beginning with "A" and not remove the one file whose name consists of an "A" and an asterisk. This characteristic is sometimes called the *principle of least surprise*.

Another thing that experienced programmers generally want is power and flexibility. This means that a system should have a small number of basic elements that can be combined in an infinite variety of ways to suit the application. One of the basic guidelines behind UNIX is that every program should do just one thing and do it well. Thus compilers do not produce listings, because other programs can do that better.

Finally, most programmers have a strong dislike for useless redundancy. Why type *copy* when *cp* is enough? To extract all the lines containing the string "ard" from the file *f*, the UNIX programmer types

　　grep ard f

The opposite approach is to have the programmer first select the *grep* program (with no arguments), and then have *grep* announce itself by saying: "Hi, I'm *grep*, I look for patterns in files. Please enter your pattern." After getting the pattern, *grep* prompts for a file name. Then it asks if there are any more file names. Finally, it summarizes what it is going to do and ask if that is correct. While this kind of user interface may or may not be suitable for rank novices, it irritates skilled programmers no end. What they want is a servant, not a nanny.

10.2.2 Interfaces to UNIX

A UNIX system can be regarded as a kind of pyramid, as illustrated in Fig. 10-1. At the bottom is the hardware, consisting of the CPU, memory, disks, terminals, and other devices. Running on the bare hardware is the UNIX operating system. Its function is to control the hardware and provide a system call interface to all the programs. These system calls allow user programs to create and manage processes, files, and other resources.

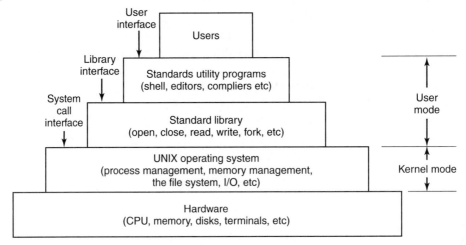

Figure 10-1. The layers in a UNIX system.

Programs make system calls by putting the arguments in registers (or sometimes, on the stack), and issuing trap instructions to switch from user mode to kernel mode to start up UNIX. Since there is no way to write a trap instruction in C, a library is provided, with one procedure per system call. These procedures are written in assembly language, but can be called from C. Each one first puts its arguments in the proper place, then executes the trap instruction. Thus to execute the read system call, a C program can call the *read* library procedure. As an aside, it is the library interface, and not the system call interface, that is specified by POSIX. In other words, POSIX tells which library procedures a conformant system must supply, what their parameters are, what they must do, and what results they must return. It does not even mention the actual system calls.

In addition to the operating system and system call library, all versions of UNIX supply a large number of standard programs, some of which are specified by the POSIX 1003.2 standard, and some of which differ between UNIX versions. These include the command processor (shell), compilers, editors, text processing programs, and file manipulation utilities. It is these programs that a user at a terminal invokes.

Thus we can speak of three different interfaces to UNIX: the true system call interface, the library interface, and the interface formed by the set of standard utility programs. While the latter is what the casual user thinks of as "UNIX," in fact, it has almost nothing to do with the operating system itself and can easily be replaced.

Some versions of UNIX, for example, have replaced this keyboard-oriented user interface with a mouse-oriented graphical user interface, without changing the operating system itself at all. It is precisely this flexibility that makes UNIX so popular and has allowed it to survive numerous changes in the underlying technology so well.

10.2.3 The UNIX Shell

Many UNIX systems have a graphical user interface of the kind made popular by the Macintosh and later Windows. However, real programmers still prefer a command line interface, called the **shell**. It is much faster to use, more powerful, easily extensible, and does not give the user RSI from having to use a mouse all the time. Below we will briefly describe the Bourne shell (*sh*). Since then, many new shells have been written (*ksh*, *bash*, etc.). Although UNIX fully supports a graphical environment (X Windows), even in this world many programmers simply make multiple console windows and act as if they have half a dozen ASCII terminals each running the shell.

When the shell starts up, it initializes itself, then types a **prompt** character, often a percent or dollar sign, on the screen and waits for the user to type a command line.

When the user types a command line, the shell extracts the first word from it, assumes it is the name of a program to be run, searches for this program, and if it finds it, runs the program. The shell then suspends itself until the program terminates, at which time it tries to read the next command. What is important here is simply the observation that the shell is an ordinary user program. All it needs is the ability to read from and write to the terminal, and the power to execute other programs.

Commands may take arguments, which are passed to the called program as character strings. For example, the command line

    cp src dest

invokes the *cp* program with two arguments, *src* and *dest*. This program interprets the first one to be the name of an existing file. It makes a copy of this file and calls the copy *dest*.

Not all arguments are file names. In

```
head –20 file
```

the first argument, *–20*, tells *head* to print the first 20 lines of *file*, instead of the default number of lines, 10. Arguments that control the operation of a command or specify an optional value are called **flags**, and by convention are indicated with a dash. The dash is required to avoid ambiguity, because the command

```
head 20 file
```

is perfectly legal, and tells *head* to first print the initial 10 lines of a file called *20*, and then print the initial 10 lines of a second file called *file*. Most UNIX commands accept multiple flags and arguments.

To make it easy to specify multiple file names, the shell accepts **magic characters**, sometimes called **wild cards**. An asterisk, for example, matches all possible strings, so

```
ls *.c
```

tells *ls* to list all the files whose name ends in *.c* If files named *x.c*, *y.c*, and *z.c* all exist, the above command is equivalent to typing

```
ls x.c y.c z.c
```

Another wild card is the question mark, which matches any one character. A list of characters inside square brackets selects any of them, so

```
ls [ape]*
```

lists all files beginning with "a", "p", or "e".

A program like the shell does not have to open the terminal in order to read from it or write to it. Instead, when it (or any other program) starts up, it automatically has access to a file called **standard input** (for reading), a file called **standard output** (for writing normal output), and a file called **standard error** (for writing error messages). Normally, all three default to the terminal, so that reads from standard input come from the keyboard and writes to standard output or standard error go to the screen. Many UNIX programs read from standard input and write to standard output as the default. For example,

```
sort
```

invokes the *sort* program, which reads lines from the terminal (until the user types a CTRL-D, to indicate end of file), sorts them alphabetically, and writes the result to the screen.

It is also possible to redirect standard input and standard output, as that is often useful. The syntax for redirecting standard input uses a less than sign (<)

followed by the input file name. Similarly, standard output is redirected using a greater than sign (>). It is permitted to redirect both in the same command. For example, the command

    sort <in >out

causes *sort* to take its input from the file *in* and write its output to the file *out*. Since standard error has not been redirected, any error messages go to the screen. A program that reads its input from standard input, does some processing on it, and writes its output to standard output is called a **filter**.

Consider the following command line consisting of three separate commands:

    sort <in >temp; head –30 <temp; rm temp

It first runs *sort*, taking the input from *in* and writing the output to *temp*. When that has been completed, the shell runs *head*, telling it to print the first 30 lines of *temp* and print them on standard output, which defaults to the terminal. Finally, the temporary file is removed.

It frequently occurs that the first program in a command line produces output that is used as the input on the next program. In the above example, we used the file *temp* to hold this output. However, UNIX provides a simpler construction to do the same thing. In

    sort <in | head –30

the vertical bar, called the **pipe symbol**, says to take the output from *sort* and use it as the input to *head*, eliminating the need for creating, using, and removing the temporary file. A collection of commands connected by pipe symbols, called a **pipeline**, may contain arbitrarily many commands. A four-component pipeline is shown by the following example:

    grep ter *.t | sort | head –20 | tail –5 >foo

Here all the lines containing the string "ter" in all the files ending in *.t* are written to standard output, where they are sorted. The first 20 of these are selected out by *head* which passes then to *tail*, which writes the last five (i.e., lines 16 to 20 in the sorted list) to *foo*. This is an example of how UNIX provides basic building blocks (numerous filters), each of which does one job, along with a mechanism for them to be put together in almost limitless ways.

UNIX is a general-purpose multiprogramming system. A single user can run several programs at once, each as a separate process. The shell syntax for running a process in the background is to follow its command with an ampersand. Thus

    wc –l <a >b &

runs the word count program, *wc*, to count the number of lines (–*l* flag) in its input, *a*, writing the result to *b*, but does it in the background. As soon as the command has been typed, the shell types the prompt and is ready to accept and handle the next command. Pipelines can also be put in the background, for example, by

    sort <x | head &

Multiple pipelines can run in the background simultaneously.

It is possible to put a list of shell commands in a file and then start a shell with this file as standard input. The (second) shell just processes them in order, the same as it would with commands typed on the keyboard. Files containing shell commands are called **shell scripts**. Shell scripts may assign values to shell variables and then read them later. They may also have parameters, and use if, for, while, and case constructs. Thus a shell script is really a program written in shell language. The Berkeley C shell is an alternative shell that has been designed to make shell scripts (and the command language in general) look like C programs in many respects. Since the shell is just another user program, various other people have written and distributed a variety of other shells.

10.2.4 UNIX Utility Programs

The user interface to UNIX consists not only of the shell, but also of a large number of standard utility programs. Roughly speaking, these programs can be divided into six categories, as follows:

1. File and directory manipulation commands.

2. Filters.

3. Program development tools such as editors and compilers.

4. Text processing.

5. System administration.

6. Miscellaneous.

The POSIX 1003.2 standard specifies the syntax and semantics of just under 100 of these, primarily in the first three categories. The idea of standardizing them is to make it possible for anyone to write shell scripts that use these programs and work on all UNIX systems. In addition to these standard utilities, there are many application programs as well, of course, such as Web browsers, image viewers, etc.

Let us consider some examples of these programs, starting with file and directory manipulation.

    cp a b

copies file *a* to *b*, leaving the original file intact. In contrast,

    mv a b

copies *a* to *b* but removes the original. In effect, it moves the file rather than really making a copy in the usual sense. Several files can be concatenated using *cat*, which reads each of its input files and copies them all to standard output, one after another. Files can be removed by the *rm* command. The *chmod* command allows the owner to change the rights bits to modify access permissions. Directories can be created with *mkdir* and removed with *rmdir*. To see a list of the files in a directory, *ls* can be used. It has a vast number of flags to control how much detail about each file is shown (e.g., size, owner, group, creation date), to determine the sort order (e.g., alphabetical, by time of last modification, reversed), to specify the layout on the screen, and much more.

We have already seen several filters: *grep* extracts lines containing a given pattern from standard input or one or more input files; *sort* sorts its input and writes it on standard output; *head* extracts the initial lines of its input; *tail* extracts the final lines of its input. Other filters defined by 1003.2 are *cut* and *paste*, which allow columns of text to be cut and pasted into files; *od* which converts its (usually binary) input to ASCII text, in octal, decimal, or hexadecimal; *tr*, which does character translation (e.g., lower case to upper case), and *pr* which formats output for the printer, including options to include running heads, page numbers, and so on.

Compilers and programming tools include *cc*, which calls the C compiler, and *ar*, which collects library procedures into archive files.

Another important tool is *make*, which is used to maintain large programs whose source code consists of multiple files. Typically, some of these are **header files**, which contain type, variable, macro, and other declarations. Source files often include these using a special *include* directive. This way, two or more source files can share the same declarations. However, if a header file is modified, it is necessary to find all the source files that depend on it, and recompile them. The function of *make* is to keep track of which file depends on which header, and similar things, and arrange for all the necessary compilations to occur automatically. Nearly all UNIX programs, except the smallest ones, are set up to be compiled with *make*.

A selection of the POSIX utility programs is listed in Fig. 10-2, along with a short description of each one. All UNIX systems have these programs, and many more.

10.2.5 Kernel Structure

In Fig. 10-1 we saw the overall structure of a UNIX system. Now let us zoom in and look more closely at the kernel before examining the various parts. Showing the kernel structure is slightly tricky since there are many different versions of UNIX, but although the diagram of Fig. 10-3 describes 4.4BSD, it also applies to many other versions with perhaps small changes here and there.

Program	Typical use
cat	Concatenate multiple files to standard output
chmod	Change file protection mode
cp	Copy one or more files
cut	Cut columns of text from a file
grep	Search a file for some pattern
head	Extract the first lines of a file
ls	List directory
make	Compile files to build a binary
mkdir	Make a directory
od	Octal dump a file
paste	Paste columns of text into a file
pr	Format a file for printing
rm	Remove one or more files
rmdir	Remove a directory
sort	Sort a file of lines alphabetically
tail	Extract the last lines of a file
tr	Translate between character sets

Figure 10-2. A few of the common UNIX utility programs required by POSIX.

System calls							Interrupts and traps	
Terminal handing		Sockets	File naming	Map-ping	Page faults	Signal handling	Process creation and termination	
Raw tty	Cooked tty	Network protocols	File systems		Virtual memory			
	Line disciplines	Routing	Buffer cache		Page cache		Process scheduling	
Character devices		Network device drivers	Disk device drivers				Process dispatching	
Hardware								

Figure 10-3. Structure of the 4.4BSD kernel.

The bottom layer of the kernel consists of the device drivers plus process dispatching. All UNIX drivers are classified as either character device drivers or block device drivers, with the main difference that seeks are allowed on block devices and not on character devices. Technically, network devices are character devices, but they are handled so differently that it is probably clearer to separate them, as has been done in the figure. Process dispatching occurs when an interrupt happens. The low-level code here stops the running process, saves its state in the kernel process table, and starts the appropriate driver. Process dispatching also happens when the kernel is finished and it is time to start up a user process again. Dispatching code is in assembler and is quite distinct from scheduling.

Above the bottom level, the code is different in each of the four "columns" of Fig. 10-3. At the left, we have the character devices. There are two ways they are used. Some programs, such as visual editors like *vi* and *emacs*, want every key stroke as it is hit. Raw terminal (tty) I/O makes this possible. Other software, such as the shell (*sh*), is line oriented and allows users to edit the current line before hitting ENTER to send it to the program. This software uses cooked mode and line disciplines.

Networking software is often modular, with different devices and protocols supported. The layer above the network drivers handles a kind of routing function, making sure the right packet goes to the right device or protocol handler. Most UNIX systems contain the full functionality of an Internet router within the kernel, although the performance is less than that of a hardware router, but this code predated modern hardware routers. Above the router code is the actual protocol stack, always including IP and TCP, but sometimes additional protocols as well. Overlaying all the network is the socket interface, which allows programs to create sockets for particular networks and protocols, getting back a file descriptor for each socket to use later.

On top of the disk drivers are the file system's buffer cache and the page cache. In early UNIX systems, the buffer cache was a fixed chunk of memory, with the rest of memory for user pages. In many modern UNIX systems, there is no longer a fixed boundary, and any page of memory can be grabbed for either function, depending on what is needed more.

On top of the buffer cache come the file systems. Most UNIX systems support multiple file systems, including the Berkeley fast file system, log-structured file system, and various System V file systems. All of these file systems share the same buffer cache. On top of the file systems come file naming, directory management, hard link and symbolic link management, and other file system properties that are the same for all file systems.

On top of the page cache is the virtual memory system. All the paging logic is here, such as the page replacement algorithm. On top of it is the code for mapping files onto virtual memory and the high-level page fault management code. This is the code that figures out what to do when a page fault occurs. It first checks if the memory reference is valid, and if so, where the needed page is located and how it can be obtained.

The last column deals with process management. Above the dispatcher is the process scheduler, which chooses which process to run next. If threads are managed in the kernel, thread management is also here, although threads are managed in user space on some UNIX systems. Above the scheduler comes the code for processing signals and sending them to the correct destination, as well as the process creation and termination code.

The top layer is the interface into the system. On the left is the system call interface. All system calls come here and are directed to one of the lower modules, depending on the nature of the call. On right part of the top layer is the entrance for traps and interrupts, including signals, page faults, processor exceptions of all kinds, and I/O interrupts.

10.3 PROCESSES IN UNIX

In the previous sections, we started out by looking at UNIX as viewed from the keyboard, that is, what the user sees at the terminal. We gave examples of shell commands and utility programs that are frequently used. We ended with a brief overview of the system structure. Now it is time to dig deeply into the kernel and look more closely at the basic concepts UNIX supports, namely, processes, memory, the file system, and input/output. These notions are important because the system calls—the interface to the operating system itself—manipulate them. For example, system calls exist to create processes, allocate memory, open files, and do I/O.

Unfortunately, with so many versions of UNIX in existence, there are some differences between them. In this chapter, we will emphasize the features common to all of them rather than focus on any one specific version. Thus in certain sections (especially implementation sections), the discussion may not apply equally to every version.

10.3.1 Fundamental Concepts

The only active entities in a UNIX system are the processes. UNIX processes are very similar to the classical sequential processes that we studied in Chap 2. Each process runs a single program and initially has a single thread of control. In other words, it has one program counter, which keeps track of the next instruction to be executed. Most versions of UNIX allow a process to create additional threads once it starts executing.

UNIX is a multiprogramming system, so multiple, independent processes may be running at the same time. Each user may have several active processes at once, so on a large system, there may be hundreds or even thousands of processes running. In fact, on most single-user workstations, even when the user is absent, dozens of background processes, called **daemons,** are running. These are started automatically when the system is booted. ("Daemon" is a variant spelling of "demon," which is a self-employed evil spirit.)

A typical daemon is the *cron daemon*. It wakes up once a minute to check if there is any work for it to do. If so, it does the work. Then it goes back to sleep until it is time for the next check.

This daemon is needed because it is possible in UNIX to schedule activities minutes, hours, days, or even months in the future. For example, suppose a user has a dentist appointment at 3 o'clock next Tuesday. He can make an entry in the cron daemon's database telling the daemon to beep at him at, say, 2:30. When the appointed day and time arrives, the cron daemon sees that it has work to do, and starts up the beeping program as a new process.

The cron daemon is also used to start up periodic activities, such as making daily disk backups at 4 A.M., or reminding forgetful users every year on October 31 to stock up on trick-or-treat goodies for Halloween. Other daemons handle incoming and outgoing electronic mail, manage the line printer queue, check if there are enough free pages in memory, and so forth. Daemons are straightforward to implement in UNIX because each one is a separate process, independent of all other processes.

Processes are created in UNIX in an especially simple manner. The fork system call creates an exact copy of the original process. The forking process is called the **parent process**. The new process is called the **child process**. The parent and child each have their own, private memory images. If the parent subsequently changes any of its variables, the changes are not visible to the child, and vice versa.

Open files are shared between parent and child. That is, if a certain file was open in the parent before the fork, it will continue to be open in both the parent and the child afterward. Changes made to the file by either one will be visible to the other. This behavior is only reasonable, because these changes are also visible to any unrelated process that opens the file as well.

The fact that the memory images, variables, registers, and everything else are identical in the parent and child leads to a small difficulty: How do the processes know which one should run the parent code and which one should run the child code? The secret is that the fork system call returns a 0 to the child and a nonzero value, the child's **PID** (**Process IDentifier**) to the parent. Both processes normally check the return value, and act accordingly, as shown in Fig. 10-4.

Processes are named by their PIDs. When a process is created, the parent is given the child's PID, as mentioned above. If the child wants to know its own PID, there is a system call, getpid, that provides it. PIDs are used in a variety of ways. For example, when a child terminates, the parent is given the PID of the child that just finished. This can be important because a parent may have many children. Since children may also have children, an original process can build up an entire tree of children, grandchildren, and further descendants.

Processes in UNIX can communicate with each other using a form of message passing. It is possible to create a channel between two processes into which one process can write a stream of bytes for the other to read. These channels are call-

```
pid = fork( );                /* if the fork succeeds, pid > 0 in the parent */
if (pid < 0) {
      handle_error( );        /* fork failed (e.g., memory or some table is full) */
} else if (pid > 0) {
                              /* parent code goes here. /*/
} else {
                              /* child code goes here. /*/
}
```

Figure 10-4. Process creation in UNIX.

ed **pipes**. Synchronization is possible because when a process tries to read from an empty pipe it is blocked until data are available.

Shell pipelines are implemented with pipes. When the shell sees a line like

    sort <f | head

it creates two processes, *sort* and *head*, and sets up a pipe between them in such a way that *sort*'s standard output is connected to *head*'s standard input. In this way, all the data that *sort* writes go directly to *head*, instead of going to a file. If the pipe fills up, the system stops running *sort* until *head* has removed some data from the pipe.

Processes can also communicate in another way: software interrupts. A process can send what is called a **signal** to another process. Processes can tell the system what they want to happen when a signal arrives. The choices are to ignore it, to catch it, or to let the signal kill the process (the default for most signals). If a process elects to catch signals sent to it, it must specify a signal handling procedure. When a signal arrives, control will abruptly switch to the handler. When the handler is finished and returns, control goes back to where it came from, analogous to hardware I/O interrupts. A process can only send signals to members of its **process group**, which consists of its parent (and further ancestors), siblings, and children (and further descendants). A process may also send a signal to all members of its process group with a single system call.

Signals are also used for other purposes. For example, if a process is doing floating-point arithmetic, and inadvertently divides by 0, it gets a a SIGFPE (floating-point exception) signal. The signals that are required by POSIX are listed in Fig. 10-5. Many UNIX systems have additional signals as well, but programs using them may not be portable to other versions of UNIX.

10.3.2 Process Management System Calls in UNIX

Let us now look at the UNIX system calls dealing with process management. The main ones are listed in Fig. 10-6. Fork is a good place to start the discussion. Fork is the only way to create a new process in UNIX systems. It creates an exact

Signal	Cause
SIGABRT	Sent to abort a process and force a core dump
SIGALRM	The alarm clock has gone off
SIGFPE	A floating-point error has occurred (e.g., division by 0)
SIGHUP	The phone line the process was using has been hung up
SIGILL	The user has hit the DEL key to interrupt the process
SIGQUIT	The user has hit the key requesting a core dump
SIGKILL	Sent to kill a process (cannot be caught or ignored)
SIGPIPE	The process has written to a pipe which has no readers
SIGSEGV	The process has referenced an invalid memory address
SIGTERM	Used to request that a process terminate gracefully
SIGUSR1	Available for application-defined purposes
SIGUSR2	Available for application-defined purposes

Figure 10-5. The signals required by POSIX.

duplicate of the original process, including all the file descriptors, registers and everything else. After the fork, the original process and the copy (the parent and child) go their separate ways. All the variables have identical values at the time of the fork, but since the entire parent core image is copied to create the child, subsequent changes in one of them do not affect the other one. The fork call returns a value, which is zero in the child, and equal to the child's PID in the parent. Using the returned PID, the two processes can see which is the parent and which is the child.

In most cases, after a fork, the child will need to execute different code from the parent. Consider the case of the shell. It reads a command from the terminal, forks off a child process, waits for the child to execute the command, and then reads the next command when the child terminates. To wait for the child to finish, the parent executes a waitpid system call, which just waits until the child terminates (any child if more than one exists). Waitpid has three parameters. The first one allows the caller to wait for a specific child. If it is −1, any old child (i.e., the first child to terminate) will do. The second parameter is the address of a variable that will be set to the child's exit status (normal or abnormal termination and exit value). The third one determines whether the caller blocks or returns if no child is already terminated.

In the case of the shell, the child process must execute the command typed by the user. It does this by using the exec system call, which causes its entire core image to be replaced by the file named in its first parameter. A highly simplified shell illustrating the use of fork, waitpid, and exec is shown in Fig. 10-7.

In the most general case, exec has three parameters: the name of the file to be executed, a pointer to the argument array, and a pointer to the environment array.

System call	Description
pid = fork( )	Create a child process identical to the parent
pid = waitpid(pid, &statloc, opts)	Wait for a child to terminate
s = execve(name, argv, envp)	Replace a process' core image
exit(status)	Terminate process execution and return status
s = sigaction(sig, &act, &oldact)	Define action to take on signals
s = sigreturn(&context)	Return from a signal
s = sigprocmask(how, &set, &old)	Examine or change the signal mask
s = sigpending(set)	Get the set of blocked signals
s = sigsuspend(sigmask)	Replace the signal mask and suspend the process
s = kill(pid, sig)	Send a signal to a process
residual = alarm(seconds)	Set the alarm clock
s = pause( )	Suspend the caller until the next signal

Figure 10-6. Some system calls relating to processes. The return code s is -1 if an error has occurred, *pid* is a process ID, and *residual* is the remaining time in the previous alarm. The parameters are what the name suggests.

```
while (TRUE) {                          /* repeat forever /*/
    type_prompt( );                     /* display prompt on the screen */
    read_command(command, params);      /* read input line from keyboard */

    pid = fork( );                      /* fork off a child process */
    if (pid < 0) {
        printf("Unable to fork0);       /* error condition */
        continue;                       /* repeat the loop */
    }

    if (pid != 0) {
        waitpid (-1, &status, 0);       /* parent waits for child */
    } else {
        execve(command, params, 0);     /* child does the work */
    }
}
```

Figure 10-7. A highly simplified shell.

These will be described shortly. Various library procedures, including *execl*, *execv*, *execle*, and *execve*, are provided to allow the parameters to be omitted or specified in various ways. All of these procedures invoke the same underlying system call. Although the system call is **exec**, there is no library procedure with this name; one of the others must be used.

Let us consider the case of a command typed to the shell such as

    cp file1 file2

used to copy *file1* to *file2*. After the shell has forked, the child locates and executes the file *cp* and passes it information about the files to be copied.

The main program of *cp* (and many other programs) contains the function declaration

    main(argc, argv, envp)

where *argc* is a count of the number of items on the command line, including the program name. For the example above, *argc* is 3.

The second parameter, *argv*, is a pointer to an array. Element *i* of that array is a pointer to the *i*-th string on the command line. In our example, *argv*[0] would point to the string "cp". Similarly, *argv*[1] would point to the 5-character string "file1" and *argv*[2] would point to the 5-character string "file2".

The third parameter of *main*, *envp*, is a pointer to the environment, an array of strings containing assignments of the form *name = value* used to pass information such as the terminal type and home directory name to a program. In Fig. 10-7, no environment is passed to the child, so the third parameter of *execve* is a zero in this case.

If **exec** seems complicated, do not despair; it is the most complex system call. All the rest are much simpler. As an example of a simple one, consider **exit**, which processes should use when they are finished executing. It has one parameter, the exit status (0 to 255), which is returned to the parent in the variable *status* of the **waitpid** system call. The low-order byte of *status* contains the termination status, with 0 being normal termination and the other values being various error conditions. The high-order byte contains the child's exit status (0 to 255), as specified in the child's call to **exit**. For example, if a parent process executes the statement

    n = waitpid(−1, &status, 0);

it will be suspended until some child process terminates. If the child exits with, say, 4 as the parameter to *exit*, the parent will be awakened with *n* set to the child's PID and *status* set to 0x0400 (0x as a prefix means hexadecimal in C). The low-order byte of *status* relates to signals; the next one is the value the child returned in its call to **exit**.

If a process exits and its parent has not yet waited for it, the process enters a kind of suspended animation called the **zombie state**. When the parent finally waits for it, the process terminates.

Several system calls relate to signals, which are used in a variety of ways. For example, if a user accidently tells a text editor to display the entire contents of a very long file, and then realizes the error, some way is needed to interrupt the editor. The usual choice is for the user to hit some special key (e.g., DEL or

CTRL-C), which sends a signal to the editor. The editor catches the signal and stops the print-out.

To announce its willingness to catch this (or any other) signal, the process can use the sigaction system call. The first parameter is the signal to be caught (see Fig. 10-5). The second is a pointer to a structure giving a pointer to the signal handling procedure, as well as some other bits and flags. The third one points to a structure where the system returns information about signal handling currently in effect, in case it must be restored later.

The signal handler may run for as long as it wants to. In practice, though, signal handlers are usually fairly short. When the signal handling procedure is done, it returns to the point from which it was interrupted.

The sigaction system call can also be used to cause a signal to be ignored, or to restore the default action, which is killing the process.

Hitting the DEL key is not the only way to send a signal. The kill system call allows a process to signal another related process. The choice of the name "kill" for this system call is not an especially good one, since most processes send signals to other ones with the intention that they be caught.

For many real-time applications, a process needs to be interrupted after a specific time interval to do something, such as to retransmit a potentially lost packet over an unreliable communication line. To handle this situation, the alarm system call has been provided. The parameter specifies an interval, in seconds, after which a SIGALRM signal is sent to the process. A process may have only one alarm outstanding at any instant. If an alarm call is made with a parameter of 10 seconds, and then 3 seconds later another alarm call is made with a parameter of 20 seconds, only one signal will be generated, 20 seconds after the second call. The first signal is canceled by the second call to alarm. If the parameter to alarm is zero, any pending alarm signal is canceled. If an alarm signal is not caught, the default action is taken and the signaled process is killed. Technically, alarm signals may be ignored, but that is a pointless thing to do.

It sometimes occurs that a process has nothing to do until a signal arrives. For example, consider a computer-aided instruction program that is testing reading speed and comprehension. It displays some text on the screen and then calls alarm to signal it after 30 seconds. While the student is reading the text, the program has nothing to do. It could sit in a tight loop doing nothing, but that would waste CPU time that a background process or other user might need. A better solution is to use the pause system call, which tells UNIX to suspend the process until the next signal arrives.

Thread Management System Calls

The first versions of UNIX did not have threads. That feature was added many years later. Initially there were many threads packages in use, but the proliferation of threads packages made writing portable code difficult. Eventually, the system calls used to manage threads were standardized as part of POSIX (P1003.1c).

The POSIX specification did not take a position on whether threads should be implemented in the kernel or in user space. The advantage of having user-space threads is that they can be implemented without having to change the kernel and thread switching is very efficient. The disadvantage of user-space threads is that if one thread blocks (e.g., on I/O, a semaphore, or a page fault), all the threads in the process block because the kernel thinks there is only one thread and does not schedule the process until the blocking thread is released. Thus the calls defined in P1003.1c were carefully chosen to be implementable either way. As long as user programs adhere carefully to the P1003.1c semantics, both implementations should work correctly. The most commonly-used thread calls are listed in Fig. 10-8. When kernel threads are used, these calls are true system calls; when user threads are used, these calls are implemented entirely in a user-space run-time library.

(For the truly alert reader, note that we have a typographical problem now. If the kernel manages threads, then calls such as "pthread_create," are system calls and following our convention should be set in Helvetica, like this: pthread_create. However, if they are simply user-space library calls, our convention for all procedure names is to use Times Italics, like this: *pthread_create*. Without prejudice, we will simply use Helvetica, also in the next chapter, in which it is never clear which Win32 API calls are really system calls. It could be worse: in the Algol 68 Report there was a period that changed the grammar of the language slightly when printed in the wrong font.)

Thread call	Description
pthread_create	Create a new thread in the caller's address space
pthread_exit	Terminate the calling thread
pthread_join	Wait for a thread to terminate
pthread_mutex_init	Create a new mutex
pthread_mutex_destroy	Destroy a mutex
pthread_mutex_lock	Lock a mutex
pthread_mutex_unlock	Unlock a mutex
pthread_cond_init	Create a condition variable
pthread_cond_destroy	Destroy a condition variable
pthread_cond_wait	Wait on a condition variable
pthread_cond_signal	Release one thread waiting on a condition variable

Figure 10-8. The principal POSIX thread calls.

Let us briefly examine the thread calls shown in Fig. 10-8. The first call, pthread_create, creates a new thread. It is called by

err = pthread_create(&tid, attr, function, arg);

This call creates a new thread in the current process running the code *function* with *arg* passed to it as a parameter. The new thread's ID is stored in memory at the location pointed to by the first parameters. The *attr* parameter can be used to specify certain attributes for the new thread, such as its scheduling priority. After successful completion, one more thread is running in the caller's address space than was before the call.

A thread that has done its job and wants to terminate calls pthread_exit. A thread can wait for another thread to exit by calling pthread_join. If the thread waited for has already exited, the pthread_join finishes immediately. Otherwise it blocks.

Threads can synchronize using locks called **mutexes**. Typically a mutex guards some resource, such as a buffer shared by two threads. To make sure that only one thread at a time accesses the shared resource, threads are expected to lock the mutex before touching the resource and unlock it when they are done. As long as all threads obey this protocol, race conditions can be avoided. Mutexes are like binary semaphores, that is, semaphores that can take on only the values of 0 and 1. The name "mutex" comes from the fact that mutexes are used to ensure mutual exclusion on some resource.

Mutexes can be created and destroyed by the calls pthread_mutex_init and pthread_mutex_destroy, respectively. A mutex can be in one of two states: locked or unlocked. When a thread needs to set a lock on an unlocked mutex (using pthread_mutex_lock), the lock is set and the thread continues. However, when a thread tries to lock a mutex that is already locked, it blocks. When the locking thread is finished with the shared resource, it is expected to unlock the corresponding mutex by calling pthread_mutex_unlock.

Mutexes are intended for short-term locking, such as protecting a shared variable. They are not intended for long-term synchronization, such as waiting for a tape drive to become free. For long-term synchronization, **condition variables** are provided. These are created and destroyed by calls to pthread_cond_init and pthread_cond_destroy, respectively.

A condition variable is used by having one thread wait on it, and another thread signal it. For example, having discovered that the tape drive it needs is busy, a thread would do pthread_cond_wait on a condition variable that all the threads have agreed to associate with the tape drive. When the thread using the tape drive is finally done with it (possibly even hours later), it uses pthread_cond_signal to release exactly one thread waiting on that condition variable (if any). If no thread is waiting, the signal is lost. In other words, condition variables do not count like semaphores. A few other operations are also defined on threads, mutexes, and condition variables.

10.3.3 Implementation of Processes in UNIX

A process in UNIX is like an iceberg: what you see is the part above the water, but there is also an important part underneath. Every process has a user part that runs the user program. However, when one of its threads makes a system call, it traps to kernel mode and begins running in kernel context, with a different memory map and full access to all machine resources. It is still the same thread, but now with more power and also its own kernel mode stack and kernel mode program counter. These are important because a system call can block part way through, for example, waiting for a disk operation to complete. The program counter and registers are then saved so the thread can be restarted in kernel mode later.

The kernel maintains two key data structures related to processes, the **process table** and the **user structure**. The process table is resident all the time and contains information needed for all processes, even those that are not currently present in memory. The user structure is swapped or paged out when its associated process is not in memory, in order not to waste memory on information that is not needed.

The information in the process table falls into the following broad categories:

1. **Scheduling parameters**. Process priority, amount of CPU time consumed recently, amount of time spent sleeping recently. Together, these are used to determine which process to run next.

2. **Memory image**. Pointers to the text, data, and stack segments, or, if paging is used, to their page tables. If the text segment is shared, the text pointer points to the shared text table. When the process is not in memory, information about how to find its parts on disk is here too.

3. **Signals**. Masks showing which signals are being ignored, which are being caught, which are being temporarily blocked, and which are in the process of being delivered.

4. **Miscellaneous**. Current process state, event being waited for, if any, time until alarm clock goes off, PID, PID of the parent process, and user and group identification.

The user structure contains information that is not needed when the process is not physically in memory and runnable. For example, although it is possible for a process to be sent a signal while it is swapped out, it is not possible for it to read a file. For this reason, information about signals must be in the process table, so they are in memory all the time, even when the process is not present in memory. On the other hand, information about file descriptors can be kept in the user structure and brought in only when the process is in memory and runnable.

The information contained in the user structure includes the following items:

1. **Machine registers**. When a trap to the kernel occurs, the machine registers (including the floating-point ones, if used) are saved here.

2. **System call state**. Information about the current system call, including the parameters, and results.

3. **File descriptor table**. When a system call involving a file descriptor is invoked, the file descriptor is used as an index into this table to locate the in-core data structure (i-node) corresponding to this file.

4. **Accounting**. Pointer to a table that keeps track of the user and system CPU time used by the process. Some systems also maintain limits here on the amount of CPU time a process may use, the maximum size of its stack, the number of page frames it may consume, and other items.

5. **Kernel stack**. A fixed stack for use by the kernel part of the process.

Bearing the use of these tables in mind, it is now easy to explain how processes are created in UNIX. When a fork system call is executed, the calling process traps to the kernel and looks for a free slot in the process table for use by the child. If it finds one, it copies all the information from the parent's process table entry to the child's entry. It then allocates memory for the child's data and stack segments, and makes exact copies of the parent's data and stack segments there. The user structure (which is often kept adjacent to the stack segment), is copied along with the stack. The text segment may either be copied or shared since it is read only. At this point, the child is ready to run.

When a user types a command, say, ls on the terminal, the shell creates a new process by forking off a clone of itself. The new shell then calls exec to overlay its memory with the contents of the executable file ls. The steps involved are shown in Fig. 10-9.

The mechanism for creating a new process is actually fairly straightforward. A new process table slot and user area are created for the child process and filled in largely from the parent. The child is given a PID, its memory map is set up, and it is given shared access to its parent's files. Then its registers are set up and it is ready to run.

In principle, a complete copy of the address space should be made, since the semantics of fork say that no memory is shared between parent and child. However, copying memory is expensive, so all modern UNIX systems cheat. They give the child its own page tables, but have them point to the parent's pages, only marked read only. Whenever the child tries to write on a page, it gets a protection fault. The kernel sees this and then allocates a new copy of the page to the child and marks it read/write. In this way, only pages that are actually written have to

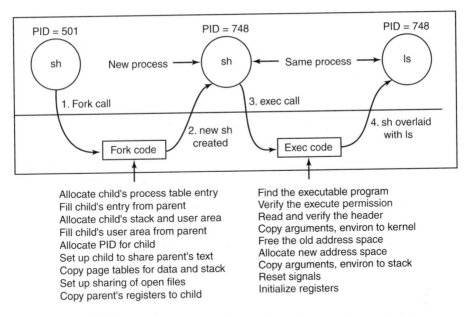

Figure 10-9. The steps in executing the command *ls* typed to the shell.

be copied. This mechanism is called **copy-on-write**. It has the additional benefit of not requiring two copies of the program in memory, thus saving RAM.

After the child process starts running, the code running there (a copy of the shell) does an exec, system call giving the command name as a parameter. The kernel now finds and verifies the executable file, copies the arguments and environment strings to the kernel, and releases the old address space and its page tables.

Now the new address space must be created and filled in. If the system supports mapped files, as System V, BSD, and most other UNIX systems do, the new page tables are set up to indicate that no pages are in memory, except perhaps one stack page, but that the address space is backed by the executable file on disk. When the new process starts running, it will immediately get a page fault, which will cause the first page of code to be paged in from the executable file. In this way, nothing has to be loaded in advance, so programs can start quickly and fault in just those pages they need and no more. Finally, the arguments and environment strings are copied to the new stack, the signals are reset, and the registers are initialized to all zeros. At this point, the new command can start running.

Threads in UNIX

The implementation of threads depends on whether they are supported in the kernel or not. If they are not, such as in 4BSD, the implementation is entirely in a user-space library. If they are, as in System V and Solaris, the kernel has some work to do. We discussed threads in a general way in Chap. 2. Here we will just make a few remarks about kernel threads in UNIX.

The main issue in introducing threads is maintaining the correct traditional UNIX semantics. First consider fork. Suppose that a process with multiple (kernel) threads does a fork system call. Should all the other threads be created in the new process? For the moment, let us answer that question with yes. Suppose that one of the other threads was blocked reading from the keyboard. Should the corresponding thread in the new process also be blocked reading from the keyboard? If so, which one gets the next line typed? If not, what should that thread be doing in the new process? The same problem holds for many other things threads can do. In a single-threaded process, the problem does not arise because the one and only thread cannot be blocked when calling fork. Now consider the case that the other threads are not created in the child process. Suppose that one of the not-created threads holds a mutex that the one-and-only thread in the new process tries to acquire after doing the fork. The mutex will never be released and the one thread will hang forever. Numerous other problems exist too. There is no simple solution.

File I/O is another problem area. Suppose that one thread is blocked reading from a file and another thread closes the file or does an lseek to change the current file pointer. What happens next? Who knows?

Signal handling is another thorny issue. Should signals be directed at a specific thread or at the process in general? A SIGFPE (floating-point exception) should probably be caught by the thread that caused it. What if it does not catch it? Should just that thread be killed, or all threads? Now consider the SIGINT signal, generated by the user at the keyboard. Which thread should catch that? Should all threads share a common set of signal masks? All solutions to these and other problems usually cause something to break somewhere. Getting the semantics of threads right (not to mention the code) is a nontrivial business.

Threads in Linux

Linux supports kernel threads in an interesting way that is worth looking at. The implementation is based on ideas from 4.4BSD, but kernel threads were not enabled in that distribution because Berkeley ran out of money before the C library could be rewritten to solve the problems discussed above.

The heart of the Linux implementation of threads is a new system call, clone, that is not present in any other version of UNIX. It is called as follows:

```
pid = clone(function, stack_ptr, sharing_flags, arg);
```

The call creates a new thread, either in the current process or in a new process, depending on *sharing_flags*. If the new thread is in the current process, it shares the address space with existing threads and every subsequent write to any byte in the address space by any thread is immediately visible to all the other threads in the process. On the other hand, if the address space is not shared, then the new thread gets an exact copy of the address space, but subsequent writes by the new thread are not visible to the old ones. These semantics are the same as fork.

In both cases, the new thread begins executing at *function*, which is called with *arg* as its only parameter. Also in both cases, the new thread gets its own private stack, with the stack pointer initialized to *stack_ptr*.

The *sharing_flags* parameter is a bitmap that allows a much finer grain of sharing than traditional UNIX systems. Five bits are defined, as listed in Fig. 10-10. Each bit controls some aspect of sharing, and each of the bits can be set independently of the other ones. The *CLONE_VM* bit determines whether the virtual memory (i.e., address space) is shared with the old threads or copied. If it is set, the new thread just moves in with the existing ones, so the clone call effectively creates a new thread in an existing process. If the bit is cleared, the new thread gets its own address space. Having its own address space means that the effect of its STORE instructions are not visible to the existing threads. This behavior is similar to fork, except as noted below. Creating a new address space is effectively the definition of a new process.

Flag	Meaning when set	Meaning when cleared
CLONE_VM	Create a new thread	Create a new process
CLONE_FS	Share umask, root, and working dirs	Do not share them
CLONE_FILES	Share the file descriptors	Copy the file descriptors
CLONE_SIGHAND	Share the signal handler table	Copy the table
CLONE_PID	New thread gets old PID	New thread gets own PID

Figure 10-10. Bits in the *sharing_flags* bitmap.

The *CLONE_FS* bit controls sharing of the root and working directories and of the umask flag. Even if the new thread has its own address space, if this bit is set, the old and new threads share working directories. This means that a call to chdir by one thread changes the working directory of the other thread, even though the other thread may have its own address space. In UNIX, a call to chdir by a thread always changes the working directory for other threads in its process, but never for threads in another process. Thus this bit enables a kind of sharing not possible in UNIX.

The *CLONE_FILES* bit is analogous to the *CLONE_FS* bit. If set, the new thread shares its file descriptors with the old ones, so calls to lseek by one thread are visible to the other ones, again as normally holds for threads within the same process but not for threads in different processes. Similarly, *CLONE_SIGHAND* enables or disables the sharing of the signal handler table between the old and new threads. If the table is shared, even among threads in different address spaces, then changing a handler in one thread affects the handlers in the others. Finally, *CLONE_PID* controls whether the new thread gets its own PID or shares its parent's PID. This feature is needed during system booting. User processes are not permitted to enable it.

This fine-grained sharing is possible because Linux maintains separate data structures for the various items listed at the start of Sec. 10.3.3 (scheduling parameters, memory image, etc.). The process table and user structure just point to these data structures, so it is easy to make a new process table entry for each cloned thread and have it either point to the old thread's scheduling, memory, and other data structures or to copies of them. The fact that such fine-grained sharing is possible does not mean that it is useful however, especially since UNIX does not offer this functionality. A Linux program that takes advantage of it is then no longer portable to UNIX.

Scheduling in UNIX

Let us now examine the UNIX scheduling algorithm. Because UNIX has always been a multiprogramming system, its scheduling algorithm was designed from the beginning to provide good response to interactive processes. It is a two-level algorithm. The low-level algorithm picks the process to run next from the set of processes in memory and ready to run. The high-level algorithm moves processes between memory and disk so that all processes get a chance to be in memory and run.

Each version of UNIX has a slightly different low-level scheduling algorithm, but most of them are close to the generic one we will describe now. The low-level algorithm uses multiple queues. Each queue is associated with a range of nonoverlapping priority values. Processes executing in user mode (the top of the iceberg) have positive values. Processes executing in kernel mode (doing system calls) have negative values. Negative values have the highest priority and large positive values have the lowest, as illustrated in Fig. 10-11. Only processes that are in memory and ready to run are located on the queues, since the choice must be made from this set.

When the (low-level) scheduler runs, it searches the queues starting at the highest priority (i.e., most negative value) until it finds a queue that is occupied. The first process on that queue is then chosen and started. It is allowed to run for a maximum of one quantum, typically 100 msec, or until it blocks. If a process uses up its quantum, it is put back on the end of its queue, and the scheduling algorithm is run again. Thus processes within the same priority range share the CPU using a round-robin algorithm.

Once a second, each process' priority is recalculated according to a formula involving three components:

$$priority = CPU\_usage + nice + base$$

Based on its new priority, each process is attached to the appropriate queue of Fig. 10-11, usually by dividing the priority by a constant to get the queue number. Let us now briefly examine each of the three components of the priority formula.

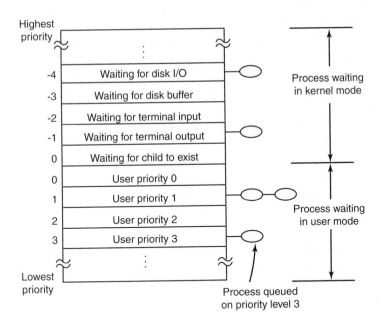

Figure 10-11. The UNIX scheduler is based on a multilevel queue structure.

CPU_usage, represents the average number of clock ticks per second that the process has had during the past few seconds. Every time the clock ticks, the CPU usage counter in the running process' process table entry is incremented by 1. This counter will ultimately be added to the process' priority giving it a higher numerical value and thus putting it on a lower-priority queue.

However, UNIX does not punish a process forever for using the CPU, so *CPU_usage* decays with time. Different versions of UNIX do the decay slightly differently. One way that has been used is to add the current value of *CPU_usage* to the number of ticks acquired in the past ΔT and divide the result by 2. This algorithm weights the most recent ΔT by ½, the one before that by ¼, and so on. This weighting algorithm is very fast because it just has one addition and one shift, but other weighting schemes have also been used.

Every process has a *nice* value associated with it. The default value is 0, but the allowed range is generally −20 to +20. A process can set *nice* to a value in the range 0 to 20 by the nice system call. A user computing π to a billion places in the background might put this call in his program to be nice to the other users. Only the system administrator may ask for *better* than normal service (meaning values from −20 to −1). Deducing the reason for this rule is left as an exercise for the reader.

When a process traps to the kernel to make a system call, it is entirely possible that the process has to block before completing the system call and returning to user mode. For example, it may have just done a waitpid system call and have to wait for one of its children to exit. It may also have to wait for terminal input or for disk I/O to complete, to mention only a few of the many possibilities. When it blocks, it is removed from the queue structure, since it is unable to run.

However, when the event it was waiting for occurs, it is put onto a queue with a negative value. The choice of queue is determined by the event it was waiting for. In Fig. 10-11, disk I/O is shown as having the highest priority, so a process that has just read or written a block from the disk will probably get the CPU within 100 msec. The relative priority of disk I/O, terminal I/O, etc. is hardwired into the operating system, and can only be modified by changing some constants in the source code and recompiling the system. These (negative) values are represented by *base* in the formula given above and are spaced far enough apart that processes being restarted for different reasons are clearly separated into different queues.

The idea behind this scheme is to get processes out of the kernel fast. If a process is trying to read a disk file, making it wait a second between read calls will slow it down enormously. It is far better to let it run immediately after each request is completed, so it can make the next one quickly. Similarly, if a process was blocked waiting for terminal input, it is clearly an interactive process, and as such should be given a high priority as soon as it is ready in order to ensure that interactive processes get good service. In this light, CPU bound processes (i.e., those on the positive queues) basically get any service that is left over when all the I/O bound and interactive processes are blocked.

Scheduling in Linux

Scheduling is one of the few areas in which Linux uses a different algorithm from UNIX. We have just examined the UNIX scheduling algorithm, so we will now look at the Linux algorithm. To start with, Linux threads are kernel threads, so scheduling is based on threads, not processes. Linux distinguishes three classes of threads for scheduling purposes:

1. Real-time FIFO.

2. Real-time round robin.

3. Timesharing.

Real-time FIFO threads are the highest priority and are not preemptable except by a newly-readied real-time FIFO thread. Real-time round-robin threads are the same as real-time FIFO threads except that they are preemptable by the clock. If multiple real-time round-robin threads are ready, each one is run for its quantum, after which it goes to the end of the list of real-time round-robin threads. Neither of these classes is actually real time in any sense. Deadlines cannot be specified and guarantees are not given. These classes are simply higher priority than threads in the standard timesharing class. The reason Linux calls them real time is that Linux is conformant to the P1003.4 standard ("real-time" extensions to UNIX) which uses those names.

Each thread has a scheduling priority. The default value is 20, but that can be altered using the nice(value) system call to a value of $20 - value$. Since *value* must be in the range −20 to +19, priorities always fall in the range: $1 \leq prior-ity \leq 40$. The intention is that the quality of service is roughly proportional to the priority, with higher priority threads getting faster response time and a larger fraction of the CPU time than lower priority threads.

In addition to a priority, each thread has a quantum associated with it. The quantum is the number of clock ticks the thread may continue to run for. The clock runs at 100 Hz by default, so each tick is 10 msec, which is called a **jiffy**. The scheduler uses the priority and quantum as follows. It first computes the **goodness** of each ready thread by applying the following rules:

```
if (class == real_time) goodness = 1000 + priority;
if (class == timesharing && quantum > 0) goodness = quantum + priority;
if (class == timesharing && quantum == 0) goodness = 0;
```

Both real-time classes count for the first rule. All that marking a thread as real time does is make sure it gets a higher goodness than all timesharing threads. The algorithm has one little extra feature: if the process that ran last still has some quantum left, it gets a bonus point, so that it wins any ties. The idea here is that all things being equal, it is more efficient to run the previous process since its pages and cache blocks are likely to be loaded.

Given this background, the scheduling algorithm is very simple: when a scheduling decision is made, the thread with the highest goodness is selected. As the selected thread runs, at every clock tick, its quantum is decremented by 1. The CPU is taken away from a thread if any of these conditions occur:

1. Its quantum hits 0.

2. The thread blocks on I/O, a semaphore, or something else.

3. A previously blocked thread with a higher goodness becomes ready.

Since the quanta keep counting down, sooner or later every ready thread will grind its quantum into the ground and they will all be 0. However, I/O bound threads that are currently blocked may have some quantum left. At this point the scheduler resets the quantum of *all* threads, ready and blocked, using the rule:

quantum = (quantum/2) + priority

where the new quantum is in jiffies. A thread that is highly compute bound will usually exhaust its quantum quickly and have it 0 when quanta are reset, giving it a quantum equal to its priority. An I/O-bound thread may have considerable quantum left and thus get a larger quantum next time. If nice is not used, the priority will be 20, so the quantum becomes 20 jiffies or 200 msec. On the other hand, for a highly I/O bound thread, it may still have a quantum of 20 left when quanta are reset, so if its priority is 20, its new quantum becomes $20/2 + 20 = 30$ jiffies. If another reset happens before it has spent 1 tick, next time it gets a quantum of $30/2 + 20 = 35$ jiffies. The asymptotic value in jiffies is twice the priority. As a consequence of this algorithm, I/O-bound threads get larger quanta and thus higher goodness than compute-bound threads. This gives I/O-bound threads preference in scheduling.

Another property of this algorithm is that when compute-bound threads are competing for the CPU, ones with higher priority get a larger fraction of it. To see this, consider two compute-bound threads, A, with priority 20 and B, with priority 5. A goes first and 20 ticks later has used up its quantum. Then B gets to run for 5 quanta. At this point the quanta are reset. A gets 20 and B gets 5. This goes on forever, so A is getting 80% of the CPU and B is getting 20% of the CPU.

10.3.4 Booting UNIX

The exact details of how UNIX is booted vary from system to system. Below we will look briefly at how 4.4BSD is booted, but the ideas are somewhat similar for all versions. When the computer starts, the first sector of the boot disk (the master boot record) is read into memory and executed. This sector contains a small (512-byte) program that loads a standalone program called *boot* from the boot device, usually an IDE or SCSI disk. The *boot* program first copies itself to a fixed high memory address to free up low memory for the operating system.

Once moved, *boot* reads the root directory of the boot device. To do this, it must understand the file system and directory format, which it does. Then it reads in the operating system kernel and jumps to it. At this point, *boot* has finished its job and the kernel is running.

The kernel start-up code is written in assembly language and is highly machine dependent. Typical work includes setting up the kernel stack, identifying the CPU type, calculating the amount of RAM present, disabling interrupts, enabling the MMU, and finally calling the C-language *main* procedure to start the main part of the operating system.

The C code also has considerable initialization to do, but this is more logical than physical. It starts out by allocating a message buffer to help debug boot problems. As initialization proceeds, messages are written here about what is happening, so they can be fished out after a boot failure by a special diagnostic program. Think of this as the operating system's cockpit flight recorder (the black box investigators look for after a plane crash).

Next the kernel data structures are allocated. Most are fixed size, but a few, such as the buffer cache and certain page table structures, depend on the amount of RAM available.

At this point the system begins autoconfiguration. Using configuration files telling what kinds of I/O devices might be present, it begins probing the devices to see which ones actually are present. If a probed device responds to the probe, it is added to a table of attached devices. If it fails to respond, it is assumed to be absent and ignored henceforth.

Once the device list has been determined, the device drivers must be located. This is one area in which UNIX systems differ somewhat. In particular, 4.4BSD cannot load device drivers dynamically, so any I/O device whose driver was not statically linked with the kernel cannot be used. In contrast, some other versions of UNIX, such as Linux, can load drivers dynamically (as can all versions of MS-DOS and Windows, incidentally).

The arguments for and against dynamically loading drivers are interesting and worth stating briefly. The main argument for dynamic loading is that a single binary can be shipped to customers with divergent configurations and have it automatically load the drivers it needs, possibly even over a network. The main argument against dynamic loading is security. If you are running a secure site, such as a bank's database or a corporate Web server, you probably want to make it impossible for anyone to insert random code into the kernel. The system administrator may keep the operating system sources and object files on a secure machine, do all system builds there, and ship the kernel binary to other machines over a local area network. If drivers cannot be loaded dynamically, this scenario prevents machine operators and others who know the superuser password from injecting malicious or buggy code into the kernel. Furthermore, at large sites, the hardware configuration is known exactly at the time the system is compiled and linked. Changes are sufficiently rare that having to relink the system when a new hardware device is added is not an issue.

Once all the hardware has been configured, the next thing to do is to carefully handcraft process 0, set up its stack, and run it. Process 0 continues initialization, doing things like programming the real-time clock, mounting the root file system, and creating *init* (process 1) and the page daemon (process 2).

Init checks its flags to see if it is supposed to come up single user or multiuser. In the former case, it forks off a process that execs the shell and waits for this process to exit. In the latter case, it forks off a process that executes the system initialization shell script, */etc/rc*, which can do file system consistency checks, mount additional file systems, start daemon processes, and so on. Then it reads */etc/ttys*, which lists the terminals and some of their properties. For each enabled terminal, it forks off a copy of itself, which does some housekeeping and then execs a program called *getty*.

Getty sets the line speed and other properties for each line (some of which may be modems, for example), and then types

login:

on the terminal's screen and tries to read the user's name from the keyboard. When someone sits down at the terminal and provides a login name, *getty* terminates by executing */bin/login*, the login program. *Login* then asks for a password, encrypts it, and verifies it against the encrypted password stored in the password file, */etc/passwd*. If it is correct, *login* replaces itself with the user's shell, which then waits for the first command. If it is incorrect, *login* just asks for another user name. This mechanism is illustrated in Fig. 10-12 for a system with three terminals.

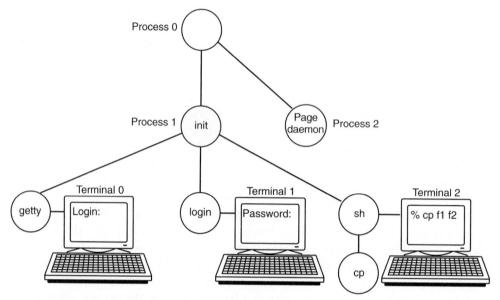

Figure 10-12. The sequence of processes used to boot some UNIX systems.

In the figure, the *getty* process running for terminal 0 is still waiting for input. On terminal 1, a user has typed a login name, so *getty* has overwritten itself with *login*, which is asking for the password. A successful login has already occurred on terminal 2, causing the shell to type the prompt (%). The user then typed

    cp f1 f2

which has caused the shell to fork off a child process and have that process exec the *cp* program. The shell is blocked, waiting for the child to terminate, at which time the shell will type another prompt and read from the keyboard. If the user at terminal 2 had typed *cc* instead of *cp*, the main program of the C compiler would have been started, which in turn would have forked off more processes to run the various compiler passes.

10.4 MEMORY MANAGEMENT IN UNIX

The UNIX memory model is straightforward, to make programs portable and to make it possible to implement UNIX on machines with widely differing memory management units, ranging from essentially nothing (e.g., the original IBM PC) to sophisticated paging hardware. This is an area of the design that has barely changed in decades. It has worked well so it has not needed much revision. We will now examine the model and how it is implemented.

10.4.1 Fundamental Concepts

Every UNIX process has an address space consisting of three segments: text, data, and stack. An example process' address space is depicted in Fig. 10-13(a) as process *A*. The **text segment** contains the machine instructions that form the program's executable code. It is produced by the compiler and assembler by translating the C, C++, or other program into machine code. The text segment is normally read-only. Self modifying programs went out of style in about 1950 because they were too difficult to understand and debug. Thus the text segment neither grows nor shrinks nor changes in any other way.

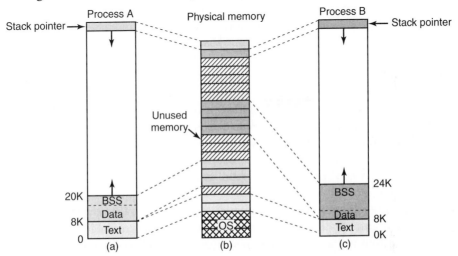

Figure 10-13. (a) Process *A*'s virtual address space. (b) Physical memory. (c) Process *B*'s virtual address space.

The **data segment** contains storage for the program's variables, strings, arrays, and other data. It has two parts, the initialized data and the uninitialized data. For historical reasons, the latter is known as the **BSS**. The initialized part of the data segment contains variables and compiler constants that need an initial value when the program is started.

For example, in C it is possible to declare a character string and initialize it at the same time. When the program starts up, it expects that the string has its initial value. To implement this construction, the compiler assigns the string a location in the address space, and ensures that when the program is started up, this location contains the proper string. From the operating system's point of view, initialized data are not all that different from program text—both contain bit patterns produced by the compiler that must be loaded into memory when the program starts.

The existence of uninitialized data is actually just an optimization. When a global variable is not explicitly initialized, the semantics of the C language say that its initial value is 0. In practice, most global variables are not initialized, and are thus 0. This could be implemented by simply having a section of the executable binary file exactly equal to the number of bytes of data, and initializing all of them, including the ones that have defaulted to 0.

However, to save space in the executable file, this is not done. Instead, the file contains all the explicitly initialized variables following the program text. The uninitialized variables are all gathered together after the initialized ones, so all the compiler has to do is put a word in the header telling how many bytes to allocate.

To make this point more explicit, consider Fig. 10-13(a) again. Here the program text is 8 KB and the initialized data is also 8 KB. The uninitialized data (BSS) is 4 KB. The executable file is only 16 KB (text + initialized data), plus a short header that tells the system to allocate another 4 KB after the initialized data and zero it before starting the program. This trick avoids storing 4 KB of zeros in the executable file.

Unlike the text segment, which cannot change, the data segment can change. Programs modify their variables all the time. Furthermore, many programs need to allocate space dynamically, during execution. UNIX handles this by permitting the data segment to grow and shrink as memory is allocated and deallocated. A system call, brk, is available to allow a program to set the size of its data segment. Thus to allocate more memory, a program can increase the size of its data segment. The C library procedure *malloc*, commonly used to allocate memory, makes heavy use of this system call.

The third segment is the stack segment. On most machines, it starts at or near the top of the virtual address space and grows down toward 0. If the stack grows below the bottom of the stack segment, a hardware fault normally occurs, and the operating system lowers the bottom of the stack segment by one page. Programs do not explicitly manage the size of the stack segment.

When a program starts up, its stack is not empty. Instead, it contains all the environment (shell) variables as well as the command line typed to the shell to invoke it. In this way a program can discover its arguments. For example, when the command

    cp src dest

is typed, the *cp* program is run with the string "cp src dest" on the stack, so it can find out the names of the source and destination files. The string is represented as an array of pointers to the symbols in the string, to make parsing easier.

When two users are running the same program, such as the editor, it would be possible, but inefficient, to keep two copies of the editor's program text in memory at once. Instead, most UNIX systems support **shared text segments**. In Fig. 10-13(a) and Fig. 10-13(c) we see two processes, *A* and *B*, that have the same text segment. In Fig. 10-13(b) we see a possible layout of physical memory, in which both processes share the same piece of text. The mapping is done by the virtual memory hardware.

Data and stack segments are never shared except after a fork, and then only those pages that are not modified. If either one needs to grow and there is no room adjacent to it to grow into, there is no problem since adjacent virtual pages do not have to map onto adjacent physical pages.

On some computers, the hardware supports separate address spaces for instructions and data. When this feature is available, UNIX can use it. For example, on a computer with 32-bit addresses, if this feature is available, there would be 2^{32} bits of address space for instructions and an additional 2^{32} bits of address space for the data and stack segments to share. A jump to 0 goes to address 0 of text space, whereas a move from 0 uses address 0 in data space. This feature doubles the address space available.

Many versions of UNIX support **memory-mapped files**. This feature makes it possible to map a file onto a portion of a process' address space so the file can be read and written as if it were a byte array in memory. Mapping a file in makes random access to it much easier than using I/O system calls such as read and write. Shared libraries are accessed by mapping them in using this mechanism. In Fig. 10-14 we see a file that is mapped into two processes at the same time, at different virtual addresses.

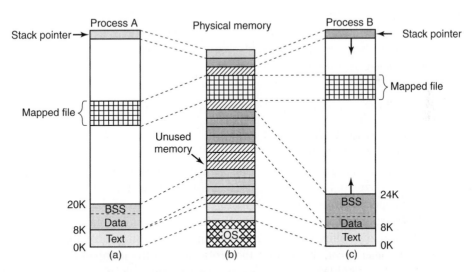

Figure 10-14. Two processes can share a mapped file.

An additional advantage of mapping a file in is that two or more processes can map in the same file at the same time. Writes to the file by any one of them are them instantly visible to the others. In fact, by mapping in a scratch file (which will be discarded after all the processes exit), this mechanism provides a high-bandwidth way for multiple processes to share memory. In the most extreme case, two or more processes could map in a file that covers the entire address space, giving a form of sharing that is partway between separate processes and threads. Here the address space is shared (like threads), but each process maintains its own open files and signals, for example, which is not like threads. In practice, making two address spaces exactly correspond is never done, however.

10.4.2 Memory Management System Calls in UNIX

POSIX does not specify any system calls for memory management. This topic was considered too machine dependent for standardization. Instead, the problem was swept under the rug by saying that programs needing dynamic memory management can use the *malloc* library procedure (defined by the ANSI C standard). How *malloc* is implemented is thus moved outside the scope of the POSIX standard. In some circles, this approach is known as passing the buck.

In practice, most UNIX systems have system calls for managing memory. The most common ones are listed in Fig. 10-15. Brk specifies the size of the data segment by giving the address of the first byte beyond it. If the new value is greater than the old one, the data segment becomes larger; otherwise it shrinks.

System call	Description
s = brk(addr)	Change data segment size
a = mmap(addr, len, prot, flags, fd, offset)	Map a file in
s = unmap(addr, len)	Unmap a file

Figure 10-15. Some system calls relating to memory management. The return code *s* is −1 if an error has occurred; *a* and *addr* are memory addresses, *len* is a length, *prot* controls protection, *flags* are miscellaneous bits, *fd* is a file descriptor, and *offset* is a file offset.

The mmap and munmap system calls control memory-mapped files. The first parameter to mmap, *addr*, determines the address at which the file (or portion thereof) is mapped. It must be a multiple of the page size. If this parameter is 0, the system determines the address itself and returns it in *a*. The second parameter, *len*, tells how many bytes to map. It, too, must be a multiple of the page size. The third parameter, *prot*, determines the protection for the mapped file. It can be marked readable, writable, executable, or some combination of these. The fourth parameter, *flags*, controls whether the file is private or sharable, and whether *addr* is a requirement or merely a hint. The fifth parameter, *fd*, is the file descriptor for the file to be mapped. Only open files can be mapped, so to map a file in, it must first be opened. Finally, *offset* tells where in the file to begin the mapping. It is not necessary to start the mapping at byte 0; any page boundary will do.

The other call, unmap, removes a a mapped file. If only a portion of the file is unmapped, the rest remains mapped.

10.4.3 Implementation of Memory Management in UNIX

Prior to 3BSD, most UNIX systems were based on swapping, which worked as follows. When more processes existed than could be kept in memory, some of them were swapped out to disk. A swapped out process was always swapped out in its entirety (except possibly for shared text). A process was thus either in memory or on disk.

Swapping

Movement between memory and disk was handled by the upper level of the two-level scheduler, known as the **swapper**. Swapping from memory to disk was initiated when the kernel ran out of free memory on account of one of the following events:

1. A fork system call needed memory for a child process.

2. A brk system call needed to expand a data segment.

3. A stack became larger and ran out of the space allocated to it.

In addition, when it was time to bring in a process that had been on disk too long, it was frequently necessary to remove another process to make room for it.

To choose a victim to evict, the swapper first looked at the processes that were blocked waiting for something (e.g., terminal input). Better to remove a process that could not run than one that could. If one or more were found, the one whose priority plus residence time was the highest was chosen. Thus a process that had consumed a large amount of CPU time recently was a good candidate, as was one that had been in memory for a long time, even if it was mostly doing I/O. If no blocked process was available, then a ready process was chosen based on the same criteria.

Every few seconds, the swapper examined the list of processes currently swapped out to see if any of them were ready to run. If any were, the one that had been on disk longest was selected. Next, the swapper checked to see if this was going to be an easy swap or a hard one. An easy swap was one for which enough free memory currently existed, so that no process had to be removed to make room for the new one. A hard swap required removing one or more processes. An easy swap was implemented by just bringing in the process. A hard one was implemented by first freeing up enough memory by swapping out one or more processes, then bringing in the desired process.

This algorithm was then repeated until one of two conditions was met: (1) no processes on disk were ready to run, or (2) memory was so full of processes that had just been brought in that there was no room left for any more. To prevent thrashing, no process was ever swapped out until it had been in memory for 2 sec.

Free storage in memory and on the swap device was kept track of by linked lists of holes. When storage was needed on either one, the appropriate hole list was read using the first fit algorithm, which returned the first sufficiently large hole it could find. The hole was then reduced in size, leaving only the residual part not needed. list.

Paging in UNIX

All versions of UNIX for the PDP-11 and Interdata machines, as well as the initial VAX implementation, were based on swapping, as just described. Starting with 3BSD, however, Berkeley added paging in order to handle the ever-larger programs that were being written. Virtually all UNIX systems now have demand paging, tracing their origins to 3BSD. Below we will describe the 4BSD design, but the System V one is closely based on 4BSD and is almost the same.

The basic idea behind paging in 4BSD is simple: a process need not be entirely in memory in order to run. All that is actually required is the user structure and the page tables. If these are swapped in, the process is deemed "in memory" and can be scheduled to run. The pages of the text, data, and stack segments are brought in dynamically, one at a time, as they are referenced. If the user structure and page table are not in memory, the process cannot be run until the swapper brings them in.

Berkeley UNIX does not use the working set model or any other form of prepaging because doing so requires knowing which pages are in use and which are not. Because the VAX did not have page reference bits, this information was not easily available (although it can be obtained in software at the cost of substantial additional overhead).

Paging is implemented partly by the kernel and partly by a new process called the **page daemon**. The page daemon is process 2 (process 0 is the swapper, and process 1 is init, as shown in Fig. 10-12). Like all daemons, the page daemon is started up periodically so it can look around to see if there is any work for it to do. If it discovers that the number of pages on the list of free memory pages is too low, it initiates action to free up more pages.

Main memory in 4BSD is organized as shown in Fig. 10-16. It consists of three parts. The first two parts, the kernel and core map, are pinned in memory (i.e., never paged out). The rest of memory is divided into page frames, each of which can contain a text, data, or stack page, a page table page, or be on the free list.

The **core map** contains information about the contents of the page frames. Core map entry 0 describes page frame 0, core map entry 1 describes page frame 1, and so forth. With 1-KB page frames and 16-byte core map entries, less than 2 percent of the memory is taken up by the core map. The first two items in the

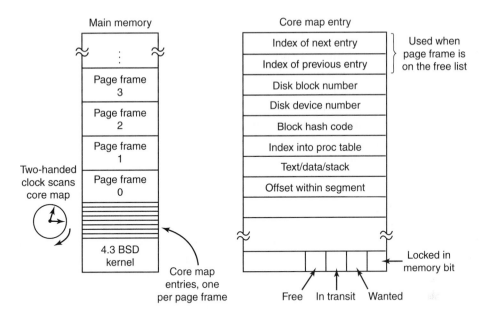

Figure 10-16. The core map in 4BSD.

core map entry shown in Fig. 10-16 are used only when the corresponding page frame is on the free list. Then they are used to hold a doubly linked list stringing together all the free page frames. The next three entries are used when the page frame contains information. Each page in memory also has a location on some disk where it is put when it is paged out. These entries are used to find the disk location where the page is stored. The next three entries give the process table entry for the page's process, which segment it is in, and where it is located in that segment. The last one shows some of the flags needed by the paging algorithm.

When a process is started, it may get a page fault because one or more of its pages are not present in memory. If a page fault occurs, the operating system takes the first page frame on the free list, removes it from the list, and reads the needed page into it. If the free list is empty, the process is suspended until the page daemon has freed a page frame.

The Page Replacement Algorithm

The page replacement algorithm is executed by the page daemon. Every 250 msec it is awakened to see if the number of free page frames is at least equal to a system parameter called *lotsfree* (typically set to 1/4 of memory). If insufficient page frames are free, the page daemon starts transferring pages from memory to disk until *lotsfree* page frames are available. If the page daemon discovers that more than *lotsfree* page frames are on the free list, it knows that it has nothing to do so it just goes back to sleep. If the machine has plenty of memory and few active processes, the page daemon sleep nearly all the time.

The page daemon uses a modified version of the clock algorithm. It is a global algorithm, meaning that when removing a page, it does not take into account whose page is being removed. Thus the number of pages each process has assigned to it varies in time.

The basic clock algorithm works by scanning the page frames circularly (as though they lay around the circumference of a clock). On the first pass, when the hand points to a page frame, the usage bit is cleared. On the second pass, any page frame that has not been accessed since the first pass will have its usage bit still cleared, and will be put on the free list (after writing it to disk, if it is dirty). A page frame on the free list retains its contents, which can be recovered if that page is needed before it is overwritten.

On a machine like the VAX that had no usage bits, when the clock hand pointed to a page frame on the first pass, the software usage bit was cleared and the page marked as invalid in the page table. When the page was next accessed, a page fault occurred, which allowed the operating system to set the software usage bit. The effect was the same as having a hardware usage bit, but the implementation was much more complicated and slower. Thus the software paid the price for poor hardware design.

Originally, Berkeley UNIX used the basic clock algorithm, but it was discovered that with large memories, the passes took too long. The algorithm was then modified to the **two-handed clock algorithm**, symbolized at the left of Fig. 10-16. With this algorithm, the page daemon maintains two pointers into the core map. When it runs, it first clears the usage bit at the front end, and then checks the usage bit at the back hand, after which it advances both hands. If the two hands are kept close together, then only very heavily used pages have much of a chance of being accessed between the time the front hand passes by and the time the back one does. If the two hands are 359 degrees apart (meaning the back hand is just ahead of the front hand), we are back to the original clock algorithm. Each time the page daemon runs, the hands rotate less than a full revolution, the amount depending on how far they have to go to get the number of pages on the free list up to *lotsfree*.

If the system notices that the paging rate is too high and the number of free pages is always way below *lotsfree*, the swapper is started to remove one or more processes from memory so that they will no longer compete for page frames. The 4BSD swap out algorithm is as follows. First the swapper looks to see if any processes have been idle for 20 sec or more. If any exist, the one that has been idle the longest is swapped out. If none exist, the four largest processes are examined and the one that has been in memory the longest is swapped out. If need be, the algorithm is repeated until enough memory has been recovered.

Every few seconds the swapper checks to see if any ready processes on the disk should be brought in. Each process on the disk is assigned a value that is a function of how long it has been swapped out, its size, the value it set using *nice* (if any), and how long it was sleeping before being swapped out. The function is weighted to usually bring in the process that has been out the longest, unless it is extremely large. The theory is that bringing in large processes is expensive, so they should not be moved too often. Swap-in only occurs if there are enough free pages, so that when the inevitable page faults start occurring, there will be page frames for them. Only the user structure and the page tables are actually brought in by the swapper. The text, data, and stack pages are paged in as they are used.

Each segment of each active process has a place on disk where it resides when it is paged or swapped out. Data and stack segments go to a scratch device, but program text is paged in from the executable binary file itself. No scratch copy is used for program text.

Paging in System V is fundamentally similar to that in 4BSD, which is not entirely surprising since the Berkeley version had been stable and running for years before paging was added to System V. Nevertheless, there are two interesting differences.

First, System V uses the original one-handed clock algorithm, instead of the two-handed one. Furthermore, instead of putting an unused page on the free list on the second pass, a page is only put there if it is unused for *n* consecutive passes. While this decision does not free pages as quickly as the Berkeley algorithm, it greatly increases the chance that a page once freed will not be needed again quickly.

Second, instead of a single variable *lotsfree*, System V has two variables, *min* and *max*. Whenever the number of free page frames falls below *min*, the page daemon is started to free up more pages. The daemon continues to run until there are *max* free page frames. This approach eliminates a potential instability in 4BSD. Consider a situation in which the number of free page frames is one less than *lotsfree*, so the page daemon runs to free one page and bring it up to *lotsfree*. Then another page fault occurs, using up one page frame, and reducing the number of available frames below *lotsfree* again, so the daemon has to run again. By setting *max* substantially above *min*, whenever the page daemon runs, it builds up a sufficient inventory so it does not have to run again for a substantial time.

Memory Management in Linux

Each Linux process on a 32-bit machine gets 3 GB of virtual address space for itself, with the remaining 1 GB reserved for its page tables and other kernel data. The kernel's 1 GB is not visible when running in user mode, but becomes accessible when the process traps into the kernel. The address space is created when the process is created and is overwritten on an **exec** system call.

The virtual address space is divided into homogeneous, contiguous, page-aligned areas or regions. That is to say, each area consists of a run of consecutive pages with the same protection and paging properties. The text segment and mapped files are examples of areas (see Fig. 10-14). There can be holes in the virtual address space between the areas. Any memory reference to a hole results in a fatal page fault. The page size is fixed, for example, 4 KB for the Pentium and 8 KB for the Alpha.

Each area is described in the kernel by a *vm_area_struct* entry. All the *vm_area_struct*s for a process are linked together in a list sorted on virtual address so all the pages can be found. When the list gets too long (more than 32 entries), a tree is created to speed up searching. The *vm_area_struct* entry lists the area's properties. These include the protection mode (e.g., read only or read/write), whether it is pinned in memory (not pageable), and which direction it grows in (up for data segments, down for stacks).

The *vm_area_struct* also records whether the area is private to the process or shared with one or more other processes. After a fork, Linux makes a copy of the area list for the child process, but sets up the parent and child to point to the same page tables. The areas are marked as read/write, but the pages are marked as read only. If either process tries to write on a page, a protection fault occurs and the kernel sees that the area is logically writable but the page is not, so it gives the process a copy of the page and marks it read/write. This mechanism is how copy-on-write is implemented.

The *vm_area_struct* also records whether the area has backing storage on disk assigned, and if so, where. Text segments use the executable binary as backing storage and memory-mapped files use the disk file as backing storage. Other areas, such as the stack, do not have backing storage assigned until they have to be paged out.

Linux uses a three-level paging scheme. Although this scheme was put into the system for the Alpha, it is also used (in degenerate form) for all architectures. Each virtual address is broken up into four fields, as shown in Fig. 10-17. The directory field is used as an index into the global directory, of which there is a private one for each process. The value found is a pointer to one of the page middle tables, which is again indexed by a field from the virtual address. The selected entry points to the final page table, which is indexed by the page field of the virtual address. The entry found here points to the page needed. On the Pentium, which uses two-level paging, each page middle directory has only one entry, so the global directory entry effectively chooses the page table to use.

Physical memory is used for various purposes. The kernel itself is fully hardwired; no part of it is ever paged out. The rest of memory is available for user pages, the buffer cache used by the file system, the paging cache, and other purposes. The buffer cache holds file blocks that have recently been read or have been read in advance in expectation of being used in the near future. It is dynamic in size and competes for the same pool of pages as the user pages. The paging cache is not really a separate cache, but simply the set of user pages that are no longer needed and are waiting around to be paged out. If a page in the paging cache is reused before it is evicted from memory, it can be reclaimed quickly.

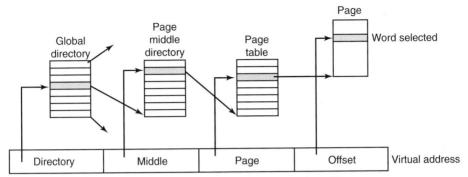

Figure 10-17. Linux uses three-level page tables.

In addition, Linux supports dynamically loaded modules, generally device drivers. These can be of arbitrary size and each one must be allocated a contiguous piece of kernel memory. As a consequence of these requirements, Linux manages physical memory in such a way that it can acquire an arbitrary-sized piece of memory at will. The algorithm it uses is known as the **buddy algorithm** and is described below.

The basic idea for managing a chunk of memory is as follows. Initially memory consists of a single contiguous piece, 64 pages in the simple example of Fig. 10-18(a). When a request for memory comes in, it is first rounded up to a power of two, say 8 pages. The full memory chunk is then divided in half, as shown in (b). Since each of these pieces is still too large, the lower piece is divided in half again (c) and again (d). Now we have a chunk of the correct size, so it is allocated to the caller, as shown shaded in (d).

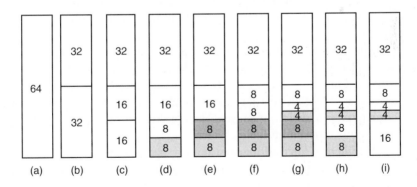

Figure 10-18. Operation of the buddy algorithm.

Now suppose that a second request comes in for 8 pages. This can be satisfied directly now (e). At this point a third request comes in for 4 pages. The smallest available chunk is split (f) and half of it is claimed (g). Next, the second of the 8-page chunks is released (h). Finally, the other 8-page chunk is released.

Since the two adjacent 8-page chunks that were just freed are buddies, that is, originated from the same 16-page chunk, they are merged to get the 16-page chunk back (i).

Linux manages memory using the buddy algorithm, with the additional feature of having an array in which the first element is the head of a list of blocks of size 1 unit, the second element is the head of a list of blocks of size 2 units, the next element points to the 4-unit blocks, etc. In this way, any power-of-2 block can be found quickly.

This algorithm leads to considerable internal fragmentation because if you want a 65-page chunk, you have to ask for and get a 128-page chunk.

To alleviate this problem, Linux has a second memory allocation that takes chunks using the buddy algorithm but then carves slabs (smaller units) from them and manages the smaller units separately. A third memory allocator is also available when the requested memory need only be contiguous in virtual space, but not in physical memory. All these memory allocators are derived from those in System V.

Linux is a demand-paged system with no prepaging and no working set concept (although there is a system call in which a user can give a hint that a certain page may be needed soon, in the hopes it will be there when needed). Text segments and mapped files are paged to their respective files on disk. Everything else is paged to either the paging partition, if present, or one of up to 8 fixed-length paging files. Paging files can be added and removed dynamically and each one has a priority. Paging to a separate partition, accessed as a raw device, is more efficient than paging to a file for several reasons. First, the mapping between file blocks and disk blocks is not needed (saves disk I/O reading indirect blocks). Second, the physical writes can be of any size, not just the file block size. Third, a page is always written contiguously to disk; with a paging file, it may or may not be.

Pages are not allocated on the paging device or partition until they are needed. Each device and file starts with a bitmap telling which pages are free. When a page without backing store has to be tossed out of memory, the highest priority paging partition or file that still has space is chosen and a page allocated on it. Normally, the paging partition, if present, has higher priority than any paging file. The disk location is written into the page table.

Page replacement works as follows. Linux tries to keep some pages free so they can be claimed as needed. Of course, this pool must be continually replenished, so the real paging algorithm is how this happens. At boot time, *init* starts up a page daemon, *kswapd*, that runs once a second. It checks to see if there are enough free pages available. If so, it goes back to sleep for another second, although it can be awakened early if more pages are suddenly needed. The page daemon's code consists of a loop that it executes up to six times, with increasingly high urgency. Why six? Probably the author of the code thought four was not enough and eight was too many. Linux is sometimes like that.

The body of the loop makes calls to three procedures, each of which tries to reclaim different kinds of pages. The urgency value is passed as a parameter telling the procedure how much effort to expend to reclaim some pages. Usually, this means how many pages to inspect before giving up. The effect of this algorithm is to first take the easy pages from each category before going after the hard ones. When enough pages have been reclaimed, the page daemon goes back to sleep.

The first procedure tries to reclaim pages from the paging cache and the file system buffer cache that have not been referenced recently, using a clock-like algorithm. The second procedure looks for shared pages that none of the users seems to be using much. The third procedure, which tries to reclaim ordinary user pages, is the most interesting, so let us take a quick look at it.

First, a loop is made over all the processes to see which one has the most pages currently in memory. Once that process is located, all of its *vm_area_struct*s are scanned and all the pages are inspected in virtual address order starting from where we left off last time. If a page is invalid, absent from memory, shared, locked in memory, or being used for DMA, it is skipped. If the page has its reference bit on, the bit is turned off and the page is spared. If the reference bit is turned off, out goes the page, so this part of the algorithm is similar to clock (except that the pages are not scanned in FIFO order).

If the page is chosen for eviction and it is clean, it is abandoned immediately. If it is dirty and has a backing store page on disk, it is scheduled for a disk write. Finally, if it is dirty and has no backing store page, it goes into the paging cache, from which it might conceivably get a reprieve later if it is reused before it is actually paged out. The idea of scanning the pages in virtual address order is based on the hope that pages near each other in virtual address space will tend to be used or not used as a group, so they should be written to disk as a group and later brought in together as a group.

One other aspect of the memory management system that we have not yet mentioned is a second daemon, *bdflush*. It wakes up periodically (and in some cases is explicitly awakened) to check if too large a fraction of the pages are dirty. If so, it starts writing them back to disk.

10.5 INPUT/OUTPUT IN UNIX

The I/O system in UNIX is fairly straightforward. Basically, all I/O devices are made to look like files and are accessed as such with the same read and write system calls that are used to access all ordinary files. In some cases, device parameters must be set, and this is done using a special system call. We will study these issues in the following sections.

10.5.1 Fundamental Concepts

Like all computers, those running UNIX have I/O devices such as disks, printers, and networks connected to them. Some way is needed to allow programs to access these devices. Although various solutions are possible, the UNIX one is to integrate the devices into the file system as what are called **special files**. Each I/O device is assigned a path name, usually in */dev*. For example, a disk might be */dev/hd1*, a printer might be */dev/lp*, and the network might be */dev/net*.

These special files can be accessed the same way as any other files. No special commands or system calls are needed. The usual read and write system calls will do just fine. For example, the command

    cp file /dev/lp

copies the *file* to printer, causing it to be printed (assuming that the user has permission to access */dev/lp*. Programs can open, read, and write special files the same way as they do regular files. In fact, *cp* in the above example is not even aware that it is printing. In this way, no special mechanism is needed for doing I/O.

Special files are divided into two categories, block and character. A **block special file** is one consisting of a sequence of numbered blocks. The key property of the block special file is that each block can be individually addressed and accessed. In other words, a program can open a block special file and read, say, block 124 without first having to read blocks 0 to 123. Block special files are typically used for disks.

Character special files are normally used for devices that input or output a character stream. Keyboards, printers, networks, mice, plotters, and most other I/O devices that accept or produce data for people use character special files. It is not possible (or even meaningful) to seek to block 124 on a mouse.

Associated with each special file is a device driver that handles the corresponding device. Each driver has what is called a **major device** number that serves to identify it. If a driver supports multiple devices, say, two disks of the same type, each disk has a **minor device** number that identifies it. Together, the major and minor device numbers uniquely specify every I/O device. In a few cases, a single driver handles two closely related devices. For example, the driver corresponding to */dev/tty* controls both the keyboard and the screen, which is often thought of as a single device, the terminal.

Although most character special files cannot be randomly accessed, they often need to be controlled in ways that block special files do not. Consider, for example, input typed on the keyboard and displayed on the screen. When a user makes a typing error and wants to erase the last character typed, he presses some key. Some people prefer to use backspace, and others prefer DEL. Similarly, to erase the entire line just typed, many conventions abound. Traditionally @ was used, but with the spread of email (which uses @ within email address), many systems have adopted CTRL-U or some other character. Likewise, to interrupt the running program, some special key must be hit. Here too, different people have different preferences.

Rather than making a choice and forcing everyone to use it, UNIX allows all these special functions and many others to be customized by the user. A special system call is generally provided for setting these options. This system call also handles tab expansion, enabling and disabling of character echoing, conversion between carriage return and line feed, and similar items. The system call is not permitted on regular files or block special files.

Networking

Another example of I/O is networking, as pioneered by Berkeley UNIX, and summarized below. The key concept in the Berkeley design is the **socket**. Sockets are analogous to mailboxes and telephone wall sockets in that they allow users to interface to the network, just as mailboxes allow people to interface to the postal system and telephone wall sockets allow them to plug in telephones and connect to the telephone system. The sockets' position is shown in Fig. 10-19.

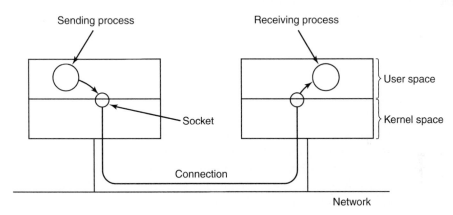

Figure 10-19. The uses of sockets for networking.

Sockets can be created and destroyed dynamically. Creating a socket returns a file descriptor, which is needed for establishing a connection, reading data, writing data, and releasing the connection.

Each socket supports a particular type of networking, specified when the socket is created. The most common types are

1. Reliable connection-oriented byte stream.

2. Reliable connection-oriented packet stream.

3. Unreliable packet transmission.

The first socket type allows two processes on different machines to establish the equivalent of a pipe between them. Bytes are pumped in at one end and they come out in the same order at the other. The system guarantees that all bytes that are sent arrive and in the same order they were sent.

The second type is similar to the first one, except that it preserves packet boundaries. If the sender makes five separate calls to write, each for 512 bytes, and the receiver asks for 2560 bytes, with a type 1 socket, all 2560 bytes will be returned at once. With a type 2 socket, only 512 bytes will be returned. Four more calls are needed to get the rest. The third type of socket is used to give the user access to the raw network. This type is especially useful for real-time applications, and for those situations in which the user wants to implement a specialized error handling scheme. Packets may be lost or reordered by the network. There are no guarantees, as in the first two cases. The advantage of this mode is higher performance, which sometimes outweighs reliability (e.g., for multimedia delivery, in which being fast counts for more than being right).

When a socket is created, one of the parameters specifies the protocol to be used for it. For reliable byte streams, the most popular protocol is **TCP** (**Transmission Control Protocol**). For unreliable packet-oriented transmission, **UDP** (**User Datagram Protocol**) is the usual choice. Both are these are layered on top of **IP** (**Internet Protocol**). All of these protocols originated with the U.S. Dept. of Defense's ARPANET, and now form the basis of the Internet. There is no common protocol for reliable packet streams.

Before a socket can be used for networking, it must have an address bound to it. This address can be in one of several naming domains. The most common domain is the Internet naming domain, which uses 32-bit integers for naming endpoints in Version 4 and 128-bit integers in Version 6 (Version 5 was an experimental system that never made it to the major leagues).

Once sockets have been created on both the source and destination computers, a connection can be established between them (for connection-oriented communication). One party makes a listen system call on a local socket, which creates a buffer and blocks until data arrive. The other one makes a connect system call, giving as parameters the file descriptor for a local socket and the address of a remote socket. If the remote party accepts the call, the system then establishes a connection between the sockets.

Once a connection has been established, it functions analogously to a pipe. A process can read and write from it using the file descriptor for its local socket. When the connection is no longer needed, it can be closed in the usual way, via the close system call.

10.5.2 Input/Output System Calls in UNIX

Each I/O device in a UNIX system generally has a special file associated with it. Most I/O can be done by just using the proper file, eliminating the need for special system calls. Nevertheless, sometimes there is a need for something that is device specific. Prior to POSIX most UNIX systems had a system call ioctl that performed a large number of device-specific actions on special files. Over the course of the years, it had gotten to be quite a mess. POSIX cleaned it up by splitting its functions into separate function calls primarily for the terminal. Whether each one is a separate system call or they share a single system call or something else is implementation dependent.

The first four listed in Fig. 10-20 are used to set and get the terminal speed. Different calls are provided for input and output because some modems operate at split speed. For example, old videotex systems allowed people to access public databases with short requests from the home to the server at 75 bits/sec with replies coming back at 1200 bits/sec. This standard was adopted at a time when 1200 bits/sec both ways was too expensive for home use. This asymmetry still persists, with some telephone companies offering inbound service at 1.5 Mbps and outbound service at 384 Kbps, often under the name of **ADSL** (**Asymmetric Digital Subscriber Line**).

Function call	Description
s = cfsetospeed(&termios, speed)	Set the output speed
s = cfsetispeed(&termios, speed)	Set the input speed
s = cfgetospeed(&termios, speed)	Get the output speed
s = cfgtetispeed(&termios, speed)	Get the input speed
s = tcsetattr(fd, opt, &termios)	Set the attributes
s = tcgetattr(fd, &termios)	Get the attributes

Figure 10-20. The main POSIX calls for managing the terminal.

The last two calls in the list are for setting and reading back all the special characters used for erasing characters and lines, interrupting processes, and so on. In addition, they enable and disable echoing, handle flow control, and other related functions. Additional I/O function calls also exist, but they are somewhat specialized so we will not discuss them further. In addition, ioctl still exists on most UNIX systems.

10.5.3 Implementation of Input/Output in UNIX

I/O in UNIX is implemented by a collection of device drivers, one per device type. The function of the drivers is to isolate the rest of the system from the idiosyncracies of the hardware. By providing standard interfaces between the drivers and the rest of the operating system, most of the I/O system can be put into the machine-independent part of the kernel.

When the user accesses a special file, the file system determines the major and minor device numbers belonging to it and whether it is a block special file or

a character special file. The major device number is used to index into one of two
internal structure arrays, *bdevsw* for block special files or *cdevsw* for character
special files. The structure thus located contains pointers to the procedures to call
to open the device, read the device, write the device, and so on. The minor device
number is passed as a parameter. Adding a new device type to UNIX means
adding a new entry to one of these tables and supplying the corresponding procedures to handle the various operations on the device.

The most important fields in the *cdevsw* array for a typical system might look
as shown in Fig. 10-21. Each row refers to a single I/O device (i.e., a single
driver). The columns represent the functions that all character drivers must support. Several other functions also exist. When an operation is performed on a
character special file, the system indexes into the *cdevsw* array to select the proper
row (structure), then calls the function in the corresponding structure member
(column) to have the work performed. Thus each row contains pointers to functions contained in one driver.

Device	Open	Close	Read	Write	Ioctl	Other
Null	null	null	null	null	null	...
Memory	null	null	mem_read	mem_write	null	...
Keyboard	k_open	k_close	k_read	error	k_ioctl	...
Tty	tty_open	tty_close	tty_read	tty_write	tty_ioctl	...
Printer	lp_open	lp_close	error	lp_write	lp_ioctl	...

Figure 10-21. Some of the fields of a typical *cdevsw* table.

Each driver is split into two parts. The top half runs in the context of the
caller and interfaces to the rest of UNIX. The bottom half runs in kernel context
and interacts with the device. Drivers are allowed to make calls to kernel procedures for memory allocation, timer management, DMA control, and other
things. The set of kernel functions that may be called is defined in a document
called the **Driver-Kernel Interface**. Writing device drivers for UNIX is covered
in detail in (Egan and Teixeira, 1992).

The I/O system is split into two major components: the handling of block special files and the handling of character special files. We will now look at each of
these components in turn.

The goal of that part of the system that does I/O on block special files (e.g.,
disks) is to minimize the number of actual transfers that must be done. To accomplish this goal, UNIX systems have a **buffer cache** between the disk drivers and
the file system, as illustrated in Fig. 10-22. The buffer cache is a table in the kernel for holding thousands of the most recently used blocks. When a block is
needed from a disk for any purpose (i-node, directory, or data), a check is first
made to see if it is in the buffer cache. If so, it is taken from there and a disk
access is avoided. The buffer cache greatly improves system performance.

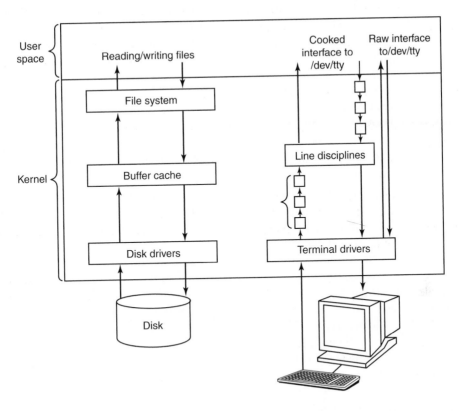

Figure 10-22. The UNIX I/O system in BSD.

If the block is not in the buffer cache, it is read from the disk into the buffer cache and from there, copied to where it is needed. Since the buffer cache has room for only a fixed number of blocks, some algorithm is needed to manage it. Usually, the blocks in the cache are linked together in a linked list. Whenever a block is accessed, it is moved to the head of the list. When a block must be removed from the cache to make room for a new block, the one at the rear of the chain is selected, since it is the least recently used block.

The buffer cache works for writes as well as for reads. When a program writes a block, it goes to the cache, not to the disk. Only when the cache fills up and the buffer must be reclaimed is the block forced out onto the disk. To avoid having blocks stay too long in the cache before being written to the disk, all the dirty blocks are written to the disk every 30 seconds.

For decades, UNIX device drivers have been statically linked into the kernel so they were all present in memory when the system was booted every time. Given the environment in which UNIX grew up, mostly departmental minicomputers and then high-end workstations, with their small and unchanging sets of I/O devices, this scheme worked well. Basically, a computer center built a kernel containing drivers for the I/O devices and that was it. If next year it bought a new disk, it relinked the kernel. No big deal.

With the arrival of Linux on the PC platform, suddenly all that changed. The number of I/O devices available on the PC is orders of magnitude larger than on any minicomputer. In addition, although all Linux users have (or can easily get) the full source code, probably the vast majority would have considerable difficulty adding a driver, updating *cdevsw* or *bdevsw*, relinking the kernel, and then instal- ling it as the bootable system (not to mention dealing with the aftermath of build- ing a kernel that does not boot).

Linux solved this problem with the concept of **loadable modules**. These are chunks of code that can be loaded into the kernel while the system is running. Most commonly these are character or block device drivers, but they can also be entire file systems, network protocols, performance monitoring tools, or anything else desired.

When a module is loaded, several things have to happen. First, the module has to be relocated on-the-fly, during loading. Second, the system has to check to see if the resources the driver needs are available (e.g., interrupt request levels) and if so, mark them as in use. Third, any interrupt vectors that are needed must be set up. Fourth, the appropriate driver switch table has to be updated to handle the new major device type. Finally, the driver is allowed to run to perform any device-specific initialization it may need. Once all these steps are completed, the driver is fully installed, the same as any statically installed driver. Some modern UNIX systems also support loadable modules now, too.

10.5.4 Streams

Since character special files deal with character streams and do not move blocks of information between memory and disk, they do not use the buffer cache. Instead, in the first versions of UNIX, each character device driver did all the work it needed for its device. However, in the course of time it became clear that many drivers were duplicating code present in other drivers such as code for buffering, flow control, and network protocols. Two different solutions were developed for structuring and modularizing the character drivers. We will now briefly examine each of them in turn.

The BSD solutions builds on data structures present in classical UNIX systems called **C-lists**, shown as small boxes in Fig. 10-22. Each one is a block of up to 64 characters, plus a count and a pointer to the next block. As characters arrive from terminals and other character devices, they are buffered in a chain of these blocks.

When a user process reads from */dev/tty* (e.g., standard input), the characters are not passed directly from the C-list to the process. Instead, they pass through a piece of kernel code called a **line discipline**. The line discipline acts like a filter, accepting the raw character stream from the terminal driver, processing it, and producing what is called a **cooked character stream**. In the cooked stream, local line editing has been done (i.e., erased characters and lines have been removed), carriage returns have been mapped onto line feeds, and other special processing has been completed. The cooked stream is passed to the process. However, if the process wants to interact on every character, it can put the line in raw mode, in which case the line discipline will be bypassed.

Output works in a similar way, expanding tabs to spaces, converting line feeds to carriage returns + line feeds, adding filler characters following carriage returns on slow mechanical terminals, and so on. Like input, output can go through the line discipline (cooked mode) or bypass it (raw mode). Raw mode is especially useful when sending binary data to other computers over a serial line and for GUIs. Here, no conversions are desired.

The System V solution, **streams**, devised by Dennis Ritchie, is more general and is shown in Fig. 10-23. (System V also has a buffer cache for block special files, but since that is essentially the same as in BSD it is not shown here.) The basic idea of a stream is to be able to connect a user process to a driver and be able to insert processing modules into the stream dynamically, during execution. To some extent, a stream is the kernel analog of pipelines in user space.

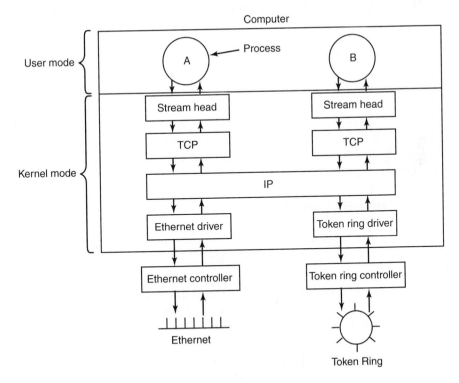

Figure 10-23. An example of streams in System V.

A stream always has a stream head on the top and connects to a driver on the bottom. As many modules as needed can be inserted into the stream. Processing can be bidirectional, so each module may need a section for reading (from the driver) and one for writing (to the driver). When a user process writes to a stream, code in the stream head interprets the system call and packs the data into stream buffers that are passed from module to module downward, with each module performing whatever transformations it is supposed to. Each module maintains a read queue and a write queue, so buffers are processed in the correct order. Modules have well-defined interfaces, defined by the streams infrastructure, so unrelated modules can be plugged together.

The example of Fig. 10-23 shows how streams are used when using the Internet TCP protocol over two different kinds of local area networks, Ethernet and Token ring. In particular, it illustrates another important feature of streams—multiplexing. A multiplexing module can take one stream and split it into multiple streams or can take multiple streams and merge them into one stream. The IP module in this configuration does both.

10.6 THE UNIX FILE SYSTEM

The most visible part of any operating system, including UNIX, is the file system. In the following sections we will examine the basic ideas behind the UNIX file system, the system calls, and how the file system is implemented. Some of these ideas derive from MULTICS, and many of them have been copied by MS-DOS, Windows, and other systems, but others are unique to UNIX. The UNIX design is especially interesting because it clearly illustrates the principle of *Small is Beautiful*. With minimal mechanism and a very limited number of system calls, UNIX nevertheless provides a powerful and elegant file system.

10.6.1 Fundamental Concepts

A UNIX file is a sequence of 0 or more bytes containing arbitrary information. No distinction is made between ASCII files, binary files, or any other kinds of files. The meaning of the bits in a file is entirely up to the file's owner. The system does not care. File names were originally restricted to 14 arbitrary characters, but Berkeley UNIX increased the limit to 255 characters, and this has been adopted by System V and most other versions as well. All the ASCII characters except NUL are allowed in file names, so a file name consisting of three carriage returns is a legal file name (but not an especially convenient one).

By convention, many programs expect file names to consist of a base name and an extension, separated by a dot (which counts as a character). Thus *prog.c* is typically a C program, *prog.f90* is typically a FORTRAN 90 program, and *prog.o* is usually an object file (compiler output). These conventions are not enforced by the operating system but some compilers and other programs expect them. Extensions may be of any length and files may have multiple extensions, as in *prog.java.Z*, which is probably a compressed Java program.

Files can be grouped together in directories for convenience. Directories are stored as files, and to a large extent can be treated like files. Directories can contain subdirectories, leading to a hierarchical file system. The root directory is called / and usually contains several subdirectories. The / character is also used to separate directory names, so that the name */usr/ast/x* denotes the file *x* located in the directory *ast*, which itself is in the */usr* directory.

Some of the major directories near the top of the tree are shown in Fig. 10-24.

Directory	Contents
bin	Binary (executable) programs
dev	Special files for I/O devices
etc	Miscellaneous system files
lib	Libraries
usr	User directories

Figure 10-24. Some important directories found in most UNIX systems.

There are two ways to specify file names in UNIX, both to the shell and when opening a file from within a program. The first way is using an **absolute path**, which means telling how to get to the file starting at the root directory. An example of an absolute path is */usr/ast/books/mos2/chap-10*. This tells the system to look in the root directory for a directory called *usr*, then look there for another directory, *ast*. In turn, this directory contains a directory *books*, which contains the directory *mos2* which contains the file *chap-10*.

Absolute path names are often long and inconvenient. For this reason, UNIX allows users and processes to designate the directory in which they are currently working as the **working directory**. Path names can also be specified relative to the working directory. A path name specified relative to the working directory is a **relative path**. For example, if */usr/ast/books/mos2* is the working directory, then the shell command

    cp chap-10 backup1

has exactly the same effect as the longer command

    cp /usr/ast/books/mos2/chap-10 /usr/ast/books/mos2/backup1

It frequently occurs that a user needs to refer to a file that belongs to another user, or at least is located elsewhere in the file tree. For example, if two users are sharing a file, it will be located in a directory belonging to one of them, so the other will have to use an absolute path name to refer to it (or change the working directory). If this is long enough, it may become irritating to have to keep typing it. UNIX provides a solution to this problem by allowing users to make a new directory entry that points to an existing file. Such an entry is called a **link**.

As an example, consider the situation of Fig. 10-25(a). Fred and Lisa are working together on a project, and each one needs frequent access to the other's files. If Fred has */usr/fred* as his working directory, he can refer to the file *x* in Lisa's directory as */usr/lisa/x*. Alternatively, Fred can create a new entry in his directory as shown in Fig. 10-25(b), after which he can use *x* to mean */usr/lisa/x*.

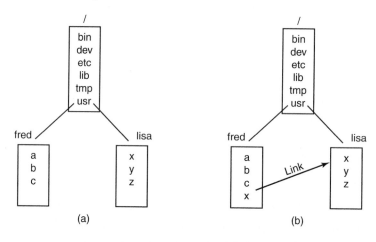

Figure 10-25. (a) Before linking. (b) After linking.

In the example just discussed, we suggested that before linking, the only way for Fred to refer to Lisa's file *x* was using its absolute path. Actually, this is not really true. When a directory is created, two entries, . and .., are automatically made in it. The former refers to the working directory itself. The latter refers to the directory's parent, that is, the directory in which it itself is listed. Thus from */usr/fred*, another path to Lisa's file *x* is *../lisa/x*.

In addition to regular files, UNIX also supports character special files and block special files. Character special files are used to model serial I/O devices such as keyboards and printers. Opening and reading from */dev/tty* reads from the keyboard; opening and writing to */dev/lp* writes to the printer. Block special files, often with names like */dev/hd1*, can be used to read and write raw disk partitions without regard to the file system. Thus a seek to byte *k* followed by a read will begin reading from the *k*-th byte on the corresponding partition, completely ignoring the i-node and file structure. Raw block devices are used for paging and swapping, by programs that lay down file systems (e.g., *mkfs*), and by programs that fix sick file systems (e.g., *fsck*), for example.

Many computers have two or more disks. On mainframes at banks, for example, it is frequently necessary to have 100 or more disks on a single machine, in order to hold the huge databases required. Even personal computers normally have at least two disks—a hard disk and a diskette drive. When there are multiple disk drives, the question arises of how to handle them.

One solution is to put a self-contained file system on each one and just keep them separate. Consider, for example, the situation depicted in Fig. 10-26(a). Here we have a hard disk, which we will call *C:*, and a diskette, which we will call *A:*. Each has its own root directory and files. With this solution, the user has to specify both the device and the file when anything other than the default is needed. For example, to copy the file *x* to the directory *d*, (assuming *C:* is the default), one would type

> cp   A:/x   /a/d/x

This is the approach taken by systems like MS-DOS, Windows 98, and VMS.

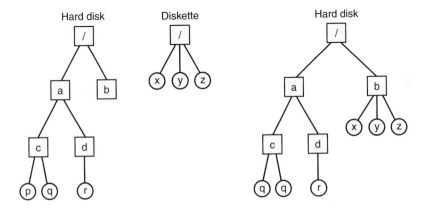

Figure 10-26. (a) Separate file systems. (b) After mounting.

The UNIX solution is to allow one disk to be mounted in another disk's file tree. In our example, we could mount the diskette on the directory */b*, yielding the file system of Fig. 10-26(b). The user now sees a single file tree, and no longer has to be aware of which file resides on which device. The above copy command now becomes

> cp   /b/x   /a/d/x

exactly the same as it would have been if everything had been on the hard disk in the first place.

Another interesting property of the UNIX file system is **locking**. In some applications, two or more processes may be using the same file at the same time, which may lead to race conditions. One solution is to program the application with critical regions. However, if the processes belong to independent users who do not even know each other, this kind of coordination is generally inconvenient.

Consider, for example, a database consisting of many files in one or more directories that are accessed by unrelated users. It is certainly possible to associate a semaphore with each directory or file and achieve mutual exclusion by having processes do a **down** operation on the appropriate semaphore before accessing the data. The disadvantage, however, is that a whole directory or file is then made inaccessible, even though only one record may be needed.

For this reason, POSIX provides a flexible and fine-grained mechanism for processes to lock as little as a single byte and as much as an entire file in one indivisible operation. The locking mechanism requires the caller to specify the file to be locked, the starting byte, and the number of bytes. If the operation succeeds, the system makes a table entry noting that the bytes in question (e.g., a database record) are locked.

Two kinds of locks are provided, **shared locks** and **exclusive locks**. If a portion of a file already contains a shared lock, a second attempt to place a shared lock on it is permitted, but an attempt to put an exclusive lock on it will fail. If a portion of a file contains an exclusive lock, all attempts to lock any part of that portion will fail until the lock has been released. In order to successfully place a lock, every byte in the region to be locked must be available.

When placing a lock, a process must specify whether it wants to block or not in the event that the lock cannot be placed. If it chooses to block, when the existing lock has been removed, the process is unblocked and the lock is placed. If the process chooses not to block when it cannot place a lock, the system call returns immediately, with the status code telling whether the lock succeeded or not.

Locked regions may overlap. In Fig. 10-27(a) we see that process A has placed a shared lock on bytes 4 through 7 of some file. Later, process B places a shared lock on bytes 6 through 9, as shown in Fig. 10-27(b). Finally, C locks bytes 2 through 11. As long as all these locks are shared, they can co-exist. Now consider what happens if a process tries to acquire an exclusive lock to byte 9 of the file of Fig. 10-27(c), with a request to block if the lock fails. Since two previous locks cover this block, the caller will block and will remain blocked until both B and C release their locks.

10.6.2 File System Calls in UNIX

Many system calls relate to files and the file system. First we will look at the system calls that operate on individual files. Later we will examine those that involve directories or the file system as a whole. To create a new file, the creat call can be used. (When Ken Thompson was once asked what he would do differently if he had the chance to reinvent UNIX, he replied that he would spell creat as create this time.) The parameters provide the name of the file and the protection mode. Thus

    fd = creat("abc", mode);

creates a file called *abc* with the protection bits taken from *mode*. These bits determine which users may access the file and how. They will be described later.

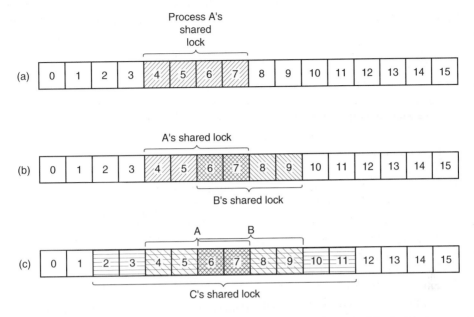

Figure 10-27. (a) A file with one lock. (b) Addition of a second lock. (c) A third lock.

The creat call not only creates a new file, but also opens it for writing. To allow subsequent system calls to access the file, a successful creat returns as its result a small nonnegative integer called a **file descriptor**, *fd* in the example above. If a creat is done on an existing file, that file is truncated to length 0 and its contents are discarded.

Now let us continue looking at the principal file system calls, which are listed in Fig. 10-28. To read or write an existing file, the file must first be opened using open. This call specifies the file name to be opened and how it is to be opened: for reading, writing, or both. Various options can be specified as well. Like creat, the call to open returns a file descriptor that can be used for reading or writing. Afterward, the file can be closed by close, which makes the file descriptor available for reuse on a subsequent creat or open. Both the creat and open calls always return the lowest numbered file descriptor not currently in use.

When a program starts executing in the standard way, file descriptors 0, 1, and 2 are already opened for standard input, standard output, and standard error, respectively. In this way, a filter, such as the *sort* program, can just read its input from file descriptor 0 and write its output to file descriptor 1, without having to know what files they are. This mechanism works because the shell arranges for these values to refer to the correct (redirected) files before the program is started.

The most heavily used calls are undoubtedly read and write. Each one has three parameters: a file descriptor (telling which open file to read or write), a

System call	Description
fd = creat(name, mode)	One way to create a new file
fd = open(file, how, ...)	Open a file for reading, writing or both
s = close(fd)	Close an open file
n = read(fd, buffer, nbytes)	Read data from a file into a buffer
n = write(fd, buffer, nbytes)	Write data from a buffer into a file
position = lseek(fd, offset, whence)	Move the file pointer
s = stat(name, &buf)	Get a file's status information
s = fstat(fd, &buf)	Get a file's status information
s = pipe(&fd[0])	Create a pipe
s = fcntl(fd, cmd, ...)	File locking and other operations

Figure 10-28. Some system calls relating to files. The return code *s* is −1 if an error has occurred; *fd* is a file descriptor, and *position* is a file offset. The parameters should be self explanatory.

buffer address (telling where to put the data or get the data from), and a count (telling how many bytes to transfer). That is all there is. It is a very simple design. A typical call is

    n = read(fd, buffer, nbytes);

Although most programs read and write files sequentially, some programs need to be able to access any part of a file at random. Associated with each file is a pointer that indicates the current position in the file. When reading (writing) sequentially, it normally points to the next byte to be read (written). If the pointer is at, say, 4096, before 1024 bytes are read, it will automatically be moved to 5120 after a successful read system call. The lseek call changes the value of the position pointer, so that subsequent calls to read or write can begin anywhere in the file, or even beyond the end of it. It is called lseek to avoid conflicting with seek, a now-obsolete call that was formerly used on 16-bit computers for seeking.

Lseek has three parameters: the first one is the file descriptor for the file; the second one is a file position; the third one tells whether the file position is relative to the beginning of the file, the current position, or the end of the file. The value returned by lseek is the absolute position in the file after the file pointer was changed. Slightly ironically, lseek is the only file system call that can never cause an actual disk seek because all it does is update the current file position, which is a number in memory.

For each file, UNIX keeps track of the file mode (regular, directory, special file), size, time of last modification, and other information. Programs can ask to see this information via the stat system call. The first parameter is the file name. The second one is a pointer to a structure where the information requested is to be put. The fields in the structure are shown in Fig. 10-29. The fstat call is the same as stat except that it operates on an open file (whose name may not be known) rather than on a path name.

Device the file is on
I-node number (which file on the device)
File mode (includes protection information)
Number of links to the file
Identity of the file's owner
Group the file belongs to
File size (in bytes)
Creation time
Time of last access
Time of last modification

Figure 10-29. The fields returned by the stat system call.

The pipe system call is used to create shell pipelines. It creates a kind of pseudofile, which buffers the data between the pipeline components, and returns file descriptors for both reading and writing the buffer. In a pipeline such as

    sort <in | head –30

file descriptor 1 (standard output) in the process running *sort* would be set (by the shell) to write to the pipe and file descriptor 0 (standard input) in the process running *head* would be set to read from the pipe. In this way, *sort* just reads from file descriptor 0 (set to the file *in*) and writes to file descriptor 1 (the pipe) without even being aware that these have been redirected. If they have not been redirected, *sort* will automatically read from the keyboard and write to the screen (the default devices). Similarly, when *head* reads from file descriptor 0, it is reading the data *sort* put into the pipe buffer without even knowing that a pipe is in use. This is a clear example where a simple concept (redirection) with a simple implementation (file descriptors 0 and 1) leads to a powerful tool (connecting programs in arbitrary ways without having to modify them at all).

The last system call in Fig. 10-28 is fcntl. It is used to lock and unlock files and perform a few other file-specific operations.

Now let us look at some system calls that relate more to directories or the file system as a whole, rather than just to one specific file. Some common ones are listed in Fig. 10-30. Directories are created and destroyed using mkdir and rmdir, respectively. A directory can only be removed if it is empty.

As we saw in Fig. 10-25, linking to a file creates a new directory entry that points to an existing file. The link system call creates the link. The parameters specify the original and new names, respectively. Directory entries are removed

System call	Description
s = mkdir(path, mode)	Create a new directory
s = rmdir(path)	Remove a directory
s = link(oldpath, newpath)	Create a link to an existing file
s = unlink(path)	Unlink a file
s = chdir(path)	Change the working directory
dir = opendir(path)	Open a directory for reading
s = closedir(dir)	Close a directory
dirent = readdir(dir)	Read one directory entry
rewinddir(dir)	Rewind a directory so it can be reread

Figure 10-30. Some system calls relating to directories. The return code s is -1 if an error has occurred; *dir* identifies a directory stream and *dirent* is a directory entry. The parameters should be self explanatory.

with unlink. When the last link to a file is removed, the file is automatically deleted. For a file that has never been linked, the first unlink causes it to disappear.

The working directory is changed by the chdir system call. Doing so has the effect of changing the interpretation of relative path names.

The last four calls of Fig. 10-30 are for reading directories. They can be opened, closed, and read, analogous to ordinary files. Each call to readdir returns exactly one directory entry in a fixed format. There is no way for users to write in a directory (in order to maintain the integrity of the file system). Files can be added to a directory using creat or link and removed using unlink. There is also no way to seek to a specific file in a directory, but rewinddir allows an open directory to be read again from the beginning.

10.6.3 Implementation of the UNIX File System

In this section we will describe the implementation of the traditional UNIX file system. Afterward, we will discuss the Berkeley improvements. Other file systems are also in use. All UNIX systems can handle multiple disk partitions, each with a different file system on it.

A classical UNIX, disk partition contains a file system with the layout illustrated in Fig. 10-31. Block 0 is not used by UNIX and often contains code to boot the computer. Block 1 is the **superblock**. It contains critical information about the layout of the file system, including the number of i-nodes, the number of disk blocks, and the start of the list of free disk blocks (typically a few hundred entries). Destruction of the superblock will render the file system unreadable.

Following the superblock are the **i-nodes** (short for index-nodes, but never called that, although some lazy people drop the hyphen and call them **inodes**).

Figure 10-31. Disk layout in classical UNIX systems.

They are numbered from 1 up to some maximum. Each i-node is 64 bytes long and describes exactly one file. An i-node contains accounting information (including all the information returned by stat, which simply takes it from the i-node), as well as enough information to locate all the disk blocks that hold the file's data.

Following the i-nodes are the data blocks. All the files and directories are stored here. If a file or directory consists of more than one block, the blocks need not be contiguous on the disk. In fact, the blocks of a large file are likely to be spread all over the disk. It is this scatter that the Berkeley improvements were designed to reduce.

A directory in the traditional (i.e., V7) file system consists of an unsorted collection of 16-byte entries. Each entry contains a file name (up to 14 arbitrary characters), and the number of the file's i-node, as shown in Fig. 6-37. To open a file in the working directory, the system just reads the directory, comparing the name to be looked up to each entry until it either finds the name or concludes that it is not present.

If the file is present, the system extracts the i-node number, and uses this as an index into the i-node table (on disk) to locate the corresponding i-node and bring it into memory. The i-node is put in the **i-node table**, a kernel data structure that holds all the i-nodes for currently open files and directories. The format of the i-node entries varies somewhat from UNIX version to UNIX version. As a bare minimum, all the fields returned by the stat system call must be present to make stat work (see Fig. 10-29). In Fig. 10-32 we show the format used by all AT&T versions from Version 7 through System V.

Looking up an absolute path name such as */usr/ast/file* is slightly more complicated. First, the system locates the root directory, which generally uses i-node 2, especially when i-node 1 is reserved for bad block handling. Then it looks up the string "usr" in the root directory, to get the i-node number of the */usr* directory. This i-node is then fetched, and the disk blocks are extracted from it, so the */usr* directory can be read and searched for the string "ast". Once this entry is found, the i-node number for the */usr/ast* directory can be taken from it. Armed with the i-node number of the */usr/ast* directory, this i-node can be read and the directory blocks located. Finally, "file" is looked up and its i-node number found. Thus the use of a relative path name is not only more convenient for the user, but it also saves a substantial amount of work for the system.

Field	Bytes	Description
Mode	2	File type, protection bits, setuid, setgid bits
Nlinks	2	Number of directory entries pointing to this i-node
Uid	2	UID of the file owner
Gid	2	GID of the file owner
Size	4	File size in bytes
Addr	39	Address of first 10 disk blocks, then 3 indirect blocks
Gen	1	Generation number (incremented every time i-node is reused)
Atime	4	Time the file was last accessed
Mtime	4	Time the file was last modified
Ctime	4	Time the i-node was last changed (except the other times)

Figure 10-32. Structure of the i-node in System V.

Let us now see how the system reads a file. Remember that a typical call to the library procedure for invoking the read system call looks like this:

```
n = read(fd, buffer, nbytes);
```

When the kernel gets control, all it has to start with are these three parameters, and the information in its internal tables relating to the user. One of the items in the internal tables is the file descriptor array. It is indexed by a file descriptor and contains one entry for each open file (up to the maximum number, usually about 20).

The idea is to start with this file descriptor and end up with the corresponding i-node. Let us consider one possible design: just put a pointer to the i-node in the file descriptor table. Although simple, unfortunately, this method does not work. The problem is as follows. Associated with every file descriptor is a file position that tells at which byte the next read (or write) will start. Where should it go? One possibility is to put it in the i-node table. However, this approach fails if two or more unrelated processes happen to open the same file at the same time because each one has its own file position.

A second possibility is to put the file position in the file descriptor table. In that way, every process that opens a file gets its own private file position. Unfortunately, this scheme fails too, but the reasoning is more subtle and has to do with the nature of file sharing in UNIX. Consider a shell script, *s*, consisting of two commands, *p1* and *p2*, to be run in order. If the shell script is called by the command line

```
s >x
```

it is expected that *p1* will write its output to *x*, and then *p2* will write its output to *x* also, starting at the place where *p1* stopped.

When the shell forks off *p1*, *x* is initially empty, so *p1* just starts writing at file position 0. However, when *p1* finishes, some mechanism is needed to make sure that the initial file position that *p2* sees is not 0 (which it would be if the file position were kept in the file descriptor table), but the value *p1* ended with.

The way this is achieved is shown in Fig. 10-33. The trick is to introduce a new table, the **open file description** table between the file descriptor table and the i-node table, and put the file position (and read/write bit) there. In this figure, the parent is the shell and the child is first *p1* and later *p2*. When the shell forks off *p1*, its user structure (including the file descriptor table) is an exact copy of the shell's, so both of them point to the same open file description table entry. When *p1* finishes, the shell's file descriptor is still pointing to the open file description containing *p1*'s file position. When the shell now forks off *p2*, the new child automatically inherits the file position, without either it or the shell even having to know what that position is.

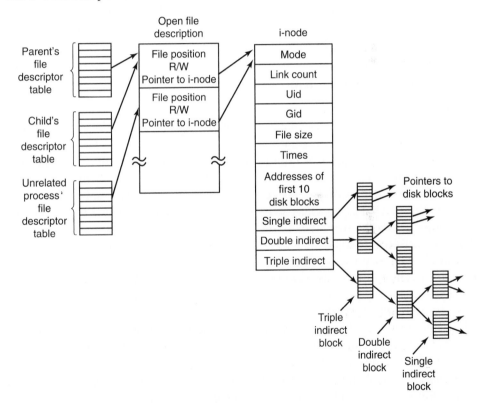

Figure 10-33. The relation between the file descriptor table, the open file description table, and the i-node table.

However, if an unrelated process opens the file, it gets its own open file description entry, with its own file position, which is precisely what is needed.

Thus the whole point of the open file description table is to allow a parent and child to share a file position, but to provide unrelated processes with their own values.

Getting back to the problem of doing the read, we have now shown how the file position and i-node are located. The i-node contains the disk addresses of the first 10 blocks of the file. If the file position falls in the first 10 blocks, the block is read and the data are copied to the user. For files longer than 10 blocks, a field in the i-node contains the disk address of a **single indirect block**, as shown in Fig. 10-33. This block contains the disk addresses of more disk blocks. For example, if a block is 1 KB and a disk address is 4 bytes, the single indirect block can hold 256 disk addresses. Thus this scheme works for files of up to 266 KB in total.

Beyond that, a **double indirect block** is used. It contains the addresses of 256 single indirect blocks, each of which holds the addresses of 256 data blocks. This mechanism is sufficient to handle files up to $10 + 2^{16}$ blocks (67,119,104 bytes). If even this is not enough, the i-node has space for a **triple indirect block**. Its pointers point to many double indirect blocks.

The Berkeley Fast File System

The description above explains how the classical UNIX file system works. Let us now take a look at the improvements Berkeley made to it. First, directories were reorganized. Instead of limiting file names to 14 characters, the limit was set to 255 characters. Of course, changing the structure of all the directories meant that programs that naively read directories (which was and is still legal) and which expected a sequence of 16-byte entries, no longer worked. To provide portability across the two kinds of directories, Berkeley provided the system calls opendir, closedir, readdir, and rewinddir to allow programs to read directories without having to know their internal structure. Long file names and these system calls for reading directories were later added to all other versions of UNIX and to POSIX.

The BSD directory structure allows file names up to 255 characters and is illustrated in Fig. 10-34. Each directory consists of some integral number of disk blocks so that directories can be written atomically to the disk. Within a directory, entries for files and directories are in unsorted order, with each entry directly following the one before it. Entries may not span disk blocks, so often there are some number of unused bytes at the end of each disk block.

Each directory entry in Fig. 10-34 consists of four fixed-length fields and one variable-length field. The first field is the i-node number, 19 for the file *colossal*, 42 for the file *voluminous*, and 88 for the directory *bigdir*. Next comes a field telling how big the entry is (in bytes), possibly including some padding after the name. This field is needed to find the next entry for the case that the file name is

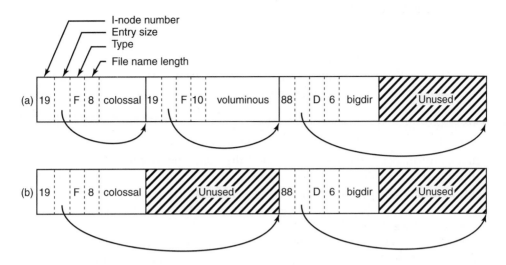

Figure 10-34. (a) A BSD directory with three files. (b) The same directory after the file *voluminous* has been removed.

padded by an unknown length. That is the meaning of the arrow in Fig. 10-34. Then comes the type field: file, directory, etc. The last fixed field is the length of the actual file name in bytes, 8, 10, and 6 in this example. Finally, comes the file name itself, terminated by a 0 byte and padded out to a 32-bit boundary. Additional padding may follow that.

In Fig. 10-34(b) we see the same directory after the entry for *voluminous* has been removed. All that is done is increase the size of the total entry field for *colossal*, turning the former field for *voluminous* into padding for the first entry. This padding can be used for a subsequent entry, of course.

Since directories are searched linearly, it can take a long time to find an entry at the end of a large directory. To improve search performance, name caching was added to BSD. Before looking up a name, the system first checks the cache. If a cache hit occurs, the linear search can be bypassed.

The second major change Berkeley made to the file system was the division of the disk up into **cylinder groups**, each with its own superblock, i-nodes, and data blocks. The idea behind this change is to keep the i-node and data blocks of a file close together, to avoid long seeks. Whenever possible, blocks are allocated in the cylinder group containing the i-node.

The third change was the introduction of two block sizes instead of just one. For storing large files, it is more efficient to have a small number of large blocks rather than many small ones. On the other hand, many UNIX files are small, so having only large blocks would be wasteful of disk space. Having two sizes allows efficient transfers for large files and space efficiency for small ones. The price paid is considerable extra complexity in the code.

The Linux File System

The initial Linux file system was the MINIX file system. However, due to the fact that it limited file names to 14 characters (in order to be compatible with UNIX Version 7) and its maximum file size was 64 MB, there was interest in better file systems almost from the beginning. The first improvement was the Ext file system, which allowed file names of 255 characters and files of 2 GB, but it was slower than the MINIX file system, so the search continued for a while. Eventually, the Ext2 file system was invented with long file names, long files, and better performance, and that has become the main file system. However, Linux still supports over a dozen file systems using the NFS file system (described in the next section). When Linux is linked, a choice is offered of which file systems should be built into the kernel. Other ones can be dynamically loaded as modules during execution, if need be.

Ext2 is very similar to the Berkeley Fast File system with some small differences. The Ext2 disk layout is shown in Fig. 10-35. Instead of using cylinder groups, which mean almost nothing with today's virtual disk geometries, it divides the disk into groups of blocks without regard to where the cylinder boundaries fall. Each block group starts with a superblock, which tells how many blocks and i-nodes there are, gives the block size, etc. Next comes the group descriptor, which contains information about the location of the bitmaps, the number of free blocks and i-nodes in the group and the number of directories in the group. This information is important since Ext2 attempts to spread directories evenly over the disk.

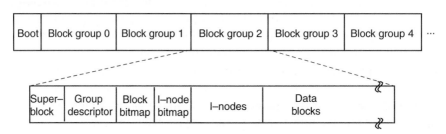

Figure 10-35. Layout of the Linux Ext2 file system.

Two bitmaps keep track of the free blocks and free i-nodes, respectively. Each map is one block long. With a 1-KB block, this design limits a block group to 8192 blocks and 8192 i-nodes. The former is a real restriction but the latter is not in practice. Next come the i-nodes themselves. Each i-node is 128 bytes, twice the size of the standard UNIX i-nodes of Fig. 10-32. The extra space is used as follows. Instead of 10 direct block addresses and 3 indirect block addresses, Linux allows 12 direct and 3 indirect addresses. Furthermore, the addresses have been extended from 3 bytes to 4 bytes, to handle disk partitions larger than 2^{24} blocks (16 GB), which was already a problem in UNIX. In addition, fields are reserved for pointers to access control lists for a finer degree of protection, but these are still on the drawing board. The rest of the i-node is reserved for future use. History shows that unused bits do not remain that way for long.

Operation of the file system is similar to the Berkeley fast file system. One difference with Berkeley, however, is the use of standard 1 KB throughout. The Berkeley fast file systems uses 8-KB blocks and then fragments them into 1-KB pieces if need be. Ext2 just does it the easy way. Like the Berkeley system, when a file grows, Ext2 tries to put the block in the same block group as the rest of the file, preferably right after the previous last block. Also, when a new file is added to a directory, Ext2 tries to put it into the same block group as its directory. New directories are scattered uniformly across the disk.

Another Linux file system is the **/proc** (process) file system, an idea originally devised in the 8th edition of UNIX from Bell Labs and later copied in 4.4BSD and System V. However, Linux extends the idea in several ways. The basic concept is that for every process in the system, a directory is created in */proc*. The name of the directory is the process PID expressed as a decimal number. for example, */proc/619* is the directory corresponding to the process with PID 619. In this directory are files that appear to contain information about the process, such as its command line, environment strings, and signal masks. In fact, these files do not exist on the disk. When they are read, the system retrieves the information from the actual process as needed and returns it in a standard format.

Many of the Linux extensions relate to other files and directories located in */proc*. They contain a wide variety of information about the CPU, disk partitions, devices, interrupt vectors, kernel counters, file systems, loaded modules, and much more. Unprivileged user programs may read much of this information to learn about system behavior in a safe way. Some of these files may be written to in order to change system parameters.

10.6.4 NFS: The Network File System

Networking has played a major role in UNIX right from the beginning (the first UNIX network was built to move new kernels from the PDP-11/70 to the Interdata 8/32 during the port to the later). In this section we will examine Sun Microsystem's **NFS** (**Network File System**), which is used on all modern UNIX systems (and some non-UNIX systems) to join the file systems on separate computers into one logical whole. Three aspects of NFS are of interest: the architecture, the protocol, and the implementation. We will now examine these in turn.

NFS Architecture

The basic idea behind NFS is to allow an arbitrary collection of clients and servers to share a common file system. In many cases, all the clients and servers are on the same LAN, but this is not required. It is also possible to run NFS over a wide area network if the server is far from the client. For simplicity we will speak of clients and servers as though they were on distinct machines, but in fact, NFS allows every machine to be both a client and a server at the same time.

Each NFS server exports one or more of its directories for access by remote clients. When a directory is made available, so are all of its subdirectories, so in fact, entire directory trees are normally exported as a unit. The list of directories a server exports is maintained in a file, often */etc/exports*, so these directories can be exported automatically whenever the server is booted. Clients access exported directories by mounting them. When a client mounts a (remote) directory, it becomes part of its directory hierarchy, as shown in Fig. 10-36.

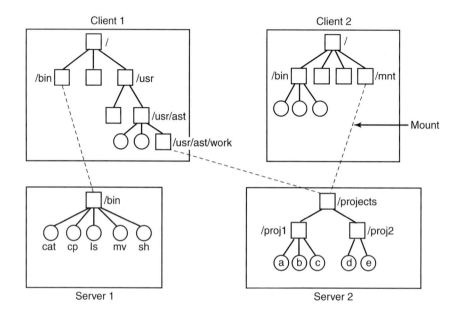

Figure 10-36. Examples of remote mounted file systems. Directories are shown as squares and files are shown as circles.

In this example, client 1 has mounted the *bin* directory of server 1 on its own *bin* directory, so it can now refer to the shell as */bin/sh* and get the shell on server 1. Diskless workstations often have only a skeleton file system (in RAM) and get all their files from remote servers like this. Similarly, client 1 has mounted server 2's directory */projects* on its directory */usr/ast/work* so it can now access file *a* as */usr/ast/work/proj1/a*. Finally, client 2 has also mounted the *projects* directory and can also access file *a*, only as */mnt/proj1/a*. As seen here, the same file can have different names on different clients due to its being mounted in a different place in the respective trees. The mount point is entirely local to the clients; the server does not know where it is mounted on any of its clients.

NFS Protocols

Since one of the goals of NFS is to support a heterogeneous system, with clients and servers possibly running different operating systems on different hardware, it is essential that the interface between the clients and servers be well defined. Only then is it possible for anyone to be able to write a new client implementation and expect it to work correctly with existing servers, and vice versa.

NFS accomplishes this goal by defining two client-server protocols. A **protocol** is a set of requests sent by clients to servers, along with the corresponding replies sent by the servers back to the clients.

The first NFS protocol handles mounting. A client can send a path name to a server and request permission to mount that directory somewhere in its directory hierarchy. The place where it is to be mounted is not contained in the message, as the server does not care where it is to be mounted. If the path name is legal and the directory specified has been exported, the server returns a **file handle** to the client. The file handle contains fields uniquely identifying the file system type, the disk, the i-node number of the directory, and security information. Subsequent calls to read and write files in the mounted directory or any of its subdirectories use the file handle.

When UNIX boots, it runs the */etc/rc* shell script before going multiuser. Commands to mount remote file systems can be placed in this script, thus automatically mounting the necessary remote file systems before allowing any logins. Alternatively, most versions of UNIX also support **automounting**. This feature allows a set of remote directories to be associated with a local directory. None of these remote directories are mounted (or their servers even contacted) when the client is booted. Instead, the first time a remote file is opened, the operating system sends a message to each of the servers. The first one to reply wins, and its directory is mounted.

Automounting has two principal advantages over static mounting via the */etc/rc* file. First, if one of the NFS servers named in */etc/rc* happens to be down, it is impossible to bring the client up, at least not without some difficulty, delay, and quite a few error messages. If the user does not even need that server at the moment, all that work is wasted. Second, by allowing the client to try a set of servers in parallel, a degree of fault tolerance can be achieved (because only one of them needs to be up), and the performance can be improved (by choosing the first one to reply—presumably the least heavily loaded).

On the other hand, it is tacitly assumed that all the file systems specified as alternatives for the automount are identical. Since NFS provides no support for file or directory replication, it is up to the user to arrange for all the file systems to be the same. Consequently, automounting is most often used for read-only file systems containing system binaries and other files that rarely change.

The second NFS protocol is for directory and file access. Clients can send messages to servers to manipulate directories and read and write files. Also, they can also access file attributes, such as file mode, size, and time of last modification. Most UNIX system calls are supported by NFS, with the perhaps surprising exception of open and close.

The omission of open and close is not an accident. It is fully intentional. It is not necessary to open a file before reading it, nor to close it when done. Instead, to read a file, a client sends the server a lookup message containing the file name, with a request to look it up and return a file handle, which is a structure that identifies the file (i.e., contains a file system identifier and i-node number, among other data). Unlike an open call, this lookup operation does not copy any information into internal system tables. The read call contains the file handle of the file to read, the offset in the file to begin reading, and the number of bytes desired. Each such message is self-contained. The advantage of this scheme is that the server does not have to remember anything about open connections in between calls to it. Thus if a server crashes and then recovers, no information about open files is lost, because there is none. A server like this that does not maintain state information about open files is said to be **stateless**.

Unfortunately, the NFS method makes it difficult to achieve the exact UNIX file semantics. For example, in UNIX a file can be opened and locked so that other processes cannot access it. When the file is closed, the locks are released. In a stateless server such as NFS, locks cannot be associated with open files, because the server does not know which files are open. NFS therefore needs a separate, additional mechanism to handle locking.

NFS uses the standard UNIX protection mechanism, with the rwx bits for the owner, group, and others (mentioned in Chap. 1 and discussed in detail below). Originally, each request message simply contained the user and group IDs of the caller, which the NFS server used to validate the access. In effect, it trusted the clients not to cheat. Several years' experience abundantly demonstrated that such an assumption was—how shall we put it?—naive. Currently, public key cryptography can be used to establish a secure key for validating the client and server on each request and reply. When this option is enabled, a malicious client cannot impersonate another client because it does not know that client's secret key.

NFS Implementation

Although the implementation of the client and server code is independent of the NFS protocols, most UNIX systems use a three-layer implementation similar to that of Fig. 10-37. The top layer is the system call layer. This handles calls like open, read, and close. After parsing the call and checking the parameters, it invokes the second layer, the Virtual File System (VFS) layer.

The task of the VFS layer is to maintain a table with one entry for each open file, analogous to the table of i-nodes for open files in UNIX. In ordinary UNIX, an i-node is indicated uniquely by a (device, i-node number) pair. Instead, the VFS layer has an entry, called a **v-node** (**virtual i-node**), for every open file. V-

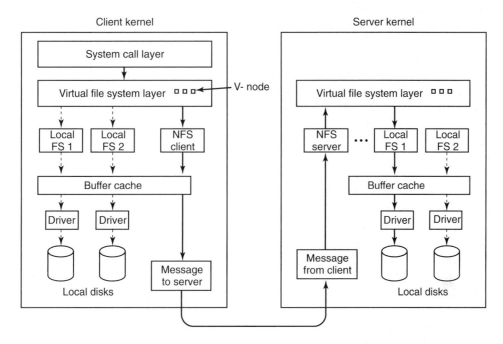

Figure 10-37. The NFS layer structure.

nodes are used to tell whether the file is local or remote. For remote files, enough information is provided to be able to access them. For local files, the file system and i-node are recorded because modern UNIX systems can support multiple file systems (e.g., V7, Berkeley FFS, ext2fs, /proc, FAT, etc.). Although VFS was invented to support NFS, most modern UNIX systems now support it as an integral part of the operating system, even if NFS is not used.

To see how v-nodes are used, let us trace a sequence of mount, open, and read system calls. To mount a remote file system, the system administrator (or */etc/rc*) calls the *mount* program specifying the remote directory, the local directory on which it is to be mounted, and other information. The *mount* program parses the name of the remote directory to be mounted and discovers the name of the NFS server on which the remote directory is located. It then contacts that machine asking for a file handle for the remote directory. If the directory exists and is available for remote mounting, the server returns a file handle for the directory. Finally, it makes a mount system call, passing the handle to the kernel.

The kernel then constructs a v-node for the remote directory and asks the NFS client code in Fig. 10-37 to create an **r-node (remote i-node)** in its internal tables to hold the file handle. The v-node points to the r-node. Each v-node in the VFS layer will ultimately contain either a pointer to an r-node in the NFS client code, or a pointer to an i-node in one of the local file systems (shown as dashed lines in Fig. 10-37). Thus from the v-node it is possible to see if a file or directory is local or remote. If it is local, the correct file system and i-node can be located. If it is remote, the remote host and file handle can be located.

When a remote file is opened on the client, at some point during the parsing of the path name, the kernel hits the directory on which the remote file system is mounted. It sees that this directory is remote and in the directory's v-node finds the pointer to the r-node. It then asks the NFS client code to open the file. The NFS client code looks up the remaining portion of the path name on the remote server associated with the mounted directory and gets back a file handle for it. It makes an r-node for the remote file in its tables and reports back to the VFS layer, which puts in its tables a v-node for the file that points to the r-node. Again here we see that every open file or directory has a v-node that points to either an r-node or an i-node.

The caller is given a file descriptor for the remote file. This file descriptor is mapped onto the v-node by tables in the VFS layer. Note that no table entries are made on the server side. Although the server is prepared to provide file handles upon request, it does not keep track of which files happen to have file handles outstanding and which do not. When a file handle is sent to it for file access, it checks the handle, and if it is valid, uses it. Validation can include verifying an authentication key contained in the RPC headers, if security is enabled.

When the file descriptor is used in a subsequent system call, for example, read, the VFS layer locates the corresponding v-node, and from that determines whether it is local or remote and also which i-node or r-node describes it. It then sends a message to the server containing the handle, the file offset (which is maintained on the client side, not the server side), and the byte count. For efficiency reasons, transfers between client and server are done in large chunks, normally 8192 bytes, even if fewer bytes are requested.

When the request message arrives at the server, it is passed to the VFS layer there, which determines which local file system holds the requested file. The VFS layer then makes a call to that local file system to read and return the bytes. These data are then passed back to the client After the client's VFS layer has gotten the 8-KB chunk it asked for, it automatically issues a request for the next chunk, so it will have it should it be needed shortly. This feature, known as **read ahead**, improves performance considerably.

For writes an analogous path is followed from client to server. Also, transfers are done in 8-KB chunks here too. If a write system call supplies fewer than 8 KB bytes of data, the data are just accumulated locally. Only when the entire 8 KB chunk is full is it sent to the server. However, when a file is closed, all of its data are sent to the server immediately.

Another technique used to improve performance is caching, as in ordinary UNIX. Servers cache data to avoid disk accesses, but this is invisible to the clients. Clients maintain two caches, one for file attributes (i-nodes) and one for file data. When either an i-node or a file block is needed, a check is made to see if it can be satisfied out of the cache. If so, network traffic can be avoided.

While client caching helps performance enormously, it also introduces some nasty problems. Suppose that two clients are both caching the same file block and that one of them modifies it. When the other one reads the block, it gets the old (stale) value. The cache is not coherent.

Given the potential severity of this problem, the NFS implementation does several things to mitigate it. For one, associated with each cache block is a timer. When the timer expires, the entry is discarded. Normally, the timer is 3 sec for data blocks and 30 sec for directory blocks. Doing this reduces the risk somewhat. In addition, whenever a cached file is opened, a message is sent to the server to find out when the file was last modified. If the last modification occurred after the local copy was cached, the cache copy is discarded and the new copy fetched from the server. Finally, once every 30 sec a cache timer expires, and all the dirty (i.e., modified) blocks in the cache are sent to the server. While not perfect, these patches make the system highly usable in most practical circumstances.

10.7 SECURITY IN UNIX

Despite the name, UNIX has been a multiuser system almost from the beginning. This history means that security and control of information was built in very early on. In the following sections, we will look at some of the security aspects of UNIX.

10.7.1 Fundamental Concepts

The user community for a UNIX system consists of some number of registered users, each of whom has a unique **UID** (**User ID**). A UID is an integer between 0 and 65,535. Files (but also processes, and other resources) are marked with the UID of their owner. By default, the owner of a file is the person who created the file, although there is a way to change ownership.

Users can be organized into groups, which are also numbered with 16-bit integers called **GIDs** Group IDs). Assigning users to groups is done manually, by the system administrator, and consists of making entries in a system database telling which user is in which group. Originally, a user could be in only one group, but some versions of UNIX now allow a user to be in more than one group at the same time. For simplicity, we will not discuss this feature further.

The basic security mechanism in UNIX is simple. Each process carries the UID and GID of its owner. When a file is created, it gets the UID and GID of the creating process. The file also gets a set of permissions determined by the creating process. These permissions specify what access the owner, the other members of the owner's group, and the rest of the users have to the file. For each of these three categories, potential accesses are read, write, and execute, designated by the letters *r*, *w*, and *x*, respectively. The ability to execute a file makes sense only if that file is an executable binary program, of course. An attempt to execute a file that has execute permission but which is not executable (i.e., does not start with a valid header) will fail with an error. Since there are three categories of users and 3 bits per category, 9 bits are sufficient to represent the access rights. Some examples of these 9-bit numbers and their meanings are given in Fig. 10-38.

Binary	Symbolic	Allowed file accesses
111000000	rwx------	Owner can read, write, and execute
111111000	rwxrwx---	Owner and group can read, write, and execute
110100000	rw-r-----	Owner can read and write; group can read
110100100	rw-r--r--	Owner can read and write; all others can read
111101101	rwxr-xr-x	Owner can do everything, rest can read and execute
000000000	---------	Nobody has any access
000000111	------rwx	Only outsiders have access (strange, but legal)

Figure 10-38. Some example file protection modes.

The first two entries in Fig. 10-38 are clear, allowing the owner and the owner's group full access, respectively. The next one allows the owner's group to read the file but not to change it, and prevents outsiders from any access. The fourth entry is common for a data file the owner wants to make public. Similarly, the fifth entry is the usual one for a publicly available program. The sixth entry denies all access to all users. This mode is sometimes used for dummy files used for mutual exclusion because an attempt to create such a file will fail if one already exists. Thus if multiple processes simultaneously attempt to create such a file as a lock, only one of them will succeed. The last example is strange indeed, since it gives the rest of the world more access than the owner. However, its existence follows from the protection rules. Fortunately, there is a way for the owner to subsequently change the protection mode, even without having any access to the file itself.

The user with UID 0 is special and is called the **superuser** (or **root**). The superuser has the power to read and write all files in the system, no matter who owns them and no matter how they are protected. Processes with UID 0 also have the ability to make a small number of protected system calls denied to ordinary users. Normally, only the system administrator knows the superuser's password, although many undergraduates consider it a great sport to try to look for security flaws in the system so they can log in as the superuser without knowing the password. Management tends to frown on such activity.

Directories are files and have the same protection modes that ordinary files do except that the *x* bits refer to search permission instead of execute permission. Thus a directory with mode *rwxr-xr-x* allows its owner to read, modify, and search the directory, but allows others only to read and search it, but not add or remove files from it.

Special files corresponding to the I/O devices have the same protection bits as regular files. This mechanism can be used to limit access to I/O devices. For example, the printer special file, */dev/lp*, could be owned by root or by a special user, daemon, and have mode *rw–––––––* to keep everyone else from directly accessing the printer. After all, if everyone could just print at will, chaos would result.

Of course, having */dev/lp* owned by, say, daemon with protection mode *rw–––––––* means that nobody else can use the printer. While this would save many innocent trees from an early death, sometimes users do have a legitimate need to print something. In fact, there is a more general problem of allowing controlled access to all I/O devices and other system resources.

This problem was solved by adding a new protection bit, the **SETUID bit** to the 9 protection bits discussed above. When a program with the SETUID bit on is executed, the **effective UID** for that process becomes the UID of the executable file's owner instead of the UID of the user who invoked it. When a process attempts to open a file, it is the effective UID that is checked, not the underlying real UID. By making the program that accesses the printer be owned by daemon but with the SETUID bit on, any user could execute it, and have the power of daemon (e.g., access to */dev/lp*) but only to run that program (which might queue print jobs for printing in an orderly fashion).

Many sensitive UNIX programs are owned by the root but with the SETUID bit on. For example, the program that allows users to change their passwords, *passwd*, needs to write in the password file. Making the password file publicly writable would not be a good idea. Instead, there is a program that is owned by the root and which has the SETUID bit on. Although the program has complete access to the password file, it will only change the caller's password and not permit any other access to the password file.

In addition to the SETUID bit there is also a SETGID bit that works analogously, temporarily giving the user the effective GID of the program. In practice, this bit is rarely used, however.

10.7.2 Security System Calls in UNIX

There are only a small number of system calls relating to security. The most important ones are listed in Fig. 10-39. The most heavily used security system call is chmod. It is used to change the protection mode. For example,

```
s = chmod("/usr/ast/newgame", 0755);
```

sets *newgame* to *rwxr–xr–x* so that everyone can run it (note that 0755 is an octal constant, which is convenient since the protection bits come in groups of 3 bits). Only the owner of a file and the superuser can change its protection bits.

System call	Description
s = chmod(path, mode)	Change a file's protection mode
s = access(path, mode)	Check access using the real UID and GID
uid = getuid( )	Get the real UID
uid = geteuid( )	Get the effective UID
gid = getgid( )	Get the real GID
gid = getegid( )	Get the effective GID
s = chown(path, owner, group)	Change owner and group
s = setuid(uid)	Set the UID
s = setgid(gid)	Set the GID

Figure 10-39. Some system calls relating to security. The return code s is -1 if an error has occurred; *uid* and *gid* are the UID and GID, respectively. The parameters should be self explanatory.

The access call tests to see if a particular access would be allowed using the real UID and GID. This system call is needed to avoid security breaches in programs that are SETUID and owned by the root. Such a program can do anything, and it is sometimes needed for the program to figure out if the user is allowed to perform a certain access. The program cannot just try it, because the access will always succeed. With the access call the program can find out if the access is allowed by the real UID and real GID.

The next four system calls return the real and effective UIDs and GIDs. The last three are only allowed for the superuser. They change a file's owner, and a process' UID and GID.

10.7.3 Implementation of Security in UNIX

When a user logs in, the login program, *login* (which is SETUID root) asks for a login name and a password. It hashes the password and then looks in the password file, */etc/passwd*, to see if the hash matches the one there (networked systems work slightly differently). The reason for using hashes is to prevent the password from being stored in unencrypted form anywhere in the system. If the password is correct, the login program looks in */etc/passwd* to see the name of the user's preferred shell, possibly *sh*, but possibly some other shell such as *csh* or *ksh*. The login program then uses setuid and setgid to give itself the user's UID and GID (remember, it started out as SETUID root). Then it opens the keyboard for standard input (file descriptor 0), the screen for standard output (file descriptor 1), and the screen for standard error (file descriptor 2). Finally, it executes the preferred shell, thus terminating itself.

At this point the preferred shell is running with the correct UID and GID and standard input, output, and error all set to their default devices. All processes that it forks off (i.e., commands typed by the user), automatically inherit the shell's UID and GID, so they also will have the correct owner and group. All files they create also get these values.

When any process attempts to open a file, the system first checks the protection bits in the file's i-node against the caller's effective UID and effective GID to see if the access is permitted. If so, the file is opened and a file descriptor returned. If not, the file is not opened and −1 is returned. No checks are made on subsequent read or write calls. As a consequence, if the protection mode changes after a file is already open, the new mode will not affect processes that already have the file open.

Security in Linux is essentially the same as in UNIX. All the UNIX security features are implemented and there is little else in this area.

10.8 SUMMARY

UNIX began life as a minicomputer timesharing system, but is now used on machines ranging from notebook computers to supercomputers. Three interfaces to it exist: the shell, the C library, and the system calls themselves. The shell allows users to type commands for execution. These may be simple commands, pipelines, or more complex structures. Input and output may be redirected. The C library contains the system calls and also many enhanced calls, such as *printf* for writing formatted output to files. The actual system call interface is lean and mean, roughly 100 calls, each of which doing what is needed and no more.

The key concepts in UNIX include the process, the memory model, I/O, and the file system. Processes may fork off subprocesses, leading to a tree of processes. Process management in UNIX uses two key data structures, the process table and the user structure. The former is always in memory, but the latter can be swapped or paged out. Process creation is done by duplicating the process table entry, and then the memory image. Scheduling is done using a priority-based algorithm that favors interactive processes.

The memory model consists of three segments per process: text, data, and stack. Memory management used to be done by swapping, but is now done by paging in most UNIX systems. The core map keeps track of the state of each page, and the page daemon uses a clock algorithm to keep enough free pages around.

I/O devices are accessed using special files, each of which has a major device number and a minor device number. Block device I/O uses a buffer cache to reduce the number of disk accesses. An LRU algorithm is used to manage the cache. Character I/O can be done in raw or cooked mode. Line disciplines or streams are used to add features to character I/O.

The file system is hierarchical with files and directories. All disks are mounted into a single directory tree starting at a unique root. Individual files can be linked into a directory from elsewhere in the file system. To use a file, it must be first opened, which yields a file descriptor for use in reading and writing the file. Internally, the file system uses three main tables: the file descriptor table, the open file description table, and the i-node table. The i-node table is the most important of these, containing all the administrative information about a file and the location of its blocks.

Protection is based on controlling read, write, and execute access for the owner, group, and others. For directories, the execute bit is interpreted to mean search permission.

PROBLEMS

1. When the kernel catches system call, how does it know which system call it is supposed to carry out?

2. A directory contains the following files:

aardvark	feret	koala	porpoise	unicorn
bonefish	grunion	llama	quacker	vicuna
capybara	hyena	marmot	rabbit	weasel
dingo	ibex	nuthatch	seahorse	yak
emu	jellyfish	ostrich	tuna	zebu

Which files will be listed by the command

    ls [abc]*e*?

3. What does the following UNIX shell pipeline do?

    grep nd xyz | wc –l

4. Write a UNIX pipeline that prints the eighth line of file z on standard output.

5. Why does UNIX distinguish between standard output and standard error, when both default to the terminal?

6. A user at a terminal types the following commands:

    a | b | c &
    d | e | f &

After the shell has processed them, how many new processes are running?

7. When the UNIX shell starts up a process, it puts copies of its environment variables, such as *HOME*, on the process' stack, so the process can find out what its home directory is. If this process should later fork, will the child automatically get these variables too?

8. About how long does it take to fork off a child process under the following conditions: text size = 100 KB, data size = 20 KB, stack size = 10 KB, process table size = 1 KB, user structure = 5 KB. The kernel trap and return takes 1 msec, and the machine can copy one 32-bit word every 50 nsec. Text segments are shared.

9. As megabyte programs became more common, the time spent executing the fork system call grew proportionally. Worse yet, nearly all of this time was wasted, since most programs call exec shortly after forking. To improve performance, Berkeley invented a new system call, vfork, in which the child shares the parent's address space, instead of getting its own copy of it. Describe a situation in which a poorly-behaved child can do something that makes the semantics of vfork fundamentally different from those of fork.

10. If a UNIX process has a *CPU_usage* value of 20, how many ΔT intervals does it take to decay to 0 if it does not get scheduled for a while? Use the simple decay algorithm given in the text.

11. Does it make sense to take away a process' memory when it enters zombie state? Why or why not?

12. To what hardware concept is a signal closely related? Give two examples of how signals are used.

13. Why do you think the designers of UNIX made it impossible for a process to send a signal to a another process that is not in its process group?

14. A system call is usually implemented using a software interrupt (trap) instruction. Could an ordinary procedure call be used as well on the Pentium hardware? If so, under what conditions and how? If not, why not?

15. In general, do you think daemons have higher priority or lower priority than interactive processes? Why?

16. When a new process is forked off, it must be assigned a unique integer as its PID. Is it sufficient to have a counter in the kernel that is incremented on each process creation, with the counter used as the new PID? Discuss your answer.

17. In every process' entry in the process table, the PID of the process' parent is stored. Why?

18. What combination of the sharing_flags bits used by the Linux clone command corresponds to a conventional Unix fork call? To creating a conventional Unix thread?

19. The Linux scheduler computes the goodness for real-time processes by adding the priority to 1000. Could a different constant have been chosen and still have the algorithm make the same choices as the regular one?

20. When booting UNIX (or most other operating systems for that matter), the bootstrap loader in sector 0 of the disk first loads a boot program which then loads the operating system. Why is the extra step needed? Surely it would be simpler to have the bootstrap loader in sector 0 just load the operating system directly.

21. A certain editor has 100 KB of program text, 30 KB of initialized data, and 50 KB of BSS. The initial stack is 10 KB. Suppose that three copies of this editor are started simultaneously. How much physical memory is needed (a) if shared text is used, and (b) if it is not?

22. In 4BSD, each core map entry contains an index for the next entry on the free list, which is used when the current entry is on the free list. This field is 16 bits. Pages are 1 KB. Do these sizes have any implications for the total amount of memory BSD can support? Explain your answer.

23. In BSD, the data and stack segments are paged and swapped to a scratch copy kept on a special paging disk or partition, but the text segment uses the executable binary file instead. Why?

24. Describe a way to use mmap and signals to construct an interprocess communication mechanism.

25. A file is mapped in using the following mmap system call:

    mmap(65536, 32768, READ, FLAGS, fd, 0)

    Pages are 8 KB. Which byte in the file is accessed by reading a byte at memory address 72,000?

26. After the system call of the previous problem has been executed, the call

    munmap(65536, 8192)

    is carried out. Does it succeed? If so, which bytes of the file remain mapped? If not, why does it fail?

27. Can a page fault ever lead to the faulting process being terminated? If so, give an example. If not, why not?

28. Is it possible that with the buddy system of memory management it ever occurs that two adjacent blocks of free memory of the same size co-exist without being merged into one block? If so, give an example of how this can happen. If not, show that it is impossible.

29. It is stated in the text that a paging partition will perform better than a paging file. Why is this so?

30. Give two examples of the advantages of relative path names over absolute ones.

31. The following locking calls are made by a collection of processes. For each call, tell what happens. If a process fails to get a lock, it blocks.

    (a) *A* wants a shared lock on bytes 0 through 10.
    (b) *B* wants an exclusive lock on bytes 20 through 30.
    (c) *C* wants a shared lock on bytes 8 through 40.
    (d) *A* wants a shared lock on bytes 25 through 35.
    (e) *B* wants an exclusive lock on byte 8.

32. Consider the locked file of Fig. 10-27(c). Suppose that a process tries to lock bytes 10 and 11 and blocks. Then, before *C* releases its lock, yet another process tries to lock

bytes 10 and 11, and also blocks. What kind of problems are introduced into the semantics by this situation. Propose and defend two solutions.

33. Suppose that an lseek system call seeks to a negative offset in a file. Given two possible ways of dealing with it.

34. If a UNIX file has protection mode 755 (octal), what can the owner, the owner's group, and everyone else do to the file?

35. Some tape drives have numbered blocks and the ability to overwrite a particular block in place without disturbing the blocks in front or behind it. Could such a device hold a mounted UNIX file system?

36. In Fig. 10-25, both Fred and Lisa have access to the file x in their respective directories after linking. Is this access completely symmetrical in the sense anything one of them can do with it the other one can too?

37. As we have seen, absolute path names are looked up starting at the root directory and relative path names are looked up starting at the working directory. Suggest an efficient way to implement both kinds of searches.

38. When the file */usr/ast/work/f* is opened, several disk accesses are needed to read i-node and directory blocks. Calculate the number of disk accesses required under the assumption that the i-node for the root directory is always in memory, and all directories are one block long.

39. A UNIX i-node has 10 disk addresses for data blocks, as well as the addresses of single, double, and triple indirect blocks. If each of these holds 256 disk addresses, what is the size of the largest file that can be handled, assuming that a disk block is 1 KB?

40. When an i-node is read in from the disk during the process of opening a file, it is put into an i-node table in memory. This table has some fields that are not present on the disk. One of them is a counter that keeps track of the number of times the i-node has been opened. Why is this field needed?

41. Why does LRU work for managing the buffer cache, whereas it rarely works for keeping track of pages in a virtual memory system?

42. UNIX has a system call, sync, that flushes the buffer cache back to disk. At boot time, a program called *update* is started. Once every 30 sec it calls sync, then goes to sleep for 30 sec. Why does this program exist?

43. After a system crash and reboot, a recovery program is usually run. Suppose that this program discovers that the link count in a disk i-node is 2, but only one directory entry references the i-node. Can it fix the problem, and if so, how?

44. Make an educated guess as to which UNIX system call is the fastest.

45. Is it possible to unlink a file that has never been linked? What happens?

46. Based on the information presented in this chapter, if a Linux ext2 file system were to be put on a 1.44 Mbyte floppy disk what is the maximum amount of user file data that could be stored on the disk? Assume that disk blocks are 1 KB.

47. In view of all the trouble that students can cause if they get to be superuser, why does this concept exist in the first place?

48. A professor shares files with his students by placing them in a publically accessible directory on the CS department's UNIX system. One day he realizes that a file placed there the previous day was left world-writable. He changes the permissions and verifies the file is identical to his master copy. The next day he finds the file has been changed. How could this have happened and how could it have been prevented?

49. Write a minimal shell that allows simple commands to be started. It should also allow them to be started in the background.

50. Using assembly language and BIOS calls, write a program that boots itself from a floppy disk on a Pentium-class computer. The program should use BIOS calls to read the keyboard and echo the characters typed, just to demonstrate that it is running.

51. Write a dumb terminal program to connect two UNIX or Linux workstations via the serial ports. Use the POSIX terminal management calls to configure the ports.

11

CASE STUDY 2: WINDOWS 2000

Windows 2000 is a modern operating system that runs on high-end desktop PCs and servers. In this chapter we will examine various aspects of it, starting with a brief history, then moving on to its architecture. After this we will look at processes, memory management, I/O, the file system, and finally, security. One thing we will not look at is networking as that could easily fill a chapter (or an entire book) all by itself.

11.1 HISTORY OF WINDOWS 2000

Microsoft operating systems for desktop and laptop PCs can be divided into three families: MS-DOS, Consumer Windows (Windows 95/98/Me), and Windows NT. Below we will briefly sketch each of these families.

11.1.1 MS-DOS

In 1981, IBM, at the time the biggest and most powerful computer company in the world, produced the 8088-based IBM PC. The PC came equipped with a 16-bit real-mode, single-user, command-line oriented operating system called MS-DOS 1.0. The operating system was provided by Microsoft, a tiny startup, mostly known at that time for its BASIC interpreter used on 8080 and Z-80 systems. This operating system consisted of 8 KB of memory resident code and was closely modeled on CP/M, a tiny operating system for the 8-bit 8080 and Z80 CPUs. Two years later, a much more powerful 24-KB operating system, MS-DOS 2.0, was released. It contained a command line processor (shell), with a number of features borrowed from UNIX.

When Intel came out with the 286 chip, IBM built a new computer around it, the PC/AT, released in 1986. AT stood for Advanced Technology, because the 286 ran at a then-impressive 8 MHz and could address—with great difficulty—all of 16 MB of RAM. In practice, most systems had at most 1 MB or 2 MB, due to the great expense of so much memory. The PC/AT came equipped with Microsoft's MS-DOS 3.0, by now 36 KB. Over the years, MS-DOS continued to acquire new features, but it was still a command-line oriented system.

11.1.2 Windows 95/98/Me

Inspired by the user interface of the Apple Lisa, the forerunner to the Apple Macintosh, Microsoft decided to give MS-DOS a graphical user interface (shell) that it called **Windows**. Windows 1.0, released in 1985, was something of a dud. Windows 2.0, designed for the PC-AT and released in 1987, was not much better. Finally, Windows 3.0 for the 386 (released in 1990), and especially its successors 3.1 and 3.11, caught on and were huge commercial successes. None of these early versions of Windows were true operating systems, but more like graphical user interfaces on top of MS-DOS, which was still in control of the machine and the file system. All programs ran in the same address space and a bug in any one of them could bring the whole system to a grinding halt.

The release of Windows 95 in August 1995 still did not completely eliminate MS-DOS, although it transferred nearly all the features from the MS-DOS part to the Windows part. Together, Windows 95 and the new MS-DOS 7.0 contained most of the features of a full-blown operating system, including virtual memory, process management, and multiprogramming. However, Windows 95 was not a full 32-bit program. It contained large chunks of old 16-bit assembly code (as well as some 32-bit code) and still used the MS-DOS file system, with nearly all its limitations. The only major change to the file system was the addition of long file names in place of the 8 + 3 character file names allowed in MS-DOS.

Even with the release of Windows 98 in June 1998, MS-DOS was still there (now called version 7.1) and running 16-bit code. Although yet more functionality migrated from the MS-DOS part to the Windows part, and a disk layout suitable for larger disks was now standard, under the hood, Windows 98 was not very different from Windows 95. The main difference was the user interface, which integrated the desktop and the Internet more closely. It was precisely this integration that attracted the attention of the U.S. Dept. of Justice, which then sued Microsoft claiming that it was an illegal monopoly, an accusation Microsoft vigorously denied. In April 2000, a U.S. Federal court agreed with the government.

In addition to containing a large lump of old 16-bit assembly code in the kernel, Windows 98 had two other serious problems. First, although it was a multiprogramming system, the kernel itself was not reentrant. If a process was busy manipulating some kernel data structure and then suddenly its quantum ran out and another process started running, the new process might find the data structure in an inconsistent state. To prevent this type of problem, after entering the kernel, most processes first acquired a giant mutex covering the whole system before doing anything. While this approach eliminated potential inconsistencies, it also eliminated much of the value of multiprogramming since processes were frequently forced to wait for unrelated processes to leave the kernel before they could enter it.

Second, each Windows 98 process had a 4-GB virtual address space. Of this, 2 GB was completely private to the process. However, the next 1 GB was shared (writably) among all other processes in the system. The bottom 1 MB was also shared among all processes to allow all of them to access the MS-DOS interrupt vectors. This sharing facility was heavily used by most Windows 98 applications. As a consequence, a bug in one program could wipe out key data structures used by unrelated processes, leading to them all crashing. Worse yet, the last 1 GB was shared (writably) with the kernel and contained some critical kernel data structures. Any rogue program that overwrote these data structures with garbage could bring down the system. The obvious solution of not putting kernel data structures in user space was not possible because this feature was essential to making old MS-DOS programs work under Windows 98.

In the millennium year, 2000, Microsoft brought out a minor revision to Windows 98 called **Windows Me** (**Windows Millennium Edition**). Although it fixed a few bugs and added a few features, under the covers it is essentially Windows 98. The new features included better ways to catalog and share images, music, and movies, more support for home networking and multiuser games, and more Internet-related features, such as support for instant messaging and broadband connections (cable modems and ADSL). One interesting new feature was the ability to restore the computer to its previous settings after a misconfiguration. If a user reconfigures the system (e.g., changing the screen from 640×480 to 1024×768) and it no longer works, this feature makes it possible to revert to the last known working configuration.

11.1.3 Windows NT

By the late 1980s, Microsoft realized that building a modern 32-bit operating system on top of the leaky 16-bit MS-DOS probably was not the best way to go. It recruited David Cutler, one of the key designers of DEC's VMS operating system, to work for Microsoft and gave him the job of leading a team to produce a brand-new 32-bit Windows compatible operating system from the ground up. This new system, later called **Windows NT (Windows New Technology)**, was intended for mission-critical business applications as well as for home users. At the time, mainframes still ruled the (business) world, so designing an operating system on the assumption that companies would use personal computers for anything important was a visionary goal, but one that history has shown to be a very good one. Features such as security and high reliability, clearly lacking on the MS-DOS-based versions of Windows, were high on the agenda for (Windows) NT. Cutler's background with VMS clearly shows in various places, with there being more than a passing similarity between the design of NT and that of VMS.

The project succeeded and the first version, called Windows NT 3.1, was released in 1993. This initial release number was chosen to match the number of Microsoft's then-popular 16-bit Windows 3.1 system. Microsoft expected that NT would rapidly replace Windows 3.1 because it was technically a far superior system.

Much to its surprise, nearly all users preferred to stick with the old 16-bit system they knew, rather than upgrade to an unknown 32-bit system they did not know, however better it might be. Furthermore, NT required far more memory than Windows 3.1 and there were no 32-bit programs for it to run, so why bother? The failure of NT 3.1 to catch on in the marketplace was the reason Microsoft decided to build a 32-bit-ish version of Windows 3.1, namely Windows 95. The continued user resistance to NT then caused Microsoft to produce Windows 98 and finally Windows Me; each one claimed to be the very last release of the MS-DOS-based systems.

Despite the fact that nearly all consumers and most businesses ignored NT 3.1 for desktop systems, it did acquire a small following in the server market. A few new 3.x releases with small changes occurred in 1994 and 1995. These slowly began to acquire more following among desktop users as well.

The first major upgrade to NT came with NT 4.0 in 1996. This system had the power, security, and reliability of the new operating system, but also sported the same user interface as the by-then very popular Windows 95. This compatibility made it much easier for users to migrate from Windows 95 to NT, and many of them did so. Some of the differences between Windows 95/98 and Windows NT are summarized in Fig. 11-1.

From the beginning, NT was designed to be portable, so it was written almost entirely in C, with only a tiny bit of assembly code for low-level functions such as interrupt handling. The initial release consisted of 3.1 million lines of C for the operating system, libraries, and the environment subsystems (discussed below). When NT 4.0 came out, the code base had grown to 16 million lines of code, still mostly C, but with a small amount of C++ in the user interface part. By this time the system was highly portable, with versions running on the Pentium, Alpha, MIPS, and PowerPC, among other CPUs. Some of these have been dropped since then. The story of how NT was developed is given in the book *Showstopper* (Zachary, 1994). The book also tells a lot about the key people involved.

Item	Windows 95/98	Windows NT
Full 32-bit system?	No	Yes
Security?	No	Yes
Protected file mappings?	No	Yes
Private addr space for each MS-DOS prog?	No	Yes
Unicode?	No	Yes
Runs on	Intel 80x86	80x86, Alpha, MIPS, ...
Multiprocessor support?	No	Yes
Re-entrant code inside OS?	No	Yes
Plug and play?	Yes	No
Power management?	Yes	No
FAT-32 file system?	Yes	Optional
NTFS file system	No	Yes
Win32 API?	Yes	Yes
Run all old MS-DOS programs?	Yes	No
Some critical OS data writable by user?	Yes	No

Figure 11-1. Some differences between Windows 98 and Windows NT.

11.1.4 Windows 2000

The release of NT following NT 4.0 was originally going to be called NT 5.0. However, in 1999, Microsoft changed the name to Windows 2000, mostly in an attempt to have a neutral name that both Windows 98 users and NT users could see as a logical next step for them. To the extent that this approach succeeds, Microsoft will have a single main operating system built on reliable 32-bit technology but using the popular Windows 98 user interface.

Since Windows 2000 really is NT 5.0, it inherits many properties from NT 4.0. It is a true 32-bit (soon to be 64-bit) multiprogramming system with individually protected processes. Each process has a private 32-bit (soon 64-bit) demand-paged virtual address space. The operating system runs in kernel mode, whereas user processes run in user mode, providing complete protection (with none of the protection flaws of Windows 98). Processes can have one or more threads, which are visible to, and scheduled by, the operating system. It has Dept. of Defense C2 security for all files, directories, processes, and other shareable objects (at least, if the floppy disk is removed and the network is unplugged). Finally, it also has full support for running on symmetric multiprocessors with up to 32 CPUs.

The fact that Windows 2000 really is NT 5.0 is visible in many places. For example, the system directory is called *winnt* and the operating system binary (in *winnt\system32*) is called *ntoskrnl.exe*. Right clicking on this file to examine its properties shows that its version number is 5.*xxx.yyy.zzz*, where the 5 stands for NT 5, *xxx* is the release number, *yyy* is the build (compilation) number, and *zzz* the minor variant. Also, many of the files in *winnt* and its subdirectories have *nt* in their names, such as *ntvdm*, NT's virtual MS-DOS emulator.

Windows 2000 is more than just a better NT 4.0 with the Windows 98 user interface. To start with, it contains a number of other features previously found only in Windows 98. These include complete support for plug-and-play devices, the USB bus, IEEE 1394 (FireWire), IrDA (the infrared link between portable computers and printers), and power management, among others. In addition, a number of new features not present in any other Microsoft operating system have been added, including active directory directory service, security using Kerberos, support for smart cards, system monitoring tools, better integration of laptop computers with desktop computers, a system management infrastructure, and job objects. Also, the main file system, NTFS, has been extended to support encrypted files, quotas, linked files, mounted volumes, and content indexing, for example. Another novel NTFS feature is the single instance store, which is a kind of copy-on-write link in which two users can share a linked file until one of them writes on it, at which time a copy is made automatically.

One other major improvement is internationalization. NT 4.0 came in separate versions for different languages with the text strings embedded in the code. Installing an English software package on a Dutch computer often caused parts of the operating system to stop using Dutch and start using English because certain files containing code and text strings were overwritten. This problem has been eliminated. Windows 2000 has a single binary that runs everywhere in the world. An installation, or even an individual user, can choose the language to use at run time because all the menu items, dialog strings, error reports, and other text strings have been removed from the operating system and put in separate directories, one per installed language. Like all previous versions of NT, Windows 2000 uses Unicode throughout the system to support languages not using the Latin alphabet, such as Russian, Greek, Hebrew, and Japanese.

One thing that Windows 2000 does not have is MS-DOS. It is simply not there in any form (nor was it there in NT). There is a command line interface, but this is a new 32-bit program that includes the old MS-DOS functionality and considerably new functionality as well.

Despite many portability features with regard to the code, hardware, language, etc., in one respect Windows 2000 is less portable than NT 4.0: it runs on only two platforms, the Pentium and the Intel IA-64. Originally NT supported additional platforms, including the PowerPC, MIPS, and Alpha, but over the years, Microsoft dropped one after another for commercial reasons.

Like previous versions of NT, Windows 2000 comes in several product levels, this time: Professional, Server, Advanced server, and Datacenter server. The differences between all these versions are minor however, with the same executable binary used for all versions. When the system is installed, the product type is recorded in an internal database (the registry). At boot time, the operating system checks the registry to see which version it is. The differences are shown in Fig. 11-2.

Version	Max RAM	CPUs	Max clients	Cluster size	Optimized for
Professional	4 GB	2	10	0	Response time
Server	4 GB	4	Unlimited	0	Throughput
Advanced server	8 GB	8	Unlimited	2	Throughput
Datacenter server	64 GB	32	Unlimited	4	Throughput

Figure 11-2. The different versions of Windows 2000.

As can be seen from the figure, the differences include the maximum memory supported, the maximum number of CPUs (for a multiprocessor configuration), and the maximum number of clients that can be served. The cluster size relates to the ability of Windows 2000 to make two or four machines look like a single server to the outside world, a useful feature for Web servers, for example. Finally, the default parameters are tuned differently on Professional, to favor interactive programs over batch work, although these can easily be changed if desired. One last difference is that some extra software is provided on the servers and some extra tools are provided on Datacenter server for managing large jobs.

The reason for having multiple versions is simply marketing: this allows Microsoft to charge big companies more than they charge individuals for what is essentially the same product. This idea is not new, however, and hardly unique to Microsoft. For years, airlines having been charging business passengers much more, not only for Business Class, but also for Cattle Class if they want the luxury of buying the ticket a day before the flight instead of a month before the flight.

Technically, the way the version differences are maintained is that in a few places in the code, two variables are read from the registry, *ProductType* and *ProductSuite*. Depending on their values, slightly different code is executed. Changing these variables is in violation of the license. In addition, the system traps any attempt to change them and records the attempt at tampering in an indelible way so it can be detected later.

In addition to the basic operating system, Microsoft has also developed several tool kits for advanced users. These include the Support Tools, the Software Development Kit, the Driver Development Kit, and the Resource Kit. These include a large number of utilities and tools for tweaking and monitoring the system. The support tools are on the Windows 2000 CD-ROM in the directory *\support\tools*. The standard installation procedure does not install them, but there is a file *setup.exe* in that directory that does. The SDK and DDK are available to developers at *msdn.microsoft.com*. The Resource Kit is a Microsoft product in a box. There are also various third-party tools available for snooping on the Windows 2000 internals, including a nice set available for free at the Web site *www.sysinternals.com.* Some of these even provide more information than the corresponding Microsoft tools.

Windows 2000 is an immensely complex system, now consisting of over 29 million lines of C code. If printed 50 lines per page and 1000 pages per bound book, the full code would occupy 580 volumes. This opus would occupy 23 running meters of shelf space (for the paperback version). If arranged in bookcases 1 m wide with 6 shelves per bookcase, the set would occupy a wall 4 m wide.

Just for fun, a comparison of a few operating system source code sizes is given in Fig. 11-3. However, this table should be taken with a grain (or better yet, a metric ton) of salt because what constitutes the operating system is different for different systems. For example, the entire window system and GUI is part of the kernel in Windows, but not in any UNIX version. It is simply a user process there. Counting X Windows adds another 1.5 million lines of code to all the UNIX versions, and that does not even count the GUI code (Motif, GNOME, etc.), which is also not part of the operating system in the UNIX world. Additionally, some systems include code for multiple architectures (e.g., five for 4.4 BSD and nine for Linux), with each architecture adding 10,000 to 50,000 lines of code. The reason Free BSD 1.0 has only 235,000 lines of code whereas 4BSD Lite, from which it is derived, has 743,000 lines is that support for all the obsolete architectures (e.g., the VAX) was dropped in Free BSD.

Also, the number of file systems, devices drivers, and libraries supplied varies greatly from system to system. In addition, Windows contains large amounts of test code that UNIX does not contain as well as some utilities and support for numerous languages besides English. Finally, the measurements were made by different people, which introduces considerable variance (e.g., did makefiles, headers, configuration files and documentation count and how much was there?). This is not like comparing apples with oranges; it is like comparing apples with telephones. However, all the counts within a single family came from the same source, so intrafamily counts are somewhat meaningful.

Despite all these disclaimers, two conclusions are fairly clear:

1. System bloat seems to be as inevitable as death and taxes.

2. Windows is much bigger than UNIX

Whether small is beautiful or big is beautiful is a matter of heated controversy. The argument for the former is that small size and a lean-and-mean mentality produces a manageable, reliable system that users can understand. The argument for the latter is that many users want lots of features. In any event, it should also be clear that any students planning to write a full-blown, state-of-the-art operating system from scratch have their work cut out for them.

Although Windows 2000 is already the world heavyweight champion in terms of pure mass, it is still growing, with bugs being fixed and new features being added. The way Microsoft manages its development is worth noting. Hundreds

Year	AT&T		BSD		MINIX		Linux		Solaris		Win NT	
1976	V6	9K										
1979	V7	21K										
1980			4.1	38K								
1982	Sys III	58K										
1984			4.2	98K								
1986			4.3	179K								
1987	SVR3	92K			1.0	13K						
1989	SVR4	280K										
1991							0.01	10K				
1993			Free 1.0	235K					5.3	850K	3.1	6M
1994			4.4 Lite	743K			1.0	165K			3.5	10M
1996							2.0	470K			4.0	16M
1997					2.0	62K			5.6	1.4M		
1999							2.2	1M				
2000			Free 4.0	1.4M					5.8	2.0M	2000	29M

Figure 11-3. A comparison of some operating system sizes. The first string in each box is the version; the second is the size measured in lines of source code, where K = 1000 and M = 1,000,000. Comparisons within a column have real meaning; comparisons across columns do not, as discussed in the text.

of programmers work on various aspects of Windows 2000 all day. Whenever a piece of code is finished, the programmer submits it electronically to the build team. At 6 P.M. every day, the door is closed and the system is rebuilt (i.e., recompiled and linked). Each build gets a unique sequence number, which can be seen by examining the version number of *ntoskrnl.exe* (the first public release of Windows 2000 was build 2195).

The new operating system is electronically distributed to thousands of machines around the Microsoft campus in Redmond, WA, where it is subjected to intense stress tests all night. Early the next morning, the results of all the tests are sent to the relevant groups, so they can see if their new code works. Each team then decides which code they want to work on that day. During the day, the programmers work on their code and at 6 P.M. the build-and-test-cycle begins anew.

11.2 PROGRAMMING WINDOWS 2000

It is now time to start our technical study of Windows 2000. However, before getting into the details of the internal structure, we will first take a look at the programming interface and the registry, a small in-memory data base.

11.2.1 The Win32 Application Programming Interface

Like all other operating systems, Windows 2000 has a set of system calls it can perform. However, Microsoft has never made the list of Windows system calls public, and it also changes them from release to release. Instead, what Microsoft has done is define a set of function calls called the **Win32 API** (**Win32 Application Programming Interface**) that are publicly known and fully documented. These are library procedures that either make system calls to get the work done, or, in some cases, do the work right in user space. The existing Win32 API calls do not change with new releases of Windows, although new API calls are added frequently.

Binary programs for the Intel x86 that adhere exactly to the Win32 API interface will run unmodified on all versions of Windows since Windows 95. As shown in Fig. 11-4, an extra library is needed for Windows 3.x to match a subset of the 32-bit API calls to the 16-bit operating system, but for the other systems no adaptation is needed. It should be noted that Windows 2000 adds substantial new functionality to Win32, so it has additional API calls not included on older versions of Win32 and which will not work on older versions of Windows.

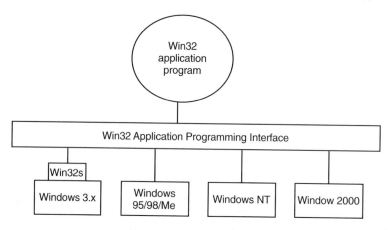

Figure 11-4. The Win32 API allows programs to run on almost all versions of Windows.

The Win32 API philosophy is completely different from the UNIX philosophy. In the latter, the system calls are all publicly known and form a minimal interface: removing even one of them would reduce the functionality of the operating system. The Win32 philosophy is to provide a very comprehensive interface, often with three or four ways of doing the same thing, and including many functions (i.e., procedures) that clearly should not be (and are not) system calls, such as an API call to copy an entire file.

Many Win32 API calls create kernel objects of one kind or another, including files, processes, threads, pipes, and so on. Every call creating an object returns a result called a **handle** to the caller. This handle can subsequently be used to perform operations on the object. Handles are specific to the process that created the object referred to by the handle. They cannot be passed directly to another process and used there (just as UNIX file descriptors cannot be passed to other processes and used there). However, under certain circumstances, it is possible to duplicate a handle and pass it to other processes in a protected way, allowing them controlled access to objects belonging to other processes. Every object also has a security descriptor associated with it, telling in detail who may and may not perform what kinds of operations on the object.

Not all system-created data structures are objects and not all objects are kernel objects. The only ones that are true kernel objects are those that need to be named, protected, or shared in some way. Every kernel object has a system-defined type, has well-defined operations on it, and occupies storage in kernel memory. Although users can perform the operations (by making Win32 calls), they cannot get at the data directly.

The operating system itself can also create and use objects and does so heavily. Most of these objects are created to allow one component of the system to store some information for a substantial period of time or to pass some data structure to another component. For example, when a device driver is loaded, an object is created for it holding its properties and pointers to the functions it contains. Within the operating system, the driver is then referred to by using its object.

Windows 2000 is sometimes said to be object-oriented because the only way to manipulate objects is by invoking operations on their handles by making Win32 API calls. On the other hand, it lacks some of the most basic properties of object-oriented systems such as inheritance and polymorphism.

The Win32 API calls cover every conceivable area an operating system could deal with, and quite a few it arguably should not deal with. Naturally, there are calls for creating and managing processes and threads. There are also many calls that relate to interprocess (actually, interthread) communication, such as creating, destroying, and using mutexes, semaphores, events, and other IPC objects.

Although much of the memory management system is invisible to programmers (fundamentally, it is just demand paging), one important feature is visible: namely the ability of a process to map a file onto a region of its virtual memory. This allows the process the ability to read and write parts of the file as though they were memory words.

An important area for many programs is file I/O. In the Win32 view, a file is just a linear sequence of bytes. Win32 provides over 60 calls for creating and destroying files and directories, opening and closing files, reading and writing them, requesting and setting file attributes, and much more.

Another area for which Win32 provides calls is security. Every process has an ID telling who it is and every object can have an access control list telling in great detail precisely which users may access it and which operations they may perform on it. This approach provides for a fine-grained security in which specific individuals can be allowed or denied specific access to every object.

Processes, threads, synchronization, memory management, file I/O, and security system calls are nothing new. Other operating systems have them too, although generally not hundreds of them, as Win32 does. But what really distinguishes Win32 are the thousands upon thousands of calls for the graphical interface. There are calls for creating, destroying, managing and using windows, menus, tool bars, status bars, scroll bars, dialog boxes, icons, and many more items that appear on the screen. There are calls for drawing geometric figures, filling them in, managing the color palettes they use, dealing with fonts, and placing icons on the screen. Finally, there are calls for dealing with the keyboard, mouse and other input devices as well as audio, printing, and other output devices. In short, the Win32 API (especially the GUI part) is immense and we could not even begin to describe it in any detail in this chapter, so we will not try. Interested readers should consult one of the many books on Win32 (e.g., Petzold, 1999; Simon, 1997; and Rector and Newcomer, 1997).

Although the Win32 API is available on Windows 98 (as well as on the consumer electronics operating system, Windows CE), not every version of Windows implements every call and sometimes there are minor differences as well. For example, Windows 98 does not have any security, so those API calls that relate to security just return error codes on Windows 98. Also, Windows 2000 file names use the Unicode character set, which is not available on Windows 98 and Windows 98 file names are not case sensitive, whereas Windows 2000 file names are case sensitive (although some kinds of searches on file names are not case sensitive). There are also differences in parameters to some API function calls. On Windows 2000, for example, all the screen coordinates given in the graphics functions are true 32-bit numbers; on Windows 98, only the low-order 16 bits are used because much of the graphics subsystem is still 16-bit code. The existence of the Win32 API on several different operating systems makes it easier to port programs between them, but since these minor variations exist, some care must be taken to achieve portability.

11.2.2 The Registry

Windows needs to keep track of a great deal of information about hardware, software, and users. In Window 3.x, this information was stored in hundreds of *.ini* (initialization) files spread all over the disk. Starting with Windows 95, nearly all the information needed for booting and configuring the system and tailoring it to the current user was gathered in a big central database called the **registry**. In this section we will give an overview of the Windows 2000 registry.

To start with, it is worth noting that although many parts of Windows 2000 are complicated and messy, the registry is one of the worst, and the cryptic nomenclature does not make it any better. Fortunately, entire books have been written describing it (Born, 1998; Hipson, 2000; and Ivens, 1998). That said, the *idea* behind the registry is very simple. It consists of a collection of directories, each of which contains either subdirectories or entries. In this respect it is a kind of file system for very small files. It has directories and entries (the files).

The confusion starts with the fact that Microsoft calls a directory a **key**, which it definitely is not. Furthermore, all the top-level directories start with the string *HKEY*, which means handle to key. Subdirectories tend to have somewhat better chosen names, although not always.

At the bottom of the hierarchy are the entries, called **values**, which contain the information. Each value has three parts: a name, a type, and the data. The name is just a Unicode string, often default if the directory contains only one value. The type is one of 11 standard types. The most common ones are Unicode string, a list of Unicode strings, a 32-bit integer, an arbitrary length binary number, and a symbolic link to a directory or entry elsewhere in the registry. Symbolic names are completely analogous to symbolic links in file systems or shortcuts on the Windows desktop: they allow one entry to point to another entry or directory. A symbolic link can also be used as a key, meaning that something that appears to be a directory is just a pointer to a different directory.

At the top level, the Windows 2000 registry has six keys, called **root keys**, as listed in Fig. 11-5. Some interesting **subkeys** (subdirectories) are also shown here. To see this list on your system, use one of the registry editors, either *regedit* or *regedt32*, which unfortunately display different information and use different formats. They can also change registry values. Amateurs should not change keys or values on any system they plan to boot again. Just looking is safe, though. You have been warned.

The first key (i.e., directory), HKEY_LOCAL_MACHINE, is probably the most important as it contains all the information about the local system. It has five subkeys (i.e., subdirectories). The HARDWARE subkey contains many subkeys telling all about the hardware and which driver controls which piece of hardware. This information is constructed on the fly by the plug-and-play manager as the system boots. Unlike the other subkeys, it is not stored on disk.

The SAM (Security Account Manager) subkey contains the user names, groups, passwords, and other account and security information needed for logging in. The SECURITY subkey contains general security policy information, such as minimum length for passwords, how many failed login attempts are tolerated before the police are called, etc.

The SOFTWARE subkey is where software manufacturers store preferences etc. For example, if a user has Adobe *Acrobat*, *Photoshop* and *Premiere* installed, there will be a subkey Adobe here, and below that further subkeys for Acrobat, Photoshop, Premiere, and any other Adobe products. The entries in these subdirectories can store anything the Adobe programmers want to put there, generally system-wide properties such as the version and build number, how to uninstall the package, drivers to use, and so forth. The registry saves them the trouble of hav-

Key	Description
HKEY_LOCAL_MACHINE	Properties of the hardware and software
HARDWARE	Hardware description and mapping of hardware to drivers
SAM	Security and account information for users
SECURITY	System-wide security policies
SOFTWARE	Generic information about installed application programs
SYSTEM	Information for booting the system
HKEY_USERS	Information about the users; one subkey per user
USER-AST-ID	User AST's profile
AppEvents	Which sound to make when (incoming email/fax, error, etc.)
Console	Command prompt settings (colors, fonts, history, etc.)
Control Panel	Desktop appearance, screensaver, mouse sensitivity, etc.
Environment	Environment variables
Keyboard Layout	Which keyboard: 102-key US, AZERTY, Dvorak, etc.
Printers	Information about installed printers
Software	User preferences for Microsoft and third party software
HKEY_PERFORMANCE_DATA	Hundreds of counters monitoring system performance
HKEY_CLASSES_ROOT	Link to HKEY_LOCAL_MACHINE\SOFTWARE\CLASSES
HKEY_CURRENT_CONFIG	Link to the current hardware profile
HKEY_CURRENT_USER	Link to the current user profile

Figure 11-5. The root keys registry keys and selected subkeys. The capitalization has no meaning but follows the Microsoft practice here.

ing to invent their own method for storing this information. User-specific information also goes in the registry, but under HKEY_USERS.

The SYSTEM subkey holds mostly information about booting the system, for example, the list of drivers that must be loaded. It also holds the list of services (daemons) that must be started after booting up and the configuration information for all of them.

The next top-level key is HKEY_USERS, which contains the profiles of all the users. All the user-specific preferences in a number of areas are stored here. When a user changes a preference using the control panel, for example, the desktop color scheme, the new settings are recorded here. In fact, many of the programs on the control panel do little more than collect user information and change the registry accordingly. Some of the subkeys under HKEY_USERS are shown in Fig. 11-5 and should need little additional comment. Some of the subkeys, such as Software, contain surprisingly large numbers of subkeys, even if no software packages are installed.

The next top-level key, HKEY_PERFORMANCE_DATA contains neither data read in from the disk nor data collected by the plug-and-play manager. Instead, it offers a window into the operating system. The system itself contains hundreds of counters for monitoring system performance. These counters are accessible via this registry key. When a subkey is queried, a specified procedure is run to collect and return the information (possibly by reading one or more counters and combining them in some way). This key is not visible using *regedit* or *regedt32*. Instead one has to use the performance tools, such as *pfmon*, *perfmon*, and *pview*. There are many such tools, some on the Windows 2000 CD-ROM, some in the resource kits, and some from third parties.

The next three top-level keys do not actually exist. Each one is a symbolic link to some place elsewhere in the registry. The HKEY_CLASSES_ROOT key is the most interesting. It points to the directory that handles COM (Component Object Model) objects and also the associations between file extensions and programs. When a user double clicks on a file ending in, say, *.doc*, the program catching the mouse click looks here to see which program to run (probably *Microsoft Word*). The complete database of recognized extensions and which program each one is owned by is under this key.

The HKEY_CURRENT_CONFIG key links to the current hardware configuration. A user can construct multiple hardware configurations, for example by disabling various devices to see if they were the cause of strange system behavior. This key points to the current configuration. Similarly, HKEY_CURRENT_USER points to the current user so that user's preferences can be found quickly.

None of the last three keys really adds anything, since the information was available elsewhere anyway (although less conveniently accessible). Thus despite the fact that *regedit* and *regedt32* list five top-level keys, there are really only three top-level directories and one of those is not shown among the five displayed.

The registry is fully available to the Win32 programmer. There are calls to create and delete keys, look up values within keys, and more. Some of the more useful ones are listed in Fig. 11-6.

Win32 API function	Description
RegCreateKeyEx	Create a new registry key
RegDeleteKey	Delete a registry key
RegOpenKeyEx	Open a key to get a handle to it
RegEnumKeyEx	Enumerate the subkeys subordinate to the key of the handle
RegQueryValueEx	Look up the data for a value within a key

Figure 11-6. Some of the Win32 API calls for using the registry

When the system is turned off, most of the registry information (but not all, as discussed above) is stored on the disk in files called **hives**. Most of them are in *\winnt\system32\config*. Because their integrity is so critical to correct system functioning, when they are updated, backups are made automatically and writes are done using atomic transactions to prevent corruption in the event of system crash during the write. Loss of the registry requires reinstalling all software.

11.3 SYSTEM STRUCTURE

In the previous sections we examined Windows 2000 as seen by the programmer. Now we are going to look under the hood to see how the system is organized internally, what the various components do, and how they interact with each other and with user programs. Although there are many books on how to use Windows 2000, there are many fewer on how it works. Far and away the best place to look for additional information on this topic is *Inside Windows 2000*, 3rd ed. by Solomon and Russinovich (2000). Some of the material in this chapter is based on information in that book and information from the authors. Microsoft was also a key source.

11.3.1 Operating System Structure

Windows 2000 consists of two major pieces: the operating system itself, which runs in kernel mode, and the environment subsystems, which run in user mode. The kernel is a traditional kernel in the sense that it handles process management, memory management, file systems, and so on. The environment subsystems are somewhat unusual in that they are separate processes that help user programs carry out certain system functions. In the following sections we will examine each of these parts in turn.

One of NT's many improvements over Windows 3.x was its modular structure. It consisted of a moderately small kernel that ran in kernel mode, plus some server processes that ran in user mode. User processes interacted with the server processes using the client-server model: a client sent a request message to a server, and the server did the work and returned the result to the client via a second message. This modular structure made it easier to port it to several computers besides the Intel line, including the DEC Alpha, IBM PowerPC, and SGI MIPS. It also protected the kernel from bugs in the server code. However, for performance reasons, starting with NT 4.0, pretty much all of the operating system (e.g., system call handling and all of the screen graphics) was put back into kernel mode. This design was carried over to Windows 2000.

Nevertheless, there is still some structure in Windows 2000. It is divided into several layers, each one using the services of the ones beneath it. The structure is illustrated in Fig. 11-7. One of the layers is divided horizontally into many modules. Each module has some particular function and a well-defined interface to the other modules.

The lowest two software layers, the HAL and the kernel, are written in C and in assembly language and are partly machine dependent. The upper ones are written entirely in C and are almost entirely machine independent. The drivers are written in C, or in a few cases C++. Below we will first examine the various components of the system starting at the bottom and working our way up.

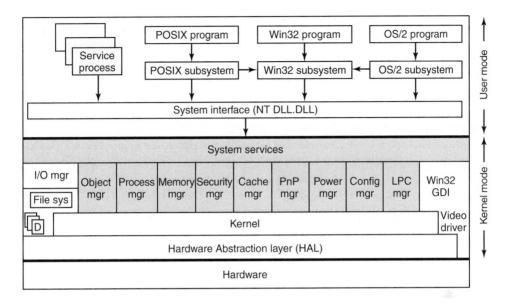

Figure 11-7. The structure of Windows 2000 (slightly simplified). The shaded area is the executive. The boxes indicated by D are device drivers. The service processes are system daemons.

The Hardware Abstraction Layer

One of the goals of Windows 2000 (and Windows NT before it) was to make the operating system portable across platforms. Ideally, when a new machine comes along, it should be possible to just recompile the operating system with the new machine's compiler and have it run the first time. Unfortunately, life is not like that. While the upper layers of the operating system can be made completely portable (because they mostly deal with internal data structures), the lower layers deal with device registers, interrupts, DMA, and other hardware features that differ appreciably from machine to machine. Even though most of the low-level code is written in C, it cannot just be scooped up from a Pentium, plopped down on, say, an Alpha, recompiled, and rebooted due to the many small hardware differences between the Pentium and the Alpha that have nothing to do with the different instruction sets and which cannot be hidden by the compiler.

Fully aware of this problem, Microsoft made a serious attempt to hide many of the machine dependencies in a thin layer at the bottom called the **HAL** (**Hardware Abstraction Layer**). (The name HAL was no doubt inspired by the computer HAL in the late Stanley Kubrick's movie *2001: A Space Odyssey*. Rumor has it that Kubrick chose the name "HAL" by taking the name of the then-dominant computer company—IBM— and subtracting 1 from each letter.)

The job of the HAL is to present the rest of the operating system with abstract hardware devices, in particular, devoid of the warts and idiosyncracies with which real hardware is so richly endowed. These devices are presented in the form of machine-independent services (procedure calls and macros) that the rest of the operating system and the drivers can use. By using the HAL services (which are identical on all Windows 2000 systems, no matter what the hardware is) and not addressing the hardware directly, drivers and the kernel require fewer changes when being ported to new hardware. Porting the HAL itself is straightforward because all the machine-dependent code is concentrated in one place and the goals of the port are well defined, namely, implement all of the HAL services.

The services chosen for inclusion in the HAL are those that relate to the chip set on the parentboard and which vary from machine to machine within reasonably predictable limits. In other words, it is designed to hide the differences between one vendor's parentboard and another one's, but not the differences between a Pentium and an Alpha. The HAL services include access to the device registers, bus-independent device addressing, interrupt handling and resetting, DMA transfers, control of the timers and real-time clock, low-level spin locks and multiprocessor synchronization, interfacing with the BIOS and its CMOS configuration memory. The HAL does not provide abstractions or services for specific I/O devices such as keyboards, mice, or disks or for the memory management unit.

As an example of what the hardware abstraction layer does, consider the issue of memory-mapped I/O versus I/O ports. Some machines have one and some have the other. How should a driver be programmed: to use memory-mapped I/O or not? Rather than forcing a choice, which would make the driver not portable to a machine that did it the other way, the hardware abstraction layer offers three procedures for driver writers to use for reading the device registers and another three for writing them:

```
uc = READ_PORT_UCHAR(port);      WRITE_PORT_UCHAR(port, uc);
us = READ_PORT_USHORT(port);     WRITE_PORT_USHORT(port, us);
ul = READ_PORT_ULONG(port);      WRITE_PORT_LONG(port, ul);
```

These procedures read and write unsigned 8-, 16-, and 32-bit integers, respectively, to the specified port. It is up to the hardware abstraction layer to decide whether memory-mapped I/O is needed here. In this way, a driver can be moved without modification between machines that differ in the way the device registers are implemented.

Drivers often need to access specific I/O devices for various purposes. At the hardware level, a device has one or more addresses on a certain bus. Since modern computers often have multiple buses (ISA, PCI, SCSI, USB, 1394, etc.), it can happen that two or more devices have the same bus address, so some way is needed to distinguish them. The HAL provides a service for identifying devices by mapping bus-relative device addresses onto system-wide logical addresses. In this way, drivers are not required to keep track of which device is on which bus.

These logical addresses are analogous to the handles the operating system gives user programs to refer to files and other system resources. This mechanism also shields higher layers from properties of alternative bus structures and addressing conventions.

Interrupts have a similar problem—they are also bus dependent. Here, too, the HAL provides services to name interrupts in a system-wide way and also provides services to allow drivers to attach interrupt service routines to interrupts in a portable way, without having to know anything about which interrupt vector is for which bus. Interrupt request level management is also handled in the HAL.

Another HAL service is setting up and managing DMA transfers in a device-independent way. Both the system-wide DMA engine and DMA engines on specific I/O cards can be handled. Devices are referred to by their logical addresses. The HAL also implements software scatter/gather (writing or reading from noncontiguous blocks of physical memory).

The HAL also manages clocks and timers in a portable way. Time is kept track of in units of 100 nsec starting at 1 January 1601, which is far more precise than MS-DOS's keeping track of time in units of 2 sec since 1 January 1980 and provides support for the many computer-related activities in the 17th, 18th, and 19th centuries. The time services decouple the drivers from the actual frequencies at which the clocks run.

Kernel components sometimes need to synchronize at a very low level, especially to prevent race conditions in multiprocessor systems. The HAL provides some primitives to manage this synchronization, such as spin locks, in which one CPU simply waits for a resource held by another CPU to be released, particularly in situations where the resource is typically only held for a few machine instructions.

Finally, after the system has been booted, the HAL talks to the BIOS and inspects the CMOS configuration memory, if any, to find out which buses and I/O devices the system contains and how they have been configured. This information is then put into the registry so other system components can look it up without having to understand how the BIOS or configuration memory work. A summary of some of the things the HAL does is given in Fig. 11-8.

Since the HAL is highly-machine dependent, it must match the system it is installed on perfectly, so a variety of HALs are provided on the Windows 2000 CD-ROM. At system installation time, the appropriate one is selected and copied to the system directory \winnt\system32 on the hard disk as hal.dll. All subsequent boots use this version of the HAL. Removing this file will make the system unbootable.

Although the HAL is reasonably efficient, for multimedia applications, it may not be fast enough. For this reason, Microsoft also produced a software package called **DirectX**, which augments the HAL with additional procedures and allows user processes much more direct access to the hardware. DirectX is somewhat specialized, so we will not discuss it further in this chapter.

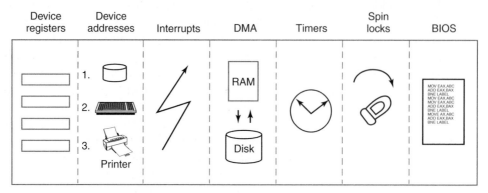

Hardware abstraction layer

Figure 11-8. Some of the hardware functions the HAL manages.

The Kernel Layer

Above the hardware abstraction layer is a layer that contains what Microsoft calls the **kernel**, as well as the device drivers. Some early documentation refers to the kernel as the "microkernel," which it really never was because the memory manager, file system, and other major components resided in kernel space and ran in kernel mode from day one. The kernel is certainly not a microkernel now since virtually the entire operating system was put in kernel space starting with NT 4.0.

In the chapter on UNIX, we used the term "kernel" to mean everything running in kernel mode. In this chapter we will (very grudgingly) reserve the term "kernel" for the part labeled as such in Fig. 11-7 and call the totality of the code running in kernel mode the "operating system." Part of kernel (and much of the HAL) is permanently resident in main memory (i.e., is not paged). By adjusting its priority, it can control whether it can tolerate being preempted by I/O interrupts or not. Although a substantial fraction of the kernel is machine specific, most of it is nevertheless written in C, except where top performance overshadows all other concerns.

The purpose of the kernel is to make the rest of the operating system completely independent of the hardware, and thus highly portable. It picks up where the HAL leaves off. It accesses the hardware via the HAL and builds upon the extremely low-level HAL services to construct higher-level abstractions. For example, the HAL has calls to associate interrupt service procedures with interrupts, and set their priorities, but does little else in this area. The kernel, in contrast, provides a complete mechanism for doing context switches. It properly saves all the CPU registers, changes the page tables, flushes the CPU cache, and so on, so that when it is done, the previously running thread has been saved in tables in memory. It then sets up the new thread's memory map and loads its registers so the new thread can start running.

The code for thread scheduling is also in the kernel. When it is time to see if a new thread can run, for example, after a quantum runs out or after an I/O interrupt completes, the kernel chooses the thread and does the context switch necessary to run it. From the point of view of the rest of the operating system, thread switching is automatically handled by lower layers without any work on their part and in a portable way. The scheduling algorithm itself will be discussed later in this chapter when we come to processes and threads.

In addition to providing a higher-level abstraction of the hardware and handling thread switches, the kernel also has another key function: providing low-level support for two classes of objects: control objects and dispatcher objects. These objects are not the objects that user processes get handles to, but are internal objects upon which the executive builds the user objects.

Control objects are those objects that control the system, including primitive process objects, interrupt objects, and two somewhat strange objects called DPC and APC. A **DPC** (**Deferred Procedure Call**) object is used to split off the non-time-critical part of an interrupt service procedure from the time critical part. Generally, an interrupt service procedure saves a few volatile hardware registers associated with the interrupting I/O device so they do not get overwritten and reenables the hardware, but saves the bulk of the processing for later.

For example, after a key is struck, the keyboard interrupt service procedure reads the key code from a register and reenables the keyboard interrupt, but does not need to process the key immediately, especially if something more important (i.e., higher priority) is currently going on. As long as the key is processed within about 100 msec, the user will be none the wiser. DPCs are also used for timer expirations and other activities whose actual processing need not be instantaneous. The DPC queue is the mechanism for remembering that there is more work to do later.

Another kernel control object is the **APC** (**Asynchronous Procedure Call**). APCs are like DPCs except that they execute in the context of a specific process. When processing a key press, it does not matter whose context the DPC runs in because all that is going to happen is that the key code will be inspected and probably put in a kernel buffer. However, if an interrupt requires copying a buffer from kernel space to a buffer in some user process' address space (e.g., as it may on completion of a read from the modem), then the copying procedure needs to run in the receiver's context. The receiver's context is needed so the page table will contain both the kernel buffer and the user buffer (all processes contain the entire kernel in their address spaces, as we will see later). For this reason, the kernel distinguishes between DPCs and APCs.

The other kind of kernel objects are **dispatcher objects**. These include semaphores, mutexes, events, waitable timers, and other objects that threads can wait on. The reason that these have to be handled (in part) in the kernel is that they are intimately intertwined with thread scheduling, which is a kernel task. As a little aside, mutexes are called "mutants" in the code because they were required to implement the OS/2 semantics of not automatically unlocking themselves when a thread holding one exited, something the Windows 2000 designers considered bizarre. (The OS/2 semantics are relevant because NT was originally conceived of as a replacement for OS/2, the operating system shipped on IBM's PC/2.)

The Executive

Above the kernel and device drivers is the upper portion of the operating system, called the **executive**, shown as the shaded area in Fig. 11-7. The executive is written in C, is architecture independent, and can be ported to new machines with relatively little effort. It consists of 10 components, each of which is just a collection of procedures that work together to accomplish some goal. There are no hard boundaries between the pieces and different authors describing the executive might even group the procedures differently into components. It should be noted that components on the same level can (and do) call each other extensively.

The **object manager** manages all objects known to the operating system. These include processes, threads, files, directories, semaphores, I/O devices, timers, and many others. The object manager allocates a block of virtual memory from kernel address space when an object is created and returns it to the free list when the object is deallocated. Its job is to keep track of all the objects.

To avoid any confusion, most of the executive components labeled "manager" in Fig. 11-7 are not processes or threads, but merely collections of procedures that other threads can execute when in kernel mode. A few of them, such as the power manager and plug-and-play manager, really are independent threads though.

The object manager also manages a name space in which newly created objects may be placed so they can be referred to later. All other components of the executive use objects heavily to do their work. Objects are so central to the functioning of Windows 2000 that they will be discussed in detail in the next section.

The **I/O manager** provides a framework for managing I/O devices and provides generic I/O services. It provides the rest of the system with device-independent I/O, calling the appropriate driver to perform physical I/O. It is also home to all the device drivers (indicated by *D* in Fig. 11-7). The file systems are technically device drivers under control of the I/O manager. Two different ones are present for the FAT and NTFS file systems, each one independent of the others and controlling different disk partitions. All the FAT file systems are managed by a single driver. We will study I/O further in Sec. 11.6 and one of the file systems, NTFS, in Sec. 11.7.

The **process manager** handles processes and threads, including their creation and termination. It deals with the mechanisms used to manage them, rather than policies about how they are used. It builds upon the kernel process and thread objects and adds extra functionality to them. It is the key to multiprogramming in Windows 2000. We will study process and thread management in Sec. 11.4.

The **memory manager** implements Windows 2000's demand-paged virtual memory architecture. It manages the mapping of virtual pages onto physical page frames. It thereby enforces the protection rules that restrict each process to only access those pages belonging to its address space and not to other processes' address spaces (except under special circumstances). It also handles certain system calls that relate to virtual memory. We will study memory management in Sec. 11.5.

The **security manager** enforces Windows 2000's elaborate security mechanism, which meets the U.S. Dept. of Defense's Orange Book C2 requirements. The Orange Book specifies a large number of rules that a conforming system must meet, starting with authenticated login through how access control is handled, to the fact that virtual pages must be zeroed out before being reused. We will study the security manager in Sec. 11.8.

The **cache manager** keeps the most recently used disk blocks in memory to speed up access to them in the (likely) event that they are needed again. Its job is to figure out which blocks are probably going to be needed again and which ones are not. It is possible to configure Windows 2000 with multiple file systems, in which case the cache manager works for all of them, so each one does not have to do its own cache management. When a block is needed, the cache manager is asked to supply it. If it does not have the block, the cache manager calls upon the appropriate file system to get it. Since files can be mapped into processes' address spaces, the cache manager must interact with the virtual memory manager to provide the necessary consistency. The amount of space devoted to caching is dynamic and can increase or decrease as demands on it change. We will study the cache manager in Sec. 11.9.

The **plug-and-play manager** is sent all notifications of newly attached devices. For some devices, a check is made at boot time and not thereafter. Other devices, for example, USB devices, can be attached at any time and their attachment triggers a message to the plug-and-play manager, which then locates and loads the appropriate driver.

The **power manager** rides herd on power usage. This consists of turning off the monitor and disks after they have been idle for a while. On laptops, the power manager monitors battery usage and takes action when the battery is about to run dry. Such action typically tells programs to save their files and prepare for a graceful shutdown. And pronto.

The **configuration manager** is in charge of the registry. It adds new entries and looks up keys when asked to.

The **local procedure call manager** provides for a highly-efficient interprocess communication used between processes and their subsystems. Since this path is needed to carry out some system calls, efficiency is critical here, which is why the standard interprocess communication mechanisms are not used.

The **Win32 GDI** executive module handles certain system calls (but not all of them). It was originally in user space but was moved to kernel space in NT 4.0 to improve performance. The **GDI** (**Graphics Device Interface**) handles image management for the monitor and printers. It provides system calls to allow user programs to write on the monitor and printers in a device-independent way. It also contains the window manager and display driver. Prior to NT 4.0, it, too, was in user space but the performance was disappointing, so Microsoft moved it into the kernel to speed it up. It is worth mentioning that Fig. 11-7 is not at all to scale. For example, the Win32 and graphics device interface module is larger than the rest of the executive combined.

At the top of the executive is a thin layer called **system services**. Its function is to provide an interface to the executive. It accepts the true Windows 2000 system calls and calls other parts of the executive to have them executed.

At boot time, Windows 2000 is loaded into memory as a collection of files. The main part of the operating system, consisting of the kernel and executive, is located in the file *ntoskrnl.exe*. The HAL is a shared library located in a separate file, *hal.dll*. The Win32 and graphics device interface are together in a third file, *win32k.sys*. Finally, many device drivers are also loaded. Most of these have extension *.sys*.

Actually, things are not quite that simple. The *ntoskrnl.exe* file comes in uniprocessor and multiprocessor versions. Also, there are versions for the Xeon processor, which can have more than 4 GB of physical memory and the Pentium, which cannot. Finally, versions can consist of a free build (sold in stores and preinstalled by computer manufacturers) or a checked build (for debugging purposes). Together there could be eight combinations, although two pairs were combined leaving only six. One of these is copied to *ntoskrnl.exe* when the system is installed.

The checked builds are worth a few words. When a new I/O device is installed on a PC, there is invariably a manufacturer-supplied driver that has to be installed to make it work. Suppose that an IEEE 1394 card is installed on a computer and appears to work fine. Two weeks later the system suddenly crashes. Who does the owner blame? Microsoft.

The bug may indeed be Microsoft's, but some bugs are actually due to flakey drivers, over which Microsoft has no control and which are installed in kernel memory and have full access to all kernel tables as well as the entire hardware. In an attempt to reduce the number of irate customers on the phone, Microsoft tries to help driver writers debug their code by putting statements of the form

        ASSERT(some condition)

throughout the code. These statements make sanity checks on all parameters to internal kernel procedures (which may be freely called by drivers) and make many other checks as well. The free builds have *ASSERT* defined as a macro that does nothing, removing all the checks. The checked builds have it defined as

        #define ASSERT(a) if (! (a)) error(...)

causing all the checks to appear in the *ntoskrnl.exe* executable code and be carried out at run time. While this slows down the system enormously, it helps driver writers debug their drivers before they ship them to customers. The checked builds also have numerous other debugging features turned on.

The Device Drivers

The last part of Fig. 11-7 consists of the **device drivers**. Each device driver can control one or more I/O devices, but a device driver can also do things not related to a specific device, such as encrypting a data stream or even just providing access to kernel data structures. Device drivers are not part of the *ntoskrnl.exe* binary. The advantage of this approach is that once a driver has been installed on a system, it is added to a list in the registry and is loaded dynamically when the system boots. In this way, *ntoskrnl.exe* is the same for everyone, but every system is configured precisely for those devices it contains.

There are device drivers for macroscopically visible I/O devices such as disks and printers, but also for many internal devices and chips that practically no one has ever heard of. In addition, the file systems are also present as device drivers, as mentioned above. The largest device driver, the one for Win32, GDI, and video, is shown on the far right of Fig. 11-7. It handles many system calls and most of the graphics. Since customers can install new device drivers, they have the power to affect the kernel and corrupt the system. For this reason, drivers must be written with great care.

11.3.2 Implementation of Objects

Objects are probably the single most important concept in Windows 2000. They provide a uniform and consistent interface to all system resources and data structures such as processes, threads, semaphores, etc. This uniformity has various facets. First, all objects are named and accessed the same way, using object handles. Second, because all accesses to objects go through the object manager, it is possible to put all the security checks in one place and ensure that no process can make an end run around them. Third, sharing of objects among processes can be handled in a uniform way. Fourth, since all object opens and closes go through the object manager, it is easy to keep track of which objects are still in use and which can be safely deleted. Fifth, this uniform model for object management makes it easy to manage resource quotas in a straightforward way.

A key to understanding objects is to realize that an (executive) object is just some number of consecutive words in memory (i.e., in kernel virtual address space). An object is a data structure in RAM, no more and no less. A file on disk is not an object, although an object (i.e., a data structure in kernel virtual address space) is created for a file when it is opened. A consequence of the fact that objects are just kernel data structures is that when the system is rebooted (or crashes) all objects are lost. In fact, when the system boots, there are no objects present at all (except for the idle and system processes, whose objects are hardwired into the *ntoskrnl.exe* file). All other objects are created on the fly as the system boots up and various initialization (and later user) programs run.

Objects have a structure, as shown in Fig. 11-9. Each object contains a header with certain information common to all objects of all types. The fields in this header include the object's name, the object directory in which it lives in object space, security information (so a check can be made when an object is opened), and a list of processes with open handles to the object (if a certain debugging flag is enabled).

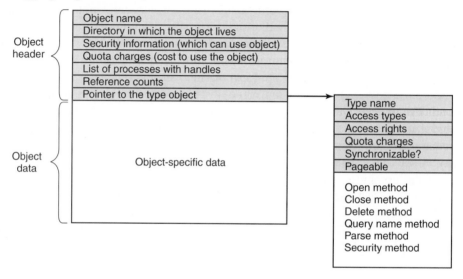

Figure 11-9. The structure of an object.

Each object header also contains a quota charge field, which is the charge levied against a process for opening the object. If a file object costs 1 point and a process belongs to a job that has 10 file points worth of quota, the processes in that job can only open 10 files in total. In this way resource limits can be enforced for each object type separately.

Objects occupy valuable real estate—pieces of kernel virtual address space—so when an object is no longer needed it should be removed and its address space reclaimed. The mechanism for reclamation is to have a reference counter in each object's header. It counts the number of open handles held by processes. This counter is incremented every time the object is opened and decremented every time it is closed. When it hits 0, no more users hold handles to the object. When an object is acquired or released by an executive component, a second counter is incremented or decremented, even though no actual handle is issued. When both counters hit 0, no user process is using the object and no executive process is using the object, so the object can be removed and its memory freed.

The object manager needs to maintain dynamic data structures (its objects), but it is not the only part of the executive with this need. Other pieces also need to allocate and release chunks of kernel memory dynamically. To meet these needs, the executive maintains two page pools in kernel address space: for objects and for other dynamic data structures. Such pools operate as heaps, similar to the C language calls *malloc* and *free* for managing dynamic data. One pool is paged and the other is nonpaged (pinned in memory). Objects that are needed often are kept in the nonpaged pool; objects that are rarely accessed, such as registry keys and some security information, are kept in the paged pool. When memory is tight, the latter can be paged out and faulted back on demand. In fact, substantial portions of the operating system code and data structures are also pageable, to reduce memory consumption. Objects that may be needed when the system is running critical code (and when paging is not permitted) must go in the nonpaged pool. When a small amount of storage is needed, a page can be taken from either pool and then broken up into units as small as 8 bytes.

Objects are typed, which means each one has certain properties common to all objects of its type. The type is indicated by a pointer in the header to a type object, as shown in Fig. 11-9. The type object information includes items such as the type name, whether a thread can wait on the object (yes for mutexes, no for open files), and whether new objects of this type go on the paged or nonpaged pool. Each object points to its type object.

The last thing a type object has is also the most important: pointers to the code for certain standard operations such as open, close, and delete. Whenever one of these operations is invoked on an object, the pointer to the type object is followed and the relevant code located and executed. This mechanism gives the system the opportunity to initialize new objects, and recover storage when they are deleted.

Executive components can create new types dynamically. There is no definitive list of object types, but some of the more common ones are listed in Fig. 11-10. Let us briefly go over the object types in Fig. 11-10. Process and thread are obvious. There is one object for every process and every thread, which holds the main properties needed to manage the process or thread. The next three objects, semaphore, mutex, and event, all deal with interprocess synchronization. Semaphores and mutexes work as expected, but with various extra bells and whistles (e.g., maximum values and timeouts). Events can be in one of two states: signaled or nonsignaled. If a thread waits on an event that is in signaled state, the thread is released immediately. If the event is in nonsignaled state, it blocks until some other thread signals the event, which releases all blocked threads. An event can also be set up, so after a signal has been successfully waited for, it automatically reverts to nonsignaled state, rather than staying in signaled state.

Port, timer, and queue objects also relate to communication and synchronization. Ports are channels between processes for exchanging messages. Timers provide a way to block for a specific time interval. Queues are used to notify threads that a previously started asynchronous I/O operation has completed.

Type	Description
Process	User process
Thread	Thread within a process
Semaphore	Counting semaphore used for interprocess synchronization
Mutex	Binary semaphore used to enter a critical region
Event	Synchronization object with persistent state (signaled/not)
Port	Mechanism for interprocess message passing
Timer	Object allowing a thread to sleep for a fixed time interval
Queue	Object used for completion notification on asynchronous I/O
Open file	Object associated with an open file
Access token	Security descriptor for some object
Profile	Data structure used for profiling CPU usage
Section	Structure used for mapping files onto virtual address space
Key	Registry key
Object directory	Directory for grouping objects within the object manager
Symbolic link	Pointer to another object by name
Device	I/O device object
Device driver	Each loaded device driver has its own object

Figure 11-10. Some common executive object types managed by object manager.

Open file objects are created when a file is opened. Files that are not opened do not have objects managed by the object manager. Access tokens are security objects; they identify a user and tell what special privileges the user has, if any. Profiles are structures used for storing periodic samples of the program counter of a running thread to see where the program is spending its time.

Sections are objects used by the memory system for handling memory-mapped files. They record which file (or part thereof) is mapped onto which memory addresses. Keys are registry keys and are used to relate names to values. Object directories are entirely local to the object manager. They provide a way to collect related objects together in exactly the same way directories work in the file system. Symbolic links are also similar to their file system counterparts: they allow a name in one part of the object name space to refer to an object in a different part of the object name space. Each known device has a device object that contains information about it and is used to refer to the device within the system. Finally, each device driver that has been loaded has an object in the object space.

Users can create new objects or open existing objects by making Win32 calls such as **CreateSemaphore** or **OpenSemaphore**. These are calls to library procedures that ultimately result in the appropriate system calls being made. The result of any successful call that creates or opens an object is a 64-bit handle table entry that is stored in the process' private handle table in kernel memory. The 32-bit index of the handle's position in the table is returned to the user to use on subsequent calls.

The 64-bit handle table entry in the kernel contains two 32-bit words. One word contains a 29-bit pointer to the object's header. The low-order 3 bits are used as flags (e.g., whether the handle is inherited by child processes). These bits are masked off before the pointer is followed. The other word contains a 32-bit rights mask. It is needed because permissions checking is done only at the time the object is created or opened. If a process has only read permission to an object, all the other rights bits in the mask will be 0s, giving the operating system the ability to reject any operation on the object other than reading it.

The handle tables for two processes and their relationships to some objects are illustrated in Fig. 11-11. In this example, process A has access to threads 1 and 2 and access to mutexes 1 and 2. Process B has access to thread 3 and mutexes 2 and 3. The corresponding entries in the handle tables hold the rights to each of these objects. For example, process A might have the rights to lock and unlock its mutexes, but not the right to destroy them. Note that mutex 2 is shared by both processes allowing threads in them to synchronize. The other mutexes are not shared, which might mean that the threads within process A use mutex 1 for their internal synchronization and the threads within process B use mutex 3 for their internal synchronization.

The Object Name Space

As objects are created and deleted during execution, the object manager needs a way to keep track of them. To do this job, it maintains a name space, in which all objects in the system are located. The name space can be used by a process to locate and open a handle for some other process' object, provided it has been granted permission to do so. The object name space is one of three name spaces maintained by Windows 2000. The other ones are the file system name space and the registry name space. All three are hierarchical name spaces with multiple levels of directories for organizing entries. The directory objects listed in Fig. 11-10 provide the means to implement this hierarchical name space for objects.

Since executive objects are volatile (i.e., vanish when the computer is shut down, unlike file system and registry entries), when the system boots up, there are no objects in memory and the object name space is empty. During booting, various parts of the executive create directories and then fill them with objects. For example, as the plug-and-play manager discovers devices out there, it creates a device object for each one and enters this object into the name space. When the system is fully booted, all I/O devices, disk partitions, and other interesting discoveries are in the object name space.

Not all objects get entered by the Columbus method—just go look and see what you find. Some executive components look in the registry to see what to do. A key example here is device drivers. During bootup, the system looks in the

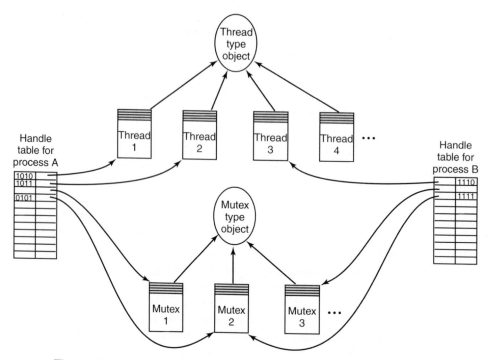

Figure 11-11. The relationship between handle tables, objects, and type objects.

registry to see which device drivers are needed. As they are loaded one by one, an object is created for each one and its name is inserted into the object space. Within the system, the driver is referred to by a pointer to its object.

Although the object name space is crucial to the entire operation of the system, few people know that it even exists because it is not visible to users without special viewing tools. One such viewing tool is *winobj*, available for free at *www.sysinternals.com*. When run, this tool depicts an object name space that typically contains the object directories listed in Fig. 11-12 as well as a few others.

The somewhat strangely named directory \?? contains the names of all the MS-DOS-style device names, such as *A:* for the floppy disk and *C:* for the first hard disk. These names are actually symbolic links to the directory *Device* where the device objects live. The name \?? was chosen to make it alphabetically first to speed up lookup of all path names beginning with a drive letter. The contents of the other object directories should be self explanatory.

11.3.3 Environment Subsystems

Going back to Fig. 11-7, we see that Windows 2000 consists of components in kernel mode and components in user mode. We have now completed our examination of the kernel mode components; now it is time to look at the user mode

Directory	Contents
??	Starting place for looking up MS-DOS devices like C:
Device	All discovered I/O devices
Driver	Objects corresponding to each loaded device driver
ObjectTypes	The type objects shown in Fig. 11-11
Windows	Objects for sending messages to all the windows
BaseNamedObjs	User-created objects such as semaphores, mutexes, etc.
Arcname	Partition names discovered by the boot loader
NLS	National language support objects
FileSystem	File system driver objects and file system recognizer objects
Security	Objects belonging to the security system
KnownDLLs	Key shared libraries that are opened early and held open

Figure 11-12. Some typical directories in the object name space.

components of which there are three kinds: DLLs, environment subsystems, and service processes. These components work together to provide each user process with an interface that is distinct from the Windows 2000 system call interface.

Windows 2000 supports three different documented APIs: Win32, POSIX, and OS/2. Each of these interfaces has a published list of library calls that programmers can use. The job of the DLLs (Dynamic Link Libraries) and environment subsystems is to implement the functionality of the published interface, thereby hiding the true system call interface from application programs. In particular, the Win32 interface is the official interface for Windows 2000, Windows NT, Windows 95/98/Me, and to a limited extent, Windows CE. By using the DLLs and Win32 environment subsystem, a program can be written to the Win32 specification and run unmodified on all these versions of Windows, even though the system calls are not the same on the various systems.

To see how these interfaces are implemented, let us look at Win32. A Win32 program normally contains many calls to Win32 API functions, for example, CreateWindow, DrawMenuBar, and OpenSemaphore. There are thousands of such calls, and most programs use a substantial number of them. One possible implementation would be to statically link every Win32 program with all the library procedures that it uses. If this were done, each binary program would contain one copy of each procedure it used in its executable binary.

The trouble with this approach is that it wastes memory if the user has multiple programs open at once and they use many of the same library procedures. For example, *Word*, *Excel*, and *Powerpoint* all use exactly the same procedures for opening dialog boxes, drawing windows, displaying menus, managing the clipboard, etc., so if a user had all of them open and active at once, there would be three (identical) copies of each of the libraries in memory.

To avoid this problem, all versions of Windows support shared libraries, called **DLLs** (**Dynamic Link Libraries**). Each DLL collects together a set of closely related library procedures and their data structures into a single file, usually (but not always) with extension *.dll*. When an application is linked, the linker sees that some of the library procedures belong to DLLs and records this information in the executable's header. Calls to procedures in DLLs are made indirectly through a transfer vector in the caller's address space. Initially this vector is filled with 0s, since the addresses of the procedures to be called are not yet known.

When the application process is started, the DLLs that are needed are located (on disk or in memory) and mapped into the process' virtual address space. The transfer vector is then filled in with the correct addresses so that the procedures can then be called via the transfer vector with only a negligible loss of efficiency. The win here is that even though multiple application programs have the same DLL mapped in, only one copy of the DLL text is needed in physical memory (but each process gets its own copy of the private static data in the DLL). Windows 2000 uses DLLs extremely heavily for all aspects of the system.

Now we have enough background to see how the Win32 and other process interfaces are implemented. Each user process generally links with a number of DLLs that together implement the Win32 interface. To make an API call, one of the procedures in a DLL is called, shown as step 1 in Fig. 11-13. What happens next depends on the Win32 API call. Different ones are implemented in different ways.

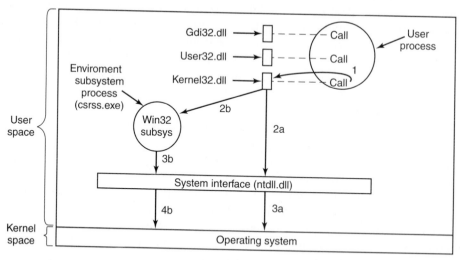

Figure 11-13. Various routes taken to implement Win32 API function calls.

In some cases, the DLL calls another DLL (*ntdll.dll*) that actually traps to the operating system. This path is shown as steps 2a and 3a in Fig. 11-13. It is also possible that the DLL does all the work itself without making a system call at all.

For other Win32 API calls a different route is taken, namely, first a message is sent to the Win32 subsystem process (*csrss.exe*), which then does some work and then makes a system call (steps 2b, 3b, and 4b). Here, too, in some cases the environment subsystem does all the work in user space and just returns immediately. The message passing between the application process and the Win32 subsystem process has been carefully optimized for performance using a special local procedure call mechanism implemented by the executive and shown as LPC in Fig. 11-7.

In the first version of Windows NT, virtually all the Win32 API calls took route 2b, 3b, 4b, putting a large chunk of the operating system in user space (e.g., the graphics). However, starting with NT 4.0, much of the code was put into kernel mode (in the Win32/GDI driver in Fig. 11-7) for performance reasons. In Windows 2000, only a small number of Win32 API calls, for example process and thread creation, take the long route. The other ones take the direct route, bypassing the Win32 environment subsystem.

As an aside, the three most important DLLs are shown in Fig. 11-13, but they are not the only ones. There are over 800 separate DLLs in the \winnt\system32 directory totalling 130 MB. To avoid any confusion, the number of DLL *files* is over 800; the number of API calls contained in them exceeds 13,000. (The 29 million lines of code had to compile into something, after all.) A few of the more important DLLs are listed in Fig. 11-14. The number of exported functions (i.e., those visible outside the file) in each one is given, but these tend to change (meaning increase) over time. The number of exported functions in the first public release of *ntdll.dll* in Windows 2000 is 1179. These are the real system calls. The 1209 calls exported by *ntoskrnl.exe* are the functions available to device drivers and other code linked with the kernel. The list of exported functions in any *.exe* or *.dll* file can be viewed using the *depends* program in the platform SDK Kit.

File	Mode	Fcns	Contents
hal.dll	Kernel	95	Low-level hardware management, e.g., port I/O
ntoskrnl.exe	Kernel	1209	Windows 2000 operating system (kernel + executive)
win32k.sys	Kernel	-	Many system calls including most of the graphics
ntdll.dll	User	1179	Dispatcher from user mode to kernel mode
csrss.exe	User	0	Win32 environment subsystem process
kernel32.dll	User	823	Most of the core (nongraphics) system calls
gdi32.dll	User	543	Font, text, color, brush, pen, bitmap, palette, drawing, etc. calls
user32.dll	User	695	Window, icon, menu, cursor, dialog, clipboard, etc. calls
advapi32.dll	User	557	Security, cryptography, registry, management calls

Figure 11-14. Some key Windows 2000 files, the mode they run in, the number of exported function calls, and the main contents of each file. The calls in *win32k.sys* are not formally exported since *win32k.sys* is not called directly.

Although the Win32 process interface is the most important one, there are also two other ones: POSIX and OS/2. The POSIX environment provides minimal support for UNIX applications. It supports only the P1003.1 functionality and little else. It does not have threads, windowing, or networking, for example. In practice, porting any real UNIX program to Windows 2000 using this subsystem is close to impossible. It was included only because parts of the U.S. government require operating systems for government computers to be P1003.1 compliant. This subsystem is not self-contained and uses the Win32 subsystem for much of its work, but without exporting the full Win32 interface to its user programs (which would have made it usable, at no extra cost to Microsoft).

To allow UNIX users to migrate to Windows 2000, Microsoft has a product called Interix that provides a better degree of UNIX compatibility than the POSIX subsystem.

The OS/2 subsystem is similarly limited in functionality and does not support any graphical applications. In practice, it, too, is completely useless. Thus the original idea of having multiple operating system interfaces implemented by different processes in user space is essentially gone. What is left is a full Win32 implementation in kernel mode and little else.

11.4 PROCESSES AND THREADS IN WINDOWS 2000

Windows 2000 has a number of concepts for managing the CPU and grouping resources together. In the following sections we will examine these, discussing some of the relevant Win32 API calls, and show how these concepts are implemented.

11.4.1 Fundamental Concepts

Windows 2000 supports traditional processes, which can communicate and synchronize with one another, just as they can in UNIX. Each process contains at least one thread, which in turn contains at least one fiber (lightweight thread). Furthermore, processes can be collected into jobs for certain resource management purposes. Together, jobs, processes, threads, and fibers provide a very general set of tools for managing parallelism and resources, both on uniprocessors (single-CPU machines) and on multiprocessors (multiCPU machines). A brief summary of these four concepts is given in Fig. 11-15.

Let us examine these concepts from the largest to the smallest. A **job** in Windows 2000 is a collection of one or more processes that are to be managed as a unit. In particular, there are quotas and resource limits associated with each job, stored in the corresponding job object. The quotas include items such as the maximum number of processes (prevents any process from generating an unbounded number of children), the total CPU time available to each process individually and

Name	Description
Job	Collection of processes that share quotas and limits
Process	Container for holding resources
Thread	Entity scheduled by the kernel
Fiber	Lightweight thread managed entirely in user space

Figure 11-15. Basic concepts used for CPU and resource management.

to all the processes combined, and the maximum memory usage, again, per process and total. Jobs can also impose security restrictions on the processes in the job, such as not being able to acquire administrator (superuser) power, even with the proper password.

Processes are more interesting than jobs and also more important. As in UNIX, processes are containers for resources. Every process has a 4-GB address space, with the user occupying the bottom 2 GB (optionally 3 GB on Advanced Server and Datacenter server) and the operating system occupying the rest. Thus the operating system is present in every process' address, although protected from tampering by the memory management unit hardware. A process has a process ID, one or more threads, a list of handles (managed in kernel mode), and an access token holding its security information. Processes are created using a Win32 call that takes as its input the name of an executable file, which defines the initial contents of the address space and creates the first thread.

Every process starts out with one thread, but new ones can be created dynamically. Threads forms the basis of CPU scheduling as the operating system always selects a thread to run, not a process. Consequently, every thread has a state (ready, running, blocked, etc.), whereas processes do not have states. Threads can be created dynamically by a Win32 call that specifies the address within the enclosing process' address space it is to start running at. Every thread has a thread ID, which is taken from the same space as the process IDs, so an ID can never be in use for both a process and a thread at the same time. Process and thread IDs are multiples of four so they can be used as byte indices into kernel tables, the same as other objects.

A thread normally runs in user mode, but when it makes a system call it switches to kernel mode and continues to run as the same thread with the same properties and limits it had in user mode. Each thread has two stacks, one for use when it is in user mode and one for use when it is in kernel mode. In addition to a state, an ID, and two stacks, every thread has a context (in which to save its registers when it is not running), a private area for its own local variables, and possibly its own access token. If it has its own access token, this one overrides the process access token in order to let client threads pass their access rights to server threads who are doing work for them. When a thread is finished executing, it can exit. When the last thread still active in a process exits, the process terminates.

It is important to realize that threads are a scheduling concept, not a resource ownership concept. Any thread is able to access all the objects that belong to its process. All it has to do is grab the handle and make the appropriate Win32 call. There is no restriction on a thread that it cannot access an object because a different thread created or opened it. The system does not even keep track of which thread created which object. Once an object handle has been put in a process' handle table, any thread in the process can use it.

In addition to the normal threads that run within user processes, Windows 2000 has a number of daemon threads that run only in kernel space and are not associated with any user process (they are associated with the special system or idle processes). Some perform administrative tasks, such as writing dirty pages to the disk, while others form a pool that can be assigned to a component of the executive or a driver that needs to get some work done asynchronously in the background. We will study some of these threads later when we come to memory management.

Switching threads in Windows 2000 is relatively expensive because doing a thread switch requires entering and later leaving kernel mode. To provide very lightweight pseudoparallelism, Windows 2000 provides **fibers**, which are like threads, but are scheduled in user space by the program that created them (or its run-time system). Each thread can have multiple fibers, the same way a process can have multiple threads, except that when a fiber logically blocks, it puts itself on the queue of blocked fibers and selects another fiber to run in the context of its thread.

The operating system is not aware of this transition because the thread keeps running, even though it may be first running one fiber, then another. In fact, the operating system knows nothing at all about fibers, so there are no executive objects relating to fibers, as there are for jobs, processes, and threads. There are also no true system calls for managing fibers. However, there are Win32 API calls. These are among the Win32 API calls that do not make system calls, which we mentioned during the discussion of Fig. 11-13. The relationship between jobs, processes, and threads is illustrated in Fig. 11-16.

Although we will not discuss it in much detail, Windows 2000 is capable of running on a symmetric multiprocessor system. This requirement means that the operating system code must be fully reentrant, that is, every procedure must be written in such a way that two or more CPUs may be changing its variables at once, without causing problems. In many cases this means that code sections have to be protected by spin locks or mutexes to keep additional CPUs at bay until the first one is done (i.e., serialize access to critical regions). The number of CPUs the system can handle is governed by the licensing restrictions and listed in Fig. 11-2. There is no technical reason why Windows Professional cannot run on a 32-node multiprocessor—it is the same binary as Datacenter Server, after all.

The upper limit of 32 CPUs is a hard limit because word-length bitmaps are used to keep track of CPU usage in various ways. For example, one word-length

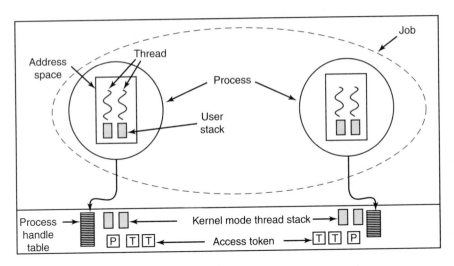

Figure 11-16. The relationship between jobs, processes, and threads.
Several fibers can also be multiplexed on one thread (not shown).

bitmap keeps track of which of the (up to) 32 CPUs are currently idle, and another bitmap is used per process to list the CPUs this process is permitted to run on. The 64-bit version of Windows 2000 should be able to effortlessly support up to 64 CPUs; beyond that requires actually changing the code substantially (to use multiple words for the bitmaps).

11.4.2 Job, Process, Thread and Fiber Management API Calls

New processes are created using the Win32 API function CreateProcess. This function has 10 parameters, each of which has many options. This design is clearly a lot more complicated than the UNIX scheme, in which fork has no parameters, and exec has just three: pointers to the name of the file to execute, the (parsed) command line parameter array, and the environment strings. Roughly speaking, the 10 parameters to CreateProcess are as follows:

1. A pointer to the name of the executable file.

2. The command line itself (unparsed).

3. A pointer to a security descriptor for the process.

4. A pointer to a security descriptor for the initial thread.

5. A bit telling whether the new process inherits the creator's handles.

6. Miscellaneous flags (e.g., error mode, priority, debugging, consoles).

7. A pointer to the environment strings.

8. A pointer to the name of the new process' current working directory.

9. A pointer to a structure describing the initial window on the screen.

10. A pointer to a structure that returns 18 values to the caller.

Windows 2000 does not enforce any kind of parent-child or other hierarchy. All processes are created equal (no processes are created more equal). However, since 1 of the 18 parameters returned to the creating process is a handle to the new process (allowing considerable control over the new process), there is an implicit hierarchy in terms of who has a handle to whom. Although these handles cannot just be passed directly to other processes, there is a way for a process to make a duplicate handle suitable for another process and then give it the handle, so the implicit process hierarchy may not last long.

Each process in Windows 2000 is created with a single thread, but a process can create more threads later on. Thread creation is simpler than process creation: CreateThread has only six parameters instead of 10:

1. The optional security descriptor.

2. The initial stack size.

3. The starting address.

4. A user-defined parameter.

5. The initial state of the thread (ready or blocked).

6. The thread's ID.

The kernel does the thread creation, so it is clearly aware of threads (i.e., they are not implemented purely in user space as is the case in some other systems).

Interprocess Communication

Threads can communicate in a wide variety of ways, including pipes, named pipes, mailslots, sockets, remote procedure calls, and shared files. Pipes have two modes: byte and message, selected at creation time. Byte-mode pipes work the same way as in UNIX. Message-mode pipes are somewhat similar but preserve message boundaries, so that four writes of 128 bytes will be read as four 128-byte messages, and not as one 512-byte message, as might happen with byte-mode pipes. Named pipes also exist and have the same two modes as regular pipes. Named pipes can also be used over a network; regular pipes cannot.

Mailslots are a feature of Windows 2000 not present in UNIX. They are similar to pipes in some ways, but not all. For one thing, they are one-way, whereas pipes are two-way. They can also be used over a network but do not provide guaranteed delivery. Finally, they allow the sending process to broadcast a message to many receivers, instead of to just one receiver.

Sockets are like pipes, except that they normally connect processes on different machines. For example, one process writes to a socket and another one on a remote machine reads from it. Sockets can also be used to connect processes on the same machine, but since they entail more overhead than pipes, they are generally only used in a networking context.

Remote procedure calls are a way for process A to have process B call a procedure in B's address space on A's behalf and return the result to A. Various restrictions on the parameters exist. For example, it makes no sense to pass a pointer to a different process.

Finally, processes can share memory by mapping onto the same file at the same time. All writes done by one process then appear in the address spaces of the other processes. Using this mechanism, the shared buffer used in producer-consumer problems can easily be implemented.

Just as Windows 2000 provides numerous interprocess communication mechanisms, it also provides numerous synchronization mechanisms, including semaphores, mutexes, critical regions, and events. All of these mechanisms work on threads, not processes, so that when a thread blocks on a semaphore, other threads in that process (if any) are not affected and can continue to run.

A semaphore is created using the CreateSemaphore API function, which can initialize it to a given value and define a maximum value as well. Semaphores are kernel objects and thus have security descriptors and handles. The handle for a semaphore can be duplicated using DuplicateHandle and passed to another process so that multiple processes can synchronize on the same semaphore. Calls for up and down are present, although they have the somewhat peculiar names of ReleaseSemaphore (up) and WaitForSingleObject (down). It is also possible to give WaitForSingleObject a timeout, so the calling thread can be released eventually, even if the semaphore remains at 0 (although timers reintroduce races).

Mutexes are also kernel objects used for synchronization, but simpler than semaphores because they do not have counters. They are essentially locks, with API functions for locking (WaitForSingleObject) and unlocking (ReleaseMutex). Like semaphore handles, mutex handles can be duplicated and passed between processes so that threads in different processes can access the same mutex.

The third synchronization mechanism is based on **critical sections**, (which we have called critical regions elsewhere in this book) which are similar to mutexes, except local to the address space of the creating thread. Because critical sections are not kernel objects, they do not have handles or security descriptors and cannot be passed between processes. Locking and unlocking is done with EnterCriticalSection and LeaveCriticalSection, respectively. Because these API functions are performed initially in user space and only make kernel calls when blocking is needed, they are faster than mutexes.

The last synchronization mechanism uses kernel objects called **events**, of which there are two kinds: **manual-reset events** and **auto-reset events**. Any event can be in one of two states: set and cleared. A thread can wait for an event to occur with WaitForSingleObject. If another thread signals an event with SetEvent, what happens depends on the type of event. With a manual-reset event, all waiting threads are released and the event stays set until manually cleared with ResetEvent. With an auto-reset event, if one or more threads are waiting, exactly one thread is released and the event is cleared. An alternative operation is Pulse-Event, which is like SetEvent except that if nobody is waiting, the pulse is lost and the event is cleared. In contrast, a SetEvent that occurs with no waiting threads is remembered by leaving the event in set state so a subsequent thread waiting on it is released immediately.

Events, mutexes, and semaphores can all be named and stored in the file system, like named pipes. Two or more processes can synchronize by opening the same event, mutex, or semaphore, rather than having one of them create the object and then make duplicate handles for the others, although the latter approach is certainly an option as well.

The number of Win32 API calls dealing with processes, threads, and fibers is nearly 100, a substantial number of which deal with IPC in one form or another. A summary of the ones discussed above as well as some other important ones are given in Fig. 11-17.

Most of the calls in Fig. 11-17 were either discussed above or should be self-explanatory. Again note that not all of these are system calls. As we mentioned earlier, Windows 2000 knows nothing about fibers. They are entirely implemented in user space. As a consequence, the CreateFiber call does its work entirely in user space without making any system calls (unless it has to allocate some memory). Many other Win32 calls have this property as well, including EnterCriticalSection and LeaveCriticalSection as we noted above.

11.4.3 Implementation of Processes and Threads

Processes and threads are more important and more elaborate than jobs and fibers, so we will concentrate on them here. A process is created when another process makes the Win32 CreateProcess call. This call invokes a (user-mode) procedure in *kernel32.dll* that creates the process in several steps using multiple system calls and other work.

1. The executable file given as a parameter is examined and opened. If it is a valid POSIX, OS/2, 16-bit Windows, or MS-DOS file, a special environment is set up for it. If it is a valid 32-bit Win32 *.exe* file, the registry is checked to see if it is special in some way (e.g., to be run under supervision of a debugger). All of this is done in user mode inside *kernel32.dll*.

2. A system call, NtCreateProcess, is made to create the empty process object and enter it into the object manager's name space. Both the kernel object and the executive object are created. In addition, the

Win32 API Function	Description
CreateProcess	Create a new process
CreateThread	Create a new thread in an existing process
CreateFiber	Create a new fiber
ExitProcess	Terminate current process and all its threads
ExitThread	Terminate this thread
ExitFiber	Terminate this fiber
SetPriorityClass	Set the priority class for a process
SetThreadPriority	Set the priority for one thread
CreateSemaphore	Create a new semapahore
CreateMutex	Create a new mutex
OpenSemaphore	Open an existing semaphore
OpenMutex	Open an existing mutex
WaitForSingleObject	Block on a single semaphore, mutex, etc.
WaitForMultipleObjects	Block on a set of objects whose handles are given
PulseEvent	Set an event to signaled then to nonsignaled
ReleaseMutex	Release a mutex to allow another thread to acquire it
ReleaseSemaphore	Increase the semaphore count by 1
EnterCriticalSection	Acquire the lock on a critical section
LeaveCriticalSection	Release the lock on a critical section

Figure 11-17. Some of the Win32 calls for managing processes, threads, and fibers.

process manager creates a process control block for the object and initializes it with the process ID, quotas, access token, and various other fields. A section object is also created to keep track of the process' address space.

3. When *kernel32.dll* gets control back, it makes another system call, NtCreateThread, to create the initial thread. The thread's user and kernel stacks are also created. The stack size is given in the header of the executable file.

4. *Kernel32.dll* now sends a message to the Win32 environment subsystem telling it about the new process and passing it the process and thread handles. The process and threads are entered into the subsystems tables so it has a complete list of all processes and threads. The subsystem then displays a cursor containing a pointer with an hourglass to tell the user that something is going on but that the cursor can be used in the meanwhile. When the process makes its first GUI

call, usually to create a window, the cursor is removed (it times out after 2 seconds if no call is forthcoming).

5. At this point, the thread is able to run. It starts out by running a run-time system procedure to complete the initialization.

6. The run-time procedure sets the thread's priority, tells loaded DLLs that a new thread is present, and does other housekeeping chores. Finally, it begins running the code of the process' main program.

Thread creation also consists of a number of steps, but we will not go into them in much detail. It starts when the running process executes CreateThread, which calls a procedure inside *kernel32.dll*. This procedure allocates a user stack within the calling process and then makes the NtCreateThread call to create an executive thread object, initialize it, and also create and initialize a thread control block. Again, the Win32 subsystem is notified and enters the new thread in its tables. Then the thread starts running and completes its own initialization.

When a process or thread is created, a handle is returned for it. This handle can be used to start, stop, kill, and inspect the process or thread. It is possible for the owner of a handle to pass the handle to another process in a controlled and secure way. This technique is used to allow debuggers to have control over the processes they are debugging.

Scheduling

Windows 2000 does not have a central scheduling thread. Instead, when a thread cannot run any more, the thread enters kernel mode and runs the scheduler itself to see which thread to switch to. The following conditions cause the currently running thread to execute the scheduler code:

1. The thread blocks on a semaphore, mutex, event, I/O, etc.

2. It signals an object (e.g., does an up on a semaphore).

3. The running thread's quantum expires.

In case 1, the thread is already running in kernel mode to carry out the operation on the dispatcher or I/O object. It cannot possibly continue, so it must save its own context, run the scheduler code to pick its successor, and load that thread's context to start it.

In case 2, the running thread is in the kernel, too. However, after signaling some object, it can definitely continue because signaling an object never blocks. Still, the thread is required to run the scheduler to see if the result of its action has released a higher priority thread that is now free to run. If so, a thread switch occurs because Windows 2000 is fully preemptive (i.e., thread switches can occur at any moment, not just at the end of the current thread's quantum).

In case 3, a trap to kernel mode occurs, at which time the thread executes the scheduler code to see who runs next. Depending on what other threads are waiting, the same thread may be selected, in which case it gets a new quantum and continues running. Otherwise a thread switch happens.

The scheduler is also called under two other conditions:

1. An I/O operation completes.

2. A timed wait expires.

In the first case, a thread may have been waiting on this I/O and is now released to run. A check has to be made to see if it should preempt the running thread since there is no guaranteed minimum run time. The scheduler is not run in the interrupt handler itself (since that may keep interrupts turned off too long). Instead a DPC is queued for slightly later, after the interrupt handler is done. In the second case, a thread has done a down on a semaphore or blocked on some other object, but with a timeout that has now expired. Again it is necessary for the interrupt handler to queue a DPC to avoid having it run during the clock interrupt handler. If a thread has been made ready by this timeout, the scheduler will be run and if nothing more important is available, the DPC will run next.

Now we come to the actual scheduling algorithm. The Win32 API provides two hooks for processes to influence thread scheduling. These hooks largely determine the algorithm. First, there is a call SetPriorityClass that sets the priority class of all the threads in the caller's process. The allowed values are: realtime, high, above normal, normal, below normal, and idle.

Second, there is a call SetThreadPriority that sets the relative priority of some thread (possibly, but not necessarily, the calling thread) compared to the other threads in its process. The allowed values are: time critical, highest, above normal, normal, below normal, lowest, and idle. With six process classes and seven thread classes, a thread can have any one of 42 combinations. This is the input to the scheduling algorithm.

The scheduler works as follows. The system has 32 priorities, numbered from 0 to 31. The 42 combinations are mapped onto the 32 priority classes according to the table of Fig. 11-18. The number in the table determines the thread's **base priority**. In addition, every thread has a **current priority**, which may be higher (but not lower) than the base priority and which we will discuss shortly.

To use these priorities for scheduling, the system maintains an array with 32 entries, corresponding to priorities 0 through 31 derived from the table of Fig. 11-18. Each array entry points to the head of a list of ready threads at the corresponding priority. The basic scheduling algorithm consists of searching the array from priority 31 down to priority 0. As soon as a nonempty slot is found, the thread at the head of the queue is selected and run for one quantum. If the quantum expires, the thread goes to the end of the queue at its priority level and the thread at the front is chosen next. In other words, when there are multiple

		Win32 process class priorities					
		Realtime	High	Above Normal	Normal	Below Normal	Idle
	Time critical	31	15	15	15	15	15
	Highest	26	15	12	10	8	6
Win32	Above normal	25	14	11	9	7	5
thread	Normal	24	13	10	8	6	4
priorities	Below normal	23	12	9	7	5	3
	Lowest	22	11	8	6	4	2
	Idle	16	1	1	1	1	1

Figure 11-18. Mapping of Win32 priorities to Windows 2000 priorities.

threads ready at the highest priority level, they run round robin for one quantum each. If no thread is ready, the idle thread is run.

It should be noted that scheduling is done by picking a thread without regard to which process that thread belongs. Thus the scheduler does *not* first pick a process and then pick a thread in that process. It only looks at the threads. It does not even know which thread belongs to which process. On a multiprocessor, each CPU schedules itself using the priority array. A spin lock is used to make sure that only one CPU at a time is inspecting the array.

The array of queue headers is shown in Fig. 11-19. The figure shows that there are actually four categories of priorities: realtime, user, zero, and idle, which is effectively −1. These deserve some comment. Priorities 16–31 are called real time, but they are not. There are no guarantees given and no deadlines are met. They are simply higher priority than 0–15. However, priorities 16 through 31 are reserved for the system itself and for threads explicitly assigned those priorities by the system administrator. Ordinary users may not run there for a good reason. If a user thread were to run at a higher priority than, say, the keyboard or mouse thread and get into a loop, the keyboard or mouse thread would never run, effectively hanging the system.

User threads run at priorities 1–15. By setting the process and thread priorities, a user can determine which threads get preference. The zero thread runs in the background and eats up whatever CPU time nobody else wants. Its job is to zero pages for the memory manager. We will discuss its role later. If there is absolutely nothing to do, not even zero pages, the idle thread runs. It is not really a full-blown thread though.

Over the course of time, some patches were made to the basic scheduling algorithm to improve system performance. Under certain specific conditions, the current priority of a user thread can be raised above the base priority (by the operating system), but never above priority 15. Since the array of Fig. 11-19 is

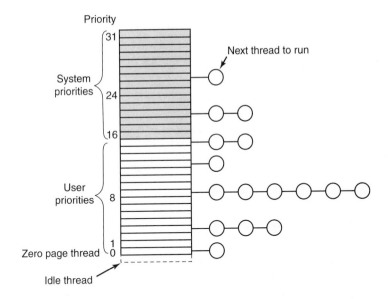

Figure 11-19. Windows 2000 supports 32 priorities for threads.

based on the current priority, changing this priority affects scheduling. No adjustments are ever made to threads running at priority 15 or higher.

Let us now see when a thread's priority is raised. First, when an I/O operation completes and releases a waiting thread, the priority is boosted to give it a chance to run again quickly and start more I/O. The idea here is to keep the I/O devices busy. The amount of boost depends on the I/O device, typically 1 for a disk, 2 for a serial line, 6 for the keyboard, and 8 for the sound card.

Second, if a thread was waiting on a semaphore, mutex, or other event, when it is released, it gets boosted by 2 units if it is in the foreground process (the process controlling the window to which keyboard input is sent) and 1 unit otherwise. This fix tends to raise interactive processes above the big crowd at level 8. Finally, if a GUI thread wakes up because window input is now available, it gets a boost for the same reason.

These boosts are not forever. They take effect immediately, but if a thread uses all of its next quantum, it loses one point and moves down one queue in the priority array. If it uses up another full quantum, it moves down another level, and so on until it hits its base level, where it remains until it is boosted again. Clearly, if a thread wants good service, it should play a lot of music.

There is one other case in which the system fiddles with the priorities. Imagine that two threads are working together on a producer-consumer type problem. The producer's work is harder, so it gets a high priority, say 12, compared to the consumer's 4. At a certain point, the producer has filled up a shared buffer and blocks on a semaphore, as illustrated in Fig. 11-20(a).

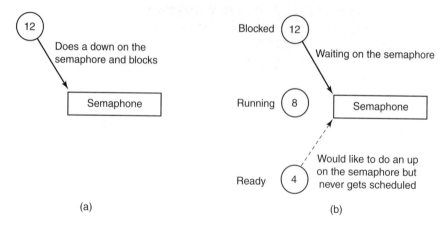

Figure 11-20. An example of priority inversion.

Before the consumer gets a chance to run again, an unrelated thread at priority 8 becomes ready and starts running, as shown in Fig. 11-20(b). As long as this thread wants to run, it will be able to, since it outguns the consumer and the producer, while higher, is blocked. Under these circumstances, the producer will never get to run again until the priority 8 thread gives up.

Windows 2000 solves this problem through what might be charitably called a big hack. The system keeps track of how long it has been since a ready thread ran last. If it exceeds a certain threshold, it is moved to priority 15 for two quanta. This may give it the opportunity to unblock the producer. After the two quanta are up, the boost is abruptly removed rather than decaying gradually. Probably a better solution would be to penalize threads that use up their quantum over and over by lowering their priority. After all, the problem was not caused by the starved thread, but by the greedy thread. This problem is well known under the name **priority inversion**.

An analogous problem happens if a priority 16 thread grabs a mutex and does not get a chance to run for a long time, starving more important system threads that are waiting for the mutex. This problem can be prevented within the operating system by having a thread that needs a mutex for a short time just disable scheduling while it is busy. On a multiprocessor, a spin lock should be used.

Before leaving the subject of scheduling, it is worth saying a couple of words about the quantum. On Windows 2000 Professional the default is 20 msec; on uniprocessor servers it is 120 msec; on multiprocessors various other values are used, depending on the clock frequency. The shorter quantum favors interactive users whereas the longer quantum reduces context switches and thus provides better efficiency. This is the meaning of the last column in Fig. 11-2. These defaults can be increased manually by 2x, 4x, or 6x if desired. As an aside, the size of the quantum was chosen a decade ago and not changed since although machines are now more than an order of magnitude faster. The numbers probably could be reduced by a factor of 5 to 10 with no harm and possibly better response time for interactive threads in a heavily loaded system.

One last patch to the scheduling algorithm says that when a new window becomes the foreground window, all of its threads get a longer quantum by an amount taken from the registry. This change gives them more CPU time, which usually translates to better service for the window that just moved to the foreground.

11.4.4 MS-DOS Emulation

One of the design goals of Windows 2000 was inherited from NT: try to run as many reasonable MS-DOS programs as possible. This goal is quite different from Windows 98's stated goal: run all old MS-DOS programs (to which we add: no matter how ill-behaved they may be).

The way Windows 2000 deals with ancient programs is to run them in a fully protected environment. When an MS-DOS program is started, a normal Win32 process is started and loaded with an MS-DOS emulation program, *ntvdm* (NT Virtual DOS Machine) that will monitor the MS-DOS program and carry out its system calls. Since MS-DOS only recognized memory up to 1 MB on the 8088 and only up to 16 MB with bank switching and other tricks on the 286, it is safe to put *ntvdm* high in the process' virtual address space where the program has no way to address it. This situation is shown in Fig. 11-21.

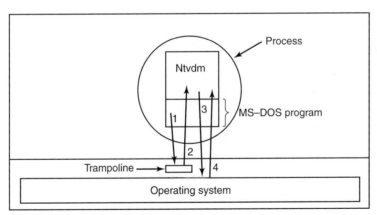

Figure 11-21. How old MS-DOS programs are run under Windows 2000.

When the MS-DOS program is just executing normal instructions, it can run on the bare hardware since the Pentium includes all the 8088 and 286 instructions as subsets. The interesting part is what happens when the MS-DOS program wants to do I/O or interact with the system. A well-behaved program just makes a system call. In expectation of this, *ntvdm* instructs Windows 2000 to reflect all MS-DOS system calls back to it. In effect, the system call just bounces off the operating system and is caught by the emulator, as shown in steps 1 and 2 in Fig. 11-21. Sometimes this technique is referred to as using a **trampoline**.

Once it gets control, the emulator figures out what the program was trying to do and issues its own Win32 calls to get the work done (step 3 and 4 in Fig. 11-21). As long as the program is well behaved and just makes legal MS-DOS system calls, this technique works fine. The trouble is that some old MS-DOS programs bypassed the operating system and wrote directly to the video RAM, read directly from the keyboard, and so on, things that are impossible in a protected environment. To the extent that the illegal behavior causes a trap, there is some hope that the emulator can figure out what the program was trying to do and emulate it. If it does not know what the program wants, the program is just killed because 100 percent emulation was not a Windows 2000 requirement.

11.4.5 Booting Windows 2000

Before Windows 2000 can start up, it must be booted. The boot process creates the initial processes that bring up the system. In this section we will briefly discuss how the boot process works for Windows 2000. The hardware boot process consists of reading in the first sector of the first disk (the master boot record) and jumping to it, as we described in Sec. 5.4.2. This short assembly language program reads the partition table to see which partition contains the bootable operating system. When it finds the operating system partition, it reads in the first sector of that partition, called the **boot sector**, and jumps to it. The program in the boot sector reads its partition's root directory, searching for a file called *ntldr* (another piece of archaeological evidence that Windows 2000 is really NT). If it finds that file, it reads the file into memory and executes it. *Ntldr* loads Windows 2000. As an aside, there are several versions of the boot sector, depending on whether the partition is formatted as FAT-16, FAT-32, or NTFS. When Windows 2000 is installed, the correct version of the master boot record and boot sector are written to disk.

Ntldr now reads a file called *Boot.ini*, which is the only configuration information not in the registry. It lists all the versions of *hal.dll* and *ntoskrnl.exe* available for booting in this partition. The file also provides many parameters, such as how many CPUs and how much RAM to use, whether to give user processes 2 GB or 3 GB, and what rate to set the real-time clock to. *Ntldr* then selects and loads *hal.dll* and *ntoskrnl.exe* files as well as *bootvid.dll*, the default video driver for writing on the display during the boot process. *Ntldr* next reads the registry to find out which drivers are needed to complete the boot (e.g., the keyboard and mouse drivers, but also dozens more for controlling various chips on the parentboard). Finally, it reads in all these drivers and passes control to *ntoskrnl.exe*.

Once started, the operating system does some general initialization and then calls the executive components to do their own initialization. For example, the object manager prepares its name space to allow other components call it to insert

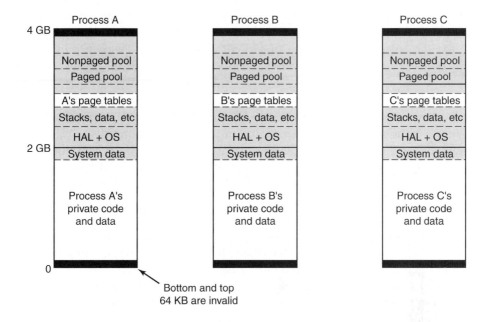

Figure 11-23. Virtual address space layout for three user processes. The white areas are private per process. The shaded areas are shared among all processes.

readable for user-mode processes. The reason for putting it here is that when a thread makes a system call, it traps into kernel mode and just keeps on running in the same thread. By making the whole operating system and all of its data structures (as well as the whole user process) visible within a thread's address space when it enters kernel mode, there is no need to change the memory map or flush the cache upon kernel entry. All that has to be done is switch to the thread's kernel stack. The trade-off here is less private address space per process in return for faster system calls. Large database servers already feel cramped, which is why the 3-GB user space option is available on Advanced Server and Datacenter Server.

Each virtual page can be in one of three states: free, reserved, or committed. A **free page** is not currently in use and a reference to it causes a page fault. When a process is started, all of its pages are in free state until the program and initial data are mapped into its address space. Once code or data is mapped onto a page, the page is said to be **committed**. A reference to a committed page is mapped using the virtual memory hardware and succeeds if the page is in main memory. If the page is not in main memory, a page fault occurs and the operating system finds and brings in the page from disk.

A virtual page can also be in **reserved** state, meaning it is not available for being mapped until the reservation is explicitly removed. For example, when a new thread is created, 1 MB of stack space is reserved in the process' virtual address space, but only one page is committed. This technique means that the stack can eventually grow to 1 MB without fear that some other thread will allocate the needed contiguous piece of virtual address space out from under it. In addition to the free, reserved, and committed attributes, pages also have other attributes, such as being readable, writable, and executable.

An interesting trade-off occurs with assignment of backing store to committed pages. A simple strategy would be to assign a page in one of the paging files to back up each committed page at the time the page was committed. This would guarantee that there was always a known place to write out each committed page should it be necessary to evict it from memory. The downside of this strategy is that the paging file might have to be as large as the union of all processes' virtual memory. On a large system that rarely ran out of memory and thus rarely paged, this approach would waste disk space.

To avoid wasting disk space, Windows 2000 committed pages that have no natural home on the disk (e.g., stack pages) are not assigned a disk page until the moment that they have to be paged out. This design makes the system more complex because the paging files maps may have to be fetched during a page fault, and fetching them may cause one or more additional page faults inside the page fault handler. On the other hand, no disk space need be allocated for pages that are never paged out.

Trade-offs like this (system complexity versus better performance or more features) tend to get resolved in favor of the latter because the value of better performance or more features is clear but the downside of complexity (a bigger maintenance headache and more crashes per year) is hard to quantify. Free and reserved pages never have shadow pages on disk and references to them always cause page faults.

The shadow pages on the disk are arranged into one or more paging files. There may be up to 16 paging files, possibly spread over 16 separate disks, for higher I/O bandwidth. Each one has an initial size and a maximum size it can grow to later if needed. These files can be created at the maximum size at system installation time in order to reduce the chances that they are highly fragmented, but new ones can be created using the control panel later on. The operating system keeps track of which virtual page maps onto which part of which paging file. For (execute only) program text, the executable binary file (i.e., *.exe* or *.dll* file) contains the shadow pages; for data pages, the paging files are used.

Windows 2000, like many versions of UNIX, allows files to be mapped directly onto regions of the virtual address spaces (i.e., runs of consecutive pages). Once a file has been mapped onto the address space, it can be read or written using ordinary memory references. Memory-mapped files are implemented in the same way as other committed pages, only the shadow pages are in the user's file instead of in the paging file. As a result, while a file is mapped in, the version in memory may not be identical to the disk version (due to recent writes to the virtual address space). However, when the file is unmapped or is explicitly flushed, the disk version is brought up to date.

Windows 2000 explicitly allows two or more processes to map onto the same part of the same file at the same time, possibly at different virtual addresses, as shown in Fig. 11-24. By reading and writing memory words, the processes can now communicate with each other and pass data back and forth at very high bandwidth, since no copying is required. Different processes may have different access permissions. Since all the processes using a mapped file share the same pages, changes made by one of them are immediately visible to all the others, even if the disk file has not yet been updated. Care is also taken that if another process opens the file for normal reading, it sees the current pages in RAM, not stale pages from the disk.

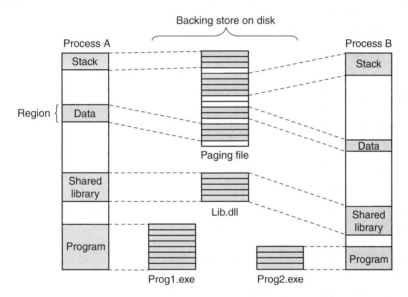

Figure 11-24. Mapped regions with their shadow pages on disk. The *lib.dll* file is mapped into two address spaces at the same time.

It is worth noting that there is a problem if two programs share a DLL file and one of them changes the file's static data. If no special action is taken, the other one will see the changed data, which is probably not what is desired. The problem is solved by mapping all pages in as read only by secretly noting that some are really writable. When a write happens to a page that is mapped read only but is really writable, a private copy of the page is made and mapped in. Now it can be written safely without affecting other users or the original copy on disk. This technique is called **copy-on-write**.

Also it is worth noting that if program text is mapped into two address spaces at different addresses, a certain problem arises with addressing. What happens if the first instruction is JMP 300? If process one maps the program in at address

65,536, the code can easily be patched to read JMP 65836. But what happens if a second process now maps it in at 131,072? The JMP 65836 will go to address 65,836 instead of 131,372 and the program will fail. The solution is to use only relative offsets, not absolute virtual addresses in code that is to be shared. Fortunately, most machines have instructions using relative offsets as well as instructions using absolute addresses. Compilers can use the relative offset instructions, but they have to know in advance whether to use them or the absolute ones. The relative ones are not used all the time because the resulting code is usually less efficient. Usually, a compiler flag tells them which to use. The technique of making it possible to place a piece of code at any virtual address without relocation is called **position independent code**.

Years ago, when 16-bit (or 20-bit) virtual address spaces were standard, but machines had megabytes of physical memory, all kinds of tricks were thought of to allow programs to use more physical memory than fit in the address space. Often these tricks went under the name of **bank switching**, in which a program could substitute some block of memory above the 16-bit or 20-bit limit for a block of its own memory. When 32-bit machines were introduced, people thought they would have enough address space forever. They were wrong. The problem is back. Large programs often need more than the 2 GB or 3 GB of user address space Windows 2000 allocates to them, so bank switching is back, now called **address windowing extensions**. This facility allows programs to map into shuffle chunks of memory in and out of the user portion of the address space (and especially above the dreaded 4-GB boundary). Since it is only used on servers with more than 2 GB of physical memory, we will defer the discussion until the next edition of this book (by which time even entry-level desktop machines will be feeling the 32-bit pinch).

11.5.2 Memory Management System Calls

The Win32 API contains a number of functions that allow a process to manage its virtual memory explicitly. The most important of these functions are listed in Fig. 11-25. All of them operate on a region consisting either of a single page or a sequence of two or more pages that are consecutive in the virtual address space.

The first four API functions are used to allocate, free, protect and query regions of virtual address space. Allocated regions always begin on 64-KB boundaries to minimize porting problems to future architectures with pages larger than current ones (up to 64 KB). The actual amount of address space allocated can be less than 64 KB, but must be a multiple of the page size. The next two give a process the ability to hardwire pages in memory so they will not be paged out and to undo this property. A real-time program might need this ability, for example. A limit is enforced by the operating system to prevent processes from getting too greedy. Actually, the pages can be removed from memory, but only if the entire

Win32 API function	Description
VirtualAlloc	Reserve or commit a region
VirtualFree	Release or decommit a region
VirtualProtect	Change the read/write/execute protection on a region
VirtualQuery	Inquire about the status of a region
VirtualLock	Make a region memory resident (i.e., disable paging for it)
VirtualUnlock	Make a region pageable in the usual way
CreateFileMapping	Create a file mapping object and (optionally) assign it a name
MapViewOfFile	Map (part of) a file into the address space
UnmapViewOfFile	Remove a mapped file from the address space
OpenFileMapping	Open a previously created file mapping object

Figure 11-25. The principal Win32 API functions for managing virtual memory in Windows 2000.

process is swapped out. When it is brought back, all the locked pages are reloaded before any thread can start running again. Although not shown in Fig. 11-25, Windows 2000 also has API functions to allow a process to access the virtual memory of a different process over which it has been given control (i.e., for which it has a handle).

The last four API functions listed are for managing memory-mapped files. To map a file, a file mapping object (see Fig. 11-10) must first be created, with CreateFileMapping. This function returns a handle to the file mapping object and optionally enters a name for it into the file system so another process can use it. The next two functions map and unmap files, respectively. The last one can be used by a process to map in a file currently also mapped in by a different process. In this way, two or more processes can share regions of their address spaces. This technique allows them to write in limited regions of each other's memory.

11.5.3 Implementation of Memory Management

Windows 2000 supports a single linear 4-GB demand-paged address space per process. Segmentation is not supported in any form. Theoretically, page sizes can be any power of two up to 64 KB. On the Pentium they are fixed at 4 KB; on the Itanium they can be 8 KB or 16 KB. In addition, the operating system itself can use 4-MB pages to reduce page table space consumed.

Unlike the scheduler, which selects individual threads to run and does not care much about processes, the memory manager deals entirely with processes and does not care much about threads. After all, processes, not threads, own the address space and that is what the memory manager deals with. When a region of virtual address space is allocated, as four of them have been for process *A* in

Fig. 11-24, the memory manager creates a **VAD (Virtual Address Descriptor)** for it, listing the range of addresses mapped, the backing store file and offset where it is mapped, and the protection code. When the first page is touched, the directory of page tables is created and a pointer to it inserted is in the VAD. In fact, an address space is completely defined by the list of its VADs. This scheme supports sparse address spaces because unused areas between the mapped regions use no resources.

Page Fault Handling

Windows 2000 does not use any form of prepaging. When a process starts, none of its pages are in memory. All of them are brought in dynamically as page faults occurs. On each page fault, a trap to the kernel (in the sense of Fig. 11-7) occurs. The kernel builds a machine-independent descriptor telling what happened and passes this to the memory manager part of the executive. The memory manager then checks it for validity. If the faulted page falls within a committed or reserved region, it looks up the address in the list of VADs, finds (or creates) the page table, and looks up the relevant entry.

The page table entries are different for different architectures. For the Pentium, the entry for a mapped page is shown in Fig. 11-26. Unmapped pages also have entries, but their format is somewhat different. For example, for an unmapped page that must be zeroed before it may be used, that fact is noted in the page table.

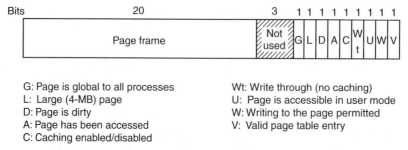

Figure 11-26. A page table entry for a mapped page on the Pentium.

The most important bits in the page table entry for purposes of the paging algorithm are the *A* and *D* bits. They are fed by the hardware and keep track of whether the page has been referenced or written on, respectively, since the last time they were cleared.

Page faults come in five categories:

1. The page referenced is not committed.

2. A protection violation occurred.

3. A shared page has been written.

4. The stack needs to grow.

5. The page referenced is committed but not currently mapped in.

The first and second cases are fatal errors from which there is no recovery for the faulting process. The third case has the same symptoms as the second one (an attempt to write to a read-only page), but the treatment is different. The solution is to copy the page to a new physical page frame and map that one in read/write. This is how copy-on-write works. (If a shared page is marked writable in all processes using it, it is not copy-on-write and no fault occurs when writing to it.) The fourth case requires allocating a new page frame and mapping it in. However, the security rules require that the page contain only 0s, to prevent the process from snooping on the previous owner of the page. Thus a page of 0s must be found, or if one is not available, another page frame must be allocated and zeroed on the spot. Finally, the fifth case is a normal page fault. The page is located and mapped in.

The actual mechanics of getting and mapping pages is fairly standard, so we will not discuss this issue. The only noteworthy feature is that Windows 2000 does not read in isolated pages from the disk. Instead, it reads in runs of consecutive pages, usually about 1–8 pages, in an attempt to minimize the number of disk transfers. The run size is larger for code pages than for data pages.

The Page Replacement Algorithm

Page replacement works like this. The system makes a serious attempt to maintain a substantial number of free pages in memory so that when a page fault occurs, a free page can be claimed on the spot, without the need to first write some other page to disk. As a consequence of this strategy, most page faults can be satisfied with at most one disk operation (reading in the page), rather than sometimes two (writing back a dirty page and then reading in the needed page).

Of course, the pages on the free list have to come from somewhere, so the real page replacement algorithm is how pages get taken away from processes and put on the free list (actually, there are four free lists, but for the moment it is simplest to think of there being just one; we will come to the details later). Let us now take a look at how Windows 2000 frees pages. To start with, the entire paging system makes heavy use of the working set concept. Each process (*not* each thread) has a working set. This set consists of the mapped-in pages that are in memory and can be thus referenced without a page fault. The size and composition of the working set fluctuates as the process' threads run, of course.

Each process' working set is described by two parameters: the minimum size and the maximum size. These are not hard bounds, so a process may have fewer pages in memory than its minimum or (under certain circumstances) more than its maximum. Every process starts with the same minimum and maximum, but these bounds can change over time. The default initial minimum is in the range 20–50 and the default initial maximum is in the range 45–345, depending on the total amount of RAM. The system administrator can change these defaults, however.

If a page fault occurs and the working set is smaller than the minimum, the page is added. On the other hand, if a page fault occurs and the working set is larger than the maximum, a page is evicted from the working set (but not from memory) to make room for the new page. This algorithm means that Windows 2000 uses a local algorithm, to prevent one process from hurting others by hogging memory. However, the system does try to tune itself to some extent. For example, if it observes that one process is paging like crazy (and the others are not), the system may increase the size of its maximum working set, so that over time, the algorithm is a mix of local and global. There is an absolute limit on the working set size, however: even if there is only one process running, it may not take the last 512 pages, to leave some slack for new processes.

So far, so good, but the story is not over yet. Once a second, a dedicated kernel daemon thread, the **balance set manager**, checks to see if there are enough free pages. If there are not enough, it starts the **working set manager** thread to examine the working sets and recover more pages. The working set manager first determines the order to examine the processes in. Large processes that have been idle for a long time are considered before small active processes and the foreground process is considered last.

The working set manager then starts inspecting processes in the chosen order. If a process' working set is currently less than its minimum or it has incurred more than a certain number of page faults since the last inspection, it is passed over. Otherwise, one or more pages are removed. The target number of pages to remove is a complicated function of the total RAM size, how tight memory is, how the current working set size compares to the process' minimum and maximum, and other parameters. All the pages are examined in turn.

On a uniprocessor, if a page's reference bit is clear, a counter associated with the page is incremented. If the reference bit is set, the counter is set to zero. After the scan, the pages with the highest counters are removed from the working set. The thread continues examining processes until it has recovered enough pages, then it stops. If a complete pass through all processes still has not recovered enough pages, it makes another pass, trimming more aggressively, even reducing working sets below their minimum if necessary.

On a multiprocessor, looking at the reference bit does not work because although the current CPU may not have touched the page recently, some other one may have. Examining another CPU's reference bits is too expensive to do. Consequently, the reference bit is not examined and the oldest pages are removed.

It should be noted that for page replacement purposes, the operating system itself is regarded as a process. It owns pages and also has a working set. This working set can be trimmed. However, parts of the code and the nonpaged pool are locked in memory and cannot be paged out under any circumstances.

Physical Memory Management

Above we mentioned that there were actually four free lists. Now it is time to see what all of them are for. Every page in memory is either in one or more working sets or on exactly one of these four lists, which are illustrated in Fig. 11-27. The standby (clean) and modified (dirty) lists hold pages that have recently been evicted from a working set, are still in memory, and are still associated with the process that was using them. The difference between them is that clean pages have a valid copy on disk and can thus be abandoned at will, whereas dirty pages do not have an up-to-date copy on disk. The free list consists of clean pages that are no longer associated with any process. The pages on the zeroed page list are not associated with any process and are also filled with zeros. A fifth list holds any physically defective RAM pages that may exist to make sure that they are not used for anything.

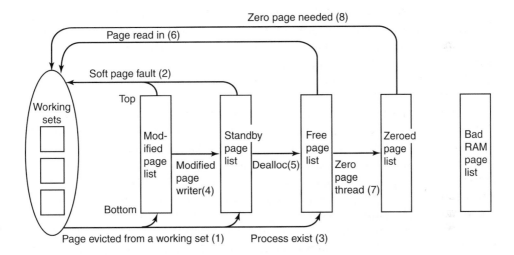

Figure 11-27. The various page lists and the transitions between them.

Pages are moved between the working sets and the various lists by the working set manager and other kernel daemon threads. Let us examine the transitions. When the working set manager removes a page from a working set, the page goes on the bottom of the standby or modified list, depending on its state of cleanliness. This transition is shown as (1). Pages on both lists are still valid pages, so if a page fault occurs and one of these pages is needed, it is removed from the list and faulted back into the working set without any disk I/O (2). When a process exits, its nonshared pages cannot be faulted back to it, so they go on the free list (3). These pages are no longer associated with any process.

Other transitions are caused by other daemon threads. Every 4 seconds the **swapper thread** runs and looks for processes all of whose threads have been idle for a certain number of seconds. If it finds any such processes, their kernel stacks are unpinned and their pages are moved to the standby or modified lists, also shown as (1).

Two other daemon threads, the **mapped page writer** and the **modified page writer**, wake up periodically to see if there are enough clean pages. If there are not, they take pages from the top of the modified list, write them back to disk, and then move them to the standby list (4). The former handles writes to mapped files and the latter handles writes to the paging files. The result of these writes is to transform dirty pages into clean pages.

The reason for having two threads is that a mapped file might have to grow as a result of the write, and growing it requires access to on-disk data structures to allocate a free disk block. If there is no room in memory to bring them in when a page has to be written, a deadlock could result. The other thread can solve the problem by writing out pages to a paging file, which never grows. Nobody ever said Windows 2000 was simple.

The other transitions in Fig. 11-27 are as follows. If a process unmaps a page, the page is no longer associated with a process and can go on the free list (5), except for the case that it is shared. When a page fault requires a page frame to hold the page about to be read in, the page frame is taken from the free list (6), if possible. It does not matter that the page may still contain confidential information because it is about to be overwritten in its entirety. The situation is different when a stack grows.

In that case, an empty page frame is needed and the security rules require the page to contain all zeros. For this reason, another kernel daemon thread, the **zero page thread**, runs at the lowest priority (see Fig. 11-19), erasing pages that are on the free list and putting them on the zeroed page list (7). Whenever the CPU is idle and there are free pages, they might as well be zeroed since a zeroed page is potentially more useful than a free page.

The existence of all these lists leads to some subtle policy choices. For example, suppose that a page has to be brought in from disk and the free list is empty. The system is now forced to choose between taking a clean page from the standby list (which might otherwise have been faulted back in later) or an empty page from the zeroed page list (throwing away the work done in zeroing it). Which is better? If the CPU is idle a lot and the zero page thread gets to run often, taking a zeroed page is better because there is no shortage of them. However, if the CPU is always busy and the disk is mostly idle, it is better to take a page from the standby list to avoid the CPU cost of having to zero another page later if a stack grows.

Another puzzle. How aggressively should the daemons move pages from the modified list to the standby list? Having clean pages around is better than having dirty pages around (since they can be reused instantly), but an aggressive cleaning policy means more disk I/O and there is some chance that a newly-cleaned page may be faulted back into a working set and dirtied again.

In general, Windows 2000 resolves these kinds of conflicts through complex heuristics, guesswork, historical precedent, rules of thumb, and administrator-controlled parameter settings. Furthermore, the code is so complex that the designers are loathe to touch parts of it for fear of breaking something somewhere else in the system that nobody really understands any more.

To keep track of all the pages and all the lists, Windows maintains a page frame database with as many entries as there are RAM pages, as shown in Fig. 11-28. This table is indexed by physical page frame number. The entries are fixed length, but different formats are used for different kinds of entries (e.g., valid versus invalid). Valid entries maintain the page's state and a count of how many page tables point to the page, so the system can tell when the page is no longer in use. Pages that are in a working set tell which one. There is also a pointer to the page table pointing to the page, if any (shared pages are handled specially), a link to the next page on the list (if any), and various other fields and flags, such as read in progress, write in progress, etc.

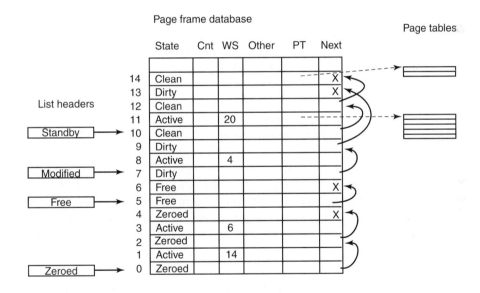

Figure 11-28. Some of the major fields in the page frame database for a valid page.

All in all, memory management is a highly complex subsystem with many data structures, algorithms, and heuristics. It attempts to be largely self tuning, but there are also many knobs that administrators can tweak to affect system performance. A number of these knobs and the associated counters can be viewed using tools in the various tool kits mentioned earlier. Probably the most important thing to remember here is that memory management in real systems is a lot more than just one simple paging algorithm like clock or aging.

11.6 INPUT/OUTPUT IN WINDOWS 2000

The goal of the Windows 2000 I/O system is to provide a framework for efficiently handling a very wide variety of I/O devices. Current input devices include various kinds of keyboards, mice, touch pads, joysticks, scanners, still cameras, television cameras, bar code readers, microphones, and laboratory rats. Current output devices include monitors, printers, plotters, beamers, CD-recorders, and sound cards. Storage devices include floppy disks, IDE and SCSI hard disks, CD-ROMs, DVDs, Zip drives, and tape drives. Finally, other devices include clocks, networks, telephones, and camcorders. No doubt many new I/O devices will be invented in the years to come, so Window 2000 has been designed with a general framework to which new devices can easily be attached. In the following sections we will examine some of the issues relating to I/O.

11.6.1 Fundamental Concepts

The I/O manager is on intimate terms with the plug-and-play manager. The basic idea behind plug and play is that of an enumerable bus. Many buses, including PC Card, PCI, USB, IEEE 1394, and SCSI, have been designed so that the plug-and-play manager can send a request to each slot and ask the device there to identify itself. Having discovered what is out there, the plug-and-play manager allocates hardware resources, such as interrupt levels, locates the appropriate drivers, and loads them into memory. As each one is loaded, a **driver object** is created for it. For some buses, such as SCSI, enumeration happens only at boot time, but for other buses, such as USB and IEEE 1394, it can happen at any moment, requiring close contact between the plug-and-play manager, the bus driver (which actually does the enumeration), and the I/O manager.

The I/O manager is also closely connected with the power manager. The power manager can put the computer into any of six states, roughly described as:

1. Fully operational.

2. Sleep-1: CPU power reduced, RAM and cache on; instant wake-up.

3. Sleep-2: CPU and RAM on; CPU cache off; continue from current PC.

4. Sleep-3: CPU and cache off; RAM on; restart from fixed address.

5. Hibernate: CPU, cache, and RAM off; restart from saved disk file.

6. Off: Everything off; full reboot required.

I/O devices can also be in various power states. Turning them on and off is handled by the power manager and I/O manager together. Note that states 2 through 6 are only used when the CPU has been idle for a shorter or longer time interval.

Somewhat surprisingly, all the file systems are technically I/O drivers. Requests for data blocks from user processes are initially sent to the cache manager. If the cache manager cannot satisfy the request from the cache, it has the I/O manager call the proper file system driver to go get the block it needs from disk.

An interesting feature of Windows 2000 is its support for **dynamic disks**. These disks may span multiple partitions and even multiple disks and may be reconfigured on the fly, without even having to reboot. In this way, logical volumes are no longer constrained to a single partition or even a single disk so that a single file system may span multiple drives in a transparent way.

Another interesting aspect of Windows 2000 is its support for asynchronous I/O. It is possible for a thread to start an I/O operation and then continue executing in parallel with the I/O. This feature is especially important on servers. There are various ways the thread can find out that the I/O has completed. One is to specify an event object at the time the call is made and then wait on it eventually. Another is to specify a queue to which a completion event will be posted by the system when the I/O is done. A third is to provide a callback procedure that the system calls when the I/O has completed.

11.6.2 Input/Output API Calls

Windows 2000 has over 100 separate APIs for a wide variety of I/O devices, including mice, sound cards, telephones, tape drives, etc. Probably the most important is the graphics system, for which there are thousands of Win32 API calls. In Sec. 5.7.3 we began our discussion of the Window graphical system. Here we will continue, mentioning a few of the Win32 API categories, each of which has many calls. A brief summary of the categories are given in Fig. 11-29. As we mentioned in Chap. 5, multiple 1500-page books have been written on the graphics portion of the Win32 API.

Win32 calls exist to create, destroy, and manage windows. Windows have a vast number of styles and options that can be specified, including titles, borders, colors, sizes, and scroll bars. Windows can be fixed or movable, of constant size or resizable. Their properties can be queried and messages can be sent to them.

Many windows contain menus, so there are Win32 calls for creating and deleting menus and menu bars. Dynamic menus can be popped up and removed. Menu items can be highlighted, dimmed out, or cascaded.

Dialog boxes are popped up to inform the user of some event or ask a question. They may contain buttons, sliders, or text fields to be filled in. Sounds can also be associated with dialog boxes, for example for warning messages.

There are hundreds of drawing and painting functions available, ranging from setting a single pixel to doing complex region clipping operations. Many calls are provided for drawing lines and closed geometric figures of various kinds, with detailed control over textures, colors, widths, and many other attributes.

API group	Description
Window management	Create, destroy, and manage windows,
Menus	Create, destroy, and append to menus and menu bars
Dialog boxes	Pop up a dialog box and collect information
Painting and drawing	Display points, lines, and geometric figures
Text	Display text in some font, size, and color
Bitmaps and icons	Placement of bitmaps and icons on the screen
Colors and palettes	Manage the set of colors available
The clipboard	Pass information from one application to another
Input	Get information from the mouse and keyboard

Figure 11-29. Some categories of Win32 API calls.

Another group of calls relates to displaying text. Actually, the text display call, **TextOut**, is straightforward. It is the management of the color, point sizes, typefaces, character widths, glyphs, kerning, and other typesetting details where the complexity comes in. Fortunately, the rasterization of text (conversion to bitmaps) is generally done automatically.

Bitmaps are small rectangular blocks of pixels that can be placed on the screen using the **BitBlt** Win32 call. They are used for icons and occasionally text. Various calls are provided for creating, destroying, and managing icon objects.

Many displays use a color mode with only 256 or 65,536 of the 2^{24} possible colors in order to represent each pixel with only 1 or 2 bytes, respectively. In these cases a color palette is needed to determine which 256 or 65,536 colors are available. The calls in this group create, destroy, and manage palettes, select the nearest available color to a given color, and try to make colors on the screen match colors on color printers.

Many Windows 2000 programs allow the user to select some data (e.g., a block of text, part of a drawing, a set of cells in a spreadsheet), put it on the clipboard, and allow it to be pasted into another application. The clipboard is generally used for this transmission. Many clipboard formats are defined, including text, bitmaps, objects, and metafiles. The latter are sets of Win32 calls that when executed draw something, allowing arbitrary drawings to be cut and pasted. This group of calls puts things on the clipboard, takes things off the clipboard, and generally manages it.

Finally, we come to input. There are no Win32 calls for GUI applications for reading input from the keyboard because GUI applications are event driven. The main program consists of a big loop getting input messages. When the user types something interesting, a message is sent to the program telling it what just came in. On the other hand, there are calls relating to the mouse, such as reading its (x, y) position and the state of its buttons. Some of the input calls are actually output calls, though, such as selecting a mouse cursor icon and moving it around the screen (basically, this is output to the screen). For nonGUI applications, it is possible to read from the keyboard.

11.6.3 Implementation of I/O

We could go on more-or-less indefinitely about the Win32 graphics calls, but now it is time to look at how the I/O manager implements graphics and other I/O functions. The main function of the I/O manager is to create a framework in which different I/O devices can operate. The basic structure of the framework is a set of device-independent procedures for certain aspects of I/O plus a set of loaded device drivers for communicating with the devices.

11.6.4 Device Drivers

To make sure that device drivers work well with the rest of Windows 2000, Microsoft has defined a **Windows Driver Model** that device drivers are expected to conform with. Furthermore, it also has provided a tool kit that is designed to help driver writers produce conformant drivers. In this section we will briefly examine this model. Conformant drivers must meet all of the following requirements as well as some others:

1. Handle incoming I/O requests, which arrive in a standard format.

2. Be as object based as the rest of Windows 2000.

3. Allow plug-and-play devices to be dynamically added or removed.

4. Permit power management, where applicable.

5. Be configurable in terms of resource usage.

6. Be reentrant for use on multiprocessors.

7. Be portable across Windows 98 and Windows 2000

I/O Requests are passed to drivers in the form of a standardized packet called an **IRP (I/O Request Packet)**. Conformant drivers must be able to handle them. Drivers must be object based in the sense of supporting a specific list of methods that the rest of the system can call. They must also correctly deal with other Windows 2000 objects when given an object handle to deal with.

Conformant drivers must fully support plug and play, which means that if a device managed by the driver is suddenly added or removed from the system, the driver must be prepared to accept this information and act on it, even in the case that the device currently being accessed is suddenly removed. Power management must also be supported for devices for which this is relevant. For example, if the system decides it is now time to go into a low-power hibernation mode, all devices that are capable of doing this must do so to save energy. They must also wake up when told to do so.

Drivers must be configurable, which means not having any built-in assumptions about which interrupt lines or I/O ports certain devices use. For example, the printer port on the IBM PC and its successors has been at address 0x378 for more than 20 years and it is unlikely to change now. But a printer driver that has this address hard coded into it is not conformant.

Being multiprocessor safe is also a requirement as Windows 2000 was designed for use on multiprocessors. Concretely, this requirement means while a driver is actively running and processing one request on behalf of one CPU, a second request may come in on behalf of a different CPU. The second CPU may begin executing the driver code simultaneously with the first one. The driver must function correctly even when being executed concurrently by two or more CPUs, which implies that all sensitive data structures may only be accessed from inside critical regions. Just assuming that there will not be any other calls until the current one is finished is not permitted.

Finally, conformant drivers must work not only on Windows 2000 but also on Windows 98. It may be necessary to recompile the driver on each system however, and use of C preprocessor commands to isolate platform dependencies is permitted.

In UNIX, drivers are located by using their major device numbers. Windows 2000 uses a different scheme. At boot time, or when a new hot pluggable plug-and-play device is attached to the computer, Windows 2000 automatically detects it and calls the plug-and-play manager. The manager queries the device to find out what the manufacturer and model number are. Equipped with this knowledge, it looks on the hard disk in a certain directory to see if it has the driver. If it does not, it displays a dialog box asking the user to insert a floppy disk or CD-ROM with the driver. Once the driver is located, it is loaded into memory.

Each driver must supply a set of procedures that can be called to get its services. The first one, called *DriverEntry*, initializes the driver. It is called just after the driver is loaded. It may create tables and data structures, but must not touch the device yet. It also fills in some of the fields of the driver object created by the I/O manager when the driver was loaded. The fields in the driver object include pointers to all the other procedures that drivers must supply. In addition, for each device controlled by the driver (e.g., each IDE disk controlled by the IDE disk driver), a **device object** is created and initialized to point to the driver object. These driver objects are entered into a special directory, \??. Given a device object, the driver object can be located easily, and hence its methods can be called.

A second required procedure is *AddDevice*, which is called once (by the plug-and-play manager) for each device to be added. Once this has been accomplished, the driver is called with the first IRP, which sets up the interrupt vector and actually initializes the hardware. Other procedures that drivers must contain are the interrupt service procedure, various timer management procedures, a fast I/O path, DMA control, a way to cancel currently executing requests, and many more. All in all, Windows 2000 drivers are so complex that multiple books have been written about them (Cant, 1999; Oney, 1999; and Viscarola and Mason, 1999).

A driver in Windows 2000 may do all the work by itself, as the printer driver does in Fig. 11-30 (just as an example). On the other hand, drivers may also be stacked, which means that a request may pass through a sequence of drivers, each doing part of the work. Two stacked drivers are also illustrated in Fig. 11-30.

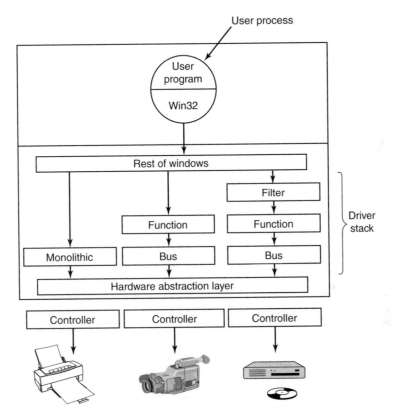

Figure 11-30. Windows 2000 allows drivers to be stacked.

One common use for stacked drivers is to separate out the bus management from the functional work of actually controlling the device. Bus management on the PCI bus is quite complicated on account of many kinds of modes and bus transactions, and by separating this work from the device-specific part, driver writers are freed from learning how to control the bus. They can just use the standard bus driver in their stack. Similarly, USB and SCSI drivers have a device-specific part and a generic part, with common drivers used for the generic part.

Another use of stacking drivers is to be able to insert **filter drivers** into the stack. A filter driver performs some transformation on the data on the way up or down. For example, a filter driver could compress data on the way to the disk or encrypt data on the way to the network. Putting the filter here means that neither the application program nor the true device driver have to be aware of it and it works automatically for all data going to (or coming from) the device.

11.7 THE WINDOWS 2000 FILE SYSTEM

Windows 2000 supports several file systems, the most important of which are **FAT-16**, **FAT-32**, and **NTFS (NT File System)**. FAT-16 is the old MS-DOS file system. It uses 16-bit disk addresses, which limits it to disk partitions no larger than 2 GB. FAT-32 uses 32-bit disk addresses and supports disk partitions up to 2 TB. NTFS is a new file system developed specifically for Windows NT and carried over to Windows 2000. It uses 64-bit disk addresses and can (theoretically) support disk partitions up to 2^{64} bytes, although other considerations limit it to smaller sizes. Windows 2000 also supports read-only file systems for CD-ROMs and DVDs. It is possible (even common) to have the same running system have access to multiple file system types available at the same time.

In this chapter we will treat the NTFS file system because it is a modern file system unencumbered by the need to be fully compatible with the MS-DOS file system, which was based on the CP/M file system designed for 8-inch floppy disks more than 20 years ago. Times have changed and 8-inch floppy disks are not quite state of the art any more. Neither are their file systems. Also, NTFS differs both in user interface and implementation in a number of ways from the UNIX file system, which makes it a good second example to study. NTFS is a large and complex system and space limitations prevent us from covering all of its features, but the material presented below should give a reasonable impression of it.

11.7.1 Fundamental Concepts

Individual file names in NTFS are limited to 255 characters; full paths are limited to 32,767 characters. File names are in Unicode, allowing people in countries not using the Latin alphabet (e.g., Greece, Japan, India, Russia, and Israel) to write file names in their native language. For example, φιλε is a perfectly legal file name. NTFS fully supports case sensitive names (so *foo* is different from *Foo* and *FOO*). Unfortunately, the Win32 API does not fully support case-sensitivity for file names and not at all for directory names, so this advantage is lost to programs restricted to using Win32 (e.g., for Windows 98 compatibility).

An NTFS file is not just a linear sequence of bytes, as FAT-32 and UNIX files are. Instead, a file consists of multiple attributes, each of which is represented by a stream of bytes. Most files have a few short streams, such as the name of the file and its 64-bit object ID, plus one long (unnamed) stream with the data. However, a file can also have two or more (long) data streams as well. Each stream has a name consisting of the file name, a colon, and the stream name, as in *foo:stream1*. Each stream has its own size and is lockable independently of all the other streams. The idea of multiple streams in a file was borrowed from the Apple Macintosh, in which files have two streams, the data fork and the resource fork. This concept was incorporated into NTFS to allow an NTFS server be able to serve Macintosh clients.

File streams can be used for purposes other than Macintosh compatibility. For example, a photo editing program could use the unnamed stream for the main image and a named stream for a small thumbnail version. This scheme is simpler than the traditional way of putting them in the same file one after another. Another use of streams is in word processing. These programs often make two versions of a document, a temporary one for use during editing and a final one when the user is done. By making the temporary one a named stream and the final one the unnamed stream, both versions automatically share a file name, security information, timestamps, etc. with no extra work.

The maximum stream length is 2^{64} bytes. To get some idea of how big a 2^{64}-byte stream is, imagine that the stream were written out in binary, with each of the 0s and 1s in each byte occupying 1 mm of space. The 2^{67}-mm listing would be 15 light-years long, reaching far beyond the solar system, to Alpha Centauri and back. File pointers are used to keep track of where a process is in each stream, and these are 64 bits wide to handle the maximum length stream, which is about 18.4 exabytes.

The Win32 API function calls for file and directory manipulation are roughly similar to their UNIX counterparts, except most have more parameters and the security model is different. Opening a file returns a handle, which is then used for reading and writing the file. For graphical applications, no file handles are predefined. Standard input, standard output, and standard error have to be acquired explicitly if needed; in console mode they are preopened, however. Win32 also has a number of additional calls not present in UNIX.

11.7.2 File System API Calls in Windows 2000

The principal Win32 API functions for file management are listed in Fig. 11-31. There are actually many more, but these give a reasonable first impression of the basic ones. Let us now examine these calls briefly. CreateFile can be used to create a new file and return a handle to it. This API function must also be used to open existing files as there is no FileOpen API function. We have not listed the

Win32 API function	UNIX	Description
CreateFile	open	Create a file or open an existing file; return a handle
DeleteFile	unlink	Destroy an existing file
CloseHandle	close	Close a file
ReadFile	read	Read data from a file
WriteFile	write	Write data to a file
SetFilePointer	lseek	Set the file pointer to a specific place in the file
GetFileAttributes	stat	Return the file properties
LockFile	fcntl	Lock a region of the file to provide mutual exclusion
UnlockFile	fcntl	Unlock a previously locked region of the file

Figure 11-31. The principal Win32 API functions for file I/O. The second column gives the nearest UNIX equivalent.

parameters for the API functions because they are so voluminous. As an example, CreateFile has seven parameters, which are roughly summarized as follows:

1. A pointer to the name of the file to create or open.

2. Flags telling whether the file can be read, written, or both.

3. Flags telling whether multiple processes can open the file at once.

4. A pointer to the security descriptor, telling who can access the file.

5. Flags telling what to do if the file exists/does not exist.

6. Flags dealing with attributes such as archiving, compression, etc.

7. The handle of a file whose attributes should be cloned for the new file.

The next six API functions in Fig. 11-31 are fairly similar to the corresponding UNIX system calls. The last two allow a region of a file to be locked and unlocked to permit a process to get guaranteed mutual exclusion to it.

Using these API functions, it is possible to write a procedure to copy a file, analogous to the UNIX version of Fig. 6-5. Such a code fragment (without any error checking) is shown in Fig. 11-32. It has been designed to mimic our UNIX version. In practice, one would not have to program a copy file program since CopyFile is an API function (which executes something close to this program as a library procedure).

Windows 2000 NTFS is a hierarchical file system, similar to the UNIX file system. The separator between component names is \ however, instead of /, a fossil inherited from MS-DOS. There is a concept of a current working directory and path names can be relative or absolute. Hard and symbolic links are supported,

```
/* Open files for input and output. */
inhandle = CreateFile("data", GENERIC_READ, 0, NULL, OPEN_EXISTING, 0, NULL);
outhandle = CreateFile("newf", GENERIC_WRITE, 0, NULL, CREATE_ALWAYS,
    FILE_ATTRIBUTE_NORMAL, NULL);

/* Copy the file. */
do {
    s = ReadFile(inhandle, buffer, BUF_SIZE, &count, NULL);
    if (s && count > 0) WriteFile(outhandle, buffer, count, &ocnt, NULL);
} while (s > 0 && count > 0);

/* Close the files. */
CloseHandle(inhandle);
CloseHandle(outhandle);
```

Figure 11-32. A program fragment for copying a file using the Windows 2000 API functions.

the former implemented by having multiple directory entries, as in UNIX, and the latter implemented using reparse points (discussed later in this chapter). In addition, compression, encryption, and fault tolerance are also supported. These features and their implementations will be discussed later in this chapter.

The major directory management API functions are given in Fig. 11-33, again along with their nearest UNIX equivalents. The functions should be self explanatory.

Win32 API function	UNIX	Description
CreateDirectory	mkdir	Create a new directory
RemoveDirectory	rmdir	Remove an empty directory
FindFirstFile	opendir	Initialize to start reading the entries in a directory
FindNextFile	readdir	Read the next directory entry
MoveFile	rename	Move a file from one directory to another
SetCurrentDirectory	chdir	Change the current working directory

Figure 11-33. The principal Win32 API functions for directory management. The second column gives the nearest UNIX equivalent, when one exists.

11.7.3 Implementation of the Windows 2000 File System

NTFS is a highly complex and sophisticated file system. It was designed from scratch, rather than being an attempt to improve the old MS-DOS file system. Below we will examine a number of its features, starting with its structure, then moving on to file name lookup, file compression, and file encryption.

File System Structure

Each NTFS volume (e.g., disk partition) contains files, directories, bitmaps, and other data structures. Each volume is organized as a linear sequence of blocks (clusters in Microsoft's terminology), with the block size being fixed for each volume and ranging from 512 bytes to 64 KB, depending on the volume size. Most NTFS disks use 4-KB blocks as a compromise between large blocks (for efficient transfers) and small blocks (for low internal fragmentation). Blocks are referred to by their offset from the start of the volume using 64-bit numbers.

The main data structure in each volume is the **MFT** (**Master File Table**), which is a linear sequence of fixed-size 1-KB records. Each MFT record describes one file or directory. It contains the file's attributes, such as its name and timestamps, and the list of disk addresses where its blocks are located. If a file is extremely large, it is sometimes necessary to use two or more MFT records to contain the list of all the blocks, in which case the first MFT record, called the **base record**, points to the other MFT records. This overflow scheme dates back to CP/M, where each directory entry was called an extent. A bitmap keeps track of which MFT entries are free.

The MFT is itself a file and as such can be placed anywhere within the volume, thus eliminating the problem with defective sectors in the first track. Furthermore, the file can grow as needed, up to a maximum size of 2^{48} records.

The MFT is shown in Fig. 11-34. Each MFT record consists of a sequence of (attribute header, value) pairs. Each attribute begins with a header telling which attribute this is and how long the value is because some attribute values are variable length, such as the file name and the data. If the attribute value is short enough to fit in the MFT record, it is placed there. If it is too long, it is placed elsewhere on the disk and a pointer to it is placed in the MFT record.

The first 16 MFT records are reserved for NTFS metadata files, as shown in Fig. 11-34. Each of the records describes a normal file that has attributes and data blocks, just like any other file. Each of these files has a name that begins with a dollar sign to indicate that it is a metadata file. The first record describes the MFT file itself. In particular, it tells where the blocks of the MFT file are located so the system can find the MFT file. Clearly, Windows 2000 needs a way to find the first block of the MFT file in order to find the rest of the file system information. The way it finds the first block of the MFT file is to look in the boot block, where its address is installed at system installation time.

Record 1 is a duplicate of the early part of the MFT file. This information is so precious that having a second copy can be critical in the event one of the first blocks of the MFT ever goes bad. Record 2 is the log file. When structural changes are made to the file system, such as adding a new directory or removing an existing one, the action is logged here before it is performed, in order to increase the chance of correct recovery in the event of a failure during the operation. Changes to file attributes are also logged here. In fact, the only changes not

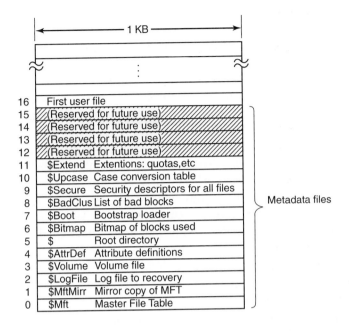

Figure 11-34. The NTFS master file table.

logged here are changes to user data. Record 3 contains information about the volume, such as its size, label, and version.

As mentioned above, each MFT record contains a sequence of (attribute header, value) pairs. The *$AttrDef* file is where the attributes are defined. Information about this file is in MFT record 4. Next comes the root directory, which itself is a file and can grow to arbitrary length. It is described by MFT record 5.

Free space on the volume is kept track of with a bitmap. The bitmap is itself a file and its attributes and disk addresses are given in MFT record 6. The next MFT record points to the bootstrap loader file. Record 8 is used to link all the bad blocks together to make sure they never occur in a file. Record 9 contains the security information. Record 10 is used for case mapping. For the Latin letters A-Z case mapping is obvious (at least for people who speak Latin). Case mapping for other languages, such as Greek, Armenian, or Georgian (the country, not the state), is less obvious to Latin speakers, so this file tells how to do it. Finally, record 11 is a directory containing miscellaneous files for things like disk quotas, object identifiers, reparse points, and so on. The last 4 MFT records are reserved for future use.

Each MFT record consists of a record header followed by a sequence of (attribute header, value) pairs. The record header contains a magic number used for validity checking, a sequence number updated each time the record is reused for a new file, a count of references to the file, the actual number of bytes in the record used, the identifier (index, sequence number) of the base record (used only for extension records), and some other miscellaneous fields. Following the record header comes the header of the first attribute, then the first attribute value, the second attribute header, the second attribute value, and so on.

NTFS defines 13 attributes that can appear in MFT records. These are listed in Fig. 11-35. Each MFT record consists of a sequence of attribute headers, each of which identifies the attribute it is heading and gives the length and location of the value field along with a variety of flags and other information. Usually, attribute values follow their attribute headers directly, but if a value is too long to fit in the MFT record, it may be put in a separate disk block. Such an attribute is said to be a **nonresident attribute**. The data attribute is an obvious candidate. Some attributes, such as the name, may be repeated, but all attributes must appear in a fixed order in the MFT record. The headers for resident attributes are 24 bytes long; those for nonresident attributes are longer because they contain information about where to find the attribute on disk.

Attribute	Description
Standard information	Flag bits, timestamps, etc.
File name	File name in Unicode; may be repeated for MS-DOS name
Security descriptor	Obsolete. Security information is now in $Extend$Secure
Attribute list	Location of additional MFT records, if needed
Object ID	64-bit file identifier unique to this volume
Reparse point	Used for mounting and symbolic links
Volume name	Name of this volume (used only in $Volume)
Volume information	Volume version (used only in $Volume)
Index root	Used for directories
Index allocation	Used for very large directories
Bitmap	Used for very large directories
Logged utility stream	Controls logging to $LogFile
Data	Stream data; may be repeated

Figure 11-35. The attributes used in MFT records.

The standard information field contains the file owner, security information, the timestamps needed by POSIX, the hard link count, the read-only and archive bits, etc. It is a fixed-length field and is always present. The file name is variable length in Unicode. In order to make files with nonMS-DOS names accessible to old 16-bit programs, files can also have an 8 + 3 MS-DOS name. If the actual file name conforms to the MS-DOS 8 + 3 naming rule, a secondary MS-DOS name is not used.

In NT 4.0, security information could be put in an attribute, but in Windows 2000 it all goes into a single file so that multiple files can share the same security descriptions. The attribute list is needed in case the attributes do not fit in the MFT record. This attribute then tells where to find the extension records. Each entry in the list contains a 48-bit index into the MFT telling where the extension record is and a 16-bit sequence number to allow verification that the extension record and base records match up.

The object ID attribute gives the file a unique name. This is sometimes needed internally. The reparse point tells the procedure parsing the file name to do something special. This mechanism is used for mounting and symbolic links. The two volume attributes are only used for volume identification. The next three attributes deal with how directories are implemented. Small ones are just lists of files but large ones are implemented using B+ trees. The logged utility stream attribute is used by the encrypting file system.

Finally, we come to the attribute that everyone has been waiting for: the data. The stream name, if present, goes in this attribute header. Following the header is either a list of disk addresses telling which blocks the file contains, or for files of only a few hundred bytes (and there are many of these), the file itself. Putting the actual file data in the MFT record is called an **immediate file** (Mullender and Tanenbaum, 1987).

Of course, most of the time the data does not fit in the MFT record, so this attribute is usually nonresident. Let us now take a look at how NTFS keeps track of the location of nonresident attributes, in particular data.

The model for keeping track of disk blocks is that they are assigned in runs of consecutive blocks, where possible, for efficiency reasons. For example, if the first logical block of a file is placed in block 20 on the disk, then the system will try hard to place the second logical block in block 21, the third logical block in 22, and so on. One way to achieve these runs is to allocate disk storage several blocks at a time, if possible.

The blocks in a file are described by a sequence of records, each one describing a sequence of logically contiguous blocks. For a file with no holes in it, there will be only one such record. Files that are written in order from beginning to end all belong in this category. For a file with one hole in it (e.g., only blocks 0–49 and blocks 60–79 are defined), there will be two records. Such a file could be produced by writing the first 50 blocks, then seeking forward to logical block 60 and writing another 20 blocks. When a hole is read back, all the missing bytes are zeros.

Each record begins with a header giving the offset of the first block within the file. Next comes the offset of the first block not covered by the record. In the example above, the first record would have a header of (0, 50) and would provide the disk addresses for these 50 blocks. The second one would have a header of (60,80) and would provide the disk addresses for these 20 blocks.

Each record header is followed by one or more pairs, each giving a disk address and run length. The disk address is the offset of the disk block from the start of its partition; the run length is the number of blocks in the run. As many pairs as needed can be in the run record. Use of this scheme for a three-run, nine-block file is illustrated in Fig. 11-36.

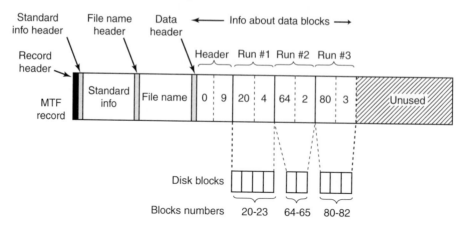

Figure 11-36. An MFT record for a three-run, nine-block file.

In this figure we have an MFT record for a short file (short here means that all the information about the file blocks fits in one MFT record). It consists of the three runs of consecutive blocks on the disk. The first run is blocks 20-23, the second is blocks 64-65, and the third is blocks 80-82. Each of these runs is recorded in the MFT record as a (disk address, block count) pair. How many runs there are depends on how good a job the disk block allocator did in finding runs of consecutive blocks when the file was created. For a n-block file, the number of runs can be anything from 1 up to and including n.

Several comments are worth making here. First, there is no upper limit to the size of files that can be represented this way. In the absence of address compression, each pair requires two 64-bit numbers in the pair for a total of 16 bytes. However, a pair could represent 1 million or more consecutive disk blocks. In fact, a 20-MB file consisting of 20 separate runs of 1 million 1-KB blocks each fits easily in one MFT record, whereas a 60-KB file scattered into 60 isolated blocks does not.

Second, while the straightforward way of representing each pair takes 2×8 bytes, a compression method is available to reduce the size of the pairs below 16. Many disk addresses have multiple high-order zero-bytes. These can be omitted. The data header tells how many are omitted, that is, how many bytes are actually used per address. Other kinds of compression are also used. In practice, the pairs are often only 4 bytes.

Our first example was easy: all the file information fit in one MFT record. What happens if the file is so large or highly fragmented that the block information does not fit in one MFT record? The answer is simple: use two or more MFT records. In Fig. 11-37 we see a file whose base record is in MFT record 102. It has too many runs for one MFT record, so it computes how many extension records it needs, say, two, and puts their indices in the base record. The rest of the record is used for the first k data runs.

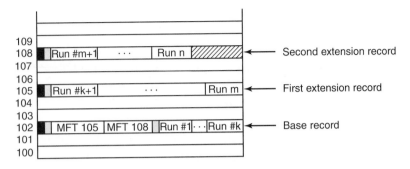

Figure 11-37. A file that requires three MFT records to store all its runs.

Note that Fig. 11-37 contains some redundancy. In theory, it should not be necessary to specify the end of a sequence of runs because this information can be calculated from the run pairs. The reason for "overspecifying" this information is to make seeking more efficient: to find the block at a given file offset, it is only necessary to examine the record headers, not the run pairs.

When all the space in record 102 has been used up, storage of the runs continues with MFT record 105. As many runs are packed in this record as fit. When this record is also full, the rest of the runs go in MFT record 108. In this way many MFT records can be used to handle large fragmented files.

A problem arises if so many MFT records are needed that there is no room in the base MFT to list all their indices. There is also a solution to this problem: the list of extension MFT records is made nonresident (i.e., stored on disk instead of in the base MFT record). Then it can grow as large as needed.

An MFT entry for a small directory is shown in Fig. 11-38. The record contains a number of directory entries, each of which describes one file or directory. Each entry has a fixed-length structure followed by a variable-length file name. The fixed part contains the index of the MFT entry for the file, the length of the file name, and a variety of other fields and flags. Looking for an entry in a directory consists of examining all the file names in turn.

Large directories use a different format. Instead of listing the files linearly, a B+ tree is used to make alphabetical lookup possible and to make it easy to insert new names in the directory in the proper place.

File Name Lookup

We now have enough information to see how file name lookup occurs. When a user program wants to open a file, it typically makes a call like

    CreateFile("C:\maria\web.htm", ...)

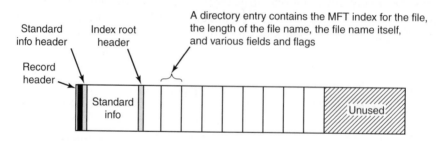

Figure 11-38. The MFT record for a small directory.

This call goes to the user-level shared library, *kernel32.dll*, where \?? is pre-pended to the file name giving

    \??\C:\maria\web.htm

It is this name that is passed as a parameter to the system call NtFileCreate.

Then the operating system starts the search at the root of the object manager's name space (see Fig. 11-12). It then looks in the directory \?? to find *C:*, which it will find. This file is a symbolic link to another part of the object manager's name space, the directory *Device*. The link typically ends at an object whose name is something like *Device\HarddiskVolume1*. This object corresponds to the first partition of the first hard disk. From this object it is possible to determine which MFT to use, namely the one on this partition. These steps are shown in Fig. 11-39.

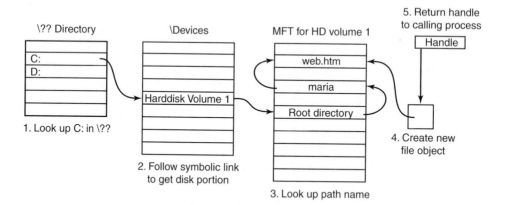

Figure 11-39. Steps in looking up the file *C:\maria\web.htm*.

The parsing of the file name continues now at the root directory, whose blocks can be found from entry 5 in the MFT (see Fig. 11-34). The string "maria" is now looked up in the root directory, which returns the index into the MFT for the directory *maria*. This directory is then searched for the string "web.htm". If successful, the result is a new object created by the object manager. The object, which is unnamed, contains the index of the MFT record for the file. A handle to this object is returned to the calling process. On subsequent ReadFile calls, the handle is provided, which allows the object manager to find the index and then the contents of the MFT record for the file. If a thread in a second process opens the file again, it gets a handle to a new file object.

In addition to regular files and directories, NTFS supports hard links in the UNIX sense, and also symbolic links using a mechanism called **reparse points**. It is possible to tag a file or directory as a reparse point and associate a block of data with it. When the file or directory is encountered during a file name parse, exception processing is triggered and the block of data is interpreted. It can do various things, including redirecting the search to a different part of the directory hierarchy or even to a different partition. This mechanism is used to support both symbolic links and mounted file systems.

File Compression

NTFS supports transparent file compression. A file can be created in compressed mode, which means that NTFS automatically tries to compress the blocks as they are written to disk and automatically uncompresses them when they are read back. Processes that read or write compressed files are completely unaware of the fact that compression and decompression are going on.

Compression works as follows. When NTFS writes a file marked for compression to disk, it examines the first 16 (logical) blocks in the file, irrespective of how many runs they occupy. It then runs a compression algorithm on them. If the resulting data can be stored in 15 or fewer blocks, the compressed data are written to the disk, preferably in one run, if possible. If the compressed data still take 16 blocks, the 16 blocks are written in uncompressed form. Then blocks 16-31 are examined to see if they can be compressed to 15 blocks or less, and so on.

Figure 11-40(a) shows a file in which the first 16 blocks have successfully compressed to eight blocks, the second 16 blocks failed to compress, and the third 16 blocks have also compressed by 50%. The three parts have been written as three runs and stored in the MFT record. The "missing" blocks are stored in the MFT entry with disk address 0 as shown in Fig. 11-40(b). Here the header (0, 48) is followed by five pairs, two for the first (compressed) run, one for the uncompressed run, and two for the final (compressed) run.

When the file is read back, NTFS has to know which runs are compressed and which are not. It sees that based on the disk addresses. A disk address of 0 indicates that it is the final part of 16 compressed blocks. Disk block 0 may not be used for storing data, to avoid ambiguity. Since it contains the boot sector, using it for data is impossible anyway.

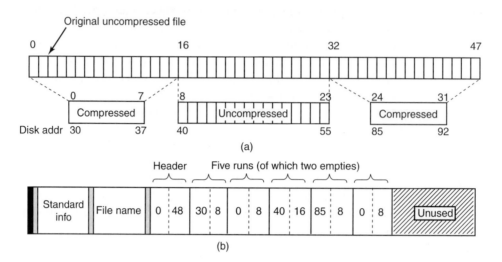

Figure 11-40. (a) An example of a 48-block file being compressed to 32 blocks. (b) The MFT record for the file after compression.

Random access to compressed files is possible, but tricky. Suppose that a process does a seek to block 35 in Fig. 11-40. How does NTFS locate block 35 in a compressed file? The answer is that it has to read and decompress the entire run first. Then it knows where block 35 is and can pass it to any process that reads it. The choice of 16 blocks for the compression unit was a compromise. Making it shorter would have made the compression less effective. Making it longer would have made random access more expensive.

File Encryption

Computers are used nowadays to store all kinds of sensitive data, including plans for corporate takeovers, tax information, and love letters (love email?), which the owners do not especially want revealed to anyone. Information loss can happen when a laptop computer is lost or stolen, a desktop system is rebooted using an MS-DOS floppy disk to bypass Windows 2000 security, or a hard disk is physically removed from one computer and installed on another one with an insecure operating system. Even the simple act of going to the bathroom and leaving the computer unattended and logged in can be a huge security breach.

Windows 2000 addresses these problem by having an option to encrypt files, so even in the event the computer is stolen or rebooted using MS-DOS, the files will be unreadable. The normal way to use Windows 2000 encryption is to mark certain directories as encrypted, which causes all the files in them to be encrypted, and new files moved to them or created in them to be encrypted as well. The actual encryption and decryption is not done by NTFS itself, but by a driver called **EFS** (**Encrypting File System**), which is positioned between NTFS and the user process. In this way, application programs are unaware of encryption and NTFS itself is only partially involved in it.

To understand how the encrypting file system works, it is necessary to understand how modern cryptography works. For this purpose, a brief review was given in Sec. 9.2. Readers not familiar with the basics of cryptography should read that section before continuing.

Now let us see how Windows 2000 encrypts files. When the user asks a file to be encrypted, a random 128-bit file key is generated and used to encrypt the file block by block using a symmetric algorithm parametrized by this key. Each new file encrypted gets a different 128-bit random file key, so no two files use the same encryption key, which increases security in case one key is compromised. The current encryption algorithm is a variant of **DES (Data Encryption Standard)**, but the EFS architecture supports the addition of new algorithms in the future. Encrypting each block independently of all the others is necessary to make random access still possible.

The file key has to be stored somewhere so the file can be decrypted later. If it were just stored on the disk in plaintext, then someone who stole or found the computer could easily decrypt the file, defeating the purpose of encrypting the files. For this reason, the file keys must all be encrypted before they are stored on the disk. Public-key cryptography is used for this purpose.

After the file is encrypted, the location of the user's public key is looked up using information in the registry. There is no danger of storing the public key's location in the registry because if a thief steals the computer and finds the public key, there is no way to deduce the private key from it. The 128-bit random file key is now encrypted with the public key and the result stored on disk along with the file, as shown in Fig. 11-41.

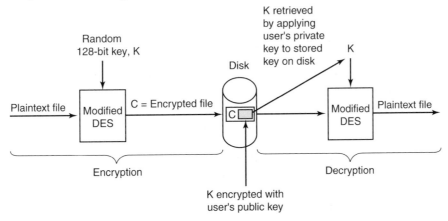

Figure 11-41. Operating of the encrypting file system.

To decrypt a file, the encrypted 128-bit random file key is fetched from disk. However, to decrypt it and retrieve the file key, the user must present the private key. Ideally, this should be stored on a smart card, external to the computer, and only inserted in a reader when a file has to be decrypted. Although Windows 2000 supports smart cards, it does not store private keys on them.

Instead, the first time a user encrypts a file using EFS, Windows 2000 generates a (private key, public key) pair and stores the private key on disk encrypted using a symmetric encryption algorithm. The key used for the symmetric algorithm is derived either from the user's login password or from a key stored on the smart card, if smart card login is enabled. In this way, EFS can decrypt the private key at login time and keep it within its own virtual address space during normal operation so it can decrypt the 128-bit file keys as needed without further disk accesses. When the computer is shut down, the private key is erased from EFS' virtual address space so anyone stealing the computer will not have access to the private key.

A complication occurs when multiple users need access to the same encrypted file. Currently the shared use of encrypted files by multiple users is not supported. However, the EFS architecture could support sharing in the future by encrypting each file's key multiple times, once with the public key of each authorized user. All of these encrypted versions of the file key could be attached to the file.

The potential need to share encrypted files is one reason why this two-key system is used. If all files were encrypted by their owner's key, there would be no way to share any files. By using a different key to encrypt each file, this problem can be solved.

Having a random file key per file but encrypting it with the owner's symmetric key does not work because having the symmetric encryption key just lying around in plain view would ruin the security— generating the decryption key from the encryption key is too easy. Thus (slow) public-key cryptography is needed to encrypt the file keys. Because the encryption key is public anyway, having it lying around is not dangerous.

The other reason the two-key system is used is performance. Using public-key cryptography to encrypt each file would be too slow. It is much more efficient to use symmetric-key cryptography to encrypt the data and public-key cryptography to encrypt the symmetric file key.

11.8 SECURITY IN WINDOWS 2000

Having just looked at encryption in the file system, this is a good time to examine security in general. NT was designed to meet the U.S. Department of Defense's C2 security requirements (DoD 5200.28-STD), the Orange Book, which we studied in Chap. 9. This standard requires operating systems to have certain properties in order to be classified as secure enough for certain kinds of military work. Although Windows 2000 was not specifically designed for C2 compliance, it inherits many security properties from NT, including the following:

1. Secure login with antispoofing measures.

2. Discretionary access controls.

3. Privileged access controls.

4. Address space protection per process.

5. New pages must be zeroed before being mapped in.

6. Security auditing.

Let us review these items briefly (none of which are met by Windows 98, incidentally).

Secure login means that the system administrator can require all users to have a password in order to log in. Spoofing is when a malicious user writes a program that displays the login prompt or screen and then walks away from the computer in the hope that an innocent user will sit down and enter a name and password. The name and password are then written to disk and the user is told that login has failed. Windows 2000 prevents this attack by instructing users to hit CTRL-ALT-DEL to log in. This key sequence is always captured by the keyboard driver, which then invokes a system program that puts up the genuine login screen. This procedure works because there is no way for user processes to disable CTRL-ALT-DEL processing in the keyboard driver.

Discretionary access controls allow the owner of a file or other object to say who can use it and in what way. Privileged access controls allow the system administrator (superuser) to override them when needed. Address space protection simply means that each process has its own protected virtual address space not accessible by any unauthorized process. The next item means that when a stack grows, the pages mapped in are initialized to zero so processes cannot find any old information put there by the previous owner (hence the zeroed page list in Fig. 11-27, which provides a supply of zeroed pages for this purpose). Finally, security auditing allows the administrator to produce a log of certain security-related events.

In the next section we will describe the basic concepts behind Windows 2000 security. After that we will look at the security system calls. Finally, we will conclude by seeing how security is implemented.

11.8.1 Fundamental Concepts

Every Windows 2000 user (and group) is identified by a **SID (Security ID)**. SIDs are binary numbers with a short header followed by a long random component. Each SID is intended to be unique worldwide. When a user starts up a process, the process and its threads run under the user's SID. Most of the security system is designed to make sure that each object can be accessed only by threads with authorized SIDs.

Each process has an **access token** that specifies its SID and other properties. It is normally assigned at login time by *winlogon* and is shown in Fig. 11-42, although processes should call *GetTokenInformation* to acquire this information since it may change in the future. The header contains some administrative information. The expiration time field could tell when the token ceases to be valid, but it is currently not used. The *Groups* fields specify the groups to which the process belongs; this is needed for POSIX conformance. The default **DACL** (**Discretionary ACL**) is the access control list assigned to objects created by the process if no other ACL is specified. The user SID tells who owns the process. The restricted SIDS are to allow untrustworthy processes to take part in jobs with trustworthy processes but with less power to do damage.

Finally, the privileges listed, if any, give the process special powers, such as the right to shut the machine down or access files to which access would otherwise be denied. In effect, the privileges split up the power of the superuser into several rights that can be assigned to processes individually. In this way, a user can be given some superuser power, but not all of it. In summary, the access token tells who owns the process and which defaults and powers are associated with it.

Header	Expiration time	Groups	Default CACL	User SID	Group SID	Restricted SIDs	Privileges

Figure 11-42. Structure of an access token .

When a user logs in, *winlogon* gives the initial process an access token. Subsequent processes normally inherit this token on down the line. A process' access token initially applies to all the threads in the process. However, a thread can acquire a different access token during execution, in which case case the thread's access token overrides the process' access token. In particular, a client thread can pass its access token to a server thread to allow the server to access the client's protected files and other objects. This mechanism is called **impersonation**.

Another basic concept is the **security descriptor**. Every object has a security descriptor associated with it that tells who can perform which operations on it. A security descriptor consists of a header followed by a DACL with one or more **ACE**s (**Access Control Elements**). The two main kinds of elements are Allow and Deny. An allow element specifies a SID and a bitmap that specifies which operations processes with that SID may perform on the object. A deny element works the same way, except a match means the caller may not perform the operation. For example, Ida has a file whose security descriptor specifies that everyone has read access, Elvis has no access. Cathy has read/write access, and Ida herself has full access. This simple example is illustrated in Fig. 11-43. The SID Everyone refers to the set of all users, but it is overridden by any explicit ACEs that follow.

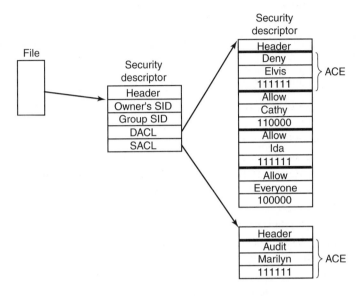

Figure 11-43. An example security descriptor for a file.

In addition to the DACL, a security descriptor also has a **SACL (System Access Control list)**, which is like a DACL except that it specifies not who may use the object, but which operations on the object are recorded in the system-wide security event log. In Fig. 11-43, every operation that Marilyn performs on the file will be logged. Windows 2000 provides additional auditing features to log sensitive accesses.

11.8.2 Security API Calls

Most of the Windows 2000 access control mechanism is based on security descriptors. The usual pattern is that when a process creates an object, it provides a security descriptor as one of the parameters to the CreateProcess, CreateFile, or other object creation call. This security descriptor then becomes the security descriptor attached to the object, as we saw in Fig. 11-43. If no security descriptor is provided in the object creation call, the default security in the caller's access token (see Fig. 11-42) is used instead.

Many of the Win32 API security calls relate to the management of security descriptors, so we will focus on those here. The most important calls are listed in Fig. 11-44. To create a security descriptor, storage for it is first allocated and then initialized using InitializeSecurityDescriptor. This call fills in the header. If the owner SID is not known, it can be looked up by name using LookupAccountSid. It can then be inserted into the security descriptor. The same holds for the group SID, if any. Normally, these will be the caller's own SID and one of the caller's groups, but the system administrator can fill in any SIDs.

Win32 API function	Description
InitializeSecurityDescriptor	Prepare a new security descriptor for use
LookupAccountSid	Look up the SID for a given user name
SetSecurityDescriptorOwner	Enter the owner SID in the security descriptor
SetSecurityDescriptorGroup	Enter a group SID in the security descriptor
InitializeAcl	Initialize a DACL or SACL
AddAccessAllowedAce	Add a new ACE to a DACL or SACL allowing access
AddAccessDeniedAce	Add a new ACE to a DACL or SACL denying access
DeleteAce	Remove an ACE from a DACL or SACL
SetSecurityDescriptorDacl	Attach a DACL to a security descriptor

Figure 11-44. The principal Win32 API functions for security.

At this point the security descriptor's DACL (or SACL) can be initialized with InitializeAcl. ACL entries can be added using AddAccessAllowedAce, and AddAccessDeniedAce. These calls can be repeated multiple times to add as many ACE entries as are needed. DeleteAce can be used to remove an entry, more like on an existing ACL than on one being constructed for the first time. When the ACL is ready, SetSecurityDescriptorDacl can be used to attach it to the security descriptor. Finally, when the object is created, the newly minted security descriptor can be passed as a parameter to have it attached to the object.

11.8.3 Implementation of Security

Security in a standalone Windows 2000 system is implemented by a number of components, most of which we have already seen (networking is a whole other story and beyond the scope of this book). Logging in is handled by *winlogon* and authentication is handled by *lsass* and *msgina.dll* as discussed in Sec. 11.4.5. The result of a successful login is a new shell with its associated access token. This process uses the SECURITY and SAM keys in the registry. The former sets the general security policy and the latter contains the security information for the individual users, as discussed in Sec. 11.2.3.

Once a user is logged in, security operations happen when an object is opened for access. Every OpenXXX call requires the name of the object being opened and the set of rights needed. During processing of the open, the security manager (see Fig. 11-7) checks to see if the caller has all the rights required. It performs this check by looking at the caller's access token and the DACL associated with the object. It goes down the list of entries in the ACL in order. As soon as it finds an entry that matches the caller's SID or one of the caller's groups, the access found there is taken as definitive. If all the rights the caller needs are available, the open succeeds; otherwise it fails.

DACLs can have Deny entries as well as Allow entries, as we have seen. For this reason, it is usual to put entries denying access ahead of entries granting access in the ACL, so that a user who is specifically denied access cannot get in via a back door by being a member of a group that has legitimate access.

After an object has been opened, a handle to it is returned to the caller. On subsequent calls, the only check that is made is whether the operation now being tried was in the set of operations requested at open time, to prevent a caller from opening a file for reading and then trying to write on it. Any log entries required by the SACL are made.

11.9 CACHING IN WINDOWS 2000

The Windows 2000 cache manager does caching for performance reasons, conceptually similar to caches in other operating systems. However, its design has some unusual properties that are worth looking at briefly.

The cache manager's job is to keep file system blocks that have been used recently in memory to reduce access time on any subsequent reference. Windows 2000 has a single integrated cache that works for all the file systems in use, including NTFS, FAT-32, FAT-16, and even CD-ROM file systems. This means that the file systems do not need to maintain their own caches.

As a consequence of the design goal to have a single integrated cache despite the presence of multiple file systems, the cache manager is located in an unusual position in the system, as we saw in Fig. 11-7. It is not part of the file system because there are multiple independent file systems that may have nothing in common. Instead it operates at a higher level than the file systems, which are technically drivers under control of the I/O manager.

The Windows 2000 cache is organized by virtual block, not physical block. To see what this means, remember that traditional file caches keep track of blocks by two-part addresses of the form (partition, block), where the first member denotes a device and partition and the second member is a block number within that partition. The Windows 2000 cache manager does not do that. Instead, it uses (file, offset) to refer to a block. (Technically, streams are cached rather than files, but we will ignore that detail below.)

The reason for this unorthodox arrangement is that when a request comes in to the cache manager, it is specified as (file, offset) because that is all the calling process knows. If cache blocks had been labeled by a (partition, block) tag, the cache manager would have no way of knowing which (file, offset) block corresponds to which (partition, block) block since it is the file systems that maintain those mappings.

Let us now examine how the cache manager works. When a file is referenced, the cache manager maps a 256-KB chunk of kernel virtual address space onto the file. If the file is larger than 256 KB, only a portion of the file is mapped. The total amount of virtual address space the cache manager can use is determined at boot time and depends on the amount of RAM present. If the cache manager runs out of 256-KB chunks of virtual address space, it must unmap an old file before mapping in a new one.

Once a file is mapped, the cache manager can satisfy requests for its blocks by just copying from kernel virtual address space to the user buffer. If the block copied is not in physical memory, a page fault will occur and the memory manager will satisfy the fault in the usual away. The cache manager is not even aware of whether the block was in the cache or not. The copy always succeeds.

The operation of the cache manager is shown in Fig. 11-45 in the case of an NTFS file system on a SCSI disk and a FAT-32 file system on an IDE disk. When a process does a read on a file, the request is directed to the cache manager. If the block needed is in the cache, it is copied to the user immediately. If it is not in the cache, the cache manager gets a page fault when trying to copy it. When the page fault has been handled, the block is copied to the calling process.

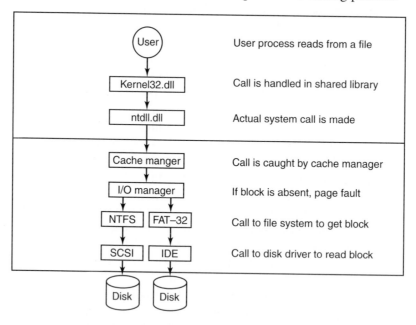

Figure 11-45. The path through the cache to the hardware.

As a consequence of this design, the cache manager does not know how many of its mapped pages are in physical memory or even how large its cache is. Only the memory manager knows for sure. This approach allows the memory manager to dynamically trade off the size of the cache against memory for user pages. If there is little file activity but there are many processes active, the memory manager can use most of physical memory for process pages. On the other hand, if there is a lot of file activity and few processes, more physical memory can be devoted to the cache.

Another property the cache manager has is that coherence is maintained between memory-mapped files and files that are open for reading and writing. Consider, for example, a situation in which one process opens some file for reading and writing and a second process maps that file onto its address space. What happens if the second process writes on the file directly and immediately thereafter the first one reads in a block that was just changed? Does it get stale data?

The answer is no. In both cases—open files and mapped files— the cache manager maps a 256-KB piece of its virtual address space onto the file. The file is only mapped once, no matter how many processes have it open or mapped. In the case of a mapped file, both the cache manager and the user process share pages in memory. When a read request has to be satisfied, the cache manager just copies the page from memory to the user buffer, which always reflects the exact current state of the file because the cache manager is using the same pages as the process that has the file mapped in.

11.10 SUMMARY

Windows 2000 is structured in the HAL, the kernel, the executive, and a thin system services layer that catches incoming system calls. In addition, there are a variety of device drivers, including the file systems and GDI. The HAL hides certain differences in hardware from the upper layers. The kernel attempts to hide the remaining differences from the executive to make it almost completely machine independent.

The executive is based on memory objects. User processes create them and get back handles to manipulate them later. Executive components can also create objects. The object manager maintains a name space into which objects can be inserted for subsequent lookup.

Windows 2000 supports processes, jobs, threads, and fibers. Processes have virtual address spaces and are containers for resources. Threads are the unit of execution and are scheduled by the operating system. Fibers are lightweight threads that are scheduled entirely in user space. Jobs are collections of processes and are used for assigning resource quotas. Scheduling is done using a priority algorithm in which the highest priority ready thread runs next.

Windows 2000 supports a demand-paged virtual memory. The paging algorithm is based on the working set concept. The system maintains several lists of free pages, so that when a page fault occurs, there is generally a free page available. The free page lists are fed by trimming the working sets using complex formulas that try to throw out pages that have not been used in a long time.

I/O is done by device drivers, which follow the Windows Device Model. Each driver starts out by initializing a driver object that contains the addresses of the procedures that the system can call to add devices or perform I/O. Drivers can be stacked to act as filters.

The NTFS file system is based on a master file table, which has one record per file or directory. Each file has multiple attributes, which can either be in the MFT record or nonresident, on the disk. NTFS supports compression and encryption, among other features.

Security is based on access control lists. Each process has an access control token that tells who it is and what special privileges it has, if any. Each object has a security descriptor associated with it. The security descriptor points to a discretionary access control list that contains access control entries that can allow or deny access to individuals or groups.

Finally, Windows 2000 maintains a single system-wide cache for all the file systems. It is a virtual cache rather than a physical one. Requests for disk blocks go first to the cache. If they cannot be satisfied, then the appropriate file system is called to fetch the needed blocks.

PROBLEMS

1. Give one advantage and one disadvantage of the registry versus having individual *.ini* files?

2. A mouse can have 1, 2, or 3 buttons. All three types are in use. Does the HAL hide this difference from the rest of the operating system? Why or why not?

3. The HAL keeps track of time starting in the year 1601. Give an example of an application where this feature is useful.

4. The POSIX subsystem needs to implement UNIX-style signals. If a user hits the key for the Quit signal, is this scheduled as a DPC or an APC?

5. Many components of the executive (Fig. 11-7) call other components of the executive. Give three examples of one component calling another one, but use (six) different components in all.

6. Win32 does not have signals. If they were to be introduced, they could be per process, per thread, both, or neither. Make a proposal and explain why it is a good idea.

7. An alternative to using DLLs is to statically link each program with precisely those library procedures it actually calls, no more and no less. If this scheme were to be introduced, would it make more sense on client machines or on server machines?

8. The file *ntdll.dll* exports 1179 function calls while *ntoskrnl.exe* exports 1209 function calls. Is this a bug? What might be the cause of this discrepancy?

9. Objects managed by the object manager are variable-sized, with different objects having different sizes. Can an object start at an arbitrary byte in the nonpaged pool? *Hint*: You do not need any information about Windows 2000 other than what was given in the text.

10. Is there any limit on the number of different operations that can be defined on an executive object? If so, where does this limit come from? If not, why not?

11. The Win32 API call WaitForMultipleObjects allows a thread to block on a set of synchronization objects whose handles are passed as parameters. As soon as any one of them is signaled, the calling thread is released. Is it possible to have the set of synchronization objects include two semaphores, one mutex, and one critical section? Why or why not? *Hint*: This is not a trick question but it does require some careful thought.

12. Name three reasons why a process might be terminated.

13. Consider the situation of Fig. 11-19 in which the system is about to schedule a thread. Assuming that each thread is compute bound, how long does it take before some thread at priority 3 gets to run on Windows 2000 Professional?

14. Suppose that the quantum is set to 20 msec and the current thread, at priority 24, has just started a quantum. Suddenly an I/O operation completes and a priority 28 thread is made ready. About how long does it have to wait to get serviced?

15. In Windows 2000, the current priority is always greater than or equal to the base priority. Are there any circumstances in which it would make sense to have the current priority be lower than the base priority? If so, give an example. If not, why not?

16. Some MS-DOS programs were written in assembly language using instructions such as IN port and OUT port. Can such programs be run under Windows 2000? If not, can you think of a way they could be supported?

17. Name two ways to give better response time to important processes.

18. Position-independent code was briefly discussed in the text. It is a technique for allowing two processes to share the same procedure at different virtual addresses. Can this problem be solved by just setting the page tables of the two processes appropriately? Explain your answer.

19. Shared libraries in Windows 2000 are contained in *.dll* files that multiple processes may map in at the same time. If two processes need to map in the same shared library at different virtual addresses, a problem will occur. How could this problem be solved on the Pentium using a property of its memory architecture? If the solution requires changes to Windows 2000 to implement, state what changes are needed.

20. If a region of virtual address space is reserved but not committed, do you think a VAD is created for it? Defend your answer.

21. Which of the transitions shown in Fig. 11-27 are policy decisions, as opposed to required moves forced by system events (e.g., a process exiting and freeing its pages)?

22. Suppose that a page is shared and in two working sets at once. If it is evicted from one of the working sets, where does it go in Fig. 11-27?

23. When a process unmaps a clean page, it makes the transition (5) in Fig. 11-27. Why is there no transition to the modified list when a dirty page is unmapped?

24. Assuming that both RAM and video RAM each can read or write a 32-bit word in 10 nsec, how long does it take to paint the background on an XGA screen in the best case?

25. A file has the following mapping. Give the MFT run entries.

Offset	0	1	2	3	4	5	6	7	8	9	10
Disk address	50	51	52	22	24	25	26	53	54	-	60

26. Consider the MFT record of Fig. 11-36. Suppose that the file grew and a 10th block was assigned to the end of the file. The number of this block is 66. What would the MFT record look like now?

27. In Fig. 11-40(b), the first two runs are each of length 8 blocks. Is it just an accident they are equal or does this have to do with the way compression works? Explain your answer.

28. Suppose that you wanted to build Windows 2000 Lite. Which of the fields of Fig. 11-42 could be removed without weakening the security of the system?

29. The *regedit* command can be used to export part or all of the registry to a text file under all current versions of Windows. Save the registry several times during a work session and see what changes. If you have access to a Windows computer on which you can install software or hardware, find out what changes when a program or device are added or removed.

30. Write a UNIX program that simulates writing an NTFS file with multiple streams. It should accept a list of one or more files as arguments and write an output file that contains one stream with the attributes of all arguments and additional streams with the contents of each of the arguments. Now write a second program for reporting on the attributes and streams and extracting all the components.

31. Write a program that generates an MS-DOS 8 + 3 filename given any file name. Use the Windows 2000 algorithm.

12

OPERATING SYSTEM DESIGN

In the past 11 chapters, we have covered a lot of ground and taken a look at many concepts and examples relating to operating systems. But studying existing operating systems is different from designing a new one. In this chapter we are going to take a quick look at some of the issues and trade-offs that operating systems designers have to take into account when designing and implementing a new system.

There is a certain amount of folklore about what is good and what is bad floating around in the operating systems community, but surprisingly little has been written down. Probably the most important book is Fred Brooks' classic (1975) book *The Mythical Man Month* in which he relates his experiences in designing and implementing IBM's OS/360. The 20th anniversary edition revises some of that material and adds four new chapters (Brooks, 1995). Probably the only operating systems textbook dealing with design in a serious way is *Operating Systems: A Design-Oriented Approach* (Crowley, 1997).

Three classic papers on operating system design are "Hints for Computer System Design" (Lampson, 1984), "On Building Systems that Will Fail" (Corbató, 1991), and "End-to-End Arguments in System Design" (Saltzer et al., 1984). Like Brooks' book, all three papers have survived the years extremely well; most of their insights are still as valid now as when they were first published.

This chapter draws upon these sources, plus the author's personal experience as designer or co-designer of three systems: Amoeba (Tanenbaum et al., 1990), MINIX (Tanenbaum and Woodhull, 1997), and Globe (Van Steen et al., 1999a).

Since no consensus exists among operating system designers about the best way to design an operating system, this chapter will thus be more personal, speculative, and undoubtedly more controversial than the previous ones.

12.1 THE NATURE OF THE DESIGN PROBLEM

Operating system design is more of an engineering project than an exact science. It is much harder to set clear goals and to meet them. Let us look at start with these points.

12.1.1 Goals

In order to design a successful operating system, the designers have to have a clear idea of what they want. Lack of a goal makes it very hard to make subsequent decisions. To make this point clearer, it is instructive to take a look at two programming languages PL/I and C. PL/I was designed by IBM in the 1960s because it was a nuisance to have to support both FORTRAN and COBOL, and embarrassing to have academics yapping in the background that Algol was better than both of them. So a committee was set up to produce a language that would be all things to all people: PL/I. It had a little bit of FORTRAN, a little bit of COBOL, and a little bit of Algol. It failed because it lacked any unifying vision. It was simply a collection of features at war with one another, and too cumbersome to be compiled efficiently, to boot.

Now consider C. It was designed by one person (Dennis Ritchie) for one purpose (system programming). It was a huge success, in no small part because Ritchie knew what he wanted and did not want. As a result, it is still in widespread use decades after its appearance. Having a clear vision of what you want is crucial.

What do operating system designers want? It obviously varies from system to system, being different for embedded systems than for server systems. However, for general-purpose operating systems four main items come to mind:

1. Define abstractions.

2. Provide primitive operations.

3. Ensure isolation.

4. Manage the hardware.

Each of these items will be discussed below.

The most important, but probably hardest task of an operating system is to define the right abstractions. Some of them, such as processes and files, have been around so long that they may seem obvious. Other ones, such as threads, are newer, and are less mature. For example, if a multithread process that has one thread blocked waiting for keyboard input forks, is there a thread in the new process also waiting for keyboard input? Other abstractions relate to synchronization, signals, the memory model, modeling of I/O and many other areas.

Each of the abstractions can be instantiated in the form of concrete data structures. Users can create processes, files, semaphores, etc. The primitive operations manipulate these data structures. For example, users can read and write files. The primitive operations are implemented in the form of system calls. From the user's point of view, the heart of the operating system is formed by the abstractions and the operations on them available via the system calls.

Since multiple users can be logged into a computer at the same time, the operating system needs to provide mechanisms to keep them separated. One user may not interfere with another. The process concept is widely used to group resources together for protection purposes. Files and other data structures generally are protected as well. Making sure each user can perform only authorized operations on authorized data is a key goal of system design. However, users also want to share data and resources, so the isolation has to be selective and under user control. This makes it much harder.

Closely related to this point is the need to isolate failures. If some part of the system goes down, most commonly a user process, it should not be able to take the rest of the system down with it. The system design should make sure that the various parts are well isolated from one another. Ideally, parts of the operating system should also be isolated from one another to allow independent failures.

Finally, the operating system has to manage the hardware. In particular, it has to take care of all the low-level chips, such as interrupt controllers and bus controllers. It also has to provide a framework for allowing device drivers to manage the larger I/O devices, such as disks, printers, and the display.

12.1.2 Why is it Hard to Design an Operating System?

Moore's law says that computer hardware improves by a factor of 100 every decade. Nobody has a law saying that operating systems improve by a factor of 100 every decade. Or even get better at all. In fact, a case can be made that some of them are worse in key respects (such as reliability) than UNIX Version 7 was back in the 1970s.

Why? Inertia and the desire for backward compatibility often get much of the blame, and the failure to adhere to good design principles is also a culprit. But there is more to it. Operating systems are fundamentally different in certain ways from small application programs sold in computer stores for $49. Let us look at eight of the issues that make designing an operating system much harder than designing an application program.

First, operating systems have become extremely large programs. No one person can sit down at a PC and dash off a serious operating system in a few months.

All current versions of UNIX exceed 1 million lines of code; Windows 2000 is 29 million lines of code. No one person can understand even 1 million lines of code, let alone 29 million lines of code. When you have a product that none of the designers can hope to fully understand, it should be no surprise that the results are often far from optimal.

Operating systems are not the most complex systems around. Aircraft carriers are far more complicated, for example, but they partition into isolated subsystems better. The people designing the toilets on a aircraft carrier do not have to worry about the radar system. The two subsystems do not interact much. In an operating system, the file system often interacts with the memory system in unexpected and unforeseen ways.

Second, operating systems have to deal with concurrency. There are multiple users and multiple I/O devices all active at once. Managing concurrency is inherently much harder than managing a single sequential activity. Race conditions and deadlocks are just two of the problems that come up.

Third, operating systems have to deal with potentially hostile users—users who want to interfere with system operation or do things that are forbidden from doing, such as stealing another user's files. The operating system needs to take measures to prevent these users from behaving improperly. Word processing programs and photo editors do not have this problem.

Fourth, despite the fact that not all users trust each other, many users do want to share some of their information and resources with selected other users. The operating system has to make this possible, but in such a way that malicious users cannot interfere. Again, application programs do not face anything like this challenge.

Fifth, operating systems live for a very long time. UNIX has been around for a quarter of a century; Windows has been around for over a decade and shows no signs of vanishing. Consequently, the designers have to think about how hardware and applications may change in the distant future and how they should prepare for it. Systems that are locked too closely into one particular vision of the world usually die off.

Sixth, operating system designers really do not have a good idea of how their systems will be used, so they need to provide for considerable generality. Neither UNIX nor Windows was designed with email or Web browsers in mind, yet many computers running these systems do little else. Nobody tells a ship designer to build a ship without specifying whether they want a fishing vessel, a cruise ship, or a battleship. And even fewer change their minds after the product has arrived.

Seventh, modern operating systems are generally designed to be portable, meaning they have to run on multiple hardware platforms. They also have to support hundreds, even thousands of I/O devices, all of which are independently designed with no regard to one another. An example of where this diversity causes problems is the need for an operating system to run on both little-endian and big-endian machines. A second example was seen constantly under MS-DOS when users attempted to install, say, a sound card and a modem that used the same I/O ports or interrupt request lines. Few programs other than operating systems have to deal with sorting out problems caused by conflicting pieces of hardware.

Eighth, and last in our list, is the frequent need to be backward compatible with some previous operating system. That system may have restrictions on word lengths, file names, or other aspects that the designers now regard as obsolete, but are stuck with. It is like converting a factory to produce next year's cars instead of this year's cars, but while continuing to produce this year's cars at full capacity.

12.2 INTERFACE DESIGN

It should be clear by now that writing a modern operating system is not easy. But where does one begin? Probably the best place to begin is to think about the interfaces it provides. An operating system provides a set of services, mostly data types (e.g., files) and operations on them (e.g., read). Together, these form the interface to its users. Note that in this context the users of the operating system are programmers who write code that use system calls, not people running application programs.

In addition to the main system call interface, most operating systems have additional interfaces. For example, some programmers need to write device drivers to insert into the operating system. These drivers see certain features and can make certain procedure calls. These features and calls also define and interface, but a very different one from one application programmers see. All of these interfaces must be carefully designed if the system is to succeed.

12.2.1 Guiding Principles

Are their any principles that can guide interface design? We believe there are. Briefly summarized, they are simplicity, completeness, and the ability to be implemented efficiently.

Principle 1: Simplicity

A simple interface is easier to understand and implement in a bug-free way. All system designers should memorize this famous quote from the pioneer French aviator and writer, Antoine de St. Exupéry:

> *Perfection is reached not when there is no longer anything to add, but when there is no longer anything to take away.*

This principle says that less is better than more, at least in the operating system itself. Another way to say this is the KISS principle: Keep It Simple, Stupid.

Principle 2: Completeness

Of course, the interface must make it possible to do everything that the users need to do, that is, it must be complete. This brings us to another famous quote, this one from Albert Einstein:

Everything should be as simple as possible, but no simpler.

In other words, the operating system should do exactly what is needed of it and no more. If users need to store data, it must provide some mechanism for storing data. If users need to communicate with each other, the operating system has to provide a communication mechanism, and so on. In his 1991 Turing Award lecture, Fernando Corbató, one of the designers of CTSS and MULTICS, combined the concepts of simplicity and completeness and said:.SP 0.25

First, it is important to emphasize the value of simplicity and elegance, for complexity has a way of compounding difficulties and as we have seen, creating mistakes. My definition of elegance is the achievement of a given functionality with a minimum of mechanism and a maximum of clarity.

The key idea here is *minimum of mechanism.* In other words, every feature, function, and system call should carry its own weight. It should do one thing and do it well. When a member of the design team proposes extending a system call or adding some new feature, the others should ask the question: "Would something awful happen if we left it out?" If the answer is: "No, but somebody might find this feature useful some day" put it in a user-level library, not in the operating system, even if it is slower that way. Not every feature has to be faster than a speeding bullet. The goal is to preserve what Corbató called minimum of mechanism.

Let us briefly consider two examples from my own experience: MINIX and A-moeba. For all intents and purposes, MINIX has three system calls: send, receive, and sendrec. The system is structured as a collection of processes, with the memory manager, the file system, and each device driver being a separate schedulable process. To a first approximation, all the kernel does is schedule processes and handle message passing between them. Consequently, only two system calls are needed: send, to send a message, and receive to receive one. The third call, sendrec is simply an optimization for efficiency reasons to allow a message to be sent and the reply to be requested with only one kernel trap. Everything else is done by requesting some other process (for example, the file system process or the disk driver) to do the work.

Amoeba is even simpler. It has only one system call: perform remote procedure call. This call sends a message and waits for a reply. It is essentially the same as MINIX' sendrec. Everything else is built on this one call.

Principle 3: Efficiency

The third guideline is efficiency of implementation. If a feature or system call cannot be implemented efficiently, it is probably not worth having. It should also be intuitively obviously to the programmer about how much a system call costs. For example, UNIX programmers expect the lseek system call to be cheaper than the read system call because the former just changes a pointer in memory while the latter performs disk I/O. If the intuitive costs are wrong, programmers will write inefficient programs.

12.2.2 Paradigms

Once the goals have been established, the design can begin. A good starting place is thinking about how the customers will view the system. One of the most important issues is how to make all the features of the system hang together well and present what is often called **architectural coherence**. In this regard, it is important to distinguish two kinds of operating system "customers." On the one hand, there are the *users*, who interact with application programs; on the other are the *programmers*, who write them. The former mostly deal with the GUI; the latter mostly deal with the system call interface. If the intention is to have a single GUI that pervades the complete system, such as in the Macintosh, the design should start there. If, on the other hand, the intention is to support many possible GUIs, such as in UNIX, the system call interface should be designed first. Doing the GUI first is essentially a top-down design. The issues are what features will it have, how will the user interact with it, and how should the system be designed to support it? For example, if most programs display icons on the screen and then wait for the user to click on one of them, this suggests an event-driven model for the GUI and probably also for the operating system. On the other hand, if the screen is mostly full of text windows, then a model in which processes read from the keyboard is probably better.

Doing the system call interface first is a bottom-up design. Here the issues are what kinds of features programmers in general need. Actually, not many special features are needed to support a GUI. For example, the UNIX windowing system, X, is just a big C program that does reads and writes on the keyboard, mouse, and screen. X was developed long after UNIX and did not require many changes to the operating system to get it to work. This experience validated that fact that UNIX was sufficiently complete.

User Interface Paradigms

For both the GUI-level interface and the system-call interface, the most important aspect is having a good paradigm (sometimes called a metaphor) to provide a way of looking at the interface. Many GUIs for desktop machines use the

WIMP paradigm that we discussed in Chap. 5. This paradigm uses point-and-click, point-and-double-click, dragging, and other idioms throughout the interface to provide an architectural coherence to the whole. Often there are additional requirements for programs, such as having a menu bar with FILE, EDIT, and other entries, each of which has certain well-known menu items. In this way, users who know one program can quickly learn another one.

However, the WIMP user interface is not the only possible one. Some palmtop computers use a stylized handwriting interface. Dedicated multimedia devices may use a VCR-like interface. And of course, voice input has a completely different paradigm. What is important is not so much the paradigm chosen, but the fact that there is a single overriding paradigm that unifies the entire user interface.

Whatever paradigm is chosen, it is important that all application programs use it. Consequently, the system designers need to provide libraries and tool kits to application developers that give them access to procedures that produce the uniform look-and-feel. User interface design is very important, but it is not the subject of this book, so we will now drop back down to the subject of the operating system interface.

Execution Paradigms

Architectural coherence is important at the user level, but equally important at the system call interface level. Here it is frequently useful to distinguish between the execution paradigm and the data paradigm, so we will do both, starting with the former.

Two execution paradigms are widespread: algorithmic and event driven. The **algorithmic paradigm** is based on the idea that a program is started to perform some function that it knows in advance or gets from its parameters. That function might be to compile a program, do the payroll, or fly an airplane to San Francisco. The basic logic is hardwired into the code with the program making system calls from time to time to get user input, obtain operating system services, etc. This approach is outlined in Fig. 12-1(a).

The other execution paradigm is the **event-driven paradigm** of Fig. 12-1(b). Here the program performs some kind of initialization, for example by displaying a certain screen, and then waiting for the operating system to tell it about the first event. The event is often a key being struck or a mouse movement. This design is useful for highly interactive programs.

Each of these ways of doing business engenders its own programming style. In the algorithmic paradigm, algorithms are central and the operating system is regarded as a service provider. In the event-driven paradigm, the operating system also provides services, but this role is overshadowed by its role as a coordinator of user activities and a generator of events that are consumed by processes.

```
main( )                         main( )
{                               {
    int ... ;                       mess_t msg;

    init( );                        init( );
    do_something( );                while (get_message(&msg)) {
    read(...);                          switch (msg.type) {
    do_something_else( );                   case 1: ... ;
    write(...);                             case 2: ... ;
    keep_going( );                          case 3: ... ;
    exit(0);                            }
}                               }
                            }
        (a)                             (b)
```

Figure 12-1. (a) Algorithmic code. (b) Event-driven code.

Data Paradigms

The execution paradigm is not the only one exported by the operating system. An equally important one is the data paradigm. The key question here is how are system structures and devices presented to the programmer. In early FORTRAN batch systems, everything was modeled as a sequential magnetic tape. Card decks read in were treated as input tapes, card decks to be punched were treated as output tapes, and output for the printer was treated as an output tape. Disk files were also treated as tapes. Random access to a file was possible only by rewinding the tape corresponding to the file and reading it again.

The mapping was done using job control cards like these:

```
MOUNT(TAPE08, REEL781)
RUN(INPUT, MYDATA, OUTPUT, PUNCH, TAPE08)
```

The first card instructed the operator to go get tape reel 781 from the tape rack and mount it on tape drive 8. The second card instructed the operating system to run the just compiled FORTRAN program, mapping *INPUT* (meaning the card reader) to logical tape 1, disk file *MYDATA* to logical tape 2, the printer (called *OUTPUT*) to logical tape 3, the card punch (called *PUNCH*) to logical tape 4. and physical tape drive 8 to logical tape 5.

FORTRAN had a syntax for reading and writing logical tapes. By reading from logical tape 1, the program got card input. By writing to logical tape 3, output would later appear on the printer. By reading from logical tape 5, tape reel 781 could be read in, and so on. Note that the tape idea was just a paradigm to integrate the card reader, printer, punch, disk files, and tapes. In this example, only logical tape 5 was a physical tape; the rest were ordinary (spooled) disk files. It was a primitive paradigm, but it was a start in the right direction.

Later came UNIX, which goes much further using the model of "everything is a file." Using this paradigm, all I/O devices are treated as files and can be opened and manipulated as ordinary files. The C statements

```
fd1 = open("file1", O_RDWR);
fd2 = open("/dev/tty", O_RDWR)'
```

open a true disk file and the user's terminal. Subsequent statements can use *fd1* and *fd2* to read and write them, respectively. From that point on, there is no difference between accessing the file and accessing the terminal, except that seeks on the terminal are not allowed.

Not only does UNIX unify files and I/O devices, but it also allows other processes to be accessed over pipes as files. Furthermore, when mapped files are supported, a process can get at its own virtual memory as though it were a file. Finally, in versions of UNIX that support the */proc* file system, the C statement

```
fd3 = open("/proc/501", O_RDWR);
```

allows the process to (try to) access process 501's memory for reading and writing using file descriptor *fd3*, something useful for, say, a debugger.

Windows 2000 goes further still and tries to make everything look like an object. Once a process has acquired a valid handle to a file, process, semaphore, mailbox, or other kernel object, it can perform operations on it. This paradigm is even more general than that of UNIX and much more general than that of FOR-TRAN.

Unifying paradigms occur in other contexts as well. One of them is worth mentioning here: the Web. The paradigm behind the Web is that cyberspace is full of documents, each of which has a URL. By typing in a URL or clicking on an entry backed by a URL, you get the document. In reality, many "documents" are not documents at all, but are generated by a program or shell script when a request comes in. For example, when a user asks an online store for a list of CDs by a particular artist, the document is generated on-the-fly by a program; it certainly did not exist before the query was made.

We have now seen four cases: namely, everything is a tape, file, object, or document. In all four cases, the intention is to unify data, devices, and other resources to make them easier to deal with. Every operating system should have such a unifying data paradigm.

12.2.3 The System Call Interface

If one believes in Corbató's dictum of minimal mechanism, then the operating system should provide as few system calls as it can get away with, and each one should be as simple as possible (but no simpler). A unifying data paradigm can play a major role in helping here. For example, if files, processes, I/O devices, and much more all look like files or objects, then they can all be read with a single read system call. Otherwise it may be necessary to have separate calls for read_file, read_proc, and read_tty, among others.

In some cases, system calls may appear to need several variants, but it is often better practice to have one system call that handles the general case, with different library procedures to hide this fact from the programmers. For example, UNIX has a system call for overlaying a process virtual address space, exec. The most general call is

    exec(name, argp, envp);

which loads the executable file *name* and gives it arguments pointed to by *argp* and environment variables pointed to by *envp*. Sometimes it is convenient to list the arguments explicitly, so the library contains procedures that are called as follows:

    execl(name, arg0, arg1, ..., argn, 0);
    execle(name, arg0, arg1, ..., argn, envp);

All these procedures do is stick the arguments in an array and then call exec to do the work. This arrangement is the best of both worlds: a single straightforward system call keeps the operating system simple, yet the programmer gets the convenience of various ways to call exec.

Of course, trying to have one call to handle every possible case can easily get out of hand. In UNIX creating a process requires two calls: fork followed by exec. The former has no parameters; the latter has three parameters. In contrast, the Win32 API call for creating a process, CreateProcess, has 10 parameters, one of which is a pointer to a structure with an additional 18 parameters.

A long time ago, someone should have asked the question: "Would something awful happen if we left some of these out?" The truthful answer would have been: "In some cases programmers might have to do more work to achieve a particular effect, but the net result would have been a simpler, smaller, and more reliable operating system." Of course, the person proposing the 10+ 18 parameter version might have added: "But users like all these features." The rejoinder to that might have been: "They like systems that use little memory and never crash even more." Trade-offs between more functionality at the cost of more memory are at least visible and can be given a price tag (since the price of memory is known). However, it is hard to estimate the additional crashes per year some feature will add and whether the users would make the same choice if they knew the hidden price. This effect can be summarized in Tanenbaum's first law of software:

Adding more code adds more bugs

Adding more features adds more code and thus adds more bugs. Programmers who believe adding new features does not add new bugs are either new to computers or believe the tooth fairy is out there watching over them.

Simplicity is not the only issue that comes out when designing system calls. An important consideration is Lampson's (1984) slogan:

Don't hide power.

If the hardware has an extremely efficient way of doing something, it should be exposed to the programmers in a simple way and not buried inside some other abstraction. The purpose of abstractions is to hide undesirable properties, not hide desirable ones. For example, suppose that the hardware has a special way to move large bitmaps around the screen (i.e., the video RAM) at high speed. It would be justified to have a new system call to get at this mechanism, rather than just providing ways to read video RAM into main memory and write it back again. The new call should just move bits and nothing else. If a system call is fast, users can always build more convenient interfaces on top of it. If it is slow, nobody will use it.

Another design issue is connection-oriented versus connectionless calls. The standard UNIX and Win32 system calls for reading a file are connection-oriented. First you open a file, then you read it, finally you close it. Some remote file access protocols are also connection-oriented. For example, to use FTP, the user first logs in to the remote machine, reads the files, and then logs out.

On the other hand, some remote file access protocols are connectionless. NFS is connectionless, as we saw in Chap. 10. Each NFS call stands on its own, so files are not opened before reading or writing. And, of course, they do not have to be closed afterward, either. The Web is also connectionless: to read a Web page you just ask for it; there is no advance setup required (a TCP connection *is* required, but this is at a lower level of protocol; the HTTP protocol for accessing the Web itself is connectionless).

The trade-off between any connection-oriented mechanism and a connectionless one is the additional work required to set up the mechanism (e.g., open the file), and the gain from not having to do it on (possibly many) subsequent calls. For file I/O on a single machine, where the setup cost is low, probably the standard way (first open, then use) is the best way. For remote file systems, a case can be made both ways.

Another issue relating to the system call interface is its visibility. The list of POSIX-mandated system calls is easy to find. All UNIX systems support these, as well as a small number of other calls, but the complete list is always public. In contrast, Microsoft has never made the list of Windows 2000 system calls public. Instead the Win32 API and other APIs have been made public, but these contain vast numbers of library calls (over 13,000 for Windows 2000), but only a small number are true system calls. The argument for making all the system calls public is that it lets programmers know what is cheap (functions performed in user space) and what is expensive (kernel calls). The argument for not making them public is that it gives the implementers the flexibility of changing the actual underlying system calls to make them better without breaking user programs.

12.3 IMPLEMENTATION

Turning away from the user and system call interfaces, let us now take a look at how to implement an operating system. In the next eight sections we will examine some general conceptual issues relating to implementation strategies. After that we will look at some low-level techniques that are often helpful.

12.3.1 System Structure

Probably the first decision the implementers have to make is what the system structure should be. We examined the main possibilities in Sec. 1.7, but will review them here. An unstructured monolithic design is really not a good idea, except maybe for a tiny operating system in, say, a refrigerator, but even there it is arguable.

Layered Systems

A reasonable approach that has been well established over the years is a layered system. Dijkstra's THE system (Fig. 1-25) was the first layered operating system. UNIX (Fig. 10-3) and Windows 2000 (Fig. 11-7) also have a layered structure, but the layering in both of them is more a way of trying to describe the system than a real guiding principle that was used in building the system.

For a new system, designers choosing to go this route should *first* very carefully choose the layers and define the functionality of each one. The bottom layer should always try to hide the worst idiosyncracies of the hardware, as the HAL does in Fig. 11-7. Probably the next layer should handle interrupts, context switching, and the MMU, so above this level, the code is mostly machine independent. Above this, different designers will have different tastes (and biases). One possibility is to have layer 3 manage threads, including scheduling and interthread synchronization, as shown in Fig. 12-2. The idea here is that starting at layer 4 we have proper threads that are scheduled normally and synchronize using a standard mechanism (e.g., mutexes).

In layer 4 we might find the device drivers, each one running as a separate thread, with its own state, program counter, registers, etc., possibly (but not necessarily) within the kernel address space. Such a design can greatly simplify the I/O structure because when an interrupt occurs, it can be converted into an unlock on a mutex and a call to the scheduler to (potentially) schedule the newly readied thread that was blocked on the mutex. MINIX uses this approach, but in UNIX, Linux, and Windows 2000, the interrupt handlers run in a kind of no-man's land, rather than as proper threads that can be scheduled, suspended, etc. Since a huge amount of the complexity of any operating system is in the I/O, any technique for making it more tractable and encapsulated is worth considering.

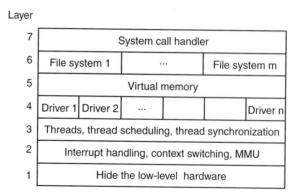

Figure 12-2. One possible design for a modern layered operating system.

Above layer 4, we would expect to find virtual memory, one or more file systems, and the system call handlers. If the virtual memory is at a lower level than the file systems, then the block cache can be paged out, allowing the virtual memory manager to dynamically determine how the real memory should be divided among user pages and kernel pages, including the cache. Windows 2000 works this way.

Exokernels

While layering has its supporters among system designers, there is also another camp that has precisely the opposite view (Engler et al., 1995). Their view is based on the **end-to-end argument** (Saltzer et al., 1984). This concept says that if something has to be done by the user program itself, it is wasteful to do it in a lower layer as well.

Consider an application of that principle to remote file access. If a system is worried about data being corrupted in transit, it should arrange for each file to be checksummed at the time it is written and the checksum stored along with the file. When a file is transferred over a network from the source disk to the destination process, the checksum is transferred, too, and also recomputed at the receiving end. If the two disagree, the file is discarded and transferred again.

This check is more accurate than using a reliable network protocol since it also catches disk errors, memory errors, software errors in the routers, and other errors besides bit transmission errors. The end-to-end argument says that using a reliable network protocol is then not necessary, since the end point (the receiving process) has enough information to verify the correctness of the file itself. The only reason for using a reliable network protocol in this view is for efficiency, that is, catching and repairing transmission errors earlier.

The end-to-end argument can be extended to almost all of the operating system. It argues for not having the operating system do anything that the user program can do itself. For example, why have a file system? Just let the user read and write a portion of the raw disk in a protected way. Of course, most users like having files, but the end-to-end argument says that the file system should be a library procedure linked with any program that needs to use files. This approach allows different programs to have different file systems. This line of reasoning says that all the operating system should do is securely allocate resources (e.g., the CPU and the disks) among the competing users. The Exokernel is an operating system built according to the end-to-end argument (Engler et al., 1995).

Client-Server Systems

A compromise between having the operating system do everything and the operating system do nothing is to have the operating system do a little bit. This design leads to a microkernel with much of the operating system running as user-level server processes as illustrated in Fig. 1-27. This is the most modular and flexible of all the designs. The ultimate in flexibility is to have each device driver also run as a user process, fully protected against the kernel and other drivers. Getting the drivers out of the kernel would eliminate the largest source of instability in any operating system—buggy third-party drivers—and would be a tremendous win in terms of reliability.

Of course, device drivers need to access the hardware device registers, so some mechanism is needed to provide this. If the hardware permits, each driver process could be given access to only those I/O devices it needs. For example, with memory-mapped I/O, each driver process could have the page for its device mapped in, but no other device pages. If the I/O port space can be partially protected, the correct portion of it could be made available to each driver.

Even if no hardware assistance is available, the idea can still be made to work. What is then needed is a new system call, available only to device driver processes, supplying a list of (port, value) pairs. What the kernel does is first check to see if the process owns all the ports in the list. If so, it then copies the corresponding values to the ports to initiate device I/O. A similar call can be used to read I/O ports in a protected way.

This approach keeps device drivers from examining (and damaging) kernel data structures, which is (for the most part) a good thing. An analogous set of calls could be made available to allow driver processes to read and write kernel tables, but only in a controlled way and with the approval of the kernel.

The main problem with this approach, and microkernels in general, is the performance hit all the extra context switches cause. However, virtually all work on microkernels was done many years ago when CPUs were much slower. Nowadays, applications that use every drop of CPU power and cannot tolerate a small loss of performance, are few and far between. After all, when running a word processor or Web browser, the CPU is probably idle 90% of the time. If a microkernel-based operating system turned an unreliable 900-MHz system into a reliable 800-MHz system, probably few users would complain. After all, most of them were quite happy only a few years ago when they got their previous computer, at the then-stupendous speed of 100 MHz.

Extensible Systems

With the client-server systems discussed above, the idea was to get as much out of the kernel as possible. The opposite approach is to put more modules into the kernel, but in a protected way. The key word here is *protected*, of course. We studied some protection mechanisms in Sec. 9.5.6 that were initially intended for importing applets over the Internet, but are equally applicable to inserting foreign code into kernel. The most important ones are sandboxing and code signing as interpretation is not really practical for kernel code.

Of course, an extensible system by itself is not a way to structure an operating system. However, by starting with a minimal system consisting of little more than a protection mechanism and then adding protected modules to the kernel one at a time until reaching the functionality desired, a minimal system can be built for the application at hand. In this view, a new operating system can be tailored to each application by including only the parts it requires. Paramecium is an example of such a system (Van Doorn, 2001).

Kernel Threads

Another issue relevant here is that of system threads, no matter which structuring model is chosen. It is sometimes convenient to allow kernel threads to exist, separate from any user process. These threads can run in the background, writing dirty pages to disk, swapping processes between main memory and disk, and so on. In fact, the kernel itself can be structured entirely of such threads, so that when a user does a system call, instead of the user's thread executing in kernel mode, the user's thread blocks and passes control to a kernel thread that takes over to do the work.

In addition to kernel threads running in the background, most operating systems start up many daemon processes in the background, too. While these are not part of the operating system, they often perform "system" type activities. These might including getting and sending email and serving various kinds of requests for remote users, such as FTP and Web pages.

12.3.2 Mechanism versus Policy

Another principle that helps architectural coherence, along with keeping things small and well structured, is that of separating mechanism from policy. By putting the mechanism in the operating system and leaving the policy to user processes, the system itself can be left unmodified, even if there is a need to change policy. Even if the policy module has to be kept in the kernel, it should be isolated from the mechanism, if possible, so that changes in the policy module do not affect the mechanism module.

To make the split between policy and mechanism clearer, let us consider two real-world examples. As a first example, consider a large company that has a payroll department, which is in charge of paying the employees' salaries. It has computers, software, blank checks, agreements with banks, and more mechanism for actually paying out the salaries. However, the policy—determining who gets paid how much—is completely separate and is decided by management. The payroll department just does what it is told to do.

As the second example, consider a restaurant. It has the mechanism for serving diners, including tables, plates, waiters, a kitchen full of equipment, agreements with credit card companies, and so on. The policy is set by the chef, namely, what is on the menu. If the chef decides that tofu is out and big steaks are in, this new policy can be handled by the existing mechanism.

Now let us consider some operating system examples. First, consider thread scheduling. The kernel could have a priority scheduler, with k priority levels. The mechanism is an array, indexed by priority level, as shown in Fig. 10-11 or Fig. 11-19. Each entry is the head of a list of ready threads at that priority level. The scheduler just searches the array from highest priority to lowest priority, selecting the first threads it hits. The policy is setting the priorities. The system may have different classes of users, each with a different priority, for example. It might also allow user processes to set the relative priority of its threads. Priorities might be increased after completing I/O or decreased after using up a quantum. There are numerous other policies that could be followed, but the idea here is the separation between setting policy and carrying it out.

A second example is paging. The mechanism involves MMU management, keeping lists of occupied pages and free pages, and code for shuttling pages to and from disk. The policy is deciding what to do when a page fault occurs. It could be local or global, LRU-based or FIFO-based, or something else, but this algorithm can (and should) be completely separate from the mechanics of actually managing the pages.

A third example is allowing modules to be loaded into the kernel. The mechanism concerns how they are inserted, how they are linked, what calls they can make, and what calls can be made on them. The policy is determining who is allowed to load a module into the kernel and which modules. Maybe only the superuser can load modules, but maybe any user can load a module that has been digitally signed by the appropriate authority.

12.3.3 Orthogonality

Good system design consists of separate concepts that can be combined independently. For example, in C, there are primitive data types including integers, characters, and floating-point numbers. There are also mechanisms for combining data types, including arrays, structures, and unions. These ideas combine independently, allowing arrays of integers, arrays of characters, structure and union members that are floating-point numbers, etc. In fact, once a new data type has been defined, such as an array of integers, it can be used as if it were a primitive data type, for example as a member of a structure or a union. The ability to combine separate concepts independently is called **orthogonality**. It is direct consequence of the simplicity and completeness principles.

The concept of orthogonality also occurs in operating systems in various disguises. One example is the Linux clone system call, which creates a new thread. The call has a bitmap as a parameter, which allows the address space, working directory, file descriptors, and signals to shared or copied individually. If everything is copied, we have a new process, the same as fork. If nothing is copied, a new thread is created in the current process. However, it is also possible to create intermediate forms of sharing not possible in traditional UNIX systems. By separating out the various features and making them orthogonal, a finer degree of control is possible.

Another use of orthogonality is the separation of the process concept from the thread concept in Windows 2000. A process is a container for resources, nothing more and nothing less. A thread is a schedulable entity. When one process is given a handle for another process, it does not matter how many threads it has. When a thread is scheduled, it does not matter which process it belongs to. These concepts are orthogonal.

Our last example of orthogonality comes from UNIX. Process creation there is done in two steps: fork plus exec. Creating the new address space and loading it with a new memory image are separate, allowing things to be done in between (such as manipulating file descriptors). In Windows 2000, these two steps cannot be separated, that is, the concepts of making a new address space and filling it in are not orthogonal there. The Linux sequence of clone plus exec is yet more orthogonal, since there are even more fine-grained building blocks available. As a general rule, having a small number of orthogonal elements that can be combined in many ways leads to a small, simple, and elegant system.

12.3.4 Naming

Most long-lived data structures used by an operating system have some kind of name or identifier by which they can be referred. Obvious examples are login names, file names, device names, process IDs, and so on. How these names are constructed and managed is an important issue in system design and implementation.

Names designed for people to use are character-string names in ASCII or Unicode and are usually hierarchical. Directory paths, for example one such as */usr/ast/books/mos2/chap-12*, are clearly hierarchical, indicating a series of directories to search starting at the root. URLs are also hierarchical. For example, *www.cs.vu.nl/~ast/* indicates a specific machine (*www*) in a specific department (*cs*) at specific university (*vu*) in a specific country (*nl*). The part after the slash indicates a specific file on the designated machine, in this case, by convention, *www/index.html* in ast's home directory. Note that URLs (and DNS addresses in general, including email addresses) are "backward," starting at the bottom of the tree and going up, unlike file names, which start at the top of the tree and go down. Another way of looking at this is whether the tree is written from the top starting at the left and going right or starting at the right and going left.

Often naming is done at two levels: external and internal. For example, files always have a character-string name for people to use. In addition, there is almost always an internal name that the system uses. In UNIX, the real name of a file is its i-node number; the ASCI name is not used at all internally. In fact, it is not even unique since a file may have multiple links to it. The analogous internal name in Windows 2000 is the file's index in the MFT. The job of the directory is to provide the mapping between the external name and the internal name, as shown in Fig. 12-3.

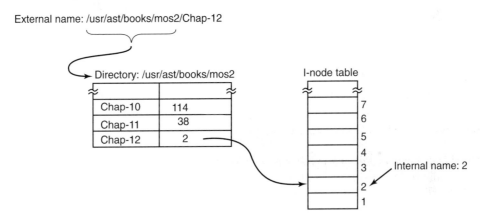

Figure 12-3. Directories are used to map external names onto internal names.

In many cases (such as the file name example given above), the internal name is an unsigned integer that serves as an index into a kernel table. Other examples of table-index names are file descriptors in UNIX and object handles in Windows 2000. Note that neither of these has any external representation. They are strictly for use by the system and running processes. In general, using table indices for transient names that are lost when the system is rebooted is a good idea.

Operating systems often support multiple name spaces, both external and internal. For example, in Chap. 11 we looked at three external name spaces supported by Windows 2000: file names, object names, and registry names (and there is also the Active Directory name space, which we did not look at). In addition, there are innumerable internal name spaces using unsigned integers, for example, object handles, MFT entries, etc. Although the names in the external name spaces are all Unicode strings, looking up a file name in the registry will not work, just as using an MFT index in the object table will not work. In a good design, considerable thought is given to how many names spaces are needed, what the syntax of names is in each one, how they can be told apart, whether absolute and relative names exist, and so on.

12.3.5 Binding Time

As we have just seen, operating systems use various kinds of names to refer to objects. Sometimes the mapping between a name and an object is fixed, but sometimes it is not. In the latter case, it may matter when the name is bound to the object. In general, **early binding** is simple, but is not flexible, whereas **late binding** is more complicated but often more flexible.

To clarify the concept of binding time, let us look at some real-world examples. An example of early binding is the practice of some colleges to allow parents to enroll a baby at birth and prepay the current tuition. When the student shows up 18 years later, the tuition is fully paid up, no matter how high it may be at that moment.

In manufacturing, ordering parts in advance and maintaining an inventory of them is early binding. In contrast, just-in-time manufacturing requires suppliers to be able to provide parts on the spot, with no advance notice required. This is late binding.

Programming languages often support multiple binding times for variables. Global variables are bound to a particular virtual address by the compiler. This exemplifies early binding. Variables local to a procedure are assigned a virtual address (on the stack) at the time the procedure is invoked. This is intermediate binding. Variables stored on the heap (those allocated by *malloc* in C or *new* in Java) are assigned virtual addresses only at the time they are actually used. Here we have late binding.

Operating systems often use early binding for most data structures, but occasionally use late binding for flexibility. Memory allocation is a case in point. Early multiprogramming systems on machines lacking address relocation hardware had to load a program at some memory address and relocate it to run there. If it was ever swapped out, it had to be brought back at the same memory address or it would fail. In contrast, paged virtual memory is a form of late binding. The actual physical address corresponding to a given virtual address is not known until the page is touched and actually brought into memory.

Another example of late binding is window placement in a GUI. In contrast to the early graphical systems, in which the programmer had to specify the absolute screen coordinates for all images on the screen, in modern GUIs, the software uses coordinates relative to the window's origin, but that is not determined until the window is put on the screen, and it may even be changed later.

12.3.6 Static versus Dynamic Structures

Operating system designers are constantly forced to choose between static and dynamic data structures. Static ones are always simpler to understand, easier to program, and faster in use; dynamic ones are more flexible. An obvious example is the process table. Early systems simply allocated a fixed array of per-process structures. If the process table consisted of 256 entries, then only 256 processes could exist at any one instant. An attempt to create a 257th one would fail for lack of table space. Similar considerations held for the table of open files (both per user and system wide), and many other kernel tables.

An alternative strategy is to build the process table as a linked list of minitables, initially just one. If this table fills up, another one is allocated from a global storage pool and linked to the first one. In this way, the process table cannot fill up until all of kernel memory is exhausted.

On the other hand, the code for searching the table becomes more complicated. For example, the code for searching a static process table to see if a given PID, *pid*, is given in Fig. 12-4. It is simple and efficient. Doing the same thing for a linked list of minitables is more work.

```
found = 0;
for (p = &proc_table[0]; p < &proc_table[PROC_TABLE_SIZE]; p++) {
    if (p->proc_pid == pid) {
        found = 1;
        break;
    }
}
```

Figure 12-4. Code for searching the process table for a given PID.

Static tables are best when there is plenty of memory or table utilizations can be guessed fairly accurately. For example, in a single-user system, it is unlikely that the user will start up more than 32 processes at once and it is not a total disaster if an attempt to start a 33rd one fails.

Yet another alternative is to use a fixed-size table, but if it fills up, allocate a new fixed-size table, say, twice as big. The current entries are then copied over to the new table and the old table is returned to the free storage pool. In this way, the table is always contiguous rather than linked. The disadvantage here is that some storage management is needed and the address of the table is now a variable instead of a constant.

A similar issue holds for kernel stacks. When a thread switches to kernel mode, or a kernel-mode thread is run, it needs a stack in kernel space. For user threads, the stack can be initialized to run down from the top of the virtual address space, so the size need not be specified in advance. For kernel threads, the size must be specified in advance because the stack takes up some kernel virtual address space and there may be many stacks. The question is: how much space should each one get? The trade-offs here are similar to those for the process table.

Another static-dynamic trade-off is process scheduling. In some systems, especially real-time ones, the scheduling can be done statically in advance. For example, an airline knows what time its flights will leave weeks before their departure. Similarly, multimedia systems know when to schedule audio, video, and other processes in advance. For general-purpose use, these considerations do not hold and scheduling must be dynamic.

Yet another static-dynamic issue is kernel structure. It is much simpler if the kernel is built as a single binary program and loaded into memory to run. The consequence of this design, however, is that adding a new I/O device requires a relinking of the kernel with the new device driver. Early versions of UNIX worked this way, and it was quite satisfactory in a minicomputer environment when adding new I/O devices was a rare occurrence. Nowadays, most operating systems allow code to be added to the kernel dynamically, with all the additional complexity that entails.

12.3.7 Top-Down versus Bottom-Up Implementation

While it is best to design the system top down, in theory it can be implemented top down or bottom up. In a top-down implementation, the implementers start with the system call handlers and see what mechanisms and data structures are needed to support them. These procedures are written and so on until the hardware is reached.

The problem with this approach is that it is hard to test anything with only the top-level procedures available. For this reason, many developers find it more practical to actually build the system bottom up. This approach entails first writing code that hides the low-level hardware, essentially the HAL in Fig. 11-7. Interrupt handling and the clock driver are also needed early on.

Then multiprogramming can be tackled, along with a simple scheduler (e.g., round-robin scheduling). At this point it should be possible to test the system to see if it can run multiple processes correctly. If that works, it is now time to begin the careful definition of the various tables and data structures needed throughout the system, especially those for process and thread management and later memory management. I/O and the file system can wait initially, except for a primitive way to read the keyboard and write to the screen for testing and debugging. In some cases, the key low-level data structures should be protected by allowing access only through specific access procedures—in effect, object-oriented programming, no matter what the programming language is. As lower layers are completed, they can be tested thoroughly. In this way, the system advances from the bottom up, much the way contractors build tall office buildings.

If a large team is available, an alternative approach is to first make a detailed design of the whole system, and then assign different groups to write different modules. Each one tests its own work in isolation. When all the pieces are ready, they are integrated and tested. The problem with this line of attack is that if nothing works initially, it may be hard to isolate whether one or more modules are malfunctioning, or one group misunderstood what some other module was supposed to do. Nevertheless, with large teams, this approach is often used to maximize the amount of parallelism in the programming effort.

12.3.8 Useful Techniques

We have just looked at some abstract ideas for system design and implementation. Now we will examine a number of useful concrete techniques for system implementation. There are numerous other ones, of course, but space limitations restrict us to just a few of them.

Hiding the Hardware

A lot of hardware is ugly. It has to be hidden early on (unless it exposes power, which most hardware does not). Some of the very low-level details can be hidden by a HAL-type layer of the type shown in Fig. 12-2. However, many hardware details cannot be hidden this way.

One thing that deserves early attention is how to deal with interrupts. They make programming unpleasant, but operating systems have to deal with them. One approach is to turn them into something else immediately. For example, every interrupt could be turned into a pop-up thread instantly. At that point we are dealing with threads, rather than interrupts.

A second approach is to convert each interrupt into an unlock operation on a mutex that the corresponding driver is waiting on. Then the only effect of an interrupt is to cause some thread to become ready.

A third approach is convert an interrupt into a message to some thread. The low-level code just builds a message telling where the interrupt came from, enqueues it, and calls the scheduler to (potentially) run the handler, which was probably blocked waiting for the message. All these techniques, and other ones like them, all try to convert interrupts into thread synchronization operations. Having each interrupt handled by a proper thread in a proper context is easier to manage than running a handler in the arbitrary context that it happened to occur in. Of course, this must be done efficiently, but deep within the operating system, everything must be done efficiently.

Most operating systems are designed to run on multiple hardware platforms. These platforms can differ in terms of the CPU chip, MMU, word length, RAM size, and other features that cannot easily be masked by the HAL or equivalent. Nevertheless, it is highly desirable to have a single set of source files that are used to generate all versions; otherwise each bug that later turns up must be fixed multiple times in multiple sources, with the danger that the sources drift apart.

Some hardware differences, such as RAM size, can be dealt with by having the operating system determine the value at boot time and keep it in a variable. Memory allocators, for example, can use the RAM size variable to determine how big to make the block cache, page tables, etc. Even static tables such as the process table can be sized based on the total memory available.

However, other differences, such as different CPU chips, cannot be solved by having a single binary that determines at run time which CPU it is running on. One way to tackle the problem of one source and multiple targets is to use conditional compilation. In the source files, certain compile-time flags are defined for the different configurations and these are used to bracket code that is dependent on the CPU, word length, MMU, etc. For example, imagine an operating system that is to run on the Pentium and UltraSPARC chips, which need different initialization code. The *init* procedure could be written as illustrated in Fig. 12-5(a). Depending on the value of *CPU*, which is defined in the header file *config.h*, one kind of initialization or other is done. Because the actual binary contains only the code needed for the target machine, there is no loss of efficiency this way.

```
#include "config.h"                          #include "config.h"

init( )                                       #if (WORD_LENGTH == 32)
{                                             typedef int Register;
#if (CPU == PENTIUM)                          #endif
/* Pentium initialization here. */
#endif                                        #if (WORD_LENGTH == 64)
                                              typedef long Register;
#if (CPU == ULTRASPARC)                       #endif
/* UltraSPARC initialization here. */
#endif                                        Register R0, R1, R2, R3;

            (a)                                           (b)
}
```

Figure 12-5. (a) CPU-dependent conditional compilation. (b) Word-length dependent conditional compilation.

As a second example, suppose there is a need for a data type *Register*, which should be 32 bits on the Pentium and 64 bits on the UltraSPARC. This could be handled by the conditional code of Fig. 12-5(b) (assuming that the compiler produces 32-bit ints and 64-bit longs). Once this definition has been made (probably in a header file included everywhere), the programmer can just declare variables to be of type *Register* and know they will be the right length.

The header file, *config.h*, has to be defined correctly, of course. For the Pentium it might be something like this:

```
#define CPU PENTIUM
#define WORD_LENGTH 32
```

To compile the system for the UltraSPARC, a different *config.h* would be used, with the correct values for the UltraSPARC, probably something like

```
#define CPU ULTRASPARC
#define WORD_LENGTH 64
```

Some readers may be wondering why *CPU* and *WORD_LENGTH* are handled by different macros. We could easily have bracketed the definition of *Register* with a test on *CPU*, setting it to 32 bits for the Pentium and 64 bits for the UltraSPARC. However, this is not a good idea. Consider what happens when we later port the system to the 64-bit Intel Itanium. We would have to add a third conditional to Fig. 12-5(b) for the Itanium. By doing it as we have, all we have to do is include the line

```
#define WORD_LENGTH 64
```

to the *config.h* file for the Itanium.

This example illustrates the orthogonality principle we discussed earlier. Those items that are CPU-dependent should be conditionally compiled based on the *CPU* macro and those things that are word-length dependent should use the *WORD_LENGTH* macro. Similar considerations hold for many other parameters.

Indirection

It is sometimes said that there is no problem in computer science that cannot be solved with another level of indirection. While something of an exaggeration, there is definitely a grain of truth here. Let us consider some examples. On Pentium-based systems, when a key is depressed, the hardware generates an interrupt and puts the key number, rather than an ASCII character code, in a device register. Furthermore, when the key is released later, a second interrupt is generated, also with the key number. This indirection allows the operating system the possibility of using the key number to index into a table to get the ASCII character, which makes it easy to handle the many keyboards used around the world in different countries. Getting both the depress and release information makes it possible to use any key as a shift key since the operating system knows the exact sequence the keys were depressed and released.

Indirection is also used on output. Programs can write ASCII characters to the screen, but these are interpreted as indices into a table for the current output font. The table entry contains the bitmap for the character. This indirection makes it possible to separate characters from fonts.

Another example of indirection is the use of major device numbers in UNIX. Within the kernel there is a table indexed by major device number for the block devices and another one for the character devices. When a process opens a special file such as */dev/hd0*, the system extracts the type (block or character) and major and minor device numbers from the i-node and indexes into the appropriate driver table to find the driver. This indirection makes it easy to reconfigure the system, because programs deal with symbolic device names, not actual driver names.

Yet another example of indirection occurs in message-passing systems that name a mailbox rather than a process as the message destination. By indirecting through mailboxes (as opposed to naming a process as the destination), considerable flexibility can be achieved (e.g., having a secretary handle her boss' messages).

In a sense, the use of macros, such as

```
#define PROC_TABLE_SIZE 256
```

is also a form of indirection, since the programmer can write code without having to know how big the table really is. It is good practice to give symbolic names to all constants (except sometimes −1, 0, and 1), and put these in headers with comments explaining what they are for.

Reusability

It is frequently possible to reuse the same code in slightly different contexts. Doing so is a good idea as it reduces the size of the binary and means that the code has to be debugged only once. For example, suppose that bitmaps are used to keep track of free blocks on the disk. Disk block management can be handled by having procedures *alloc* and *free* that manage the bitmaps.

As a bare minimum, these procedures should work for any disk. But we can go further than that. The same procedures can also work for managing memory blocks, blocks in the file system's block cache, and i-nodes. In fact, they can be used to allocate and deallocate any resources that can be numbered linearly.

Reentrancy

Reentrancy refers for the ability of code to be executed two or more times simultaneously. On a multiprocessor, there is always the danger than while one CPU is executing some procedure, another CPU will start executing it as well, before the first one has finished. In this case, two (or more) threads on different CPUs might be executing the same code at the same time. This situation must be protected against by using mutexes or some other means to protect critical regions.

However, the problem also exists on a uniprocessor. In particular, most of any operating system runs with interrupts enabled. To do otherwise, would lose many interrupts and make the system unreliable. While the operating system is busy executing some procedure, P, it is entirely possible that an interrupt occurs and that the interrupt handler also calls P. If the data structures of P were in an inconsistent state at the time of the interrupt, the handler will see them in an inconsistent state and fail.

An obvious example where this can happen is if P is the scheduler. Suppose that some process used up its quantum and the operating system was moving it to the end of its queue. Part way through the list manipulation, the interrupt occurs, makes some process ready, and runs the scheduler. With the queues in an inconsistent state, the system will probably crash. As a consequence even on a uniprocessor, it is best that most of the operating system is reentrant, critical data structures are protected by mutexes, and interrupts are disabled at moments when they cannot be tolerated.

Brute Force

Using brute force to solve a problem has acquired a bad name over the years, but it is often the way to go in the name of simplicity. Every operating system has many procedures that are rarely called or operate with so little data that optimizing them is not worthwhile. For example, it is frequently necessary to search various tables and arrays within the system. The brute force algorithm is just leave the table in the order the entries are made and search it linearly when something has to be looked up. If the number of entries is small (say, under 100), the gain from sorting the table or hashing it is small, but the code is far more complicated and more likely to have bugs in it.

Of course, for functions that are on the critical path, say, context switching, everything should be done to make them fast, possibly even writing them in (heaven forbid) assembly language. But large parts of the system are not on the critical path. For example, many system calls are rarely called. If there is one fork every 10 sec, and it takes 10 msec to carry out, then even optimizing it to 0 wins only 0.1%. If the optimized code is bigger and buggier, a case can be made not to bother with the optimization.

Check for Errors First

Many system calls can potentially fail for a variety of reasons: the file to be opened belongs to someone else; process creation fails because the process table is full; or a signal cannot be sent because the target process does not exist. The operating system must painstakingly check for every possible error before carrying out the call.

Many system calls also require acquiring resources such as process table slots, i-node table slots, or file descriptors. A general piece of advice that can save a lot of grief is to first check to see if the system call can actually be carried out before acquiring any resources. This means putting all the tests at the beginning of the procedure that executes the system call. Each test should be of the form

```
if (error_condition) return(ERROR_CODE);
```

If the call gets all the way through the gauntlet of tests, then it is certain that it will succeed. At that point resources can be acquired.

Interspersing the tests with resource acquisition means that if some test fails along the way, all the resources acquired up to that point must be returned. If an error is made here and some resource is not returned, no damage is done immediately. For example, one process table entry may just become permanently unavailable. However, over a period of time, this bug may be triggered multiple times. Eventually, most or all the process table entries may become unavailable, leading to a system crash in an extremely unpredictable and difficult to debug way.

Many systems suffer from this problem in the form of memory leaks. Typically, the program calls *malloc* to allocate space but forgets to call *free* later to release it. Ever so gradually, all of memory disappears until the system is rebooted.

Engler et al. (2000) have proposed an interesting way to check for some of these errors at compile time. They observed that the programmer knows many invariants that the compiler does not know, such as when you lock a mutex, all paths starting at the lock must contain an unlock and no more locks of the same mutex. They have devised a way for the programmer to tell the compiler this fact and instruct it to check all the paths at compile time for violations of the invariant. The programmer can also specify that allocated memory must be released on all paths and many other conditions as well.

12.4 PERFORMANCE

All things being equal, a fast operating system is better than a slow one. However, a fast unreliable operating system is not as good as a reliable slow one. Since complex optimizations often lead to bugs, it is important to use them sparingly. This notwithstanding, there are places where performance is critical and optimizations are well worth the effort. In the following sections, we will look at some general techniques that can be used to improve performance in places where that is called for.

12.4.1 Why Are Operating Systems Slow?

Before talking about optimization techniques, it is worth pointing out that the slowness of many operating systems is to a large extent self-inflicted. For example, older operating systems, such as MS-DOS and UNIX Version 7, booted within a few seconds. Modern UNIX systems and Windows 2000 can take minutes to boot, despite running on hardware that is 100 times as fast. The reason is that they are doing much more, wanted or not. A case in point. Plug and play makes it somewhat easier to install a new hardware device, but the price paid is that on *every* boot, the operating system has to go out and inspect all the hardware to see if there is anything new out there. This bus scan takes time.

An alternative (and in the author's opinion, better) approach would be to scrap plug-and-play altogether and have an icon on the screen labeled "Install new hardware." Upon installing a new hardware device, the user would click on this icon to start the bus scan, instead of doing it on every boot. The designers of current systems were well aware of this option, of course. They rejected it, basically, because they assumed that the users were too stupid to be able to do this correctly (although they would word it more kindly). This is only one example, but there are many more where the desire to make the system "user-friendly" (or "idiot-proof," depending on your viewpoint) slows the system down all the time for everyone.

Probably the biggest single thing system designers can do to improve performance is to be much more selective about adding new features. The question to ask is not: "Will the users like this?" but "Is this feature worth the inevitable price in code size, speed, complexity, and reliability?" Only if the advantages clearly outweigh the drawbacks should it be included. Programmers have a tendency to assume that code size and bug count will be 0 and speed will be infinite. Experience shows this view to be a bit optimistic.

Another factor that plays a role is product marketing. By the time version 4 or 5 of some product has hit the market, probably all the features that are actually useful have been included and most of the people who need the product already have it. To keep sales going, many manufacturers nevertheless continue to produce new versions, with more features, just so they can sell their existing customers upgrades. Adding new features just for the sake of adding new features may help sales but rarely helps performance.

12.4.2 What Should Be Optimized?

As a general rule, the first version of the system should be as straightforward as possible. The only optimizations should be things that are so obviously going to be a problem that they are unavoidable. Having a block cache for the file system is such an example. Once the system is up and running, careful measurements should be made to see where the time is *really* going. Based on these numbers, optimizations should be made where they will help most.

Here is a true story of where an optimization did more harm than good. One of the author's students (who shall here remain nameless) wrote the MINIX *mkfs* program. This program lays down a fresh file system on a newly formatted disk. The student spent about 6 months optimizing it, including putting in disk caching. When he turned it in, it did not work and it required several additional months of debugging. This program typically runs once on the hard disk during the life of the computer, when the system is installed. It also runs once for each floppy disk that is formatted. Each run takes about 2 sec. Even if the unoptimized version had taken 1 minute, it was a poor use of resources to spend so much time optimizing a program that is used so infrequently.

A slogan that has considerable applicability to performance optimization is

Good enough is good enough.

By this we mean that once performance has achieved a reasonable level, it is probably not worth the effort and complexity to squeeze out the last few percent. If the scheduling algorithm is reasonably fair and keeps the CPU busy 90% of the time, it is doing its job. Devising a far more complex one that is 5% better is probably a bad idea. Similarly, if the page rate is low enough that it is not a bottleneck, jumping through hoops to get optimal performance is usually not worth it. Avoiding disaster is far more important than getting optimal performance, especially since what is optimal with one load may not be optimal with another.

12.4.3 Space-Time Trade-offs

One general approach to improving performance is to trade off time versus space. It frequently occurs in computer science that there is a choice between an algorithm that uses little memory but is slow and an algorithm that uses much more memory but is faster. When making an important optimization, it is worth looking for algorithms that gain speed by using more memory or conversely save precious memory by doing more computation.

One technique that is often helpful is to replace small procedures by macros. Using a macro eliminates the overhead normally associated with a procedure call. The gain is especially significant if the call occurs inside a loop. As an example, suppose we use bitmaps to keep track of resources and frequently need to know how many units are free in some portion of the bitmap. For this purpose we need a procedure, *bit_count*, that counts the number of 1 bits in a byte. The straightforward procedure is given in Fig. 12-6(a). It loops over the bits in a byte counting them one at a time.

This procedure has two sources of inefficiency. First, it must be called, stack space must be allocated for it, and it must return. Every procedure call has this overhead. Second, it contains a loop, and there is always some overhead associated with a loop.

A completely different approach is to use the macro of Fig. 12-6(b). It is an inline expression that computes the sum of the bits by successively shifting the argument, masking out everything but the low-order bit, and adding up the eight terms. The macro is hardly a work of art, but it appears in the code only once. When the macro is called, for example, by

```
sum = bit_count(table[i]);
```

the macro call looks identical to the call of the procedure. Thus other than one somewhat messy definition, the code does not look any worse in the macro case

```
#define BYTE_SIZE 8                      /* A byte contains 8 bits */

int bit_count(int byte)
{                                        /* Count the bits in a byte. */
    int i, count = 0;

    for (i = 0; i < BYTE_SIZE; i++)      /* loop over the bits in a byte */
        if ((byte >> i) & 1) count++;    /* if this bit is a 1, add to count */
    return(count);                       /* return sum */
}
```

(a)

```
/*Macro to add up the bits in a byte and return the sum. */
#define bit_count(b) (b&1) + ((b>>1)&1) + ((b>>2)&1) + ((b>>3)&1) + \
                ((b>>4)&1) + ((b>>5)&1) + ((b>>6)&1) + ((b>>7)&1)
```

(b)

```
/*Macro to look up the bit count in a table. */
char bits[256] = {0, 1, 1, 2, 1, 2, 2, 3, 1, 2, 2, 3, 2, 3, 3, 4, 1, 2, 2, 3, 2, 3, 3, ...};
#define bit_count(b) (int) bits[b]
```

(c)

Figure 12-6. (a) A procedure for counting bits in a byte. (b) A macro to count the bits.

than in the procedure case, but it is much more efficient since it eliminates both the procedure call overhead and the loop overhead.

We can take this example one step further. Why compute the bit count at all? Why not look it up in a table? After all, there are only 256 different bytes, each with a unique value between 0 and 8. We can declare a 256-entry table, *bits*, with each entry initialized (at compile time) to the bit count corresponding to that byte value. With this approach no computation at all is needed at run time, just one indexing operation. A macro to do the job is given in Fig. 12-6(c).

This is a clear example of trading computation time against memory. However, we could go still further. If the bit counts for whole 32-bit words are needed, using our *bit_count* macro, we need to perform four lookups per word. If we expand the table to 65,536 entries, we can suffice with two lookups per word, at the price of a much bigger table.

Looking answers up in tables can be used in other ways. For example, in Chap. 7 we saw how JPEG image compression works, with fairly complex discrete cosine transformations. An alternative compression technique, GIF, uses table lookup to encode 24-bit RGB pixels. However, GIF only works on images with 256 or fewer colors. For each image to be compressed, a palette of 256 entries is constructed, each entry containing one 24-bit RGB value. The compressed image then consists of an 8-bit index for each pixel instead of a 24-bit color value, a gain of a factor of three. This idea is illustrated for a 4×4 section of an image in Fig. 12-7. The original compressed image is shown in Fig. 12-7(a). Each value here is a 24-bit value, with 8 bits each giving the intensity for red, green, and blue. The GIF image is shown in Fig. 12-7(b). Here each value is an 8-bit index into the color palette. The color palette is stored as part of the image file, and is shown in Fig. 12-7(c). Actually, there is more to GIF, but the core of the idea is table lookup.

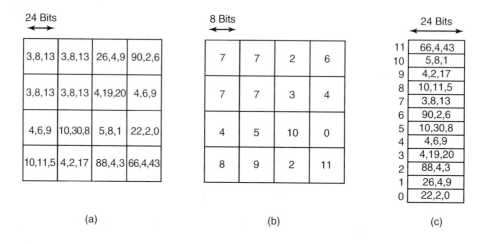

(a)   (b)   (c)

Figure 12-7. (a) Part of an uncompressed image with 24 bits per pixel. (b) The same part compressed with GIF, with 8 bits per pixel. (c) The color palette.

There is another way to reduce image size, and it illustrates a different trade-off. PostScript is a programming language that can be used to describe images. (Actually, any programming language can describe images, but PostScript is tuned for this purpose.) Many printers have a PostScript interpreter built into them to be able to run PostScript programs sent to them.

For example, if there is a rectangular block of pixels all the same color in an image, a PostScript program for the image would carry instructions to place a rectangle at a certain location and fill it with a certain color. Only a handful of bits are needed to issue this command. When the image is received at the printer, an interpreter there must run the program to construct the image. Thus PostScript achieves data compression at the expense of more computation, a different trade-off than table lookup, but a valuable one when memory or bandwidth is scarce.

Other trade-offs often involve data structures. Doubly-linked lists take up more memory than singly-linked lists, but often allow faster access to items. Hash tables are even more wasteful of space, but faster still. In short, one of the main things to consider when optimizing a piece of code is whether using different data structures would make the best time-space tradeoff.

12.4.4 Caching

A well-known technique for improving performance is caching. It is applicable any time it is likely the same result will be needed multiple times. The general approach is to d[Ho the full work the first time, and then save the result in a cache. On subsequent attempts, the cache is first checked. If the result is there, it is used. Otherwise, the full work is done again.

We have already seen the use of caching within the file system to hold some number of recently used disk blocks, thus saving a disk read on each hit. However, caching can be used for many other purposes as well. For example, parsing path names is surprising expensive. Consider the UNIX example of Fig. 6-39 again. To look up */usr/ast/mbox* requires the following disk accesses:

1. Read the i-node for the root directory (i-node 1).

2. Read the root directory (block 1).

3. Read the i-node for */usr* (i-node 6).

4. Read the */usr* directory (block 132).

5. Read the i-node for */usr/ast* (i-node 26).

6. Read the */usr/ast* directory (block 406).

It takes six disk accesses just to discover the i-node number of the file. Then the i-node itself has to be read to discover the disk block numbers. If the file is smaller than the block size (e.g., 1024 bytes), it takes eight disk accesses to read the data.

Some systems optimize path name parsing by caching (path, i-node) combinations. For the example of Fig. 6-39, the cache will certainly hold the first three entries of Fig. 12-8 after parsing */usr/ast/mbox*. The last three entries come from parsing other paths.

Path	I-node number
/usr	6
/usr/ast	26
/usr/ast/mbox	60
/usr/ast/books	92
/usr/bal	45
/usr/bal/paper.ps	85

Figure 12-8. Part of the i-node cache for Fig. 6-39.

When a path has to be looked up, the name parser first consults the cache and searches it for the longest substring present in the cache. For example, if the path

/usr/ast/grants/stw is presented, the cache returns the fact that */usr/ast* is i-node 26, so the search can start there, eliminating four disk accesses.

A problem with caching paths is that the mapping between file name and i-node number is not fixed for all time. Suppose that the file */usr/ast/mbox* is removed from the system and its i-node reused for a different file owned by a different user. Later, the file */usr/ast/mbox* is created again, and this time it gets i-node 106. If nothing is done to prevent it, the cache entry will now be wrong and subsequent lookups will return the wrong i-node number. For this reason, when a file or directory is deleted, its cache entry and (if it is a directory) all the entries below it must be purged from the cache.

Disk blocks and path names are not the only items that can be cached. I-nodes can be cached, too. If pop-up threads are used to handle interrupts, each one of them requires a stack and some additional machinery. These previously-used threads can also be cached, since refurbishing a used one is easier than creating a new one from scratch (to avoid having to allocate memory). Just about anything that is hard to produce can be cached.

12.4.5 Hints

Cache entries are always correct. A cache search may fail, but if it finds an entry, that entry is guaranteed to be correct and can be used without further ado. In some systems, it is convenient to have a table of **hints**. These are suggestions about the solution, but they are not guaranteed to be correct. The caller must verify the result itself.

A well-known example of hints are the URLs embedded on Web pages. Clicking on a link does not guarantee that the Web page pointed to is there. In fact, the page pointed to may have been removed years ago. Thus the information on the pointing page is really only a hint.

Hints are also used in connection with remote files. The information is the hint tells something about the remote file, such as where it is located. However, the file may have moved or been deleted since the hint was recorded, so a check is always needed to see if it is correct.

12.4.6 Exploiting Locality

Processes and programs do not act at random. They exhibit a fair amount of locality in time and space, and this information can be exploited in various ways to improve performance. One well-known example of spatial locality is the fact that processes do not jump around at random within their address spaces. They tend to use a relatively small number of pages during a given time interval. The pages that a process is actively using can be noted as its working set and the operating system can make sure that when the process is allowed to run, its working set is in memory, thus reducing the number of page faults.

The locality principle also holds for files. When a process has selected a particular working directory, it is likely that many of its future file references will be to files in that directory. By putting all the i-nodes and files for each directory close together on the disk, performance improvements can be obtained. This principle is what underlies the Berkeley Fast File System (McKusick et al., 1984).

Another area in which locality plays a role is in thread scheduling in multiprocessors. As we saw in Chap. 8, one way to schedule threads on a multiprocessor is to try to run each thread on the CPU it last used, in hopes that some of its memory blocks will still be in the memory cache.

12.4.7 Optimize the Common Case

It is frequently a good idea to distinguish between the most common case and the worst possible case and treat them differently. Often the code for the two is quite different. It is important to make the common case fast. For the worst case, if it occurs rarely, it is sufficient to make it correct.

As a first example, consider entering a critical region. Most of the time, the entry will succeed, especially if processes do not spend a lot of time inside critical regions. Windows 2000 takes advantage of this expectation by providing a Win32 API call EnterCriticalSection that atomically tests a flag in user mode (using TSL or equivalent). If the test succeeds, the process just enters the critical region and no kernel call is needed. If the test fails, the library procedure does a down on a semaphore to block the process. Thus in the normal case, no kernel call is needed.

As a second example, consider setting an alarm (using signals in UNIX). If no alarm is currently pending, it is straightforward to make an entry and put it on the timer queue. However, if an alarm is already pending, it has to be found and removed from the timer queue. Since the alarm call does not specify whether there is already an alarm set, the system has to assume worst case, that there is. However, since most of the time there is no alarm pending, and since removing an existing alarm is expensive, it is a good idea to distinguish these two cases.

One way to do this is to keep a bit in the process table that tells whether an alarm is pending. If the bit is off, the easy path is followed (just add a new timer queue entry without checking). If the bit is on, the timer queue must be checked.

12.5 PROJECT MANAGEMENT

Programmers are perpetual optimists. Most of them think that the way to write a program is to run to the keyboard and start typing. Shortly thereafter the fully debugged program is finished. For very large programs, it does not quite work like that. In the following sections we have a bit to say about managing large software projects, especially large operating system projects.

12.5.1 The Mythical Man Month

In his classic book, Fred Brooks, one of the designers of OS/360, who later moved to academia, addresses the question of why it is so hard to build big operating systems (Brooks, 1975, 1995). When most programmers see his claim that programmers can produce only 1000 lines of debugged code per *year* on large projects, they wonder whether Prof. Brooks is living in outer space, perhaps on Planet Bug. After all, most of them can remember an all nighter when they produced a 1000-line program in one night. How could this be the annual output of anybody with an IQ > 50?

What Brooks pointed out is that large projects, with hundreds of programmers, are completely different than small projects and that the results obtained from small projects do not scale to large ones. In a large project, a huge amount of time is consumed planning how to divide the work into modules, carefully specifying the modules and their interfaces, and trying to imagine how the modules will interact, even before coding begins. Then the modules have to be coded and debugged in isolation. Finally, the modules have to be integrated and system as a whole has to be tested. The normal case is that each module works perfectly when tested by itself, but the system crashes instantly when all the pieces are put together. Brooks estimated the work as being

1/3 Planning
1/6 Coding
1/4 Module testing
1/4 System testing

In other words, writing the code is the easy part. The hard part is figuring out what the modules should be and making module *A* correctly talk to module *B*. In a small program written by a single programmer, all that is left over is the easy part.

The title of Brooks' book comes from his assertion that people and time are not interchangeable. There is no such unit as a man-month (or a person-month). If a project takes 15 people 2 years to build, it is inconceivable that 360 people could do it in one month and probably not possible to have 60 people do it in 6 months.

There are three reasons for this effect. First, the work cannot be fully parallelized. Until the planning is done and it has been determined what modules are needed and what their interfaces will be, no coding can be even started. On a two-year project, the planning alone may take 8 months.

Second, to fully utilize a large number of programmers, the work must be partitioned into large numbers of modules so everyone has something to do. Since every module may potentially interact with every other module, the number of module-module interactions that need to be considered grows as the square of the number of modules, that is, as the square of the number of programmers. This complexity quickly gets out of hand. Careful measurements of 63 software projects have confirmed that the trade-off between people and months is far from linear on large projects (Boehm, 1981).

Third, debugging is highly sequential. Setting ten debuggers on a problem does not find the bug ten times as fast. In fact, ten debuggers are probably slower than one because they will waste so much time talking to each other.

Brooks sums up his experience with trading-off people and time in Brooks' law:

Adding manpower to a late software project makes it later.

The problem with adding people is that they have to be trained in the project, the modules have to be redivided to match the larger number of programmers now available, many meetings will be needed to coordinate all the efforts and so on. Abdel-Hamid and Madnick (1991) confirmed this law experimentally. A slightly irreverent way of restating Brooks law is

It takes 9 months to bear a child, no matter how many women you assign to the job.

12.5.2 Team Structure

Commercial operating systems are large software projects and invariably require large teams of people. The quality of the people matters immensely. It has been known for decades that top programmers are 10× more productive than bad programmers (Sackman et al., 1968). The trouble is, when you need 200 programmers, it is hard to find 200 top programmers; you have to settle for a wide spectrum of qualities.

What is also important in any large design project, software or otherwise, is the need for architectural coherence. There should be one mind controlling the design. Brooks cites the Reims cathedral as an example of a large project that took decades to build, and in which the architects who came later subordinated their desire to put their stamp on the project to carry out the initial architect's plans. The result is an architectural coherence unmatched in other European cathedrals.

In the 1970s, Harlan Mills combined the observation that some programmers are much better than others with the need for architectural coherence to propose the **chief programmer team** paradigm (Baker, 1972). His idea was to organize a programming team like a surgical team rather than like a hog-butchering team. Instead of everyone hacking away like mad, one person wields the scalpel. Everyone else is there to provide support. For a 10-person project, Mills suggested the team structure of Fig. 12-9.

Three decades have gone by since this was proposed and put into production. Some things have changed (such as the need for a language lawyer—C is simpler

Title	Duties
Chief programmer	Performs the architectural design and writes the code
Copilot	Helps the chief programmer and serves as a sounding board
Administrator	Manages the people, budget, space, equipment, reporting, etc.
Editor	Edits the documentation, which must be written by the chief programmer
Secretaries	The administrator and editor each need a secretary
Program clerk	Maintains the code and documentation archives
Toolsmith	Provides any tools the chief programmer needs
Tester	Tests the chief programmer's code
Language lawyer	Part timer who can advise the chief programmer on the language

Figure 12-9. Mills' proposal for populating a 10-person chief programmer team.

than PL/I), but the need to have only one mind controlling the design is still true. And that one mind should be able to work 100% on designing and programming, hence the need for the support staff, although with help from the computer, a smaller staff will suffice now. But in its essence, the idea is still valid.

Any large project needs to be organized as a hierarchy. At the bottom level are many small teams, each headed by a chief programmer. At the next level, groups of teams must be coordinated by a manager. Experience shows that each person you manage costs you 10% of your time, so a full-time manager is needed for each group of 10 teams. These managers must be managed, and so on up the tree.

Brooks observed that bad news does not travel up the tree well. Jerry Saltzer of M.I.T. called this effect the **bad-news diode**. No chief programmer or manager wants to tell his boss that the project is 4 months late and has no chance whatsoever of meeting the deadline because there is a 1000-year old tradition of beheading the messenger who brings bad news. As a consequence, top management is generally in the dark about the state of the project. When it becomes obvious that the deadline cannot be met, top management responds by adding people, at which time Brooks' law kicks in.

In practice, large companies, which have had long experience producing software and know what happens if it is produced haphazardly, have a tendency to at least try to do it right. In contrast, smaller, newer companies, which are in a huge rush to get to market, do not always take the care to produce their software carefully. This haste often leads to far from optimal results.

Neither Brooks nor Mills foresaw the growth of the open source movement. Although it has had some successes, it remains to be seen if this is a viable model for producing large amounts of quality software once the novelty wears off. Recall that in its early days, radio was dominated by ham radio operators, but that soon gave way to commercial radio and later to commercial television. What is noticeable is that the open source software projects that have been most successful have clearly used the chief programmer model of having one mind control the architectural design (e.g., Linus Torvalds for the Linux kernel and Richard Stallman for the GNU C compiler).

12.5.3 The Role of Experience

Having experienced designers is critical to an operating systems project. Brooks points out that most of the errors are not in the code, but in the design. The programmers correctly did what they were told to do. What they were told to do was wrong. No amount of test software will catch bad specifications.

Brooks' solution is to abandon the classical development model of Fig. 12-10(a) and use the model of Fig. 12-10(b). Here the idea is to first write a main program that merely calls the top-level procedures, which are initially dummies. Starting on day 1 of the project, the system will compile and run, although it does nothing. As time goes on, modules are inserted into the full system. The result of this approach is that system integration testing is performed continuously, so errors in the design show up much earlier. In effect, the learning process caused by bad design decisions starts much earlier in the cycle.

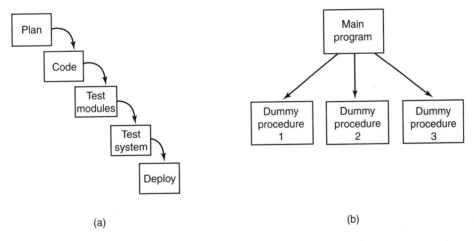

(a)   (b)

Figure 12-10. (a) Traditional software design progresses in stages. (b) Alternative design produces a working system (that does nothing) starting on day 1.

A little knowledge is a dangerous thing. Brooks observed what he called the **second system effect**. Often the first product produced by a design team is minimal because the designers are afraid it may not work at all. As a result, they are hesitant to put in many features. It the project succeeds, they build a follow-up system. Impressed by their own success, the second time the designers include all the bells and whistles that were intentionally left out the first time. As a result, the second system is bloated and performs poorly. The third time around they are sobered by the failure of the second system and are cautious again.

The CTSS-MULTICS pair is a clear case in point. CTSS was the first general-purpose timesharing system and was a huge success despite having minimal functionality. Its successor, MULTICS was too ambitious and suffered badly for it. The ideas were good, but there were too many new things so the system performed poorly for years and was never a big commercial success. The third system in this line of development, UNIX, was much more cautious and much more successful.

12.5.4 No Silver Bullet

In addition to *The Mythical Man Month*, Brooks also wrote an influential paper called "No Silver Bullet" (Brooks, 1987). In it, he argued that none of the many nostrums being hawked by various people at the time was going to generate an order-of-magnitude improvement in software productivity within a decade. Experience shows that he was right.

Among the silver bullets that were proposed were better high-level languages, object-oriented programming, artificial intelligence, expert systems, automatic programming, graphical programming, program verification, and programming environments. Perhaps the next decade will see a silver bullet, but maybe we will have to settle for gradual, incremental improvements.

12.6 TRENDS IN OPERATING SYSTEM DESIGN

Making predictions is always difficult—especially about the future. For example, in 1899, the head of the U.S. Patent Office, Charles H. Duell, asked then-President McKinley to abolish the Patent Office (and his job!), because, as he put it: "Everything that can be invented, has been invented" (Cerf and Navasky, 1984). Nevertheless, Thomas Edison showed up on his doorstep within a few years with a couple of new items, including the electric light, the phonograph, and the movie projector. Let us put new batteries in our crystal ball and venture a guess on where operating systems are going in the near future.

12.6.1 Large Address Space Operating Systems

As machines move from 32-bit address spaces to 64-bit address spaces, major shifts in operating system design become possible. A 32-bit address space is not really that big. If you tried to divide up 2^{32} bytes by giving everybody on earth his or her own byte, there would not be enough bytes to go around. In contrast, 2^{64} is about 2×10^{19}. Now everybody gets his or her personal 3 GB chunk.

What could we do with an address space of 2×10^{19} bytes? For starters, we could eliminate the file system concept. Instead, all files could be conceptually held in (virtual) memory all the time. After all, there is enough room in there for over 1 billion full-length movies, each compressed to 4 GB.

Another possible use is a persistent object store. Objects could be created in the address space and kept there until all references to them were gone, at which time they would be automatically deleted. Such objects would be persistent in the address space, even over shutdowns and reboots of the computer. With a 64-bit address space, objects could be created at a rate of 100 MB/sec for 5000 years before we run out of address space. Of course, to actually store this amount of data, a lot of disk storage would be needed for the paging traffic, but for the first time in history, the limiting factor would be disk storage, not address space.

With large numbers of objects in the address space, it becomes interesting to allow multiple processes to run in the same address space at the same time, to share the objects in a general way. Such a design would clearly lead to very different operating systems than we now have. Some thoughts on this concept are contained in (Chase et al., 1994).

Another operating system issue that will have to be rethought with 64-bit addresses is virtual memory. With 2^{64} bytes of virtual address space and 8-KB pages we have 2^{51} pages. Conventional pages tables do not scale well to this size, so something else is needed. Inverted page tables are a possibility, but other ideas have been proposed as well (Talluri et al., 1995). In any event there is plenty of room for new research on 64-bit operating systems.

12.6.2 Networking

Current operating systems were designed for standalone computers. Networking was an afterthought and is generally accessed through special programs, such as Web browsers, FTP, or telnet. In the future, networking will probably be the basis for all operating systems. A standalone computer without a network connection will be as rare as a telephone without a connection to the network. And it is likely that multimegabit/sec connections will be the norm.

Operating systems will have to change to adapt to this paradigm shift. The difference between local data and remote data may blur to the point that virtually no one knows or cares where data are stored. Computers anywhere may be able to treat data anywhere as local data. To a limited extent, this is already true with NFS, but it is likely to become far more pervasive and better integrated.

Access to the Web, which now requires special programs (browsers) may also become completely integrated into the operating system in a seamless way. The standard way to store information may become Web pages, and these pages may contain a wide variety of nontext items, including audio, video, programs, and more, all managed as the operating system's fundamental data.

12.6.3 Parallel and Distributed Systems

Another area that is up and coming is parallel and distributed systems. Current operating systems for multiprocessors and multicomputers are just standard uniprocessor operating systems with minor adjustments to the scheduler to handle parallelism a bit better. In the future, we may see operating systems where parallelism is much more central than it now is. This effect will be enormously stimulated if desktop machines soon have two, four, or more CPUs in a multiprocessor configuration. This may lead to many application programs being designed for multiprocessors, with the concurrent demand for better operating system support for them.

Multicomputers are likely to dominant large-scale scientific and engineering supercomputers in the coming years, but the operating systems for them are still fairly primitive. Process placement, load balancing, and communication need a lot of work.

Current distributed systems are often built as middleware because existing operating systems do not provide the right facilities for distributed applications. Future ones may be designed with distributed systems in mind, so all the necessary features are already present in the operating system from the start.

12.6.4 Multimedia

Multimedia systems are clearly a rising star in the computer world. It would surprise no one if computers, stereos, televisions, and telephones all merged into a single device capable of supporting high-quality still images, audio and video, and connected to high-speed networks so these files could easily be downloaded, exchanged, and accessed remotely. The operating systems for these devices, or even for standalone audio and video devices, will have to be substantially different from current ones. In particular, real-time guarantees will be needed, and these will drive the system design. Also, consumers will be very intolerant of hourly crashes of their digital television sets, so better software quality and fault tolerance will be required. Also, multimedia files tend to be very long, so file systems will have to change to be able to handle them efficiently.

12.6.5 Battery-Powered Computers

Powerful desktop PCs, probably with 64-bit address spaces, high-bandwidth networking, multiple processors, and high-quality audio and video will no doubt be commonplace soon. Their operating systems will have to be appreciably different from current ones to handle all these demands. However, an even faster growing segment of the market is battery-powered computers, including laptops, palmtops, Webpads, and various telephone hybrids. Some of these will have wireless connections to the outside world; others will run in disconnected mode when not docked at home. They will need different operating systems that are smaller, faster, more flexible, and more reliable than current ones. Various kinds of microkernel and extensible systems may form the basis here.

These operating systems will have to handle fully connected (i.e., wired), weakly connected (i.e., wireless), and disconnected operation, including data hoarding before going offline and consistency resolution when going back online better than current systems. They will also have to handle the problems of mobility better than current systems (e.g., find a laser printer, log onto it, and send it a file by radio). Power management, including extensive dialogs between the operating system and applications about how much battery power is left and how it can be best used, will be essential. Dynamic adaptation of applications to handle the limitations of tiny screens may become important. Finally, new input and output modes, including handwriting and speech, may require new techniques in the operating system to improve the quality. It is unlikely the operating system for a battery-powered, handheld wireless, voice-operated computer will have much in common with that of a desktop 64-bit four-CPU multiprocessor with a gigabit fiber-optic network connection. And of course, there will be innumerable hybrid machines with their own requirements.

12.6.6 Embedded Systems

One final area in which new operating systems will proliferate is embedded systems. The operating systems inside washing machines, microwave ovens, dolls, transistor (Internet?) radios, MP3 players, camcorders, elevators, and pacemakers will differ from all of the above and most likely from each other. Each one will probably be carefully tailored for its specific application, since it is unlikely anyone will ever stick a PCI card into a pacemaker to turn it into an elevator controller. Since all embedded systems run only a limited number of programs, known at design time, it may be possible to make optimizations not possible in general-purpose systems.

A promising idea for embedded systems are the extensible operating systems (e.g., Paramecium and Exokernel). These can be made as lightweight or heavyweight as the application in question demands, but in a consistent way across applications. Since embedded systems will be produced by the hundreds of millions, this will be a major market for new operating systems.

12.7 SUMMARY

Designing an operating system starts with determining what it should do. The interface should be simple, complete, and efficient. It should have a clear user interface paradigm, execution paradigm, and data paradigm.

The system should be well structured, using one of several known techniques, such as layering or client-server. The internal components should be orthogonal to one another and clearly separate policy from mechanism. Considerable thought should be given to issues such as static versus dynamic data structure, naming, binding time, and order of implementing modules.

Performance is important, but optimizations should be chosen carefully so as not to ruin the system's structure. Space-time trade-offs, caching, hints, exploiting locality, and optimizing the common case are often worth doing.

Writing a system with a couple of people is different than producing a big system with 300 people. In the latter case, team structure and project management play a crucial role in the success or failure of the project.

Finally, operating systems will have to change in the coming years to follow new trends and meet new challenges. These may include 64-bit address spaces, massive connectivity, desktop multiprocessors, multimedia, handheld wireless computers, and a huge variety of embedded systems. The coming years will be exciting times for operating system designers.

PROBLEMS

1. Moore's law describes a phenomenon of exponential growth similar to the population growth of an animal species introduced into a new environment with abundant food and no natural enemies. In nature, an exponential growth curve is likely eventually to become a sigmoid curve with an asymptotic limit when food supplies become limiting or predators learn to take advantage of new prey. Discuss some factors that may eventually limit the rate of improvement of computer hardware.

2. In Fig. 12-1, two paradigms are shown, algorithmic and event driven. For each of the following kinds of programs, which paradigm is likely to be easiest to use:
   (a) A compiler.
   (b) A photo editing program.
   (c) A payroll program.

3. On some of the early Apple Macintoshes, the GUI code was in ROM. Why?

4. Hierarchical file names always start at the top of the tree. Consider, for example, the file name */usr/ast/books/mos2/chap-12* rather than *chap-12/mos2/books/ast/usr*. In contrast, DNS names start at the bottom of the tree and work up. Is there some fundamental reason for this difference?

5. Corbató's dictum is that the system should provide minimal mechanism. Here is a list of POSIX calls that were also present in UNIX Version 7. Which ones are redundant, that is, could be removed with no loss of functionality because simple combinations of other ones could do the same job with about the same performance? Access, alarm, chdir, chmod, chown, chroot, close, creat, dup, exec, exit, fcntl, fork, fstat, ioctl, kill, link, lseek, mkdir, mknod, open, pause, pipe, read, stat, time, times, umask, unlink, utime, wait, and write.

6. Suppose that layers 3 and 4 in Fig. 12-2 were exchanged. What implications would that have for the design of the system?

7. In a microkernel-based client-server system, the microkernel just does message passing and nothing else. Is it possible for user processes to nevertheless create and use semaphores? If so, how? If not, why not?

8. Careful optimization can improve system call performance. Consider the case in which one system call is made every 10 msec. The average time of a call is 2 msec. If the system calls can be speeded up by a factor of two, how long does a process that took 10 sec to run now take?

9. Give a short discussion of mechanism versus policy in the context of retail stores.

10. Operating systems often do naming at two different levels: external and internal. What are the differences between these names with respect to

   (a) Length
   (b) Uniqueness
   (c) Hierarchies

11. One way to handle tables whose size is not known in advance is to make them fixed, but when one fills up, to replace it with a bigger one, copy the old entries over to the new one, then release the old one. What are the advantages and disadvantages of making the new one 2× the size of the original one, as compared to making it only 1.5× as big?

12. In Fig. 12-4, a flag, *found*, is used to tell whether the PID was located. Would it have been possible to forget about *found* and just test p at the end of the loop to see whether it got to the end or not?

13. In Fig. 12-5, the differences between the Pentium and the UltraSPARC are hidden by conditional compilation. Could this same approach be used to hide the difference between Pentiums with an IDE disk as the only disk and Pentiums with a SCSI disk as the only disk? Would it be a good idea?

14. Indirection is a way of making an algorithm more flexible. Does it have any disadvantages, and if so, which ones?

15. Can reentrant procedures have private static global variables? Discuss your answer.

16. The macro of Fig. 12-6(b) is clearly much more efficient than the procedure of Fig. 12-6(a). One disadvantage, however, is that it is hard to read. Are there any other disadvantages? If so, what are they?

17. Suppose that we need a way of computing whether the number of bits in a 32-bit word is odd or even. Devise an algorithm for performing this computation as fast as possible. You may use up to 256 KB of RAM for tables if need be. Write a macro to carry out your algorithm. *Extra Credit*: Write a procedure to do the computation by looping over the 32 bits. Measure how many times faster your macro is than the procedure.

18. In Fig. 12-7, we saw how GIF files use 8-bit values to index into a color palette. The same idea can be used with a 16-bit-wide color palette. Under what circumstances, if any, might a 24-bit color palette be a good idea?

19. One disadvantage of GIF is that the image must include the color palette, which increases the file size. What is the minimum image size for which an 8-bit-wide color palette breaks even? Now repeat this question for a 16-bit-wide color palette.

20. In the text we showed how caching path names can result in a significant speedup when looking up path names. Another technique that is sometimes used is having a daemon program that opens all the files in the root directory and keeps them open permanently, in order to force their i-nodes to be in memory all the time. Does pinning the i-nodes like this improve the path lookup even more?

21. Even if a remote file has not been removed since a hint was recorded, it may have been changed since the last time it was referenced. What other information might it be useful to record?

22. Consider a system that hoards references to remote files as hints, for example as (name, remote-host, remote-name). It is possible that a remote file will quietly be removed and then replaced. The hint may then retrieve the wrong file. How can this problem be made less likely to occur?

23. In the text it is stated that locality can often be exploited to improve performance. But consider a case where a program reads input from one source and continuously outputs to two or more files. Can an attempt to take advantage of locality in the file system lead to a decrease in efficiency here? Is there a way around this?

24. Fred Brooks claims that a programmer can write 1000 lines of debugged code per year, yet the first version of MINIX (13,000 lines of code) was produced by one person in under three years. How do you explain this discrepancy?

25. Using Brooks' figure of 1000 lines of code per programmer per year, make an estimate of the amount of money it took to produce Windows 2000. Assume that a programmer costs $100,000 per year (including overhead, such as computers, office space, secretarial support, and management overhead). Do you believe this answer? If not, what might be wrong with it?

26. As memory gets cheaper and cheaper, one could imagine a computer with a big battery-backed up RAM instead of a hard disk. At current prices, how much would a low-end RAM-only PC cost? Assume that a 1-GB RAM-disk is sufficient for a low-end machine. Is this machine likely to be competitive?

27. Name some features of a conventional operating system that are not needed in an embedded system used inside an appliance.

28. Write a procedure in C to do a double precision addition on two given parameters. Write the procedure using conditional compilation in such a way that it works on 16-bit machines and also on 32-bit machines.

29. Write programs that enter randomly generated short strings into an array and then can search the array for a given string using (a) a simple linear search (brute force), and (b) a more sophisticated method of your choice. Recompile your programs for array sizes ranging from small to as large as you can handle on your system. Evaluate the performance of both approaches). Where is the breakeven point?

30. Write a program to simulate an in-memory file system.

13

READING LIST AND BIBLIOGRAPHY

In the previous 12 chapters we have touched upon a variety of topics. This chapter is intended as an aid to readers interested in pursuing their study of operating systems further. Section 13.1 is a list of suggested readings. Section 13.2 is an alphabetical bibliography of all books and articles cited in this book.

In addition to the references given below, the *Proceedings of the n-th ACM Symposium on Operating Systems Principles* (ACM) held every other year and the *Proceedings of the n-th International Conference on Distributed Computing Systems* (IEEE) held every year are good places to look for recent papers on operating systems. So is the USENIX *Symposium on Operating Systems Design and Implementation*. Furthermore, *ACM Transactions on Computer Systems* and *Operating Systems Review* are two journals that often have relevant articles.

13.1 SUGGESTIONS FOR FURTHER READING

In the following sections, we give some suggestions for further reading. Unlike the papers cited in the sections entitled "RESEARCH ON ..." in the text, which were about current research, these references are mostly introductory or tutorial in nature. They can serve to present material present in this book from a different perspective or with a different emphasis, however.

13.1.1 Introduction and General Works

Kavi et al., "Computer Systems Research: The Pressure is On"
Where is systems research going? What is important now? How about developing robust, predictable systems? How about billion-transistor chips and billion-user worldwide systems? These are some of the questions and answers presented in this paper.

Milojicic, "Operating Systems: Now and in the Future,"
Suppose you were to ask six of the world's leading experts in operating systems a series of questions about the field and where it was going. Would you get the same answers? *Hint*: No. Find out what they said here.

Silberschatz et al., *Applied Operating System Concepts*
A general textbook on operating systems. It covers processes, storage management, distributed systems, and protection. Three case studies are given: UNIX, Linux, and Windows NT. The cover is full of dinosaurs. What, if anything, this has to do with operating systems anno 2000 is unclear.

Stallings, *Operating Systems, 4th Ed.*
Still another textbook on operating systems. It covers all the traditional topics, and also includes a small amount of material on distributed systems.

Stevens, *Advanced Programming in the UNIX Environment*
This book tells how to write C programs that use the UNIX system call interface and the standard C library. Examples are based on the System V Release 4 and the 4.4BSD versions of UNIX. The relationship of these implementations to POSIX is described in detail.

13.1.2 Processes and Threads

Andrews and Schneider, "Concepts and Notations for Concurrent Programming"
A tutorial and survey of processes and interprocess communication, including busy waiting, semaphores, monitors, message passing, and other techniques. The article also shows how these concepts are embedded in various programming languages.

Ben-Ari, *Principles of Concurrent Programming*
This little book is entirely devoted to the problems of interprocess communication. There are chapters on mutual exclusion, semaphores, monitors, and the dining philosophers problem, among others.

Silberschatz et al., *Applied Operating System Concepts*
Chapters 4 through 6 cover processes and interprocess communication, including scheduling, critical sections, semaphores, monitors, and classical interprocess communication problems.

13.1.3 Deadlocks

Coffman et al., "System Deadlocks"
A short introduction to deadlocks, what causes them, and how they can be prevented or detected.

Holt, "Some Deadlock Properties of Computer Systems"
A discussion of deadlocks. Holt introduces a directed graph model that can be used to analyze some deadlock situations.

Isloor and Marsland, "The Deadlock Problem: An Overview"
A tutorial on deadlocks, with special emphasis on database systems. A variety of models and algorithms are covered.

13.1.4 Memory Management

Denning, "Virtual Memory"
A classic paper on many aspects of virtual memory. Denning was one of the pioneers in this field, and was the inventor of the working set concept.

Denning, "Working Sets Past and Present"
A good overview of numerous memory management and paging algorithms. A comprehensive bibliography is included.

Knuth, *The Art of Computer Programming* Vol. 1
First fit, best fit, and other memory management algorithms are discussed and compared in this book.

Silberschatz et al, *Applied Operating System Concepts*
Chapters 9 and 10 deal with memory management, including swapping, paging, and segmentation. A variety of paging algorithms are mentioned.

13.1.5 Input/Output

Chen et al., "RAID: High Performance Reliable Secondary Storage"
The use of multiple disk drives in parallel for fast I/O is a trend in high-end systems. The authors discuss this idea and examine different organizations in terms of performance, cost, and reliability.

Computer, March 1994
   This issue of *Computer* contains eight articles on advanced I/O, and covers simulation, high performance storage, caching, I/O for parallel computers, and multimedia.

Geist and Daniel, "A Continuum of Disk Scheduling Algorithms"
   A generalized disk arm scheduling algorithm is presented. Extensive simulation and experimental results are given.

Gibson and Van Meter, "Network Attached Storage"
   The Internet is driving the need for vast amounts of storage for Web, database, and other servers. This situation has led to various designs in which freestanding storage can be attached to a network. In this paper, several architectures to accomplish this goal are discussed.

Ng, "Advances in Disk Technology: Performance Issues"
   The various factors in disk performance, such as linear bit density, rpm, number of heads, and number of sectors/track can be traded off in various ways to affect system performance. These issues and their impact on performance are covered in this easy-to-read paper on disk technology.

Ruemmler and Wilkes, "An Introduction to Disk Drive Modeling"
   The first part of this article is about modern disk drives and how they work inside, including topics such as seeking, zoning, track skewing, sparing, caching, read ahead, and much more. The second part is about modeling disk drives.

Walker and Cragon, "Interrupt Processing in Concurrent Processors"
   Implementing precise interrupts on superscalar computers is a challenging activity. The trick is to serialize the state and do it quickly. A number of the design issues and trade-offs are discussed here.

13.1.6 File Systems

Harbron, *File Systems*
   A book on file system design, applications, and performance. Both structure and algorithms are covered.

McKusick et al., "A Fast File System for UNIX"
   The UNIX file system was completely redone for 4.2 BSD. This paper describes the design of the new file system, with emphasis on its performance.

Silberschatz et al., *Applied Operating System Concepts*
   Chapter 11 is about file systems. It covers file operations, access methods, directories, and implementation, among other topics.

Stallings, *Operating Systems, 2nd Ed.*

Chapter 14 contains a fair amount of material about the security environment especially about hackers, viruses, and other threats.

13.1.7 Multimedia Operating Systems

ACM Computing Surveys, Dec. 1995

This issue of *ACM Computing Surveys* contains 21 short papers on various aspects of multimedia, ranging from low-level technical issues to high-level applications issues.

Computer, May 1995

The theme of this issue of *Computer* is multimedia and it contains six articles on the subject. After a brief introduction, the papers cover interactive television, multimedia servers, research management, and applications in medicine and education.

Lee, "Parallel Video Servers: A Tutorial"

Many organizations want to offer video on demand, which creates a need for scalable, fault-tolerant parallel video servers. The major issues of how to build them are covered here, including server architecture, striping, placement policies, load balancing, redundancy, protocols, and synchronization.

Leslie et al., "The Design and Implementation of an Operating System to Support Distributed Multimedia Applications,"

Many attempts at implementing multimedia have been based on adding features to an existing operating system. An alternative approach is to start all over again, as described here, and build a new operating system for multimedia from scratch, with no need to be backward compatible for anything. The result is a fairly different design than conventional systems.

Reddy, "I/O Issues in a Multimedia System"

When people talk about computer performance, they usually mean CPU performance. However, for multimedia, I/O performance is at least as important and that is the subject of this paper. Disk scheduling, buffer space trade-offs, and admission control are among the topics covered here.

Sitaram and Dan, "Multimedia Servers"

Multimedia servers have many differences with regular file servers. The authors discuss the differences in detail, especially in the areas of scheduling, the storage subsystem, and caching.

13.1.8 Multiple Processor Systems

Ahmad, "Gigantic Clusters: Where Are They and What Are They Doing?"

To get an idea of the state-of-the-art in large multicomputers, this is a good place to look. It describes the idea and gives an overview of some of the larger systems currently in operation. Given the working of Moore's law, it is a reasonable bet that the sizes mentioned here will double about every 2 years or so.

Bhoedjang et al., "User-Level Network Interface Protocols"

More and more multicomputers are putting the network interface board in user space to improve performance. Doing so raises many design issues, eleven of which are discussed here. A number of actual systems are also compared.

Computer, Dec 1996

This issue of *Computer* contains eight papers on multiprocessors. One of them is a tutorial on the semantics of shared memory, but the other seven deal with multiprocessor applications and performance.

Dubois et al., "Synchronization, Coherence, and Event Ordering in Multiprocessors"

A tutorial on synchronization in shared-memory multiprocessor systems. However, some of the ideas are equally applicable to single processor and distributed memory systems as well.

Kwok and Ahmad "Static Scheduling Algorithms for Allocating Directed Task Graphs to Multiprocessors"

Optimal job scheduling of a multicomputer or multiprocessor is possible when the characteristics of all the jobs are known in advance. The problem is that optimal scheduling takes far too long to compute. In this paper, the authors discuss and compare 27 known algorithms for attacking this problem in different ways.

Langendoen et al., "Models for Asynchronous Message Handling"

High performance in multicomputers depends critically on the performance of the message-passing system, especially how incoming messages are handled. The main choices are active messages, upcalls, and pop-up threads. The authors describe all three of them in this paper and then present experimental results comparing them on the same hardware platform.

Protic et al., *Distributed Shared Memory: Concepts and Systems*

For an introduction to distributed shared memory, this collection of 28 previously published papers is a good start. It collects many of the classic papers on models, algorithms, and implementations into a single convenient book.

Stenstrom et al., "Trends in Shared Memory Multiprocessing,"

Which way are multiprocessors going? The authors believe the future lies more in small-scale multiprocessors than large-scale ones. They also discuss models, architectures, and parallel software.

Waldo, "Alive and Well: Jini Technology Today"

For a quick introduction to Jini, its components, and how they fit together, this paper is a good starting place. Perhaps indicative of how information will be disseminated in the future, it has no bibliography of published papers, but instead provides the URLs of many Web resources on Jini.

13.1.9 Security

Computer, Feb 2000

The theme of this issue of *Computer* is biometrics, with six papers on the subject. They range from an introduction to the subject, through various specific technologies, to a paper dealing with the legal and privacy issues.

Denning, "The United States vs. Craig Neidorf"

When a young hacker discovered and published information about how the telephone system works, he was indicted for computer fraud. This article describes the case, which involved many fundamental issues, including freedom of speech. The article is followed by some dissenting views and a rebuttal by Denning.

Denning, *Information Warfare and Security*

Information has become a weapon of war, both military and corporate. The participants not only try to attack the other side's information systems, but safeguard their own as well. In this fascinating book, the author covers every conceivable topic relating to offensive and defensive strategy, from data diddling to packet sniffers. A must read for anyone seriously interested in computer security.

Hafner and Markoff, *Cyberpunk*

Three compelling tales of young hackers breaking into computers around the world are told here by the *New York Times* computer reporter who broke the Internet worm story (Markoff). *Computer*, Feb 2000

Johnson and Jajodia, "Exploring Steganography: Seeing the Unseen"

Steganography has a long history, going back to the days when the writer would shave the head of a messenger, write a message on the shaved head, and send him off after the hair grew back. Although current techniques are often hairy, they are also digital. For a thorough introduction to the subject as currently practiced, this paper is the place to start.

Ludwig, *The Giant Black Book of Computer Viruses, 2nd ed.*

If you want to write antivirus software and need to understand how viruses work down to the bit level, this is the book for you. Every kind of virus is discussed at length and actual code for most of them is supplied on a floppy disk. A thorough knowledge of programming the Pentium in assembly language is a must, however.

Milojicic, "Security and Privacy,"

Security has many facets including operating systems, networks, implications for privacy, and more. In this article, six security experts are interviewed on their thoughts on the subject.

Nachenberg, "Computer Virus-Antivirus Coevolution"

As soon as the antivirus developers find a way to detect and neutralize some class of computer virus, the virus writers go them one better and improve the virus. The cat-and-mouse game played by the virus and antivirus sides is discussed here. The author is not optimistic about the antivirus writers winning the war, which is bad news for computer users.

Pfleeger, *Security in Computing, 2nd ed.*

Although a number of books on computer security have been published, most of them cover only network security. This book does that, but also has three chapters on operating systems security, which make it a good reference for more background on that subject.

13.1.10 UNIX and Linux

Bovet and Cesati, *Understanding the Linux Kernel*

This book is probably the best overall discussion of the Linux kernel. It covers processes, memory management, file systems, signals, and much more.

IEEE, *Information Technology—Portable Operating System Interface (POSIX), Part 1: System Application Program Interface (API) [C Language]*

This is the standard. Some parts are actually quite readable, especially Annex B, "Rationale and Notes," which often sheds light on why things are done as they are. One advantage of referring to the standards document is that, by definition, there are no errors. If a typographical error in a macro name makes it through the editing process it is no longer an error, it is official.

Lewine, *POSIX Programmer's Guide*

This book describes the POSIX standard in more detail than the standards document, and includes discussions on how to convert older programs to POSIX and how to develop new programs for the POSIX environment, with examples.

Maxwell, *Linux Core Kernel Commentary*

The first 400 pages of this book contain a subset of the Linux kernel code. The last 150 pages consists of comments on the code, very much in the style of John Lions' classic book (1996). If you want to understand the Linux kernel in all its gory detail, this is the place to begin, but be warned: reading 40,000 lines of C is not for everyone.

McKusick et al., *The Design and Implementation of the 4.4 BSD Operating System*

The title says it all. But actually, the book is more general than that since all UNIX systems are fairly similar internally. This is an excellent reference for anyone wanting to learn about the internal workings of UNIX in general.

13.1.11 Windows 2000

Cusumano and Selby, "How Microsoft Builds Software"

Have you ever wondered how anyone could write a 29-million-line program (like Windows 2000) and have it work at all? To find out how Microsoft's build and test cycle is used to manage very large software projects, take a look at this paper.

Norton et al., *Complete Guide to Windows 2000 Professional*

If you are looking for a book that discusses how to set up and use Windows 2000 but also discusses many of the advanced features in some detail, such as the registry, FAT and NTFS file systems, ActiveX, DCOM, and networking this is a good choice. It lies in between the mass of books that tell where to click to get which effect and Solomon and Russinovich's book

Rector and Newcomer, *Win32 Programming*

If you are looking for one of those 1500-page books giving a summary of how to write Windows programs, this is not a bad start. It covers windows, devices, graphical output, keyboard and mouse input, printing, memory management, libraries, and synchronization, among many other topics. It requires knowledge of C or C++.

Solomon and Russinovich, *Inside Windows 2000, 3rd ed.*

If you want to learn how to use Windows 2000, there are hundreds of books out there. If you want to know how Windows 2000 works inside, this is your best bet. It covers numerous internal algorithms and data structures and in considerable technical detail. No other book comes close.

13.1.12 Design Principles

Brooks, "The Mythical Man Month: Essays on Software Engineering"
  Fred Brooks was one of the designers of IBM's OS/360. He learned the hard way what works and what does not work. The advice given in this witty, amusing, and informative book is as valid now as it was a quarter of a century ago when he first wrote it down.

Cooke et al., "UNIX and Beyond: An Interview with Ken Thompson"
  Designing an operating system is much more of an art than a science. Consequently, listening to experts in the field is a good way to learn about the subject. They do not come much more expert than Ken Thompson, co-designer of UNIX, Inferno, and Plan 9. In this wide-ranging interview, Thompson gives his thoughts on where we came from and where we are going in the field.

Corbató, "On Building Systems That Will Fail"
  In his Turing Award lecture, the father of timesharing addresses many of the same concerns that Brooks does in the *Mythical Man-Month*. His conclusion is that all complex systems will ultimately fail, and that to have any chance for success at all, it is absolutely essential to avoid complexity and strive for simplicity and elegance in design.

Crowley, *Operating Systems: A Design-Oriented Approach*
  Most textbooks on operating systems just describe the basic concepts (processes, virtual memory, etc.) and a few examples, but say nothing about how to design an operating system. This one is unique in devoting four chapters to the subject.

Lampson, "Hints for Computer System Design"
  Butler Lampson, one of the world's leading designers of innovative operating systems, has collected many hints, suggestions, and guidelines from his years of experience and put them together in this entertaining and informative article. Like Brooks' book, this is required reading for every aspiring operating system designer.

Wirth, "A Plea for Lean Software"
  Niklaus Wirth, a famous and experienced system designer, makes the case here for lean and mean software based on a few simple concepts, instead of the bloated mess that much commercial software is. He makes his point by discussing his Oberon system, a network-oriented, GUI-based operating system that fits in 200 KB, including the Oberon compiler and text editor.

13.2 ALPHABETICAL BIBLIOGRAPHY

ABDEL-HAMID, T., and MADNICK, S.: *Software Project Dynamics: An Integrated Approach*, Upper Saddle River, NJ: Prentice Hall, 1991.

ABRAM-PROFETA, E.L., and SHIN, K.G.: "Providing Unrestricted VCR Functions in Multicast Video-on-Demand Servers," *Proc. Int'l Conf. on Multimedia Comp. Syst.*, IEEE, pp. 66-75, 1998.

ABUTALEB, A., and LI, V.O.K.: "Paging Strategy Optimization in Personal Communication Systems Wireless Networks," *Wireless Networks*, vol. 3, pp. 195-204, Aug. 1997.

ACCETTA, M., BARON, R., GOLUB, D., RASHID, R., TEVANIAN, A., and YOUNG, M.: "Mach: A New Kernel Foundation for UNIX Development," *Proc. Summer 1986 USENIX Conf.*, USENIX, pp. 93-112, 1986.

ADAMS, G.B. III, AGRAWAL, D.P., and SIEGEL, H.J.: "A Survey and Comparison of Fault-Tolerant Multistage Interconnection Networks," *Computer*, vol. 20, pp. 14-27, June 1987.

ADAMS, A., and SASSE, M.A.: "Taming the Wolf in Sheep's Clothing," *Proc. Seventh Int'l Conf. on Multimedia*, ACM, pp. 101-107, 1999.

AHMAD, I.: "Gigantic Clusters: Where Are They and What Are They Doing?" *IEEE Concurrency*, vol. 8, pp. 83-85, April-June 2000.

ALEXANDROV, A.D., IBEL, M., SCHAUSER, K.E., and SCHEIMAN, C.J.: "UFO: a Personal Global File System Based on User-Level Extensions to the Operating System," *Trans. on Computer Systems*, vol. 16, pp. 207-233, Aug. 1998.

ALFIERI, R.A.: "An Efficient Kernel-Based Implementation of POSIX Threads," *Proc. Summer 1994 USENIX Tech. Conf.*, USENIX, pp. 59-72, June 1994.

ALVAREZ, G.A., BURKHARD, W.A., and CRISTIAN, F.: "Tolerating Multiple Failures in RAID Architectures with Optimal Storage And Uniform Declustering," *Proc. 24th Int'l Symp. on Computer Architecture*, ACM, pp. 62-72, 1997.

ANDERSON, T.E.: "The Performance of Spin Lock Alternatives for Shared-Memory Multiprocessors," *IEEE Trans. on Parallel and Distr. Systems*, vol. 1, pp. 6-16, Jan. 1990.

ANDERSON, T.E., BERSHAD, B.N., LAZOWSKA, E.D., and LEVY, H.M.: "Scheduler Activations: Effective Kernel Support for the User-level Management of Parallelism," *ACM Trans. on Computer Systems*, vol. 10, pp. 53-79, Feb. 1992.

ANDREWS, G.R.: *Concurrent Programming—Principles and Practice*, Redwood City, CA: Benjamin/Cummings, 1991.

ANDREWS, G.R., and SCHNEIDER, F.B.: "Concepts and Notations for Concurrent Programming," *Computing Surveys*, vol. 15, pp. 3-43, March 1983.

ARON, M., and DRUSCHEL, P.: "Soft Timers: Efficient Microsecond Software Timer Support for Network Processing," *Proc. 17th Symp. on Operating Systems Principles*, ACM, pp. 223-246, 1999.

ARORA, A.S., BLUMOFE, R.D., and PLAXTON, C.G.: "Thread Scheduling for Multiprogrammed Multiprocessors," *Proc. Tenth Symp. on Parallel Algorithms and Architectures*, ACM, pp. 119-129, 1998.

BAKER, F.T.: "Chief Programmer Team Management of Production Programming," *IBM Systems Journal*, vol. 11, pp. 1, 1972.

BAKER-HARVEY, M.: "ETI Resource Distributor: Guaranteed Resource Allocation and Scheduling in Multimedia Systems," *Proc. Third Symp. on Operating Systems Design and Implementation*, USENIX, pp. 131-144, 1999.

BALA, K., KAASHOEK, M.F., WEIHL, W.: "Software Prefetching and Caching for Translation Lookaside Buffers," *Proc. First Symp. on Operating System Design and Implementation*, USENIX, pp. 243-254, 1994.

BALLINTIJN, G., VAN STEEN, M., and TANENBAUM, A.S.: "Scalable Naming in Global Middleware," *Proc. 13th Int'l Conf. on Parallel and Distributed Systems*, ISCA, pp. 624-631, 2000.

BAYS, C.: "A Comparison of Next-Fit, First-Fit, and Best-Fit," *Commun. of the ACM*, vol. 20, pp. 191-192, March 1977.

BECK, M., BOHME, H., DZIADZKA, M., KUNITZ, U., MAGNUS, R., VERWORNER, D.: *Linux Kernel Internals, 2nd ed.*, Reading, MA: Addison-Wesley, 1998.

BELADY, L.A., NELSON, R.A., and SHEDLER, G.S.: "An Anomaly in Space-Time Characteristics of Certain Programs Running in a Paging Machine," *Commun. of the ACM*, vol. 12, pp. 349-353, June 1969.

BELL, D., and LA PADULA, L.: "Secure Computer Systems: Mathematical Foundations and Model," Technical Report MTR 2547 v2, Mitre Corp., Nov. 1973.

BEN-ARI, M.: *Principles of Concurrent Programming*, Upper Saddle River, NJ: Prentice Hall International, 1982.

BERNHARDT, C., and BIERSACK, E.W.: "The Server Array: A Scalable Video Server Architecture," in *High-Speed Networking for Multimedia Applications*, Amsterdam: Kluwer Publishers, 1996.

BERSHAD, B.N., SAVAGE, S., PARDYAK, P., BECKER, D., FIUCZYNSKI, M., and SIRER, E.G.: "Protection is a Software Issue," *Proc. Hot Topics in Operating Systems V*, IEEE, pp. 62-65, 1995a.

BERSHAD, B.N., SAVAGE, S., PARDYAK, P., SIRER, E.G.., FIUCZYNSKI, M., BECKER, D., CHAMBERS, C., and EGGERS, S.: "Extensibility, Safety, and Performance in the SPIN Operating System," *Proc. 15th Symp. on Operating Systems Principles*, ACM, pp. 267-284, 1995b.

BHOEDJANG, R.A.F.: *Communication Architectures for Parallel-Programming Systems*, Ph.D. Thesis, Vrije Universiteit, Amsterdam, The Netherlands, 2000.

BHOEDJANG, R.A.F., RUHL, T., and BAL, H.E.: "User-Level Network Interface Protocols," *Computer*, vol. 31, pp. 53-60, Nov. 1998.

BHUYAN, L.N., YANG, Q., and AGRAWAL, D.P.: "Performance of Multiprocessor Interconnection Networks," *Computer*, vol. 22, pp. 25-37, Feb. 1989.

BIBA, K.: "Integrity Considerations for Secure Computer Systems," Technical Report 76-371, U.S. Air Force Electronic Systems Division, 1977.

BIRRELL, A.D., and NELSON, B.J.: "Implementing Remote Procedure Calls," *ACM Trans. on Computer Systems*, vol. 2, pp. 39-59, Feb. 1984.

BISDIKIAN, C.C., and PATEL, B.V.: "Issues on Movie Allocation in Distributed Video-on-Demand Systems," *Proc. Int'l Conf. on Commun.*, IEEE, pp. 250-255, 1995.

BLAUM, M., BRADY, J., BRUCK, J., and MENON, J.: "EVENODD: An Optimal Scheme for Tolerating Double Disk Failures in RAID Architectures," *Proc. 21st Int'l Symp. on Computer Architecture*, ACM, pp. 245-254, 1994.

BLUMOFE, R.D., and LEISERSON, C.E.: "Scheduling Multithreaded Computations by Work Stealing," *Proc. 35th Annual Symp. on Foundations of Computer Science*, IEEE, pp. 356-368, Nov. 1994.

BOEHM, B.W.: *Software Engineering Economics*, Upper Saddle River, NJ: Prentice Hall, 1981.

BOLOSKY, W.J., FITZGERALD, R.P., and DOUCEUR, J.R.: "Distributed Schedule Management in the Tiger Video Fileserver," *Proc. 16th Symp. on Operating Systems Principles*, ACM, pp. 212-223, 1997.

BORN, G.,: *Inside the Microsoft Windows 98 Registry*, Redmond, WA: Microsoft Press, 1998.

BOVET, D.P., and CESATI, M.: *Understanding the Linux Kernel*, Sebastopol, CA: O'Reilly & Associates, 2000.

BRANDWEIN, R., KATSEFF, H., MARKOWITZ, R., MORTENSON, R., and ROBINSON, B.: "Nemesis: Multimedia Information Delivery," *Proc. Second ACM Int'l Conf. on Multimedia*, ACM, pp. 473-481, 1994.

BRICKER, A., GIEN, M., GUILLEMONT, M., LIPKIS, J., ORR, D., and ROZIER, M.: "A New Look at Microkernel-Based UNIX Operating Systems: Lessons in Performance and Compatibility," *Proc. EurOpen Spring '91 Conf.*, EurOpen, pp. 13-32, 1991.

BRINCH HANSEN, P.: "The Programming Language Concurrent Pascal," *IEEE Trans. on Software Engineering*, vol. SE-1, pp. 199-207, June 1975.

BROOKS, F. P., Jr.: *The Mythical Man-Month: Essays on Software Engineering*, Reading, MA: Addison-Wesley, 1975.

BROOKS, F.P., Jr. "No Silver Bullet—Essence and Accident in Software Engineering," *Computer*, vol. 20, pp. 10-19, April 1987.

BROOKS, F. P., Jr.: *The Mythical Man-Month: Essays on Software Engineering*, 20th Anniversary edition, Reading, MA: Addison-Wesley, 1995.

BUCHANAN, M., and CHIEN, A.: "Coordinated Thread Scheduling for Workstation Clusters Under Windows NT," *The USENIX Windows NT Workshop*, USENIX, pp. 47-??, 1997.

BUGNION, E., DEVINE, S., GOVIL, K., and ROSENBLUM, M.: "Disco: Running Commodity Operating Systems on Scalable Multiprocessors," *Trans. on Computer Systems*, vol. 15, pp. 412-447, Nov. 1997.

BUZZARD, G., JACOBSON, D., MACKEY, M., MAROVICH, S., and WILKES, J.: "An Implementation of the Hamlyn Sender-Managed Interface Architecture," *Proc. Second Symp. on Operating System Design and Implementation*, USENIX, pp. 245-259, Oct. 1996.

CANT, C.: *Writing Windows WDM Device Drivers*, Lawrence, KS: R&D Books, 1999.

CAO, P., LIN, S.B., VENKATARAMAN, S., and WILKES, J.: "The TickerTAIP Parallel RAID Architecture," *Trans. on Computer Systems*, vol. 12, pp. 236-269, Aug. 1994.

CAO, P., FELTEN, E.W., KARLIN, A.R., and LI, K.: "A Study of Integrated Prefetching and Caching Strategies," *Proc. SIGMETRICS Joint Int'l Conf. on Measurement and Modeling of Computer Systems*, ACM, pp. 188-197, 1995.

CARLEY, L.R., GANGER, G.R., and NAGLE, D.F.: "MEMS-Based Integrated Circuit Mass Storage Systems," *Commun. of the ACM*, vol. 43. pp. 73-80, Nov. 2000.

CARR, R.W., and HENNESSY, J.L.: "WSClock—A Simple and Effective Algorithm for Virtual Memory Management," *Proc. Eighth Symp. on Operating Systems Principles*, ACM, pp. 87-95, 1981.

CARRIERO, N., and GELERNTER, D.: "The S/Net's Linda Kernel," *ACM Trans. on Computer Systems*, vol. 4, pp. 110-129, May 1986.

CARRIERO, N., and GELERNTER, D.: "Linda in Context," *Commun. of the ACM*, vol. 32, pp. 444-458, April 1989.

CARTER, J.B., BENNETT, J.K., and ZWAENEPOEL, W.: "Techniques for Reducing Consistency-Related Communication in Distributed Shared-Memory Systems," *Trans. on Computer Systems*, vol. 13, pp. 205-243, Aug. 1995.

CERF, C., and NAVASKY, V.: *The Experts Speak*, New York: Random House, 1984.

CHANDRA, A., ADLER, M., GOYAL, P., and SHENOY, P.:s10 "Surplus Fair Scheduling: A Proportional-Share CPU Scheduling Algorithm for Symmetric Multiprocessors," *Proc. Fourth Symp. on Operating Systems Design and Implementation*, USENIX, pp. 45-58, 2000.

CHASE, J.S., LEVY, H.M., FEELEY, M.J., and LAZOWSKA, E.D.: "Sharing and Protection in a Single-Address-Space Operating System," *Trans. on Computer Systems*, vol. 12, pp. 271-307, Nov. 1994.

CHEN, P.M., LEE, E.K., GIBSON, G.A., KATZ, R.H., and PATTERSON, D.A.: "RAID: High Performance Reliable Storage," *Comp. Surv.*, vol. 26, pp. 145-185, June 1994.

CHEN, P.M., NG, W.T., CHANDRA,S., AYCOCK, C., RAJAMANI, G., and LOWELL, D.: "The Rio File Cache: Surviving Operating System Crashes," *Proc. Seventh Int'l Conf. on Architectural Support for Programming Languages and Operating Systems*, ACM, pp. 74-83, 1996.

CHEN, S., and THAPAR, M.: "A Novel Video Layout Strategy for Near-Video-on-Demand Servers," *Proc. Int'l Conf. on Multimedia Computing and Systems*, IEEE, pp. 37-45, 1997.

CHEN, S., and TOWSLEY, D.: "A Performance Evaluation of RAID Architectures," *IEEE Trans, on Computers*, vol. 45, pp. 1116-1130, Oct. 1996.

CHERITON, D.R.: "An Experiment Using Registers for Fast Message-Based Interprocess Communication," *Operating Systems Review*, vol. 18, pp. 12-20, Oct. 1984.

CHERITON, D.: "The V Distributed System," *Commun. of the ACM*, vol. 31, pp. 314-333, March 1988.

CHERVENAK, A., VELLANKI, V., and KURMAS, Z.: "Protecting File Systems: A Survey of Backup Techniques," *Proc. 15th IEEE Symp. on Mass Storage Systems*, IEEE, 1998.

CHOW, T.C.K., and ABRAHAM, J.A.: "Load Balancing in Distributed Systems," *IEEE Trans. on Software Engineering*, vol. SE-8, pp. 401-412, July 1982.

CLARK, P.C., and HOFFMAN, L.J.: "BITS: A Smartcard Protected Operating System," *Commun. of the ACM*, vol. 37, pp. 66-70, Nov. 1994.

COFFMAN, E.G., ELPHICK, M.J., and SHOSHANI, A.: "System Deadlocks," *Computing Surveys*, vol. 3, pp. 67-78, June 1971.

COMER, D.: *Operating System Design. The Xinu Approach*, Upper Saddle River, NJ: Prentice Hall, 1984.

COOKE, D., URBAN, J., and HAMILTON, S.: "Unix and Beyond: An Interview with Ken Thompson," *Computer*, vol. 32, pp. 58-64, May 1999.

CORBALAN, J., MARTORELL, X., and LABARTA, J.: "Performance-Driven Processor Allocation," *Proc. Fourth Symp. on Operating Systems Design and Implementation*, **USENIX, pp. 59-71, 2000.**

CORBATO, F.J.: "On Building Systems That Will Fail," *Commun. of the ACM*, vol. 34, pp. 72-81, June 1991.

CORBATO, F.J., MERWIN-DAGGETT, M., and DALEY, R.C.: "An Experimental Time-Sharing System," *Proc. AFIPS Fall Joint Computer Conf.*, AFIPS, pp. 335-344, 1962.

CORBATO, F.J., SALTZER, J.H., and CLINGEN, C.T.: "MULTICS—The First Seven Years," *Proc. AFIPS Spring Joint Computer Conf.*, AFIPS, pp. 571-583, 1972.

CORBATO, F.J., and VYSSOTSKY, V.A.: "Introduction and Overview of the MULTICS System," *Proc. AFIPS Fall Joint Computer Conf.*, AFIPS, pp. 185-196, 1965.

COURTOIS, P.J., HEYMANS, F., and PARNAS, D.L.: "Concurrent Control with Readers and Writers," *Commun. of the ACM*, vol. 10, pp. 667-668, Oct. 1971.

CRANOR, C.D., and PARULKAR, G.M.: "The UVM Virtual Memory System," *Proc. USENIX Annual Tech. Conf.*, USENIX, pp. 117-130, 1999.

CROWLEY, C:. *Operating Systems: A Design-Oriented Approach*, Chicago: Irwin, 1997.

CUSUMANO, M.A., and SELBY, R.W.: "How Microsoft Builds Software," *Commun. of the ACM*, vol. 40, pp. 53-61, June 1997.

DALEY, R.C., and DENNIS, J.B.: "Virtual Memory, Process, and Sharing in MULTICS," *Commun. of the ACM*, vol. 11, pp. 306-312, May 1968.

DAN, A., SITARAM, D., and SHAHABUDDIN, P: "Scheduling Policies for an On-Demand Video Server with Batching," *Proc. Second Int'l Conf. on Multimedia*, ACM, pp. 15-23, 1994.

DANDAMUDI, S.P.: "Reducing Run Queue Contention in Shared Memory Multiprocessors," *Computer*, vol. 30, pp. 82-89, March 1997.

DE JONGE, W., KAASHOEK, M.F., and HSIEH, W.C.: "The Logical Disk: A New Approach to Improving File Systems," *Proc. 14th Symp. on Operating Systems Principles*, ACM, pp. 15-28, 1993.

DENNING, D.: "A Lattice Model of Secure Information Flow," *Commun. of the ACM*, vol. 19, pp. 236-243, 1976.

DENNING, D.: "The United States vs. Craig Neidorf," *Commun. of the ACM*, vol. 34, pp. 22-43, March 1991.

DENNING, D.: *Information Warfare and Security*, Reading, MA: Addison-Wesley, 1999.

DENNING, P.J.: "The Working Set Model for Program Behavior," *Commun. of the ACM*, vol. 11, pp. 323-333, 1968a.

DENNING, P.J.: "Thrashing: Its Causes and Prevention," *Proc. AFIPS National Computer Conf.*, AFIPS, pp. 915-922, 1968b.

DENNING, P.J.: "Virtual Memory," *Computing Surveys*, vol. 2, pp. 153-189, Sept. 1970.

DENNING, P.J.: "Working Sets Past and Present," *IEEE Trans. on Software Engineering*, vol. SE-6, pp. 64-84, Jan. 1980.

DENNIS, J.B., and VAN HORN, E.C.: "Programming Semantics for Multiprogrammed Computations," *Commun. of the ACM*, vol. 9, pp. 143-155, March 1966.

DEVARAKONDA, M., KISH, B., and MOHINDRA, A.: "Recovery in the Calypso File System," *Trans. on Computer Systems*, vol. 14, pp. 287-310, Aug. 1996.

DIFFIE, W., and HELLMAN, M.E.: "New Directions in Cryptography," *IEEE Trans. on Information Theory*, vol. IT-22, pp. 644-654, Nov. 1976.

DIJKSTRA, E.W.: "Co-operating Sequential Processes," in *Programming Languages*, Genuys, F. (Ed.), London: Academic Press, 1965.

DIJKSTRA, E.W.: "The Structure of THE Multiprogramming System," *Commun. of the ACM*, vol. 11, pp. 341-346, May 1968.

DUBOIS, M., SCHEURICH, C., and BRIGGS, F.A.: "Synchronization, Coherence, and Event Ordering in Multiprocessors," *Computer*, vol. 21, pp. 9-21, Feb. 1988.

DOUCEUR, J.R., and BOLOSKY, W.J.: "A Large-Scale Study of File-System Contents," *Proc. Int'l Conf. on Measurement and Modeling of Computer Systems*, ACM, pp. 59-70, 1999.

DRUSCHEL, P., PAI, V.S., and ZWAENEPOEL, W.: "Extensible Systems are Leading OS Research Astray," *Proc. Hot Topics in Operating Systems VI*, IEEE, pp. 38-42, 1997.

DUDA, K.J., and CHERITON, D.R.: "Borrowed-Virtual-Time (BVT) Scheduling: Supporting Latency-Sensitive Threads in a General-Purpose Scheduler," *Proc. 17th Symp. on Operating Systems Principles*, ACM, pp. 261-276, 1999.

EAGER, D.L., LAZOWSKA, E.D., and ZAHORJAN, J.: "Adaptive Load Sharing in Homogeneous Distributed Systems," *IEEE Trans. on Software Engineering*, vol. SE-12, pp. 662-675, May 1986.

EAGER, D.L., VERNON, M., and ZAHORJAN, J.: "Optimal and Efficient Merging Schedules for Video-on-Demand Servers," *Proc. Seventh Int'l Conf. on Multimedia*, ACM, pp. 199-202, 1999.

EDLER, J., LIPKIS, J., and SCHONBERG, E.: "Process Management for Highly Parallel UNIX Systems," *Proc. USENIX Workshop on UNIX and Supercomputers*, USENIX, pp. 1-17, Sept. 1988.

EGAN, J.I., and TEIXEIRA, T.J.: *Writing a UNIX Device Driver, 2nd ed.*, New York: John Wiley, 1992.

EL GAMAL, A.: "A Public Key Cryptosystem and Signature Scheme Based on Discrete Logarithms," *IEEE Trans. on Information Theory*, vol. IT-31, pp. 469-472, July 1985.

ELLIS, C.S.: "The Case for Higher-Level Power Management," *Proc. Hot Topics in Operating Systems VII*, IEEE, pp. 162-167, 1999.

ENGLER, D.R., GUPTA, S.K., and KAASHOEK, M.F.: "AVM: Application-Level Virtual Memory," *Proc. Hot Topics in Operating Systems V*, IEEE, pp. 72-77, 1995a.

ENGLER, D., CHELF, B., CHOU, A., HALLEM, S.: "Checking System Rules Using System-Specific Programmer-Written Compiler Extensions," *Proc. Fourth Symp. on Operating Systems Design and Implementation*, USENIX, pp. 1-16, 2000.

ENGLER, D.R., and KAASHOEK, M.F.: "Exterminate All Operating System Abstractions," *Proc. Hot Topics in Operating Systems V*, IEEE, pp. 78-83, 1995.

ENGLER, D.R., KAASHOEK, M.F., and O'TOOLE, J. Jr.: "Exokernel: An Operating System Architecture for Application-Level Resource Management," *Proc. 15th Symp. on Operating Systems Principles*, ACM, pp. 251-266, 1995.

EVEN, S.: *Graph Algorithms*, Potomac, MD: Computer Science Press, 1979.

FABRY, R.S.: "Capability-Based Addressing," *Commun. of the ACM*, vol. 17, pp. 403-412, July 1974.

FEELEY, M.J., MORGAN, W.E., PIGHIN, F.H., KARLIN, A.R., LEVY, H.M., and THEK-KATH, C.A.: "Implementing Global Memory Management in a Workstation Cluster," *Proc. 15th Symp. on Operating Systems Principles*, ACM, pp. 201-212, 1995.

FERGUSON, D., YEMINI, Y., and NIKOLAOU, C.: "Microeconomic Algorithms for Load Balancing in Distributed Computer Systems," *Proc. Eighth Int'l Conf. on Distributed Computing Systems*, IEEE, pp. 491-499, 1988.

FEUSTAL, E.A.: "The Rice Research Computer—A Tagged Architecture," *Proc. AFIPS Conf.*, AFIPS, 1972.

FLINN, J., and SATYANARAYANAN, M.: "Energy-Aware Adaptation for Mobile Applications," *Proc. 17th Symp. on Operating Systems Principles*, ACM, pp. 48-63, 1999.

FLUCKIGER, F.: *Understanding Networked Multimedia*, Upper Saddle River, NJ: Prentice Hall, 1995.

FORD, B., HIBLER, M., LEPREAU, J., TULLMAN, P., BACK, G., CLAWSON, S.: "Micro-kernels Meet Recursive Virtual Machines," *Proc. Second Symp. on Operating Systems Design and Implementation*, USENIX, pp. 137-151, 1996.

FORD, B., and SUSARLA, S.: "CPU Inheritance Scheduling," *Proc. Second Symp. on Operating Systems Design and Implementation*, USENIX, pp. 91-105, 1996.

FORD, B., BACK, G., BENSON, G., LEPREAU, J., LIN, A., SHIVERS, O.: "The Flux OSkit: A Substrate for Kernel and Language Research," *Proc. 17th Symp. on Operating Systems Principles*, ACM, pp. 38-51, 1997.

FOTHERINGHAM, J.: "Dynamic Storage Allocation in the Atlas Including an Automatic Use of a Backing Store," *Commun. of the ACM*, vol. 4, pp. 435-436, Oct. 1961.

GAFSI, J., and BIERSACK, E.W.: "A Novel Replica Placement Strategy for Video Servers," *Proc. Sixth Int'l Workshop on Interactive and Distrib. Multimedia Systems*, ACM, pp. 321-335.

GEIST, R., and DANIEL, S.: "A Continuum of Disk Scheduling Algorithms," *ACM Trans. on Computer Systems*, vol. 5, pp. 77-92, Feb. 1987.

GELERNTER, D.: "Generative Communication in Linda," *ACM Trans. on Programming Languages and Systems*, vol. 7, pp. 80-112, Jan. 1985.

GHORMLEY, D., PETROU, D., RODRIGUES, S., VAHDAT, A., and ANDERSON, T.E.: "SLIC: An Extensible System for Commodity Operating Systems," *Proc. USENIX Annual Tech. Conf.*, USENIX, pp. 39-46, 1998.

GIBSON, G.A., and VAN METER, R.: "Network Attached Storage," *Commun. of the ACM*, vol. 43, pp. 37-45, Nov. 2000.

GILL, D.S., ZHOU, S., and SANDHU, H.S.: "A Case Study of File System Workload in a Large-Scale Distributed Environment," *Proc. 1994 Conf. on Measurement and Modeling of Computer Systems*, ACM, pp. 276-277, 1994.

GOLDBERG, L.A., GOLDBERG, P.W., PHILLIPS, C.A., and SORKIN, G.B.: "Constructing Virus Phylogenies," *Journal of Algorithms*, vol. 26, pp. 188-208, Jan. 1998.

GOLDEN, D., and PECHURA, M.: "The Structure of Microcomputer File Systems," *Commun. of the ACM*, vol. 29, pp. 222-230, March 1986.

GONG, L.: *Inside Java 2 Platform Security*, Reading, MA: Addison-Wesley, 1999.

GOODHEART, B., and COX, J.: *The Magic Garden Explained*, Upper Saddle River, NJ: Prentice Hall, 1994.

GOVIL, K., TEODOSIU, D., HUANG, Y., and ROSENBLUM. M.: "Cellular Disco: Resource Management Using Virtual Clusters on Shared-Memory Multiprocessors," *Proc. 17th Symp. on Operating Systems Principles*, ACM, 1999, pp. 154-169 .

GOYAL, P., GUO, X., and VIN, H.M.: "A Hierarchical CPU Scheduler for Multimedia Operating Systems," *Proc. Second Symp. on Operating Systems Design and Implementation*, USENIX, pp. 107-121, 1996.

GRAHAM, R.: "Use of High-Level Languages for System Programming," Project MAC Report TM-13, M.I.T., Sept. 1970.

GRIFFIN, J.L., SCHLOSSER, S.W., GANGER, G.R., and NAGLE, D.F.: "Operating System Management of MEMS-based Storage Devices," *Proc. Fourth Symp. on Operating Systems Design and Implementation*, USENIX, pp. 87-102, 2000.

GRIMM, R., and BERSHAD, B: "Security for Extensible Systems," *Proc. Hot Topics in Operating Systems VI*, IEEE, pp. 62-66, 1997

GRIWODZ, C., BAR. M., and WOLF, L.C.: "Long-Term Movie Popularity Models in Video-on-Demand Systems," *Proc. Fifth Int'l Conf. on Multimedia*, ACM, pp. 349-357, 1997.

GROPP, W., LUSK, E., and SKJELLUM, A.: *Using MPI: Portable Parallel Programming with the Message Passing Interface*, Cambridge, MA: M.I.T. Press, 1994.

GROSSMAN, D., and SILVERMAN, H.: "Placement of Records on a Secondary Storage Device to Minimize Access Time," *Journal of the ACM*, vol. 20, pp. 429-438, 1973

HAFNER, K., and MARKOFF, J.: *Cyberpunk*, New York: Simon and Schuster, 1991.

HAND, S.M.: "Self-Paging in the Nemesis Operating System," *Proc. Third Symp. on Operating Systems Design and Implementation*, USENIX, pp. 73-86, 1999.

HARBRON, T.R.: *File Systems*, Upper Saddle River, NJ: Prentice Hall, 1988.

HARCHOL-BALTER, M., and DOWNEY, A.B.: "Exploiting Process Lifetime Distributions for Dynamic Load Balancing," *Proc. SIGMETRICS Conf. on Measurement and Modeling of Computer Systems*, ACM, pp. 13-24, 1996.

HARRISON, M.A., RUZZO, W.L., and ULLMAN, J.D.: "Protection in Operating Systems," *Commun. of the ACM*, vol. 19, pp. 461-471, Aug. 1976.

HART, J.M.: *Win32 System Programming*, Reading, MA: Addison-Wesley, 1997.

HARTIG, H., HOHMUTH, M., LIEDTKE, J., and SCHONBERG, S.: "The Performance of Kernel-Based Systems," *Proc. 16th Symp. on Operating Systems Principles*, ACM, pp. 66-77, 1997.

HARTMAN, J.H., and OUSTERHOUT, J.K.: "The Zebra Striped Network File System," *Trans. on Computer Systems*, vol. 13, pp. 274-310, Aug. 1995.

HAUSER, C., JACOBI, C., THEIMER, M., WELCH, B., and WEISER, M.: "Using Threads in Interactive Systems: A Case Study," *Proc. 14th Symp. on Operating Systems Principles*, ACM, pp. 94-105, 1993.

HAVENDER, J.W.: "Avoiding Deadlock in Multitasking Systems," *IBM Systems Journal*, vol. 7, pp. 74-84, 1968.

HEBBARD, B., et al.: "A Penetration Analysis of the Michigan Terminal System," *Operating Systems Review*, vol. 14, pp. 7-20, Jan. 1980.

HEIDEMANN, J.S., and POPEK, G.J.: "File-System Development with Stackable Layers," *Trans. on Computer Systems*, vol. 12, pp. 58-89, Feb. 1994.

HEYBEY, A., SULLIVAN, M., ENGLAND, P.: "Calliope: A Distributed Scalable Multimedia Server," *Proc. USENIX Annual Tech. Conf.*, USENIX, pp. 75-86, 1996.

HIPSON, P.D.: *Mastering Windows 2000 Registry*, Alameda, CA: Sybex, 2000.

HOARE, C.A.R.: "Monitors, An Operating System Structuring Concept," *Commun. of the ACM*, vol. 17, pp. 549-557, Oct. 1974; Erratum in *Commun. of the ACM*, vol. 18, p. 95, Feb. 1975.

HOLT, R.C.: "Some Deadlock Properties of Computer Systems," *Computing Surveys*, vol. 4, pp. 179-196, Sept. 1972.

HONEYMAN, P., ADAMSON, A., COFFMAN, K., JANAKIRAMAN, J., JERDONEK, R., and REES, J.: "Secure Videoconferencing," *The Seventh USENIX Security Symp.*, USENIX, pp. 123-133, 1998.

HOWARD, J.H., KAZAR, M.J., MENEES, S.G., NICHOLS, D.A., SATYANARAYANAN, M., SIDEBOTHAM, R.N., and WEST, M.J.: "Scale and Performance in a Distributed File System," *ACM Trans. on Computer Systems*, vol. 6, pp. 55-81, Feb. 1988.

HUCK, J., and HAYS, J.: "Architectural Support for Translation Table Management in Large Address Space Machines," *Proc. 20th Int'l Symp. on Computer Architecture*, ACM, pp. 39-50, 1993.

HUTCHINSON, N.C., MANLEY, S., FEDERWISCH, M., HARRIS, G., HITZ, D., KLEIMAN, S., and O'MALLEY, S.: "Logical vs. Physical File System Backup," *Proc. Third Symp. on Operating Systems Design and Implementation*, USENIX, pp. 239-249, 1999.

IEEE: *Information Technology—Portable Operating System Interface (POSIX), Part 1: System Application Program Interface (API) [C Language]*, New York: Institute of Electrical and Electronics Engineers, Inc., 1990

ISLOOR, S.S., and MARSLAND, T.A.: "The Deadlock Problem: An Overview," *Computer*, vol. 13, pp. 58-78, Sept. 1980.

ITZKOVITZ, A., and SCHUSTER, A.: "MultiView and Millipage—Fine-Grain Sharing in Page-Based DSMs," *Proc. Third Symp. on Operating Systems Design and Implementation*, USENIX, pp. 215-228, 1999.

IVENS, K.: *Optimizing the Windows Registry*, Foster City, CA: IDG Books Worldwide, 1998.

JOHNSON, K.L., KAASHOEK, M.F., and WALLACH, D.A.: "CRL: High-Performance All-Software Distributed Shared Memory," *Proc. 15th Symp. on Operating Systems Principles*, ACM, pp. 213-226, 1995.

JOHNSON, N.F., and JAJODIA, S.: "Exploring Steganography: Seeing the Unseen," *Computer*, vol. 31, pp. 26-34, Feb. 1998.

JONES, M.B., ROSU, D., and ROSU, M.-C.: "CPU Reservations and Time Constraints Efficient, Predictable Scheduling of Independent Activities," *Proc. 16th Symp. on Operating Systems Principles*, ACM, pp. 198-211, 1997.

KAASHOEK, M.F., ENGLER, D.R., GANGER, G.R., BRICENO, H., HUNT, R., MAZIERES, D., PINCKNEY, T., GRIMM, R., JANNOTTI, J., and MACKENZIE, K.: "Application Performance and Flexibility on Exokernel Systems," *Proc. 16th Symp. on Operating Systems Principles*, ACM, pp. 52-65, 1997.

KABAY, M.: "Flashes from the Past," *Information Security*, p. 17, 1997.

KALLAHALLA, M., and VARMAN, P.J.: "Optimal Read-Once Parallel Disk Scheduling," *Proc. Sixth Workshop on I/O in Parallel and Distributed Systems*, ACM, pp. 68-77, 1999.

KARACALI, B., TAI, K.C., and VOUK, M.A.: "Deadlock Detection of EFSMs Using Simultaneous Reachability Analysis," *Proc. Int'l Conference on Dependable Systems and Networks (DSN 2000)*, IEEE, pp. 315-324, 2000.

KARLIN, A.R., LI, K., MANASSE, M.S., and OWICKI, S.: "Empirical Studies of Competitive Spinning for a Shared-Memory Multiprocessor," *Proc. 13th Symp. on Operating Systems Principles*, ACM, pp. 41-54, 1991.

KARLIN, A.R., MANASSE, M.S., McGEOCH, L., and OWICKI, S.: "Competitive Randomized Algorithms for Non-Uniform Problems," *Proc. First Annual ACM Symp. on Discrete Algorithms*, ACM, pp. 301-309, 1989.

KARPOVICH, J.F., GRIMSHAW, A.S., and FRENCH, J.C.: "Extensible File System (ELFS): An Object-Oriented Approach to High Performance File I/O," *Proc. Ninth Annual Conf. on Object-Oriented Programming Systems, Language, and Applications*, ACM, pp. 191-204, 1994.

KATCHER, D.I., KETTLER, K.A., and STROSNIDER, J.K.: "Real-Time Operating Systems for Multimedia Processing," *Proc. Hot Topics in Operating Systems V*, IEEE, 1995.

KAUFMAN, C., PERLMAN, R., and SPECINER, M.: *Network Security*, Upper Saddle River, NJ: Prentice Hall, 1995.

KAVI, K., BROWNE, J.C., and TRIPATHI, A.: "Computer Systems Research: The Pressure is On," *Computer*, vol. 32, pp. 30-39, Jan 1999.

KELEHER, P., COX, A., DWARKADAS, S., and ZWAENEPOEL, W.: "TreadMarks: Distributed Shared Memory on Standard Workstations and Operating Systems," *Proc. USENIX Winter 1994 Conf.*, USENIX, pp. 115-132, 1994.

KERNIGHAN, B.W., and PIKE, R.: *The UNIX Programming Environment*, Upper Saddle River, NJ: Prentice Hall, 1984.

KHALIDI, Y.A., and NELSON, M.N.: "Extensible File Systems in Spring," *Proc. 14th Symp. on Operating Systems Principles*, ACM, pp. 1-14, 1993.

KLEIN, D.V.: "Foiling the Cracker: A Survey of, and Improvements to, Password Security," *Proc. UNIX Security Workshop II*, USENIX, Summer 1990.

KLEINROCK, L.: *Queueing Systems. Vol. 1*, New York: John Wiley, 1975.

KLINE, R.L., and GLINERT, E.P.: "Improving GUI Accessibility for People with Low Vision," *Proc. Conf. on Human Factors in Computing Systems*, ACM, pp. 114-121, 1995.

KNUTH, D.E.: *The Art of Computer Programming, Volume 1: Fundamental Algorithms, 2nd Ed.*, Reading, MA: Addison-Wesley, 1973.

KOCHAN, S.G., and WOOD, P.H.: *UNIX Shell Programming*, Indianapolis, IN: Hayden Books, 1990.

KRAVETS, R., and KRISHNAN, P.: "Power Management Techniques for Mobile Communication," *Proc. Fourth ACM/IEEE Int'l Conf. on Mobile Computing and Networking*, ACM/IEEE, pp. 157-168, 1998.

KRISHNAN, R.: "Timeshared Video-on-Demand: A Workable Solution," *IEEE Multimedia*, vol. 6, Jan.-March 1999, pp. 77-79.

KRUEGER, P., LAI, T.-H., and DIXIT-RADIYA, V.A.: "Job Scheduling is More Important than Processor Allocation for Hypercube Computers," *IEEE Trans. on Parallel and Distr. Systems*, vol. 5, pp. 488-497, May 1994.

KUMAR, V.P., and REDDY, S.M.: "Augmented Shuffle-Exchange Multistage Interconnection Networks," *Computer*, vol. 20, pp. 30-40, June 1987.

KWOK, Y.-K., AHMAD, I.: "Static Scheduling Algorithms for Allocating Directed Task Graphs to Multiprocessors," *Computing Surveys*, vol. 31, pp. 406-471, Dec. 1999.

LAMPORT, L.: "Password Authentication with Insecure Communication," *Commun. of the ACM*, vol. 24, pp. 770-772, Nov. 1981.

LAMPSON, B.W.: "A Scheduling Philosophy for Multiprogramming Systems," *Commun. of the ACM*, vol. 11, pp. 347-360, May 1968.

LAMPSON, B.W.: "A Note on the Confinement Problem," *Commun. of the ACM*, vol. 10, pp. 613-615, Oct. 1973.

LAMPSON, B.W.: "Hints for Computer System Design," *IEEE Software*, vol. 1, pp. 11-28, Jan. 1984.

LAMPSON, B.W., and STURGIS, H.E.: "Crash Recovery in a Distributed Data Storage System," Xerox Palo Alto Research Center Technical Report, June 1979.

LANDWEHR, C.E.: "Formal Models of Computer Security," *Computing Surveys*, vol. 13, pp. 247-278, Sept. 1981.

LANGENDOEN, K., BHOEDJANG, R., and BAL, H.E.: "Models for Asynchronous Message Passing," *IEEE Concurrency*, vol. 5, pp. 28-37, April-June 1997.

LEBECK, A.R., FAN, X., ZENG, H., ELLIS, C.S.: "Power Aware Page Allocation," *Proc. Ninth Int'l Conf. on Architectural Support for Programming Languages and Operating Systems*, ACM, 2000.

LEE, J.Y.B.: "Parallel Video Servers: A Tutorial," *IEEE Multimedia*, vol. 5, pp. 20-28, April-June 1998.

LEE, W., SU, D., WIJESEKERA, D., SRIVASTAVA, J., KENCHAMMANA-HOSEKOTE, D., and FORESTI, M.: "Experimental Evaluation of PFS Continuous Media File System," *Proc. Sixth Int'l Conf. on Information and Knowledge Management*, ACM, pp. 246-253, 1997.

LESLIE, I., McAULEY, D., BLACK, R., ROSCOE, T., BARHAM, P., EVERS, D., FAIRBAIRNS, R., and HYDEN, E.: "The Design and Implementation of an Operating System to Support Distributed Multimedia Applications," *IEEE Journal on Selected Areas in Commun.*, vol. 14, pp. 1280-1297, July 1996.

LEVIN, R., COHEN, E.S., CORWIN, W.M., POLLACK, F.J., and WULF, W.A.: "Policy/Mechanism Separation in Hydra," *Proc. Fifth Symp. on Operating Systems Principles*, ACM, pp. 132-140, 1975.

LEWINE, D.: *POSIX Programmer's Guide*, Sebastopol, CA: O'Reilly & Associates, 1991.

LI, K.: "Shared Virtual Memory on Loosely Coupled Multiprocessors," Ph.D. Thesis, Yale Univ., 1986.

LI, K., and HUDAK, P.: "Memory Coherence in Shared Virtual Memory Systems," *ACM Trans. on Computer Systems*, vol. 7, pp. 321-359, Nov. 1989.

LI, K., KUMPF, R., HORTON, P., and ANDERSON, T.: "A Quantitative Analysis of Disk Drive Power Management in Portable Computers," *Proc. 1994 Winter Conf.*, USENIX, pp. 279-291, 1994.

LIEDTKE, J.: "Improving IPC by Kernel Design," *Proc. 14th Symp. on Operating Systems Principles*, ACM, pp. 175-188, 1993.

LIEDTKE, J.: "On Micro-Kernel Construction," *Proc. 15th Symp. on Operating Systems Principles*, ACM, pp. 237-250, 1995.

LIEDTKE, J.: "Toward Real Microkernels," *Commun. of the ACM*, vol. 39, pp. 70-77, Sept. 1996.

LINDE, R.R.: "Operating System Penetration," *Proc. AFIPS National Computer Conf.*, AFIPS, pp. 361-368, 1975.

LIONS, J.: *Lions' Commentary on Unix 6th Edition, with Source Code*, San Jose, CA: Peer-to-Peer Communications, 1996.

LIU, C.L., and LAYLAND, J.W.: "Scheduling Algorithms for Multiprogramming in a Hard Real-Time Environment," *Journal of the ACM*, vol. 20, pp. 46-61, Jan. 1973.

LO, V.M.: "Heuristic Algorithms for Task Assignment in Distributed Systems," *Proc. Fourth Int'l Conf. on Distributed Computing Systems*, IEEE, pp. 30-39, 1984.

LORCH, J.R., and SMITH, A.J.: "Reducing Processor Power Consumption by Improving Processor Time Management In a Single-User Operating System," *Proc. Second Int'l Conf. on Mobile Computing and Networking*, ACM, pp. 143-154, 1996.

LORCH, J., and SMITH, A.J.: "Apple Macintosh's Energy Consumption," *IEEE Micro*, vol. 18, pp. 54-63, Nov./Dec. 1998.

LOUGHER, P., PEGLER, D., and SHEPHERD, D.: "Scalable Storage Servers for Digital Audio and Video," *Proc. IEE Int'l Conf. on Storage and Recording Systems*, London: IEE, pp. 140-143, 1994.

LU, Y.-H., SIMUNIC, T., DE MICHELI, G.: "Software Controlled Power Management," *Proc. Seventh Int'l Workshop on Hardware/Software Codesign*, ACM, pp. 157-161, 1999.

LUDWIG, M.A.: *The Giant Black Book of Computer Viruses, 2nd ed.*, Show Low, AZ: American Eagle Publications, 1998.

LUMB, C.R., SCHINDLER, J., GANGER, G.R., and NAGLE, D.F.: "Towards Higher Disk Head Utilization: Extracting Free Bandwidth from Busy Disk Drives," *Proc. Fourth Symp. on Operating Systems Design and Implementation*, USENIX, pp. 87-102, 2000.

MAEKAWA, M., OLDEHOEFT, A.E., and OLDEHOEFT, R.R.: *Operating Systems: Advanced Concepts*, Menlo Park, CA: Benjamin/Cummings, 1987.

MALKEWITZ, R.: "Head Pointing and Speech Control as a hands-free interface to Desktop Computing," *Proc. Third Int'l Conf. on Assistive Technologies*, ACM, pp. 182-188, 1998.

MANARIS, B., and HARKREADER, A.: "SUITEKeys: A Speech Understanding Interface for the Motor-Control Challenged," *Proc. Third Int'l Conf. on Assistive Technologies*, ACM, pp. 108-115, 1998.

MARK, A.R.: "The Development of Destination-Specific Biometric Authentication," *Proc. Tenth Conf. on Computers, Freedom and Privacy*, ACM. pp. 77-80, 2000.

MARKOWITZ, J.A.: "Voice Biometrics," *Commun. of the ACM*, vol. 43, pp. 66-73, Sept. 2000.

MARSH, B.D., SCOTT, M.L., LEBLANC, T.J., and MARKATOS, E.P.: "First-Class User-Level Threads," *Proc. 13th Symp. on Operating Systems Principles*, ACM, pp. 110-121, 1991.

MATTHEWS, J.N., ROSELLI, D., COSTELLO, A.M., WANG, R.Y., and ANDERSON, T.E.: "Improving the Performance of Log-Structured File Systems with Adaptive Methods," *Proc. 16th Symp. on Operating Systems Prin.*, ACM, pp. 238-251, 1997.

MAXWELL, S.E.: *Linux Core Kernel Commentary*, Scottsdale, AZ: Coriolis, 1999.

MAZIERES, D., KAMINSKY, M., KAASHOEK, M.F., and WITCHEL, E.: "Separating Key Management from File System Security," *Proc. 17th Symp. on Operating Systems Principles*, ACM, pp. 124-139, 1999.

McDANIEL, T.: "Magneto-Optical Data Storage," *Commun. of the ACM*, vol. 43, pp. 57-63, Nov. 2000.

McKUSICK, M.K., BOSTIC, K., KARELS, M.J., and QUARTERMAN, J.S.: *The Design and Implementation of the 4.4 BSD Operating System*, Reading, MA: Addison-Wesley, 1996.

McKUSICK, M.J., JOY, W.N., LEFFLER, S.J., and FABRY, R.S.: "A Fast File System for UNIX," *ACM Trans. on Computer Systems*, vol. 2, pp. 181-197, Aug. 1984.

MEDINETS,D.: *UNIX Shell Programming Tools*, New York, NY: McGraw-Hill, 1999.

MELLOR-CRUMMEY, J.M., and SCOTT, M.L.: "Algorithms for Scalable Synchronization on Shared-Memory Multiprocessors," *ACM Trans. on Computer Systems*, vol. 9, pp. 21-65, Feb. 1991.

MERCER, C.W.: "Operating System Support for Multimedia Applications," *Proc. Second Int'l Conf on Multimedia*, ACM, pp. 492-493, 1994.

MILLER, F.W.: "pk: A POSIX Threads Kernel," *FREENIX Track: USENIX Annual Technical Conference*, USENIX, pp. 179-182, 1999.

MILOJICIC, D.: "Operating Systems: Now and in the Future," *IEEE Concurrency*, vol. 7, pp. 12-21, Jan.-March 1999.

MILOJICIC, D.: "Security and Privacy," *IEEE Concurrency*, vol. 8, pp. 70-79, April-June 2000.

MONROSE, F., and RUBIN, A.: "Authentication Via Keystroke Dynamics," *Proc. Conf. on Computer and Communications Security*, ACM, pp. 48-56, 1997.

MORRIS, J.H., SATYANARAYANAN, M., CONNER, M.H., HOWARD, J.H., ROSENTHAL, D.S., and SMITH, F.D.: "Andrew: A Distributed Personal Computing Environment," *Commun. of the ACM*, vol. 29, pp. 184-201, March 1986.

MORRIS, R., and THOMPSON, K.: "Password Security: A Case History," *Commun. of the ACM*, vol. 22, pp. 594-597, Nov. 1979.

MULLENDER, S.J., and TANENBAUM, A.S.: "Immediate Files," *Software—Practice and Experience*, vol. 14, pp. 365-368, April 1984.

MYERS, A.C., and LISKOV, B.: "A Decentralized Model for Information Flow Control," *Proc. 16th Symp. on Operating Systems Principles*, ACM, pp. 129-142, 1997.

NACHENBERG, C.: "Computer Virus-Antivirus Coevolution" *Commun. of the ACM*, vol. 40, pp. 46-51, Jan. 1997.

NEMETH, E., SNYDER, G., SEEBASS, S., and HEIN, T.R.: *UNIX System Administration Handbook, 2nd ed.*, Upper Saddle River, NJ: Prentice Hall, 2000.

NEWHAM, C., and ROSENBLATT, B.: *Learning the Bash Shell*, Sebastopol, CA: O'Reilly & Associates, 1998.

NEWTON, G.: "Deadlock Prevention, Detection, and Resolution: An Annotated Bibliography," *Operating Systems Review*, vol. 13, pp. 33-44, April 1979.

NIEH, J., and LAM, M.S.: "The Design, Implementation and Evaluation of SMART a Scheduler for Multimedia Applications," *Proc. 16th Symp. on Operating Systems Principles*, ACM, pp. 184-197, 1997.

NIST (National Institute of Standards and Technology): FIPS Pub. 180-1, 1995.

NG, S.W.: "Advances in Disk Technology: Performance Issues," *Computer*, vol. 31, pp. 75-81, May 1998.

NORTON, P., MUELLER, J., and MANSFIELD, R.: *Complete Guide to Windows 2000 Professional*, Indianapolis, IN: Sams, 2000.

OKI, B., PFLUEGL, M., SIEGEL, A., and SKEEN, D.: "The Information Bus—An Architecture for Extensible Distributed Systems," *Proc. 14th Symp. on Operating Systems Principles*, ACM, pp. 58-68, 1993.

ONEY, W.: *Programming the Microsoft Windows Driver Model*, Redmond, WA: Microsoft Press, 1999.

ORGANICK, E.I.: *The Multics System*, Cambridge, MA: M.I.T. Press, 1972.

ORLOV, S.S.: "Volume Holographic Data Storage," *Commun. of the ACM*, vol. 43, pp. 47-54, Nov. 2000.

OUSTERHOUT, J.K.: "Scheduling Techniques for Concurrent Systems," *Proc. Third Int'l Conf. on Distrib. Computing Systems*, IEEE, pp. 22-30, 1982.

PAI, V.S., DRUSCHEL, P., and ZWAENEPOEL, W.: "IO-Lite: A Unified I/O Buffering and Caching System," *Trans. on Computer Systems*, vol. 18, pp. 37-66, Feb. 2000.

PAKIN, S., KARAMCHETI, V., CHIEN, A.A.: "Fast Messages (FM): Efficient, Portable Communication for Workstation Clusters and Massively Parallel Processors," *IEEE Concurrency*, vol. 5, pp. 60-73, April-June 1997.

PANKANTI, S., BOLLE, R.M., and JAIN, A.: "Biometrics: The Future of Identification," *Computer*, vol. 33, pp. 46-49, Feb. 2000.

PATE, S.D.: *UNIX Internals A Practical Approach*, Reading, MA: Addison-Wesley, 1996.

PATTERSON, R.H., GIBSON, G.A., GINTING, E., STODOLSKY, D., and ZELENKA, J.: "Informed Prefetching and Caching," *Proc. 15th Symp. on Operating Systems Principles*, ACM, pp. 79-95, 1995.

PATTERSON, D.A., GIBSON, G., and KATZ, R.: "A Case for Redundant Arrays of Inexpensive Disks (RAID)," *Proc. ACM SIGMOD Int'l. Conf. on Management of Data*, ACM, pp. 109-166,1988.

PENTLAND, A., and CHOUDHURY, T.: "Face Recognition for Smart Environments," *Computer*, vol. 33, pp. 50-55, Feb. 2000

PETERSON, G.L.: "Myths about the Mutual Exclusion Problem," *Information Processing Letters*, vol. 12, pp. 115-116, June 1981.

PETROU, D., MILFORD, J., and GIBSON, G.: "Implementing Lottery Scheduling," *Proc. USENIX Annual Tech. Conf.*, USENIX, pp. 1-14, 1999.

PETZOLD, C.: *Programming Windows, 5th ed.*, Redmond, WA: Microsoft Press, 1999.

PFLEEGER, C.P.: *Security in Computing, 2nd ed.*, Upper Saddle River, NJ: Prentice Hall, 1997.

PHILBIN, J., EDLER, J., ANSHUS, O.J., DOUGLAS, C.C., and LI, K.: "Thread Scheduling for Cache Locality," *Proc. Seventh Int'l Conf. on Architectural Support for Programming Languages and Operating Systems*, ACM, pp. 60-71, 1996.

PRECHELT, L.: "An Empirical Comparison of Seven Programming Languages," *Computer*, vol. 33, pp. 23-29, Oct. 2000.

PROTIC, J., TOMASEVIC, M., and MILUTINOVIC, V.: *Distributed Shared Memory: Concepts and Systems*, Los Alamitos, CA: IEEE Computer Society, 1998.

RAWSON, F.L. III: "Experience with the Development of a Microkernel-Based, Multi-Server Operating System," *Proc. Hot Topics in Operating Systems VI*, IEEE, pp. 2-7, 1997.

RECTOR, B.E., and NEWCOMER, J.M.: *Win32 Programming*, Reading, MA: Addison-Wesley, 1997.

REDDY, A.L.N., and WYLLIE, J.C.: "Disk Scheduling in a Multimedia I/O System," *Proc. ACM Multimedia Conf.*, ACM, pp. 225-233, 1992.

REDDY, A.L.N., and WYLLIE, J.C.: "I/O Issues in a Multimedia System," *Computer*, vol. 27, pp. 69-74, March 1994.

RITCHIE, D.M.: "Reflections on Software Research," *Commun. of the ACM*, vol. 27, pp. 758-760, Aug. 1984.

RITCHIE, D.M., and THOMPSON, K.: "The UNIX Timesharing System," *Commun. of the ACM*, vol. 17, pp. 365-375, July 1974.

RIVEST, R.L.: "The MD5 Message-Digest Algorithm," RFC 1320, April 1992.

RIVEST, R.L., SHAMIR, A., and ADLEMAN, L.: "On a Method for Obtaining Digital Signatures and Public Key Cryptosystems," *Commun. of the ACM*, vol. 21, pp. 120-126, Feb. 1978.

ROBBINS, A.: *UNIX in a Nutshell: A Desktop Quick Reference for SVR4 and Solaris 7*, Sebastopol, CA: O'Reilly & Associates, 1999.

ROMPOGIANNAKIS, Y., NERJES, G., MUTH, P., PATERAKIS, M., TRIANTAFILLOU, P., and WEIKUM, G.: "Disk Scheduling for Mixed-Media Workloads in a Multimedia Server," *Proc. Sixth Int'l Conf. on Multimedia*, ACM, pp. 297 -302, 1998.

ROSENBLUM, M., and OUSTERHOUT, J.K.: "The Design and Implementation of a Log-Structured File System," *Proc. 13th Symp. on Oper. Sys. Prin.*, ACM, pp. 1-15, 1991.

ROSELLI, D., and LORCH, J.R.: "A Comparison of File System Workloads," *Proc. USENIX Annual Tech. Conf.*, USENIX, pp. 41-54, 2000.

ROZIER, M., ABBROSSIMOV, V., ARMAND, F., BOULE, I., GIEN, M., GUILLEMONT, M., HERRMANN, F., KAISER, C., LEONARD, P., LANGLOIS, S., and NEUHAUSER, W.: "Chorus Distributed Operating Systems," *Computing Systems*, vol. 1, pp. 305-379, Oct. 1988.

RUEMMLER, C., and WILKES, J.: "An Introduction to Disk Drive Modeling," *Computer*, vol. 27, pp. 17-28, March 1994.

SACKMAN, H., ERIKSON, W.J., and GRANT, E.E.: "Exploratory Experimental Studies Comparing Online and Offline Programming Performance," *Commun. of the ACM*, vol. 11, pp. 3-11, Jan. 1968.

SALTZER, J.H.: "Protection and Control of Information Sharing in MULTICS," *Commun. of the ACM*, vol. 17, pp. 388-402, July 1974.

SALTZER, J.H., REED, D.P., and CLARK, D.D.: "End-to-End Arguments in System Design," *Trans. on Computer Systems*, vol. 2, pp. 277-277, Nov. 1984.

SALTZER, J.H., and SCHROEDER, M.D.: "The Protection of Information in Computer Systems," *Proc. IEEE*, vol. 63, pp. 1278-1308, Sept. 1975.

SALUS, P.H.: "UNIX At 25," *Byte*, vol. 19, pp. 75-82, Oct. 1994.

SANDHU, R.S.: "Lattice-Based Access Control Models," *Computer*, vol. 26, pp. 9-19, Nov. 1993.

SANTRY, D., FEELEY, M.J., HUTCHINSON, N.C., VEITCH, A.C. : "Elephant: The File System That Never Forgets," *Proc. Hot Topics in Operating Systems VII*, IEEE, pp. 2-7, 1999a.

SANTRY, D., FEELEY, M., HUTCHINSON, N., VEITCH, A.C., CARTON, R.W., and OFIR, J.: "Deciding When to Forget in the Elephant File System," *Proc. 17th Symp. on Operating Systems Principles*, ACM, pp. 110-123, 1999b.

SATYANARAYANAN, M., HOWARD, J.H., NICHOLS, D.N., SIDEBOTHAM, R.N., SPECTOR, A.Z., and WEST, M.J.: "The ITC Distributed File System: Principles and Design," *Proc. of the Tenth Symp. on Operating System Prin.*, ACM, pp. 35-50, 1985.

SAVAGE, S., BURROWS, M., NELSON, G., SOBALVARRO, P., and ANDERSON, T.: "Eraser: A Dynamic Data Race Detector for Multithreaded Programs," *Trans. on Computer Systems*, vol. 15, pp. 391-411, Nov. 1997.

SCALES, D.J., and GHARACHORLOO, K.: "Towards Transparent and Efficient Software Distributed Shared Memory," *Proc. 16th Symp. on Operating Systems Principles*, ACM, pp. 157-169, 1997.

SCHMIDT, B.K., LAM, M.S., and NORTHCUTT, J.D.: "The Interactive Performance of Slim: A Stateless, Thin-Client Architecture," *Proc. 17th Symp. on Operating Systems Principles*, ACM, pp. 32-47, 1999.

SCOTT, M., LeBLANC, T., and MARSH, B.: "Multi-model Parallel Programming in Psyche," *Proc. Second ACM Symp. on Principles and Practice of Parallel Programming*, ACM, pp. 70-78, 1990.

SEAWRIGHT, L.H., and MACKINNON, R.A.: "VM/370—A Study of Multiplicity and Usefulness," *IBM Systems Journal*, vol. 18, pp. 4-17, 1979.

SEGARRA, M.-T., and ANDRI, F.: "MFS: a Mobile File System Using Generic System Services," *Proc. 1999 Symp. on Applied Computing*, ACM, pp. 419-420, 1999.

SELTZER, M., ENDO, Y., SMALL, C., and SMITH, K.: "Dealing with Disaster: Surviving Misbehaved Kernel Extensionsm". *Proc. Second Symp. on Operating System Design and Implementation*, USENIX, pp. 213-227, 1994.

SHENOY, P.J., and VIN, H.M.: "Efficient Striping Techniques for Variable Bit Rate Continuous Media File Servers," *Perf. Eval. Journal*, vol. 38, pp. 175-199, 1999.

SHENOY, P.J., GOYAL, P., and VIN, H.M.: "Architectural Considerations for Next Generation File Systems," *Proc. Seventh Int'l Conf. on Multimedia*, ACM, pp. 457-467, 1999.

SILBERSCHATZ, A., GALVIN, P.B., and GAGNE, G: *Applied Operating System Concepts*, New York: Wiley, 2000.

SIMON, R.J.: *Windows NT Win32 API SuperBible*, Corte Madera, CA: Sams Publishing, 1997.

SITARAM, D., and DAN, A.: *Multimedia Servers*, San Francisco, CA: Morgan Kaufman, 2000.

SLAUGHTER, L., OARD, D.W., WARNICK, V.L., HARDING, J.L., and WILKERSON, G.J.: "A Graphical Interface for Speech-Based Retrieval," *Proc. Third ACM Conf. on Digital Libraries*, ACM, pp. 305-306, 1998.

SMALL, C., and SELTZER, M.: "MiSFIT: constructing Safe Extensible Systems," *IEEE Concurrency*, vol. 6, pp. 34-41, July-Sept. 1998.

SMITH, D,K., and ALEXANDER, R.C.: *Fumbling the Future: How Xerox Invented, Then Ignored, the First Personal Computer*, New York: William Morrow, 1988.

SNIR, M., OTTO, S.W., HUSS-LEDERMAN, S., WALKER, D.W., and DONGARRA, J.: *MPI: The Complete Reference Manual*, Cambridge, MA: M.I.T. Press, 1996.

SOLOMON, D.A., and RUSSINOVICH, M.E.: *Inside Windows 2000, 3rd ed.*, Redmond, WA: Microsoft Press, 2000

SPAFFORD, E., HEAPHY, K., and FERBRACHE, D.: *Computer Viruses*, Arlington, VA: ADAPSO, 1989.

STALLINGS, W.: *Operating Systems, 4th Ed.*, Upper Saddle River, NJ: Prentice Hall, 2001.

STEENKISTE, P.A.: "A Systematic Approach to Host Interface Design for High-Speed Networks," *Computer*, vol. 27, pp. 47-57, March 1994.

STEINMETZ, R., and NAHRSTEDT, K.: *Multimedia: Computing, Communications and Applications*, Upper Saddle River, NJ: Prentice Hall, 1995.

STENSTROM, P., HAGERSTEN, E., LILJA, D.J., MARTONOSI, M., and VENUGOPAL, M.: "Trends in Shared Memory Multiprocessing," *Computer*, vol. 30, pp. 44-50, 1997.

STETS, R., DWARKADAS, S., HARDAVELLAS, N., HUNT, G., KONTOTHANASSIS, L., PARTHASARATHY, S., and SCOTT, M.: "Cashmere—2L Software Coherent Shared Memory on a Clustered Remote-Write Network," *Proc. 16th Symp. on Operating Systems Principles*, ACM, pp. 170-183, 1997.

STEVENS, W.R.: *Advanced Programming in the UNIX Environment*, Reading, MA: Addison-Wesley, 1992.

STOLL, C.: *The Cuckoo's Egg: Tracking a Spy through the Maze of Computer Espionage*, New York: Doubleday, 1989.

STONE, H.S., and BOKHARI, S.H.: "Control of Distributed Processes," *Computer*, vol. 11, pp. 97-106, July 1978.

TAI, K.C., and CARVER, R.H.: "VP: A New Operation for Semaphores," *Operating Systems Review*, vol. 30, pp. 5-11, July 1996.

TALLURI, M., and HILL, M.D.: "Surpassing the TLB Performance of Superpages with Less Operating System Support," *Proc. Sixth Int'l Conf. on Architectural Support for Programming Languages and Operating Systems*, ACM, pp. 171-182, 1994.

TALLURI, M., HILL, M.D., and KHALIDI, Y.A.: "A New Page Table for 64-bit Address Spaces," *Proc. 15th Symp. on Operating Systems Prin.*, ACM, pp. 184-200, 1995.

TANENBAUM, A.S.: *Operating Systems: Design and Implementation*, Upper Saddle River, NJ: Prentice Hall, 1987.

TANENBAUM, A.S.: *Computer Networks*, Upper Saddle River, NJ: Prentice Hall, 1996.

TANENBAUM, A.S., VAN RENESSE, R., VAN STAVEREN, H., SHARP, G.J., MULLENDER, S.J., JANSEN, J., and VAN ROSSUM, G.: "Experiences with the Amoeba Distributed Operating System," *Commun. of the ACM*, vol. 33, pp. 46-63, Dec. 1990.

TANENBAUM, A.S., and VAN STEEN, M.R.: *Distributed Systems*, Upper Saddle River, NJ: Prentice Hall, 2002.

TANENBAUM, A.S., and WOODHULL, A.S.: *Operating Systems: Design and Implementation, 2nd ed.*, Upper Saddle River, NJ: Prentice Hall, 1997.

TAYLOR, R.N, MEDVIDOVIC, N., ANDERSON, K.M., WHITEHEAD, E.J., and ROBBINS, J.E.: "A Component- and Message-Based Architectural Style for GUI Software," *Proc. 17th Int'l Conf. on Software Engineering*, ACM, pp. 295-304, 1995.

TEORY, T.J.: "Properties of Disk Scheduling Policies in Multiprogrammed Computer Systems," *Proc. AFIPS Fall Joint Computer Conf.*, AFIPS, pp. 1-11, 1972.

THEKKATH, C.A., MANN, T., and LEE, E.K.: "Frangipani: A Scalable Distributed File System," *Proc. 16th Symp. on Operating Systems Principles*, ACM, pp. 224-237, 1997.

THOMPSON, K.: "Reflections on Trusting Trust," *Commun. of the ACM*, vol. 27, pp. 761-763, Aug. 1984.

TRONO, J.A.: "Comments on Tagged Semaphores," *Operating Systems Review*, vol. 34, pp. 7-11, Oct. 2000.

TUCKER, A., and GUPTA, A.: "Process Control and Scheduling Issues for Multiprogrammed Shared-Memory Multiprocessors," *Proc. 12th Symp. on Operating Systems Principles*, ACM, pp. 159-166, 1989.

UHLIG, R., NAGLE, D., STANLEY, T., MUDGE, T., SECREST, S., and BROWN, R.: "Design Tradeoffs for Software-Managed TLBs," *ACM Trans. on Computer Systems*, vol. 12, pp. 175-205, Aug. 1994.

VAHALIA, U.: *UNIX Internals—The New Frontiers*, Upper Saddle River, NJ: Prentice Hall, 1996.

VAN BUSKIRK, R., and LALOMIA, M.: "A Comparison of Speech and Mouse/Keyboard GUI Navigation," *Conference Companion on Human Factors in Computing Systems*, ACM, p. 96, 1995.

VAN DOORN, L.: *The Design and Application of an Extensible Operating System*, Ph.D. Thesis, Vrije Universiteit, Amsterdam, The Netherlands, 2001.

VAN DOORN, L., HOMBURG, P., and TANENBAUM, A.S.: "Paramecium: An Extensible Object-Based Kernel," *Proc. Hot Topics in Operating Systems V*, IEEE, pp. 86-89, 1995.

VAN STEEN, M., HAUCK, F.J., BALLINTIJN, G., and TANENBAUM, A.S.: "Algorithmic Design of the Globe Wide-Area Location Service," *Computer Journal*, vol. 41, pp. 207-310, 1998a.

VAN STEEN, M., HAUCK, F.J., HOMBURG, P., and TANENBAUM, A.S.: "Locating Objects in Wide-Area Systems," *IEEE Communications Magazine*, vol. 36, pp. 104-109, Jan. 1998b.

VAN STEEN, M., HOMBURG, P., and TANENBAUM, A.S.: "Globe: A Wide-Area Distributed System," *IEEE Concurrency*, vol. 7, pp. 70-78, Jan.-March 1999a.

VAN STEEN, M., TANENBAUM, A.S., KUZ, I., and SIPS, H.J.: "A Scalable Middleware Solution for Advanced Wide-Area Web Services," *Distributed Systems Engineering*, vol. 7, pp. 34-42, 1999b.

VASWANI, R., and ZAHORJAN, J.: "The Implications of Cache Affinity on Processor Scheduling for Multiprogrammed Shared-Memory Multiprocessors," *Proc. 13th Symp. on Operating Systems Principles*, ACM, pp. 26-40, 1991.

VENKATASUBRAMANIAN, N., and RAMANATHAN, S: "Load Management in Distributed Video Servers," *Proc. 17th Int'l Conf. on Distrib. Computing Systems*, IEEE, pp. 528-535, 1997.

VINOSKI, S.: "CORBA: Integrating Diverse Applications within Distributed Heterogeneous Environments," *IEEE Communications Magazine*, vol. 35, pp. 46-56, Feb 1997.

VISCAROLA, P.G., and MASON, W.A.: *Windows NT Device Driver Development*, Indianapolis, IN: Macmillan Technical Publishing, 1999.

VOGELS, W.: "File System Usage in Windows NT 4.0," *Proc. 17th Symp. on Operating Systems Principles*, ACM, pp. 93-109, 1999.

VON EICKEN, T., BASU, A., BUCH, V., and VOGELS, W.: "U-Net: a User-Level Network Interface for Parallel and Distributed Computing," *Proc. 15th Symp. on Operating Systems Principles*, ACM, pp. 40-53, 1995.

VON EICKEN, T., CULLER, D., GOLDSTEIN, S.C., SCHAUSER, K.E.: "Active Messages: A Mechanism for Integrated Communication and Computation," *Proc. 19th Int'l Symp. on Computer Architecture*, ACM, pp. 256-266, 1992.

WAHBE, R., LUCCO, S., ANDERSON, T., and GRAHAM, S.: "Efficient Software-Based Fault Isolation," *Proc. 14th Symp. on Operating Systems Principles*, ACM, pp. 203-216, 1993.

WALDO, J.: "The Jini Architecture for Network-Centric Computing," *Commun. of the ACM*, vol. 42, pp. 76-82, July 1999.

WALDO, J.: "Alive and Well: Jini Technology Today," *Computer*, vol. 33, pp. 107-109, June 2000.

"Lottery Scheduling: Flexible Proportional-Share Resource Management," *Proc. First Symp. on Operating System Design and Implementation*, **USENIX, pp. 1-12, 1994.**

WALKER, W., and CRAGON, H.G.: "Interrupt Processing in Concurrent Processors," *Computer*, vol. 28, pp. 36-46, June 1995.

WAN, G., and LIN, E.: "A Dynamic Paging Scheme for Wireless Communication Systems," *Proc. Third Int'l Conf. on Mobile Computing and Networking*, ACM/IEEE, pp. 195-203, 1997

WANG, C., GOEBEL, V., and PLAGEMANN, T.: "Techniques to Increase Disk Access Locality in the Minorca Multimedia File System," *Proc. Seventh Int'l Conf. on Multimedia*, ACM, pp. 147-150, 1999.

WANG, R.Y., ANDERSON, T.E., and PATTERSON, D.A.: "Virtual Log Based File Systems for a Programmable Disk," *Proc. Third Symp. on Operating Systems Design and Implementation*, USENIX, pp. 29-43, 1999.

WEISER, M., WELCH, B., DEMERS, A., and SHENKER, S.: "Scheduling for Reduced CPU Energy," *Proc. First Symp. on Operating System Design and Implementation*, USENIX, pp. 13-23, 1994.

WILKES, J., GOLDING, R., STAELIN, C, and SULLIVAN, T.: "The HP AutoRAID Hierarchical Storage System," *ACM Trans. on Computer Systems*, vol. 14, pp. 108-136, Feb. 1996.

WIRTH, N.: "A Plea for Lean Software," *Computer*, vol. 28, pp. 64-68, Feb. 1995.

WOLMAN, A., VOELKER, M., SHARMA, N., CARDWELL, N., KARLIN, A., and LEVY, H.M.: "On the Scale and Performance of Cooperative Web Proxy Caching," *Proc. 17th Symp. on Operating Systems Principles*, ACM, pp. 16- 31, 1999.

WONG, C.K.: *Algorithmic Studies in Mass Storage Systems*, New York: Computer Science Press, 1983.

WONG, P.C., and LEE, Y.B.: "Redundant Array of Inexpensive Servers (RAIS)," *Proc. Int'l Conf. on Commun.*, IEEE, pp. 787-792, 1997.

WORTHINGTON, B.L., GANGER, G.R., and PATT, Y.N.: "Scheduling Algorithms for Modern Disk Drives," *Proc. 1994 Conf. on Measurement and Modeling of Computer Systems*, pp. 241-251, 1994.

WU, M., and SHU, W.: "Scheduling for Large-Scale Parallel Video Servers," *Proc. Sixth Symp. on Frontiers of Massively Parallel Computation*, IEEE, pp. 126-133, 1996.

WULF, W.A., COHEN, E.S., CORWIN, W.M., JONES, A.K., LEVIN, R., PIERSON, C., and POLLACK, F.J.: "HYDRA: The Kernel of a Multiprocessor Operating System," *Commun. of the ACM*, vol. 17, pp. 337-345, June 1974.

YOUNG, M., TEVANIAN, A., Jr., RASHID, R., GOLUB, D., EPPINGER, J., CHEW, J., BOLOSKY, W., BLACK, D., and BARON, R.: "The Duality of Memory and Communication in the Implementation of a Multiprocessor Operating System," *Proc. 11th Symp. on Operating Systems Principles*, ACM, pp. 63-76, 1987.

ZACHARY, G.P.: *Showstopper*, New York: Maxwell MacMillan, 1994.

ZAHORJAN, J., LAZOWSKA, E.D., and EAGER, D.L.: "The Effect of Scheduling Discipline on Spin Overhead in Shared Memory Parallel Systems," *IEEE Trans. on Parallel and Distr. Systems*, vol. 2, pp. 180-198, April 1991.

ZEKAUSKAS, M.J., SAWDON, W.A., and BERSHAD, B.N.: "Software Write Detection for a Distributed Shared Memory," *Proc. First Symp. on Operating System Design and Implementation*, USENIX, pp. 87-100, 1994.

ZOBEL, D.: "The Deadlock Problem: A Classifying Bibliography," *Operating Systems Review*, vol. 17, pp. 6-16, Oct. 1983.

ZUBERI, K.M., PILLAI, P., and SHIN, K.G.: "EMERALDS: A Small-Memory Real-Time Microkernel," *Proc. 17th Symp. on Operating Systems Principles*, ACM, pp. 277-299, 1999.

ZWICKY, E.D.: "Torture-Testing Backup and Archive Programs: Things You Ought to Know but Probably Would Rather Not," *Proc. Fifth Conf. on Large Installation Systems Admin.*, USENIX, pp. 181-190, 1991.

INDEX

O

P

X

Y

Z

ABOUT THE AUTHOR

Andrew S. Tanenbaum has an S.B. degree from M.I.T. and a Ph.D. from the University of California at Berkeley. He is currently a Professor of Computer Science at the Vrije Universiteit in Amsterdam, The Netherlands, where he heads the Computer Systems Group. He is also Dean of the Advanced School for Computing and Imaging, an interuniversity graduate school doing research on advanced parallel, distributed, and imaging systems. Nevertheless, he is trying very hard to avoid turning into a bureaucrat.

In the past, he has done research on compilers, operating systems, networking, and local-area distributed systems. His current research focuses primarily on the design of wide-area distributed systems that scale to a billion users. These research projects have led to over 85 refereed papers in journals and conference proceedings and five books.

Prof. Tanenbaum has also produced a considerable volume of software. He was the principal architect of the Amsterdam Compiler Kit, a widely-used toolkit for writing portable compilers, as well as of MINIX, a small UNIX clone intended for use in student programming labs. Together with his Ph.D. students and programmers, he helped design the Amoeba distributed operating system, a high-performance microkernel-based distributed operating system. The MINIX and Amoeba systems are now available for free via the Internet.

His Ph.D. students have gone on to greater glory after getting their degrees. He is very proud of them. In this respect he resembles a mother hen.

Prof. Tanenbaum is a Fellow of the ACM, a Fellow of the the IEEE, a member of the Royal Netherlands Academy of Arts and Sciences, winner of the 1994 ACM Karl V. Karlstrom Outstanding Educator Award, and winner of the 1997 ACM/SIGCSE Award for Outstanding Contributions to Computer Science Education. He is also listed in *Who's Who in the World*. His home page on the World Wide Web can be found at URL *http://www.cs.vu.nl/~ast/* .